ELEVENTH EDITION

Management

LEADING & COLLABORATING IN A COMPETITIVE WORLD

Thomas S. Bateman
McIntire School of Commerce
University of Virginia

Scott A. Snell
Darden Graduate School of Business
University of Virginia

McGraw Hill Education

MANAGEMENT: LEADING & COLLABORATING IN A COMPETITIVE WORLD,
ELEVENTH EDITION
Published by McGraw-Hill Education, 2 Penn Plaza, New York, NY 10121. Copyright © 2015 by
McGraw-Hill Education. All rights reserved. Printed in the United States of America. Previous editions
© 2013, 2011, and 2009. No part of this publication may be reproduced or distributed in any form or by
any means, or stored in a database or retrieval system, without the prior written consent of McGraw-Hill
Education, including, but not limited to, in any network or other electronic storage or transmission, or
broadcast for distance learning.

Some ancillaries, including electronic and print components, may not be available to customers outside
the United States.

This book is printed on acid-free paper.

1 2 3 4 5 6 7 8 9 0 DOW/DOW 1 0 9 8 7 6 5 4

ISBN 978-1-259-25422-2
MHID 1-259-25422-4

www.mhhe.com

For my parents, Tom and Jeanine Bateman,
and Mary Jo, Lauren, T.J., and James

and

My parents, John and Clara Snell,
and Marybeth, Sara, Jack, and Emily

About the Authors

THOMAS S. BATEMAN

Thomas S. Bateman is Bank of America Professor and management area coordinator in the McIntire School of Commerce at the University of Virginia. He teaches leadership courses and is director of a new leadership minor open to undergraduate students of all majors. Prior to joining the University of Virginia, he taught organizational behavior at the Kenan-Flagler Business School of the University of North Carolina to undergraduates, MBA students, PhD students, and practicing managers. He also taught for two years in Europe as a visiting professor at the Institute for Management Development (IMD), one of the world's leaders in the design and delivery of executive education. Professor Bateman completed his doctoral program in business administration in 1980 at Indiana University. Prior to receiving his doctorate, Dr. Bateman received his BA from Miami University. In addition to Virginia, UNC–Chapel Hill, and IMD, Dr. Bateman has taught at Texas A&M, Tulane, and Indiana universities.

Professor Bateman is an active management researcher, writer, and consultant. He serves on the editorial boards of the *Academy of Management Review*, the *Academy of Management Journal*, and the *Asia Pacific Journal of Business and Management*. His articles have appeared in professional journals such as the *Academy of Management Journal*, *Academy of Management Review*, *Journal of Applied Psychology*, *Organizational Behavior and Human Decision Processes*, *Journal of Management*, *Business Horizons*, *Journal of Organizational Behavior*, and *Decision Sciences*.

Tom's current consulting and research center on practical wisdom in business executives, leadership in the form of problem solving at all organizational levels, various types of proactive behavior by employees at all levels, and the successful pursuit of long-term work goals. He works with organizations including Singapore Airlines, the Brookings Institution, the U.S. Chamber of Commerce, the Nature Conservancy, and LexisNexis.

SCOTT A. SNELL

 Scott Snell is Professor of Business Administration at the University of Virginia's Darden Graduate School of Business. He teaches courses in leadership, developing organizational capability, and human capital consulting. His research focuses on human resources and the mechanisms by which organizations generate, transfer, and integrate new knowledge for competitive advantage. He is co-author of four books: *Managing People and Knowledge in Professional Service Firms*, *Management: Leading and Collaborating in a Competitive World*, *M: Management*, and *Managing Human Resources*. His work has been published in a number of journals such as the *Academy of Management Journal*, *Academy of Management Review*, *Strategic Management Journal*, *Journal of Management*, *Journal of Management Studies*, *and Human Resource Management*, and he was recently listed among the top 100 most-cited authors in scholarly journals of management. He has served on the boards of the Strategic Management Society's human capital group, the Society for Human Resource Management Foundation, the Academy of Management's human resource division, the *Human Resource Management Journal, the Academy of Management Journal and the Academy of Management Review*. Professor Snell has worked with companies such as AstraZeneca, Deutsche Telekom, Shell, and United Technologies to align strategy, capability, and investments in talent. Prior to joining the Darden faculty in 2007, he was professor and director of executive education at Cornell University's Center for Advanced Human Resource Studies and a professor of management in the Smeal College of Business at Pennsylvania State University. He received a B.A. in psychology from Miami University, as well as M.B.A. and Ph.D. degrees in business administration from Michigan State University.

Preface

Welcome to our 11th edition! Thank you to everyone who has used and learned from previous editions. We are proud to present to you our newest and most exciting edition.

Our Goals

Our mission with this text hasn't changed from that of our previous editions: to inform, instruct, and inspire. We hope to inform by providing descriptions of the important concepts and practices of modern management. We hope to instruct by describing how you can take action on the ideas discussed. We hope to inspire not only by writing in an interesting and optimistic way but also by providing a real sense of the opportunities ahead of you. Whether your goal is starting your own company, leading a team to greatness, building a strong organization, delighting your customers, or generally forging a positive future, we want to inspire you to take constructive actions.

We hope to inspire you to be both a thinker and a doer. We want you to think about the issues, think about the impact of your actions, think before you act. But being a good thinker is not enough; you also must be a doer. Management is a world of action. It is a world that requires timely and appropriate action. It is a world not for the passive but for those who commit to positive accomplishments.

Keep applying the ideas you learn in this course, read about management in sources outside of this course, and keep learning about management after you leave school and continue your career. Make no mistake about it: Learning about management is a personal voyage that will last years, an entire career.

Competitive Advantage

Today's world is competitive. Never before has the world of work been so challenging. Never before has it been so imperative to your career that you learn the skills of management. Never before have people had so many opportunities and challenges with so many potential risks and rewards.

You will compete with other people for jobs, resources, and promotions. Your organization will compete with other firms for contracts, clients, and customers. To survive the competition, and to thrive, you must perform in ways that give you an edge over your competitors, that make the other party want to hire you, buy from you, and do repeat business with you. You will want them to choose you, not your competitor.

To survive and thrive, today's managers have to think and act strategically. Today's customers are well educated, aware of their options, and demanding of excellence. For this reason, managers today must think constantly about how to build a capable workforce and manage in a way that delivers the goods and services that provide the best possible value to the customer.

By this standard, managers and organizations must perform. Six essential types of performance, on which the organization beats, equals, or loses to the competition, are *cost, quality, speed, innovation, service,* and *sustainability*. These six performance dimensions, when managed well, deliver value to the customer and competitive advantage to you and your organization. We will elaborate on all of these topics throughout the book.

The idea is to keep you focused on a type of bottom line to make sure you think continually about delivering the goods that make both you and your organization a competitive success. This results-oriented approach is unique among management textbooks.

Leading & Collaborating

Yes, business is competitive. But it's not that simple. In fact, to think strictly in terms of competition is overly cynical, and such cynicism can sabotage your performance. The other fundamental elements in the success equation are collaboration and leadership. People working with, rather than against, one another are essential to competitive advantage. Put another way, you can't do it alone—the world is too complex, and business is too challenging.

You need to work with your teammates. Leaders and followers need to work as collaborators more than as adversaries. Work groups throughout your organization need to cooperate with one another. Business and government, often viewed as antagonists, can work productively together. And today more than ever, companies that traditionally were competitors engage in joint ventures and find other ways to collaborate on some things even as they compete in others. Leadership is needed to make these collaborations happen.

How does an organization create competitive advantage through collaboration? It's all about the people, and it derives from good leadership. Three stereotypes of leadership are that it comes from the top of the company, that it comes from one's immediate boss, and that it means being decisive and issuing commands. These stereotypes may contain grains of truth, but the reality is much more complex. First, the person at the top may or may not provide effective leadership—in fact, many observers believe that good leadership is far too rare. Second, organizations need leaders at all levels, in every team and work unit. This includes you, beginning early in your career, and this is why leadership is an important theme in this book. Third, leaders should be capable of decisiveness and of giving commands, but relying too much on this traditional approach isn't enough. Great leadership is far more inspirational than this and helps people both to think differently and to work differently—including working collaboratively with a focus on results.

Leadership—from your boss as well as from you—generates collaboration, which in turn creates results that are good for the company and good for the people involved.

As Always, Currency and Variety in the 11th Edition

It goes without saying that this textbook, in its 11th edition, remains on the cutting edge of topical coverage, updated via both current business examples and recent management research. Chapters have been thoroughly updated, and students are exposed to a broad array of important current topics. As but two examples, we have expanded and strengthened our coverage of sustainability and social enterprise, topics on which we were early leaders and that we continue to care about as much as today's students.

We have done our very best to draw from a wide variety of subject matter, sources, and personal experiences. We continue to emphasize throughout the book themes such as real results, ethics, cultural considerations, and leadership and collaboration. Here is just a sampling of new highlights in the 11th edition—enough to convey the wide variety of people, organizations, issues, and contexts represented throughout the text.

Chapter 1

- New Management Connection about Jeff Bezos of Amazon

- New text example of collaborating with customers via social media, focusing on L.L. Bean

- New example of car makers expanding production in the United States

- New In Practice about Mark Little, chief technology officer at GE

- New example of the importance of people skills to management success, beginning early in one's career

- New In Practice about Anne Ackerley, chief marketing officer of BlackRock, a money management firm

Chapter 2

- New Management Connection about Facebook and Mark Zuckerberg

- New Figure 2.3 on employment trends following recent recessions

- New examples throughout chapter on cola wars and efforts, especially at PepsiCo, to include more healthful products in the mix

- New example of e-readers and eBooks as complementary products

- New In Practice about the growth and challenges of using contingent workers

- New In Practice about Google's organizational culture

Chapter 3

- New Management Connection about decisions related to Boeing Dreamliner

- New example of logistics decisions to help Toys "R" Us compete with online-only retailers

- New Henry Ford example from *The Greatest Business Decisions of All Time*

- New text describing the significance of big data for decision making

- New In Practice about decision to launch Apple Maps

- New In Practice about GE and Virgin Airlines using social media to gather ideas for a "social airplane"

- New example of Pixar's ideas for boosting creative thinking

- New Concluding Case: Soaring Eagle Skate Company

Chapter 4

- New Management Connection about Walt Disney Company

- New example of New York Community Bancorp
- New In Practice about the Bill and Melinda Gates Foundation
- New example of Procter & Gamble, including A. G. Lafley on importance of strategy
- New example of Zappos.com
- New example of QlikTech, including sample graphic for a SWOT analysis
- New example of General Electric
- New In Practice about Valve's online distribution of video games at the Steam website
- New example of Bloomin' Brands
- New example of Spirit Airlines
- New Concluding Case: Wish You Wood

Chapter 5

- New Management Connection about IBM (including Smarter Planet initiative)
- New In Practice fictional example of an ethical dilemma at a sign company
- New example applying ethical principles to decisions about fracking
- New Table 5.2 with updated current examples of ethical issues in business, including health care, social media, and telework
- New In Practice about Red Frog Events
- New Table 5.4 of Unisys Corporation's code of ethics
- New example of Siemens

Chapter 6

- New Management Connection about Lenovo
- New examples (e.g., General Motors) of Chinese manufacturing shifting toward more skilled manufacturing aimed at serving its growing middle class
- South America information updated to include growth beyond Brazil
- New example of IBM finding opportunities in Africa
- New example of Cinnabon in the Middle East and Russia
- New In Practice about Starbucks
- New example of Panasonic
- New example of U.S. tariffs on Chinese solar panels
- New In Practice about Celtel
- New Concluding Case: Net-Work Docs

Chapter 7

- New Management Connection about Popchips
- New list of entrepreneurs in their 20s (Table 7.2)
- New example of Limor Fried, founder of Adafruit Industries
- New examples of SpaceX and Bigelow Aerospace
- New examples of itMD and Care at Hand—health care technology companies receiving grants in an area of new demand
- New In Practice about 3Cinteractive
- New example of Zipcar
- Material on financial needs of a start-up collected in one section, with the addition of material about crowdfunding expansion under the JOBS Act of 2012
- New In Practice about David Karp, founder of Tumblr
- New example of Neema Bahramzad and Caitlin Bales, founders of Locabal
- New Concluding Case: ScrollCo

Chapter 8

- New Management Connection about General Motors
- New In Practice about Coca-Cola's board of directors
- New example of outside directors helping companies during the Great Recession
- New example of Time Warner Cable
- New example of San Francisco Federal Credit Union
- New In Practice about enterprise social networks

Chapter 9

- New Management Connection about General Electric
- Updated Walmart example
- New In Practice about Hewlett-Packard
- New example of DreamWorks Animation
- New In Practice about clothing customization by eShakti and Bow & Drape
- New example of Toyota
- New example of Japanese companies revisiting their approach to just-in-time, following the earthquake and tsunami's impact
- New example of R. A. Jones & Co.

Chapter 10

- Updated Management Connection about Google
- New examples of Johnson & Johnson, Colgate
- New example of Ford Motor Company
- Updated Figure 10.2
- New In Practice about use of big data by Xerox and Catalyst IT Services
- Updated Table 10.1
- New example of Verizon
- Updated Figure 10.4
- Updated information about CEO pay
- New In Practice about Royal Dutch Shell

Chapter 11

- New Management Connection about NASCAR
- New Figure 11.2 about extent of diversity initiatives
- Updated information on gender gap in pay
- New information for Tables 11.1 and 11.2
- New Table 11.4
- New ranking of DiversityInc's Best Companies for Diversity
- New In Practice about CVS Caremark
- New example of Etsy
- New In Practice about Ingersoll Rand
- New Concluding Case: Niche Hotel Group

Chapter 12

- New Management Connection about Meg Whitman as leader of Hewlett-Packard
- New example of Maria Green at Illinois Tool Works
- New In Practice about Barbara Corcoran as leader of Corcoran Group
- New example of Jeff Bezos as leader of Amazon
- New In Practice about David Novak as leader of Yum Brands
- New example of John Heer as leader of Mississippi Health Services
- New Concluding Case: Breitt, Starr & Diamond LLC

Chapter 13

- New Management Connection about SAS
- New example of QuikTrip convenience-store chain

- New example of Northeast Georgia Health System
- New In Practice about RescueTime auto-analytics for performance feedback
- New example of Parasole restaurant group
- New example of Plante Moran accounting firm
- New In Practice about Mars Inc.

Chapter 14

- New Management Connection about Whole Foods Market
- New example of FLEXcon
- New example of Game Freak
- New example of Lockheed Martin
- New example of trend toward rapid team formation
- New In Practice about Menlo Innovations
- New example of National Information Solutions Cooperative
- New In Practice about Stand Up to Cancer Dream Teams
- New Concluding Case: Excel Pro Drilling Systems

Chapter 15

- New Management Connection about Yahoo
- New example of Cisco
- New example of misperception when communicating with high-tech workers
- Updated emphasis on social media in discussion of electronic media as a communications channel
- New IBM example of managing excessive e-mail
- New In Practice about Automattic
- New example of Exelon
- New In Practice about communications by Kaiser Permanente's CEO
- New example of listening
- New example of horizontal communication at National Public Radio

Chapter 16

- New Management Connection about Best Buy
- New example of La-Z-Boy
- New example of BP
- New In Practice about McDonald's
- New description of after-action reviews
- New example of Virginia Mason Medical Center

- New description of sustainability audits and the triple bottom line
- Updated In Practice about the Ritz Carlton
- New example of Ethicon

Chapter 17

- New Management Connection about Tesla Motors
- New paragraph on disruptive innovation
- New example of forces for innovation in higher education
- New In Practice about Square mobile payments
- New example of Rethink Robotics
- New example of GE's ultra-tiny electronics cooling system
- New In Practice about manufacturing transformed by 3D printers
- New description of innovations as competency enhancing or competency destroying
- New example of acquisitions by Twitter
- New example of open innovation at Elmer's Products

Chapter 18

- New Management Connection about Time Warner
- New example of resistance to a change in banking: use of universal agents with broad job descriptions
- New In Practice about change to open workspaces at American Express and other companies
- New example of Envision
- New paragraph updating Kotter's model of change leadership for turbulent times
- New Concluding Case: EatWell Technologies

A Team Effort

This book is the product of a fantastic McGraw-Hill team. Moreover, we wrote this book believing that we are part of a team with the course instructor and with students. The entire team is responsible for the learning process.

Our goal, and that of your instructor, is to create a positive learning environment in which you can excel. But in the end, the raw material of this course is just words. It is up to you to use them as a basis for further thinking, deep learning, and constructive action.

What you do with the things you learn from this course, and with the opportunities the future holds, *counts*. As a manager, you can make a dramatic difference for yourself and for other people. What managers do matters *tremendously*.

Acknowledgments

This book could not have been written and published without the valuable contributions of many individuals.

Ingrid Benson and her colleagues at Words & Numbers were instrumental in creating a strong 11th edition. Many thanks for their meticulous attention to detail, ideas, and contributions. Ingrid has become a valued friend throughout the process; we couldn't have done it, or had as much fun, without Ingrid.

Special thanks to Lily Bowles, Taylor Gray, and Meg Nexsen for contributing their knowledge, insights, and research to Appendix B: Managing in Our Natural Environment.

Our reviewers over the last ten editions contributed time, expertise, and terrific ideas that significantly enhanced the quality of the text. The reviewers of the 11th edition are

Laura L. Alderson
University of Memphis
Daniel Arturo Cernas Ortiz
University of North Texas
Claudia S. Davis
Sam Houston State University
Greg Dickens
Sam Houston State University
Michael Drafke
College of DuPage
Judson Faurer
Metropolitan State University of Denver
Shirley Fedorovich
Embry-Riddle Aeronautical University
Randall Fletcher
Sinclair Community College
Rebecca M. Guidice
University of North Carolina-Wilmington
Dan Hallock
University of North Alabama
Ivan Franklin Harber, Jr.
Indian River State College
David Lynn Hoffman
Metropolitan State University of Denver
Cathleen Hohner
College of DuPage
Carrie Hurst
Tennessee State University
Jacquelyn D. Jacobs
University of Tennessee
Donald E. Kreps
Kutztown University
Christopher McChesney
Indian River State College

Jeffrey E. McGee
University of Texas at Arlington
Jane Murtaugh
College of DuPage
Mansour Sharifzadeh
Cal State Poly University-Pomona
Qiumei Xu
Northeastern Illinois University

Many individuals contributed directly to our development as textbook authors. Dennis Organ provided one of the authors with an initial opportunity and guidance in textbook writing. John Weimeister has been a friend and adviser from the very beginning. The entire McGraw-Hill Education team, starting with Executive Brand Manager Mike Ablassmeir (who spontaneously and impressively knew *Rolling Stone*'s top three drummers of all time) provided great support and expertise to this new edition. Many thanks to Managing Development Editor Christine Scheid for so much good work on previous editions and for continued friendship.

And to our superb Senior Development Editor Laura Griffin, and to Elizabeth Trepkowski, marketing manager, thank you for your skills, professionalism, collegiality, good fun, and for making the new edition *rock!* What a team!

Finally, we thank our families. Our parents, Jeanine and Tom Bateman and Clara and John Snell, provided us with the foundation on which we have built our careers. They continue to be a source of great support. Our wives, Mary Jo and Marybeth, demonstrated great encouragement, insight, and understanding throughout the process. Our children, Lauren, T. J., and James Bateman and Sara, Jack, and Emily Snell, inspire us in every way.

Thomas S. Bateman
Charlottesville, VA

Scott A. Snell
Charlottesville, VA

Bottom Line

Bottom Line

With increased competition from foreign and domestic companies, managers must pay particular attention to cost.
Does low cost mean low quality? Why or why not?

Bottom Line

The Internet lets customers quickly find products with the cost and quality features they want.
What might "flexible processes" mean for a fast-food restaurant? For an auto company?

Bottom Line

The ability to manufacture even customized products quickly has become a competitive requirement.
To meet this requirement, what qualities would a company need in its employees?

Bottom Line

Most creative ideas come not from the lone genius in the basement laboratory, but from people talking and working together.
Why is listening part of stimulating creativity?

Bottom Line

In all businesses—services as well as manufacturing—strategies that emphasize good customer service provide a critical competitive advantage.
Name a company that has delivered good customer service to you.

Bottom Line

As in this example, when you want to pursue sustainability, think in terms of the *long-term consequences* of your decisions.
What might be the long-term consequences of not investing in energy efficiency?

In this ever more competitive environment, there are six essential types of performance on which the organization beats, equals, or loses to the competition: cost, quality, speed, innovation, service, and sustainability. These six performance dimensions, when done well, deliver value to the customer and competitive advantage to you and your organization.

Throughout the text, Bateman and Snell remind students of these six dimensions and their impact on the bottom line with marginal icons. This results-oriented approach is a unique hallmark of this textbook.

Questions have also now been added to this edition to emphasize the bottom line further. Answers to these questions can be found in the Instructor's Manual.

In CASE You Haven't Noticed . . .

Bateman and Snell have once again put together an outstanding selection of case studies of various lengths that highlight companies' ups and downs, stimulate learning and understanding, and challenge students to respond.

Instructors will find a wealth of relevant and updated cases in every chapter, using companies—big and small—that students will enjoy learning about.

CHAPTER UNFOLDING CASES

Each chapter begins with a "Management Connection: Manager's Brief" section that describes an actual organizational situation, leader, or company. The Manager's Brief is referred to again within the chapter in the "Progress Report" section, showing the student how the chapter material relates back to the company, situation, or leader highlighted in the chapter opener. At the end of the chapter, the "Onward" section ties up loose ends and brings the material full circle for the student. Answers to Management Connection section questions can be found in the Instructor's Manual.

IN PRACTICE

In Practice boxes have been added to this edition to reinforce concepts learned in the chapter. Answers to In Practice box questions are also included in the Instructor's Manual.

CONCLUDING CASES

Each chapter ends with a case based on disguised but real companies and people that reinforces key chapter elements and themes.

SUPPLEMENTARY CASES

At the end of each part, an additional case is provided for professors who want students to delve further into part topics.

Assurance of Learning

① This 11th edition contains revised learning objectives for each chapter, and ② learning objectives are called out within the chapter where the content begins. ③ The summary for each chapter ties the learning objectives back together as well. ④ Our test bank provides tagging for the learning objective that the question covers, so instructors will be able to test material covering all learning objectives, thus ensuring that students have mastered the important topics.

ASSURANCE OF LEARNING READY

Many educational institutions today are focused on the notion of *assurance of learning*, an important element of some accreditation standards. The edition of *Management: Leading & Collaborating in a Competitive World* is designed specifically to support your assurance of learning initiatives with a simple yet powerful solution.

Each test bank question for *Management: Leading & Collaborating in a Competitive World*, 11e, maps to a specific chapter learning outcome/objective listed in the text. You can use our test bank software, EZ Test and EZ Test Online, or *Connect Management* to query easily for learning outcomes/objectives that directly relate to the learning objectives for your course. You can then use the reporting features of EZ Test to aggregate student results in similar fashion, making the collection and presentation of assurance of learning data simple and easy.

AACSB STATEMENT

The McGraw-Hill Companies are a proud corporate member of AACSB International. Understanding the importance and value of AACSB accreditation, *Management: Leading & Collaborating in a Competitive World*, 11e, recognizes the curricula guidelines detailed in the AACSB standards for business accreditation by connecting selected questions in the text and/or the test bank to the six general knowledge and skill guidelines in the AACSB standards.

The statements contained in *Management: Leading & Collaborating in a Competitive World*, 11e, are provided only as a guide for the users of this textbook. The AACSB leaves content coverage and assessment within the purview of individual schools, the mission of the school, and the faculty. Although this book and the teaching package make no claim of any specific AACSB qualification or evaluation, we have within *Management: Leading & Collaborating in a Competitive World*, 11e, labeled selected questions according to the six general knowledge and skills areas.

Outstanding Pedagogy

Management: Leading & Collaborating in a Competitive World is pedagogically stimulating and is intended to maximize student learning. With this in mind, we used a wide array of pedagogical features—some tried and true, others new and novel:

END-OF-CHAPTER ELEMENTS

- **Key terms** are page-referenced to the text and are part of the vocabulary-building emphasis. These terms are defined again in the glossary at the end of the book.

- A **Summary of Learning Objectives** provides clear, concise responses to the learning objectives, giving students a quick reference for reviewing the important concepts in the chapter.

- **Discussion Questions,** which follow the Summary of Learning Objectives, are thought-provoking questions on concepts covered in the chapter and ask for opinions on controversial issues.

- **Experiential Exercises** in each chapter bring key concepts to life so students can experience them firsthand.

Comprehensive Supplements

INSTRUCTOR'S MANUAL

Authored by Carrie Hurst, Tennessee State University, the Instructor's Manual was revised and updated to include thorough coverage of each chapter as well as time-saving features such as an outline, key student questions, class prep work assignments, guidance for using the unfolding cases, video supplements, and, finally, PowerPoint slides.

TEST BANK

The Test Bank includes more than 100 questions per chapter in a variety of formats. It has been revised for accuracy and expanded to include a greater variety of comprehension and application (scenario-based) questions as well as tagged with Bloom's Taxonomy levels and AACSB requirements. **EZ Test** is a flexible and easy-to-use electronic testing program that allows instructors to create tests from book-specific items. A downloadable desktop version can be found on the IRCD. And **EZ Test Online** (www.eztestonline. com) allows you to access the test bank from the OLC virtually anywhere and anytime. EZ Test–created exams and quizzes can be administered online, providing instant feedback for students.

POWERPOINT PRESENTATION SLIDES

Prepared by Brad Cox, Midlands Technical College, the PowerPoint presentation collection contains an easy-to-follow outline including figures downloaded from the text. In addition to providing lecture notes, the slides also include questions for class discussion as well as company examples not found in the textbook. This versatility allows you to create a custom presentation suitable for your own classroom experience.

MCGRAW-HILL *CONNECT MANAGEMENT*

LESS MANAGING. MORE TEACHING. GREATER LEARNING

McGraw-Hill *Connect Management* is an online assignment and assessment solution that connects students with the tools and resources they'll need to achieve success.

McGraw-Hill *Connect Management* helps prepare students for their future by enabling faster learning, more efficient studying, and higher retention of knowledge.

MCGRAW-HILL *CONNECT MANAGEMENT* FEATURES

Connect Management offers a number of powerful tools and features to make managing assignments easier, so faculty can spend more time teaching. With *Connect Management*, students can engage with their coursework anytime and anywhere, making the learning process more accessible and efficient. *Connect Management* offers you the features described next.

Diagnostic and Adaptive Learning of Concepts: LearnSmart Students want to make the best use of their study time. The LearnSmart adaptive self-study technology within *Connect Management* provides students with a seamless combination of practice, assessment, and remediation for every concept in the textbook. LearnSmart's intelligent software adapts to every student response and automatically delivers concepts that advance the student's understanding while reducing time devoted to the concepts already mastered. The result for every student is the fastest path to mastery of the chapter concepts.

- Applies an intelligent concept engine to identify the relationships between concepts and to serve new concepts to each student only when he or she is ready.

- Adapts automatically to each student, so students spend less time on the topics they understand and practice more those they have yet to master.

- Provides continual reinforcement and remediation but gives only as much guidance as students need.

- Integrates diagnostics as part of the learning experience.

- Enables you to assess which concepts students have efficiently learned on their own, thus freeing class time for more applications and discussion.

Online Interactives Online Interactives are engaging tools that teach students to apply key concepts in practice. These interactives provide them with immersive, experiential learning opportunities. Students will engage in a variety of interactive scenarios to deepen critical knowledge of key course topics. They receive immediate feedback at intermediate steps throughout each exercise as well as comprehensive feedback at the end of the assignment. All interactives are automatically scored and entered into the instructor grade book.

Lecture Capture via Tegrity Campus Increase the attention paid to lecture discussion by decreasing the attention paid to note taking. For an additional charge, Lecture Capture offers new ways for students to focus on the in-class discussion, knowing they can revisit important topics later.

McGraw-Hill *Connect Plus Management* McGraw-Hill reinvents the textbook learning experience for the modern student with *Connect Plus Management*. A seamless integration of an eBook and *Management*, *Connect Plus Management* provides all of the *Connect Management* features plus the following:

- An integrated eBook, allowing for anytime, anywhere access to the textbook.
- Dynamic links between the problems or questions you assign to your students and the location in the eBook where that problem or question is covered.
- A powerful search function to pinpoint and connect key concepts in a snap.

In short, *Connect Management* offers you and your students powerful tools and features that optimize your time and energies, enabling you to focus on course content, teaching, and student learning. *Connect Management* also offers a wealth of content resources for both instructors and students. This state-of-the-art, thoroughly tested system supports you in preparing students for the world that awaits.

For more information about *Connect*, go to www.mcgrawhillconnect.com or contact your local McGraw-Hill sales representative.

TEGRITY CAMPUS

Lectures 24/7: Tegrity Campus is a service that makes class time available 24/7 by automatically capturing every lecture in a searchable format for students to review when they study and complete assignments. With a simple one-click start-and-stop process, you capture all computer screens and corresponding audio. Students can replay any part of any class with easy-to-use browser-based viewing on a PC or Mac.

Educators know that the more students can see, hear, and experience class resources, the better they learn. In fact, studies prove it. With Tegrity Campus, students quickly recall key moments by using Tegrity Campus's unique search feature. This search helps students efficiently find what they need, when they need it, across an entire semester of class recordings. Help turn all your students' study time into learning moments immediately supported by your lecture. Lecture Capture enables you to

- Record and distribute your lecture with a click of a button.
- Record and index PowerPoint presentations and anything shown on your computer so it is easily searchable, frame by frame.
- Offer access to lectures anytime and anywhere by computer, iPod, or mobile device.
- Increase intent listening and class participation by easing students' concerns about note taking. Lecture Capture will make it more likely you will see students' faces, not the tops of their heads.

To learn more about Tegrity, watch a two-minute Flash demo at http://tegritycampus.mhhe.com.

Student Progress Tracking *Connect Management* keeps instructors informed about how each student, section, and class is performing, allowing for more productive use of lecture and office hours. The progress-tracking function enables you to

- View scored work immediately and track individual or group performance with assignment and grade reports.
- Access an instant view of student or class performance relative to learning objectives.
- Collect data and generate reports required by many accreditation organizations, such as AACSB.

Smart Grading When it comes to studying, time is precious. *Connect Management* helps students learn more efficiently by providing feedback and practice material when they need it, where they need it. When it comes to teaching, your time also is precious. The grading function enables you to

- Have assignments scored automatically, giving students immediate feedback on their work and side-by-side comparisons with correct answers.

- Access and review each response; manually change grades or leave comments for students to review.

- Reinforce classroom concepts with practice tests and instant quizzes.

Simple Assignment Management With *Connect Management*, creating assignments is easier than ever, so you can spend more time teaching and less time managing. The assignment management function enables you to

- Create and deliver assignments easily with selectable end-of-chapter questions and test bank items.

- Streamline lesson planning, student progress reporting, and assignment grading to make classroom management more efficient than ever.

- Go paperless with the eBook and online submission and grading of student assignments.

Instructor Library The *Connect Management* Instructor Library is your repository for additional resources to improve student engagement in and out of class. You can select and use any asset that enhances your lecture. The *Connect Management* Instructor Library includes

- Instructor Manual.
- PowerPoint files.
- Test Bank.
- Management Asset Gallery.
- eBook.

Student Study Center The *Connect Management* Student Study Center is the place for students to access additional resources. The Student Study Center

- Offers students quick access to lectures, practice materials, eBooks, and more.

- Provides instant practice material and study questions, easily accessible on the go.

- Gives students access to self-assessments, video materials, Manager's Hot Seat, and more.

eBOOK OPTIONS

eBooks are an innovative way for students to save money and to go green. McGraw-Hill's eBooks are typically 40 percent of the bookstore price. Students have the choice between an online and a downloadable CourseSmart eBook.

Through CourseSmart, students have the flexibility to access an exact replica of their textbook from any computer that has Internet service without plug-ins or special software via the online version or create a library of books on their hard drive via the downloadable version. Access to the CourseSmart eBooks lasts for one year.

Features CourseSmart eBooks allow students to highlight, take notes, organize notes, and share the notes with other CourseSmart users. Students can also search terms across all eBooks in their purchased CourseSmart library. CourseSmart eBooks can be printed (five pages at a time).

More Info and Purchase Please visit www.coursesmart.com for more information and to purchase access to our eBooks. CourseSmart allows students to try one chapter of the eBook, free of charge, before purchase.

Create

Craft your teaching resources to match the way you teach! With McGraw-Hill *Create*, www.mcgrawhillcreate.com, you can easily rearrange chapters, combine material from other content sources, and quickly upload content you have written, like your course syllabus or teaching notes. Find the content you need in *Create* by searching through thousands of leading McGraw-Hill textbooks. Arrange your book to fit your teaching style. *Create* even allows you to personalize your book's appearance by selecting the cover and adding your name, school, and course information. Order a *Create* book and you'll receive a complimentary print review copy in three to five business days or a complimentary electronic review copy (eComp) via e-mail in about one hour. Go to www.mcgrawhillcreate.com today and register. Experience how McGraw-Hill *Create* empowers you to teach *your* students *your* way.

McGraw-Hill Higher Education and Blackboard

McGraw-Hill Higher Education and Blackboard have teamed up. What does this mean for you?

1. **Your life, simplified.** Now you and your students can access McGraw-Hill's *Connect* and *Create* right from within your Blackboard course—all with one single sign-on. Say goodbye to the days of logging into multiple applications.

2. **Deep integration of content and tools.** Not only do you get single sign-on with *Connect* and *Create*, you also get deep integration of McGraw-Hill content and content engines right in Blackboard. Whether you're choosing a book for your course or building Connect assignments, all the tools you need are right where you want them—inside of Blackboard.

3. **Seamless gradebooks.** Are you tired of keeping multiple gradebooks and manually synchronizing grades into Blackboard? We thought so. When a student completes an integrated Connect assignment, the grade for that assignment automatically (and instantly) feeds your Blackboard grade center.

4. **A solution for everyone.** Whether your institution is already using Blackboard or you just want to try Blackboard on your own, we have a solution for you. McGraw-Hill and Blackboard can now offer you easy access to industry-leading technology and content, whether your campus hosts it or we do. Be sure to ask your local McGraw-Hill representative for details.

McGraw-Hill Customer Experience

At McGraw-Hill, we understand that getting the most from new technology can be challenging. That's why our services don't stop after you purchase our products. You can e-mail our product specialists 24 hours a day to get product training online. Or you can search our knowledge bank of frequently asked questions on our support website. For customer support, call **800-331-5094**, submit a support request using our contact us form, **http://mpss.mhhe.com/contact.php**, or visit **www.mhhe.com/support**. One of our technical support analysts will be able to assist you in a timely fashion.

The Management Asset Gallery

McGraw-Hill Management still provides a one-stop shop for our wealth of assets, making it quick and easy for instructors to locate specific materials to enhance their courses.

The Asset Gallery is intuitively organized and designed, allowing instructors ease of use in previewing our wealth of resources. These resources correlate with specific asset categories and more than 40 topics in management.

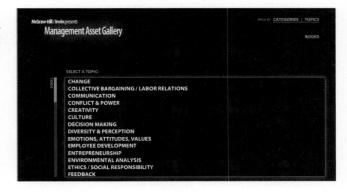

The Asset Gallery includes all of our non-text-specific management resources (Self-Assessments, Test Your Knowledge exercises, videos and information, additional group and individual exercises) along with supporting PowerPoint and Instructor Manual materials. Additionally, to help incorporate the assets in the classroom, a guide is provided specific to McGraw-Hill texts. Instructors can reach the Asset Gallery through a link from the Instructor area of the Online Learning Center or on the Connect library.

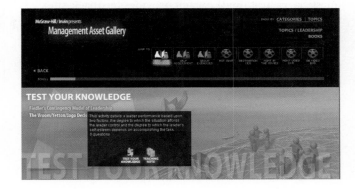

All of the following can be accessed within the Asset Gallery:

MANAGER'S HOT SEAT

This interactive, video-based application puts students in the manager's hot seat, building critical thinking and decision-making skills and allowing students to apply concepts to real managerial challenges. Students watch as 21 real managers apply their years of experience when confronting unscripted issues such as bullying in the workplace, cyber loafing, globalization, intergenerational work conflicts, workplace violence, and leadership versus management. In addition, Manager's Hot Seat interactive applications, featuring video cases and accompanying quizzes, can be found in Connect.

SELF-ASSESSMENT GALLERY

Unique among publisher-provided self-assessments, our 23 self-assessments provide students with background information to ensure that students understand the purpose of the assessment. Students test their values, beliefs, skills, and interests in a wide variety of areas allowing them to apply chapter content to their own lives and careers.

Every self-assessment is supported with PowerPoints and an instructor's manual in the Instructor & Student Asset Gallery, making it easy for the instructor to create an engaging classroom discussion surrounding the assessments.

TEST YOUR KNOWLEDGE

To help reinforce students' understanding of key management concepts, Test Your Knowledge activities give students a review of the conceptual materials followed by application-based questions to work through. Students can choose practice mode, which provides them with detailed feedback after each question, or test mode, which provides feedback after the entire test has been completed. Every Test Your Knowledge activity is supported by instructor notes in the Instructor & Student Asset Gallery to make it easy for the instructor to create engaging classroom discussions surrounding the materials students have completed.

MANAGEMENT HISTORY TIMELINE

This web application allows instructors to present and students to learn the history of management in an engaging and interactive way. Management history is presented along an intuitive timeline that can be traveled through sequentially or by selected decade. With the click of a mouse students learn the important dates, see the people who influenced the field, and understand the general management theories that have molded and shaped management as we know it today.

PRINCIPLES OF MANAGEMENT VIDEO DVD VOLUMES 1, 2, AND 3

More than 95 video clips from sources such as *BusinessWeek* Online, BBC, CBS, FiftyLessons, NBC, PBS, and McGraw-Hill are provided on three DVD sets. These company videos are organized by the four functions of management and feature companies such as AFLAC, Goldman Sachs, Google, IDEO, Zappos, PlayStation, Panera Bread, Patagonia, Mini Cooper, the Greater Chicago Food Depository, Employer-Subsidized Commuting, Grounded: Are U.S. Airlines Safe?, Using Facebook at Work, Adult Bullies, and Encore Careers in 2½- to 15-minute clips. Corresponding video cases and a guide that ties the videos closely to the chapter can be found in the Instructor's Manual and online.

Online Learning Center

WWW.MHHE.COM/BATEMAN11E

More and more students are studying online and on the go.

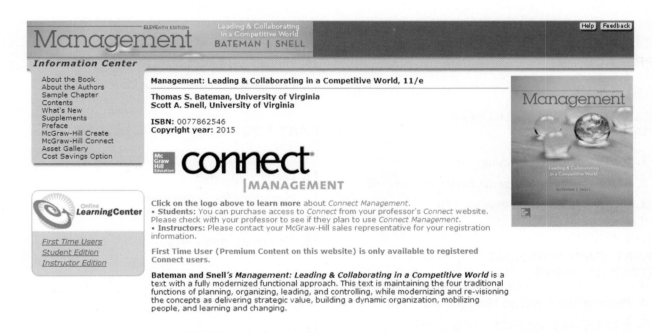

To obtain an instructor login for this Online Learning Center, ask your local sales representative. If you're an instructor thinking about adopting this textbook, request a free copy for review.

©2015 McGraw-Hill Higher Education
Any use is subject to the Terms of Use and Privacy Notice.
McGraw-Hill Higher Education is one of the many fine businesses of The McGraw-Hill Companies.

Brief Contents

Contents

PART ONE FOUNDATIONS OF MANAGEMENT

PART TWO PLANNING: DELIVERING STRATEGIC VALUE

PART THREE ORGANIZING: BUILDING A DYNAMIC ORGANIZATION

CHAPTER 11
Managing the Diverse Workforce 368

PART FOUR LEADING: MOBILIZING PEOPLE

CHAPTER 12
Leadership 404

CHAPTER 13
Motivating for Performance 438

PART FIVE   CONTROLLING: LEARNING AND CHANGING

The Management Process

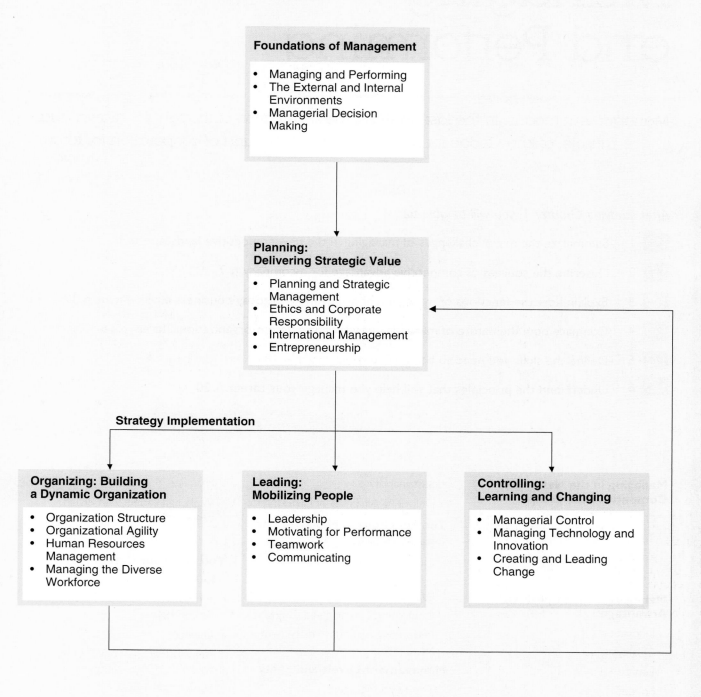

Foundations of Management

- Managing and Performing
- The External and Internal Environments
- Managerial Decision Making

Planning:
Delivering Strategic Value

- Planning and Strategic Management
- Ethics and Corporate Responsibility
- International Management
- Entrepreneurship

Strategy Implementation

Organizing: Building a Dynamic Organization

- Organization Structure
- Organizational Agility
- Human Resources Management
- Managing the Diverse Workforce

Leading:
Mobilizing People

- Leadership
- Motivating for Performance
- Teamwork
- Communicating

Controlling:
Learning and Changing

- Managerial Control
- Managing Technology and Innovation
- Creating and Leading Change

CHAPTER I

Managing and Performing

Management means, in the last analysis, the substitution of thought for brawn and muscle, of knowledge for folklore and tradition, and of cooperation for force.

— PETER DRUCKER

2

Management Connection

INTRODUCING THE BEST: AMAZON'S JEFF BEZOS

What does a well-run company look like? You might say that it is popular or that its sales are high, but these can be fleeting things. You could say that it has a famous brand or a prominent leader, but familiar brands and well-publicized leaders can fall from grace. You can say that a well-managed company makes a big profit, but most business experts agree that a better measure of success is the company's long-term value.

Using long-term value as the performance measure, three professors writing for *Harvard Business Review* identified the best-performing chief executive officers (CEOs), or top managers. For each company's CEO, they looked at how the company's value changed while that person held the top job. By that measure, the best living CEO was Jeffrey P. Bezos of online retailer Amazon (number two after Apple's Steve Jobs, who recently succumbed to cancer). Since 1996, Amazon under Bezos has delivered returns of 12,266 percent on shareholders' investments, and the company's value has risen by $111 billion.

To generate such breathtaking growth, Bezos has to get a lot of things right. As an early entrant into the then-revolutionary online marketplace, he was a visionary about the Internet's potential. At the same time, Bezos has consistently insisted to investors and employees that the company would take a long-term view, recognizing that the smartest innovations may take time to pay off. (This is especially true given Amazon's practice of keeping costs and prices as low as possible.)

But innovation alone isn't Amazon's secret. Bezos sets the tone for the company by insisting on a customers-first outlook. Putting customers first has led to some decisions that at first seemed a little crazy to outsiders.

Why would a bookseller offer an e-reader, the Kindle, if it would reduce book sales? Why would an online store create the Amazon Marketplace, where competing retailers can sell their products? The answer, says Bezos, is that those innovations benefit customers. And so far, they seem to drive ever more shoppers to Amazon, where they download e-books *and* buy print books and where they enjoy the convenience of buying an extremely broad range of goods from many sellers without Amazon needing to build more warehouses.

If you listen to Bezos, this story is all about the customer. If you are a store owner, it also is about a formidable, game-changing global competitor that didn't exist two decades ago but today sells more than $48 billion a year. And, finally, it is a story about managers like Bezos figuring out how to build something amazing in a fast-changing world.[1]

As you read this chapter, notice the wide variety of skills that Jeff Bezos needs to help Amazon meet its goals. Also, think about how managing people, money, and other resources enables Amazon and other organizations to accomplish far more than individuals acting independently could ever achieve.

Amazon's CEO, Jeff Bezos, is one of the most interesting leaders in business today. He is an innovator who combines financial know-how with a vision for the future of technology and an unswerving drive to serve customers. Together, those qualities have helped him build a business idea into a major corporation that continues to transform industry.

Bezos and the other top business leaders identified by *Harvard Business Review* are chief executives who have been far more than a flashy presence in the media; they have delivered strong performance over years at the helm. In the 2013 rankings, number one was no surprise: Steve Jobs, who took over Apple in 1997 when the company was in bad shape and then led the company to sterling returns and market value year after year. After Jobs and Bezos, other top CEOs on the list were Samsung's Yun Jong-Yong (number 3), eBay's Meg Whitman (number 9), and Cisco Systems' John Chambers (number 10).[2]

Consider Groupon as a contrasting example. You might have been one of its many fans if you like low prices for local goods and services. The new company was booming as it strived to become the Amazon.com of local commerce, but then its performance collapsed, and the board in 2013 fired CEO and cofounder Andrew Mason. Why did the popular company fall into such disfavor? Answers to questions like this are rarely simple, but Groupon's great deals brought businesses new one-time customers wanting rock-bottom prices, angering customers who paid full price. Not enough customers returned.

In business, there is no alternative to managing well. Companies may fly high for a while, but they cannot do well for very long without good management. It's the same for individuals: the best managers succeed by focusing on fundamentals, knowing what's important, and managing well. The aim of this book is to help you succeed in those pursuits.

Managing in the New Competitive Landscape

When the economy is soaring, business seems easy. Starting an Internet company looked easy in the 1990s, and ventures related to the real estate boom looked like a sure thing just a few years ago. But investors grew wary of dot-com start-ups, and the demand for new homes dropped off the table when the economy crashed in late 2008. At such times, it becomes evident that management is a challenge requiring knowledge and skills to adapt to new circumstances.

What defines the competitive landscape of today's business? You will be reading about many relevant issues in the coming chapters, but we begin here by highlighting four ongoing challenges that characterize the current business landscape: globalization, technological change, the importance of knowledge and ideas, and collaboration across organizational boundaries.

> Management is a challenge requiring knowledge and skills to adapt to new circumstances.

Globalization

Far more than in the past, today's enterprises are global, with offices and production facilities in countries all over the world. Corporations operate worldwide, transcending national borders. Companies that want to grow often need to tap international markets, where incomes are rising and demand is increasing. The change from a local to a global marketplace is gaining momentum and is irreversible.[3]

Fortune magazine annually publishes a list of the world's most admired companies. Whereas U.S. companies used to dominate, Switzerland-based Nestlé was the most admired maker of consumer food products in 2012, and Germany's Volkswagen was the most admired producer of motor vehicles. The company rated best in global competitiveness was Spain's Gas Natural Fenosa, followed by McDonald's and Nestlé.[4] Who are other or more recent leaders?

Globalization also means that a company's talent and competition can come from anywhere. As with its sales, more than half of GE's employees live outside the United States.[5] Hollywood film studios now hire actors and choose locations in markets outside the United States; two-thirds of total box office receipts now often come from overseas (for *Life of Pi*, it was four-fifths). Bollywood movies produced in India are competing and performing at record levels, and Nollywood (Nigerian Hollywood) is now bigger than Bollywood on a per capita basis.[6]

Globalization has changed the face of the workforce. Management in this new competitive landscape will need to attract and effectively manage a talent pool from all over the globe.

PepsiCo's chief executive, Indra Nooyi, brings a much-needed global viewpoint to a company whose international business has been growing three times faster than sales in the United States. Nooyi, who was raised in India and educated there and in the United States, has steered the company toward more "better for you" and "good for you" snacks with acquisitions including a nut packager in Bulgaria and a hummus producer in Israel.[7]

Meanwhile Coca-Cola has higher sales in Mexico than in any other country at 665 servings per year per capita. In Kenya, the rate is 39 servings per year per capita. Coca-Cola is already Africa's largest employer, and the continent is a key to Coke's future growth. Coke's CEO Muhtar Kent says, "Africa is the untold story, and could be the big story, of the next decade, like India and China were this past decade."[8]

Globalization affects small companies as well as large. Many small companies export their goods. Many domestic firms assemble their products in other countries. And companies are under pressure to improve their products in the face of intense competition from foreign manufacturers. Firms today must ask themselves, "How can we be the best in the world?"

For students, it's not too early to think about the personal ramifications. In the words of CEO Jim Goodnight of SAS, the largest privately held software company in the world, "The best thing business schools can do to prepare their students is to encourage them to look beyond their own backyards. Globalization has opened the world for many opportunities, and schools should encourage their students to take advantage of them."[9]

Technological Change

The Internet's impact on globalization is only one of the ways that technology is vitally important in the business world. Technology both complicates things and creates new opportunities. The challenges come from the rapid rate at which communication, transportation, information, and other technologies change.[10] For example, after just a couple of decades of widespread desktop use, customers switched to laptop models, which require different accessories.[11] Any company that served desktop users had to rethink its customers' wants and needs, not to mention the possibility that these customers are now working at the airport or a local Starbucks outlet rather than in an office.

Later chapters discuss technology further, but here we highlight the rise of the Internet and its effects. Why is the Internet so important to business?[12] It is a marketplace, a means for manufacturing goods and services, a distribution channel, an information service, and more. It drives down costs and speeds up globalization. It improves efficiency of decision making. It facilitates design of new products, from pharmaceuticals to financial services. Managers can watch and learn what other companies are doing—on the other side of the world. Although these advantages create business opportunities, they also create threats as competitors sometimes capitalize on new developments more than you do.

Things continue to change at breakneck speed. In 2003, tech guru Tim O'Reilly coined the term "Web 2.0" to describe the exciting new wave of social networking start-ups that allow users to publish and share information. But most failed or are stalled; very few, other than Facebook, make a profit.[13] Nevertheless, Web 2.0 not only is a continuing reality, it is redefining the ways that customers and sellers, employees and employers are sharing knowledge. (And the saying is true: knowledge really is power.) Looking forward, the managers of the future will take Web 2.0 for granted and must be ready for Web 3.0, whatever that might turn out to be.

Knowledge Management

Companies and managers need good new ideas. Because companies in advanced economies have become so efficient at producing physical goods, most workers have been freed up to provide services or "abstract goods" such as software, entertainment, data, and advertising. Efficient factories with fewer workers produce the cereals and cell phones the market demands; meanwhile, more and more workers create software and invent new goods and services. These workers, whose primary contributions are ideas and problem-solving expertise, are often referred to as *knowledge workers*. Managing these workers poses some particular challenges, which we examine throughout this book. For example, determining whether they are doing a good job can be difficult because the manager cannot simply count or measure a knowledge worker's output. Also, these workers often are most motivated to do their best when the work is interesting, not because of a carrot or stick dangled by the manager.[14]

knowledge management

Practices aimed at discovering and harnessing an organization's intellectual resources.

Because the success of modern businesses so often depends on the knowledge used for innovation and the delivery of services, organizations need to manage that knowledge. **Knowledge management** is the set of practices aimed at discovering and harnessing an organization's intellectual resources—fully using the intellects of the organization's people. Knowledge management is about finding, unlocking, sharing, and altogether capitalizing on the most precious resources of an organization: people's expertise, skills, wisdom, and relationships.

Knowledge managers find these human assets, help people collaborate and learn, help people generate new ideas, and harness those ideas into successful innovations.

In hospitals, important knowledge includes patients' histories, doctors' orders, billing information, dietary requirements, prescriptions administered, and much more. With lives at stake, many hospitals have embraced knowledge management. For example, at Virginia Commonwealth University (VCU) Health System, a single information system lets doctors write prescriptions, look up patient information and lab results, and consult with one another. Billing also is automated as part of VCU's knowledge management system, making the process more efficient and connecting with patient data so that it can remind the physician of all the conditions being treated—and billed for.[15] Hospitals can also give patients access to the knowledge management system so that they can schedule appointments, request prescription refills, and send questions to their doctors.

Collaboration across Boundaries

One of the most important processes of knowledge management is to ensure that people in different parts of the organization collaborate effectively with one another. This requires productive communications among different departments, divisions, or other subunits of the organization. For example, "T-shaped" managers break out of the traditional corporate hierarchy to share knowledge freely across the organization (the horizontal part of the T) while remaining committed to the bottom-line performance of their individual business units (the vertical part). This emphasis on dual responsibilities for performance and knowledge sharing occurs at pharmaceutical giant GlaxoSmithKline, large German industrial company Siemens, and London-based steelmaker Ispat International.[16]

For example, Toyota keeps its product development process efficient by bringing together design engineers and manufacturing employees from the very beginning. Often, manufacturing employees can see ways to simplify a design so that it is easier to make without defects or unnecessary costs. Toyota expects its employees to listen to input from all areas of the organization, so this type of collaboration is a natural part of the organization's culture. Employees use software to share their knowledge—best practices they have developed for design and manufacturing.[17] Thus, at Toyota, knowledge management supports collaboration and vice versa.

Collaboration across boundaries occurs even beyond the boundaries of the organization itself. Companies today must motivate and capitalize on the ideas of people outside the organization. Customers, for instance, can be collaborators. Companies must realize that the need to serve the customer drives everything else.

In the Web 2.0 era, customers *expect* to share their ideas and be heard. Companies collaborate with their customers by actively and continuously listening and responding. L.L. Bean, for example, tracks customer comments and reviews on its website; if any product averages fewer than three stars out of five, the company removes it and directs the product manager to resolve the problem.[18] Businesses also pay attention to customer comments on Amazon, Zappos, Yelp, TripAdvisor, Facebook, Twitter, and many more. Customer feedback management software can search these and other sites and generate statistics and reports.

Managing for Competitive Advantage

The rise of the Internet turned careers (and lives) upside down. Students dropped out of school to join Internet start-ups or start their own. Managers in big corporations quit their jobs to do the same. Investors salivated, and invested heavily. The risks were often ignored or downplayed—sometimes tragically as the boom went bust. Or consider an earlier industry with similar transforming power: automobiles. There have been at least 2,000 car makers—how many remain?

What is the lesson to be learned from the failures in these important transformational industries? A key to understanding the success of a company—whether traditional, Internet-based, or a combination of both—is not just how much the industry in which it operates will affect society or how much it will grow. The key is the competitive advantage a particular company holds and how well it can sustain that advantage.

To survive and win over time, you have to gain and sustain advantages over your competitors. You gain competitive advantage by being better than your competitors at doing valuable things for your customers. But what does this mean, specifically? To succeed, managers must deliver performance. The fundamental success drivers of performance are innovation, quality, service, speed, cost competitiveness, and sustainability.

Innovation

Companies must continually innovate. **Innovation** is the introduction of new goods and services. Your firm must adapt to changes in consumer demands and to new competitors. Products don't sell forever; in fact, they don't sell for nearly as long as they used to because so many competitors are introducing so many new products all the time. Your firm must innovate, or it will die. Likewise, you have to be ready with new ways to communicate with customers and deliver the products to them. When the internet allowed merchants to bypass traditional distribution channels and reach buyers directly, traditional marketers had to learn how to innovate to remain competitive.

Innovation isn't all about tech products. Dunkin' Brands Culinary Innovation Team is a group of 18 chefs led by executive chef Stan Frankenthaler. They send out about 20 new product launches to market each year for Dunkin' Donuts and

 LO 2

Bottom Line
Because it's easy for managers to get so caught up in being busy, get distracted, and lose sight of what really drives performance, you will periodically see icons as bottom-line reminders of the need for innovation, quality, service, speed, cost competitiveness, and sustainability.
Which of these advantages do you think would be hard to deliver at the same time?

innovation

The introduction of new goods and services.

Baskin-Robbins in a constant effort to boost revenues and profits. Bagel twists are a recent success; whole wheat donuts are not. The team is working long-term to create a zero-grams trans-fat menu.[19]

The need for innovation is driven in part by globalization. One obvious reason is that facilities in other countries can manufacture appliances or write software code at a lower cost than facilities in the United States; U.S. facilities thus operate at a disadvantage. Therefore, they must provide something their foreign competitors can't—and often that requires delivering something new. This is a challenge as developing nations such as China increase their engineering prowess. Philips, which started out making light bulbs in the Netherlands in the 1890s, has set up research as well as manufacturing operations in China because that country is becoming a key source of technical know-how, not just cheap labor.[20] Nevertheless, as labor and other costs rise overseas, and as U.S. companies find ways to improve efficiency at home, the future for North American facilities is brightening. Nissan, for example, has expanded production in Smyrna, Tennessee, including assembly of its Infiniti JX luxury car and Leaf electric car. Other companies that have announced plans to expand in the U.S., especially in the South, include Toyota, General Motors, Ford, and Honda.[21]

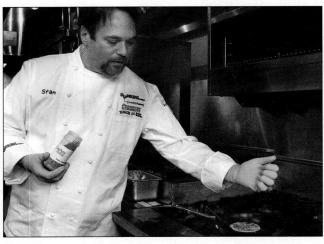

Stan Frankenthaler, executive chef at Dunkin' Brands, tests omelette recipes in the test kitchen. The Culinary Innovation Team is constantly trying out new ideas.

Innovation is today's holy grail (2013's number one most admired company in *Fortune*'s innovativeness category was Apple, and number two was Amazon).[22] Like the other sources of competitive advantage, innovation comes from people, it must be a strategic goal, and it must be managed properly. Later chapters show you how great companies innovate.

Quality

When Spectrum Health, a hospital chain based in Grand Rapids, Michigan, asked patients how well they were served, patients rated staff low on helpfulness and their attitude toward visitors and said they didn't get good information about procedures or how to take care of themselves after being released to go home. Spectrum set up an advisory council of patients and family members, making visiting hours more flexible, getting patient input into who was allowed to hear medical information and make decisions about treatment, and calling discharged patients at home to make sure they understood the directions they had received. Satisfaction scores of Spectrum patients improved dramatically.[23]

quality

The excellence of your product (goods or services).

Spectrum Health's efforts reflect a commitment to quality. In general, **quality** is the excellence of your product. The importance of quality and the standards for acceptable quality have increased dramatically in recent years. Customers now demand high-quality goods and services, and often they will accept nothing less.

Historically, quality pertained primarily to the physical goods that customers bought, and it referred to attractiveness, lack of defects, reliability, and long-term dependability. The traditional approach to quality was to check work after it was completed and then eliminate defects, using inspection and statistical data to determine whether products were up to standards. But then W. Edwards Deming, J. M. Juran, and other quality gurus convinced managers to take a more complete approach to achieving *total* quality. This includes *preventing* defects before they occur, *achieving zero defects* in manufacturing, and *designing* products for quality. The goal is to solve and eradicate from the beginning all quality-related problems and to live a philosophy of *continuous improvement* in the way the company operates.[24]

ed t gotg

Quality is further provided when companies customize goods and services to the wishes of the individual consumer. Choices at Starbucks give consumers thousands of variations on the drinks they can order, whether it's half-caff or all caffeine, skim milk or soy milk, or shots of espresso and any of a variety of flavored syrups. For a premium price, candy lovers can select M&M's candies bearing the message of their own creation.[25] Similarly, Jones Soda Company lets visitors to its website order a 12-pack of soda with their photo on the bottles. They upload the photo to the myJones website (www.myjones.com) and choose a soda flavor.[26]

Providing world-class quality requires a thorough understanding of what quality really is.[27] Quality can be measured in terms of product performance, customer service, reliability (avoidance of failure or breakdowns), conformance to standards, durability, and aesthetics. Only when you move beyond broad, generic concepts such as "quality" and identify specific quality requirements can you identify problems, target needs, set performance standards more precisely, and deliver world-class value.

> Providing world-class quality requires a thorough understanding of what quality really is.

By the way, *Fortune* magazine's 2013 number one company for quality of products and services was Apple; Norstrom was number two.

Service

As noted, important quality measures often pertain to the service customers receive. This dimension of quality is particularly important because the service sector has come to dominate the U.S. economy. In recent years, the fastest-growing job categories have been almost entirely services and retailing jobs, and the jobs with the greatest declines are primarily in manufacturing (although some manufacturing is returning to the U.S.).[28] Services include intangible products such as insurance, hotel accommodations, medical care, and haircuts.

Service means giving customers what they want or need, when they want it. So service is focused on continually meeting the needs of customers to establish mutually beneficial long-term relationships. Thus software companies, in addition to providing the actual programs, may help their customers identify requirements, set up computer systems, and perform maintenance.

An important dimension of service quality is making it easy and enjoyable for customers to experience a service or to buy and use products. The Detroit Institute of Arts recently hired a manager formerly with the Ritz-Carlton hotel chain, noted for its exceptional level of service, to be vice president of museum operations. As the art museum prepared for a grand reopening following a major renovation, the manager analyzed the types of customer interactions that occur in a museum, identifying ways to make the experience more pleasant. He also worked with his staff to identify ways to customize services, such as offering tours tailored to the interests of particular groups.[29]

service

The speed and dependability with which an organization delivers what customers want.

Speed

Google constantly improves its search product at a rapid rate. In fact, its entire culture is based on rapid innovation. Sheryl Sandberg, a Google vice president, once made a mistake because she was moving too fast to plan carefully. Although the mistake cost the company a few million dollars, Google cofounder Larry Page responded to her explanation and apology by saying he was actually glad she had made the mistake. It showed that she appreciated the company's values. Page told Sandberg, "I want to run a company where we are moving too quickly and doing too much, not being too cautious and doing too little. If we don't have any of these mistakes, we're just not taking enough risks."[30]

Although it's unlikely that Google actually favors mistakes over moneymaking ideas, Page's statement expressed an appreciation that in the modern business

speed

Fast and timely execution, response, and delivery.

environment, **speed**—rapid execution, response, and delivery—often separates the winners from the losers. How fast can you develop and get a new product to market? How quickly can you respond to customer requests? You are far better off if you are faster than the competition—and if you can respond quickly to your competitors' actions.

Speed isn't everything—you can't get sloppy in your quest to be first. But other things being equal, faster companies are more likely to be the winners, slow ones the losers. Even pre-Internet, companies were getting products to market and in the hands of customers faster than ever. Now the speed requirement has increased exponentially. Everything, it seems, is on fast-forward.

Speed is no longer just a goal of some companies; it is a strategic imperative. In the auto industry, getting faster is essential just for keeping up with the competition. A recent study found that employees at Ford's assembly plant in Atlanta needed just 15.4 hours to assemble a vehicle. Compare that with the 1980s, when GM employees needed 40 hours to assemble a vehicle.[31] Another important measure of speed in the auto industry is the time the company takes to go from product concept to availability of the vehicle in the showroom. During the 1980s, that time was about 30 or 40 months. Today, Toyota has cut the process to an average of 24 months.[32]

Walmart's goal is to provide products at low costs to retain its large customer base. To remain successful and cost competitive, it has devised and followed through with many plans to lower its operational costs.

Cost Competitiveness

Walmart keeps driving hard to find new ways to cut billions of dollars from its already very low distribution costs. It leads the industry in efficient distribution, but competitors are copying Walmart's methods, so the efficiency no longer gives it as much of an advantage.[33] Walmart has sought to keep costs down by scheduling store employees more efficiently. It introduced a computerized system that schedules employees based on each store's sales, transactions, units sold, and customer traffic. The system is intended to schedule just enough workers, with full staffing only at the busiest times of day and days of the week, so it requires more flexibility from Walmart's employees.[34]

Walmart's efforts are aimed at **cost competitiveness,** which means keeping costs low enough so that the company can realize profits and price its products (goods or services) at levels that are attractive to consumers. Needless to say, if you can offer a desirable product at a lower price, it is more likely to sell.

Singapore Airlines, one of the world's most admired companies, kept profiting during the economic recession while the global airline industry lost money. It did so by cutting costs more strategically than the competition. While competitors cut prices and still didn't fill their planes (and risked a backlash to later price hikes), SA slashed flights, parked planes, and reduced salaries, including the CEO's.[35]

In contrast to the high-quality, even luxurious flying experience offered by Singapore Airlines, Ryanair is a European low-cost airline. *Bloomberg BusinessWeek* reported that CEO Michael O'Leary was "remaking commercial air travel in his image: shabby, crabby, and cheap, cheap, cheap." O'Leary thought that short flights need only one toilet, and every flight needs only one pilot because the computer or a trained member of the cabin crew can fly if necessary. Less frighteningly, he believed that commercial air passengers do not need free pillows, blankets, and snacks; they just want to arrive at their destination cheaply and with their luggage. His vision is for profits to come

cost competitiveness

Keeping costs low to achieve profits and be able to offer prices that are attractive to consumers.

from inflight sales, high luggage fees, low-cost secondary airports, and commissions on travel products sold through the airline's website.[36]

One reason every company must worry about cost is that consumers can easily compare prices on the Internet from thousands of competitors. Consumers looking to buy popular items, such as cameras, printers, and plane fares, can go online to research the best models and the best deals. If you can't cut costs and offer attractive prices, you can't compete.

Sustainability

Avoiding wasteful use of energy can bolster a company's financial performance while being kind to the environment. Efforts to cut energy waste are just one way to achieve an important form of competitive advantage: **sustainability,** which at its most basic is the effort to minimize the use and loss of resources, especially those that are polluting and nonrenewable.

Although sustainability means different things to different people,[37] in this text, we emphasize a long-term perspective on sustaining the natural environment and building tomorrow's business opportunities while managing today's business.[38] In the United States, corporate efforts aimed at sustainability have fluctuated somewhat as environmental laws are strengthened or loosened; overall, the worldwide trend has been in the direction of greater concern for sustainability. The clashes among the rising demand for resources, limited supplies, and changing social attitudes toward environmental protection mean that the coming decade is likely to have greater focus on resource productivity, the emergence of clean-tech industries, and regulation.[39]

As many companies have discovered, addressing that concern often produces bottom-line benefits. Companies with strong sustainability performance that have also become financial winners include athletic-shoe maker Adidas, Spanish fashion group Inditex, French luxury-goods maker Hermès International, and Eaton, a power management company.[40]

sustainability

The effort to minimize the use and loss of resources, especially those that are polluting and nonrenewable.

In Practice

GE'S ENERGY EFFICIENCY EFFORTS

As GE's chief technology officer, Mark Little is charged with finding ways to make the company and its customers more energy-efficient. Although these improvements save money and boost profits, they also help the planet.

Under Little, the 2,600 employees in GE's global research division have found ways that technology can lower emissions and make more efficient use of electricity. In addition, clean-energy projects are improving the ability to get power from wind and solar energy. In the case of wind energy, for example, Little notes that over the past decade, GE has improved what was an expensive, low-performing technology to the point of building a $7.5 billion business. And its products for electric vehicles such as the Nissan Leaf and vehicle charging stations are positioning the company to be part of what Little expects will become an important business in the long term.

With a big corporation such as GE, small improvements in performance can multiply to generate huge savings. When GE improves the fuel efficiency of a jet engine by 15 percent, that savings is spread to every aircraft using the engine. In the case of electric vehicles, Little recently noted that when GE invests $1 in an electric vehicle, that translates to about 10 cents of content. Ten cents isn't much, but 10 percent of every electric vehicle could become a fortune.[41]

- How can the other performance factors—innovation, quality, service, speed, and cost competitiveness—help GE gain a sustainability advantage?

Patagonia Sur is a for-profit company that has created the first private land trust in Patagonia to protect the company's land permanently; it plans to create up to 10 profitable, environmentally sustained businesses on that land.[42] The goals are to apply free-market forces to develop the land for profit, do no harm, and spread this radically different land management model to developing nations around the world.

Sustainability is about protecting our options.[43] Done properly, sustainability allows people to live and work in ways that can be maintained over the long term (generations) without depleting or harming our environmental, social, and economic resources. In 2012, the number one company for responsibility to the community and environment was GDF Suez, an energy company headquartered in France. What companies can you think of that are great, and not so great, in their sustainability practices?

Delivering All Types of Performance

Don't assume that you can settle for delivering just one of the six competitive advantages: low cost alone, or quality alone, for example. The best managers and companies perform on all of these criteria.

Virginia Mason Medical Center, like many hospitals, felt challenged in delivering low costs along with high quality and superior services. Virginia Mason has a reputation for high-quality care, but it was losing money treating certain patients. So Virginia Mason collaborated with Aetna, an insurer that pays for 10 percent of the medical center's business, and found ways to treat some of the most expensive conditions so that they became more economical to insure but were paid for at higher rates that would be profitable for Virginia Mason. The medical center has also improved quality through measures that enhance speed—in this case, cutting waiting times for patients, such as a reduction in the four-hour wait for chemotherapy to 90 minutes.[44]

Trade-offs may occur among the six sources of competitive advantage, but this doesn't need to be a zero-sum game in which one has to suffer at the expense of another.

Bottom Line

Don't focus on one aspect of performance and neglect the others. You might be better at or more interested in one than the others, but you should strive for all six.

Imagine you're in your first management job, supervising a team. What would be your natural tendency? Which performance measures would you focus on, and why? How can you be sure to pay attention to all of them?

The Functions of Management

management

The process of working with people and resources to accomplish organizational goals.

Management is the process of working with people and resources to accomplish organizational goals. Good managers do those things both effectively and efficiently. To be *effective* is to achieve organizational goals. To be *efficient* is to achieve goals with minimal waste of resources—that is, to make the best possible use of money, time, materials, and people. Some managers fail on both criteria, or focus on one at the expense of another. The best managers achieve high performance by focusing on both effectiveness *and* efficiency. These definitions have been around for a long time. But as you know, business is changing radically. The real issue is how to *do* these things.[45]

Although the context of business and the specifics of doing business are changing, there are still plenty of timeless principles that make great managers, and great companies, great. While fresh thinking and new approaches are required now more than ever, much of what has already been learned about successful management practices remains relevant, useful, and adaptable, with fresh thinking, to the 21st century business environment.

In the business world today, great executives not only adapt to changing conditions but also apply—fanatically, rigorously, consistently, and with discipline—the fundamental management principles.

These fundamentals include the four traditional functions of management: *planning, organizing, leading,* and *controlling.* They remain as relevant as ever, and they still provide the fundamentals that are needed in start-ups as much as in established corporations. But their form has evolved.

Planning: Delivering Strategic Value

Planning is specifying the goals to be achieved and deciding in advance the appropriate actions needed to achieve those goals. Planning activities include analyzing current situations, anticipating the future, determining objectives, deciding in what types of activities the company will engage, choosing corporate and business strategies, and determining the resources needed to achieve the organization's goals. Plans set the stage for action and for major achievements.

The planning function for the new business environment, discussed in Part 2 of this book, is more dynamically described as *delivering strategic value.* **Value** is a complex concept.[46] Fundamentally, it describes the monetary amount associated with how well a job, task, good, or service meets users' needs. Those users might be business owners, customers, employees, society, and even nations. The better you meet those needs (in terms of quality, speed, efficiency, and so on), the more value you deliver. That value is strategic when it contributes to meeting the organization's goals. On a personal level, you will do well when you periodically ask yourself and your boss, "How can I add value?" Answering that question will enhance your contributions, your job performance, and your career.

Historically, planning described a top-down approach in which top executives establish business plans and tell others to implement them. Now and in the future, delivering strategic value is a continual process in which people throughout the organization use their brains and the brains of customers, suppliers, and other stakeholders to identify opportunities to create, seize, strengthen, and sustain competitive advantage. This dynamic process swirls around the objective of creating more and more value for the customer. Effectively creating value requires fully considering a new and changing set of stakeholders and issues, including the government, the natural environment, globalization, and the dynamic economy in which ideas are king and entrepreneurs are both formidable competitors and potential collaborators. You learn about these and related topics in Chapter 4 (planning and strategic management), Chapter 5 (ethics and corporate responsibility), Chapter 6 (international management), and Chapter 7 (entrepreneurship).

> You will do well when you periodically ask yourself and your boss, "How can I add value?"

Organizing: Building a Dynamic Organization

Organizing is assembling and coordinating the human, financial, physical, informational, and other resources needed to achieve goals. Organizing activities include attracting people to the organization, specifying job responsibilities, grouping jobs into work units, marshaling and allocating resources, and creating conditions so that people and things work together to achieve maximum success.

Part 3 of the book describes the organizing function as *building a dynamic organization.* Historically, organizing involved creating an organization chart by identifying business functions, establishing reporting relationships, and having a personnel department that administered plans, programs, and paperwork. Now and in the

planning

The management function of systematically making decisions about the goals and activities that an individual, a group, a work unit, or the overall organization will pursue.

value

The monetary amount associated with how well a job, task, good, or service meets users' needs.

organizing

The management function of assembling and coordinating human, financial, physical, informational, and other resources needed to achieve goals.

future, effective managers will be using new forms of organizing and viewing their people as perhaps their most valuable resources. They will build organizations that are flexible and adaptive, particularly in response to competitive threats and customer needs. Progressive human resource practices that attract and retain the very best of a highly diverse population will be essential aspects of the successful company. You learn about these topics in Chapter 8 (organization structure), Chapter 9 (organizational agility), Chapter 10 (human resources management), and Chapter 11 (managing the diverse workforce).

Shona Brown, now a consultant after 10 years at Google, says, "The company's goal is to determine precisely the amount of management it needs—and then use a little bit less."

leading

The management function that involves the manager's efforts to stimulate high performance by employees.

Leading: Mobilizing People

Leading is stimulating people to be high performers. It includes motivating and communicating with employees, individually and in groups. Leading involves close day-to-day contact with people, helping to guide and inspire them toward achieving team and organizational goals. Leading takes place in teams, departments, and divisions as well as at the tops of large organizations.

In earlier textbooks, the leading function described how managers motivate workers to come to work and execute top management's plans by doing their jobs. Today and in the future, managers must be good at mobilizing people to contribute their ideas—to use their brains in ways never needed or dreamed of in the past.

As described in Part 4, managers must rely on a very different kind of leadership (Chapter 12) that empowers and motivates people (Chapter 13). Far more than in the past, great work must be done via great teamwork (Chapter 14), both within work groups and across group boundaries. Ideally, underlying these processes will be effective interpersonal and organizational communication (Chapter 15).

controlling

The management function of monitoring performance and making needed changes.

Controlling: Learning and Changing

Planning, organizing, and leading do not guarantee success. The fourth function, **controlling,** monitors performance and implements necessary changes. By controlling, managers make sure the organization's resources are being used as planned and that the organization is meeting its goals such as quality and safety.

When managers implement their plans, they often find that things are not working out as planned. The controlling function makes sure that goals are met. It asks and answers the question, "Are our actual outcomes consistent with our goals?" It then makes adjustments as needed.

Successful organizations, large and small, pay close attention to the controlling function. But Part 5 of the book makes it clear that today and for the future, the key managerial challenges are far more dynamic than in the past; they involve continually *learning and changing.* Controls must still be in place, as described in Chapter 16. But new technologies and other innovations (Chapter 17) make it possible to achieve controls in more effective ways and to help all the people throughout the company, and across company boundaries (including customers and suppliers), to use their brains, learn, make a variety of new contributions, and help the organization change in ways that forge a successful future (Chapter 18).

The four management functions apply to you personally as well. You must find ways to create value; organize for your own personal effectiveness; mobilize your own talents and skills as well as those of others; monitor performance; and constantly learn, develop, and change for the future. As you proceed through this book and this course, we encourage you not merely to do your textbook learning of an impersonal course subject but to think about these issues from a personal perspective as well, using the ideas for your own personal development.

Performing All Four Management Functions

As a manager, your typical day will not be neatly divided into the four functions. You will be doing many things more or less simultaneously.[47] Your days will be busy and fractionated, spent dealing with interruptions, meetings, and firefighting. There will be plenty to do that you wish you could be doing but can't seem to get to. These activities will include all four management functions.

Some managers are particularly interested in, devoted to, or skilled in one or two of the four functions but not in the others. But you should devote adequate attention and resources to *all four* functions. You can be a skilled planner and controller, but if you organize your people improperly or fail to inspire them to perform at high levels, you will not be realizing your potential as a manager. Likewise, it does no good to be the kind of manager who loves to organize and lead, but who doesn't really understand where to go or how to determine whether you are on the right track. Good managers don't neglect any of the four management functions. Knowing what they are, you can periodically ask yourself whether you are devoting adequate attention to *all* of them.

Management Connection

HOW BEZOS BUILT A BUSINESS

Amazon CEO Jeff Bezos has quantitative skills, computer expertise, and formal training in management. After earning a bachelor's degree in computer science and a master's in business administration, he worked as a hedge fund manager. As he pursued that career during the 1990s, he observed some of the early changes the Internet was making in the way people did business.

Bezos decided that this new technology offered an opportunity to sell books in a new way, offering a far bigger selection than any bricks-and-mortar store could hold. In 1994, he wrote a business plan for a company he wanted to launch. He would call it Amazon, and it would be the world's largest bookstore, serving U.S. customers from its website. In his plan, he estimated that the company could achieve sales of $100 million a year within a decade. As it turned out, Bezos was wrong. He started Amazon and was selling that much in just a few years. In 1997, he took the company public, raising funds by selling shares to investors. And his idea for a U.S. bookstore became a global enterprise employing 70,000 people and selling music, games, tools, kitchen gadgets, and far more.

Bezos sets clear priorities. He insists on excellent services but at a low cost. That requires seeking efficiency and avoiding frills in the company's operations. He seizes new opportunities when they offer a chance to meet customer needs. For example, when hardware makers began to create e-readers, Bezos saw a way for readers to have access to even more titles. Initially, consumers were reluctant to try the new technology, so Amazon got involved in developing a more enticing model. From the start, the Kindle was priced so low it just covered the cost. The goal wasn't to make money on the hardware but to make it available to consumers so they could buy electronic books, magazines, and more. Incidentally, the low-price strategy also makes it harder for computer companies to beat Amazon at the e-reader game.[48]

- What are Amazon's areas of competitive advantage? How does Jeff Bezos help the company compete in those areas?
- Give an example of something Bezos does or would need to do to carry out each of the four functions of management.

MANAGER'S BRIEF

PROGRESS REPORT

ONWARD

Management Levels and Skills

 Organizations—particularly large organizations—have many levels. In this section, you learn about the types of managers found at three broad organizational levels: top level, middle level, and frontline.

Top-Level Managers

top-level managers

Senior executives responsible for the overall management and effectiveness of the organization.

Top-level managers are the senior executives of an organization and are responsible for its overall management. Top-level managers, often referred to as *strategic managers*, are supposed to focus on long-term issues and emphasize the survival, growth, and overall effectiveness of the organization.

Top managers are concerned not only with the organization as a whole but also with the interaction between the organization and its external environment. This interaction often requires managers to work extensively with outside individuals and organizations.

The chief executive officer (CEO) is one type of top-level manager found in large corporations. This individual is the primary strategic manager of the firm and has authority over everyone else. Others include the chief operating officer (COO), company presidents, and other members of the top management team. In the 1970s, finance was by far the most common single function represented in the top management team (TMT). The top team now typically includes the CEO, COO, chief information (or technology, or knowledge) officer, and other chiefs in the C-suite, including strategy (or corporate development) and marketing (or branding). Functional chiefs sometimes have the title of senior vice president (SVP).[49] A role for the C-suite of the future could well be Chief Sustainability Officer or even Climate Change Officer.[50]

Traditionally, the role of top-level managers has been to set overall direction by formulating strategy and controlling resources. But now top managers are more commonly called on to be not only strategic architects but also true organizational leaders. As leaders, they must create and articulate a broader corporate purpose with which people can identify—and one to which people will enthusiastically commit.

> Top managers are more commonly called on to be not only strategic architects but also true organizational leaders.

Middle-Level Managers

middle-level managers

Managers located in the middle layers of the organizational hierarchy, reporting to top-level executives.

As the name implies, **middle-level managers** are located in the organization's hierarchy below top-level management and above the frontline managers. Sometimes called *tactical managers*, they are responsible for translating the general goals and plans developed by strategic managers into more specific objectives and activities.

Traditionally, the role of the middle manager is to be an administrator who bridges the gap between higher and lower levels. Middle-level managers break down corporate objectives into business unit targets; put together separate business unit plans from the units below them for higher-level corporate review; and serve as linchpins of internal communication, interpreting and broadcasting top management's priorities downward and channeling and translating information from the front lines upward.

As a stereotype, the term *middle manager* connotes mediocrity: unimaginative people behaving like bureaucrats and defending the status quo. But middle managers are closer than top managers to day-to-day operations, customers, frontline managers, and employees—so they know the problems and opportunities. They also have many creative ideas—often better than their bosses'. Middle managers play crucial roles in determining which entrepreneurial ideas are blocked and which are supported,[51] and how well they integrate with top management is crucial to formulating and implementing strategy.[52] Good middle managers provide the operating skills and practical problem solving that keep the company working.[53]

In Practice

BEST PRACTICES RESEARCH

A clear look at the benefits contributed by capable middle-level managers comes from a study of factories that weren't implementing the basic practices that managers should, such as recording quality defects, specifying job requirements, and tracking inventory. A group of Stanford researchers visited randomly selected textile factories in India to evaluate their use of basic practices of good management. At many of the facilities, managers were simply unfamiliar with controls that are widely used in developed economies. Consequently, the factories were in disarray, and waste was the norm. Unsorted yarn rotted in storerooms, dirty machinery blocked hallways, and tools were strewn about.

The researchers then dispatched a locally based team of management consultants to spend several months teaching management basics to managers at most of the factories they visited (leaving the rest as a control group, which received just one month of consulting services). The newly trained managers began requiring employees to sort and stack yarn, clean workspaces, and post schedules of workflows. Defect rates tumbled, as did the amount of raw materials and finished goods taking up space in inventory. Information flow increased, so the factories set up computers, enabling managers to keep better track of what was happening day by day and freeing them to delegate more work. According to the researchers' estimates, the improvements added more than $200,000 to profits at each factory they assisted—an average increase of about 11 percent.[56]

- Managers at the textile factories initially doubted that the changes would have practical benefits. Why might this be so? How common or unusual do you think this attitude is?

Frontline Managers

Frontline managers, or *operational managers*, are lower-level managers who supervise the operations of the organization. These managers often have titles such as *supervisor* or *sales manager*. They are directly involved with nonmanagement employees, implementing the specific plans developed with middle managers. This role is critical in the organization because operational managers are the link between management and nonmanagement personnel. Your first management position probably will fit into this category.

Traditionally, frontline managers have been directed and controlled from above to make sure that they successfully implement operations in support of company strategy. But in leading companies, the role has expanded. Whereas the operational execution aspect of the role remains vital, in leading companies frontline managers are increasingly called on to be innovative and entrepreneurial, managing for growth and new business development.

Managers on the front line are crucial to creating and sustaining quality, innovation, and other drivers of financial performance.[54] In outstanding organizations, talented frontline managers are not only *allowed* to initiate new activities but are *expected* to by their top- and middle-level managers. And they are given freedom, incentives, and support to find ways to do so.[55]

Table 1.1 elaborates on the changing aspects of different management levels. You learn about these aspects of management throughout this course.

frontline managers

Lower-level managers who supervise the operational activities of the organization.

TABLE 1.1
Transformation of
Management Roles and
Activities

	Frontline Managers	Middle-Level Managers	Top-Level Managers
Changing Roles	• From operational implementers to aggressive entrepreneurs.	• From administrative controllers to supportive coaches.	• From resource allocators to institutional leaders.
Key Activities	• Creating and pursuing new growth opportunities for the business.	• Developing individuals and supporting their activities.	• Establishing high performance standards.
	• Attracting and developing resources.	• Linking dispersed knowledge and skills across units.	• Institutionalizing a set of norms and values to support cooperation and trust.
	• Managing continuous improvement within the unit.	• Managing the tension between short-term purpose and long-term ambition.	• Creating an overarching corporate purpose and ambition.

SOURCE: Adapted from C. Bartlett and S. Goshal, "The Myth of the Generic Manager: New Personal Competencies for New Management Roles," *California Management Review* 40, no. 1, Fall 1997, pp. 92–116.

Working Leaders with Broad Responsibilities

In small firms—and in those large companies that have adapted to the times—managers have strategic, tactical, *and* operational responsibilities. They are *complete* businesspeople; they have knowledge of all business functions, are accountable for results, and focus on serving customers both inside and outside their firms. All of this requires the ability to think strategically, translate strategies into specific objectives, coordinate resources, and do real work with lower-level people.

In short, today's best managers can do it all; they are working leaders.[57] They focus on relationships with other people and on achieving results. They don't just make decisions, give orders, wait for others to produce, and then evaluate results. They get dirty, do hard work themselves, solve problems, and produce value.

What does all of this mean in practice? How do managers spend their time—what do they actually do? A classic study of top executives found that they spend their time engaging in 10 key activities or roles, falling into three categories: interpersonal, informational, and decisional.[58] Table 1.2 summarizes these roles. Even though the study was done decades ago, it remains highly relevant as a description of what executives do. And even though the study focused on top executives, managers at all levels engage in all these activities. As you study the table, you might ask yourself, "Which of these activities do I enjoy most (and least)? Where do I excel (and not excel)? Which would I like to improve?" Whatever your answers, you will be learning more about these activities throughout this course.

Management Skills

Performing management functions and roles, and achieving competitive advantage, are the cornerstones of a manager's job. However, understanding this fact does not ensure success. Managers need a variety of skills to do these things well. Skills are specific abilities that result from knowledge, information, practice, and aptitude. Although managers need many individual skills, which you will learn about throughout this textbook, there are three essential categories: technical skills, conceptual and decision skills, and interpersonal and communication skills.[59]

Interpersonal Roles	*Leader:* Staffing, training, and motivating people.
	Liaison: Maintaining a network of outside contacts who provide information and favors.
	Figurehead: Performing symbolic duties (ceremonies and serving other social and legal demands).
Informational Roles	*Monitor:* Seeking and receiving information to develop a thorough understanding of the organization and its environment; serving as the nerve center of communication.
	Disseminator: Transmitting information from source to source, sometimes interpreting and integrating diverse perspectives.
	Spokesperson: Speaking on behalf of the organization about plans, policies, actions, and results.
Decisional Roles	*Entrepreneur:* Searching for new business opportunities and initiating new projects to create change.
	Disturbance handler: Taking corrective action during crises or other conflicts.
	Resource allocator: Providing funding and other resources to units or people; includes making or approving significant organizational decisions.
	Negotiator: Engaging in negotiations with parties outside the organization as well as inside (for example, resource exchanges).

TABLE 1.2
Managerial Roles: What Managers Do

SOURCE: Adapted from H. Mintzberg, *The Nature of Managerial Work* (New York: Harper & Row, 1973), pp. 92–93.

First-timers can underestimate the challenges of the many technical, human, and conceptual competencies required.[60] But when the key management functions are performed by managers who have these critical management skills, the result is high performance.

A **technical skill** is the ability to perform a specialized task that involves a certain method or process. Most people develop a set of technical skills to complete the activities that are part of their daily work lives. The technical skills you learn in school will provide you with the opportunity to get an entry-level position; they will also help you as a manager. For example, your accounting and finance courses will develop the technical skills you need to understand and manage the financial resources of an organization.

Conceptual and decision skills involve the ability to identify and resolve problems for the benefit of the organization and everyone concerned. Managers use these skills when they consider the overall objectives and strategy of the firm, the interactions among different parts of the organization, and the role of the business in its external environment. As you acquire greater responsibility, you must exercise your conceptual and decision skills with increasing frequency. You will confront issues that involve all aspects of the organization and must consider a larger and more interrelated set of decision factors. Much of this book is devoted to enhancing your conceptual and decision skills, but experience also plays an important part in their development.

Interpersonal and communication skills influence the manager's ability to work well with people. These skills are often called *people skills*. Managers spend the great majority of their time interacting with people,[61] and they must develop their abilities to lead, motivate, and communicate effectively with those around them.

The importance of these skills varies by managerial level. Technical skills are most important early in your career. Conceptual and decision skills become more important

technical skill

The ability to perform a specialized task involving a particular method or process.

conceptual and decision skills

Skills pertaining to the ability to identify and resolve problems for the benefit of the organization and its members.

interpersonal and communication skills

People skills; the ability to lead, motivate, and communicate effectively with others.

than technical skills as you rise higher in the company. But interpersonal skills are important throughout your career, at every level of management. Several biomedical companies in California's Orange County collaborated to provide training because they observed that managers originally hired for their technical expertise needed to develop their people skills so that they could handle higher-level assignments successfully.[62]

An example of a manager with these skills is Mark Bertolini, chief executive of Aetna, which provides health insurance and related services. As a young man doing assembly work for Ford Motor Company, Bertolini acquired an interest in union management, so he decided to study business and earned a degree in accounting and then a master's degree in finance. Those two specialties involve valuable technical skills, but Bertolini rose through the management ranks at a series of insurance companies because he also has a passion for people. He recently told an interviewer that he is constantly engaged in learning about people and forging networks with them. He sees tapping into those networks and figuring out how to lead people as the kinds of skills that allow managers to get results. At Aetna, Bertolini is not only an expert at insurance matters, but also a promoter of employee diversity. Furthermore, challenges in his personal life—he survived a spinal cord injury and donated a kidney to his son—have placed him in a position to empathize with others, including clients who use his company's services.[63]

You and Your Career

 LO 6

At the beginning of your career, your contribution to your employer depends on your own performance; that's all you're responsible for. But on becoming a manager, you are responsible for a whole group. To use an orchestra analogy, instead of playing an instrument, you're a conductor, coordinating others' efforts.[64] The challenge is much greater than most first-time managers expect it to be.

Throughout your career, you'll need to lead teams effectively as well as influence people over whom you have no authority; thus the human skills are especially important. Businesspeople often talk about **emotional intelligence,**[65] or EQ—the skills of understanding yourself (including strengths and limitations), managing yourself (dealing with emotions, making good decisions, seeking and using feedback, exercising self-control), and dealing effectively with others (listening, showing empathy, motivating, leading, and so on). The common phrase "emotional intelligence" is controversial.[66] For instance, you should *not* consider it as a type of intelligence but as a set of skills that you can learn and develop—but these skills do matter in many ways, as you will learn in future chapters.

A common complaint about leaders, especially newly promoted ones who had been outstanding individual performers, is that they lack what is perhaps the most fundamental of EQ skills: empathy. The issue is not lack of ability to change (you can), but the lack of motivation to change.[67] William George, former chair and CEO of Medtronic, says some people can go a long way in their careers based on sheer determination and aggressiveness, but personal development—including EQ—ultimately becomes essential.[68] Executives who score low on EQ are less likely to be rated as excellent on their performance reviews, and their divisions tend not to perform as well.[69] A vice president at an aerospace company underwent a program to improve her EQ after colleagues kept complaining that she was overly demanding and inclined to put people down. An assessment found that she lacked social awareness. The vice president eventually learned to respond after calming herself as well as to explore colleagues' ideas rather than demeaning them. Before long, her colleagues began to appreciate the change, and her career took a more successful path.[70]

What should you do to forge a successful, gratifying career? You are well advised to be both a specialist and a generalist, to be self-reliant and connected, to actively manage your relationship with your organization actively, and to know what is required not only to survive but also to thrive in today's world.

emotional intelligence

The skills of understanding yourself, managing yourself, and dealing effectively with others.

Be Both a Specialist and a Generalist

If you think your career will be as a specialist, think again. Chances are, you will not want to stay forever in strictly technical jobs with no managerial responsibilities. Accountants are promoted to accounting department heads and team leaders, sales representatives become sales managers, writers become editors, and nurses become nursing directors. As your responsibilities increase, you must deal with more people, understand more about other aspects of the organization, and make bigger and more complex decisions. Beginning to learn now about these managerial challenges will yield benefits sooner than you think.

So it will help if you can become both a specialist and a generalist.[71] Seek to become a *specialist:* you should be an expert in something useful. This will give you specific skills that help you provide concrete, identifiable value to your firm and to customers. And over time, you should learn to be a *generalist*, knowing enough about a variety of disciplines so that you can think strategically and work with different perspectives. Table 1.3 gives you career advice from experts.

Be Self-Reliant

To be self-reliant means to take full responsibility for yourself and your actions. You cannot count on your boss or your company to take care of you. A useful metaphor is to think of yourself as a business, with you as president and sole employee.

To be self-reliant, find new ways to make your overall performance better. Take responsibility for change; be an innovator.[72] Don't just do your work and wait for orders; look for opportunities to contribute in new ways, to develop new products and processes, and to generate constructive change that strengthens the company and benefits customers and colleagues. Success requires more than talent; you also have to be willing to work hard. The elite, world-class performers in many fields reach the top tier only after 10 years or more of hard work.[73] The key is to engage in consistent practice, looking at the results and identifying where to improve.

> Don't just do your work and wait for orders; look for opportunities to contribute in new ways.

Escape the industry-specific silo.	Develop a skill set that transcends a single function, industry, or career path.
Know what you know.	And find ways to apply it.
Keep learning throughout life.	No one can rest on what they already know.
Never compromise your integrity.	Succumbing to temptations can destroy a career.
Be willing to take on tough jobs.	Continually challenge yourself.
Build a global perspective.	Understanding other cultures creates opportunities.
Take a long view.	Look at your career as a whole, and stay true to yourself.
Zig-zag strategically.	Job changing can be high risk, but not if you have measurable accomplishments.
Prevent obsolescence.	Job security comes from transportable skills.
Pay attention.	Seriously evaluate where you are and where you want to be.

TABLE 1.3
Career Advice from the Experts

Career advice is readily available to you; all you have to do is search and ask. Here's a sampling of good career tips from Joyce Lain Kennedy, Hilary Lovelle, David Calhoun, and Dan Kadler.

SOURCE: Joyce Lain Kennedy, "Best Career Advice for 2013," *Chicago Tribune,* December 23, 2012, http://www.chicagotribune.com; Lorraine Sanders, "Hilary Novelle Hahn's Zig-Zag Career Guide," *Fast Company,* November 13, 2012, http://www.fastcompany.com; Dan Kadlec, "Graduation Day Advice: 5 Steps to a Great Career," *Time,* May 9, 2012, http://business.time.com.

It's easy to see how this works for violinists or basketball players, but what about business managers? The answer is to focus on getting better results each time you try any business task, whether it's writing a report, chairing a meeting, or interpreting a financial statement. To know whether you're getting better, make a point of asking for feedback from customers, colleagues, and bosses.

To develop your full potential, assess yourself, including your interests, aptitudes, and personal character strengths. Think about it, ask others who know you well, conduct a formal exercise in which you learn what others consider to be your "best self,"[74] and use the resources of recent advances in psychology to identify your signature strengths.[75] Consider the professional image and reputation you would like to develop,[76] and continue building your capabilities. Consider the suggestions found throughout this book, and your courses, as you pursue these objectives.

In Practice

TAKING RESPONSIBILITY FOR YOUR CAREER

By any measure, Anne Ackerley has built a successful career in investments. She is chief marketing officer (CMO) for BlackRock, a money management firm that handles $3.6 trillion worth of investments for clients in more than two dozen countries. To get there, Ackerley had to take charge of managing her own career, not just her clients' money.

After managing fund groups for Merrill Lynch and then for BlackRock, Ackerley had risen to the number two job in the unit responsible for client relationships at BlackRock. Landing a higher-level position would require her skills to be recognized throughout the company, not just in her particular group. Ackerley gained that visibility by helping with the establishment and expansion of an employee group called the Women's Initiative Network.

The Women's Initiative Network helps BlackRock develop the talent of its female employees. It hosts small-group meetings at which members can converse directly with company executives, and it coaches employees in how to advance in their careers. The network also invites speakers to tell about how BlackRock is addressing key issues facing the company and the industry. Through her participation, Ackerley got to know Ken Wilson, a member of BlackRock's executive committee. He became impressed with her, advised her on important career experiences, and eventually supported her efforts to become CMO.[77]

- How did Ackerley take responsibility for meeting people who could help with her career? Where can *you* go to meet people with common career interests? (Like Ackerley, think about how you can meet people by serving others, not just how to get something from someone.)

Connect

Being connected means having many good working relationships and interpersonal contacts and being a team player with strong interpersonal skills. For example, those who want to become partners in professional service organizations such as accounting, advertising, and consulting firms strive constantly to build a network of contacts. Their connectedness goal is to work not only with lots of clients but also with a half dozen or more senior partners, including several from outside their home offices and some from outside their country. A study of new auditors showed that social relationships improved newcomers' knowledge of the organization and their jobs, their social integration into the firm, and their commitment to the organization.[78] Networks of diverse individuals can make huge contributions to your professional development no matter what your career—including if you hope to be inducted into the Major League Baseball Hall of Fame on the first ballot.[79]

Social capital is the goodwill stemming from your social relationships, and you can mobilize it on your behalf. It aids career success, compensation, employment, team

Bottom Line

If you want people who see your Facebook profile to think of you as a future manager, what should *not* be on the profile?

social capital

Goodwill stemming from your social relationships.

effectiveness, successful entrepreneurship, and relationships with suppliers and other outsiders.[80] Today much of that social capital can be tapped online at social networking websites. Besides the purely social sites such as Facebook, some of these sites are aimed at helping people tap business networks. For example, LinkedIn has more than 200 million registered users, with membership growing rapidly.

States *Fortune*, "Facebook is for fun . . . If you're serious about managing your career, the only social site that really matters is LinkedIn."[81]

All business is a function of human relationships.[82] Building competitive advantage depends not only on you but on other people. Management is personal. Commercial dealings are personal. Purchase decisions, repurchase decisions, and contracts all hinge on relationships. Even the biggest business deals—takeovers—are intensely personal and emotional. Without good work relationships, you are an outsider, not an effective manager and leader.

Actively Manage Your Relationship with Your Organization

Many of the previous comments suggest the importance of taking responsibility for your own actions and your own career. Unless you are self-employed and your own boss, one way to do this is to think about the nature of the relationship between you and your employer. Figure 1.1 shows two possible relationships—and you have some control over which relationship you will be in.

Relationship #1 is one in which you view yourself as an employee and passively expect your employer to tell you what to do and give you pay and benefits. Your employer is in charge, and you are a passive recipient of its actions. Your contributions are likely to be adequate but minimal—you won't make the added contributions that strengthen your organization, and if all organizational members take this perspective, the organization is not likely to be strong for the long run. Personally, you may lose your job, or keep your job in a declining organization, or receive few positive benefits from working there and either quit or become cynical and unhappy in your work.

In contrast, relationship #2 is a two-way relationship in which you and your organization both benefit from one another. The mind-set is different: Instead of doing what you are told, you think about how you can contribute—and you act accordingly. To the extent that your organization values your contributions, you are likely to benefit in return by receiving full and fair rewards, support for further personal development, and a more gratifying work environment. If you think in broad terms about how you can help your company, and if others think like this as well, there is likely to be continuous improvement in the company's ability to innovate, cut costs, and deliver quality products quickly to an expanding customer base. As the company's bottom line strengthens, benefits accrue to shareholders as well as to you and other employees.

What contributions can you make? You can do your basic work. But you can, and should, go further. You can also figure out new ways to add value—by thinking of and implementing new ideas that improve processes and results. You can do this by using your technical knowledge and skills, as in developing a better information system, accounting technique, or sales strategy.

You also can contribute with your conceptual and human skills and your managerial actions (see Figure 1.2). You can execute the essential management functions and

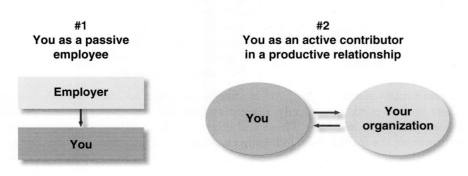

#1
You as a passive employee

Employer

You

#2
You as an active contributor in a productive relationship

You ⇄ **Your organization**

FIGURE 1.1
Two Relationships: Which Will You Choose?

FIGURE 1.2

Managerial Action Is Your Opportunity to Contribute

You

Your organization

Managerial actions

1. Delivering strategic value
2. Building a dynamic organization
3. Mobilizing people
4. Learning and changing

deliver competitive advantage. You can deliver strategic value (Part 2 of this book). You can take actions that help build a more dynamic organization (Part 3). You can mobilize people to contribute to their fullest potential (Part 4). And you can learn and change—and help your colleagues and company learn and change—to adapt to changing realities and forge a successful future (Part 5).

Survive and Thrive

Now more than ever, you will be accountable for your actions and for results. In the past, people at many companies could show up, do an OK job, get a decent evaluation, and get a raise equal to the cost of living and maybe higher. Today, managers must do more, better. Eminent management scholar Peter Drucker, in considering what makes managers effective, noted that some are charismatic whereas some are not, and some are visionary whereas others are more numbers-oriented.[83] But successful executives do share some common practices:

- They ask "What needs to be done?" not just "What do I want to do?"
- They write an action plan. They don't just think, they do, based on a sound, ethical plan.
- They take responsibility for decisions. This requires checking up, revisiting, and changing if necessary.
- They focus on opportunities rather than problems. Problems have to be solved, and problem solving prevents more damage. But exploiting opportunities is what creates great results.

Social networking via websites such as Facebook and LinkedIn is an important way to stay "connected" and build social relationships within and outside of the workplace.

Career success is most likely if you are flexible, creative, and motivated. You need to learn how to think strategically, discern and convey your business vision, make decisions, and work in teams. These and other topics, essential to your successful career, provide the focus for the following chapters.

Management Connection Onward

WORKING FOR BEZOS AT AMAZON

To be a manager at Amazon, you must thrive under the leadership of an intensely driven CEO. Like many successful company founders, Jeff Bezos is supremely committed to his company and his customers. Nadia Shouraboura, a former Amazon vice president, recalled attending meetings in which Bezos seemed less interested in the discussion than in reading e-mail from customers. When he received a complaint, he could be relentless about fixing it. Eventually, Shouraboura realized that, for Bezos, fixing the problem behind one complaint would improve the company's processes for all its customers.

To succeed, Amazon managers have to get used to defining problems in terms of customer needs and benefits. For example, the Amazon Prime service grew out of efforts to improve customers' ordering experience. Subscribers to Amazon Prime pay to get special offers and free shipping (which then makes Amazon their first and last stop for shopping). Anthony Bay, an Amazon vice president, has said that when the company was planning Amazon Prime, "Bezos just kept asking everyone questions like: 'How will this serve the customer?'" Bezos pressed for details about customer benefits and forecasts of new customers. Whether your job involves acquiring Kiva Systems, whose robot technology makes warehouses more efficient, or setting up Amazon Web Services, based on skills learned from making music and videos available to customers on any web-linked device, innovations aim to improve the customer experience.

Amazon managers also must appreciate that the company's low-price strategy requires minimizing every expense. The company lacks some perks workers have come to expect in the high-tech industry, such as free meals and fancy workspaces. Even pay scales are lower than at other e-commerce businesses, and there are no bonuses. The primary financial reward comes from owning Amazon stock, and managers have to find other ways to motivate employees. For many, the lure is the chance to be part of an exciting, innovative enterprise.

Innovation would be a constant consideration if you worked as an Amazon manager. Bezos says, "We think of ourselves as explorers." The goal is less about beating the competition, and more about discovering new ways to please customers and recognizing or creating the next big thing.[84]

- How would a middle manager's job at Amazon differ from the job of CEO Jeff Bezos?
- How could you manage your career to be a successful middle manager at Amazon?

KEY TERMS

SUMMARY OF LEARNING OBJECTIVES

Now that you have studied Chapter 1, you should be able to:

LO 1 Summarize the major challenges of managing in the new competitive landscape.

Managers today must deal with dynamic forces that create greater change than ever before. Among many forces that are creating a need for managers to rethink their approaches, there have recently been four major waves of change: globalization, technological change including the development and applications of the Internet, knowledge management, and collaboration across organizational boundaries.

LO 2 Describe the sources of competitive advantage for a company.

Because business is a competitive arena, you need to deliver value to customers in ways that are superior to what your competitors do. Competitive advantages result from innovation, quality, service, speed, cost, and sustainability.

LO 3 Explain how the functions of management are evolving in today's business environment.

Despite massive change, management retains certain foundations that will not disappear. The primary functions of management are planning, organizing, leading, and controlling. Planning is analyzing a situation, determining the goals that will be pursued, and deciding in advance the actions needed to pursue these goals. Organizing is assembling the resources needed to complete the job and coordinating employees and tasks for maximum success. Leading is motivating people and stimulating high performance. Controlling is monitoring the progress of the organization or the work unit toward goals and then taking corrective action, as necessary. In today's business environment, these functions more broadly require creating strategic value, building a dynamic organization, mobilizing people, and learning and changing.

LO 4 Compare how the nature of management varies at different organizational levels.

Top-level, strategic managers are the senior executives responsible for the organization's overall management. Middle-level, tactical managers translate general goals and plans into more specific objectives and activities. Frontline, operational managers are lower-level managers who supervise operations. Today, managers at all levels must perform a variety of interpersonal, informational, and decisional roles. Even at the operational level, the best managers think strategically and operate like complete businesspeople.

LO 5 Define the skills you need to be an effective manager.

To execute management functions successfully, managers need technical skills, conceptual and decision skills, and interpersonal and communication skills. A technical skill is the ability to perform a specialized task involving certain methods or processes. Conceptual and decision skills help the manager recognize complex and dynamic issues, analyze the factors that influence those issues or problems, and make appropriate decisions. Interpersonal and communication skills enable the manager to interact and work well with people. As you rise to higher organizational levels, technical skills tend to become less important and conceptual skills become more important, whereas interpersonal and communication skills remain extremely important at every level.

LO 6 Understand the principles that will help you manage your career.

You are more likely to succeed in your career if you become both a specialist and a generalist. You should be self-reliant but also connected. You should actively manage your relationship with your organization and continuously improve your skills so you can perform in the ways demanded in the changing work environment.

DISCUSSION QUESTIONS

1. Identify and describe a great manager. What makes him or her stand out from the crowd?

2. Have you ever seen or worked for an ineffective manager? Describe the causes and the consequences of the ineffectiveness.

3. Describe in as much detail as possible how the Internet and globalization affect your daily life.

4. Identify some examples of how different organizations collaborate across boundaries.

5. Name a great organization. How do you think management contributes to making it great?

6. Name an ineffective organization. What can management do to improve it?

7. Give examples you have seen of firms that are outstanding and weak on each of the six pillars of competitive advantage. Why do you choose the firms you do?

8. Describe your use of the four management functions in the management of your daily life.

9. Discuss the importance of technical, conceptual, and interpersonal skills at school and in jobs you have held.

10. What are your strengths and weaknesses as you contemplate your career? How do they correlate with the skills and behaviors identified in the chapter?

11. Devise a plan for developing yourself and making yourself attractive to potential employers. How would you go about improving your managerial skills?

12. Consider the managers and companies discussed in the chapter. Have they been in the news lately, and what is the latest? If their image, performance, or fortunes have gone up or down, what has changed to affect how they have fared?

13. Who are *Bloomberg Businessweek*'s most recent "best and worst managers," and why were they selected?

EXPERIENTIAL EXERCISES

1.1   PERSONAL ASSESSMENT OF MANAGEMENT SKILLS (PAMS)

To get an overall profile of your level of skill competence, respond to the following statements using the following rating scale. Please rate your behavior as it is, not as you would like it to be. If you have not engaged in a specific activity, answer according to how you think you would behave based on your experience in similar activities. Be honest; this instrument is designed to help you tailor your learning to your specific needs.

RATING SCALE

1 Strongly disagree

2 Disagree

3 Slightly disagree

4 Slightly agree

5 Agree

6 Strongly agree

In regard to my level of self-knowledge:

_____   1. I seek information about my strengths and weaknesses from others as a basis for self-improvement.

_____   2. To improve, I am willing to be self-disclosing to others (that is, to share my beliefs and feelings).

_____   3. I am aware of my preferred style in gathering information and making decisions.

_____   4. I understand how I cope with situations that are ambiguous and uncertain.

_____   5. I have a well-developed set of personal standards and principles that guide my behavior.

When faced with stressful or time-pressured situations:

_____   6. I use effective time management methods such as keeping track of my time, making to-do lists, and prioritizing tasks.

_____   7. I reaffirm my priorities so that less important things don't drive out more important things.

_____   8. I maintain a program of regular exercise for fitness.

_____   9. I maintain an open, trusting relationship with someone with whom I can share my frustrations.

_____ 10. I know and practice several temporary relaxation techniques such as deep breathing and muscle relaxation.

_____ 11. I maintain balance in my life by pursuing a variety of interests outside work.

When I approach a typical, routine problem:

_____ 12. I state clearly and explicitly what the problem is. I avoid trying to solve it until I have defined it.

_____ 13. I generate more than one solution to the problem instead of identifying only one obvious solution.

_____ 14. I keep steps in the problem-solving process distinct; that is, I define the problem before proposing alternative solutions, and I generate alternatives before selecting a single solution.

When faced with a complex or difficult problem that does not have an easy solution:

_____ 15. I define a problem in multiple ways. I don't limit myself to just one problem definition.

_____ 16. I unfreeze my thinking by asking lots of questions about the nature of the problem before considering ways to solve it.

_____ 17. I think about the problem from both the left (logical) side of my brain and the right (intuitive) side of my brain.

_____ 18. I avoid selecting a solution until I have developed many possible alternatives.

_____ 19. I have specific techniques that I use to help develop creative and innovative solutions to problems.

When trying to foster more creativity and innovation among those with whom I work:

_____ 20. I make sure divergent points of view are represented or expressed in every complex problem-solving situation.

_____ 21. I try to acquire information from individuals outside the problem-solving group who will be affected by the decision, mainly to determine their preferences and expectations.

_____ 22. I provide recognition not only for those who come up with creative ideas (the idea champions) but also for those who support others' ideas (supporters) and who provide resources to implement them (orchestrators).

_____ 23. I encourage informed rule breaking in pursuit of creative solutions.

When I have to provide negative feedback or offer corrective advice:

_____ 24. I help others recognize and define their own problems when I counsel them.

_____ 25. I am clear about when I should coach someone and when I should provide counseling instead.

_____ 26. When I give feedback to others, I avoid referring to personal characteristics and focus on problems or solutions instead.

_____ 27. When I try to correct someone's behavior, our relationship is strengthened.

_____ 28. I am descriptive in giving negative feedback to others. That is, I objectively describe events, their consequences, and my feelings about them.

_____ 29. I take responsibility for my statements and point of view—for example, "I have decided" instead of "They have decided."

_____ 30. I identify some area of agreement in a discussion with someone who has a different point of view.

_____ 31. I don't talk down to those who have less power or less information than I do.

_____ 32. When discussing someone's problem, I respond with a reply that indicates understanding rather than advice.

When it is important to obtain more power:

_____ 33. I put forth more effort and take more initiative than expected in my work.

_____ 34. I am continually upgrading my skills and knowledge.

_____ 35. I support organizational ceremonial events and activities.

_____ 36. I form a broad network of relationships with people throughout the organization at all levels.

_____ 37. In my work, I strive to generate new ideas, initiate new activities, and minimize routine tasks.

_____ 38. I send personal notes to others when they accomplish something significant or when I pass along important information to them.

_____ 39. I refuse to bargain with individuals who use high-pressure negotiation tactics.

_____ 40. I avoid using threats or demands to impose my will on others.

When another person needs to be motivated:

_____ 41. I determine whether the person has the necessary resources and support to succeed in a task.

_____ 42. I use a variety of rewards to reinforce exceptional performances.

_____ 43. I design task assignments to make them interesting and challenging.

_____ 44. I make sure the person gets timely feedback from those affected by task performance.

_____ 45. I help the person establish performance goals that are challenging, specific, and time bound.

_____ 46. Only as a last resort do I attempt to reassign or release a poorly performing individual.

_____ 47. I discipline when effort is below expectations and capabilities.

_____ 48. I make sure that people feel fairly and equitably treated.

_____ 49. I provide immediate compliments and other forms of recognition for meaningful accomplishments.

When I see someone doing something that needs correcting:

_____ 50. I avoid making personal accusations and attributing self-serving motives to the other person.

_____ 51. I encourage two-way interaction by inviting the respondent to express his or her perspective and to ask questions.

_____ 52. I make a specific request, detailing a more acceptable option.

When someone complains about something I've done:

_____ 53. I show genuine concern and interest, even when I disagree.

_____ 54. I seek additional information by asking questions that provide specific and descriptive information.

_____ 55. I ask the other person to suggest more acceptable behaviors.

When two people are in conflict and I am the mediator:

_____ 56. I do not take sides but remain neutral.

_____ 57. I help the parties generate multiple alternatives.

_____ 58. I help the parties find areas on which they agree.

When I have an opportunity to empower others:

_____ 59. I help people feel competent in their work by recognizing and celebrating their small successes.

_____ 60. I provide regular feedback and needed support.

_____ 61. I provide all the information that people need to accomplish their tasks.

_____ 62. I highlight the important impact that a person's work will have.

When delegating work to others:

_____ 63. I specify clearly the results I desire.

_____ 64. I specify clearly the level of initiative I want others to take (for instance, wait for directions, do part of the task and then report, do the whole task and then report).

_____ 65. I allow participation by those accepting assignments regarding when and how work will be done.

_____ 66. I avoid upward delegation by asking people to recommend solutions, rather than merely asking for advice or answers, when a problem is encountered.

_____ 67. I follow up and maintain accountability for delegated tasks on a regular basis.

When I am in the role of leader in a team:

_____ 68. I know how to establish credibility and influence among team members.

_____ 69. I am clear and consistent about what I want to achieve.

_____ 70. I build a common base of agreement in the team before moving forward with task accomplishment.

_____ 71. I articulate a clear, motivating vision of what the team can achieve along with specific short-term goals.

When I am in the role of team member:

_____ 72. I know a variety of ways to facilitate task accomplishment in the team.

_____ 73. I know a variety of ways to help build strong relationships and cohesion among team members.

When I desire to make my team perform well, regardless of whether I am a leader or member:

_____ 74. I am knowledgeable about the different stages of team development experienced by most teams.

_____ 75. I help the team avoid groupthink by making sure that sufficient diversity of opinions is expressed in the team.

_____ 76. I diagnose and capitalize on my team's core competencies or unique strengths.

_____ 77. I encourage exceptionally high standards of performance and outcomes that far exceed expectations.

When I am leading change:

_____ 78. I usually emphasize a higher purpose or meaning associated with the work I do.

_____ 79. I keep track of things that go right, not just things that go wrong.

_____ 80. I frequently give other people positive feedback.

_____ 81. I work to close performance gaps—the difference between good performance and great performance.

_____ 82. I express gratitude frequently and conspicuously, even for small acts.

_____ 83. I know how to get people to commit to my vision of positive change.

_____ 84. I know how to unlock the positive energy in other people.

_____ 85. I express compassion toward people who are facing pain or difficulty.

SOURCE: David A. Whetten and Kim S. Cameron, *Developing Management Skills*, 6th ed. pp. 23–27. Copyright 2005. Reproduced by permission of Pearson Education, Inc., Upper Saddle River, New Jersey.

1.2   YOUR PERSONAL NETWORK

1. See the figure on page 30. Working on your own, write down all of your primary contacts—individuals you know personally who can support you in attaining your professional goals. Then begin to explore their secondary connections. Make assumptions about possible secondary connections that can be made for you by contacting your primary connections. For example, through one of your teachers (primary), you might be able to obtain some names of potential employers (secondary). (10–15 min.)

2. Then meet with your partner or small group to exchange information about your primary and secondary networks and to exchange advice and information on how best to use these connections as well as how you could be helpful to them. (about 5 min. per person; 10–30 min. total, depending on group size)

3. Add names or types of names to your list based on ideas you get by talking with others in your group. (2–5 min.)

4. Discuss with your large group or class, using the following discussion questions. (10 min.)

QUESTIONS

1. What were some of the best primary sources identified by your group?

2. What were some of the best sources for secondary contacts identified by your group?

3. What are some suggestions for approaching primary contacts?

4. What are some suggestions for approaching secondary contacts, and how is contacting secondary sources different from contacting primary contacts?

5. What did you learn about yourself and others from this exercise?

SOURCE: Suzanne C. de Janasz, Karen O'Dowd, and Beth Z. Schneider, *Interpersonal Skills in Organizations* (New York: McGraw-Hill, 2002), p. 211. © 2002 The McGraw-Hill Companies, Inc. Reprinted with permission.

1.3   EFFECTIVE MANAGERS

OBJECTIVES

1. To understand better what behaviors contribute to effective management.

2. To conceive a ranking of critical behaviors that you personally believe reflects their importance to your success as a manager.

INSTRUCTIONS

1. Following is a partial list of behaviors in which managers may engage. Rank these items in terms of their importance for effective performance as a manager. Put a 1 next to the item that you think is most important, 2 for the next most important, down to 10 for the least important.

2. Bring your rankings to class. Be prepared to justify your results and rationale. If you can add any behaviors to this list that might lead to success or greater management effectiveness, write them in.

Effective Managers Worksheet

_____ Communicates and interprets policy so that it is understood by the members of the organization.

_____ Makes prompt and clear decisions.

_____ Assigns subordinates to the jobs for which they are best suited.

_____ Encourages associates to submit ideas and plans.

_____ Stimulates subordinates by means of competition among employees.

Primary and Secondary
Connections

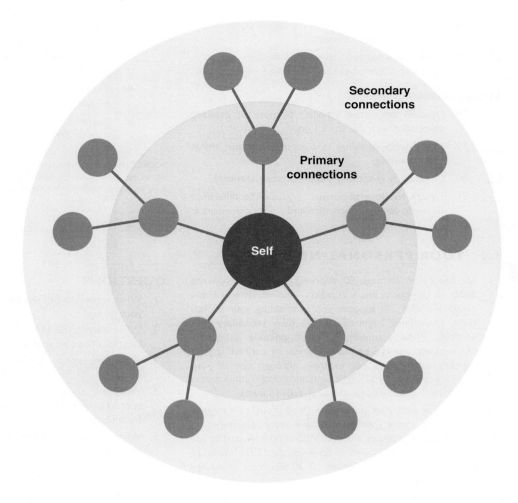

_____ Seeks means of improving management capabilities and competence.

_____ Fully supports and carries out company policies.

_____ Participates in community activities as opportunities arise.

_____ Is neat in appearance.

_____ Is honest in all matters pertaining to company property or funds.

SOURCE: Excerpted from Lawrence R. Jauch, Arthur G. Bedeian, Sally A. Coltrin, and William F. Glueck, _The Managerial Experience: Cases, Exercises, and Readings_, 5th ed. © 1989 South-Western, a part of Cengage Learning, Inc. Reproduced with permission. www.cengage.com/permissions.

1.4   CAREER PLANNING

OBJECTIVES

1. To explore your career thinking.
2. To visualize your ideal job in terms as concrete as possible.
3. To summarize the state of your career planning and to become conscious of the main questions you have about it at this point.

INSTRUCTIONS

Read the instructions for each activity, reflect on them, and then write your response. Be as brief or extensive as you like.

Career Planning Worksheet

1. Describe your ideal occupation in terms of responsibilities, skills, and how you would know whether you were successful.

_____

_____

_____

_____

_____

_____

_____

_____

2. Identify 10 statements you can make today about your current career planning. Identify 10 questions you need answered for career planning.

10 statements	**10 questions**
1. _____	1. _____
_____	_____
2. _____	2. _____
_____	_____
3. _____	3. _____
_____	_____
4. _____	4. _____
_____	_____
5. _____	5. _____
_____	_____
6. _____	6. _____
_____	_____
7. _____	7. _____
_____	_____
8. _____	8. _____
_____	_____

<table>
<tr><td align="center">**10 statements**</td><td align="center">**10 questions**</td></tr>
<tr><td>9. _____
_____
_____</td><td>9. _____
_____
_____</td></tr>
<tr><td>10. _____
_____
_____</td><td>10. _____
_____
_____</td></tr>
</table>

SOURCE: Judith R. Gordon, *Diagnostic Approach to Organizational Behavior.* © 1983 Pearson Education, Inc. Reprinted by permission of Pearson Education, Inc., Upper Saddle River, NJ.

CONCLUDING CASE

A NEW MANAGER AT USA HOSPITAL SUPPLY

As Charlie Greer drove to work, he smiled, recalling the meeting at the end of the previous day. Inez Rodriguez, the owner of the company where he worked, USA Hospital Supply, had summoned him to her office, where she warmly shook his hand and exclaimed, "Congratulations!" As they settled into chairs, Inez reviewed the conversation she'd had with the company's board of directors that morning: USA Hospital had been growing steadily for the past 10 years despite the economy's ups and downs. As the company's founder, Inez had always been an insightful and enthusiastic leader of the five-person sales team, but the level of activity was becoming too much of a distraction. Inez needed to think about the long-range vision of the company, so she needed a leader who could focus on sales. She had interviewed several candidates outside the firm as well as Charlie and two of the other sales representatives. In the end, Inez told Charlie, the choice was obvious: Charlie was far and away the best sales rep on the team, he had extensive knowledge of the company's product mix, and if anyone could help the sales team achieve its goals, it was Charlie. She offered him the job as the company's first sales manager. He eagerly accepted. When he left work that evening, his head was full of ideas, and his heart was full of confidence.

Now Charlie pulled into the office park where USA Hospital Supply was located and easily found a parking space in the lot outside the one-story office and warehouse facility. As usual, he was one of the first employees to arrive. By habit, he strode toward his cubicle, but after a second, he recalled that Inez had arranged for the small firm's accountant and computer systems manager to share an office so he could have an office of his own. Charlie entered his new domain and settled into the swivel chair behind his desk.

At that instant, the eagerness to enjoy his new status and responsibility began to give way to nervousness. Charlie realized that although he knew a lot about selling supplies to hospitals and doctor's offices, he had never given much thought to managing. Obviously, he mused, his job was to see that his department met or exceeded its sales targets. But how?

Charlie started his computer and then opened his e-mail and his word-processing software, intending to get some ideas into writing. He typed out a list of the four sales reps: Cindy, Paula, John, and Doreen. Cindy handled the large corporate accounts, Paula covered the East Coast, John called on accounts in the South, and Doreen handled the Midwest. Until today, Charlie had been building a fast-growing territory west of the Mississippi. Now who was going to do that? Charlie was tempted to keep that work for himself; he knew he could build a base of loyal clients better than anyone else. Still, he wondered whether he could excel as a manager and as a sales rep at the same time.

While he was pondering that challenge, Cindy walked past the office door and, without stopping, politely called, "Congratulations!" through the doorway. Charlie's heart sank as he realized that Cindy had also wanted this job. They had always enjoyed a friendly rivalry as talented salespeople; now what would happen to the fun of being team members? It was easier to think about the other representatives at the moment. Charlie scanned his e-mail inbox and saw status reports from John and Doreen, both of them out of the office to call on clients. What about Paula? Charlie wasn't quite sure he remembered her plans for this week. Obviously he needed to catch up on what everyone was doing, and that gave him a new idea. He could build on his strengths by traveling with each of the sales reps and coaching them. That way, he could show them all his proven methods for closing a sale, and they could learn to sell as well as he did. Charlie thought, "That's what a good manager does: shows employees how to do the job right." He was starting to feel less nervous as he began to compose an e-mail to Paula.

DISCUSSION QUESTIONS

1. How will Charlie's approach to quality and service affect his company's performance?

2. Which of the basic functions of management has Charlie considered? How well is he preparing to carry out these functions?

3. Which management skills does Charlie have? In what areas do you think he has the greatest need to develop skills? How can he actively manage his development as a manager?

The Evolution of Management

For thousands of years, managers have wrestled with the same issues and problems confronting executives today. Around 1100 BC, the Chinese practiced the four management functions—planning, organizing, leading, and controlling—discussed in Chapter 1. Between 400 BC and 350 BC, the Greeks recognized management as a separate art and advocated a scientific approach to work. The Romans decentralized the management of their vast empire before the birth of Christ. During medieval times, the Venetians standardized production through the use of an assembly line, building warehouses and using an inventory system to monitor the contents.[1]

But throughout history, most managers operated strictly on a trial-and-error basis. The challenges of the Industrial Revolution changed that. Management emerged as a formal discipline at the turn of the century. The first university programs to offer management and business education, the Wharton School at the University of Pennsylvania and the Amos Tuck School at Dartmouth, were founded in the late 19th century. By 1914, 25 business schools existed.[2]

Thus, the management profession as we know it today is relatively new. This appendix explores the roots of modern management theory. Understanding the origins of management thought will help you grasp the underlying contexts of the ideas and concepts presented in the chapters ahead.

Although this appendix is titled "The Evolution of Management," it might be more appropriately called "The Revolutions of Management" because it documents the wide swings in management approaches over the past 100 years. Out of the great variety of ideas about how to improve management, parts of each approach have survived and been incorporated into modern perspectives on management. Thus, the legacy of past efforts, triumphs, and failures has become our guide to future management practice.

EARLY MANAGEMENT CONCEPTS AND INFLUENCES

Communication and transportation constraints hindered the growth of earlier businesses. Therefore, improvements in management techniques did not substantially improve performance. However, the Industrial Revolution changed that. As companies grew and became more complex, minor improvements in management tactics produced impressive increases in production quantity and quality.[3]

The emergence of **economies of scale**—reductions in the average cost of a unit of production as the total volume produced increases—drove managers to strive for further growth. The opportunities for mass production created by the Industrial Revolution spawned intense and systematic thought about management problems and issues—particularly efficiency, production processes, and cost savings.[4]

Figure A.1 provides a time line depicting the evolution of management thought through the decades. This historical perspective is divided into two major sections: classical approaches and contemporary approaches. Many of these approaches overlapped as they developed, and they often had a significant impact on one another. Some approaches were a direct reaction to the perceived deficiencies of previous approaches. Others developed as the needs and issues confronting managers changed over the years. All the approaches attempted to explain the real issues facing managers and provide them with tools to solve future problems.

Figure A.1 will reinforce your understanding of the key relationships among the approaches and place each perspective in its historical context.

CLASSICAL APPROACHES

The classical period extended from the mid-19th century through the early 1950s. The major approaches that emerged during this period were systematic management, scientific

FIGURE A.1   The Evolution of Management Thought

management, administrative management, human relations, and bureaucracy.

Systematic Management

During the 19th century, growth in U.S. business centered on manufacturing.[5] Early writers such as Adam Smith believed the management of these firms was chaotic, and their ideas helped to systematize it. Most organizational tasks were subdivided and performed by specialized labor. However, poor coordination caused frequent problems and breakdowns of the manufacturing process.

The **systematic management** approach attempted to build specific procedures and processes into operations to ensure coordination of effort. Systematic management emphasized economical operations, adequate staffing, maintenance of inventories to meet consumer demand, and organizational control. These goals were achieved through

- Careful definition of duties and responsibilities.
- Standardized techniques for performing these duties.
- Specific means of gathering, handling, transmitting, and analyzing information.
- Cost accounting, wage, and production control systems to facilitate internal coordination and communications.

Systematic management emphasized internal operations because managers were concerned primarily with meeting the explosive growth in demand brought about by the Industrial Revolution. In addition, managers were free to focus on internal issues of efficiency, in part because the government did not constrain business practices significantly. Finally, labor was poorly organized. As a result, many managers were oriented more toward things than toward people.

Systematic management did not address all the issues 19th-century managers faced, but it tried to raise managers' awareness about the most pressing concerns of their job.

Production costs dropped as mass manufacturing lowered unit costs. Thus economies of scale were born—a concept that persists in the modern manufacturing era.

An Early Labor Contract

The following rules, taken from the records of Cocheco Company, were typical of labor contract provisions in the 1850s.

1. The hours of work shall be from sunrise to sunset, from the 21st of March to the 20th of September inclusively; and from sunrise until eight o'clock, p.m., during the remainder of the year. One hour shall be allowed for dinner, and half an hour for breakfast during the first mentioned six months; and one hour for dinner during the other half of the year; on Saturdays, the mill shall be stopped one hour before sunset, for the purpose of cleaning the machinery.

2. Every hand coming to work a quarter of an hour after the mill has been started shall be docked a quarter of a day; and every hand absenting him or herself, without absolute necessity, shall be docked in a sum double the amount of the wages such hand shall have earned during the time of such absence. No more than one hand is allowed to leave any one of the rooms at the same time—a quarter of a day shall be deducted for every breach of this rule.

3. No smoking or spiritous liquors shall be allowed in the factory under any pretense whatsoever. It is also forbidden to carry into the factory, nuts, fruits, etc. books, or papers during the hours of work.

SOURCE: W. Sullivan, "The Industrial Revolution and the Factory Operative in Pennsylvania," *The Pennsylvania Magazine of History and Biography* 78 (1954), pp. 478–79.

Scientific Management

Systematic management failed to lead to widespread production efficiency. This shortcoming became apparent to a young engineer named Frederick Taylor, who was hired by Midvale Steel Company in 1878. Taylor discovered that production and pay were poor, inefficiency and waste were prevalent, and most companies had tremendous unused potential. He concluded that management decisions were unsystematic and that no research to determine the best means of production existed.

In response, Taylor introduced a second approach to management, known as **scientific management.**[6] This approach advocated the application of scientific methods to analyze work and to determine how to complete production tasks efficiently. For example, U.S. Steel's contract with the United Steel Workers of America specified that sand shovelers should move 12.5 shovelfuls per minute; shovelfuls should average 15 pounds of river sand composed of 5.5 percent moisture.[7]

Taylor identified four principles of scientific management:

1. Management should develop a precise, scientific approach for each element of one's work to replace general guidelines.

2. Management should scientifically select, train, teach, and develop each worker so that the right person has the right job.

3. Management should cooperate with workers to ensure that jobs match plans and principles.

4. Management should ensure an appropriate division of work and responsibility between managers and workers.

To implement this approach, Taylor used techniques such as time-and-motion studies. With this technique, a task was divided into its basic movements, and different motions were timed to determine the most efficient way to complete the task.

After the "one best way" to perform the job was identified, Taylor stressed the importance of hiring and training the proper worker to do that job. Taylor advocated the standardization of tools, the use of instruction cards to help workers, and breaks to eliminate fatigue.

Another key element of Taylor's approach was the use of the differential piecerate system. Taylor assumed workers were motivated by receiving money. Therefore, he implemented a pay system in which workers were paid additional wages when they exceeded a standard level of output for each job. Taylor concluded that both workers and management would benefit from such an approach.

Scientific management principles were widely embraced. Other proponents, including Henry Gantt and Frank and Lillian Gilbreth, introduced many refinements and techniques for applying scientific management on the factory floor. One of the most famous examples of the application of scientific management is the factory Henry Ford built to produce the Model T.[8]

The legacy of Taylor's scientific management approach is broad and pervasive. Most important, productivity and efficiency in manufacturing improved dramatically. The concepts of scientific methods and research were introduced to manufacturing. The piecerate system gained wide acceptance because it more closely aligned effort and reward. Taylor also emphasized the need for cooperation between management and workers. And the concept of a management specialist gained prominence.

Despite these gains, not everyone was convinced that scientific management was the best solution to all business problems. First, critics claimed that Taylor ignored many job-related social and psychological factors by emphasizing only money as a worker incentive. Second, production tasks were reduced to a set of routine, machinelike procedures that led to boredom, apathy,

Scientific Management and the Model T

At the turn of the century, automobiles were a luxury that only the wealthy could afford. They were assembled by craftspeople who put an entire car together at one spot on the factory floor. These workers were not specialized, and Henry Ford believed they wasted time and energy bringing the needed parts to the car. Ford took a revolutionary approach to automobile manufacturing by using scientific management principles.

After much study, machines and workers in Ford's new factory were placed in sequence so that an automobile could be assembled without interruption along a moving production line. Mechanical energy and a conveyor belt were used to take the work to the workers.

The manufacture of parts likewise was revolutionized. For example, formerly it had taken one worker 20 minutes to assemble a flywheel magneto. By splitting the job into 29 operations, putting the product on a mechanical conveyor, and changing the height of the conveyor, Ford cut production time to 5 minutes.

By 1914, chassis assembly time had been trimmed from almost 13 hours to 1½ hours. The new methods of production required complete standardization, new machines, and an adaptable labor force. Costs dropped significantly, the Model T became the first car accessible to the majority of Americans, and Ford dominated the industry for many years.

SOURCE: H. Kroos and C. Gilbert, *The Principles of Scientific Management* (New York: Harper & Row, 1911).

and quality control problems. Third, unions strongly opposed scientific management techniques because they believed management might abuse its power to set the standards and the piecerates, thus exploiting workers and diminishing their importance. Finally, although scientific management resulted in intense

Frederick Taylor (left) and Dr. Lillian Gilbreth (right) were early experts in management efficiency.

scrutiny of the internal efficiency of organizations, it did not help managers deal with broader external issues such as competitors and government regulations, especially at the senior management level.

Administrative Management

The **administrative management** approach emphasized the perspective of senior managers within the organization and argued that management was a profession and could be taught.

An explicit and broad framework for administrative management emerged in 1916, when Henri Fayol, a French mining engineer and executive, published a book summarizing his management experiences. Fayol identified five functions and 14 principles of management. The five functions, which are very similar to the four functions discussed in Chapter 1, are planning, organizing, commanding, coordinating, and controlling. Table A.1 lists and defines the 14 principles. Although some critics claim Fayol treated the principles as universal truths for management, he actually wanted them applied flexibly.[9]

A host of other executives contributed to the administrative management literature. These writers discussed a broad spectrum of management topics, including the social responsibilities of management, the philosophy of management, clarification of business terms and concepts, and organizational principles. Chester Barnard's and Mary Parker Follet's contributions have become classic works in this area.[10]

Barnard, former president of New Jersey Bell Telephone Company, published his landmark book *The Functions of the Executive* in 1938. He outlined the role of the senior executive: formulating the purpose of the organization, hiring key individuals, and maintaining organizational communications.[11] Mary Parker Follet's 1942 book *Dynamic Organization* extended Barnard's work by emphasizing the continually changing situations that managers face.[12] Two of her key contributions—the notion that managers desire flexibility and the differences between motivating groups and individuals—laid the groundwork for the modern contingency approach discussed later in the chapter.

All the writings in the administrative management area emphasize management as a profession along with fields such as law and medicine. In addition, these authors offered many recommendations based on their personal experiences, which often included managing large corporations. Although these perspectives and recommendations were considered sound, critics noted that they might not work in all settings. Different types of personnel, industry conditions, and technologies may affect the appropriateness of these principles.

Human Relations

A fourth approach to management, **human relations**, developed during the 1930s. This approach aimed at understanding how psychological and social processes interact with the work situation to influence performance. Human relations was the first major approach to emphasize informal work relationships and worker satisfaction.

This approach owes much to other major schools of thought. For example, many of the ideas of the Gilbreths (scientific management) and Barnard and Follet (administrative management) influenced the development of human relations from 1930 to

TABLE A.1

Fayol's 14 Principles of Management

1. *Division of work*—divide work into specialized tasks and assign responsibilities to specific individuals.
2. *Authority*—delegate authority along with responsibility.
3. *Discipline*—make expectations clear and punish violations.
4. *Unity of command*—each employee should be assigned to only one supervisor.
5. *Unity of direction*—employees' efforts should be focused on achieving organizational objectives.
6. *Subordination of individual interest to the general interest*—the general interest must predominate.
7. *Remuneration*—systematically reward efforts that support the organization's direction.
8. *Centralization*—determine the relative importance of superior and subordinate roles.
9. *Scalar chain*—keep communications within the chain of command.
10. *Order*—order jobs and material so they support the organization's direction.
11. *Equity*—fair discipline and order enhance employee commitment.
12. *Stability and tenure of personnel*—promote employee loyalty and longevity.
13. *Initiative*—encourage employees to act on their own in support of the organization's direction.
14. *Esprit de corps*—promote a unity of interests between employees and management.

1955. In fact, human relations emerged from a research project that began as a scientific management study.

Western Electric Company, a manufacturer of communications equipment, hired a team of Harvard researchers led by Elton Mayo and Fritz Roethlisberger. They were to investigate the influence of physical working conditions on workers' productivity and efficiency in one of the company's factories outside Chicago. This research project, known as the *Hawthorne Studies,* provided some of the most interesting and controversial results in the history of management.[13]

The Hawthorne Studies were a series of experiments conducted from 1924 to 1932. During the first stage of the project (the illumination experiments), various working conditions, particularly the lighting in the factory, were altered to determine the effects of those changes on productivity. The researchers found no systematic relationship between the factory lighting and production levels. In some cases, productivity continued to increase even when the illumination was reduced to the level of moonlight. The researchers concluded that the workers performed and reacted differently because the researchers were observing them. This reaction is known as the **Hawthorne Effect.**

This conclusion led the researchers to believe productivity may be affected more by psychological and social factors than by physical or objective influences. With this thought in mind, they initiated the other four stages of the project. During these stages, the researchers performed various work group experiments and had extensive interviews with employees. Mayo and his team eventually concluded that productivity and employee behavior were influenced by the informal work group.

Human relations proponents argued that managers should stress primarily employee welfare, motivation, and communication. They believed social needs had precedence over economic needs. Therefore, management must gain the cooperation of the group and promote job satisfaction and group norms consistent with the goals of the organization.

Another noted contributor to the field of human relations was Abraham Maslow.[14] In 1943, Maslow suggested that humans have five levels of needs. The most basic needs are the physical needs for food, water, and shelter; the most advanced need is for self-actualization, or personal fulfillment. Maslow argued that people try to satisfy their lower-level needs and then progress upward to the higher-level needs. Managers can facilitate this process and achieve organizational goals by removing obstacles and encouraging behaviors that satisfy people's needs and organizational goals simultaneously.

Although the human relations approach generated research into leadership, job attitudes, and group dynamics, it drew heavy criticism.[15] Critics believed that one result of human relations— a belief that a happy worker was a productive worker—was too simplistic. Whereas scientific management overemphasized the economic and formal aspects of the workplace, human relations ignored the more rational side of the worker and the important characteristics of the formal organization. However, human relations was a significant step in the development of management thought because it prompted managers and researchers to consider the psychological and social factors that influence performance.

Bureaucracy Max Weber, a German sociologist, lawyer, and social historian, showed how management itself could be more efficient and consistent in his book, *The Theory of Social and Economic Organizations.*[16] The ideal model for management, according to Weber, is the **bureaucracy** approach.

Weber believed bureaucratic structures can eliminate the variability that results when managers in the same organization have different skills, experiences, and goals. Weber advocated that the jobs themselves be standardized so that personnel changes would not disrupt the organization. He emphasized a structured, formal network of relationships among specialized positions in an organization. Rules and regulations standardize behavior, and authority resides in positions rather than in individuals. As a result, the organization need not rely on a particular individual but will realize efficiency and success by following the rules in a routine and unbiased manner.

According to Weber, bureaucracies are especially important because they allow large organizations to perform the many

A Human Relations Pioneer

In 1837, William Procter, a ruined English retailer, and James Gamble, son of a Methodist minister, formed a partnership in Cincinnati to make soap and candles. Both were known for their integrity, and soon their business was thriving.

By 1883, the business had grown substantially. When William Cooper Procter, grandson of the founder, left Princeton University to work for the firm, he wanted to learn the business from the ground up. He started working on the factory floor. "He did every menial job from shoveling rosin and soap to pouring fatty mixtures into crutchers. He brought his lunch in a paper bag . . . and sat on the floor [with the other workers] and ate with them, learning their feelings about work."

By 1884, Cooper Procter believed, from his own experience, that increasing workers' psychological commitment to the company would lead to higher productivity. His passion to increase employee commitment to the firm led him to propose a scandalous plan: share profits with workers to increase their sense of responsibility and job satisfaction. The surprise was audible on the first dividend day, when workers held checks equivalent to seven weeks' pay.

Still, the plan was not complete. Workers saw the profit sharing as extra pay rather than as an incentive to improve. In addition, Cooper Procter recognized that a fundamental issue for the workers, some of whom continued to be his good friends, was the insecurity of old age. Public incorporation in 1890 gave Procter a new idea. After trying several versions, by 1903 he had discovered a way to meet all his goals for labor: a stock purchase plan. For every dollar a worker invested in P&G stock, the company would contribute four dollars' worth of stock.

Finally, Cooper Procter had resolved some key issues for labor that paid off in worker loyalty, improved productivity, and an increasing corporate reputation for caring and integrity. He went on to become CEO of the firm, and P&G today remains one of the most admired corporations in the United States.

SOURCES: O. Schisgall, *Eyes on Tomorrow* (Chicago: J. G. Ferguson, 1981); T. Welsh, "Best and Worst Corporate Reputations," *Fortune*, February 7, 1994, pp. 58–66.

routine activities necessary for their survival. Also, bureaucratic positions foster specialized skills, eliminating many subjective judgments by managers. In addition, if the rules and controls are established properly, bureaucracies should be unbiased in their treatment of people—both customers and employees.

Many organizations today are bureaucratic. Bureaucracy can be efficient and productive. However, bureaucracy is not the appropriate model for every organization. Organizations or departments that need rapid decision making and flexibility may suffer under a bureaucratic approach. Some people may not perform their best with excessive bureaucratic rules and procedures.

Other shortcomings stem from a faulty execution of bureaucratic principles rather than from the approach itself. Too much authority may be vested in too few people; the procedures may become the ends rather than the means; or managers may ignore appropriate rules and regulations. Finally, one advantage of a bureaucracy—its permanence—can also be a problem. Once a bureaucracy is established, dismantling it is difficult.

CONTEMPORARY APPROACHES

The contemporary approaches to management include quantitative management, organizational behavior, systems theory, and the contingency perspective. The contemporary approaches have developed at various times since World War II, and they continue to represent the cornerstones of modern management thought.

Quantitative Management Although Taylor introduced the use of science as a management tool early in the 20th century, most organizations did not adopt the use of quantitative techniques for management problems until the 1940s and 1950s.[17] During World War II, military planners began to apply mathematical techniques to defense and logistics problems. After the war, private corporations began assembling teams of quantitative experts to tackle many of the complex issues confronting large organizations. This approach, referred to as **quantitative management**, emphasizes the application of quantitative analysis to management decisions and problems.

Quantitative management helps a manager make a decision by developing formal mathematical models of the problem. Computers facilitated the development of specific quantitative methods. These include such techniques as statistical decision theory, linear programming, queuing theory, simulation, forecasting, inventory modeling, network modeling, and break-even analysis. Organizations apply these techniques in many areas, including production, quality control, marketing, human resources, finance, distribution, planning, and research and development.

Despite the promise quantitative management holds, managers do not rely on these methods as the primary approach to decision making. Typically, they use these techniques as a supplement or tool in the decision process. Many managers will use results that are consistent with their experience, intuition, and judgment, but they often reject results that contradict their beliefs. Also, managers may use the process to compare alternatives and eliminate weaker options.

Several explanations account for the limited use of quantitative management. Many managers have not been trained in using these techniques. Also, many aspects of a management decision cannot be expressed through mathematical symbols and formulas. Finally, many of the decisions managers face are nonroutine and unpredictable.

Organizational Behavior During the 1950s, a transition took place in the human relations approach. Scholars began to recognize that worker productivity and organizational success are based on more than the satisfaction of economic or social needs. The revised perspective, known as **organizational behavior**, studies and identifies management activities that promote employee effectiveness through an understanding of the complex nature of individual, group, and organizational processes. Organizational behavior draws from a variety of disciplines, including psychology and sociology, to explain the behavior of people on the job.

During the 1960s, organizational behaviorists heavily influenced the field of management. Douglas McGregor's Theory X and Theory Y marked the transition from human relations.[18] According to McGregor, Theory X managers assume workers are lazy and irresponsible and require constant supervision and external motivation to achieve organizational goals. Theory Y managers assume employees *want* to work and can direct and control themselves. McGregor advocated a Theory Y perspective, suggesting that managers who encourage participation and allow opportunities for individual challenge and initiative would achieve superior performance.

Other major organizational behaviorists include Chris Argyris, who recommended greater autonomy and better jobs for workers,[19] and Rensis Likert, who stressed the value of participative management.[20] Through the years, organizational behavior has consistently emphasized development of the organization's human resources to achieve individual and organizational goals. Like other approaches, it has been criticized for its limited perspective, although more recent contributions have a broader and more situational viewpoint. In the past few years, many of the primary issues addressed by organizational behavior have experienced a rebirth with a greater interest in leadership, employee involvement, and self-management.

Systems Theory The classical approaches as a whole were criticized because they (1) ignored the relationship between the organization and its external environment, and (2) usually stressed one aspect of the organization or its employees at the expense of other considerations. In response to these criticisms, management scholars during the 1950s stepped back from the details of the organization to attempt to understand it as a whole system. These efforts were based on a general scientific approach called **systems theory**.[21] Organizations are open systems, dependent on inputs from the outside world, such as raw materials, human resources, and capital. They transform these inputs into outputs that (ideally) meet the market's needs for goods and services. The environment reacts to the outputs through a feedback loop; this feedback provides input for the next cycle of the system. The process repeats itself for the life of the system and is illustrated in Figure A.2.

Systems theory also emphasizes that an organization is one system in a series of subsystems. For instance, Southwest Airlines is a subsystem of the airline industry, and the flight crews are a subsystem of Southwest. Systems theory points out that each subsystem is a component of the whole and is interdependent with other subsystems.

Contingency Perspective Building on systems theory ideas, the **contingency perspective** refutes universal principles of management by stating that a variety of factors, both internal and external to the firm, may affect the organization's

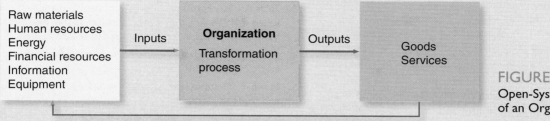

EXTERNAL ENVIRONMENT

Raw materials
Human resources
Energy
Financial resources
Information
Equipment

Inputs →

Organization
Transformation process

→ Outputs

Goods
Services

performance.[22] Therefore, there is no one best way to manage and organize because circumstances vary.

Situational characteristics are called **contingencies**. Understanding contingencies helps a manager know which sets of circumstances dictate which management actions. You will learn recommendations for the major contingencies throughout this text. The contingencies include

1. Circumstances in the organization's external environment.

2. The internal strengths and weaknesses of the organization.

3. The values, goals, skills, and attitudes of managers and workers in the organization.

4. The types of tasks, resources, and technologies the organization uses.

With an eye to these contingencies, a manager may categorize the situation and then choose the proper competitive strategy, organization structure, or management process for the circumstances.

Researchers continue to identify key contingency variables and their effects on management issues. As you read the topics covered in each chapter, you will notice similarities and differences among management situations and the appropriate responses. This perspective should represent a cornerstone of your own approach to management. Many of the things you will learn about throughout this course apply a contingency perspective.

2008–2009 U.S. auto industry collapses
2010–2012 Gulf Oil Spill
    Troubled Asset Relief Program
    General Motors comeback
    Occupy Wall Street
    U.S. and European debt crisis
    Facebook IPO
2013 – Manufacturing comeback?
    Economic recovery, U.S. and global?

AN EYE ON THE FUTURE

This appendix has summarized the major schools of management thought. Some schools offer more general courses in business history, and the subject is well worth knowing. What goes on today derives from what went on yesterday, which stemmed from what began years, decades, even centuries ago. It is reasonable to believe that if decision makers paid more attention to history, the subprime mortgage crisis of 2007 and the more general financial panic of 2008 could have been avoided.[23] It helps to examine the past for help in making good decisions today and in the future.

Knowledge of history could help with the economic recovery and mitigate or prevent future fiascos. Knowing history *could*–if used properly—have a positive effect on the future.[24]

KEY TERMS

administrative management A classical management approach that attempted to identify major principles and functions that managers could use to achieve superior organizational performance, p. 36.

bureaucracy A classical management approach emphasizing a structured, formal network of relationships among specialized positions in the organization, p. 37.

contingencies Factors that determine the appropriateness of managerial actions, p. 39.

contingency perspective An approach to the study of management proposing that the managerial strategies, structures, and processes that result in high performance depend on the characteristics, or important contingencies, of the situation in which they are applied, p. 38.

economies of scale Reductions in the average cost of a unit of production as the total volume produced increases, p. 33.

Hawthorne Effect People's reactions to being observed or studied resulting in superficial rather than meaningful changes in behavior, p. 37.

human relations A classical management approach that attempted to understand and explain how human psychological and social processes interact with the formal aspects of the work situation to influence performance, p. 36.

organizational behavior A contemporary management approach that studies and identifies management activities that promote employee effectiveness by examining the complex and dynamic nature of individual, group, and organizational processes, p. 38.

quantitative management A contemporary management approach that emphasizes the application of quantitative analysis to managerial decisions and problems, p. 38.

scientific management A classical management approach that applied scientific methods to analyze and determine the one best way to complete production tasks, p. 34.

systematic management A classical management approach that attempted to build into operations the specific procedures and processes that would ensure coordination of effort to achieve established goals and plans, p. 34.

systems theory A theory stating that an organization is a managed system that changes inputs into outputs, p. 38.

DISCUSSION QUESTIONS

1. How does today's business world compare with the one of 40 years ago? What is different about today, and what is not so different?

2. What is scientific management? How might today's organizations use it?

3. Table A.1 lists Fayol's 14 principles of management, first published in 1916. Are they as useful today as they were then? Why or why not? *When* are they most, and least, useful?

4. What are the advantages and disadvantages of a bureaucratic organization?

5. In what situations are quantitative management concepts and tools applicable?

6. Choose any organization and describe its system of inputs and outputs.

7. Why did the contingency perspective become such an important approach to management? Generate a list of contingencies that might affect the decisions you make in your life or as a manager.

8. For each of the management approaches discussed in the appendix, give examples you have seen. How effective or ineffective were they?

Experiential Exercises

A.1 APPROACHES TO MANAGEMENT

OBJECTIVES

1. To help you conceive a wide variety of management approaches.
2. To clarify the appropriateness of different management approaches in different situations.

INSTRUCTIONS

Your instructor will divide your class randomly into groups of four to six people. Acting as a team, with everyone offering ideas and one person serving as official recorder, each group will be responsible for writing a one-page memo to your present class. The subject matter of your group's memo will be "My advice for managing people today is . . ." The fun part of this exercise (and its creative element) involves writing the memo from the viewpoint of the person assigned to your group by your instructor.

Among the memo viewpoints your instructor may assign are

- An ancient Egyptian slave master (building the great pyramids).
- Henri Fayol.
- Frederick Taylor.
- Mary Parker Follet.
- Douglas McGregor.
- A contingency management theorist.
- A Japanese auto company executive.
- The chief executive officer of IBM in the year 2030.
- Commander of the Starship Enterprise II in the year 3001.
- Others as assigned by your instructor.

Use your imagination, make sure everyone participates, and try to be true to any historical facts you've encountered. Attempt to be as specific and realistic as possible. Remember, the idea is to provide advice about managing people from another point in time (or from a particular point of view at the present time).

Make sure you manage your 20-minute time limit carefully. A recommended approach is to spend 2 to 3 minutes putting the exercise into proper perspective. Next, take about 10 to 12 minutes brainstorming ideas for your memo, with your recorder jotting down key ideas and phrases. Have your recorder use the remaining time to write your group's one-page memo, with constructive comments and help from the others. Pick a spokesperson to read your group's memo to the class.

SOURCE: R. Krietner and A. Kinicki, *Organization Behavior,* 3rd ed. (New York: Richard D. Irwin, 1994), pp. 30–31.

A.2 THE UNIVERSITY GRADING SYSTEM ANALYSIS

OBJECTIVES

1. To learn to identify the components of a complex system.

2. To understand organizations as systems better.

3. To visualize how a change in policy affects the functioning of an organization system.

INSTRUCTIONS

1. Assume that your university has decided to institute a pass–fail system of grading instead of the letter-grade system it presently has. Apply the systems perspective learned from this chapter to understanding this decision.

2. Answer the questions on the Grading System Analysis Worksheet individually, or in small groups, as directed by your instructor.

DISCUSSION QUESTIONS

Share your own or your group's responses with the entire class. Then answer the following questions:

1. Did you diagram the system in the same way?

2. Did you identify the same system components?

3. Which subsystems will be affected by the change?

4. How do you explain differences in your responses?

Grading System Analysis Worksheet

DESCRIPTION

1. What subsystems compose the system (the university)? Diagram the system.

_____

_____

_____

2. Identify the following in this system: inputs, outputs, transformations.

_____

_____

_____

DIAGNOSIS

3. Which of the subsystems will be affected by the change; that is, what changes are likely to occur throughout the system as a result of the policy change?

_____

_____

_____

SOURCE: J. Gordon, *A Diagnostic Approach to Organizational Behavior* (Englewood Cliffs, NJ: Prentice Hall, 1983), p. 38. Reprinted with permission of Prentice Hall, Inc., Englewood Cliffs, NJ.

CHAPTER 2

The External and Internal Environments

The essence of a business is outside itself.

— PETER DRUCKER

LEARNING OBJECTIVES

CHAPTER OUTLINE

Management Connection

CAN MARK ZUCKERBERG STEER FACEBOOK THROUGH A TURBULENT ENVIRONMENT?

Some managers transform an industry; many others are swept up by change. Some do both. In the unprecedented pace of the Internet era, a few managers do both within a mere decade. One of those is Facebook founder Mark Zuckerberg.

Zuckerberg started Facebook in 2004, when as a Harvard student, he developed a way for his classmates to connect online. The service quickly spread from Harvard to other universities, then high schools, and eventually to anyone with an e-mail address. Today, Facebook, with more than a billion active users a month, is the largest online social network.

To carry out its mission to "make the world more open and connected," Facebook added capabilities making it easier to post photos, video clips, and links to websites. The ever-present Like button encourages users to signal their opinions to all their friends—and to Facebook's database. Facebook's user database thus becomes its most precious resource. For users, Facebook can deliver more relevant links, ads, and services. It also can sell highly targeted advertising.

Driven by Zuckerberg's vision to connect individuals more and more, Facebook has redefined how we communicate socially. When we want to share a thought or pictures of our vacation, we don't write e-mail or print photos, we post to our Timeline or use Facebook's messaging service. As Facebook became part of everyday life, the only thing holding back even more enormous growth seemed to be cash from eager investors. So Facebook made an initial public offering of stock.

Yet technology almost left Facebook behind. The Internet underwent a mobile revolution. Spurred by the launch of the powerful iPhone and iPad tablet computer, people began wanting to be online always, everywhere. While Facebook continued adding features and advertising to its

main website, people were switching to mobile devices; in 2013, for the first time, the number of mobile devices in use exceeded the number of personal computers (desktops and laptops). More people now access Facebook via its mobile app—the most-downloaded app for the iPhone—than at computers. Unfortunately for Facebook, most of its ads were displaying on the computer website—and what mobile advertising it sold went for a lower rate. Therefore, just as the company began selling stock, investors were seeing trouble.

In the initial days of trading, Facebook's stock price fell. However, Facebook's managers scrambled to catch up to the mobile Internet. They improved their mobile site and began pushing up ad rates; in less than a year, mobile ad revenues went from 0 percent of revenues to 23 percent. Stock prices have begun to trend upward. Does this mean the uncertainty is over for Facebook's managers? Far from it. Technology will continue advancing, and computer users will keep looking for the next big thing.[1]

Technology and social behavior are just two of the forces shaping the environment in which Facebook operates. As you study this chapter, consider what other forces Facebook's managers should be monitoring and engaging with.

FIGURE 2.1

Organization Inputs and
Outputs

Inputs

Raw materials
Services
Equipment
Capital
Information

Organization

Outputs

Products
Services

open systems

Organizations that are affected
by, and that affect, their
environment.

inputs

Goods and services
organizations take in and use
to create products or services.

outputs

The products and services
organizations create.

external environment

All relevant forces outside
a firm's boundaries, such as
competitors, customers, the
government, and the economy.

**competitive
environment**

The immediate environment
surrounding a firm; includes
suppliers, customers, rivals,
and the like.

As a technology leader, Facebook is affecting how people play, shop, and communicate today, as well as preparing for how they might want to do so in the future. Its management must therefore keep a sharp watch on a broad spectrum of influences and events that can affect its operations. In this chapter, we discuss in detail how pressures from outside the organization help create the context in which managers and their companies must operate.

As we suggested in the first chapter, organizations are **open systems**—that is, they are affected by and in turn affect their external environments. For example, they take in **inputs** such as goods or services from their environment and use them to create products and services that are **outputs** to their environment, as shown in Figure 2.1. But when we use the term **external environment** here, we mean more than an organization's clients or customers; the external environment includes *all* relevant forces outside the organization's boundaries.

Many of these factors are uncontrollable. Companies large and small are buffeted or battered by recession, government regulations, competitors' actions, and other factors. But their lack of control does not mean that managers can ignore such forces, use them as excuses for poor performance, and try to just get by. Managers must stay abreast of external developments and react effectively. Moreover, as we will discuss later in this chapter, sometimes managers can influence components of the external environment. We will examine ways in which organizations can do just that.

Figure 2.2 shows the external environment of a business organization. The organization exists in its **competitive environment,** which is composed of the firm and its

FIGURE 2.2

The External Environment

Environments

Macroenvironment

Economy

Technology

Legal and regulations

Demographics

Social issues

Natural ecology

**Competitive
Environment**

Rivals

Suppliers

Buyers

New entrants

Substitutes
and complements

**Internal
Environment**

Culture

Values

Climate

rivals, suppliers, customers (buyers), new entrants, and substitute or complementary products. At the more general level is the **macroenvironment,** which includes legal, political, economic, technological, demographic, and social and natural factors that generally affect all organizations.

macroenvironment

The general environment; includes governments, economic conditions, and other fundamental factors that generally affect all organizations.

A Look Ahead

This chapter discusses the basic characteristics of an organization's environment and the importance of that environment for strategic management. We also examine the *internal environment,* or *culture,* of the organization and the way that culture may influence the organization's response to its environment. Later chapters elaborate on many of the basic environmental forces introduced here. For example, technology will be discussed again in Chapter 17. The global environment gets a thorough treatment in Chapter 6, which is devoted to international management. Other chapters focus on ethics, social responsibility, and the natural environment. Chapter 18 reiterates the theme that recurs throughout this text: Organizations must change continually because environments change continually.

The Macroenvironment

All organizations operate in a macroenvironment, which is defined by the most general elements in the external environment that potentially can influence strategic decisions. Although a top executive team may have unique internal strengths and ideas about its goals, it must consider external factors before taking action.

LO 2

The Economy

Although most Americans think in terms of the U.S. economy, the economic environment for organizations is much larger—created by complex interconnections among the economies of different countries. Wall Street investment analysts begin their workday thinking not just about what the New York Stock Exchange did yesterday but also about how the London and Tokyo exchanges did overnight. Growth and recessions occur worldwide as well as domestically.

LO 3

The economic environment dramatically affects managers' ability to function effectively and influences their strategic choices. Interest and inflation rates affect the availability and cost of capital, growth opportunities, prices, costs, and consumer demand for products. Steeply rising energy and health care costs have had a great effect on companies' ability to hire and their cost of doing business. Changes in the value of the dollar on world exchanges may make American products cheaper or more expensive than their foreign competitors. Unemployment rates affect labor availability and the wages the firm must pay as well as product demand.

During boom times, hiring accelerates, and unemployment rates fall. Generally, unemployment rises as workers are laid off in a recession (a period of falling economic output). During the Great Recession of 2007–2009, the drop-off in employment was especially severe. Figure 2.3 shows how long it has taken the United States to recover jobs lost during each of the past four recessions. Five years after the start of the Great Recession, there continued to be fewer people working than when the recession began, even though economic output had been growing for several years. The ability to grow with little or no hiring suggests profit opportunities for some businesses but poses difficult challenges for societies and their governments.

An important economic influence is the government where a business is operating. In the United States, the federal government is a major employer and customer

FIGURE 2.3

Percent Change in Nonfarm Payroll Employment since Start of Each Recession

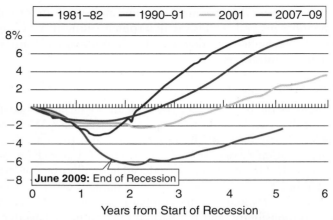

SOURCE: Center on Budget and Policy Priorities, "Chart Book: The Legacy of the Great Recession," Special Series: Economic Recovery Watch, updated February 21, 2013, http://www.cbpp.org.

for business and military goods and services. When it spends more money than it is receiving, it also is a major borrower in the financial markets (adding to the national debt). These government activities can increase or decrease a nation's economic activity. The pros and cons of government spending and borrowing decisions are important topics that are beyond the scope of this book. However, to be effective, managers educate themselves about the impact of the government on the societies in which they work.

Another important economic influence is the stock market. When investors bid up stock prices, they are paying more to own shares in companies, which means the companies have more capital to fuel their strategies. Observers of the stock market watch trends in major indexes such as the Dow Jones Industrial Average, Standard and

In Practice

ECONOMIC FORCES ON ETHANOL PRODUCERS

Economic forces have caused the fortunes of corn-based ethanol producers to swing wildly. For a time, soaring gasoline prices intensified the demand for alternative fuel sources for automobiles. That fact, coupled with a belief that ethanol fuel would reduce emissions of greenhouse gases, inspired the U.S. government to mandate the use of ethanol. Farmers responded by planting more corn, and energy companies built ethanol refineries.

But soon other forces pummeled the ethanol producers. First flooding in the Midwest led to forecasts of high corn prices, and many ethanol producers tried to protect themselves by signing contracts for a generous $7 and more per bushel. Then fields dried and prospects for a good harvest improved, so corn prices started falling, leaving ethanol producers with contracts for overpriced corn.

More recently, the economy swung downward. A bubble of inflated real estate prices burst, contributing to problems for mortgage lenders that quickly spread to the entire financial industry. As credit dried up, the overall pace of business slowed dramatically, and oil prices fell, erasing some of ethanol's competitive advantage in the marketplace for fuel. But prices for corn also fell, keeping production costs down. Ethanol producers are hopeful that in the long run, drivers will need to rely more and more on alternative fuels. Meanwhile, ethanol companies need steady and farsighted management to guide them through the ups and downs of commodity prices and demand.[2] Besides corn, what are some other products for which prices have swung dramatically?

Poor's 500, and NASDAQ Composite, which combine many companies' performance into a single measurement. Stock indexes tell managers about overall expectations for business value. Of course, managers also follow trends in stocks for their industry and their own company.

The stock market may have a profound effect on the behavior of individual managers. In publicly held companies, managers throughout the organization may feel required to meet Wall Street's earnings expectations. It is quite likely that you, too, at some point in your career, will be asked to improve a budget or estimate because your company does not want to disappoint "the Street." Such external pressures usually have a positive effect—they help make many firms more efficient and profitable. But failure to meet those expectations can cause a company's stock price to drop, making it more difficult for the firm to raise additional capital for investment. The compensation of managers may also be affected, particularly if they have been issued stock options. The net effect of these pressures may sometimes be that managers focus on short-term results at the expense of the long-term success of their organizations. Even worse, a few managers may be tempted to engage in unethical or unlawful behavior that misleads investors.[3] We will discuss managerial ethics in Chapter 5 and stock options in Chapter 10.

Economic conditions change over time and are difficult to predict. Bull and bear markets come and go. Periods of dramatic growth may be followed by a recession. Every trend undoubtedly will end—but when? Even when times seem good, budget deficits or other considerations create concern about the future.

> Economic conditions change over time and are difficult to predict.

Technology

Today a company cannot succeed without incorporating into its strategy the astonishing technologies that exist and continue to evolve. Technological advances create new products, advanced production techniques, and better ways of managing and communicating. In addition, as technology evolves, new industries, markets, and competitive niches develop. For example, early entrants in biotechnology are trying to establish dominant positions, whereas later entrants work on technological advances that will give them a competitive niche. Advances in technology also permit companies to enter markets that would otherwise be unavailable to them, such as when cable TV companies adapted their technology to enter the market for Internet services.

New technologies also provide new production techniques. In manufacturing, sophisticated robots perform jobs without suffering fatigue, requiring vacations or weekends off, or demanding wage increases. New methods, such as injecting steam into oil fields at high pressure (popularly known as fracking), are enabling Shell, ExxonMobil, and other oil companies to extract that valuable resource from locations that had once been considered depleted. In this case, technological and economic forces overlap: the rising price of oil has made it worthwhile for companies to develop and try the new technology.[4]

In addition, new technologies provide new ways to manage and communicate. Computerized management information systems (MISs) make information available when needed, and networking via the Internet makes that information available where it is needed. Computers monitor productivity and note performance deficiencies. Telecommunications allow conferences to take place without requiring people to travel to the same location. Such technological advances create innovations in business. Strategies developed around the cutting edge of technological advances create a competitive advantage; strategies that ignore or lag behind competitors' technology lead to obsolescence and extinction. This issue is so important that we devote an entire chapter (Chapter 17) to the topic.

Laws and Regulations

U.S. government policies impose strategic constraints on organizations but may also provide opportunities.[5] In the United States, the Affordable Care Act of 2010 is a relevant example because it contains such a variety of provisions that some managers have identified mainly costs of compliance whereas others have identified opportunities for their companies.[6] Some provisions of this law impose requirements for insurance coverage (for example, covering dependent children up to age 26 and covering preventive services without charging the patient a copay or deductible). Giving employees more generous benefits could add to the cost of compensating them. Other provisions, such as insurance exchanges and tax credits for small businesses, may help smaller firms compete in the market for talent. Some consequences of the law will differ by industry: a retailer that needs to add an insurance benefit would see a new expense, whereas hospitals are hoping that broader insurance coverage will lower their expense of providing services to patients who cannot pay. As members of society, many of us have strong views about whether the law is beneficial or harmful. As businesspeople, managers also need to sort through the details, plan how to limit any harm, and build on any opportunities.

The government can affect business opportunities through tax laws, economic policies, and international trade rulings. An example of restraint on business action is the U.S. government's standards regarding bribery. In some countries, bribes and kickbacks are common and expected ways of doing business, but for U.S. firms, they are illegal practices. Some U.S. businesses have, in fact, been fined for using bribery when competing internationally. But laws can also assist organizations. Because U.S. federal and state governments protect property rights, including copyrights, trademarks, and patents, it is economically more attractive to start businesses in the United States than in countries where laws and law enforcement offer less protection.

Regulators are specific government organizations in a firm's more immediate task environment. Regulatory agencies such as the Occupational Safety and Health Administration (OSHA), the Interstate Commerce Commission (ICC), the Federal Aviation Administration (FAA), the Equal Employment Opportunity Commission (EEOC), the National Labor Relations Board (NLRB), the Office of Federal Contract Compliance Programs (OFCCP), and the Environmental Protection Agency (EPA) have the power to investigate company practices and take legal action to ensure compliance with laws.

The Securities and Exchange Commission (SEC) regulates U.S. financial markets. Its regulations are intended to protect investors. For instance, the SEC has proposed regulations requiring companies to disclose more details about the total compensation paid to executives, including deferred compensation (pensions, severance pay) and perks (such as free housing and personal use of a corporate jet). The objective of the regulations is to help investors in a company evaluate whether executives are being compensated at an appropriate level.[7]

Another example of a regulatory body is the Food and Drug Administration (FDA), which can prevent a company from selling an unsafe or ineffective product to the public. Following recent highly publicized incidents of illness from people who ate tainted peanuts, lettuce, spinach, and green onions, the FDA came under pressure to tighten its regulations for food safety.

Often, the corporate community sees government as an adversary. However, many organizations realize that government can be a source of competitive advantages for an individual company or an entire industry. Public policy may prevent or limit new foreign or domestic competitors from entering an industry. Government may subsidize failing companies or provide tax breaks to some. Federal patents protect innovative products or production process technologies. Legislation may be passed to support industry prices, thereby guaranteeing profits or survival. The government may even intervene to ensure the survival of certain key industries or companies, as it has done to help auto companies, airlines, and agricultural businesses.

Demographics

Demographics are measures of various characteristics of the people who make up groups or other social units. Work groups, organizations, countries, markets, and societies can be described statistically by referring to demographic measures such as their members' age, gender, family size, income, education, occupation, and so forth.

Managers must consider workforce demographics in formulating their human resources strategies. Population growth influences the size and composition of the labor force. In the decade from 2008 to 2018, the U.S. civilian labor force is expected to grow at a rate of 8.2 percent, reaching 166.9 million.[8] This growth is slower than during the previous decade, partly because young workers—those between the ages of 16 and 24—are declining in numbers. The fastest-growing age group will be workers who are 55 and older, who are expected to represent close to one-fourth of the labor force in 2018. What does this mean for employers? They will need to find ways to retain and fully use the talents of their experienced workers while competing for relatively scarce entry-level workers. They may find that many of their older employees are willing to work past the traditional retirement age of 65; one reason is that research suggests that a lack of pensions and adequate savings will make retirement unaffordable for many of today's baby boomers.[9] Eventually, however, declining participation in work by older persons will require managers to find replacements for these highly experienced workers.

The education and skill levels of the workforce are another demographic factor managers must consider. The share of the U.S. labor force with at least some college education has been increasing steadily over the past several decades, from less than one-fourth of the workforce in 1970 to more than three-fourths today.[10] Even so, many companies find that they must invest heavily in training their entry-level workers, who may not have been adequately prepared for some of the more complex tasks the modern workplace requires. (We discuss training in greater detail in Chapter 10.) Also, as college has become a more popular option, employers are finding it difficult to recruit employees for jobs that require knowledge of a skilled trade, such as machinists and toolmakers, especially in areas where the cost of living is so high that most residents are professionals.[11] However, as education levels improve around the globe, more managers find they are able to send even technical tasks to lower-priced but highly trained workers overseas, which we discuss further in Chapter 6.

Another factor that significantly influences the U.S. population and labor force is immigration. Immigrants represent over 15 percent of the U.S. workforce, although they are a stronger presence in the West (almost 24 percent of the workforce) than in the Midwest (less than 8 percent).[12] Immigrants are frequently of working age but have different educational and occupational backgrounds from the rest of the labor force. Immigration is one reason the labor force in the future will be more ethnically diverse than it is today. The biggest percentage employment increases will be by Hispanics and Asian Americans, followed by African Americans. The demographic importance of immigration intersects with legal issues governing who is permitted to work in the United States. For example, the federal government has recently cracked down not only on undocumented workers but also on the managers who hired them. Other companies have asked the government to admit more foreign workers with technical expertise that may be hard to find in the United States.

Since the last quarter of the 20th century, women have joined the U.S. labor force in record numbers. Throughout the 1970s and 1980s, they became much more likely to take paying jobs. In the 1970s, only about one-third of women were in the labor

As the number of people in the workforce with a college education increases, managers must consider how this affects their work.

demographics

Measures of various characteristics of the people who make up groups or other social units.

Immigration is one reason the labor force in the future will be more ethnically diverse than it is today.

force, but 60 percent had jobs in 1999. Since then, women's labor force participation rate has stayed near that level, declining only slightly. Women's participation contrasts with a participation rate of 72 percent for men, also declining gradually as the workforce ages and more adults retire.[13]

A more diverse workforce has many advantages, but managers have to make certain they provide equality for women and minorities with respect to employment, advancement opportunities, and compensation. They must make strategic plans to recruit, retain, train, motivate, and effectively use people of diverse demographic backgrounds who have the skills to achieve the company's mission. We discuss the issue of managing the diverse workforce in detail in Chapter 11.

Social Issues

Societal trends regarding how people think and behave have major implications for management of the labor force, corporate social actions, and strategic decisions about products and markets. For example, during the 1980s and 1990s, women in the workforce often chose to delay having children as they focused on their careers, but today more women are having children and then returning to the workforce. As a result, companies have introduced more supportive policies, including family leave, flexible working hours, and child care assistance. Many firms also extend these benefits to all employees or allow them to design their own benefits packages, where they can choose from a menu of available benefits that suit their individual situations. Domestic partners, whether they are in a marital relationship or not, also are covered by many employee benefit programs. Firms provide these benefits as a way of increasing a source of competitive advantage: an experienced workforce.

How companies respond to these and other social issues may also affect their reputation in the marketplace, which in turn may help or hinder their competitiveness. For companies in the soft-drink industry, one of the issues demanding a response is the epidemic of obesity and associated health problems such as diabetes. The New York City Board of Health has gone as far as banning sales of sweetened drinks in containers larger than 16 ounces at restaurants and other establishments inspected by the agency. In this social environment, Coke has run ads pointing out that soft drinks aren't the only source of the problem and encouraging consumers to engage in calorie-burning exercise. PepsiCo has been exploring ways to make its soft drinks and snacks "better for you," including research into tastier low-calorie sweeteners. All the major soft-drink makers have introduced reduced-calorie sodas, including Coca-Cola's Sprite Select and PepsiCo's Pepsi Next, which they hope will appeal to consumers who dislike diet drinks.[14]

Sustainability and the Natural Environment

Directly or indirectly, organizations depend on the natural environment to provide them with resources. Depending on their processes, they may need trees for paper, steel for manufacturing goods, petroleum to fuel transportation or make plastics, and adequate air and water quality to maintain a healthy workforce. In addition, the ways in which organizations operate will have some impact on the quantity and quality of natural resources available. When the quantity is depleted or the quality is damaged, costs for resources skyrocket. Furthermore, the impact on natural resources—whether negatively by poisoning wells or positively by restoring forests—affects the quality of life for citizens in the areas where companies operate. Decisions that affect the natural environment therefore shape the climate of social issues and the political and legal environment in which organizations operate.

A dramatic example was the explosion of BP's Deepwater Horizon drilling rig in the Gulf of Mexico, which killed 11 workers and caused millions of barrels of oil to gush into the gulf and spread toward the coastlands of Mississippi and Louisiana. During the weeks that followed, fisheries closed, and tourists vacationed elsewhere. BP was forced to set aside tens of billions of dollars to cover all costs of the spill and its cleanup. In addition, the U.S. government assessed billions of dollars in fines against the company; and to prevent similar accidents in the future, it imposed additional regulations on any oil companies that want to drill in the Gulf.[15]

Protecting the natural environment has become so important to managerial decisions that we devote Appendix B following Chapter 5 to that subject.

The Competitive Environment

All managers are affected by the components of the macroenvironment we just discussed. But each organization also functions in a closer, more immediate competitive environment. The competitive environment includes the organizations with which the organization directly interacts. As shown in Figure 2.4, the competitive environment includes rivalry among current competitors and the impact of new entrants, substitute and complementary products, suppliers, and customers. This model was originally developed by Michael Porter, a Harvard professor and a noted authority on strategic management. According to Porter, successful managers do more than simply react to the environment; they act in ways that actually shape or change the organization's environment. In strategic decision making, Porter's model is an excellent method to help managers analyze the competitive environment and adapt to or influence the nature of their competition.

Competitors

Among the various components of the competitive environment, competitors within the industry must first deal with one another. When organizations compete for the same customers and try to win market share at the others' expense, all must react to and anticipate their competitors' actions.

The first question to consider is this: Who is the competition? Sometimes the answer is obvious. The major competitors in the market for soft drinks are Coca-Cola and PepsiCo. But consumer tastes have shifted away from soda to bottled water and other beverages. Young people, who in the past were the main consumers of soft drinks, increasingly prefer to buy water, coffee, or energy drinks, so for years, sales of soda have been declining. Therefore, Coca-Cola and PepsiCo have had to compete in introducing new products, not just in winning consumers over to their brand of cola.[16]

FIGURE 2.4
The Competitive Environment

The competition between Coke and Pepsi products is intense. Often, the products are found side by side, as is the case with these vending machines.

Thus, as a first step in understanding their competitive environment, organizations must identify their competitors. Competitors may include (1) small domestic firms, especially their entry into tiny, premium markets; (2) strong regional competitors; (3) big new domestic companies exploring new markets; (4) overseas firms, especially those that either try to solidify their position in small niches (a traditional Japanese tactic) or are able to draw on an inexpensive labor force on a large scale (as in China); and (5) newer entries, such as firms offering their products on the web. The growth in competition from other countries has been especially significant in recent years with the worldwide reduction in international trade barriers. For example, the North American Free Trade Agreement (NAFTA) sharply reduced tariffs on trade between the United States, Canada, and Mexico. Managers today confront a particular challenge from low-cost producers abroad (see Chapter 6).

Once competitors have been identified, the next step is to analyze how they compete. Competitors use tactics such as price reductions, new product introductions, and advertising campaigns to gain advantage over their rivals. In its competition against PepsiCo, Coca-Cola outdoes its rival with much heavier spending on advertising. The emphasis on promotion helps the company win a larger share of not only the cola market but also juices (its Minute Maid outsells PepsiCo's Tropicana) and sports drinks (its Powerade is beating PepsiCo's Gatorade). PepsiCo has tried to catch up by spending more on advertising, but this is a difficult game to win.[17]

It's essential to understand what competitors are doing when you are honing your own strategy. If soft-drink consumption continues to fall, Coke will have to be careful not to be complacent about its leadership role versus Pepsi. Most of Coke's sales are beverages. PepsiCo, in contrast, has expanded into a broader range of products, hoping to grow sales whether consumers are looking for a fun treat or a healthful snack. In beverages, PepsiCo's CEO Indra Nooyi says the company's success should be measured in terms of its share of "total liquid refreshment." And besides reducing salt and sugar in traditional snacks such as chips, the company is expanding healthful options under its Quaker brand (for example, Real Medleys multigrain cereal) and in a joint venture called Müller Quaker Dairy, which is rolling out a line of yogurt with tasty mix-ins. These are areas in which Coke lacks a presence— but also are less profitable than soft drinks.[18]

> It's essential to understand what competitors are doing when you are honing your own strategy.

Competition is most intense when there are many direct competitors (including foreign contenders), when industry growth is slow, and when the product or service cannot be differentiated in some way. New, high-growth industries offer enormous opportunities for profits. When an industry matures and growth slows, profits drop. Then intense competition causes an industry shakeout: weaker companies are eliminated, and the strong companies survive.[19] We will discuss the issue of competitors and strategy in further detail in Chapter 4.

New Entrants

New entrants into an industry compete with established companies. New entrants in the market for entertainment have come from unexpected quarters as increasing broadband speeds and more powerful microprocessors have enabled a whole host of ways to enjoy videos and games online. Cable and satellite television saw viewers flock to Hulu, Blockbuster lost movie sales to Netflix, and the makers of game consoles have watched sales dry up as consumers switched to playing Farmville via Facebook and downloading the Angry Birds app for their smart phones.

If many factors prevent new companies from entering an industry, the threat to established firms is less serious. If there are few such **barriers to entry,** the threat of

barriers to entry

Conditions that prevent new companies from entering an industry.

new entrants is more serious. Some major barriers to entry are government policy, capital requirements, brand identification, cost disadvantages, and distribution channels. The government can limit or prevent entry, as occurs when the FDA forbids a new drug entrant. Some industries, such as liquor retailing, are regulated; more subtle government controls operate in fields such as mining and ski area development. Patents are also entry barriers. When a patent expires, other companies can then enter the market. For example, the patents have recently expired on several drugs made by Pfizer, including antidepressant Zoloft, allergy medicine Zyrtec, and blood pressure medicine Norvasc. At the same time, several research projects to introduce new, patented medicines have failed, so Pfizer was forced to lay off employees and close some facilities to cut costs.[20]

Other barriers are less formal but can have the same effect. Capital requirements may be so high that companies won't risk or try to raise such large amounts of money. Brand identification forces new entrants to spend heavily to overcome customer loyalty. Imagine, for example, the costs involved in trying to launch a new cola against Coke or Pepsi. The cost advantages established companies hold—due to large size, favorable locations, existing assets, and so forth—can also be formidable entry barriers.

Finally, existing competitors may have such tight distribution channels that new entrants have difficulty getting their goods or services to customers. For example, established food products already have supermarket shelf space. New entrants must displace existing products with promotions, price breaks, intensive selling, and other tactics.

> ### Bottom Line
> Cost is often a major barrier to entry.
> *Would cost be a bigger barrier for a soft-drink maker or an operator of hot dog stands? Why?*

In Practice

TATA MOTORS ENTERS THE FIELD

The barriers to entry are so high in the automotive industry that it's rare to see a new entrant. A notable exception has been India's Tata Motors, the country's largest maker of commercial vehicles, which a few years ago promised to become a leading car maker in the fast-growing economies of the developing world. Tata announced it was developing a "people's car." Priced at $2,000 to $2,500 (or 1 lakh in Indian currency), the Nano would become the standard transportation for Indian families working their way up to the middle class.

However, it is not yet clear whether Tata will overcome the industry's barriers to success. The promised launch was so ambitious that Tata could not realistically meet expectations. Production was postponed for about a year and a half, and then the company determined it couldn't afford to sell the Nano profitably at the promised price. The first Nanos to roll off assembly lines were priced just $800 below Suzuki's competing Alto, which offers more storage space and a bigger engine. The Nano's safety performance also ran into embarrassing problems; some reportedly caught fire.

Tata has responded with price adjustments, maintenance contracts, test drives, and safety improvements. It has revenues from its commercial vehicles and its Jaguar Land Rover operations to stay afloat. Perhaps the Nano will still become the people's car. Start-ups often make mistakes, and some of them recover brilliantly. What made Tata's stumble remarkable was its grand scale.[21]

- What barriers to entry would you expect for entering the auto market at the low end, as Tata did with the Nano?

Substitutes and Complements

Besides products that directly compete, other products can affect a company's performance by being substitutes for or complements of the company's offerings. A *substitute* is a potential threat; customers use it as an alternative, buying less of one kind of

TABLE 2.1
Potential Substitutes for
and Complements of
Products

If the Product Is . . .	The Substitute Might Be . . .
Coca-Cola Classic	Starbucks mocha
HP laptop computer	iPad tablet computer
Nissan Sentra (purchased)	Nissan Sentra and Honda CR-V (shared via Zipcar)
SanDisk USB flash drive	CrashPlan online backup service
If the Product Is . . .	**The Complement Might Be . . .**
Starbucks coffee	Starbucks Cake Pops
Netflix streaming video	Orville Redenbacher's popcorn
iTouch media player	iTunes music store
Apartment rental	IKEA furniture

product but more of another. A *complement* is a potential opportunity because customers buy more of a given product if they also demand more of the complementary product. Table 2.1 lists a dozen products and their potential substitutes and complements.

Technological advances and economic efficiencies are among the ways that firms can develop substitutes for existing products. After Amazon introduced the Kindle e-reader and Barnes & Noble introduced the competing Nook—and even more so as the companies were able to lower the price of these devices—consumers began treating e-books as an attractive substitute for printed books. But even as consumers were still gravitating toward e-readers, Apple launched the iPad tablet computer. Because it is lightweight and versatile, consumers are treating it as a substitute not only for e-readers but also in some cases as a substitute for a basic laptop computer.

Companies don't have to be at the mercy of customers switching to a substitute. To avoid losing out when others create a new supplement, some companies try to create their own supplementary products. PepsiCo's investment in development of new sweeteners and more healthful snacks is a way to offer substitutes for consumers avoiding the calories, fat, and sugar of its "fun for you" products. Anticipating that a growing share of consumers will care about healthful snacking, PepsiCo CEO Nooyi believes the company's products should include many choices that are "better for you" or "good for you."[22]

Besides identifying and planning for substitutes, companies must consider complements for their products. When people are buying new homes, they are also buying appliances and landscaping products. When they buy a car, they buy insurance for it. When they buy a Kindle, they buy e-books, and when they buy an iPad, they buy a variety of apps for playing games, reading the news, and many other activities. And when consumers munch on Lays, Doritos, or Cheetos snacks, they are bound to get thirsty and need a complementary product—say, an ice-cold Pepsi or Sierra Mist. PepsiCo owns all these food and drink brands; the company sells products that are complements as well as supplements. If PepsiCo meets its goal to shift more of its product line to healthier fare, it may become known for complementary products there, too—say, some Tropicana juice with your Quaker oatmeal or some Aquafina water with your Müller by Quaker yogurt.[23]

> Organizations are at a disadvantage if they become overly dependent on any powerful supplier.

As with substitutes, a company needs to watch for new complements that can change the competitive landscape. Publishers that originally saw e-readers and tablet computers as a threat—as substitutes for their print publications—have tried to develop profitable ways of providing complements for the devices: electronic books and magazines as well as apps for reading content online. Textbook and cookbook publishers have teamed up with a software company called Inkling to prepare e-book versions of titles that support the use of multimedia and interactive features. In this case, the books offer capabilities that would be impossible in the print version of the book and therefore sell at a higher price.[24]

Suppliers

Recall from our earlier mention of open systems that organizations must acquire resources (inputs) from their environment and convert those resources into products or services (outputs) to sell. Suppliers provide the resources needed for production, and those resources may come in the form of people (supplied by trade schools and universities), raw materials (from producers, wholesalers, and distributors), information (supplied by researchers and consulting firms), and financial capital (from banks and other sources). But suppliers are important to an organization for reasons that go beyond the resources they provide. Suppliers can raise their prices or provide poor-quality goods and services. Workers may produce either outstanding or defective work. Powerful suppliers, then, can reduce an organization's profits, particularly if the organization cannot pass on price increases to its customers.

Organizations are at a disadvantage if they become overly dependent on any powerful supplier. A supplier is powerful if the buyer has few other sources of supply or if the supplier has many other buyers. Dependence also results from high **switching costs**—the fixed costs buyers face if they change suppliers. For example, once a buyer learns how to operate a supplier's equipment, such as computer software, the buyer faces both economic and psychological costs in changing to a new supplier. Of course, close supplier relationships can also be a source of advantages. Food and beverage companies work closely with the makers of the flavorings and additives that make their products appealing to consumers. With companies such as PepsiCo and Coca-Cola looking to offer more healthful and natural versions of their soft drinks, suppliers such as Archer Daniels Midland and Wild Flavors are coming up with blends of vitamins and minerals, sweeteners based on the stevia plant, energy boosters extracted from coffee beans, and new flavors such as ginger and chili.[25]

In recent years, supply chain management has become an increasingly important contributor to a company's competitiveness and profitability. By **supply chain management,** also known as the extended enterprise, we mean the managing of the entire network of facilities and people that obtain raw materials from outside the organization, transform them into products, and distribute them to customers.[26] In the past, managers did not have to pay as much attention to supply chain management as they do today. Products tended to be standardized, overseas competition was still years in the future, and the pace of change was slower. But increased competition has required managers to pay very close attention to their costs. For example, they can no longer afford to hold large and costly inventories, waiting for orders to come in. Also, once orders do come in, some products still sitting in inventory might well be out of date.

With the emergence of the Internet, customers look for products built to their specific needs and preferences—and they want them delivered quickly at the lowest available price. This requires the supply chain to be not only efficient but also *flexible*, so that the organization's output can quickly respond to changes in demand.

Today, the goal of effective supply chain management is to have the right product in the right quantity available at the right place at the right cost. Boeing, the aircraft and defense systems company, provides a good example of effective supply chain management. Boeing forges partnerships with its suppliers to share knowledge that will help them learn how to operate more efficiently. For example, at Boeing Integrated Defense Systems (IDS), Rick Behrens is senior manager of

switching costs

Fixed costs buyers face when they change suppliers.

supply chain management

The managing of the network of facilities and people that obtain materials from outside the organization, transform them into products, and distribute them to customers.

Bottom Line

The ability to manufacture even customized products quickly has become a competitive requirement.
To meet this requirement, what qualities would a company need in its employees?

A Keurig single-serving coffee maker is shown at the Green Mountain Coffee Roasters outlet store in Waterbury, Vermont. Green Mountain Coffee Roasters was granted approval by the Federal Trade Commission to buy single-cup brewing systems maker Keurig Incorporated. Green Mountain already owned 35 percent of Keurig and announced that it would acquire the company outright. Do you think this collaboration will benefit the company or the customers?

supplier development, charged with building close supplier relationships and help-ing them understand Boeing's commitment to lean operations, aimed at eliminat-ing waste. Behrens tailors the supplier relationships to each supplier's familiarity with lean processes. He educates some suppliers in the basics of how to run lean operations; for others, he sends a supplier development team to the organization to help it streamline certain activities. He also identifies Boeing specialists who can help suppliers with particularly challenging problems. Along the way, Behrens helps suppliers develop their abilities so that they can move from simply selling parts to providing complete subassemblies. In Behrens's words, "We need suppliers that can grow with us."[27]

In sum, choosing the right supplier is an important strategic decision. Suppliers can affect manufacturing time, product quality, and inventory levels. The relationship between suppliers and the organization is changing in many companies. The close supplier relationship has become a new model for many organizations that are using a just-in-time manufacturing approach (discussed further in Chapters 16 and 17). And in some companies, innovative managers are forming strategic partnerships with their key suppliers in developing new products or new production techniques. We describe this kind of strategic partnership in more detail in Chapter 9.

In Practice

NATURAL FORCES DISRUPT SUPPLY CHAINS

Highly efficient supply chains depend on reliable suppliers, and recent events have shown that the external environment can break those chains. The 2011 earthquake and tsunami that devastated Japan created supply chain headaches for automakers in the United States, which depend on Japanese suppliers for a variety of components, including microchips, LCD panels, and optical sensors.

One response was to cut production processes that depend on parts from Japan. For example, in a facility north of Tokyo, Hitachi Automotive Systems makes an electronic part used in mass airflow sensors. Hitachi's share of the market for airflow sensors is about 60 percent, so when its facility was damaged, automakers feared they wouldn't have enough of these sensors to meet production goals. General Motors stopped production at facto-ries in Louisiana, Germany, and Spain, and Peugeot-Citroën reduced production of several models. Ford initially announced no production cuts but said it was monitoring its supply of sensors on an hourly basis.

Other companies have spotted opportunities to solve supply chain problems. Gage Prod-ucts Company, located near Detroit, cleans and maintains painting systems for automakers. When the earthquake shut down a paint-manufacturing plant in Japan, auto companies were limited in the paints they could use. Before switching from a paint from Japan to an available alternative, they had to clean out their equipment. Gage quickly filled up its schedule with jobs to clean out paint machines.[28]

- Given these problems, why would auto companies want close relationships with a few suppliers?

Customers

Customers purchase the goods or services an organization offers. Without cus-tomers, a company won't survive. Customers can be intermediate (wholesalers and retailers) or final (end users), depending on where they are in the value chain. You are a **final consumer** when you buy a McDonald's hamburger or a pair of jeans from

Aéropostale. **Intermediate consumers** buy raw materials or wholesale products and then sell to final consumers, as when Sony buys components from IBM and ATI Technologies and uses them to make PS3 consoles. Intermediate customers actually make more purchases than individual final consumers do. Types of intermediate customers include retailers, who buy clothes from wholesalers and manufacturers' representatives before selling them to their customers, and industrial buyers, who buy raw materials (such as chemicals) before converting them into final products. Selling to intermediate customers is often called *business-to-business* (B2B) selling. Notice in these B2B examples that the intermediate customer eventually goes on to become a seller.

Like suppliers, customers are important to organizations for reasons other than the money they provide for goods and services. Customers can demand lower prices, higher quality, unique product specifications, or better service. They also can play competitors against one another, as occurs when a car buyer (or a purchasing agent) collects different offers and negotiates for the best price. Many companies are finding that today's customers want to be actively involved with their products, as when the buyer of an iPhone customizes it with ring tones, wallpaper, and a variety of apps. Dell Inc. took customer input a step further by asking customers what they want the company to develop next. At Dell's IdeaStorm website (www.ideastorm.com), visitors can post ideas and comments about products. One of IdeaStorm's most enthusiastic customer-users became so involved with the resulting community that he was eventually hired as the project's manager and helped expand the site's customer interactions.[29]

The Internet has further empowered customers. It provides an easy source of information—both about product features and about pricing. In addition, today's Internet users informally create and share messages about a product, which provides flattering free "advertising" at best or embarrassing and even erroneous bad publicity at worst. Companies try to use this to their advantage by creating opportunities for consumers and the brand to interact. For example, PepsiCo created the Pepsi Pulse website (www.pepsi.com) to lure consumers with features such as top-ten rankings of pop-culture interests. Celebrities go on the site to offer challenges such as an invitation to post photos related to a theme. A research company collects data about what people say and do on the site, and this helps Pepsi learn more about its customers' interests.[30]

As we discussed in Chapter 1, customer service means giving customers what they want or need, the way they want it, the first time. This usually depends on the speed and dependability with which an organization can deliver its products. Actions and attitudes that provide excellent customer service include the following:

Speed of filling and delivering normal orders.
Willingness to meet emergency needs.
Merchandise delivered in good condition.
Readiness to take back defective goods and resupply quickly.
Availability of installation and repair services and parts.
Service charges (that is, whether services are free or priced separately).[31]

An organization is at a disadvantage if it depends too heavily on powerful customers. Customers are powerful if they make large purchases or if they can easily find alternative places to buy. If you are the largest customer of a firm and you can buy from others, you have power over that firm, and you most likely can negotiate with it successfully. Your firm's biggest customers—especially if they can buy from other sources—will have the greatest negotiating power over you. Customer relationship management is discussed more fully in Chapter 9. As you read "Management Connection: Progress Report," consider how Facebook distinguishes itself with customers by seeking advantages in its relationships with other parties in the competitive environment.

intermediate consumer

A customer who purchases raw materials or wholesale products before selling them to final customers.

Bottom Line

In all businesses—services as well as manufacturing—strategies that emphasize good customer service provide a critical competitive advantage. *Name a company that has delivered good customer service to you.*

Management Connection

FACEBOOK'S FIERCELY COMPETITIVE ENVIRONMENT

Even as technology transformed the macroenvironment for Facebook, its competitive environment is shifting almost as rapidly. Four Internet-era giants—Facebook, Amazon, Apple, and Google—once ruled separate domains but now are increasingly fighting for the same territory. Amazon started as a bookstore but now sells information for its Kindle e-reader, making it a competitor with Apple. Google created a social-networking service (Google+), and Facebook launched a search tool for its site. Some observers predict Google and Facebook will be players in the market for mobile devices, to drive more usage of their services.

As they seek ever-larger shares of online activity, Facebook and these competitors rely on their customer data. As you saw at the beginning of this chapter, details about consumers and their behavior make advertising on Facebook valuable. Facebook has commissioned studies of the value of social marketing. In one case, it found that if Facebook users were fans of Starbucks (by "liking" the brand's page and therefore getting messages from the brand), they and their friends bought from Starbucks more often. Promoting such results helps Facebook charge more for promotions on its site. The other Internet giants gather different kinds of data. Amazon has information about product searches and purchases. Google knows what a person is searching for but not necessarily the person's

opinions about the content. Until it launched Google+, Google would not have known personal details such as age, interests, and relationships; adding a social network delivers a powerful combination of information sources.

No wonder, then, that Facebook launched its own search tool. But can a social search engine compete with Google? It's handy for discovering what restaurants your friends like. But it won't give you a weather forecast or directions to your job interview; for that, Facebook's search engine has partnered with Microsoft's Bing. Facebook's hope is that the tools will be helpful enough to keep people from leaving Facebook. If it can do so, it will have succeeded against a formidable competitor. So far, Google is taking in three-quarters of the ad spending on search ads (the links that show up beside users' search results). Some people see Facebook at a disadvantage because it waited until recently to offer a search function; others see Google+ as far behind Facebook in the social-networking arena.[32]

- Are Amazon, Apple, and Google competitors in Facebook's competitive environment or sellers of complements? Explain.
- Facebook has two major kinds of customers: the users of its site and the advertisers on its site. What challenges does Facebook face from Google in serving each customer group?

Environmental Analysis

If managers do not understand how the environment affects their organizations or cannot identify opportunities and threats that are likely to be important, their ability to make decisions and execute plans will be severely limited. For example, if little is known about customer likes and dislikes, organizations will have a difficult time designing new products, scheduling production, or developing marketing plans. In short, timely and accurate environmental information is critical for running a business.

But information about the environment is not always readily available. For example, even economists have difficulty predicting whether an upturn or a downturn in the economy is likely. Moreover, managers find it difficult to forecast how well their own products will sell, let alone how a competitor might respond. In other words, managers often operate under conditions of uncertainty. **Environmental uncertainty** means that managers do not have enough information about the environment to understand or predict the future. Uncertainty arises from two related factors: complexity and dynamism. Environmental *complexity* refers to the number of issues to which a manager must attend as well as their interconnectedness. For example, industries that have many firms that compete in vastly different ways tend to be more complex—and uncertain—than industries with only a few key competitors. Similarly, environmental dynamism refers to the degree of discontinuous change that occurs within the industry. High-growth industries with products and technologies that change rapidly tend to be more uncertain than stable industries where change is less dramatic and more predictable.[33]

As environmental uncertainty increases, managers must develop techniques and methods for collecting, sorting through, and interpreting information about the environment. We discuss some of these approaches in this section of the chapter. (In the next chapter, we will

> Managers often operate under conditions of uncertainty.

also discuss how managers make decisions under conditions of uncertainty.) By analyzing environmental forces—in both the macroenvironment and the competitive environment—managers can identify opportunities and threats that might affect the organization.

Environmental Scanning

Perhaps the first step in coping with uncertainty in the environment is pinning down what might be important. Frequently, organizations and individuals act out of ignorance, only to regret those actions in the future. IBM, for example, had the opportunity to purchase the technology behind xerography but turned it down. Xerox saw the potential, and the rest is history. However, Xerox researchers later developed the technology for the original computer mouse, but not seeing the potential, the company missed an important market opportunity.

To understand and predict changes, opportunities, and threats, organizations such as Monsanto, Weyerhaeuser, and Union Carbide spend a good deal of time and money monitoring events in the environment. **Environmental scanning** means both searching out information that is unavailable to most people and sorting through that information to interpret what is important and what is not. Managers can ask questions such as these:

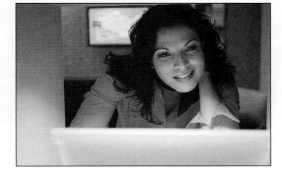

As a manager, you will likely be involved in budgeting. Using what you have learned in this chapter, how would you approach this task?

Who are our current competitors?
Are there few or many entry barriers to our industry?
What substitutes exist for our product or service?
Is the company too dependent on powerful suppliers?
Is the company too dependent on powerful customers?[34]

Answers to these questions help managers develop **competitive intelligence,** the information necessary to decide how best to manage in the competitive environment they have identified. Porter's competitive analysis, discussed earlier, can guide environmental scanning and help managers evaluate the competitive potential of different environments. Table 2.2 describes two extreme environments: an attractive environment, which gives a firm a competitive advantage, and an unattractive environment, which puts a firm at a competitive disadvantage.[35]

Scenario Development

As managers attempt to determine the effect of environmental forces on their organizations, they frequently develop **scenarios** of the future. Scenarios create alternative combinations of different factors into a total picture of the environment and the firm. For example, when Congress and the president must forecast the size of the federal budget deficit, they develop several scenarios about what the economy is likely to do over the next decade or so. Frequently, organizations develop a *best-case scenario* (the occurrence of events that are favorable to the firm), a *worst-case scenario* (the

environmental scanning

Searching for and sorting through information about the environment.

competitive intelligence

Information that helps managers determine how to compete better.

scenario

A narrative that describes a particular set of future conditions.

TABLE 2.2
Attractive and Unattractive
Environments

Environmental Factor	Unattractive	Attractive
Competitors	Many; low industry growth; equal size; commodity	Few; high industry growth; unequal size; differentiated
Threat of entry	High threat; few entry barriers	Low threat; many entry barriers
Substitutes	Many	Few
Suppliers	Few; high bargaining power	Many; low bargaining power
Customers	Few; high bargaining power	Many; low bargaining power

occurrence of unfavorable events), and some middle-ground alternatives. The formal practice of scenario development was pioneered by Royal/Dutch Shell.

The value of scenario development is that it helps managers develop contingency plans for what they might do given different outcomes.[36] For example, as a manager, you will quite likely be involved in budgeting for your area. You will almost certainly be asked to list initiatives that you would eliminate in case of an economic downturn and new investments you would make if your firm does better than expected.

Effective managers regard the scenarios they develop as living documents, not merely prepared once and put aside. Instead they constantly update the scenarios to take into account relevant new factors that emerge, such as significant changes in the economy or actions by competitors.

Forecasting

forecasting

Method for predicting how variables will change the future.

Whereas environmental scanning is used to identify important factors, and scenario development is used to develop alternative pictures of the future, **forecasting** is used to predict exactly how some variable or variables will change in the future. For example, in making capital investments, firms may try to forecast how interest rates will change. In deciding to expand or downsize a business, firms may try to forecast the demand for goods and services or forecast the supply and demand of labor they probably would use. Publications such as *Bloomberg Businessweek*'s *Business Outlook* provide forecasts to businesses both large and small.

Although forecasts are designed to help executives make predictions about the future, their accuracy varies from application to application. Because they extrapolate from the past to project the future, forecasts tend to be most accurate when the future ends up looking a lot like the past. Of course, we don't need sophisticated forecasts in those instances. Forecasts are most useful when the future will look radically different from the past. Unfortunately, that is when forecasts tend to be less accurate. The more things change, the less confidence we tend to have in our forecasts. The best advice for using forecasts might include the following ideas:

Use multiple forecasts, and perhaps average their predictions.
Remember that accuracy decreases the further into the future you are trying to predict.
Forecasts are no better than the data used to construct them.
Use simple forecasts (rather than complicated ones) when possible.
Keep in mind that important events often are surprises and represent a departure from predictions.[37]

Benchmarking

benchmarking

The process of comparing an organization's practices and technologies with those of other companies.

In addition to trying to predict changes in the environment, firms can undertake intensive study of the best practices of various firms to understand their sources of competitive advantage. **Benchmarking** means identifying the best-in-class performance by a company in a given area, say, product development or customer service, and then comparing your processes to theirs. To accomplish this, a benchmarking team would collect information on its own company's operations and those of the other firm to determine gaps. These gaps serve as a point of entry to learn the underlying causes of performance differences. Ultimately, the team would map out a set of best practices that lead to world-class performance. We will discuss benchmarking further in Chapter 4.

Responding to the Environment

For managers and organizations, responding effectively to their environments is almost always essential. Clothing retailers who pay no attention to changes in the public's style preferences, or manufacturers who don't make sure they have steady sources of supply, are soon out of business. To respond to their environment, managers and companies have a number of options, which can be grouped into three categories: (1) selecting a new environment, (2) influencing the environment, and (3) adapting to the environment. This section describes the options briefly; we will elaborate on them in Chapter 4.

Changing the Environment You Are In

Organizations need not be stuck within some given environment; they have options for defining where they operate. We refer to this category of responses as **strategic maneuvering.** By making a conscious effort to change the boundaries of its competitive environment, a firm can maneuver around potential threats and capitalize on arising opportunities.[38] Managers can use several strategic maneuvers, including domain selection, diversification, merger and acquisition, and divestiture.[39]

strategic maneuvering

An organization's conscious efforts to change the boundaries of its task environment.

Domain selection is the entrance by a company into another suitable market or industry. For example, the market may have limited competition or regulation, ample suppliers and customers, or high growth. PepsiCo's decision to begin selling yogurt was based on the company's goal of selling more healthful snacks coupled with the recent growing popularity of yogurt in the United States. The company also saw an opportunity to do more with its Quaker brand by offering varieties with granola and other tidbits to mix in.[40]

domain selection

Entering a new market or industry with an existing expertise.

Diversification occurs when a firm invests in different types of businesses or products or when it expands geographically to reduce its dependence on a single market or technology. Apple successfully diversified its product line when it added the iPod, iTouch, iPad, and iPhone to its offerings of personal computers. As the popularity of the devices has spread, Apple has identified an opportunity to diversify its customer base as well. Apple recently partnered with Unisys to provide tech support so that Apple can serve organizational customers better. Besides maintaining systems, Unisys will write business- and government-related apps. For example, Unisys provides border patrol agents with an iPhone app that lets them easily look up border-crossing data.[41]

diversification

A firm's investment in a different product, business, or geographic area.

A **merger** or **acquisition** takes place when two or more firms combine, or one firm buys another, to form a single company. Mergers and acquisitions can offer greater efficiency from combined operations or can give companies relatively quick access to new markets or industries. After Bayer acquired Schering, it announced plans to cut more than 6,000 jobs to "create an internationally successful pharmaceutical company with competitive cost structures," in the words of Werner Wenning, Bayer Schering Pharma's board chairman.[42] Acquisitions can also give a company quick expertise in an area where it wants to grow. PepsiCo's drive to expand into healthier foods has been helped by acquisitions such as Quaker Oats in 2000 and Wimm-Bill-Dann, a Russian dairy company, in 2012.[43]

merger

One or more companies combining with another.

acquisition

One firm buying another.

divestiture

A firm selling one or more businesses.

prospectors

Companies that continually change the boundaries for their task environments by seeking new products and markets, diversifying and merging, or acquiring new enterprises.

defenders

Companies that stay within a stable product domain as a strategic maneuver.

independent strategies

Strategies that an organization acting on its own uses to change some aspect of its current environment.

Divestiture occurs when a company sells one or more businesses. At Ford Motor Company, recent operating losses and the costs of restructuring its workforce have brought about a cash shortage. To raise cash, Ford sold its Aston Martin sports car brand and its Hertz rental car unit.[44]

Organizations engage in strategic maneuvering when they move into different environments. Some companies, called **prospectors,** are more likely than others to engage in strategic maneuvering.[45] Aggressive companies continuously change the boundaries of their competitive environments by seeking new products and markets, diversifying, and merging or acquiring new enterprises. In these and other ways, corporations put their competitors on the defensive and force them to react. **Defenders,** in contrast, stay within a more limited, stable product domain.

Influencing Your Environment

In addition to redefining the boundaries of their environment, managers and organizations can develop proactive responses aimed at changing the environment. Two general types of proactive responses are independent action and cooperative action.

Independent Action   A company uses **independent strategies** when it acts on its own to change some aspect of its current environment.[46] Table 2.3 shows the definitions and uses of these strategies. For example, Southwest Airlines demonstrates competitive aggression by cutting fares when it enters a new market, and Apple uses competitive aggression whenever it launches a new product such as the iPhone or iTunes with great fanfare to establish its dominance as a technological leader. In contrast, when Kellogg Company promotes the cereal industry as a whole, it demonstrates competitive pacification. Weyerhaeuser Company advertises its reforestation efforts (public relations). The Gap, Motorola, Nike, American Express, Converse, and other companies have signed on to Product Red, a program in which they market special Red-themed products and donate a percentage of the profits to the Global

TABLE 2.3   Independent Action

Strategy	Definition	Examples
Competitive aggression	Exploiting a distinctive competence or improving internal efficiency for competitive advantage	Aggressive pricing, comparative advertising (e.g., Walmart)
Competitive pacification	Independent action to improve relations with competitors	Helping competitors find raw materials
Public relations	Establishing and maintaining favorable images in the minds of those making up the environment	Sponsoring sporting events
Voluntary action	Voluntary commitment to various interest groups, causes, and social problems	Johnson & Johnson donating supplies to tsunami victims
Legal action	Engaging company in private legal battle	Warner Music lawsuits against illegal music copying
Political action	Efforts to influence elected representatives to create a more favorable business environment or limit competition	Issue advertising; lobbying at state and national levels

SOURCE: Adapted from *Journal of Marketing,* published by the American Marketing Association. C. Zeithaml and V. Zeithaml, "Environmental Management: Revising the Marketing Perspective," Spring 1984.

Fund, a project to help end AIDS in Africa (voluntary action). Viacom sued Google for allowing users to post copyrighted video clips on the Google-owned YouTube website (legal action). In a recent year, pharmaceutical companies spent $1.1 billion to lobby members of Congress (political action); insurers, the second biggest spenders on lobbying, paid out almost $900 million.[47] Each of these examples shows how organizations—on their own—can have an impact on the environment.

Cooperative Action   In some situations, two or more organizations work together using **cooperative strategies** to influence the environment.[48] Table 2.4 shows several examples of cooperative strategies. An example of contracting occurs when suppliers and customers, or managers and labor unions, sign formal agreements about the terms and conditions of their future relationships. These contracts are explicit attempts to make their future relationship predictable. An example of cooptation might occur when universities invite wealthy alumni to join their boards of directors.

cooperative strategies
Strategies used by two or more organizations working together to manage the external environment.

Finally, an example of coalition formation might be when local businesses band together to curb the rise of employee health care costs and when organizations in the same industry form industry associations and special interest groups. You may have seen cooperative advertising strategies, such as when dairy producers, beef producers, orange growers, and the like jointly pay for television commercials. Life Is Good, a New England–based T-shirt company, used the latest economic downturn as an opportunity to strengthen cooperative action with the retailers that stock its products. According to cofounder Bert Jacobs, employees at Life Is Good began calling retailers to ask how they could help them through the slow times. Based on the feedback, Jacobs identified a need to establish online networks that retailers—his company's customers—could use for sharing ideas.[49]

How did T-shirt company Life Is Good use the economic downturn as an opportunity?

At the organizational level, firms establish strategic alliances, partnerships, joint ventures, and mergers with competitors to deal with environmental uncertainties. Cooperative strategies such as these make most sense when (1) taking joint action will reduce the organizations' costs and risks and (2) cooperation will increase their power—that is, their ability to accomplish the changes they desire successfully.

Strategy	Definition	Examples
Contraction	Negotiation of an agreement between the organization and another group to exchange goods, services, information, patents, and so on	Contractual marketing systems
Cooptation	Absorbing new elements into the organization's leadership structure to avert threats to its stability or existence	Consumer and labor representatives and bankers on boards of directors
Coalition	Two or more groups that coalesce and act jointly with respect to some set of issues for some period of time	Industry associations; political initiatives of the Business Roundtable and the U.S. Chamber of Commerce

TABLE 2.4
Cooperative Action

SOURCE: Reprinted from *Journal of Marketing*, published by the American Marketing Association. C. Zeithaml and V. Zeithaml, "Environmental Management: Revising the Marketing Perspective," Spring 1984.

Adapting to the Environment: Changing Yourself

To cope with environmental uncertainty, organizations frequently make adjustments in their structures and work processes. When uncertainty arises from environmental complexity, organizations tend to adapt by decentralizing decision making. For example, if a company faces a growing number of competitors in various markets, if different customers want different things, if the dissimilar characteristics of different products keep increasing, and if production facilities are being built in different regions of the world, it may be impossible for the chief executive (or a small group of top executives) to keep abreast of all activities and understand all the operational details of a business. In these cases, the top management team is likely to give authority to lower-level managers to make decisions that benefit the firm. The term **empowerment** is used frequently today to talk about this type of decentralized authority. We will address empowerment and decision making in more detail in Chapters 3 and 9.

In response to uncertainty caused by change (dynamism) in the environment, organizations tend to establish more flexible structures. In today's business world, the term *bureaucracy* generally has a bad connotation. Most of us recognize that bureaucratic organizations tend to be formal and very stable; frequently they are unable to adjust to change or exceptional circumstances that "don't fit the rules." And although bureaucratic organizations may be efficient and controlled if the environment is stable, they tend to be slow-moving and plodding when products, technologies, customers, or competitors are changing over time. In these cases, more *organic* structures give organizations the flexibility to adjust to change. We will discuss organic structures in more detail in Chapter 9, but we can simply say here that they are less formal than bureaucratic organizations—making decisions through interaction and mutual adjustment among individuals rather than from a set of predefined rules. Table 2.5 shows four approaches that organizations can take in adapting to environmental uncertainty.

Adapting at the Boundaries   Because they are open systems, organizations are exposed to uncertainties from both their inputs and outputs. To help them compete, they can create buffers on both the input and output boundaries with the environment. **Buffering** creates supplies of excess resources to meet unpredictable needs. On the input side, organizations establish relationships with employment agencies to hire part-time and temporary help during rush periods when labor demand is difficult to predict. In the U.S. labor force, these workers, known as *contingent workers*, include 2.5 million on-call workers, 1.2 million temporary help agency workers, and more than 800,000 workers provided by contract firms, suggesting widespread use of this approach to buffering labor input uncertainties.[50] On the output side of the system, most organizations use some type of ending inventories that allow them to keep merchandise on hand in case a rush of customers decide to buy their products. Auto dealers are a common example of this use of buffers, but we can see similar use of buffer inventories in fast-food restaurants, bookstores, clothing stores, and even real estate agencies.[51]

---

empowerment

The process of sharing power with employees, thereby enhancing their confidence in their ability to perform their jobs and their belief that they are influential contributors to the organization.

---

buffering

Creating supplies of excess resources in case of unpredictable needs.

In today's business world, the term *bureaucracy* generally has a bad connotation.

TABLE 2.5
Four Approaches for Managing Uncertainty

		Stable	Dynamic
Complex		Decentralized	Decentralized
		Bureaucratic (standardized skills)	Organic (mutual adjustment)
Simple		Centralized	Centralized
		Bureaucratic (standardized work processes)	Organic (direct supervision)

In Practice

CONTINGENT WORK OPPORTUNITIES GROWING

According to Adecco, a firm that places workers in temporary assignments, the number of positions for contingent workers will grow at least three times as fast as the number of traditional (full-time, permanent) jobs. The demand for temporary workers in finance, administrative support, health care, engineering, and information technology is especially strong. A significant reason is that companies still in shock from the Great Recession are cautious about expanding payrolls. This is good news for people who do contingent work because they want to. Reasons for choosing contingent work include exposure to a variety of assignments, enjoyment of independence, and the ability to design work arrangements that fit with personal needs.

Businesses seeking contingent workers not only turn to firms such as Adecco; they also can use talent websites to help them find a good match. For example, YourEncore offers a network of scientists and engineers, many of whom are retired but interested in taking on projects. InnoCentive puts a new twist on project work: it hosts competitions in which a client-specified network of would-be problem solvers is invited to compete to offer a solution to a particular problem; the client pays only for winning ideas.

For companies using contingent workers, it is critical to manage them as effectively as traditional employees. Managers need to be clear about the talents these employees bring to the organization. And they must take the time to provide orientation and performance feedback so the workers are clear about what is expected of them. Good communication is essential.[52]

- What do you think would be the greatest challenges of managing contingent workers rather than full-time employees?

In addition to buffering, organizations may try **smoothing,** or leveling normal fluctuations at the boundaries of the environment. For example, during winter months in the north, when automobile sales drop off, it is not uncommon for dealers to cut the price of their in-stock vehicles to increase demand. At the end of each clothing season, retailers discount their merchandise to clear it out to make room for incoming inventories. These are examples of smoothing environmental cycles to level off fluctuations in demand.

Adapting at the Core   Although buffering and smoothing manage uncertainties at the boundaries of the organization, firms also can establish **flexible processes** that allow for adaptation in their technical core. For example, firms increasingly try to customize their goods and services to meet the varied and changing demands of customers. Even in manufacturing, where it is difficult to change basic core processes, firms are adopting techniques of mass customization that help them create flexible factories. Instead of mass-producing large quantities of a "one-size-fits-all" product, organizations can use mass customization to produce individually customized products at an equally low cost. Whereas Henry Ford used to claim that "you could have a Model T in any color you wanted, as long as it was black," auto companies now offer a wide array of colors and trim lines, with different options and accessories. The process of mass customization involves the use of a network of independent operating units in which each performs a specific process or task such as making a dashboard assembly on an automobile. When an order comes in, different modules join forces to deliver the product or service as specified by the customer.[53] We will discuss mass customization and flexible factories in more depth in Chapter 9.

smoothing

Leveling normal fluctuations at the boundaries of the environment.

flexible processes

Methods for adapting the technical core to changes in the environment.

Bottom Line

The Internet lets customers quickly find products with the cost and quality features they want.
What might "flexible processes" mean for a fast-food restaurant? For an auto company?

Choosing a Response Approach

Three general considerations help guide management's response to the environment. First, organizations should attempt to change appropriate elements of the environment. Environmental responses are most useful when aimed at elements of the environment that (1) cause the company problems, (2) provide it with opportunities, and (3) allow the company to change successfully. Thus, PepsiCo recognized that public concern about the obesity epidemic and its impact on health could be a problem for the sales and reputation of a company that makes snacks and soft drinks. CEO Nooyi believed it would be irresponsible to try to change that concern, so she focused on what the company could do: change its product mix to include more healthful alternatives without abandoning the idea that an occasional fun snack is fine to enjoy. In terms of success, the company has been able to develop alternative products; the jury is still out on whether this approach will be profitable.

Second, organizations should choose responses that focus on pertinent elements of the environment. If a company wants to manage its competitive environment better , competitive aggression and pacification are viable options. Political action influences the legal environment, and contracting helps manage customers and suppliers.

Third, companies should choose responses that offer the most benefit at the lowest cost. Return-on-investment calculations should incorporate short-term financial considerations as well as long-term impact. Strategic managers who consider these factors carefully will guide their organizations to competitive advantage more effectively.

The Internal Environment of Organizations: Culture and Climate

LO 6 Of course an organization is more than a collection of responses to the external environment. The ways people in an organization behave, including the goals they set and the manner in which they treat their customers, are also shaped by forces within the organization. These forces, which include an organization's culture and its climate,

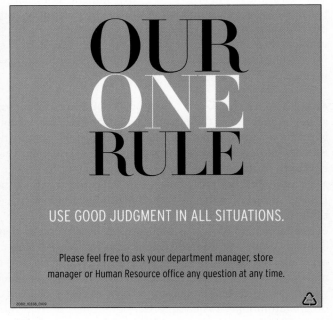

At Nordstrom, the fashion retailer, new employees are given a five-by-eight-inch card with one rule on it, along with a full handbook containing policies and legal regulations.

are sets of conditions that influence the decisions and behavior of employees at all levels of the organization. On a day-to-day basis, an employee's experience of an organization's culture and climate may feel hard to sort out, much as your experience of a hot summer day may result from a combination of your region's climate and the day's weather or your experience of happiness from a combination of your general personality and your mood in response to recent events.

Organization Culture

One of the most important factors that influence an organization's response to its external environment is its culture. **Organization culture** is the set of important assumptions about the organization and its goals and practices that members of the company share. It is a system of shared values about what is important and beliefs about how the world works. In this way, a company's culture provides a framework that organizes and directs people's behavior on the job.[54] The culture of an organization may be difficult for an observer to define easily, yet like an individual's personality, it can often be sensed almost immediately. For example, the way people dress and behave, the way they interact with each other and with customers, and the qualities that are likely to be valued by their managers are usually quite different at a bank than they are at a rock music company, and different again at a law firm or an advertising agency.

Cultures can be strong or weak; strong cultures can have great influence on how people think and behave. A strong culture is one in which everyone understands and believes in the firm's goals, priorities, and practices. A strong culture can be a real advantage to the organization if the behaviors it encourages and facilitates are appropriate ones. For example, the Walt Disney Company's culture encourages extraordinary devotion to customer service; the culture at Apple Inc. encourages innovation. Employees in these companies don't need rule books to dictate how they act because

organization culture

The set of important assumptions about the organization and its goals and practices that members of the company share.

In Practice

GOOGLE ANALYZES EMPLOYEE TURNOVER

Google is well known for having a strong culture that supports technical excellence and innovation. Its skill at manipulating data is not just a feature of its software and services; it is a valued way of approaching every problem from marketing to employee retention. When Google's managers want to improve in any area, they take an analytic approach.

Take the case of employee turnover. Many companies can tell you an overall turnover rate, but by tracking the details of employee-related data, Google's Director, Global Security Operations, Shannon Deegan, noticed that the departure rate of women who had recently given birth was twice the company's average. So the company crafted a more generous and flexible plan for maternity leave. This wasn't just a matter of generosity. The company tracked the outcome of the change and determined that turnover fell by 50 percent, and the savings in recruitment cost canceled out the cost of the expanded employee benefits.

Often, the company creates more formal experiments. Its People and Innovation Lab investigates the best ways to encourage participation in retirement plans and the most effective forms of performance-based pay. It improved the effectiveness of its managers by investigating which behaviors were associated with the highest performance in the company and then delivering training to managers with weaknesses in areas identified. Employees, most of them engineers, are trained to study problems objectively by collecting and analyzing data, so this kind of approach is well received. It reinforces a culture that values learning highly.[55]

- How would Google's culture affect its sales management? Could someone who makes decisions based on hunches and intuition succeed as a sales manager at Google? Explain.

these behaviors are conveyed as "the way we do things around here"; they are rooted in their companies' cultures.

In contrast, a strong culture that encourages inappropriate behaviors can severely hinder an organization's ability to deal effectively with its external environment—particularly if the environment is undergoing change, as is almost always the case today. A culture that was suitable and even advantageous in a prior era may become counterproductive in a new environment. For instance, a small start-up may have an informal culture that becomes less suitable when the company grows, faces more competition, and requires decision making by a wide range of specialized employees spread out over many locations.

Similarly, when a merger or acquisition brings together organizations with strong cultures, cultural differences can encourage behaviors that are harmful to the combined organization. After Sprint acquired Nextel, conflicts arose because the two wireless carriers had different cultures. Sprint moved cautiously, whereas Nextel's culture was more entrepreneurial. Such differences in style can be unsettling to employees on both sides and may help to explain why research has found much higher turnover rates among managers at companies that have been acquired.[56]

In contrast to strong cultures, weak cultures have the following characteristics: different people hold different values, there is confusion about corporate goals, and it is not clear from one day to the next what principles should guide decisions. Some managers may pay lip service to some aspects of the culture ("we would never cheat a customer") but behave very differently ("don't tell him about the flaw"). As you can guess, such a culture fosters confusion, conflict, and poor performance. Most managers would agree that they want to create a strong culture that encourages and supports goals and useful behaviors that will make the company more effective. In other words, they want to create a culture that is appropriately aligned with the organization's competitive environment.[57]

Diagnosing Culture   Let's say you want to understand a company's culture. Perhaps you are thinking about working there and you want a good fit, or perhaps you are working there right now and want to deepen your understanding of the organization and determine whether its culture matches the challenges it faces. How would you go about making the diagnosis? A variety of things will give you useful clues about culture:

Corporate mission statements and official goals are a starting point because they will tell you the firm's desired public image. Most companies have a mission statement—even the CIA, as shown in Figure 2.5. Your school has one, and you can probably find it online. But are these statements a true expression of culture? A study of hospital employees and their managers found that managers rated their mission statement more positively than nonmanagers (even though employees had participated in developing it), and 3 out of 10 employees were not even aware that the hospital had a mission statement (even though the hospital had processes for communicating about it).[58] So, even after reading statements of mission and goals, you still need to figure out whether the statements truly reflect how the firm conducts business.

Business practices can be observed. How a company responds to problems, makes strategic decisions, and treats employees and customers tells a lot about what top management really values. The Tribune Company's repeated efforts to cut costs at the *Los Angeles Times* and consolidate its Washington bureau with that of the chain's other newspapers told the acquired company's employees about the parent company's priorities.

Symbols, rites, and ceremonies give further clues about culture. For instance, status symbols can give you a feel for how rigid the hierarchy is and for the nature of relationships between lower and higher levels. Who is hired and fired—and why—and the activities that are rewarded indicate the firm's real values.

FIGURE 2.5

Vision	We will provide knowledge and take action to ensure the national security of the United States and the preservation of American life and ideals.
Mission	We are the eyes and ears of the nation and at times its hidden hand. We accomplish this mission by:
	• Collecting intelligence that matters.
	• Providing relevant, timely, and objective all-source analysis.
	• Conducting covert action at the direction of the president to preempt threats or achieve United States policy objectives.
Values	In pursuit of our country's interests, we put Nation before Agency, Agency before unit, and all before self. What we do matters.
	• Our success depends on our ability to act with total discretion and an ability to protect sources and methods.
	• We provide objective, unbiased information and analysis.
	• Our mission requires complete personal integrity and personal courage, physical and intellectual.
	• We accomplish things others cannot, often at great risk. When the stakes are highest and the dangers greatest, we are there and there first.
	• We stand by one another and behind one another. Service, sacrifice, flexibility, teamwork, and quiet patriotism are our hallmarks.

CIA Vision, Mission, and Values
SOURCE: CIA website at www.cia.gov/information/mission.html.

The stories people tell carry a lot of information about the company's culture. Every company has its myths, legends, and true stories about important past decisions and actions that convey the company's main values. The stories often feature the company's heroes: people once or still active who possessed the qualities and characteristics that the culture especially values and who act as models for others about how to behave.

A strong culture combines these measures in a consistent way. The Ritz-Carlton hotel chain gives each employee a laminated card listing its 12 service values. Each day it carries out a type of ceremony: a 15-minute meeting during which employees from every department resolve problems and discuss areas of potential improvement. At these meetings, the focus is on the day's "wow story," which details an extraordinary way that a Ritz-Carlton employee lived up to one of the service values. For example, a family arrived at the Bali Ritz-Carlton with special eggs and milk because of their son's allergies, but the food had spoiled. The manager and dining staff couldn't find replacements in town, so the executive chef called his mother-in-law in Singapore and asked her to buy the necessary products and fly with them to Bali.[59]

In general, cultures can be categorized according to whether they emphasize flexibility or control and whether their focus is internal or external to the organization. By juxtaposing these two dimensions, we can describe four types of organizational cultures, depicted in Figure 2.6:

Group culture. A group culture is internally oriented and flexible. It tends to be based on the values and norms associated with affiliation. An organizational member's compliance with organizational directives flows from trust, tradition, and long-term commitment. It tends to emphasize member development and values participation in decision making. The strategic orientation associated with this cultural type is one of implementation through consensus building. Leaders tend to act as mentors and facilitators.

Flexible

Type: Group
Dominant attributes:
  Cohesiveness, participation,
  teamwork, sense of family
Leadership style: Mentor,
  facilitator, parent figure
Bonding: Loyalty, tradition,
  interpersonal cohesion
Strategic emphasis: Toward
  developing human resources,
  commitment, and morale

Type: Adhocracy
Dominant attributes:
  Entrepreneurship, creativity,
  adaptability, dynamism
Leadership style: Innovator,
  entrepreneur, risk taker
Bonding: Flexibility, risk,
  entrepreneur
Strategic emphasis: Toward
  innovation, growth, new
  resources

Internal maintenance ——————————————————— **External positioning**

Type: Hierarchy
Dominant attributes: Order, rules
  and regulations, uniformity,
  efficiency
Leadership style: Coordinator,
  organizer, administrator
Bonding: Rules, policies and
  procedures, clear expectations
Strategic emphasis: Toward
  stability, predictability, smooth

Type: Rational
Dominant attributes: Goal
  achievement, environment
  exchange, competitiveness
Leadership style: Production-
  and achievement-oriented,
  decisive
Bonding: Goal orientation,
  production, competition
Strategic emphasis: Toward
  competitive advantage and
  market superiority

Control–oriented

FIGURE 2.6
Competing Values Model of Culture
SOURCE: Kim S. Cameron and Robert E. Quinn, *Diagnosing and Changing Organizational Culture* 3rd Edition (San Francisco: Jossey Bass, 2011). Used by permission of the authors.

Hierarchical culture. The hierarchical culture is internally oriented by more focus on control and stability. It has the values and norms associated with a bureaucracy. It values stability and assumes that individuals will comply with organizational mandates when roles are stated formally and enforced through rules and procedures.

Rational culture. The rational culture is externally oriented and focused on control. Its primary objectives are productivity, planning, and efficiency. Organizational members are motivated by the belief that performance that leads to the desired organizational objectives will be rewarded.

Adhocracy. The adhocracy is externally oriented and flexible. This culture type emphasizes change in which growth, resource acquisition, and innovation are stressed. Organizational members are motivated by the importance or ideological appeal of the task. Leaders tend to be entrepreneurial and risk takers. Other members tend to have these characteristics as well.[60]

This type of diagnosis is important when two companies are considering combining operations, as in a merger, acquisition, or joint venture, because as we noted, cultural differences can sink these arrangements. In some cases, organizations investigating this type of change can benefit from setting up a clean team of third-party experts who investigate the details of each company's culture. For example, they might conduct employee focus groups to learn about leadership styles, the way policies are established, and the kinds of behavior that are rewarded. They can look for systems that indicate employees are empowered to make independent decisions or that directions are handed down from above. They can note how management talks about the company's founder, customers, and employees. In this way, the clean team can identify for the organizations' leaders the types of issues they will have to resolve and the values they must choose among as they try to establish a combined culture.[61]

Managing Culture   We mentioned earlier in this chapter that one important way organizations have of responding to the environment is to *adapt* to it by changing the organization itself. One of the most important tools managers have for implementing such a change lies in their management of their organization's culture. A culture that is inwardly instead of customer focused, for example, when the new competitive environment requires excellence in customer service, can delay or even defeat a manager's efforts to effect change. Simple directives alone are often ineffective; the underlying values of the organization also have to be shifted in the desired direction. Most companies today know that adopting a customer orientation, improving quality, and making other moves necessary to remain competitive are so essential that they require deep-rooted cultural changes. When that kind of change occurs, organization members may then begin to internalize the new values and display the appropriate behaviors on their own.

Top managers can take several approaches to managing culture. First, they should espouse lofty ideals and visions for the company that will inspire organization members. (We will discuss vision more fully in Chapter 4, on strategy, and in Chapter 12, on leadership.) That vision—whether it concerns quality, integrity, innovation, or whatever—should be articulated over and over until it becomes a tangible presence throughout the organization.

Second, executives must give constant attention to the mundane details of daily affairs such as communicating regularly, being visible and active throughout the company, and setting examples. Not only should the CEO talk about the vision, but he or she should also embody it day in and day out. This makes the CEO's pronouncements credible, creates a personal example others can emulate, and builds trust that the organization's progress toward the vision will continue over the long run.

Important here are the moments of truth when hard choices must be made. Imagine top management trumpeting a culture that emphasizes quality and then discovering that a part used in a batch of assembled products is defective. Whether to replace the part at great expense in the interest of quality or to ship the defective part just to save time and money is a decision that will go a long way toward reinforcing or destroying a quality-oriented culture.

To reinforce the organization's culture, the CEO and other executives should routinely celebrate and reward those who exemplify the new values. Another key to managing culture involves hiring, socializing newcomers, and promoting employees on the basis of the new corporate values. In this way, the new culture will begin to permeate the organization. Although this may seem a time-consuming approach to building a new culture, effective managers recognize that replacing a long-term culture of traditional values with one that embodies the competitive values needed in the future can take years. But the rewards of that effort will be an organization much more effective and responsive to its environmental challenges and opportunities.

Organizational Climate

In contrast to a culture's deeply held beliefs, values, and so on, an organization's climate can be measured more readily. **Organizational climate** consists of the patterns of attitudes and behavior that shape people's experience of an organization.[62] For example, an organization's climate might include clear performance standards, frequent conflict, great trust in leaders, and open communication between supervisors and their employees. Researchers have developed and tested surveys for measuring organizational climate in terms of factors such as morale, employees' relationships with managers and coworkers, handling of conflicts, openness and effectiveness of communication, methods for measuring and rewarding performance, and the clarity of one's role in the organization.

Bottom Line
A culture aligned with its environment helps the organization succeed. *To be aligned with its environment, what values should an oil company have?*

organizational climate

The patterns of attitudes and behavior that shape people's experience of an organization.

An organization's climate and its culture both shape the experience of working there and the organization's effectiveness. However, because organizational climate is easier to measure, managers often find that dimensions of organizational climate are more manageable. Later chapters explore a variety of management responsibilities that shape organizational climate, including ethical conduct (Chapter 5), creating a structure for the organization (Chapter 8), appraising and rewarding performance (Chapter 10), valuing diversity (Chapter 11), leading (Chapter 12), motivating employees (Chapter 13), fostering teamwork (Chapter 14), communicating (Chapter 15), and leading change (Chapter 18). An organization is most effective when it has a climate that motivates and enables workers to achieve the organization's strategy. As you read "Management Connection: Onward," consider how a healthy organizational climate would strengthen Facebook under the leadership of Mark Zuckerberg.

MANAGER'S BRIEF

PROGRESS REPORT

ONWARD

Management Connection—Onward

FACEBOOK'S WAY FORWARD

Several actions by Mark Zuckerberg and his management team suggest the future they have forecast for Facebook. At the Facebook-sponsored f8 conference for developers of the social web a few years ago, Zuckerberg said, "Our development is guided by the idea that every year, the amount that people want to add, share, and express is increasing."

Facebook has addressed this expectation by making it easier for web users to share what they are doing. Using Facebook's Open Graph service, media providers such as ESPN.com and Hulu let users share with their social network what articles they're reading or TV shows they're watching. The benefit for Facebook members is that they can get involved in the same interests. The objective for Facebook and its partners is getting minute-by-minute details of computer users' activities. It also helps keep members engaged on Facebook longer—important in markets such as the United States and Britain, where so many people already use Facebook that there is little potential for membership growth.

Another goal is to improve Facebook's revenues. Facebook members don't have to pay to post status updates or send messages—yet. And as we saw earlier, more users are accessing Facebook with mobile devices, where advertising rates are lower. By one account, ad revenue per mobile user is only about one-fifth of ad revenue per desktop user. To explore the possibility of revenue from members, Facebook has experimented with paid messages. One test involved the option to send paid messages to people outside a member's own network; for example, sending a message to Zuckerberg or chief operating officer Sheryl Sandburg would cost $100. In another test, members could pay $7 to broadcast pictures or announcements to a wider audience. Concerning ad revenues, Zuckerberg remains optimistic. He expects that as members use Facebook more and more from their mobile devices, the frequency of use will drive up revenues.

In addition, Facebook takes a global view of its marketplace. Recall that its mission is to make the *world* more open and connected. After the United States, Facebook's largest group of members is in Brazil, where social-media use has been soaring. (Brazil is also the number two market for Twitter and for Google-owned YouTube.) Brazil is an attractive market for social media because it has an outgoing culture, large population, and expanding economy. So far, Brazilian marketers are not spending much for online advertising, but eMarketer, a research firm, expects online ad spending in Brazil to double over four years.[63]

- How well do you think Facebook has been responding to its fast-changing environment? Name one or two actions it could take to improve its response.

- How can Mark Zuckerberg strengthen Facebook's culture to help the company fulfill its mission?

KEY TERMS

acquisition, p. 61	empowerment, p. 64	open systems, p. 44
barriers to entry, p. 52	environmental scanning, p. 59	organizational climate, p. 71
benchmarking, p. 60	environmental uncertainty, p. 58	organization culture, p. 67
buffering, p. 64	external environment, p. 44	outputs, p. 44
competitive environment, p. 44	final consumer, p. 56	prospectors, p. 62
competitive intelligence, p. 59	flexible processes, p. 65	scenario, p. 59
cooperative strategies, p. 63	forecasting, p. 60	smoothing, p. 65
defenders, p. 62	independent strategies, p. 62	strategic maneuvering, p. 61
demographics, p. 49	inputs, p. 44	supply chain management, p. 55
diversification, p. 61	intermediate consumer, p. 57	switching costs, p. 55
divestiture, p. 62	macroenvironment, p. 45	
domain selection, p. 61	merger, p. 61	

SUMMARY OF LEARNING OBJECTIVES

Now that you have studied Chapter 2, you should be able to:

 Describe how environmental forces influence organizations and how organizations can influence their environments.

Organizations are open systems that are affected by, and in turn affect, their external environments. Organizations receive financial, human, material, and information resources from the environment; transform those resources into finished goods and services; and then send those outputs back into the environment.

LO 2 Distinguish between the macroenvironment and the competitive environment.

The macroenvironment is composed of economic, legal and political, technological, demographic, social, and natural environment forces that influence strategic decisions. The competitive environment is composed of forces closer to the organization, such as current competitors, new entrants, substitute and complementary products, suppliers, and customers. Perhaps the simplest distinction between the macroenvironment and the competitive environment is in the amount of control a firm can exert on external forces. Macroenvironmental forces such as the economy and social trends are much less controllable than are forces in the competitive environment such as suppliers and customers.

LO 3 Explain why managers and organizations should attend to economic and social developments.

Developments outside the organization can have a profound effect on the way managers and their companies operate. For example, higher energy costs or increased spending on security may make it harder for managers to keep their prices low. The growing diversity of the labor force gives managers access to a much broader range of talent but also requires them to make sure different types of employees are treated equally. Effective managers stay aware of trends like these and respond to them appropriately.

 Identify elements of the competitive environment.

Elements in the environment can range from favorable to unfavorable. To determine how favorable a competitive environment is, managers should consider the nature of the competitors, potential new entrants, threat of substitutes, opportunities from complements, and relationships with suppliers and customers. Analyzing how these forces influence the organization provides an indication of potential threats and opportunities. Effective management of the firm's supply chain is one way to achieve a competitive advantage. Attractive environments tend to be those with high industry growth, few competitors, products that can be differentiated, few potential entrants, many barriers to entry, few substitutes, many suppliers (none with much power), and many customers. After identifying and analyzing competitive forces, managers must formulate a strategy that minimizes the power external forces have over the organization.

 Summarize how organizations respond to environmental uncertainty.

Responding effectively to the environment often requires devising proactive strategies to change the environment. Strategic maneuvering involves changing the boundaries of the competitive environment through domain selection, diversification, mergers, and the like. Independent strategies require not moving into a new environment but rather changing some aspect of the current environment through competitive aggression, public relations, legal action, and so on. Cooperative strategies, such as contracting, cooptation, and coalition building, involve the working together of two or more organizations. Organizations also may make themselves better able to handle environmental change by decentralizing authority, buffering or smoothing, and establishing flexible processes.

LO 6 **Define elements of an organization's culture.**

An organization's culture is its set of shared values and practices related to what is important and how the world works. The culture provides a framework that organizes and directs people's behavior at work. Elements of the culture may be expressed in corporate mission statements and official goals, assuming these reflect how the organization actually operates. Business practices are a basic measure of culture. Symbols, rites, ceremonies, and the stories people tell express and reinforce their cultural values.

LO 7 **Discuss how an organization's culture and climate affect its response to its external environment.**

A culture may be strong or weak and may be one of four types: group, hierarchical, rational, or adhocracy. These cultures shape whether they are flexible and whether the focus is on the external or internal environment. Managing and changing the culture to align it with the organization's environment will require strong, long-term commitment by the CEO and other managers. Managers should espouse high ideals and pay constant attention to conveying values by communicating and modeling them, making decisions that are consistent with cultural values, and rewarding those who demonstrate the organization's values. In addition, an organization's climate shapes the attitudes and behaviors of its people. When the climate is positive, employees want to and are able to carry out its strategy for responding to the external environment.

DISCUSSION QUESTIONS

1. This chapter's opening quote by Peter Drucker said, "The essence of a business is outside itself." What do you think this means? Do you agree?

2. What are the most important forces in the macroenvironment facing companies today?

3. What are the main differences between the macroenvironment and the competitive environment?

4. What kinds of changes do companies make in response to environmental uncertainty?

5. We outlined several proactive responses that organizations can make to the environment. What examples have you seen recently of an organization's responding effectively to its environment? Did the effectiveness of the response depend on whether the organization was facing a threat or an opportunity?

6. Select two organizations that you are interested in. Research information about the firms or talk with an employee, if possible. What types of cultures do they have? Write a paragraph that describes each culture.

7. When you visited colleges to select one to attend, were there cultural differences in the campuses that made a difference in your choice? Did these differences help you decide which college to attend?

EXPERIENTIAL EXERCISES

2.1   EXTERNAL ENVIRONMENT ANALYSIS

OBJECTIVE

To give you the experience of performing an analysis of a company's external environment

INSTRUCTIONS

Select a company you want to learn more about. Using online and/or library resources, including websites on the company's industry and its website and annual report, fill out the following External Environment Worksheet for that company:

External Environment Worksheet

Laws and regulations

What are some key laws and regulations under which this company and industry must operate?

_____

_____

The economy

How does the state of the economy influence the sales of this company's products?

_____

_____

Technology

What new technologies strongly affect the company you have selected?

_____

_____

Demographics

What changes in the population might affect the company's customer base?

_____

_____

Social issues

What changes in society affect the market for your company's products?

_____

_____

Suppliers

How does your company's relationship with suppliers affect its profitability?

_____

_____

Competitors

What companies compete with the firm you have selected? Do they compete on price, on quality, or on other factors?

_____

_____

New entrants

Are new competitors to the company likely? Possible?

_____

_____

Substitutes and complements

Is there a threat of substitutes for the industry's existing products? Are there complementary products that suggest an opportunity for collaboration?

_____

_____

Customers

What characteristics of the company's customer base influence the company's competitiveness?

_____

_____

DISCUSSION QUESTIONS

1. What has the company done to adapt to its environment?

2. How does the company attempt to influence its environment?

SOURCE: From Steven L. McShane and Mary Ann Von Glinow, _Organizational Behavior_ 3rd edition, 2005, p. 499. Reprinted with permission of The McGraw-Hill Companies.

2.2 CORPORATE CULTURE PREFERENCE SCALE

OBJECTIVE

This self-assessment is designed to help you identify a corporate culture that fits most closely with your personal values and assumptions.

INSTRUCTIONS

Read each pair of the statements in the Corporate Culture Preference Scale and circle the statement that describes the organization you would prefer to work in. This exercise is completed alone so students assess themselves honestly without concerns of social comparison. However, class discussion will focus on the importance of matching job applicants to the organization's dominant values.

Corporate Culture Preference Scale

I would prefer to work in an organization:

1a.	Where employees work well together in teams.	**OR**	1b.	That produces highly respected products or services.
2a.	Where top management maintains a sense of order in the workplace.	**OR**	2b.	Where the organization listens to customers and responds quickly to their needs.
3a.	Where employees are treated fairly.	**OR**	3b.	Where employees continuously search for ways to work more efficiently.
4a.	Where employees adapt quickly to new work requirements.	**OR**	4b.	Where corporate leaders work hard to keep employees happy.
5a.	Where senior executives receive special benefits not available to other employees.	**OR**	5b.	Where employees are proud when the organization achieves its performance goals.
6a.	Where employees who perform the best get paid the most.	**OR**	6b.	Where senior executives are respected.
7a.	Where everyone gets his or her job done like clockwork.	**OR**	7b.	That is on top of new innovations in the industry.
8a.	Where employees receive assistance to overcome any personal problems.	**OR**	8b.	Where employees abide by company rules.
9a.	That is always experimenting with new ideas in the marketplace.	**OR**	9b.	That expects everyone to put in 110 percent for peak performance.
10a.	That quickly benefits from market opportunities.	**OR**	10b.	Where employees are always kept informed of what's happening in the organization.
11a.	That can quickly respond to competitive threats.	**OR**	11b.	Where most decisions are made by the top executives.
12a.	Where management keeps everything under control.	**OR**	12b.	Where employees care for each other.

SOURCE: Steven L. McShane and Mary Ann Von Glinow, *Organizational Behavior*, 3rd ed., McGraw-Hill, 2005, p. 499. Copyright. © 2005 The McGraw-Hill Companies, Inc. Reprinted with permission.

Scoring Key for the Corporate Culture Preference Scale

Scoring instructions: In each space, write in a "I" if you circled the statement and "0" if you did not. Then add up the scores for each subscale.

Control culture $\dfrac{}{(2a)} + \dfrac{}{(5a)} + \dfrac{}{(6b)} + \dfrac{}{(8b)} + \dfrac{}{(11b)} + \dfrac{}{(12a)} = \underline{\quad}$

Performance culture $\dfrac{}{(1b)} + \dfrac{}{(3b)} + \dfrac{}{(5b)} + \dfrac{}{(6a)} + \dfrac{}{(7a)} + \dfrac{}{(9a)} = \underline{\quad}$

Relationship culture $\dfrac{}{(1a)} + \dfrac{}{(3a)} + \dfrac{}{(4b)} + \dfrac{}{(8a)} + \dfrac{}{(10b)} + \dfrac{}{(12b)} = \underline{\quad}$

Responsive culture $\dfrac{}{(2b)} + \dfrac{}{(4a)} + \dfrac{}{(7b)} + \dfrac{}{(9a)} + \dfrac{}{(10a)} + \dfrac{}{(11a)} = \underline{\quad}$

Interpreting your score: These corporate cultures may be found in many organizations, but they represent only four of many possible organizational cultures. Also, keep in mind none of these subscales is inherently good or bad. Each is effective in different situations. The four corporate cultures are defined here, along with the range of scores for high, medium, and low levels of each dimension based on a sample of MBA students:

Corporate Culture Dimension and Definition	**Score Interpretation**
Control culture: This culture values the role of senior executives to lead the organization. Its goal is to keep everyone aligned and under control.	High: 3 to 6 Medium: 1 to 2 Low: 0

Performance culture: This culture values individual and organizational performance and strives for effectiveness and efficiency.

High: 5 to 6
Medium: 3 to 4
Low: 0 to 2

Relationship culture: This culture values nurturing and well-being. It considers open communication, fairness, teamwork, and sharing a vital part of organizational life.

High: 6
Medium: 4 to 5
Low: 0 to 3

Responsive culture: This culture values its ability to keep in tune with the external environment, including being competitive and realizing new opportunities.

High: 6
Medium: 4 to 5
Low: 0 to 3

CONCLUDING CASE

WILD WATER GETS SOAKED

Jason and Marie Salerno, brother and sister, have been running their family business, a water park called Wild Water, since they both graduated from college. The Salernos operate the park, which is located near the New Jersey shore, with help from their parents. Marie's husband and Jason's wife are also involved in the business. Wild Water has now been in business for more than 40 years—it is a landmark to both locals and summer tourists. The water park features such attractions as a wave pool, several water slides, a flume ride, a kiddie pool, and a tube ride. A picnic park, shaded petting zoo, aquarium, snack bar, and restaurant called the Seafood Shack round out the park's offerings.

The park opens on Memorial Day and cuts back to weekends only after Labor Day, typically closing in the fall. With just a few months to accumulate revenue, the family and employees of the park work extremely hard. Marie oversees the financial aspects of the business; Jason manages the staff. The staff—ride operators, ticket takers, lifeguards, and the like—are very loyal. Some have parents who once worked at the water park, and many have siblings who also work there. By its very nature, the organization culture of Wild Water is hierarchical—but most who work there, including Jason and Marie, would refer to their employees as part of the family. Jason holds weekly staff meetings, where employees are encouraged to voice their ideas about any aspect of the park's operations. Photos of workers and customers line the walls of Jason and Marie's tiny office, and stories about the park and its people abound, including sightings of celebrity visitors and near-disasters such as a close call with a hurricane.

Although the organization culture has remained largely unchanged for the past four decades, the environment in which the park operates is changing. A new state safety law requires some expensive updating to meet the code. The Salernos recently learned that some of the smaller beach cottages in the area are going to be torn down to make way for a development

of expensive condominiums. Vacationers who rent the condos are more likely to be looking for entertainment in the form of golf, deep-sea fishing trips, and exclusive restaurants. One of the major amusement park chains has been looking at a piece of real estate nearby. This chain is well known for its high-end rides, shows, and eating establishments. The Salernos point out that an entire family could enter Wild Water for the cost of one ticket at one of the chain's parks.

Although the Salernos acknowledge that they have serious challenges ahead, they remain upbeat. Wild Water has been a favorite of families for more than two generations, and they expect it to continue to be a destination for local residents as well as vacationers. But they need to make some changes to keep those visitors—and the new condo owners—coming through the turnstile.

DISCUSSION QUESTIONS

1. Imagine that you are a management consultant hired by the Salernos to help them navigate the choppy waters ahead. First, describe the elements of the macroenvironment and competitive environment that affect Wild Water now. Then describe elements that you anticipate will affect the water park in the next few years.

2. Next, describe the organization's culture. Discuss how the current culture affects the way it responds to the organization's external environment.

3. Now create a plan for Wild Water. In your plan, describe what changes the organization needs to make in its culture to meet upcoming challenges in the external environment. Then describe steps that Wild Water can take to compete successfully against the new amusement park. How can the Salernos keep their loyal customers happy while attracting new ones?

CHAPTER 3

Managerial Decision Making

> The business executive is by profession a decision maker. Uncertainty is his opponent. Overcoming it is his mission.
>
> — John McDonald

Management Connection

HOW HIGH-STAKES DECISIONS MAKE BOEING AN INDUSTRY LEADER

When the first Boeing 787 Dreamliners soared into the sky, they looked like the greatest advance in passenger aircraft in decades. Lightweight materials and efficient engine technology meant they would fly farther on less fuel. Besides being less expensive to operate, the planes had interiors offering passengers greater comfort. Airlines eagerly placed orders, and Boeing's major competitor, Airbus, hastened to improve its own product designs.

Within months, however, Boeing acknowledged problems with the aircraft's performance. Particularly troubling, fires started in power distribution panels and in batteries installed to provide auxiliary power. Boeing grounded the 787s until the battery problem could be resolved, and some people wondered whether the Dreamliner was actually a nightmare.

Why did Boeing have so much trouble with implementing its decision to produce the 787? Was the decision a mistake? For answers, we must look at Boeing's history as an innovator. Under the forceful leadership of engineer George Schairer, the company after World War II studied a German idea to increase speed by angling the wings toward the back of the plane. It was a risky, difficult change to the earlier designs of propeller aircraft, but Boeing created first the B-47 bomber and then the 707 jet airliner. The 707 put Boeing far ahead of its competitors, Douglas and Lockheed. A few decades later, the company again offered an impressive development, the first jumbo jet—its 747, introduced in 1970.

Based on its commitment to technology, Boeing dominated the commercial aircraft market until the 1980s, when a European consortium called Airbus launched its

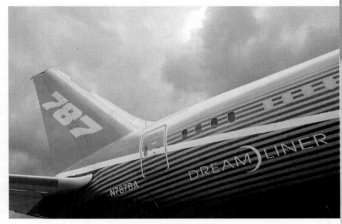

A320 with a highly automated cockpit and began stealing market share from Boeing. Under the leadership of Alan Mulally, who headed the commercial-aircraft division until 2006, the company decided to make its next daring move into the future. The complex undertaking that became the Dreamliner was approved unanimously by Boeing's board of directors in 2003.

Today, Boeing's management insists that the decision was sound. Although the plane was completed behind schedule and over budget, customers have been placing orders at a record pace. And observers note that innovative planes often have problems that must be fixed as they are identified. Airbus has had problems with its own recent launch, the A380 superjumbo jet. Tom Enders, CEO of Airbus's parent company, noted that innovation in the aircraft business is risky, but "if you're too risk-averse, the competition will kill you."[1]

Developing the 787 Dreamliner was a complex decision for Boeing, but it seemed worthwhile because of the potential to remain at the forefront of aircraft technology. As you read this chapter, consider what makes managers' decisions difficult and what skills and resources can help managers overcome those difficulties and make the right choices.

The best managers make decisions constantly. Some are big, difficult, and strategic, such as the decision to spend billions of dollars building an innovative type of jetliner—especially knowing that many lives depend on the aircraft being safe. But managers also make countless smaller decisions that affect day-to-day operations and procedures. Marie Robinson, the chief logistics officer at Toys "R" Us, draws on her experience with army logistics to make sure toys get to the retailer's 600 U.S. stores and to online customers' homes efficiently and on schedule. In the struggle to compete with Amazon, Robinson is using stores as a tool for making logistics more efficient and speedier than an Internet-only retailer can. For routine decisions, she set up a decision-making system in which toys are shipped from either warehouses or stores based on which locations are most economical and have enough of the item in stock. Other decisions must be made in crisis mode. When superstorm Sandy shut down transportation systems in the New York City region in October 2012, Robinson learned that a ship loaded with merchandise for the holidays was being rerouted from New Jersey to the Bahamas. She worked with the shipper to arrange a stop in Baltimore instead, so that the toys could still reach stores in time for Black Friday.[2]

The typical organization has the potential to more than double its decision effectiveness in terms of impact on financial results.[3] If you can't make decisions, you won't be an effective manager. This chapter discusses what kinds of decisions managers face, how they are made, and how they *should* be made.

Bottom Line

You'll be making decisions constantly. It may seem obvious, but it's worth stating: If you know how to make good decisions, you'll deliver good results.

What qualities or results of a management decision make it a "good" decision?

Characteristics of Managerial Decisions

Managers face problems and opportunities constantly. Some situations that require a decision are relatively simple; others seem overwhelming. Some demand immediate action; others take months or even years to unfold.

Actually, managers often ignore challenges.[4] For several reasons, they avoid taking action.[5] First, managers can't be sure how much time, energy, or trouble lies ahead once they start working on a challenge. Second, getting involved is risky; tackling a problem but failing to solve it successfully can hurt a manager's track record. Third, because problems can be so perplexing, it is easier to procrastinate or to get busy with less demanding activities. For these reasons, managers may lack the insight, courage, or will to decide.

It is important to understand why decision making can be so challenging. Figure 3.1 illustrates several characteristics of managerial decisions that contribute to their difficulty and pressure. Most managerial decisions lack structure and entail risk, uncertainty, and conflict.

Lack of Structure

Lack of structure is the usual state of affairs in managerial decision making.[6] Although some decisions are routine and clear-cut, for most there is no automatic procedure to follow. Problems are novel and unstructured, leaving the decision maker uncertain about how to proceed.

An important distinction illustrating this point is between programmed and nonprogrammed decisions. **Programmed decisions** have been encountered and made before. They have objectively correct answers and can be solved by using simple rules, policies, or numerical computations. If you face a programmed decision, a clear procedure or structure exists for arriving at the right decision. For example, if you are a small business owner and must decide the amounts for your employees' paychecks, you can use a formula—and if the amounts are wrong, your employees will prove it to you. Table 3.1 gives some other examples.

programmed decisions

Decisions encountered and made before, having objectively correct answers, and solvable by using simple rules, policies, or numerical computations.

FIGURE 3.1

Characteristics of
Managerial Decisions

If most important decisions were programmed, managerial life would be much easier. But managers typically face **nonprogrammed decisions:** new, novel, complex decisions having no certain outcomes. They have a variety of possible solutions, all of which have merits and drawbacks. The decision maker must create or impose a method for making the decision; there is no predetermined structure on which to rely. As Table 3.1 suggests, important, difficult decisions tend to be nonprogrammed, and they demand creative approaches.

nonprogrammed decisions

New, novel, complex decisions having no proven answers.

Uncertainty and Risk

If you have all the information you need and can predict precisely the consequences of your actions, you are operating under a condition of **certainty.**[7] Managers are expressing their preference for certainty when they are not satisfied hearing about what might have happened or may happen and insist on hearing what did or will happen.[8] But

certainty

The state that exists when decision makers have accurate and comprehensive information.

	Programmed Decisions	Nonprogrammed Decisions
Problem	Frequent, repetitive, routine. Much certainty regarding cause-and-effect relationships.	Novel, unstructured. Much uncertainty regarding cause-and-effect relationships.
Procedure	Dependence on policies, rules, and definite procedures.	Necessity for creativity, intuition, tolerance for ambiguity, creative problem solving.
Examples		
Business firm	Periodic reorders of inventory.	Diversification into new products and markets.
University	Necessary grade point average for good academic standing.	Construction of new classroom facilities.
Health care	Procedure for admitting patients.	Purchase of experimental equipment.
Government	Merit system for promotion of state employees.	Reorganization of state government agencies.

TABLE 3.1

Comparison of Types of
Decisions

uncertainty

The state that exists when decision makers have insufficient information.

risk

The state that exists when the probability of success is less than 100 percent and losses may occur.

conflict

Opposing pressures from different sources, occurring on the level of psychological conflict or of conflict between individuals or groups.

perfect certainty is rare. For important, nonprogrammed managerial decisions, uncertainty is the rule.

Uncertainty means the manager has insufficient information to know the consequences of different actions. Decision makers may have strong opinions—they may feel sure of themselves—but they are still operating under conditions of uncertainty if they lack pertinent information and cannot estimate accurately the likelihood of different results of their actions. Businesspeople do not like uncertainty; it can hold them back from taking action. For example, uncertainty about the strength and timing of the economic recovery made businesses slow to start hiring.[9] But economies don't strengthen until consumer demand picks up, which doesn't happen until employment rises.

When you can estimate the likelihood of various consequences but still do not know with certainty what will happen, you are facing **risk.** Risk exists when the probability of an action being successful is less than 100 percent and losses may occur. If the decision is the wrong one, you may lose money, time, reputation, or other important assets.

Risk, like uncertainty, is a fact of life in managerial decision making. But this is not the same as taking a risk. Although it sometimes seems as though risk takers are admired and entrepreneurs and investors thrive on taking risks, the reality is that good decision makers prefer to manage risk. They accept the fact that decisions have consequences entailing risk, but they do everything they can to anticipate the risk, minimize it, and control it.

The stories detailed in *The Greatest Business Decisions of All Time* are creative approaches to managing risk. One classic was Henry Ford's decision in 1914 to increase workers' pay. He had met the fast-growing demand for the Model T by setting up assembly lines. The process was efficient, but the work was mind-numbing and exhausting, so workers were quitting after only months on the job. Ford made a decision that seemed sure to send costs through the roof: He would reduce the workers' hours by going from two nine-hour shifts to three eight-hour shifts per day, and he would more than double their wages. Although the decision cost Ford an additional $10 million per year, employee turnover plummeted and productivity soared, enabling the company to lower the price of the Model T and earn billions selling to a larger market.[10] Ford could not have known with certainty that productivity would improve, but he assessed his options and concluded that the risk was worth taking.

A more recent example is a T-shirt company called Threadless, which reduces uncertainty and manages risk by basing its whole marketing model on collaboration with customers. Professional and amateur graphic designers submit their ideas for T-shirt designs at the Threadless website, where customers vote on the designs they like. From hundreds of submissions, the company selects four to six of the top vote getters each week and pays their designers $1,000. But it makes and sells them only after a minimum number of customers have already ordered the shirt design.[11]

T-shirt designers have a chance to get their designs printed through the Threadless website, but only after enough customers have given them high ratings and ordered a shirt.

Conflict

Important decisions are even more difficult because of the conflict managers face. **Conflict,** which exists when a manager must consider opposing pressures from different sources, occurs at two levels.

First, individual decision makers experience psychological conflict when several options are attractive or when none of the options is attractive. For instance, a manager may have to decide whom to lay off when she doesn't want to lay off anyone. Or she may have three promising job applicants for one position—but choosing one means she has to reject the other two.

Second, conflict arises between people. A chief financial officer argues in favor of increasing long-term debt to finance an acquisition. The chief executive officer, however, prefers to minimize such debt and find the funds elsewhere. A marketing department wants more product lines to sell, and the engineers want higher-quality products. But the production people want to lower costs by having longer production runs of fewer products with no changes. Few decisions are without conflict.

The Phases of Decision Making

Faced with these challenges, how can you make good decisions? The ideal decision-making process includes six phases. As Figure 3.2 illustrates, decision makers should (1) identify and diagnose the problem, (2) generate alternative solutions, (3) evaluate alternatives, (4) make the choice, (5) implement the decision, and (6) evaluate the decision.

LO 2

Identifying and Diagnosing the Problem

The first phase in the decision-making process is to recognize that a problem exists and must be solved. Typically, a manager realizes some discrepancy between the current state (the way things are) and a desired state (the way things ought to be). Such discrepancies—say, in organizational or unit performance—may be detected by comparing current performance against (1) *past* performance, (2) the *current* performance of other organizations or units, or (3) *future* expected performance as determined by plans and forecasts.[12] Michael Ortner and Rakesh Chilakapati cofounded a company called Capterra, which created an online directory of companies that sell business software. Their problem was that they wanted to bring more traffic to their website; more listings would make the site more valuable to buyers, and more buyers would make the site more attractive to vendors.[13] We will refer to this example throughout this section.

The problem may be an opportunity that needs to be exploited: a gap between what the organization is doing now and what it can do to create a more positive future. In that case, decisions involve choosing how to seize the opportunity. To recognize important opportunities as a manager, you will need to understand your company's macro- and competitive environments (described in Chapter 2).

Recognizing that a problem or opportunity exists is only the beginning of this phase. The decision maker must dig in deeper and attempt to diagnose the situation. For example, a sales manager knows that sales have dropped drastically. If he is leaving the company

FIGURE 3.2

The Phases of Decision Making

soon or believes the decreased sales volume is due to the economy (which he can't do anything about), he won't take action. But if he does try to solve the problem, he should not automatically reprimand his sales staff, add new people, or increase the advertising budget. He must analyze *why* sales are down and then develop a solution appropriate to his analysis. Asking why, of yourself and others, is essential to understanding the real problem. In the case of Capterra, the company had asked *why* traffic was low by conducting surveys of the directory's users. The results showed that buyers wanted to find reviews of the vendors—a feature that the directory was not offering. To Capterra's founders, it seemed plausible that the underlying problem was that their website lacked a key feature that would make it helpful.[14]

The following questions are useful to ask and answer in this phase:[15]

> Is there a difference between what is actually happening and what should be happening?
>
> How can you describe the deviation as specifically as possible?
>
> What is/are the cause(s) of the deviation?
>
> What specific goals should be met?
>
> Which of these goals are absolutely critical to the success of the decision?

Generating Alternative Solutions

The second phase of decision making links problem diagnosis to the development of alternative courses of action aimed at solving the problem. Managers generate at least some alternative solutions based on past experiences.[16]

ready-made solutions

Ideas that have been seen or tried before.

custom-made solutions

New, creative solutions designed specifically for the problem.

Solutions range from ready-made to custom-made.[17] Decision makers who search for **ready-made solutions** use ideas they have tried before or follow the advice of others who have faced similar problems. **Custom-made solutions,** by contrast, must be designed for specific problems. This technique often combines ideas into new, creative solutions. For example, Yamaha Corporation drew on ideas from its customer community, which said that hobby guitarists were interested in an instrument they could play without a lot of practice. Designers at Yamaha created an idea for a guitar that could read electronically entered songs and display lights on the fingerboard showing users where to put their fingers. Customers provided ideas for modifications, and the back and forth eventually generated more than the minimum number of orders for the company to produce the innovative product.[18] Potentially, custom-made solutions can be devised for any challenge. Later in the chapter, we will discuss how to generate creative ideas.

Often, many more alternatives are available than managers may realize. For example, what would you do if one of your competitors reduced prices? Managers sometimes assume that cutting prices in response to a competitor's price cuts is their only option, but it is not. Alternatives include emphasizing consumer risks to low-priced products, building awareness of your products' features and overall quality, and communicating your cost advantage to your competitors so they realize that they can't win

Often, many more alternatives are available than managers may realize.

a price war. If you do decide to cut your price as a last resort, do it fast—if you do it slowly, your competitors will gain sales in the meantime, which may embolden them to employ the same tactic again in the future.[19]

Returning to the example of Capterra, Michael Ortner, whose background was in sales, was eager to launch the product reviews, but his colleague, Rakesh Chilakapati, the company's technology manager, wanted to proceed cautiously because of the time and expense required to add the feature, along with fear that some vendors would get bad reviews and leave the directory. So to generate alternatives, the two partners studied existing websites with product reviews (for example, Amazon, eBay, and Edmunds. com). They identified a variety of ways to offer some kind of reviewing feature. They could simply post testimonials from satisfied customers. They could allow or forbid anonymous comments. They could require reviewers to list both positive and negative points. The big question that remained was whether the features attractive to buyers would repel sellers.[20]

Evaluating Alternatives

The third phase of decision making involves determining the value or adequacy of the alternatives that were generated. In other words, which solution will be the best?

Especially when decisions are important, alternatives should be evaluated with careful thought and logic. Fundamental to this process is to predict the consequences that will occur if the various options are put into effect. Managers should consider several types of consequences, including quantifiable measures of success such as lower costs, higher sales, lower employee turnover, and higher profits. The evaluation of alternatives at Capterra weighed the expected impact of reviews on buyers against the expected impact on vendors. Posting testimonials instead of inviting reviews seemed likely to protect the goodwill of vendors, but this one-sided approach seemed unlikely to satisfy buyers, so the founders doubted it would have much impact on traffic to the website. Anonymous reviews seemed risky because vendors' competitors could abuse the system, so that alternative was easily abandoned. Requiring both pros and cons in the reviews would encourage balanced information about vendors, an apparent plus. One issue that remained was that any review feature opened the possibility that vendors would be upset by negative comments. Ortner investigated further by sending a survey to the site's vendors, and he learned that many, in fact, did worry about that risk.[21]

An important technological change affecting the analysis of alternatives is the ability to collect and analyze big data. The term refers to massive amounts of data that exceed the capabilities of a traditional computer database. Businesses today can gather details about Internet usage, consumer behavior, and employee skills and activities, among many other things. Computer technology enables organizations of all sizes to store the data, search it for patterns or trends, and analyze the information to identify alternatives that previously would have gone unnoticed. Evaluation that would have relied heavily on intuition or experience now can be data-driven. For example, companies are using big data to make more effective decisions about pay. Pricewaterhouse-Coopers assumed that pay raises would help it keep consultants from leaving early in their careers, but evaluating big data showed a larger effect from helping employees balance their work and personal commitments.[22]

To evaluate alternatives, refer to your original goals, defined in the first phase. Which goals does each alternative meet and fail to meet? Which alternatives are most acceptable to you and to other important stakeholders? If several alternatives may solve the problem, which can be implemented at the lowest cost or greatest profit? If no alternative achieves all your goals, perhaps you can combine two or more of the best ones. Several additional questions help:[23]

> Is our information about alternatives complete and current? If not, can we get more and better information?
> Does the alternative meet our primary objectives?
> What problems could we have if we implement the alternative?

Of course, results cannot be forecast with perfect accuracy. But sometimes decision makers can build in safeguards against an uncertain future by considering the potential consequences of several scenarios. Then they generate **contingency plans**—alternative courses of action that can be implemented depending on how the future unfolds.

For example, during an economic crisis when it is unclear when a recovery might begin and how strong it will be or what shape it will take, the range of potential

contingency plans

Alternative courses of action that can be implemented based on how the future unfolds.

Some decisions do not work out. Although it can be surprising and frustrating, you will need to create alternative courses of action, or contingency plans, that will allow you to achieve your desired goals.

outcomes is very large, and many companies will not survive. Firms could consider at least four scenarios:[24]

1. A most optimistic scenario in which trade and capital flows resume, further recession is averted, globalization stays on course, and developed and emerging economies continue to integrate as confidence rebounds quickly.
2. A battered-but-resilient scenario in which the recession continues for a long period, recovery is slow, confidence is shaken but does rebound, and globalization slowly gets back on course.
3. Stalled globalization, in which the global recession is significant, the intensity varies greatly from nation to nation (for example, with China and the United States proving resilient), but the integration of the world's economies stalls and growth is slow.
4. A long freeze, in which the recession lasts more than five years, economies everywhere stagnate, and globalization goes into reverse.

As you read this, what economic scenario is unfolding? What are the important current events and trends? What scenarios could evolve six or eight years from now? How will *you* prepare?

Making the Choice

Once you have considered the possible consequences of your options, it is time to make your decision. Quantitatively inclined people can easily tweak the assumptions behind every scenario in countless ways. But the temptation can lead to paralysis by analysis—that is, indecisiveness caused by too much analysis rather than the assertive decision making that can help an organization seize new opportunities or thwart challenges. This kind of indecisiveness became a risk at Capterra because Ortner and Chilakapati had conflicting worries. Ortner continued to see the lack of reviews as a missed opportunity, whereas Chilakapati remained focused on the risks of adding this feature. Ortner further researched the situation by calling vendors who had expressed concerns about reviews; he became convinced that they, too, were simply failing to see the opportunities of this additional feature and would come around when experience showed them the value of reviews. Finally, after three months of debate, Ortner was enjoying his regular five-mile run when he concluded that the analysis had to end, and a decision must be made. As president, he made the final call, respecting Chilakapati's concerns but announcing that it was time to try the reviews.[25]

> The process of considering multiple scenarios raises important "what if" questions for decision makers and highlights the need for preparedness and contingency plans.

As you make your decision, important concepts include maximizing, satisficing, and optimizing.[26]

maximizing

A decision realizing the best possible outcome.

Maximizing is achieving the best possible outcome. The maximizing decision realizes the greatest positive consequences and the fewest negative consequences. In other words, maximizing results in the greatest benefit at the lowest cost, with the largest expected total return. Maximizing requires searching thoroughly for a complete range of alternatives, carefully assessing each alternative, comparing one to another, and then choosing or creating the very best.

satisficing

Choosing an option that is acceptable, although not necessarily the best or perfect.

Satisficing is choosing the first option that is minimally acceptable or adequate. When you satisfice, you compare your choice against your goal, not against other options. Satisficing means that a search for alternatives stops after you find one that is okay. You do not expend the time or energy to gather more information. Instead you make the expedient decision based on readily available information.

Let's say you are purchasing new equipment, and your goal is to avoid spending too much money. You would be maximizing if you checked out all your options and their prices and then bought the cheapest one that met your performance requirements. But you would be satisficing if you bought the first adequate option that was within your budget and failed to look for less expensive options.

Satisficing is sometimes a result of laziness; other times, there is no other known option because time is short, information is unavailable, or other constraints make maximizing impossible. When the consequences are not huge, satisficing can even be the ideal approach. But in other situations, when managers satisfice, they fail to consider options that might be better.

Optimizing means that you achieve the best possible balance among several goals. Perhaps, in purchasing equipment, you are interested in quality and durability as well as price. So instead of buying the cheapest piece of equipment that works, you buy the one with the best combination of attributes, even though there may be options that are better on the price criterion and others that are better on the quality and durability criteria. The same idea applies to achieving business goals: One marketing strategy could maximize sales, whereas a different strategy might maximize profit. An optimizing strategy is the one that achieves the best balance among multiple goals.

optimizing

Achieving the best possible balance among several goals.

In Practice

REPLACING GOOGLE WITH APPLE MAPS

The first versions of the Apple iPhone included Google Maps as a default app—a logical choice, given that people often use their mobile devices to get directions and Google Maps was the most popular mapping software. However, Google became more of a competitor after it financially backed and later purchased the Android operating system for smart phones.

That created a tough decision for Apple when it prepared to launch iOS 6, its operating system for mobile phones. Apple terminated its agreement with Google and replaced Google Maps with its own Apple Maps. Unfortunately, Apple Maps was far from ready for the big time. Information was missing and incorrect. For example, Apple Maps users posted photos of places such as the Washington Monument tagged blocks from the satellite image of it and creepy 3D images of roads surging into the air or bridges dipping into the river. The Australian government even warned people not to use Apple Maps after police were called to rescue people misdirected into arid wilderness. Consumers also complained about the lack of directions for public transit systems.

Why did Apple release its mapping application? Managers evidently concluded that competing with Google outweighed the technical problems. Some believe that Google was unwilling to share data needed for the app to offer turn-by-turn directions, a feature Apple considered essential. Yet state-of-the-art mapping software requires so much data, so many functions, and so many licensing agreements on a global scale that creating a fully functional product would have taken years longer. In the end, Apple added Google Maps to its App Store.[27]

• Where and how did Apple fail in its decision-making processes in this example?

Implementing the Decision

The decision-making process does not end once a choice is made. The chosen alternative must be implemented. Sometimes the people involved in making the choice must put it into effect. At other times, they delegate the responsibility for implementation to others, such as when a top management team changes a policy or operating procedure and has operational managers carry out the change. At Capterra, implementation of the decision to add customer reviews included 10 months of software development, followed by invitations to vendors to encourage their customers to submit reviews. Notice that the implementation took into account the concerns about negative reviews by giving the vendors some control over who submitted the initial reviews.[28]

Unfortunately, sometimes people make decisions but don't take action. Implementing may fail to occur when talking a lot is mistaken for doing a lot; if people just assume that a decision will happen; when people forget that merely making a decision changes nothing; when meetings, plans, and reports are seen as actions, even if they have no effect on what people actually do; and if managers don't check to ensure that what was decided was actually done.[29]

Managers should plan implementation carefully. Adequate planning requires several steps:[30]

1. Determine how things will look when the decision is fully operational.
2. Chronologically order, perhaps with a flow diagram, the steps necessary to achieve a fully operational decision.
3. List the resources and activities required to implement each step.
4. Estimate the time needed for each step.
5. Assign responsibility for each step to specific individuals.

Decision makers should assume that things will *not* go smoothly during implementation. It is useful to take a little extra time to *identify potential problems* and *identify potential opportunities* associated with implementation. Then you can take actions to prevent problems and be ready to seize unexpected opportunities. The following questions are useful:

What problems could this action cause?
What can we do to prevent the problems?
What unintended benefits or opportunities could arise?
How can we make sure they happen?
How can we be ready to act when the opportunities come?

> Decision makers should assume that things will *not* go smoothly during implementation.

Many of the chapters in this book are concerned with implementation issues: how to implement strategy, allocate resources, organize for results, lead and motivate people, manage change, and so on. View the chapters from that perspective and learn as much as you can about how to implement properly.

Evaluating the Decision

The final phase in the decision-making process is evaluating the decision. It involves collecting information on how well the decision is working. Quantifiable goals—a 20 percent increase in sales, a 95 percent reduction in accidents, 100 percent on-time deliveries—can be set before the solution to the problem is implemented. Then objective data can be gathered to determine its success or failure accurately.

Decision evaluation is useful whether the conclusion is positive or negative. Feedback that suggests the decision is working implies that the decision should be continued and perhaps applied elsewhere in the organization. Negative feedback means that either (1) implementation will require more time, resources, effort, or thought or (2) the decision was a bad one. The feedback for Capterra was positive. In the first year of offering customer reviews, the site gathered about 500 reviews. Another year after that, the site had 2,000 reviews, with about 40 percent of them unsolicited. Most of the reviews are positive. Even though some are less than glowing, traffic to the site has grown so much that vendors see the review feature as a benefit because they are getting more business. Revenues to Capterra have jumped and Ortner and Chilakapati are finally in agreement: Customer reviews were a great idea.[31]

If the decision appears inappropriate, it's back to the drawing board. Then the process cycles back to the first phase: (re)defining the problem. The decision-making process begins anew, preferably with more information, new suggestions, and an approach that attempts to eliminate the mistakes made the first time around.

The Best Decision

How can managers tell whether they have made the best decision? Although nothing can guarantee a "best" decision, managers should at least be confident that they followed proper *procedures* that will yield the best possible decision under the circumstances. This means that the decision makers were appropriately vigilant in making the decision. **Vigilance** occurs when the decision makers carefully and conscientiously execute all six phases of decision making, including making provisions for implementation and evaluation.[32]

Author and CEO Luda Kopeikina says managers can learn to make better decisions by improving the processes they use. First, your decisions will get better if you learn to manage stress, get enough rest, and put distractions aside when you need to make important decisions. Next, you should define the consequences you are trying to achieve and make sure the data you gather match the goals for your decision. Along with this comes the vision of how your decision can play out when you implement it. Finally, you need to develop the strength of character to take responsibility for the consequences of your decision. Encourage debate so you can see all the alternatives; but if you are the decision maker, you must eventually end the debate, exercise courage, and act on your responsibility as decision maker.[33]

Even if managers reflect on their decision-making activities and conclude that they executed each step conscientiously, they still will not know whether the decision will work; after all, nothing guarantees a good outcome. But they *will* know that they did their best to make the best possible decision. As you read "Management Connection: Progress Report," ask yourself whether you think this is how the managers at Boeing felt about their decision to develop the Dreamliner.

vigilance

A process in which a decision maker carefully executes all stages of decision making.

Barriers to Effective Decision Making

Vigilance and full execution of the six-phase decision-making process are the exception rather than the rule. But when managers use such rational processes, better decisions result.[34] Managers who make sure they engage in these processes are more effective.

But, it is easy to neglect or improperly execute these processes. The problem may be improperly defined or goals misidentified. Not enough solutions may be generated, or they may be evaluated incompletely. A satisficing rather than maximizing choice may be made. Implementation may be poorly planned or executed, or monitoring may be inadequate or nonexistent. And decisions are influenced by subjective psychological biases, time pressures, and social realities.

Psychological Biases

Decision makers are far from objective in the way they gather, evaluate, and apply information in making their choices. People have biases that interfere with objective rationality. The examples that follow represent only a few of the many documented subjective biases.[35]

Management Connection

BOEING'S DECISION TO INNOVATE

For Alan Mulally, getting the approval from Boeing's board of directors to build the 787 Dreamliner was far from a sure thing. Boeing had made cutbacks in new-product investments, and Mulally's previous project, development of the 777, had run far over budget (although it did make money for the company). However, the Dreamliner's design was so impressive that the directors believed the project would succeed even if Mulally's projections turned out to be too rosy.

Mulally recognized, however, that he must address concerns about cost overruns. He had an idea to minimize that risk: Design and construction wouldn't be centralized within Boeing. Rather, the company would work with a global network of suppliers. They would share in the costs and use their own investments in factories and equipment to build components of the aircraft. With this arrangement, Boeing hoped to keep the costs of developing the aircraft around $5 billion. With the average jetliner selling for around $100 million, the program could cost far more and still make money.

Implementing the decision was both difficult and rewarding. Coordinating the work of a network of suppliers proved to be far more difficult to manage than anyone seems to have anticipated. Meanwhile, leadership at the top changed: Boeing hired James McNerney, a board member with broad business experience, to be its new CEO, rather than Mulally, whose background was in aircraft engineering. Shortly afterward, Mulally left Boeing to run Ford. Without Mulally, who pushed hard to keep work on schedule, the plane's development fell further and further behind. McNerney struggled to find a successful replacement at the head of the commercial-aircraft division, appointing three managers to that post.

Nevertheless, airline customers loved the idea of a plane that would please passengers while saving money. Robert Milton was CEO of Air Canada's parent company when it ordered 60 Dreamliners. Milton noted that "issues" are bound to arise whenever a company introduces "an airplane so radically different." Customers placed orders totaling 848, a record for a new jetliner.[36]

- Evaluate how well Boeing's managers performed at each phase of the decision-making process. How could they have improved the process?
- Do you think the board's decisions about the Dreamliner were the best it could have made? Explain.

illusion of control

People's belief that they can influence events even when they have no control over what will happen.

The **illusion of control** is a belief that one can influence events even when one has no control over what will happen. Gambling is one example: some people believe they have the skill to beat the odds, even though most of the time they cannot. In business, such overconfidence can lead to failure because decision makers ignore risks and fail to evaluate the odds of success objectively.

In addition, managers may believe they can do no wrong or hold a general optimism about the future that can lead them to believe they are immune to risk and failure.[37] In addition, managers may overrate the value of their experience. They may believe that a previous project met its goals because of their decisions, so they can succeed by doing everything the same way on the next project. Rohit Girdhar admits that he held this type of bias until he tried a computer simulation that he assumed would confirm his skills as an experienced manager of software programmers. In the simulation, the workload increased and he hired more workers, as he had in his prior jobs. But the added workers weren't as productive as his experience told him they would be, and his project fell behind. Girdhar learned to question his assumptions before making decisions.[38]

framing effects

A decision bias influenced by the way in which a problem or decision alternative is phrased or presented.

Framing effects refer to how problems or decision alternatives are phrased or presented and how these subjective influences can override objective facts. In one example, managers indicated a desire to invest more money in a course of action that was reported to have a 70 percent chance of profit than in one said to have a 30 percent chance of loss.[39] The choices were equivalent in their chances of success; it was the way the options were framed that determined the managers' choices.

Managers may be quick to frame a problem as being similar to problems they have already handled, so they don't search for new alternatives. For example, when CEO Richard Fuld tackled financial problems at Lehman Brothers as the mortgage market tumbled, he assumed that the situation was much the same as when he had handled a previous financial crisis in the late 1990s. Unfortunately for Lehman Brothers, the recent crisis was far worse. In late 2008, the firm declared bankruptcy—the largest in U.S. history—helping to send global financial markets into a tailspin. Similarly, when the head of the operations center of the Department of Homeland Security prepared for Hurricane Katrina as it headed for New Orleans, he assumed the storm would be like Florida hurricanes he had prepared for in the past. As information came in, he focused on the data that fit his expectations, but Katrina turned out to be far more devastating.[40]

Often, decision makers **discount the future.** That is, in their evaluation of alternatives, they weigh short-term costs and benefits more heavily than longer-term costs and benefits. Consider your own decision about whether to go for a dental checkup. The choice to go poses short-term financial costs, anxiety, and perhaps physical pain. The choice not to go will inflict even greater costs and more severe pain if dental problems worsen. How do you choose? Many people decide to avoid the short-term costs by not going for regular checkups, but end up facing greater pain in the long run.

The same bias applies to students who don't study, weight watchers who sneak dessert or skip an exercise routine, and people who take the afternoon off to play golf when they really need to work. It can also affect managers who hesitate to invest funds in research and development programs that may not pay off until far into the future. In all these cases, the avoidance of short-term costs or the seeking of short-term rewards results in negative long-term consequences.

Asian managers tend to think with a longer-term outlook than do American managers, and many believe that this provides competitive advantage for long-term success.[41] Western myopia is driven in part by Wall Street's focus on quarterly earnings, causing managers to make decisions based primarily on short-run considerations and to neglect long-term problems and opportunities.

In contrast, when U.S. companies sacrifice present value to invest for the future—such as when Weyerhaeuser incurs enormous costs for its reforestation efforts that won't lead to harvest until 60 years in the future—it seems the exception rather than the rule. Discounting the future partly explains governmental budget deficits, environmental destruction, and decaying urban infrastructure.[42]

Time Pressures

In today's rapidly changing business environment, the premium is on acting quickly and keeping pace. The most conscientiously made business decisions can become irrelevant and even disastrous if managers take too long to make them.

How can managers make decisions quickly? Some natural tendencies, at least for North Americans, might be to skimp on analysis (not be too vigilant), suppress conflict, and make decisions on one's own without consulting other managers.[43] These strategies may speed up decision making, but they reduce decision quality. Carl Camden, CEO of Kelly Services, believed that rapid-fire decisions were the sign of a dynamic executive until he saw how this approach could hurt decision quality.[44]

The speed trap can be as dangerous as moving too slowly.[45] In an Internet start-up that went bankrupt, fast decisions initially helped the firm achieve its growth objectives. Early on, the founders did everything they could to create a sense of urgency: They planned a meeting to "light a fire under the company," calling it a "state-of-emergency address" with the purpose of creating "the idea of

discounting the future
A bias weighting short-term costs and benefits more heavily than longer-term costs and benefits.

Bottom Line
As in this example, when you want to pursue sustainability, think in terms of the *long-term consequences* of your decisions. *What might be the long-term consequences of not investing in energy efficiency?*

Delaying dental checkups can have a negative impact on the future. It may save money today but lead to larger costs later.

panic with an emerging deadline." Speed became more important than content. They failed to consider multiple alternatives, used little information, didn't fully acknowledge competing views, and didn't consult outside advisers. They never considered slowing down to be an option.

Can managers under time pressure make decisions that are timely and of high quality? A study of effective decision-making processes in microcomputer firms—a high-tech, fast-paced industry—revealed the tactics that such companies use.[46] First, instead of relying on old data, long-range planning, and futuristic forecasts, they focus on real-time information: current information obtained with little or no time delay. For example, they constantly monitor daily operating measures such as work in process rather than checking periodically the traditional accounting-based indicators such as profitability.

Second, they involve people more effectively and efficiently in the decision-making process. They rely heavily on trusted experts, and this yields both good advice and the confidence to act quickly despite uncertainty. They also take a realistic view of conflict; they value differing opinions, but they know that if disagreements are not resolved, the top executive must make the final choice in the end. Slow-moving firms, in contrast, are stymied by conflict. Like the fast-moving firms, they seek consensus; but when disagreements persist, they fail to decide.

> The speed trap can be as dangerous as moving too slowly.

Bottom Line

You'll feel pressure to make quick decisions, but then it becomes easier to make mistakes. Fortunately, you can be vigilant while moving quickly, and you can avoid the speed trap.

When you are under time pressure, what can you do to avoid mistakes?

In Practice

POOR DECISIONS AT BP

The explosion of leaking gas at BP's Deepwater Horizon oil rig caused 11 deaths and the worst-ever oil spill off the shores of the United States. Even before the oil leak was contained, questions were emerging about what kinds of decisions and actions led to this catastrophe. The answers have been complex and not always consistent. However, they illustrate significant barriers to effective decision making.

Initial investigations and a later report by BP suggest that the disaster arose from a unique series of poor decisions. On the final day of the rig's operation, employees were feeling intense time and cost pressure. The well had posed a series of problems that were driving the drilling project behind schedule and over budget. However, the well was finally drilled and lined with cement to prevent gas from escaping and causing an explosion, so it was ready for testing. On the day of the test, BP engineers decided to modify the typical testing procedures. Crew members who were to implement the procedure weren't clear about the rationale, but they went ahead. The test results were mixed, so workers consulted managers on the rig. Those managers divided their time between trying to make sense of the results and giving a tour to a delegation of managers from the rig's owner, Transocean. They decided the well was OK. Transocean workers who were monitoring the well then missed further indications of trouble. Gas escaped from the well, and attempts to trigger a blowout preventer failed.

A report by the presidential commission charged with investigating the spill found that all the companies involved in the project failed to evaluate risks and communicate problems adequately. The commission's report implied that the disaster was the result of a flawed system, not just a unique set of decisions. In fact, the trend toward more deepwater drilling has been making drilling operations more complex, and the rate of drilling spills has been rising in recent years.[47]

• What barriers to effective decision making can you identify in this situation?

Social Realities

Many decisions are made by a group rather than by an individual manager. In slow-moving firms, interpersonal factors decrease decision-making effectiveness. Even the manager acting alone is accountable to the boss and to others and must consider the preferences and reactions of many people. Important managerial decisions are marked by conflict among interested parties. Therefore, many decisions are the result of intensive social interactions, bargaining, and politicking.

The remainder of this chapter focuses on the social context of decisions, including decision making in groups and the realities of decision making in organizations.

Decision Making in Groups

Sometimes a manager finds it necessary to convene a group of people for the purpose of making an important decision. Some advise that in today's complex business environment, significant problems should *always* be tackled by groups.[48] As a result, managers must understand how groups operate and how to use them to improve decision making. You will learn much more about how groups work later in the book.

The basic philosophy behind using a group to make decisions is captured by the adage, "two heads are better than one." But is this statement really valid? Yes, it is—potentially.

If enough time is available, groups usually make higher-quality decisions than most individuals acting alone. However, groups often are inferior to the *best* individual.[49]

How well the group performs depends on how effectively it capitalizes on the potential advantages and minimizes the potential problems of using a group. Table 3.2 summarizes these issues.

Potential Advantages of Using a Group

If other people have something to contribute, using groups to make a decision offers at least five potential advantages:[50]

1. More information is available when several people are making the decision. If one member doesn't have all the facts or the pertinent expertise, another member might.
2. A greater number of perspectives on the issues, or different approaches to solving the problem, are available. The problem may be new to one group member but familiar to another. Or the group may need to consider other viewpoints—financial, legal, marketing, human resources, and so on—to achieve an optimal solution.
3. Group discussion provides an opportunity for intellectual stimulation. It can get people thinking and unleash their creativity to a far greater extent than would be possible with individual decision making.

Bottom Line

Using a group may seem to slow down decision making. If one person dominates the discussion, it may feel like you're speeding up the decision making. But one dominant person reduces decision quality, and most of you will have wasted your time.
When you're meeting with a group, how can you help to make sure everyone is contributing?

Potential Advantages	Potential Disadvantages
1. Larger pool of information.	1. One person dominates.
2. More perspectives and approaches.	2. Satisficing.
3. Intellectual stimulation.	3. Groupthink.
4. People understand the decision.	4. Goal displacement.
5. People are committed to the decision.	

TABLE 3.2

Pros and Cons of Using a Group to Make Decisions

These three potential advantages of using a group improve the odds that a more fully informed, higher-quality decision will result. Thus managers should involve people with different backgrounds, perspectives, and access to information. They should not involve only their cronies who think the same way they do.

4. People who participate in a group discussion are more likely to understand why the decision was made. They will have heard the relevant arguments both for the chosen alternative and against the rejected alternatives.

5. Group discussion typically leads to a higher level of commitment to the decision. Buying into the proposed solution translates into high motivation to ensure that it is executed well.

The last two advantages improve the chances that the decision will be implemented successfully. Therefore, managers should involve the people who will be responsible for implementing the decision as early in the deliberations as possible.

In Practice

PROS AND CONS OF SOCIAL INTELLIGENCE

Social media such as Facebook and Twitter are providing an avenue to expand the group contributing to a decision. Businesses can use social intelligence, the ideas and opinions collected from social media, to generate alternatives, identify relevant criteria for evaluating ideas, and select options that are most likely to appeal to members of the communities they serve.

As part of its Ecomagination-branded commitment to sustainability, General Electric and Virgin Airlines partnered to learn their Twitter followers' "innovative ideas for the future of flight." Ideas for what the companies began to call this "social plane" included such environmentally friendly options as installing LED lighting and using solar energy at facilities where engines are manufactured. Other ideas suggested ways to make the flight more social, comfortable, or convenient: assigning a Twitter hashtag to each flight and letting passengers receive mobile-phone messages when they could board. As ideas streamed in, Virgin prompted more contributions by offering free flights to participants with interesting contributions. In a matter of hours, GE had thousands of ideas it had not previously considered.

GE and Virgin applied some of those ideas to a test flight. And yes, the flight had a hashtag: #nerdbird. The aircraft was powered by GE's fuel-efficient Leading Edge Aviation Propulsion (LEAP) engine.[51]

• What pros and cons of using social intelligence to support business decisions can you think of?

Potential Problems of Using a Group

Things can go wrong when groups make decisions. Most of the potential problems concern the process through which group members interact with one another:[52]

1. Sometimes one group member dominates the discussion. When this occurs—such as when a strong leader makes his or her preferences clear—the result is the same as it would be if the dominant individual made the decision alone. Individual dominance has two disadvantages. First, the dominant person does not necessarily have the most valid opinions—and may even have the most unsound ideas. Second, even if that person's preference leads to a good decision, convening as a group will have been a waste of everyone else's time.

2. Satisficing is more likely with groups. Most people don't like meetings and will do what they can to end them. This may include criticizing members who want to continue exploring new and better alternatives. The result is a satisficing rather than an optimizing or maximizing decision.

3. Pressure to avoid disagreement can lead to a phenomenon called groupthink. **Groupthink** occurs when people choose not to disagree or raise objections because they don't want to break up a positive team spirit. Some groups want to think as one, tolerate no dissension, and strive to remain cordial. Such groups are overconfident, complacent, and perhaps too willing to take risks. Pressure to go along with the group's preferred solution stifles creativity and the other behaviors characteristic of vigilant decision making.

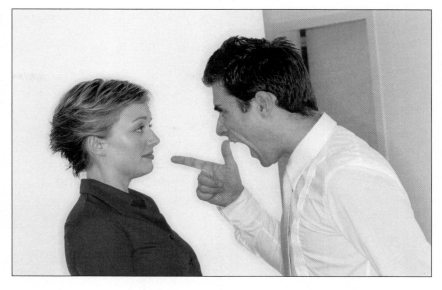

Heated arguments can arise when team members have differing opinions and are more concerned with winning the dispute than resolving the initial problem.

groupthink

A phenomenon that occurs in decision making when group members avoid disagreement as they strive for consensus.

4. Goal displacement often occurs in groups. The goal of group members should be to come up with the best possible solution to the problem. But when **goal displacement** occurs, new goals emerge to replace the original ones. It is common for two or more group members to have different opinions and present their conflicting cases. Attempts at rational persuasion become heated disagreement. Winning the argument becomes the new goal. Saving face and defeating the other person's idea become more important than solving the problem.

Effective managers pay close attention to the group process; they manage it carefully. You have just read about the pros and cons of using a group to make decisions, and you are about to read how to manage the group's decision-making process. Chapter 12, on leadership, helps you decide when to use groups to make decisions.

goal displacement

A decision-making group loses sight of its original goal and a new, less important goal emerges.

Managing Group Decision Making

As Figure 3.3 illustrates, effectively managing group decision making has three requirements: (1) an appropriate leadership style, (2) the constructive use of disagreement and conflict, and (3) the enhancement of creativity.

Leadership Style

The leader of a decision-making group must attempt to minimize process-related problems. The leader should avoid dominating the discussion or allowing another individual to dominate. Less vocal group members should be encouraged to air their opinions and suggestions, and all members should be asked for dissenting viewpoints.

At the same time, the leader should not allow the group to pressure people into conforming. The leader should be alert to the dangers of groupthink and satisficing.

FIGURE 3.3
Managing Group Decision
Making

First, don't lose sight of the problem and
your goals. Second, make a decision!

Also, she should be attuned to indications that group members are losing sight of the primary objective: to come up with the best possible solution to the problem.

These suggestions have two implications. First, don't lose sight of the problem and your goals. Second, make a decision! Slow-moving organizations whose group members can't come to an agreement will be standing still while their competitors move ahead.

Constructive Conflict

Total and consistent agreement among group members can be destructive. It can lead to groupthink, uncreative solutions, and a waste of the knowledge and diverse viewpoints that individuals bring to the group. Therefore, a certain amount of constructive conflict should exist.[53] Pixar, which depends on creativity to make its animated films great, encourages constructive conflict with a standard for production meetings: Whenever someone wants to criticize an idea, the critic must attach an idea for improvement. In this way, good ideas can become great, and great ideas can become amazing. The practice is so much a part of Pixar's culture, it even has a name, "plussing."[54]

The most constructive type of conflict is **cognitive conflict,** or differences in perspectives or judgments about issues. In contrast, **affective conflict** is emotional and directed at other people. Affective conflict is likely to be destructive to the group because it can lead to anger, bitterness, goal displacement, and lower-quality decisions. Cognitive conflict, in contrast, can air legitimate differences of opinion and develop better ideas and problem solutions. Conflict, then, should be task-related rather than personal.[55] But even task-related conflict is good only when managed properly.[56]

Conflict can be generated formally through structured processes.[57] Two techniques that purposely program cognitive conflict into the decision-making process are devil's advocacy and the dialectic method.

cognitive conflict

Issue-based differences in perspectives or judgments.

affective conflict

Emotional disagreement directed toward other people.

A **devil's advocate** has the job of criticizing ideas. The group leader can formally assign people to play this role. Requiring people to point out problems can lessen inhibitions about disagreeing and make the conflict less personal and emotional.

An alternative to devil's advocacy is the dialectic. The **dialectic** goes a step beyond devil's advocacy by requiring a structured debate about two conflicting courses of action.[58] The philosophy of the dialectic stems from Plato and Aristotle, who advocated synthesizing the conflicting views of a thesis and an antithesis. Structured debates between plans and counterplans can be useful prior to making a strategic decision. For example, one team might present the case for acquiring a firm while another team advocates not making the acquisition.

Constructive conflict does not need to be generated on such a formal basis and is not solely the leader's responsibility. Any team member can introduce cognitive conflict by being honest with opinions, by being unafraid to disagree with others, by pushing the group to action if it is taking too long or making the group slow down if necessary, and by advocating long-term considerations if the group is too focused on short-term results. Introducing constructive conflict is a legitimate and necessary responsibility of all group members interested in improving the group's decision-making effectiveness.

Encouraging Creativity

As you've already learned, ready-made solutions to a problem can be inadequate or unavailable. In such cases, custom-made solutions are necessary, so the group must be creative in generating ideas.

Some have said we are in the midst of the next great business revolution: the "creative revolution."[59] Said to transcend the agricultural, industrial, and information revolutions, the most fundamental unit of value in the creativity revolution is ideas. Creativity is more than just an option; it is essential to survival. Allowing people to be creative may be one of the manager's most important and challenging responsibilities.

You might be saying to yourself, "I'm not creative." But even if you are not an artist or a musician, you do have potential to be creative in countless other ways. You are being creative if you (1) bring a new thing into being (*creation*); (2) join two previously unrelated things (*synthesis*); or (3) improve something or give it a new application (*modification*). You don't need to be a genius in school either—Thomas Edison and Albert Einstein were not particularly good students. Nor does something need to change the world to be creative; the little things can always be done in new, creative ways that add value to the product and for the customer.

How do you get creative?[60] Recognize the almost infinite little opportunities to be creative. Assume you can be creative if you give it a try. Escape from work once in a while. Read widely and try new experiences. Take a course or find a good book about creative thought processes; plenty are available. Exchange information and seek feedback about your ideas.[61] And be aware that creativity is social; your creativity will be affected by your social relationships at work, including your connections with other people outside your immediate close network.[62] Talk to people, often, about the issues and ideas with which you are wrestling.

How do you get creativity out of other people?[63] Give creative efforts the credit they are due and don't punish creative failures. Avoid extreme time pressure if possible.[64] Stimulate and challenge people intellectually. Listen to employees' ideas and allow enough time to explore different ideas. Put together groups of people with different styles of thinking and behaving. Get your people in touch with customers. Experiment with ways to stimulate fresh modes of thinking: Some companies are asking employees to put down their electronic devices and doodle on paper or whiteboards, and a software company called Citrix Systems stocks its meeting room with craft supplies for modeling ideas.[65] And strive to be creative yourself—you'll set a good example.

People are likely to be more creative if they believe they are capable, if they know that their coworkers expect creativity, and if they believe that their employer values

---

devil's advocate

A person who has the job of criticizing ideas to ensure that their downsides are fully explored.

---

dialectic

A structured debate comparing two conflicting courses of action.

Bottom Line

Most creative ideas come not from the lone genius in the basement laboratory, but from people talking and working together.
Why is listening part of stimulating creativity?

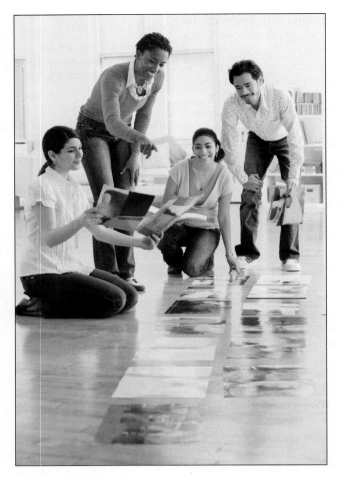

Brainstorming is a technique used to generate as many ideas as possible to solve a problem. You have probably engaged in brainstorming sessions for various class or work projects.

creativity.[66] As a manager, you can do much to help employees develop these beliefs by how you listen, what you allow, and what you reward and punish. At a large consumer products company, management signals that it values creativity by inviting managers to post stories on the company's intranet about ideas their employees have suggested and the results of implementation. The company also awards innovation bonuses linked to how these innovations have benefited the organization.[67]

Brainstorming

A common technique used to elicit creative ideas is brainstorming. In **brainstorming**, group members generate as many ideas about a problem as they can. As the ideas are presented, they are posted so that everyone can read them, and people can use the ideas as building blocks. The group is encouraged to say anything that comes to mind, with one exception: no criticism of other people or their ideas is allowed.

In the proper brainstorming environment—free of criticism—people are less inhibited and more likely to voice their unusual, creative, or even wild ideas. By the time people have exhausted their ideas, a long list of alternatives has been generated. Only then does the group turn to the evaluation stage. At that point, many ideas can be considered, modified, or combined into a creative, custom-made solution to the problem.

Brainstorming isn't necessarily as effective as some people think. Sometimes in a brainstorming session, people are inhibited and anxious, they conform to others' ideas, they set low standards, and they engage in noncreative behaviors including cocktail party–type conversations—complimenting one another, repeating ideas, telling stories—that are nice but don't promote creativity. Fortunately, there are techniques that help, including brainwriting (taking time to write down ideas silently), using trained facilitators, setting high performance goals, brainstorming electronically so that people aren't competing for air time, and even building a playground with fun elements that can foster creativity.[68]

Organizational Decision Making

LO 7   Individuals and groups make decisions constantly throughout every organization. To understand decision making in organizations, a manager must consider (1) the constraints decision makers face, (2) organizational decision processes, and (3) decision making during a crisis.

Constraints on Decision Makers

Organizations—or, more accurately, the people who make important decisions—cannot do whatever they wish. They face various constraints—financial, legal, market, human, and organizational—that inhibit certain actions. Capital or product markets may make an expensive new venture impossible. Legal restrictions may constrain the kinds of international business activities in which a firm can participate. Labor unions may defeat a contract proposed by management, and managers and investors may block a takeover attempt. In strategic alliances, the allies should pursue rational decisions collaboratively, not separately.[69] Even brilliant ideas must take into account the practical matters of implementation.[70]

Suppose you have a great idea that will provide a revolutionary service for your bank's customers. You won't be able to put your idea into action immediately. You will have to sell it to the people who can give you the go-ahead and to those whose help you will need to carry out the project. You might start by convincing your boss of your idea's merit. Next, the two of you may have to hash it out with a vice president. Then maybe the president has to be sold. At each stage, you must listen to these individuals' opinions and suggestions and often incorporate them into your original concept. Ultimately, you will have to derive a proposal acceptable to others.

In addition, ethical and legal considerations must be thought out carefully. Decision makers must consider ethics and the preferences of many constituent groups—the realities of life in organizations. You will have plenty of opportunity to think about ethical issues in Chapter 5.

Organizational Decision Processes

Just as with individuals and groups, organizational decision making historically was described with rational models like the one depicted earlier, in Figure 3.2. But Nobel laureate Herbert Simon challenged the rational model and proposed an important alternative called bounded rationality. According to Simon's **bounded rationality,** decision makers cannot be truly rational because (1) they have imperfect, incomplete information about alternatives and consequences; (2) the problems they face are so complex; (3) human beings simply cannot process all the information to which they are exposed; (4) there is not enough time to process all relevant information fully; and (5) people, including managers within the same firm, have conflicting goals.

When these conditions hold—and they do for most consequential managerial decisions—perfect rationality will give way to more biased, subjective, messier decision processes. For example, the **incremental model** of decision making occurs when decision makers make small decisions, take little steps, move cautiously, and move in piecemeal fashion toward a bigger solution. The classic example is the budget process, which traditionally begins with the budget from the previous period and makes incremental decisions from that starting point.

The **coalitional model** of decision making arises when people disagree on goals or compete with one another for resources. The decision process becomes political as groups of individuals band together and try collectively to influence the decision. Two or more coalitions form, each representing a different preference, and each tries to use power and negotiations to sway the decision.

Organizational politics, in which people try to influence organizational decisions so that their own interests will be served, can reduce decision-making effectiveness.[71] One of the best ways to reduce such politics is to create common goals for members of the team—that is, make the decision-making process a collaborative, rather than a competitive, exercise by establishing a goal around which the group can rally. In one study, top management teams with stated goals such as "build the biggest financial war chest" for an upcoming competitive battle, or "create *the* computer firm of the decade," or "build the best damn machine on the market" were less likely to have dysfunctional conflict and politics between members.[72] On a personal level, if you find yourself in a conflict, you and your adversary may be focused on the wrong goals. Work to find common ground in the form of an important goal that you both want to achieve.

The **garbage can model** of decision making occurs when people aren't sure of their goals, or disagree about the goals, and likewise are unsure of or in disagreement about what to do. This situation occurs because some problems are so complex that they are not well understood and because decision makers move in and out of the

Bottom Line

You may be an innovator if you come up with a creative idea. But you're not yet, until you implement it.

Say you're a manager who dreamed up a great process for cutting costs. Whose buy-in might you need to implement this innovation?

---

bounded rationality

A less-than-perfect form of rationality in which decision makers cannot be perfectly rational because decisions are complex, and complete information is unavailable or cannot be fully processed.

---

incremental model

Model of organizational decision making in which major solutions arise through a series of smaller decisions.

---

coalitional model

Model of organizational decision making in which groups with differing preferences use power and negotiation to influence decisions.

---

garbage can model

Model of organizational decision making depicting a chaotic process and seemingly random decisions.

decision process because they have so many other things to attend to as well. This model implies that some decisions are chaotic and almost random. You can see that this is a dramatic departure from rationality in decision making.

LO 8   Decision Making in a Crisis

In crises, managers must make decisions under a great deal of pressure.[73] You may know some of the most famous recent crises: the explosion of BP's oil rig in the Gulf of Mexico, the devastation of hurricanes along the East Coast, the financial crisis that brought turmoil to the housing industry, and the political crises that have shaken many governments in the Middle East and northern Africa.

Superstorm Sandy hit the East Coast with fierce devastation. Managers had to make critical decisions to keep people safe.

In two famous cases from the past, Union Carbide's gas leak in Bhopal, India, killed thousands of people, and several people were killed in the cyanide poisonings from using Johnson & Johnson's Tylenol. As outlined in Table 3.3, Union Carbide and J&J handled their crises in very different ways. Today, J&J is still known for its effective handling of the crisis, as outlined in the table.

Information technology is a new arena for crises. Businesses, homes, government agencies, hospitals, and other organizations send critical information through the Internet and private networks around the clock, and any technical failure—sometimes accidental, sometimes maliciously intentional—could be magnified by the speed and widespread use of information technology. One vulnerable area is the electrical grid, which links utilities and carries power to each user. Information technology systems allow utility employees to control the grid remotely. Hackers have gained access to the U.S. electrical grid, enabling them to interfere with the grid's operations.[74] Such programs can be purged, but the biggest challenge is preventing or catching each attempt to gain unauthorized access to the system.

The response to IT-related crises must involve senior executives in online communication, both to protect the firm's reputation and to communicate with outside experts, news sources, and key external and internal stakeholders. Managers can use IT to monitor and respond immediately to problems, including scandals, boycotts, rumors, cyberattacks, and other crises.[75]

Although many companies don't concern themselves with crisis management, it is imperative for it to be on management's agenda. An effective plan for crisis management (CM) should include the following elements:[76]

1. *Strategic actions* such as integrating CM into strategic planning and official policies.
2. *Technical and structural actions* such as creating a CM team and dedicating a budget to CM.
3. *Evaluation and diagnostic actions* such as conducting audits of threats and liabilities and establishing tracking systems for early warning signals.
4. *Communication actions* such as providing training for dealing with the media, local communities, and police and government officials.
5. *Psychological and cultural actions* such as showing a strong top management commitment to CM and providing training and psychological support services regarding the human and emotional impacts of crises.

Union Carbide	Johnson & Johnson
Failed to identify as a crisis the public perception that the company was a negligent, uncaring killer.	Identified the crisis of public perception that Tylenol was unsafe and J&J was not in control.
No planning before reacting: CEO immediately went to India to inspect damage. All executives involved.	Planned before reacting: CEO picked one executive to head crisis team. Rest of company involved only on a need-to-know basis.
Set no goals	Set goals: Stop the killings. Find reasons for the killings. Provide assistance to the victims. Restore Tylenol's credibility.
Action: Damage control/stonewalling. Distanced itself. Misrepresented safety conditions. Did not inform spokespeople Adopted bunker mentality	Action: Gave complete information. Worked with authorities. Pulled Tylenol from shelves (first-year cost: $150 million). Used strong marketing program. Reissued Tylenol with tamper-proof packaging.
Chronic problems continued: Public confidence low. Costly litigation. No formal crisis plan resulted.	Crisis resolved: Public confidence high. Sales high again. Well-documented crisis management plan.

TABLE 3.3
Two Disasters

Ultimately, management should be able to answer the following questions:[77]

What kinds of crises could your company face?
Can your company detect a crisis in its early stages?
How will it manage a crisis if one occurs?
How can it benefit from a crisis after it has passed?

The last question makes an important point: a crisis, managed effectively, can have benefits. For example, a prison riot helped Jerry Heftler create a firm bond with one of his company's first clients. Heftler set up Integrated Medical Solutions (IMS) to manage medical care for prison inmates who need to visit doctors, hospitals, and rehabilitation centers outside prison walls. The company contacts providers located near prisons to identify who will be willing to serve inmates, and then it makes appointments and handles insurance paperwork for prisons that sign contracts with his company. A few days after IMS had signed a contract with its second customer but a week before the contract was to go into effect, Heftler learned that prisoners at his new client's facility were rioting. Heftler called the prison's health services director and offered to be of assistance immediately. Drawing on earlier experience in hostage negotiation, Heftler kept cool as he worked overtime to locate injured prisoners who had been loaded onto medevac helicopters without identification and sent to any hospital that would take them. He set up a system to track them by their tattoos until they could be properly identified, and he stayed in constant touch with the health services director. In the years since then, that prison's management has had unfailing confidence in IMS's abilities.[78]

> And if someone steps in and manages the crisis well, a hero is born.

With effective crisis management, old as well as new problems can be resolved, new strategies and competitive advantages may appear, and positive change can emerge. And if someone steps in and manages the crisis well, a hero is born. As you read "Management Connection: Onward," ask yourself who emerged as heroes during Boeing's management of the battery fire crisis.

As a leader during a crisis, don't pretend that nothing happened (as did managers at one firm after a visitor died in the hallway despite employees' efforts to save him).[79] Communicate and reinforce the organization's values. Try to find ways for people to support one another and remember that people will take cues from your behavior. You should be optimistic but brutally honest. Show emotion, but not fear. "You have to be cooler than cool," says Gene Krantz of *Apollo 13* ground control fame. But don't ignore the problems or downplay them and reassure too much; don't create false hopes. Give people the bad news straight—you'll gain credibility, and when the good news comes, it will really mean something.

Management Connection

BOEING CONTENDS WITH A CRISIS

To reduce fuel consumption, Boeing designed its Dreamliner with lightweight but strong composite materials and with many systems running on electricity instead of hydraulic and pneumatic controls. Unfortunately, the complex electrical systems had problems. Most dramatically, in a 787 sold to Japan Airlines, the 63-pound lithium-ion battery caught fire while the plane was parked in Boston, and an All Nippon Airways plane experienced a battery fire during a flight. Following cockpit warnings, the pilot was able to land the second aircraft safely.

The Dreamliners were grounded by the Federal Aviation Administration (FAA), and the Japanese and the U.S. governments launched investigations. Deborah Hersman, chairman of the National Transportation Safety Board, said the NTSB would review the design and the testing that had led to FAA approval for the Dreamliner to carry passengers. Today's safety standard for onboard fires is zero. The FAA approval was based on Boeing's estimate that the chance of a battery meltdown was about one in 10 million flights—not exactly zero but much safer than industry-standard jet engines that malfunction once out of about 100,000 flights. (So far, the actual performance has been two battery fires in fewer than 50,000 flights.)

Boeing, too, responded with an investigation. It assigned engineers and technical experts to focus on identifying and correcting the problems so the aircraft could be returned to service as soon as possible. Boeing also stated its commitment to cooperate fully with investigators.

Boeing's decision to produce the Dreamliner using a network of suppliers complicated its decision making during this crisis. Boeing did not make the batteries in question; they came from GS Yuasa Corporation, a Japanese supplier. Another complication was the technology's sophistication. The first weeks of study yielded no clear answers about the cause of the fires, and few people at the NTSB and Japan Transport Safety Board had expertise in the technology, so they were learning about the batteries while investigating them. Even if Boeing solved the problem itself, it would have to convince these investigators that its solution was valid.

As the investigation continued, so did management decisions. CEO James McNerney reportedly sent handwritten letters of apology to the heads of the affected airlines. Separately, he said he was doing the one thing that would make him confident: "dive in deeply with the people doing the scientific and technical work." Meanwhile, Boeing maintained its production schedule.[80]

- Compare Boeing's decision making during a crisis (the battery fire) with its process of deciding to make the Dreamliner. How does a crisis make the process harder?
- What principles of group decision making could help Boeing make decisions during this crisis?

MANAGER'S BRIEF   PROGRESS REPORT   ONWARD

KEY TERMS

SUMMARY OF LEARNING OBJECTIVES

Now that you have studied Chapter 3, you should be able to:

LO 1 Describe the kinds of decisions you will face as a manager.

Most important managerial decisions are ill-structured and characterized by uncertainty, risk, and conflict. Yet managers are expected to make rational decisions in the face of these challenges.

LO 2 Summarize the steps in making "rational" decisions.

The ideal decision-making process involves six phases. The first, identifying and diagnosing the problem (or opportunity), requires recognizing a discrepancy between the current state and a desired state and then delving below surface symptoms to uncover the underlying causes of the problem. The second phase, generating alternative solutions, requires adopting ready-made or designing custom-made solutions. The third, evaluating alternatives, means predicting the consequences of different alternatives, sometimes through building scenarios of the future. Fourth, a solution is chosen; the solution might maximize, satisfice, or optimize. Fifth, people implement the decision; this phase requires more careful planning than it often receives. Finally, managers should evaluate how well the decision is working. This means gathering objective, valid information about the impact the decision is having. If the evidence suggests the problem is not getting solved, either a better decision or a better implementation plan must be developed.

LO 3 Recognize the pitfalls you should avoid when making decisions.

Situational and human limitations lead most decision makers to satisfice rather than maximize. Psychological biases, time pressures, and the social realities of organizational life may prevent rational execution of the six decision-making stages. But vigilance and an understanding of how to manage decision-making groups and organizational constraints will improve the process and result in better decisions.

LO 4 Evaluate the pros and cons of using a group to make decisions.

Advantages of using groups include more information, perspectives, and approaches brought to bear on problem solving; intellectual stimulation; greater understanding by all of the final decision; and higher commitment to the decision once it is made. Potential dangers or disadvantages of using groups include individual domination of discussions, satisficing, groupthink, and goal displacement.

LO 5 Identify procedures to use in leading a decision-making group.

Effective leaders in decision-making teams avoid dominating the discussion; encourage people's input; avoid groupthink and satisficing; and stay focused on the group's goals. They encourage constructive conflict via devil's advocacy and the dialectic, posing opposite sides of an issue or solutions to a problem. They also encourage creativity through a variety of techniques.

LO 6 Explain how to encourage creative decisions.

When creative ideas are needed, leaders should set a good example by being creative themselves. They should recognize the almost infinite little opportunities for creativity and have confidence in their own creative abilities. They can inspire creativity in others by pushing for creative freedom, rewarding creativity, and not punishing creative failures. They should encourage interaction with customers, stimulate discussion, and protect people from managers who might squelch the creative process. Brainstorming is one of the most popular techniques for generating creative ideas.

LO 7 Discuss the processes by which decisions are made in organizations.

Decision making in organizations is often a highly complex process. Individuals and groups are constrained by a variety of factors and constituencies. In practice, decision makers are boundedly rational rather than purely rational. Some decisions are made on an incremental basis. Coalitions form to represent different preferences. The process is often chaotic, as depicted in the garbage can model. Politics can also enter the process, decisions are negotiated, and crises come and go.

LO 8 Describe how to make decisions in a crisis.

Crisis conditions make sound, effective decision making more difficult. However, it is possible for crises to be managed well. A strategy for crisis management can be developed beforehand, and the mechanisms readied, so that if crises do arise, decision makers are prepared.

DISCUSSION QUESTIONS

1. Discuss Boeing's Dreamliner in terms of risk, uncertainty, and how its managers handled the company's challenges. What is the current news on this company?

2. Identify some risky decisions you have made. Why did you take the risks? How did they work out? Looking back, what did you learn?

3. Identify a decision you made that had important unexpected consequences. Were the consequences good, bad, or both? Should you, and could you, have done anything differently in making the decision?

4. What effects does time pressure have on your decision making? In what ways do you handle it well and not so well?

5. Recall a recent decision that you had difficulty making. Describe it in terms of the characteristics of managerial decisions.

6. What do you think are some advantages and disadvantages to using computer technology in decision making?

7. Do you think that when managers make decisions they follow the decision-making steps as presented in this chapter? Which steps are apt to be overlooked or given inadequate attention? What can people do to make sure they do a more thorough job?

8. Discuss the potential advantages and disadvantages of using a group to make decisions. Give examples from your experience.

9. Suppose you are the CEO of a major corporation and one of your company's oil tanks has ruptured, spilling thousands of gallons of oil into a river that empties into the ocean. What do you need to do to handle the crisis?

10. Identify some problems you want to solve. Brainstorm with others a variety of creative solutions.

EXPERIENTIAL EXERCISES

3.1   COMPETITIVE ESCALATION: THE DOLLAR AUCTION

OBJECTIVE

To consider some psychological and interpersonal influences on decisions in a social and financial context.

INSTRUCTIONS

Step 1: *5 minutes.* The instructor will play the role of auctioneer. In this auction, the instructor will auction off $1 bills. (The instructor will inform you whether this money is real or imaginary.) All members of the class may participate in the auction at the same time.

The rules for this auction are slightly different from those of a normal auction. In this version, both the highest bidder and the next highest bidder will play their last bids even though the dollar is awarded only to the highest bidder. For example, if Bidder A bids 15 cents for the dollar and Bidder B bids 10 cents, and there is no further bidding, then A pays 15 cents for the dollar and receives the dollar, and B pays 10 cents and receives nothing. The auctioneer will lose 75 cents on the dollar just sold.

Bids must be made in multiples of 5 cents. The dollar will be sold when there is no further bidding. If two individuals bid the same amount at the same time, ties are resolved in favor of the bidder located physically closest to the auctioneer. During each round, there is to be no talking except for making bids.

Step 2: *15 minutes.* The instructor (auctioneer) will auction off five individual dollars to the class. Any student may bid in an effort to win the dollar. A record sheet of the bidding and winners can be kept in the worksheet that follows.

DISCUSSION QUESTIONS

1. Who made the most money in this exercise—one of the bidders or the auctioneer? Why?

2. As the auction proceeded, did bidders become more competitive or more cooperative? Why?

3. Did two bidders ever pay more for the money being auctioned than the value of the money itself? Explain how and why this happened.

4. Did you become involved in the bidding? Why?

   a. If you became involved, what were your motivations? Did you accomplish your objectives?

   b. If not, why didn't you become involved? What did you think were the goals and objectives of those who did become involved?

5. Did people say things to one another during the bidding to influence their actions? What was said, and how was it influential?

Dollar Auction Worksheet

	Amount Paid by Winning Bidder	Amount Paid by Second Bidder	Total Paid for This Dollar
First dollar			
Second dollar			
Third dollar			
Fourth dollar			
Fifth dollar			

SOURCE: Excerpted from R. Lewicki, *Experiences in Management and Organizational Behavior,* 3rd ed. 1991. Reprinted with permission of John Wiley and Sons, Inc.

3.2   GROUP PROBLEM-SOLVING MEETING AT THE COMMUNITY AGENCY

OBJECTIVE

To understand the interactions in group decision making through role playing a meeting between a chairman and his subordinates.

INSTRUCTIONS

1. Gather role sheets for each character and instructions for observers.

2. Set up a table in front of the room with five chairs around it arranged in such a way that participants can talk comfortably and have their faces visible to observers.

3. Read the introduction and cast of characters.

4. Five members from the class are selected to role-play the five characters. All other members act as observers. The participants study the roles. All should play their roles without referring to the role sheets.

5. The observers read the instructions for observers.

6. When everyone is ready, John Cabot enters his office, joins the others at the table, and the scene begins. Allow 20 minutes to complete the meeting. The meeting is carried to the point of completion unless an argument develops and no progress is evident after 10 or 15 minutes of conflict.

DISCUSSION QUESTIONS

1. Describe the group's behavior. What did each member say? Do?

2. Evaluate the effectiveness of the group's decision making.

3. Did any problems exist in leadership, power, motivation, communication, or perception?

4. How could the group's effectiveness be increased?

INTRODUCTION

The Community Agency is a role-play exercise of a meeting between the chairman of the board of a social service agency and four of his subordinates. Each character's role is designed to re-create the reality of a business meeting. Each character comes to the meeting with a unique perspective on a major problem facing the agency as well as some personal impressions of the other characters developed over several years of business and social associations.

CAST OF CHARACTERS

John Cabot, the chairman, was the principal force behind the formation of the Community Agency, a multiservice agency. The agency employs 50 people and, during its 19 years of operations, has enjoyed better client relations, a better service record, and a better reputation than other local agencies because of a reputation for high-quality service at a moderate cost to funding agencies. Recently, however, competitors have begun to overtake the Community Agency, resulting in declining contracts. John Cabot is expending every possible effort to keep his agency comfortably at the top.

Ron Smith, director of the agency, reports directly to Cabot. He has held this position since he helped Cabot establish the agency 19 years ago.

Joan Sweet, head of client services, reports to Smith. She has been with the agency 12 years, having worked before that for the government as a contracting officer.

Tom Lynch, head community liaison, reports to Joan Sweet. He came to the Community Agency at Sweet's request, having worked with Sweet previously.

Jane Cox, lead case worker, also works for Joan Sweet. Cox was promoted to this position two years ago. Prior to that time, Jane had gone through a year's training program after receiving an MSW from a large urban university.

TODAY'S MEETING

John Cabot has called the meeting with these four managers to solve some problems that have developed in meeting service schedules and contract requirements. Cabot must catch a plane to Washington in half an hour; he has an appointment to negotiate a key contract that means a great deal to the future of the Community Agency. He has only 20 minutes to meet with his managers and still catch the plane. Cabot feels that getting the Washington contract is absolutely crucial to the future of the agency.

SOURCE: Judith R. Gordon, *A Diagnostic Approach to Organizational Behavior.* Copyright © 1983 Pearson Education, Inc. Reprinted by permission of Pearson Education, Inc., Upper Saddle River, NJ.

CONCLUDING CASE

SOARING EAGLE SKATE COMPANY

As a child, Stan Eagle just knew he loved riding his skateboard and doing tricks. By the time he was a teenager, he was so proficient at the sport that he began entering professional contests and taking home prize money. By his twenties, Eagle was so successful and popular that he could make skateboarding his career. A skateboard maker sponsored him in competitions and demonstrations around the world.

The sponsorship and prize money paid enough to support him for several years. But then interest in the sport waned, and Eagle knew he would have to take his business in new directions. He believed skateboarding would return to popularity, so he decided to launch into designing, building, and selling skateboards under his own brand. To finance Soaring Eagle Skate Company, he pooled his own personal savings with money from a friend, Pete Williams, and came up with $75,000. Sure enough, new young skaters began snapping up the skateboards, attracted in part by the products' association with a star.

As the company prospered, Eagle considered ideas for expansion. Another friend had designed a line of clothing he thought would appeal to Eagle's skateboarding fans, and Eagle's name on the product would lend it credibility. At the friend's urging, Eagle branched out into clothing for skateboarders. However, he discovered that the business of shorts and shirts is far different from the business of sports equipment. The price markups were tiny, and the sales channels were entirely different. Three years into the expansion, Soaring Eagle had invested millions of dollars in the line but was still losing money. Eagle decided to sell off that part of the business to a clothing company and cut his losses.

Soon after that experiment, cofounder Williams proposed another idea: They should begin selling other types of sports equipment—inline roller skates and ice skates. Selling equipment for more kinds of sports would produce more growth than the company could obtain by focusing on just one sport. Eagle was doubtful. He was considered one of the most knowledgeable people in the world about skateboarding. He knew nothing about inline skating and ice skating. Eagle argued that the company would be better off focusing on the sport in which it offered the most expertise. Surely there were ways to seek growth within that sport—or at least to avoid the losses that came from investing in industries in which the company lacked experience.

Williams continued to press Eagle to try his idea. He pointed out that unless the company took some risks and expanded into new areas, there was little hope that Williams and Eagle could continue to earn much of a return on the money they had invested. Eagle was troubled. The attempt at clothing delivered, he thought, a message that they needed to be careful about expansion. But he seemed unable to persuade Williams to accept his point of view. He could go along with Williams and take the chance of losing money again, or he could use money he had earned from his business to buy Williams's ownership share in the company and then continue running Soaring Eagle on his own.

DISCUSSION QUESTIONS

1. How do the characteristics of management decisions—uncertainty, risk, conflict, and lack of structure—affect the decision facing Stan Eagle?

2. What steps can Eagle take to increase the likelihood of making the best decision in this situation?

PART ONE   SUPPORTING CASE

SSS Software In-Basket Exercise

One way to assess your own strengths and weaknesses in management skills is to engage in an actual managerial work experience. The following exercise gives you a realistic glimpse of the tasks faced regularly by practicing managers. Complete the exercise and then compare your own decisions and actions with those of classmates.

SSS Software designs and develops customized software for businesses. It also integrates this software with the customer's existing systems and provides system maintenance. SSS Software has customers in the following industries: airlines, automotive, finance/banking, health/hospital, consumer products, electronics, and government. The company has also begun to attract important international clients. These include the European Airbus consortium and a consortium of banks and financial firms based in Kenya.

SSS Software has grown rapidly since its inception just over a decade ago. Its revenue, net income, and earnings per share have all been above the industry average for the past several years.

However, competition in this technologically sophisticated field has grown very rapidly. Recently, it has become more difficult to compete for major contracts. Moreover, although SSS Software's revenue and net income continue to grow, the rate of growth declined during the past fiscal year.

SSS Software's 250 employees are divided into several operating divisions with employees at four levels: nonmanagement, technical/professional, managerial, and executive. Nonmanagement employees take care of the clerical and facilities support functions. The technical/professional staff perform the core technical work for the firm. Most managerial employees are group managers who supervise a team of technical/professional employees working on a project for a particular customer. Staff who work in specialized areas such as finance, accounting, human resources, nursing, and law are also considered managerial employees. The executive level includes the 12 highest-ranking employees at SSS Software. The organization chart in Figure A illustrates SSS Software's structure. There is also an employee

classification report that lists the number of employees at each level of the organization.

In this exercise, you will play the role of Chris Perillo, vice president of operations for health and financial services. You learned last Wednesday, October 13, that your predecessor, Michael Grant, has resigned and gone to Universal Business Solutions, Inc. You were offered his former job, and you accepted it. Previously, you were the group manager for a team of 15 software developers assigned to work on the Airbus consortium project in the airline services division. You spent all of Thursday and Friday and most of the weekend finishing up parts of the project, briefing your successor, and preparing for an interim report you will deliver in Paris on October 21.

It is now 7 a.m. Monday, and you are in your new office. You have arrived at work early so you can spend the next two hours reviewing material in your in-basket (including some memos and messages to Michael Grant) as well as your voice mail and e-mail. Your daily planning book indicates that you have no appointments today or tomorrow but will have to catch a plane for Paris early Wednesday morning. You have a full schedule for the remainder of the week and all of next week.

ASSIGNMENT

During the next two hours, review all the material in your in-basket as well as your voice mail and e-mail. Take only two hours. Using the following response form as a model, indicate how you want to respond to each item (that is, via letter/memo, e-mail, phone/voice mail, or personal meeting). If you decide not to respond to an item, check "no response" on the response form. All of your responses must be written on the response forms. Write your precise, detailed response (do not merely jot down a few notes). For example, you might draft a memo or write out a message that you will deliver via phone/voice mail. You may also decide to meet with an individual (or individuals) during the limited time available on your calendar today or tomorrow. If so, prepare an agenda for a personal meeting and list your goals for the meeting. As you read through the items, you may occasionally observe some information that you think is relevant and want to remember (or attend to in the future) but that you decide not to include in any of your responses to employees. Write down such information on a sheet of paper titled "note to self."

SOURCE: D. Whetten and K. Cameron, *Developing Management Skills*, 6th ed. Copyright 2005. Reproduced by permission of Pearson Education, Inc., Upper Saddle River, New Jersey.

SAMPLE RESPONSE FORM

Relates to:

Memo # _____   E-mail # _____   Voice mail # _____

Response form:

_____ Letter/memo   _____ Meet with person (when, where)

_____ E-mail   _____ Note to self

_____ Phone call/voice mail   _____ No response

ITEM 1 MEMO

TO: All employees
FROM: Roger Steiner, chief executive officer
DATE: October 15

I am pleased to announce that Chris Perillo has been appointed as vice president of operations for health and financial services. Chris will immediately assume responsibility for all operations previously managed by Michael Grant. Chris will have end-to-end responsibility for the design, development, integration, and maintenance of custom software for the health and finance/banking industries. This responsibility includes all technical, financial, and staffing issues. Chris will also manage our program of software support and integration for the recently announced merger of three large health maintenance organizations (HMOs). Chris will be responsible for our recently announced project with a consortium of banks and financial firms operating in Kenya. This project represents an exciting opportunity for us, and Chris's background seems ideally suited to the task.

Chris comes to this position with an undergraduate degree in computer science from the California Institute of Technology and an MBA from the University of Virginia. Chris began as a member of our technical/professional staff six years ago and has most recently served for three years as a group manager supporting domestic and international projects for our airlines industry group, including our recent work for the European Airbus consortium.

I am sure you all join me in offering congratulations to Chris for this promotion.

ITEM 2 MEMO

TO: All managers
FROM: Hal Harris, vice president, community and public relations
DATE: October 15

For your information, the following article appeared on the front page of the business section of Thursday's *Los Angeles Times*.

In a move that may create problems for SSS Software, Michael Grant and Janice Ramos have left SSS Software and moved to Universal Business Solutions Inc. Industry analysts see the move as another victory for Universal Business Solutions Inc. in their battle with SSS Software for share of the growing software development and integration business. Both Grant and Ramos had been with SSS Software for over seven years. Grant was most recently vice president of operations for all SSS Software's work in two industries: health and hospitals, and finance and banking. Ramos brings to Universal Business Solutions Inc. her special expertise in the growing area of international software development and integration.

Hillary Collins, an industry analyst with Merrill Lynch, said "The loss of key staff to a competitor can often create serious problems for a firm such as SSS Software. Grant and Ramos have an insider's understanding of SSS Software's strategic and technical limitations. It will be interesting to see if they can exploit this knowledge to the advantage of Universal Business Solutions Inc."

ITEM 3 MEMO

TO: Chris Perillo

FROM: Paula Sprague, executive assistant to Roger Steiner

DATE: October 15

Chris, I know that in your former position as a group manager in the airline services division, you probably have met most of the group managers in the health and financial services division, but I thought you might like some more personal information about them. These people will be your direct reports on the management team.

Group #1: Bob Miller, 55-year-old white male, married (Anne) with two children and three grandchildren. Active in local Republican politics. Well regarded as a "hands-off" manager heading a high-performing team. Plays golf regularly with Mark McIntyre, John Small, and a couple of V.P.s from other divisions.

Group #2: Wanda Manners, 38-year-old white female, single with one school-age child. A fitness "nut," has run in several marathons. Some experience in Germany and Japan. Considered a hard-driving manager with a constant focus on the task at hand. Will be the first person to show up every morning.

Group #3: William Chen, 31-year-old male of Chinese descent, married (Harriet), two young children from his first marriage. Enjoys tennis and is quite good at it. A rising star in the company, he is highly respected by his peers as a "man of action" and a good friend.

Group #4: Leo Jones, 36-year-old white male, married (Janet) with an infant daughter. Recently returned from paternity leave. Has traveled extensively on projects because he speaks three languages. Has liked hockey ever since the time he spent in Montreal. Considered a strong manager who gets the most out of his people.

Group #5: Mark McIntyre, 45-year-old white male, married (Mary Theresa) to an executive in the banking industry. No children. A lot of experience in Germany and Eastern Europe. Has been writing a mystery novel. Has always been a good "team player," but several members of his technical staff are not well respected, and he hasn't addressed the problem.

Group #6: John Small, 38-year-old white male, recently divorced. Three children living with his wife. A gregarious individual who likes sports. He spent a lot of time in Mexico and Central America before he came to SSS Software. Recently has been doing mostly contract work with the federal government. An average manager, has had some trouble keeping his people on schedule.

Group #7: This position has been vacant since Janice Ramos left. Roger thinks we ought to fill this position quickly. Get in touch with me if you want information on any in-house candidates for any position.

Group #8: Marcus Harper, 42-year-old black male, married (Tamara) with two teenage children. Recently won an award in a local photography contest. Considered a strong manager who gets along with peers and works long hours.

Customer Services: Armand Marke, 38-year-old Armenian male, divorced. A basketball fan. Originally from Armenia. Previously a group manager. Worked hard to establish the technical services phone line, but now has pretty much left it alone.

Office administrator: Michelle Harrison, 41-year-old white female, single. Grew up on a ranch and still rides horses whenever she can. A strict administrator.

There are a number of good folks here, but they don't function well as a management team. I think Michael played favorites, especially with Janice and Leo. There are a few cliques in this group, and I'm not sure how effectively Michael dealt with them. I expect you will find it a challenge to build a cohesive team.

ITEM 4 MEMO

TO: Chris Perillo

FROM: Wanda Manners, Group 2 manager

DATE: October 15

CONFIDENTIAL AND RESTRICTED

Although I know you are new to your job, I feel it is important that I let you know about some information I just obtained concerning the development work we recently completed for First National Investment. Our project involved the development of asset management software for managing their international funds. This was a very complex project due to the volatile exchange rates and the forecasting tools we needed to develop.

As part of this project, we had to integrate the software and reports with all their existing systems and reporting mechanisms. To do this we were given access to all of their existing software (much of which was developed by Universal Business Solutions Inc.). Of course, we signed an agreement acknowledging that the software to which we were given access was proprietary and that our access was solely for the purpose of our system integration work associated with the project.

Unfortunately, I have learned that some parts of the software we developed actually "borrow" heavily from complex application programs developed for First National Investment by Universal Business Solutions Inc. It seems obvious to me that one or more of the software developers from Group 5 (that is, Mark McIntyre's group) inappropriately "borrowed" algorithms developed by Universal Business Solutions Inc. I am sure that doing so saved us significant development time on some aspects of the project. It seems very unlikely that First National Investment or Universal Business Solutions Inc. will ever become aware of this issue.

Finally, First National Investment is successfully using the software we developed and is thrilled with the work we did. We brought the project in on time and under budget. You probably know that they have invited us to bid on several other substantial projects.

I'm sorry to bring this delicate matter to your attention, but I thought you should know about it.

ITEM 5A MEMO

TO: Chris Perillo

FROM: Paula Sprague, executive assistant to Roger Steiner

DATE: October 15

RE: Letter from C.A.R.E. Services (copies attached)

Roger asked me to work on this C.A.R.E. project and obviously wants some fast action. A lot of the staff are already booked solid for the next couple of weeks. I knew that Elise Soto and Chu Hung Woo have the expertise to do this system, and when I checked with them, they were relatively free. I had them pencil in the next two weeks and wanted to let you know. Hopefully, it will take a "hot potato" out of your hands.

ITEM 5B COPY OF FAX

C.A.R.E.
Child and Adolescent Rehabilitative and Educational Services
A United Way Member Agency
200 Main Street
Los Angeles, California 90230

DATE: October 11

Mr. Roger Steiner, CEO
SSS Software
13 Miller Way
Los Angeles, California 90224

Dear Roger,

This letter is a follow-up to our conversation after last night's board meeting. I appreciated your comments during the board meeting about the need for sophisticated computer systems in nonprofit organizations, and I especially appreciate your generous offer of assistance to have SSS Software provide assistance to deal with the immediate problem with our accounting system. Since the board voted to fire the computer consultant, I am very worried about getting our reports done in time to meet the state funding cycle.

    Thanks again for your offer of help during this crisis.

Sincerely yours,

Janice Polocizwic

Janice Polocizwic
Executive Director

ITEM 5C COPY OF LETTER

SSS SOFTWARE
13 Miller Way
Los Angeles, CA 90224
213-635-2000

DATE: October 12

Janice Polocizwic
Executive Director, C.A.R.E. Services
200 Main Street
Los Angeles, California 90230

Dear Janice,

I received your fax of October 11. I have asked Paula Sprague, my executive assistant, to line up people to work on your accounting system as soon as possible. You can expect to hear from her shortly.

Sincerely,
Roger Steiner
Roger Steiner

cc: Paula Sprague, Executive Assistant

ITEM 6 MEMO

TO: Michael Grant

FROM: Harry Withers, Group 6 technical staff

DATE: October 12

PERSONAL AND CONFIDENTIAL

Our team is having difficulty meeting the submission deadline of November 5 for the Halstrom project. Kim, Fred, Peter, Kyoto, Susan, Mala, and I have been working on the project for several weeks, but are experiencing some problems and may need additional time. I hesitate to write this letter, but the main problem is that our group manager, John Small, is involved in a relationship with Mala. Mala gets John's support for her ideas and brings them to the team as required components of the project. Needless to say, this has posed some problems for the group. Mala's background is especially valuable for this project, but Kim and Fred, who have both worked very hard on the project, do not want to work with her. In addition, one member of the team has been unavailable recently because of child care needs. Commitment to the project and team morale have plummeted. However, we'll do our best to get the project finished as soon as possible. Mala will be on vacation the next two weeks, so I'm expecting that some of us can complete it in her absence.

ITEM 7 VOICE MAIL

Hello, Michael. This is Jim Bishop of United Hospitals. I wanted to talk with you about the quality assurance project that you are working on for us. When José Martinez first started talking with us, I was impressed with his friendliness and expertise. But recently he doesn't seem to be getting much accomplished and has seemed distant and on-edge in conversations. Today I asked him about the schedule, and he seemed very defensive and not entirely in control of his emotions. I am quite concerned about our project. Please give me a call at 213-951-1234.

ITEM 8 VOICE MAIL

Hi, Michael. This is Armand. I wanted to talk with you about some issues with the technical services phone line. I've recently received some complaint letters from phone line customers whose complaints have included long delays while waiting for a technician to answer the phone; technicians who are not knowledgeable enough to solve problems; and, on occasion, rude service. Needless to say, I'm quite concerned about these complaints.

I believe that the overall quality of the phone line staff is very good, but we continue to be understaffed, even with the recent hires. The new technicians look strong but are working on the help line before being fully trained. Antolina, our best tech, often brings her child to work, which is adding to the craziness around here.

I think you should know that we're feeling a lot of stress here. I'll talk to you soon.

ITEM 9 VOICE MAIL

Hi Chris, it's Pat. Congratulations on your promotion. They definitely picked the right person. It's great news—for me, too. You've been a terrific mentor so far, so I'm expecting to learn a lot from you in your new position. How about lunch next week?

ITEM 10 VOICE MAIL

Chris, this is Bob Miller. Just thought you'd like to know that John's joke during our planning meeting has disturbed a few of the women in my group. Frankly, I think the thing's being blown out of proportion, especially since we all know this is a good place for both men and women to work. Give me a call if you want to chat about this.

ITEM 11 VOICE MAIL

Hello. This is Lorraine Adams from Westside Hospital. I read in today's Los Angeles Times *that you will be taking over from Michael Grant. We haven't met yet, but your division has recently finished two large million-dollar projects for Westside. Michael Grant and I had some discussion about a small conversion of a piece of existing software to be compatible with the new systems. The original vendor had said that they would do the work but has been stalling, and I need to move quickly. Can you see if Harris Wilson, Chu Hung Woo, and Elise Soto are available to do this work as soon as possible? They were on the original project and work well with our people. You can call me at 213-555-3456.*

Um . . . (long pause) I guess I should tell you that I got a call from Michael offering to do this work. But I think I should stick with SSS Software. Give me a call.

ITEM 12 VOICE MAIL

Hi, Chris. This is Roosevelt Moore calling. I'm a member of your technical/professional staff. I used to report to Janice Ramos, but since she left the firm, I thought I'd bring my concerns directly to you. I'd like to arrange some time to talk with you about my experience since returning from six weeks of paternity leave. Some of my major responsibilities have been turned over to others. I seem to be out of the loop and wonder if my career is at risk. Also, I am afraid that I won't be supported or seriously considered for the opening created by Janice's departure. Frankly, I feel I'm being screwed for taking my leave. I'd like to talk with you this week.

ITEM 13 E-MAIL

TO: Michael Grant

FROM: José Martinez, Group 1 technical staff

DATE: October 12

I would like to set up a meeting with you as soon as possible. I suspect that you will get a call from Jim Bishop of United Hospitals and want to be sure that you hear my side of the story first. I have been working on a customized system design for quality assurance for them using a variation of the J-3 product we developed several years ago. They had a number of special requirements and some quirks in their accounting systems, so I have had to put in especially long hours. I've worked hard to meet their demands, but they keep changing the ground rules. I keep thinking, this is just another J-3 I'm working on, but they have been interfering with an elegant design I have developed. It seems I'm not getting anywhere on this project. Then Mr. Bishop asked me if the system was running yet. I was worn out from dealing with the controller, and I made a sarcastic comment to Mr. Bishop. He gave me a funny look and just walked out of the room.

I would like to talk with you about this situation at your earliest convenience.

ITEM 14 E-MAIL

TO: Chris Perillo

FROM: John Small, Group 6 manager

DATE: October 15

Welcome aboard, Chris. I look forward to meeting with you. I just wanted to put a bug in your ear about finding a replacement for Janice Ramos. One of my technical staff, Mala Abendano, has the ability and drive to make an excellent group manager. I have encouraged her to apply for the position. I'd be happy to talk with you further about this at your convenience.

ITEM 15 E-MAIL

TO: Chris Perillo

FROM: Paula Sprague, executive assistant to Roger Steiner

DATE: October 15

Roger asked me to let you know about the large contract we have gotten in Kenya. It means that a team of four managers will be making a short trip to determine current needs. They will assign their technical staff the task of developing a system and software here over the next six months, and then the managers and possibly some team members will be spending about 10 months on site in Kenya to handle the implementation. Roger would appreciate an e-mail of your thoughts about the issues to be discussed at this meeting, additional considerations about sending people to Kenya, and about how you will put together an effective team to work on this project. The October 15 memo I sent to you will provide you with some information you'll need to start making these decisions.

ITEM 16 E-MAIL

TO: Chris Perillo

FROM: Sharon Shapiro, V.P. of Human Resources

DATE: October 15

RE: Upcoming meeting

I want to update you on the rippling effect of John Small's sexual joke at last week's planning meeting. Quite a few women have been very upset and have met informally to talk about it. They have decided to call a meeting of all the people concerned about this kind of behavior throughout the firm. I plan to attend, so I'll keep you posted.

ITEM 17 E-MAIL

TO: All SSS Software managers

FROM: Sharon Shapiro, Vice President, Human Resources

DATE: October 14

RE: Promotions and External Hires

Year-to-date (January through September) promotions and external hires

	Race					Sex		
Level	White	Black	Asian	Hispanic	Native American	M	F	Total
Hires into executive level	0 (0%)	0 (0%)	0 (0%)	0 (0%)	0 (0%)	0 (0%)	0 (0%)	0
Promotions to executive level	0 (0%)	0 (0%)	0 (0%)	0 (0%)	0 (0%)	0 (0%)	0 (0%)	0
Hires into management level	2 (67%)	1 (33%)	0 (0%)	0 (0%)	0 (0%)	2 (67%)	1 (33%)	3
Promotions to management level	7 (88%)	0 (0%)	1 (12%)	0 (0%)	0 (0%)	7 (88%)	1 (12%)	8
Hires into technical/professional level	10 (36%)	6 (21%)	10 (36%)	2 (7%)	0 (0%)	14 (50%)	14 (50%)	28
Promotions to technical/professional level	0 (0%)	0 (0%)	0 (0%)	0 (0%)	0 (0%)	0 (0%)	0 (0%)	0
Hires into nonmanagement	4 (20%)	10 (50%)	2 (10%)	4 (20%)	0 (0%)	6 (30%)	14 (70%)	20
Promotions to nonmanagement level	NA	NA	NA	NA	NA	NA	NA	NA

SSS Software employee (EEO) classification report as of June 30

	Race					Sex		
Level	White	Black	Asian	Hispanic	Native American	M	F	Total
Executive level	11 (92%)	0 (0%)	1 (8%)	0 (0%)	0 (0%)	11 (92%)	1 (8%)	12
Management level	43 (90%)	2 (4%)	2 (4%)	1 (2%)	0 (0%)	38 (79%)	10 (21%)	48
Technical/professional level	58 (45%)	20 (15%)	37 (28%)	14 (11%)	1 (1%)	80 (62%)	50 (38%)	130
Nonmanagement level	29 (48%)	22 (37%)	4 (7%)	4 (7%)	1 (2%)	12 (20%)	48 (80%)	60
Total	141 (56%)	44 (18%)	44 (18%)	19 (8%)	2 (1%)	141 (56%)	109 (44%)	250

Employee Raiding

Litson Cotton Yarn Manufacturing Company, located in Murray, New Jersey, decided as a result of increasing labor costs to relocate its plant in Fairlee, a southern community of 4,200. Plant construction was started, and a human resources office was opened in the state employment office, located in Fairlee.

Because of ineffective HR practices in the other three textile mills located within a 50-mile radius of Fairlee, Litson was receiving applications from some of the most highly skilled and trained textile operators in the state. After receiving applications from approximately 500 people, employment was offered to 260 male and female applicants. These employees would be placed immediately on the payroll with instructions to await final installation of machinery, which was expected within the following six weeks.

The managers of the three other textile companies, faced with resignations from their most efficient and best-trained employees, approached the Litson managers with the complaint that their labor force was being "raided." They registered a strong protest to cease such practices and demanded an immediate cancellation of the employment of the 260 people hired by Litson.

Litson managers discussed the ethical and moral considerations involved in offering employment to the 260 people. Litson clearly faced a tight labor market in Fairlee, and management thought that if the 260 employees were discharged, the company would face cancellation of its plans and large construction losses. Litson management also felt obligated to the 260 employees who had resigned from their previous employment in favor of Litson.

The dilemma was compounded when the manager of one community plant reminded Litson that his plant was part of a nationwide chain supplied with cotton yarn from Litson. He implied that Litson's attempts to continue operations in Fairlee could result in cancellation of orders and the possible loss of approximately 18 percent market share. It was also suggested to Litson managers that actions taken by the nationwide textile chain could result in cancellation of orders from other textile companies. Litson's president held an urgent meeting of his top subordinates to (1) decide what to do about the situation in Fairlee, (2) formulate a written policy statement indicating Litson's position regarding employee raiding, and (3) develop a plan for implementing the policy.

How would you prepare for the meeting, and what would you say at the meeting?

SOURCE: J. Champion and J. James, *Critical Incidents in Management: Decision and Policy Issues*, 6th ed. McGraw-Hill/Irwin, 1989. Copyright © 1989 The McGraw-Hill Companies.

Effective Management

Dr. Sam Perkins, a graduate of the Harvard University College of Medicine, had a private practice in internal medicine for 12 years. Fourteen months ago, he was persuaded by the Massachusetts governor to give up private practice to be director of the State Division of Human Services.

After one year as director, Perkins recognized he had made little progress in reducing the considerable inefficiency in the division. Employee morale and effectiveness seemed even lower than when he had assumed the position. He realized his past training and experiences were of a clinical nature with little exposure to effective management techniques. Perkins decided to research literature on the subject of management available to him at a local university.

Perkins soon realized that management scholars are divided on the question of what constitutes effective management. Some believe people are born with certain identifiable personality traits that make them effective managers. Others believe a manager can learn to be effective by treating subordinates with a personal and considerate approach and by giving particular attention to their need for favorable working conditions. Still others emphasize the importance of developing a management style characterized by an authoritarian, democratic, or laissez-faire approach. Perkins was further confused when he learned that a growing number of scholars advocate that effective management is contingent on the situation.

Because a state university was located nearby, Perkins contacted the dean of its college of business administration. The dean referred him to the director of the college's management center, Professor Joel McCann. Discussions between Perkins and McCann resulted in a tentative agreement that the management center would organize a series of management training sessions for the State Division of Human Services. Before agreeing on the price tag for the management conference, Perkins asked McCann to prepare a proposal reflecting his thoughts on the following questions:

1. How will the question of what constitutes effective management be answered during the conference?
2. What will be the specific subject content of the conference?
3. Who will the instructors be?
4. What will be the conference's duration?
5. How can the conference's effectiveness be evaluated?
6. What policies should the State Division of Human Services adopt regarding who the conference participants should be and how they should be selected? How can these policies be implemented best?

SOURCE: J. Champion and J. James, *Critical Incidents in Management: Decision and Policy Issues*, 6th ed. McGraw-Hill/Irwin, 1989. Copyright © 1989 The McGraw-Hill Companies.

CHAPTER 4

Planning and Strategic Management

Manage your destiny, or someone else will.

— Jack Welch, Former CEO, General Electric

Management Connection

HOW WALT DISNEY COMPANY SCRIPTS ITS OWN SUCCESS

Mickey Mouse, mascot of the Walt Disney Company, may be a tiny creature, but the company he represents might be better portrayed as the massive and many-tentacled giant squid. With revenues exceeding $40 billion per year, the company is the largest in the entertainment industry, well ahead of News Corporation and Time Warner.

Walt Disney is not merely huge in terms of sales volume; it has five business divisions, involved in nearly every kind of commercial entertainment. It all began with Walt Disney Studios, which today produces movies, music, and stage shows under the banners of Disney, Pixar, Marvel Studios, Touchstone Pictures, and Hollywood Records. The Media Networks group covers publishing, radio, and broadcast and cable television, including Disney/ABC Television and ESPN. The Parks and Resorts group encompasses 11 theme parks and 43 resorts around the world as well as a cruise line. Disney Interactive offers entertainment on digital platforms, including console games and the Internet. And Disney Consumer Products extends the business value of characters and story lines by operating Disney Stores and licensing its creations for use on toys, clothing, art objects, and a wide variety of other consumer goods.

The man in charge of keeping the magic alive through activities carried out by more than 160,000 employees is Disney's chief executive officer, Robert Iger. Iger and his executive team must define an overall direction and goal for the company and keep an eye on how well each business group is contributing to achievement of that goal. Iger, whose experience was in running sports and entertainment broadcasting for ABC, does this by spotting opportunities for growth in the industry—hence the expansion into cable television and, more recently, into interactive entertainment. He also looks for characters and brands Disney can make more valuable because of its access to more channels. For example, Disney could pay generously for Pixar and Marvel because those companies' characters generate sales in products as diverse as theme parks, videogames, and sweatshirts. Another coup for Iger was the purchase of ESPN, the most valuable cable channel in terms of revenues.

Iger meets weekly over lunch with the heads of the business units. Although he keeps an eye on the company's overall direction, he gives each unit's head wide latitude. This pattern was evident when he planned the purchase of Pixar in 2006. Acknowledging that Pixar had become the dominant animation studio, he not only left its executives in charge after the acquisition but also placed them at the helm of the Disney animation studios. However, challenges remain for Iger. Disney Interactive is struggling to turn a profit. Somehow, the CEO from the television era has to ensure that Mickey remains a star of the Internet age.[1]

As you read this chapter, think about the challenge of providing direction to a massive enterprise offering entertainment to all ages around the globe. What planning methods could help managers at all levels zero in on the best opportunities?

To imagine the global Disney—or any organization—dealing with the significant challenges it faces without developing a plan beforehand is almost impossible. Planning is a formal expression of managerial intent. It describes what managers decide to do and how they will do it. It provides the framework, focus, and direction required for a meaningful effort. Without planning, any improvements in an organization's innovation, speed, quality, service, and cost will be accidental, if they occur at all. This chapter examines the most important concepts and processes involved in planning and strategic management. By learning these concepts and reviewing the steps outlined, you will be on your way to understanding the current approaches to the strategic management of today's organizations.

An Overview of Planning Fundamentals

The importance of formal planning in organizations has grown dramatically. Until the mid-1900s, most planning was unstructured and fragmented, and formal planning was restricted to a few large corporations. Although management pioneers such as Alfred Sloan of General Motors instituted formal planning processes, planning became a widespread management function only during the past few decades. Initially, larger organizations adopted formal planning, but today even small firms operated by aggressive, opportunistic entrepreneurs engage in formal planning.[2]

Planning is the conscious, systematic process of making decisions about goals and activities that an individual, group, work unit, or organization will pursue in the future. Planning is not an informal or haphazard response to a crisis; it is a purposeful effort that is directed and controlled by managers and often draws on the knowledge and experience of employees throughout the organization. Planning provides individuals and work units with a clear map to follow in their future activities; at the same time, this map may be flexible enough to allow for individual circumstances and changing conditions.

The Basic Planning Process

LO 1

Because planning is a decision process—you're deciding what to do and how to go about doing it—the important steps followed during formal planning are similar to the basic decision-making steps we discussed in Chapter 3. Figure 4.1 summarizes the similarities between decision making and planning—including the fact that both move not just in one direction but in a cycle. The outcomes of decisions and plans are evaluated, and if necessary, they are revised.

We now describe the basic planning process in more detail. Later in this chapter, we will discuss how managerial decisions and plans fit into the larger purposes of the organization—its ultimate strategy, mission, vision, and goals.

situational analysis

A process planners use, within time and resource constraints, to gather, interpret, and summarize all information relevant to the planning issue under consideration.

Step 1: Situational Analysis   As the contingency approach advocates, planning begins with a **situational analysis.** Within their time and resource constraints, planners should gather, interpret, and summarize all information relevant to the planning issue in question. A thorough situational analysis studies past events, examines current conditions, and attempts to forecast future trends. It focuses on the internal forces at work in the organization or work unit and, consistent with the open-systems approach (see Chapter 2), examines influences from the external environment. The outcome of this step is the identification and diagnosis of planning assumptions, issues, and problems.

A thorough situational analysis will provide information about the planning decisions you need to make. For example, if you are a manager in a magazine company

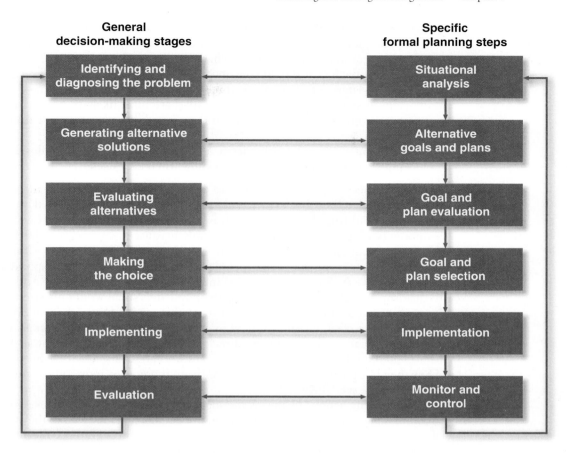

General decision-making stages

Identifying and diagnosing the problem

Generating alternative solutions

Evaluating alternatives

Making the choice

Implementing

Evaluation

Specific formal planning steps

Situational analysis

Alternative goals and plans

Goal and plan evaluation

Goal and plan selection

Implementation

Monitor and control

FIGURE 4.1
Decision-Making Stages (Chapter 3) and Formal Planning Steps (Chapter 4)

considering the launch of a sports publication for the teen market, your analysis will include such factors as the number of teens who subscribe to magazines, the appeal of the teen market to advertisers, your firm's ability to serve this market effectively, current economic conditions, the level of teen interest in sports, and any sports magazines already serving this market and their current sales. Such a detailed analysis will help you decide whether to proceed with the next step in your magazine launch.

Step 2: Alternative Goals and Plans   Based on the situational analysis, the planning process should generate alternative goals that may be pursued in the future and the alternative plans that may be used to achieve those goals. This step in the process should stress creativity and encourage managers and employees to think in broad terms about their jobs. Once a range of alternatives has been developed, the merits of these different plans and goals will be evaluated. Continuing with our magazine publishing example, the alternatives you might want to consider could include whether the magazine should be targeted at young men, young women, or both groups, and whether it should be sold mainly online, through subscriptions, or on newsstands.

Goals are the targets or ends the manager wants to reach. To be effective, goals should have certain qualities, which are easy to remember with the acronym SMART:

goal

A target or end that management desires to reach.

Specific—When goals are precise, describing particular behaviors and outcomes, employees can more easily determine whether they are working toward the goals.

Measurable—As much as possible, each goal should quantify the desired results so there is no doubt whether it has been achieved.

Attainable (but challenging)—Employees need to recognize that they can attain the goals they are responsible for, or else they are likely to become discouraged. However, they also should feel challenged to work hard and be creative.

Relevant—Each goal should contribute to the organization's overall mission (discussed later in this chapter) while being consistent with its values, including ethical standards (see Chapter 5). Goals are most likely to be relevant to the organization's overall objectives if they are consistent within and among work groups.

Time-bound—Effective goals specify a target date for completion. Besides knowing what to do, employees should know when they need to deliver results.

General Electric met at least some of these criteria with its goal to increase sales in India to $8 billion by 2010 from $1.9 billion in 2006.[3] The goal was clearly measurable and time-bound. It also was relevant because the fast-growing Indian economy is a logical source of sales, not only because of its size, but also because a developing economy needs many of the kinds of products GE sells. Although the sales number was specific, GE's people would need to settle on many details of how to achieve it: $8 billion from selling which products to whom? And the goal to quadruple sales was challenging to the point that some would question whether it was achievable. In fact, GE did not meet this target, but perhaps it could have done so with a clearer vision of how to achieve it. Ideally, SMART goals not only point individual employees in the direction they should be going but also tend to be accepted by the managers and employees who are charged with achieving them. Thus they both direct employees and motivate them. (For more on the importance of motivation, see Chapter 13.)

plans

The actions or means managers intend to use to achieve organizational goals.

Plans are the actions or means the manager intends to use to achieve goals. At a minimum, planning should outline alternative actions that may lead to the attainment of each goal, the resources required to reach the goal through those means, and the obstacles that may develop. After General Motors declared bankruptcy and borrowed billions from the U.S. government in 2009, management made plans for a return to profitability. The plans included reducing costs by producing fewer trucks, eliminating several brands, introducing smaller vehicles, keeping fewer vehicles in inventory, and closing hundreds of dealerships. GM had relied on trucks to generate comfortable profits, but those plans were no longer effective as a poor economy and high gas prices shifted demand toward fuel-efficient models. So besides cutting costs, GM introduced cars it hoped would be more popular, including the Cruze compact and the Sonic subcompact. Despite obstacles such as difficulty meeting demand with a reduced workforce and the lower profitability of smaller vehicles, the company moved back into the black a year after the bankruptcy, and in two years it reported its strongest financial performance in over a decade.[4]

Bottom Line

Contingency plans that keep service levels high during a crisis can seal a company's reputation for caring about customers. But this commitment requires highly dedicated and creative employees, and access to the necessary resources can be expensive. Managers must decide how crucial service is to their strategy—and how willing customers will be to forgive them for service lapses under pressure.

During a major storm, what services do you expect to be able to receive without interruption? Would you pay more to make these services more reliable?

In this chapter, we will talk about various types of plans. Some plans, called *contingency plans*, might be referred to as "what if" plans. They include sets of actions to be taken when a company's initial plans have not worked well or if events in the external environment require a sudden change. Disasters of recent years, including the 2001 terrorist attacks and Hurricanes Katrina and Rita, have reminded many businesses how important contingency planning can be.

Most major corporations now have contingency plans in place to respond to a major disaster—to make sure vital data are backed up and can be recovered in an emergency, for instance, or that employees know what to do when a crisis occurs. But contingency plans are important for more common situations as well. For example, many businesses are affected by snowstorms, increases in gasoline prices, computer breakdowns, or changes in consumer tastes. JetBlue initially achieved success as an airline that would "bring humanity back to air travel" by caring about its customers and employees. But the airline was humiliated by its inability to cope with a February snowstorm during which at least one plane notoriously sat on a runway for 10 hours; the company took days to recover, canceling a thousand flights.[5]

Step 3: Goal and Plan Evaluation   Next, managers will evaluate the advantages, disadvantages, and potential effects of each alternative goal and plan. They must prioritize those goals and even eliminate some of them. Also, managers will consider carefully the implications of alternative plans for meeting high-priority goals. In particular, they will pay a great deal of attention to the cost of any initiative and the investment return that is likely to result. In our magazine publishing example, your evaluation might determine that newsstand sales alone wouldn't be profitable enough to justify the launch. Perhaps you could improve profits with an online edition supplemented by podcasts. To decide, you would estimate the costs and expected returns of such alternatives, trying to follow the decision steps advised in Chapter 3.

Step 4: Goal and Plan Selection   Once managers have assessed the various goals and plans, they will select the one that is most appropriate and feasible. The evaluation process will identify the priorities and trade-offs among the goals and plans. For example, if your plan is to launch a number of new publications, and you're trying to choose among them, you might weigh the different up-front investment each requires, the size of each market, which one fits best with your existing product line or company image, and so on. Experienced judgment always plays an important role in this process. However, as you will discover later in the chapter, relying on judgment alone may not be the best way to proceed.

Typically, a formal planning process leads to a written set of goals and plans that are appropriate and feasible for a particular set of circumstances. In some organizations, the alternative generation, evaluation, and selection steps generate planning **scenarios,** as discussed in Chapter 2. A different contingency plan is attached to each scenario. The manager pursues the goals and implements the plans associated with the most likely scenario. However, the manager will also be prepared to switch to another set of plans if the situation changes and another scenario becomes relevant. This approach helps the firm anticipate and manage crises and allows greater flexibility and responsiveness.

The Hard Rock Café carries its strategy—to be identified with rock 'n' roll—through to its hotel signs.

scenario

A narrative that describes a particular set of future conditions.

Step 5: Implementation   Once managers have selected the goals and plans, they must implement the plans designed to achieve the goals. Even the best plans are useless if they are not implemented properly. Managers and employees must understand the plan, have the resources to implement it, and be motivated to do so. Including employees in the previous steps of the planning process paves the way for the implementation phase. As we mentioned earlier, employees usually are better informed, more committed, and more highly motivated when a goal or plan is one they helped develop.

Finally, successful implementation requires a plan to be linked to other systems in the organization, particularly the budget and reward systems. If the manager does not have a budget with financial resources to execute the plan, the plan is probably doomed. Similarly, goal achievement must be linked to the organization's reward system. Many organizations use incentive programs to encourage employees to achieve goals and to implement plans properly. Commissions, salaries, promotions, bonuses, and other rewards are based on successful performance.

> Even the best plans are useless if they are not implemented properly.

New York Community Bancorp (NYCB) looked at the possible ways to compete for customers: convenient locations, interest rates on savings, and customer service. With branches expensive to open and interest rates highly competitive, NYCB decided it would become known for exceptional customer service. NYCB's training department used service standards to create a classroom training program that teaches employees how to deliver excellent service. The trainers also visit NYCB's business units to practice the jobs and see firsthand what issues are important to success, using these experiences to make improvements to the employee training program. NYCB reinforces the program with coaching, and it has a system of rewards and recognition for meeting the service standards. Since implementing the goal-oriented training, coaching, and rewards, NYCB has seen its overall score for customer service rise from 89.5 percent to 97.5 percent.[6]

Step 6: Monitor and Control   Although it is sometimes ignored, the sixth step in the formal planning process—monitoring and controlling—is essential. Without it, you will never know whether your plan is succeeding. As we mentioned earlier, planning works in a cycle; it is an ongoing, repetitive process. Managers must continually monitor the actual performance of their work units against the units' goals and plans. They also need to develop control systems to measure that performance and allow them to take corrective action when the plans are implemented improperly or when the situation changes. In our magazine publishing example, newsstand and subscription sales reports are essential for letting you know how well your new magazine launch is going. If subscription sales aren't doing as well as expected, you may need to revise your marketing plan. We will discuss the important issue of control systems in greater detail later in this chapter and in Chapter 16.

In Practice

PLANNING AT THE BILL AND MELINDA GATES FOUNDATION

Careful planning is essential for the Bill and Melinda Gates Foundation, which directs the resources of a $36.4 billion trust. This much money can make an enormous difference, but only if it is spent wisely on programs that deliver results. Planning begins with the broad objective to "help all people lead healthy, productive lives." To accomplish this, the foundation makes grants to programs internationally, with a focus on improving health and education so that people are enabled to feed themselves and provide for their basic needs.

The Gates Foundation is extraordinarily committed to measuring results. It requires "actionable measurement": Every program must define goals in terms of actions intended to achieve the program's purpose. Funded programs must collect data and assess whether they are performing those actions and accomplishing the purpose.

Consider the foundation's goal to eradicate polio. The number of cases fell by 99 percent from 1988 to 2000, leaving the most difficult 1 percent. In Nigeria, for example, less than half of children were regularly vaccinated, and an investigation showed data so poor that the program didn't even know why it was failing. The foundation sent an independent team to remote areas to visit homes and see whether the children had been vaccinated. The team learned that maps were inaccurate, so team members were unaware of villages or couldn't make all their visits in the time allotted. The foundation had people walk through all the high-risk areas and prepare new, detailed maps. It also installed GPS on health workers' mobile phones to verify that the workers were actually visiting the locations. Finally, the polio program is sharing its experience with other health care programs, so they can improve their performance, too.[7]

- How do data collection and analysis improve planning at the Gates Foundation?

Levels of Planning

LO 2

In Chapter 1, you learned about the three major types of managers: top-level (strategic managers), middle-level (tactical managers), and frontline (operational managers). Because planning is an important management function, managers at all three levels use it. However, the scope and activities of the planning process at each level of the organization often differ.

Strategic Planning

Strategic planning involves making decisions about the organization's long-term goals and strategies. Strategic plans have a strong external orientation and cover major portions of the organization. Senior executives are responsible for the development and execution of the strategic plan, although they usually do not formulate or implement the entire plan personally.

Strategic goals are major targets or results that relate to the long-term survival, value, and growth of the organization. Strategic managers—top-level managers—usually establish goals that reflect both effectiveness (providing appropriate outputs) and efficiency (a high ratio of outputs to inputs). Typical strategic goals include growth, increasing market share, improving profitability, boosting return on investment, fostering both quantity and quality of outputs, increasing productivity, improving customer service, and contributing to society.

Organizations usually have a number of mutually reinforcing strategic goals. For example, a computer manufacturer may have as its strategic goals the launch of a specified number of new products in a particular time frame, of higher quality, with a targeted increase in market share. Each of these goals supports and contributes to the others.

A strategy is a pattern of actions and resource allocations designed to achieve the goals of the organization. An effective strategy provides a basis for answering five broad questions about how the organization will meet its objectives: (1) Where will we be active? (2) How will we get there (e.g., by increasing sales or acquiring another company)? (3) How will we win in the marketplace (e.g., by keeping prices low or offering the best service)? (4) How fast will we move and in what sequence will we make changes? (5) How will we obtain financial returns (low costs or premium prices)?[8] Former Procter & Gamble CEO A. G. Lafley and consultant Roger Martin emphasize that the answers to the "where" and "how" questions should be aimed at winning (question 3), which requires offering a better "value proposition" than the competition. Merely matching the competition, they say, is neither strategic nor a path to success. For example, P&G gave new life to its Oil of Olay skin care brand by addressing the concerns of middle-aged women and by improving the active ingredients in its product. In addition, P&G used its strength in selling to mass-market retailers to persuade them to set up attractive displays for Oil of Olay. With the value proposition of an affordable, attractive, widely available product serving a previously ignored market segment, P&G could meet its strategic goal of leadership in the skin care market.[9]

In setting a strategy, managers try to match the organization's skills and resources to the opportunities found in the external environment. Every organization has certain strengths and weaknesses, so the actions, or strategies, the organization implements should help build on strengths in areas that satisfy the wants and needs of consumers and other key factors in the organization's external environment. Also, some organizations may implement strategies that change or influence the external environment, as discussed in Chapter 2.

Tactical and Operational Planning

Once the organization's strategic goals and plans are identified, they serve as the foundation for planning done by middle-level and frontline managers. As you can see in

strategic planning

A set of procedures for making decisions about the organization's long-term goals and strategies.

strategic goals

Major targets or results relating to the organization's long-term survival, value, and growth.

strategy

A pattern of actions and resource allocations designed to achieve the organization's goals.

FIGURE 4.2
Hierarchy of Goals and
Plans

	Managerial Level	Level of Detail	Time Horizon
Strategic	Top	Low	Long (3–7 years)
Tactical	Middle	Medium	Medium (1–2 years)
Operational	Frontline	High	Short (<1 year)

tactical planning

A set of procedures for translating broad strategic goals and plans into specific goals and plans that are relevant to a distinct portion of the organization, such as a functional area like marketing.

operational planning

The process of identifying the specific procedures and processes required at lower levels of the organization.

Bottom Line

Ideally, strategic plans integrate all the bottom-line practices of the firm.
What could be the consequences if a company's innovation practices were not aligned with its strategy?

Figure 4.2, goals and plans become more specific and involve shorter periods of time as they move from the strategic level to the tactical level and then to the operational level. A strategic plan will typically have a time horizon of from three to seven years—but sometimes even decades, as with the successful plan to land a probe on Titan, Saturn's moon. Tactical plans may have a time horizon of a year or two, and operational plans may cover a period of months.

Tactical planning translates broad strategic goals and plans into specific goals and plans that are relevant to a definite portion of the organization, often a functional area like marketing or human resources, as discussed in Chapter 10. Tactical plans focus on the major actions a unit must take to fulfill its part of the strategic plan. For example, if the strategy calls for the rollout of a new product line, the tactical plan for the manufacturing unit might involve the design, testing, and installation of the equipment needed to produce the new line.

Operational planning identifies the specific procedures and processes required at lower levels of the organization. Frontline managers usually focus on routine tasks such as production runs, delivery schedules, and human resource requirements, as we discuss in Chapters 16 and 17.

The planning model we have been describing is a hierarchical one, with top-level strategies flowing down through the levels of the organization into more specific goals and plans and an ever-more-limited timetable. But in today's complex organizations, the planning sequence is often not as rigid as this traditional view. As we will see later in this chapter, managers throughout an organization may be involved in developing the strategic plan and contributing critical elements to it. Also, in practice, lower-level managers may be making decisions that shape strategy, whether or not top executives realize it. When Intel senior adviser Andy Grove suggested that the company exit the computer memory business, Intel was directing about one-third of its research dollars to memory-related projects. However, on a practical level, the company had already been exiting the business; only 4 percent of its total sales were for computer memory products. Why was this occurring if it wasn't yet a defined strategy? Manufacturing managers had been directed by finance executives to set up factories in a way that would generate the biggest margins (revenues minus costs) per square inch of microchips produced. As computer memory became a money-losing commodity, manufacturing made fewer of those products. So when Intel announced it would get out of the memory business, its strategy was catching up with its operational planning, which had been driven by tactical plans.[10] The lesson for top managers is to make sure they are communicating strategy to all levels of the organization *and* paying attention to what is happening at all levels in the organization.

Aligning Tactical, Operational, and Strategic Planning

To be fully effective, the organization's strategic, tactical, and operational goals and plans must be aligned—that is, they must be consistent, mutually supportive, and focused on achieving the common purpose and direction. Whole Foods Market, for example, links its tactical and operational planning directly to its strategic planning. The firm describes itself on its website as a mission-driven company that aims to set the standards for excellence for food retailers. The firm measures its success in fulfilling its vision by "customer satisfaction, team member excellence and happiness, return on capital investment, improvement in the state of the environment, and local and larger community support."

Whole Foods's strategic goal is "to sell the highest-quality products that also offer high value for our customers." Its operational goals focus on ingredients, freshness, taste, nutritional value, safety, and appearance that meet or exceed its customers' expectations, including guaranteeing product satisfaction. Tactical goals include store environments that are "inviting, fun, unique, informal, comfortable, attractive, nurturing, and educational" and safe and inviting work environments for its employees.

One method for aligning the organization's strategic and operational goals is a *strategy map*. A strategy map provides a tool managers can use to communicate their strategic goals and enable members of the organization at every level to understand the parts they will play in helping to achieve them. The map illustrates the four key drivers (or "balanced scorecard") of a firm's long-term success: the skills of its people and their ability to grow and learn; the effectiveness of its internal processes; its ability to deliver value to customers; and ultimately its ability to grow its financial assets. The map shows how specific plans and goals in each area link to the others and can generate real improvements in an organization's performance.

Figure 4.3 shows how a strategy map might be built and how the various goals of the organization relate to each other to create long-term value for the firm. As an example, let us assume that a company's primary financial goal is "to increase revenues by enhancing the value we offer to existing customers by making our prices the lowest available." (Target and Walmart might be good examples of companies with this kind of strategy.) The company will then have corresponding goals and plans in the other sections of the map to support that strategy. Its learning and growth goals might include bringing in the most efficient production technologies or work processes and training the staff to use them. These in turn will lead to the internal goals of improved production speed and lower cost, which in turn lead to the customer goal of competitive pricing, making the original financial goal feasible. On the other hand, a financial strategy of revenue growth through new products might lead to people and technology goals that speed up product design, to internal processes that lead to innovation, and to a customer goal of perceived product leadership. Whatever the strategy, the strategy map can be used to develop the appropriate measures and standards in each operational area for that strategy and to show how they are all linked.[11]

As you read "Management Connection: Progress Report," consider how well tactical, operational, and strategic planning are aligned at Walt Disney Company, particularly with regard to its Disney Interactive unit.

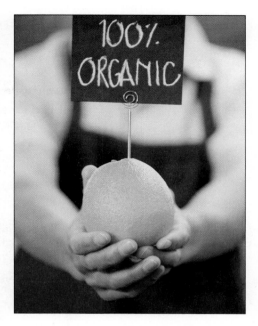

Whole Foods has operational goals that focus on high quality and appearance among other qualities.

Bottom Line

The strategy map shows the relationship between a firm's practices and its long-term success.
Where do a company's quality practices show up in the strategy map (Figure 4.3)?

Strategic Planning

Strategic decision making is one of the most exciting and controversial topics in management today. In fact, many organizations currently are changing the ways they develop and execute their strategic plans.

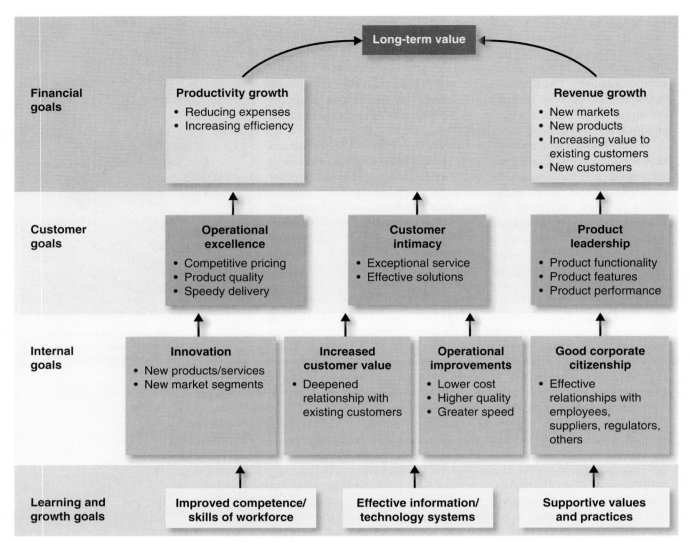

FIGURE 4.3
The Strategy Map: Creating Value by Aligning Goals

SOURCE: Adapted from R. Kaplan and D. Norton, "Plotting Success with Strategy Maps," *Optimize*, February 2004, online; and R. Kaplan and D. Norton, "Having Trouble with Your Strategy? Then Map It," *Harvard Business Review*, September–October 2000.

Traditionally, strategic planning emphasized a top-down approach—senior executives and specialized planning units developed goals and plans for the entire organization. Tactical and operational managers received those goals and plans, and their own planning activities were limited to specific procedures and budgets for the units.

Over the years, managers and consulting firms innovated with a variety of analytical techniques and planning approaches, many of which have been critical for analyzing complex business situations and competitive issues. In many instances, however, senior executives spent too much time with their planning specialists to the exclusion of line managers in the rest of the organization. As a result, a gap often developed between strategic managers and tactical and operational managers, and managers and employees throughout the organization became alienated and uncommitted to the organization's success.[12]

Today, however, senior executives increasingly are involving managers throughout the organization in the strategy formation process.[13] The problems just described and the rapidly changing environment of the past 25 years have forced executives to look to all levels of the organization for ideas and innovations to make their firms more competitive. Although the CEO and other top managers continue to furnish the strategic direction, or "vision," of the organization, tactical and even operational

Bottom Line

New ideas from managers throughout the organization can contribute to a plan's effectiveness.

What experiences might give frontline managers ideas that top-level executives haven't thought of?

Management Connection

PLANNING A TURNAROUND FOR DISNEY INTERACTIVE

Walt Disney Company's corporate strategy is to lead in providing entertainment and information. The company's top ranking in the industry and recent profits of $9 billion suggest it is succeeding. However, Disney Interactive posted an operating loss—which came after several years' worth of quarterly losses.

Disney Interactive, founded in 2008, has as its ambitious goal to "entertain kids, families, and Disney enthusiasts everywhere with world-class products that push the boundaries of technology and imagination." Its tactical plans include development of games for every digital media platform, including mobile and social media as well as the major gaming consoles.

Measured by those standards, performance has been less than perfect. The slow pace at which it crafts movies is unsuitable for game creation. The six years required to go from concept to release of Epic Mickey, created only for the Nintendo Wii, meant the release came in 2010, after that console's popularity had peaked. At one point, Disney ran six development studios creating games for consoles, which became a problem when players switched to online games and began using mobile devices.

A basic element of Disney's digital strategy has been its entertainment website, Disney.com, successor to the Go.com web portal, which closed in 2001. However, the company has struggled to make it relevant. One challenge is that the brand aims to serve the diverse interests of toddlers and parents as well as game players of all ages in between. Mostly, the site has focused on cross-promoting its entertainment and licensed merchandise.

To become more agile, Disney acquired Playdom, a social gaming company, and made its CEO, John Pleasants, co-president of Disney Interactive along with James Pitaro, recruited from Yahoo. Pleasants and Pitaro cut costs by laying off employees and closing some of its studios (including the studio that created Epic Mickey). They planned to increase sales by strengthening Disney.com with exclusive content, creating popular characters in its games, and making games playable across platforms. For example, the company is offering a mobile version of Club Penguin, a virtual world designed for children. Disney Interactive also is getting out of its less-popular businesses. For example, it shut down Disney Movies Online, a service that allowed streaming (but not downloading) only Disney and Pixar films through a web browser. Consumers had preferred movie services offering greater flexibility.[14]

- At which steps of the planning process would you say Disney Interactive most needs improvement? Why?
- How can Pleasants and Pitaro ensure that tactical, operational, and strategic management are well aligned?

managers often provide valuable inputs to the organization's strategic plan. In some cases, these managers also have substantial autonomy to formulate or change their own plans. This authority increases flexibility and responsiveness, critical requirements for success in today's organizations.

Because of these trends, firms often use the term *strategic management* to describe the process. **Strategic management** involves managers from all parts of the organization in the formulation and implementation of strategic goals and strategies. It integrates strategic planning and management into a single process. Strategic planning becomes an ongoing activity in which all managers are encouraged to think strategically and focus on long-term, externally oriented issues as well as short-term tactical and operational issues.

As shown in Figure 4.4, the strategic management process has six major components:

1. Establishment of mission, vision, and goals.
2. Analysis of external opportunities and threats.
3. Analysis of internal strengths and weaknesses.
4. SWOT (strengths, weaknesses, opportunities, and threats) analysis and strategy formulation.

strategic management

A process that involves managers from all parts of the organization in the formulation and implementation of strategic goals and strategies.

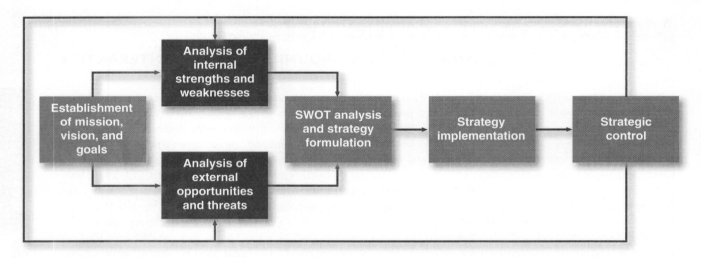

FIGURE 4.4

The Strategic Management Process

5. Strategy implementation.
6. Strategic control.

Because this process is a planning and decision process, it is similar to the planning framework discussed earlier. Although organizations may use different terms or emphasize different parts of the process, the components and concepts described in this section are found either explicitly or implicitly in every organization. Even a small entrepreneurial firm can benefit from the kind of planning framework we describe here.

Step 1: Establishment of Mission, Vision, and Goals

The first step in strategic planning is establishing a mission, a vision, and goals for the organization. The **mission** is a clear and concise expression of the basic purpose of the organization. It describes what the organization does, for whom it does it, its basic good or service, and its values. Here are some mission statements from firms you will recognize:[15]

mission

An organization's basic purpose and scope of operations.

> *McDonald's:* "To be our customers' favorite place and way to eat."
> *Google:* "To organize the world's information and make it universally accessible and useful."
> *U.S. Air Force:* "To fly, fight, and win . . . in air, space, and cyberspace."

Smaller organizations, of course, may have missions that aren't as broad as these. For example, the local bar found next to most campuses has this implicit mission: "to sell large quantities of inexpensive beer to college students in a noisily enjoyable environment."

The mission describes the organization as it currently operates. The **strategic vision** points to the future—it provides a perspective on where the organization is headed and what it can become. Ideally, the vision statement clarifies the long-term direction of the company and its strategic intent. Here are some actual vision statements:[16]

strategic vision

The long-term direction and strategic intent of a company.

> *DuPont:* "To be the world's most dynamic science company, creating sustainable solutions essential to a better, safer, and healthier life for people everywhere."
> *City of Redmond, Washington:* "Together we create a community of good neighbors."
> *Great Lakes Naval Museum:* "To enhance and become an integral part of the training mission of the Naval Service Training Command, Great Lakes, by instilling in our newest sailors a strong sense of tradition and heritage of naval service in the United States."

The strategic vision points to the future— where the organization is headed and what it can become.

The most effective vision statements inspire organization members. They offer a worthwhile target for the entire organization to work together to achieve. Often these statements are not strictly financial because financial targets alone may not motivate all organization members. For example, DuPont's vision refers to being a "dynamic science company" that works toward a "better, safer, and healthier life" for people. This vision inspires innovation aimed at making the world better—the type of work that is likely to motivate the scientists and other knowledge workers who can give the company an edge, ultimately improving DuPont's competitive position. Likewise, "instilling . . . a strong sense of tradition and heritage" provides an inspirational basis for operating the Great Lakes Naval Museum, in contrast to planning based only on budgets and historical artifacts.

Strategic goals evolve from the mission and vision of the organization. The chief executive officer of the organization, with the input and approval of the board of directors, establishes the mission, vision, and major strategic goals. The concepts and information within the mission statement, vision statement, and strategic goals statement may not be identified as such, but they should be communicated to everyone who has contact with the organization. Large firms generally provide public formal statements of their missions, visions, goals, and even values. For example, in support of its vision that "creating a community of good neighbors" is best done "together" with all sectors of the community, the City of Redmond has established goals such as these:

- Enhance citizen engagement in city issues.
- Sustain the natural systems and beauty of the community.
- Sustain a safe community with a coherent, comprehensive, cohesive approach to safety.
- Maintain economic vitality.

Different city departments would contribute to various aspects of this vision in the way they carry out their operational plans with an emphasis on collaborating with local businesses and residents.

Lofty words in a vision and mission statement cannot be meaningful without strong leadership support. At McDonald's, the commitment of past and present CEOs has played a large role in the success of the company's strategy implementation. Several years ago, the company was floundering as it lost sight of its commitment to quality, value, speed, and convenience. Under the leadership of James Cantalupo, the company created the mission statement quoted earlier, which placed the emphasis on the customer's experience. In a "Plan to Win," strategic goals such as revamping restaurants for a better drive-through experience and improving the quality of the menu supported the mission. When Jim Skinner took the job of chief executive, he enthusiastically backed the mission statement and its supporting Plan to Win, not hesitating to share credit for the company's continued success.[17]

Where leadership is strong, statements of visions and goals clarify the organization's purpose to key constituencies outside the organization. They also help employees focus their talent, energy, and commitment in pursuit of the organization's goals. When the time comes for you to seek employment with a firm, reviewing the firm's statements of mission, vision, and goals is a good first step in determining whether the firm's purposes and values will be compatible with your own.

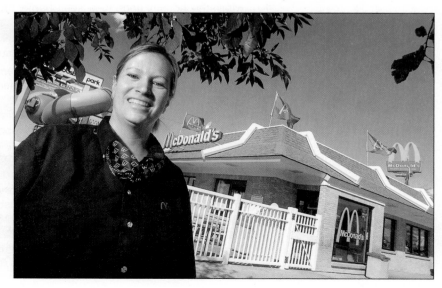

The mission statement at McDonald's is "to be our customers' favorite place and way to eat." How do you see that translated into the atmosphere at your local McDonald's?

Step 2: Analysis of External Opportunities and Threats

The mission and vision drive the second component of the strategic management process: analysis of the external environment. Successful strategic management depends on an accurate and thorough evaluation of the competitive environment and macroenvironment. The various components of these environments were introduced in Chapter 2.

The important activities in an environmental analysis include the ones listed in Table 4.1. The analysis begins with an examination of the industry. Next, organizational stakeholders are examined. **Stakeholders** are groups and individuals who affect and are affected by the achievement of the organization's mission, goals, and strategies. They include buyers, suppliers, competitors, government and regulatory agencies, unions and employee groups, the financial community, owners and shareholders, and trade associations. The environmental analysis provides a map of these stakeholders and the ways they influence the organization.[18]

stakeholders

Groups and individuals who affect and are affected by the achievement of the organization's mission, goals, and strategies.

TABLE 4.1

Environmental Analysis

Industry and Market Analysis
• *Industry profile:* major product lines and significant market segments in the industry.
• *Industry growth:* growth rates for the entire industry, growth rates for key market segments, projected changes in patterns of growth, and the determinants of growth.
• *Industry forces:* threat of new industry entrants, threat of substitutes, economic power of buyers, economic power of suppliers, and internal industry rivalry (recall Chapter 2).

Competitor Analysis
• *Competitor profile:* major competitors and their market shares.
• *Competitor analysis:* goals, strategies, strengths, and weaknesses of each major competitor.
• *Competitor advantages:* the degree to which industry competitors have differentiated their products or services or achieved cost leadership.

Political and Regulatory Analysis
• *Legislation and regulatory activities* and their effects on the industry.
• *Political activity:* the level of political activity that organizations and associations within the industry undertake (see Chapter 5).

Social Analysis
• *Social issues:* current and potential social issues and their effects on the industry.
• *Social interest groups:* consumer, environmental, and similar activist groups that attempt to influence the industry (see Chapters 5 and 6).

Human Resources Analysis
• *Labor issues:* key labor needs, shortages, opportunities, and problems confronting the industry (see Chapters 10 and 11).

Macroeconomic Analysis
• *Macroeconomic conditions:* economic factors that affect supply, demand, growth, competition, and profitability within the industry.

Technological Analysis
• *Technological factors:* scientific or technical methods that affect the industry, particularly recent and potential innovations (see Chapter 17).

In Practice

COLLABORATION AT INTUIT

Collaborating with key stakeholders can help organizations successfully develop and implement their strategic plans. At software company Intuit, CEO Brad Smith launched strategy development by learning what was on the minds of some key stakeholders. He visited with his board of directors and investors and set up meetings with groups of employees who work directly with Intuit's customers.

Smith asked each group of stakeholders some key questions related to strategic analysis: "What is Intuit's biggest untapped opportunity? What is the biggest risk facing Intuit that keeps you up at night? What is the biggest mistake I can make as a CEO in my first year?" From the answers, Smith gained insights that helped him establish priorities for Intuit's strategy.

Smith learned that a sizable number of Intuit's business customers have international activities, so he determined that Intuit would have to become a more global company. Its QuickBooks financial software now handles multiple currencies for international transactions. In response to the competitive threat of a new release of financial software from Microsoft, Smith assembled managers to craft a marketing strategy that would convince customers to wait two more months for the next version of QuickBooks. That campaign caused QuickBooks sales to jump despite Microsoft's efforts.[19]

- Now that Smith has launched his strategy development process, what can he do to continue learning from environmental analysis?

The environmental analysis also should examine other forces in the environment, such as economic conditions and technological factors. One critical task in environmental analysis is forecasting future trends. As noted in Chapter 2, forecasting techniques range from simple judgment to complex mathematical models that examine systematic relationships among many variables. Even simple quantitative techniques outperform the intuitive assessments of experts. Judgment is susceptible to bias, and managers have a limited ability to process information. Managers should use subjective judgments as inputs to quantitative models or when they confront new situations.

Since some states require the use of renewable sources to generate power, it is up to these companies to turn the negative aspect of higher costs into an overall positive outcome.

Frequently, the difference between an opportunity and a threat depends on how a company positions itself strategically. For example, some states have required electric utilities to get a certain share of their power from renewable sources such as wind and solar energy rather than from fossil fuels, including coal, oil, and natural gas. This requirement poses an obvious threat to utilities because the costs of fossil fuel energy are less, and customers demand low prices. However, some companies see strategic opportunities in renewable power. For example, the German conglomerate Schott has developed a solar thermal technology in which sunlight heats oil in metal tubes enclosed in coated glass; the heated oil makes steam, which powers a turbine and generates electricity. Solar thermal energy, although it now costs more than fossil fuels, is more efficient than the solar panels installed on buildings, and it can store extra power to be used on cloudy days.[20] Similarly, overflowing landfills are an expensive challenge for many municipalities, but a growing number are seeing an opportunity in the form of energy generation. As garbage decomposes, it produces methane gas, which is used as a fuel to power generators. In East Brunswick, New Jersey, for example, the Edgeboro landfill generates electricity that powers the county's wastewater treatment plant.[21]

In some environments, it takes an especially creative mind to see opportunities among severe threats. For Farif Ali Abood, who opened a shop to make commercial signs in his hometown of Najaf, Iraq, the difficulties have included sporadic electrical service, lack of funds to borrow, and even occasional sniper fire in the area. Despite these challenges, Abood has managed to keep the business running by using a generator when the power goes out. As conditions in the city have stabilized, business has grown enough for Abood to hire several full-time employees and earn a modest profit.

Halfway across the world in Haiti, the potentially devastating threat to businesses was the massive earthquake of 2010. Mathias Pierre had launched an information technology company to serve schools and the government. When his client base was effectively wiped out or at least disabled by the quake, Pierre managed to locate his key managers, and together they worked tirelessly to ensure communications for all the organizations at work on the relief effort. Eventually, these agencies became the new clients for Pierre's business.[22] The brave few who, like Pierre and Abood, can fill needs amidst such difficult threats are well positioned to benefit from the business relationships they create with loyal customers.

Step 3: Analysis of Internal Strengths and Weaknesses

As managers conduct an external analysis, they will also assess the strengths and weaknesses of major functional areas inside their organization. Table 4.2 lists some of the major components of this internal resource analysis. For example, is your firm strong enough financially to handle the lengthy and costly investment new projects often require? Can your existing staff carry out its part of the plan, or will additional training or hiring be needed? Is your firm's image compatible with the strategy, or will it have to persuade key stakeholders that a change in direction makes sense? This kind of internal analysis gives strategic decision makers an inventory of the organization's existing functions, skills, and resources as well as its overall performance level. Many of your other business courses will prepare you to conduct an internal analysis.

resources

Inputs to a system that can enhance performance.

Resources and Core Capabilities   Without question, strategic planning has been strongly influenced in recent years by a focus on internal resources. **Resources** are inputs to production (recall systems theory) that can be accumulated over time to enhance the performance of a firm. Resources can take many forms, but they tend to fall into two broad categories: (1) tangible assets such as real estate, production facilities, raw materials, and so on, and (2) intangible assets such as company reputation, culture, technical knowledge, and patents as well as accumulated learning and experience. The Walt Disney Company, for example, has developed its strategic plan on combinations of tangible assets (e.g., hotels and theme parks) as well as intangible assets (brand recognition, talented craftspeople, culture focused on customer service).[23]

Effective internal analysis provides a clearer understanding of how a company can compete through its resources. Resources are a source of competitive advantage only under certain circumstances. First, if the resource is instrumental for creating customer value—that is, if it increases the benefits customers derive from a good or service relative to the costs they incur—the resource can lead to a competitive advantage.[24]

TABLE 4.2
Internal Resource Analysis

Financial Analysis
Examines financial strengths and weaknesses through financial statements such as a balance sheet and an income statement and compares trends to historical and industry figures (see Chapter 18).
Marketing Audit
Examines strengths and weaknesses of major marketing activities and identifies markets, key market segments, and the competitive position (market share) of the organization within key markets.
Operations Analysis
Examines the strengths and weaknesses of the manufacturing, production, or service delivery activities of the organization (see Chapters 9, 16, and 17).
Other Internal Resource Analyses
Examine, as necessary and appropriate, the strengths and weaknesses of other organizational activities, such as research and development (product and process), management information systems, engineering, and purchasing.
Human Resources Assessment
Examines strengths and weaknesses of all levels of management and employees and focuses on key human resources activities, including recruitment, selection, placement, training, labor (union) relationships, compensation, promotion, appraisal, quality of work life, and human resources planning (see Chapters 10 and 11).

For example, Amazon's powerful search technology and its ability to track customer preferences and offer personalized recommendations each time its site is accessed, as well as its quick product delivery system, are clearly valuable resources that enhance Amazon's competitiveness.

Second, resources are a source of advantage if they are rare and not equally available to all competitors. Even for extremely valuable resources, if all competitors have equal access, the resource cannot provide a source of competitive advantage. For companies such as Merck, DuPont, Dow Chemical, and others, patented formulas represent important resources that are both rare and valuable. Amazon, too, sought a patent for its one-click shopping technique.

Third, if resources are difficult to imitate, they provide a source of competitive advantage. Online retailer Zappos.com seeks a competitive advantage in the form of service that makes customers say "Wow!" The company hires customer service employees based on their match with its values, gives them seven weeks of training, and empowers them to do whatever it takes to delight a customer, whether that be spending hours on the phone, issuing a refund, or sending a package of free cookies. Zappos frees reps from using scripted replies, promotes positive relationships with colleagues through mentoring programs and fun activities, and provides on-site coaching to help employees achieve their career and personal goals.[25] As in this example, where success relies on a combination of hiring, training, motivation, and job design, not just a policy of free returns, resources tend to be harder to imitate if they are complex, with many interdependent variables and no obvious links between easily explained behaviors and desired outcomes.[26]

Finally, resources can enhance a firm's competitive advantage when they are well organized. For example, Coca-Cola's well-organized and global network of bottlers allows the company to introduce a new soft drink worldwide quickly and to distribute it more efficiently than any competitor. IBM, known primarily for computer hardware until it became more of a commodity than a source of competitive advantage,

Bottom Line
Amazon's key customer benefits are speed and excellence of service.
What are some resources Amazon needs to deliver these benefits?

has organized its staff and systems to produce a consolidated technology product efficiently for its corporate clients—hardware, software, and service in one package. This spares its clients the cost of managing technology on their own.

As shown in Figure 4.5, when resources are valuable, rare, inimitable, and organized, they can be viewed as a company's core capabilities. Simply stated, a **core capability** (also referred to as "competence") is something a company does especially well relative to its competitors. Honda, for example, has a core competence in small engine design and manufacturing; Sony has a core competence in miniaturization; Federal Express has a core competence in logistics and customer service. As in these examples, a core competence typically refers to a set of skills or expertise in some activity rather than physical or financial assets.

Benchmarking   To assess and improve performance, some companies use benchmarking, the process of assessing how well one company's basic functions and skills compare with those of another company or set of companies. The goal of benchmarking is to understand the "best practices" of other firms thoroughly and to undertake actions to achieve both better performance and lower costs. Benchmarking programs have helped a myriad of companies, such as Ford, Corning, Hewlett-Packard, Xerox, and Anheuser-Busch, make great strides in eliminating inefficiencies and improving competitiveness.

Depending on how it is applied, benchmarking may be of limited help in that it only helps a company perform as well as its competitors; strategic management ultimately is about surpassing those companies. Besides benchmarking against leading organizations in other industries, companies may address this problem by engaging in internal benchmarking. That approach involves benchmarking their different internal operations and departments against one another to disseminate the company's best practices throughout the organization and thereby gain a competitive advantage.

One company that has experienced the pros and cons of benchmarking is AXA Canada, an insurance company. The company turned to benchmarking as a way to identify how it could improve its processes and lower its costs. AXA Canada used internal benchmarking to compare results among its regions. However, employees objected that in a country as vast as Canada, the differences among regions were so great that performance couldn't really be compared. More energy went to arguing about the numbers than looking for ways to close performance gaps. The company

---

core capability

A unique skill and/or knowledge an organization possesses that gives it an edge over competitors.

Bottom Line

Aligning a firm's bottom-line practices with best practices can improve its competitiveness. *In some famous benchmarking examples, businesses have learned from pit crews for race car teams. What kinds of bottom-line practices could such an organization demonstrate?*

FIGURE 4.5
Resources and Core Capability

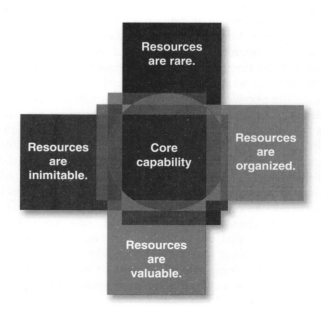

made similar efforts to compare Canadian performance with insurers in other countries, and it ran into even greater difficulty making comparisons. The most success came from an arrangement with the Ward Group to gather performance data from several insurance companies, analyze it, and report on areas of strength and weakness. Using this benchmarking information, AXA Canada has found areas where it can operate more efficiently by applying other companies' practices. The company uses the benchmarking data primarily for cutting costs and identifying potential new markets.[27]

Step 4: SWOT Analysis and Strategy Formulation

Once managers have analyzed the external environment and the internal resources of the organization, they will have the information they need to assess the organization's strengths, weaknesses, opportunities, and threats. Such an assessment normally is referred to as a **SWOT analysis.** Strengths and weaknesses refer to internal resources. For example, an organization's strengths might include skilled management, positive cash flow, and well-known and highly regarded brands. Weaknesses might be lack of spare production capacity and the absence of reliable suppliers. Opportunities and threats arise in the macroenvironment and competitive environment. Examples of opportunities are a new technology that could make the supply chain more efficient and a market niche that is currently underserved. Threats might include the possibility that competitors will enter the underserved niche once it has been shown to be profitable.

SWOT analysis helps managers summarize the relevant, important facts from their external and internal analyses. Based on this summary, they can identify the primary and secondary strategic issues their organization faces. The managers then formulate a strategy that will build on the SWOT analysis to take advantage of available opportunities by capitalizing on the organization's strengths, neutralizing its weakness, and countering potential threats.

To take an example, consider how SWOT analysis might be carried out by Qlik-Tech, a Swedish maker of business intelligence software, which is designed to retrieve, analyze, and report data in formats useful to businesspeople. QlikTech has grown fast, building on strong marketing, a user-friendly product, and relatively low prices. However, it originally aimed at relatively small customers, which has raised questions about whether the company and the software can handle the needs of big organizations. If QlikTech can keep ahead of competitors, it should be able to continue expanding in new markets, particularly the United States. Figure 4.6 summarizes these points in a format commonly used for a basic SWOT analysis. Based on these and other points, the company's strategy calls for it to continue improving its software, offering the latest features, such as data discovery, an application that enables users without statistical training to look up data and create various tables and charts for fast and personalized analysis.[28] In the real world, as a company is formulating strategy, so are its competitors. As a result, the process must be continually evolving through contingency planning. The more uncertainty that exists in the external environment, the more the strategy needs to focus on building internal capabilities through practices such as knowledge sharing and continuous process improvement.[29] Yet at a basic level, strategy formulation moves from analysis to devising a coherent course of action, such as Microsoft's plan to purchase (and eventually operate) DoubleClick. In this way, the organization's corporate, business, and functional strategies will begin to take shape.

Before we continue our strategy discussion, we note that many individuals seeking a job or a career change can find a self-SWOT analysis helpful. What are you particularly good at? What weaknesses might you need to overcome to improve your employment chances? What firms offer the best opportunity to market your skills to full advantage? Will you have a lot of competition from other job seekers? As with companies, this kind of analysis can be the beginning of a plan of action and can improve the plan's effectiveness.

SWOT analysis

A comparison of strengths, weaknesses, opportunities, and threats that helps executives formulate strategy.

FIGURE 4.6
Sample SWOT Analysis:
QlikTech

Strengths	Weaknesses
• Effective sales and marketing • User-friendly software • Relatively low price	• Experience limited to smaller companies • Need to prove capabilities for larger customers

Opportunities	Threats
• Geographical expansion • More markets • New services (e.g., data discovery)	• Large vendors with similar software • Pressure on price • Possibility of software becoming standard

Source: Based on information from Erica Driver, "QlikTech Comes Out Strong in Gartner SWOT Analysis," *QlikCommunity Business Discovery Blog*, October 15, 2010, http://community.qlikview.com; Erica Driver, "QlikTech: A Leader in the Gartner MQ for Third Year in a Row," *QlikCommunity Business Discovery Blog*, February 28, 2013, http://community.qlikview.com.

corporate strategy

The set of businesses, markets, or industries in which an organization competes and the distribution of resources among those entities.

concentration

A strategy employed for an organization that operates a single business and competes in a single industry.

vertical integration

The acquisition or development of new businesses that produce parts or components of the organization's product.

concentric diversification

A strategy used to add new businesses that produce related products or are involved in related markets and activities.

Corporate Strategy   A **corporate strategy** identifies the set of businesses, markets, or industries in which the organization competes and the distribution of resources among those businesses. Figure 4.7 shows four basic alternatives for a corporate strategy, ranging from very specialized to highly diverse. A **concentration** strategy focuses on a single business competing in a single industry. In the food retailing industry, Kroger, Safeway, and A&P all pursue concentration strategies. Frequently, companies pursue concentration strategies to gain entry into an industry when industry growth is good or when the company has a narrow range of competencies. An example is C. F. Martin & Company, which pursues a concentration strategy by focusing on making the best possible guitars and guitar strings, a strategy that has enabled the family-owned business to operate successfully for more than 150 years.

A **vertical integration** strategy involves expanding the domain of the organization into supply channels or to distributors. At one time, Henry Ford had fully integrated his company from the ore mines needed to make steel all the way to the showrooms where his cars were sold. Vertical integration generally is used to eliminate uncertainties and reduce costs associated with suppliers or distributors.

A strategy of **concentric diversification** involves moving into new businesses that are related to the company's original core business. William Marriott expanded his original restaurant business outside Washington, DC, by moving into airline catering, hotels, and fast food. Each of these businesses within the hospitality industry is related in terms of the services it provides, the skills necessary for success, and the customers it attracts. Often companies such as Marriott pursue a strategy of concentric diversification to take advantage of their strengths in one business to gain advantage in another. Because the businesses are related, the products, markets, technologies, or capabilities used in one business can be transferred to another. Success in a concentric diversification strategy requires adequate management and other resources for operating more than one business. Guitar maker C. F. Martin once tried expanding through purchases of other instrument companies, but management was stretched too thin to run them all well, so the company eventually divested the acquisitions and returned to its concentration strategy.[30]

In contrast to concentric diversification, **conglomerate diversification** is a corporate strategy that involves expansion into unrelated businesses. For example, General

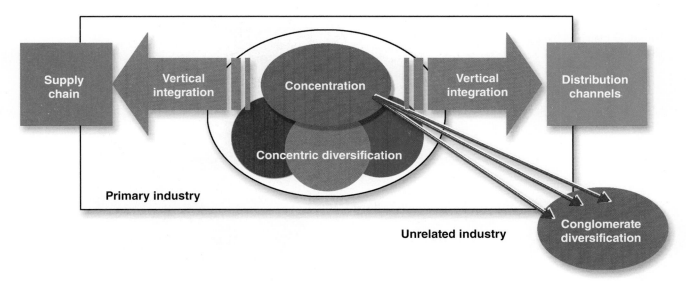

FIGURE 4.7
Summary of Corporate Strategies

Electric Corporation has diversified from its original base in electrical and home appliance products to such wide-ranging industries as health, finance, insurance, truck and air transportation, and even media with its ownership of NBC (now owned with Comcast). Typically, companies pursue a conglomerate diversification strategy to minimize risks due to market fluctuations in one industry.

The diversified businesses of an organization are sometimes called its business *portfolio.* One of the most popular techniques for analyzing a corporation's strategy for managing its portfolio is the BCG matrix, developed by the Boston Consulting Group. The BCG matrix is shown in Figure 4.8. Each business in the corporation is plotted on the matrix on the basis of the growth rate of its market and the relative strength of its competitive position in that market (market share). The business is represented by a circle whose size depends on the business's contribution to corporate revenues.

High-growth, weak-competitive-position businesses are called *question marks.* They require substantial investment to improve their position; otherwise divestiture is recommended. High-growth, strong-competitive-position businesses are called *stars.* These businesses require heavy investment, but their strong position allows them to generate the needed revenues. Low-growth, strong-competitive-position businesses are called *cash cows.* These businesses generate revenues in excess of their investment needs and therefore fund other businesses. Finally, low-growth, weak-competitive-position businesses are called *dogs.* The remaining revenues from these businesses are realized, and then the businesses are divested.

The BCG matrix is not intended as a substitute for management judgment, creativity, insight, or leadership. But it is a tool that can, along with other techniques, help managers of the firm as a whole and of its individual businesses evaluate their strategy alternatives.[31] This approach can help a company such as General Electric that needs to weigh the relative merits of many business units and product lines. When GE struggled to generate acceptable returns in some of its widely diversified businesses, such as NBC Universal and GE Capital, the company refocused on its strength as a manufacturer, targeting three industries: energy, health care, and transportation. Not only do these industries offer significant growth potential, but GE already dominates the markets for electric turbines and jet engines. Therefore, besides selling the NBC unit and scaling back the financial business, GE has acquired wind farms in Europe and purchased Avio, an Italian aerospace company with jet engine expertise and customers beyond the aviation industry.[32]

conglomerate diversification

A strategy used to add new businesses that produce unrelated products or are involved in unrelated markets and activities.

Bottom Line

Companies that integrate vertically often do so to reduce their costs.
Why might buying from a division of your company be less costly than buying on the open market?

FIGURE 4.8
The BCG Matrix

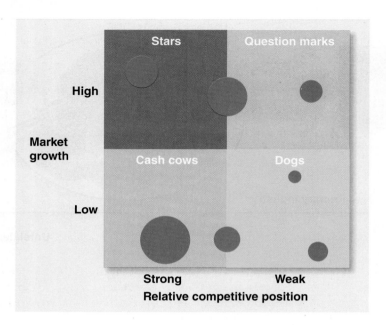

In Practice

CISCO'S EXPANSION DECISIONS

Cisco Systems has struggled with decisions about how to expand. Cisco is primarily known as the world's largest producer of computer networking equipment. That expertise has won the company respect and a sizable income as customers pay a premium for it when they set up computer networks. However, as more customers shift to wireless modes of connecting, Cisco's management has seen less demand for its hardware in the future and has had to make tough choices about where the company will find success.

Cisco tried to get involved in video technology. It acquired Pure Digital, which makes the Flip camera, and it tried developing the idea of using separate networks for video and other kinds of information traffic in computer networks. Also in the video arena, Cisco began offering a technology called TelePresence, which delivers high-quality video messages to others on a network; for example, colleagues in different cities can participate in a meeting by viewing each other on screens. However, the Flip camera flopped when consumers found that it was handier to record videos on their smart phones, and the expense of setting up Cisco's TelePresence system in special locations was less attractive to businesses than using a service such as Skype on their laptop computers.

In light of these missteps, Cisco has refocused on five priorities related to the company's deep knowledge of computer networks and business customers: routing and switching, user collaboration, cloud computing, network architectures, and video. The company also decided to move out of less profitable areas of businesses aimed at serving consumers, such as set-top boxes and digital cameras.[33]

• What type of corporate strategy is Cisco following in this example?

Trends in Corporate Strategy   Corporate America is periodically swept by waves of mergers and acquisitions (M&As). The targets chosen for mergers and acquisitions depend on the organization's corporate strategy of either concentrating in one industry or diversifying its portfolio. Many of the most recent deals, including US Airways' acquisition of American Airlines, have been aimed at helping the companies enjoy the cost advantages of consolidating their marketing, customer service, and other operations. In contrast, during the 1990s, many deals—including the merger of America Online and Time Warner—were made to help traditional businesses enter the hot Internet market.

The value of implementing a diversified corporate strategy depends on individual circumstances. Many critics have argued that unrelated diversification hurts a company more often than it helps it. In recent years, many diversified companies have sold their peripheral businesses so they could concentrate on a more focused portfolio. In contrast, the diversification efforts of an organization competing in a slow-growth, mature, or threatened industry often are applauded. Although the merits of diversification are an issue for continued study, most observers agree that organizations usually perform better if they implement a more concentric diversification strategy, in which businesses are related somehow or similar to one another.

Within the various types of corporate strategies, other trends are shaping the ways that today's companies are seeking growth. One huge trend affecting almost every company's strategy is the degree to which business today takes place across national boundaries. Today, there is hardly any organization that does not buy at least some of its supplies and equipment from, or sell at least some of its products to, individuals and organizations in other countries. In terms of strategy, companies are often finding the best opportunities for growth where economies are expanding the fastest, as in Brazil, India, and China. Chapter 6 explores this trend, known as globalization.

Other trends are related to the business arrangements used to carry out the strategy. Rather than expanding through organic growth—that is, adding employees, equipment, offices, and so on—an organization can find a partner that already has the expertise it needs in a particular market, technology, or product. Choosing such partners in support of a strategy and entering a business arrangement with them can be called a joint venture, strategic partnership, or strategic alliance, depending on the details of the arrangement. Chapter 9 describes how some organizations use strategic alliances to become more agile, and Chapter 17 tells how joint ventures can give companies quick access to new technology.

Business Strategy   After the top management team and board make the corporate strategic decisions, executives must determine how they will compete in each business area. **Business strategy** defines the major actions by which an organization builds and strengthens its competitive position in the marketplace. A competitive advantage typically results from one of two generic business strategies introduced here and elaborated in Chapter 7.[34]

First, organizations such as Walmart and Southwest Airlines pursue competitive advantage through **low-cost strategies.** Businesses using a low-cost strategy attempt to be efficient and offer a standard, no-frills product. Walmart Stores expresses its low-price strategy with the slogan "save money, live better." The company uses the power of its giant size to negotiate favorable prices from suppliers, enabling it to sell at prices below those of most competing retailers. Recently, when gasoline prices soared, the company promoted its stores as a place where consumers can save on transportation costs by purchasing everything they need at low prices in one trip.[35] Companies that succeed with a low-cost strategy often are large and try to take advantage of economies of scale in production or distribution. In many cases, their scale allows them to buy and sell their goods and services at a lower price, which leads to higher market share, volume, and ultimately profits. To succeed, an organization using this strategy generally must be the cost leader in its industry or market segment. However, even a cost leader must offer a product that is acceptable to customers compared with competitors' products.

Second, an organization may pursue a **differentiation strategy.** With a differentiation strategy, a company attempts to be unique in its industry or market segment along some dimensions that customers value. This unique or differentiated position within the industry often is based on high product quality, excellent marketing and distribution, or superior service.

business strategy

The major actions by which a business competes in a particular industry or market.

low-cost strategy

A strategy an organization uses to build competitive advantage by being efficient and offering a standard, no-frills product.

Bottom Line

Low-price strategies usually require low production costs. *How do you think Walmart keeps costs low?*

differentiation strategy

A strategy an organization uses to build competitive advantage by being unique in its industry or market segment along one or more dimensions.

In Practice

PRICE STRATEGY AT VALVE

Valve, a video game development and distribution company known for the Half-Life, Portal, and Team Fortress games, has a successful low-price strategy for its Steam online distribution network. Developers offer downloads of their games on Steam, and game players join Steam to buy games, read and write reviews, and form groups to play together online.

Some of the greatest excitement on the site occurs when Steam hosts a sale. Markdowns can be drastic—75 to 90 percent off the list price. Suddenly, instead of debating whether to buy a game costing $20 to $40, players make impulse purchases for $5 or even less. The result is a snowball effect: Curious players try a game and, if they love it, rave about it; other members of the community add the title to their wish lists or make it their next purchase. This approach to game distribution has lured more than 50 million players in the United States, Brazil, and around the world to set up accounts to access Steam's 2,000-plus titles.

Some game developers worry that Valve's strategy devalues games. Others point out that a low-cost, high-volume strategy makes perfect sense for a product that is essentially software code. Once a developer has earned back the cost to create the software, there is essentially zero cost for every additional copy of the game that is downloaded. And evidence suggests that the volume generated by the price markdowns is massive. Valve runs pricing experiments on the site, and it once found that a price reduction of 75 percent increased revenues by 40 *times* (not just 40 percent). That kind of jump can place a game on Steam's list of most-popular games, essentially becoming advertising that drives even more sales.[36]

• Does a low-cost strategy such as Valve's hurt product quality? Why or why not?

Nordstrom's commitment to quality and customer service in the retail apparel industry is an excellent example of a differentiation strategy. For example, Nordstrom's personal shoppers are available online, by phone, or in stores to select items for shoppers' consideration at no charge. Innovation, too, is an important ingredient of a differentiation strategy. In the market for toilet paper, Scott Paper Company once determined that it could not afford to compete for institutional sales based on price. Instead, the company began offering institutions a free dispenser that would hold larger rolls of paper, saving its customers the labor cost of replacing empty rolls more frequently. Scott initially was the only company selling the larger rolls, so it gained market share while competitors scrambled to catch up.[37]

Whatever strategy managers adopt, the most effective strategy is one that competitors are unwilling or unable to imitate. If the organization's strategic plan is one that could easily be adopted by industry competitors, it may not be sufficiently distinctive or, in the long run, contribute significantly to the organization's competitiveness. For example, a strategy to gain market share and profits by being the first mover to offer an innovative product may or may not succeed, depending in part on competitive responses. In some industries, such as computers, technology advances so fast that the first company to provide a new product is quickly challenged by later entrants offering superior products.[38]

Bottom Line

A high-quality strategy is often more difficult for competitors to imitate.

What would be hard about imitating Nordstrom's strategy for top-quality service?

functional strategies

Strategies implemented by each functional area of the organization to support the organization's business strategy.

Functional Strategy   The final step in strategy formulation is to establish the major functional strategies. **Functional strategies** are implemented by each functional area of the organization to support the business strategy. The typical functional areas include production, human resources, marketing, research and development, finance, and distribution. For example, Bloomin' Brands, the parent company of restaurant chains including Outback Steakhouse, Bonefish Grill, and Carrabba's Italian

Grill, recently set a business strategy with targets for aggressive growth and greater efficiency built on the chains' reputation for offering good food at affordable prices. To achieve this, functional strategies include creation of a lunch menu, methods aimed at improving the productivity of its employees, and deals signed in advance for large purchases of beef, a major expense for the Outback restaurants. Another functional strategy is the use of a team of data analysts to keep an eye on consumer behavior, environmental trends, and other information that can support informed decisions about menu items, new restaurant locations, and more.[39]

Employees at Bonefish Grill strive to meet the company's business strategy to achieve greater efficiency.

Functional strategies typically are developed by functional area executives with input of and approval from the executives responsible for business strategy. Senior strategic decision makers review the functional strategies to ensure that each major department is operating consistently with the business strategies of the organization. For example, automated production techniques—even if they saved money—would not be appropriate for a piano company like Steinway, whose products are strategically positioned (and priced) as high-quality and handcrafted. At companies that compete based on product innovation, strategies for research and development are especially critical. But in the recession of 2001, General Electric cut back on research in lighting technology just as other companies were making advances in LED lighting. When the economy recovered, customers were looking for innovative lighting, but GE had fallen behind. Based on that experience, GE committed itself to an R&D strategy of maintaining budgets even when sales slow down. In the latest economic downturn, the company continued to fund a project in which it is developing new aircraft engines with Honda Motor Company.[40]

Step 5: Strategy Implementation

As with any plan, simply formulating a good strategy is not enough. Strategic managers also must ensure that the new strategies are implemented effectively and efficiently. Recently, corporations and strategy consultants have been paying more attention to implementation. They realize that clever techniques and a good plan do not guarantee success. This greater appreciation is reflected in two major trends.

First, organizations are adopting a more comprehensive view of implementation. The organization structure, technology, human resources, employee reward systems, information systems, organization culture, and leadership style must all support the strategy. Just as an organization's strategy must be matched to the external environment, so must it also fit the multiple factors through which it is implemented. The remainder of this section discusses these factors and the ways they can be used to implement strategy.

Second, many organizations are extending the more participative strategic management process to implementation. Managers at all levels are involved with formulating strategy and identifying and executing ways to implement it. Senior executives still may oversee the implementation process, but they are placing much greater responsibility and authority in the hands of others. In general, strategy implementation involves four related steps:

LO 7

> Step 1: Define strategic tasks. Articulate in simple language what a particular business must do to create or sustain a competitive advantage. Define strategic tasks to help employees understand how they contribute to the organization, including redefining relationships among the parts of the organization.
>
> Step 2: Assess organization capabilities. Evaluate the organization's ability to implement the strategic tasks. A task force typically interviews employees and managers to identify specific issues that help or hinder effective implementation. Then the results are summarized for top management. In the course of your

career, you will likely be asked to participate in a task force. We discuss working effectively in teams in Chapter 14.

Step 3: Develop an implementation agenda. Management decides how it will change its own activities and procedures; how critical interdependencies will be managed; what skills and individuals are needed in key roles; and what structures, measures, information, and rewards might ultimately support the needed behavior. A philosophy statement, communicated in terms of value, is the outcome of this process.

Step 4: Create an implementation plan. The top management team, the employee task force, and others develop the implementation plan. The top management team then monitors progress. The employee task force continues its work by providing feedback about how others in the organization are responding to the changes.

This process, though straightforward, does not always go smoothly. Table 4.3 shows six barriers to strategy implementation and provides a description of some key principles for overcoming these silent killers. By paying closer attention to the processes by which strategies are implemented, executives, managers, and employees can make sure that strategic plans are actually carried out.[41]

Step 6: Strategic Control

The final component of the strategic management process is strategic control. A **strategic control system** is designed to support managers in evaluating the organization's progress with its strategy and, when discrepancies exist, taking corrective action.

strategic control system

A system designed to support managers in evaluating the organization's progress regarding its strategy and, when discrepancies exist, taking corrective action.

TABLE 4.3
Attacking the Six Barriers to Strategy Implementation

Change starts with the leader	
The Silent Killers	**Principles for Engaging and Changing the Silent Killers**
Top-down or laissez-faire senior management style	With the top team and lower levels, the CEO/general manager creates a partnership built around the development of a compelling business direction, the creation of an enabling organizational context, and the delegation of authority to clearly accountable individuals and teams.
Unclear strategy and conflicting priorities	The top team, as a group, develops a statement of strategy, and priorities that members are willing to stand behind are developed.
An ineffective senior management team	The top team, as a group, is involved in all steps in the change process so that its effectiveness is tested and developed.
Poor vertical communication	An honest, fact-based dialogue is established with lower levels about the new strategy and the barriers to implementing it.
Poor coordination across functions, businesses, or borders	A set of businesswide initiatives and new organizational roles and responsibilities are defined that require "the right people to work together on the right things in the right way" to implement the strategy.
Inadequate down-the-line leadership skills and development	Lower-level managers develop skills through newly created opportunities to lead change and drive key business initiatives. They are supported with just-in-time coaching, training, and targeted recruitment. Those who still are not able to make the grade must be replaced.

The system must encourage efficient operations that are consistent with the plan while allowing flexibility to adapt to changing conditions. As with all control systems, the organization must develop performance indicators, an information system, and specific mechanisms to monitor progress. Spirit Airlines has a low-cost strategy that depends on cutting costs wherever possible so the airline can remain profitable while winning passengers with the lowest fare. According to Spirit's CEO, Ben Baldanza, this makes productivity a key performance indicator for every function. For example, the company purchases airplanes with the maximum number of seats allowed by the Federal Aviation Administration, so it minimizes the amount of fuel required to transport each passenger. In marketing, it tracks the percentage of revenue spent to advertise. Spirit relies heavily on e-mail advertising because that medium costs relatively little, yet recipients will pass along messages they find funny or thought-provoking.[42]

Most strategic control systems include a budget to monitor and control major financial expenditures. In fact, as a first-time manager, you will most likely confront your work unit's budget—a key aspect of your organization's strategic plan. Your executive team may give you budget assumptions and targets for your area, reflecting your part in the overall plan, and you may be asked to revise your budget once all the budgets in your organization have been consolidated and reviewed.

The dual responsibilities of a control system—efficiency and flexibility—often seem contradictory with respect to budgets. The budget usually establishes spending limits, but changing conditions or the need for innovation may require different financial commitments during the period. To solve this dilemma, some companies have created two budgets: strategic and operational. For example, managers at Texas Instruments control two budgets under the OST (objectives–strategies–tactics) system. The strategic budget is used to create and maintain long-term effectiveness, and the operational budget is tightly monitored to achieve short-term efficiency. In "Management Connection: Onward," consider the significance of budgets and budgetary controls to Disney's decisions about its portfolio of businesses. The topic of control in general—and budgets in particular—is discussed in more detail in Chapter 16.

Management Connection

WALT DISNEY COMPANY'S STRATEGY UNDER ROBERT IGER

Reportedly, Walt Disney Company's mission statement once was "Make people happy." The corporate website now offers a longer statement: "to be one of the world's leading producers and providers of entertainment and information, using its portfolio of brands to differentiate its content, services and consumer products." The statement adds, "The company's primary financial goals are to maximize earnings and cash flow, and to allocate capital toward growth initiatives that will drive long-term shareholder value."

In pursuit of this two-part objective, Disney has made decisions about its large portfolio of businesses. As it repositions itself for a global marketplace and a social, mobile Internet, it continues making strategic decisions about where to invest and what to divest.

Disney's largest sources of revenues are cable networks and theme parks, with cable providing by far the greatest profits. ESPN alone delivers 45 percent of operating income. Under Robert Iger, Disney closed down its ABC Sports channel to focus on ESPN, which also has an online presence. The company has rolled out apps based on WatchESPN to let cable subscribers watch programming on mobile devices. In the theme park arena, profitability during a sluggish economy lets Disney build when construction costs are low, so it has renovated Disney California Adventure, expanded Hong Kong Disneyland, and added a cruise ship to its fleet.

Disney Interactive is by far the smallest business unit in terms of revenues and has not been profitable. Still, it matters because children are spending ever more time online, and winning the hearts of children has been the basis for the company's growth. Disney Interactive has therefore acquired Playdom, which produces social-media games.

MANAGER'S BRIEF

PROGRESS REPORT

ONWARD

Disney's movie studios, though a relatively small unit, are a core business. To increase the brand's appeal with teenage boys, this unit purchased Lucasfilm, producer of *Star Wars*. Disney also signed a deal giving Netflix the right to stream movies soon after release on DVD, when cable channels air movies. Dealing directly with Netflix signals that movie streaming is an important trend for Disney. And Disney created Keychest, which gives buyers of its DVDs and Blu-ray discs automatic access to streamed versions.

China is a huge growth market, so Iger is heavily investing in a new theme park, Shanghai Disney. The venture is risky; Disney's resort in Hong Kong is just breaking even after a 2005 opening. But it offers access to a billion consumers, and the effort is supported by use of the Disney Channel to build consumer relationships in China and 166 other countries.[43]

- How clear is Walt Disney Company's mission? How well does its strategy support the mission?
- In the BCG matrix (Figure 4.8), where would you place Disney's main businesses? How well is Disney matching its strategic moves to businesses' positions in the matrix?

KEY TERMS

business strategy, p. 141	low-cost strategy, p. 141	strategic goals, p. 125
concentration, p. 138	mission, p. 130	strategic management, p. 129
concentric diversification, p. 138	operational planning, p. 126	strategic planning, p. 125
conglomerate diversification, p. 139	plans, p. 122	strategic vision, p. 130
core capability, p. 136	resources, p. 134	strategy, p. 125
corporate strategy, p. 138	scenario, p. 123	SWOT analysis, p. 137
differentiation strategy, p. 141	situational analysis, p. 120	tactical planning, p. 126
functional strategy, p. 142	stakeholders, p. 132	vertical integration, p. 138
goal, p. 121	strategic control system, p. 144	

SUMMARY OF LEARNING OBJECTIVES

Now that you have studied Chapter 4, you should be able to:

 Summarize the basic steps in any planning process.

The planning process begins with a situation analysis of the external and internal forces affecting the organization. This examination helps identify and diagnose issues and problems and may bring to the surface alternative goals and plans for the firm. Next, the advantages and disadvantages of these goals and plans should be evaluated against one another. Once a set of goals and a plan have been selected, implementation involves communicating the plan to employees, allocating resources, and making certain that other systems such as rewards and budgets support the plan. Finally, planning requires instituting control systems to monitor progress toward the goals.

 Describe how strategic planning should be integrated with tactical and operational planning.

Strategic planning is different from operational planning in that it involves making long-term decisions about the entire organization. Tactical planning translates broad goals and strategies into specific actions to be taken within parts of the organization. Operational planning identifies the specific short-term procedures and processes required at lower levels of the organization.

 Identify elements of the external environment and internal resources of the firm to analyze before formulating a strategy.

Strategic planning is designed to leverage the strengths of a firm while minimizing the effects of its weaknesses. It is difficult to know the potential advantage a firm may have unless external analysis is done well. For example, a company may have a talented marketing department or an efficient production system. However, the organization cannot determine whether these internal characteristics are sources of competitive advantage until it knows something about how well the competitors stack up in these areas.

 Define core capabilities and explain how they provide the foundation for business strategy.

A core competence is something a company does especially well relative to its competitors. When this competence, say, in engineering or marketing, is in some area important to market success, it becomes the foundation for developing a competitive advantage. It can provide a sustainable advantage if it is valuable, rare, difficult to imitate, and well organized.

5 **Summarize the types of choices available for corporate strategy.**

Corporate strategy identifies the breadth of a firm's competitive domain. Corporate strategy can be kept narrow, as in a concentration strategy, or can move to suppliers and buyers via vertical integration. Corporate strategy also can broaden a firm's domain via concentric (related) diversification or conglomerate (unrelated) diversification.

LO **6** **Discuss how companies can achieve competitive advantage through business strategy.**

Companies gain competitive advantage in two primary ways. They can attempt to be unique in some way by pursuing a differentiation strategy, or they can focus on efficiency and price by pursuing a low-cost strategy.

 7 **Describe the keys to effective strategy implementation.**

Many good plans are doomed to failure because they are not implemented correctly. Strategy must be supported by structure, technology, human resources, rewards, information systems, culture, leadership, and so on. Ultimately, the success of a plan depends on how well employees at low levels are able and willing to implement it. Participative management is one of the more popular approaches executives use to gain employees' input and ensure their commitment to strategy implementation.

DISCUSSION QUESTIONS

1. This chapter opened with a quote from former CEO of GE Jack Welch: "Manage your destiny, or someone else will." What does this mean for strategic management? What does it mean when Welch adds, "or someone else will"?

2. List the six steps in the formal planning process. Suppose you are a top executive of a home improvement chain and you want to launch a new company website. Provide examples of activities you would carry out during each step to create the site.

3. Your friend is frustrated because he's having trouble selecting a career. He says, "I can't plan because the future is too complicated. Anything can happen, and there are too many choices." What would you say to him to change his mind?

4. How do strategic, operational, and tactical planning differ? How might the three levels complement one another in an organization?

5. How might an organization such as Urban Outfitters use a strategy map? With your classmates and using Figure 4.3 as a guide, develop a possible strategy map for the company.

6. What accounts for the shift from strategic planning to strategic management? In which industries would you be most likely to observe these trends? Why?

7. Review Table 4.1, which lists the components of an environmental analysis. Why would this analysis be important to a company's strategic planning process?

8. In your opinion, what are the core capabilities of Harley-Davidson Motor Company motorcycles? How do these capabilities help Harley-Davidson compete against foreign competitors such as Yamaha and Suzuki?

9. How could SWOT analysis help newspaper companies remain competitive in the new media environment?

10. What are the key challenges in strategy implementation? What barriers might prevent strategy implementation?

EXPERIENTIAL EXERCISES

4.1   STRATEGIC PLANNING

OBJECTIVE
To study the strategic planning of a corporation recently in the news.

INSTRUCTIONS
Bloomberg Businessweek magazine frequently has articles on the strategies of various corporations. Find a recent article on a corporation in an industry of interest to you. Read the article and answer the following questions.

Follow your instructor's directions for turning in the responses with a copy of the article or a link to the article online.

Strategic Planning Worksheet

1. Has the firm clearly identified what business it is in and how it is different from its competitors? Explain.

_____

_____

_____

_____

_____
_____
_____

2. What key assumptions about the future have shaped the firm's new strategy?

_____
_____
_____
_____
_____
_____

3. What key strengths and weaknesses of the firm influenced the selection of the new strategy?

_____
_____
_____
_____
_____
_____
_____

4. What specific objectives has the firm set in conjunction with the new strategy?

_____
_____
_____
_____
_____
_____

4.2   FORMULATING BUSINESS STRATEGY

OBJECTIVES

1. To illustrate the complex interrelationships central to the formulation of business strategy.

2. To demonstrate the use of SWOT (strengths, weaknesses, opportunities, and threats) analysis in a business situation.

INSTRUCTIONS

1. Your instructor will divide the class into small groups and assign each group a well-known organization for analysis.

2. Each group will
   a. Study the SWOT Introduction and the SWOT Worksheet to understand the work needed to complete the assignment.
   b. Obtain the needed information about the organization under study through library research, interviews, and so on.
   c. Complete the SWOT Worksheet.
   d. Prepare group responses to the discussion questions.

3. After the class reconvenes, group spokespersons will present group findings.

DISCUSSION QUESTIONS

1. Why would most organizations not develop strategies for matches between opportunities and strengths?

2. Why would most organizations not develop strategies for matches between opportunities and weaknesses?

3. Why do most organizations want to deal from strength?

SWOT INTRODUCTION

One of the more commonly used strategy tools is SWOT (strengths, weaknesses, opportunities, and threats) analysis, which is accomplished in four steps:

Step 1: Analyze the organization's internal environment, identifying its strengths and weaknesses.

Step 2: Analyze the organization's external environment, identifying its opportunities and threats.

Step 3: Match (a) strengths with opportunities, (b) weaknesses with threats, (c) strengths with threats, and (d) weaknesses with opportunities.

Step 4: Develop strategies for those matches that appear to be of greatest importance to the organization. Most organizations give top priority to strategies that involve the matching of strengths with opportunities and second priority to strategies that involve the matching of weaknesses with threats. The key is to exploit opportunities in areas where the organization has a strength and to defend against threats in areas where the organization has a weakness.

SWOT Worksheet

Organization being analyzed: _____

Internal Analysis	External Analysis
Strengths	Opportunities
_____	_____
_____	_____
_____	_____
_____	_____
_____	_____
_____	_____
_____	_____
_____	_____
_____	_____

Internal Analysis	External Analysis
Weaknesses	Threats

_____   _____
_____   _____
_____   _____
_____   _____
_____   _____
_____   _____
_____   _____
_____   _____

Strategies That Match Strengths with Opportunities	Strategies That Match Weaknesses with Threats

_____   _____
_____   _____
_____   _____
_____   _____
_____   _____
_____   _____
_____   _____
_____   _____
_____   _____
_____   _____
_____   _____
_____   _____
_____   _____

Strategies That Match Strengths with Threats	Strategies That Match Weaknesses with Opportunities

_____   _____
_____   _____
_____   _____
_____   _____
_____   _____
_____   _____
_____   _____
_____   _____
_____   _____
_____   _____
_____   _____
_____   _____
_____   _____

CONCLUDING CASE

WISH YOU WOOD TOY STORE

Wish You Wood is a toy boutique located in the main shopping strip of a resort town near Piney Lake. People who own cabins near the lake or come to visit the local state park enjoy browsing through the town's stores, where they pick up pottery, landscape paintings, and Wish You Wood's beautifully crafted wooden toys. For these shoppers, Wish You Wood is more than a store; it is a destination they associate with family and fun.

The store's owners, Jim and Pam Klein, personally select the toys from craftspeople and toymakers around the world. They enjoy their regular customers but believe selling mostly to vacationers has limited the company's growth. They decided that the lowest-cost way to expand would be to sell toys online. However, after several years, they had to admit that traffic to the store's website was unimpressive. Thanks to e-mail and Facebook reminders, they were luring some of their loyal in-store shoppers to the site to make off-season purchases, but few other people looking for toys ever found Wish You Wood online.

Jim and Pam concluded that the next-best way to sell online would be to partner with Amazon.com. Amazon's Marketplace service lets other retailers sell products on Amazon. The Kleins signed an agreement to list the store's most popular items with Amazon. For example, if a shopper is searching for wooden dollhouses, Wish You Wood's dollhouses will be included in the search results. A customer who chooses to buy from Wish You Wood places the order right on Amazon's website. Under Amazon's participation agreement, the listings must be honest and may not link to Wish You Wood's own website or invite phone calls from customers. In exchange for giving the products exposure on the site, Amazon charges a monthly fee plus a commission on each sale.

Initially, Jim and Pam were thrilled about their decision to partner with Amazon. They tracked each month's sales and compared them with in-store sales. In the first five months, sales jumped 45 percent, mainly because of sales on Amazon. Then, suddenly, sales of popular toy train sets, which were particularly profitable, stopped altogether. Puzzled, Jim visited Amazon to make sure the train sets were still listed. To his surprise, he found that the train set was there, at the usual price of $149, listed right after the same set available directly from Amazon, at $129. He and Pam concluded that shoppers were now buying the product directly from Amazon. It appeared that their store had helped Amazon identify a product consumers value.

The Kleins worried that they needed a new strategy. If they matched Amazon's price, they would lose most of the profit on their most popular items. Wish You Wood was too small of a business to negotiate better prices from its suppliers. If the store didn't match Amazon's price, it would continue to lose sales at the Amazon site. Jim and Pam wondered whether they should pull out of Amazon altogether or find a way to continue working with the partner that had become a competitor. They also considered rethinking which toys to offer on Amazon.

DISCUSSION QUESTIONS

1. Prepare a SWOT analysis for Wish You Wood, based on the information given.
2. Using the SWOT analysis, what general corporate strategy would you recommend for Wish You Wood? Should the store continue or change its current approach?

CHAPTER 5

Ethics, Corporate Responsibility, and Sustainability

It is truly enough said that a corporation has no conscience; but a corporation of conscientious men is a corporation with a conscience.

— HENRY DAVID THOREAU

Management Connection

HOW CAN GINNI ROMETTY ENSURE THAT IBM DOES WELL WHILE DOING GOOD?

The standard for principled leadership is set high for IBM's chief executive, Ginni Rometty. She took charge of IBM upon the retirement of the widely admired Sam Palmisano, who saw an opportunity for the company to distinguish itself by applying its data-processing expertise to delivering customized business solutions. Rather than jumping straight into corporate restructuring or marketing campaigns, Palmisano started with values. In 2003, he set up a three-day "values jam," during which employees throughout the global company were asked to contribute thoughts about what IBM's values should be. Out of that process came a commitment to helping clients and building relationships based on trust and personal responsibility.

In a further expression of Palmisano's vision, IBM began to use the tagline, "Smarter Planet." Employees would not just be fulfilling contracts; they would be helping companies, cities, and communities around the world make better decisions aimed at improving business results, living conditions, and even the health of planet Earth. This goal was based on the realization that computers have extraordinary power to gather and analyze data, but applying the data also requires creative thinking, productive processes, and open communication. IBM would offer not just computer hardware but also decision-making and analytic expertise to bring all these requirements together.

Palmisano's vision set IBM on course for years of strong growth as businesses, city governments, and non-governmental organizations saw how the company could help them meet their goals. When he prepared to retire, Palmisano threw his support behind Rometty, who had started as a systems engineer at IBM in the 1980s and

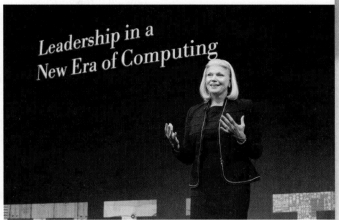

worked her way up to senior vice president and group executive for sales, marketing, and strategy. In a recent speech, Rometty signaled that she sees the Smarter Planet strategy as positioning IBM for a future in which data will drive more decisions, and social media will be the normal way to accomplish knowledge-related work.

Rometty's strategy expertise and technical background prepared her to continue leading IBM on an already-successful path. In her first year as CEO, IBM—for the 20th year in a row—filed more patent applications in the United States than any other company. Although revenue growth slipped 2 percent, profits rose, and sales related to the Smarter Planet strategy posted double-digit gains. Apparently, there is money to be made in caring about the needs of cities, the business community, and the planet.[1]

For IBM's Sam Palmisano and Ginni Rometty, business success can grow out of values that emphasize focusing on the needs of others. As you read this chapter, think about how well IBM's values-driven approach positions the company to be both ethical and successful.

How would you measure the success of a company such as IBM? By this quarter's profits and its value in the stock market? By the quality and market share of its computer systems? By the degree of trust people place in its managers and consultants? By the good it does in improving quality of life by helping people make better decisions? Although a company might enjoy high profits in one quarter without quality, trust, or contributions to society, many people would argue that in the long run, all these measures of success are interdependent.

This chapter addresses the values and manner of doing business adopted by managers as they carry out their corporate and business strategies. In particular, we will explore ways of applying **ethics,** the system of rules that governs the ordering of values. We do so based on the premise that managers, their organizations, and their communities thrive over the long term when the managers apply ethical standards that direct them to act with integrity.

In addition, we consider the idea that organizations may have a responsibility to meet social obligations beyond earning profits within legal and ethical constraints. As you study this chapter, consider what kind of manager you want to be. What reputation do you hope to have? How would you like others to describe your behavior as a manager?

ethics

The system of rules that governs the ordering of values.

It's a Big Issue

Recent scandals have engulfed company executives, independent auditors, politicians and regulators, and shareholders and employees.[2] In some, executives at public companies have made misleading statements to inflate stock prices, undermining the public's trust in the integrity of the financial markets. Often the scandals are perpetrated by a number of people cooperating with one another, and many of the guilty parties had been otherwise upstanding individuals. Lobbyists have been accused—and some convicted—of buying influence with lavish gifts to politicians. Executives have admitted they received huge bonuses or stock options that were backdated to guarantee they would make money from investing in their company, regardless of whether their performance caused the stock's value to rise or fall. What other news disturbs you about managers' behavior? Tainted products in the food supply . . . actions that harm the environment . . . Internet scams . . . employees pressured to meet sales or production targets by any means? The list goes on, and the public becomes cynical. According to a survey by the public relations firm Edelman, only about one-fifth of people trust business leaders to make ethical decisions and tell uncomfortable truths.[3] Try to imagine the challenge of leading employees who don't trust you.

Temptations exist in every organization.

Sadly, when corporations behave badly, it's often not the top executives but the rank-and-file employees who suffer most. When companies such as energy trader Enron and insurance brokerage firm Marsh & McLennan saw their stocks tumble following scandals, executives had millions invested from generous pay and bonus packages. In contrast, employees, who had been encouraged to invest their retirement packages heavily in their company's stock, saw their savings disappear along with their company's reputation.

Still, simply talking about Enron and other famous cases as examples of lax company ethics doesn't get at the heart of the problem. Clearly, these cases involve bad guys, and the ethical lapses are obvious. But saying, "I would never do things like that," becomes too easy. The fact is that temptations exist in every organization. Many of the decisions you will face as a manager will pose ethical dilemmas, and the right thing to do is not always evident.

It's a Personal Issue

"Answer true or false: 'I am an ethical manager.' If you answered 'true,' here's an uncomfortable fact: You're probably not."[4] These sentences are the first in a *Harvard Business Review* article called "How (Un)Ethical Are You?" The point is that most of us think we are good decision makers, ethical, and unbiased. But the fact is, most people have unconscious biases that favor themselves and their own group. For example, managers often hire people who are like them, think they are immune to conflicts of interest, take more credit than they deserve, and blame others when they deserve some blame themselves. Knowing that you have biases may help you try to overcome them, but usually that's not enough.

Knowing that you have biases may help you try to overcome them, but usually that's not enough. Consider the basic ethical issue of telling a lie. Many people lie—some more than others, and in part depending on the situation, usually presuming that they will benefit from the lie. At a basic level, we all can make ethical arguments against lying and in favor of honesty. Yet it is useful to think thoroughly about the real consequences of lying.[5] Table 5.1 summarizes the possible outcomes of telling the truth or lying in different situations. People often lie or commit other ethical transgressions somewhat mindlessly, without realizing the full array of negative personal consequences.

Ethics issues are not easy, and they are not just for newsworthy corporate CEOs. For example, people at work use computers with Internet access. If the employer pays for the computer and the time you spend sitting in front of it, is it ethical for you to use the computer to do tasks unrelated to your work?

But what if you stream video of games for your own and your coworkers' enjoyment or take a two-hour lunch to locate the best deal on a flat-panel TV?

TABLE 5.1   Telling the Truth and Lying: Possible Outcomes

Reason and Context of the Lie	Results of Lying	Results of Truth Telling
Conflicting expectations	• Easier to lie than to address the underlying conflict. • Offers quick relief of the issue. • Leaves the underlying problem unresolved. • May have no meaningful consequences, good or bad. • Liar must rationalize the action to preserve positive self-concept.	• Emotionally more difficult than lying. • May correct underlying problem. • May provoke further conflict. • Sometimes difficult to have an impact on an impermeable structure. • Develops one's reputation as an honest person.
Negotiation	• Short-term gain. • Economically positive. • Harms long-term relationship. • Must rationalize to oneself.	• Supports high-quality, long-term relationship. • Develops reputation of integrity. • Models behavior to others.
Keeping a confidence (that may require at least a lie of omission)	• Protects whatever good reason there is for the confidence. • Maintains a long-term relationship with the party for whom confidence is kept. • May project deceitfulness to the deceived party.	• Violates a trust to the confiding party. • Makes one appear deceitful to all parties in the long run. • Creates the impression of honesty beyond utility.
Reporting your own performance within an organization	• Might advance oneself or one's cause. • Develops dishonest reputation over time. • Must continue the sequence of lies to appear consistent.	• Creates reputation of integrity. • May not always be positive.

SOURCE: From *Academy of Management Executive: The Thinking Manager's Source* by S. L. Gover, "The Truth, the Whole Truth, and Nothing but the Truth: The Causes and Management of Workplace Lying." Copyright © 2005. Reproduced with permission of Academy of Management via Copyright Clearance Center.

Besides lost productivity, employers are most concerned about computer users introducing viruses, leaking confidential information, and creating a hostile work environment by downloading inappropriate web content.

Sometimes employees write blogs or post comments online about their company and its products. Obviously, companies do not want their employees to say bad things about them, but some companies are concerned about employees who are overly enthusiastic. When employees plug their companies and products on comments pages, this practice is considered spamming at best and deceptive if the employees don't disclose their relationship with their company. Another practice considered deceptive is when companies create fictional blogs as a marketing tactic without disclosing their sponsorship. And in a practice known as Astroturfing—because the "grassroots" interest it builds is fake—businesses pay bloggers to write positive comments about them. A Florida company known as PayPerPost will match advertisers with bloggers but now requires bloggers to disclose the relationship. Companies such as Coca-Cola, UPS, and IBM have established guidelines directing employees to identify themselves accurately in online communications so that they can participate in online conversations about their companies without being accused of deception.[6]

Are these examples too small to worry about? This chapter will help you think through decisions with ethical ramifications.

Ethics

The aim of ethics is to identify both the rules that should govern people's behavior and the "goods" that are worth seeking. Ethical decisions are guided by the underlying values of the individual. Values are principles of conduct such as caring, being honest, keeping promises, pursuing excellence, showing loyalty, being fair, acting with integrity, respecting others, and being a responsible citizen.[7]

Most people would agree that all of these values are admirable guidelines for behavior. However, ethics becomes a more complicated issue when a situation dictates that one value overrules others. An **ethical issue** is a situation, problem, or opportunity in which an individual must choose among several actions that must be evaluated as morally right or wrong.[8]

> Ethics becomes a more complicated issue when a situation dictates that one value overrules others.

Ethical issues arise in every facet of life; we concern ourselves here with business ethics in particular. **Business ethics** comprises the moral principles and standards that guide behavior in the world of business.[9]

 Ethical Systems

Moral philosophy refers to the principles, rules, and values people use in deciding what is right or wrong. This is a simple definition in the abstract but often terribly complex and difficult when facing real choices. How do you decide what is right and wrong? Do you know what criteria you apply and how you apply them?

---

ethical issue

Situation, problem, or opportunity in which an individual must choose among several actions that must be evaluated as morally right or wrong.

business ethics

The moral principles and standards that guide behavior in the world of business.

moral philosophy

Principles, rules, and values people use in deciding what is right or wrong.

Ethics scholars point to various major ethical systems as guides.[10] The first ethical system, **universalism,** states that all people should uphold certain values, such as honesty, that society needs to function. Universal values are principles so fundamental to human existence that they are important in all societies—for example, rules against murder, deceit, torture, and oppression.

Some efforts have been made to establish global, universal ethical principles for business. The Caux Roundtable, a group of international executives based in Caux, Switzerland, worked with business leaders from Japan, Europe, and the United States to create the **Caux Principles.** Two basic ethical ideals underpin the Caux Principles: *kyosei* and human dignity. *Kyosei* means living and working together for the common good, allowing cooperation and mutual prosperity to coexist with healthy and fair competition. Human dignity concerns the value of each person as an end, not a means to the fulfillment of others' purposes.

Employees sometimes feel that "borrowing" a few office supplies from their company helps compensate for any perceived inequities in pay or other benefits.

Universal principles can be powerful and useful, but what people say, hope, or think they would do is often different from what they *really* do, faced with conflicting demands in real situations. Before we describe other ethical systems, consider the following "In Practice" example and think about how you or others would resolve it.

In Practice

ETHICAL DILEMMA AT SIGN OF THE TIMES

At Sign of the Times Company, salespeople turn over their orders to a small team of schedulers, who provide the production department with details of the materials and parts to use in filling the order. Madison is a new scheduler; her supervisor, Ron, has been reviewing each work order to help her learn the details of a job. Madison carefully filled an order for 112 signs for an amusement park, making sure to match all of the quality standards the salesperson had promised to the customer. But when Ron reviewed the work order, he asked her to change the type of paint she called for to a lower grade.

"But that's not what we promised the customer," Madison pointed out. Ron explained, "We can't be limited by what some sales rep says. The PF92 line is the industry standard; it will look exactly the same. The customer won't have any problems with peeling or cracking for at least five years, and by then, they won't attribute any problems to us. Heck, the contractor will be out of the picture, and the park owner will just replace the signs."

"Are you sure?" asked Madison. Ron looked annoyed. "Sure, I'm sure! I've been doing this for 12 years. You can't just use the top of the line for everything and meet our division's profit targets for the quarter. I thought you said you're a team player. The whole group's bonus depends on meeting our targets. Do you want to make this the first quarter in three years we've missed our bonus? Because if you do, you won't have much of a future around here."

Now Madison was nervous. This job was her first full-time position since Alexis turned five and her husband filed for divorce. And if Ron was right, this little tweak to the work order wouldn't even be noticed—at least not for a few years.[11]

• What should Madison do? Is that what you believe you would do in this situation?

---

universalism

The ethical system stating that all people should uphold certain values that society needs to function.

Caux Principles

Ethical principles established by international executives based in Caux, Switzerland, in collaboration with business leaders from Japan, Europe, and the United States.

Not everyone would behave the same in this scenario. Different individuals would apply different moral philosophies. Consider each of the following moral philosophies and the actions to which they might lead in the "In Practice" example.[12]

egoism

An ethical system defining acceptable behavior as that which maximizes consequences for the individual.

utilitarianism

An ethical system stating that the greatest good for the greatest number should be the overriding concern of decision makers.

Egoism and Utilitarianism   According to **egoism,** acceptable behavior is that which maximizes benefits for the individual. "Doing the right thing," the focus of moral philosophy, is defined by egoism as "do the act that promotes the greatest good for oneself." If everyone follows this system, according to its proponents, the well-being of society as a whole should increase. This notion is similar to Adam Smith's concept of the invisible hand in business. Smith argued that if every organization follows its own economic self-interest, the total wealth of society will be maximized.

Unlike egoism, **utilitarianism** directly seeks the greatest good for the greatest number of people. Consider whether utilitarianism would help guide ethical decision making with regard to student loan programs. New York's attorney general investigated 100 colleges and half a dozen lenders for arrangements in which the lenders allegedly offered payments, stock grants, and perks to schools, and the schools listed the companies as "preferred lenders" in information given to students who wanted to borrow tuition money from private sources. The attorney general called the arrangements "kickbacks"; some schools replied that they were not being corrupted but used the money to add to the financial aid they could award to students.[13]

Whereas ethics based on egoism would accept actions that allow the lenders to maximize their earnings and the financial aid officers to pursue whatever arrangements benefit themselves and their schools, utilitarianism requires a broader view. Most obviously, there is the question of what these arrangements cost students who make borrowing decisions on the possibly mistaken assumption that preferred lenders will give students the best deals. But other students benefited if payments from lenders were used to augment the financial aid given to other students. The utilitarian approach might consider how many students benefited—and by how much—and how many students paid extra for loans and how much more they paid. One company responded to the allegations by agreeing to a code of conduct that forbids gifts in exchange for preferred status.[14]

relativism

Philosophy that bases ethical behavior on the opinions and behaviors of relevant other people.

Relativism   Perhaps it seems that an individual makes ethical choices on a personal basis, applying personal perspectives. But this is not necessarily the case. **Relativism** defines ethical behavior based on the opinions and behaviors of relevant other people. In the previous example of student loans, U.S. business, government, and society largely agree that bribes, kickbacks, and conflicts of interest would not be acceptable behaviors for people in the lending industry—perhaps even less so for those charged with serving students. Those standards help explain the rapid actions taken by the organizations when they found out about the situation.

Relativism acknowledges the existence of different ethical viewpoints. For example, *norms,* or standards of expected and acceptable behavior, vary from one culture to another. A study of Russian versus U.S. managers found that all followed norms of informed consent about chemical hazards in work situations and paying wages on time. But in Russia more than in the United States, businesspeople were likely to consider the interests of a broader set of stakeholders (in this study, keeping factories open for the sake of local employment), to keep double books to hide information from tax inspectors and criminal organizations, and to make personal payments to government officials in charge of awarding contracts.[15] Relativism defines ethical behavior according to how others behave.

virtue ethics

Classification of people based on their level of moral judgment.

Virtue ethics   The moral philosophies just described apply different types of rules and reasoning. **Virtue ethics** is a perspective that goes beyond the conventional rules of society by suggesting that what is moral must also come from what a mature person with good "moral character" would deem right. Society's rules provide a moral minimum, and then moral individuals can transcend rules by applying their personal virtues such as faith, honesty, and integrity.

Individuals differ in this regard. **Kohlberg's model of cognitive moral development** classifies people into categories based on their level of moral judgment.[16] People in the *preconventional* stage make decisions based on rewards and punishments and immediate self-interest. People in the *conventional* stage conform to the expectations of ethical behavior held by groups or institutions such as society, family, or peers. People in the *principled* stage see beyond authority, laws, and norms and follow their self-chosen ethical principles.[17] Some people forever reside in the preconventional stage, some move into the conventional stage, and some develop further yet into the principled stage. Over time, and through education and experience, people may change their values and ethical behavior.[18]

Returning to the "In Practice" example about Madison and the scheduler at Sign of the Times, egoism would probably lead her to comply with her supervisor's instructions unless she sees a greater benefit from becoming known for her integrity. Utilitarianism would dictate a more thorough cost–benefit analysis; Madison would need to weigh the consequences not only for herself and her daughter but also for her co-workers, the company as a whole, the customer, and perhaps the visitors to the amusement park. A simple analysis might see her co-workers as the greatest number to satisfy; a more thoughtful analysis would also weigh the long-term benefits of the company having a reputation for quality and integrity. The relativist perspective might prompt Madison to look at company policy and general industry practice and to seek opinions from colleagues and perhaps trade journals and ethics codes; or she might consult with family members, who urge her to remember their cultural norm that family comes first. Whatever she perceives to be a consensus or normal practice would dictate her action. Finally, virtue ethics, applied by people in the principled stage of moral development, would lead to efforts to treat all the parties fairly and honestly—perhaps conferring with the salesperson about whether he might offer the paint recommended by Madison's boss, but at a discount that benefits the customer while preserving some additional profits for the company.[19]

These major ethical systems underlie personal moral choices and ethical decisions in business.

Business Ethics

Insider trading, sweatshops and modern slavery,[20] bribery and kickbacks, famous court cases, and other scandals have created a perception that business leaders use illegal means to gain competitive advantage, increase profits, or improve their personal positions. Neither young managers nor consumers believe top executives are doing a good job of establishing high ethical standards.[21] Some even joke that *business ethics* is a contradiction in terms.

Most employees rate their supervisors' performance as ethical and professional.[22] However, many people feel ethically conflicted, stressed, and exhausted as companies sometimes encourage them to behave in ways that differ from their own sense of right and wrong.[23] Many managers and their organizations must deal frequently with ethical dilemmas, and the issues are becoming increasingly complex. For example, many people seek spiritual renewal in the workplace, in part reflecting a broader religious awakening in America, whereas others argue that this trend violates religious freedom and the separation of church and boardroom.[24]

Table 5.2 shows some other important examples of ethical dilemmas in business. Think about how you would address each of these issues as a manager. What ethical principles are you applying?

Kohlberg's model of cognitive moral development

Perspective that what is moral comes from what a mature person with "good" moral character would deem right.

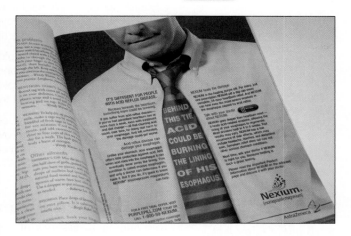

Should pharmaceutical companies be allowed to advertise directly to the consumer if the medicine can be obtained only with a prescription from a doctor? When patients request a particular product, doctors are more likely to prescribe it—even if the patients haven't reported the corresponding symptoms.

TABLE 5.2
Current Ethical Issues in Business

CEO pay	What is a fair level of pay for a top executive? Twenty times what the average company worker earns? Four hundred times? Whatever other companies pay their top executives?
Climate	What is a company's responsibility for its impact on the climate? For example, if operations in one country contribute to rising global temperatures that lead to greater floods in another country, how should the company respond? Does it matter whether a particular impact can be traced to the company?
Globalization	When a company operates in countries with lower costs, what are its obligations, if any, to workers in higher-cost countries? If lower-cost locations have looser protections for workers and the environment, what standards should the company meet there? What standards should it meet for pay rates?
Health care	With health care costs outpacing inflation, employers struggle to cover the cost of health insurance for workers. Are they ethically obligated to provide this benefit? Is it ethical to move full-time workers to part-time status to avoid paying for insurance or paying a fine? How should managers handle legal requirements to provide insurance that covers medical procedures in conflict with their moral principles (e.g., birth control)?
Obesity	As an obesity epidemic threatens health and adds to health care costs, what role, if any, should employers play in encouraging healthy employee lifestyles? What ethical obligations do businesses have if they sell products that contribute to obesity?
Online privacy	What obligations do employers have in protecting the privacy of employee information and information about customers? With the increasing sophistication of cyber-attacks, all online databases are vulnerable; what should companies do when security systems fail?
Politics	Since 2010, businesses and labor unions in the United States have wide latitude for making anonymous contributions to political candidates. What are the ethical limits of such contributions? When is it ethical for a company or union to take sides on a political issue?
Social media	What ethical obligations do employees have in commenting about their employer on social media? What ethical obligations do employers have concerning their employees' privacy on social media?
Telework	When employees work at home or in other remote locations, how can they and their employer ensure that these arrangements are fair to the employees, their co-workers, and the company? How can they build trust?
Wages	When adjusted for inflation, the median wage in the United States has fallen over the past few decades. What should employers do to promote a sense that their compensation is fair?

The Ethics Environment

Sarbanes-Oxley Act

An act passed into law by Congress in 2002 to establish strict accounting and reporting rules to make senior managers more accountable and to improve and maintain investor confidence.

Responding to a series of corporate scandals—particularly the high-profile cases of Enron and WorldCom—Congress passed the **Sarbanes-Oxley Act** in 2002 to improve and maintain investor confidence. The law requires companies to have more independent board directors (not just company insiders), to adhere strictly to accounting rules, and to have senior managers personally sign off on financial results. Violations can result in heavy fines and criminal prosecution. One of the biggest impacts of the law was the requirement for companies and their auditors to provide reports to financial statement users about the effectiveness of internal controls over the financial reporting process.

Companies that make the effort to meet or exceed these requirements can reduce their risks by lowering the likelihood of misdeeds and the consequences if an employee does break the law.[25] But some executives say Sarbanes-Oxley distracts from their real work and makes them more risk-averse. Some complain about the time and money needed to comply with the internal control reporting—millions of dollars at big businesses. But as companies have implemented tighter controls, many have discovered that the effort is helping them avoid mistakes and improve efficiency. Regardless of managers' attitudes toward Sarbanes-Oxley, it creates legal requirements intended to improve ethical behavior.

Ethics are not shaped only by laws and by individual virtue. They also may be influenced by the company's work environment. Unethical corporate behavior may be the responsibility of an unethical individual, but it often also reveals a company culture that is ethically lax.[26]

Maintaining a positive ethical climate is always challenging, but it is especially complex for organizations with international activities. Different cultures and countries may have different standards of behavior, and managers have to decide when relativism is appropriate, rather than adherence to firm standards. Table 5.3 gives examples of real situations when ethics-related decisions have arisen in an international context.

The **ethical climate** of an organization refers to the processes by which decisions are evaluated and made on the basis of right and wrong.[27] For example, General Electric's top executives have demonstrated a commitment to promoting high levels of integrity without sacrificing the company's well-known commitment to business results. The measures taken by GE to maintain a positive ethical climate include establishing global standards for behavior to prevent ethical problems such as conflicts of interest and money laundering. As managers monitor the external environment, they are expected to consider legal and ethical developments, along with other concerns, so that the company can be prepared for new issues as they arise. Managers at all levels are rewarded for their performance in meeting both integrity and business standards, and when violations occur, even managers who were otherwise successful are disciplined, sending a powerful message that ethical behavior is truly valued at GE.[28]

ethical climate

In an organization, the processes by which decisions are evaluated and made on the basis of right and wrong.

TABLE 5.3
Ethical Decision Making in the International Context

What would you do in each of these true-life situations, and why?

- You are a sales representative for a construction company in the Middle East. Your company wants very much to land a particular project. The cousin of the minister who will award the contract informs you that the minister wants $20,000 in addition to the standard fees. If you do not make this payment, your competition certainly will—and will get the contract.

- You are the international vice president of a multinational chemical corporation. Your company is the sole producer of an insecticide that will effectively combat a recent infestation of West African crops. The minister of agriculture in a small, developing African country has put in a large order for your product. Your insecticide is highly toxic and is banned in the United States. You inform the minister of the risks of using your product, but he insists on using it and claims it will be used "intelligently." The president of your company believes you should fill the order, but the decision ultimately is yours.

- You are a new marketing manager for a large automobile tire manufacturer. Your company's advertising agency has just presented plans for introducing a new tire into the Southeast Asia market. Your tire is a truly good product, but the proposed advertising is deceptive. For example, the "reduced price" was reduced from a hypothetical amount that was established only so it could be "reduced," and claims that the tire was tested under the "most adverse" conditions ignore the fact that it was not tested in prolonged tropical heat and humidity. Your superiors are not concerned about deceptive advertising, and they are counting on you to see that the tire does extremely well in the new market. Will you approve the ad plan?

SOURCE: N. Adler, *International Dimensions of Organizational Behavior*, 2nd ed. (Boston: Kent, 1997).

In Practice

ETHICAL CLIMATE AT RED FROG EVENTS

The ethical climate at Red Frog Events is rooted in a high level of trust in its employees, which is reinforced by the workers' enthusiasm for the company and its goals. The Chicago-based company organizes weekend events. Great Urban Races, Warrior Dashes, and Beach Dashes have participants completing scavenger hunts and racing around obstacle courses. For the less athletic, the company puts together Red Frog Bar Crawls, the Firefly Music Festival, and Farm to Fork chef-prepared dinners featuring locally grown produce served on a farm.

A Red Frog–organized event might include a Warrior Dash.

At headquarters, the company has about 80 full-time employees, but hundreds of people are needed to work on a race event. So for each event, Red Frog partners with local nonprofits. For every 25 volunteers from the organization, Red Frog donates $1,000 to the organization. The company also donates a portion of the proceeds from each Great Urban Race to St. Jude Children's Hospital. The combination of charity and fun inspires employees as well as event participants, and it doesn't seem to hurt business: Red Frog earned a profit on its first race and saw revenues skyrocket, with growth of more than 10,000 percent between 2008 and 2011.

Red Frog's founder and co-CEO, Joe Reynolds, believes that because he hires enthusiastic people who are devoted the company's mission, he can trust them to manage their time responsibly. So Red Frog's policy for time off allows unlimited vacation days. As long as employees meet their goals and arrange for someone to cover for them during an absence, they can take as many days as they want. Reynolds insists that in the company's first five years, no one has abused the policy.[29]

- As Red Frog grows, how should it reinforce its ethical climate to ensure ethical behavior?

Danger Signs   Maintaining consistent ethical behavior by all employees is an ongoing challenge. What are some danger signs that an organization may be allowing or even encouraging unethical behavior? Many factors create a climate conducive to unethical behavior:

1. Excessive emphasis on short-term revenues over longer-term considerations
2. Failure to establish a written code of ethics
3. A desire for simple, quick-fix solutions to ethical problems
4. An unwillingness to take an ethical stand that may impose financial costs
5. Consideration of ethics solely as a legal issue or a public relations tool
6. Lack of clear procedures for handling ethical problems
7. Responding to the demands of shareholders at the expense of other constituencies[30]

Regardless of your employer's ethical climate, you are responsible for the decisions you make.

It's been said that your reputation is your most precious asset. Here's a suggestion: Set a goal for yourself to be seen by others as both a moral person and as a moral manager, someone who influences others to behave ethically. When you are both personally moral and a moral manager, you will truly be an **ethical leader.**[31] You can have strong personal character, but if you pay more attention to other things, and ethics is managed by benign neglect, you won't have a reputation as an ethical leader.

Corporate Ethical Standards   To create a culture that encourages ethical behavior, managers must be more than ethical people. They also should lead others to behave ethically.[32] At General Electric, chief executive Jeffrey Immelt demonstrates his concern for ethical leadership by beginning and ending each annual meeting with a statement of the company's integrity principles, emphasizing that "GE's business success is built on our reputation with all stakeholders for lawful and ethical behavior."[33]

IBM uses a guideline for business conduct that asks employees to determine whether, under the full glare of examination by associates, friends, and family, they would remain comfortable with their decisions. One suggestion is to imagine how you would feel if you saw your decision and its consequences on the front page of the newspaper.[34] This "light of day" or "sunshine" ethical framework can be powerful.

Such fear of exposure compels people more strongly in some cultures than in others. In some Asian countries, anxiety about losing face often makes executives resign immediately if they are caught in ethical transgressions or if their companies are embarrassed by revelations in the press. By contrast, in the United States, exposed executives might respond with indignation, intransigence, pleading the Fifth Amendment, stonewalling, and an everyone-else-does-it self-defense or by not admitting wrongdoing and giving no sign that resignation ever crossed their minds. Partly because of legal tradition, the attitude often is never explain, never apologize, don't admit the mistake, and do not resign, even if the entire world knows exactly what happened.[35]

> Fear of exposure compels people more strongly in some cultures than in others.

Ethics Codes   The Sarbanes-Oxley Act requires public companies periodically to disclose whether they have adopted a code of ethics for senior financial officers—and if not, why not. Often the statements are just for show, but when implemented well, they can change a company's ethical climate for the better and truly encourage ethical behavior. Executives say they pay most attention to their company's code of ethics when they feel that stakeholders (customers, investors, lenders, and suppliers) try to influence them to do so, and their reasons for paying attention to the code are that doing so will help create a strong ethical culture and promote a positive image.[36]

Ethics codes must be carefully written and tailored to individual companies' philosophies. Table 5.4 reprints the introduction to Unisys Corporation's code, which is based on four values that serve as the basis for key ethical principles. Most ethics codes address subjects such as employee conduct, community and environment, shareholders, customers, suppliers and contractors, political activity, and technology. The nonprofit Ethics Resource Center assists companies interested in establishing a corporate code of ethics.[37]

To make an ethics code effective, do the following: (1) involve those who have to live with it in writing the statement; (2) focus on real-life situations that employees can relate to; (3) keep it short and simple, so it is easy to understand and remember; (4) write about values and shared beliefs that are important and that people can really believe in; and (5) set the tone at the top, having executives talk about and live up to the statement.[38] When reality differs from the statement—as when a motto says people are our most precious asset or a product is the finest in the world, but in fact people are treated poorly or product quality is weak—the statement becomes a joke to employees rather than a guiding light.

Ethics Programs   Corporate ethics programs commonly include formal ethics codes that articulate the company's expectations regarding ethics; ethics committees that develop policies, evaluate actions, and investigate violations; ethics communication systems that give employees a means of reporting problems or getting guidance; ethics

---

ethical leader

One who is both a moral person and a moral manager influencing others to behave ethically.

TABLE 5.4

Unisys Corporation's Code of Ethics and Business Conduct: Introduction

As a Unisys employee or director, you are expected to always act in accordance with our Code of Ethics and Business Conduct. Four key principles form the basis for our Code:	
Integrity	We are honest in all our dealings and stand for what is right.
Respect	We show respect for one another by treating everyone with dignity and fairness.
Accountability	We are accountable for our actions and honor our commitments.
Responsibility	We conduct our business as responsible citizens in accordance with applicable laws and regulations in each country where we operate.

While the Code does not cover every situation you may encounter, it provides general guidance. If you have questions about how to handle a work situation, refer to the Code and, most importantly, seek guidance from the Corporate Ethics Officer or the Office of the General Counsel.

As a Unisys employee you have the obligation and responsibility to report any suspected potential or actual violation of the Code to your manager, the Corporate Ethics Office or the Office of General Counsel. As a manager, if you receive such a report, you must immediately notify the Corporate Ethics Office or the Office of the General Counsel. The Corporate Ethics Office, working with the Office of the General Counsel, has the responsibility to review and investigate every ethics matter.

If in doubt, contact the Corporate Ethics Office.

SOURCE: Unisys Corporation, "Code of Ethics and Business Conduct," effective December 7, 2011, http://www.app3.unisys.com/investors/other/Code_of_Ethics.pdf. Reprinted with permission.

officers or ombudspersons who investigate allegations and provide education; ethics training programs; and disciplinary processes for addressing unethical behavior.[39]

Ethics programs can range from compliance-based to integrity-based.[40] **Compliance-based ethics programs** are designed by corporate counsel to prevent, detect, and punish legal violations. Program elements include establishing and communicating legal standards and procedures, assigning high-level managers to oversee compliance, auditing and monitoring compliance, reporting criminal misconduct, punishing wrongdoers, and taking steps to prevent offenses in the future.

Such programs should reduce illegal behavior and help a company stay out of court. But Richard Breeden, former chairman of the Securities and Exchange Commission, said, "It is not an adequate ethical standard to aspire to get through the day without being indicted."

Integrity-based ethics programs go beyond the mere avoidance of illegality; they are concerned with the law but also with instilling in people a personal responsibility for ethical behavior. With such a program, companies and people govern themselves through a set of guiding principles that they embrace.

For example, the Americans with Disabilities Act (ADA) required companies to change the physical work environment so it will allow people with disabilities to function on the job. Mere compliance would involve making the changes necessary to avoid legal problems. Integrity-based programs would go further by training people to understand and perhaps change attitudes toward people with disabilities and sending clear signals that people with disabilities also have valued abilities. This effort goes far beyond taking action to stay out of trouble with the law.[41]

compliance-based ethics programs

Company mechanisms typically designed by corporate counsel to prevent, detect, and punish legal violations.

integrity-based ethics programs

Company mechanisms designed to instill in people a personal responsibility for ethical behavior.

Ethical Decision Making

LO 3

We've said it's not easy to make ethical choices. Such decisions are complex. For starters, you may face pressures that are difficult to resist. Furthermore, it's not always clear that a problem has ethical dimensions; they don't hold up signs that say "Hey, I'm an ethical issue, so think about me in moral terms!"[42]

Making ethical decisions takes moral awareness (realizing the issue has ethical implications), moral judgment (knowing what actions are morally defensible), and moral character (the strength and persistence to act in accordance with your ethics despite the challenges).[43]

The philosopher John Rawls created a thought experiment based on the "veil of ignorance."[44] Imagine that you are making a decision about a policy that will benefit or disadvantage some groups more than others. For example, a policy might provide extra vacation time for all employees but eliminate flextime, which allows parents of young children to balance their work and family responsibilities. Or you're a university president considering raising tuition or cutting financial support for study abroad.

Now pretend that you belong to one of the affected groups, but you don't know which one—for instance, those who can afford to study abroad or those who can't, or a young parent or a young single person. You won't find out until after the decision is made. How would you decide? Would you be willing to risk being in the disadvantaged group? Would your decision be different if you were in a group other than your own? Rawls maintained that only a person ignorant of his own identity can make a truly ethical decision. A decision maker can apply the veil of ignorance to help minimize personal bias.

Thinking before deciding, and having an ethics-oriented conversation with others, can help you and others make more ethical decisions.[45] You can use the process illustrated in Figure 5.1. Understand the various moral standards (universalism, relativism, etc.), as described on pp. 158–159. Go through the problem-solving model from Chapter 3 and recognize the

> Excuses are often bogus.

impacts of your alternatives: Which people do they benefit and harm, which are able to exercise their rights, and whose rights are denied? You now know the full scope of the moral problem.

Excuses are often bogus.[46] "I was told to do it" implies a person has no thought and blindly obeys. "Everybody's doing it" often really means that someone is doing it, but it's rarely everybody; regardless, following convention doesn't mean correctness. "Might equals right" is just a rationalization. "It's not my problem" is sometimes a wise perspective, if it's a battle you can't win, but sometimes it's a cop-out. "I didn't mean for that to happen, it just felt right at the time" can be prevented with more forethought and analysis.

You must also consider legal requirements to ensure full compliance, and the economic outcomes of your options, including costs and potential profits.[47] Some are

Bottom Line

"Costs" aren't exactly synonymous with "ethics." But by considering all costs to all parties, you can make high-quality ethical decisions that you can more convincingly sell to others who might otherwise balk. *What are some costs of treating employees unethically?*

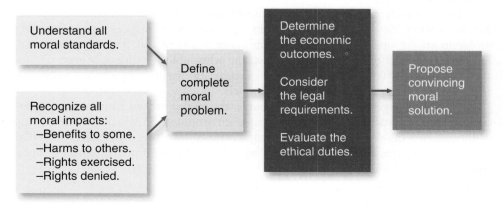

FIGURE 5.1

A Process for Ethical Decision Making

Understand all moral standards.

Recognize all moral impacts:
–Benefits to some.
–Harms to others.
–Rights exercised.
–Rights denied.

Define complete moral problem.

Determine the economic outcomes.

Consider the legal requirements.

Evaluate the ethical duties.

Propose convincing moral solution.

SOURCE: L. T. Hosmer, *The Ethics of Management,* 4th ed. McGraw-Hill/Irwin, 2003, p. 32. Fig. 5.1A. © 2003 The McGraw-Hill Companies. Reprinted with permission.

obvious: fines and penalties. Others, such as corrective actions and lower morale, are less obvious. Ultimately, the effects on customers, employees, and government reactions can be huge. Being fully aware of the potential costs can help prevent people from straying into unethical terrain.

Courage

Behaving ethically requires not just moral awareness and moral judgment but also moral character, including the courage to take actions consistent with your ethical decisions. Think about how hard it can be to do the right thing.[48] On the job, how hard would it be to walk away from lots of money just to stick to your ethics? To tell colleagues or your boss that you believe they've crossed an ethical line? To disobey a boss's order? To go over your boss's head to someone in senior management with your suspicions about accounting practices? To go outside the company to alert others if someone is being hurt and management refuses to correct the problem?

Courage plays a role in the moral awareness involved in identifying an act as unethical, the moral judgment to consider the repercussions fully, and the moral character to take the ethical action. Consider, for example, how difficult it is to deliver unpleasant news, even if you agree that honesty is important and is the way you would want to be treated. This was a hurdle for some Hilton Worldwide managers as they made staffing decisions for their call centers. Hilton, which operates call centers in five countries and contracts with call centers in the Philippines, reportedly sent employees from its Hemet, California, center to a new call center in Manila to train employees in handling reservation changes and other customer service activities. Only afterward were the California employees told that the company would be closing the Hemet facility, located southeast of Los Angeles, and laying off the workers there unless they chose to relocate to jobs in Texas or Florida. Perhaps the managers feared that telling employees they were training their replacements would have hurt performance; honesty takes courage when it is risky, and the risks of complete honesty are real.[49]

The road for whistleblowers is rocky.

Behaving ethically in an ethical climate is complicated enough, but even more courage is necessary when you decide that the only ethical course of action is *whistleblowing*—telling others, inside or outside the organization, of wrongdoing. The road for whistleblowers is rocky. When whistleblowers go public, they are often seen as acting against the company's interests. Many, perhaps most, whistleblowers suffer consequences such as being ostracized, treated rudely, or given undesirable assignments.

For this reason, and in response to the revised sentencing guidelines under the Sarbanes-Oxley Act, organizations set up channels for employees to report ethics problems so the organization can respond without the matter becoming a scandal. Ideally, the reporting method should keep the whistleblower's identity secret, management should investigate and respond quickly, and there should be no retaliation against whistleblowers who use proper channels.[50]

From the manager's perspective, of course, the goal is to lead employees to maintain high ethical standards, which creates an environment in which whistleblowing is unnecessary. As you read "Management Connection: Progress Report," consider how IBM promotes ethical conduct and how this might reinforce employees' moral courage.

Management Connection

THE STATE OF ETHICS AT IBM

One advantage IBM has in meeting its standards for trust is that it is part of a relatively trusted industry. In the Edelman Trust Barometer, an annual survey of public attitudes toward a variety of institutions, people from around the world rated the technology industry as the industry they most often trust to do what is right—mainly because they see tech companies as able to benefit society. People are, however, concerned about data security and privacy.

IBM is addressing these issues. It has a set of policies aimed at building trust, including a policy for business conduct and ethics and a policy for protecting data privacy. The ethics policy states, "It is IBM's policy to conduct itself ethically and lawfully in all matters and to maintain IBM's high standards of business integrity." It puts employees on notice that there are consequences for unethical conduct. IBM's policies call for fairness, equity, a commitment to quality, and compliance with laws, including employment and anti-corruption laws. Its data privacy laws call for employees to collect only relevant personal information, keep it as accurate as possible, and take measures to keep it secure, among other requirements.

Compliance with ethical standards is most likely when managers and employees at all levels are committed to the standards. Thus, it should help IBM that its strategy and culture changes under Sam Palmisano started with an all-employee values jam. An outcome of that process was a statement of three values:

1. Dedication to every client's success
2. Innovation that matters, for our company and the world
3. Trust and personal responsibility in all relationships

These statements appear on the company's website, where any employee or concerned citizen can be reminded of what IBM is striving to achieve.

Even with formal statements and consequences for behavior, maintaining ethical conduct is a challenge, especially for a global company, because employees encounter differences in standards and practices in other countries. Thus, IBM was charged by the Securities and Exchange Commission with bribing government officials in South Korea and China over more than 10 years. In its settlement, IBM must file monthly reports with the SEC to demonstrate its efforts to avoid future violations of the Foreign Corrupt Practices Act. Living up to its own code of ethics will require continued vigilance at IBM.[51]

- Besides the measures described, how else can IBM promote ethical conduct by its employees?
- In a company operating where bribing government officials is expected, how can employees find the moral courage to forgo bribery at the risk of losing a big sale?

Corporate Social Responsibility

 LO 4

Consider the following examples:

- Burt's Bees helped develop the Natural Standard for personal products, which created guidelines for what can be deemed natural.
- Kenneth Cole actively encourages and supports service volunteerism.
- Pedigree dog food built its brand by focusing on the need to adopt homeless dogs.
- Whole Foods created Whole Planet Foundation to fight poverty through microlending to microentrepreneurs in rural communities around the world.
- Ford Motor Company fights HIV/AIDS in South Africa.
- Levi Strauss fights racism.
- Green Mountain Coffee promotes fair trade coffee around the world.
- Bank Boston fosters economic development in communities of moderate income and in the inner city.
- McDonald's and Bank of America support sustainable development in a variety of strategic ways.[52]

Green Mountain Coffee promotes fair trade coffee around the world as part of its corporate social responsibility.

corporate social responsibility (CSR)

Obligation toward society assumed by business.

triple bottom line

Economic, social, and environmental performance.

economic responsibilities

To produce goods and services that society wants at a price that perpetuates the business and satisfies its obligations to investors.

Should business be responsible for social concerns beyond its own economic well-being? Do social concerns affect a corporation's financial performance? The extent of business's responsibility for noneconomic concerns has been hotly debated for years. In the 1960s and 1970s, the political and social environment became more important to U.S. corporations as society turned its attention to issues such as equal opportunity, pollution control, energy and natural resource conservation, and consumer and worker protection.[53] Public debate addressed these issues and the ways business should respond to them. This controversy focused on the concept of corporate social responsibility (CSR).

Corporate social responsibility is the obligation toward society assumed by business.[54] Corporate social responsibility reflects the social imperatives and the social consequences of business success and consists broadly of policies and practices that reflect business responsibility for some of the wider societal good. CSR actions and policies take into account stakeholders' expectations and often consider the **triple bottom line** of economic, social, and environmental performance.[55] The precise policies and practices underlying this responsibility lie at the discretion of the corporation. Some companies refer to their CSR practices in terms of sustainability, on the grounds that these efforts maintain positive long-term relationships with communities, employees, customers, governments, and the natural environment.[56]

Social responsibilities can be categorized[57] as shown in Figure 5.2. The **economic responsibilities** of business are to produce goods and services that society wants at a price that perpetuates the business and satisfies its obligations to investors. For Smithfield Foods, the largest pork producer in the United States, this means selling bacon, ham, and other products to customers at prices that maximize Smithfield's profits and keep the company growing over the long term. Economic responsibility may also extend to offering certain products to needy consumers at a reduced price.

Legal responsibilities are to obey local, state, federal, and relevant international laws. Laws affecting Smithfield cover a wide range of requirements, from filing tax returns to meeting worker safety standards. **Ethical responsibilities** include meeting other societal expectations, not written as law. Smithfield took on this level of responsibility when it responded to requests by major customers, including McDonald's and Walmart, that it discontinue the practice of using gestation crates to house its sows. The customers were reacting to pressure from animal rights advocates who consider it cruel for sows to live in the two-foot by seven-foot crates during their entire gestation period, which means they cannot walk, turn around, or stretch their legs for months at a time.[58] Smithfield was not legally required to make the change (except in two states), and the arrangement was costly, but the company's decision helped its public image—that is, until it backed out of the plan, citing economic woes.

Finally, **philanthropic responsibilities** are additional behaviors and activities that society finds desirable and that the values of the business support. Examples include supporting community projects and making charitable contributions. Philanthropic activities can be more than mere altruism; managed properly, strategic philanthropy can become not an oxymoron but a way to build goodwill in a variety of stakeholders and even add to shareholder wealth.[59]

Robert Giacalone, who teaches business ethics at Temple University, believes that a 21st century education must help students think about responsibilities beyond

legal responsibilities

To obey local, state, federal, and relevant international laws.

ethical responsibilities

Meeting other social expectations, not written as law.

philanthropic responsibilities

Additional behaviors and activities that society finds desirable and that the values of the business support.

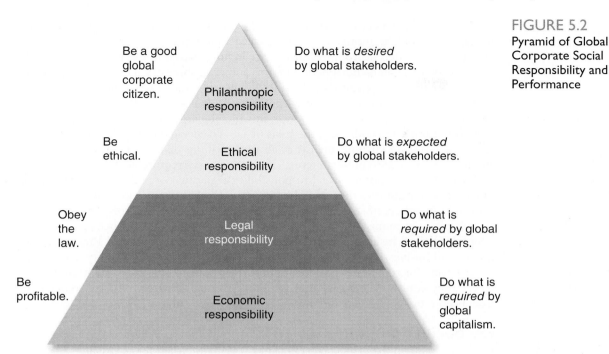

FIGURE 5.2
Pyramid of Global Corporate Social Responsibility and Performance

SOURCE: From *Academy of Management Executive: The Thinking Manager's Source* by A. Carroll, "Management Ethically with Global Stakeholders: A Present and Future Challenge." Copyright © 2004. Reproduced with permission of Academy of Management via Copyright Clearance Center.

self-interest and profitability. A real education, he says, teaches students to leave a legacy that extends beyond the bottom line—a transcendent education.[60] A **transcendent education** has five higher goals that balance self-interest with responsibility to others: *empathy* (feeling your decisions as potential victims might feel them, to gain wisdom); *generativity* (learning how to give as well as take, to others in the present as well as to future generations); *mutuality* (viewing success not merely as personal gain, but a common victory); *civil aspiration* (thinking not just in terms of don'ts [lie, cheat, steal, kill], but also in terms of positive contributions); and *intolerance of ineffective humanity* (speaking out against unethical actions).

> A real education, he says, teaches students to leave a legacy that extends beyond the bottom line—a transcendent education.

transcendent education

An education with five higher goals that balance self-interest with responsibility to others.

Contrasting Views

Two basic and contrasting views describe principles that should guide managerial responsibility. The first holds that managers act as agents for shareholders and, as such, are obligated to maximize the present value of the firm. This tenet of capitalism is widely associated with the early writings of Adam Smith in *The Wealth of Nations* and more recently with Milton Friedman, the Nobel Prize–winning economist of the University of Chicago. With his now-famous dictum, "The social responsibility of business is to increase profits," Friedman contended that organizations may help improve the quality of life as long as such actions are directed at increasing profits.

Some considered Friedman to be "the enemy of business ethics," but his position was ethical: he believed that it was unethical for unelected business leaders to decide what was best for society and unethical for them to spend shareholders' money on projects unconnected to key business interests.[61] Furthermore, the context of Friedman's famous statement includes the qualifier that business should increase its profits while conforming to society's laws and ethical customs.

The second perspective, different from the profit maximization perspective, is that managers should be motivated by principled moral reasoning. Adam Smith wrote about a world different from the one we are in now, driven in the 18th century by the self-interest of small owner-operated farms and craft shops trying to generate a living income for themselves and their families. This self-interest was quite different from that of top executives of modern corporations.[62] It is noteworthy that Adam Smith also wrote *A Theory of Moral Sentiments*, in which he argued that "sympathy," defined as a proper regard for others, is the basis of a civilized society.[63] Smith argued further that "the wise and virtuous man is at all times willing that this own private interest should be sacrificed to public interest" if circumstances require it.[64]

Advocates of corporate social responsibility argue that organizations have a wider range of responsibilities that extend beyond the production of goods and services at a profit. As members of society, organizations should actively and responsibly participate in the community and in the larger environment. From this perspective, many people criticized insurance companies after Hurricanes Katrina and Rita devastated homes and businesses along the Gulf Coast. From a social responsibility perspective, it was wrong for companies to watch out for their bottom line and avoid paying claims where they could make a case that the damage wasn't covered; the insurers should have been more concerned about their devastated customers.

Reconciliation

Profit maximization and corporate social responsibility used to be regarded as antagonistic, leading to opposing policies. But the two views can converge.[65] The Coca-Cola Company has set up dozens of charitable projects to provide clean water in countries. These projects are helping some of the 1.2 billion people without access to safe drinking water. The company is constructing structures to harvest rainwater in India, building extensions of the municipal water supply in Mali, and delivering water purification systems and storage urns to Kenya. These projects are aimed at burnishing the company's image and resolving complaints that the company is using up too much of the world's water supply to manufacture its beverages. From a practical perspective, Coca-Cola's strategic planners have identified water shortages as a strategic risk; from a values perspective, water is, in the words of executive Neville Isdell, "at the very core of our ethos," so "responsible use of that resource is very important to us."[66]

Earlier attention to corporate social responsibility focused on alleged wrongdoing and how to control it. More recently, attention has also been centered on the possible competitive advantage of socially responsible actions. DuPont has been incorporating care for the environment into its business in two ways it hopes will put it ahead of the competition. First, the company has been reducing its pollution. It hopes these efforts will give it an advantage in a future when the government more heavily regulates emissions, requiring competitors to play catch-up. In addition, reducing emissions goes hand in hand with reducing waste and unnecessary use of energy, saving the company money and directly benefiting the bottom line. Second, DuPont has been developing products that are sustainable, meaning they don't deplete the earth's resources. Examples include corn-based fabrics and new applications of its Tyvek material to make buildings more energy-efficient. DuPont expects these innovations to give the company profitable access to the growing market for environmentally friendly products.[67]

The real relationship between corporate social performance and corporate financial performance is highly complex; socially responsible organizations are not necessarily more or less successful in financial terms.[68] But on net, the accumulated evidence indicates that social responsibility is associated with better financial performance.[69] Some advantages are clear. For example, socially responsible actions can have long-term benefits. Companies can avoid unnecessary and costly regulation if they are socially responsible. Honesty and fairness may pay great dividends to the conscience, to the personal reputation, and to the public image of the company as well as in the market response.[70] In addition, society's problems can offer business opportunities, and profits can be made from systematic and vigorous efforts to solve these problems. Firms can perform cost–benefit analyses to identify actions that will maximize profits while satisfying the demand for corporate social responsibility from multiple stakeholders.[71] In other words, managers can treat corporate social responsibility as they would treat all investment decisions. This has been the case as firms attempt to reconcile their business practices with their effect on the natural environment.

The Natural Environment and Sustainability

Most large corporations developed in an era of abundant raw materials, cheap energy, and unconstrained waste disposal.[72] But many of the technologies developed during this era are contributing to the destruction of ecosystems. Industrial-age systems follow a linear flow of extract, produce, sell, use, and discard—what some call a take–make–waste approach.[73] But perhaps no time in history has offered greater possibilities for a change in business thinking than the 21st century. Some maintain that ecological sustainability is now the key driver of innovation.[74] And, whereas some are pessimistic about the planet's future, many are both resolute about creating a healthier planet, and more optimistic now than in recent years for many of the reasons to follow.[75]

Business used to look at environmental issues as a no-win situation; you either help the environment and hurt your business or help your business at a cost to the environment. But now a paradigm shift is taking place in corporate environmental management: the deliberate incorporation of environmental values into competitive strategies and into the design and manufacturing of products.[76] Why? In addition to philosophical reasons, companies go green to satisfy consumer demand, to react to a competitor's actions, to meet requests from customers or suppliers, to comply with guidelines, and to create competitive advantage.

> Business used to look at environmental issues as a no-win situation, but now a paradigm shift is taking place.

General Electric CEO Jeff Immelt used to view environmental rules as a burden and a cost. Now he sees environmentally friendly technologies as one of the global economy's most significant business opportunities. Under a business initiative called Ecomagination, GE is looking for business opportunities from solving environmental problems. Ecomagination solutions include wind turbines, materials for solar energy cells, and energy-efficient home appliances. Ecomagination has delivered many billions in revenues. It also has built a green image for the GE brand and positioned the company as a leader in many rapidly growing markets, including high-efficiency jet engines and locomotives.[77]

A Risk Society

We live in a risk society. That is, the creation and distribution of wealth generate by-products that can cause injury, loss, or danger to people and the environment. The fundamental sources of risk in modern society are the excessive production of hazards and ecologically unsustainable consumption of natural resources.[78] Risk has proliferated through population explosion, industrial pollution, and environmental degradation.[79]

Industrial pollution risks include air pollution, smog, global warming, ozone depletion, acid rain, toxic waste sites, nuclear hazards, obsolete weapons arsenals, industrial accidents, and hazardous products. Tens of thousands of uncontrolled toxic waste sites have been documented in the United States alone. The situation is far worse in other parts of the world. The pattern, for toxic waste and many other risks, is one of accumulating risks and inadequate remedies.

The institutions that create environmental and technological risk (corporations and government agencies) are responsible for controlling and managing the risks.[80] For example, as a manufacturer, 3M acknowledges that its activities result in pollution, so the company has committed itself to reducing its impact on the environment. A combination of reduced energy use, improvements in manufacturing processes, redesign of products, and the use of pollution control equipment have enabled the company to cut its global emissions of greenhouse gases dramatically. 3M recently installed charging stations for electric vehicles at its headquarters in St. Paul, Minnesota.[81]

Some of the world's worst environmental problems are in China because of its rapid industrialization and its huge population and size. About one-third of China's rural population—hundreds of millions of people—drink unhealthful, unclean water. At least the problem is recognized; local authorities are beginning to experience pressure from the central government to clean up or shut down dirty factories.[82] Still, most cleanup efforts focus on big cities while rural areas get worse.

Developing countries are often seen as sustainability laggards, focused solely on raising people out of poverty. Regulatory agencies can be weak and hesitant to impose restrictions, but visionary individuals the world over can pioneer successful sustainability efforts.[83]

Ecocentric Management

ecocentric management

Its goal is the creation of sustainable economic development and improvement of quality of life worldwide for all organizational stakeholders.

sustainable growth

Economic growth and development that meet present needs without harming the needs of future generations.

life-cycle analysis (LCA)

A process of analyzing all inputs and outputs, through the entire cradle-to-grave life of a product, to determine total environmental impact.

carbon footprint

The output of carbon dioxide and other greenhouse gases.

Ecocentric management has as its goal the creation of sustainable economic development and improvement of quality of life worldwide for all organizational stakeholders.[84] **Sustainable growth** is economic growth and development that meet the organization's present needs without harming the ability of future generations to meet their needs.[85] Sustainability is fully compatible with the natural ecosystems that generate and preserve life.[86]

Businesses are both a cause of and a solution to environmental degradation, and clearly have a major role to play in sustainability debates and strategies.[87]

Increasingly, firms are paying attention to the total environmental impact throughout the life cycle of their products.[88] **Life-cycle analysis (LCA)** is a process of analyzing all inputs and outputs, through the entire cradle-to-grave life of a product, to determine the total environmental impact of the production and use of a product. LCA quantifies the total use of resources and the releases into the air, water, and land. Reporting worldwide **carbon footprints** is a big step in environmental reporting in that industry.

LCA considers the extraction of raw materials, product packaging, transportation, and disposal. Consider packaging alone. Goods make the journey from manufacturer to wholesaler to retailer to customer; then they are recycled back to the manufacturer. They may be packaged and repackaged several times, from bulk transport, to large crates, to cardboard boxes, to individual consumer sizes. Repackaging not only creates waste but also costs time. The design of initial packaging in sizes and formats adaptable to the final customer can minimize the need for repackaging, cut waste, and realize financial benefits.

Rather than the linear take–make–waste production model described earlier, a fully sustainable model applies a circular borrow–use–return approach.[89] Whereas the former model engages in harmful extraction, generates huge quantities of waste and pollution, and depletes natural resources (a process in which resources move from cradle to grave), the cradle-to-cradle approach is ecologically benign and restorative. In its ideal form, this sustainable approach extracts energy and raw materials without harm, phases out the use of nonrenewable resources, designs processes and products that recirculate so they don't cause environmental or socioeconomic harm, keeps toxic substances in closed-loop industrial cycles, and recirculates biological materials back into nature without harm.[90]

Profitability need not suffer and may be positively affected by ecocentric philosophies and practices. Some, but not all, research has shown a positive relationship between corporate environmental performance and profitability.[91] Of course, whether the relationship is positive, negative, or neutral depends on the strategies chosen and the effectiveness of implementation.

Companies can integrate green practices with strategy in a variety of ways. Certainly they develop and market green products; Toyota's bold move to develop the Prius paid off handsomely with market dominance.[92] Companies also can emphasize green attributes in their marketing but need to avoid misleading claims (greenwashing) and public backlash. For instance, Arm & Hammer positioned its baking soda brand as "the number one environmentally sensible alternative for cleaning and deodorizing" and "committed to the environment since 1846." On the other hand, the company ignored a major problem: it used animal testing. The blogosphere began touting equally green but cruelty-free Bob's Red Mill baking soda.[93]

Companies also can acquire other companies with sustainability (and image) in mind. L'Oreal bought The Body Shop, Colgate-Palmolive bought Tom's of Maine, Unilever bought Ben & Jerry's, and Group Danone bought Stonyfield's.[94] When Clorox bought Burt's Bees, which had decades of leadership and experience with sustainability, it did so for growth and to convince environmental stakeholders that the company's strategic change was genuine, but also to acquire knowledge about the green product space.[95]

For those interested in reading more about this subject, Appendix B of this chapter discusses in greater detail the reasons for managing with the environment in mind, some history of the environmental movement, economic issues, and a wide array of green examples pertaining to strategy, public affairs, legal issues, operations, marketing, accounting, and finance.

You also can check out the Global Reporting Initiatives list of sustainability performance indicators. This useful resource, at www.gri.com, aims to help companies improve their sustainability practices, including transparent reporting.

Timberland has paid particular attention to life cycle analysis, as implied by what is printed on their recycled material shoe boxes.

Environmental Agendas for the Future

In the past, most companies were oblivious to their negative environmental impact. More recently, many began striving for low impact. Now some strive for positive impact, eager to sell solutions to the world's problems. Siemens, a major electronics and electrical engineering company headquartered in Switzerland, produces energy-efficient equipment for power generation and transmission, including smart grids. In addition, Siemens Building Technologies is tackling energy efficiency in buildings, which account for 40 percent of energy consumption. For example, in Oregon, a Siemens project is helping Sky Lakes Medical Center save $3 million in energy expenses over 12 years with advanced lighting, heating, and cooling systems.[96]

Or consider climate change and the world's shortage of clean water. When Dow Chemical's Freeport, Texas, site had trouble getting enough water to run its processes during droughts, it installed technology to monitor the water system 24/7 and reduced water consumption by a billion gallons a year.[97] Coca-Cola pursues its water neutrality pledge, aiming to replenish watersheds to the full extent of the water it extracts. And for Nestlé, a major strategic challenge is water security for farmers who supply factories (and people) the world over.[98] Nestlé saves up to 1,375 cubic meters of water per year since improving how it collects and transports milk from farmers.

You don't have to be a manufacturer or a utility to jump on the green bandwagon. Web search giant Google is working hard to reduce its carbon footprint and purchasing offsets—funding projects that reduce greenhouse gas emissions elsewhere.[99]

Collaborative efforts will be essential—for example, the energy industry and environmentalists working with rather than against one another.[100] Webs of companies

Bottom Line

Packaging isn't the most glamorous of business topics, but it holds great potential for reducing costs and increasing speed while helping the environment. You can always find opportunities to improve results in unexpected places where others haven't tried. *Think of a product you recently purchased. How could its packaging have been more environmentally friendly?*

with a common ecological vision can combine their efforts into high-leverage, impactful action.[101] In cities such as San Antonio, Texas, and Columbus, Ohio, federal partner agencies work closely with city governments, utilities, and multiple manufacturers to reduce pollutants and energy consumption and to increase energy savings. In Kalundborg, Denmark, such a collaborative alliance exists among an electric power generating plant, an oil refiner, a biotech production plant, a plasterboard factory, cement producers, heating utilities, a sulfuric acid producer, and local agriculture and horticulture. Chemicals, energy (for both heating and cooling), water, and organic materials flow among companies. Resources are conserved, waste materials generate revenues, and water, air, and ground pollution all are reduced.

Mark Tercek, CEO of the Nature Conservancy and former managing director and partner at Goldman Sachs, states, "individuals, businesses, and nations have long acted as if 'society will always have the resources it needs, and if anything runs short, then creative businesses can simply replace it with something else that is not so scarce.' [But] for the first time in human history, these assumptions are open to serious question at a global scale."[102] Natural resources no longer are free goods.[103]

In 2010, the World Bank launched a project to help developing countries arrive at valuations of their natural capital. Then-president Robert Zoellik said, "The natural wealth of nations should be a capital asset, valued in combination with its financial capital, manufactured capital, and human capital."[104] Now, nonprofit organizations and accounting firm PriceWaterhouseCoopers offer methodologies that value ecosystems. Dow Chemical pledged $10 million for scientists from the Nature Conservancy to help Dow develop ecosystem service valuation methods.

States Dow CEO Andrew Liveris, "Companies that value and integrate biodiversity and ecosystem services into their strategic plans are best positioned for the future."[105] In addition to the benefits to the world of sustainable practices, many now believe that preparing for and adapting to climate change is a big and fast-arriving challenge,[106] and that solving environmental problems is one of the biggest opportunities in the history of commerce.[107]

MANAGER'S BRIEF

PROGRESS REPORT

ONWARD

Management Connection

IBM TAKES RESPONSIBILITY

Given that disclosure builds the kind of trust IBM wants as the basis for its relationships, the company publishes its values and policies online along with an annual Corporate Responsibility Report. IBM's understanding of its role in corporate citizenship includes practices related to the natural environment and the communities it serves. IBM defines its social role this way:

1. We identify and act upon new opportunities to apply our technology and expertise to societal problems.
2. We scale our existing programs and initiatives to achieve maximum benefit.
3. We empower our employees and others to serve their communities.
4. We integrate corporate citizenship and social responsibility into every aspect of our company.

These statements apply IBM's resources as a large global technology company (over 425,000 employees in almost 170 countries) to the communities where it operates.

Especially in its concern for the natural environment, IBM unites a commitment to be responsible with the business opportunities available to a company specializing in data analysis and planning. In fact, IBM has had policies for protecting the environment and conserving resources since 1967. Its equipment-recycling program has 22 facilities worldwide refurbishing, dismantling, and culling materials from used electronics. And its efforts to conserve electricity saved the company $442 million between 1990 and 2011. The company also requires its suppliers to demonstrate that they are taking responsibility for their impact on the environment.

Moreover, environmental protection is now part of IBM's Smarter Planet strategy. IBM's consultants and systems help cities, businesses, and building owners manage the data required to operate as efficiently as possible. For example, IBM is helping San Francisco figure out how to keep all of its waste out of landfills by directing it to recycling and other uses. IBM's Smarter Building initiative installs sensors and building automation software to gather data on building systems and uses, applying the data to conserve energy and water.

IBM's corporate citizenship also involves supporting selected nonprofit causes, including economic development, education, and health. Its biggest philanthropy is its Smarter Cities challenge, which awards grants to cities to help them improve in a specified area of performance. IBM sends a six-member team of its own experts to each city to help leaders analyze problems and develop solutions. By the end of 2012, IBM had sent teams to 62 cities to work on reducing asthma, managing traffic, encouraging entrepreneurship, improving energy efficiency, and much more.[108]

- How is IBM's commitment to corporate social responsibility good for IBM as a business? Explain.
- Improving energy efficiency saves IBM millions of dollars, but recycling its used electronics requires hiring hundreds of people. Is the recycling program justifiable? Why or why not?

KEY TERMS

business ethics, p. 156	ethical climate, p. 161	moral philosophy, p. 156
carbon footprint, p. 172	ethical issue, p. 156	philanthropic responsibilities, p. 168
Caux Principles, p. 157	ethical leader, p. 163	relativism, p. 158
compliance-based ethics programs, p. 164	ethical responsibilities, p. 168	Sarbanes-Oxley Act, p. 160
corporate social responsibility (CSR), p. 168	ethics, p. 154	sustainable growth, p. 172
	integrity-based ethics programs, p. 164	transcendent education, p. 169
ecocentric management, p. 172	Kohlberg's model of cognitive moral development, p. 159	triple bottom line, p. 168
economic responsibilities, p. 168	legal responsibilities, p. 168	universalism, p. 157
egoism, p. 158	life-cycle analysis (LCA), p. 172	utilitarianism, p. 158
		virtue ethics, p. 158

SUMMARY OF LEARNING OBJECTIVES

Now that you have studied Chapter 5, you should be able to:

 Describe how different ethical perspectives guide decision making.

The purpose of ethics is to identify the rules that govern human behavior and the "goods" that are worth seeking. Ethical decisions are guided by the individual's values or principles of conduct such as honesty, fairness, integrity, respect for others, and responsible citizenship. Different ethical systems include universalism, egoism and utilitarianism, relativism, and virtue ethics. These philosophical systems, as practiced by different individuals according to their level of cognitive moral development and other factors, underlie the ethical stances of individuals and organizations.

LO 2 Explain how companies influence their ethics environment.

Different organizations apply different ethical perspectives and standards. Ethics codes sometimes are helpful, although they must be implemented properly. Ethics programs can range from compliance-based to integrity-based. Ethics codes address employee conduct, community and environment, shareholders, customers, suppliers and contractors, political activity, and technology.

 Outline a process for making ethical decisions.

Making ethical decisions requires moral awareness, moral judgment, and moral character. When faced with ethical dilemmas, the veil of ignorance is a useful metaphor. More precisely, you can know various moral standards (universalism, relativism, and so on), use the problem-solving model described in Chapter 3, identify the positive and negative effects of your alternatives on different parties, consider legal requirements and the costs of unethical actions, and then evaluate your ethical duties.

LO 4 Summarize the important issues surrounding corporate social responsibility.

Corporate social responsibility is the extension of the corporate role beyond economic pursuits. It includes not only economic but also legal, ethical, and philanthropic responsibilities. Advocates believe managers should consider societal and human needs in their business decisions because corporations are members of society and carry a wide range of responsibilities. Critics of corporate responsibility believe managers' first responsibility is to increase profits for the shareholders who own the corporation. The two perspectives are potentially reconcilable, especially if managers choose to address areas of social responsibility that contribute to the organization's strategy.

| LO | 5 | Discuss reasons for businesses' growing interest in the natural environment. |

In the past, most companies viewed the natural environment as a resource to be used for raw materials and profit. But consumer, regulatory, and other pressures arose. Executives often viewed these pressures as burdens, constraints, and costs to be borne. Now more companies view the interface between business and the natural environment as a potential win–win opportunity. Some are adopting a greener agenda for philosophical reasons and personal commitment to sustainable development. Many also are recognizing the potential financial benefits of managing with the environment in mind and are integrating environmental issues into corporate and business strategy. Some see entering businesses that help rather than harm the natural environment as one of the great commercial opportunities in history.

| LO | 6 | Identify actions managers can take to manage with the environment in mind. |

Organizations have contributed risk to society and have some responsibility for reducing risk to the environment. They also have the capability to help solve environmental problems. Eco-centric management attempts to minimize negative environment impact, create sustainable economic development, and improve the quality of life worldwide. Relevant actions are described in the chapter, including strategic initiatives, life-cycle analysis, and interorganizational alliances. A chapter appendix provides a wide variety of specific examples of strategic, operations, finance, legal and public affairs, marketing, and accounting practices that are environmentally friendly.

DISCUSSION QUESTIONS

1. Consider the various ethical systems described early in the chapter. Identify concrete examples from your own past decisions or the decisions of others you have seen or read about.

2. Choose one or more topics from Table 5.2 and discuss their current status and the ethical issues surrounding them.

3. What would you do in each of the scenarios described in Table 5.3?

4. Identify and discuss illegal, unethical, and socially responsible business actions in the current news.

5. Does your school have a code of ethics? If so, what does it say? Is it effective? Why or why not?

6. You have a job you like at which you work 40 to 45 hours per week. How much off-the-job volunteer work would you do? What kinds of volunteer work? How will you react if your boss makes it clear he or she wants you to cut back on the outside activities and devote more hours to your job?

7. What are the arguments for and against the concept of corporate social responsibility? Where do you stand and why? Give your opinions, specifically, with respect to the text examples.

8. What do you think of the concept of a transcendent education as described in the chapter? What can be done to implement such a vision for education?

9. What is the current status of the Sarbanes-Oxley Act? What do executives think of it now? What impact has it had?

10. A company in England slaughtered 70,000 baby ostrich chicks each year for their meat. It told a teen magazine that it would stop if it received enough complaints. Analyze this policy, practice, and public statement using the concepts discussed in the chapter.

11. A Nike ad in the U.S. magazine *Seventeen* showed a picture of a girl, aged perhaps 8 or 9. The ad read,

    If you let me play . . .
    I will like myself more.
    I will have more self-confidence.
    I will suffer less depression.
    I will be 60 percent less likely to get breast cancer.
    I will be more likely to leave a man who beats me.
    I will be less likely to get pregnant before I want to.
    I will learn what it means to be strong.
    If you let me play sports.

    Assess this ad in terms of chapter concepts surrounding ethics and social responsibility. What questions would you ask in doing this analysis?

12. Should companies be held accountable for actions of decades past, then legal but since made illegal, as their harmful effects became known? Why or why not?

13. Discuss courage as a requirement for ethical behavior. What personal examples can you offer, either as an actor or as an observer? What examples are in the news?

14. See additional discussion questions in Appendix B.

EXPERIENTIAL EXERCISES

5.1   MEASURING YOUR ETHICAL WORK BEHAVIOR

OBJECTIVES

1. To explore a range of ethically perplexing situations.

2. To understand your own ethical attitudes.

INSTRUCTIONS

Make decisions in the situations described in the Ethical Behavior Worksheet. You will not have all the background information on each situation; instead, you should make whatever assumptions you feel you would make if you were actually confronted with the decision choices described. Select the decision choice that most closely represents the decision you feel you would make personally. You should choose decision options even though you can envision other creative solutions that were not included in the exercise.

Ethical Behavior Worksheet

Situation 1. You are taking a very difficult chemistry course, which you must pass to maintain your scholarship and to avoid damaging your application for graduate school. Chemistry is not your strong suit, and, because of a just-below-failing average in the course, you will have to receive a grade of 90 or better on the final exam, which is two days away. A janitor, who is aware of your plight, informs you that he found the master for the chemistry final in a trash barrel and has saved it. He will make it available to you for a price, which is high but which you could afford. What would you do?

_____ (a) I would tell the janitor thanks, but no thanks.

_____ (b) I would report the janitor to the proper officials.

_____ (c) I would buy the exam and keep it to myself.

_____ (d) I would not buy the exam myself, but I would let some of my friends, who are also flunking the course, know that it is available.

Situation 2. You have been working on some financial projections manually for two days now. It seems that each time you think you have them completed, your boss shows up with a new assumption or another what-if question. If you only had a copy of a spreadsheet software program for your personal computer, you could plug in the new assumptions and revise the estimates with ease. Then a colleague offers to let you make a copy of some software that is copyrighted. What would you do?

_____ (a) I would accept my friend's generous offer and make a copy of the software.

_____ (b) I would decline to copy it and plug away manually on the numbers.

_____ (c) I would decide to go buy a copy of the software myself, for $300, and hope I would be reimbursed by the company in a month or two.

_____ (d) I would request another extension on an already overdue project date.

Situation 3. Your small manufacturing company is in serious financial difficulty. A large order of your products is ready to be delivered to a key customer when you discover that the product is simply not right. It will not meet all performance specifications, will cause problems for your customer, and will require rework in the field; however, this, you know, will not become evident until after the customer has received and paid for the order. If you do not ship the order and receive the payment as expected, your business may be forced into bankruptcy. And if you delay the shipment or inform the customer of these problems, you may lose the order and go bankrupt. What would you do?

_____ (a) I would not ship the order and place my firm in voluntary bankruptcy.

_____ (b) I would inform the customer and declare voluntary bankruptcy.

_____ (c) I would ship the order and inform the customer after I received payment.

_____ (d) I would ship the order and not inform the customer.

Situation 4. You are the cofounder and president of a new venture, manufacturing products for the recreational market. Five months after launching the business, one of your suppliers informs you it can no longer supply you with a critical raw material because you are not a large-quantity user. Without the raw material, the business cannot continue. What would you do?

_____ (a) I would grossly overstate my requirements to another supplier to make the supplier think I am a much larger potential customer to secure the raw material from that supplier, even though this would mean the supplier will no longer be able to supply another, noncompeting small manufacturer who may thus be forced out of business.

_____ (b) I would steal raw material from another firm (noncompeting) where I am aware of a sizable stockpile.

_____ (c) I would pay off the supplier because I have reason to believe that the supplier could be persuaded to meet my needs with a sizable under-the-table payoff that my company could afford.

_____ (d) I would declare voluntary bankruptcy.

Situation 5. You are on a marketing trip for your new venture for the purpose of calling on the purchasing agent of a major prospective client. Your company is manufacturing an electronic system that you hope the purchasing agent will buy. During your conversation, you notice on the cluttered desk of the purchasing agent several copies of a cost proposal for a system from one of your direct competitors. This purchasing agent has previously reported mislaying several of your own company's proposals and has asked for additional copies. The purchasing agent leaves the room momentarily to get you a cup of coffee, leaving you alone with your competitor's proposals less than an arm's length away. What would you do?

_____ (a) I would do nothing but await the man's return.

_____ (b) I would sneak a quick peek at the proposal, looking for bottom-line numbers.

_____ (c) I would put the copy of the proposal in my briefcase.

_____ (d) I would wait until the man returns and ask his permission to see the copy.

SOURCE: Jeffry A. Timmons, *New Venture Creation*, 3rd ed. 1994, pp. 160–161. Copyright 1994 The McGraw-Hill Companies. Reprinted with permission.

5.2   ETHICAL STANCE

Are the following actions ethical or unethical in your opinion? Why? Consider the actions individually and discuss them in small groups.

- Calling in sick when you really are not
- Taking office supplies home for personal use
- Cheating on a test
- Turning someone in for cheating on a test or paper
- Overcharging on your company expense report
- Trying to flirt your way out of a speeding ticket
- Splicing cable from your neighbor
- Surfing the net on company time

- Cheating on income tax
- Lying (exaggerating) about yourself to influence someone of the opposite sex
- Looking at pornographic sites on the web through the company network
- Lying about your education on a job application
- Lying about experience in a job interview
- Making a copy of a rental DVD before returning it to the store

SOURCE: Suzanne C. de Janasz, Karen O'Dowd, and Beth Z. Schneider, *Interpersonal Skills in Organizations*, McGraw-Hill, 2002, p. 211. Copyright 2002 The McGraw-Hill Companies. Reprinted with permission.

CONCLUDING CASE

MA EARTH SKIN CARE TRIES TO STAY NATURAL

Heather Franklin is a marketing manager for Ma Earth Skin Care. Four years ago, when she was hired to help with the paperwork for promotional campaigns, she was thrilled to become a part of this company because she loved Ma Earth's lotions, soaps, and cosmetics. Besides smelling heavenly and offering exquisite colors for eye shadow and lipstick, the products spoke to Heather's values: Ma Earth promised to use all natural ingredients, sustainably grown or mined, and to operate with minimal adverse impact on the planet. So for Heather, going to work was almost like carrying out a mission, promoting both beauty and concern for the planet's well-being. No doubt, her commitment and enthusiasm helped pave the way when the position of marketing manager opened up.

Currently, Heather and her team are preparing a promotional campaign for a new product line, Oré Essentials, which includes lipsticks, foundation, and eye shadows tinted with a plant extract called orellana. The exciting feature of Oré Essentials is that orellana is harvested deep in the Amazon rain forest, and because of its sustainable practices, Ma Earth will obtain this special ingredient in a socially responsible manner. The company set up a contract with a tribe living in a remote village. The people of the tribe are supposed to grow and harvest the orellana, which is naturally part of the area's ecosystem, and Ma Earth has promised to pay a fair price to the whole tribe so the people can use the money to maintain their village and their way of life. Consumers will get a beautiful product and the pleasure of knowing that they are helping preserve an endangered ecology—and an endangered way of life for the rain forest people.

But when Heather sat down for a meeting with the photography crew that traveled to the village, some concerns began to surface. She was looking at stunning photos of tribe members arrayed in grass skirts as they stood behind a pile of fruit from the orellana tree. As she was selecting her favorite shots, one of the photographers commented that the translator had made some surprising remarks on the return trip from the village. Apparently the pile of orellana fruit had been gathered just for the photo shoot. The tribe doesn't really bother with growing and harvesting orellana; the people of this area aren't primarily farmers, and there aren't actually many orellana trees within a day's walk of the village. The first year they had tried selling orellana to Ma Earth, they grew only enough to earn a few hundred dollars, not really worth the effort. Heather felt confused by these statements and planned to take a closer look at spending on her product later that day.

Hours later, when the other employees had gone home, Heather finally had a chance to spend some time researching her product on the company's employee website. She found purchasing transactions for "orellana/annatto," and after a little research learned that under either name, the product is just an inexpensive dye. Under the latter name, it is used as a common food coloring. It turns out that Ma Earth made most of its purchases from a mainstream supplier, which is cheaper than persuading remote villagers to provide orellana.

That evening Heather went home feeling betrayed and upset. The next day she asked her boss, the divisional vice president, why the company pretended to care about a remote village if it was just a front for a brand. Heather's boss, Megan McDonough, said, "But we *do* care! We send them tens of thousands of dollars every year. Sure, they don't actually grow that stuff for us, but they could, and we'll buy it if they do. Anyway, our aid has provided a school and a health clinic, not to mention food and clothing. We've helped the tribe members stay healthy and preserve their language and culture."

Heather considered what Megan said. "So," she asked, "does this mean we're using their culture to build an image for our brand, and in exchange, they get money from us to keep that culture alive?" She thought about the traditional designs the marketing department had copied from the tribe as decorations for the Oré Essentials packaging.

Megan nodded encouragingly. "That's exactly what I'm saying. It's a win–win situation." Heather felt relieved but not quite sure that her original idealism would withstand her deeper knowledge of how Ma Earth defined its mission.

DISCUSSION QUESTIONS

1. What ethical issues is Heather facing in this situation? What possible marketing claims about the company's relationship with the Amazonian tribe would cross a line into unethical territory? What claims could it make ethically?

2. How could Ma Earth create an ethical climate that would help managers such as Heather ensure that they are behaving ethically?

3. How effectively do you think Ma Earth is practicing corporate social responsibility in this situation? Explain the reasoning behind your evaluation.

Managing in Our Natural Environment

BUSINESS AND THE ENVIRONMENT: CONFLICTING VIEWS

Some people believe everyone wins when business tackles environmental issues.[1] Others disagree.

Business used to look at environmental issues as a no-win situation; you either help the environment and hurt your business or help your business only at a cost to the environment. Fortunately, things have changed. "When Americans first demanded a cleanup of the environment during the early 1970s, corporations threw a tantrum. Their response ran the psychological gamut from denial to hostility, defiance, obstinacy, and fear. But today, when it comes to green issues, many U.S. companies have turned from rebellious underachievers to active problem solvers."[2] This appendix gives examples of things U.S. corporations are doing to help solve environmental problems.

Johan Piet said, "Only win–win companies will survive, but that does not mean that all win–win ideas will be successful."[3] In other words, rigorous analysis is essential. Thus some companies maintain continuous improvement in environmental performance but fund only projects that meet financial objectives.

Most people understand that business has the resources and the competence to bring about constructive change and that this creates great opportunity—if well managed—for both business and the environment.

WHY MANAGE WITH THE ENVIRONMENT IN MIND?

Business is turning its full attention to environmental issues for many reasons, including legal compliance, cost effectiveness, competitive advantage, public opinion, and long-term thinking.

Legal Compliance Government regulations and liability for damages provide strong economic incentives to comply with environmental guidelines. Most industries already have made environmental protection regulation and liability an integral part of their business planning.[4] The U.S. Justice Department has handed out tough prison sentences to executives whose companies violate hazardous waste requirements.

Some businesspeople consider the regulations to be too rigid, inflexible, and unfair. In response to this concern, regulatory reform may become more creative. The Aspen Institute Series on the Environment in the Twenty-First Century has tried to increase the cost-effectiveness of compliance measures through more flexibility in meeting standards and relying on market-based incentives. Such mechanisms, including tradable permits, pollution charges, and deposit refund systems, provide positive financial incentives for good environmental performance.[5]

Cost Effectiveness Environmentally conscious strategies can be cost-effective.[6] In the short run, company after company is realizing cost savings from repackaging, recycling, and other approaches. Union Carbide faced costs of $30 a ton for disposal of solid wastes and $2,000 a ton for disposal of hazardous wastes. By recycling, reclaiming, or selling its waste, it avoided $8.5 million in costs *and* generated $3.5 million in income during a six-month period. Dow Chemical launched a 10-year program to improve its environmental, health, and safety performance worldwide. Dow projected savings of $1.8 billion over the 10-year period.[7]

Environmentally conscious strategies offer long-run cost advantages as well. Companies that are functioning barely within legal limits today may incur big costs—being forced to pay damages or upgrade technologies and practices—when laws change down the road.

A few of the other cost savings include fines, cleanups, and litigation; lower raw materials costs; reduced energy use; less expensive waste handling and disposal; lower insurance rates; and possibly higher interest rates.

Competitive Advantage Corporations gain a competitive advantage by channeling their environmental concerns into entrepreneurial opportunities and by producing higher-quality products that meet consumer demand. Business opportunities abound in pollution protection equipment and processes, waste cleanup, low-water-use plumbing, new light bulb technology, and marketing of environmentally safe products such as biodegradable plastics. With new pools of venture capital, government funding, and specialized investment funds available, environmental technology has become a major sector of the venture capital industry.[8]

In addition, companies that fail to innovate in this area will be at a competitive disadvantage. Environmental protection is not only a universal need; it is also a major export industry. U.S. trade suffered as other countries—notably Germany—took the lead in patenting and exporting anti–air pollution and other environmental technologies. If the United States does not produce innovative, competitive new technologies, it will forsake a growth industry and see most of its domestic spending for environmental protection go to imports.[9]

In short, competitive advantage can be gained by maintaining market share with old customers and by creating new products for new market opportunities. And if you are an environmental leader, you may set the standards for future regulations—regulations that you are prepared to meet while your competitors are not.

Public Opinion The majority of the U.S. population believes business must clean up; few people think it is doing its job well. Gallup surveys have shown that more than 80 percent of U.S. consumers consider environmentalism in making purchases. An international survey found that majorities gave priority to environmental protection even at the risk of slowing economic growth. Consumers seem to have reached the point of routinely expecting companies to come up with environmentally friendly alternatives to current products and practices.[10]

Companies also receive pressure from local communities and from their own employees. Sometimes the pressure is informal and low-key, but much pressure is exerted by environmental organizations; aroused citizen groups, societies and associations; international codes of conduct; and environmentally conscious investors.[11]

Another important reason for paying attention to environmental impact is TRI, the Toxic Release Inventory.[12] Starting in 1986, the EPA required all the plants of approximately 10,000 U.S. manufacturers to report annual releases of 317 toxic chemicals into the air, ground, and water. The substances include Freon, PCBs, asbestos, and lead compounds. Hundreds of others have been added to the list. The releases are not necessarily illegal, but they provide the public with an annual environmental benchmark. TRI continues to provide a powerful incentive to reduce emissions.

Finally, it is useful to remember that companies recover very slowly in public opinion from the impact of an environmental disaster. Adverse public opinion may affect sales as well as the firm's ability to attract and retain talented people. You can see why companies such as P&G consider concern for the environment a consumer need, making it a basic and critical business issue.

Long-Term Thinking

Long-term thinking about resources helps business leaders understand the nature of their responsibilities with regard to environmental concerns. For example, you read about sustainable growth in the chapter.[13] Seventh Generation is named after, and operates under, the ideals set by the Iroquois Indians—every decision must consider the impact it will have on the next (seven) generations. Economic arguments and the tragedy of the commons highlight the need for long-term thinking.

Economic arguments In Chapter 3, we discussed long-term versus short-term decision making. We stated that it is common for managers to succumb to short-term pressure for profits and to avoid spending now when the potential payoff is years down the road. In addition, some economists maintain that it is the responsibility of management to maximize returns for shareholders, implying the preeminence of the short-term profit goal.

But other economists argue that such a strategy caters to immediate profit maximization for stock speculators and neglects serious investors who are with the company for the long haul. Attention to environmental issues enhances the organization's long-term viability because the goal is the long-term creation of wealth for the patient, serious investors in the company[14]—not to mention the future state of our planet and the new generations of humans and other species who will inhabit it.

The tragedy of the commons In a classic article in *Science*, Garrett Hardin described a situation that applies to all business decisions and social concerns regarding scarce resources such as clean water, air, and land.[15] Throughout human history, a commons was a tract of community land on which people grazed their animals. A commons has limited **carrying capacity,** or the ability to sustain a population, because it is a finite resource. For individual herders, short-term interest lies in adding as many animals to the commons as they can. But problems develop as more herders add more animals to graze the commons. This leads to tragedy: As each herder acts in his short-term interest, the long-run impact is the destruction of the commons. The solution is to make choices according to long-run rather than short-run consequences.

In many ways, we are witnessing this **tragedy of the commons.** Carrying capacities are shrinking as precious resources, water chief among them, become scarcer. Inevitably, conflict arises—and solutions are urgently needed.

The Environmental Movement

The 1990s were labeled the earth decade, when a new environmentalism with new features emerged.[16] For example, proponents of the new environmentalism asked companies to reduce their wastes, use resources prudently, market safe products, and take responsibility for past damages. These requests are updated and formalized in the CERES Roadmap of the 21st Century.

The new environmentalism combined many diverse viewpoints, but initially it did not blend easily with traditional business values. Some of the key aspects of this philosophy are noted in the following discussion of the history of the movement.[17]

Conservation and Environmentalism

A strand of environmental philosophy that is not at odds with business management is **conservation.** The conservation movement is anthropocentric (human centered), technologically optimistic, and concerned chiefly with the efficient use of resources. The movement seeks to avoid waste, promote the rational and efficient use of natural resources, and maximize long-term yields, especially of renewable resources.

The **environmental movement,** in contrast, historically has posed dilemmas for business management. Following the lead of early thinkers such as George Perkins Marsh (1801–1882), it has shown that the unintended negative effects of human economic activities on the environment often are greater than the benefits. For example, there are links between forest cutting and soil erosion and between the draining of marshes and lakes and the decline of animal life.

Other early environmentalists, such as John Muir (1838–1914) and Aldo Leopold (1886–1948), argued that humans are not above nature but a part of it. Nature is not for humans to subdue but is sacred and should be preserved not simply for economic use but for its own sake—and for what people can learn from it.

Science and the Environment

Rachel Carson's 1962 best-selling book, *Silent Spring,* helped ignite the modern environmental movement by alerting the public to the dangers of unrestricted pesticide use.[18] Carson brought together the findings of toxicology, ecology, and epidemiology in a form accessible to the public. Blending scientific, moral, and political arguments, she connected environmental politics and values with scientific knowledge.

Barry Commoner's *Science and Survival* (1963) continued in this vein. Commoner expanded the scope of ecology to include everything in the physical, chemical, biological, social, political, economic, and philosophical worlds.[19] He argued that all of these elements fit together and have to be understood as a whole. According to Commoner, the symptoms of environmental problems are in the biological world, but their source lies in economic and political organizations.

Economics and the Environment Economists promote growth for many reasons: to restore the balance of payments, to make nations more competitive, to create jobs, to reduce the deficit, to provide for the elderly and the sick, and to reduce poverty. Environmentalists criticize economics for its notions of efficiency and its emphasis on economic growth.[20] For example, environmentalists argue that economists do not adequately consider the unintended side effects of efficiency such as negative production externalities, which occur when a firm's production harms the environment or reduces the well-being of others who receive no benefit. Environmentalists hold that economists need to supplement estimates of the economic costs and benefits of growth with estimates of other factors that historically were not measured in economic terms.[21]

Economists and public policy analysts argue that the benefits of eliminating risk to the environment and to people must be balanced against the costs. Reducing risk involves determining how effective the proposed methods of reduction are likely to be and how much they will cost. There are many ways to consider cost factors. Analysts can perform cost-effectiveness analyses, in which they attempt to figure out how to achieve a given goal with limited resources, or they can conduct more formal risk–benefit and cost–benefit analyses, in which they quantify both the benefits and the costs of risk reduction.[22]

Qualitative Judgments in Cost–Benefit Analysis Formal, quantitative approaches to balancing costs and benefits do not eliminate the need for qualitative judgments. For example, how does one assess the value of a magnificent vista obscured by air pollution? What is the loss to society if a particular genetic strain of grass or animal species becomes extinct? How does one assess the lost opportunity costs of spending vast amounts of money on air pollution that could have been spent on productivity enhancement and global competitiveness?

Fairness cannot be ignored when doing cost–benefit analysis.[23] For example, the costs of air pollution reduction may have to be borne disproportionately by the poor in the form of higher gasoline and automobile prices. Intergenerational fairness also plays a role.[24] Future generations have no representatives in the current market and political processes. To what extent should the current generation hold back on its own consumption for the sake of posterity? This question is particularly poignant because few people in the world today are well off. To ask the poor to reduce their life's chances for the sake of a generation yet to come is asking for a great sacrifice.

International Perspectives Environmental problems present a different face in various countries and regions of the world. The United States and Great Britain lagged behind Germany and Japan in mandated emissions standards.[25] In Europe, the Dutch, the Germans, and the Danes are among the most environmentally conscious. Italy, Ireland, Spain, Portugal, and Greece are in earlier stages of developing environmental policies. Poland, Hungary, the Czech Republic, and former East Germany are among the most polluted of the world's industrialized nations.[26]

U.S. companies need to realize that there is a large market in western Europe for environmentally friendly products.

U.S. managers also need to be fully aware of the environmental movement in western Europe. Environmentalists in Europe have been successful in halting many projects, and consumers generally have been much more resistant to genetically modified foods than in the United States.[27] China has been paying a high ecological price for its rapid economic growth. But the government has begun recognizing the problem and is creating some antipollution laws.[28]

WHAT MANAGERS CAN DO

To be truly green—that is, a cutting-edge company with respect to environmental concerns—legal compliance is not enough. Progressive companies stay abreast and ahead of the laws by going beyond marginal compliance and anticipating future requirements and needs.[29] But companies can go further still by experimenting continually with innovations that protect the environment. McDonald's, for example, conducted tests and pilot projects in composting food scraps and in offering refillable coffee mugs and starch-based (biodegradable) cutlery.[30]

Systems Thinking The first thing managers can do to understand environmental issues in their companies better is to engage in systems thinking. Environmental considerations relate to the organization's inputs, processes, and outputs.[31] Inputs include raw materials and energy. Environmental pressures are causing prices of some raw materials, such as metals, to rise. This greatly increases the costs of production. Higher energy costs are causing firms to switch to more efficient sources.

Firms are considering new processes or methods of production that will reduce water pollution, air pollution, noise and vibration, and waste. They are incorporating technologies that sample and monitor (control) these by-products of business processes. Chemical plants have computerized systems that flash warnings when a maximum allowable pollution level is soon to be reached. Many companies keep only minimal stocks of hazardous materials, making serious accidents less likely.

Outputs have environmental impact, whether the products themselves or the waste or by-products of processes. To reduce the impact of its outputs, Herman Miller recycles or reuses nearly all waste from the manufacturing process. It sells fabric scraps to the auto industry, leather trim to luggage makers, and vinyl to stereo and auto manufacturers. It buys back its old furniture, refurbishes it, and resells it. Its corporatewide goal is to send zero waste to landfills. As their environmental manager stated, "There is never an acceptable level of waste at Miller. There are always new things we can learn."[32]

Strategic Integration Systems thinking reveals that environmental issues permeate the firm and therefore should be addressed in a comprehensive, integrative fashion. Start with the proper mind-set. Does your firm see environmental concerns merely in terms of a business versus environment trade-off, or does it see a potential source of competitive advantage and an important part of a strategy for long-term success? The latter attitude, of course, is more likely to set the stage for the following strategic actions.

These ideas help integrate environmental considerations strategically into the firm's ongoing activities:[33]

1. *Develop a mission statement and strong values supporting environmental advocacy.* See P&G, Genworth, Bayer, or other examples online.

2. *Establish a framework for managing environmental initiatives.* Some industries have created voluntary codes of environmental practice, such as the chemical industry's Responsible Care Initiative. Not all standard practices are adopted by all companies, however.[34] At J&J, Environmental Regulatory Affairs uses external audit teams to conduct environmental audits.[35] The Community Environmental Responsibility Program includes strategy and planning and the development of products and processes with neutral environmental impact.

3. *Engage in green process and design.* Herman Miller's leading Aeron desk chair had 200 components made from more than 800 chemical compounds. Upon learning this, they created the award-winning Mirra desk chair, using far fewer materials that are 96 percent recyclable.[36] The surface of Chicago City Hall's landscaped green roof is 70 degrees cooler in the summer than those of nearby buildings, and the air temperature just above is 15 degrees cooler. Green roofs help clean the air, serve as a wildlife habitat, and absorb and filter rain that would otherwise flood storm drains and streets.[37]

4. *Establish environmentally focused stakeholder relationships.* The E3 Initiative is a coordinated federal and local technical assistance initiative that helps manufacturers adapt and thrive in a sustainability era. It became official in September 2010. To defray costs as well as develop new ideas, small companies such as WHYCO Chromium Company establish environmental management partnerships with firms such as IBM and GM.[38]

5. *Provide internal and external education.* Engage employees in environmental actions. Dow's WRAP program has cut millions of pounds of hazardous and solid waste and emissions and achieved annual cost savings of over $10 million, all through employee suggestions.[39] At the same time, inform the public of your firm's environmental initiatives. For example, ecolabeling can urge consumers to recycle and communicate the environmental friendliness of your product. But don't greenwash—that is, engage in deceptive communication practices that do not accurately reflect the company's behavior.[40]

Implementation How can companies implement greening strategies? One tactic you read about in the chapter is life-cycle analysis.[41] That and other approaches begin with a commitment by top management. Specific actions could include commissioning an environmental audit in which an outside company checks for environmental hazards, drafting (or reviewing) the organization's environmental policy, communicating the policy and making it highly visible throughout the organization, having environmental professionals within the company report directly to the president or CEO, allocating sufficient resources to support the environmental effort, and building bridges between the organization and other companies, governments, environmentalists, and local communities.

Companies can employ all areas of the organization to meet the challenges posed by pollution and environmental challenges. A variety of companies have responded creatively to these challenges[42] and may serve as models for other organizations. The following sections describe specific actions companies can take to address environmental issues.

Strategy Actions companies can take in the area of strategy include the following:

1. *Cut back on environmentally unsafe businesses.* Du Pont, the leading producer of CFCs, voluntarily pulled out of this $750 million business.[43]

2. *Carry out R&D on environmentally safe activities.* GM is spending millions to develop hydrogen-powered cars that don't emit carbon dioxide. GE is doing research on earth-friendly hydrogen and lower-emission locomotives and jet engines.[44]

3. *Develop and expand environmental cleanup services.* Building on the expertise gained in cleaning up its own plants, Du Pont formed a safety and environmental resources division to help industrial customers clean up their toxic wastes.[45] Global Research Technologies LLC is trying to use solvents to grab carbon dioxide out of the air to isolate it for disposal.[46]

4. *Compensate for environmentally risky projects.* AES has a long-standing policy of planting trees to offset its power plants' carbon emission.[47]

5. *Make your company accountable to others.* Royal Dutch Shell and Bristol-Myers Squibb are trendsetters in green reporting.[48] Danish health care and enzymes company Novo Nordisk purposely asked for feedback from environmentalists, regulators, and other interested bodies from around Europe. Its reputation has been enhanced, its people have learned a lot, and new market opportunities have been identified.[49]

6. *Make every new product environmentally better than the last.* Intel is developing ultra-energy-efficient chips.[50] IBM uses recyclable materials, reduces hazardous materials, reduces emissions, and uses natural energy and resources in packaging.[51]

7. *Invest in green businesses.* American Electric Power Co. invested in renewable energy in Chile and retrofitted Bulgarian schools for greater efficiency.[52]

Public affairs In the area of public affairs, companies can take a variety of actions:

1. *Attempt to gain environmental legitimacy and credibility.* The cosponsors of Earth Day included Apple Computer, Hewlett-Packard, and the Chemical Manufacturers Association. McDonald's has tried to become a corporate environmental educator. Ethel M. Chocolates, in public tours of its Las Vegas factory, showcases effective handling of its industrial wastes. 1% for the Planet has inspired members of the business community to contribute 1 percent of sales to environmental groups around the world.[53]

2. *Work to improve standing in the Dow Jones Sustainability Index,* which assesses the sustainability performance of the largest companies on the Dow Jones Global Total Stock Market

Index. Companies are evaluated on long-term economic, social, and environmental asset management plans.

3. *Try to avoid losses caused by insensitivity to environmental issues.* As a result of Exxon's apparent lack of concern after the *Valdez* oil spill, 41 percent of Americans polled said they would consider boycotting the company.[54] MacMillan Bloedel lost a big chunk of sales almost overnight when it was targeted publicly as a clear-cutter and chlorine user.[55] The BP Gulf oil spill in 2010 was a disaster on many levels, including the company's inadequate and insensitive communications with the public.

4. *Collaborate with environmentalists.* Executives at Pacific Gas & Electric seek discussions and joint projects with any willing environmental group.

The legal area Actions companies can take in the legal area include the following:

1. *Try to avoid confrontation with state or federal pollution control agencies.* Browning-Ferris, Waste Management Inc. and Louisiana-Pacific were charged with pollution control violations, damaging their reputations.

2. *Comply early.* Because compliance costs only increase over time, the first companies to act will have lower costs. The European Union's Restriction of Hazardous Substances Directive, which regulates the use of lead in electronics products, took effect in July 2006. Hewlett-Packard realized in the previous decade that lead is toxic and governments would one day ban lead solders. Experiments begun in the early 1990s led to new solders that are an amalgam of tin, silver, and copper. HP was able to comply with the directive immediately, long before others. HP and Cisco try to comply with the most stringent legal standards in the world, thus positioning themselves to be ahead of the requirements of other countries.[56]

3. *Take advantage of innovative compliance programs.* The EU started a carbon-cutting and trading system in 2005.[57] Instead of source-by-source reduction, the EPA's bubble policy allows factories to reduce pollution at different sources by different amounts, provided the overall result is equivalent. Therefore, 3M installed equipment on only certain production lines at its tape-manufacturing facility in Pennsylvania, thereby lowering its compliance costs.[58] *Joint implementation* involves companies in industrialized nations working with businesses in developing countries to help them reduce greenhouse gas emissions. The company lending a hand then receives credit toward fulfilling its environmental obligations at home. The developing country receives investment, technology, and jobs; the company giving a lending hand receives environmental credits; and the world gets cleaner air.[59]

4. *Don't deal with fly-by-night subcontractors for waste disposal.* They are more likely to cut corners, break laws, and do a poor job. Moreover, the result for you could be bad publicity and legal problems.[60]

Operations The actions companies can take in the area of operations include the following:

1. *Promote new manufacturing technologies.* Louisville Gas and Electric took the lead in installing smokestack scrubbers, Consolidated Natural Gas pioneered the use of clean-burning technologies, and Nucor developed state-of-the-art steel mills.

2. *Practice reverse logistics.* Firms move packaging and other used goods from the consumer back up the distribution channel to the firm. Make them not just costs but a source of revenue—inputs to production. Fuji Australia believes that remanufacturing has generated returns in the tens of millions of dollars.[61]

3. *Encourage technological advances that reduce pollution from products and manufacturing processes.* Cinergy and AEP are working on technologies that capture carbon as coal is burned and pump it deep into the ground to be stored for thousands of years.[62] 3M's Pollution Prevention Pays has saved the company more than $1 billion.[63] Pollution prevention, more than pollution control, is related to both better environmental performance and better manufacturing performance, including cost and speed.[64]

4. *Develop new product formulations.* The Chicago Transit Authority and Union Pacific Corporation replaced traditional wood railroad ties with plastic ties. Other companies experimented with making recycled cross-ties of old tires, grocery bags, milk jugs, and Styrofoam cups.[65] Weyerhaeuser, recognizing the decreasing supply of timber and growing demand, is working to produce high-quality wood on fewer, continuously regenerated acres.[66] Electrolux has developed a sun-powered lawn mower and a chainsaw that runs on vegetable oil.[67]

5. *Eliminate manufacturing wastes.* The city of San Francisco has targeted zero waste by 2020. 3M replaced volatile solvents with water-based ones, thereby eliminating the need for costly air pollution control equipment. DuPont, consistent with its "zero waste" commitment, shed its carpet and nylon businesses, in part because of their big eco-footprints.[68] Walmart's Sustainability 360 established goals to purchase 100 percent renewable energy, create zero waste, and slash greenhouse gas emissions.[69]

6. *Reduce waste and recycle.* In Canada, most beer bottles are refillable, and return rates approach 100 percent.[70] Most bottles are reused 15 to 20 times before recycling. FedEx has developed dozens of software programs to optimize aircraft schedules and flight routes and uses hybrid vans and efficient aircraft to reduce fuel consumption.

7. *Find alternative uses for wastes.* When DuPont halted ocean dumping of acid iron salts, it discovered that the salts could be sold to water treatment plants at a profit. A Queensland sugarcane facility powers production via sugarcane waste.[72]

8. *Insist that your suppliers have strong environmental performance.* Scott Paper discovered that many of its environmental problems were imported through the supply chain. Scott dropped the worst performers and announced that the best performers would in the future receive preference in its purchasing decisions.[73] Unilever will soon be purchasing palm oil and tea exclusively from sustainable sources.[74] Staples gets materials for most of its paper-based products from sustainable-yield forests.[75] McDonald's shows its commitment to global fish stocks because the Marine Stewardship Council certifies that its Filet-O-Fish sandwiches use fish from sustainable fisheries.[76]

9. *Assemble products with the environment in mind.* Make them easy to snap apart, sort, and recycle, and avoid glues and screws.

Marketing Companies can also take action in the marketing area:

1. *Cast products in an environment-friendly light.* Most Americans believe a company's environmental reputation influences what they buy.[77] Seventh Generation Products are not tested on animals, are kosher-certified, and use hydrogen peroxide rather than chlorine bleach and plant-derived cleaning agents rather than petroleum-based cleaners. A Chinese entrepreneur is making underwear out of soybean by-products.[78] Other eco-friendly fibers are made from hemp and bamboo, which require little pesticide.

2. *Avoid attacks by environmentalists for unsubstantiated or inappropriate claims.* When Hefty marketed biodegradable garbage bags, that claim was technically true, but it turned out that landfill conditions didn't allow decomposition to occur.[79] The extensive public backlash affected not only Hefty bags but also other Hefty products. Hefty didn't lie, but it did exaggerate. Its tactics overshadowed well-intentioned greening actions.

3. *Differentiate your product via environmental services.* Teach customers how to use and dispose of products; for instance, farmers inadvertently abuse pesticides. Make education part of a firm's after-sales service. Waste Management, formerly just a waste-trucking company, set up a unit to generate value from waste; it now shows customers how to reduce waste and recover value from waste.[80]

4. *Take advantage of the net.* The EcoMall (www.ecomall.com/biz/) promotes a number of environmentally oriented firms. Firms can target green consumers globally, effectively, and efficiently.[81]

Accounting Actions companies can take in the accounting area include the following:

1. *Collect useful data.* The best reporters of environmental information include Dow Europe, Danish Steel, BSO/Origin, 3M, and Monsanto.[82]

2. *Make polluters pay.* CIBA-GEIGY has a "polluter pays" principle throughout the firm, so managers have the incentive to combat pollution at the sources they can influence.[83]

3. *Demonstrate that antipollution programs pay off.* 3M's Pollution Prevention Pays program is based on the premise that only if the program pays will there be the motivation to carry it out. Every company needs to be cost-effective in its pollution reduction efforts.

4. *Use an advanced waste accounting system.* Do this in addition to standard management accounting, which can hinder investment in new technologies. Waste accounting makes sure all costs are identified and better decisions can be made.

5. *Adopt full-cost accounting.* This approach ensures that the price of a product reflects its full environmental cost.[84] Puma, of the French PPR Group (which includes Yves Saint Laurent and Stella McCartney among others), commissioned Price-

WaterhouseCoopers to develop the EP&L statement, calling it "hard-nosed economics."[85]

6. *Show the overall impact of the pollution reduction program.* Companies have an obligation to account for the costs and benefits of their pollution reduction programs. 3M has saved billions from pollution prevention efforts.

Finance In the area of finance, companies can do the following:

1. *Gain the respect of the socially responsible investment community.* Deutsche Asset Management, CalPERS, and Nikko Asset management are integrating sustainability into investment decision making in all asset classes.[86] The Ariel Fund screens for environmental impact, tobacco, weapons, nuclear energy, and lack of diversity. Orientation has shifted from negative (problem companies) to positive (companies that are most environmentally viable in the long run). Terminology has shifted from "socially responsible" companies to "sustainable investing."[87]

2. *Recognize true liability.* Investment houses often employ environmental analysts who search for companies' true environmental liability in evaluating their potential performance. Bankers look at environmental risks and environmental market opportunities when evaluating a company's credit rating.[88] The Securities and Exchange Commission in New York requires some companies to report certain environmental costs.

3. *Fund and then assist green companies.* Ann Winblad was one of the first venture capitalists to coach green entrepreneurs to increase their business skills and chances of success.[89]

4. *Recognize financial opportunities.* Worldwide, one of these great opportunities is water. Water must be purified and delivered reliably to everyone worldwide. Billions of people lack sanitary sewage facilities and have poor access to drinking water. Infrastructures in big cities, including those in the United States, are seriously deteriorating. Supplying clean water to people and companies is a huge industry. Companies are aggressively pursuing this market. They are betting that water in the 21st century will be like oil in the 20th century.

KEY TERMS

carrying capacity   The ability of a finite resource to sustain a population. p. 180

conservation   An environmental philosophy that seeks to avoid waste, promote the rational and efficient use of natural resources, and maximize long-term yields, especially of renewable resources. p. 180

environmental movement   An environmental philosophy postulating that the unintended negative effects of human economic activities on the environment are often greater than the benefits, and that nature should be preserved. p. 180

tragedy of the commons   The environmental destruction that results as individuals and businesses consume finite resources (the commons) to serve their short-term interests without regard for the long-term consequences. p. 180

DISCUSSION QUESTIONS

1. To what extent can and should we rely on government to solve environmental problems? What are some of government's limitations? Take a stand on the role and usefulness of government regulations on business activities.

2. To what extent should managers today be responsible for cleaning up mistakes from years past that have hurt the environment?

3. How would you characterize the environmental movement in western Europe? How does it differ from the U.S. movement? What difference will this make to a multinational company that wants to produce and market goods in many countries?

4. What business opportunities can you see in meeting environmental challenges? Be specific.

5. You are appointed environmental manager of XYZ Company. Describe some actions you will take to address environmental challenges. Discuss obstacles you are likely to encounter in the company and how you will manage them.

6. Interview a businessperson about environmental regulations and report your findings to the class. How would you characterize his or her attitude? How constructive is his or her attitude?

7. Interview a businessperson about actions he or she has taken that have helped the environment. Report your findings to the class and discuss.

8. Identify and discuss some examples of the tragedy of the commons. How can the tragedies be avoided?

9. Discuss the status of recycling efforts in your community or school, your perspectives on it as a consumer, and what business opportunities could be available.

10. What companies currently come to mind as having the best and worst reputations with respect to the environment? Why do they have these reputations?

11. Choose one product and discuss its environmental impact through its entire life cycle.

12. What are you, your college or university, and your community doing about the environment? What would you recommend doing?

CHAPTER 6

International Management

It was once said that the sun never set on the British Empire. Today, the sun does set on the British Empire, but not on the scores of global empires, including those of IBM, Unilever, Volkswagen, and Hitachi.

— LESTER BROWN

LEARNING OBJECTIVES

CHAPTER OUTLINE

Managing in a (Sometimes) Flat World
Implications of a Flat World
The Role of Outsourcing

The Global Environment
European Unification
Asia: China and India's Ascent
The Americas
Africa and the Middle East

Global Strategy
Pressures for Global Integration
Pressures for Local Responsiveness
Choosing a Global Strategy

Entry Mode
Exporting
Licensing
Franchising

Joint Ventures
Wholly Owned Subsidiaries

Managing across Borders
Skills of the Global Manager
Understanding Cultural Issues
Ethical Issues in International Management

Management Connection

HOW LENOVO IS BECOMING A GLOBAL BRAND

Sales in China have fueled growth that propelled Lenovo onto the world stage. Today, the electronics company led by chief executive Yang Yuanqing is fighting a close battle with Hewlett-Packard for first place in market share for personal computers, with plans to become a leader in smart phone sales as well. *The Wall Street Journal* has called Lenovo "the first Chinese global consumer brand."

Until 2005, Lenovo was a Chinese manufacturer serving Chinese customers. But China is a huge marketplace, and sales there brought in a lot of revenue as the company developed its expertise in the high-tech sector. That cash came in handy when IBM decided to get out of the business of selling laptop computers. Lenovo surprised the Western world by purchasing IBM's laptop division, including the ThinkPad brand name.

Lenovo assumed it would need Western-style management to compete in the West, so it hired an American executive to run the laptop business. But by 2009, sales had slumped. Businesses, which had been the ThinkPad's main customers, were cutting back in the Great Recession, and Lenovo lacked strong relationships with retailers. Yang, who rose through the ranks after starting as a Lenovo salesperson, took back the reins with one of Lenovo's founders, Liu Chuanzhi, who returned as chairman. Together, they crafted Lenovo's strategy for international expansion—start by targeting fast-growing developing economies and use the revenues to enter additional markets as the brand and company strengthened.

Lenovo focused on expanding its presence through retailers in China, India, Russia, and Brazil. This strategy generated sales growth in computers even while the worldwide market for PCs slumped as consumers in North America switched to tablet computers and European customers struggled with economic stagnation

in their region. Lenovo is the top brand in the high-potential market of India, where less than 10 percent of the population owns a personal computer. Brazil, too, has a large population with rising incomes, and Lenovo expects that market to represent one of its biggest in the future.

Lenovo's strategy for smart phones is similar. In China, Lenovo is among the top brands in the biggest market for the devices. In just one recent quarter, Lenovo sold 9 million smart phones in China. The company has recently moved into India, Indonesia, and Russia, where the market for smart phones, like the market for PCs, is potentially huge. While others in the PC industry are struggling in mature markets, Lenovo has recently boasted record profits, even profiting in the highly competitive market for smart phones.[1]

How well can Lenovo's commitment to meeting the needs of developing economies appeal to consumers around the world? As you read this chapter, consider what qualities of the international business environment present threats and opportunities for this company.

The direction of Lenovo's growth resembles that of many successful businesses in recent decades. The company started out by satisfying customers in a local market. As sales increased, the company began serving a larger region. Eventually, it began selling goods to and running operations in other countries. Now it boasts sales and develops managers around the globe.

Today's corporate giants—and many ambitious, creative small businesses—need employees and sales in other countries to meet their objectives. U.S. multinational corporations now employ almost one-third of their workers outside the United States, and the overseas share is growing. Sales of some product categories also are growing faster outside the United States. That's why GE, for example, earns 60 percent of its revenues outside the United States (versus 30 percent in 2000) and has over half its workforce outside the United States (54 percent, up from 46 percent in 2000).[2] Or consider Walt Disney Company. After years of negotiations, the iconic U.S. company began construction of a theme park and resort in Shanghai. The deal is complex because the Chinese government insisted on Chinese ownership, but for Disney it was worthwhile because it wants to bring its brand of entertainment to China's vast population and rapidly developing economy.[3]

Because of such trends, today's managers need to be able to plan how their company will enter markets around the world. That planning begins with understanding the importance of the global economy and the opportunities and threats of the fast-changing global environment.

Managing in a (Sometimes) Flat World

The global economy matters precisely because it *is* global—because your customers, employees, and suppliers could be located anywhere in the world. Several years ago, *New York Times* columnist Thomas Friedman wrote a best seller about this phenomenon. His book, *The World Is Flat*, described how such trends as the Internet and trade agreements between more and more nations have made international business the norm today. Whether you are a large or small company looking for financing, supplies, employees, machinery, natural resources, or transportation services, you can readily go online and find the mix of price and quality that is right for you. In that way, according to Friedman, the business environment has become a level playing field—in a word, flat.

But if "flat" is taken to mean everyone has the same advantages or buys the same products, it hardly describes the real world. Internet connectivity doesn't necessarily make us more aware of every idea or interested in every global trend. Sometimes individuals go online to connect with people they already know and to buy products that are tailored to their own particular tastes. And sometimes a local government still makes it hard for a business to grow, or a community lacks the resources to encourage development. In that sense, the world is not always flat; it is often bumpy.[4] For managers, that makes the business environment more complex and exciting than ever: a global economy with threats and opportunities around the world, accompanied by a requirement to know their customers' specific needs and values, which may vary considerably from place to place.

Later in this chapter, we will describe how managers can select strategies for the world's bumpiness. But first, let's see how the ever-greater interconnection, or integration, of the world economy is shaping the way business is done today.

Implications of a Flat World

LO 1

As you will see later in the chapter, increasing prosperity and the lowering of trade barriers have increased the extent to which the economies of different nations are integrated into one global economy. The increasing integration of the global economy has had many consequences. First, even as the world's economic output has grown, the volume of exports has increased much faster. The severe global recession of 2009 caused a one-year dip in output and trade, but exports surged the following year and have continued to climb since then.[5] Years of emphasis on international commerce by major industrial countries, liberalized trading brought about by free trade agreements, and market reforms in China have resulted in lowering the barriers to the free flow of goods, services, and capital among nation–states. The impact of these trends is staggering. The dollar value of international trade (merchandise exports and commercial services) is over $17.7 trillion—up from just a few hundred billion dollars in the 1960s and 1970s. For example, Figure 6.1 shows how the international trade of the United States (exports of goods and services) increased relative to the country's output since the 1990s. Despite some dips during recessions, the percentage of goods and services exported to other countries has risen from 10 percent to 14 percent of U.S. gross domestic product. And for durable goods (manufactured goods such as computers and machinery designed to last for several years), more than 20 percent of these products shipped are now exports. Most experts expect competition to increase as trade is liberalized, and as is often the case, the more efficient players will survive. To succeed in this industrial climate, managers need to study opportunities in existing markets as well as work to enhance the competitiveness of their firms.

A second consequence of increased global integration is that foreign direct investment (FDI) is playing an ever-increasing role in the global economy as companies of all sizes invest overseas. In particular, the foreign direct investment flows to less developed countries from firms in developed countries have risen substantially.[6] Investment by foreign companies and individuals in U.S. firms is also huge: $2.3 trillion, close to double the 2000 level, with the majority coming from European investors. In recent years, the United States has received more foreign direct investment than any other country.[7] To give two examples, Deutsche Boerse, a German provider of securities trading, arranged to buy the parent company of the New York Stock Exchange, and a Chinese company called Geely bought the Volvo business unit from Ford Motor Company.[8] In recent years, China's role as an export powerhouse has allowed the Chinese government to amass about $1 trillion in foreign exchange reserves, of which it is expected to invest hundreds of billions of dollars.[9]

A third consequence of an increasingly integrated global economy is that imports are penetrating deeper into the world's largest economies. For example, high percentages of the clothing and textile products, paper, cut diamonds, and electronics

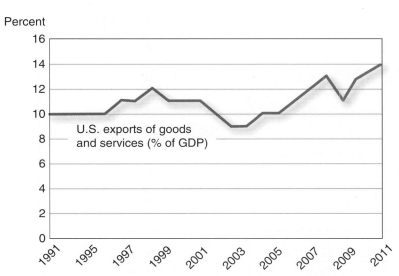

Percent

FIGURE 6.1

U.S. Exports as a Share of U.S. Output (goods and services)

U.S. exports of goods and services (% of GDP)

Source: World Bank, "World Development Indicators," *World DataBank*, http://databank.worldbank.org.

consumed in the United States are imported. Until recently, most of the canned peaches sold in the United States were cling peaches grown in California, but China's share of this market has been skyrocketing and now represents more than 1 out of every 10 cans sold. And in the automobile industry, over half of the new cars sold in the United States in 2010 were from automakers based in other countries, primarily in Asia.[10] Figure 6.2 shows how the world trade of manufactured merchandise has grown relative to other product groups. The growth of imports is a natural by-product of the growth of world trade and the trend toward the manufacture of component parts, or even entire products, overseas before shipping them back home for final sale.

Finally, the growth of world trade, FDI, and imports implies that companies around the globe are finding their home markets under attack from foreign competitors. This is true in the United States, where Japanese automakers have captured market share from General Motors, Ford, and Chrysler, and in western Europe, where the once-dominant Dutch company Philips N. V. has lost market share in the consumer electronics industry to Japan's JVC, Matsushita, and Sony.

> Companies both large and small now view the world as their marketplace.

What does all this mean for today's managers? Compared with only a few years ago, opportunities are greater because the movement toward free trade has opened up many formerly protected national markets. The potential for export and for making direct investments overseas is greater today than ever before. The environment is more complex because today's manager often has to deal with the challenges of doing business in countries with radically different cultures and coordinating globally dispersed operations. The environment is more competitive because in addition to domestic competitors, the manager must deal with cost-efficient overseas competitors.

Companies both large and small now view the world, rather than a single country, as their marketplace. As Figure 6.3 shows, the United States has no monopoly on

FIGURE 6.2

Relative Growth in World Merchandise Exports by Major Product Group, 1950–2011

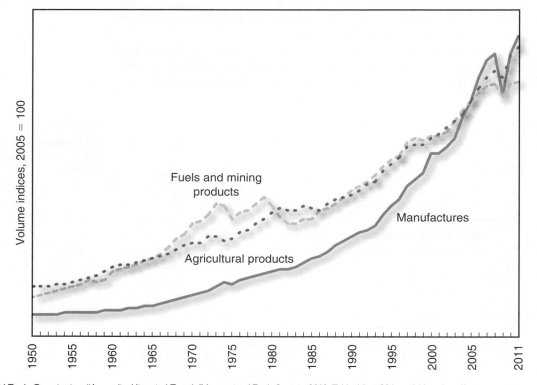

Source: World Trade Organization, "Appendix: Historical Trends," *International Trade Statistics 2012*, Table A1, p. 204, available at http://www.wto.org.

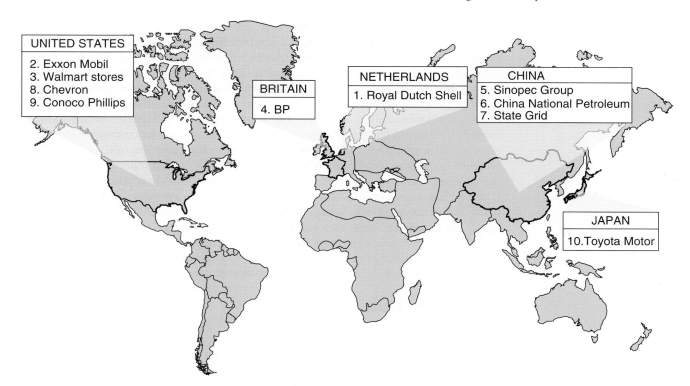

UNITED STATES

2. Exxon Mobil
3. Walmart stores
8. Chevron
9. Conoco Phillips

BRITAIN

4. BP

NETHERLANDS

1. Royal Dutch Shell

CHINA

5. Sinopec Group
6. China National Petroleum
7. State Grid

JAPAN

10. Toyota Motor

Source: "Global 500," *Fortune*, July 23, 2012, http://money.cnn.com/magazines/fortune/global500/2012/full_list.

FIGURE 6.3
Top 10 Global Firms

international business. Of the top 25 corporations in the world, 16 are based in countries outside the United States. Also, companies have dispersed their manufacturing, marketing, and research facilities to those locations around the globe where cost and skill conditions are most favorable. This trend is now so pervasive in industries such as automobiles, aerospace, and electronics that it is becoming increasingly irrelevant to talk about "American products" or "Japanese products" or "German products."

For example, the headquarters of an automaker no longer says much about where a particular car is made. According to the National Highway Traffic Safety Administration, despite the Jeep Patriot's red-white-and-blue name, only 66 percent of its components are made in the United States. In contrast, although Toyota is a Japanese-headquartered company, 80 percent of the parts in a Toyota Sequoia are produced in the United States. A U.S. headquarters doesn't limit a U.S. car company either. General Motors reports that it employs more people, sells more cars, and sees its best growth prospects outside the United States.[11]

Such internationalization is not limited to the largest corporations. An increasing number of medium-size and small firms also engage in international trade. Some companies have limited their involvement to exporting, whereas others set up production facilities overseas. Jade Corporation, which started out as a tool and die maker, operates three facilities with a few hundred employees. The company found it difficult to compete as U.S. manufacturing operations moved overseas, but creative management continued to find opportunities. As the company moved into making more specialized products, it developed its engineering capabilities and its experience in working with a Singapore manufacturer. Eventually, Jade began working with clients to set up manufacturing facilities in Asia. Jade employees first learn about the customer's product and the way to make it, and then they use their overseas connections to get the customer's foreign plant running.[12] Responding to the dominance of English on the Internet, an Israeli software start-up developed a program called WhiteSmoke, which uses artificial intelligence to analyze written English, not only checking for spelling and grammar errors but also suggesting ways to make the writing clearer and more natural. The company originally found a customer base among Israeli lawyers and tech workers. Since then, the ease of downloading a program online has expanded the market to computer users in the United States. The company next began negotiating with distributors to sell WhiteSmoke in China and India. The global nature of the Internet has provided both the need and a major means of distributing WhiteSmoke.[13]

Some of the reasons managers collaborate with their overseas counterparts on trade are obvious. Other countries offer expanded markets for one's own products. In turn, they might have natural resources, products, or cost structures that managers need but that aren't available in the home country. But there are other, perhaps less obvious, benefits to collaborating with other countries on trade. Because trade allows each country to obtain more efficiently what it cannot as easily produce on its own, it lowers prices overall and makes more goods more widely available. This in turn raises living standards—and may broaden the market for a manager's own products, both locally and abroad. Trade also makes new technologies and methods more widely available, again raising the standard of living and improving efficiency. Finally, collaborating with others on trade creates links between people and cultures that, particularly over the long run, can lead to cooperation in other areas.

The Role of Outsourcing

outsourcing

Contracting with an outside provider to produce one or more of an organization's goods or services.

offshoring

Moving work to other countries.

In recent years, the issues of offshoring and outsourcing have become sources of controversy. **Outsourcing** occurs when an organization contracts with an outside provider to produce one or more of its goods or services. **Offshoring** occurs when companies move jobs to another country, typically where wages are lower. This practice does not necessarily require using an outside provider. Companies with large workforces can resource globally. However, most of the concerns expressed about offshoring refer to outsourcing because people conclude that high-paying U.S. jobs are being lost to low-cost countries overseas. The concern is prompted by widespread reports of major corporations relocating assembly lines, computer programming, help centers, and other parts of their operations to India or China. One study has estimated that by 2015, more than 3 million U.S. jobs will be sent abroad.[14] Economist Alan Blinder raised the possibility that communication technology will lead to the offshoring of at least 30 million jobs over the longer term. For example, the work of bookkeepers, accounting clerks, computer programmers, data entry keyers, and financial analysts can be performed anywhere and submitted to the customer or employer electronically.[15]

The decline in manufacturing employment in the United States is evident. During the previous decade, the United States lost 2 million manufacturing jobs as well as 1.6 million office and administrative support jobs. During the recession in 2009, more workers in the United States were laid off than abroad. Some economists blame certain conditions in the United States for making the business climate relatively unfavorable: taxes, declining infrastructure, inadequate education, and barriers to hiring skilled immigrant workers.[16] However, considerable evidence suggests that the cause of this job decline is not offshoring but innovation. Because of new technology and processes, managers simply need fewer workers to produce the same quantity of goods. Even as manufacturing employment has declined, manufacturing output in the United States has grown. In addition, technology and trade enable the creation of new jobs. Even as manufacturing jobs have been lost, the United States has gained millions of new jobs, including 3.2 million service jobs, 2.5 million professional jobs, and 1.3 million managerial jobs. Thus the important question may not be how to prevent offshoring from taking jobs but how to prepare the workforce for the types of jobs that will be needed in the United States of the future—jobs requiring personal interaction (such as the work of doctors or counselors), hands-on activity (plumbers, janitors), and tailoring to particular situations (identifying clients' needs rather than following a routine).[17]

The statistics on offshoring often overlook that the job transfers from offshoring represent a small fraction of the 135 million jobs in the United States. Most jobs require workers to be close to their markets—people still shop at their local supermarkets and appliance dealers, visit their doctors, and attend a community school. Perhaps most important, as offshoring increases efficiency, it frees funds for expansion and additional employment. The challenge is primarily one in which individual workers are deeply affected when their jobs are lost. Some organizations determine that they have a social responsibility to participate in retraining programs to help these displaced workers identify and prepare for jobs that are less likely to move overseas. The controversy over offshoring also overlooks the extent to which foreign companies hire workers in the United States—for example, when Germany's BMW runs a South Carolina assembly plant for its X5 sport utility vehicle.

An increasing number of American companies are outsourcing and off-shoring divisions and departments of their organizations to save money. Many call centers are now located in India, where wages are still much lower than in the United States. Here is a photo of a typical call center in Hyderabad, India.

One less positive effect of offshoring has been wage stagnation in industries where offshoring is common because workers in those areas compete with their lower-wage counterparts abroad. On the other hand, wages, energy costs, and other expenses in some of those other countries have started to rise, reducing the benefits of offshoring.[18] Some firms have looked for lower costs outside India and China by heading for Bangladesh, Vietnam, and Indonesia, whereas others are testing the potential of operations in African countries.

In recent years, automation has reduced the percentage of product costs that can be attributed to labor, making it less necessary to consider moving jobs overseas. Also, managers who offshore to achieve wage savings alone often incur unexpected additional costs in travel, training, quality control, language barriers, and the resistance of some customers who prefer to deal with local personnel. However, offshoring is a continuing trend because in some cases it delivers advantages other than cost. For some types of work, companies use offshoring as a way to find talent that is in short supply at home. A survey of software firms found that the main reasons for offshoring were to enable the company to grow and to get products to market faster. The companies either have difficulty finding enough programmers in the United States or determine that they can keep a project moving ahead around the clock as U.S. and overseas teams hand the project back and forth. Similarly, by outsourcing a project to a specialist firm, a company can quickly have hundreds of people devoted to it, dramatically shortening the turnaround time.[19]

In short, in deciding whether to offshore, managers should not start out with the assumption that it will be cheaper for them to do so. Instead, here are some of the factors they might take into account:

What is the competitive advantage of the products they offer? If, say, rapid delivery, reliability, and customer contact are paramount, then offshoring is a less attractive option. But if the product is widely available and standardized, like a calculator, and the only competitive advantage is price, the lowest possible production cost becomes essential and offshoring becomes something managers will consider.

Is the business in its early stages? If so, offshoring may well be inappropriate because managers need to stay close to the business and its customers to solve problems and make sure everything is going according to plan. When the business is more mature, managers can afford to consider moving some operations overseas.

Can production savings be achieved locally? Automation can often achieve significant labor cost savings and eliminate the advantage of moving production abroad. Where automation savings are not feasible, as with computer call centers, then offshoring becomes a more attractive option.

Can the entire supply chain be improved? As we discussed in Chapter 2, enormous productivity savings are possible when managers develop an efficient supply chain, from suppliers to manufacturing to customers. These improvements permit both lower cost and high customer responsiveness. If the supply chain is not a major consideration, or is already highly efficient or routine, and more savings are needed, then offshoring may be one way for managers to achieve additional efficiencies.[20]

These considerations lead to a variety of decisions about where to operate. The high costs of transporting heavy appliances are one reason GE decided to move some of its appliance manufacturing back to the United States. Master Lock, based in Milwaukee, Wisconsin, also found that returning production to the United States from China had become more cost-effective. Fortunately for the company, it still had some production facilities and employees in the United States; companies that previously outsourced all production have found that their options for bringing manufacturing home are now more limited.[21]

The Global Environment

LO 2

The global economy is becoming more integrated than ever before.

As we saw in Chapter 2, an organization's external environment includes its economic, technological, legal/regulatory, demographic, social, and natural environments. When today's managers think about, for example, the economic potential of a market, the laws that both protect their property and restrain their conduct, and the resources they need for making products, they should be thinking about these in terms of where the best opportunities lie anywhere in the world. The simple fact is that technology and an integrated economy are making international business inescapable. Table 6.1 provides examples of current issues we will consider in each area of this international environment.

The global economy is becoming more integrated than ever before. For example, the World Trade Organization (WTO), formed in 1995, now has 159 member countries involved in most of the world's trade. The newest members are Laos, Montenegro, the Russian Federation, Samoa, Tajikistan, and Vanuatu. (The International Monetary Fund, set up by the United Nations in 1945, serves a similar purpose and includes 188 countries.) The WTO provides a forum for nations to negotiate trade agreements and procedures for administering the agreements and resolving disputes. Issues that are currently under negotiation because they have been difficult for the parties to resolve include objections to environmental regulations and subsidies to

TABLE 6.1
Key Issues of the Global Environment

Economic environment	Foreign investment; growth of developing nations; rising wages in developing nations
Technological environment	Internet and wireless technology
Legal/regulatory environment	Free trade agreements; anticorruption laws
Demographics	Aging population in developed nations; growing population worldwide, especially in the developing world
Social issues	Cultural differences; bribery concerns
Natural environment	Intensifying demand for resources, including oil, water, and food; growing desire for sustainable products and operations; increasingly endangered species; climate change

farmers in developed countries, on the grounds that they conflict with free trade. To follow how these issues are playing out, you can explore the "Trade Topics" section of the WTO website, http://www.wto.org.

The global economy is dominated by countries in three regions: North America, western Europe, and Asia. However, other developing countries and regions represent important areas for economic growth as well.

European Unification

Europe is integrating economically to form the biggest market in the world. Under the Maastricht Treaty, which formally established the European Union (EU), the euro was adopted as a common currency among 13 member countries. Currencies with a long history like the franc and the mark are now relics of the past. The EU allows most goods, services, capital, and human resources to flow freely across its national borders. The EU was originally formed after World War II to foster cooperation through trade in place of military conflict, but the efforts have also created an economic superpower. Its 27 members now boast a population of more than 495 million and a GDP (gross domestic product) exceeding that of the United States.[22]

The pace of European unification accelerated in 2004 with the addition of former Eastern-bloc countries, including Poland and Hungary, and in 2007 Bulgaria and Romania joined. Many of these new members offer a particular challenge to full integration because as former communist countries they do not have extensive experience as modern market economies. Other even less wealthy countries—Croatia, Macedonia, and Turkey—have also applied to join the EU.

In addition to the difficulty of integrating widely divergent economies, certain structural issues within Europe need to be corrected for the EU to function effectively. In particular, western Europeans on average work fewer hours, earn more pay, take longer vacations, and enjoy far more social entitlements than do their counterparts in North America and Asia. To be competitive in a global economy, Europeans must increase their level of productivity. Other problems will present even greater challenges, such as Europe's aging population, low birthrates, and low immigration, all of which are threatening to cause Europe's population to drop, even as America's is increasing. Recently, EU relationships were tested by the global financial crisis and recession, which hit some member nations harder than others. For example, Ireland, which had been enjoying impressive growth in the banking and insurance sectors, suffered the near-collapse of those industries. With tax revenues falling even as citizens needed more help, the governments of Portugal, Ireland, and Greece found themselves petitioning other EU nations for financial assistance. The economically stronger nations were reluctant to ask their own citizens to support a bailout of other countries but eventually agreed to provide loans through the EU and International Monetary Fund. That assistance is accompanied by requirements that the less stable governments bring more discipline to their spending habits. That, in the end, may make the EU even more potent than it was before.[23]

Still, unification is creating a more competitive Europe, one that U.S. managers will increasingly have to take into account. The economic difficulties in the region have brought down the costs of investing and hiring workers there, and the region boasts a highly skilled workforce. Dow Chemical, for example, has taken advantage of the opportunity to build a research center to study water desalination in Spain; in Ireland, Microsoft is building a data center, and Eli Lilly expects to erect a facility for making biopharmaceuticals. Companies such as these are hoping Europe will recover from its financial woes, and they will be ready for the next surge in demand.[24]

The EU also presents a regulatory challenge to the United States and other countries. For example, the EU has supported excluding genetically engineered food products from American firms, over objections from the WTO. It has fined Microsoft for what it says are unreasonable prices Microsoft charges rival software firms to give

Bottom Line
Globalization requires improvements in all bottom-line practices. *Why might innovation be important for a U.S. company in a global market?*

them the information and documentation they need to develop products compatible with the Windows operating system. The EU required the documentation as a remedy to remove its antitrust charges.[25]

The EU's more competitive and regulatory environment clearly presents new challenges to managers and their employees. Managers in U.S. companies that wish to export to that market must become more knowledgeable about the new business environment the EU is creating. Management and labor will have to work cooperatively to achieve high levels of quality to make U.S. goods and services attractive to consumers in Europe and other markets around the world. The United States needs managers who will stay on top of worldwide developments and manage high-quality, efficient organizations as well as a well-educated, well-trained, and continually *retrained* labor force to remain competitive with the Europeans and other formidable competitors.

Asia: China and India's Ascent

Among the Pacific Rim countries, and particularly in the United States, Japan dominated world attention toward the end of the last century. Today Japan is America's fourth-largest export market, after Canada, China, and Mexico, as you can see in Figure 6.4. And Japan is in fourth place as a source of U.S. imports. Japanese companies such as Toyota are both a major source of goods and, as competitors, a growing influence in the ways U.S. managers seek quality and efficiency.

Today, however, a bigger force is rising in Asia: China. With the world's largest population and increasing industrialization, China is on its way to becoming the largest producer and consumer of many of the world's goods. Its large and growing demand for oil is a cost factor that managers everywhere must consider in their long-range planning. The country has also become the world's largest consumer of basic raw materials, such as steel and cement, as well as the world's largest cell phone market. Not only is China the largest source of imports to the United States (see Figure 6.4), but it has surged ahead of Germany to become the world's largest exporter and is the number two importer after the United States.[26]

As a consuming nation, China's appeal to managers lies in its large population of 1.3 billion people and its rapid economic growth. As more and more Chinese people earn engineering and science degrees and as labor demand pushes up wages, Chinese

FIGURE 6.4

Top U.S. Trading Partners, Based on Total Imports and Exports

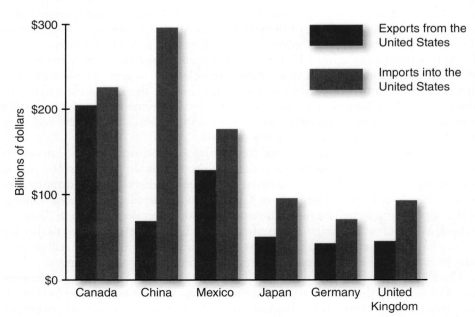

SOURCE: U.S. Bureau of the Census, *Statistical Abstract of the United States: 2011*, Table 1306, http://www.census.gov.

companies are branching out into more complex manufacturing operations, such as auto parts, optical devices,
and other advanced electronics. Rising incomes create
a paradox for business expansion: Newly middle-class
consumers in China are purchasing more products,
both foreign and domestic, and low-cost manufacturers
are now looking away from China to set up operations
in lower-wage countries, such as Vietnam.[27] Other
companies are staying in China to serve the huge market there. General Motors, for example, is setting up
research and design facilities in China so it can introduce innovations aimed at satisfying the demands of
Chinese consumers, starting with battery power.[28]

Even with its growing consumption, China has had
an even greater global impact in its role as an export-
ing nation. The enormous size of its labor force, combined with its low labor costs,
has given it a competitive advantage in manufacturing. Just a few years ago, estimates

This Chevy Volt electric car is
charging in the parking lot in
Shanghai at General Motors
headquarters.

In Practice

DISNEY'S ENGLISH SCHOOLS IN SHANGHAI

Several U.S. and European companies have sensed opportunity in the estimated 300 million
Chinese people learning English—and presumably many millions more who want to learn,
given the chance. British publisher Pearson PLC and Sweden-based school operator English
First SV have emphasized adult education, but Walt Disney Company sees a profitable
niche market in teaching children.

Disney has opened a chain of Disney English schools in Shanghai and has drawn up
plans to operate in Beijing. Managers insist that the mission of the schools is simply to
teach English to Chinese children, but that mission requires books and worksheets, and
they just happen to be populated with Buzz Lightyear, Ariel the Mermaid, and other characters from Disney's movies. Young students can earn rewards such as stickers and CDs
featuring Disney characters and productions. Rather than being repelled by the marketing
angle, Chinese parents see a chance for their children to learn from a company that is
familiar and truly international.

For Disney, the schools offer an opportunity to connect with families in an environment that is otherwise politically tricky. Although the Chinese government limits movie
and television distribution of Disney productions, Disney English can offer students all the
Disney-themed worksheets, backpacks, and toys they need to develop a lasting love for
Mickey Mouse.[29]

• What threats and opportunities did Disney identify in China?

placed labor costs in China at less than $1 an hour, compared with $2.92 for manufacturing workers in Mexico and $24.59 for manufacturing workers in the United
States.[30] These low wage rates led many managers to relocate operations to China or
to import an increasing number and variety of Chinese products instead of continuing
to do business with local manufacturers. This trend is one reason the value of U.S.
imports from China is more than five times the value of U.S exports to China.

This type of trade imbalance may well have contributed to the loss of manufacturing
jobs in the United States and Europe. But it has also led to the continuing availability of
comparatively low-priced goods, helping consumers everywhere and leading to overall
economic and job growth at home. Yet jobs in certain industries, such as textiles, may

have been transferred abroad permanently to lower-cost producers such as China and India. Those affected workers and communities experience real hardships. We will be discussing the effects of outsourcing or offshoring in more detail later in this chapter.

Threats to China's growing dominance include political instability as the growing prosperity of its cities and industrial enclaves leaves millions of poor rural residents further behind. Also, countries that have experienced job loss may face growing pressure to restrict Chinese imports, particularly in the EU, with its strong labor unions. But for the foreseeable future, China's growing presence in the world economy, as an importer *and* exporter, is one that you as a manager will increasingly have to take into account.

Besides China, India has become an important player in the global marketplace. The nation is still developing, and its poverty is often severe, but its 1.2 billion people (the world's second-largest population), many of them entering the working and professional classes, make India an essential market for more and more companies. For many U.S. companies, India is seen as a provider of online support for computer software, software development, and other services. In fact, so many companies have set up shop there that the demand for Indian workers with strong technical and English language skills is exceeding the supply. Companies such as Wipro and Tata Group are responding with expanded training programs.[31] Thanks to India's fast-growing economy and huge population, more U.S. businesses are beginning to see the country as a source of customers as well as workers. Citigroup, for example, has made plans to open more branches in India and expand service such as microfinance (small loans), as well as to add thousands more staff members there.[32]

Other rapidly growing countries in the region that have strong trade relationships with the United States include South Korea, Taiwan, and Singapore. These countries are important trading partners not merely because of their wage rates but because many of their companies have developed competitive advantages in areas such as engineering and technological know-how. South Korea's Samsung has the largest share of the world's markets for flat-screen televisions and flash memory cards, and Taiwan's Hon Hai is the leader in contract manufacturing of electronics. The reason you may not have heard of Hon Hai is that it specializes in making components for brand-name products of other companies, including Sony (PlayStations), Apple (iPods), and Dell (computers).[33]

These Asian countries and others have joined with the United States, Australia, and Russia to form the 21-member Asia-Pacific Economic Cooperation (APEC) trade group. Combined, APEC members' economies account for more than half of world output (GDP) and 44 percent of world trade.[34] In recent years, the APEC countries have been working to establish policies that encourage international commerce and reduce trade barriers. APEC members address these objectives through dialogue and nonbinding commitments rather than treaties.

Another international organization, the Association of Southeast Asian Nations (ASEAN), brings together 10 developing nations, including Indonesia, Malaysia, and the Philippines. Along with economic development, ASEAN is aimed at promoting cultural development and political security.

The Americas

North and South America constitute a mix of industrialized countries, such as Canada and the United States, as well as countries with growing economies, such as Argentina, Brazil, Chile, and Mexico. The winter fruit you eat may come from Chile, the coffee you drink from Jamaica, and the shirt you wear from Honduras. Increasingly, businesses are looking to establish freer trade among countries in the Western Hemisphere—and with other parts of the world.

The **North American Free Trade Agreement (NAFTA)** combined the economies of the United States, Canada, and Mexico into the world's largest trading bloc with nearly 450 million U.S., Canadian, and Mexican consumers and a total output of $17 trillion. By 2008, virtually all U.S. industrial exports into Mexico and Canada were duty-free. Although the United States has had a longer-standing agreement with Canada, Mexico has quickly emerged as the United States's third largest trading partner as a result of

North American Free Trade Agreement (NAFTA)

An economic pact that combined the economies of the United States, Canada, and Mexico into one of the world's largest trading blocs.

NAFTA. U.S. industries that have benefited in the short run include capital goods suppliers, manufacturers of consumer durables, grain producers and distributors, construction equipment manufacturers, the auto industry, and the financial industry, which now has privileged access into a previously protected market. Besides importing and exporting, companies in the NAFTA countries have invested in facilities across national borders. Mexico-based CEMEX, the world's third-largest cement company, is actually the largest cement supplier in the United States. Twenty-two percent of CEMEX's employees and 27 percent of its sales are in the United States, and it conducts management meetings in English because the majority of its employees do not speak Spanish.[35]

Leading the growth following the Great Recession was Brazil, especially in the agricultural and energy sectors. Bright spots in Brazil have included the production of ethanol and potential leadership in wind power from harnessing its steady trade winds at wind farms built on land being auctioned by the government. As Brazil's economy matures, investors looking for fresh growth are turning their attention to other South American markets, including Colombia and Peru, both of which have posted solid economic growth in recent years.[36] As in Asia, more South American companies are relying on innovation and technology rather than simply cost to compete in the global marketplace. For example, one reason that Argentina's Tenaris is the global leader in the market for oil pipes is that management of a predecessor company, Siderca, decided to focus on building a global network of facilities that could research customer needs, develop products, and deliver pipes just as needed by their customers. This focus gave Siderca, now part of Tenaris, a competitive advantage.[37]

Other agreements have been proposed to promote trade with Central and South America. In 2005, President George W. Bush signed into law U.S. participation in a Central America–Dominican Republic–United States Free Trade Agreement (CAFTA-DR). Other nations that have agreed to participate include Costa Rica, the Dominican Republic, El Salvador, Guatemala, Honduras, and Nicaragua. CAFTA-DR creates the second-largest free trade zone with the United States (NAFTA being the largest). As part of the negotiations for CAFTA-DR, Central American nations promised to protect workers' rights in their countries. Complaints that some countries have not delivered on this promise have led the U.S. government to request consultations with Guatemala on "apparent violations of its obligations."[38] Other trade agreements have been negotiated on a country-by-country basis with Chile, Peru, Colombia, and Panama. In addition, the countries of South America formed their own trading bloc, called Mercosur, to promote trade among nations of that continent.

Africa and the Middle East

We can't begin to discuss fully all the important developments, markets, and competitors shaping the global environment. These trends leave huge and promising areas of the world—the Middle East, parts of South America, and much of Africa—that have not yet participated as much in globalization. These regions account for a major share of the world's natural resources, and managers are watching the global environment, looking for areas with potential.

The economy of the Middle East is, of course, best known for its export of oil. Although oil exploration and drilling take place in many parts of the world, the oil-rich countries of the Middle East supply by far the most oil to the world's buyers, most of it going to buyers in Asia. The Middle East is not, however, the largest supplier of oil to the United States. About half of the petroleum consumed in the United States comes from imports, slightly more than half of which comes from the Western Hemisphere, mainly Canada, Venezuela, and Mexico. The main Middle Eastern supplier of U.S. oil imports is Saudi Arabia.[39] Nevertheless, U.S. businesses are concerned about the Middle East because activities there can shape the price of oil, which is important not only for transportation but also for the manufacture of many products, including fertilizer and plastic. Recently, for example, many Middle Eastern and North African governments have been shaken by public protests, overthrown leaders, and even civil war; the turmoil has been blamed as one cause of a spike in oil prices.

Africa has long been seen only as a place of dire poverty. Indeed, the continent is still plagued by an epidemic of AIDS and many unstable political situations, including outright wars. Nevertheless, a reduction in severe poverty and growth in the middle class in many countries have provided exciting opportunities for businesses willing to learn the needs of the population and make the effort of navigating a sometimes challenging environment. As part of its Smarter Planet initiative (described in the "Management Connection" for Chapter 5), IBM learns about the continent's huge potential by sending in teams to help local governments solve problems. As it gets to know the region, IBM has begun selling services, setting up partnerships with local companies, and opening research facilities in Kenya, Senegal, South Africa, and other countries. Although African sales are still a small part of IBM's total, the company expects them to double over the next few years.[40]

Global Strategy

 LO 3

One of the critical tasks an international manager faces is to identify the best strategy for competing in a global marketplace. To approach this issue, managers can plot a company's position on an integration–responsiveness grid, such as that shown in Figure 6.5. The vertical axis measures pressures for global integration, and the horizontal axis measures pressures for local responsiveness. Borrowing language from early in this chapter, we might say that much of the pressure for global integration comes from today's business world being flat, whereas the pressure for local responsiveness reflects the world's bumpiness.

Pressures for Global Integration

Managers may have several reasons to want or need a common global strategy rather than one tailored to individual markets. These factors include the existence of universal needs, pressures to reduce costs, or the presence of competitors with a global strategy.

Universal needs create strong pressure for a global strategy. Universal needs exist when the tastes and preferences of consumers in different countries with regard to a product are similar. Products that serve universal needs require little adaptation across national markets; thus global integration is facilitated. This is the case in many industrial markets. For

Universal needs create strong pressure for a global strategy.

FIGURE 6.5
Organizational Models

SOURCES: C. A. Bartlett and S. Ghoshal, *Managing across Borders: The Transnational Solution* (Boston: Harvard Business School Press, 1991); and A. W. Harzing, "An Empirical Analysis and Extension of the Bartlett and Ghoshal Typology of Multinational Companies," *Journal of International Business Studies* 31, no. 1 (2000), pp. 101–20.

example, electronic products such as semiconductor chips meet universal needs. Certain basic foodstuffs (such as colas) and appliances (such as can openers) are also increasingly available and regarded in similar ways globally.

Competitive pressures to reduce costs may cause managers to seek to integrate manufacturing globally. Cost can be particularly important in industries in which price is the main competitive weapon and competition is intense (e.g., as with smart phones). It is also important if key international competitors are based in countries where labor and other operating costs are low. In these cases, products are more likely to be standardized and perhaps produced in a few locations to capture economies of scale.

The presence of competitors engaged in global strategic coordination is another factor that creates pressures for global integration. For example, a competitor that centrally coordinates the purchase of raw materials worldwide may achieve significant price reductions compared with firms that allow subsidiaries to handle purchases locally. Global competition can often create pressures to centralize in corporate headquarters certain decisions being made by different national subsidiaries. And once one multinational company adopts global strategic coordination, its competitors may be forced to do the same.

Bottom Line

The need to lower costs is a key globalization driver. *What is one way in which a global strategy can help reduce costs?*

Pressures for Local Responsiveness

In some circumstances, managers need to make sure their companies can adapt to different needs in different locations. Strong pressures for local responsiveness emerge when consumer tastes and preferences differ significantly among countries. In such cases, products and/or marketing messages have to be customized. In the automobile industry, for example, U.S. consumers' demand for pickup trucks is strong in the South and West, where many families have a pickup truck as a second or third vehicle. In contrast, in Europe pickup trucks are viewed as utility vehicles and are purchased primarily by companies rather than by individuals. As a result, automakers must tailor their marketing messages to these differences in consumer demand.

Pressures for local responsiveness also emerge when there are differences in traditional practices among countries. For example, in Great Britain people drive on the

In Practice

IGNIGHTER.COM GAINS TRACTION IN INDIA

Ignighter.com is an Internet start-up that surprised its founders by appealing to traditional practices far from its home base in New York City. Dan Osit, Kevin Owocki, and Adam Sachs created Ignighter.com as a dating site that would make dating "safer, less awkward, and more fun." Its distinction was the founders' assumption that dating would be more comfortable if the individuals met up with others in a group. Thus one customer coordinates a date by inviting a group of people to join him or her for an outing.

After a year, 50,000 people in the United States had registered for the service—not an embarrassing start, but also not enough for a viable business. It turned out that many people in the target group—singles in their twenties—were confused by the concept. But Osit studied user data and picked up on an unexpected trend: the site was generating a lot of traffic from Singapore, Malaysia, India, and South Korea. At first the founders brushed off that information as just a quirk.

The trend persisted, however, especially in India, where hundreds of users were signing up for Ignighter every day. After another year, the founders acknowledged that they had accidentally created a website for dating Indian-style. In many parts of India, young people are not supposed to be out with someone from the opposite sex; but from their exposure to Western media, the idea of dating appeals to them. Group outings meet their desire in a socially acceptable way. With that realization, Ignighter's founders laid plans to hire employees in India and let the U.S. website coast.[41]

• How might Ignighter's founders have prepared better for local responsiveness?

left side of the road, creating a demand for right-hand-drive cars, whereas in neighboring France, people drive on the right side of the road. Obviously, automobiles must be customized to accommodate this difference in traditional practices.

Differences in distribution channels and sales practices among countries also may create pressures for local responsiveness. In India, people are used to buying their groceries at small, local shops, creating challenges for Walmart as it develops plans to open supermarkets and larger stores in that country.[42] Cinnabon had to adjust its approach to retailing when it moved into the Middle East and Russia. The company had found customers in the United States by setting up in malls, but Middle Eastern and Russian consumers have less of a culture of entertaining themselves with a visit to the mall. So in those locations, Cinnabon shops are more likely to be storefronts in shopping districts.[43]

Finally, economic and political demands that host-country governments impose may necessitate a degree of local responsiveness. Most important, threats of protectionism, economic nationalism, and local content rules (rules requiring that a certain percentage of a product be manufactured locally) dictate that international companies manufacture locally. For example, countries may impose tariffs (taxes on imports) or quotas (restrictions on the number of imports allowed into a country) to protect domestic industries from foreign competition perceived to be unfair or not in the nation's interests. Recently, the United States began imposing tariffs on paper imported from China. The U.S. government justified the tariffs as a response to complaints that the Chinese companies were selling the paper below the cost of the raw materials, presumably because the Chinese government was subsidizing the industry. Others interpret this and other protectionist actions as being motivated primarily by political objectives.[44] Whatever the reasons for them, tariffs and quotas influence managers' decisions about whether it is economically advantageous, or even possible, to operate locally or rely on exporting.

Choosing a Global Strategy

As Figure 6.5 shows, managers can use four approaches to international competition, depending on their company's position on the integration–responsiveness grid: the international model, the multinational model, the global model, and the transnational model. Organizations in each model compete globally, but they differ in the strategy they use and in the structure and systems that drive their operations.

The International Model   In the **international model,** managers use their organization's existing core capabilities to expand into foreign markets. As the grid suggests, it is most appropriate when there are few pressures for economies of scale *or* local responsiveness. Pfizer is an example of a company operating in the international model. It is in an industry that doesn't compete on cost, and its drugs obviously don't need to be tailored for local tastes. The international model uses subsidiaries in each country in which the company does business, with ultimate control exercised by the parent company. In particular, although subsidiaries may have some latitude to adapt products to local conditions, core functions such as research and development tend to be centralized in the parent company. Consequently, the dependence of subsidiaries on the parent company for new products, processes, and ideas requires a great deal of coordination and control by the parent company.

The advantage of this model is that it facilitates the transfer of skills and know-how from the parent company to subsidiaries around the globe. For example, IBM and Xerox profited from the transfer of their core skills in technology and research and development (R&D) overseas. The overseas successes of Kellogg, Coca-Cola, Heinz, and Procter & Gamble are based more on marketing know-how than on technological

international model

An organizational model that is composed of a company's overseas subsidiaries and characterized by greater control by the parent company over the research function and local product and marketing strategies than is the case in the multinational model.

Bottom Line

The international model helps spread quality and service standards globally. *Give an example of a product for which quality standards would apply globally.*

expertise. Toyota and Honda successfully penetrated U.S. markets from
their base in Japan with their core
competencies in manufacturing relative to local competitors. Still other
companies have based their competitive advantage on general management skills. These factors explain the
growth of international hotel chains
such as Hilton International, Intercontinental, and Sheraton.

One disadvantage of the international model is that it does not provide
maximum latitude for responding to
local conditions. In addition, it frequently does not provide the opportunity to achieve a low-cost position
via scale economies.

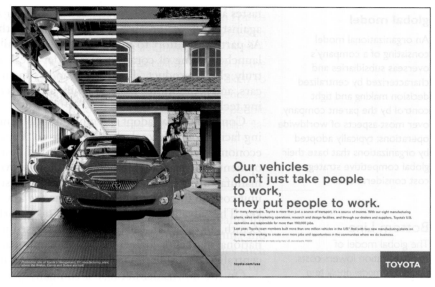

Our vehicles
don't just take people
to work,
they put people to work.

TOYOTA

In this ad, Toyota counters the perception that foreign auto companies take jobs from Americans. The production line above is actually its Georgetown, KY, manufacturing plant. According to the organizational model in Figure 6.5, what type of company is Toyota?

The Multinational Model   Where global efficiency is not required but
adapting to local conditions offers advantages, the multinational model is appropriate. The **multinational model,** sometimes referred to as *multidomestic*, uses
subsidiaries in each country in which the company does business and provides a
great deal of discretion to those subsidiaries to respond to local conditions. Each
local subsidiary is a self-contained unit with all the functions required for operating in the host market. Thus each subsidiary has its own manufacturing, marketing, research, and human resources functions. Because of this autonomy, each
multinational subsidiary can customize its products and strategies according to the
tastes and preferences of local consumers; the competitive conditions; and political,
legal, and social structures.

A good example of a multinational firm is Heineken, a Netherlands-based brewing
company. Heineken has three major global brands—Heineken, Amstel, and Murphy's
Stout—but it also offers regional and local brands. The company understands that
every country is unique, with its own culture and business practices. So it attempts
to adapt its products to local attitudes and tastes while maintaining its high quality.
As a result, the company produces more than 170 brands around the world, from
its international brands to local and specialty brews. The localized portfolio includes
such brands as Primus and Star in Africa, Vitamalt and Piton in the Caribbean, and
Tiger in Asia. Individual countries have considerable autonomy in the beer that is
brewed locally.[45]

A major disadvantage of the multinational form is higher manufacturing costs and
duplication of effort. Although a multinational can transfer core skills among its international operations, it cannot realize scale economies from centralizing manufacturing facilities and offering a standardized product to the global marketplace. Moreover,
because a multinational approach tends to decentralize strategy decisions (discussed
further in Chapters 8 and 9), launching coordinated global attacks against competitors
is difficult. This can be a significant disadvantage when competitors have this ability.

The Global Model   The **global model** is designed to enable a company to market
a standardized product in the global marketplace and to manufacture that product in
a limited number of locations where the mix of costs and skills is most favorable. The
global model has been adopted by companies that view the world as one market and
assume that no tangible differences exist among countries with regard to consumer

multinational model
An organizational model that consists of the subsidiaries in each country in which a company does business and provides a great deal of discretion to those subsidiaries to respond to local conditions.

Bottom Line
The multinational model helps speed up local response. *What kind of product might experience rapid changes in local demand?*

TABLE 6.4   Identifying International Executives

End-State Dimensions	Sample Items
1. Sensitivity to cultural differences	When working with people from other cultures, works hard to understand their perspective.
2. Business knowledge.	Has a solid understanding of the company's products and services.
3. Courage to take a stand.	Is willing to take a stand on issues.
4. Brings out the best in people.	Has a special talent for dealing with people.
5. Acts with integrity.	Can be depended on to tell the truth regardless of circumstances.
6. Is insightful.	Is good at identifying the most important part of a complex problem.
7. Is committed to success.	Clearly demonstrates commitment to seeing the organization succeed.
8. Takes risks.	Takes personal as well as business risks.
Learning-Oriented Dimensions	**Sample Items**
1. Uses feedback.	Has changed as a result of feedback.
2. Is culturally adventurous.	Enjoys the challenge of working in countries other than his or her own.
3. Seeks opportunities to learn.	Takes advantage of opportunities to do new things.
4. Is open to criticism.	Does not appear brittle—as if criticism might cause him or her to break.
5. Seeks feedback.	Pursues feedback even when others are reluctant to give it.
6. Is flexible.	Doesn't get so invested in things that he or she cannot change when something doesn't work.

SOURCE: Copyright © 1997 by the American Psychological Association. G. M. Spreitzer, M. W. McCall, and J. D. Mahoney, "Early Identification of International Executive Potential," *Journal of Applied Psychology* 82, no. 1 (1997), pp. 6–29.

Companies such as BPAmoco, Global Hyatt, and others with large international staffs have extensive training programs to prepare employees for international assignments. Table 6.5 suggests ways to improve their likelihood of success. Other organizations, such as Coca-Cola, Motorola, Chevron, and Mattel, have extended this training to include employees who may be located in the United States but who also deal in international markets. These programs focus on areas such as language, culture, and career development.

Managers who are sent on an overseas assignment usually wonder about the effect such an assignment will have on their careers. Certainly their selection for a post overseas is usually an indication that they are being groomed to become more effective managers in an era of globalization. In addition, they will often have more responsibility, challenge, and operating leeway than they might have at home. Yet they may

TABLE 6.5   How to Prevent Failed Global Assignments

- Structure assignments clearly: Develop clear reporting relationships and job responsibilities.
- Create clear job objectives.
- Develop performance measurements based on objectives.
- Use effective, validated selection and screening criteria (both personal and technical attributes).
- Prepare expatriates and families for assignments (briefings, training, support).
- Create a vehicle for ongoing communication with expatriates.
- Anticipate repatriation to facilitate reentry when they come back home.
- Consider developing a mentor program that will help monitor and intervene in case of trouble.

be concerned that they will soon be out of the loop on key developments back home. Good companies and managers address that issue with effective communication between subsidiaries and headquarters and by a program of visitations to and from the home office. Communication technology now makes it easy for expatriates to keep in touch with colleagues in their home country on a daily or even more frequent basis, through e-mail and phone calls. Alan Paul, an American journalist working in China, says Internet phone service, a webcam, and podcasts of favorite radio programs also enable him to stay in touch with family and friends back home, even to the extent that he has to work hard to have "a fully engaged existence in China."[66]

Understanding Cultural Issues

In many ways, cultural issues represent the most elusive aspect of international business. In an era when modern transportation and communication technologies have created a global village, it is easy to forget how deep and enduring the differences among nations can be. The fact that people everywhere drink Coke, wear blue jeans, and drive Toyotas doesn't mean we are all becoming alike. Each country is unique for reasons rooted in history, culture, language, geography, social conditions, race, and religion. These differences complicate any international activity and represent the fundamental issues that inform and guide how a company should conduct business across borders. For example, while working in Hong Kong, Geoffrey Fowler discovered that his coworkers there choose topics for small talk—people's weight, salary, and the size of their apartment—that would horrify Americans. At the same time, Chinese workers are put off by the American custom of combining lunch with a business meeting, meaning junior employees are chewing away while a superior in the company is talking.[67]

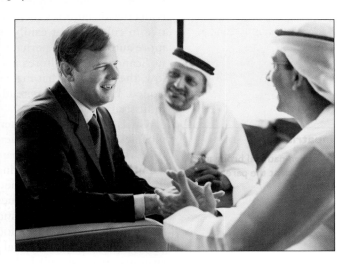

In this era, when people from all over the globe are collaborating on business issues, it is important to continue learning about and respecting different cultures in order to succeed.

Ironically, although most of us would guess that the trick to working abroad is learning about a foreign culture, in reality our problems often stem from our being oblivious to our own cultural conditioning. Most of us pay no attention to how culture influences our everyday behavior, and because of this, we tend to adapt poorly to situations that are unique or foreign to us. Without realizing it, some managers may even act out of **ethnocentrism**—a tendency to judge foreign people or groups by the standards of one's own culture or group and to see one's own standards as superior. Such tendencies may be totally unconscious—for example, the assumption that "in England, they drive on the *wrong* side of the road" rather than merely on the left. Or they may reflect a lack of awareness of the values underlying a local culture—for example, an assumption that the culture is backward because it does not air American or European television programming, when it is actually focused on maintaining its traditional values and norms.

ethnocentrism

The tendency to judge others by the standards of one's group or culture, which are seen as superior.

Assumptions such as these are one reason people traveling abroad frequently experience **culture shock**—the disorientation and stress associated with being in a foreign environment. Managers are better able to navigate this transition if they are sensitive to their surroundings, including social norms and customs, and readily able to adjust their behavior to such circumstances.[68] Employers can help by identifying some of the cultural norms to expect and by establishing performance measures for behaviors that contribute to success in the host country (for example, the types of communication and direction employees will expect from their manager).

culture shock

The disorientation and stress associated with being in a foreign environment.

A wealth of cross-cultural research has been conducted on the differences and similarities among various countries. Geert Hofstede, for example, has identified on weekends. Obviously, matters such as these are most helpfully raised and addressed at the beginning of the work assignment.

E-mail: Parts of the world have not yet embraced e-mail and voice mail the way U.S. workers have. Often others prefer to communicate face to face. Particularly when potential language difficulties exist, managers will probably want to avoid using e-mail for important matters at the outset.

Fast-trackers: Although U.S. companies may put a young MBA graduate on the fast track to management, most other cultures still see no substitute for the wisdom gained through experience. (This is something U.S. managers working abroad will also want to keep in mind.) More experienced managers are often a better choice for mentoring inpatriates.

Feedback: Everyone likes praise, but the use of excessive positive feedback tends to be less prevalent in other cultures than in the United States—a useful fact for managers when they give foreign nationals their performance reviews.[70]

Ethical Issues in International Management

If managers are to function effectively in a foreign setting, they must understand how culture influences both how they are perceived and how others behave. One of the most sensitive issues in this regard is how culture plays out in terms of ethical behavior.[71] Issues of right and wrong get blurred as we move from one culture to another, and actions that may be normal and customary in one setting may be unethical—even illegal—in another. The use of bribes, for example, is perceived to be an accepted part of commercial transactions in many Asian, African, Latin American, and Middle Eastern cultures; and even in cultures that view bribery as a form of corruption, some companies offer bribes when they think that it is part of the culture.[72]

In Practice

CELTEL'S START IN AFRICA

Mo Ibrahim had to address the expectation of bribery when he set up Celtel to bring cellular service to underserved countries in Africa. Ibrahim saw enormous untapped demand for mobile communications on a continent with a billion people where many regions lacked fixed telephone lines, but he couldn't persuade any established companies to operate in African countries. Ibrahim decided he could do what others wouldn't, and he raised enough funds to start Celtel.

Ibrahim assembled a board of directors experienced in the telecommunications industry. They decided that the company's long-term success required a sterling reputation. Celtel defined requirements for doing business: Licenses to operate must be granted in an open bidding process, and the entire board had to approve any expense greater than $30,000. One of the directors, Salim Ahmed

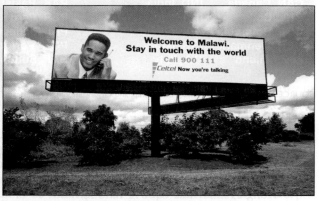

This billboard advertising Celtel's service is located in Malawi.

Salim, formerly prime minister of Tanzania, even offered a personal touch. Whenever a local official hinted to a Celtel employee that a bribe might be helpful, Salim would contact an appropriate authority and explain that bribery would taint Africa's reputation. Generally, this diplomacy returned the deal to a transparent course.

Celtel's ethical approach prevailed. By targeting low-cost markets with low-priced mobile devices, Celtel opened up as much demand as it could meet. The decision to avoid bribery actually helped because Celtel instead used its money to invest openly in communities through fair wages, employee training, and construction of schools and health clinics, thereby winning customers' goodwill. Today Celtel's operations are part of Bharti Airtel, an Indian company whose corporate vision is to be "the most loved brand, enriching the lives of millions"—a vision requiring an ongoing commitment to ethics.[73]

• What were the risks and rewards of Ibraham's insistence on ethical practices at Celtel?

In the United States, of course, such behavior is illegal, but what should a U.S. businessperson do when working abroad? Failure to sweeten the deal with bribes can result in lost business. Although the Foreign Corrupt Practices Act of 1977 prohibits U.S. employees from bribing foreign officials, one study published in the United States found that fewer than half of U.S. managers said bribes were unacceptable, and 20 percent actually said they were always acceptable. (Small business gifts or grease payments to lower-level officials are permissible under the act if the dollar amount of the payments would not influence the outcome of the negotiations.) Internationally, countries of the Organization for Economic Cooperation and Development, including the United States, have also prohibited bribes since 1977.[74] Companies that conduct business in Britain are also subject to that country's Bribery Act, which prohibits not only bribes of foreign officials but also bribes between businesspeople.[75] That sweeping law took effect in 2011; as of this writing, it is not yet clear how aggressive the British government will be in pursuing cases involving small bribes and companies based outside Britain.

Britain's law comes at a time when other governments are getting tough on bribery and other forms of corruption. Other European countries have recently strengthened their laws against bribery, and China has begun to prosecute corporations for bribery. In the United States, the Justice Department has been charging more firms with violating the Foreign Corrupt Practices Act (FCPA). In one case, for example, IBM paid $10 million to settle charges by the Securities and Exchange Commission that its people had been engaging in bribery to win contracts. (That settlement was actually small; fines in FCPA cases can exceed $100 million.) In this case, IBM neither admitted wrongdoing nor denied it, and the company said it was taking remedial action to ensure that violations didn't occur in the future.[76]

Without an understanding of local customs, ethical standards, and applicable laws, an expatriate may be woefully unprepared to work internationally. To safeguard against the problems and mitigate the punishment if an organization should be found guilty of bribery, the U.S. Sentencing Commission has deemed it essential for firms to establish effective ethics programs and see that they are enforced. Companies such as Caterpillar, General Dynamics, and United Technologies established official codes of conduct for their employees years ago. In addition, many other companies have hired official ethics officers and increased their efforts to ensure ethical conduct. UPS couples an international code of conduct (available in 12 languages) with tools to ensure compliance: a corporate compliance department headed by a senior vice president, ethics training for all managers and employees, a toll-free line for requesting guidance or reporting problems, and regular audits of compliance with the code. In developing the international code of ethics, the compliance department sought input from employees in many positions and countries to ensure that the policies would be relevant throughout the company. Employees are invited to submit any ideas they have for improving the code's current language.[77]

To put teeth into the corporate ethics initiative, companies with global operations should be at least as engaged in establishing and enforcing standards for ethical behavior as domestic corporations. In Chapter 5, we identified a number of steps organizations should take. They include establishing and communicating the company's values, measuring performance in meeting ethical standards, rewarding employees at all levels for meeting those standards, and taking swift but fair action when violations occur. The primary difference in the international context is that these activities must be carried out with foreign business partners and employees in any subsidiary, franchise, or other company operation.

Interestingly, despite some obvious differences across cultures, research suggests that regardless of nationality or religion, most people embrace a set of five core values: compassion, fairness, honesty, responsibility, and respect for others. These values lie at the heart of human rights issues and seem to transcend more superficial differences among Americans, Europeans, and Asians. Finding shared values such as these allows companies to build more effective partnerships and alliances, especially across cultures. Perhaps as long as people understand that there is a set of core values, they can permit all kinds of differences in strategy and tactics.[78]

To a large extent, the challenge of managing across borders comes down to the philosophies and systems used to manage people. In moving from domestic to international management, managers need to develop a wide portfolio of behaviors along with the capacity to adjust their behavior for a particular situation. This adjustment, however, should not compromise the values, integrity, and strengths of their home country. When managers can transcend national borders and move among different cultures, they can leverage the strategic capabilities of their organization and take advantage of the opportunities that our global economy has to offer.

Taking these management principles beyond national borders is an exciting challenge that should be irresistible to today's and tomorrow's leaders. As we saw in the early sections of this chapter, the business environment is spreading wider. The implications are evident at Lenovo, as described in "Management Connection: Onward" and the earlier parts of this continuing case. People around the world are seizing the chance to get an education, launch a business, and enjoy a higher standard of living. The opportunities to serve their needs are enormous. Thanks to modern technology, the ability to learn about needs and meet them globally is available even to small, local businesses. Whether you are addressing unique desires in a bumpy world or delivering your product to all continents in a flat one, you must pay attention to what is happening far beyond your neighborhood.

MANAGER'S BRIEF · PROGRESS REPORT · ONWARD

Management Connection

MANAGING LENOVO ACROSS NATIONAL BOUNDARIES

To implement its strategy of keeping production in-house and expanding to new markets as it builds market share, Lenovo needs managers who understand local markets and can run an efficient manufacturing operation. Examples include host-country nationals such as Amar Babu, the managing director of Lenovo's business in India, and third-country nationals such as American Dan Stone, whose background in business strategy helps him succeed as the head of Lenovo's Brazilian business unit. In India, Babu notes that consumers are just beginning to make the move from a basic cell phone to a smart phone, whereas demand for PCs is likely to remain strong because people want a computer with a full screen for educational applications.

Of course, electronics companies also need to dream up, or at least keep up with, the next great ideas. Lenovo's chief executive, Yang Yuanqing, admits that Lenovo has not exactly been a leader in design, but he has plenty of experience in catching up. In the 1980s, when Yang was a Lenovo salesperson, he used a bicycle to deliver products, and support services such as advertising agencies were unavailable. As he persevered then, he is persevering today in leading innovation. A recent attempt includes the IdeaPad Yoga, whose keyboard can be positioned for using the computer as a tablet or laptop.

China, where the market is huge and the brand is already respected and popular, provides fertile ground for launching new ideas such as the K91 Smart TV, an

Internet-connected television. China is an important locale for the move into smart phones. Lenovo, which until recently had just one model, unveiled a line of 19 phones, helping it gain the second-largest share of the world's biggest smart phone market. From there, Lenovo took its smart phones to India, Russia, and Indonesia, with plans for expansion into Latin America and the Middle East.

Yang is patient in building Lenovo's brand in the United States. According to Yang, the company intends to use its reputation as the maker of business computers as the basis for selling high-end PCs to consumers. Yang said recent prototypes have been exciting, but the final versions suffered from compromises made to lower costs. Yang intends to shift the focus toward favoring the design. Also, during some recent quarters, Lenovo has ranked as the world's biggest seller of PCs, which Lenovo hopes will further raise the brand's profile worldwide.[79]

- What advantages does Lenovo have from its choice of entry modes?
- What cultural issues should an American-born manager at Lenovo be prepared to handle?

KEY TERMS

culture shock, p. 213

ethnocentrism, p. 213

expatriates, p. 210

failure rate, p. 210

global model, p. 203

host-country nationals, p. 210

inpatriate, p. 214

international model, p. 202

multinational model, p. 203

North American Free Trade Agreement (NAFTA), p. 198

offshoring, p. 192

outsourcing, p. 192

third-country nationals, p. 210

transnational model, p. 204

SUMMARY OF LEARNING OBJECTIVES

Now that you have studied Chapter 6, you should be able to:

 Discuss what integration of the global economy means for individual companies and their managers.

In recent years, rapid growth has occurred in world trade, foreign direct investment, and imports. One consequence is that companies around the globe are now finding their home markets under attack from international competitors. The global competitive environment is becoming a much tougher place in which to do business. However, companies now have access to markets that previously were denied to them.

 Describe how the world economy is becoming more integrated than ever before.

The gradual lowering of barriers to free trade is making the world economy more integrated. This means that the modern manager operates in an environment that offers more opportunities but is also more complex and competitive than that faced by the manager of a generation ago.

 Define the strategies organizations use to compete in the global marketplace.

The international corporation builds on its existing core capabilities in R&D, marketing, manufacturing, and so on to penetrate overseas markets. A multinational is a more complex form that usually has fully autonomous units operating in multiple countries. Subsidiaries are given latitude to address local issues such as consumer preferences, political pressures, and economic trends in different regions of the world. The global organization pulls control of overseas operations back into the headquarters and tends to approach the world market as a unified whole by combining activities in each country to maximize efficiency on a global scale. A transnational attempts to achieve both local responsiveness and global integration by using a network structure that coordinates specialized facilities positioned around the world.

 Compare the various entry modes organizations use to enter overseas markets.

There are five ways to enter an overseas market: exporting, licensing, franchising, entering into a joint venture, and setting up a wholly owned subsidiary. Each mode has advantages and disadvantages.

Explain how companies can approach the task of staffing overseas operations.

Most executives use a combination of expatriates, host-country nationals, and third-country nationals. Expatriates sometimes are used to establish new country operations quickly, transfer the company's culture, and bring in a specific technical skill. Host-country nationals have the advantages that they are familiar with local customs and culture, may cost less, and are viewed more favorably by local governments. Third-country nationals often are used as a compromise in politically touchy situations or when home-country expatriates are not available.

 Summarize the skills and knowledge managers need to manage globally.

The causes for failure overseas extend beyond technical capability and include personal and social issues as well. Success depends on a manager's core skills, such as having a multidimensional perspective; having proficiency in line management and decision making; and having resourcefulness, cultural adaptability, sensitivity, team-building skills, and mental maturity. In addition, helpful augmented skills include computer literacy, negotiating skills, strategic vision, and the ability to delegate.

LO 7   Identify ways in which cultural differences across countries influence management.

Culture influences our actions and perceptions as well as the actions and perceptions of others. Unfortunately, we are often unaware of how culture influences us, and this can cause problems. Today, managers must be able to change their behavior to match the needs and customs of local cultures. For example, in various cultures, employees expect a manager to be either more or less autocratic or participative. By recognizing their cultural differences, people can find it easier to work together collaboratively and benefit from the exchange.

DISCUSSION QUESTIONS

1. Why is the world economy becoming more integrated? What are the implications of this integration for international managers?

2. Imagine you were the CEO of a major company. What approach to global competition would you choose for your firm: international, multinational, global, or transnational? Why?

3. Why have franchises been so popular as a method of international expansion in the fast-food industry? Contrast this with high-tech manufacturing, where joint ventures and partnerships have been more popular. What accounts for the differences across industries?

4. What are the pros and cons of using expatriates, host-country nationals, and third-country nationals to run overseas operations? If you were expanding your business, what approach would you use?

5. If you had entered into a joint venture with a foreign company but knew that women were not treated fairly in that culture, would you consider sending a female expatriate to handle the start-up? Why or why not?

6. What are the biggest cultural obstacles that we must overcome if we are to work effectively in Mexico? Are there different obstacles in France? Japan? China?

EXPERIENTIAL EXERCISES

6.1   UNDERSTANDING MULTINATIONAL CORPORATIONS

OBJECTIVE

To gain a more thorough picture of how a multinational corporation operates.

INSTRUCTIONS

Perhaps the best way to gain an understanding of multinational corporations is to study a specific organization and how it operates throughout the world. Select a multinational corporation, find several articles on that company, and answer the questions on the Multinational Worksheet.

Multinational Worksheet

1. What is the primary business of this organization?

_____

2. To what extent does the company engage in multinational operations? For example, does it market its products and/or services only in other countries, or does it also have overseas manufacturing facilities? What portion of the firm's operating income comes from overseas operations?

_____

3. What percentage of the managers in international activities are American (or from the country the corporation considers home)? Are these managers given any special training before their international assignment?

_____

4. What characteristics of the organization have contributed to its success or lack of success in the international marketplace?

_____

SOURCE: R. R. McGrath Jr., *Exercises in Management Fundamentals*, p. 177. Copyright 1985. Reproduced by permission of Pearson Education, Inc., Upper Saddle River, New Jersey.

6.2 CROSS-CULTURAL COMMUNICATION SIMULATION

In this simulation, you will play the part of a manager employed by one of three firms—a commercial bank, a construction firm, and a hotel development company—that are planning a joint venture to build a new hotel and retail shopping complex in Perth, Australia. They come from three cultures: Blue, Green, and Red. Each has specific cultural values, traits, customs, and practices.

You are a manager in the company to which you have been assigned. You will attend the kickoff get-together for the three-day meeting during which the three companies will negotiate the details of the partnership. Your management team consists of a vice president and a number of other managers. Consider the types of topics that would be discussed by the various corporations at an initial meeting.

INSTRUCTIONS

Your instructor will provide you with information pertaining to your culture. You will be given about 15 minutes to meet with your fellow corporate members, during which you should

1. Select a leader.
2. Discuss what your objectives and approaches will be at the opening get-together.
3. Use the description of your assigned culture to practice how you will talk and behave until you are reasonably familiar with your cultural orientation. Be sure to practice conversation distance, greeting rituals, and nonverbal behavior.

You will then return to the kick-off meeting, where you will meet with the other firms. As the social proceeds, interact with the managers from the other companies. Maintain the role you have been assigned, but do not discuss it explicitly. Notice how other people react to you and how you react to them. You will discuss the experience after it is over.

Upon completing this activity, answer the following questions:

1. In what ways did your perceptions of others and their differences influence how you interacted with them and your ability to achieve your goals?

_____

2. What did you learn about yourself and others through this activity? Discuss your strengths and weaknesses in cross-cultural interaction.

_____

3. What were things you or others did or said that enabled or hindered you from adjusting to other people and their culture (a) in this activity? (b) in similar real-life situations?

_____

4. What lessons did you learn from this activity? What steps can you take to improve your ability to understand and appreciate differences?

_____

SOURCE: D. A. Jameson, "Using a Simulation to Teach Intercultural Communication in Business Communication Courses," *Business Communication Quarterly*, Vol. 55, No. 4, March 1993, pp. 1–10. Copyright 1993. Reprinted by permission of Sage Publications, Inc., via Copyright Clearance Center.

CONCLUDING CASE

A GLOBAL LAUNCH FOR NET-WORK DOCS

Nina Jones and Matt Smith have been raising capital for their start-up, Net-Work Docs. The company will help business clients create and manage their documents electronically. Net-Work Docs will help companies create easily searchable electronic versions of their safety manuals, human resource manuals, training guides, operating instructions, and more. For clients who wish, the company will help in embedding video, audio, and pop-up content along with the basic text and will develop apps for companies that want to make the content available through mobile devices. They also will provide consulting services such as helping clients shop for cloud storage of their documents.

As Nina and Matt developed their business plan, they found themselves expanding their idea of the geographic market they could serve. Initially, they intended to start by working with businesses in their city. But they realized they will be selling a product that can be made anywhere and shipped anywhere. Software and electronic documents can be transported over the Internet at essentially no cost, and a website gives a company an immediate global presence. With that in mind, Nina and Matt have concluded that they are unnecessarily limiting themselves by targeting geographic markets.

Thus, the plan is now to launch Net-Work Docs as a global company, serving clients in any country. After all, reason Nina and Matt, companies everywhere have policies and procedures they need to document. They will describe their services on their website, make initial contacts via e-mail, and set up a PayPal service to handle online payments. They can travel to meet major clients, but routine jobs may not require face-to-face meetings, and cost-conscious clients should appreciate the savings of conducting business online.

One hitch with this plan is that some potential investors have expressed doubts about operating globally before the company

CHAPTER 7

Entrepreneurship

> A man is known by the company he organizes.
>
> —AMBROSE BIERCE

LEARNING OBJECTIVES

CHAPTER OUTLINE

Management Connection

HOW POPCHIPS BECAME KEITH BELLING'S NEXT BIG IDEA

Keith Belling was no stranger to business start-ups when he got an idea for making snacks better. A corporate attorney until age 27, Belling had already built and run the Oh La La chain of coffee stores and the Paragon restaurant group; in addition, his web portal for small companies, Allbusiness.com, earned him and his business partner $225 million when he eventually sold it to NBC Interactive. After the experience of running those enterprises, it might not seem so crazy to take on industry giants such as PepsiCo to sell a new line of snacks, branded Popchips.

Belling had been looking for a healthy-food company to run with his business partner, Pat Turpin. They toured a possible facility, a factory for making rice cakes, located near Los Angeles. Belling was intrigued by the process, cooking rice under high pressure to make it pop the way popcorn does. He investigated the possibility of popping other starchy foods and concluded that making snacks this way preserved flavor in a reduced-fat snack. It sounded like the next great thing for diet-conscious Americans, so he and Turpin had the idea they were looking for.

Belling and Turpin bought the Los Angeles rice cake factory in 2005, and two years later, Popchips, with Belling as CEO, was making popped, seasoned potato chips and selling them at Safeway stores on the West Coast. (Later, the company introduced triangular popped tortilla chips.) By 2008, Popchips was reporting sales of $6.5 million. To expand, Popchips generated publicity. The company sent samples to all the employees at selected companies (for example, Amazon.com and J. Crew) and to influential people at Mercedes-Benz Fashion Week. With the attention earned, Popchips won shelf space in Jamba Juice, Target, and Whole Foods.

Along the way, Belling pursued a creative idea for publicity: Sign agreements with celebrities in which they not only pitch the brand in advertisements but actually become investors. Each celebrity invests in Popchips, gets involved in developing a new flavor, and becomes a spokesperson for the flavor. First was Ashton Kutcher, who also was a party to the company's first big marketing embarrassment: In one ad, he portrayed an awkward Indian stereotype of a Bollywood producer to promote the snack's chili-lime flavor. After complaints of racism, the ads were canceled. Meanwhile, however, sales continued rising, and Popchips has signed up other celebrities, including Jillian Michaels, Heidi Klum, Sean "Diddy" Combs, David Ortiz of the Red Sox, and Katy Perry. Sales have continued to soar—to $40.9 million in 2010, $73 million in 2011, and more than $93 million in 2012. By a recent count, Popchips snacks are now available for sale in 25,000 stores in the United States and beyond.[1]

Keith Belling took an existing method for preparing snacks and built a company by applying that method in tasty new ways. As you read about the qualities of successful entrepreneurs and the challenges they must overcome, think about which of these you see in Belling and his experience with Popchips.

entrepreneurship

The pursuit of lucrative opportunities by enterprising individuals.

Bottom Line

Entrepreneurship is inherently about innovation—creating a new venture where one didn't exist before.

How is entrepreneurship different from inventing a new product?

small business

A business having fewer than 100 employees, independently owned and operated, not dominant in its field, and not characterized by many innovative practices.

entrepreneurial venture

A new business having growth and high profitability as primary objectives.

As Keith Belling and countless others have demonstrated, great opportunity is available to talented entrepreneurs who are willing to work hard to achieve their dreams. **Entrepreneurship** occurs when an enterprising individual pursues a lucrative opportunity.[2] To be an entrepreneur is to initiate and build an organization rather than being only a passive part of one.[3] The entrepreneurial process involves discovering, evaluating, and capitalizing on opportunities to create new and future goods and services.[4]

Creating value is a central objective of entrepreneurship, just as it is in strategic management. Wealth may be an entrepreneur's ultimate goal, but it won't come without providing value for other individuals, organizations, and/or society.[5]

How does entrepreneurship differ from managing a small business?[6] A **small business** is often defined as having fewer than 100 employees, being independently owned and operated, not dominant in its field, and not characterized by many innovative practices. Small-business owners tend not to manage particularly aggressively, and they expect normal, moderate sales, profits, and growth. In contrast, an **entrepreneurial venture** has growth and high profitability as primary objectives. Entrepreneurs manage aggressively and develop innovative strategies, practices, and products. They and their financial backers usually seek rapid growth, immediate and high profits, and sometimes a quick sellout with large capital gains.

The Excitement of Entrepreneurship   Consider these words from Jeffry Timmons, a leading entrepreneurship scholar and author: "During the past 30 years, America has unleashed the most revolutionary generation the nation has experienced since its founding in 1776. This new generation of entrepreneurs has altered permanently the economic and social structure of this nation and the world. . . . It will determine more than any other single impetus how the nation and the world will live, work, learn, and lead in this century and beyond."[7] Timmons had written previously, "We are in the midst of a silent revolution—a triumph of the creative and entrepreneurial spirit of humankind throughout the world. I believe its impact on the 21st century will equal or exceed that of the Industrial Revolution on the 19th and 20th."[8]

Overhype? Well, partly, because the rate of new business formation may be slowing down.[9] But let's hope the slowdown is temporary, because entrepreneurship has transformed economies all over the world and the global economy in general.[10] In the United States in the quarter century since 1980, more than 95 percent of the wealth was created by entrepreneurs.[11] It's been estimated that since World War II, small entrepreneurial firms have generated 95 percent of all radical innovation in the United States. The Small Business Administration has found that in states with more small-business start-ups, statewide economies tend to grow faster, and employment levels tend to be higher than in states with less entrepreneurship.[12]

The self-employed love the entrepreneurial process, and they report the highest levels of pride, satisfaction, and income. Importantly, entrepreneurship is not about the privileged descendants of the Rockefellers and the Vanderbilts—it provides opportunity and upward mobility for anyone who performs well.[13]

Myths about Entrepreneurship   Simply put, entrepreneurs generate new ideas and turn them into business ventures.[14] But entrepreneurship is not simple, and it is frequently misunderstood. Read Table 7.1 to start thinking about the myths and realities of this important career option.

Here is another myth, not in the table: Being an entrepreneur is great because you can get rich quick and enjoy a lot of leisure time while your employees run the company. But the reality is much more difficult. During the start-up period, you are likely to have a lot of bad days. It's exhausting. Even if you don't have employees, you should expect communications breakdowns and other people problems with agents, vendors, distributors, family, subcontractors, lenders, and whomever. Software entrepreneur Dan Bricklin advises that the most important thing to remember is this: "You are

TABLE 7.1   Some Myths about Entrepreneurs

Myth 1—Entrepreneurs are born, not made.
Reality—Although entrepreneurs are born with certain native intelligence, a flair for creating, and energy, these talents by themselves are like unmolded clay or an unpainted canvas. The making of an entrepreneur occurs by accumulating the relevant skills, know-how, experiences, and contacts over a period of years and includes large doses of self-development. The creative capacity to envision and then pursue an opportunity is a direct descendant of at least 10 or more years of experience that lead to pattern recognition.
Myth 2—Anyone can start a business.
Reality—Entrepreneurs who recognize the difference between an idea and an opportunity, and who think big enough, start businesses that have a better chance of succeeding. Luck, to the extent it is involved, requires good preparation. And the easiest part is starting. What is hardest is surviving, sustaining, and building a venture so its founders can realize a harvest. Perhaps only one in 10 to 20 new businesses that survive five years or more results in a capital gain for the founders.
Myth 3—Entrepreneurs are gamblers.
Reality—Successful entrepreneurs take very careful, calculated risks. They try to influence the odds, often by getting others to share risk with them and by avoiding or minimizing risks if they have the choice. Often they slice up the risk into smaller, quite digestible pieces; only then do they commit the time or resources to determine whether that piece will work. They do not deliberately seek to take more risk or to take unnecessary risk, nor do they shy away from unavoidable risk.
Myth 4—Entrepreneurs want the whole show to themselves.
Reality—Owning and running the whole show effectively puts a ceiling on growth. Solo entrepreneurs usually make a living. It is extremely difficult to grow a higher-potential venture by working single-handedly. Higher-potential entrepreneurs build a team, an organization, and a company. Besides, 100 percent of nothing is nothing, so rather than taking a large piece of the pie, they work to make the pie bigger.
Myth 5—Entrepreneurs are their own bosses and completely independent.
Reality—Entrepreneurs are far from independent and have to serve many masters and constituencies, including partners, investors, customers, suppliers, creditors, employees, families, and those involved in social and community obligations. Entrepreneurs, however, can make free choices of whether, when, and what they care to respond to. Moreover, it is extremely difficult, and rare, to build a business beyond $1 million to $2 million in sales single-handedly.
Myth 6—Entrepreneurs work longer and harder than managers in big companies.
Reality—There is no evidence that all entrepreneurs work more than their corporate counterparts. Some do, some do not. Some actually report that they work less.
Myth 7—Entrepreneurs experience a great deal of stress and pay a high price.
Reality—Being an entrepreneur is stressful and demanding. But there is no evidence that it is any more stressful than numerous other highly demanding professional roles, and entrepreneurs find their jobs very satisfying. They have a high sense of accomplishment, are healthier, and are much less likely to retire than those who work for others. Three times as many entrepreneurs as corporate managers say they plan never to retire.
Myth 8—Start a business and fail and you'll never raise money again.
Reality—Talented and experienced entrepreneurs—because they pursue attractive opportunities and are able to attract the right people and necessary financial and other resources to make the venture work—often head successful ventures. Further, businesses fail, but entrepreneurs do not. Failure is often the fire that tempers the steel of an entrepreneur's learning experience and street savvy.
Myth 9—Money is the most important start-up ingredient.
Reality—If the other pieces and talents are there, the money will follow, but it does not follow that an entrepreneur will succeed if he or she has enough money. Money is one of the least important ingredients in new venture success. Money is to the entrepreneur what the paint and brush are to the artist—an inert tool that in the right hands can create marvels.

(continued)

Myth 10—Entrepreneurs should be young and energetic.
Reality—Although these qualities may help, age is no barrier. The average age of entrepreneurs starting high-potential businesses is in the mid-30s, and there are numerous examples of entrepreneurs starting businesses in their 60s. What is critical is possessing the relevant know-how, experience, and contacts that greatly facilitate recognizing and pursuing an opportunity.
Myth 11—Entrepreneurs are motivated solely by the quest for the almighty dollar.
Reality—Entrepreneurs seeking high-potential ventures are more driven by building enterprises and realizing long-term capital gains than by instant gratification through high salaries and perks. A sense of personal achievement and accomplishment, feeling in control of their own destinies, and realizing their vision and dreams are also powerful motivators. Money is viewed as a tool and a way of keeping score rather than an end in itself. Entrepreneurs thrive on the thrill of the chase; and, time and again, even after an entrepreneur has made a few million dollars or more, he or she will work on a new vision to build another company.
Myth 12—Entrepreneurs seek power and control over others.
Reality—Successful entrepreneurs are driven by the quest for responsibility, achievement, and results rather than for power for its own sake. They thrive on a sense of accomplishment and of outperforming the competition rather than a personal need for power expressed by dominating and controlling others. By virtue of their accomplishments, they may be powerful and influential, but these are more the by-products of the entrepreneurial process than a driving force behind it.
Myth 13—If an entrepreneur is talented, success will happen in a year or two.
Reality—An old maxim among venture capitalists says it all: The lemons ripen in two and a half years, but the pearls take seven or eight. Rarely is a new business established solidly in less than three or four years.
Myth 14—Any entrepreneur with a good idea can raise venture capital.
Reality—Of the ventures of entrepreneurs with good ideas who seek out venture capital, only 1 to 3 out of 100 are funded.
Myth 15—If an entrepreneur has enough start-up capital, he or she can't miss.
Reality—The opposite is often true; that is, too much money at the outset often creates euphoria and a spoiled-child syndrome. The accompanying lack of discipline and impulsive spending usually lead to serious problems and failure.
Myth 16—Entrepreneurs are lone wolves and cannot work with others.
Reality—The most successful entrepreneurs are leaders who build great teams and effective relationships working with peers, directors, investors, key customers, key suppliers, and the like.
Myth 17—Unless you attained 600 + on your SATs or GMATs, you'll never be a successful entrepreneur.
Reality—Entrepreneurial IQ is a unique combination of creativity, motivation, integrity, leadership, team building, analytical ability, and ability to deal with ambiguity and adversity.

SOURCE: From S. Spinelli, Jr., and R. J. Adams *New Venture Creation: Entrepreneurship for the 21st Century,* 9th ed, 2012, pp. 46–47. Copyright 2012 The McGraw Hill Companies, Inc. Reprinted with permission.

entrepreneur

Individual who establishes a new organization without the benefit of corporate sponsorship.

---

intrapreneurs

New venture creators working inside big companies.

not your business. On those darkest days when things aren't going so well—and trust me, you will have them—try to remember that your company's failures don't make you an awful person. Likewise, your company's successes don't make you a genius or superhuman."[15]

As you read this chapter, you will learn about two primary sources of new venture creation: independent entrepreneurship and intrapreneurship. **Entrepreneurs** are individuals who establish a new organization without the benefit of corporate support. **Intrapreneurs** are new venture creators working inside big companies; they are corporate entrepreneurs, using their company's resources to build a profitable line of business based on a fresh new idea.[16] Thus, although people tend to think of new, young ventures when they consider entrepreneurship, really it is an activity that should contribute to mature organizations as well. Entrepreneurship is vitally important across the entire life cycle of an organization.[17]

Entrepreneurship

Table 7.2 lists some extraordinary entrepreneurs. The companies they founded are famously successful—and all of the founders started in their 20s. Two young entrepreneurs who started a highly successful business are Tony Hsieh and Nick Swinmurn. In 1999, Swinmurn had the then-new idea to sell shoes online, but he needed money to get started. Hsieh, who at age 24 had already just sold his first start-up (LinkExchange, sold to Microsoft for $265 million), agreed to take a chance on the new venture. Swinmurn has moved on, but Hsieh remains at the helm of the company as the CEO of Zappos.com. In a recent year, Zappos.com enjoyed sales of $1 billion.[18] The real, more complete story of entrepreneurship is not about the famous people in Table 7.2—it's mostly about people you've probably never heard of. Often it's about young people, and definitely it's about people of all ages and ethnic groups.[19]

They have built companies, thrived personally, created jobs, and made positive contributions to their communities through their businesses. Or they're just starting out.

Why Become an Entrepreneur?

Jessica Mah was an entrepreneur before she even finished school. At the age of 13, she went into business using eBay to sell computer parts and templates for websites. While in college at the University of California–Berkeley, she and another student, Andy Su, founded a business they called InternshipIN, which provided information about internship opportunities. When she graduated, Mah was ready to launch another venture. With support from Y Combinator, which provides funds and advice to selected start-ups, Mah again partnered with Su, this time founding inDinero, a company that helps small business owners manage their money. Customers give inDinero their bank and credit card account numbers, and inDinero keeps track of transactions and analyzes where their money is going. The idea for inDinero came from Mah's own experience that for some people excited about starting a new business, working with customers and products is more exciting and easier to learn than handling money.[20]

Why do Jessica Mah and other entrepreneurs do what they do? Entrepreneurs start their own firms because of the challenge, the profit potential, and the enormous satisfaction they hope lie ahead. People starting their own businesses are seeking a better quality of life than they might have at big companies. They seek independence and a

Bottom Line

Today's concern for sustainability presents a tremendous variety of opportunities to entrepreneurs who care about the environment.
What are some environmentally friendly start-ups you've heard about? Do you think they have great profit potential?

Entrepreneurial Company	Founder(s)
Apple	Steve Jobs and Steve Wozniak
Facebook	Mark Zuckerberg
Foursquare	Naveen Selvadurai and Dennis Crowley
Google	Sergey Brin and Larry Page
Instagram	Kevin Systrom
Microsoft	Bill Gates and Paul Allen
Pinterest	Ben Silbermann and Evan Sharp
Rent the Runway	Jennifer Hyman and Jenny Fleiss
Spotify	Daniel Ek
Tumblr	David Karp
Wal-Mart	Sam Walton

TABLE 7.2

Successful Entrepreneurs Who Started in Their 20s

Sources: Brock Blake, "Why 20-Somethings Are the Most Successful Entrepreneurs," *Forbes*, November 30, 2012, http://www.forbes.com; Burt Helm, "Inside Spotify's U.S. Invasion," *Inc.*, July 2, 2012, http://www.inc.com; "30 under 30 2011: Where Are They Now?" *Inc.*, 2011, http://www.inc.com (slideshow); Lizette Chapman, "'Pivoting' Pays Off for Tech Entrepreneurs," *The Wall Street Journal*, April 26, 2012, http://online.wsj.com; Christine Lagorio, "Introducing the Two Young Men Who Made Pinterest," *Inc.*, July 2, 2012, http://www.inc.com.

Shoppers who stay on top of the latest fashion trends can go to www.renttherunway.com to rent apparel and accessories for special occasions. No dry cleaning required. Photos in ensemble can also be uploaded to the website's runway.

feeling of being part of the action. They feel tremendous satisfaction in building something from nothing, seeing it succeed, and watching the market embrace their ideas and products.

People also start their own companies when they see their progress or ideas blocked at big corporations. When people are laid off, they often try to start businesses of their own. And when employed people believe they will not receive a promotion or are frustrated by bureaucracy or other features of corporate life, they may quit and become entrepreneurs. Years ago, Philip Catron became disillusioned with his job as a manager at ChemLawn because he concluded that the lawn care company's reliance on pesticides contributed to illness in its employees, its customers' pets, and even in the lawns themselves. Catron left the company to start NaturaLawn of America, based on the practice of integrated pest management, which uses natural and nontoxic products as much as possible, reducing pesticide use on lawns by 85 percent. Catron built NaturaLawn into 66 franchises in 23 states—and helped integrated pest management become mainstream, as even his former employer, now part of TruGreen, has changed many of its practices.[21]

Immigrants also may find conventional paths to economic success closed to them and turn to entrepreneurship.[22] For example, the Cuban community in Miami has produced many successful entrepreneurs, as has the Vietnamese community throughout the United States. Sometimes the immigrant's experience gives him or her useful knowledge about foreign suppliers or markets that present an attractive business opportunity. Rakesh Kamdar immigrated to the United States from India to study computer science, but he saw a way he could meet the huge U.S. demand for nursing talent. He set up DB Healthcare to recruit nurses from India to work in the United States. Unlike U.S. competitors that had failed, Kamdar set up meetings at DB's Indian offices, and he invited nurses to attend with their husbands, parents, and in-laws. His staff discussed family and individual questions related to the American jobs. With this strategy, DB Healthcare was earning millions of dollars within a few years.[23]

What Does It Take to Succeed?

What can we learn from the people who start their own companies and succeed? What enables entrepreneurs to succeed? We show this in general terms with Figure 7.1. Successful entrepreneurs are innovators who also have good knowledge and skills in management, business, and networking.[24] In contrast, inventors

FIGURE 7.1
Who Is the Entrepreneur?

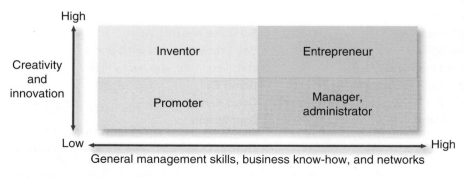

SOURCE: J. A. Timmons and S. Spinelli, Jr., *New Venture Creation: Entrepreneurship for the 21st Century*, 7th ed., 2007, pp. 67–68. Copyright 2007 The McGraw-Hill Companies, Inc. Reprinted with permission.

may be highly creative but often lack the skills to turn their ideas into a successful business. Manager–administrators may be great at ensuring efficient operations but aren't necessarily innovators. Promoters have a different set of marketing and selling skills—useful for entrepreneurs, but those skills can be hired, whereas innovativeness and business management skills remain the essential combination for successful entrepreneurs.

What Business Should You Start?

You need a good idea, and you need to find or create the right opportunity. The following discussion offers some general considerations for choosing a type of business.

LO 2

The Idea   Many entrepreneurs and observers say that in contemplating your business, you must start with a great idea. A great product, a viable market, and good timing are essential ingredients in any recipe for success.

Many great organizations have been built on a different kind of idea: the founder's desire to build a great organization rather than to offer a particular product.[25] Examples abound. Bill Hewlett and David Packard decided to start a company and then figured out what to make. J. Willard Marriott knew he wanted to be in business for himself but didn't have a product in mind until he opened an A&W root beer stand. Masaru Ibuka had no specific product idea when he founded Sony in 1945. Sony's first product attempt, a rice cooker, didn't work, and its first product (a tape recorder) didn't sell. The company stayed alive by making and selling crude heating pads.

Many now-great companies had early failures. But the founders persisted; they believed in themselves and in their dreams of building great organizations. Be prepared to kill or revise an idea, but never give up on your company—this has been a prescription for success for many great entrepreneurs and business leaders. Think about Sony, Disney, Hewlett-Packard, Procter & Gamble, IBM, and Walmart: their founders' greatest achievements—their greatest ideas—are their organizations.[26]

The Opportunity   Entrepreneurs spot, create, and exploit opportunities in a variety of ways.[27] Entrepreneurial companies can explore domains that big companies avoid and introduce goods or services that capture the market because they are simpler, cheaper, more accessible, or more convenient. Limor Fried spotted her opportunity when she got involved with a hobby that flew under the radar of most traditional businesses: building clever do-it-yourself electronic gadgets. When Fried was at MIT, earning a master's degree in computer science and electrical engineering, she relaxed by ordering parts to build homemade MP3 players, programmable jewelry, and other fun gadgets. As she posted her creations on her personal website, she began attracting requests from people wanting her to sell them kits so they could make the same items themselves. Fried took some personal funds and started Adafruit Industries, now a 50-employee business racking up $10 million in sales annually.[28]

Limor Fried, Adafruit Industries, combined both her academic knowledge and personal interests to prove her capabilities as an entrepreneur.

To spot opportunities, think carefully about events and trends as they unfold. Consider, for example, the following possibilities:[29]

Technological discoveries. Start-ups in biotechnology, microcomputers, and nanotechnology followed technological advances.
Demographic changes. All kinds of health care organizations have sprung up to serve an aging population, from exercise studios to assisted-living facilities.

One business that targets both the aging American population and the growth in single-parent and dual-career households is Errands Done Right. The service assists those who are pressed for time or have difficulty getting around.[30]

Lifestyle and taste changes. Start-ups have capitalized on new clothing and music trends, desire for fast food, and growing interest in sports. In recent years, more consumers want to help take care of the environment, and more businesses are concerned about showing consumers that they care, too.

Economic dislocations, such as booms or failures. Rising oil prices spurred a variety of developments related to alternative energy or energy efficiency.

Calamities such as wars and natural disasters. The terrorist attacks of September 2001 spurred concern about security, and entrepreneurs today are still pursuing ideas to help government agencies prevent future attacks. The hurricanes on the Gulf Coast raised awareness of the importance of preparing for emergencies.

Government initiatives and rule changes. Deregulation spawned new airlines and trucking companies. Whenever the government tightens energy efficiency requirements, opportunities become available for entrepreneurs developing ideas for cutting energy use.

Franchises   One important type of opportunity is the franchise. You may know intuitively what franchising is. Or you can at least name some prominent franchises: Chipotle, Jiffy Lube, Dunkin' Donuts—add your favorites here. **Franchising** is an entrepreneurial alliance between two organizations: the franchisor and the franchisee.[31] The franchisor is the innovator who has created at least one successful store and seeks partners to operate the same concept in other local markets. For the franchisee, the opportunity is wealth creation via a proven (but not failureproof) business concept, with the added advantage of the franchisor's expertise. For the franchisor, the opportunity is wealth creation through growth. The partnership is manifest in a trademark or brand, and together the partners' mission is to maintain and build the brand. The Noodles & Company chain of fast casual restaurants first grew by opening 79 company-owned locations. Management concluded that it could grow at a faster pace through franchising. Establishing standard menus and prices took a year, but franchising helped the company almost double its revenues in just two years.[32]

People often assume that buying a franchise is less risky than starting a business from scratch, but the evidence is mixed. One study that followed businesses for six years found the opposite of the popular assumption: 65 percent of the franchises studied were operating at the end of the period, whereas 72 percent of independent businesses were still operating. One reason may be that the franchises involved mostly a few, possibly riskier, industries. A study that compared only restaurants over a three-year period found that 43 percent of the franchises and 39 percent of independent restaurants remained in business.[33]

If you are contemplating a franchise, consider its market presence (local, regional, or national), market share and

franchising

An entrepreneurial alliance between a franchisor (an innovator who has created at least one successful store and wants to grow) and a franchisee (a partner who manages a new store of the same type in a new location).

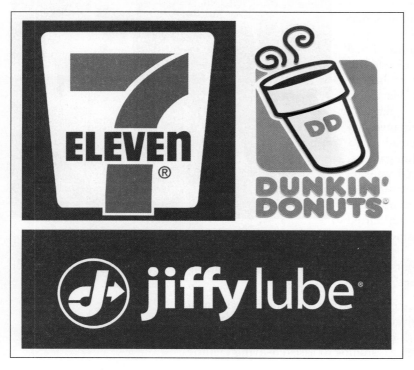

profit margins, national programs for marketing and purchasing, the nature of the business, including required training and degree of field support, terms of the license agreement (e.g., 20 years with automatic renewal versus less than 10 years or no renewal), capital required, and franchise fees and royalties.[34]

Although some people think success with a franchise is a no-brainer, would-be franchisees have a lot to consider. Luckily, plenty of useful sources exist for learning more, including the International Franchise Association (http://www.franchise.org), the Small Business Administration (http://www.sba.gov), Franchise Chat (http://www.franchise-chat.com), and *Entrepreneur* magazine's online Franchises page (http://www.entrepreneur.com), which includes rankings as well as articles profiling franchisors and franchisees. In addition, the Federal Trade Commission investigates complaints of deceptive claims by franchisors and publishes information about those cases. Take your time in investigating business opportunities, consulting with an accountant or lawyer who has experience.

The Next Frontiers   The next frontiers for entrepreneurship—where do they lie? Throughout history, aspiring entrepreneurs have asked this question. The editors of *Entrepreneur* magazine recently identified opportunities arising from new technology and changing consumer tastes.[35] The powerful potential of big data to improve decision making is opening up tremendous opportunities for businesses that can help their clients collect, store, manage, and analyze data. Sectors and product categories that have recently enjoyed huge growth are health care, education, and, of course, mobile apps.[36]

One fascinating opportunity for entrepreneurs is outer space. Historically, the space market was driven by the government and was dominated by big defense contractors such as Boeing and Lockheed Martin. But now, with demand for satellite launches and potential profits skyrocketing, smaller entrepreneurs are entering the field. SpaceX has been transporting cargo to the International Space Station for NASA and is developing the capability to transport astronaut crews. NASA also has granted a cargo-shuttling contract to Orbital Sciences Corporation. More futuristic still is the concept of entrepreneur Robert Bigelow. His company, Bigelow Aerospace, has created a residence module for living in space. The module is made out of a synthetic fiber rather than a metal structure, so it can be compressed for more efficient transportation and then expanded upon its arrival. Bigelow has a contract to test a 13-foot by 10-foot version of the module at the International Space Station.[37]

Changes have been coming fast in the health care sector in the United States, and where there is change, smart entrepreneurs spot opportunities. Driven by advances in technology coupled with incentives in the Affordable Care Act, health care providers have been digitizing their data for patient care, medication management, and treatment outcomes—a trend that yields opportunities for hardware and software businesses that understand the needs of these clients. In addition, rising costs for health care and health insurance create

The International Space Station is a habitable artificial satellite. Currently the largest artificial body in orbit, it can be seen at certain times with the naked eye from earth.

opportunities for entrepreneurs with ideas for restraining those costs. For example, mobile-device apps that promote fitness or help patients manage chronic conditions can appeal to consumers, insurance companies, and employers. GE's healthymagination program recently partnered with an entrepreneurship support group called Startup Health to fund promising start-ups in the health care field. Among the companies the partners funded are itMD, which developed a system for sharing and storing medical images online, and Care at Hand, which analyzes data about elderly patients receiving home care to alert nurses when data signal a possible disease requiring attention.[38]

In Practice

SWITCHBLADE: HELPING CUSTOMERS' CUSTOMERS

The mobile Internet is another important business frontier for companies such as 3Cinteractive. While many entrepreneurs rushed to offer mobile apps for consumers, 3Cinteractive founders John Duffy, Mike FitzGibbon, and Mark Smith saw profit potential in serving business customers. They formed their company to provide software that helps companies connect with *their* customers on mobile devices.

Basically, 3Cinteractive created a software platform called Switchblade, which resides on the company's computer servers and is accessed online. Then 3Cinteractive helps business customers identify what kinds of tasks they want to do with this platform—say, sending text messages or collecting payments. For example, Walgreens uses a 3Cinteractive app to analyze customer data and automatically text customers to remind them when it's time to refill a prescription, and Boca Raton Regional Hospital uses the service to remind patients of their appointments. The hospital app also includes a database patients can use to look up general medical advice associated with particular symptoms. Newer applications aim to monitor social media for company-related posts and prompt an appropriate response—say, a customer service representative phoning after a major customer complains.

Along with Walgreens, other big clients include Best Buy, Disney, and ESPN. In its first seven years, 3Cinteractive has grown to a $28.7 million business by showing its customers how they can retain and engage consumers better via mobile devices. Cofounders Duffy and FitzGibbon both have backgrounds in sales, so they understand that success is about more than jumping on the latest fad; they have to help their customers achieve their goals.[39]

- What other opportunities might the popularity of mobile devices offer to 3Cinteractive?

transaction fee model

Charging fees for goods and services.

advertising support model

Charging fees to advertise on a site.

intermediary model

Charging fees to bring buyers and sellers together.

affiliate model

Charging fees to direct site visitors to other companies' sites.

subscription model

Charging fees for site visits.

The Internet The Internet is a business frontier that continues to expand. With Internet commerce, as with any start-up, entrepreneurs need sound business models and practices. During the heady days of the Internet rush, many entrepreneurs and investors thought revenues and profits were unimportant and all that mattered was to attract visitors to their websites (capture eyeballs). But you need to watch costs carefully, and you want to break even and achieve profitability as soon as possible.[40]

At least five successful business models have proven successful in the e-commerce market: transaction fee, advertising support, intermediary, affiliate, and subscription models.[41] In the **transaction fee model**, companies charge a fee for goods or services. Amazon.com and online travel agents are prime examples. In the **advertising support model**, advertisers pay the site operator to gain access to the demographic group that visits the operator's site.

The **intermediary model** has eBay as the premier example, bringing buyers and sellers together and charging a commission for each sale. With the **affiliate model**, sites pay commissions to other sites to drive business to their own sites. Zazzle.com, Spreadshirt.com, and CafePress.com are variations on this model. They sell custom-decorated gift items such as mugs and T-shirts. Designers are the affiliates; they choose basic, undecorated products (such as a plain shirt) and add their own designs, creating the customized products offered to consumers.[42] Finally, websites using the **subscription model** charge a monthly or annual fee for site visits or access to site content. Newspapers and magazines are good examples.

What about businesses whose primary focus is not e-commerce? Start-ups and established small companies can create attractive websites that add to their professionalism, give them access to more customers, and bring them closer to suppliers, investors, and service providers. Companies can move much more quickly than in the past and save money on activities including customer service/support, technical support, data retrieval, public relations, investor relations, selling, requests for product literature, and purchasing. Setting up shop online costs less than it ever did.

Social Entrepreneurship   Social entrepreneurship has been around for decades, but is surging in popularity and impact and as a focus for academic research.[43] **Social entrepreneurship** has been defined in many ways, but most fundamentally it refers to leveraging resources to address social problems.[44]

It does so by using market-based methods.[45] Organizations that do this are **social enterprises.** Social entrepreneurship creates social value by stimulating social change or meeting social needs.[46]

One of the best-known examples of social entrepreneurship is the Nobel Prize–winning work of Dr. Muhammad Yunus, formerly of Grameen Bank, which began helping women in South Asia obtain microloans.[47] Another is Fabio Rosa's Agroelectric System of Appropriate Technology (STA), which established low-cost electrification and irrigation in rural Brazil.[48] Additional examples include Nuru Energy, which uses local entrepreneurs to sell high-efficiency LED lighting in Rwanda;[49] the EMR Project, which developed an electronic medical records system to improve patient care in Botswana;[50] the Cookie Project, which trained women to make high-quality cookies with natural ingredients in distressed areas of South Africa;[51] and the Feeds Project, which produces low-cost, high-quality animal feed in Zambia for small-scale chicken farmers, thereby alleviating unemployment and starvation.[52]

Social entrepreneurship is not charity, and it is different from corporate social responsibility (CSR),[53] which you read about in Chapter 5. CSR is not necessarily practiced with profit as a guiding principle, and corporations often relegate it to a side activity. Social entrepreneurship fully incorporates social as well as economic value into mainstream thinking and decision making. It provides dual, shared value: creating economic value plus social or societal benefit simultaneously.[54] See Table 7.3 for examples.

social entrepreneurship

Leveraging resources to address social problems.

social enterprise

Organization that engages in social entrepreneurship.

TABLE 7.3   Examples of Social Entrepreneurship Companies

Company Name	Description
Kopo Kopo	Offers software that enables 30 million SMEs in emerging markets to accept, process, and manage mobile money payments (e.g., Safaricom M-Pesa, Airtel Money). Kopo Kopo is the first company to offer this service on a subscription basis and is positioning itself to be a leader in providing merchant services in emerging markets.
Lipisha	Provides financial services technology that facilitates and tracks transactions between mobile money accounts and bank accounts for small and medium-sized businesses that interact with consumers at the base of the pyramid (BoP). Over 15 million people in Kenya use mobile money services such as M-Pesa. Through Lipisha, businesses can also compile and analyze business reports, assess consumer trends, and advertise to customers via SMS.
Simpa Networks	Offers a secure, prepaid payment platform that makes clean energy solutions affordable and investable for the base of the pyramid. Simpa sells a mobile meter that enables distributed energy on a progressive purchase basis to underserved consumers in emerging markets. Customers make a small initial down payment for a high-quality solar PV system and pre-pay for energy service in affordable, user-defined increments using a mobile phone. Each payment is applied toward the purchase price of a system. Once fully paid, the system unlocks and produces energy on an ongoing basis.
Waste Capital Partners	Cleans urban areas by providing integrated solid waste management services that also meaningfully employ marginalized individuals. Waste Capital Partners provides doorstep waste collection to residential households in small and medium-sized cities and towns in India for a nominal monthly fee. They also compost organic waste to sell to farmers and sell recyclable waste to processors.
viaCycle	Provides fleets of bicycles that can be rented instantly via SMS, voice, or mobile app to build more sustainable communities. They have developed a proprietary system (including hardware and software) to monitor and control access to each bike remotely and seamlessly manage billing and data collection.

(continued)

Company Name	Description
Save Energy Systems	Improves the energy efficiency of small to mid-size businesses by controlling their heating, ventilation, and air conditioning (HVAC) systems through proprietary software. Save Energy Systems' Demand Limiting Controller (DLC) is integrated with building thermostat systems to provide automated demand response, kWh reductions, and peak-rate power shifts, resulting in reduced energy use and cost savings.
CleanNG	Aims to increase natural gas fuel storage and efficiency for natural-gas vehicles through the manufacture and distribution of high-pressure fuel storage systems. CleanNG has developed a proprietary, high-efficiency fuel storage system that carries 30% more fuel than traditional tanks, is 60% lighter, and is created through a sustainable manufacturing process. By making it easier to switch to compressed natural gas, CleanNG is contributing to major reductions in pollution.
Eco Fuels Kenya	Uses Kenya's indigenous croton nuts to produce environmentally friendly green biofuels and organic fertilizers. EFK contracts with local communities in western Kenya to harvest and deposit the nuts in locally owned and operated collection centers. The liquid biofuel they process can be used as a direct replacement for diesel, and the residue from the oil extraction process is used to produce organic fertilizers for commercial agricultural use.
SevaMob	Provides basic health care, insurance, and legal advisory services to populations at the base of the pyramid through an affordable subscription of $2-3/month. They leverage a network of mobile field officers, a 24/7 call center, and appointments with third-party specialists for advanced needs.
Saútil	A web-based platform that provides free health care information to Brazilians. Saútil is serving 100,000 Brazilians living below the poverty line per month and has raised $1 million in follow-on capital from commercial investors.
Kickboard	Founded by Teach for America alumna Jen Medbery, enables teachers to use data to improve student performance in high-poverty areas of the United States. It has raised $2 million in investment and is now serving 25,000 students across the United States.
Mobile Works	Enables home-based workers, primarily women living in poverty, in the United States and India to earn extra cash performing micro-tasks on a mobile phone. It has processed over 2 million tasks, graduated Y-Combinator, and raised $1.7 million.
Takamoto Biogas	Sells affordable household biogas systems, including stoves, water heaters, and power generators. They are delivered and financed as a utility with remote GSM metering. The biogas systems pay for themselves in 2 years and have a lifespan of over 30 years. They have generated $15K in revenue to date.

Source: Courtesy of Village Capital.

Combining social and commercial goals isn't new; consider hospitals, universities, and arts organizations.[55] And, not all social problems can be solved by entrepreneurial solutions. But pursuing the dual goal of both economic and social value may be developing as the new norm, with positive social outcomes as key to long-term success. States Pierre Omidyar, founder of eBay: "you really can make the world better in any sector—in nonprofits, in business, or in government. It's not a question of one sector's struggling against another, or of 'giving back' versus 'taking away.' That's old thinking. A true philanthropist will use every tool he can to make an impact. Today business is a key part of the equation, and the sectors are learning to work together."[56]

Opportunities exist to make substantial positive impact on virtually every societal need and to make a profit doing so. Profit is likely to make societal value creation more sustainable over the long run.

What Does It Take, Personally?

Many people assume that there is an entrepreneurial personality. No single personality type predicts entrepreneurial success, but you are more likely to succeed as an entrepreneur if you exhibit certain characteristics:[57]

1. *Commitment and determination:* Successful entrepreneurs are decisive, tenacious, disciplined, willing to sacrifice, and able to immerse themselves in their enterprises. Entrepreneurial passion[58] can play an important role in all of these things.
2. *Leadership:* They are self-starters, team builders, superior learners, and teachers. Communicating a vision for the future of the company—an essential component of leadership that you'll learn more about in Chapter 12—has a direct impact on venture growth.[59]
3. *Opportunity obsession:* They have an intimate knowledge of customers' needs, are market driven, and are obsessed with value creation and enhancement.
4. *Tolerance of risk, ambiguity, and uncertainty:* They are calculated risk takers and risk managers, tolerant of stress, and able to resolve problems.
5. *Creativity, self-reliance, and ability to adapt:* They are open-minded, restless with the status quo, able to learn quickly, highly adaptable, creative, skilled at conceptualizing, and attentive to details.
6. *Motivation to excel:* They have a clear results orientation, set high but realistic goals, have a strong drive to achieve, know their own weaknesses and strengths, and focus on what can be done rather than on the reasons things can't be done.

Making Good Choices   Success is a function not only of personal approaches but also of making good choices about the business you start. Figure 7.2 presents a model for conceptualizing entrepreneurial ventures and making the best possible choices. It depicts ventures along two dimensions: innovation and risk. The new venture may involve high or low levels of innovation or the creation of something new and different. It can also be characterized by low or high risk. Risk refers primarily to the probability of major financial loss. But it also is more than that; it is psychological risk as perceived by the entrepreneur, including risk to reputation and ego.[60]

The upper-left quadrant, high innovation/low risk, depicts ventures of truly novel ideas with little risk. As examples, the inventors of Lego building blocks and Velcro fasteners could build their products by hand at little expense. A pioneering product idea from Procter & Gamble might fit here if there are no current competitors and because, for a company of that size, the financial risks of new product investments can seem relatively small.

In the upper-right quadrant, high innovation/high risk, novel product ideas are accompanied by high risk because the financial investments are high and the competition is great. A new drug or a new automobile would likely fall into this category.

FIGURE 7.2
Entrepreneurial Strategy Matrix

Most small business ventures are in the low innovation/high risk cell (lower right). They are fairly conventional entries in well-established fields. New restaurants, retail shops, and commercial outfits involve high investment for the small business entrepreneur and face direct competition from similar businesses. Finally, the low innovation/low risk category includes ventures that require minimal investment and/or face minimal competition for strong market demand. Examples are some service businesses having low start-up costs and those involving entry into small towns if there is no competitor and demand is adequate.

How is this matrix useful? It helps entrepreneurs think about their ventures and decide whether they suit their particular objectives. It also helps identify effective and ineffective strategies. You might find one cell more appealing than others. The lower-left cell is likely to have relatively low payoffs but to provide more security. The higher risk/return trade-offs are in other cells, especially the upper right. So you might place your new venture idea in the appropriate cell and determine whether that cell is the one in which you would prefer to operate. If it is, the venture is one that perhaps should be pursued, pending fuller analysis. If it is not, you can reject the idea or take steps to move it toward a different cell.

The matrix also can help entrepreneurs remember a useful point: successful companies do not always require a cutting-edge technology or an exciting new product. Even companies offering the most mundane products—the type that might reside in the lower-left cell—can gain competitive advantage by doing basic things differently from and better than competitors.

In Practice

For Max Arndt, the choice of a business idea was a requirement for his entrepreneurship class at the University of Minnesota. Pondering what problems of modern society have yet to be solved, it occurred to Arndt that many people hate touching the door handle when they leave a public restroom. How else could they make a sanitary exit? Arndt figured you would need to come up with some kind of metal piece that could be bolted to the bottom of the inside of the door, and that way, you could pull the door open with the toe of your shoe.

That thinking gave birth to the Toepener—basically a metal plate with an L-shaped hook for pulling the door open. Arndt's class loved the idea and voted to make it the one they would back. The school provided a $15,000 loan, and Arndt led his team in setting up the business, with the goal of repaying the loan and earning a profit by the end of the semester. They built a website, set the price at $49.95, and contracted with a manufacturer. Soon they had hundreds of orders and were on track to meet their goals. The editors of *Inc.* magazine also fell in love with the idea, naming the Toepener one of the coolest college start-ups.[61]

- Would you rate this business idea as high or low on innovation? As high or low on risk?

Success and Failure

Success or failure lies ahead for entrepreneurs starting their own companies as well as for those starting new businesses within bigger corporations. Entrepreneurs succeed or fail in private, public, and not-for-profit sectors; in nations at all stages of development; and in all nations, regardless of their politics.[62]

Estimated failure rates for start-ups vary. Most indicate that failure is more the rule than the exception. The failure rate is high for certain businesses such as restaurants and lower for successful franchises. Start-ups have at least two major liabilities: newness and smallness.[63] New companies are relatively unknown and need to learn how to be better than established competitors at something that customers value. Regarding smallness, the odds of surviving improve if the venture reaches a critical mass of at least 10 or 20 people, has revenues of $2 million or $3 million, and is pursuing opportunities with growth potential.[64]

To understand further the factors that influence success and failure, we'll consider risk, the economic environment, various management-related hazards, and initial public stock offerings (IPOs).

Risk   You learned about risk in Chapter 3. It's a given: starting a new business is risky. Entrepreneurs with plenty of business experience are especially aware of this. When Chris McGill was evaluating his idea for Mixx.com, a news website that could be personalized based on recommendations by users, he was *USA Today*'s vice president of strategy. To make Mixx succeed, McGill knew he would be leaving a well-paying job for an uncertain future in which he had to line up financing and hire talented people in a turbulent business environment. But McGill also concluded that his experience at *USA Today* and prior management experience with *Yahoo News* gave him the knowledge and connections for a successful Internet business.[65] He sold Mixx.com in 2011 to UberMedia.

Successful entrepreneurs are realistic about risk. They anticipate difficulties and cushion their business to help it weather setbacks. In downtown Seattle, entrepreneurs Ben and Cindi Raykovich saw a risk when a major construction project began disrupting traffic around their store, Sound Sports. The Raykoviches had built their business around serving running enthusiasts who worked downtown and would stop by on their lunch hour or after work. Concerned that the construction would drive away so much business that the store couldn't survive, they opened a second location in the nearby community of Poulsbo. If they needed to close the first store, they could continue to build their business in Poulsbo. Ben Raykovich is hardly cavalier about the situation: "My life is invested in this business. We need to spread out the risk."[66]

Richard Foos (left), Bob Emmer (center), and Garson Foos are successful entrepreneurs due to their creativity, innovation, and knowledge of their target customers' desires. They are shown here with a circa 1966–1967 Batmobile children's arcade ride in their Shout! Factory headquarters in Los Angeles. As CEO of the Shout! Factory, Richard Foos runs an emporium filled with nostalgia-type collectibles.

The Role of the Economic Environment   Entrepreneurial activity stems from the economic environment as well as the behavior of individuals. For example, money is a critical resource for all new businesses. Increases in the money supply and the supply of bank loans, real economic growth, and improved stock market performance lead to both improved prospects and increased sources of capital. In turn, the prospects and the capital increase the rate of business formation. Under favorable conditions, many aspiring entrepreneurs find early success. But economic cycles can quickly change favorable conditions into downturns. To succeed, entrepreneurs must have the foresight and talent to survive when the environment becomes more hostile.

> Economic cycles can quickly change favorable conditions into downturns.

Although good economic times may make it easier to start a company and to survive, bad times can offer an opportunity to expand. Ken Hendricks of ABC Supply found a business opportunity in a grim economic situation: a serious downturn in the manufacturing economy of the Midwest contributed to the shutdown of his town's largest employer, the Beloit Corporation. Hendricks purchased the company's buildings and lured a diverse group of new employers to town despite the economic challenges. In fact, Hendricks turned around struggling suppliers that ABC acquired.[67] Another silver lining in difficult economic times is that it's easier to recruit talent.

Business Incubators   The need to provide a nurturing environment for fledgling enterprises led to the creation of business incubators. **Business incubators,** often located in industrial parks or abandoned factories, are protected environments for new, small businesses. Incubators offer benefits such as low rents and shared costs. Shared staff costs, such as for receptionists and secretaries, avoid the expense of a full-time employee but still provide convenient access to services. The staff manager is usually an experienced businessperson or consultant who advises the new business owners. Incubators often are associated with universities, which provide technical and business services for the new companies.

The heyday of business incubators came in the 1990s, when around 700 of them were financing start-ups, mainly emphasizing technology. Eight out of 10 shut down following the collapse of the Internet bubble, but the idea of nurturing new businesses persists. Naval Ravikant, for example, is developing a company tentatively named Hit Forge, which resembles the dot-com incubators. Hit Forge hired four engineers with experience in launching successful Internet concepts. The engineers have wide latitude to try ideas, but they work under strict deadlines. They must go from concept to product within 90 days, and any enterprises that aren't growing after a year will be terminated. Unlike the older-style incubator, Hit Forge lets engineers work from the locations of their choice, and the engineers retain half ownership in the ventures they develop. Also, whereas incubators in the 1990s might have spent $2 million developing an idea, today's launches might cost just $50,000.[68]

Business incubators hatch new businesses. Once a young business begins gaining a foothold and establishing itself, **business accelerators** can provide additional support and advice. These still-young firms are more mature but still in their formative years, and they now face the challenges of sustaining growth and achieving their full market potential.[69]

 Common Management Challenges   As an entrepreneur, you are likely to face several common challenges that you should understand before you face them and then manage effectively when the time comes. We next discuss several such challenges.

You Might Not Enjoy It   Some managers and employees can specialize in what they love, whether it's selling or accounting. But entrepreneurs usually have to do it all, at least in the beginning. If you love product design, you also have to sell what you invent. If you love marketing, get ready to manage the money too. This last challenge was almost a stumbling block for Elizabeth Busch, Anne Frey-Mott, and Beckie Jankiewicz when they launched The Event Studio to run business conferences for their clients. All three women had experience with some aspect of running conferences, but when they started their company, they didn't fully think out all the accounting decisions they would need for measuring their income and cash flow. With some practical advice, they learned some basic accounting lessons that helped them avoid tax troubles later on.[70] If they hadn't been willing to learn new skills, entrepreneurship might not have been the right career path for them.

Survival Is Difficult   Companies without much of a track record tend to have more trouble lining up lenders, investors, and customers. When economic conditions cool or competition heats up, a small start-up serving a niche market may have limited options for survival. Failure can be devastating.

Founders of a start-up must make key decisions in so many areas of business that mistakes are a potentially devastating risk. Several months after starting Zipcar, a car-sharing service, founder Robin Chase evaluated the early financial data and discovered

business incubators

Protected environments for new, small businesses.

business accelerator

An organization that assists young firms in achieving faster and sustainable growth as they move into the next phase of their development.

that the company had made a mistake in setting prices. The daily rental fees had been set too low to make the company profitable. Chase concluded that the only way she could keep Zipcar in business was to own up to her error, disclose it to her customers, and explain that the rate would be rising by 25 percent. Only two customers complained, and Zipcar grew into a multimillion-dollar business.[71]

Growth Creates New Challenges   Just one in three *Inc.* 500 companies keeps growing fast enough to make this list of fastest-growing companies two years running. The reason: They are facing bigger challenges, competing with bigger firms, stretching the founders' capacities, and probably burning cash. Consultant Doug Tatum calls this phase of a company's growth "no man's land."[72] It's a difficult transition.

In the beginning, entrepreneurs keep their business afloat with dogged determination to win customers and keep them happy. They work long hours at low pay, deliver great service, and get good word-of-mouth advertising, and their business grows. When keeping up with all the work becomes physically impossible, entrepreneurs feel they need to bring in help. Julie Ladd, founder of CopyShark.net, says she got ready to contract for help after she spent six months doing everything alone: "I was working 70-plus hours a week and wasn't able to get the turnaround time that my clients needed."[73] The challenge, of course, is that you not only have to come up with the money to keep paying people for the long haul but also have to figure out who will bring the necessary skills and a level of motivation that can bring them close to the business owner's commitment to the company.

Growth seems to be a consuming goal for most entrepreneurs. But some company founders reach the size where they're happy and don't want to grow any further. Reaching a golden mean is possible.[74] Also, sometimes growth needs to be restrained until the company is ready. Only a year after Gregory Wynn, Komichel Johnson, and Robert A. Jones III set up their homebuilding business, JLW Homes and Communities, they had an opportunity to build a 70-unit condominium project called Heritage Pointe. They determined that getting the job done would require a master builder, two assistants, and at least 100 workers. JLW had two master builders, who were already assigned to projects, and too few workers, so the partners reluctantly decided not to take the job. Jones recalls, "It was way too early for us to do this type of deal, . . . and I'm glad we did [turn it down] because if we didn't, we may have lost our shirts."[75] By carefully planning growth at a sustainable pace, JLW has become a successful Atlanta firm.

It's Hard to Delegate   As the business grows, entrepreneurs often hesitate to delegate to other people work that they are used to doing. Leadership deteriorates into micromanagement, in which managers monitor too strictly, to the minutest detail. For example, during the Internet craze, many company founders with great technical knowledge but little experience became instant experts in every phase of business, including branding and advertising.[76] Turns out, they didn't know as much as they thought, and their companies crashed. Fortunately, many entrepreneurs observe the consequences of their behavior and figure out how to manage more effectively. Albert Ko, who founded a coupon website called DealPerk, used to handle employees' mistakes by yelling at them, but after he realized he was creating a fear-driven workplace, he began discussing problems privately with an emphasis on improvement. And after losing $500 to mistakes made by an employee who didn't understand directions, Jimmy Tomczak, founder of sandal maker Paper-Feet, has learned to verify that employees understand directions before they get started.[77]

Misuse of Funds   Many unsuccessful entrepreneurs blame their failure on inadequate financial resources. Yet failure due to a lack of financial resources doesn't necessarily indicate a real lack of money; it could mean a failure to use the available money properly. A lot of start-up capital may be wasted—on expensive locations, great furniture,

Bottom Line

Entrepreneurs can stabilize their companies' size, but they still have to keep a high-value business model and provide great customer service. *What might be a sign that a small company is growing too fast?*

and fancy stationery. Entrepreneurs who fail to use their resources wisely usually make one of two mistakes: They apply financial resources to the wrong uses, or they maintain inadequate control over their resources.

This problem may be more likely when a lucky entrepreneur gets a big infusion of cash from a venture capital firm or an initial offering of stock. For most start-ups, where the money on the line comes from the entrepreneur's own assets, he or she has more incentive to be careful. Tripp Micou, founder of Practical Computer Applications, says, "If all the money you spend is based on what you're bringing in [through sales], you very quickly focus on the right things to spend it on."[78] Micou, an experienced entrepreneur, believes that this financial limitation is actually a management advantage.

Poor Controls   Entrepreneurs, in part because they are very busy, often fail to use formal control systems. One common entrepreneurial malady is an aversion to record keeping. Expenses mount, but records do not keep pace. Pricing decisions are based on intuition without adequate reference to costs. As a result, the company earns inadequate margins to support growth.

Sometimes an economic slowdown provides a necessary alarm, warning business owners to pay attention to controls. When Servatii Pastry Shop and Deli's sales deteriorated even as the prices of ingredients were rising, owner Gary Gottenbusch set goals and monitored progress. One problem Gottenbusch tackled was the price of baking commodities, such as shortening and flour. He partnered with other local bakeries to form a purchasing association that buys in bulk and passes along the savings. Keeping costs down helped Servatii stay profitable when customers were trimming their budgets for baked goods.[79] Blinded by the light of growing sales, many entrepreneurs fail to maintain vigilance over other aspects of the business.

Even in high-growth companies, great numbers can mask brewing problems. In the absence of controls, the business veers out of control. So don't get overconfident; keep asking critical questions. Is our success based on just one big customer? Is our product just a fad that can fade away? Can other companies easily enter our domain and hurt our business? Are we losing a technology lead? Do we really understand the numbers, know where they come from, and have any hidden causes for concern?

Mortality and Succession   One long-term measure of an entrepreneur's success is the fate of the venture after the founder's death. Founding entrepreneurs often fail to plan for succession. When death occurs, estate tax problems or the lack of a skilled replacement for the founder can lead to business failure. In the United States and around the world, the large majority of family-owned businesses fail before the founder's grandchildren have taken charge.[80]

Management guru Peter Drucker offered the following advice to help family-managed businesses survive and prosper.[81] Family members working in the business must be at least as capable and hard-working as other employees; at least one key position should be filled by a nonfamily member; and someone outside the family and the business should help plan succession. Family members who are mediocre performers are resented by others; outsiders can be more objective and contribute expertise the family might not have. Issues of management succession are often the most difficult of all, causing serious conflict and possible breakup of the firm.

Going Public   Sometimes companies reach a point at which the owners want to go public. **Initial public stock offerings (IPOs)** offer a way to raise capital through federally registered and underwritten sales of shares in the company.[82] You need lawyers and accountants who know current regulations. The reasons for going public include raising more capital, reducing debt or improving the balance sheet and enhancing net worth, pursuing otherwise unaffordable opportunities, and improving credibility with customers and other stakeholders—you're in the big leagues now. Disadvantages

Bottom Line

You probably will pay close attention to costs at the beginning, but success sometimes brings neglect. Don't fall into that trap.

An entrepreneur who loves selling delegates bookkeeping to an accountant. What danger does this pose to the business?

---

initial public offering (IPO)

Sale to the public, for the first time, of federally registered and underwritten shares of stock in the company.

include the expense, time, and effort involved; the tendency to become more interested in the stock price and capital gains than in running the company properly; and the creation of a long-term relationship with an investment banking firm that won't necessarily always be a good one.[83]

Many entrepreneurs prefer to avoid going public, feeling they'll lose control if they do. That's a viewpoint that has persisted into the second generation of ownership at Half Price Books, a retail chain that was founded four decades ago by Pat Anderson and Ken Gjemre and remains a family business run by Anderson's daughter, Sharon Anderson Wright. Wright sees retaining private ownership as a necessary part of maintaining the company's commitment to employees, pointing out that "not everyone comes out well" when a business is sold. The company, which has more than 100 stores in 16 states, prides itself on hiring bright people and rewarding them with training, a good benefits package, and opportunities for advancement. Concern for employees fits in well with Half Price Books' general commitment to sustainability: 70 percent of the stores' inventory consists of used books, magazines, and music, a business model that promotes reusing rather than throwing out these items. Wright's desire to run an ecofriendly business is another value she can insist on when she is both owner and CEO of the company.[84]

Executing IPOs and other approaches to acquiring capital are complex, legalistic, and beyond the scope of this chapter. Sources for more information include the National Venture Capital Association (www.nvca.org), the Small Business Administration's Community page (http://www.sba.gov/community), and the SBA's Small Business Learning Center (http://www.sba.gov/sba-learning-center).

In the case of Popchips founder Keith Belling, he didn't opt for an IPO with his earlier venture, Allbusiness.com; instead, he exited after selling it to NBC. As you read "Management Connection: Progress Report," think about whether Popchips would be a good candidate for an IPO.

Management Connection

CAN POPCHIPS STAY HEALTHY?

Although founders Keith Belling and Kara Nielsen can be proud to see Popchips generate $93.7 million in sales after just a few years, their company does face some formidable challenges. For one thing, although $93 million is a lot of money, it represents roughly 0.1 percent of the $90 *billion* global market for snacks. Among the hundreds of snack makers in the United States alone, Popchips is competing with such giants as PepsiCo's Frito-Lay products and Mondelez (formerly part of Kraft Foods). In fact, Kellogg's has introduced Popcorn Chips, and Quaker has introduced its Popped brand of snacks. Consumers who are now snapping up Popchips as a way to enjoy crunchy snacks without the fat could abandon the brand as soon as someone new offers an alternative.

Belling tries to address the challenge by being personally engaged in helping to keep excitement for Popchips high. Five years after the start-up, Belling told a reporter that he personally answers 25 customer e-mails every

day. He does it because he wants to learn about what customers are thinking. It also puts him in a position to respond more dramatically than a big-company customer relations agent could ever do. In one case, after an enthusiastic New Yorker wrote in about her love of the product, Belling invited her to meet with a marketing manager—and sent her about 200 bags of Popchips for an event she was hosting.

To get out the message that his chips are not just low-fat but also delicious, Belling experiments with marketing. As is often the case when people get creative, some of the ideas backfire. The most notable flop was Ashton Kutcher's attempt to portray a Bollywood producer on a dating show, using an obviously fake Indian accent. After an uproar dominated by a blogger named Anil Dash, the company pulled the ad, and Keith Belling apologized on the company's website. Reflecting on the incident later, Belling noted that the experience had taught him about the powerful impact that social media can make and had prompted the company to consider consumers' perceptions more carefully.

Popchips has forged ahead with other celebrity-based marketing efforts. It recently lined up singer Katy Perry to launch tortilla chips in four flavors (Nacho, Ranch, Salsa, and Chili Limón) in 2012 and Katy's Kettle Corn in 2013. Even if consumers haven't always appreciated

the taste of Popchips advertising, the company hopes they will continue to get excited about the taste of its popped snacks.[85]

- What do you think are the most significant risks affecting Popchips?
- Do you think Popchips would be a good candidate for an initial public offering (IPO)? Why or why not?

Increasing Your Chances of Success

Entrepreneurs need to think through their business idea carefully to help ensure its success. We discuss here the importance of good planning and a variety of resources.

Planning   So you think you have identified a business opportunity. And you have the personal drive to make it a success. Now what? Where should you begin?

The Business Plan   Your excitement and intuition may convince you that you are on to something. But they might not convince anyone else. You need more thorough planning and analysis. This effort will help convince other people to get on board and help you avoid costly mistakes.

The first formal planning step is to do an opportunity analysis. An **opportunity analysis** includes a description of the good or service, an assessment of the opportunity, an assessment of the entrepreneur (you), a specification of activities and resources needed to translate your idea into a viable business, and your source(s) of capital.[86] Table 7.4 shows the questions you should answer in an opportunity analysis.

The opportunity analysis, or opportunity assessment plan, focuses on the opportunity, not the entire venture. It provides the basis for making a decision on whether to act. Then the **business plan** describes all the elements involved in starting the new venture.[87] The business plan describes the venture and its market, strategies, and future directions. It often has functional plans for marketing, finance, manufacturing, and human resources.

Table 7.5 shows an outline for a typical business plan. The business plan (1) helps determine the viability of your enterprise, (2) guides you as you plan and organize, and (3) helps you obtain financing. It is read by potential investors, suppliers, customers, and others. Get help in writing up a sound plan!

opportunity analysis

A description of the good or service, an assessment of the opportunity, an assessment of the entrepreneur, specification of activities and resources needed to translate your idea into a viable business, and your source(s) of capital.

business plan

A formal planning step that focuses on the entire venture and describes all the elements involved in starting it.

TABLE 7.4
Opportunity Analysis

What market need does my idea fill?
What personal observations have I experienced or recorded with regard to that market need?
What social condition underlies this market need?
What market research data can be marshaled to describe this market need?
What patents might be available to fulfill this need?
What competition exists in this market? How would I describe the behavior of this competition?
What does the international market look like?
What does the international competition look like?
Where is the money to be made in this activity?

SOURCE: R. Hisrich and M. Peters, *Entrepreneurship: Starting, Developing, and Managing a New Enterprise*, p. 41. Copyright © 1998 by The McGraw-Hill Companies, Inc. Reprinted with permission.

TABLE 7.5   Outline of a Business Plan

I. EXECUTIVE SUMMARY

Description of the Business Concept and the Business

Opportunity and Strategy

Target Market and Projections

Competitive Advantages

Costs

Sustainability

The Team

The Offering

II. THE INDUSTRY AND THE COMPANY AND ITS PRODUCT(S) OR SERVICE(S)

The Industry

The Company and the Concept

The Product(s) or Service(s)

Entry and Growth Strategy

III. MARKET RESEARCH AND ANALYSIS

Customers

Market Size and Trends

Competition and Competitive Edges

Estimated Market Share and Sales

Ongoing Market Evaluation

IV. THE ECONOMICS OF THE BUSINESS

Gross and Operating Margins

Profit Potential and Durability

Fixed, Variable, and Semivariable Costs

Months to Breakeven

Months to Reach Positive Cash Flow

V. MARKETING PLAN

Overall Marketing Strategy

Pricing

Sales Tactics

Service and Warranty Policies

Advertising and Promotion

Distribution

VI. DESIGN AND DEVELOPMENT PLANS

Development Status and Tasks

Difficulties and Risks

Product Improvement and New Products

Costs

Proprietary Issues

VII. MANUFACTURING AND OPERATIONS PLAN

Operating Cycle

Geographical Location

Facilities and Improvements

Strategy and Plans

Regulatory and Legal Issues

VIII. MANAGEMENT TEAM

Organization

Key Management Personnel

Management Compensation and Ownership

Other Investors

Employment and Other Agreements and Stock Option and Bonus Plans

Board of Directors

Other Shareholders, Rights, and Restrictions

Supporting Professional Advisers and Services

IX. OVERALL SCHEDULE

X. CRITICAL RISKS, PROBLEMS, AND ASSUMPTIONS

XI. THE FINANCIAL PLAN

Actual Income Statements and Balance Sheets

Pro Forma Income Statements

Pro Forma Balance Sheets

Pro Forma Cash Flow Analysis

Breakeven Chart and Calculation

Cost Control

Highlights

XII. PROPOSED COMPANY OFFERING

Desired Financing

Offering

Capitalization

Use of Funds

Investor's Return

XIII. APPENDIXES

SOURCE: J. A. Timmons and S. Spinelli, Jr., *New Venture Creation: Entrepreneurship for the 21st Century*, 7th ed., 2007, p. 229. Copyright 2007 The McGraw-Hill Companies. Reprinted with permission.

Key Planning Elements   A successful business needs enough cash to cover start-up expenses and keep the company running during slow periods. The initial budget should cover one-time costs, such as the fee to form a corporation, and ongoing expenses such as supplies and rent for the first few months. The company's founders may start the business with their own money, or they may seek financing in the form of debt (taking out a loan from family, friends, or a bank) or equity (taking money in exchange for an ownership share in the company). Typically, start-ups get most of their money from the owners, their families, and loans and credit lines from banks. Other kinds of investors, such as venture capital firms, generate a lot of publicity for splashy deals but provide a very small share of start-up funds.[88]

Under these circumstances, raising money to start a business can be one of the entrepreneur's greatest challenges. When Eaton Corporation decided to close down the Massillon, Ohio, factory where Tony Lee worked, the ambitious foreman decided he would rather learn to run it than watch it go out of business. Lee studied business books at the library, wrote a detailed plan, and convinced a group of investors that his ideas could work; however, the investors insisted he also raise $25,000 of his own money and become a part-owner. Lee saved every penny he could, sold his motorcycle, and took out a second mortgage on his house. Since then, he has rebuilt the manufacturing company, now called Ring Masters, has earned a tidy return on his investment, and is planning to expand.[89]

Just as the Internet has transformed every other aspect of business, it is poised to remake the challenge of raising start-up money. This trend started with the use of social-media tools to link would-be entrepreneurs with people who want to make great ideas happen. At crowdfunding websites, such as AngelList, Crowdfunder.com, FundersClub, and Kickstarter, the entrepreneurs post their ideas, and anyone can donate to the cause. Until recently, crowdfunding was mostly limited to small contributions from people who gave in exchange for a company-provided experience, discount, or product sample; the funders don't receive equity in the business. The main reason is that the Securities and Exchange Commission, which regulates investing, needs to ensure that investors on these sites have the same protections available to traditional investors. In 2012, however, Congress passed the Jumpstart Our Business Startups Act (JOBS Act), which allows crowdfunding sites to begin accepting equity investors after the SEC has prepared rules for this type of financing. As of this writing, the rules were expected to be ready before the end of 2013. If crowdfunding takes off, as some observers expect, entrepreneurs could have access to a huge new source of funds and new ways to convert customers into fans of the company, but they should be careful not to rely on the crowd to the exclusion of seasoned investors who might also provide valuable advice.[90]

Most business plans devote so much attention to financial projections that they neglect other important information—information that matters greatly to astute investors. In fact, financial projections tend to be overly optimistic. Investors know this and discount the figures. In addition to the numbers, the best plans convey—and make certain that the entrepreneurs have carefully thought through—five key factors: the people, the opportunity, the competition, the context, and risk and reward.[91]

The people should be energetic and have skills and expertise directly relevant to the venture. For many astute investors, the people are the most important variable, more important even than the idea. Arthur Rock, a legendary venture capitalist who helped start Intel, Teledyne, and Apple, stated, "I invest in people, not ideas. If you can find good people, if they're wrong about the product, they'll make a switch."[92]

The opportunity should provide a competitive advantage that can be defended. Customers are the focus here: Who is the customer? How does the customer make decisions? How will the product be priced? How will the venture reach all customer segments? How much does it cost to acquire and support a customer and to produce and deliver the product? How easy or difficult is it to retain a customer?

> The opportunity should provide a competitive advantage that can be defended.

It is also essential to consider the competition fully. The plan must identify current competitors and their strengths and weaknesses, predict how they will respond to the new venture, indicate how the new venture will respond to the competitors' responses, identify future potential competitors, and consider how to collaborate with or face off against actual or potential competitors. The original plan for Zappos was for its website to compete with other online shoe retailers by offering a wider selection than they did. However, most people buy shoes in stores, so Zappos cofounders Nick Swinmurn and Tony Hsieh soon realized that they needed a broader view of the competition. They began focusing more on service and planning a distribution method that would make online shopping as successful as visiting a store.[93]

The environmental context should be a favorable one from regulatory and economic perspectives. Such factors as tax policies, rules about raising capital, interest rates, inflation, and exchange rates will affect the viability of the new venture. The context can make it easier or harder to get backing and to succeed. Importantly, the plan should make clear that you know that the context inevitably will change, forecast how the changes will affect the business, and describe how you will deal with the changes.

The risk must be understood and addressed as fully as possible. The future is always uncertain, and the elements described in the plan will change over time. Although you cannot predict the future, you must contemplate head-on the possibilities of key people leaving, interest rates changing, a key customer leaving, or a powerful competitor responding ferociously. Then describe what you will do to prevent, avoid, or cope with such possibilities. You should also speak to the end of the process: how to get money out of the business eventually. Will you go public? Will you sell or liquidate? What are the various possibilities for investors to realize their ultimate gains?[94]

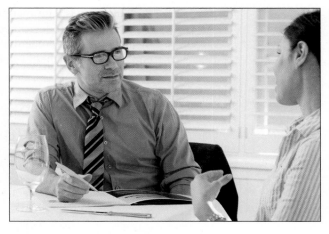

Entrepreneurs should carefully consider the five key factors when developing a business plan: the people, the opportunity, the competition, the context, and risk and reward. Typically, financial projections dominate the plan while these other important factors are overlooked or undervalued.

Selling the Plan   Your goal is to get investors to support the plan, so the elements of a great plan, as just described, are essential. It's also important whom you decide to try to convince to back your plan.

Many entrepreneurs want passive investors who will give them money and let them do what they want. Doctors and dentists generally fit this image. Professional venture capitalists do not—they demand more control and more of the returns. But when a business goes wrong—and chances are, it will—nonprofessional investors are less helpful and less likely to advance more (needed) money. Sophisticated investors have seen sinking ships before and know how to help. They are more likely to solve problems, provide more money, and navigate financial and legal waters.[95]

View the plan as a way for you to figure out how to reduce risk, maximize reward, and convince others that you understand the entire new venture process. Don't put together a plan built on naïveté or overconfidence or one that cleverly hides major flaws. You might not fool others, and you certainly would be fooling yourself.

Nonfinancial Resources   Also crucial to the success of a new business are nonfinancial resources, including legitimacy in the minds of the public and the various ways in which other people can help.

Legitimacy   An important resource for the new venture is **legitimacy**—people's judgment of a company's acceptance, appropriateness, and desirability.[96] When the market confers legitimacy, it helps overcome the liability of newness that creates a high percentage of new venture failure.[97] Legitimacy helps a firm acquire other resources such as top managers, good employees, financial resources, and government support. In a three-year study tracking business start-ups, the likelihood that a company would succeed at selling products, hiring employees, and attracting investors depended most on how skillfully entrepreneurs demonstrated that their business was legitimate.[98]

legitimacy

People's judgment of a company's acceptance, appropriateness, and desirability, generally stemming from company goals and methods that are consistent with societal values.

A business is legitimate if its goals and methods are consistent with societal values. You can generate legitimacy by visibly conforming to rules and expectations created by governments, credentialing associations, and professional organizations; by visibly endorsing widely held values; and by visibly practicing widely held beliefs.[99]

In Practice

TUMBLRS' LEGITIMACY

Tumblr, a blogging platform with social-media features, quickly gained legitimacy because it is beautifully designed and easy to use. Founder David Karp was concerned about creating a genuine sense of community among users and a place where people could enjoy being creative. At Tumblr's dashboard, users can prepare blog posts, follow other blogs, and share one another's work. Users who want to comment on another blog do so by reblogging it and commenting on their own page; this avoids anonymity and the ugly behavior that has sometimes followed it. With this approach, Tumblr has attracted more than 86 million blogs and almost 170 million visitors.

The challenge, as has so often been the case with online enterprises, is how to make money without losing sight of the original vision that gave Tumblr its legitimacy. Karp initially downplayed the importance of advertising in Tumblr's business model—it didn't even run ads for five years. Then, rather than collect user metrics that would help advertisers target humdrum messages, Karp focused on the creativity of Tumblr and its users. He hoped advertisers with a particularly creative message would consider Tumblr's blogs a desirable medium. But as the company has grown beyond 100 employees, Karp seems to have accepted that advertising must be a greater part of Tumblr's future, perhaps as a way to build the advertiser's image more than close a sale. One compromise he is testing is to include especially creative paid messages in its list of the best Tumblr content.[100]

- How can Tumblr maintain its legitimacy as a creative outlet if it accepts advertising? (Or if it can't have both ads and legitimacy, how else might Tumblr be profitable?)

social capital

A competitive advantage in the form of relationships with other people and the image other people have of you.

Networks   The entrepreneur is aided greatly by having a strong network of people. **Social capital**—being part of a social network and having a good reputation—helps entrepreneurs gain access to useful information, gain trust and cooperation from others, recruit employees, form successful business alliances, receive funding from venture capitalists, and become more successful.[101] Social capital provides a lasting source of competitive advantage.[102]

Top Management Teams   The top management team is another crucial resource. For example, Sudhin Shahani's start-ups include MyMPO, whose digital media services include Musicane, which lets musicians sell audio and video files and ringtones online at storefronts they create for themselves. The company's head of marketing was singer Will.i.am.[103] Having a musician in that top spot may help Musicane build client relationships with other artists. Also, in companies that have incorporated, a board of directors improves the company's image, develops longer-term plans for expansion, supports day-to-day activities, and develops a network of information sources.

Advisory Boards   Whether or not the company has a formal board of directors, entrepreneurs can assemble a group of people willing to serve as an advisory board. Board members with business experience can help an entrepreneur learn basics such as how to do cash flow analysis; identify needed strategic changes; and build relationships with bankers, accountants, and attorneys.

Partners Often two people go into business together as partners. Partners can help one another access capital, spread the workload, share the risk, and share expertise. One of the strengths of JLW Homes and Communities, the Atlanta construction business described earlier, is that the three founding partners bring different areas of expertise to the business. Gregory Wynn was a master homebuilder, Komichel Johnson was a financial expert, and Robert A. Jones III was a successful salesperson. Johnson explains the advantage this way: "We don't all agree on the same issues, and we've had some heated arguments. . . . But we realize that through communication and laying out the facts, we can overcome any issues that may arise within our organization."[104]

Partnerships are not always marriages made in heaven.

Despite the potential advantages of finding a compatible partner, partnerships are not always marriages made in heaven. "Mark" talked three of his friends into joining him in starting his own telecommunications company because he didn't want to try it alone. He learned quickly that while he wanted to put money into growing the business, his three partners wanted the company to pay for their cars and meetings in the Bahamas. The company collapsed. "I never thought a business relationship could overpower friendship, but this one did. Where money's involved, people change."

To be successful, partners need to acknowledge one another's talents, let each other do what they do best, communicate honestly, and listen to one another. Partners also must learn to trust each other by making and keeping agreements. If they must break an agreement, it is crucial that they give early notice and clean up after their mistakes.

Corporate Entrepreneurship

Large corporations are more than passive bystanders in the entrepreneurial explosion. Even established companies try to find and pursue new and profitable ideas—and they need in-house entrepreneurs (sometimes called intrapreneurs) to do so.

LO 6

Building Support for Your Idea

A manager who has a new idea to capitalize on a market opportunity will need to get others in the organization to buy in or sign on. In other words, you need to build a network of allies who support and will help implement the idea.

If you need to build support for a project idea, the first step involves clearing the investment with your immediate boss or bosses.[105] At this stage, you explain the idea and seek approval to look for wider support.

Higher executives often want evidence that the project is backed by your peers before committing to it. This involves making cheerleaders—people who will support the manager before formal approval from higher levels.

Next, horse trading begins. You can offer promises of payoffs from the project in return for support, time, money, and other resources that peers and others contribute.

Finally, you should get the blessing of relevant higher-level officials. This usually involves a formal presentation. You will need to guarantee the project's technical and political feasibility. Higher management's endorsement of the project and promises of resources help convert potential supporters into an enthusiastic team. At this point, you can go back to your boss and make specific plans for going ahead with the project. Along the way, expect resistance and frustration—and use passion and persistence, as well as business logic, to persuade others to get on board.

Bottom Line
Recall from Chapter 3 that creativity spawns good new ideas, but innovation requires actually implementing those ideas so they become realities. If you work in an organization and have a good idea, you must convince other people to get on board.
What skills would you need to get people on board with a new idea?

Building Intrapreneurship

Success in fostering a culture in which intrapreneurs flourish comes from making an intentional decision to foster entrepreneurial thinking and behavior, creating new venture teams, and changing the compensation system so that it encourages, supports, and rewards creative and innovative behaviors. In other words, building intrapreneurship derives from careful and deliberate strategy.

skunkworks

A project team designated to produce a new, innovative product.

Two common approaches used to stimulate intrapreneurial activity are skunkworks and bootlegging. **Skunkworks** are project teams designated to produce a new product. A team is formed with a specific goal within a specified time frame. A respected person is chosen to be manager of the skunkworks. In this approach to corporate innovation, risk takers are not punished for taking risks and failing—their former jobs are held for them. The risk takers also have the opportunity to earn large rewards.

bootlegging

Informal work on projects, other than those officially assigned, of employees' own choosing and initiative.

Bootlegging refers to informal efforts—as opposed to official job assignments—in which employees work to create new products and processes of their own choosing and initiative. Informal can mean secretive, such as when a bootlegger believes the company or the boss will frown on those activities. But companies should tolerate some bootlegging, and some even encourage it. To a limited extent, they allow people freedom to pursue pet projects without asking what they are or monitoring progress, figuring bootlegging will lead to some lost time but also to learning and to some profitable innovations.

Merck, desiring entrepreneurial thinking and behavior in research and development, explicitly rejects budgets for planning and control. New product teams don't get a budget. They must persuade people to join the team and commit their resources. This creates a survival-of-the-fittest process, mirroring the competition in the real world.[106] At Merck, as elsewhere, intrapreneurship derives from deliberate strategic thinking and execution.

Management Challenges

Organizations that encourage intrapreneurship face an obvious risk: the effort can fail. One author noted, "There is considerable history of internal venture development by large firms, and it does not encourage optimism."[107] However, this risk can be managed. In fact, failing to foster intrapreneurship may represent a subtler but greater risk than encouraging it. The organization that resists entrepreneurial initiative may lose its ability to adapt when conditions dictate change.

The most dangerous risk in corporate entrepreneurship is the risk of overreliance on a single project. Many companies fail while awaiting the completion of one large, innovative project.[108] The successful entrepreneurial organization avoids overcommitment to a single project and relies on its entrepreneurial spirit to produce at least one winner from among several projects.

Organizations also court failure when they spread their entrepreneurial efforts over too many projects.[109] If there are many projects, each effort may be too small in scale. Managers will consider the projects unattractive because of their small size. Or those recruited to manage the projects may have difficulty building power and status within the organization.

The hazards in intrapreneurship, then, are related to scale. One large project is a threat, as are too many underfunded projects. But a carefully managed approach to this strategically important process will upgrade an organization's chances for long-term survival and success.

Entrepreneurial Orientation

Earlier in this chapter, we described the characteristics of individual entrepreneurs. To conclude the chapter, we do the same for companies: we describe how companies that are highly entrepreneurial differ from those that are not. CEOs play a crucial role in promoting entrepreneurship within large corporations.[110]

Entrepreneurial orientation is the tendency of an organization to engage in activities designed to identify and capitalize successfully on opportunities to launch new ventures by entering new or established markets with new or existing goods or services.[111] Entrepreneurial orientation is determined by five tendencies: to allow independent action, innovate, take risks, be proactive, and be competitively aggressive. Entrepreneurial orientation should enhance the likelihood of success and may be particularly important for conducting business internationally.[112]

To allow independent action is to grant to individuals and teams the freedom to exercise their creativity, champion promising ideas, and carry them through to completion. Innovativeness requires the firm to support new ideas, experimentation, and creative processes that can lead to new products or processes; it requires a willingness to depart from existing practices and venture beyond the status quo. Risk taking comes from a willingness to commit significant resources, and perhaps borrow heavily, to venture into the unknown. The tendency to take risks can be assessed by considering whether people are bold or cautious, whether they require high levels of certainty before taking or allowing action, and whether they tend to follow tried-and-true paths.

To be proactive is to act in anticipation of future problems and opportunities. A proactive firm changes the competitive landscape; other firms merely react. Proactive firms are forward thinking and fast to act and are leaders rather than followers. Similarly, some individuals are more likely to be proactive, to shape and create their own environments, than others who more passively cope with the situations in which they find themselves.[113] Proactive firms encourage and allow individuals and teams to be proactive.

Finally, competitive aggressiveness is the tendency of the firm to challenge competitors directly and intensely to achieve entry or improve its position. In other words, it is a competitive tendency to outperform one's rivals in the marketplace. This might take the form of striking fast to beat competitors to the punch, to tackle them head-to-head, and to analyze and target competitors' weaknesses.

What makes a firm entrepreneurial is its engagement in an effective combination of independent action, innovativeness, risk taking, proactiveness, and competitive aggressiveness.[114] The relationship between these factors and the performance of the firm is a complicated one that depends on many things. Still, you can imagine how the opposite profile—too many constraints on action, business as usual, extreme caution, passivity, and a lack of competitive fire—will undermine entrepreneurial activities. And without entrepreneurship, how would firms survive and thrive in a constantly changing competitive environment?

Thus management can create environments that foster more entrepreneurship. If your bosses are not doing this, consider trying some entrepreneurial experiments on your own.[115] Seek out others with an entrepreneurial bent. What can you learn from them, and what can you teach others? Sometimes it takes individuals and teams of experimenters to show the possibilities to those at the top. Ask yourself and ask others: Between the bureaucrats and the entrepreneurs, who is having a more positive impact? And who is having more fun?

entrepreneurial orientation

The tendency of an organization to identify and capitalize successfully on opportunities to launch new ventures by entering new or established markets with new or existing goods or services.

Management Connection

THE PEOPLE AND PASSION OF POPCHIPS

Despite his own track record as a successful entrepreneur, Keith Belling never tried to start Popchips alone. He partnered with Pat Turpin, whose experience included investment banking and management of Costco's private-label (store brand) products. Before the Popchips venture, she had worked for Belling at the Allbusiness.com portal. As president of Popchips, Turpin focuses on manufacturing and finance.

Belling's experience also gave him time to build a network of valuable relationships. A key contact early on was someone he knew socially, Alex Panos, managing director of an investment firm called TSG Consumer Partners. When Panos heard about Belling's idea for Popchips, he thought it sounded similar to another product TSG had successfully invested in, Vitaminwater, so he was interested in a financial stake in the start-up. TSG eventually took 30 percent ownership in exchange for a $25 million investment. It helped that Panos knew Belling as an entrepreneur who had successfully started companies in the past.

But networking was hardly just about money. Through TSG, Belling met Rohan Oza, who had been the chief marketing officer at Vitaminwater. Oza, too, loved the idea for Popchips, so he invested, offered advice, and helped the company recruit former Vitaminwater employees to market Popchips.

As Popchips has built its sales, the value of the business has grown. TSG recently sold its ownership share to another investment firm, Verlinvest, based in Brussels. Verlinvest paid $670 million—a handsome return for TSG and a vote of confidence in the future of Popchips.

With experienced advice and consistent access to funds, can Popchips keep growing, or will it be gobbled up by another business? So far, Belling has shown no signs of stopping. He told a *USA Today* reporter that entrepreneurs like him need "a ton of passion" because the job is so hard—"probably twice as hard as you think it's going to be." But, he added, "The good news is that it's probably twice as much fun when it's going well."[116]

- What actions described in this case increase Popchips' chances of long-term success?
- Why do you think the innovation of popped snacks came from an entrepreneur like Keith Belling instead of from a big snack company? How could a large company increase the odds that it will be the source of the next great snack idea?

KEY TERMS

SUMMARY OF LEARNING OBJECTIVES

Now that you have studied Chapter 7, you should be able to:

LO 1 Describe why people become entrepreneurs and what it takes, personally.

People become entrepreneurs because of the profit potential, the challenge, and the satisfaction they anticipate (and often receive) from participating in the process, and sometimes because they are blocked from more traditional avenues of career advancement. Successful entrepreneurs are innovators, and they have good knowledge and skills in management, business, and networking. Although there is no single entrepreneurial personality, certain characteristics are helpful: commitment and determination; leadership skills; opportunity obsession; tolerance of risk, ambiguity, and uncertainty; creativity; self-reliance; the ability to adapt; and motivation to excel.

LO 2 Summarize how to assess opportunities to start new businesses.

You should always be on the lookout for new ideas, monitoring the current business environment and other indicators of opportunity. Franchising offers an interesting opportunity, and the potential of the Internet is being tapped (after entrepreneurs learned some tough lessons from the dot-bomb era). Trial and error and preparation play important roles. Assessing the business concept on the basis of how innovative and risky it is, combined with your personal interests and tendencies, will also help you make good choices. Ideas should be carefully assessed via opportunity analysis and a thorough business plan.

LO 3 Identify common causes of success and failure.

New ventures are inherently risky. The economic environment plays an important role in the success or failure of the business, and the entrepreneur should anticipate and be prepared to adapt in the face of changing economic conditions. How you handle a variety of common management challenges also can mean the difference between success and failure, as can the effectiveness of your planning and your ability to mobilize nonfinancial resources, including other people who can help.

LO 4 Discuss common management challenges.

When new businesses fail, the causes often can be traced to some common challenges that entrepreneurs face and must manage well. You might not enjoy the entrepreneurial process. Survival—including getting started and fending off competitors—is difficult. Growth creates new challenges, including reluctance to delegate work to others. Funds may be put to improper use, and financial controls may be inadequate. Many entrepreneurs fail to plan well for succession. When needing or wanting new funds, initial public offerings provide an option, but they represent an important and difficult decision that must be considered carefully.

LO 5 Explain how to increase your chances of success, including good business planning.

The business plan helps you think through your idea thoroughly and determine its viability. It also convinces (or fails to convince) others to participate. The plan describes the venture and its future, provides financial projections, and includes plans for marketing, manufacturing, and other business functions. The plan should describe the people involved in the venture, a full assessment of the opportunity (including customers and competitors), the environmental context (including regulatory and economic issues), and the risk (including future risks and how you intend to deal with them). Successful entrepreneurs also understand how to develop social capital, which enhances legitimacy and helps develop a network of others including customers, talented people, partners, and boards.

LO 6 Describe how managers of large companies can foster entrepreneurship.

Intrapreneurs work within established companies to develop new goods or services that allow the corporation to reap the benefits of innovation. To facilitate intrapreneurship, organizations use skunkworks—special project teams designated to develop a new product—and allow bootlegging—informal efforts beyond formal job assignments in which employees pursue their own pet projects. Organizations should select projects carefully, have an ongoing portfolio of projects, and fund them appropriately. Ultimately, a true entrepreneurial orientation in a company comes from encouraging independent action, innovativeness, risk taking, proactive behavior, and competitive aggressiveness.

DISCUSSION QUESTIONS

1. On a 1 to 10 scale, what is your level of personal interest in becoming an entrepreneur? Why did you rate yourself as you did?

2. How would you assess your capability of being a successful entrepreneur? What are your strengths and weaknesses? How would you increase your capability?

3. Most entrepreneurs learn the most important skills they need after age 21. How does this affect your outlook and plans?

4. Identify and discuss new ventures that fit each of the four cells in the entrepreneurial strategy matrix.

5. Brainstorm a list of ideas for new business ventures. Where did you get the ideas? Which ones are most and least viable, and why?

6. Identify some businesses that recently opened in your area. What are their chances of survival, and why? How would you advise the owners or managers of those businesses to ensure their success?

7. Assume you are writing a story about what it's really like to be an entrepreneur. To whom would you talk, and what questions would you ask?

8. Conduct interviews with two entrepreneurs, asking whatever questions most interest you. Share your findings with the class. How do the interviews differ from one another, and what do they have in common?

9. Read Table 7.1. Which myths did you believe? Do you still? Why or why not? Interview two entrepreneurs by asking each myth as a true-or-false question. Then ask them to elaborate on their answers. What did they say? What do you conclude?

10. With your classmates, form small teams of skunkworks. Your charge is to identify an innovation that you think would benefit your school and to outline an action plan for bringing your idea to reality.

11. Identify a business that recently folded. What were the causes of the failure? What could have been done differently to prevent the failure?

12. Does franchising appeal to you? What franchises would most and least interest you, and why?

13. The chapter specified some of the changes in the external environment that can provide business opportunity (technological discoveries, lifestyle and taste changes, and so on).

Identify some important recent changes or current trends in the external environment and the business opportunities they might offer.

14. Choose an Internet company with which you are familiar and brainstorm ideas for how its services or approach to business can be improved. How about starting a new Internet company altogether—what would be some possibilities?

15. Find some inspiring examples of social entrepreneurship and describe them to your class.

16. Brainstorm some new ideas for social enterprise. What challenges do you foresee, and how would you proceed?

EXPERIENTIAL EXERCISES

7.1   TAKE AN ENTREPRENEUR TO DINNER

OBJECTIVES

1. To get to know what an entrepreneur does, how she or he got started, and what it took to succeed.

2. To interview a particular entrepreneur in depth about his or her career and experiences.

3. To acquire a feeling for whether you might find an entrepreneurial career rewarding.

INSTRUCTIONS

1. Identify an entrepreneur in your area you would like to interview.

2. Contact the person you have selected and make an appointment. Be sure to explain why you want the appointment and to give a realistic estimate of how much time you will need.

3. Identify specific questions you would like to have answered and the general areas about which you would like information. (See the following suggested interview questions, although there probably won't be time for all of them.)

Using a combination of open-ended questions—such as general questions about how the entrepreneur got started, what happened next, and so forth—and closed-ended questions—such as specific questions about what his or her goals were, if he or she had to find partners, and so forth—will help keep the interview focused yet allow for unexpected comments and insights.

4. Conduct the interview. If both you and the person you are interviewing are comfortable, using a small voice recorder during the interview can be of great help to you later. Remember, too, that you most likely will learn more if you are an interested listener.

5. Evaluate what you have learned. Write down the information you have gathered in some form that will be helpful to you later on. Be as specific as you can. Jotting down direct quotes is more effective than statements such as "highly motivated individual." Also be sure to make a note of what you did not find out.

6. Write a thank-you note. This is more than a courtesy; it will also help the entrepreneur remember you favorably should you want to follow up on the interview.

Suggested Interview

QUESTIONS FOR GATHERING INFORMATION

- *Would you tell me about yourself before you started your first venture?*

  Were your parents, relatives, or close friends entrepreneurial? How so?

  Did you have any other role models?

  What was your education/military experience? In hindsight, was it helpful? In what specific ways?

  What was your previous work experience? Was it helpful? What particular chunks of experience were especially valuable or relevant?

  In particular, did you have any sales or marketing experience? How important was this in starting your company?

- *How did you start your venture?*

  How did you spot the opportunity? How did it surface?

  What were your goals? What were your lifestyle or other personal requirements? How did you fit these factors together?

  How did you evaluate the opportunity in terms of the critical elements for success? The competition? The market?

  Did you find or have partners? What kind of planning did you do? What kind of financing did you have?

  Did you have a start-up business plan of any kind? Please tell me about it.

  How much time did it take from conception to the first day of business? How many hours a day did you spend working on it?

  How much capital did it take? How long did it take to reach a positive cash flow and break-even sales volume? If you did not have enough money at the time, what were some ways in which you "bootstrapped" the venture (i.e., bartering, borrowing, and the like)? Tell me about the pressures and crises during that early survival period.

What outside help did you get? Did you have experienced advisers? Lawyers? Accountants? Tax experts? Patent experts? How did you develop these networks and how long did it take?

What was your family situation at the time?

What did you perceive to be your own strengths? Weaknesses?

What did you perceive to be the strengths of your venture? Weaknesses?

What was your most triumphant moment? Your worst moment?

Did you want to have partners or do it solo? Why?

• *Once you got going . . .*

What were the most difficult gaps to fill and problems to solve as you began to grow rapidly?

When you looked for key people as partners, advisers, or managers, were there any personal attributes or attitudes you were especially seeking because you knew they would fit with you and were important to success? How did you find them?

Are there any attributes among partners and advisers that you would definitely try to avoid?

Have things become more predictable? Or less?

Do you spend more/same/less time with your business now than in the early years?

Do you feel more managerial and less entrepreneurial now?

In terms of the future, do you plan to harvest? To maintain? To expand?

Do you plan ever to retire? Would you explain?

Have your goals changed? Have you met them?

QUESTIONS FOR CONCLUDING (CHOOSE ONE)

• What do you consider your most valuable asset—the thing that enabled you to make it?
• If you had it to do over again would you do it again in the same way?
• Looking back, what do you feel are the most critical concepts, skills, attitudes, and know-how you needed to get your company started and grown to where it is today? What will be needed for the next five years? To what extent can any of these be learned?
• Some people say there is a lot of stress being an entrepreneur. What have you experienced? How would you say it compares with other hot-seat jobs, such as the head of a big company or a partner in a large law, consulting, or accounting firm?
• What are the things that you find personally rewarding and satisfying as an entrepreneur? What have been the rewards, risks, and trade-offs?
• Who should try to be an entrepreneur? Can you give me any ideas there?
• What advice would you give an aspiring entrepreneur? Could you suggest the three most important lessons you have learned? How can I learn them while minimizing the tuition?

SOURCE: J. A. Timmons, *New Venture Creation*, 3rd ed. 1994. Copyright © 1994 The McGraw-Hill Companies. Reprinted with permission.

7.2 STARTING A NEW BUSINESS

OBJECTIVES

1. To introduce you to the complexities of going into business for yourself.
2. To provide hands-on experience in making new business decisions.

INSTRUCTIONS

1. Your instructor will divide the class into teams and assign each team the task of investigating the start-up of one of the following businesses:
   a. Submarine sandwich shop
   b. Day care service
   c. Bookstore
   d. Gasoline service station
   e. Other

2. Each team should research the information necessary to complete the New Business Start-Up Worksheet. The following agencies or organizations might be of assistance:
   a. Small Business Administration
   b. Local county/city administration agencies
   c. Local chamber of commerce
   d. Local small business development corporation
   e. U.S. Department of Commerce
   f. Farmer's Home Administration
   g. Local realtors
   h. Local businesspeople in the same or a similar business
   i. Banks and S&Ls

3. Each team presents its findings to the class.

New Business Start-Up Worksheet

1. *Product*   _____

    What customer need will we satisfy?   _____

    How can our product be unique?   _____

2. *Customer*   _____

    Who are our customers? What are their profiles?   _____

    Where do they live/work/play?   _____

    What are their buying habits?   _____

    What are their needs?   _____

3. *Competition*   _____

    Who/where is the competition?   _____

    What are their strengths and weaknesses?   _____

    How might they respond to us?   _____

4. *Suppliers*   _____

    Who/where are our suppliers?   _____

    What are their business practices?   _____

    What relationships can we expect?   _____

5. *Location*   _____

    Where are our customers/competitors/suppliers?   _____

    What are the location costs?   _____

    What are the legal limitations to location?   _____

6. *Physical Facilities/Equipment*   _____

    Rent/own/build/refurbish facilities?   _____

    Rent/lease/purchase equipment?   _____

    Maintenance?   _____

7. *Human Resources*   _____

    Availability?   _____

    Training?   _____

    Costs?   _____

8. *Legal/Regulatory Environment*   _____

    Licenses/permits/certifications?   _____

    Government agencies?   _____

    Liability?   _____

9. *Cultural/Social Environment*   _____

    Cultural issues?   _____

    Social issues?   _____

10. *International Environment*   _____

    International issues?   _____

11. *Other*   _____

CONCLUDING CASE
ROLLING OUT SCROLLCO

Mandy Toberman had enjoyed her engineering job at Acme Electronics, but she began to grow restless. Most of her work for the past five years had involved designing minor adjustments to existing products. She worried she would lose her edge in a fast-changing industry, and work just didn't engage her imagination or problem-solving skills the way it once did. In the evenings, she found herself pursuing new ideas, researching some of the latest technology, and testing out some possible inventions. As the weeks passed, Mandy became increasingly interested in one idea: an e-reader made with flexible materials that could be rolled up and stuffed into a satchel, backpack, or purse. At first she doubted it could be made, but with some investigation, Mandy began to develop a design for the device, which she called the Scroll.

The more Mandy considered the Scroll, the more she thought it would be an exciting new product for Acme to offer. It would open up a whole new area of sales for the company, which had not seen much growth for the past few years. It would generate tremendous publicity for Acme and excitement in her division. So Mandy collected a few of the drawings she had created, estimated the manufacturing costs, and prepared a proposal. She invited her supervisor, Tom Ringsack, and two of her colleagues to a meeting, saying only that she had an idea she wanted to bring up.

At the meeting, Mandy started her laptop to show her drawings and describe her idea for the Scroll. The other engineers' eyes were wide, and Mandy could sense their eagerness to explore the concept. However, Tom sighed and said, "Mandy, you know our situation, right? In the present economy, we can't get a lot of financing for risky new projects. We have to focus on the product enhancements that will increase our profit margins, and the budget for anything else is tight—well, really, non-existent." Mandy could tell the discussion was over, so she shut down her computer with a quiet sigh.

That weekend, Mandy spent hours at her desk at home, beginning to plan her escape from Acme Electronics. She perused the Small Business Administration website, looking for advice on writing a business plan, and explored her LinkedIn network, looking for contacts who might give her advice—and possibly funding—for her start-up, which she intended to name ScrollCo. By the end of the weekend, feeling more than a little nervous, Mandy had drafted the outline of a business plan.

DISCUSSION QUESTIONS

1. What actions could Acme Electronics take to foster intrapreneurship? What consequences does it suffer from failing to foster it?

2. What information should Mandy include in her business plan?

3. Describe three nonfinancial resources likely to be important for the future of ScrollCo. How can Mandy ensure that her business has those resources?

PART TWO   SUPPORTING CASE

Can Foxconn Deliver for Apple?

Apple is famous for its attractive and highly prized electronics, including iPhone and iTouch portable devices, iPod and iTunes for music, and iMac and iPad computers. However, Apple doesn't actually make any of its products. Rather, it develops ideas, designs devices, and promotes the products and its brand. To put the devices together, Apple relies on a set of contractors.

One of those contractors is an electronics company called Foxconn, based in Taiwan. With factories located in China, Foxconn has combined manufacturing expertise with low-cost labor to win deals to make computers and key components such as motherboards. As consumers have slowed their spending on laptop computers in favor of smaller devices such as the iPad tablet computer and smartphones, Foxconn has benefited. As of this writing, it was the only company making Apple's iPad and one of just two makers of Apple's iPhone. Workers at Foxconn facilities also produce the Sony PlayStation 3, the Nintendo Wii, Dell and Hewlett-Packard computers, and Nokia cell phones. In China alone, Foxconn employs almost a million workers, making it one of the largest employers in the world. Many of those workers live in on-site dormitories, eat in company-run dining halls, and relax in bookstores and gyms located right at their workplace.

Recently, Foxconn has been running into some tragic problems. In 2010, the company drew international media attention when it came to light that several workers at Foxconn's plant in Shenzhen (a city in southern China) had committed suicide. Questions arose about whether working conditions were so horrible as to drive workers to kill themselves. Apple sent executives accompanied by suicide prevention experts to the plant to investigate. Although Apple requires its contract partners to meet specific standards in its code of conduct, and it visits over 100 facilities a year to ensure compliance, it had failed to uncover any problems at Foxconn before the suicides came to light.

In the following year, Foxconn was again in the news about a tragedy when an explosion in its Chengdu, China, plant killed 3 workers and injured 15. Initial investigations suggested that the explosion was the result of a fairly basic manufacturing safety problem: because of improper ventilation, dust collected in the air of a metal-polishing shop, and the dust ignited. If such a problem occurred in the United States, regulators would quickly shut down the facility for violating safety requirements.

Embarrassed by the media and pressured by important customers such as Apple, Foxconn acted to improve working conditions. At the Shenzhen plant, it brought in counselors, improved training of managers and the staff answering calls on the employee hotline, and launched a morale-boosting program called Care–Love, which sponsors employee outings. In the factories in Chengdu and elsewhere, the company took measures to improve ventilation. Along with these changes, Foxconn began giving out raises. In Shenzhen, workers' wages more than doubled.

Since Foxconn launched the effort to improve morale, employee turnover has fallen, and the suicides seem to have ended. Unfortunately, the payoff for the company is difficult to measure. Higher costs have erased profits, and Foxconn's stock price has tumbled. So now the company is looking for lower-cost locations. It opened facilities in China's interior cities, where wage rates are about one-third below those of Shenzhen, and is investigating sites in Slovakia, Turkey, and Brazil. Besides saving money, the additional facilities in China may contribute to morale by allowing workers to live closer to their hometowns and families; many of the workers at the Shenzhen facility had traveled far to work there and were homesick.

QUESTIONS

1. What threats, opportunities, strengths, and weaknesses can you identify at Foxconn? How is it addressing these with its strategy?

2. If Foxconn's management hired you to offer advice on improving its ethical decision making and corporate social responsibility, what measures would you suggest? Why?

3. For Foxconn, what management challenges arise from running an exporting business based in China and serving developed nations such as the United States? What management skills does it need under these circumstances?

SOURCES: T. Culpan, Z. Lifei, and B. Einhorn, "Foxconn: How to Beat the High Cost of Happy Workers," Bloomberg Businessweek, May 5, 2011, http://www.businessweek.com; D. Nystedt, "Apple: Foxconn 'Saved Lives' with Suicide Prevention Efforts," PC World, February 15, 2011, http://www.pcworld.com; J. Bussey, "Measuring the Human Cost of an iPad Made in China," The Wall Street Journal, June 3, 2011, http://online.wsj.com; "Apple Report Details Response to Foxconn Suicides," eWeek, February 15, 2011, Business & Company Resource Center, http://galenet.galegroup.com; and J. Dalrymple, "Apple Reports on Foxconn, Supplier Workplace Standards," CNET News, February 14, 2011, http://news.cnet.com.

Information for Entrepreneurs

If you are interested in starting or managing a small business, you have access to many sources of useful information.

PUBLISHED SOURCES

The first step is a complete search of materials in libraries and on the Internet. You can find a huge amount of published information, databases, and other sources about industries, markets, competitors, and personnel. Some of this information will have been uncovered when you searched for ideas. Listed here are additional sources that should help get you started.

Guides and Company Information Valuable information is available in special issues and the websites of *Business-Week, Forbes, Inc., The Economist, Fast Company,* and *Fortune,* as well as online in the following:

- Hoovers.com
- ProQuest.com
- Investext.com
- RDS Bizsuite.com

Valuable Sites on the Internet

- Entreworld (http://www.entreworld.org), the website of the Kauffman Center for Entrepreneurial Leadership, Ewing Marion Kauffman Foundation
- *Fast Company* (http://www.fastcompany.com)
- Ernst & Young (http://www.ey.com)
- Global Access—SEC documents through a subscription-based website (http://www.primark.com)
- *Inc.* magazine (http://www.inc.com)
- Entrepreneur.com and magazine (http://www.entrepreneur.com).
- EDGAR database (http://www.sec.gov)—subscription sources, such as ThomsonResearch (http://www.thomsonfinancial.com), provide images of other filings as well.
- Venture Economics (http://www.ventureeconomics.com).

Journal Articles via Computerized Indexes

- Factiva with Dow Jones, *Reuters, The Wall Street Journal*
- EBSCOhost
- FirstSearch
- Ethnic News Watch
- LEXIS/NEXIS
- *The New York Times*
- InfoTrac from Gale Group
- ABI/Inform and other ProQuest databases
- RDS Business Reference Suite
- *The Wall Street Journal*

Statistics

- Stat-USA (http://www.stat-usa.gov)—U.S. government subscription site for economic, trade, and business data and market research
- U.S. Bureau of the Census (http://www.census.gov)—the source of many statistical data, including
  - Statistical Abstract of the United States
  - American FactFinder—population data
  - Economic programs (http://www.census.gov/econ/www/index.html)—data by sector
  - County business patterns
  - Zip code business patterns
- Knight Ridder . . . CRB Commodity Year Book
- Manufacturing USA, Service Industries USA, and other sector compilations from Gale Group
- Economic Statistics Briefing Room (http://www.whitehouse.gov/fsbr/esbr.html)
- Federal Reserve Bulletin
- Survey of Current Business
- FedStats (http://www.fedstats.gov/)
- Labstat (http://stats.bls.gov/labstat.htm)
- Global Insight, formerly DRI-WEFA
- International Financial Statistics—International Monetary Fund
- World Development Indicators—World Bank
- Bloomberg Database

Consumer Expenditures

- New Strategist Publications

Projections and Forecasts

- ProQuest
- InfoTech Trends
- Guide to Special Issues and Indexes to Periodicals (*Grey House Directory of Special Issues*)
- RDS Business Reference Suite
- Value Line Investment Survey

Market Studies

- LifeStyle Market Analyst
- MarketResearch.com
- Scarborough Research
- Simmons Market Research Bureau

Consumer Expenditures

- New Strategist Publications
- Consumer Expenditure Survey
- Euromonitor

Other Sources

- Wall Street transcript
- Brokerage house reports from Investext, Multex and so on
- Company annual reports and websites

OTHER INTELLIGENCE

Everything entrepreneurs need to know will not be found in libraries because this information needs to be highly specific and current. This information is most likely available from people—industry experts, suppliers, and the like. Summarized here are some useful sources of intelligence.

Trade Associations Trade associations, especially the editors of their publications and information officers, are good sources of information. Trade shows and conferences are prime places to discover the latest activities of competitors.

Employees Employees who have left a competitor's company often can provide information about the competitor, especially if the employee departed on bad terms. Also, a firm can hire people away from a competitor. Although consideration of ethics in this situation is important, the number of experienced people in any industry is limited, and competitors must prove that a company hired a person intentionally to get specific trade secrets to challenge any hiring legally. Students who have worked for competitors are another source of information.

Consulting Firms Consulting firms frequently conduct industry studies and then make this information available. Frequently, in such fields as computers or software, competitors use the same design consultants, and these consultants can be sources of information.

Market Research Firms Firms doing market studies, such as those listed under the previously mentioned published sources, can be sources of intelligence.

Key Customers, Manufacturers, Suppliers, Distributors, and Buyers These groups are often a prime source of information.

Public Filings Federal, state, and local filings, such as filings with the Securities and Exchange Commission (SEC), Patent and Trademark Office, or Freedom of Information Act filings, can reveal a surprising amount of information. There are companies that process inquiries of this type.

Reverse Engineering Reverse engineering can be used to determine costs of production and sometimes even manufacturing methods. An example of this practice is the experience of Advanced Energy Technology, Inc., of Boulder, Colorado, which learned firsthand about such tactics. No sooner had it announced a new product, which was patented, than it received 50 orders, half of which were from competitors asking for only one or two of the items.

Networks The networks mentioned in this chapter can be sources of new venture ideas and strategies.

Other Classified ads, buyers' guides, labor unions, real estate agents, courts, local reporters, and so on can all provide clues.

The U.S. government is engaging in new and more extensive outreach efforts so that small business owners will use government resources more and understand them more easily. In 2009, the U.S. Small Business Administration launched a community forum, the first government-sponsored online community built specifically for small business owners, on the Business Gateway site of Business.gov. The forum combines discussion threads, blogs, and resource articles. The goals for the SBA and 21 other federal agencies that cosponsor the site are to engage in dialogue with the public, leverage the expertise that exists in both the public and private sectors, and help government serve entrepreneurs better.

SOURCES: J. A. Timmons and S. Spinelli, *New Venture Creation,* 7th ed. (Burr Ridge, IL: McGraw-Hill/Irwin, 2007), pp. 103–4; K. Klein, "Government Resources for Entrepreneurs," *Business Week,* March 3, 2009.

CHAPTER 8

Organization Structure

> Take my assets—but leave me my organization and in five years
> I'll have it all back.
>
> —ALFRED P. SLOAN JR.

Management Connection

HOW GENERAL MOTORS' DAN AKERSON TRIES TO MAKE A GIANT NIMBLE

The history of General Motors shows that size and longevity do not guarantee success. GM once dominated the U.S. auto industry with a "price ladder" strategy in which Chevrolet, Pontiac, GMC, Oldsmobile, Buick, and Cadillac catered to specific slices of the consumer market. But after GM's U.S. market share peaked in 1962 at 51 percent, the company steadily began losing share to smaller, more nimble, and more innovative competition. By 2008, GM's U.S. market share was less than half what it was in 1962, and when customer demand and bank lending dried up in the 2008 financial crisis, GM neared collapsed. The federal government stepped in with money to keep GM alive through a Chapter 11 managed bankruptcy. In July 2009, after restructuring, the old General Motors Corporation reemerged as General Motors Company. Daniel Akerson, a Navy veteran with experience turning around companies in other industries, was named to the new company's Board of Directors. In September 2010, Akerson was named Chairman and CEO and led the company's initial public offering—the largest in U.S. history—in November of that year.

In 2011, GM posted record earnings and reclaimed its spot as the world's automotive sales leader, but its stock price slid as investors questioned the company's long-term potential. In the years leading up to bankruptcy, GM had become known for a culture in which managers were slow to act and reluctant to embrace change. Akerson set out to change that. In his 2012 letter to stockholders, he wrote, "It has never been far from my mind that U.S. and Canadian taxpayers rightfully expected us to change the way we do business in exchange for a second chance." Among Akerson's challenges has been teaching a 213,000-employee multinational company selling millions of vehicles annually to be more nimble, more innovative, and more customer-centric.

Akerson has driven change by assembling a management team of seasoned industry insiders (including Mark Reuss, president, GM North America, and Mary Barra,

executive vice president, Global Product Development, Purchasing & Supply Chain) and outside expertise (including chief financial officer Dan Ammann, chief information officer Randy Mott, and chief infotainment officer Mary Chan). GM has also assembled a diverse board of 14 directors, mostly current and retired executives from other organizations, including representatives from Fortune 100 companies (Walmart, Coca-Cola, Conoco-Phillips, Burlington Northern Santa Fe, etc.), the financial and telecom industries, academia, and a former chairman of the U.S. Joint Chiefs of Staff.

As GM strives to return to greatness, some signs are hopeful. The company reported 2012 earnings of $7.9 billion on revenue of more than $152 billion, enabling significant reinvestments for growth. GM also boasted the largest market share in the industry's two biggest markets, the United States and China, fueled by record sales of 2.8 million vehicles in China (the 2.6 million sold in the United States actually represented a slip in market share). Whether GM can meet its goals will depend on its ability to roll out enticing new products while continuing to improve vehicle quality, customer service, and global efficiency.[1]

Chairman and CEO Dan Akerson thinks that the way employees are organized into departments and divisions plays a role in how fast and effectively they can seize new opportunities. As you read this chapter, notice the options available for an organization's structure, and consider whether GM's management has made the right choices to enable continued growth.

Since its emergence from bankruptcy, General Motors has been running neck and neck with Toyota and Volkswagen to keep its spot as the world's biggest auto company, even as its U.S. market share slips and it struggles with investor doubts about its ability to operate efficiently. How could the company respond to this situation? The way in which a company organizes itself to address an issue such as declining market share may well be the most important factor in determining whether its strategy will succeed. GM, like many other companies, is working hard to make certain that its strategy and structure are aligned.

This chapter focuses on the vertical and horizontal dimensions of organization structure. We begin by covering basic principles of differentiation and integration. Next we discuss the vertical structure, which includes issues of authority, hierarchy, delegation, and decentralization. We continue on to describe the horizontal structure, which includes functional, divisional, and matrix forms. Finally, we illustrate the ways in which organizations can integrate their structures: coordination by standardization, coordination by plan, and coordination by mutual adjustment.

In the next chapter, we continue with the topic of organization structure but take a different perspective. In that chapter, we focus on the flexibility and responsiveness of an organization—that is, how capable it is of changing its form and adapting to strategy, technology, the environment, and other challenges it confronts.

Fundamentals of Organizing

organization chart

The reporting structure and division of labor in an organization.

To get going, let's start simple. We often begin to describe a firm's structure by looking at its organization chart. The **organization chart** depicts the positions in the firm and the way they are arranged. The chart provides a picture of the reporting structure (who reports to whom) and the various activities that are carried out by different individuals. Most companies have official organization charts drawn up to give people this information.

Figure 8.1 shows a traditional organization chart. Note the various types of information that are conveyed in a very simple way:

1. The boxes represent different work.
2. The titles in the boxes show the work performed by each unit.
3. Reporting and authority relationships are indicated by solid lines showing superior–subordinate connections.
4. Levels of management are indicated by the number of horizontal layers in the chart. All persons or units that are at the same rank and report to the same person are on one level.

differentiation

An aspect of the organization's internal environment created by job specialization and the division of labor.

Although the organization chart presents some important structural features, other design issues related to structure—while not so obvious—are no less significant. Two fundamental concepts around which organizations are structured are differentiation and integration. **Differentiation** means that the organization is composed of many units that work on different kinds of tasks, using different skills and work methods. **Integration** means that these differentiated units are put back together so that work is coordinated into an overall product.[2]

integration

The degree to which differentiated work units work together and coordinate their efforts.

Differentiation

Several related concepts underlie the idea of structural differentiation. For example, differentiation is created through division of labor and job specialization. **Division of labor** means the work of the organization is subdivided into smaller tasks. Various individuals and units throughout the organization perform different tasks.

division of labor

The assignment of different tasks to different people or groups.

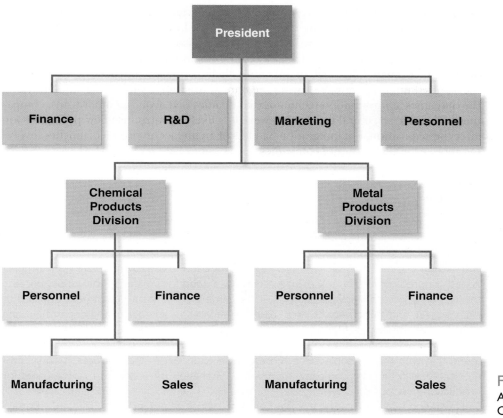

FIGURE 8.1
A Conventional
Organization Chart

Specialization refers to the fact that different people or groups often perform specific parts of the larger task. The two concepts are, of course, closely related. Administrative assistants and accountants specialize in, and perform, different jobs; similarly, marketing, finance, and human resources tasks are divided among the respective departments. The many tasks that must be carried out in an organization make specialization and division of labor necessities. Otherwise, the complexity of the overall work of the organization would be too much for any individual.[3]

Differentiation is high when an organization has many subunits and many kinds of specialists who think differently. Harvard professors Lawrence and Lorsch found that organizations in complex, dynamic environments (plastics firms in their study) developed a high degree of differentiation to cope with the complex challenges. Companies in simple, stable environments (container companies) had low levels of differentiation. Companies in intermediate environments (food companies) had intermediate differentiation.[4]

> As organizations differentiate their structures, managers must simultaneously consider issues of integration.

specialization

A process in which different individuals and units perform different tasks.

Integration

As organizations differentiate their structures, managers must simultaneously consider issues of integration. All the specialized tasks in an organization cannot be performed completely independently. Because the different units are part of the larger organization, some degree of communication and cooperation must exist among them. Integration and its related concept, **coordination**, refer to the procedures that link the various parts of the organization to achieve the organization's overall mission.

Integration is achieved through structural mechanisms that enhance collaboration and coordination. Any job activity that links different work units performs an

coordination

The procedures that link the various parts of an organization for the purpose of achieving the organization's overall mission.

integrative function. Remember, the more highly differentiated your firm, the greater the need for integration among the different units. Lawrence and Lorsch found that highly differentiated firms were successful if they also had high levels of integration. Organizations are more likely to fail if they exist in complex environments and are highly differentiated but fail to integrate their activities adequately.[5] In contrast, focusing on integration may slow innovation, at least for a while. In a study tracking the outcomes at information technology companies that acquired other firms, companies with more structural integration were less likely to introduce new products soon after the acquisition, but integration had less of an impact on product launches involving more experienced target companies.[6]

In Practice

Even though companies are in the same industry, they might take very different approaches to differentiation and integration. Consider two successful developers of video games, Harmonix Music Systems and Valve Software.

Harmonix, known for "Guitar Hero" and "Rock Band," has grown rapidly. As Harmonix added hundreds of employees, management saw a need for greater specialization. Because the company develops several projects at the same time, it has a department devoted to each project, and these departments share the services of an engineering department and an audio department. Each project department has a pair of leaders, one responsible for the game's creative vision and the other for managing the schedule and budget. Also, Harmonix found that with more people came more diverse experiences and practices, making communication difficult. The company improved coordination by setting formal standards for production methods.

Integration is far less formal at Valve Software, whose games include "Half-Life," "Portal," and "Team Fortress." Valve's structure is based on its organizational culture, which values cooperation and adaptability. The "creative" and "production" roles that Harmonix assigns to its developers are unknown distinctions at Valve, where each employee is a team member who focuses on whatever aspect of the game requires attention. Valve's role is to hire employees it can trust to make the right decisions. The team members working on a project frequently test it and meet to discuss it, and the test results and group input are required to drive any decisions about the product.[7]

- Which company has the higher level of differentiation?

These concepts permeate the rest of the chapter. First we discuss vertical differentiation within organization structure. This concept includes issues pertaining to authority within an organization, the board of directors, the chief executive officer, and hierarchical levels as well as issues pertaining to delegation and decentralization. Next we turn to horizontal differentiation in an organization's structure, exploring issues of departmentalization that create functional, divisional, and matrix organizations. Finally, we cover issues pertaining to structural integration, including coordination, organizational roles, interdependence, and boundary spanning.

The Vertical Structure

LO 2   To understand issues such as reporting relationships, authority, responsibility, and the like, we need to begin with the vertical dimension of a firm's structure.

Authority in Organizations

At the most fundamental level, the functioning of every organization depends on the use of **authority,** the legitimate right to make decisions and to tell other people what to do. For example, a boss has the authority to give an order to a subordinate.

Traditionally, authority resides in positions rather than in people. Thus the job of vice president of a particular division has authority over that division, regardless of how many people come and go in that position and who currently holds it.

In private business enterprises, the owners have ultimate authority. In most small, simply structured companies, the owner also acts as manager. Sometimes the owner hires another person to manage the business and its employees. The owner gives this manager some authority to oversee the operations, but the manager is accountable to—that is, reports and defers to—the owner. Thus the owner still has the ultimate authority.

Formal position authority is generally the primary means of running an organization. An order that a boss gives to a lower-level employee is usually carried out. As this occurs throughout the organization day after day, the organization can move forward and achieve its goals.[8] However, authority in an organization is not always position-dependent. People with particular expertise, experience, or personal qualities may have considerable *informal* authority—for example, people who carry themselves with confidence, can deliver valuable information, or work face to face with those who have high positions.[9] Effective managers are aware of informal authority as a factor that can help or hinder their achievement of the organization's goals; we will say more about informal authority in the next chapter and Chapter 12. For now, we discuss the formal authority structure of the organization from the top down, beginning with the board of directors.

authority

The legitimate right to make decisions and to tell other people what to do.

Board of Directors In corporations, the owners are the stockholders. But because there are numerous stockholders and these individuals generally lack timely information, few are directly involved in managing the organization. Stockholders elect a board of directors to oversee the organization. The board, led by the chair, makes major decisions affecting the organization, subject to corporate charter and bylaw provisions. Boards perform at least three major sets of duties: (1) selecting, assessing, rewarding, and perhaps replacing the CEO; (2) determining the firm's strategic direction and reviewing financial performance; and (3) ensuring ethical, socially responsible, and legal conduct.[10]

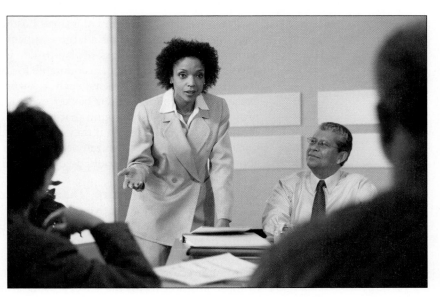

The job of CEO typically consists of leading the board of directors, encouraging employees, and promoting positive change while being accountable for the overall success of the company.

The board's membership usually includes some top executives—called *inside directors.* Outside members of the board tend to be executives at other companies. The trend in recent years has been toward reducing the number of insiders and increasing the number of outsiders. Today, most companies have a majority of outside directors. Boards made up of strong, independent outsiders are more likely to provide different information and perspectives and to prevent big mistakes. Successful boards tend to be those who are active, critical participants in determining company strategies. Even so, in the wake of scandals and lawsuits, many boards have shifted their focus to compliance issues, such as audits, financial reporting, and laws against discrimination. These issues are critically important, but a board staffed mainly with legal and regulatory experts cannot always give management the necessary direction on strategy.[11]

In Practice

Surprisingly, at a company that made its brand a worldwide symbol of American youthful energy and fun, Coca-Cola has a board of directors dominated by senior citizens. A recent look at Coke's board found that the average age of its members was 67—even older than the year before, when the average was 62.6 years. Of the board's 17 directors elected that year, 9 were at least 70 years old, including a pair of members aged 80 and 86.

Is that a problem? Certainly, great age brings great experience. This advantage has to be balanced against the question of whether board members accustomed to the explosion in cola's popularity during the twentieth century are ready for consumers' shifting tastes in the twenty-first. In fact, the board of directors vetoed a former CEO's idea to acquire Quaker Oats with its Gatorade brand. (PepsiCo bought it.) Coke's oldest board member, Donald Keough, reportedly joined others in resisting an idea to acquire Monster, whose energy drinks are popular but controversial. Nevertheless, even with an older-than-average board, Coke has added new products and extended its marketing presence into social media.

Coke expresses no intention of putting an age cap on board membership. But as its oldest members retire, it is nominating new members for the vacancies. One recent addition in his fifties is Robert Kotick, CEO of Activision Blizzard, which develops entertainment software. And with the recent decision of Coke's two 80-year-olds to retire, the company nominated 57-year-old Helene Gayle, chief executive of the nonprofit Care USA, who also has experience with the Centers for Disease Control and Prevention and the Bill and Melinda Gates Foundation.[12]

- Besides years of experience, what other qualifications are important in board members of Coca-Cola Company?

The owner and managers of a small business may need the expertise of a board of directors at least as much as a large company does. To obtain some of these benefits without the expense or loss of day-to-day control, small-business leaders may seek advisers who will hold them accountable for their goals and performance. Some owners set up a board of advisers, such as owners of noncompeting companies, retired executives, and perhaps their banker or accountant. University of Windsor, Canada, professor Roger Hussey found that privately owned companies were more profitable during the recent recession if they had a board of directors that included people from outside the company. One important reason was their ability to be more objective about what the company could do during difficult times.[13]

Chief Executive Officer   The authority officially vested in the board of directors is assigned to a chief executive officer (CEO), who occupies the top of the organizational pyramid. The CEO is personally accountable to the board and to the owners for the organization's performance.

In some corporations, one person holds all three positions of CEO, chair of the board of directors, and president.[14] More commonly, however, one person holds two of those positions, with the CEO serving also as either the chair of the board or the president of the organization. When the CEO is president, the chair may be honorary and may do little more than conduct meetings. In other cases, the chair may be the CEO, and the president is second in command.

In recent years, the trend has been to separate the position of CEO and chairman of the board. Sometimes this change is related to improved corporate governance;

board oversight is easier when the CEO is not quite as dominant a figure. In other cases, the board has acted to reduce an unpopular CEO's power or to help prepare for a successor to the CEO.

Top Management Team   Increasingly, CEOs share their authority with other key members of the top management team. Top management teams typically are composed of the CEO, president, chief operating officer, chief financial officer, and other key executives. Rather than make critical decisions on their own, CEOs at companies such as Shell, Honeywell, and Merck regularly meet with their top management teams to make decisions as a unit.[15]

Hierarchical Levels

In Chapter 1, we discussed the three broad levels of the organizational pyramid, commonly called the **hierarchy.** The CEO occupies the top position and is the senior member of top management. The top managerial level also includes presidents and vice presidents. They are the strategic managers in charge of the entire organization.

The key responsibilities at this top level include **corporate governance**—a term describing the oversight of the firm by its executive staff and board of directors. In recent years, as a result of corporate scandals and extremely generous executive pay packages, the public's trust in corporate governance has eroded significantly. As we mentioned in Chapter 5, Congress responded by passing the Sarbanes-Oxley Act, which, along with requirements by the Securities and Exchange Commission, imposed much tighter corporate governance rules. For example, company CEOs and CFOs (chief financial officers) now have to certify the accuracy of their firm's financial statements personally.

The second broad level of the organization is middle management. At this level, managers are in charge of plants or departments. The lowest level is made up of lower management and workers. It includes office managers, sales managers, supervisors, and other first-line managers as well as the employees who report directly to them. This level is also called the *operational level* of the organization.

An authority structure is the glue that holds these levels together. Generally, but not always, people at higher levels have the authority to make decisions and tell lower-level people what to do. For example, middle managers can give orders to first-line supervisors; first-line supervisors, in turn, direct operative-level workers.

A powerful trend for U.S. businesses over the past few decades has been to reduce the number of hierarchical layers. General Electric used to have 29 levels; today it has only a handful of layers, and its hierarchical structure is basically flat. Most executives today believe that fewer layers create a more efficient, fast-acting, and cost-effective organization. This also holds true for the **subunits** of major corporations. A study of 234 branches of a financial services company found that branches with fewer layers tended to have higher operating efficiency than did branches with more layers.[16]

This trend and research might seem to suggest that hierarchy is a bad thing, but it offers benefits as well. A hierarchy provides management career paths that help organizations retain and develop ambitious, talented people, giving them gradually more challenging experiences as they prepare for executive positions. In contrast, where there is little hierarchy, employees who see no chance of promotion may leave to find better opportunities elsewhere. Also, a well-designed hierarchy can ensure that managers have a reasonable number of people to monitor, as described in the next section.[17]

Span of Control

The number of people under a manager is an important feature of an organization's structure. The number of subordinates who report directly to an executive or supervisor is called the **span of control.** The implications of differences in the span of control for the shape of an organization are straightforward. Holding size constant, narrow spans build a tall organization that has many reporting levels. Wide spans

hierarchy

The authority levels of the organizational pyramid.

corporate governance

The role of a corporation's executive staff and board of directors in ensuring that the firm's activities meet the goals of the firm's stakeholders.

Bottom Line

A structure with fewer horizontal layers saves time and money.
Why not eliminate all middle layers to save the most time and money?

subunits

Subdivisions of an organization.

span of control

The number of subordinates who report directly to an executive or supervisor.

 LO 4

create a flat organization with fewer reporting levels. The span of control can be too narrow or too wide. The optimal span of control maximizes effectiveness because it is (1) narrow enough to permit managers to maintain control over subordinates but (2) not so narrow that it leads to overcontrol and an excessive number of managers who oversee a small number of subordinates.

What is the optimal number of subordinates? Five, according to Napoleon Bonaparte.[18] Some managers today still consider five a good number. At one Japanese bank, in contrast, several hundred branch managers report to the same boss. In a study by the Corporate Executive Board, the average span of control at large companies increased from 7 direct reports to 12 between 2008 and 2012.

Actually, the optimal span of control depends on a number of factors. The span should be wider when (1) the work is clearly defined and unambiguous, (2) subordinates are highly trained and have access to information, (3) the manager is highly capable and supportive, (4) jobs are similar and performance measures are comparable, and (5) subordinates prefer autonomy to close supervisory control. If the opposite conditions exist, a narrow span of control may be more appropriate.[19]

Delegation

delegation

The assignment of new or additional responsibilities to a subordinate.

As we look at organizations and recognize that authority is spread out over various levels and spans of control, the issue of delegation becomes paramount. **Delegation** is the assignment of authority and responsibility to a subordinate at a lower level. It often requires the subordinate to report back to his or her boss about how effectively the assignment was carried out. Delegation is perhaps the most fundamental feature of management because it entails getting work done through others. Thus delegation is important at all hierarchical levels. The process can occur between any two individuals in any type of structure with regard to any task.

Some managers are comfortable fully delegating an assignment to subordinates; others are not. Consider how the two office managers in the following "In Practice" box gave out the same assignment. Are both of these statements examples of delegation?

In Practice

Manager A: "Call Tom Burton at Cavalier Computer. Ask him to give you the price list on an upgrade for our personal computers. I want to move up to a quad-core processor with 8 gigs of RAM and at least a 1.5-terabyte hard drive. Ask them to give you a demonstration of the Windows 8 operating system and Microsoft Office 365. I want to be able to establish collaboration capability for the entire group. Invite Cochran and Snow to the demonstration and let them try it out. Have them write up a summary of their needs and the potential applications they see for the new systems. Then prepare me a report with the costs and specifications of the upgrade for the entire department. Oh, yes, be sure to ask for information on service costs."

Manager B: "I'd like to do something about our personal computer system. I've been getting some complaints that the current systems are too slow, can't run current software, and don't allow for networking. Could you evaluate our options and give me a recommendation on what we should do? Our budget is around $2,000 per person, but I'd like to stay under that if we can. Feel free to talk to some of the managers to get their input, but we need to have this done as soon as possible."

responsibility

The assignment of a task that an employee is supposed to carry out.

Responsibility, Authority, and Accountability   When delegating work, it is helpful to keep in mind the important distinctions among the concepts of authority, responsibility, and accountability. **Responsibility** means that a person is assigned a task that he or she is supposed to carry out. When delegating work responsibilities, the manager also should delegate to the subordinate enough authority to get the job done. Authority, recall, means that the person has the power and the right to make decisions, give orders, draw on resources, and do whatever else is necessary to fulfill the responsibility. Ironically, it is quite common for people to have more responsibility than authority; they must perform as well as they can through informal influence tactics instead of relying purely on authority. More will be said about informal power and how to use it in Chapter 12.

As the manager delegates responsibilities, subordinates are held accountable for achieving results. **Accountability** means that the subordinate's manager has the right to expect the subordinate to perform the job and the right to take corrective action if the subordinate fails to do so. The subordinate must report upward on the status and quality of his or her performance of the task.

However, the ultimate responsibility—accountability to higher-ups—lies with the manager doing the delegating. Managers remain responsible and accountable not only for their own actions but also for the actions of their subordinates. Managers should not resort to delegation to others as a means of escaping their own responsibilities. In many cases, however, managers refuse to accept responsibility for subordinates' actions. Managers often pass the buck or take other evasive action to ensure they are not held accountable for mistakes.[20] Ideally, however, empowering employees to make decisions or take action results in an increase in employee responsibility.

accountability

The expectation that employees will perform a job, take corrective action when necessary, and report upward on the status and quality of their performance.

Advantages of Delegation   Delegating work offers important advantages, particularly when it is done effectively. Effective delegation leverages the manager's energy and talent and those of his or her subordinates. It allows managers to accomplish much more than they would be able to do on their own. Conversely, lack of delegation, or ineffective delegation, sharply reduces what a manager can achieve. The manager also saves one of his or her most valuable assets—time—by giving some of his or her responsibility to somebody else. He or she is then free to devote energy to important, higher-level activities such as planning, setting objectives, and monitoring performance.

Another very important advantage of delegation is that it helps develop effective subordinates. Look again at the different ways the two office managers gave out the same assignment. The approach that is more likely to empower subordinates and help them develop will be obvious to you. (You may also quickly conclude which of the two managers you would prefer to work for.) Delegation essentially gives the subordinate a more important job. The subordinate acquires an opportunity to develop new skills and to demonstrate potential for additional responsibilities and perhaps promotion. In essence, the subordinate receives a vital form of on-the-job training that could pay off in the future. In addition, there is evidence that, at least for some employees, delegation promotes a sense of being an important, contributing member of the organization, so these employees tend to feel a stronger commitment, perform their tasks better, and engage in more innovation.[21]

Through delegation, the organization also receives payoffs. Allowing managers to devote more time to important managerial functions while lower-level employees carry out assignments means that jobs are done more efficiently and cost-effectively. In addition, as subordinates develop and grow in their own jobs, their ability to contribute to the organization increases as well.

Bottom Line

Effective delegation raises the quality of subordinates and the service they provide to customers or co-workers. *Under what conditions might an effort at delegation backfire?*

How Should Managers Delegate?   To achieve the advantages we have just discussed, delegation must be done properly. As Figure 8.2 shows, effective delegation proceeds through several steps.[22]

The first step in the delegation process, defining the goal, requires the manager to have a clear understanding of the outcome he or she wants. Then the manager should select a person who is capable of performing the task. Delegation is especially

FIGURE 8.2
The Steps in Effective
Delegation

beneficial if you can identify an employee who would benefit from developing skills through the experience of taking on the additional responsibility.

The person who gets the assignment should be given the authority, time, and resources to carry out the task successfully. The required resources usually involve people, money, and equipment, but often they may also involve critical information that will put the assignment in context. ("Review every cost item carefully, because if we're the low bidder, we'll get the account.") Throughout the delegation process, the manager and the subordinate must work together and communicate about the project. The manager should know the subordinate's ideas at the beginning and inquire about progress or problems at periodic meetings and review sessions. Thus, even though the subordinate performs the assignment, the manager is available and aware of its current status. These checkups also provide an important opportunity to offer encouragement and praise.

Some tasks, such as disciplining subordinates and conducting performance reviews, should not be delegated. But when managers err, it usually is because they delegated too little rather than too much. The manager who wants to learn how to delegate more effectively should remember this distinction: If you are not delegating, you are merely doing things; but the more you delegate, the more you are truly building and managing an organization.[23]

Decentralization

The delegation of responsibility and authority *decentralizes* decision making. In a **centralized organization,** important decisions usually are made at the top. In **decentralized organizations,** more decisions are made at lower levels. Ideally, decision making occurs at the level of the people who are most directly affected and have the most intimate knowledge about the problem. This is particularly important when the business environment is fast-changing and decisions must be made quickly and well. Balanced against these criteria, centralization may be valuable when departments have different priorities or conflicting goals, which need to be mediated by top management. For example, when researchers modeled the search for new ideas in organizations, they found that the worst performance occurred in decentralized organizations where the search for new ideas was carried out at lower levels, because ideas were presented for approval only if they benefited the particular department doing the search.[24]

> The delegation of responsibility and authority *decentralizes* decision making.

Sometimes organizations change their degree of centralization, depending on the particular challenges they face. Tougher times often cause senior managements to take charge, whereas in times of rapid growth, decisions are pushed further down the chain of command. Time Warner Cable (TWC) tried to decentralize marketing as a way to let regional teams move quickly in response to opportunities in local markets. However, competition for online entertainment and from satellite companies is putting cable companies such as TWC in an increasingly tight spot. In that environment, TWC reversed its decision and returned to a centralized marketing

centralized organization
An organization in which high-level executives make most decisions and pass them down to lower levels for implementation.

decentralized organization
An organization in which lower-level managers make important decisions.

structure.[25] Unfortunately for TWC, research suggests that decentralizing tends to go more smoothly than a change toward greater centralization; in that study, teams that became more centralized failed to make the efficiency gains typically associated with a centralized organization.[26]

Most American executives today understand the advantages of pushing decision-making authority down to the point of the action. The level that deals directly with problems and opportunities has the most relevant information and can foresee the consequences of decisions best. Executives also see how the decentralized approach allows people to take timelier action.[27]

At times, decentralizing decision making or allowing decisions to be made by middle and lower-level managers can be an advantage to higher-level executives. These are the managers who deal directly with the problem and know the best solution for the company and the employees.

According to Raj Gupta, president of Environmental Systems Design (ESD), the engineering design firm decentralized as a necessary response to growth. A traditional command-and-control approach to management worked fine when the company was starting out, but now with 240 engineering and design professionals designing for diverse clients working on commercial, transportation, residential, manufacturing, energy, and other projects, it would be impossible for a few people at the top to dictate solutions. In fact, it wouldn't even be desirable, given the diverse expertise of its employees. So instead of grouping staff into functional departments such as sustainable design or electrical work, ESD has a structure in which studios of professionals serve particular clients, making decisions to meet their specialized needs.[28]

Bottom Line

Decentralization often speeds decision making.
What makes centralized decision making slower?

The Horizontal Structure

Up to this point, we've talked primarily about vertical aspects of organization structure. Issues of authority, span of control, delegation, and decentralization are important because they give us an idea of how managers and employees relate to one another at different levels. Yet separating discussion of vertical differentiation from horizontal differentiation is a bit artificial because the elements work simultaneously.

As the tasks of organizations become increasingly complex, the organization inevitably must be subdivided—that is, *departmentalized*—into smaller units or departments. One of the first places this can be seen is in the distinction between line and staff departments. **Line departments** are those that have responsibility for the principal activities of the firm. Line units deal directly with the organization's primary goods or services; they make things, sell things, or provide customer service. At General Motors, for example, line departments include product design, fabrication, assembly, distribution, and the like. Line managers typically have much authority and power in the organization. They have the ultimate responsibility for making major operating decisions. They also are accountable for the bottom-line results of their decisions.

Staff departments are those that provide specialized or professional skills that support line departments. They include research, legal, accounting, public relations,

line departments

Units that deal directly with the organization's primary goods and services.

staff departments

Units that support line departments.

and human resources departments. Each of these specialized units often has its own vice president, and some are vested with a great deal of authority, as when accounting or finance groups approve and monitor budgetary activities.

In traditionally structured organizations, conflicts could arise between line and staff departments. One reason was that career paths and success in many staff functions have depended on being an expert in that particular functional area, whereas success in line functions is based more on knowing the organization's industry. Thus, although line managers might be eager to pursue new products and customers, staff managers might seem to stifle these ideas with a focus on requirements and procedures. Line managers might seem more willing to take risks for the sake of growth, whereas staff managers seem more focused on protecting the company from risks. But in today's organizations, staff units tend to be less focused on monitoring and controlling performance and more interested in moving toward a new role focused on strategic support and expert advice.[29] For example, human resource managers have broadened their focus from merely creating procedures that meet legal requirements to helping organizations plan for, recruit, develop, and keep the kinds of employees who will give the organization a long-term competitive advantage. This type of strategic thinking not only makes staff managers more valuable to their organizations but also can reduce the conflict between line and staff departments.

In Practice

To foster coordination by mutual adjustment, the libraries that serve some organizations are closing down the traditional book-filled rooms and moving librarians onto the teams that need their research skills.

For example, at Johns Hopkins University, the Welch Medical Library has switched from print journals and reference books to a fully digital system. This frees librarians to be wherever they are needed. The Welch librarians, now called informationists, are assigned to the departments that formerly came to them for information. They work in their assigned department's facility, where they can readily get to know the doctors and other staff members. Library scientist David Shumaker notes that this type of arrangement is becoming more common in medical settings, where librarians sometimes participate in rounds, equipped with a computer to look up research literature whenever questions arise about a diagnosis.

CH2M HILL, an engineering, construction, and project management firm, also has begun embedding librarians in project teams. Librarian Amy Maule is embedded in a team of engineers investigating new technologies such as renewable energy applications. As they learn about potential new applications, Maule manages the information and suggests additional sources. The longer she works with the team, the more she learns about the technologies and the more she can contribute her own ideas. Being an embedded librarian has made Maule a subject matter expert as well as a functional expert, increasing her value to the organization.[30]

- How might this approach of embedding librarians in line departments help reduce line-staff conflicts in these organizations?
- How else could an organization increase the integration of its library services?

departmentalization

Subdividing an organization into smaller subunits.

As organizations divide work into different units, we can detect patterns in the way departments are clustered and arranged. The three basic approaches to **departmentalization** are functional, divisional, and matrix. We will talk about each and highlight some of their similarities and differences.

FIGURE 8.3
The Functional
Organization

The Functional Organization

In a **functional organization,** jobs (and departments) are specialized and grouped according to business functions and the skills they require: production, marketing, human resources, research and development, finance, accounting, and so forth. Figure 8.3 illustrates a basic functional organization chart.

Functional departmentalization is common in both large and small organizations. Large companies may organize along several functional groupings, including groupings unique to their businesses. For example, Carmike Cinema, which operates more than 2,200 screens in 240 theaters in 36 states, has vice presidents of finance, concessions, film, and entertainment and digital cinema as well as a general manager of theater operations.

The traditional functional approach to departmentalization has a number of potential advantages for an organization:[31]

1. Economies of scale can be realized. When people with similar skills are grouped, more efficient equipment can be purchased, and discounts for large purchases can be used.
2. Monitoring of the environment is more effective. Each functional group is more closely attuned to developments in its own field and therefore can adapt more readily.
3. Performance standards are better maintained. People with similar training and interests may develop a shared concern for performance in their jobs.
4. People have greater opportunity for specialized training and in-depth skill development.
5. Technical specialists are relatively free of administrative work.
6. Decision making and lines of communication are simple and clearly understood.

The functional form does have disadvantages, however. People may care more about their own function than about the company as a whole, and their attention to functional tasks may make them lose focus on overall product quality and customer satisfaction. Managers develop functional expertise but do not acquire knowledge of the other areas of the business; they become specialists but not generalists. Between functions, conflicts arise, and communication and coordination fall off. In short, although functional differentiation may exist, functional integration may not.

As a consequence, the functional structure may be most appropriate in rather simple, stable environments. If the organization becomes fragmented (or *dis*integrated), it may have difficulty developing and bringing new products to market and responding quickly to customer demands and other changes. Particularly when companies are growing and business environments are changing, organizations need to integrate work areas more effectively so they can be more flexible and responsive. Other forms of departmentalization can be more flexible and responsive than the functional structure.

functional organization

Departmentalization around specialized activities such as production, marketing, and human resources.

Bottom Line

When like functions are grouped, savings often result. *Why might a company centralize its information technology (IT) department?*

One organization that has capitalized on the benefits of integrating functions is San Francisco Federal Credit Union (SFFCU). Several years ago, management could see the organization was losing members but didn't have the tools to understand why or to plan for growth. So SFFCU purchased a software system called Connections Online that gives employees in all functions access to information about the credit union's strategy and its progress toward goals. That visibility pushed management to launch regular cross-functional discussions about SFFCU's strategic plan. With everyone understanding priorities and engaged in getting results, the credit union has upgraded its technology, improved its marketing, and is watching membership and lending rates climb again.[32]

Demands for total quality, customer service, innovation, and speed have made clear the shortcomings of the functional form for some firms. Functional organizations are highly differentiated and create barriers to coordination across functions. Cross-functional coordination is essential for total quality, customer service, innovations, and speed. The functional organization will not disappear, in part because functional specialists will always be needed, but functional managers will make fewer decisions. The more important units will be cross-functional teams that have integrative responsibilities for products, processes, or customers.[33]

The Divisional Organization

divisional organization

Departmentalization that groups units around products, customers, or geographic regions.

The discussion of a functional structure's weaknesses leads us to the **divisional organization.** As organizations grow and become increasingly diversified, they find that functional departments have difficulty managing a wide variety of products, customers, and geographic regions. In this case, organizations may restructure to group all functions into a single division and duplicate each of the functions across all the divisions. In the divisional organization chart in Figure 8.4, Division A has its own operations, marketing, and finance departments, Division B has its own operations, marketing, and finance departments, and so on. In this structure, separate divisions may act almost as separate businesses or profit centers and work autonomously to accomplish the goals of the entire enterprise. Table 8.1 presents examples of how the same tasks would be organized under functional and divisional structures.

FIGURE 8.4
The Divisional Organization

Functional Organization	Divisional Organization
Magazine publisher with editorial, sales, production, web design, and fulfillment departments handling their functions for all magazines.	Magazine publisher with separate teams for each magazine, with editorial, sales, production, web design, and fulfillment employees on each team.
Chain of movie theaters with departments for concessions, films, theater operations, and finance, responsible for all theaters.	Chain of movie theaters with one division for each region of the country handling all functions in that region.
Manufacturer with departments of engineering, production, purchasing, distribution, and sales handling all products.	Manufacturer with product groups each staffed with people to handle that product's engineering, production, purchasing, distribution, and sales.
One human resources department serving the needs of an entire multinational firm, reporting to the corporate leadership.	A human resources group at the offices of each country in which a multinational firm operates, reporting to the vice president in charge of that country's operations.

TABLE 8.1

Examples of Functional and Divisional Organization

SOURCE: George Strauss and Leonard R. Sayles, *Strauss and Sayles's Behavioral Strategies for Managers,* © 1980, p. 221. Reprinted by permission of Prentice Hall, Inc., Englewood Cliffs, New Jersey.

Organizations create a divisional structure in several ways. It can be created around products, customers, or geographic regions. Each of these is described in the following sections.

Product Divisions   In the product organization, all functions that contribute to a given product are organized under one manager. In the product organization, managers in charge of functions for a particular product report to a product manager. Johnson & Johnson is one example of this form. J&J has more than 250 independent company divisions, many of which are responsible for particular product lines. For example, its subsidiary, Cordis Corporation, has divisions that develop and sell products for treating vascular diseases, whereas McNeil-PPC's products include Listerine and Plax mouthwashes.

The product approach to departmentalization offers a number of advantages:[34]

1. *Information needs are managed more easily.* Less information is required because people work closely on one product and need not worry about other products.
2. *People have a full-time commitment to a particular product line.* They develop a greater awareness of how their jobs fit into the broader scheme.
3. *Task responsibilities are clear.* When things go wrong in a functional organization, functional managers can pass the buck ("That other department is messing up, making it harder for us to do our jobs"). In a product structure, managers are more independent and accountable because they usually have the resources they need to perform their tasks. Also, the performances of different divisions can be compared by contrasting their profits and other measures.
4. *People receive broader training.* General managers develop a wide variety of skills, and they learn to be judged by results. Many top executives received crucial early experience in product structures.

Because the product structure is more flexible than the functional structure, it is best suited for unstable environments in which an ability to adapt rapidly to change is important. But the product structure also has disadvantages. It is difficult to coordinate across product lines and divisions. And although managers learn to become generalists, they may not acquire the depth of functional expertise that develops in the functional structure.

Furthermore, functions are not centralized at headquarters, where they are done for all product lines or divisions. Such duplication of effort is expensive. Also, decision making is decentralized in this structure, so top management can lose some control over decisions made in the divisions. Proper management of all the issues surrounding decentralization and delegation, as discussed earlier, is essential for this structure to be effective.[35]

Customer and Geographic Divisions Some companies build divisions around groups of customers or around different geographic areas. Pfizer recently replaced divisions based on location with three based on customer groups: primary care, specialty care, and emerging markets. The pharmaceutical company hopes that this structure will make the company more responsive to the needs of doctors and their patients in each group.[36] Similarly, a hospital may organize its services around child, adult, psychiatric, and emergency cases. Bank loan departments commonly have separate groups handling consumer and business needs.

In contrast to customers, divisions can be structured around geographic regions. Sears, for example, was a pioneer in creating geographic divisions. Geographic distinctions include district, territory, region, and country. Macy's Group, formerly Federated Department Stores, has geographic divisions for its operations serving particular states or regions of the United States: Macy's East, Macy's Florida, Macy's Midwest, Macy's North, Macy's Northwest, Macy's South, and Macy's West as well as Macys.com for online shoppers. Avon Products recently restructured into two major business units divided in terms of geography (and economics). Its developed market group will serve customers in North America and Western Europe, whereas its developing market group will serve customers in Latin America, Central and Eastern Europe, and the Asia-Pacific region.[37]

The primary advantage of both the product and customer/regional approaches to departmentalization is the ability to focus on customer needs and provide faster, better service. But again, duplication of activities across many customer groups and geographic areas is expensive. As you read "Management Connection: Progress Report," consider how well the advantages and drawbacks of these divisional structures might apply to General Motors.

The Matrix Organization

A **matrix organization** is a hybrid form of organization in which functional and divisional forms overlap. Managers and staff personnel report to two bosses—a functional manager and a divisional manager. Thus matrix organizations have a dual rather than a single line of command. In Figure 8.5, for example, each project manager draws employees from each functional area to form a group for the project. The employees working on those projects report to the individual project manager as well as to the manager of their functional area.

A good example of the matrix structure can be found at Time Inc., the top magazine publisher in the United States and United Kingdom. At major Time Inc. titles such as *Time*, *Sports Illustrated*, and *People*, production managers who are responsible for getting the magazines printed report both to the individual publishers and editors of each title *and* to a senior corporate executive in charge of production. At the corporate level, Time Inc. achieves enormous economies of scale by buying paper and printing in bulk and making sure production activities in the company as a whole are coordinated. At the same time, production managers working at each title make sure the different needs and schedules of their individual magazines are being met. Similar matrix arrangements are in place for other key managers such as circulation and finance. In this way, the company attempts to gain the benefits of both the divisional and functional organization structure.

Bottom Line

Customer and geographic divisions often serve customers faster.

Suppose your international company sells scientific equipment to high schools, universities, and businesses. Would you set up customer divisions or geographic divisions? Why?

LO 8

matrix organization

An organization composed of dual reporting relationships in which some employees report to two superiors—a functional manager and a divisional manager.

Management Connection

GENERAL MOTORS PLOTS A NEW STRUCTURE

CEO Daniel Akerson's plans to make General Motors more nimble reportedly include a corporate reorganization to create more of a functional structure. Over the past few decades, GM had moved from a structure based on product lines (Chevrolet, Buick, Cadillac, and so on) toward one based on regions (North America, South America, Europe, and International Operations). But the main result seems to have been that the company moved from one set of independently operating groups (the brand groups) to another (the geographic groups), and the company still was not operating as a unified whole with a common mission. Efforts to save money by globally applying product designs broke down as regional executives insisted on making their own decisions for their regions.

A functional structure would place more authority in the hands of the functional executives, who could set up companywide systems and identify designs to use for models created to sell in several or all geographic markets. Evidence for a change in this direction includes some of Akerson's hiring decisions. Chief Financial Officer Dan Ammann was charged with upgrading the accounting system to track financial performance more clearly, and Chief Information Officer Randy Mott is upgrading GM's information technology to become a core competency that supports decision making. Joel Ewanick was placed in charge of marketing, and he set to work reviewing GM's

many advertising deals (70 contracts for Chevrolet alone), combining the best-performing ideas into one marketing package. Akerson promoted Timothy Lee from head of international operations to vice president of global manufacturing.

Finally, Akerson placed Mary Barra in charge of GM's global product development, in charge of 29,000 employees. She then put the development of each vehicle program under the control of one chief engineer. Formerly, the responsibility for developing a vehicle was shared by a vehicle line executive, vehicle line director, and vehicle chief engineer; Barra's change eliminated a layer of management, including about 20 positions. The product development group is also working to use fewer underlying architectures in the design of its vehicles, so more parts and processes can be standardized across models. In 2010, 30 percent of the company's vehicles sold had one of these core vehicle platforms; the share rose to 61 percent in 2012, and the company's goal is to reach 90 percent by 2018.[38]

- Review the advantages and drawbacks of functional organizations and geographic divisions. Which ones apply to the situation General Motors is facing?
- What do you think will be the impact of GM's effort to create more centralized structure based on functional groups?

The matrix form originated in the aerospace industry, first with TRW in 1959 and then with NASA. Applications now occur in hospitals and health care agencies, entrepreneurial organizations, government laboratories, financial institutions, and multinational corporations.[39] Other companies that have used or currently use the matrix form include IBM, Boeing, Xerox, Wellpoint, Texas Instruments, Bechtel, and Dow Corning.

Pros and Cons of the Matrix Form   Like other organization structures, the matrix has both strengths and weaknesses. Table 8.2 summarizes the advantages of using a matrix structure. The major potential advantage is a higher degree of flexibility and adaptability.

Table 8.2 also summarizes the potential shortcomings of the matrix form. Many of the disadvantages stem from the matrix's inherent violation of the **unity-of-command principle,** which states that a person should have only one boss. Reporting to two superiors can create confusion and a difficult interpersonal situation unless steps are taken to prevent these problems from arising.

Matrix Survival Skills   The value of collaboration is particularly pronounced in a matrix organization. For example, in the kind of structure illustrated in Figure 8.5, project group members may not be permanently assigned to the project manager.

unity-of-command principle

A structure in which each worker reports to one boss, who in turn reports to one boss.

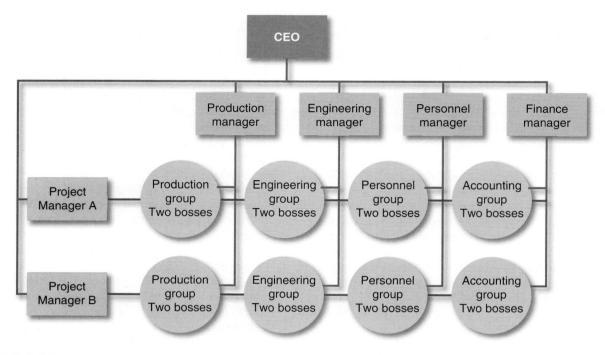

FIGURE 8.5

Matrix Organizational Structure

They will return to their functional area once the project has been completed. For this group to work effectively, the traditional command-and-control management style may not be the most appropriate; it might gain compliance from group members but not their full commitment, making it harder to achieve the project's goals. Also, because the matrix organization draws on members of functional groups to tap their expertise, it is very important to get their full contribution. A collaborative process,

TABLE 8.2

Advantages and Disadvantages of the Matrix Design

Advantages
• Linkage of employees at all levels and in all functions to the company's goals and strategy.
• More information shared across functions.
• Communication fostered—especially valuable for complex assignments where different groups depend on each other.
• Greater responsiveness to customers from bringing together information about customer needs and organizational capabilities.
• Creative ideas from cross-functional work.
• Loyalty to the organization as a whole rather than to a function or division.

Disadvantages
• Unclear responsibilities and competing priorities.
• Violation of the unity-of-command principle.
• Accountability difficult to define.
• Accountability for results under other matrix members' control.
• Possible conflict and stress for employees who must manage a dual reporting role.
• Additional time required for meetings and other communications to coordinate work.
• Extensive collaboration needed but not always easy to reward.

Sources: Based on E. Krell, "Managing the Matrix," *HR Magazine,* April 2011, pp. 69–71; R. Lash, "Cracking the Matrix Code," *Canadian HR Reporter,* March 28, 2011, pp. 16, 18; and M. North and C. Coors, "Avoiding Death by Dotted Line," *Healthcare Financial Management,* January 2010, pp. 120–21.

in which the manager and participants develop a shared sense of ownership for the work they are doing, will generate better ideas, participation, and commitment to the project and its outcomes.

To a large degree, problems can be avoided if the key managers in the matrix learn the behavioral skills demanded in the matrix structure.[40] These skills vary depending on the job in the four-person diamond structure shown in Figure 8.6.

The top executive, who heads the matrix, must learn to balance power and emphasis between the product and functional orientations. Product or division managers and functional managers must learn to collaborate and manage their conflicts constructively. Finally, the two-boss managers or employees at the bottom of the diamond must learn how to be responsible to two superiors. This means prioritizing multiple demands and sometimes even reconciling conflicting orders. Some people function poorly under this ambiguous, conflictual circumstance; sometimes this signals the end of their careers with the company. Others learn to be proactive, communicate effectively with both superiors, rise above the difficulties, and manage these work relationships constructively.

> The key to managing today's matrix is the realization that the matrix is a process.

The Matrix Form Today   The popularity of the matrix form waned during the late 1980s, when many companies had difficulty implementing it. But recently it has come back strong. Reasons for this resurgence include pressures to consolidate costs and be faster to market, creating a need for better coordination across functions in the business units and a need for coordination across countries for firms with global business strategies. Many of the challenges created by the matrix are particularly acute in an international context, mainly because of the distances involved and the differences in local markets.[41]

The key to managing today's matrix is not the formal structure itself but the realization that the matrix is a process. Managers who have appropriately adopted the matrix structure because of the complexity of the challenges they confront, but have had trouble implementing it, often find that they haven't changed the employee and managerial relationships within their organizations in ways that make the matrix effective. It is not enough to create a flexible organization merely by changing its structure. To create an environment that allows information to flow freely throughout

Bottom Line

The matrix structure can speed decisions and cut costs. *How might a matrix structure increase speed?*

FIGURE 8.6
The Matrix Diamond

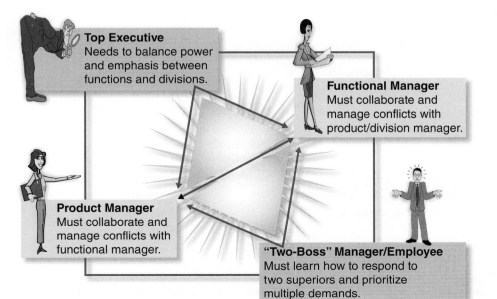

the organization, managers must also attend to the norms, values, and attitudes that shape how people within their organizations behave.[42] We will address these issues in the next chapter and in Part 4 of the book, which focuses on how to lead and manage people.

The Network Organization

So far, the structures we have been discussing are variations of the traditional, hierarchical organization, within which all the business functions of the firm are performed. In contrast, the **network organization** is a collection of independent, mostly single-function firms that collaborate to produce a good or service. As depicted in Figure 8.7, the network organization describes not one organization but the web of relationships among many firms. Network organizations are flexible arrangements among designers, suppliers, producers, distributors, and customers where each firm is able to pursue its own distinctive competence yet work effectively with other members of the network. Often, members of the network communicate electronically and share information to be able to respond quickly to customer demands. In effect, the normal boundary of the organization becomes blurred or porous as managers within the organization interact closely with network members outside it. The network as a whole, then, can display the technical specialization of the functional structure, the market responsiveness of the product structure, and the balance and flexibility of the matrix.[43]

A very flexible version of the network organization is the **dynamic network**—also called the *modular* or *virtual* corporation. It is composed of temporary arrangements among members that can be assembled and reassembled to meet a changing competitive environment. The members of the network are held together by contracts that stipulate results expected (market mechanisms) rather than by hierarchy and authority. Poorly performing firms can be removed and replaced.

Such arrangements are common in the electronics, toy, and apparel industries, each of which creates and sells trendy products at a fast pace. Dynamic networks also are suited to organizations in which much of the work can be done independently by experts. For example, Philip Rosedale set up a virtual company called LoveMachine to commercialize a software tool of the same name: an online communication system that allows users to send one another brief messages. The primary difference from a microblogging service like Twitter is that the system is completely transparent; everyone in the system sees the messages. Thus in a company using LoveMachine for

network organization

A collection of independent, mostly single-function firms that collaborate on a good or service.

dynamic network

Temporary arrangements among partners that can be assembled and reassembled to adapt to the environment.

Bottom Line

Networks can improve cost, quality, service, speed, sustainability, and innovation. *Which functions would you include in a network to improve sustainability?*

FIGURE 8.7
A Network Organization

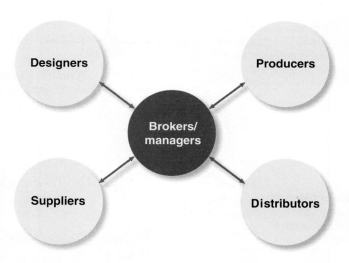

SOURCE: From Raymond E. Miles and Charles C. Snow, "Organizations: New Concepts for New Forms," in *California Management Review* 28, no. 3 (Spring 1986), pp. 62–73. Copyright 1986 by the Regents of the University of California. Reprinted by permission of University of California Press.

employee recognition, everyone sees a message of appreciation, with the intent that public acknowledgment builds morale. For such a transparent application, Rosedale and his partners decided to build a completely transparent company. They launched an online bulletin board where they posted a list of all the tasks to be done for LoveMachine. Freelancers bid on a job by describing how they would carry out the task and what they would charge. For any collaboration required, the freelancers communicate online at the company's chat room or via e-mail and Skype. Rosedale started this virtual arrangement for programming tasks, and it was so successful in delivering great prices and fast turnaround that the company expanded to support tasks such as recruiting contracts and processing payments. One regular contractor is an American who lives in Belgium; other contractors are in India, Russia, and Australia. However, Rosedale acknowledges that he sometimes misses that camaraderie of a face-to-face work team, so he is setting up a San Francisco work space where local workers can gather if they wish.[44]

Successful networks potentially offer flexibility, innovation, quick responses to threats and opportunities, and reduced costs and risk. But for these arrangements to be successful, several things must occur:

The firm must choose the right specialty. It must be something (good or service) that the market needs and that the firm is better at providing than other firms.

The firm must choose collaborators that also are excellent at what they do and that provide complementary strengths.

The firm must make certain that all parties fully understand the strategic goals of the partnership.

Each party must be able to trust all the others with strategic information and trust that each collaborator will deliver quality products even if the business grows quickly and makes heavy demands.

The role of managers shifts in a network from that of command and control to more like that of a **broker**. Broker/managers serve several important boundary roles that aid network integration and coordination:

broker

A person who assembles and coordinates participants in a network.

Designer role. The broker serves as a network architect who envisions a set of groups or firms whose collective expertise could be focused on a particular good or service.

Process engineering role. The broker serves as a *network co-operator* who takes the initiative to lay out the flow of resources and relationships and makes certain that everyone shares the same goals, standards, payments, and the like.

Nurturing role. The broker serves as a network developer who nurtures and enhances the network (like team building) to make certain the relationships are healthy and mutually beneficial.[45]

Organizational Integration

At the beginning of this chapter, we said organizations are structured around differentiation and integration. So far, our discussion has focused on *differentiation*—the way the organization is composed of different jobs and tasks and the way they fit on an organization chart. But as organizations differentiate their structures, they also need to be concerned about *integration* and *coordination*—the way all parts of the organization will work together. Often, the more differentiated the organization, the more difficult integration may be. Because of specialization and the division of labor, different groups of managers and employees develop different orientations. Depending

> Often the more differentiated the organization, the more difficult integration may be.

on whether employees are in a functional department or a divisional group, are line or staff, and so on, they will think and act in ways that are geared toward their particular work units. In short, people working in separate functions, divisions, and business units literally tend to forget about one another. When this happens, it is difficult for managers to combine all their activities into an integrated whole.

A variety of approaches are available to managers to help them make certain that interdependent units and individuals will work together to achieve a common purpose. In some situations, managers might see that employees need to work closely to achieve joint objectives, so they build mutual trust, train employees in a common set of skills, and reward teamwork. In other situations, the organization might rely more on individuals with unique talents and ideas, so they set up flexible work arrangements and reward individual achievements to inspire the best from each individual while encouraging individual employees to share knowledge and develop respect for one another's contributions.[46] In general, however, coordination methods include standardization, plans, and mutual adjustment.[47]

Coordination by Standardization

When organizations coordinate activities by establishing routines and standard operating procedures that remain in place over time, we say that work has been standardized. **Standardization** constrains actions and integrates various units by regulating what people do. People often know how to act—and how to interact—because standard operating procedures spell out what they should do. For example, managers may establish standards for which types of computer equipment the organization will use. This simplifies the purchasing and computer-training process—everyone will be on a common platform—and makes it easier for the different parts of the organization to communicate with each other.

standardization

Establishing common routines and procedures that apply uniformly to everyone.

To improve coordination, organizations may also rely on **formalization**—the presence of rules and regulations governing how people in the organization interact. Simple, often written, policies regarding attendance, dress, and decorum, for example, may help eliminate a good deal of uncertainty at work. But an important assumption underlying both standardization and formalization is that the rules and procedures should apply to most (if not all) situations. These approaches, therefore, are most appropriate in situations that are relatively stable and unchanging. In some cases, when the work environment requires flexibility, coordination by standardization may not be very effective. Who hasn't experienced a time when rules and procedures—frequently associated with a slow bureaucracy—prevented timely action to address a problem? In these instances, we often refer to rules and regulations as red tape.[48]

formalization

The presence of rules and regulations governing how people in the organization interact.

Coordination by Plan

If laying out the exact rules and procedures by which work should be integrated is difficult, organizations may provide more latitude by establishing goals and schedules for interdependent units. **Coordination by plan** does not require the same high degree of stability and routinization required for coordination by standardization. Interdependent units are free to modify and adapt their actions as long as they meet the deadlines and targets required for working with others.

coordination by plan

Interdependent units are required to meet deadlines and objectives that contribute to a common goal.

In writing this textbook, for example, we (the authors) sat down with a publication team that included the editors, the marketing staff, the production group, and support staff. Together, we ironed out a schedule for developing this book that covered approximately a two-year period. That development plan included dates and deliverables that specified what was to be accomplished and forwarded to the others in the organization. The plan allowed for a good deal of flexibility on each subunit's part, and the overall approach allowed us to work together effectively.

Coordination by Mutual Adjustment

Ironically, the simplest and most flexible approach to coordination may just be to have interdependent parties talk to one another. **Coordination by mutual adjustment** involves feedback and discussions to figure out jointly how to approach problems and devise solutions that are agreeable to everyone. The popularity of teams today is in part because they allow flexible coordination; teams can operate under the principle of mutual adjustment.

But the flexibility of mutual adjustment as a coordination device does not come without some cost. Hashing out every issue takes time and may not be the most expedient approach for organizing work. Imagine how long it would take to accomplish even the most basic tasks if subunits had to talk through every situation. At the same time, mutual adjustment can be very effective when problems are novel and cannot be programmed in advance with rules, procedures, or plans. Particularly during crises, in which rules and procedures don't apply, mutual adjustment is likely to be the most effective approach to coordination.

coordination by mutual adjustment

Units interact with one another to make accommodations to achieve flexible coordination.

Coordination and Communication

Today's environments tend to be complex, dynamic, and therefore uncertain. Huge amounts of information flow from the external environment to the organization and back to the environment. To cope, organizations must acquire, process, and respond to that information. Doing so has direct implications for how firms organize. To function effectively, organizations need to develop structures for processing information.

To cope with high uncertainty and heavy information demands, managers can use the two general strategies shown in Figure 8.8. First, management can act to reduce the need for information. Second, it can increase its capacity to handle more information.[49]

Information sharing is vital at the National Counterterrorism Center, shown here. Technology is used to enable the efficient and safe sharing of this information.

FIGURE 8.8
Managing High Information-Processing Demands

Option 1: Reducing the Need for Information   Managers can reduce the need for information in two ways: (a) creating slack resources and (b) creating self-contained tasks. Slack resources are simply extra resources on which organizations can rely in a pinch so that if they get caught off guard, they can still adjust. Inventory, for example, is a type of slack resource that provides extra stock on hand in case it is needed. With extra inventory, an organization does not need as much information about sales demand, lead time, and the like. Employees also can be a type of slack resource. For example, many companies augment their full-time staffs with part-time and temporary employees. This way, they do not have to forecast sales peaks perfectly but can rely on supplementary workers to handle irregularities.

Like slack resources, creating self-contained tasks allows organizations to reduce the need for some information. Creating self-contained tasks refers to changing from a functional organization to a product or project organization and giving each unit the resources it needs to perform its task. Information-processing problems are reduced because each unit has its own full complement of specialties instead of functional specialties that have to share their expertise among a number of different product teams. Communications then flow within each team rather than among a complex array of interdependent groups.

Option 2: Increasing Information-Processing Capability   Instead of reducing the need for information, an organization may take the approach of increasing its information-processing capability. It can invest in information systems, which usually means employing or expanding computer systems. But increasing an organization's information-processing capability also means what we referred to in Chapter 1 as knowledge management—capitalizing on the intellect and experience of the organization's human assets to increase collaboration and effectiveness. One way to do that is by creating horizontal relationships between units to foster coordination. Such horizontal relationships are effective because they increase integration, which Lawrence and Lorsch suggest is necessary for managing complex environments. As uncertainty increases, the following horizontal processes may be used, ranging from the simplest to the most complex:[50]

Bottom Line

Cross-unit coordination can lead to effective problem solutions.

Why does more information tend to improve solutions?

1. *Direct contact (mutual adjustment)* among managers who share a problem. In a university, for example, a residence hall adviser might call a meeting to resolve differences between two feuding students who live in adjacent rooms.
2. *Liaison roles,* or specialized jobs to handle communications between two departments. A fraternity representative is a liaison between the fraternity and the interfraternity council, the university, or the local community.
3. *Task forces,* or groups of representatives from different departments, brought together temporarily to solve a common problem. For example, students, faculty, and administrators may be members of a task force charged with bringing distinguished speakers to campus for a current events seminar.
4. *Teams,* or permanent interdepartmental decision-making groups. An executive council made up of department heads might meet regularly to make decisions affecting a college of engineering or liberal arts.
5. *Product, program, or project managers* who direct interdisciplinary groups with a common task to perform. In a college of business administration, a faculty administrator might head an executive education program of professors from several disciplines.
6. *Matrix organizations,* composed of dual relationships in which some managers report to two superiors. Your instructors, for example, may report to department heads in their respective disciplines and to a director of undergraduate or graduate programs.

Several of these processes are discussed further in Chapter 14, where we examine managing teams and intergroup relations.

In Practice

Just as individuals have learned that it is easy to keep in touch with family and friends on social networks such as Facebook, Pinterest, and Twitter, organizations are learning that enterprise social networks are a powerful tool for sharing information among employees. Instead of posting photos of their dogs and links to music videos, users of enterprise social networks are sharing project documents, posting ideas for improving efficiency, and looking up tips for solving problems previously tackled by their co-workers. These networks have the potential to help employees take control over their time: Instead of getting a stream of e-mail updates about a project, an employee can check the project's page to see what others have posted, or instead of calling a meeting every time a problem arises, an employee can post a question seeking experts in the subject matter.

A variety of software companies offer the tools for enterprise social networks; IBM's platform, IBM Connections, has the biggest market share. Customers of IBM Connections include Prudential Insurance, Lowe's Home Improvement, and Electrolux, but most big corporations now have or are installing the networking tools. However, simply offering the tools will not automatically lead to participation by employees. Organizations that want to get the most out of the systems need to show employees how to use the tools and what benefits can result. Those that do so can get knowledge flowing to the employees who need it, when they need it, regardless of their function or geographic location.[51]

- Why do you think an organization would set up an enterprise social network for its employees instead of encouraging them to use existing tools, such as Tumblr (for blogging) or LinkedIn (for building a network)?

Looking Ahead

The organization chart, differentiation, integration, authority, delegation, coordination, and the like convey fundamental information about an organization's structure. However, the information so far has provided only a snapshot. The real organization is more like a motion picture—it moves! More flexible and innovative—even virtual—forms of organizations are evolving. Today's organizations are far removed, in many of their fundamental characteristics, from the traditional forms they once had. They may be more networked, flexible, and global, using electronic sharing of information to move faster than 20th century managers could have envisaged.

No organization is merely a set of static work relationships. Because organizations are composed of people, they are hotbeds of social relationships. Networks of individuals cutting across departmental boundaries interact with one another. Various friendship groups or cliques band together to form *coalitions*—members of the organization who jointly support a particular issue and try to ensure that their viewpoints determine the outcome of policy decisions.

Thus the formal organization structure does not describe everything about how the company really works. Even if you know departments and authority relationships, you still have much to understand. How do things really get done? Who influences whom, and how? Which managers are the most powerful? How effective is the top leadership? Which groups are most and which are least effective? What is the nature of communication patterns throughout the organization? These issues are discussed throughout the rest of the book.

Now you are familiar with the basic organizing concepts discussed in this chapter. In the next chapter, we will discuss the current challenges of designing the modern organization with which the modern executive constantly grapples. As you read "Management Connection: Onward," consider how the organizing concepts from the chapter help you evaluate the challenges facing General Motors, but also notice where personal relationships and other human factors come into play.

Management Connection

GETTING WORK INTEGRATED AT GENERAL MOTORS

In GM's 2012 annual report, CEO Dan Akerson said management aims to "make GM the world's most valuable automotive company." For this, everyone must pull together to restore the struggling Opel division in Europe, introduce more than 10 new products a year in China, and create better vehicles to woo former customers in the United States. Those measures are complicated at a corporation where people customarily defend their own turf. Anecdotes of Akerson's tenure describe middle managers insisting on old ways, such as requiring that executives' office furniture not be too cheap.

Reorganizing therefore involves more than redrawing lines on an organization chart; GM's managers must build cooperation across the old divisional boundaries. Board member Robert Krebs told a Bloomberg reporter that Akerson had changed the culture at the top of the organization but the sense of urgency needed time to move down through the vast company's hierarchy. Changes such as the revamped accounting system and centralized information technology are aimed at speeding the transition. Chief Financial Officer Dan Ammann backs that up by keeping his presentations understandable and free of mind-numbing detail.

One key player in implementing these changes is Mary Barra, senior vice president of global product development, whose decisions shape how fast new products come to market. Her streamlining of the product development group's structure was an important first step. Barra, who joined GM as an electrical engineer and worked her way up, also has simplified systems. Instead of letting managers constantly tweak their four-year plans, she holds twice-yearly meetings at which the plans are reviewed. Her audit of processes in product development showed that the people in her own group were the ones slowing development by coming up with a stream of revision ideas. It found fiefdoms within the group, too. In a compact car, for example, the seat controls were poorly placed because the designer of the seat belt and the designer of the seat control were fighting for the best location rather than thinking of the driver's needs. Under Barra, such conduct is not tolerated.

Changing a company's culture is difficult, and past efforts at reorganizing GM have not always gone as planned. Recent declines in GM's stock price (even as the U.S. government is selling its shares) show that investors continue to worry. But executives remain confident that they have begun matching GM's structure to its strategy.[52]

- In its effort to improve integration, how is GM addressing the need for communication? What else could the company do to improve coordination through communication?
- What personal factors are likely to affect GM's success in achieving greater organizational integration?

KEY TERMS

SUMMARY OF LEARNING OBJECTIVES

Now that you have studied Chapter 8, you should be able to:

LO 1 Explain how differentiation and integration influence an organization's structure.

Differentiation means that organizations have many parts. Specialization means that various individuals and units throughout the organization perform different tasks. The assignment of tasks to different people or groups often is referred to as the division of labor. But the specialized tasks in an organization cannot all be performed independently of one another. Coordination links the various tasks to achieve the organization's overall mission. An organization with many specialized tasks and work units is highly differentiated; the more differentiated the organization is, the more integration or coordination is required.

LO 2 Summarize how authority operates.

Authority is the legitimate right to make decisions and tell other people what to do. Authority is exercised throughout the hierarchy because bosses have the authority to give orders to subordinates. Through the day-to-day operation of authority, the organization proceeds toward achieving its goals. Owners or stockholders have ultimate authority.

LO 3 Define the roles of the board of directors and the chief executive officer.

Boards of directors report to stockholders. The board of directors controls or advises management, considers the firm's legal and other interests, and protects stockholders' rights. The chief executive officer reports to the board and is accountable for the organization's performance.

LO 4 Discuss how span of control affects structure and managerial effectiveness.

Span of control is the number of people who report directly to a manager. Narrow spans create tall organizations, and wide spans create flat ones. No single span of control is always appropriate; the optimal span is determined by characteristics of the work, the subordinates, the manager, and the organization.

LO 5 Explain how to delegate effectively.

Delegation—the assignment of tasks and responsibilities—has many potential advantages for the manager, the subordinate, and the organization. But to be effective, the process must be managed carefully. The manager should define the goal, select the person, solicit opinions, provide resources, schedule checkpoints, and discuss progress periodically.

LO 6 Distinguish between centralized and decentralized organizations.

In centralized organizations, most important decisions are made by top managers. In decentralized organizations, many decisions are delegated to lower levels.

LO 7 Summarize ways organizations can be structured.

Organizations can be structured on the basis of function, division (product, customers, or geographic), matrix, and network. Each form has advantages and disadvantages.

LO 8 Identify the unique challenges of the matrix organization.

The matrix is a complex structure with a dual authority organization. A well-managed matrix enables organizations to adapt to change. But it can also create confusion and interpersonal difficulties. People in all positions in the matrix—top executives, product and function managers, and two-boss employees—must acquire unique survival skills.

LO 9 Describe important integrative mechanisms.

Managers can coordinate interdependent units through standardization, plans, and mutual adjustment. Standardization occurs when routines and standard operating procedures are put in place. They typically are accompanied by formalized rules. Coordination by plan is more flexible and allows more freedom in how tasks are carried out but keeps interdependent units focused on schedules and joint goals. Mutual adjustment involves feedback and discussions among related parties to accommodate each other's needs. It is at once the most flexible and simple to administer, but it is time-consuming.

DISCUSSION QUESTIONS

1. Based on the description of General Motors in this chapter, give some examples of differentiation in that organization. In other words, what specialized tasks have to be performed, and how is labor divided at General Motors? Also, how does General Motors integrate the work of these different units? Based on what you have learned in this chapter, would you say General Motors has an effective structure? Why or why not?

2. What are some advantages and disadvantages of being in the CEO position?

3. Would you like to sit on a board of directors? Why or why not? If you did serve on a board, what kind of organization would you prefer? As a board member, in what kinds of activities do you think you would most actively engage?

4. Interview a member of a board of directors, and discuss that member's perspectives on his or her role.

5. Pick a job you have held and describe it in terms of span of control, delegation, responsibility, authority, and accountability.

6. Why do you think managers have difficulty delegating? What can be done to overcome these difficulties?

7. Consider an organization in which you have worked, draw its organization chart, and describe it by using terms in this chapter. How did you like working there, and why?

8. Would you rather work in a functional or divisional organization? Why?

9. If you learned that a company had a matrix structure, would you be more or less interested in working there? Explain your answer. How would you prepare yourself to work effectively in a matrix?

10. Brainstorm a list of methods for integrating interdependent work units. Discuss the activities that need to be undertaken and the pros and cons of each approach.

EXPERIENTIAL EXERCISES

8.1   THE BUSINESS SCHOOL ORGANIZATION CHART

OBJECTIVES

1. To clarify the factors that determine organization structure.

2. To provide insight into the workings of an organization.

3. To examine the working relationships within an organization.

INSTRUCTIONS

1. Draw an organization chart for your school of business. Be sure to identify all the staff and line positions in the school. Specify the chain of command and the levels of administration. Note the different spans of control. Are there any advisory groups, task forces, or committees to consider?

2. Review the chapter material on organization structure to help identify both strong and weak points in your school's organization. Now draw another organization chart for the school, incorporating any changes you believe would improve the quality of the school. Support the second chart with a list of recommended changes and reasons for their inclusion.

DISCUSSION QUESTIONS

1. Is your business school well organized? Why or why not?

2. In what ways is the school's structure designed to suit the needs of students, faculty, staff, the administration, and the business community?

8.2   DESIGNING A STUDENT-RUN ORGANIZATION THAT PROVIDES CONSULTING SERVICES

OBJECTIVES

1. To appreciate the importance of the total organization on group and individual behavior.

2. To provide a beginning organization design experience that will be familiar to students.

BACKGROUND

The Industry Advisory Council for your school has decided to sponsor a student-run organization that will provide business consulting services to nonprofit groups in your community. The council has donated $20,000 toward start-up costs and has agreed to provide office space, computer equipment, and other materials as needed. The council hopes that the organization will establish its own source of funding after the first year of operation.

Task 1

The dean of the school wants you to develop alternative designs for the new organization. Your task is to identify the main design dimensions or factors to be dealt with in establishing such an organization and to describe the issues that must be resolved for each factor. For example, you might provide an organization chart to help describe the structural issues involved. Before jumping ahead with your design, you may also have to think about (1) groups in the community that could use your help and (2) problems they face. Remember, though, your task is to create the organization that will provide services, not to provide an in-depth look at the types of services provided.

You and your team are to brainstorm design dimensions to be dealt with and to develop a one- or two-page outline that can be shared with the entire class. You have one hour to develop the outline. Select two people to present your design.

Assume that you will all be involved in the new organization, filling specific positions.

Task 2

After the brainstorming period, the spokespersons will present the group designs or preferred design and answer questions from the audience.

Task 3

The instructor will comment on the designs and discuss additional factors that might be important for the success of this organization.

SOURCE: A. B. (Rami) Shani and James B. Lau, *Behavior in Organizations: An Experimental Approach,* p. 369. Copyright 2005 The McGraw-Hill Companies. Reprinted with permission.

8.3 DECENTRALIZATION: PROS AND CONS

OBJECTIVE

To explore the reasons for, as well as the pros and cons of, decentralizing.

INSTRUCTIONS

The following Decentralization Worksheet contains some observations on decentralization. As you review each of the statements, provide an example that illustrates why this statement is important and related problems and benefits of the situation or condition indicated in the statement.

Decentralization Worksheet

A large number of factors determine the extent to which a manager should decentralize. Clearly, anything that increases a manager's workload creates pressure for decentralization because only a finite level of work can be accomplished by a single person. As with many facets of management, there are advantages and disadvantages to decentralization.

1. The greater the diversity of products, the greater the decentralization.

_____

_____

_____

2. The larger the size of the organization, the more the decentralization.

_____

_____

_____

3. The more rapidly changing the organization's environment, the more decentralization.

_____

_____

_____

4. Developing adequate, timely controls is the essence of decentralizing.

_____

_____

_____

5. Managers should delegate decisions that involve large amounts of time but minimal erosions of their power and control.

_____

_____

_____

6. Decentralizing involves delegating authority, and therefore, the principles of delegation apply to decentralization. (List the principles of delegation before you start your discussion.)

_____

_____

_____

SOURCE: R. R. McGrath Jr., *Exercises in Management Fundamentals* (Englewood Cliffs, NJ: Prentice Hall, 1985), pp. 59–60. Reprinted by permission of Prentice Hall, Inc.

CONCLUDING CASE

STANLEY LYNCH INVESTMENT GROUP

The Stanley Lynch Investment Group is a large investment firm headquartered in New York. The firm has 12 major investment funds, each with analysts operating in a separate department. Along with knowledge of the financial markets and the businesses it analyzes, Stanley Lynch's competitive advantage comes from its advanced and reliable computer systems. Thus an effective information technology (IT) division is a strategic necessity, and the company's chief information officer (CIO) holds a key role at the firm.

When the company hired J. T. Kundra as a manager of technology, he learned that the IT division at Stanley Lynch consists of 68 employees, most of whom specialize in serving the needs of a particular fund. The IT employees serving a fund operate as a distinct group, each of them led by a manager who supervises several employees. (Five employees report to J. T.)

He also learned that each group sets up its own computer system to store information about its projects. The problems with that arrangement quickly became evident. As J. T. tried to direct his group's work, he would ask for documentation of one program or another. Sometimes, no one was sure where to find the documentation; it might turn out to be stored in an obscure place such as only on someone's flash drive. Other times, he would quickly get three different responses from three different people with three versions of the documentation. And if he was interested in another group's project or a software program used in another department, getting information was next to impossible. He lacked the authority to ask employees in another group to drop what they were doing to hunt down information he needed.

J. T. concluded that the entire IT division could serve the firm much better if all authorized people had easy access to the work that had already been done and the software that was available. The logical place to store that information was online. From experience at a previous company, he believed that the easiest way to compile the information would be to set up a shared web project called a wiki—an online document created through the collaboration of its users, who can look up or contribute information according to their knowledge and needs. The challenge would be how to get everyone to contribute, given that he had authority over so few of the IT workers.

J. T. started by working with his five employees to build a wiki offering basic information presented in a consistent format. Then he met with two higher-level managers who report to the CIO. He showed them the wiki and explained that fast access to information would improve the IT group's quality and efficiency. He suggested that the managers require all the IT employees to put their documentation on the wiki, and he even persuaded them that this behavior should be measured for performance appraisals. This last tactic was especially significant because at an investment company, bonuses for meeting performance targets are a big part of employees' compensation.

The IT employees quickly came to appreciate that the wiki would help them perform better. When they visited it, they could see from the original information that it would be useful. Adoption of the wiki was swift, and before long, the IT employees came to think of it as one of their most important software systems.

DISCUSSION QUESTIONS

1. Give an example of differentiation in Stanley Lynch's organization structure and an example of integration in this structure.
2. What role did authority play in the adoption of the wiki by the IT division at Stanley Lynch?
3. Describe how the IT division used coordination to achieve greater integration.

CHAPTER 9

Organizational Agility

> I came to the conclusion long ago that limits to innovation have less to do with technology or creativity than organizational agility. Inspired individuals can only do so much.
>
> —Ray Stata, founder of Analog Devices

After studying Chapter 9, you will be able to:

LO **1**   Discuss why it is critical for organizations to be responsive. p. 296

LO **2**   Describe the qualities of an organic organization structure. p. 298

LO **3**   Identify strategies and dynamic organizational concepts that can improve an organization's responsiveness. p. 299

LO **4**   Explain how a firm can be both big and small. p. 302

LO **5**   Summarize how firms organize to meet customer requirements. p. 306

LO **6**   Identify ways that firms organize around different types of technology. p. 312

Management Connection

HOW JEFFREY IMMELT TRIES TO KEEP GENERAL ELECTRIC NIMBLE

As General Electric's CEO, Jeffrey Immelt once was asked to identify GE's core capability. Immelt's reply echoed his predecessor, the legendary Jack Welch: "Evaluating people." Evaluation—needed for identifying, developing, and keeping the best leaders—is a powerful core capability, especially for GE, which requires excellence in so many areas. Unlike specialized or regional companies, GE operates seven large industrial businesses and a financial business, all operating worldwide. It has to be able to do *many* things right.

Recently, however, some observers have wondered whether GE has been losing its core capability. The recent financial crisis hit GE hard, especially because it had relied heavily on GE Capital's lending and investments for a significant part of GE's earnings. Although GE Capital managed to turn a profit every year, 2009's profits were less than one-sixth of 2008's, and the numbers climbed back slowly over the next few years. The recession slowed purchases from GE's business and government customers, and in the United States, the rising cost of health care hit demand for GE's imaging equipment such as X-ray machines and MRI scanners. GE's stock price tumbled, and its credit rating slipped. Immelt responded by focusing the company more on infrastructure, such as transportation and energy systems, and scaling back GE Capital, especially its real estate investments.

Can a behemoth such as GE be nimble enough for today's business world? Immelt says yes. He sees GE as a 305,000-employee team with operations in 160 countries, united by a mission to "build, move, power and cure the world." He expects strong growth from its oil and gas and its power and water business units, especially as

a result of demand for infrastructure in developing economies. As economies compete for increasingly scarce (and costly) energy resources, Immelt sees potential for GE's energy management business, which helps customers conserve energy. The company hopes efficiency projects will also spur demand in its other industrial businesses: aviation, transportation, healthcare, and home and business solutions.

Few businesses could maintain a lead in so many arenas, but Immelt sees GE as having the resources to do just that. In recessions as well as expansions, customers want to save money, so GE invests heavily in research for making jet engines more efficient, cutting waste from energy systems, and upgrading its equipment for the era of big data. In a recent letter to shareholders, Immelt maintains, "Our ability to create our own future is why GE can win in any environment."[1]

> GE is trying to maintain its position as one of the world's great industrial companies with an organization that enables innovation and demands high performance. As you read this chapter, consider whether GE can remain competitive in a fast-changing world.

Like GE, today's successful companies can't afford to stand still. They cannot rest on their previous accomplishments. If they do, they can all too easily become vulnerable—to a competitor's new product, shifts in customer preferences, or other changes in their environment. Instead they use their current successes to continue to build a competitive advantage for the future, constantly seeking new ways to remain flexible, innovative, efficient, and responsive to their customers. One of the most important ways they have of doing that is to make sure that their organization structures and systems remain *adaptable*—prepared to meet the complex and ever-changing challenges that managers and their organizations constantly confront.

In Chapter 8, we described the formal structure of the organization. Businesses and other organizations are complex; they use the elements of the formal structure, including hierarchical levels, division of labor, and coordination, to manage that complexity. However, concentration on formal structure might leave the false impression that organizations are static structures, in which case they would be ill suited for today's fast-changing environment. But in fact, organizations are complex systems in which many people do many things at the same time. The behavior of organizations does not just pop out of a chart; it emerges from the processes, systems, and relationships.

Therefore, the task of organizing extends to the issues described in this chapter: the design of processes, information flows, and technology. When these are well designed, the organization is flexible and agile enough to succeed in a changing world. Such an organization is often called ambidextrous. As some people have the gift of writing with either hand, an ambidextrous organization is simultaneously good at *exploitation* (efficiently and quickly meeting needs in areas where it currently excels) and *exploration* (seeking and recognizing new ways to meet future needs).[2] In this chapter, we will see ways to organize people, information, and work that have helped organizations excel at both exploitation and exploration.

The Responsive Organization

The formal structure is put in place to control people, decisions, and actions. But in today's fast-changing business environment, responsiveness—quickness, agility, the ability to adapt to changing demands—is more vital than ever to a firm's survival.[3]

Many years after Max Weber wrote about the concept of bureaucracy, two British management scholars (Burns and Stalker) described what they called the **mechanistic organization**.[4] The common mechanistic structure they described was similar to Weber's bureaucracy, but they went on to suggest that in the modern corporation, the mechanistic structure is not the only option. The **organic structure** stands in stark contrast to the mechanistic organization. It is much less rigid and, in fact, emphasizes flexibility. The organic structure can be described as follows:

1. Jobholders have broader responsibilities that change as the need arises.
2. Communication occurs through advice and information rather than through orders and instructions.
3. Decision making and influence are more decentralized and informal.
4. Expertise is highly valued.
5. Jobholders rely more heavily on judgment than on rules.
6. Obedience to authority is less important than commitment to the organization's goals.
7. Employees depend more on one another and relate more informally and personally.

Figure 9.1 contrasts the formal structure of an organization—epitomized by the organization chart—to the informal structure, which is much more organic. As you

Bottom Line

Speed is vital to an organization's survival. *How can lack of speed kill an organization?*

mechanistic organization

A form of organization that seeks to maximize internal efficiency.

organic structure

An organizational form that emphasizes flexibility.

Leers
(CEO)

O'Hara (SVP)	Calder (SVP)	Long (SVP)	Stern (SVP)
Blair	Harris	Fiola	Huttle
Stewart	Benson	Muller	Atkins
Ruiz	Flemming	Jules	Kibler
	Church	Baker	
	Martin	Daven	
	Lee	Thomas	
	Wilson	Zonado	
	Swinney		
	Carlson		
	Hoberman		
	Fiola		

FIGURE 9.1
Two Ways to Describe an Organization

compare these two charts, what do you notice that should concern this company's managers? Astute managers are keenly aware of the network of interactions among the organization's members, and they structure around this network to increase agility. People in organic organizations work more as teammates than as subordinates who take orders from the boss, thus breaking away from the traditional bureaucratic form.[5]

The ideas underlying the organic structure and networks are the foundation for the newer forms of organization described in this chapter. The more organic a firm is, the more responsive it will be to changing competitive demands and market realities. Managers in progressive companies place a premium on being able to act fast. They want to act in accordance with customer needs and other outside pressures. They want to take actions to correct past mistakes and to prepare for an uncertain future. They want to be able to respond to threats and opportunities. The particular form—and degree—of organic structure the organization adopts to accomplish these goals will depend on its strategy, its size, its customers, and its technology. We will consider each of these in turn.

Strategy and Organizational Agility

LO 2

Certain strategies, and the structures, processes, and relationships that accompany them, seem particularly well suited to improving an organization's ability to respond quickly and effectively to the challenges it faces. They reflect its managers' determination to leverage its people and assets fully to make the firm more agile and competitive. These strategies and structures are based on the firm's core capabilities, its strategic alliances, its ability to learn, and its ability to engage all the people in the organization in achieving its objectives.

Organizing around Core Capabilities

A recent, different, and important perspective on strategy and organization hinges on the concept of *core capabilities*.[6] As you learned in Chapter 4, a core capability is the knowledge, expertise, or skill that underlies a company's ability to be a leader in providing a range of specific goods or services. It allows the company to compete on the basis of its core strengths and expertise, not just on what it produces. For example, Barnes & Noble's core capability is book merchandising. A core capability gives value to customers, makes the company's products different from—and better than—those of competitors, and can be used in creating new products. Think of core capabilities as the roots of competitiveness and products as the fruits.

Successfully developing a world-class core capability opens the door to a variety of future opportunities; failure means being foreclosed from many markets. Thus a well-understood, well-developed core capability can enhance a company's responsiveness and competitiveness. Strategically, this means that companies should commit to excellence and leadership in capabilities, and strengthen them, before they commit to winning market share for specific products. Organizationally, this means that the corporation should be viewed as a portfolio of capabilities, not just a portfolio of specific businesses. Companies should strive for core competence leadership, not just product leadership.

Managers who want to strengthen their firms' competitiveness via core capabilities need to focus on several related issues:

Identify existing core capabilities.
Acquire or build core capabilities that will be important for the future.
Keep investing in capabilities so that the firm remains world class and better than competitors.
Extend capabilities to find new applications and opportunities for the markets of tomorrow.[7]

Keep in mind that it's not enough for an organization to have valuable resources that provide capabilities; those resources have to be managed in a way that gives the organization an advantage over competitors.[8] That means managers have to do three things. First, they must accumulate the right resources (such as talented people) by determining what resources they need, acquiring and developing those resources, and eliminating resources that don't provide value. Next, they combine the resources in ways that give the organization capabilities, such as researching new products or resolving problems for customers. These combinations may involve knowledge sharing and alliances between departments or with other organizations. Finally, managers need to leverage or exploit their resources. They do this by identifying the opportunities where their competencies deliver value to customers—say, by creating new products or by delivering existing products better than competitors—and then by coordinating and deploying the employees and other resources needed to respond to those opportunities.

In Practice

PFIZER'S CORE CAPABILITIES

At Pfizer, Jordan Cohen has helped the pharmaceutical company build on core capabilities by freeing employees from getting bogged down in activities that are not related to those capabilities. Although some companies have a strategy of outsourcing activities outside of their core capabilities, Cohen applied this kind of strategic decision to the level of individual employees by creating a system called pfizerWorks.

Cohen arrived at his idea for pfizerWorks at a time when Pfizer was encouraging its employees to look for ways to boost efficiency. Cohen noticed that highly trained colleagues were devoting hours to clerical tasks such as creating graphs, transcribing notes from meetings, and conducting data searches. They could be more productive if they focused on the analytical and strategic roles for which they had been hired.

So Cohen recruited several of his coworkers to try a new system for six months: Whenever they had a task that was outside their core responsibilities, they could click a pfizerWorks icon on their computer screens, which would take them to a request form to buy outside services. Within an hour, a Pfizer-trained contractor would phone the employee to clarify the details of the assignment and submit a cost estimate. If the employee accepted the arrangement, the contractor would perform the job, and the employee would rate the work.

The trial was a success, and the system was rolled out to the company with Cohen in charge. In its first year, it saved Pfizer almost 70,000 hours of time spent on lower-value work that could be handled more economically by outsiders.[9]

- What would you expect Pfizer's core capabilities to be? How does pfizerWorks help Pfizer invest in these?

Strategic Alliances

As we discussed in Chapter 8, the modern organization has a variety of links with other organizations. These links are more complex than the standard relationships with traditional stakeholders such as suppliers and clients. Today even fierce competitors are working together at unprecedented levels to achieve their strategic goals. For example, Federal Express has drop-off boxes at U.S. Postal Service facilities. The New York Times Company and Monster Worldwide formed an alliance in which job advertisements for 19 newspapers will carry the Monster.com brand. The arrangement gives the newspaper company, whose papers include the *New York Times* and *Boston Globe*, a stronger online presence and gives Monster better visibility in local job markets, which have traditionally been dominated by local papers.[10] In these and other examples, strategic alliances allow participants to respond to customer demands or environmental threats far faster and less expensively than each would be able to do on its own.

strategic alliance

A formal relationship created among independent organizations with the purpose of joint pursuit of mutual goals.

Bottom Line

Alliances can increase speed and innovation and lower costs. *How might an alliance increase innovation?*

A **strategic alliance** is a formal relationship created with the purpose of joint pursuit of mutual goals. In a strategic alliance, individual organizations share administrative authority, form social links, and accept joint ownership. Such alliances are blurring firms' boundaries. They occur between companies and their competitors, governments, and universities. Such partnering often crosses national and cultural boundaries. Companies form strategic alliances to develop new technologies, enter new markets, and reduce manufacturing costs. Not only can alliances enable companies to move ahead faster and more efficiently, but they also are sometimes the only practical way to bring together the variety of specialists needed for operating in today's complex and fast-changing environment. Rather than hiring experts who understand the technology and market segments for each new product, companies can form alliances with partners that already have those experts on board.[11]

Managers typically devote plenty of time to screening potential partners in financial terms. But for the alliance to work, the partners also must consider one another's areas of expertise and the incentives involved in the structure of the alliance. A comparison of research and development alliances found that the most innovation occurred when the partners were experts in moderately different types of research. If the partners were very different, they shared ideas and innovated more when the alliance was set up through equity (stock) ownership; for similar partners, a contract to do the research was associated with more innovation.[12]

Managers also must foster and develop the human relationships in the partnership. Asian companies seem to be the most comfortable with the nonfinancial, people side of alliances; European companies the next so; and U.S. companies the least. Thus U.S. companies may need to pay extra attention to the human side of alliances. Table 9.1 shows some recommendations for how to do this. In fact, most of the ideas apply not only to strategic alliances but to any type of relationship.[13]

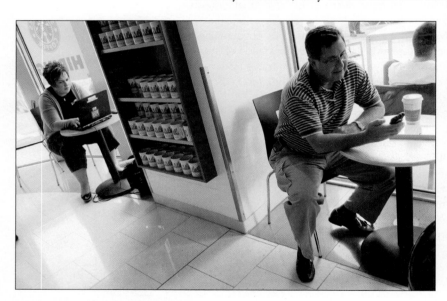

Music and coffee—a harmonious strategic alliance! Apple and Starbucks created a partnership that allows Apple customers to sync to the Starbucks wireless Internet network instantly from their iPod Touch, iPads, Macs, and iPhones to download music. Shown here is a Starbucks customer, Steve Carpenter (right), using his iPhone to capture a song at a Starbucks in Miami Beach, Florida.

learning organization

An organization skilled at creating, acquiring, and transferring knowledge and at modifying its behavior to reflect new knowledge and insights.

The Learning Organization

Being responsive requires continually changing and learning new ways to act. Some experts have stated that the only sustainable advantage is learning faster than the competition. This has led to a new term that is now part of the vocabulary of most managers: the learning organization.[14] A **learning organization** is an organization skilled at creating, acquiring, and transferring knowledge and at modifying its behavior to reflect new knowledge and insights.[15] Google, Toyota, and IDEO are good examples of learning organizations. Such organizations are skilled at solving problems, experimenting with new approaches, learning from their own experiences, learning from other organizations, and spreading knowledge quickly and efficiently.

How do firms become true learning organizations? They make sure a few important activities are happening at all levels and in all functions:[16]

1. Engaging in disciplined thinking and paying attention to details, so decisions are based on data and evidence, not guesswork and assumptions
2. Searching constantly for new knowledge and ways to apply it, looking for broader horizons and opportunities, not just quick fixes for current problems

TABLE 9.1
How I's Can Become We's

The best alliances are true partnerships that meet these criteria:
1. *Individual excellence:* Both partners add value, and their motives are positive (pursue opportunity) rather than negative (mask weaknesses).
2. *Importance:* Both partners want the relationship to work because it helps them meet long-term strategic objectives.
3. *Interdependence:* The partners need each other; each helps the other reach its goal.
4. *Investment:* The partners devote financial and other resources to the relationship.
5. *Information:* The partners communicate openly about goals, technical data, problems, and changing situations.
6. *Integration:* The partners develop shared ways of operating; they teach each other and learn from each other.
7. *Institutionalization:* The relationship has formal status with clear responsibilities.
8. *Integrity:* Both partners are trustworthy and honorable.

SOURCE: Reprinted by permission of *Harvard Business Review.* Adapted from "Collaborative Advantage: The Art of Alliances," by R. M. Kanter, July–August 1994, pp. 96–108. Copyright © 1994 by the Harvard Business School Publishing Corporation; all rights reserved.

3. Valuing and rewarding individuals who expand their knowledge and skill in areas that benefit the organization
4. Reviewing successes and failures carefully to find lessons and deeper understanding
5. Benchmarking—that is, identifying and implementing the best business practices of other organizations, stealing ideas shamelessly
6. Sharing ideas throughout the organization via reports, information systems, informal discussions, site visits, education, training, and mentoring of less experienced employees by more experienced ones

These efforts are ideally aimed at the two areas of learning we mentioned at the beginning of this chapter.[17] The first is exploitation, or continuously learning ways to operate more efficiently and effectively in the company's first domain. We will see ideas for this kind of learning throughout the remainder of this chapter. The second is exploration, or uncovering new areas in which the company can excel. Chapter 17 will say more about this kind of learning with regard to technology and innovation.

The High-Involvement Organization

Participative management is becoming increasingly popular as a way to create a competitive advantage. Particularly in high-technology companies facing stiff international competition, the aim is to generate high levels of commitment and involvement as employees and managers work together to achieve organizational goals.

In a **high-involvement organization**, top management ensures that there is a consensus about the direction in which the business is heading. The leader seeks input from his or her top management team and from lower levels of the company. Task forces, study groups, and other techniques are used to foster participation in decisions that affect the entire organization. Also fundamental to the high-involvement organization is continual feedback to participants regarding how they are doing compared with the competition and how effectively they are meeting the strategic agenda.

high-involvement organization

A type of organization in which top management ensures that there is consensus about the direction in which the business is heading.

Participative management is becoming increasingly popular as a way to create competitive advantage.

Structurally, this usually means that even lower-level employees have a direct relationship with a customer or supplier and thus receive feedback and are held accountable for a good or service delivery. The organizational form is a flat, decentralized structure built around a customer, good, or service. Employee involvement is particularly powerful when the environment changes rapidly, work is creative, complex activities require coordination, and firms need major breakthroughs in innovation and speed—in other words, when companies need to be more responsive.[18]

Organizational Size and Agility

One of the most important characteristics of an organization—and one of the most important factors influencing its ability to respond effectively to its environment—is its size. Large organizations are typically less organic and more bureaucratic. For example, Unilever, whose many consumer brands include Hellman's, Ben & Jerry's, Lipton, Vaseline, Dove, and Slim-Fast, has more than 200,000 employees worldwide. In many countries, the company has operated as three independent business lines—food, personal care, and ice cream and frozen food—each with its own supply chain and marketing budget.[19]

In large organizations, jobs become more specialized. More distinct groups of specialists get created because large organizations can add a new specialty at lower proportional expense. The complexity created by these numerous specialties makes the organization harder to control. As a result, in the past, management added more levels to keep spans of control from becoming too large. To cope with complexity, large companies tend to become more bureaucratic. Rules, procedures, and paperwork are introduced.

Thus with size comes greater complexity, and complexity brings a need for increased control. In response, organizations adopt bureaucratic strategies of control. The conventional wisdom is that bureaucratization increases efficiency but decreases a company's ability to innovate. So are larger companies more responsive to competitive demands or not? Let's see.

Bottom Line

Large size often leads to scale economies. *How has General Motors's large size affected its ability to compete?*

The Case for Big

Bigger was better after World War II, when foreign competition was limited and growth seemed limitless. To meet high demand for its products, U.S. industry embraced high-volume, low-cost manufacturing methods. IBM, General Motors (GM), and Sears all grew into behemoths during those decades.

Alfred Chandler, a pioneer in strategic management, noted that big companies were the engine of economic growth throughout the 20th century.[20] Size creates scale economies—that is, lower costs per unit of production. And size can offer specific advantages such as lower operating costs, greater purchasing power, and easier access to capital. Walmart, among the largest companies in America, has the purchasing power to buy merchandise in larger volumes and sell it at lower prices than its competitors can. Size also creates **economies of scope;** materials and processes employed in one product can be used to make related products. With such advantages, huge companies with lots of money may be the best at taking on large foreign rivals in huge global markets.

economies of scope

Economies in which materials and processes employed in one product can be used to make related products.

The Case for Small

But a huge, complex organization can find it hard to manage relationships with customers and among its own units. Bureaucracy can run rampant. Too much success can breed complacency, and the resulting inertia hinders change. Experts suggest that this is a surefire formula for being left in the dust by hungry competitors. As consumers demand a more diverse array of high-quality, customized products supported by excellent service, giant companies have begun to stumble. Some evidence exists, for example, that as firms get larger and their market share grows, customers begin to view their products as having lower quality. Also, once a company has captured a big share of the market, future growth is complicated because winning over more customers requires costlier efforts or a fresh approach. Walmart's low-price strategy helped it become the largest U.S. corporation in terms of sales, but sales growth has flattened out. The company's response—cutting labor costs—has helped profits in the short term but may drive away shoppers frustrated with unstocked shelves and difficulty finding help. Walmart recently placed last in the American Customer Satisfaction Index for department and discount stores.[21]

Larger companies also are more difficult to coordinate and control. Although size may enhance efficiency by spreading fixed costs over more units, it also may create administrative difficulties that inhibit efficient performance. Unilever not only has three organizations selling different product lines in each country it serves, but until recently it was run by two chairmen–CEOs, an artifact of a merger that took place decades ago. This cumbersome structure has held back Unilever's efficiency and agility, making competition more difficult.[22] To describe this type of problem, a new term has entered the business vocabulary: *diseconomies of scale,* or the costs of being too big. "Small is beautiful" has become a favorite phrase of entrepreneurial business managers.[23]

Smaller companies can move fast, provide quality goods and services to targeted market niches, and inspire greater involvement from their people. Nimble small firms frequently outmaneuver big bureaucracies. They introduce new and better products, and they steal market share. The premium now is on flexibility and responsiveness—the unique potential strengths of the small firm. An extreme example is Kobold Watch, staffed by founder Michael Kobold and three employees. The small company makes and sells premium mechanical wristwatches priced at thousands of dollars each. Kobold advertises online and through word of mouth generated by sales to celebrities, including former president Bill Clinton and actors Kiefer Sutherland and James Gandolfini. When sales surge, Kobold calls on two other watchmakers to help out as needed. He intentionally limits production to 2,500 watches a year—not just to keep his company lean but also to maintain the prestige of his brand.[24]

This Kobold watch workshop in Nepal opened after the owners received intensive training from Kobold in the U.S.

Being Big and Small

Small *is* beautiful for unleashing energy and speed. But in buying and selling, size offers market power. The challenge, then, is to be both big and small to capitalize on the advantages of each.

When Intuit grew from a software start-up to an established company selling popular accounting software, the company brought in a CEO recruited from General Electric, Steve Bennett, to mesh big-company skills with Intuit's entrepreneurial energy. Managers had plenty of new ideas but needed to build their skill in choosing and implementing the best ideas. Bennett helped the company reevaluate its strategy to find areas of new growth. Popular Intuit products such as QuickBooks have already captured most of the market for accounting software, so the company needs to focus less on competitors for its existing products and more on areas of untapped opportunity, which is why Intuit has begun to develop new areas such as online banking and software for managing health care expenses.[25]

The challenge is to be both big and small to capitalize on the advantages of each.

Bottom Line
Small size may improve speed. *A salesperson learns about a customer's new challenge. Why might a small company be able to react to this information faster?*

From a different angle, companies such as Starbucks and Amazon are very large companies that work hard to act small and maintain a sense of intimacy with employees and customers. Both are considered among the best-managed companies in the world. To avoid problems of growth and size, they decentralize decision making and organize around small, adaptive, team-based work units.

In Practice

HP USES IT TO ACT SMALL

Hewlett-Packard is using information technology to stay big but act small. That effort started at the top, with the decision to bring in John Hinshaw as executive vice president of technology and operations. Usually, the top technology position in a large corporation is the chief information officer (CIO), but Hinshaw is more than CIO. He also is responsible for HP's Global Business Services Group, which provides all the services needed to keep the business units running—payroll, marketing, real estate, data security, and so on. That means Hinshaw thinks about technology in terms of how it helps HP get things done, and when he thinks of how HP gets things done, he sees where technology can help.

To see how this plays out, consider how HP got information flowing to and from its 30,000-member sales team. The company decided to adopt software from Salesforce.com, which allows easy sharing and retrieval of data about customers and their orders. In a traditional functional organization, the information technology (IT) department would have focused on all the steps required to change over to a new software system. But at HP, the changeover started with a study of its sales process, and the system was adapted to the needs of the salespeople and their customers. This approach gets enthusiastic buy-in from employees, and rolling out the new system happened in record time.

Hinshaw is applying similar principles to HP's other functions. His goal is to find ways that IT can make all its processes more efficient, eventually contributing to savings of $3.5 billion. Beyond mere savings, Hinshaw sees himself creating a better corporation—one that people will want to buy from and work for.[26]

• How might easy access to information help a big company be as agile as a small one?

downsizing

The planned elimination of positions or jobs.

Downsizing   As large companies attempt to regain the responsiveness of small companies, they often face the dilemma of downsizing. **Downsizing** is the planned elimination of positions or jobs. Common approaches to downsizing include eliminating functions, hierarchical levels, or even whole units.[27] Another growing trend has been to replace full-time employees with less expensive part-time or temporary workers.

Recognizing that people will be unemployed, frightened, and perhaps unable to pay their bills, managers usually opt for downsizing only in response to some kind of pressure. Traditionally, companies have downsized when demand falls and seems unlikely to rebound in the short run. Laying off workers is a way to avoid paying people who aren't needed to produce and ship goods, as well as to lower costs so that the company remains profitable—or at least viable—until the next upturn in business. More recently, however, global competition forced companies to cut costs even when sales were strong, and technological advances made it possible to produce the same amount of work with fewer employees. As a result, in recent decades, many companies have used downsizing as a way to become more efficient. This trend changed the types of positions that were eliminated. Downsizing in response to a slowdown in demand has tended to have the most impact on operating-level jobs in manufacturing firms. Downsizing to improve efficiency has focused on eliminating layers of management and bureaucratic structures, so those layoffs target white-collar middle managers.

The recent recession has forced widespread downsizing across a variety of industries, not just manufacturing. Although companies have rehired workers during the recovery, many find that tough competition requires them to stay as lean as possible. In the movie industry, the success or failure of a few releases can drastically affect the amount of money available to pay employees to work on new films. In 2012, DreamWorks Animation was overly optimistic about the audience size for holiday releases, including *Rise of the Guardians*. After disappointing results came in, DreamWorks announced layoffs of hundreds of employees as it postponed releases scheduled for the year ahead.[28]

Done appropriately, with inefficient layers eliminated and resources focused more on adding customer value than on wasteful internal processes, downsizing can indeed lead to a more agile, flexible, and responsive firm. In that case, downsizing can be called **rightsizing**—arrival at the size at which the company performs most effectively. But even under the best circumstances, downsizing can be traumatic for an organization and its employees. What can be done to manage downsizing effectively, to help make it more effective?

First, firms should avoid excessive (cyclical) hiring to help reduce the need to engage in major or multiple downsizings. But beyond that, firms must avoid common mistakes such as making slow, small, frequent layoffs; implementing voluntary early retirement programs that entice the best people to leave; and laying off so many people that the company's work can no longer be performed. Instead firms can engage in a number of positive practices to ease the pain and increase the effectiveness of downsizing:[29]

> Use downsizing only as a last resort, when other methods of improving performance by innovating or changing procedures have been exhausted.
>
> Choose positions to be eliminated by engaging in careful analysis and strategic thinking.
>
> Train people to cope with the new situation.
>
> Identify and protect talented people.
>
> Give special attention and help to those who have lost their jobs.
>
> Communicate constantly with people about the process and invite ideas for alternative ways to operate more efficiently.
>
> Identify how the organization will operate more effectively in the future and emphasize this positive future and the remaining employees' new roles in attaining it.

The management practices of high-involvement organizations, described earlier in this chapter, also play a role. In general, the negative consequences of downsizing are greater at high-involvement organizations—but not as bad if the organization continues the high employee involvement after the layoffs.[30]

Interestingly, the people who lose their jobs because of downsizing are not the only ones deeply affected. Those who survive the process—who keep their jobs—tend to exhibit what has become known as **survivor's syndrome**.[31] They struggle with heavier workloads; wonder who will be next to go; try to figure out how to survive; lose commitment to the company and faith in their bosses; and become narrow-minded, self-absorbed, and risk-averse. As a consequence, morale and productivity usually drop.

You will learn more about some of these ideas in later chapters on human resources management, leadership, motivation, communication, and managing change. You might also refer back to our discussion in Chapter 1 about some of the things you can do to manage your own career successfully in an era where downsizing is a normal occurrence. And for an example of a company that has made downsizing one element of its efforts to enjoy the advantages of being both big and small, see "Management Connection: Progress Report."

rightsizing
A successful effort to achieve an appropriate size at which the company performs most effectively.

survivor's syndrome
Loss of productivity and morale in employees who remain after a downsizing.

Management Connection

GE'S ADVANTAGES OF BEING BIG—AND TRYING TO ACT SMALL(ER)

Writing to shareholders, GE chief executive Jeffrey Immelt stated, "Few companies can do what GE does." Immelt was referring to GE's global customer relationships and enormous pool of assets. The company operates in several industries, and when it wants to launch new products, it has the resources to do so. Thanks to its 50,000 engineers and scientists, GE ranks in the top 10 companies for U.S. patent applications. In terms of the total value of its stock, GE is the world's seventh largest company.

Consider GE's response to the role big data has begun to play. Companies are analyzing detailed data about their customers, employees, and operations so they can identify how to make significant improvements in efficiency and quality. GE got on board by setting up its Software and Analytical Center of Excellence in California, near Silicon Valley, and hiring hundreds of software and statistical experts to make GE's equipment and systems part of the big-data revolution. Applications include jet engines that monitor their own performance, sensors on hospital equipment to streamline operations, and systems for automating train traffic.

Another example is GE's creation of an energy-efficient battery for heavy-duty use. Applying technology from more than 30 patents it already owned, GE set up a team Immelt calls "a start-up within the Company." GE staffed the team with its own experts from several industries and consulted with customers around the globe. Potential applications such as powering cell phone towers and storing energy at wind farms could make the battery a billion-dollar business.

Despite the advantages of bigness, Immelt is concerned about the downside, that people in a giant corporation can be more attuned to its rules and habits than to customers' needs. His solution is to focus on measuring whether GE is delivering on its purpose—its mission to "build, move, power and cure the world." GE sold unrelated businesses, such as NBC Universal, and downsized others, such as GE Capital. The focused approach is also shaping the way GE develops managers. In the past, high-potential managers moved from one industry to another on their way up GE's hierarchy. Today they are likelier to specialize in an industry. GE's recent split of its energy business into three units (Power and Water, Oil and Gas, and Energy Management) opened up more paths for developing leaders within those related industries, even as it removed layers of management from the former energy unit.[32]

- How does GE benefit from being large?
- How can GE also reap some of the benefits of smallness?

Customers and the Responsive Organization

LO 5

So far we have discussed how an organization's agility, adaptability, and structure are influenced by its strategy and size. But in the end, the point of structuring a responsive, agile organization lies in enabling it to meet and exceed the expectations of its customers—the people it must attract to purchase a good or service and whose continued patronage and involvement with the organization constitute the fundamental driver of sustained, long-term competitiveness and success.

Recall from Chapter 2 that an organization's environment is composed of many parts—government, suppliers, competitors, and the like. Perhaps no other aspect of the environment has had a more profound impact on organizing in recent years than a focus on customers. Dr. Kenichi Ohmae points out that any business unit must take into account three key players: the company itself, the competition, and the customer. These components form what Ohmae refers to as the *strategic triangle*, as shown in Figure 9.2. Managers need to balance the strategic triangle, and successful organizations use their strengths to create value by meeting customer requirements better than competitors do. In this section, we will discuss in some depth how organizations maintain and extend a competitive advantage with their customers.

Bottom Line

Today's customers demand excellent service and new high-quality, low-cost products—fast. *How does a rigid bureaucracy make it difficult to meet all these challenges at once?*

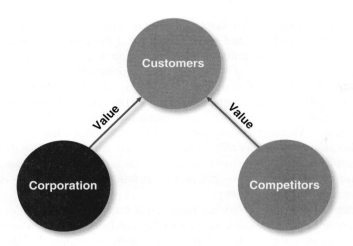

FIGURE 9.2
The Strategic Triangle

Customer Relationship Management

Customer relationship management (CRM) is a multifaceted process, typically mediated by a set of information technologies, that focuses on creating two-way exchanges with customers so that firms have an intimate knowledge of their needs, wants, and buying patterns. The use of a particular technology to conduct CRM—for example, using cell phone applications to track consumers' locations or social networking to measure what topics they chat about—is less important than figuring out how the organization can use the information to deliver exactly what customers want. Thus at companies that use CRM effectively, it helps them understand, as well as anticipate, the needs of current and potential customers. And in that way, it is part of a business strategy for managing customers to maximize their long-term value to an enterprise.[33]

customer relationship management (CRM)

A multifaceted process focusing on creating two-way exchanges with customers to foster intimate knowledge of their needs, wants, and buying patterns.

In Practice

TOYOTA FRIEND HELPS CUSTOMERS

One of the industry leaders in providing CRM software is San Francisco–based Salesforce.com. The company recently arranged with Toyota to provide a private social network for buyers of new electric and plug-in hybrid vehicles. The network, called Toyota Friend, links drivers in the network to each other, Toyota, dealerships, and their cars. Customers can use Toyota Friend to send short messages to other drivers on the network and communicate with local dealers. Using a technology called telematics, drivers on the network can receive remote diagnostic information, such as battery usage or tire pressure, or direct the car to, for example, start the engine and warm the seats as they head for the parking lot.

The plan was to launch Toyota Friend first in Japan, with a global rollout of the service about a year later. Where the network is available, Toyota customers can access it through any wireless mobile device such as a smartphone or computer. Toyota anticipates that customers will be interested in looking up information such as where the nearest charging station is located and whether the battery needs to be charged. They also can look up maintenance tips provided by Toyota.[34]

- How might Toyota apply the information generated by Toyota Friend to improve how it anticipates and meets customer needs?

As discussed throughout this book, customers want quality goods and services, low cost, innovative products, and speed. Traditional thinking considered these basic customer wants as a set of potential trade-offs. For instance, customers wanted high quality or low costs passed along in the form of low prices. But world-class companies today know that the trade-off mentality no longer applies. Customers want it *all*, and they are learning that an organization exists somewhere that will provide it all.

But if all companies seek to satisfy customers, how can a company realize a competitive advantage? World-class companies have learned that almost any advantage is temporary because competitors will strive to catch up. Simply stated—although obviously not simply done—a company attains and retains competitive advantage by continuing to improve. This concept—*kaizen*, or continuous improvement—is an integral part of Japanese operations strategy.

In the realm of customer relations, continuous improvement includes continually changing to connect with customers, even without waiting for customers to make the first move. Comcast Cable, Dell, and other companies have adopted Salesforce.com's

> World-class companies know that the trade-off mentality no longer applies.

Service Cloud application, which lets companies find customers who take their questions and problems to Facebook, Twitter, or other social networking communities. Customer service agents can locate messages about their products and then offer to help, potentially saving a customer relationship. Chase Paymentech Solutions is using collaboration software called Greenhouse to invite customers into conversations about new product ideas. Customers can critique and vote on ideas; their feedback not only helps Chase figure out which ideas have potential but also strengthens customer commitment.[35]

As organizations focus on responding to customer needs, they soon find that the traditional meaning of a customer expands to include internal customers. The word *customer* now refers to the next process, or wherever the work goes next.[36] This highlights the idea of interdependence among related functions and means that all functions of the organization—not just marketing people—have to be concerned with customer satisfaction. Any recipient of a person's work, whether coworker, boss, subordinate, or external party, should be viewed as the customer.

A deeper way to understand how organizations can add customer value to their products has been provided by Michael Porter, who popularized the concept of the value chain. A **value chain** is the sequence of activities that flow from raw materials to the delivery of a good or service, with additional value created at each step. You can see a generic value chain illustrated in Figure 9.3. Each step in the chain adds value to the product or service:

value chain

The sequence of activities that flow from raw materials to the delivery of a good or service, with additional value created at each step.

Research and development focus on innovation and new products.
Inbound logistics receive and store raw materials and distribute them to operations.
Operations transform the raw materials into final product.
Outbound logistics warehouse the product and handle its distribution.
Marketing and sales identify customer requirements and get customers to purchase the product.
Service offers customer support, such as repair, after the item has been bought.

When the total value created—that is, what customers are willing to pay—exceeds the cost of providing the good or service, the result is the organization's profit margin.[37]

Managers can add customer value and build competitive advantage by paying close attention to their organization's value chain—not only each step in it, but the way each step interacts with the others. For example, they can achieve economies of scale, as Walmart has, so that their materials and operations costs are lowered, or they can develop innovative distribution channels, as Amazon has done, and add customer value that way. They can also create structures and systems that link the elements of the value chain in innovative ways.

SOURCE: M. Porter, *Competitive Advantage: Creating and Sustaining Superior Performance* (New York: Free Press, 1985).

FIGURE 9.3
Generic Value Chain

One of the most effective ways to leverage an organization's value chain is to bring together elements of the chain to collaborate to add customer value and build competitive advantage. For example, long-term relationships can be established with suppliers to encourage investment in new technologies and practices that speed product development and turnaround. Nike chooses its suppliers—what it calls its strategic partners—to that end and shares its business plans and strategies with them to reinforce close collaboration. Sales staff can communicate with operations staff, before the manufacturing process even starts, to develop products jointly that customers will value highly. Service managers can constantly report back to operations about defects and work with operations and suppliers to reduce and eliminate them. When managers create that type of collaboration, their organization's agility and responsiveness increase significantly.

Quality Initiatives

Often the effort to be more responsive has brought managers face to face with the need to ensure consistently high quality. Systematic ways of meeting that need include total quality management, six sigma, and ISO 9001 standards.

Total quality management (TQM) is a way of managing in which everyone is committed to continuous improvement of his or her part of the operation. In business, success depends on having high-quality products. As described in Chapter 1 and throughout the book, TQM is a comprehensive approach to improving product quality and thereby customer satisfaction. It is characterized by a strong orientation toward customers (external and internal) and has become an umbrella theme for organizing work. TQM reorients managers toward involving people across departments in improving all aspects of the business. Continuous improvement requires integrative mechanisms that facilitate group problem solving, information sharing, and cooperation across business functions. As a consequence, the walls that separate stages and functions of work tend to come down, and the organization operates more in a team-oriented manner.[38]

One of the founders of the quality management movement was W. Edwards Deming. When he started, his work was largely ignored by American companies, but it was adopted eagerly by Japanese firms that wanted to shed their products of their post–World War II reputation for shoddiness. The quality emphasis of Japanese car

total quality management (TQM)

An integrative approach to management that supports the attainment of customer satisfaction through a wide variety of tools and techniques that result in high-quality goods and services.

Bottom Line

High quality requires organizationwide commitment. *What happens when the commitment to quality is weak at the top of an organization?*

manufacturing was one direct result of Deming's work, which has since been adopted by many American and other companies worldwide. Deming's "14 points" of quality emphasized a holistic approach to management that demands intimate understanding of the process—the delicate interaction of materials, machines, and people that determines productivity, quality, and competitive advantage:

1. Create constancy of purpose—strive for long-term improvement rather than short-term profit.
2. Adopt the new philosophy—don't tolerate delays and mistakes.
3. Cease dependence on mass inspection—build quality into the process on the front end.
4. End the practice of awarding business on price tag alone—build long-term relationships.
5. Improve constantly and forever the system of production and service—at each stage.
6. Institute training and retraining—continually update methods and thinking.
7. Institute leadership—provide the resources needed for effectiveness.
8. Drive out fear—people must believe it is safe to report problems or ask for help.
9. Break down barriers among departments—promote teamwork.
10. Eliminate slogans, exhortations, and arbitrary targets—supply methods, not buzzwords.
11. Eliminate numerical quotas—they are contrary to the idea of continuous improvement.
12. Remove barriers to pride in workmanship—allow autonomy and spontaneity.
13. Institute a vigorous program of education and retraining—people are assets, not commodities.
14. Take action to accomplish the transformation—provide a structure that enables quality.

> At six sigma, a product or process is defect-free 99.99966 percent of the time.

six sigma quality

A method of systematically analyzing work processes to identify and eliminate virtually all causes of defects, standardizing the processes to reach the lowest practicable level of any cause of customer dissatisfaction.

One of the most important contributors to total quality management has been the introduction of statistical tools to analyze the causes of product defects, in an approach called **six sigma quality**. Sigma is the Greek letter used to designate the estimated standard deviation or variation in a process. (The higher the sigma level, the lower the amount of variation.) The product defects analyzed may include anything that results in customer dissatisfaction—for example, late delivery, wrong shipment, or poor customer service as well as problems with the product itself. When the defect has been identified, managers then engage the organization in a determined, comprehensive effort to eliminate its causes and reduce it to the lowest practicable level. At six sigma, a product or process is defect-free 99.99966 percent of the time—fewer than 3.4 defects or mistakes per million. Reaching that goal almost always requires managers to restructure their internal processes and relationships with suppliers and customers in fundamental ways. For example, managers may have to create teams from all parts of the organization to implement the process improvements that will prevent defects from arising. Motorola, where six sigma was developed, and General Electric, whose success with six sigma helped to make the technique popular, credit the method with helping them improve efficiency and quality. Today many companies are combining six sigma's drive to improve quality with a method of improving efficiency known as lean manufacturing, described later in this chapter. This hybrid effort, often called *lean six sigma*, is powerful because it helps an organization to be simultaneously responsive and agile. We will discuss six sigma in more detail in Chapter 16.

Commitment to total quality requires a thorough, extensive, integrated approach to organizing. To encourage American companies to make that commitment and achieve excellence, the Malcolm Baldrige National Quality Award was established in

1987. Named after a former U.S. Secretary of Commerce, the award is given every year to companies and nonprofit organizations that have met specified criteria in seven areas: (1) leadership; (2) strategic planning; (3) customer and market focus; (4) measurement, analysis, and knowledge management; (5) workforce focus; (6) process management; and (7) business results. Recent winners include Nestlé Purina PetCare Company, which outperforms its pet food competitors in customer satisfaction and boasts exceptional performance in worker safety and employee turnover, and K&N Management, a Texas restaurant operator where managers carry handheld computers that deliver daily performance information and any guest comments or complaints so they can make quick course corrections.[39]

A company can both improve its responsiveness to customers and demonstrate to them that it has done so by being certified for meeting widely recognized standards set by outside organizations. For example, the International Organization for Standardization (known globally as ISO) sets a wide variety of exacting standards for parts, materials, products, and organizational processes, each identified by number.

In the quality arena, a particularly important family of standards is ISO 9000, which defines good quality management practices. The requirements for a quality management system that will ensure such practices are spelled out in **ISO 9001**. Meeting this standard enables any type or size of organization to improve its total quality for the benefit of producers and consumers by addressing eight principles:[40]

Nestlé Purina PetCare Company has recently won the Malcolm Baldrige National Quality Award.

ISO 9001

A series of quality standards developed by a committee working under the International Organization for Standardization to improve total quality in all businesses for the benefit of producers and consumers.

1. *Customer focus*—learning and addressing customer needs and expectations.
2. *Leadership*—establishing a vision and goals, establishing trust, and providing employees with the resources and inspiration to meet goals.
3. *Involvement of people*—establishing an environment in which employees understand their contribution, engage in problem solving, and acquire and share knowledge.
4. *Process approach*—defining the tasks needed to carry out each process successfully and assigning responsibility for them.
5. *System approach to management*—putting processes together into efficient systems that work together effectively.
6. *Continual improvement*—teaching people how to identify areas for improvement and rewarding them for making improvements.
7. *Factual approach to decision making*—gathering accurate performance data, sharing the data with employees, and using the data to make decisions.
8. *Mutually beneficial supplier relationships*—working in a cooperative way with suppliers.

U.S. companies first became interested in ISO 9001 because overseas customers, particularly those in the European Union, embraced it. Companies that comply with the quality guidelines of ISO 9001 can apply for official certification; some countries and companies demand certification as an acknowledgment of compliance before they will do business. Now some U.S. customers as well are making the same demand.

Certification is not the end of the quality effort but a beginning step. Rather than defining how to operate perfectly, ISO 9001 standards establish practices that enable the organization to keep improving—assuming that it continues to follow those practices.

Reengineering

Extending from TQM and a focus on organizing around customer needs, organizations also have embraced the notion of reengineering (introduced in Chapter 1). The principal idea of reengineering is to revolutionize key organizational systems and processes to answer this question: "If you were the customer, how would you like us to operate?" The answer to this question forms a vision for how the organization should run, and then decisions are made and actions are taken to make the organization operate like the vision. Processes such as product development, order fulfillment,

Bottom Line

Effective reengineering can cut costs significantly. *What other drivers of success can reengineering improve?*

Reengineering often requires a fundamental change in the way the parts of the organization work together.

customer service, inventory management, billing, and production are redesigned from scratch as if the organization were brand new and just starting out.

For example, Procter & Gamble used reengineering to make its products more competitive. The company learned that the average family buying its products rather than private-label or lower-price brands paid an extra $725 per year. That figure, P&G realized, was far too high and warned that the company's high prices could drive the company to extinction. Other data also signaled the need for P&G to change. Market shares of famous brands such as Comet, Mr. Clean, and Ivory had been dropping for 25 years. P&G was making 55 price changes *daily* on about 80 brands, and inaccurate billings were common. Its plants were inefficient, and the company had the highest overhead in the business. It clearly had to cut prices, and to do that, it had to cut costs.

In response, P&G reengineered. The company tore down and rebuilt nearly every activity that contributed to its high costs. It redesigned the way it develops, manufactures, distributes, prices, markets, and sells products. The reengineering was difficult, time-consuming, and expensive. But after the changes, price changes became rare, factories became far more efficient, inventory levels fell, and sales and profits rose. P&G was able to price its brands nearer to the prices of store brands. P&G might have reinvented itself as a leader in the industry once again and created for itself a long-term competitive advantage that others have scrambled to match.[41]

The kind of reengineering that P&G undertook requires much more than a management directive from the top, a change in the formal organization structure, the introduction of new technology, or even a well-communicated change in strategy. Rather, to be fully effective and successful, reengineering often requires a fundamental change in the way the parts of the organization work together. They need to see each other as partners in a common effort rather than as members of a particular department or unit. Teams made up of all levels of the organization may be involved in the reengineering effort, and information on problems and possible solutions needs to be fully shared between them. Customers and other stakeholders may be interviewed to get their contributions. Often several teams will be working simultaneously. In this way, all the information that is available within and outside the organization can be brought to bear on a problem—and the solution developed will have wider acceptance and can be implemented faster.

As you can see, reengineering is not about making minor organizational changes here and there. It is about completely overhauling the operation, in revolutionary ways, to achieve the greatest possible benefits to the customer and to the organization.

Technology and Organizational Agility

LO 6

We have discussed the strategic, size, and customer influences on organizational design and agility. We now turn to one more critical factor affecting an organization's structure and responsiveness: its technology.

technology

The systematic application of scientific knowledge to a new product, process, or service.

Broadly speaking, **technology** can be viewed as the methods, processes, systems, and skills used to transform resources (inputs) into products (outputs). Although we will discuss technology—and innovation—more fully in Chapter 17, in this chapter we want to highlight some of the important influences technology has on organizational design.

Types of Technology Configurations

Research by Joan Woodward laid the foundation for understanding technology and structure. According to Woodward, three basic technologies characterize how work is done: small batch, large batch, and continuous process technologies. These three classifications are equally useful for describing either service or manufacturing technologies. Each differs in terms of volume produced and variety of goods/services offered. Each also has a different influence on how managers organize and structure the work of their organizations.[42]

Small Batch Technologies   When goods or services are provided in very low volume or **small batches**, a company that does such work is called a *job shop*. A fairly typical example of a job shop is PMF Industries, a small custom metalworking company in Williamsport, Pennsylvania, that produces stainless steel assemblies for medical and other uses. Less formally, in the service industry, restaurants or doctors' offices are examples of job shops because they provide a high variety of low-volume, customized services.

In a small batch organization, structure tends to be very organic. There tend not to be a lot of rules and formal procedures, and decision making tends to be decentralized. The emphasis is on mutual adjustment among people.

Large Batch Technologies   As volume increases, product variety usually decreases. Companies with higher volumes and lower varieties than a job shop tend to be characterized as **large batch**, or mass production technologies. Examples of large batch technologies include the auto assembly operations of General Motors, Ford, and Chrysler. In the service sector, McDonald's and Burger King are good examples. Their production runs tend to be more standardized, and all customers receive similar (if not identical) products. Machines tend to replace people in the physical execution of work. People run the machines.

With a large batch technology, structure tends to be more mechanistic. There tend to be more rules and formal procedures, and decision making tends to be centralized with higher spans of control. Communication tends to be more formal in companies where hierarchical authority is more prominent.

Continuous Process Technologies   At the very-high-volume end of the scale are companies that use **continuous process** technologies—technologies that do not stop and start. Domino Sugar and Shell Chemical, for example, use continuous process technologies by which a very limited number of products are produced. People are completely removed from the work itself. It is done entirely by machines and/or computers. In some cases, people run the computers that run the machines.

Ironically, with continuous process technology, structure can return to a more organic form because less monitoring and supervision are needed. Communication tends to be more informal in companies where fewer rules and regulations are established.

Organizing for Flexible Manufacturing

Although issues of volume and variety often have been seen as trade-offs in a technological sense, today organizations are trying to produce both high-volume and high-variety products at the same time. This is referred to as **mass customization**.[43] Automobiles, clothes, computers, and other products are increasingly being manufactured to match each customer's taste, specifications, and budget. Although this seemed

small batch

Technologies that produce goods and services in low volume.

large batch

Technologies that produce goods and services in high volume.

continuous process

A process that is highly automated and has a continuous production flow.

mass customization

The production of varied, individually customized products at the low cost of standardized, mass-produced products.

Dell has revolutionized the concept of mass customization. The production process from order to delivery is managed electronically, which allows Dell to build servers very efficiently and its customers to know where their server is during each step of the process.

only a fantasy a few years ago, mass customization is quickly becoming more prevalent among leading firms. You can now buy clothes cut to your proportions, supplements with the exact blend of the vitamins and minerals you like, CDs with the music tracks you choose, and textbooks whose chapters are picked out by your professor.

In Practice

TECHNOLOGY FOR CLOTHING COMPANIES

Some enterprising clothing companies are figuring out how to make mass customization work for the average consumer, who may not have an average body. One of them is eShakti, a women's apparel company with headquarters in Seattle, designers in California and New York, factories in India, and a shopping site online. At the most basic level of customization, the customer chooses a dress, skirt, or top design and enters her size (from 0 to 36) and height and may choose variations in length as well as neck and sleeve styles. Customers also have the option to submit a full set of body measurements (about half of them do). Computers in Delhi automatically modify the dress design to fit and then print out the pattern for a dress to be made to order. Customizing adds just $7.50 to the cost of a dress.

For customers who can afford to spend a little more, there's Bow & Drape, which serves busy, quality-driven business professionals by offering classic styles of women's apparel they can customize in a variety of ways. Rather than ask for a set of measurements, Bow & Drape offers several silhouettes, so women can choose the look that works for them. For each item, menus offer choices of hemlines, sleeves, trims, colors, and more. Customers have the option to try out a muslin version in up to three sizes to make sure it will fit. Bow & Drape, which has facilities in Boston and New York City, then has the order produced by small garment-making businesses, which fit in these small orders between their big production runs.[44]

- Which basic technology configuration do these companies use? Based on the configuration, what kind of structure would suit these organizations best?

Bottom Line

Today's technologies offer customization at low cost. *Give an example of a product you'd like to have customized for your personal preferences. Have you found a customized version yet? If not, you may someday.*

computer-integrated manufacturing (CIM)

The use of computer-aided design and computer-aided manufacturing to sequence and optimize a number of production processes.

How do companies organize to pull off this type of customization at low cost? As shown in Table 9.2, they organize around a dynamic network of relatively independent operating units.[45] Each unit performs a specific process or task—called a *module*—such as making a component, performing a credit check, or performing a particular welding method. Some modules may be performed by outside suppliers or vendors.

Different modules join forces to make the good or provide a service. How and when the various modules interact with one another are dictated by the unique requests of each customer. The manager's responsibility is to make it easier and less costly for modules to come together, complete their tasks, and then recombine to meet the next customer demand. The ultimate goal of mass customization is a never-ending campaign to expand the number of ways a company can satisfy customers. The Internet has also made it easy for customers to choose their product preferences online and for companies to take an order straight to the manufacturing floor.

Computer-Integrated Manufacturing   One technological advance that has helped make mass customization possible is **computer-integrated manufacturing (CIM)**, which links computerized production efforts. Two major elements are computer-aided design and computer-aided manufacturing, which share data needed for product design, testing, manufacturing, and quality control.

These systems can produce high-variety and high-volume products at the same time.[46] They may also offer greater control and predictability of production processes, reduced waste, faster throughput times, and higher quality. But managers cannot buy their way

TABLE 9.2
Key Features in Mass
Customization

Products	High variety and customization
Product design	Collaborative design; significant input from customers
	Short product development cycles
	Constant innovation
Operations and processes	Flexible processes
	Business process reengineering (BPR)
	Use of modules
	Continuous improvement (CI)
	Reduced setup and changeover times
	Reduced lead times
	JIT delivery and processing of materials and components
	Production to order
	Shorter cycle times
	Use of information technology (IT)
Quality management	Quality measured in customer delight
	Defects treated as capability failures
Organizational structure	Dynamic network of relatively autonomous operating units
	Learning relationships
	Integration of the value chain
	Team-based structure
Workforce management	Empowerment of employees
	High value on knowledge, information, and diversity of employee capabilities
	New product teams
	Broad job descriptions
Emphasis	Low-cost production of high-quality, customized products

SOURCE: Reprinted with permission of APICS—The Educational Society for Resource Management, *Production and Inventory Management* 41, no. 1, 2000, pp. 56–65.

out of competitive trouble simply by investing in superior technology alone. They must also ensure that their organization has the necessary strategic and people strengths.

Flexible Factories   CIM can make it practical to set up **flexible factories**, which serve customers needing fast turnaround on relatively small orders. In contrast to traditional factories, flexible factories have short production runs, organize work flow around products, and use decentralized scheduling.[47] Instead of moving large orders of standard products through assembly lines, flexible factories set up work cells or teams to focus on one product at a time. Scheduling decisions are made on the shop floor by the people doing the work, which aims to keep the schedules adaptable to change.

Lean Manufacturing   Another organizing approach is **lean manufacturing**, based on a commitment to making an operation both efficient and effective; it strives to achieve the highest possible productivity and total quality, cost-effectively, by eliminating unnecessary steps in the production process and continually striving for improvement. Rejects are unacceptable, and staff, overhead, and inventory are

flexible factories

Manufacturing plants that have short production runs, are organized around products, and use decentralized scheduling.

lean manufacturing

An operation that strives to achieve the highest possible productivity and total quality, cost-effectively, by eliminating unnecessary steps in the production process and continually striving for improvement.

Bottom Line

Lean manufacturing strives for high quality, speed, sustainability, and low cost. *Which of the quality improvement approaches is often combined with lean manufacturing?*

considered wasteful. In a lean operation, the emphasis is on quality, speed, and flexibility more than on cost, efficiency, and hierarchy. If an employee spots a problem, the employee is authorized to halt the operation and signal for help to correct the problem at its source so that processes can be improved and future problems avoided. With a well-managed lean production process, a company can develop, produce, and distribute products with half or less of the human effort, space, tools, time, and overall cost.[48]

Toyota receives much of the credit for modeling and teaching a commitment to think lean. Many manufacturing companies have tried to adopt a similar lean approach, but Toyota and others have also applied lean methods to nonmanufacturing processes, including product development. For example, early in the design process, teams bring together experts from various functions to identify potential problems and identify as many solutions as they can to avoid the need to make design changes later in the process. Further adding to efficiency and quality, the company uses standard parts, procedures, and skill sets wherever possible; detailed checklists help engineers ensure they are using best practices. As technology has advanced, Toyota has used these advances in the service of its lean approach. What makes Toyota's use of lean so effective is that when a new technology, such advanced bar coding for keeping track of components, comes along, the company does not simply assume more automation or more data collection will be better. Rather, it looks at the entire process to see whether technology, with or without other changes, will make it more efficient.[49]

For the lean approach to result in more effective operations, the following conditions must be met:[50]

People are broadly trained rather than specialized.

Communication is informal and horizontal among line workers.

Equipment is general-purpose.

Work is organized in teams, or cells, that produce a group of similar products.

Supplier relationships are long-term and cooperative.

Product development is concurrent, not sequential, and is done by cross-functional teams.

In recent years, many companies have tried to become leaner by cutting overhead costs, laying off operative-level workers, eliminating layers of management, and utilizing capital

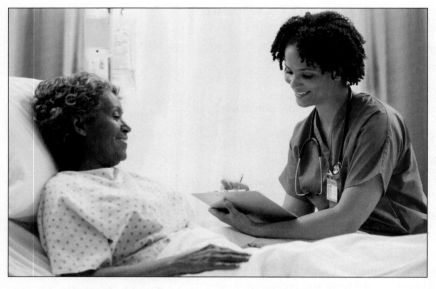

Some hospitals have been using lean principles to reduce costs and patient waiting times while improving safety.

equipment more efficiently. But if the move to lean manufacturing is simply a harsh, haphazard cost-cutting approach, the result will be chaos, overworked people, and low morale.

In Practice

LEAN MANUFACTURING ORGANIZATIONS

Getting lean makes each employee more valuable to the organization because in lean processes, each employee's activities are essential. With waste already eliminated, companies have little to cut if demand falls. In the first recession following widespread use of lean manufacturing, manufacturers did lay off workers, but not as many as an equally severe downturn would have caused in the past, when companies weren't so streamlined.

An example is Parker Hannifin Corporation's factory in Spartanburg, South Carolina, where workers produce a variety of plastic parts. Lean operations and high-tech manufacturing systems enable the company to operate with a few skilled workers. For example, to make seals for aerosol cans, just five workers operate high-speed machinery, each handling a different step of the process. If demand slows, work can be divided so that two workers start the production on one day and the other three finish on a second day, or everyone can work only part of the week. Laying off any of the five workers would be difficult because someone would have to be trained to run that person's machine. Similarly, only two workers are needed to run each shift that produces plastic tubes for blasting caps, down from eight a decade ago. If the company doesn't have enough demand to run two shifts, fewer jobs are at risk.

Parker Hannifin's production levels also are more closely tied to order volume, so fewer goods sit around in inventory. That means staffing is more closely matched to demand as well.[51]

• What would be the consequences of layoffs in a lean organization?

Organizing for Speed: Time-Based Competition

Companies worldwide have devoted so much energy to improving product quality that high quality is now the standard attained by all top competitors. Competition has driven quality to such heights that quality products no longer are enough to distinguish one company from another. Time has emerged as the key competitive advantage that can separate market leaders from also-rans.[52]

> Time has emerged as the key competitive advantage that can separate market leaders from also-rans.

Companies today must learn what the customer needs and meet those needs as quickly as possible. **Time-based competition (TBC)** refers to strategies aimed at reducing the total time needed to deliver the good or service. TBC has several key organizational elements: logistics, just-in-time (JIT), and concurrent engineering. JIT production systems reduce the time to manufacture products. Logistics speed the delivery of products to customers. Both are essential steps toward bringing products to customers in the shortest time possible. In today's world, speed is essential.

time-based competition (TBC)

Strategies aimed at reducing the total time needed to deliver a good or service.

Logistics   The movement of resources into the organization (inbound) and products from the organization to its customers (outbound) is called **logistics**. Like the supply chain, which we discussed in Chapter 2, an organization's logistics are often a critical element in its responsiveness and competitive advantage.

The world of logistics includes the great mass of parts, materials, and products moving via trucks, trains, planes, and ships from and to every region of the globe. Depending on the product, duplication and inefficiency in distribution can cost far more than making the product itself, and slowdowns can cause products to go out of stock so that consumers choose alternatives. One technological advance that is helping some companies improve logistics efficiency and speed is the use of radio frequency identification (RFID) tags. When manufacturers label their products with RFID tags, automated readers can easily track where each product is in the distribution system, including which particular items are selling in each store. Best Buy has had great success with RFID tagging; stores using the system are seeing sales increases as employees more efficiently keep track of which products need to be restocked and where they are located. Walmart, in contrast, is trying to keep its well-known leadership role in distribution by asking suppliers to use RFID, but many of them are finding they cannot afford to institute the new system at this stage of its development while also meeting Walmart's demands to keep prices at a minimum.[53]

logistics

The movement of the right goods in the right amount to the right place at the right time.

In some industries, speedy logistics are essential because products are perishable. For example, Flora-Holland, a flower auctioneer based in the Netherlands, acquires flowers from 8,000 suppliers and stores them in a massive warehouse for auction and distribution to buyers. Using RFID tagging on each cart of flowers, the company can process more than 60,000 transactions within hours. Whenever a pallet of flowers is sorted or moved, the RFID chip transmits the information about its place in the distribution system, along with data about its freshness.[54]

just-in-time (JIT)

A system that calls for subassemblies and components to be manufactured in very small lots and delivered to the next stage of the production process just as they are needed.

Just-in-Time Operations   An additional element of TBC involves **just-in-time (JIT)** operations. JIT calls for subassemblies and components to be manufactured in very small lots and delivered to the next stage in the process precisely at the time needed, or just in time. A customer order triggers a factory order and the production process. The supplying work centers do not produce the next lot of product until the consuming work center requires it. Even external suppliers deliver to the company just in time.

Just-in-time is a companywide philosophy oriented toward eliminating waste throughout all operations and improving materials throughout. In this way, excess inventory is eliminated and costs are reduced. The ultimate goal of JIT is to serve the customer better by providing higher levels of quality and service. An example of an effective just-in-time operation is provided by Dell, which does not begin production of a computer customized to a consumer's specifications until after the customer's order has been received. Contrast this approach with traditional production methods, which require extremely costly warehousing of inventory and parts, uncertain production runs, considerable waste, no customizing capability, and lengthy delivery times.

JIT represents a number of key production and organizational concepts, including the following:

Elimination of waste. Eliminate all waste from the production process, including waste of time, people, machinery, space, and materials.

Perfect quality. Produce perfect parts even when lot sizes are reduced, and produce the product exactly when it is needed in the exact quantities that are needed.

Reduced cycle times. Accomplish the entire manufacturing process more rapidly. Reduce setup times for equipment, move parts only short distances (machinery is placed in closer proximity), and eliminate all delays. The goal is to reduce action to the time spent working on the parts. For most manufacturers today, the percentage of time parts are worked on is about 5 percent of the total production time. JIT seeks to eliminate the other 95 percent—that is, to reduce to zero the time spent not working on the parts.

Employee involvement. In JIT, employee involvement is central to success. The workers are responsible for production decisions. Managers and supervisors are coaches. Top management pledges that there will never be layoffs due to improved productivity.

Value-added manufacturing. Do only those things (actions, work, etc.) that add value to the finished product. If it doesn't add value, don't do it. For example, inspection does not add value to the finished product, so make the product correctly the first time and inspection will not be necessary.

Discovery of problems and prevention of recurrence. Foolproofing, or fail-safing, is a key component of JIT. To prevent problems from arising, their cause(s) must be known and acted on. Thus, in JIT operations, people try to find the weak link in the chain by forcing problem areas to the surface so that preventive measures may be determined and implemented.

As organizations have seen the advantages of JIT, they have found applications beyond the factory floor. For example, in the area of information technology, BMC Software used JIT principles to reduce lead times to fulfill orders.[55]

However, JIT has limits. It's not the most efficient choice when the costs of delivery exceed the costs of storage. And if suppliers have any problems fulfilling orders, the whole system breaks down. JIT requires close ties with suppliers, so finding replacements can be difficult. These weaknesses became painfully clear when a massive earthquake and tsunami hit Japan in 2011. Big manufacturers there, including Toyota, Canon, and Sony, began experiencing supply disruptions not only from their suppliers but from the supplier's suppliers. With the potential to lose millions of sales, the companies quickly began learning more about the entire supply chains feeding into their companies and diversifying their networks of suppliers.[56] The Automotive Experience group at Johnson Controls used to have arrangements in which one plant served one customer to deliver products just in time to the customer's assembly plant. But now the company's Lerma, Mexico, facility designs standard seats that a variety of customers can use; robots switch between the assembly of seats for the Dodge Journey, Ford Fiesta, and Chrysler PT Cruiser.[57]

Concurrent Engineering   JIT is a vital component of TBC, but JIT traditionally concentrates on reducing time in only one function: manufacturing. TBC attempts to deliver speed in *all* functions—product development, manufacturing, logistics, and customer service. Customers will not be impressed if you manufacture quickly but it takes weeks for them to receive their products or get a problem solved.

Many companies are turning to concurrent (sometimes called simultaneous) engineering as the cornerstone of their TBC strategy. **Concurrent engineering**—also an important component of total quality management—is a major departure from the old development process in which tasks were assigned to various functions in sequence. When R&D completed its part of the project, the work was passed over the wall to engineering, which completed its task and passed it over the wall to manufacturing, and so on. This process was highly inefficient, and errors took a long time to correct.

In contrast, concurrent engineering incorporates the issues and perspectives of all the functions—and customers and suppliers—from the beginning of the process. This team-based approach results in a higher-quality product that is designed for efficient manufacturing *and* customer needs.[58] When concurrent engineering brings the perspective of manufacturing employees into the design process, the company can find significant cost savings and reduce error rates. Every time manufacturing employees can identify how to reduce the use of different parts, they reduce the need to order those parts, maintain an inventory of them, and keep track of which parts to use in which application. R. A. Jones & Co., which makes machines used for packaging, found a way to realize these benefits. Every time the company's engineers would design a new model of its machines, they would devise all new parts for the machine. Jones & Co. moved the engineers' work stations to the factory floor, so the engineers would routinely interact with the production employees. With more communication during the design process, they found they could readily use many standard parts in their new designs.[59]

Some managers resist the idea of concurrent engineering. Why should marketing, product planning and design, and R&D allow manufacturing to get involved in their work? The answer is because the decisions made during the early, product concept stage determine most of the manufacturing cost and quality. Furthermore, manufacturing can offer ideas about the product because of its experience with the prior generation of the product and with direct customer feedback. Also, the other functions must know early on what manufacturing can and cannot do. Finally, when manufacturing is in from the start, it is a full and true partner and will be more committed to decisions it helped make.

concurrent engineering

A design approach in which all relevant functions cooperate jointly and continually in a maximum effort aimed at producing high-quality products that meet customers' needs.

When relevant functions interact with each other on a regular basis, the greater the opportunity to improve processes, maximize efficiency, and reduce cost.

Final Thoughts on Organizational Agility

As we pointed out in the previous chapter, *any* approach to organizing has its strengths and limitations. The advantages of even the innovative, leading-edge structures and systems we have discussed in this chapter are likely to be short-lived if they become fixed rather than remain flexible. Smart managers and smart competitors soon catch up. Today's advantages are tomorrow's table stakes—the minimum requirements that need to be met if an organization expects to be a major player.

To retain or gain a competitive edge, managers may want to keep in mind the principle with which we opened this chapter: successful organizations—and that includes the successful managers within them—do not sit still. They do not follow rigid models but maintain structures, systems, organizational designs, and relationships that are adaptive—always sensitive to changes in their environment and able to respond quickly, efficiently, and effectively to them. Their managers focus constantly on exceeding customer expectations and on continuous quality improvement, designing their systems and structures to help them do just that.

The emphasis on agility, quality, flexibility, learning, and leanness to which you have been exposed in this chapter is likely to be a constant in your managerial career—ideally in your own organization, but perhaps as well in the competition you confront. When Jack Welch was chairman of GE, he saw his goal as the creation of the boundaryless organization, one in which there were no meaningful barriers between the organization and its environment. In such an organization, structures, technologies, and systems are perfectly aligned with the external challenges and opportunities it confronts. Many forward-thinking managers have embraced this goal.[60]

Management Connection

GE'S PURSUIT OF HIGH QUALITY AND LEANNESS

According to Tom Gentile, chief executive of GE Healthcare Systems, the company tries to be responsive in multiple ways. To improve quality, GE applies six sigma, and to improve efficiency by eliminating waste, it uses the lean initiative methods. These methods are not just for manufacturing, either; Gentile's experience includes leading six sigma for finance.

GE considers six sigma part of its culture, not just a process tacked on. Employees must apply the concepts of six sigma to all GE's processes and in the design of its products. Six sigma is the latest initiative in a series of efforts beginning in the 1980s. Then it launched a program called Work-Out to empower employees, hear ideas from employees at all levels, and eliminate bureaucracy and boundaries that got in the way of making improvements. The Work-Out initiative continues to create a learning environment in which quality improvement can proceed more effectively. GE trains all its employees in the six sigma practices, with the most basic training being quality overview seminars. Employees also learn to participate on six sigma teams, and some learn the statistical and quality-control techniques needed to become six sigma Green Belts, Black Belts, and Master Black Belts.

Lean gets credit for enabling GE to move some of its appliance manufacturing back to the United States from China and Mexico, according to Chip Blankenship, chief executive of GE Appliances. GE seeks input from employees at all levels about how to make its processes more efficient. At the GE Appliances facility in Louisville, Kentucky, one outcome of the lean initiative is that all functions related to manufacturing—design, product development, engineering, production, and quality control—are located at the same facility. When an employee learns of customer concerns or a production problem, everyone is at hand to respond.

GE continues experimenting with methods for being more responsive. For example, GE Aviation used a concurrent engineering process, working with its suppliers, to develop wing components for the Airbus A350 XWB. And a few years ago, GE software developers began trying out a technique known as Agile software development. This method basically involves breaking a big project into components and working on one component at a time, with frequent meetings and collaboration to get the component finished quickly. In one project for GE Healthcare, the Agile process cut development time by about half.[61]

- How else might GE become more responsive to its customers?
- Based on the information in the three parts of this case, how would you rate GE's organizational agility? Summarize your reasons for this rating.

KEY TERMS

computer-integrated manufacturing (CIM), p. 314

concurrent engineering, p. 319

continuous process, p. 313

customer relationship management, (CRM), p. 307

downsizing, p. 304

economies of scope, p. 302

flexible factories, p. 315

high-involvement organization, p. 301

ISO 9001, p. 311

just-in-time (JIT), p. 318

large batch, p. 313

lean manufacturing, p. 315

learning organization, p. 300

logistics, p. 317

mass customization, p. 313

mechanistic organization, p. 296

organic structure, p. 296

rightsizing, p. 305

six sigma quality, p. 310

small batch, p. 313

strategic alliance, p. 300

survivor's syndrome, p. 305

technology, p. 312

time-based competition (TBC), p. 317

total quality management, (TQM), p. 309

value chain, p. 308

SUMMARY OF LEARNING OBJECTIVES

Now that you have studied Chapter 9, you should be able to:

LO 1 Discuss why it is critical for organizations to be responsive.

Organizations have a formal structure to help control what goes on within them. But to survive today, firms need more than control—they need responsiveness. They must act quickly and adapt to fast-changing demands.

LO 2 Describe the qualities of an organic organization structure.

The organic form emphasizes flexibility. Organic organizations are decentralized, informal, and dependent on the judgment and expertise of people with broad responsibilities. The organic form is not a single formal structure but a concept that underlies all the new forms discussed in this chapter.

LO 3 Identify strategies and dynamic organizational concepts that can improve an organization's responsiveness.

New and emerging organizational concepts and forms include core capabilities, strategic alliances, learning organizations, and high-involvement organizations.

LO 4 Explain how a firm can be both big and small.

Historically, large organizations have had important advantages over small organizations. Today small size has advantages, including the ability to act quickly, respond to customer demands, and serve small niches. The ideal firm today combines the advantages of both. It creates many small, flexible units, while the corporate levels add value by taking advantage of its size and power.

LO 5 Summarize how firms organize to meet customer requirements.

Firms have embraced principles of continuous improvement, total quality management, and six sigma quality (often combined with lean manufacturing) to respond to customer needs. Baldrige criteria and ISO 9001 standards help firms organize to meet better quality specifications. Extending these, reengineering efforts are directed at completely overhauling processes to provide world-class customer service.

LO 6 Identify ways that firms organize around different types of technology.

Organizations tend to move from organic structures to mechanistic structures and back to organic structures as they transition from small batch to large batch and continuous process technologies. To organize for flexible manufacturing, organizations pursue mass customization via computer-integrated manufacturing and lean manufacturing. To organize for time-based competition, firms emphasize their logistics operations, just-in-time operations, and concurrent engineering.

DISCUSSION QUESTIONS

1. Discuss evidence you have seen of the imperatives for change, flexibility, and responsiveness faced by today's firms.

2. Describe large, bureaucratic organizations with which you have had contact that have not responded flexibly to customer demands. Also describe examples of satisfactory responsiveness. What do you think accounts for the differences between the responsive and nonresponsive organizations?

3. Considering the potential advantages of large and small size, would you describe the feel of your college or university as big, small, or small within big? Why? What might make it feel different?

4. What is a core capability? What would you say are the core capabilities of Toyota, Walmart, and Apple? Brainstorm some creative new products and markets to which these capabilities could be applied.

5. If you were going into business for yourself, what would be your core capabilities? What capabilities do you have now, and what capabilities are you going to develop? Describe what your role would be in a network organization and the capabilities and roles of other firms you would want in your network.

6. Using an Internet search engine, search for "strategic alliance" and identify three recently formed alliances. For each alliance, identify whether the companies' other products are generally competitors or complementary products. What are the goals of each alliance? What brought them together? Discuss whether you think a strategic alliance is an effective way for these organizations to meet their goals.

7. What skills will you need to work effectively in (a) a learning organization and (b) a high-involvement organization? Be specific, generating long lists. Would you enjoy working in these environments? Why or why not? What can you do to prepare yourself for these eventualities?

EXPERIENTIAL EXERCISES

9.1 MECHANISTIC AND ORGANIC STRUCTURES

OBJECTIVES

1. To think about your own preferences when it comes to working in a particular organizational structure.

2. To examine aspects of organizations by using as an example this class you are a member of.

INSTRUCTIONS

1. Complete the Mechanistic and Organic Worksheet here.

2. Meet in groups of four to six persons. Share your data from the worksheet. Discuss the reasons for your responses and analyze the factors that probably encouraged your instructor to choose the type of structure that now exists.

Mechanistic and Organic Worksheet

1. Indicate your general preference for working in one of these two organizational structures by circling the appropriate response:

| **Mechanistic** | 1 | 2 | 3 | 4 | 5 | 6 | 7 | 8 | 9 | 10 | **Organic** |

2. Indicate your perception of the form of organization that is used in this class by circling the appropriate response for each item:

A. Task role definition

| **Rigid** | 1 | 2 | 3 | 4 | 5 | 6 | 7 | 8 | 9 | 10 | **Flexible** |

B. Communication

| **Vertical** | 1 | 2 | 3 | 4 | 5 | 6 | 7 | 8 | 9 | 10 | **Multidirectional** |

C. Decision making

| **Centralized** | 1 | 2 | 3 | 4 | 5 | 6 | 7 | 8 | 9 | 10 | **Decentralized** |

D. Sensitivity to the environment

| **Closed** | 1 | 2 | 3 | 4 | 5 | 6 | 7 | 8 | 9 | 10 | **Open** |

SOURCE: From Keith Davis and John W. Newstrom, *Human Behavior at Work*, p. 346. Copyright 1993. Reprinted with permission of the McGraw-Hill Companies.

9.2   THE WOODY MANUFACTURING COMPANY

OBJECTIVE

To apply the concepts learned about structure and agility at the individual, group, and organizational levels in designing the Woody Manufacturing Company.

TASK 1 (INDIVIDUAL ASSIGNMENT)

a. Read the following case study of the Woody Manufacturing Company.

b. Review the chapter carefully and choose the organizational design orientation that you feel can best guide you in developing the design for Mr. Woody.

c. Write down your thoughts on alternative management structures, pay systems, and allocation of work to individuals and groups.

TASK 2 (TEAM ASSIGNMENT)

a. Get together with your team and develop a proposal for Mr. Woody that, if followed, would help him fulfill his vision.

b. Prepare a five-minute presentation. Your typewritten team proposal is due prior to your team presentation in Mr. Woody's conference room.

Designing a New Furniture Company

Mr. Woody, the owner/operator of a small furniture company specializing in the manufacture of high-quality bar stools, has experienced a tremendous growth in demand for his products. He has standing orders for $750,000. Consequently, Mr. Woody has decided to expand his organization and attack the market aggressively. His stated mission is "to manufacture world-class products that are competitive in the world market in quality, reliability, performance, and profitability." He would like to create a culture where "pride, ownership, employment security, and trust" are a way of life. He just finished a set of interviews, and he has hired 32 new workers with the following skills:

Four skilled craftspeople.

Ten people with some woodworking experience.

Twelve people with no previous woodworking experience or other skills.

One nurse.

One schoolteacher.

One bookkeeper.

Three people with some managerial experience in nonmanufacturing settings.

Mr. Woody (with your help) must now decide how to design his new organization. This design will include the management structure, pay system, and the allocation of work to individuals and groups. The bar stool–making process has 15 steps:

1. Wood is selected.
2. Wood is cut to size.
3. Defects are removed.
4. Wood is planed to exact specifications.
5. Joints are cut.
6. Tops are glued and assembled.
7. Legs/bases are prepared.
8. Legs/bases are attached to tops.
9. Bar stools are sanded.
10. Stain is applied.
11. Varnish is applied.
12. Bar stools are sanded.
13. Varnish is reapplied.
14. Bar stools are packaged.
15. Bar stools are delivered to the customer.

Mr. Woody currently manufactures three kinds of bar stools (pedestal, four-legged corner, and four-legged recessed). There is no difference in the difficulty of making the three types of bar stools. Major cost variations have been associated with defective wood, imprecise cuts, and late deliveries to customers. Mr. Woody must decide how to organize his company to maintain high quality and profits.

He has thought about several options. He could have some individuals perform the first step for all types of bar stools; he could have an individual perform several steps for one type of bar stool; or he could have a team perform some combination of steps for one or more bar stools. He wonders whether how he organized would affect quality or costs. He's also aware that although the demand for all types of bar stools has been roughly equal over the long run, there were short periods where one type of bar stool was in greater demand than the others. Because Mr. Woody wants to use his people effectively, he has committed an expert in work design to help him set up an optimal organization.

SOURCE: A. B. (Rami) Shani and James B. Lau, *Behavior in Organizations: An Experimental Approach,* 2005, p. 370. Copyright 2005 Reprinted with permission of The McGraw-Hill Companies.

CONCLUDING CASE

DIY STORES

DIY Stores is a nationwide chain that offers every tool and supply for repairing and maintaining a home. Shoppers at DIY can find paints and paintbrushes, screwdrivers and lumber, pliers and electrical conduit, spades and shrubs, and much more. Besides the wide variety under one roof, what sets DIY apart is its sales associates. The company hires avid do-it-yourselfers and retired trade workers, assigns them to work in departments where their know-how is relevant, provides training in new products and creative methods, and pays them a little more than they could earn by working for another retailer. The company also makes available fact sheets and lists of tips and building ideas. Together these efforts make DIY Stores a place where shoppers can go to get ideas and advice, so they get more than supplies for a project—they get all the ingredients they need for their project to succeed.

Over the past couple of decades, however, consumers have found an alternative to getting advice in a store: many prefer to do their research online, comfortably seated at a computer. If consumers can use a search engine or chat in an online community to figure out the best way to fix a leaky toilet or make a small bedroom look airy and bright, why would they trek into a store to ask? The answer, DIY's management feared, was that they wouldn't bother. If true, that trend placed DIY's competitive advantage at risk. The retailer needed to change with the times.

DIY's solution was to go where the consumers were: online. Management decided the company needed to supplement its in-store experts with online experts, employees who shared the same kinds of information on the Internet as they did in the stores. The company's corporate communications department was charged with developing a plan for this effort.

The department's people were used to thinking of corporate communications as something that originates at headquarters, so they initially thought the most efficient approach would be to hire a team of writers to work in offices at headquarters, blogging about new products and maintenance tips. But when they presented this plan to top management, one of the vice presidents raised a question: The company's salespeople were its base of knowledge. Why bring in new people? Why not figure out a way to use the human assets the company already had?

The corporate communications people went back to work on the plan. Probably some of the sales associates already were using the Internet themselves and knew how to write a blog and participate in social networking. Probably some of them had the necessary combination of helpfulness and writing skills. So they considered identifying those employees and inviting them to take jobs at headquarters. But as the group discussed this idea, they realized it had a flaw. If employees left the stores, they would no longer be seeing, selling, and watching customers' reactions to products. They would lose the hands-on and face-to-face experiences that kept them up to date and in touch with consumers. Also, consumers would quickly figure out that the online exchanges were not with a real DIY sales associate but with someone who had become a call center employee or professional communicator.

So the team arrived at an unusual plan. The company would identify Internet-savvy sales associates, but it wouldn't remove them from the stores. Rather, the associates who accepted the new position would work three days a week in a store and two days a week in an office, with their schedules staggered so that the online community would be active seven days a week. The company's executives were enthusiastic about this plan.

DIY contacted store managers in cities where it has regional offices. The store managers recommended employees they thought would deliver effective help online, and a team of recruiters interviewed these candidates and selected two dozen to provide an online presence. The typical employee selected had eight years of experience with DIY and submitted an excellent writing sample. Meanwhile, the company built an online "Do It with Us" web page where customers can submit questions, read tips, share ideas, and find links to information about new products available at DIY's stores.

After a three-day training program, the sales associates started the online conversation with DIY. Within months, they and the site's visitors had started thousands of conversation threads. And in an unexpected development, the sales associates have also become a valued source of knowledge for DIY's other employees. In stores, at headquarters, and in the regional offices, if someone wants product or project information, they often start their search at the "Do It with Us" web page.

DISCUSSION QUESTIONS

1. As DIY Stores built its online presence, how well did it organize around its core capabilities?

2. DIY Stores is a large national chain. What impact did its size have on its agility?

3. How could DIY increase its agility in responding to the importance of the Internet?

Human Resources Management

> You can get capital and erect buildings, but it takes people to build a business.
>
> — THOMAS J. WATSON, FOUNDER, IBM

After studying Chapter 10, you should be able to:

LO 1 Discuss how companies use human resources management to gain competitive advantage. p. 328

LO 2 Give reasons companies recruit both internally and externally for new hires. p. 333

LO 3 Identify various methods for selecting new employees. p. 334

LO 4 Evaluate the importance of spending on training and development. p. 344

LO 5 Explain alternatives for who appraises an employee's performance. p. 347

LO 6 Describe the fundamental aspects of a reward system. p. 351

LO 7 Summarize how unions and labor laws influence human resources management. p. 358

Management Connection

HOW GOOGLE LANDS THE BEST EMPLOYEES IN A TOUGH JOB MARKET

Year after year, we hear that U.S. schools are not preparing enough engineers and software developers to meet employers' demand for skilled technology workers. Yet Google, the software company known for its popular search engine, gets about a million job applicants a year and hires the cream of the crop.

How does Google win the competition for talent? An obvious place to find answers is in how the 28,000-employee company treats its workers. It pays them well, and knowing they hold demanding jobs, it makes the workplace comfortable. Uncommon benefits include exercise facilities, a free laundry service, and free food in all company cafeterias. Google offers flexibility with on-site child care and arrangements for job sharing and telecommuting. These qualities help Google land at the top of *Fortune*'s list of the 100 Best Companies to Work For.

More significant is the excitement of being part of something meaningful. At least since the name Google became synonymous with searching the web, people with a passion for technology have considered the company a cool place to work, both because its software is advanced and because it makes the Internet a powerful tool. In a survey of young professionals, Google was by far the top choice for an ideal employer. Universum, which conducted the survey, noted that young professionals value working for companies they already like as consumers.

Because Google is an attractive employer, it can be picky about whom it hires. The company selects people who are excited about what computers can do and value intellectual excellence. It retains them by creating a work environment in which employees can contribute

creatively and continue to develop. Such people appreciate the hours of training Google provides its employees each year.

These decisions about hiring, training, and employee benefits are far from random. Rather, under the leadership of Chief People Officer Laszlo Bock, Google applies its prowess in analyzing data to figure out how to acquire, develop, and keep talented people. Every year, Google conducts its Googlegeist employee survey to measure employee attitudes about work, and the company carefully tracks all kinds of people-related measures such as managers' effectiveness. Prasad Setty, who as the head of people analytics reports to Bock, says Google tries to "bring the same level of rigor to people decisions that we do to engineering decisions," so all decisions are based on hard data.[1]

> In receiving roughly 20,000 job applications every week, Google has a huge challenge as well as an opportunity. It has to figure out which of these people to hire, how to bring out the best in them, and how to keep them around. As you read this chapter, think about how the strategic use of people is essential to Google's success.

327

human resources management (HRM)

Formal systems for the management of people within an organization.

The opening quote by Thomas Watson, founder of IBM, summarizes our view of the importance of people to any organization. Google's practice of wooing bright people with exciting challenges and generous perks has differentiated the company in important ways. **Human resources management (HRM),** historically known as personnel management, deals with formal systems for managing people at work. For that reason, it is one of the fundamental aspects of organizational and managerial life. Your first formal interaction with an organization you wish to join will likely involve some aspect of its human resources function, and throughout your career as a manager you will be a part of, as well as be affected by, your organization's human resources management.

We begin this chapter by describing HRM as it relates to strategic management. We will also discuss more of the nuts and bolts of HRM: staffing, training, performance appraisal, rewards, and labor relations. Throughout the chapter, we discuss legal issues that influence each aspect of HRM. In the next chapter, we expand this focus to address related issues of managing a diverse workforce.

Strategic Human Resources Management

LO 1

HRM has assumed a vital strategic role in recent years as organizations attempt to compete through people. Recall from Chapter 4 that firms can create a competitive advantage when they possess or develop resources that are valuable, rare, inimitable, and organized. We can use the same criteria to talk about the strategic impact of human resources:

1. *Creates value.* People can increase value through their efforts to decrease costs or provide something unique to customers or some combination of the two. Empowerment programs, total quality initiatives, and continuous improvement efforts at companies such as Corning and Xerox are intentionally designed to increase the value that employees bring to the bottom line.

2. *Is rare.* People are a source of competitive advantage when their skills, knowledge, and abilities are not equally available to all competitors. Top companies invest a great deal to hire and train the best and the brightest employees to gain advantage over their competitors. Dow Chemical went to court to stop General Electric from hiring away its engineers. This case shows that some companies recognize both the value and the rarity of certain employees.

> People are a source of competitive advantage when their skills, knowledge, and abilities are not equally available to all competitors.

3. *Is difficult to imitate.* People are a source of competitive advantage when their capabilities and contributions cannot be copied by others. Disney, Southwest Airlines, and Whole Foods are known for creating unique cultures that get the most from employees (through teamwork) and are difficult to imitate.

4. *Is organized.* People are a source of competitive advantage when organizations know how to deploy them as needed based on their experience, skills, and potential. Johnson & Johnson, Colgate, and other companies have formal systems for identifying future management needs and developing high-potential employees so the company can promote from within. This way, they fill openings with people who are well acquainted with the company's culture, customers, and industry.

These four criteria highlight the importance of people and show the closeness of HRM to strategic management. At a growing number of companies, HR experts are participating in strategy meetings to identify key issues where they can analyze data and propose how new methods of acquiring, training, and keeping talent will help the company meet its goals.[2] The evidence is growing that this focus brings positive business results. For example, a study by Deloitte associated the use of effective human resources practices with higher valuation of a company in the stock market.[3] Global trends make this focus even more important. Competition is intensifying. Rising educational standards and access to technology are increasingly available worldwide. *Innovation*—useful new ideas that emerge from the focused creativity of organization members—has become ever more critical to gaining and maintaining

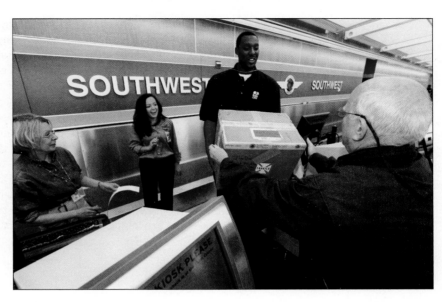

competitive advantage. Because employee skills, knowledge, and abilities are among the most distinctive and renewable resources on which a company can draw, their strategic management is more important than ever. Increasingly, organizations are recognizing that their success depends on what people know—that is, their knowledge and skills. The term **human capital** (or, more broadly, *intellectual capital*) often is used today to describe the strategic value of employee knowledge and abilities.

As more executives have come to appreciate that their employees can be their organization's most valuable resources, human resources managers have played a greater role in contributing to the organization's strategic planning. That means human resources (HR) specialists are challenged to know their organization's business, and line managers are challenged to excel at selecting and motivating the best people. As contributors to the organization's strategy, HR managers also face greater ethical challenges. When they were merely a specialized staff function, they could focus on, say, legal requirements for hiring decisions. But strategy decisions require them to be able to link decisions about staffing, training, and other HR matters to the organization's business success. For example, as members of the top management team, HR managers may be faced with the need for drastic downsizing of the workforce while still retaining top executives through generous salaries or bonuses, or they may fail to investigate and challenge corrupt practices of colleagues aggressively. Such dilemmas are complex and challenging. In the long run, however, organizations are best served when HR leaders are a strong advocate for at least four sets of values: strategic, ethical, legal, and financial.[4]

Southwest Airlines is known for creating a unique culture that gets the most from employees. Southwest rewards its employees for excellent performance and maintains loyalty by offering free airfare, profit sharing, and other incentives. What benefits would you need to stay motivated?

human capital

The knowledge, skills, and abilities of employees that have economic value.

In Practice

PRICESPECTIVE MANAGES HR CHALLENGES

Tough economic times deliver exciting HR opportunities as well as tough HR challenges. Well-managed firms seize the opportunities and meet the challenges.

One company that prepares well for a slowdown is PriceSpective, a consulting firm. The company's four co-owners meet monthly with senior managers to determine whether their current staffing levels are appropriate for their coming needs. Whenever sales are slow, PriceSpective institutes a temporary hiring freeze. Because these actions are part of a regular planning process, employees don't worry; they know managers are simply making course adjustments to keep the company efficient. Also, even when clients are not signing up for services, PriceSpective keeps talking to prospective employees. For the firm's specialized practice serving pharmaceutical firms, it needs many employees with doctoral degrees, who would be difficult to find and hire quickly when business picks up. Of course, when interviewing during a hiring freeze, managers are careful to explain the company's situation and plans for the future.

Other firms are able to hire during a recession, gaining access to a huge pool of talented people. The recent recession drove more shoppers from higher-priced retailers to Family Dollar Stores, so the company opened more stores, receiving applications from workers with better-than-usual credentials. The company also needed specialists for its information technology department; it found experienced IT workers who left Circuit City when that chain went out of business. Companies that, like Family Dollar, build up their staff when talented people are hungry for work can boost sales, improve efficiency, and gain an advantage over competitors—if they can keep and motivate these employees.[5]

- How would you expect these companies to adjust their HR strategy when the economy is booming?

Managing human capital to sustain a competitive advantage is perhaps the most important part of an organization's HR function. But on a day-to-day basis, HR managers also have many other concerns regarding their workers and the entire personnel puzzle. These concerns include attracting talent; maintaining a well-trained, highly motivated, and loyal workforce; managing diversity; devising effective compensation systems; managing layoffs; and containing health care and pension costs. Balancing these issues is difficult, and the best approach varies depending on the circumstances of the organization. A steel producer facing a cutback in business may need human resources activities to assist with layoffs, whereas a semiconductor company may need more staff to produce enough microchips to meet the demands of the consumer electronics market. The emphasis on different HR activities depends on whether the organization is growing, declining, or standing still. This leads to the practical issues involved in HR planning.

The HR Planning Process

"Get me the right kind and the right number of people at the right time." It sounds simple enough, but meeting an organization's staffing needs requires strategic human resources planning: an activity with a strategic purpose derived from the organization's plans.

The HR planning process occurs in three stages: planning, programming, and evaluating. First, HR managers need to know the organization's business plans to ensure that the right number and types of people are available—where the company is headed, in what businesses it plans to be, what future growth is expected, and so forth. Few actions are more damaging to morale than having to lay off recently hired college graduates because of inadequate planning for future needs. Second, the organization conducts programming of specific human resources activities, such as recruitment, training, and layoffs. In this stage, the company's plans are implemented. Third, human resources activities are evaluated to determine whether they are producing the results needed to contribute to the organization's business plans. Figure 10.1 illustrates the components of the human resources planning process. In this chapter, we focus on human resources planning and programming. Many of the other factors listed in Figure 10.1 are discussed in later chapters.

Demand Forecasts Perhaps the most difficult part of human resources planning is conducting demand forecasts—that is, determining how many and what type

PLANNING **PROGRAMMING** **EVALUATING**

Organizational strategic planning

HRM environmental scanning

Human resources planning

Human resources activities

Results

- Labor markets
- Technology
- Legislation
- Competition
- Economy

- Demand forecast
- Internal labor supply
- External labor supply
- Job analysis

- Employee recruitment
- Employee selection
- Outplacement
- Training and development
- Performance appraisal
- Reward systems
- Labor relations

- Productivity
- Quality
- Innovation
- Satisfaction
- Turnover
- Absenteeism
- Health

FIGURE 10.1
An Overview of the HR Planning Process

of people are needed. Demand forecasts for people needs are derived from organizational plans. As Ford Motor Company increased production and prepared to launch new products following the recession of 2009, it hired more than 8,100 workers for manufacturing and engineering positions associated with the greater production volume. It then planned to hire 2,200 salaried workers to carry out work related to introducing new models, including engineering and software jobs. Similarly, companies selling an existing product consider current sales and projected future sales growth as they estimate the plant capacity needed to meet future demand, the sales force required, the support staff needed, and so forth. They calculate the number of labor-hours required to operate a plant, sell the product, distribute it, serve customers, and so forth. These estimates are used to determine the demand for different types of workers.

Labor Supply Forecasts   Along with forecasting demand, managers must forecast the *supply of labor*—that is, how many and what types of employees the organization actually will have. In performing a supply analysis, the organization estimates the number and quality of its current employees as well as the available external supply of workers. To estimate internal supply, the company typically relies on its experiences with turnover, terminations, retirements, promotions, and transfers. A computerized human resources information system assists greatly in supply forecasting.

Externally, organizations have to look at workforce trends to make projections. Worldwide, as we discussed in Chapter 6, the highly skilled, higher-paid jobs have been generated mostly in the cities of the industrialized world, where companies have scrambled to find enough qualified workers. At the same time, companies in industrialized nations have used offshoring to move much of their routine and less skilled work to nations with a large population willing to work for lower pay.

In the United States, demographic trends have contributed to a shortage of workers with the appropriate skills and education level. Traditional labor-intensive jobs, in agriculture, mining, and assembly-line manufacturing, are making way for jobs in technical, financial, and customized goods and service industries. These jobs often require much more training and schooling than the jobs they are replacing—or that the education system may currently be producing. Demand for highly qualified employees continues to outpace supply—one reason some jobs are being transferred overseas. Some demographic trends we discussed in Chapter 2 may worsen this situation. For example, the upcoming retirement of the baby boomer generation will remove a large number of educated and trained employees from the workforce. And in math, science, and engineering graduate schools, fewer than half of the students receiving graduate degrees are American born. (To fill U.S. jobs, companies must hire U.S. citizens or immigrants with permission to work in the United States.)

One response managers have made to deal with this skills shortage has been to increase significantly the remedial and training budgets within their own organizations.[6] For example, Caspers Company, which operates 50 McDonald's stores in Tampa, Florida, pays for its non-English-speaking employees to take an intensive English language class. Employees who choose to participate not only provide better customer service but also are able to move into positions of greater responsibility. And Bayer's Baytown, Texas, plant set up an internship program because it can't find enough employees to run its complex chemical-processing equipment and has decided to train them itself. A related approach to training current employees is to retrain and hire workers who were downsized.

Another response has been to increase the labor supply by recruiting workers from other countries. The supply of legal immigrant labor is restricted by various laws and regulations. For example, each year the U.S. government awards H-1B visas to 65,000 college-educated workers in high-skilled, highly demanded jobs such as engineers and college instructors. Those people are permitted to work temporarily in the United States. Managers at high-tech companies, including Microsoft and Google, complain that the number of H-1B visas is too small to enable companies to meet the demand for science and technology workers, and some companies address that challenge by aggressively hiring early each year, before the quota has been met.[7] Immigrant workers are also attractive to companies with a low-cost strategy because strong labor demand in the United States enables U.S. workers to insist on higher pay.

On the plus side, earlier forecasts of a diverse workforce have become fact, adding greatly to the pool of available talent. The business world is no longer the exclusive domain of white males. In fact, two-career families have become the norm. Minorities, women, immigrants, older and disabled workers, and other groups have made the management of diversity a fundamental activity of the modern manager. Because of the importance of managing the new workforce, the next chapter is devoted entirely to this topic.

Reconciling Supply and Demand   Once managers have a good idea of the supply of and the demand for various types of employees, they can start developing approaches for reconciling the two. In some cases, organizations find they need more people than they currently have (i.e., a labor deficit). In such cases, organizations can hire new employees, promote current employees to new positions, or outsource work to contractors. In other cases, organizations may find that they have more people than they need (i.e., a labor surplus). If this is detected far enough in advance, organizations can use attrition—the normal turnover of employees—to reduce the surplus. In other instances, the organization may lay off employees or transfer them to other areas.

When managers do need to hire, one tool they can use is their organization's compensation policy. Large companies in particular spend a lot of time gathering information about pay scales for the various jobs they have available and making sure their compensation system is fair and competitive. We discuss pay issues later in this chapter.

Job Analysis   Although issues of supply and demand are fairly macro activities—conducted at an organizational level—HR planning also has a micro side called *job analysis*. **Job analysis** does two things.[8] First, it tells the HR manager about the job itself: the essential tasks, duties, and responsibilities involved in performing the job. This information is called a *job description*. The job description for an accounting manager might specify that the position will be responsible for monthly, quarterly, and annual financial reports, getting bills issued and paid, preparing budgets, ensuring the company's compliance with laws and regulations, working closely with line managers on financial issues, and supervising an accounting department of 12 people.

Second, job analysis describes the skills, knowledge, abilities, and other characteristics needed to perform the job. This is called the *job specification*. For our accounting manager example, the job requirements might include a degree in accounting or business, knowledge of computerized accounting systems, prior managerial experience, and excellent communication skills.

Job analysis provides the information required by virtually every human resources activity. It assists with the essential HR programs: recruitment, training, selection, appraisal, and reward systems. It may also help organizations defend themselves in lawsuits involving employment practices—for example, by clearly specifying what a job requires if someone claims unfair dismissal.[9] Ultimately, job analysis helps increase the value added by employees to the organization because it clarifies what is really required to perform effectively.

> **job analysis**
>
> A tool for determining what is done on a given job and what should be done on that job.

> Job analysis provides the information required by virtually every human resources activity.

Staffing the Organization

Once HR planning is completed, managers can focus on staffing the organization. The staffing function consists of three related activities: recruitment, selection, and outplacement.

LO 2

Recruitment

Recruitment activities help increase the pool of candidates that might be selected for a job. Recruitment may be internal to the organization (considering current employees for promotions and transfers) or external. Each approach has advantages and disadvantages.[10]

Internal Recruiting   The advantages of internal recruiting are that employers know their employees, and employees know their organization. External candidates who are unfamiliar with the organization may find they don't like working there. Also, the opportunity to move up within the organization may encourage employees to remain with the company, work hard, and succeed. Recruiting from outside the company can be demoralizing to employees. Many companies, such as Sears and Eli Lilly, prefer internal to external recruiting for these reasons.

Internal staffing has some drawbacks. If existing employees lack skills or talent, internal recruitment yields a limited applicant pool, leading to poor selection decisions. Also, an internal recruitment policy can inhibit a company that wants to change the nature or goals of the business by bringing in outside candidates. In changing from a rapidly growing, entrepreneurial organization to a mature business with more stable growth, Dell went outside the organization to hire managers who better fit those needs.

> **recruitment**
>
> The development of a pool of applicants for jobs in an organization.

> **Bottom Line**
>
> Outside hires often bring new ideas to the organization. *How might an organization identify candidates with innovative ideas?*
>
>

Many companies that rely heavily on internal recruiting use a job-posting system. A *job-posting system* is a mechanism for advertising open positions, typically on a bulletin board or the company's intranet. Texas Instruments uses job posting. Employees complete a request form indicating interest in a posted job. The posted job description includes a list of duties and the minimum skills and experience required.

External Recruiting   External recruiting brings in new blood to a company and can inspire innovation. Among the most frequently used sources of outside applicants are Internet job boards, company websites, employee referrals, newspaper advertisements, and college campus recruiting.

Recent surveys suggest that employers place the greatest emphasis on referrals by current employees and online job boards.[11] Some companies actively encourage employees to refer their friends by offering cash rewards. In fact, surveys show word-of-mouth recommendations are the way most job positions get filled. Not only is this recruitment method relatively inexpensive, but employees also tend to know who will be a good fit with the company. Web job boards such as CareerBuilder and Monster are widely used because they easily reach a large pool of job seekers. For specialized positions, however, a growing number of companies are opting to look on professional networking sites such as LinkedIn or to hire a recruiter because the job boards generate many unqualified leads that are overwhelming to process. Many companies accept applications and may post job openings at their corporate websites. When it is worthwhile to pay an outside organization to narrow down the pool of applicants, employers may turn to employment agencies or, for important management positions, an executive search firm. Campus recruiting can be helpful for companies looking for applicants who have up-to-date training and innovative ideas. However, companies that rely heavily on campus recruiting and employee referrals have to take extra care to ensure that these methods do not discriminate by generating pools of applicants who are, say, mostly women or primarily white.[12]

Most companies use some combination of the methods we have been discussing, depending on the particular job or situation. For example, they might use internal recruiting for existing jobs that need replacements and external recruiting when the firm is expanding or needs to acquire some new skill.

Selection

selection

Choosing from among qualified applicants to hire into an organization.

Selection builds on recruiting and involves decisions about whom to hire. As important as these decisions are, they are—unfortunately—at times made in careless or cavalier ways. In this section we describe a number of selection instruments to which you may soon be exposed in your own career.

Applications and Résumés   Application blanks and résumés provide basic information to prospective employers. To make a first cut through candidates, employers review the profiles and backgrounds of various job applicants. Applications and résumés typically include information about the applicant's name, educational background, citizenship, work experiences, certifications, and the like. Their appearance and accuracy also say something about the applicant—spelling mistakes, for example, are almost always immediately disqualifying (something to keep in mind when preparing your own). Although providing important information, applications and résumés tend not to be extremely useful for making final selection decisions.

Interviews   The most popular selection tool is interviewing, and every company uses some type of interview. However, employment interviewers must be careful about what they ask and how they ask it. As we will explain later in the chapter, federal law requires employers to avoid discriminating against people based on criteria such as sex and race; questions that distinguish candidates according to protected categories may be seen as evidence of discrimination.

In an unstructured (or nondirective) interview, the interviewer asks different interviewees different questions. The interviewer may also use probes—that is, ask follow-up questions to learn more about the candidate.[13]

In a **structured interview,** the interviewer conducts the same interview with each applicant. There are two basic types of structured interview. The first approach—called the *situational interview*—focuses on hypothetical situations. Zale Corporation, a major jewelry chain, uses this type of structured interview to select sales clerks. Here is a sample question: "A customer comes into the store to pick up a watch he had left for repair. The watch is not back yet from the repair shop, and the customer becomes angry. How would you handle the situation?" An answer that says "I would refer the customer to my supervisor" might suggest that the applicant felt incapable of handling the situation on his or her own. The second approach—called the *behavioral description interview*—explores what candidates have actually done in the past. In selecting accountants, Bill Bufe of Plante & Moran asks candidates how they handled a difficult person they have worked with, and Art King asks how candidates have handled a stressful situation because he believes this shows how candidates "think on their feet."[14] Because behavioral questions are based on real events, they often provide useful information about how the candidate will actually perform on the job.

Each of these interview techniques offers a manager different advantages and disadvantages, and many interviewers use more than one technique during the same interview. Unstructured interviews can help establish rapport and provide a sense of the applicant's personality, but they may not provide the manager with specific information about the candidate's ability. Structured interviews tend to be more reliable predictors of job performance because they are based on the job analysis that has been done for the position. They are also more likely to be free of bias and stereotypes. And because the same questions are being asked of all candidates for the job, an interview that is at least partially structured allows the manager to compare responses across different candidates.[15]

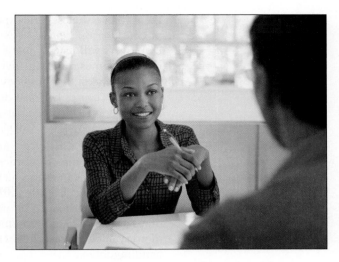

During an interview, employers may opt to hold unstructured interviews, where they ask each potential employee different questions, or they may choose to hold structured interviews where the employer asks all potential employees the same questions.

structured interview

Selection technique that involves asking all applicants the same questions and comparing their responses to a standardized set of answers.

> Many interviewers use more than one technique during the same interview.

Reference Checks Résumés, applications, and interviews rely on the honesty of the applicant. To make an accurate selection decision, employers have to be able to trust the words of each candidate. Unfortunately, some candidates may hide criminal backgrounds that could pose a risk to the employer or exaggerate their qualifications. In a highly publicized incident, the dean of admissions at the Massachusetts Institute of Technology resigned after nearly three decades on the job because the school learned that she had provided false information about her educational background.[16] Although she had certainly demonstrated an ability to perform the job functions, she could no longer claim the level of integrity required by that position. Once lost, a reputation is hard to regain.

Because these and more ambiguous ethical gray areas arise, employers supplement candidate-provided information with other screening devices, including reference checks. Virtually all organizations contact references or former employers and educational institutions listed by candidates. Although checking references makes sense, reference information is becoming increasingly difficult to obtain because individuals have won costly lawsuits against former employers who spoke negatively about them. Nevertheless, HR experts encourage prospective employers to make a practice of checking references.[17] One reason is that it does occasionally raise a red flag: past employers will usually just verify dates of employment, job title, and sometimes pay, but sometimes they will advise caution when asked if the candidate is hirable. Checking references also provides a defense for an employer in the event that one of its employees causes harm. It demonstrates that the company was diligent about making the decision to hire that person.

Background Checks   For a higher level of scrutiny, background investigations also have become standard procedure for many companies. Some state courts have ruled that companies can be held liable for negligent hiring if they fail to do adequate background checks. The different types of checks include Social Security verification, past employment and education verification, and a criminal records check. A number of other checks can be conducted if they pertain to the job being hired for, including a motor vehicle record check (for jobs involving driving) and a credit check (for money-handling jobs).

Internet tools have made basic background checks fast and easy to perform. Recent surveys of hiring managers found that roughly half are using social networking sites, especially Facebook and LinkedIn, to learn about job candidates; some prospective employers even ask candidates for user names and passwords.[18] Many companies have chosen not to extend job offers to candidates based on content they have found online. Internet users are advised to remember that anything that carries their name online may become information for potential employers, even years down the road.

Figure 10.2 shows which screening tools are used most often.

Personality Tests   The popularity of using tests to measure candidates' personalities has risen and fallen, but it currently seems to be on the upswing.[19] Concerns that have discouraged the use of personality tests include the possibility they might be seen as discriminatory or might not accurately predict job performance—perhaps because candidates will cheat by trying to guess the right answers or even retaking

FIGURE 10.2
Online Tools Used to
Screen Job Applicants

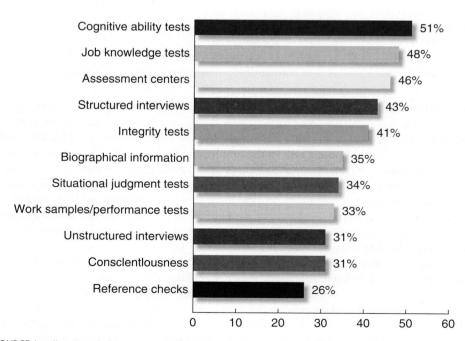

- Cognitive ability tests — 51%
- Job knowledge tests — 48%
- Assessment centers — 46%
- Structured interviews — 43%
- Integrity tests — 41%
- Biographical information — 35%
- Situational judgment tests — 34%
- Work samples/performance tests — 33%
- Unstructured interviews — 31%
- Conscientiousness — 31%
- Reference checks — 26%

SOURCE: http://answers.mheducation.com/management/human-resource-management/personnel-selection.

the test with different answers later if they fail the first screening. However, tests can be constructed using past performance data to find associations between traits and job performance. Some personality types have been associated with greater job satisfaction and performance, especially in situations in which the organization can build groups of people with similar positive traits.[20]

A number of well-known inventories measure personality traits such as sociability, adjustment, and energy. Typical questions are "Do you like to socialize with people?" and "Do you enjoy working hard?" Some personality tests try to determine the type of working conditions that the candidate prefers, to see whether he or she would be motivated and productive in the particular job. For example, if the candidate prefers making decisions on his or her own but the job requires gaining the cooperation of others, another candidate might be a better fit. Today many personality tests are taken online rather than with paper and pencil. These online tests can be constructed to deliver certain questions based on answers to preceding questions, so that the test is tailored to the individual test taker.

Drug Testing   Drug testing is now a frequently used screening instrument. Since the passage of the Drug-Free Workplace Act of 1988, applicants and employees of federal contractors and Department of Defense contractors and those under Department of Transportation regulations have been subject to testing for illegal drugs. To avoid discrimination against individuals with disabilities, companies typically wait to conduct drug testing until after they have made a conditional job offer. According to statistics from the federal government, about one in four full-time employees is tested when hired, and almost one in three is subject to random drug tests once they have started working.[21]

Drug testing has become more complicated for employers in the growing number of states that have legalized the use of marijuana for medical purposes.[22] Companies that fire a worker for failing a drug test because of medical marijuana use worry that they could be found guilty of discriminating against a disabled person. For many jobs, however, it is also critical that workers not be under the influence of any substance, legal or illegal. So far, most state medical marijuana laws do not include employment protections for workers, but because these developments are new and the laws vary from state to state, employers are in a legal gray area for the time being.

Cognitive Ability Tests   Among the oldest employment selection devices are cognitive ability tests. These tests measure a range of intellectual abilities, including verbal comprehension (vocabulary, reading) and numerical aptitude (mathematical calculations). About 20 percent of U.S. companies use cognitive ability tests for selection purposes.[23] Figure 10.3 shows some examples of cognitive ability test questions.

Performance Tests   In a performance test, the test taker performs a sample of the job. Most companies use some type of performance test, typically for administrative assistant and clerical positions. The most widely used performance test is the typing test. However, performance tests have been developed for almost every occupation, including managerial positions. Assessment centers are the most notable offshoot of the managerial performance test.[24]

Assessment centers originated during World War II. A typical **assessment center** consists of 10 to 12 candidates who participate in a variety of exercises or situations; some of the exercises involve group interactions, and others are performed individually. Each exercise taps a number of critical managerial dimensions, such as leadership, decision-making skills, and communication ability. Assessors, generally line managers from the organization, observe and record information about the candidates' performance in each exercise. The first organization to use assessment centers was AT&T. Since then, a number of large organizations have used or currently are using the assessment center technique, including the FBI and Sears.

assessment center

A managerial performance test in which candidates participate in a variety of exercises and situations.

Verbal	1. What is the meaning of the word surreptitious?
	a. covert c. lively
	b. winding d. sweet

1. What is the meaning of the word surreptitious?
   - a. covert
   - b. winding
   - c. lively
   - d. sweet

2. How is the noun clause used in the following sentence:
   "I hope that I can learn this game."
   - a. subject
   - b. predicate nominative
   - c. direct object
   - d. object of the preposition

Quantitative

3. Divide 50 by .5 and add 5. What is the result?
   - a. 25
   - b. 30
   - c. 95
   - d. 105

4. What is the value of 144^2?
   - a. 12
   - b. 72
   - c. 288
   - d. 20736

Reasoning

5. _____ is to boat as snow is to _____
   - a. sail, ski
   - b. water, winter
   - c. water, ski
   - d. engine, water

6. Two women played 5 games of chess. Each woman won the same number of games, yet there were no ties. How can this be so?
   - a. There was a forfeit.
   - b. One player cheated.
   - c. They played different people.
   - d. One game was still in progress.

Mechanical

7. If gear A and gear C are both turning counterclockwise, what is happening to gear B?
   - a. It is turning counterclockwise.
   - b. It is turning clockwise.
   - c. It remains stationary.
   - d. The whole system will jam.

A   B   C

Answers: 1a, 2c, 3d, 4d, 5c, 6c, 7b.

SOURCE: Snell, S.A., and Bohlander, G.W. *Managing Human Resources*, 16th ed. Copyright © 2012. Cincinnati, OH: Cengage Learning, Inc. Reproduced by permission. www.cengage.com/permissions

FIGURE 10.3
Sample Measures of Cognitive Ability

Integrity Tests To assess job candidates' honesty, employers may administer integrity tests. Two forms of integrity tests are polygraphs and paper-and-pencil honesty tests. Polygraphs, or lie detector tests, have been banned for most employment purposes.[25] Paper-and-pencil honesty tests are more recent instruments for measuring integrity. These tests include questions such as whether a person has ever thought about stealing and whether he or she believes other people steal ("What percentage of people take more than $1 from their employer?"). Although companies, including Payless ShoeSource, reported that losses due to theft declined following the introduction of integrity tests, the accuracy of these tests is still debatable.[26]

Reliability and Validity Regardless of the method used to select employees, two crucial issues that need to be addressed are a test's reliability and its validity. **Reliability** refers to the consistency of test scores over time and across alternative measurements. For example, if three interviewers talked to the same job candidate but drew very different conclusions about the candidate's abilities, we might suspect that there were problems with the reliability of one or more of the selection tests or interview procedures.

reliability

The consistency of test scores over time and across alternative measurements.

Validity moves beyond reliability to assess the accuracy of the selection test. The most common form of validity, *criterion-related validity*, refers to the degree to which a test actually predicts or correlates with job performance. Questions about validity are one reason (along with ethical and public policy concerns) employers were recently criticized for making current employment a requirement for being hired. At a time when unemployment rates were high and employers were flooded with applications, some companies were screening out people based on their unemployed status. Critics of this practice doubted that being jobless during a recession was highly correlated with poor performance.[27] In general, validity is usually established through studies comparing test performance and job performance for a large enough sample of employees to enable a fair conclusion to be reached. For example, if a high score on a cognitive ability test is strongly predictive of good job performance, then candidates who score well will usually be preferred over those who do not. Still, no test by itself perfectly predicts performance. Managers usually rely on other criteria as well before making a final selection.

validity

The degree to which a selection test predicts or correlates with job performance.

Another form of validity, *content validity*, concerns the degree to which selection tests measure a representative sample of the knowledge, skills, and abilities required for the job. The best-known example of a content-valid test is a keyboarding test for administrative assistants, because keyboarding is a task a person in that position almost always performs. However, to be completely content-valid, the selection process also should measure other skills the assistant would be likely to perform, such as answering the telephone, duplicating and faxing documents, and dealing with the public. Content validity is more subjective (less statistical) than evaluations of criterion-related validity but is no less important, particularly when one is defending employment decisions in court.

Due to tough economic times, workforce reductions in companies throughout the United States have become commonplace. Job seekers are shown here standing in line to attend a job fair in Chicago.

In Practice

COMPANIES USE BIG DATA TO SELECT EMPLOYEES

Today companies are using big data to predict which job candidates will perform best. They use software that analyzes data about their current employees and identifies which qualities are associated with the success. Analysis might find that employees with certain personality traits are less likely to quit or that people who approach a problem in a certain way get better customer satisfaction scores. Then the employer looks for those qualities in its selection process.

Before applying big data, Xerox Corporation had selected workers for its call center based on their having similar job experiences. But data analysis showed that other qualities were at least as important. For example, turnover was lower among people who scored as having creative but not highly inquisitive or empathic personalities. Xerox now tests for these personality traits plus other characteristics of loyal call center workers. In the first six months of using big data for hiring, Xerox's employee turnover dropped by about 20 percent.

Catalyst IT Services uses big data to select candidates for technology teams that work on software for its clients. Programmers applying to Catalyst take an online test that measures not only their answers but *how* they approach complex math and programming problems. Someone who dives into a challenging problem and labors over it until it is solved would bring a different work style to a team than someone who hops around the test, picking off the easiest solutions first. Based on the type of task and client, some teams would need one kind of worker; others would benefit from a different kind. Gathering detailed data about its candidates has helped Catalyst keep employee turnover to about half of the U.S. industry norm.[28]

- What methods should Xerox and Catalyst combine with data analysis for selecting employees? Why?

Workforce Reductions

Unfortunately, staffing decisions do not simply focus on hiring employees. As organizations evolve and markets change, the demand for certain employees rises and falls. Also, some employees simply do not perform at a level required to justify continued employment. For these reasons, managers sometimes must make difficult decisions to terminate their employment.

Layoffs   As a result of the massive restructuring of American industry brought about by mergers and acquisitions, divestiture, and increased competition, many organizations have been downsizing—laying off large numbers of managerial and other employees. As mentioned in Chapter 9, dismissing any employee is tough, but when a company lays off a substantial portion of its workforce, the results can rock the foundations of the organization.[29] The victims of restructuring face all the difficulties of being let go—loss of self-esteem, demoralizing job searches, and the stigma of being out of work. To some extent, employers can help employees with these problems by offering **outplacement,** the process of helping people who have been dismissed from the company regain employment elsewhere. Even then, the impact of layoffs goes further than the employees who leave. For many of the employees who remain with the company, disenchantment, distrust, and lethargy overshadow the comfort of still having a job. In many respects, how management deals with dismissals will affect the productivity and satisfaction of those who remain. A well-thought-out dismissal process eases tensions and helps remaining employees adjust to the new work situation.

Organizations with strong performance evaluation systems benefit because the survivors are less likely to believe the decision was arbitrary. In addition, if care is taken during the actual layoff process—that is, if workers are offered severance pay and help in finding a new job—remaining workers will be comforted. Companies also should avoid stringing out layoffs by dismissing a few workers at a time.

outplacement

The process of helping people who have been dismissed from the company regain employment elsewhere.

Termination   People sometimes get fired for poor performance or other reasons. Should an employer have the right to fire a worker? In 1884, a Tennessee court ruled, "All may dismiss their employee(s) at will for good cause, for no cause, or even for cause morally wrong." The concept that an employee may be fired for any reason is known as **employment-at-will** or *termination-at-will* and was upheld in a 1908 Supreme Court ruling.[30] The logic is that if the employee may quit at any time, the employer is free to dismiss at any time.

Since the mid-1970s, courts in most states have made exceptions to this doctrine. Under the public policy exception (i.e., a ruling designed to protect the public from harm), employees cannot be fired for such actions as refusing to break the law, taking time off for jury duty, or whistleblowing to report illegal company behavior. For example, if a worker reports an environmental violation to a regulatory agency and the company fires him or her, the courts may argue that the firing was unfair because the employee acted for the good of the community. Union contracts that limit an employer's ability to fire without cause are another major exception to the employment-at-will doctrine.

employment-at-will

The legal concept that an employee may be terminated for any reason.

> How management deals with dismissals will affect the productivity and satisfaction of those who remain.

Employers can avoid the pitfalls associated with dismissal by developing progressive and positive disciplinary procedures.[31] By *progressive,* we mean that a manager takes graduated steps in attempting to correct a workplace behavior. For example, an employee who has been absent receives a verbal reprimand for the first offense. A second offense invokes a written reprimand. A third offense results in employee counseling and probation, and a fourth results in a paid leave day to think over the consequences of future rule infractions. The employer is signaling to the employee that this is the last straw. Arbitrators are more likely to side with an employer that fires someone when they believe the company has made sincere efforts to help the person correct his or her behavior.

The **termination interview,** in which the manager discusses the company's position with the employee, is a stressful situation for both parties. Most experts believe that the immediate superior should be the one to deliver the bad news to employees. However, it is a wise precaution to have a third party, such as an HR manager, present to provide guidance and take notes on the meeting. Because announcing a termination is likely to upset the employee and occasionally leads to a lawsuit, the manager should prepare carefully. Preparation should include knowing all the facts of the situation and reviewing any documents to make sure they are consistent with the reason for the termination. During the termination interview, ethics and common sense dictate that the manager should be truthful but respectful, stating the facts and avoiding arguments.[32] Table 10.1 provides some other guidelines for conducting a termination interview.

Legal Issues and Equal Employment Opportunity   Many laws have been passed governing employment decisions and practices. They will directly affect a good part of your day-to-day work as a manager as well as the human resource function of your organization. Most of these laws are designed to protect job candidates and employees against discrimination or sexual harassment and to establish standards of pay and hours worked for certain classes of employee. For example, the 1938 *Fair Labor Standards Act* (FLSA), among other provisions, creates two

termination interview

A discussion between a manager and an employee about the employee's dismissal.

Do's	Don'ts
• Make termination the last step in a clear and fair process, being certain you have the facts.	• Don't spring a termination on an employee as a total surprise.
• Be sure the person terminating the employee is the employee's direct supervisor.	• Don't start a meeting unprepared, causing the terminated employee to wait awkwardly while you find answers or call in an HR representative.
• Be prepared with answers to basic questions such as the official end date and any severance benefits.	• Don't beat around the bush; state the termination simply and briefly.
• Consult with the human resource department to identify any benefits available; give the employee a written list of information about benefits and policies.	• Don't get caught up in responding to the employee's emotions or views about fairness; focus on practical realities—the need to move on.
• Invite a trained HR representative to attend the meeting.	• Don't argue with the employee or apologize.
• Listen respectfully.	• Don't offer to help the employee find another job, assuming you cannot honestly give a glowing reference.

TABLE 10.1
Advice on Termination

SOURCES: Ron Ashkenas, "If You Have to Fire an Employee—Here's How to Do It Right," *Forbes,* March 11, 2013, http://www.forbes.com; Jeff Haden, "The Best Way to Fire an Employee," *Inc.,* March 19, 2012, http://www.inc.com; Melissa Korn, "The Best Ways to Fire Somebody," *The Wall Street Journal,* October 26, 2012, http://online.wsj.com.

employee categories: exempt and nonexempt. Employees are normally exempt from overtime pay if they have considerable discretion in how they carry out their jobs and if their jobs require them to exercise independent judgment. Managers usually fall in this category. Nonexempt employees are usually paid by the hour and must be paid overtime if they work more than 40 hours in a week. As a manager, you will almost certainly need to specify the exempt or nonexempt status of anyone you hire.

The 1964 *Civil Rights Act* prohibits discrimination in employment based on race, sex, color, national origin, and religion. Title VII of the act specifically forbids discrimination in such employment practices as recruitment, hiring, discharge, promotion, compensation, and access to training.[33] The *Americans with Disabilities Act*, passed in 1990, prohibits employment discrimination against people with disabilities. Recovering alcoholics and drug abusers, cancer patients in remission, and AIDS patients are covered by this legislation. The 1991 *Civil Rights Act* strengthened all these protections and permitted punitive damages to be imposed on companies that violate them.

Failure to comply with any of these laws may expose the organization to charges of unfair practices, expensive lawsuits, and civil and even criminal penalties in some cases. For example, Walmart recently paid $17.5 million to settle a lawsuit in which employees said the company had discriminated against African American workers seeking positions as truck drivers. According to these workers, the company had placed stiffer requirements on African American job candidates. In another case, Union Pacific Railroad paid $75,000 to settle a sex discrimination lawsuit in which a woman was not hired as system material foreman, even though she had more experience than men who applied for the position. And Nordstrom paid $292,500 to settle a lawsuit in which Florida workers said their manager had harassed them because of their race.[34]

adverse impact

When a seemingly neutral employment practice has a disproportionately negative effect on a protected group.

One common reason employers are sued is **adverse impact**—when a seemingly neutral employment practice has a disproportionately negative effect on a group protected by the Civil Rights Act.[35] For example, if equal numbers of qualified men and women apply for jobs but a particular employment test results in far fewer women being hired, the test may be considered to cause an adverse impact and, therefore, be subject to challenge on that basis.

Because of the importance of these issues, many companies have established procedures to ensure compliance with labor and equal opportunity laws. For example, companies frequently monitor and compare salaries by race, gender, length of service, and other categories to make sure employees across all groups are being fairly paid. Written policies can also help ensure fair and legal practices in the workplace, although the company may also have to demonstrate a record of actually following those procedures and making sure they are implemented. In this sense, smart and effective management practices not only help managers motivate employees to do their best work but often help provide legal protection as well. For example, managers who provide their employees with regular, specific evaluations can often prevent misunderstandings that can lead to lawsuits. And a written record of those evaluations is often useful in demonstrating fair and objective treatment.

Many other important staffing laws affect employment practices. For example, the *Age Discrimination in Employment Act* of 1967 and its amendments in 1978 and 1986 prohibit discrimination against people age 40 and over. One reason for this legislation was the common practice of dismissing older workers to replace them with younger workers who were not as highly paid. The *Worker Adjustment and Retraining Notification Act* of 1989, commonly known as the *WARN Act* or *Plant Closing Bill*, requires covered employers to give affected employees 60 days' written notice of plant closings or mass layoffs. Table 10.2 summarizes many of these major employment laws.

TABLE 10.2   U.S. Equal Employment Laws

Act	Major Provisions	Enforcement and Remedies
Fair Labor Standards Act (1938)	Creates exempt (salaried) and nonexempt (hourly) employee categories, governing overtime and other rules; sets minimum wage, child labor laws.	Enforced by Department of Labor, private action to recover lost wages; civil and criminal penalties also possible.
Equal Pay Act (1963)	Prohibits gender-based pay discrimination between two jobs substantially similar in skill, effort, responsibility, and working conditions.	Fines up to $10,000, imprisonment up to 6 months, or both; enforced by Equal Employment Opportunity Commission (EEOC); private actions for double damages up to 3 years' wages, liquidated damages, reinstatement, or promotion.
Title VII of Civil Rights Act (1964)	Prohibits discrimination based on race, sex, color, religion, or national origin in employment decisions: hiring, pay, working conditions, promotion, discipline, or discharge.	Enforced by EEOC; private actions, back pay, front pay, reinstatement, restoration of seniority and pension benefits, attorneys' fees and costs.
Executive Orders 11246 and 11375 (1965)	Requires equal opportunity clauses in federal contracts; prohibits employment discrimination by federal contractors based on race, color, religion, sex, or national origin.	Established Office of Federal Contract Compliance Programs (OFCCP) to investigate violations; empowered to terminate violator's federal contracts.
Age Discrimination in Employment Act (1967)	Prohibits employment discrimination based on age for persons over 40 years; restricts mandatory retirement.	EEOC enforcement; private actions for reinstatement, back pay, front pay, restoration of seniority and pension benefits; double unpaid wages for willful violations; attorneys' fees and costs.
Vocational Rehabilitation Act (1973)	Requires affirmative action by all federal contractors for persons with disabilities; defines disabilities as physical or mental impairments that substantially limit life activities.	Federal contractors must consider hiring disabled persons capable of performance after reasonable accommodations.
Americans with Disabilities Act (1990)	Extends affirmative action provisions of Vocational Rehabilitation Act to private employers; requires workplace modifications to facilitate disabled employees; prohibits discrimination against disabled.	EEOC enforcement; private actions for Title VII remedies.
Civil Rights Act (1991)	Clarifies Title VII requirements: disparate treatment impact suits, business necessity, job relatedness; shifts burden of proof to employer; permits punitive damages and jury trials.	Punitive damages limited to sliding scale only in intentional discrimination based on sex, religion, and disabilities.
Family and Medical Leave Act (1991)	Requires 12 weeks' unpaid leave for medical or family needs: paternity, family member illness.	Private actions for lost wages and other expenses, reinstatement.

Developing the Workforce

Bottom Line

Training improves employee quality. *How might you measure quality improvements from training salespeople?*

Today's competitive environment requires managers to upgrade the skills and performance of employees continually—and their own. Such constant improvement increases both personal and organizational effectiveness. It makes organization members more useful in their current jobs and prepares them to take on new responsibilities. And it helps the organization as a whole handle new challenges and take advantage of new methods and technologies that emerge. Developing the workforce in this way involves training and development activities. It also involves appraising employees' performance and giving them effective feedback so they will be motivated to perform at their best. We will discuss each of these activities in turn.

Cold Stone Creamery spends a portion of its training budget in developing computerized simulations to show how employee actions affect store performance. The company uses computer games because they are familiar and attractive to its young employees.

Training and Development

U.S. businesses spend more than $125 billion annually to provide their employees with formal training. The greatest share of that spending goes to training that the organization itself delivers to its employees. The remainder is spent on training by outsiders, including payments for training companies and tuition reimbursement.[36]

Fortune 500 companies such as General Electric and Procter & Gamble have invested heavily in training. IBM's annual training costs have at times exceeded Harvard University's annual operating expenses. But competitive pressures require companies to consider the most efficient training methods. That means traditional classroom settings are often giving way to computerized methods.

The American Society for Training and Development has argued that as a percentage of total payroll, the average organizational investment in training is too small.[37] This lack of commitment is a great concern because today's jobs require more education, but the education level of U.S. workers has not kept pace. What's more, companies need to ensure that employees who have survived layoffs can lead their organizations through tough times.

Overview of the Training Process Although we use the general term *training* here, training sometimes is distinguished from development. **Training** usually refers to teaching lower-level employees how to perform their present jobs, whereas **development** involves teaching managers and professional employees broader skills needed for their present and future jobs.

Phase one of training usually starts with a **needs assessment**. Managers conduct an analysis to identify the jobs, people, and departments for which training is necessary. Job analysis and performance measurements are useful for this purpose.

Phase two involves the design of training programs. Based on needs assessment, training objectives and content can be established. For example, in support of Verizon's corporate goals for operational excellence, the company's learning and development team set a goal to make the sales support team "an industry-leading technical sales support team capable of selling/supporting complex solutions" for Verizon's business customers. The team would do this by developing and presenting a training program in which the employees earn a Data Solutions Certification by mastering 11 competencies—technical skills needed for selling data solutions to businesses.[38]

Phase three involves decisions about the training methods to be used and whether the training will be provided on or off the job. Common training methods include

training

Teaching lower-level employees how to perform their present jobs.

development

Helping managers and professional employees learn the broad skills needed for their present and future jobs.

needs assessment

An analysis identifying the jobs, people, and departments for which training is necessary.

lectures, role-playing, business simulation, behavior modeling (watching a video and imitating what is observed), conferences, vestibule training (practicing in a simulated job environment), and apprenticeships. The method should be well suited to the objectives defined in phase two. Verizon sales support employees earning a Data Solutions Certificate participated in 45 hours of technical training presented through a combination of instructor-led training (both in classrooms and virtually, over the Internet) and online training, and they prepared a sales presentation, which they presented to management. Besides this, the employees had to meet or exceed their sales quota for the period.[39] As shown in Figure 10.4, a major share of training is conducted electronically (for example, with online videos, games, and quizzes). Computer-based training is easy and inexpensive to deliver, can be provided anywhere an employee has access to a computer, and can be tailored to a trainee's responses. Well-designed computer training also can get trainees highly involved in learning. A recent study found that trainees learned better from an interactive video game than they did from other forms of instruction.[40] Another popular training method is job rotation, by which employees are assigned to different jobs in the organization to broaden their experience and improve their skills. It is frequently applied to managers as well as lower-level employees. In fact, smart managers often request assignment to jobs where they can be challenged and their skills broadened.

Finally, *phase four* of training should evaluate the program's effectiveness. Measures of effectiveness include employee reactions (surveys), learning (tests), improved behavior on the job, and bottom-line results (e.g., an increase in sales or reduction in defect rates following the training program).

Types of Training   Companies invest in training to enhance individual performance and organizational productivity. Programs to improve an employee's computer, technical, or communication skills are quite common, and some types of training have become fairly standard across many organizations. **Orientation training** is typically used to familiarize new employees with their new jobs, work units, and the organization in general. Done well, orientation training has a number of benefits, including lower employee turnover, increased morale, better productivity, and lower recruiting and training costs.

   Team training has taken on more importance as organizations reorganize to facilitate individuals working together. Team training teaches employees the skills they need to work together and facilitates their interaction. After General Mills acquired Pillsbury, it used a team training program called Brand Champions to combine the marketing expertise of the two companies and share knowledge among employees handling various functions such as sales and research and development. Most of the time, trainees engaged in team exercises to analyze brands, target customers, and develop marketing messages.[41]

orientation training

Training designed to introduce new employees to the company and familiarize them with policies, procedures, culture, and the like.

team training

Training that provides employees with the skills and perspectives they need to collaborate with others.

FIGURE 10.4
Training Delivery Methods: Percent of Total Hours

1.1%   2.0%
24.7%
45.2%
27.0%

■ Classroom, instructor-led
■ Blended learning (classroom plus computer methods)
■ Computer-based or online
■ Mobile devices
■ Not specified

SOURCE: Based on data from "2012 Training Industry Report," *Training*, November/December 2012, EBSCOhost, http://web. ebscohost.com.

diversity training

Programs that focus on identifying and reducing hidden biases against people with differences and developing the skills needed to manage a diversified workforce.

Diversity training focuses on building awareness of diversity issues and providing the skills employees need to work with others who are different from them. This topic is so important that the next chapter is devoted solely to managing diversity.

Today's decentralized and leaner organizations put more demands and responsibility on managers, as has an increasingly competitive environment. And as managers rise in the organization, their technical skills generally become less important than their ability to motivate others. For these reasons, management training programs have become another widely used development tool. Such programs often seek to improve managers' people skills—their ability to delegate effectively, increase the motivation of their subordinates, and communicate and inspire the achievement of organization goals. Coaching—being trained by a superior—is usually the most effective and direct management development tool. Managers may also participate in training programs that are used for all employees, such as job rotation, or attend seminars and courses specifically designed to help them improve their supervisory skills or prepare them for future promotion. As you read "Management Connection: Progress Report," consider how Google's management training and coaching complement its methods for hiring.

MANAGER'S BRIEF

PROGRESS REPORT

ONWARD

Management Connection

HOW GOOGLE HIRES AND TRAINS

The Google search engine provides a model for how the company has successfully grown and continued attracting the best talent. Much as the search engine sorts through vast amounts of data to deliver the most relevant information, its human resource strategy involves analyzing data about employees and the impact of how they are managed.

In terms of hiring, Google's strategy is to position the company as a highly attractive place to work, receive a flood of applications, and make collaborative decisions about which applicants will fit best with Google's demanding and creative culture. In the tight labor market for experts in computer programming and online marketing, even a popular employer such as Google must recruit actively. Google has expanded its recruiting on college campuses and offers generously paid summer internships. It hosts regular open houses, provides speakers about its projects, and posts information about Google jobs on YouTube, blogs, and Twitter feeds.

The selection process is famously demanding and occasionally quirky. Candidates interview with several Google employees. The interviewers compile an extensive file of information to use in making a group decision, a process aimed at avoiding selection of candidates that merely resemble the interviewer. To select creative and intellectually talented people, the interviews include questions aimed at stimulating creative thinking—say, why manhole covers are round or how you would escape if you were

shrunk to a tiny size and dropped into a blender. Data analysis helps Google refine the process. In the past, a candidate might undergo a dozen interviews or more; data showed that interviews beyond four provide little value, so five is now the maximum number.

With regard to training, data-driven decisions match topics to particular employees for whom the training will deliver meaningful results. For management training, Laszlo Bock's People Operations group studied data from employee surveys, managers' performance appraisals, and nominations for best-manager awards. They identified eight management behaviors associated with success in leading teams and retaining employees. They developed training programs for each behavior, and they recommend programs to individual managers based on each manager's performance. Management training courses also are recommended based on data showing the skills that are relevant in particular functions or at particular stages of a manager's career. Formal training sessions are backed up with customized reminders and recommendations related to events in the manager's department.[42]

- Discuss your impression of the reliability and validity of Google's selection methods.
- How could Google's approach to management training address the training needs of its nonmanagement employees?

Performance Appraisal

One of the most important responsibilities you will have as a manager is **performance appraisal (PA),** the assessment of an employee's job performance. Done well, it can help employees improve their performance, pay, and chances for promotion; foster communication between managers and employees; and increase the employees' and the organization's effectiveness. Done poorly, it actually can have a negative effect—it can cause resentment, reduce motivation, diminish performance, and even expose the organization to legal action.

Performance appraisal has two basic purposes. First, appraisal serves an administrative purpose. It provides managers with the information they need to make salary, promotion, and dismissal decisions; helps employees understand and accept the basis of those decisions; and, if necessary, provides documentation that can justify those decisions in court. Second, and at least as important, appraisal serves a developmental purpose. The information gathered in the appraisal can be used to identify and plan the additional training, learning, experience, or other improvement employees require. In addition, the manager's feedback and coaching based on the appraisal help employees improve their day-to-day performance and can help prepare them for greater responsibilities in the future.

What Do You Appraise?

Performance appraisals can assess three basic categories of employee performance: traits, behaviors, and results. Trait appraisals involve subjective judgments about employee characteristics related to performance. They contain dimensions such as initiative, leadership, and attitude, and they ask raters to indicate how much of each trait an employee possesses. Usually the manager will use a numerical ratings scale to specify the extent to which an employee possesses the particular traits being measured. For example, if the measured trait is attitude, the employee might be rated anywhere from 1 (very negative attitude) to 5 (very positive attitude). Trait scales are quite common because they are simple to use and provide a standard measure for all employees. But they are often not valid as performance measures. Because they tend to be ambiguous as well as highly subjective—does the employee really have a bad attitude, or is he or she just shy?—they often lead to personal bias and may not be suitable for providing useful feedback.

Behavioral appraisals, although still subjective, focus more on observable aspects of performance. They were developed in response to the problems of trait appraisals. These scales focus on specific, prescribed behaviors that can help ensure that all parties understand what the ratings are really measuring. Because they are less ambiguous, they also can help provide useful feedback. Figure 10.5 contains an example of a behaviorally anchored rating scale (BARS) for evaluating quality.

Another common behaviorally focused approach is the critical incident technique. In this technique, the manager keeps a regular log and records each significant behavior by the subordinate that reflects the quality of his or her performance. ("Juanita impressed the client with her effective presentation today." "Joe was late with his report.") This approach can be subjective as well as time-consuming, and it may give some employees the feeling that everything they do is being recorded. But it does have the advantage of reminding managers in advance of a performance review what the employee actually did.

Results appraisals tend to be more objective and can focus on production data such as sales volume (for a salesperson), units produced (for a line worker), or profits (for a manager). One approach to results appraisals—called **management by objectives (MBO)**—involves a subordinate and a supervisor agreeing in advance on specific performance

---

LO 5

performance appraisal (PA)

Assessment of an employee's job performance.

management by objectives (MBO)

A process in which objectives set by a subordinate and a supervisor must be reached within a given time period.

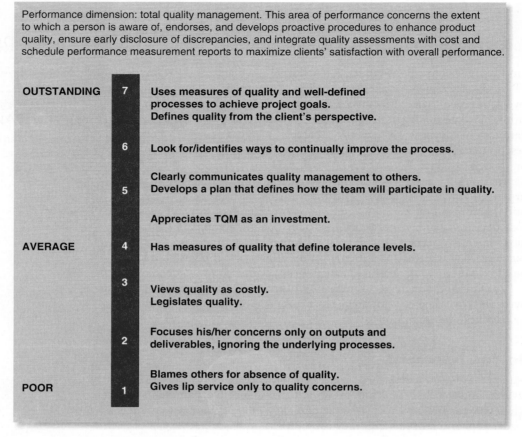

Performance dimension: total quality management. This area of performance concerns the extent to which a person is aware of, endorses, and develops proactive procedures to enhance product quality, ensure early disclosure of discrepancies, and integrate quality assessments with cost and schedule performance measurement reports to maximize clients' satisfaction with overall performance.

OUTSTANDING   7   Uses measures of quality and well-defined processes to achieve project goals.
Defines quality from the client's perspective.

6   Look for/identifies ways to continually improve the process.

5   Clearly communicates quality management to others.
Develops a plan that defines how the team will participate in quality.

Appreciates TQM as an investment.

AVERAGE   4   Has measures of quality that define tolerance levels.

3   Views quality as costly.
Legislates quality.

2   Focuses his/her concerns only on outputs and deliverables, ignoring the underlying processes.

Blames others for absence of quality.
POOR   1   Gives lip service only to quality concerns.

SOURCE: Landy, Jacobs, and Associates. Used with permission.

FIGURE 10.5
Example of BARS Used for Evaluating Quality

goals (objectives). They then develop a plan that describes the time frame and criteria for determining whether the objectives have been reached. The aim is to agree on a set of objectives that are clear, specific, and reachable. For example, an objective for a salesperson might be "Increase sales by 25 percent during the following year." An objective for a computer programmer might be "Complete two projects within the next six months."

MBO has several important advantages. First, it avoids the biases and measurement difficulties of trait and behavioral appraisals. At the end of the review period, the employee either has or has not achieved the specified objective. The employee is judged on actual job performance. Second, because the employee and manager have agreed on the objective at the outset, the employee is likely to be more committed to the outcome, and there is less chance for misunderstanding. Third, because the employee is directly responsible for achieving the objective, MBO can be useful when managers want to empower employees to adapt their behavior to achieve the desired results. But the approach has disadvantages as well. It can result in unrealistic objectives being set, frustrating the employee and the manager. The objectives can also be too rigid, leaving the employee with insufficient flexibility should circumstances change. Finally, MBO often focuses too much on short-term achievement at the expense of long-term goals.

None of these performance appraisal systems is easy to conduct properly, and all have drawbacks that must be guarded against. In choosing an appraisal method, the following guidelines may prove helpful:

1. Base performance standards on job analysis.
2. Communicate performance standards to employees.

3. Evaluate employees on specific performance-related behaviors rather than on a single global or overall measure.
4. Document the PA process carefully.
5. If possible, use more than one rater (discussed in the next section).
6. Develop a formal appeal process.
7. Always take legal considerations into account.[43]

Who Should Do the Appraisal?

Just as multiple methods can be used to gather performance appraisal information, several sources can provide PA information. Managers and supervisors are the traditional source of appraisal information because they are often in the best position to observe an employee's performance. However, companies are also turning to peers and team members to provide input to the performance appraisal. Peers and team members often see different dimensions of performance and are often best at identifying leadership potential and interpersonal skills.

One increasingly popular source of appraisal is a person's subordinates. Appraisal by subordinates has been used by companies such as Xerox and IBM to give superiors feedback on how their employees view them. Often this information is given in confidence to the manager and not shared with superiors. Even so, this approach can make managers uncomfortable initially, but the feedback they get is often extremely useful and can help them significantly improve their management style. Because this process gives employees power over their bosses, it is generally used for development purposes only, not for salary or promotion decisions.

Internal and external customers also are used as sources of performance appraisal information, particularly for companies, such as Ford and Honda, that are focused on total quality management. External customers have been used for some time to appraise restaurant employees, but internal customers can include anyone inside the organization who depends on an employee's work output. Finally, it is usually a good idea for employees to evaluate their own performance. Although self-appraisals may be biased upward, the process of self-evaluation helps increase the employee's involvement in the review process and is a starting point for establishing future goals.

Because each source of PA information has some limitations, and because different people may see different aspects of performance, Shell, Eastman Kodak, and many other companies have used approaches that involve more than one source for appraisal information. In a process known as **360-degree appraisal,** feedback is obtained from subordinates, peers, and superiors—every level involved with the employee. Often the person being rated can select the appraisers, subject to a manager's approval, with the understanding that the individual appraisals are kept confidential; returned forms might not include the name of the appraiser, for example, and the results may be consolidated for each level.

The 360-degree appraisal offers many advantages. It provides a much fuller picture of the employee's strengths and weaknesses, and it often captures qualities other appraisal methods miss. For example, an employee may have a difficult relationship with his or her supervisor yet be highly regarded by peers and subordinates. The approach can lead to significant improvement, with employees often very motivated to improve their ratings. Improvements in management performance following 360-degree appraisals have been observed in various countries, but cultural differences can affect the impact of this method. Using the cultural measures defined by Geert Hofstede (described in Chapter 6), researchers found that 360-degree appraisals were most effective with managers in cultures that were individualistic and had relatively low power distance.[44] On the downside,

During 360-degree appraisals, every level involved with the employee provides feedback.

360-degree appraisal

Process of using multiple sources of appraisal to gain a comprehensive perspective on one's performance.

employees are often unwilling to rate their colleagues harshly, so a certain uniformity of ratings may result. In addition, the 360-degree appraisal is less useful than more objective criteria, such as financial targets, in measuring performance. Its objective is usually the employee's development, not to provide a basis for administrative decisions such as raises. For those, appraisal methods like MBO are more appropriate.[45]

How Do You Give Employees Feedback?

Appraisals are most effective when they are based on an ongoing relationship with employees and not just a top-down formal judgment issued once a year. Managers of sports teams do not wait until the season is over to perform an appraisal. Instead they work with team members throughout the season, and with the team as a whole, to improve the team's performance. Similarly, in high-functioning organizations informal appraisal and feedback are constantly taking place. Managers discuss the goals of the organization regularly and often to create a shared understanding of the job performance those goals require. They try to create an atmosphere in which they and their employees are working together on a common agenda. And they communicate with their employees on a day-to-day basis, praising or coaching as appropriate and together assessing progress toward goals. When managers and employees have open communication and employees feel fairly and effectively managed, the kind of appraisal they receive should rarely come as a surprise to them.

> In high-functioning organizations, informal appraisal and feedback are constantly taking place.

Giving PA feedback can be a stressful task for both managers and subordinates. The purposes of PA conflict to some degree. Providing growth and development requires understanding and support; however, the manager must be impersonal and be able to make tough decisions. Employees want to know how they are doing, but typically they are uncomfortable about getting feedback. Finally, the organization's need to make HR decisions conflicts with the individual employee's need to maintain a positive image.[46] These conflicts often make a PA interview difficult; therefore, managers should conduct such interviews thoughtfully.

There is no one best way to do a PA interview. In general, appraisal feedback works best when it is specific and constructive—related to clear goals or behaviors and clearly intended to help the employee rather than simply criticize. Managers have an interest not just in rating performance but in raising it, and effective appraisals take that into account. In addition, the appraisal is likely to be more meaningful and satisfying when the manager gives the employee an opportunity to discuss his or her performance and respond to the appraisal.

One of the most difficult interviews takes place with an employee who is performing poorly. Here is a useful PA interview format to use when an employee is performing below acceptable standards:

1. Summarize the employee's specific performance. Describe the performance in behavioral or outcome terms, such as sales or absenteeism. Don't say the employee has a poor attitude; rather, explain which employee behaviors indicate a poor attitude.
2. Describe the expectations and standards and be specific.
3. Determine the causes for the low performance; get the employee's input.
4. Discuss solutions to the problem and have the employee play a major role in the process.
5. Agree to a solution. As a supervisor, you have input into the solution. Raise issues and questions but also provide support.
6. Agree to a timetable for improvement.
7. Document the meeting.

Bottom Line

Effective feedback raises employee performance. *What kind of feedback is most likely to be effective?*

Follow-up meetings may be needed. Here are some guidelines for giving feedback to an average employee:

1. Summarize the employee's performance and be specific.
2. Explain why the employee's work is important to the organization.
3. Thank the employee for doing the job.
4. Raise any relevant issues, such as areas for improvement.
5. Express confidence in the employee's future good performance.

Designing Reward Systems

Another major set of HRM activities involves reward systems. Most of this section will be devoted to monetary rewards such as pay and fringe benefits. (We discuss other motivational tools in Chapter 13.) Although traditionally pay has been the primary monetary reward considered, in recent years benefits have received increased attention. Benefits currently make up a far greater percentage of the total payroll than they did in past decades.[47] The typical employer today pays about 30 percent of payroll costs in benefits. Throughout most of the past two decades, benefits costs have risen faster than wages and salaries, fueled by the rapidly rising cost of medical care. Accordingly, employers are attempting to reduce benefits costs, even as their value to employees is rising. Benefits are also receiving more management attention because of their increased complexity. Many new types of benefits are now available, and tax laws affect myriad fringe benefits such as health insurance and pension plans.

LO 6

> The typical employer today pays about 30 percent of payroll costs in benefits.

Pay Decisions

Reward systems can serve the strategic purposes of attracting, motivating, and retaining people. The wages paid to employees are based on a complex set of forces. Beyond the body of laws governing compensation, a number of basic decisions must be made in choosing the appropriate pay plan. Figure 10.6 illustrates some of the factors that influence the wage mix.

Three types of decisions are crucial for designing an effective pay plan: pay level, pay structure, and individual pay.

Pay level refers to the choice of whether to be a high-, average-, or low-paying company. Compensation is a major cost for any organization, so low wages can be

Internal factors

Compensation policy of organization

Worth of job

Employee's relative worth

Employer's ability to pay

Wage mix

External factors

Conditions of the labor market

Area wage rates

Cost of living

Collective bargaining

Legal requirements

FIGURE 10.6

Factors Affecting the Wage Mix

SOURCE: Snell, S.A., and Bohlander, G.W. *Managing Human Resources*, 16th ed. Copyright © 2012. Cincinnati, OH: Cengage Learning, Inc. Reproduced by permission. www.cengage.com/permissions

justified on a short-term financial basis. But being the high-wage employer—the highest-paying company in the region—ensures that the company will attract many applicants. Being a wage leader may be important during times of low unemployment or intense competition.

The *pay structure* decision is the choice of how to price different jobs within the organization. Jobs that are similar in worth usually are grouped into job families. A pay grade, with a floor and a ceiling, is established for each job family. Figure 10.7 illustrates a hypothetical pay structure.

Finally, *individual pay decisions* concern different pay rates for jobs of similar worth within the same family. Differences in pay within job families are decided in two ways. First, some jobs are occupied by individuals with more seniority than others. Second, some people may be better performers who are therefore deserving of a higher level of pay. Setting an individual's pay lower than that of coworkers—like choosing an overall low pay level—may become more difficult for employers to sustain in the future as more employees use online resources such as Salary.com and PayScale to check whether their pay is above or below the average amount for similar job titles.[48]

Unlike many other types of decisions in organizations, decisions about pay, especially at the individual level, often are kept confidential. Is that practice advantageous for organizations? Surprisingly, there is little evidence about this practice even though it affects almost every private sector employee.[49] Some possible ways the organization may benefit from keeping pay decisions secret are by avoiding conflicts, protecting individuals' privacy, and reducing the likelihood that employees will leave to seek better pay if they are earning less than the average for their position. However, if decisions about pay are kept secret, employees may worry that decisions are unfair and may be less motivated because the link between performance and pay is unclear. Also, in an economic sense, labor markets are less efficient when information is unavailable, which can reduce organizations' ability to get the best workers at the optimum rate

FIGURE 10.7
Pay Structure

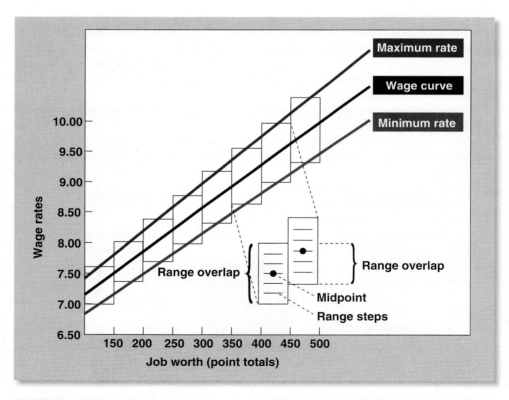

SOURCE: From Arthur Sherman, George Bohlander, and Scott Snell, *Managing Human Resources,* 11th ed. Copyright 1998 South-Western, a part of Cengage Learning, Inc. Reproduced by permission. www.cengage.com/permissions

of pay. Finally, as a practical matter, younger employees today are used to living in a world where most data are readily retrievable online (including pay data on websites such as Glassdoor.com), and many are dismissive of requests for confidentiality. Given these possible pros and cons of pay secrecy, do you think this practice is wise? Is it ethical? And what about you—do you want to know how much your coworkers earn?

Incentive Systems and Variable Pay

Various incentive systems have been devised to encourage and motivate employees to be more productive.[50] (See Chapter 13 for more discussion of rewarding performance.) Individual incentive plans are the most common type of incentive plan. An individual incentive system consists of an objective standard against which a worker's performance is compared. Pay is determined by the employee's performance. Individual incentive plans are used frequently in sales jobs—for example, a salesperson will receive extra compensation for exceeding a sales target. Another widely used individual incentive tool is management bonuses. If effectively designed, individual incentive plans can be highly motivating. Some companies, including Walmart, are even beginning to apply them for nonmanagers. Walmart hopes that using bonuses to reward hourly employees for meeting sales, profit, and inventory targets at their stores each quarter will build employees' job satisfaction and reduce turnover.[51]

Several types of group incentive plans, in which pay is based on group performance, are increasingly used today. The idea behind these plans is to give employees a sense of shared participation and even ownership in the performance of the firm. Gainsharing plans concentrate on rewarding employees for increasing productivity or saving money in areas under their direct control.[52] For example, if the usual waste allowance in a production line has been 5 percent and the company wants production employees to try to reduce that number, the company may offer to split any savings gained with the employees.

Profit-sharing plans are usually implemented in the division or organization as a whole, although some incentives may still be tailored to unit performance. In most companies, the profit-sharing plan is based on a formula for allocating an annual amount to each employee if the company exceeds a specified profit target. One disadvantage of profit-sharing plans is that they do not reward individual performance. However, they do give all employees a stake in the company's success and motivate efforts to improve the company's profitability.

Bottom Line
Incentives can help raise all aspects of organization performance. *Think about the activities of a store employee. What could a Walmart employee do to earn a bonus for meeting quarterly profit goals?*

In Practice

LARGE BONUSES FOR HIGHER-LEVEL EMPLOYEES

Sprint CEO Dan Hesse wants all his employees to be clear about what matters and what they should focus on. He defined a three-pronged strategy for the wireless provider: (1) improve the customer experience; (2) strengthen the brand; and (3) generate cash, increase profits. The HR department works with managers to ensure that everyone's objectives are in line with this strategy because part of each employee's pay is tied to meeting his or her goals. The size of this annual bonus rises with experience and level in the company. For entry-level employees, the bonus is 5 percent of their total pay; for senior executives, that share rises to 50 percent or more.

To make the incentive pay fair, managers no longer have a subjective 5-point rating scale to measure whether employees are eligible. Rather, each employee is scored as having met or not met each of three objectives linked to the strategy. Employees who don't meet an objective are supposed to receive coaching on how to do better next time—and managers' own performance reviews include whether they coached all their employees.[53]

- Why do you think bonuses are larger for higher-level employees? How does that relate to the incentive this kind of pay is intended to provide?

When objective performance measures are not available but the company still wants to base pay on performance, it uses a merit pay system. Individuals' pay raises and bonuses are based on the merit rating they receive from their boss. In Rochester, Minnesota, the school superintendent's bonus is an example of merit pay. The school board rates the superintendent's performance in several predetermined areas, such as promoting teamwork between the board and school district staff and supporting the board in developing a strategic plan. In a recent year, the superintendent received an average score of 3 on a four-point scale, so the board awarded him three-quarters of the maximum bonus.[54]

Executive Pay and Stock Options

In recent years, the issues of executive pay and stock options, particularly for CEOs, have become major sources of controversy. One reason is that the gap between the pay of top executives and the average pay of employees has widened considerably. In the mid-1960s in the United States, the average company paid its CEO roughly 20 times as much as it paid its average nonmanagement worker. Since then, the ratio of CEO pay to average-worker pay soared to a peak of around 400-to-1 in 2000 and more recently has been around 200-to-1. Further adding to concern is a widespread belief that the pay difference is much wider in the United States. However, some of those claims may be exaggerated. A recent analysis of companies in countries where corporations must disclose executive pay found a difference among countries, but it was a relatively modest 26 percent advantage for U.S. CEOs, down from 58 percent in 2003.[55]

Besides the difference between executive and average-worker pay, the sheer size and growth of CEO compensation have also contributed to criticism by shareholders and the general public. Top-earning CEOs today can make tens of millions of dollars a year—sometimes even at companies that have performed poorly and even, recently, at companies that received government help during the financial crisis. Still, it's important to keep in mind that the huge awards that make headlines are not necessarily typical. In a recent year, CEOs of companies in the Standard & Poor's stock index earned on average $4.5 million, but the median was $2.5 million because a few executives with far higher earnings pushed the average higher. Also, if we consider only the biggest companies, those in the Standard & Poor's 500, CEO pay averaged $9 million because CEOs of the biggest companies tend to earn more than most CEOs.[56]

Even with these considerations, $9 million or even $2.5 million is a lot of money to earn in one year, and the amount of compensation paid to top executives is growing. Although salaries and bonuses have risen at a moderate pace, the fastest-growing part of executive compensation comes from stock grants and stock options. Such options give the holder the right to purchase shares of stock at a specified price. For example, if the company's stock price is $8 a share, the company may award a manager the right to purchase a specific number of shares of company stock at that price. If the price of the stock rises to, say, $10 a share after a specified holding period—usually three years or more—the manager can exercise the option. He or she can purchase the shares from the company at $8 per share, sell the shares on the stock market at $10, and keep the difference. (Of course, if the stock price never rises above $8, the options will be worthless.) For many top managers, large option grants became a major source of additional compensation. Adding to the scrutiny over this practice is the striking number of situations in which options were dated just before the company's stock price rose, increasing their value—and the suspicion that at least some of these options were backdated unethically to make them more valuable rather than give executives the incentive to improve the company's performance in the stock market.[57]

Companies issue options to managers to align their interests with those of the company's owners, the shareholders. The assumption is that managers will become even more focused on making the company successful, leading to a rise in its stock price. Assuming that the executives continue to own their stock year after year, the amount of their wealth that is tied to the company's performance—and their incentive to work hard for the company—should continually increase.[58] However, many critics have suggested that excessive use of options encouraged executives to focus on short-term results to drive up the price of their stock at the expense of their firm's long-run competitiveness. Others suggested that lucrative options motivated questionable or even unethical behavior, as we mentioned in Chapter 2. More recently, a plunging stock market highlighted another problem with stock options: many options became essentially worthless, so they failed to reward employees.[59] Evidence suggests, however, that corporations readily adjust executives' total compensation packages accordingly. A review of compensation to the five highest-paid executives at 3,000 companies found that after the financial crisis, performance-based pay continued to rise, becoming a majority of the pay package, but shifted away from options toward stock grants and bonuses.

Traditionally, companies incurred no expense when they issued stock options. This was another reason options were considered an attractive incentive tool and were sometimes even issued to nonmanagers. However, because of corporate scandals and to curb excessive use of options, the rules were changed in 2004 so that options have to be treated as an expense by companies that issue them. This means that compensation committees have to focus more on whether options motivate executives to focus on what is important for the company's future.

Employee Benefits

Like pay systems, employee benefit plans are subject to regulation. Employee benefits are divided into those required by law and those optional for an employer.

The three basic required benefits are workers' compensation, Social Security, and unemployment insurance. Workers' compensation provides financial support to employees suffering a work-related injury or illness. Social Security, as established in the Social Security Act of 1935, provides financial support to retirees; in subsequent amendments, the act was expanded to cover disabled employees. The funds come from payments made by employers, employees, and self-employed workers. Unemployment insurance provides financial support to employees who are laid off for reasons they cannot control. Companies that have terminated fewer employees pay less into the unemployment insurance fund; thus organizations have an incentive to keep terminations at a minimum.

A large number of benefits are not required to be employer-provided. The most common are pension plans and medical and hospital insurance. Both of these are undergoing significant change. For decades, most Americans under the retirement age were covered by health insurance plans provided by their employers. But as the cost of providing this benefit has soared far faster than other compensation costs, employers started dropping it or providing very limited policies. In 2010 the federal government responded to concern about the rising number of uninsured people and the high cost of care by passing the Affordable Care Act. Among its many provisions, the law requires that, starting in 2014, employers (except small businesses) must either provide their employees with health insurance or pay a fee to offset the cost of government subsidies for individuals buying their own insurance. As the deadline approaches, organizations have begun considering whether to continue offering health insurance benefits. In one survey, in which respondents were invited to compare the costs of insurance versus fees, about 30 percent of managers said they expected to discontinue health insurance benefits. However, most surveys by economists and public policy analysts have predicted a much smaller shift, based on the assumption that employers will consider other factors beyond a cost comparison of fees and insurance. A key reason for expecting continuation of this benefit is that

Bottom Line

Organizations today seek new ways to reduce benefits costs. *What benefits have you received from an employer? Did you ever consider the cost of those benefits?*

Employee benefits include those required by law, such as workers' compensation, Social Security, and unemployment insurance, and those decided by the employer. Retirement plans and paid vacation time are examples of employer-provided, nonrequired benefits.

employees place a high value on health insurance, so employers view it as a necessary means of attracting and retaining employees—and of enabling them to stay healthy and productive.[60]

At the same time, retirement benefits have been shifting away from guaranteed pension payments. Whereas a promised monthly payout used to be the norm, almost no company offers this approach to new employees today.[61] Instead, in many companies, the employer, and perhaps the employee, may contribute to an individual retirement account or 401(k) plan, which is invested. When the employee retires, he or she gets the total amount that has accumulated in the account.

Because of the wide variety of possible benefits and the considerable differences in employee preferences and needs, companies often use **cafeteria** or **flexible benefit programs**. In this type of program, employees are given credits that they spend on benefits they desire. Then employees use their credits toward individualized packages of benefits—medical and dental insurance, dependent care, life insurance, and so on.

cafeteria benefit program

An employee benefit program in which employees choose from a menu of options to create a benefit package tailored to their needs.

flexible benefit programs

Benefit programs in which employees are given credits to spend on benefits that fit their unique needs.

comparable worth

Principle of equal pay for different jobs of equal worth.

Legal Issues in Compensation and Benefits

Several laws affect employee compensation and benefits. We have already mentioned the FLSA, which in addition to distinguishing between exempt and nonexempt employees also sets minimum wage, maximum hour, and child labor provisions.[62] The *Equal Pay Act (EPA)* of 1963, now enforced by the EEOC, prohibits unequal pay for men and women who perform equal work. Equal work means jobs that require equal skill, effort, and responsibility and are performed under similar working conditions. The law does permit exceptions in which the difference in pay is due to a seniority system, a merit system, an incentive system based on quantity or quality of production, or any other factor other than sex, such as market demand. Although equal pay for equal work may sound like common sense, many employers have fallen victim to this law by rationalizing that men, traditionally the breadwinners, deserve more pay than women or by giving equal jobs different titles (senior assistant versus office manager) as the sole basis for pay differences.

One controversy concerns male and female pay differences within the same company. **Comparable worth** doctrine implies that women who perform *different* jobs of *equal* worth as those performed by men should be paid the same wage.[63] In contrast to the equal-pay-for-equal-work notion, comparable worth suggests that the jobs need *not* be the same to require the same pay. For example, nurses (predominantly female) were found to be paid considerably less than skilled craftworkers (predominantly male), even though the two jobs were found to be of equal value or worth.[64] Under the Equal Pay Act, this would not constitute pay discrimination because the jobs are very different. But under the comparable worth concept, these findings would indicate discrimination because the jobs are of equal worth. To date, no federal law requires comparable worth, and the Supreme Court has made no decisive rulings about it. However, some states, including Iowa, Minnesota, and Washington have comparable worth laws for public sector employees.

Some laws influence mostly benefit practices. The *Pregnancy Discrimination Act* of 1978 states that pregnancy is a disability and qualifies a woman to receive the same benefits that she would with any other disability. The *Employee Retirement Income Security Act (ERISA)* of 1974 protects private pension programs from mismanagement. ERISA requires that retirement benefits be paid to those who vest or earn a right to draw benefits and ensures retirement benefits for employees whose companies go bankrupt or who otherwise cannot meet their pension obligations.

Health and Safety

The *Occupational Safety and Health Act (OSHA)* of 1970 requires employers to pursue workplace safety. Employers must maintain records of injuries and deaths caused by workplace accidents and submit to onsite inspections. Large-scale industrial accidents and nuclear power plant disasters worldwide have focused attention on the importance of workplace safety.

Coal mining is one of many industries that benefit from safety laws. Mining is one of the five most dangerous jobs to perform, according to the U.S. Bureau of Labor Statistics. Nearly every coal miner can name a friend or family member who has been killed, maimed, or stricken with black lung disease. "You die quick or you die slow," reports one mine worker. Mine safety tragically returned to American consciousness in April 2010, when a coal mine explosion at the Massey Energy Company's Upper Big Branch Mine killed 29 workers. An independent investigation found that the accident could have been prevented by standard mine safety practices that evidently had been disregarded by management and missed by regulators.[65] However, according to the Mine Safety and Health Administration, mines have become safer. In the 1960s, hundreds of coal miners died in mine accidents every year; beginning in the mid-1980s, that number fell below 100 per year. During the past decade, even in the year of the Massey disaster, the number of annual fatalities was less than 50.[66]

Another area of concern is the safety of young workers, who may lack the confidence to speak up if they see health or safety problems. A recent study of teenage workers found that many were exposed to hazards and used equipment that should have been off-limits to teens under federal regulations. For example, almost half of teenaged grocery store employees said they had performed prohibited tasks such as using box crushers and dough mixers.[67]

In Practice

SHELL ENSURES WORKER SAFETY

As the world was reminded a few years ago by the deaths of 11 workers in the *Deepwater Horizon* accident in the Gulf of Mexico, workers in the oil industry face enormous safety risks. But Royal Dutch Shell is seeking a very different kind of record: Its goal is to have zero fatalities and zero significant safety incidents. It's an impressive goal for any organization, especially one with almost 90,000 employees, many of them working in harsh conditions, in more than 90 countries.

Shell's approach is to make its rules simple. It has three Golden Rules: (1) comply with the law, standards, and procedures; (2) intervene in situations that are unsafe or out of compliance; and (3) "respect our neighbors." For Shell, neighbors are the people in the communities where it operates—people who would be endangered by an oil leak or impaired truck driver. Respecting neighbors means keeping them safe. Shell knows that this is both the responsible way to act and essential for winning public and government support for new ventures it wants to undertake, such as drilling in the Arctic Ocean near Alaska.

In support of its Golden Rules, Shell teaches its employees "12 life-saving rules." These are basic safety practices, such as wearing a seat belt, not using a cell phone while driving, and not walking under suspended loads. The rules themselves aren't unusual; what is distinctive about Shell's approach is to distill its safety program into easy-to-understand guidelines about the day-to-day actions that make a practical difference in safety performance. The company also says it holds managers accountable for enforcing the rules. Since it began using the 12 life-saving rules, Shell reports a significant drop in fatalities.[68]

- To ensure worker safety, what does Shell need to do beyond teaching safety rules?

Labor Relations

Labor relations is the system of relations between workers and management. Labor unions recruit members, collect dues, and ensure that employees are treated fairly with respect to wages, working conditions, and other issues. When workers organize for the purpose of negotiating with management to improve their wages, hours, or working conditions, two processes are involved: unionization and collective bargaining. These processes have evolved since the 1930s in the United States to provide important employee rights.[69]

labor relations

The system of relations between workers and management.

Labor Laws

Try to imagine what life would be like with unemployment at 25 percent. Pretty grim, you would say. Legislators in 1935 felt that way too. Therefore, organized labor received its Magna Carta with the passage of the National Labor Relations Act.

The *National Labor Relations Act* (also called the *Wagner Act* after its legislative sponsor) ushered in an era of rapid unionization by (1) declaring labor organizations legal, (2) establishing five unfair employer labor practices, and (3) creating the National Labor Relations Board (NLRB). Prior to the act, employers could fire workers who favored unions, and federal troops were often provided to put down strikes. Today the NLRB conducts unionization elections, hears complaints of unfair labor practices, and issues injunctions against offending employers. The Wagner Act greatly assisted the growth of unions by enabling workers to use the law and the courts to organize and collectively bargain for better wages, hours, and working conditions. Many of the improvements all of us take for granted in the workplace, including minimum wages, health benefits, maternity leave, the 35-hour workweek, and worker protections in general were largely the result of collective bargaining over many years by unions.

Since 2000, unions have aggressively tried to organize workers at Walmart, the world's largest employer with over 2 million employees. So far, the company remains union-free except in China. For a manager, what would be the pros and cons of a union?

Public policy began on the side of organized labor in 1935, but over the next 25 years, the pendulum swung toward the side of management. The *Labor-Management Relations Act*, or *Taft-Hartley Act* (1947), protected employers' free speech rights, defined unfair labor practices by unions, and permitted workers to decertify (reject) a union as their representative.

Finally, the *Labor-Management Reporting and Disclosure Act*, or *Landrum-Griffin Act* (1959), swung the public policy pendulum midway between organized labor and management. By declaring a bill of rights for union members, establishing control over union dues increases, and imposing reporting requirements for unions, Landrum-Griffin was designed to curb abuses by union leadership and rid unions of corruption.

Unionization

How do workers join unions? Through a union organizer or local union representative, workers learn what benefits they may receive by joining.[70] The union representative distributes authorization cards that permit workers to indicate whether they want an election to be held to certify the union to represent them. The National Labor Relations Board will conduct a certification election if at least 30 percent of the employees sign authorization cards. Management has several choices at this stage: to recognize the union without an election, to consent to an election, or to contest the number of cards signed and resist an election.

If an election is warranted, an NLRB representative will conduct the election by secret ballot. A simple majority of those voting determines the winner. Thus apathetic workers who do not show up to vote in effect support the union. If the union wins the election, it is certified as the bargaining unit representative.

During the campaign preceding the election, management and the union each try to persuade the workers how to vote. Most workers, though, are somewhat resistant to campaign efforts, having made up their minds well before the NLRB appears on the scene. If the union wins the election, management and the union are legally required to bargain in good faith to obtain a collective bargaining agreement or contract.

Why do workers vote for a union? The four factors that play a significant role are presented in Figure 10.8.[71] First, economic factors are important, especially for workers in low-paying jobs; unions attempt to raise the average wage rate for their members. Second, job dissatisfaction encourages workers to seek out a union. Poor supervisory practices, favoritism, lack of communication, and perceived unfair or arbitrary discipline and discharge are specific triggers of job dissatisfaction. Third, the belief that the union can obtain desired benefits can generate a pro-union vote. Finally, the image of the union can determine whether a dissatisfied worker will seek out the union. Headline stories of union corruption and dishonesty can discourage workers from unionization.

Collective Bargaining

In the United States, management and unions engage in a periodic ritual (typically every three years) of negotiating an agreement over wages, benefits, hours, and working conditions. Two types of disputes can arise during this process. First, before an

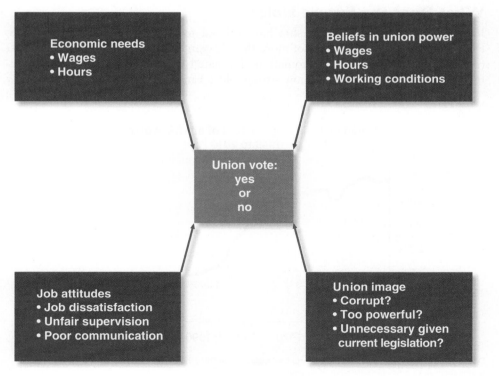

FIGURE 10.8
Determinants of Union Voting Behavior

agreement is reached, the workers may go on strike to compel agreement on their terms. Such an action is known as an *economic strike* and is permitted by law. However, strikes today are less likely to be used as a bargaining tool, although they sometimes occur as a last resort. Strikers are not paid if they are on strike, and few workers want to undertake this hardship unnecessarily. In addition, managers may legally hire replacement workers during a strike, offsetting some of the strike's effect. Finally, workers are as aware as managers of the tougher competition companies face today, and if treated fairly, they will usually share management's interest in coming to an agreement.

Once an agreement is signed, management and the union sometimes disagree over *interpretation* of the agreement. Usually they settle their disputes through arbitration. **Arbitration** is the use of a neutral third party, typically jointly selected, to resolve the dispute. U.S. companies use arbitration while an agreement is in effect to avoid *wildcat strikes* (in which workers walk off the job in violation of the contract) or unplanned work stoppages.

What does a collective bargaining agreement contain? In a **union shop,** a union security clause specifies that workers must join the union after a set period of time. **Right-to-work** states, through restrictive legislation, do not permit union shops; that is, workers have the right to work without being forced to join a union. The southern United States has many right-to-work states. The wage component of the contract spells out rates of pay, including premium pay for overtime and paid holidays. Individual rights usually are specified in terms of the use of seniority to determine pay increases, job bidding, and the order of layoffs.

A feature of any contract is the grievance procedure. Through the grievance procedure, unions perform a vital service for their membership by giving workers a voice in what goes on during contract negotiations and administration.[72] In about 50 percent of discharge cases that go to arbitration, the arbitrator overturns management's decision and reinstates the worker.[73] Unions have a legal duty of fair representation, which means they must represent all workers in the bargaining unit and ensure that workers' rights are protected.

What Does the Future Hold?

In recent years, union membership has declined to about 11 percent of the U.S. labor force—down from a peak of more than 33 percent at the end of World War II (see Figure 10.9). Increased automation eliminated many of the types of manufacturing jobs that used to be union strongholds. Employees in today's white-collar

arbitration

The use of a neutral third party to resolve a labor dispute.

union shop

An organization with a union and a union security clause specifying that workers must join the union after a set period of time.

right-to-work

Legislation that allows employees to work without having to join a union.

FIGURE 10.9
Decline in Union Membership—1948 to 2010

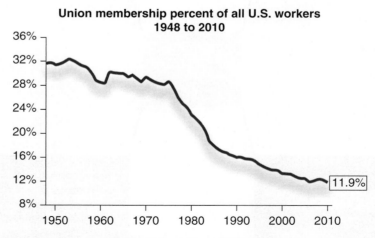

Union membership percent of all U.S. workers 1948 to 2010

11.9%

Data adapted from: Bureau of Labor Statistics, http://dailycapitalist.com/2012/02/03/unions-continue-to-drive-themselves-out-of-business/.

office jobs are less interested in joining unions and are also more difficult to organize. Tough global competition has made managers much less willing to give in to union demands, and as a result, the benefits of unionization are less clear to many workers—particularly young, skilled workers who no longer expect to stay with one company all their lives. Some people applaud unions' apparent decline. Others hope for an eventual reemergence. Unions may play a different role in the future, one that is less adversarial and more cooperative with management. Unions are adapting to changing workforce demographics; they are paying more attention to women, older workers, government employees, and people who work at home. Elimination of inefficient work rules, the introduction of profit sharing, and a guarantee of no layoffs were seen as big steps toward a fundamentally different, cooperative long-term relationship.

> In recent years, union membership has declined to about 11 percent of the U.S. labor force.

What seems clear is that when companies recognize that their success depends on the talents and energies of employees, the interests of unions and managers may begin to converge. Rather than one side exploiting the other, unions and managers can find common ground in developing, valuing, and involving employees. Particularly in knowledge-based companies, the balance of power is shifting toward employees. Whether or not employees belong to a union, they, not companies, own their own human capital. And these employees are free, within limits, to leave the organization, taking their human capital with them. This leaves organizations in a particularly vulnerable position if they manage poorly. To establish a strong competitive capability, organizations are searching for ways to obtain, retain, and engage their most valuable resources: human resources. "Management Connection: Onward" explores why and how this is a critical issue for Google today. The processes and practices outlined in this chapter form the foundation for effective people management. In the next chapter, we discuss one particularly important people-related issue: managing a diverse workforce.

Management Connection

GOOGLE GEARS UP FOR MORE LABOR MARKET COMPETITION

Google's recruiting and selection practices have contributed to its mystique, helping it meet its goals for hiring the best talent, but that human resource strategy has been shaken by the appeal of up-and-coming high-tech firms. Google risks becoming the boring, established brand. High-tech workers still love Google, but many are drawn to opportunities at Twitter, Dropbox, and other rising stars. Thus, even as Google is adding thousands to its ranks, it must keep current employees from leaving.

One way to keep people is to ensure that they feel well compensated. Google has increased its budget for compensation. For Google, this is an investment: to enter new, growing areas of the high-tech industry, it needs talented people.

But it's not just about money. One reason tech workers leave for start-ups is that they want to enjoy the excitement of building something new. Big-company bureaucracy can be boring. Google's founders originally

held weekly meetings during which engineers presented their projects to the leaders. As the company grew, the list of presenters got so long that the founders lost interest and limited technical reviews to a select group.

Google therefore tries to be worker-friendly in its own data-driven way. The effort to measure and improve management effectiveness was conceived partly as a way to create a more positive work environment. It helps that managers' performance is measured both by the manager's boss and by his or her employees. The same goal and approach apply to decisions about employee benefits. For example, Google determines what kind of advice helps employees get the most value from their retirement plans and how to structure an increase in pay so employees will appreciate it most. (It concluded that a raise in base pay is better than a bonus.)

Or consider the case of the disappearing women. Google's People Operations (POPS) department tracked

MANAGER'S BRIEF

PROGRESS REPORT

ONWARD

turnover rates and noticed that female employees were leaving at a high rate—an expensive problem, given the costs to recruit, hire, and train replacements. Digging deeper, POPS analysts determined that the attrition was led by women quitting after giving birth. Google's parental-leave policy was standard for its industry, but the evidence showed that was not enough. So Google began offering mothers five months off at full pay—time they may schedule however they want. Turnover among new mothers dropped by half, matching the rate of all employees. That improvement lowered the expense of replacing employees enough to make up for the cost of the benefit.[74]

- How is Google's approach to employee benefits more effective than a simple decision to offer the biggest benefits package?
- Do you think Google's HR strategy will enable it to maintain a competitive advantage? Why or why not?

KEY TERMS

adverse impact, p. 342

arbitration, p. 360

assessment center, p. 337

cafeteria benefit programs, p. 356

comparable worth, p. 356

development, p. 344

diversity training, p. 346

employment-at-will, p. 340

flexible benefit programs, p. 356

human capital, p. 329

human resources management (HRM), p. 328

job analysis, p. 333

labor relations, p. 358

management by objectives (MBO), p. 347

needs assessment, p. 344

orientation training, p. 345

outplacement, p. 340

performance appraisal (PA), p. 347

recruitment, p. 333

reliability, p. 338

right-to-work, p. 360

selection, p. 334

structured interview, p. 335

360-degree appraisal, p. 349

team training, p. 345

termination interview, p. 341

training, p. 344

union shop, p. 360

validity, p. 339

SUMMARY OF LEARNING OBJECTIVES

Now that you have studied Chapter 10, you should be able to:

 Discuss how companies use human resources management to gain competitive advantage.

To succeed, companies must align their human resources to their strategies. Effective planning is necessary to make certain that the right number and type of employees are available to implement a company's strategic plan. It is clear that hiring the most competent people is a very involved process. Companies that compete on cost, quality, service, and so on also should use their staffing, training, appraisal, and reward systems to elicit and reinforce the kinds of behaviors that underlie their strategies.

 Give reasons companies recruit both internally and externally for new hires.

Some companies prefer to recruit internally to make certain that employees are familiar with organizational policies and values. In other instances, companies prefer to recruit externally, such as through employee referrals, job boards, newspaper advertising, and campus visits, to find individuals with new ideas and fresh perspectives. External recruiting is also necessary to fill positions when the organization is growing or needs skills that do not exist among its current employees.

 Identify various methods for selecting new employees.

There are myriad selection techniques from which to choose. Interviews and reference checks are the most common. Personality tests and cognitive ability tests measure an individual's aptitude and potential to do well on the job. Other selection techniques include assessment centers and integrity tests. Background and reference checks verify that the information supplied by employees is accurate. Regardless of the approach used, any test should be able to demonstrate reliability (consistency across time and different interview situations) and validity (accuracy in predicting job performance). In addition, selection methods must comply with equal opportunity laws, which are intended to ensure that companies do not discriminate in any employment practices.

 Evaluate the importance of spending on training and development.

People cannot depend on a set of skills for all of their working lives. In today's changing, competitive world, old skills quickly become obsolete, and new ones become essential for success. Refreshing or updating an individual's skills requires a great deal of continuous training, designed with measurable goals and methods that will achieve those goals. Companies understand that gaining a competitive edge in quality of service depends on having the most talented, flexible workers in the industry.

LO 5 Explain alternatives for who appraises an employee's performance.

Many companies are using multiple sources of appraisal because different people see different sides of an employee's performance. Typically, a superior is expected to evaluate an employee, but peers and team members are often well positioned to see aspects of performance that a superior misses. Even an employee's subordinates are being asked more often today to give their input to get yet another perspective on the evaluation. Particularly in companies concerned about quality, internal and external customers also are surveyed. Finally, employees should evaluate their own performance, if only to get them thinking about their own performance as well as to engage them in the appraisal process.

LO 6 Describe the fundamental aspects of a reward system.

Reward systems include pay and benefits. Pay systems have three basic components: pay level, pay structure, and individual pay determination. To achieve an advantage over competitors, executives may want to pay a generally higher wage to their company's employees, but this decision must be weighed against the need to control costs. (Pay level decisions often are tied to strategic concerns such as these.) To achieve internal equity (paying people what they are worth relative to their peers within the company), managers must look at the pay structure,

making certain that pay differentials are based on knowledge, effort, responsibility, working conditions, seniority, and so on. Individual pay determination is often based on merit or the different contributions of individuals. In these cases, it is important to make certain that men and women receive equal pay for equal work, and managers may wish to base pay decisions on the idea of comparable worth (equal pay for an equal contribution). Also, the Occupational Safety and Health Act requires employees to have a safe and healthful work environment.

LO 7 Summarize how unions and labor laws influence human resources management.

Labor relations involve the interactions between workers and management. One mechanism by which this relationship is conducted is unions. Unions seek to present a collective voice for workers, to make their needs and wishes known to management. Unions negotiate agreements with management regarding a range of issues such as wages, hours, working conditions, job security, and health care. One important tool that unions can use is the grievance procedure established through collective bargaining. This mechanism gives employees a way to seek redress for wrongful action on the part of management. In this way, unions make certain that the rights of all employees are protected. Labor laws seek to protect the rights of both employees and managers so that their relationship can be productive and agreeable.

DISCUSSION QUESTIONS

1. How will changes in the labor force affect HRM practices for the next decade?
2. Describe the major regulations governing HRM practices.
3. Define job analysis. Why is job analysis relevant to each of the six key HRM activities discussed in the chapter (i.e., planning, staffing, training, performance appraisal, reward systems, labor relations)?
4. What are the various methods for recruiting employees? Why are some better than others? In what sense are they better?
5. What is a test? Give some examples of tests used by employers.

6. What purpose does performance appraisal serve? Why are there so many methods of appraisal?
7. What are some key ideas to remember when conducting a performance appraisal?
8. How would you define an effective reward system? What role do benefits serve in a reward system?
9. Why do workers join unions? What implications would this have for an organization that wishes to remain nonunion?
10. Discuss the advantages and disadvantages of collective bargaining for the employer and the employee.

EXPERIENTIAL EXERCISES

10.1 THE LEGAL INTERVIEW

OBJECTIVES

1. To introduce you to the complexities of employment law.
2. To identify interview practices that might lead to discrimination in employment.

INSTRUCTIONS

1. Working alone, review the text material on interviewing and discrimination in employment.
2. In small groups, complete the Legal Interview Worksheet.
3. After the class reconvenes, group spokespersons present group findings.

Legal Interview Worksheet

The employment interview is one of the most critical steps in the employment selection process. It also may be an occasion for discriminating against individual employment candidates.

The following represents questions that interviewers often ask job applicants. Identify the legality of each question by circling *L* (legal) or *I* (illegal) and briefly explain your decision.

Interview Question	Legality	Explanation
1. Could you provide us with a photo for our files?	L I	_____
2. Have you ever used another name (previous married name or alias)?	L I	_____
3. What was your maiden name?	L I	_____
4. What was your wife's maiden name?	L I	_____
5. What was your mother's maiden name?	L I	_____
6. What is your current address?	L I	_____
7. What was your previous address?	L I	_____
8. What is your Social Security number?	L I	_____
9. Where was your place of birth?	L I	_____
10. Where were your parents born?	L I	_____
11. What is your national origin?	L I	_____
12. Are you a naturalized citizen?	L I	_____
13. What languages do you speak?	L I	_____
14. What is your religious/church affiliation?	L I	_____
15. What is your racial classification?	L I	_____
16. How many dependents do you have?	L I	_____
17. What are the ages of your dependent children?	L I	_____
18. What is your marital status?	L I	_____
19. How old are you?	L I	_____
20. Do you have proof of your age (birth certificate or baptismal record)?	L I	_____
21. Whom do we notify in case of an emergency?	L I	_____
22. What are your height and weight?	L I	_____
23. Have you ever been arrested?	L I	_____
24. Do you own your own car?	L I	_____
25. Do you own your own house?	L I	_____
26. Do you have any charge accounts?	L I	_____
27. Have you ever had your salary garnished?	L I	_____
28. To what organizations do you belong?	L I	_____
29. Are you available to work on Saturdays and Sundays?	L I	_____
30. Do you have any form of disability?	L I	_____

10.2   THE PAY RAISE

OBJECTIVES

1. To further your understanding of salary administration.
2. To examine the many facets of performance criteria, performance criteria weighting, performance evaluation, and rewards.

INSTRUCTIONS

1. Working in small groups, complete the Pay Raise Worksheet.
2. After the class reconvenes, group spokespersons present group findings.

Pay Raise Worksheet

April Knepper is the new supervisor of an assembly team. It is time for her to make pay raise allocations for her subordinates. She has been budgeted $30,000 to allocate among her seven subordinates as pay raises. There have been some ugly grievances in other work teams over past allocations, so Knepper has been advised to base the allocations on objective criteria that can be quantified, weighted, and computed in numerical terms. After she makes her allocations, Knepper must be prepared to justify her decisions. All of the evaluative criteria available to Knepper are summarized as follows:

Employee	Seniority	Output Rating*	Absent Rate	Skills	Initiative	Attitude	Personal
				Skills	Initiative	Attitude	Personal
David Bruce	15 yrs.	0.58	0.5%	Good	Poor	Poor	Nearing retirement. Wife just passed away. Having adjustment problems.
Eric Cattalini	12 yrs.	0.86	2.0	Excellent	Good	Excellent	Going to night school to finish his BA degree.
Chua Li	7 yrs.	0.80	3.5	Good	Excellent	Excellent	Legally deaf.
Marilee Miller	1 yr.	0.50	10.0	Poor	Poor	Poor	Single parent with three children.
Victor Munoz	3 yrs.	0.62	2.5	Poor	Average	Good	Has six dependents. Speaks little English.
Derek Thompson	11 yrs.	0.64	8.0	Excellent	Average	Average	Married to rich wife. Personal problems.
Sarah Vickers	8 yrs.	0.76	7.0	Good	Poor	Poor	Women's activist. Wants to create a union.

*Output rating determined by production rate less errors and quality problems.

CONCLUDING CASE

INVINCIBILITY SYSTEMS

The 17,000 employees of Invincibility Systems design and make aerospace and defense equipment such as rockets, spacecraft propulsion systems, and missile propulsion systems. Along with cutting-edge engineering, the company stands out for its cutting-edge human resource management. Invincibility has hired quantitative experts to analyze HR data with the same care it uses to analyze rocket trajectories.

A few years ago, the company hired a statistician and an HR planner to join a team that would collect and analyze data, looking for factors that would predict human resource needs. The team started by looking for ways to improve recruiting. They collected data on the various sources of candidates that the company was using and the candidates actually selected. Then they used a statistical method called regression analysis to identify which sources of candidates generated the most hires—as well as the sources that generated hires who went on to perform well. Using the results of the analysis, Invincibility made its recruiting effort more efficient. By focusing on the most productive sources of top employees, it saves time and money that formerly had gone toward recruiting through channels that were less fruitful.

Next the HR team turned its efforts toward workforce planning. For each department of Invincibility, the team collects data describing the workforce—for example, job categories, years with the company, and labor force projections. It runs regression analysis to predict the likelihood that employees will leave the company in the coming year. The results, coupled with sales forecasts, enable the company to predict how many new employees will need to be hired in each department.

Other companies do this kind of planning, but the extent of the analysis at Invincibility is unusual. For one thing, the analysis is conducted on the level of individual employees. Thus it shows not only that turnover may rise or fall, but also which employees are most likely to leave. That level of analysis is important to Invincibility because unlike organizations where many people perform the same type of work and can step in when someone leaves, employees at Invincibility typically fill highly specialized, highly skilled roles. If an engineer with years of experience in developing high-caliber ammunition suddenly departs, there may be no one else on the team with that person's knowledge and skill set.

Another unusual quality of Invincibility's HR planning is the variety of factors that the planners consider when they run their regression analyses. For example, the company has run regressions to determine whether turnover is related to changes in employee benefits and even the month of the year. If the analysis shows that a factor has been significant in the past, the planners take it into account in their forecasts. In one situation, the planners found that retirements in a department rose after the company announced that it would be phasing out health insurance benefits for retirees. More experienced workers left before the phase-out took effect. When the company prepared to phase out similar benefits in another division, the planners knew they would need to step up recruiting efforts there in preparation for an uptick in retirements.

Some of the data Invincibility uses for planning are unsuitable for other kinds of HR decisions. For example, the company has found that employees' ages and marital status are relevant for predicting whether they are likely to leave the company. Turnover rates are higher among unmarried employees and recently hired employees (who tend to be younger). Thus the company plans greater recruiting efforts in departments where it has higher levels of young and unmarried employees. It also may consider stepping up its efforts to mentor and train employees in these departments. However, it does not make employment decisions such as hiring and promotion based on these factors.

DISCUSSION QUESTIONS

1. Besides the factors identified, what other factors should Invincibility Systems take into account in its HR planning?

2. What legal concerns does the data analysis at Invincibility raise? How should the company address those issues?

3. Besides its use for HR planning and recruiting, how might Invincibility's data analysis be applied to improving the company's training programs?

Managing the Diverse Workforce

Management Connection

HOW BRIAN FRANCE IS CHANGING THE FACE OF NASCAR

What does a NASCAR fan look like? A NASCAR driver? If you pictured a white, male Southerner in answer to both questions, you have just illustrated a concern of NASCAR's chief executive, Brian France. Even as America's population is becoming more diverse, the sport of auto racing has tended to draw its drivers and fans from one segment of the population. If a sport is off the radar of the rest of the population, its growth potential is limited.

But France sees a different future. Years ago, he told Richard Lapchick, founder of the National Consortium for Academics and Sports, that he wanted NASCAR to "look like America." And since then, he has moved aggressively to begin making that happen.

Under France's leadership, NASCAR established its Drive for Diversity (D4D) development program to recruit female and minority group drivers and members of pit crews. The program hosts its three-day Drive for Diversity Combine each fall to see the candidates in action and select the best for training and support, which includes guidance in marketing and media opportunities. Participants enter D4D's Rev Racing competitions, seeking to move up to other competitive levels, including the top level, the Sprint Cup Series. Since the program was established in 2004, NASCAR has supported more than 30 drivers in competitions at the grassroots level. In 2013, Kyle Larson, who is Japanese-American, became the first Drive for Diversity driver to win a national series race (the Truck Series race held at Rockingham Speedway). Other graduates of D4D have signed developmental contracts with NASCAR teams.

In the pit crew training program, participants develop the technical and athletic skills to serve as tire changers, fuelers, and jackmen.

Diversity efforts are not just for show out on the track. NASCAR also seeks to develop talent for its business and leadership roles. It partners with about 20 universities to identify talented students for internships and jobs in marketing and other business areas. It also brought in the Teamwork Leadership Institute, a program of the National Consortium for Academics and Sports, to train all its employees in valuing and managing diversity. The institute's program supports NASCAR's goal of making diversity a value in all of NASCAR's relationships—within the organization and with its fans, vendors, and sponsors.[1]

When Brian France talks about NASCAR "looking like America," he may be thinking of a variety of the characteristics that define people—their age and sex, their place of birth and economic status, their racial and ethnic identities. As you read this chapter, think about how bringing together a diverse group and leading it toward a common purpose can be challenging but also a source of opportunity.

In Chapter 10, we described the laws that require equal opportunity and fair treatment in the workplace. In this chapter, we discuss why a proactive approach to developing and managing a diverse workforce has become not only a legal or moral obligation but a fundamental business requirement as well. NASCAR's Brian France considers diversity an essential ingredient for his sport's future growth. Managers who lack the ability to work with and effectively manage men and women of different colors, cultures, ages, abilities, and backgrounds will be at a significant disadvantage in their careers. And organizations that do not take the issue of managing diversity seriously will leave their organizations not only open to legal challenge but also far less able to compete effectively at home and abroad.

In the United States, as we shall see, the number of racial and ethnic minorities is increasing at a far faster rate than the growth in the white, nonminority population, and women make up a sizable share of the workforce. American workers, customers, and markets are already highly diverse and becoming even more so every day. In addition, as we discussed in Chapter 6, businesses are increasingly global. Managers need to be much more aware of, and sensitive to, cultural differences to succeed in a world economy. We have also discussed throughout this book how vital creativity and innovation have become for organization success. These qualities are fostered in an atmosphere where different perspectives and bright people from all walks of life are celebrated. Few societies have access to the range of talents available in the United States, with its immigrant tradition and racially and ethnically diverse population. Yet getting people from widely divergent backgrounds to work together effectively is not easy. For this reason, managing diversity is one of America's biggest challenges—and opportunities.

managing diversity

Managing a culturally diverse workforce by recognizing the characteristics common to specific groups of employees while dealing with such employees as individuals and supporting, nurturing, and using their differences to the organization's advantage.

Managing diversity involves, first, such basic activities as recruiting, training, promoting, and using to full advantage individuals with different backgrounds, beliefs, capabilities, and cultures. But it means more than just hiring women and minorities and making sure they are treated equally and encouraged to succeed. It also means understanding and deeply valuing employee differences to build a more effective and profitable organization.

This chapter examines the meaning of diversity and the management skills and organizational processes involved in managing the diverse workforce effectively. We also explore the social and demographic changes and economic and employment shifts that are creating this changing U.S. workforce.

Diversity: A Brief History

Managing diversity is not a new management issue. From the late 1800s to the early 1900s, most of the groups that immigrated to the United States were from Italy, Poland, Ireland, and Russia. Members of those groups were considered outsiders because most did not speak English and had different customs and work styles. They struggled, often violently, to gain acceptance in industries such as steel, coal, automobile manufacturing, insurance, and finance. In the 1800s, it was considered poor business practice for white Protestant–dominated insurance companies to hire Irish, Italians, Catholics, or Jews. As late as the 1940s, and in some cases even later than that, colleges routinely discriminated against immigrants, Catholics, and Jews, establishing strict quotas that limited their number, if any were admitted at all. The employment prospects of these groups were severely diminished by this kind of discrimination, and it wasn't until the 1960s that the struggle for acceptance by the various white ethnic and religious groups had on the whole succeeded.

Women's struggle for acceptance in the workplace was in some ways even more difficult. When the women's rights movement was launched in Seneca Falls in 1848, most occupations were off-limits to women, and colleges and professional schools were totally closed to them. Women could not vote and lost all property rights once they were married. In the first part of the 20th century, when women began to be accepted into professional schools, they were subject to severe quotas. There was also a widespread, persistent assumption that certain jobs were done only by men, and other jobs only by women. Even into the 1970s, less than 40 years ago, classified ad sections in newspapers listed different jobs by sex, with sections headed "Help Wanted—Males" and "Help Wanted—Females." Women who wanted a bank loan needed a male cosigner, and married women were not issued credit cards in their own name.[2] Only when the Civil Rights Act of 1964 (see Chapter 10) and other legislation began to be enforced was this kind of sex discrimination gradually eliminated. As we shall see, women

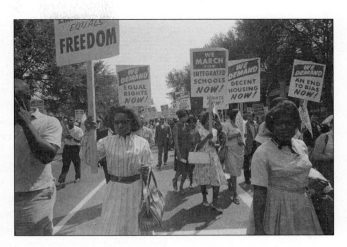

Many of the rights all of us take for granted today—equal opportunity, fair treatment in housing, the illegality of religious, racial, and sex discrimination—received their greatest impetus from the civil rights movement.

are still underrepresented at the most senior levels of corporate life, and major disparities in other areas, such as pay, still exist. But most jobs today once considered the exclusive province of men—including frontline military units as well as the executive suite—are now open to and occupied by increasing numbers of women.

The most difficult and wrenching struggle for equality involved America's nonwhite minorities. Rigid racial segregation remained a fact of American life for 100 years after the end of the Civil War. Black voting rights, particularly in the South, were often viciously suppressed, and racial discrimination in education, employment, and housing throughout the United States was a harsh daily reality. Years of difficult, courageous protest and struggle gradually began to eat away at both legal and social barriers to equality. Organizations such as the NAACP, formed by a group of blacks and whites, began to use America's court system and the Constitution to bring equality to African Americans and other people of color. The unanimous *Brown v. Board of Education* Supreme Court decision in 1954 declared segregation unconstitutional, setting the stage for other legislation we discussed in the previous chapter, including the Civil Rights Act of 1964. The consequences of America's bitter racial legacy are still with us; the struggle for equality is far from complete. But many of the rights all of us take for granted today—equal opportunity, fair treatment in housing, the illegality of religious, racial, and sex discrimination—received their greatest impetus from the civil rights movement.

Today nearly half of the U.S. workforce consists of women, 14 percent of U.S. workers identify themselves as Hispanic or Latino, and 11 percent are black. Two-thirds of all global migration is into the United States. One-third of all businesses in the United States are owned by women, employing about 20 percent of America's workers.[3]

The traditional American image of diversity has been one of assimilation. The United States was considered the melting pot of the world, a country in which ethnic and racial differences were blended into an American purée. In real life, many ethnic and most racial groups retained their identities, but they did not express them at work. Employees often abandoned most of their ethnic and cultural distinctions while at work to keep their jobs and get ahead. Many Europeans came to the United States, Americanized their names, perfected their English, and tried to enter the mainstream as quickly as possible.

> The traditional American image of diversity has been one of assimilation.

Today's immigrants typically want to be part of an integrated team, but they understandably do not want to sacrifice their cultural identities to get ahead. Nor will they have to do so. Companies are recognizing that they should be more accommodating of differences, and that doing so pays off in business. Managers are also realizing that their customers have become increasingly diverse and that retaining a diversified workforce can provide a significant competitive advantage in the marketplace.

Diversity Today

LO 1 Today *diversity* refers to far more than skin color and gender. It is a broad term used to refer to all kinds of differences, as summarized in Figure 11.1. These differences include religious affiliation, age, disability status, military experience, sexual orientation, economic class, educational level, and lifestyle in addition to gender, race, ethnicity, and nationality.[4]

Although members of different groups (white males, people born during the Depression, homosexuals, Iraq war veterans, Hispanics, Asians, women, African Americans, etc.) share within their groups many common values, attitudes, and perceptions, much diversity also exists within each of these categories. Every group is made up of individuals who are unique in personality, education, and life experiences. There may be more differences among, say, three Asians from Thailand, Hong Kong, and Korea than among a white, an African American, and an Asian all born in Chicago. And not all white males share the same personal or professional goals and values or behave alike.

Thus managing diversity may seem a contradiction within itself. It means being acutely aware of characteristics common to a group of employees while also managing these employees as individuals. Managing diversity means not just tolerating or accommodating all sorts of differences, but supporting, nurturing, integrating, and using these differences to the organization's advantage. Borders Books, for example, tries to match up the demographics of its workforce with the demographics of the communities in which its stores operate. Top managers at the company say that sales are better as a result. U.S. businesses will not have a choice of whether to have a diverse workforce; if they want to survive, they must learn to manage a diverse workforce sooner or better than their competitors do.

Although many companies initially instituted diversity programs to prevent discrimination, more are seeing these programs as a crucial way to expand their pool of talent and customer bases worldwide. These potential benefits are making diversity initiatives standard practice among industry-leading companies. A recent study of the large, mostly multinational companies in the Standard & Poor's 100 stock index found that 95 percent have at least one or two initiatives to develop a diverse workforce. Figure 11.2 shows how widespread those initiatives are.

FIGURE 11.1

Components of a Diversified Workforce

At least 1 diversity initiative

Diversity training for managers/leaders

Mentoring programs

Mandatory diversity training

Executive compensation linked to diversity

Demonstrated evidence of robust commitment*

0%   20%   40%   60%   80%   100%

FIGURE 11.2
Examples of Diversity Programs in S&P 100 Companies

SOURCE: Based on data in Christine DeGroot, Aditi Mohapatra, and Jamie Lippman, "Examining the Cracks in the Ceiling: A Survey of Corporate Diversity Practices of the S&P 100," Calvert Investments, March 2013, http://www.calvert.com.
*Extent to which diversity and inclusion are integrated into company's policies and strategies (for example, with executive-level involvement and oversight)

The Workforce of the Future

Until recently, white American-born males dominated the U.S. workforce. Businesses catered to their needs. However, although this group still constitutes the largest percentage of workers—about 80 percent of U.S. workers are white, and more than half of them are male—its share of the labor force is declining. Although the number of white male workers is expected to continue growing, the number of women and the numbers of Asian American, African American, and Hispanic workers are expected to grow faster.[5] This significant change in the workforce parallels trends in the overall U.S. population. Recently the census bureau announced that, for the first time, about one in three residents of the United States is a racial or ethnic minority—a unique milestone in the nation's history. The largest and fastest-growing minority group is Hispanics, closely followed by African Americans. In several states—California, Hawaii, New Mexico, and Texas—and the District of Columbia, these minority groups plus Asians, Native Americans, and Pacific Islanders combine to make a population that is "majority minority."[6] These population trends affect not only the nature of the workforce but also the varied customers and markets managers must attract.

Gender Issues   One of the most important developments in the U.S. labor market has been the growing number of women working outside the home. Social changes during the 1960s and 1970s coupled with financial necessity caused women to enter the workforce and redefine their roles. Consider this:

Women make up about 47 percent of the workforce.
The overall labor force participation rate of women rose throughout the 1970s through the 1990s and is now holding steady even as the participation rate of men gradually declines.
Almost 60 percent of marriages are dual-earner marriages.
One of every four married women in two-income households earns more than her husband does.[7]

For many women, as well as their spouses, balancing work life with family responsibilities and parenting presents an enormous challenge. Although men's roles in our society have been changing, women still adopt the bulk of family responsibilities, including

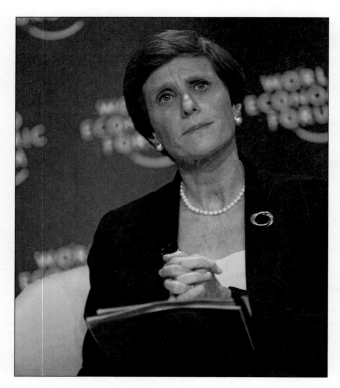

Irene Rosenfeld has broken through the glass ceiling as CEO of Mondelez International, overseeing the company with revenues of over $35 billion.

homemaking, child care, and care of elderly parents. Yet some companies may still expect their employees, particularly at the managerial level, to put in long hours and sacrifice their personal lives for the sake of their jobs, organizations, and careers. Not only may these expectations put many women at a disadvantage in the workplace, but they also may cause companies to lose valuable talent. Companies that offer their employees the opportunity to balance work and family commitments are better able to recruit and retain women. These companies are offering family-friendly benefits such as onsite child care, in-home care for elderly family members, and flexible work schedules, and they are taking advantage of newer technologies to permit more work from home. Still, weighing employees' needs for flexibility against the organization's need for productivity entails complex decisions that take into account different job requirements as well as each employee's contributions and motivation to meet goals under the flexible arrangement. Michele Coleman Mayes, senior vice president and general counsel of Pitney Bowes, agreed to let one attorney leave promptly at five o'clock each evening; the attorney works on her laptop at night as needed to meet her deadlines. But Mayes refused another employee's request to work part-time because the person in that position needed to be available each day to handle requests for other departments. Mayes tells her employees that scheduling decisions "may not always be equal, but I will try to be fair."[8]

The desire for flexible scheduling is often cited as a reason significant pay disparities still exist between men and women. The average full-time working woman earns about 82 percent as much as men in the same job (recall the discussion in Chapter 10 about equal pay and comparable worth). However, the gap has shrunk most years since the 1970s; women's earnings were just 62 percent of men's in 1979. Still, research by the AAUW has found a persistent gap between male and female workers' earnings that grows over time, even after adjusting for age, marital status, geographic region, college major and GPA, type and selectivity of undergraduate school, type of occupation, economic sector, number of hours worked, and months between graduation and starting work. One possible explanation for the wage gap is that women are not negotiating pay as effectively as men seeking the same positions. This hurdle is complicated by evidence that some negotiation tactics that work for men can backfire when women use them, but women may benefit from greater skill at researching pay scales and expressing their pay requirements in a pleasant tone, backed up with evidence of their worth.[9]

> The average full-time working woman earns about 82 percent as much as men in the same job.

Another concern involving female workers is the low representation of women in top jobs. As women—along with minorities—move up the corporate ladder, they encounter a glass ceiling. The *glass ceiling* is an invisible barrier that makes it difficult for women and minorities to move beyond a certain level in the corporate hierarchy. For example, just 12 women are chief executives of *Fortune* 500 companies—that's 12 out of 500. Looking at all board members of those companies, 13 percent are white women, and 3 percent are minority women.[10] Still, one positive trend is that women's leadership is beginning to be seen at a broader range of companies. Besides Ginni Rometty at the helm of IBM and Indra Nooyi at PepsiCo, the executive ranks now include the likes of Xerox CEO Ursula Burns and Facebook chief operating officer Sheryl Sandberg. Table 11.1 lists top women executives and the companies for which they work.

TABLE 11.1   The A-List: Top Women Executives

Rank	Name	Company	Title
1	Ginni Rometty	IBM	President and CEO
2	Indra Nooyi	PepsiCo	Chairman and CEO
3	Meg Whitman	Hewlett-Packard	President and CEO
4	Irene Rosenfeld	Mondelez International (formerly Kraft Foods)	Chairman and CEO
5	Ellen Kullman	DuPont	Chair and CEO
6	Patricia Woertz	ADM	Chairman and CEO
7	Ursula Burns	Xerox	Chairman and CEO
8	Sheryl Sandberg	Facebook	Chief operating officer
9	Abigail Johnson	Fidelity Investments	President, Fidelity Financial Services
10	Safra Catz	Oracle	President and chief financial officer
11	Melanie Healey	P&G	Group president, North America
12	Anne Sweeney	Disney/ABC Television Group	Co-chair, Disney Media Network; president, ABC Television Group
13	Rosalind Brewer	Wal-Mart Stores	President and CEO, Sam's Club
14	Marissa Mayer	Yahoo	CEO
15	Carol Meyrowitz	TJX Companies	CEO
16	Phebe Novakovic	General Dynamics	President and chief operating officer
17	Sheri McCoy	Avon Products	CEO
18	Susan Wojcicki	Google	Senior vice president, Product Management & Engineering
19	Marillyn Hewson	Lockheed Martin	Executive vice president, Electronic Systems
20	Denise Morrison	Campbell Soup Company	President and CEO

SOURCE: From "50 Most Powerful Women in Business," *Fortune*, October 8, 2012, http://money.cnn.com.

Some companies are helping women break through the glass ceiling. Accenture sponsors monthly networking events for its female employees and offers flexible schedules and part-time arrangements. Employers also sometimes match employees with mentors to help the employees navigate the business environment. Frustratingly, the very roadblocks that can make this guidance important may come from female managers. Researchers have observed what they call the queen bee syndrome, in which a female manager, perhaps out of insecurity, insults and demeans women who report to her.[11] Of course, managerial bullies are as likely to be men, but there is evidence that a queen bee targets mainly women. Whatever the source of the obstacles, corporate efforts to empower female employees may be behind the results of a survey of managers in which 79 percent of female respondents said they could envision themselves holding a senior management post, compared with only 66 percent feeling that

TABLE 11.2
Top 10 Companies for
Executive Women

Abbott	KPMG
Astra Zeneca	Marriott International
General Mills	Procter & Gamble
IBM	Prudential Financial
Johnson & Johnson	State Farm

SOURCE: Based on National Association for Female Executives, "2013 NAFE Top 50 Companies for Executive Women," *Working Mother*, February/March 2013, http://www.workingmother.com.

way at the start of their careers.[12] Table 11.2 shows the best companies for women executives according to the National Association of Female Executives.

sexual harassment

Conduct of a sexual nature that has negative consequences for employment.

As women have gained more presence and power in the workforce, some have drawn attention to the problem of **sexual harassment**, which is unwelcome sexual conduct that is a term or condition of employment. Sexual harassment falls into two categories. The first, *quid pro quo harassment*, occurs when submission to or rejection of sexual conduct is used as a basis for employment decisions. The second type of harassment, *hostile environment*, occurs when unwelcome sexual conduct "has the purpose or effect of unreasonably interfering with job performance or creating an intimidating, hostile, or offensive working environment." Behaviors that can cause a hostile work environment include persistent or pervasive displays of pornography, lewd or suggestive remarks, or demeaning taunts or jokes. Both categories of harassment violate Title VII of the Civil Rights Act of 1964, regardless of the sex of the harasser and the victim; in a recent year, more than 15 percent of complaints filed with the federal

In Practice

ADDRESSING MALE AND FEMALE STYLE DIFFERENCES AT CH2M

CH2M Hill, based in Denver, manages major engineering and construction projects as far afield as London, Abu Dhabi, and the Panama Canal. But one project looked impossible: how to get women into top jobs in a male-dominated industry. CH2M was hiring plenty of talented female engineers, but they never seemed to rise very far.

Determined to find answers, the company investigated and found that although formal policies were equitable, male and female engineers tended to behave in ways that gave the edge to men. Male engineers more actively sought positions involving greater responsibility. Women tended to focus on gaining experience and accomplishing goals, figuring they would eventually be rewarded if they were productive. But they tended to get less helpful coaching because their male managers focused on being polite to them.

To expose and address these style differences, CH2M Hill set up a women's network and began hosting two-day annual meetings at which female managers are encouraged to be assertive in controlling their careers. The meetings include training sessions on negotiation and opportunities to meet with mentors. Eventually the annual meetings were expanded to include men, so the learning can flow both ways.

Along with strengthening the female managers' career strategies, CH2M established a policy that for senior management jobs, any pool of candidates considered for an opening must include at least one woman. Since instituting these changes, the share of women in top jobs at CH2M has grown to 30 percent.[13]

- In breaking its glass ceiling, did CH2M look for a need for change in its female employees' behavior, in its own practices, or both?

1.	Develop a comprehensive organizationwide policy on sexual harassment and present it to all current and new employees. Stress that sexual harassment will not be tolerated under any circumstances. Emphasis is best achieved when the policy is publicized and supported by top management.
2.	Hold training sessions with supervisors to explain Title VII requirements, their role in providing an environment free of sexual harassment, and proper investigative procedures when charges occur.
3.	Establish a formal complaint procedure in which employees can discuss problems without fear of retaliation. The complaint procedure should spell out how charges will be investigated and resolved.
4.	Act immediately when employees complain of sexual harassment. Communicate widely that investigations will be conducted objectively and with appreciation for the sensitivity of the issue.
5.	When an investigation supports employee charges, discipline the offender at once. For extremely serious offenses, discipline should include penalties up to and including discharge. Discipline should be applied consistently across similar cases and among managers and hourly employees alike.
6.	Follow up on all cases to ensure a satisfactory resolution of the problem.

TABLE 11.3

Basic Components of an Effective Sexual Harassment Policy

SOURCE: Snell, S.A., and Bohlander, G.W. *Managing Human Resources*, 16th ed. Copyright © 2012. Cincinnati, OH: Cengage Learning, Inc. Reproduced by permission. www.cengage.com/permissions.

government came from males. If an employee files a complaint of sexual harassment with the Equal Employment Opportunity Commission (EEOC), the commission may investigate and, if it finds evidence for the complaint, may request mediation, seek a settlement, or file a lawsuit with the potential for stiff fines—and negative publicity that may damage the company's ability to recruit the best employees in the future.

Harassment by creation of a hostile work environment is now more typical than quid pro quo harassment. But because it may involve more subjective standards of behavior, it puts an extra burden on managers to maintain an appropriate work environment by ensuring that all employees know what conduct is and is not appropriate and that there are serious consequences for this behavior. In fact, even when managers do not themselves engage in harassment, if they fail to prevent it or to take appropriate action after receiving legitimate complaints about it, they may still be held liable, along with their companies, if a lawsuit is filed. It is also important for managers to know that the "hostile work environment" standard applies to same-sex harassment as well as to non-gender-related cases, such as a pattern of racial or ethnic slurs. Teenaged workers are a particularly vulnerable population because they are inexperienced, tend to hold lower-status jobs, and often feel hesitant or embarrassed to speak up. The federal EEOC has made this concern a priority and launched a teen-focused page called "Youth at Work" on its website (at http://www.youth.eeoc.gov). The National Restaurant Association and National Retail Federation also have stepped up efforts to protect teens from harassment.[14]

One way managers can help their companies prevent harassment from arising, or avoid punitive damages if a lawsuit is filed, is to make sure their organizations have an effective and comprehensive policy on harassment in place. Table 11.3 shows the basic components of such a policy. Companies such as Avon, Corning, and PwC have found that a strong commitment to diversity leads to fewer problems with sexual harassment.[15]

Before moving on, it is important to note that gender issues and the changing nature of work do not apply just to women. In some ways, the changing status of women has given men the opportunity to redefine their roles, expectations, and lifestyles. Some men are deciding that there is more to life than corporate success and are choosing to scale back work hours and commitments to spend time with their families.

> A strong commitment to diversity leads to fewer problems with sexual harassment.

Worker values are shifting toward personal time, quality of life, self-fulfillment, and family. Workers today, both men and women, are looking to achieve a balance between career and family.

In addition, a growing number of employers are thinking about gender in terms of the issues facing their employees who are gay, lesbian, bisexual, or transgender (LGBT). These employees may be concerned about work-related issues such as avoiding harassment, obtaining benefits for a same-sex spouse or domestic partner, or simply feeling free not to be secretive about this aspect of who they are. Treatment of LGBT employees is an area of ongoing change, both in societal attitudes and in the law. For example, a few years ago, a person in a same-sex relationship would automatically be legally categorized as single, but today some states have laws allowing these people to marry or register as domestic partners and to adopt children together. And the U.S. military has changed policies from banning homosexual service members to a policy of "don't ask, don't tell" in 1993, to a phased-in repeal of that policy beginning in 2011 that aims at an end of the ban on gay persons serving openly. In situations such as this, where laws, policies, and social norms are in a state of flux, employers must be especially attentive to understand what is required and how employees, customers, and other stakeholders are affected by company policies and practices.

Minorities and Immigrants   In addition to gender issues, the importance and scope of diversity are evident in the growth of racial minorities and immigrants in the workforce. Consider these facts:

> African American, Asian, and Hispanic workers are about one-fifth of the labor force in the United States.
>
> Asian and Hispanic workforces are growing the fastest in the United States, followed by the African American workforce.
>
> By 2020, more than 18 percent of the workforce is expected to be people of Hispanic origin.
>
> In 2012, for the first time, the census bureau estimated that a majority of children under age 1 in the United States were members of racial or ethnic minority groups.
>
> Four states (California, Hawaii, New Mexico, and Texas) and the District of Columbia have become majority minority, meaning a majority of the population consists of members of racial and ethnic minorities.
>
> Foreign-born workers make up more than 16 percent of the U.S. civilian labor force. Close to half of these workers are Hispanic, and nearly one-fourth are Asian.[16]

These numbers indicate that the term *minority*, as it is used typically, may soon become outdated. Particularly in urban areas where white males do not predominate, managing diversity means more than eliminating discrimination; it means capitalizing on the wide variety of skills available in the labor market. Organizations that do not take full advantage of the skills and capabilities of minorities and immigrants are severely limiting their potential talent pool and their ability to understand and capture minority markets. Those markets are growing rapidly. As the minority share of the population expands, so does its share of purchasing power. And if you sell to businesses, you are likely to deal with some minority-owned companies because the number of businesses started by Asian American, African American, and Hispanic entrepreneurs is growing much faster than the overall growth in new companies in the United States. For example, more than half of the companies that started in California's high-tech Silicon Valley were founded by immigrants, and in a recent year, one-fourth of patent applications in the United States identified an immigrant as the inventor or a co-inventor.[17]

In many urban areas with large Asian, Hispanic, or African American populations, banks have deliberately increased the diversity of their managers and tellers to reflect the population mix in the community and attract additional business. If they did not, customers would readily notice and switch to other banks in the area where they would feel more welcome and comfortable. Such diversity—and collaboration

TABLE 11.4   Executives of Color: Selected Examples

Name	Company	Title
Ajay Banga	MasterCard	President and CEO
David P. Bozeman	Caterpillar	Senior vice president, Caterpillar Enterprise System Group
Ursula Burns	Xerox Corp.	Chairman and CEO
Jin Sook and Do Won Chang	Forever 21	Cofounders and owners
Kenneth Chenault	American Express	Chairman and CEO
Paul Diaz	Kindred Healthcare	CEO
Linda Gooden	Lockheed Martin	Executive vice president, Information Systems and Global Solutions
Paul Fabara	American Express	Executive vice president, head of Global Credit Administration
Tony Hsieh	Zappos.com	CEO
Sanjay Jha	Motorola Mobility	CEO
Oscar Munoz	CSX	Executive vice president and chief operating officer
Kenneth C. Frazier	Merck	CEO
Gisel Ruiz	Wal-Mart Stores	Executive vice president, Wal-Mart US
Don Thompson	McDonald's	President and CEO
Oprah Winfrey	OWN	Chairman and CEO

SOURCES: "50 Most Powerful Women in Business," *Fortune,* October 8, 2012, http://money.cnn.com; Derek T. Dingle, "The Business Trailblazers and Titans of Black America," *Black Enterprise,* April 6, 2013, http://www.blackenterprise.com; Derek T. Dingle, "Black Enterprise's 100 Most Powerful Executives Honored," *Black Enterprise,* October 3, 2012, http://www.blackenterprise.com; "Top Six Indian CEOs in America," *SiliconIndia News,* March 15, 2012, http://www.siliconindia.com; "The 2013 Corporate Elite: Top 25 Executives," *Hispanic Business,* January 4, 2013, http://www.hispanicbusiness.com.

among employees—permits increased customer service, helping banks maintain their competitiveness. For example, tellers approached by new immigrants who do not yet speak English immediately call on their bilingual colleagues for help. The bilingual colleagues are also in a better position to assist the bank customers with special problems such as income transfers from abroad.

Even so, the evidence shows some troubling disparities in employment and earnings. Unemployment rates are higher for black and Hispanic workers than for whites—twice as high in the case of black men. Earnings of black and Hispanic workers have consistently trailed those of white workers; recent figures put the median earnings for African American employees at 79 percent of median earnings for white workers and the median earnings of Hispanics at just 71 percent. African Americans and Hispanic Americans are also underrepresented in management and professional occupations.[18] This underrepresentation may itself help perpetuate the problem because it can leave many aspiring young minorities with fewer role models or mentors that are so helpful in an executive career.

This disparity may exist even for similar jobs. There is also considerable evidence that discrimination may account for at least some of the disparities in employment and earnings. For example, in one recent study, fictitious résumés were used to respond to help-wanted ads in Boston and Chicago newspapers. Each résumé used either African American names such as Lakisha and Jamal or white-sounding names such as Emily and Greg. The résumés with white-sounding names were 50 percent more likely to get a callback for an interview than the same résumés with African American names. Despite equivalence in credentials, the often unconscious assumptions about different racial groups are very difficult to overcome.[19]

Nevertheless, significant progress has been made. As you can see from the examples in Table 11.4, talented members of minority groups are among the executives running companies and their divisions in a wide variety of industries. And some individuals

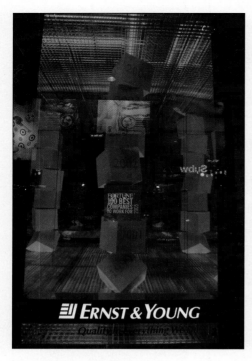

and groups are highly successful. Average pay and employment rates for Asian Americans actually exceed those for white workers.

In addition, virtually every large organization today has policies and programs dedicated to increasing minority representation—including compensation systems that reward managers for increasing the diversity of their operations. Major companies such as FedEx, Xerox, Morgan Stanley Shell, and Sun Microsystems have corporate diversity officers who assist organization managers in their efforts to attract, retain, and promote minority and women executives. Many organizations are also working to ensure a continuing supply of minority candidates by supporting minority internships and MBA programs. Dun and Bradstreet, for example, sponsors summer internship programs for minority MBA students. Lockheed Martin has partnered with the American Management Association's Operation Enterprise to establish two-week paid summer internship programs for high school and college students. These internship programs help students and organizations learn about one another and, ideally, turn into full-time employment opportunities. Table 11.5 shows the top 10 companies for diversity according to DiversityInc.com. For all these companies, developing, hiring, and retaining minority executives is critical for their ability to manage an ever-more-diverse workforce and to serve an increasing number of clients and customers with varied backgrounds.

According to a recent survey, Ernst & Young has been named as one of the best companies for valuing diversity, based on how it ranked in four key areas—CEO commitment, human capital, corporate and organizational communications, and supplier diversity.

Mentally and Physically Disabled People   The largest unemployed minority population in the United States is people with disabilities. It is composed of people of all ethnic backgrounds, cultures, and ages. The share of the population with a disability is growing as the average worker gets older and heavier.[20] According to U.S. government statistics, people with disabilities represent 10 percent of the working-age civilian population. Many of these people are not in the labor force (meaning they are neither working nor looking for a job), but of the more than 6 million disabled persons who are in the labor force, 14.5 percent were unemployed in 2009. That rate was far above the 9.3 percent unemployment rate for the general population. Persons with a disability are more likely to have jobs if they have higher levels of education, and they are more likely than nondisabled workers to have a part-time job because they can't find full-time work.[21]

The Americans with Disabilities Act (ADA), mentioned in Chapter 10, defines a disability as a physical or mental impairment that substantially limits one or more major life activities. Examples of such physical or mental impairments include those resulting from conditions such as orthopedic, visual, speech, and hearing impairments; cerebral palsy; epilepsy; multiple sclerosis; HIV infections; cancer; heart disease; diabetes; mental retardation; psychological illness; specific learning disabilities; drug addiction; and alcoholism.[22]

New assistive technologies are making it easier for companies to comply with the ADA and for those with disabilities to be productive on the job. In many cases, state

TABLE 11.5
Top 10 Companies for Diversity

1. Sodexo	6. Novartis Pharmaceuticals
2. PricewaterhouseCoopers (PwC)	7. Procter & Gamble
3. Kaiser Permanente	8. Prudential Financial
4. Ernst & Young	9. Accenture
5. MasterCard Worldwide	10. Johnson & Johnson

SOURCE: "The DiversityInc Top 50 Companies for Diversity," *DiversityInc*, 2013, http://www.diversityinc.com.

governments will pay for special equipment or other accommodations that workers need. Companies are discovering that making these accommodations can result in unanticipated fringe benefits, too. The National Industries for the Blind (NIB), a Wisconsin company that markets products under the Skilcraft brand name, is a case in point. Seventy-five percent of NIB employees are visually impaired. Because the company's warehouse pickers have trouble reading instructions on paper, NIB installed a voice technology system that conveys instructions to workers through headsets. An added benefit is that the technology has raised the productivity of the entire operation. Accuracy has improved, and workers—both blind and sighted—are able to pick and ship orders faster using the headsets.

For most businesses, mentally and physically disabled people represent an unexplored but fruitful labor market. Frequently employers have found that disabled employees are more dependable than other employees, miss fewer days of work, and exhibit lower turnover. Tax credits are also available to companies that hire disabled workers. In addition, managers who hire and support employees with disabilities are signaling to other employees and outside stakeholders their strong interest in creating an inclusive organization culture.

Education Levels   When the United States was primarily an industrial economy, many jobs required physical strength, stamina, and skill in a trade, rather than college and professional degrees. In today's service and technology economy, more positions require a college education and even a graduate or professional degree. Today's prospective employees have responded by applying to college in record numbers. The proportion of the workforce with at least some college education has been growing steadily. In 1947, about 5 percent of workers had at least a bachelor's degree; the percentage passed 15 percent in the 1970s and stands at 30 percent today. These numbers include rising shares of African American, Hispanic, and female graduates. People with degrees in science and technology are in especially high demand. Employers often expand their search for scientists and computer professionals overseas, but visa requirements limit that supply. At the other end of the spectrum, in the current labor pool, almost 25 percent of foreign-born workers have not completed high school, compared with just 5 percent of native-born workers.[23]

> The share of workers with a bachelor's degree has more than doubled since 1970.

The Age of the Workforce

The baby boom generation (those born between 1946 and 1964) is aging. Today almost 4 out of 10 workers are age 45 or older, and the median age of America's workforce is rising as the number of older workers swells, whereas the number of young workers grows only slightly. Industries such as nursing and manufacturing are already facing a tremendous loss of expertise as a result of downsizing and a rapidly aging workforce. Other industries will soon be in similar straits.[24] As a result of these trends, the Bureau of Labor Statistics projects that entry-level workers will be in short supply.

On the plus side, almost 70 percent of workers between the ages of 45 and 74 told researchers with AARP (formerly the American Association of Retired Persons) that they intend to work in retirement. Retirees often return to the workforce at the behest of their employers, who can't afford to lose the knowledge accumulated by longtime employees, their willingness to work nontraditional shifts, and their reliable work habits, which have a positive effect on the entire work group.

To prevent an exodus of talent, employers need strategies to help retain and attract skilled and knowledgeable older workers. Phased retirement plans that allow older employees to work fewer hours per week is one such strategy. Almost one-third of retiring faculty members at 16 University of North Carolina campuses take advantage of phased retirement, and the concept is catching on in many other public and private

TABLE 11.6
Top Five Approaches for
Using Older Employees
More Fully

Approaches to Using Older Employees More Fully	Approaches Considered Very or Moderately Effective	Businesses That Have Implemented the Approach
Benefit packages targeted toward older employees	68%	18%
Part-time work arrangements with continuation of benefits	64	30
Educating managers about ways to use older employees	60	25
Increased availability of part-time work for older employees (regardless of benefits)	55	36
Skill training for older employees	55	44

SOURCE: From "American Business and Older Employees: A Survey of Findings," Copyright © 2002 AARP.

organizations.[25] Other strategies include making workplace adaptations to help older workers cope with the physical problems they experience as they age, such as poorer vision, hearing, and mobility. This trend is a significant change from the practice in recent decades, when older workers were given incentives to leave to allow companies to reduce overhead and perhaps hire less expensive replacements. Table 11.6 shows how creative companies are rethinking their retirement policies and solving their skilled labor shortage by finding ways to attract and retain people over 55. These companies save on turnover and training costs and capitalize on the experience of their older employees.

In Practice

HIRING WORKERS 50 AND OLDER AT CVS

For CVS Caremark, hiring workers aged 50 and older is a way to get the best people. The drugstore chain has found that employees in the upper age brackets are just as productive as their younger coworkers and less likely to quit. Furthermore, because with one-fourth of its customers are older than 65, CVS Caremark hopes the one-fifth of its employees who are 50 or older will have a knack for sensing and meeting their needs.

The company actively recruits older workers for its entry-level positions through a program it calls Talent Is Ageless. To find candidates, it partners with groups such as AARP, the National Council on Aging, and Experience Works. CVS Caremark offers part-time, flexible schedules, which are attractive to people easing their way into retirement or supplementing retirement income.

One way the company retains these older workers is by offering a snowbird program. Because some older people enjoy living in northern climates during the summer and southern climates during the winter, CVS Caremark sees geographic shifts in its workers and customers as the seasons change. The snowbird program lets workers, including pharmacists, cosmetics consultants, and photo supervisors, hold jobs at one store for part of the year and another store during the rest of the year. This enables the chain to meet geographic shifts in demand using experienced workers. A few hundred employees sign up as snowbirds every year. CVS Caremark credits the program with helping it keep employee retention rates above the average for its industry.[26]

- How might the effort to hire older workers affect the four-fifths of employees who are *under* age 50? How can CVS Caremark foster a good working environment for all?

At the same time, companies need to compete hard for the smaller pool of young talent, being prepared for applicants who know the job market and are ready to demand the working conditions they value and the praise they were raised to expect. Bruce Tulgan, founder of Rainmaker Thinking, which specializes in researching generational differences, says Generation Y—today's young workers—tend to be "high-maintenance" but also "high-performing," having learned to process the flood of information that pours in over the Internet.[27] Many of these workers were raised by highly involved parents who filled their lives with quality experiences, so employers are scrambling to design work arrangements that are stimulating, involve teamwork, keep work hours reasonable to allow for outside activities, and provide for plenty of positive feedback. Employers are also updating their recruiting tactics to reach young workers where they are—online. Intermedia, which operates computer centers to host large-scale web and e-mail software for small companies, says the social networking site LinkedIn helps the company reach well-qualified information technology workers. In the government sector, the Central Intelligence Agency and National Security Agency have set up pages on Facebook, where members who register for access can read information about job openings.[28]

Managing Diversity versus Affirmative Action

For many organizations, the original impetus to diversify their workforces was social responsibility and legal necessity (recall Chapters 5 and 10). To correct the past exclusion of women and minorities, companies introduced **affirmative action**—special efforts to recruit and hire qualified members of groups that have been discriminated against in the past. The intent is not to prefer these group members to the exclusion of others but to correct for the long history of discriminatory practices and exclusion. Viewed from this perspective, amending these wrongs is seen as the moral, ethical, and legal approach.

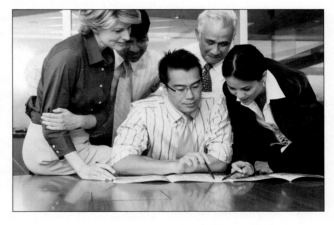

affirmative action

Special efforts to recruit and hire qualified members of groups that have been discriminated against in the past.

Such efforts, along with legal remedies to end discrimination, have had a powerful impact, transforming our society and organizations in positive ways that would have been unimaginable only a few decades ago. Today the immigrant nature of American society is virtually taken for granted—even seen as a source of pride. And women, African Americans, Hispanics, and other minorities routinely occupy positions that in years past would have been totally closed to them.

Nevertheless, as we have seen, a legislated approach tends to result in fragmented efforts that have not yet fully achieved the integrative goals of diversity. Employment discrimination still persists, and even after decades of government legislation, equal employment opportunity (EEO) and affirmative action laws have not adequately improved the upward mobility of women and

Managing diversity involves organizations making changes to remove obstacles that may keep people from reaching their full potential.

minorities. To move beyond correcting past wrongs to truly inclusive organizations requires a change in organization culture—one in which diversity is seen as contributing directly to the attainment of organization goals.

Seen in this way, affirmative action and diversity are complementary, not the same. In contrast to EEO and affirmative action programs, managing diversity means moving beyond legislated mandates to embrace a proactive business philosophy that sees differences as a positive value. In the end, *all* employees are different. These differences may include the fundamental attributes of race, ethnicity, age, and gender we have been discussing, but they also may include less obvious attributes such as employees' place of origin, their education, or their life experience. All these elements add to the richness of talents and perspectives managers can draw on. Managing diversity in this broader sense involves organizations making changes in their systems, structures, and practices to eliminate barriers that may keep people from reaching their full potential. It means treating people as individuals—*equally* but not necessarily the *same*—recognizing that each employee has different needs and will need different things to succeed. But it also asks managers to recognize and value the uniqueness of each employee and to see the different ideas and perspectives each brings to the organization as a source of competitive advantage. In short, managing diversity is not just about getting more minorities and women into the organization. It is about creating an environment in which employees from *every* background listen to each other and work better together so that the organization as a whole will become more effective. This emphasis on coming together to benefit the whole has led many companies now to refer to diversity and *inclusion* as their objectives.

Affirmative action and diversity are complementary, not the same.

LO 3 Competitive Advantage through Diversity and Inclusion

Today many organizations are approaching diversity and inclusion from a more practical, business-oriented perspective. Increasingly, diversity can be a powerful tool for building competitive advantage. Various studies have found links between diversity in an organization's upper ranks and superior financial performance. Some evidence suggests that this correlation may result from investors' preferences for organizations with a policy of inclusion rather than from superior management of diverse companies. Nevertheless, diversity does not stand in the way of high performance, and it may provide an organizational strength—especially if organizations know how to leverage it.[29]

There are many advantages—and some obvious challenges—to managing a diverse workforce. We discuss some of them in this section.

Ability to Attract and Retain Motivated Employees   For companies facing changing demographics and business needs, diversity makes good sense. Companies with a reputation for providing opportunities for diverse employees will have a competitive advantage in the labor market and will be sought out by the most qualified employees. In addition, when employees believe their differences are not merely tolerated but valued, they may become more loyal, productive, and committed.

Better Perspective on a Differentiated Market   Companies such as Elizabeth Arden, IBM, Target, and Kroger are committed to diversity because as the composition of the American workforce changes, so does the customer base of these companies. Just as women and minorities may prefer to work for an employer that values diversity, they may prefer to patronize such organizations.

Many Asian Americans, African Americans, Hispanic Americans, and women have entered the middle class and now control consumer dollars. Similarly, each new generation has its own set of values and experiences, so diversity in ages can help the organization relate to more age groups of customers. A diverse workforce can provide a company with greater knowledge of the preferences and consuming habits of this diversified marketplace. This knowledge can assist companies in designing products and developing marketing campaigns to meet those consumers' needs. In addition, for at least some goods and services, a multicultural sales force may help an organization sell to diverse groups. A diverse workforce also can give a company a competitive edge in a global economy by facilitating understanding of other customs, cultures, and marketplace needs.

Ability to Leverage Creativity and Innovation in Problem Solving   Work team diversity promotes creativity and innovation because people from different backgrounds hold different perspectives on issues. Diverse groups have a broader

Bottom Line

Diversity can help an organization succeed in new markets. *What are some new or diverse markets that Toys "R" Us can serve best with a diverse workforce?*

base of experience from which to approach a problem; when effectively managed, they invent more options and create more solutions than homogeneous groups do. In addition, diverse work groups are freer to deviate from traditional approaches and practices. The presence of diversity also can help minimize "groupthink" (recall Chapter 3).[30]

Many law firms now routinely have diverse legal teams working together on a case. Fresh "out of the box" ideas are often required in complex cases, and a group of lawyers from the same background who all think the same way may not be able to be as innovative as a team that is more diverse. In addition, in jury trials, the impression that a legal team makes on a jury can help or badly hurt the client, and diverse jurors are more likely to be receptive to a visibly diverse team, with different kinds of lawyers participating. The increased importance of legal team diversity has caused some law firms to form alliances with minority firms so they can collaborate on cases.

Enhancement of Organizational Flexibility   A diverse workforce can enhance organizational flexibility because managing diversity successfully requires a corporate culture that tolerates many styles and approaches. Less restrictive policies and procedures and less standardized operating methods enable organizations to become more flexible and thus better able to respond quickly to environmental changes (recall Chapters 2 and 9). J. P. Morgan, for example, sees valuing diversity as a necessary part of a strategy based on superior talent: "We can only win by creating and encouraging a culture of inclusion, where everyone's opinion counts and all employees have the freedom to deliver their absolute best."[31]

Bottom Line

Diversity can bring new ideas to the organization. *What kinds of innovation are a strength in your generation? In a generation older than yours?*

Bottom Line

A diverse workforce can lead to greater responsiveness. *Why might a customer who wants something new get a faster response from a company that tolerates different styles?*

In Practice

RESPECT FOR DIVERSITY AT P&G

Procter & Gamble considers employee diversity a source of competitive advantage. At a global company, recruiting diversity opens up the largest possible pool of talent and brings in people who understand all customer groups and their needs. Respect for diversity also is a way to ensure the greatest innovation because people feel confident about drawing on their skills and sharing their ideas.

This commitment to diversity is reflected in corporate programs. P&G has established seven affinity groups, including the African American Leadership Network, Hispanic Leadership Team, and People with Disabilities group. By participating in these voluntary groups, employees can bring up issues of concern, find mentors, and enjoy mutual support. Also, a training program called the Clay Street Project sends employees offsite to practice working effectively on diverse teams.

Commitment to diversity is also reflected in P&G's talented people. The 11-member board of directors is unusually diverse for a big U.S. corporation; it includes five women and a prominent African-American man, American Express CEO Ken Chenault. P&G's 135,000 employees in 80 countries include Linda Clement-Holmes, the chief diversity officer, who reports directly to the CEO. Clement-Holmes is a 27-year veteran of P&G, an African-American woman who started in the information technology department. Another successful African-American woman is Monique Picou, who leads supply operations in the United Kingdom. She started her P&G career in 1989, working in manufacturing and process engineering in Kansas and Louisiana and then holding supply management roles at the Ohio headquarters and in Geneva, Switzerland.[32]

• What strengths does P&G gain from adding these managers into the mix with the white, male, Cincinnati-based managers who dominated the company in the past?

Challenges of Diversity and Inclusion

We have discussed the laws guaranteeing equal opportunity and the significant and growing business advantages of diversity and inclusion. Yet every year thousands of lawsuits are filed over issues of discrimination and fair treatment, some involving even the largest and most respected firms.[33] Even when there is no overt discrimination in hiring and pay, managing diversity can be difficult. Often minorities and women who have been hired find themselves in an organization culture or environment that does not give them the opportunity to do their best work. And managers with all the goodwill in the world find it harder than they expected to get people from different backgrounds to work together for a common goal.[34]

To become effective managers of the diverse organization, we first have to identify and overcome a number of challenges. These include unexamined assumptions, lower cohesiveness, communication problems, mistrust and tension, and stereotyping.

Unexamined Assumptions   For most of us, seeing the world from someone else's perspective is difficult because our own assumptions and viewpoints seem so normal and familiar. For example, heterosexuals may not even think about whether to put a picture of their loved ones on their desks; it is a routine, even automatic decision, repeated in a million workplaces across the country. But for gay employees in many companies, displaying such a picture may cause considerable anxiety—if they feel able to consider it at all. Other unexamined assumptions involve the roles of men and women; for example, many people assume that women will shoulder the burden of caring for children, even if it conflicts with the demands of work. In a recent study, researchers sent employers résumés that were identical except that some bore a male name and others a female name, and half implied that the person submitting the résumé was a parent. Employers were less likely to invite the fictional candidate for an interview when the résumé implied the candidate was a parent—but only if the name was female.[35] Because the résumés were otherwise identical, the results suggest that people make assumptions about mothers that do not apply to fathers or to childless women.

In an organization that is oblivious to these different perspectives and does not take an active role in making people from diverse backgrounds feel welcome and valued, managers may find it more difficult to develop an enthusiastically shared sense of purpose.

Lower Cohesiveness   Diversity can create a lack of cohesiveness. *Cohesiveness* refers to how tightly knit the group is and the degree to which group members perceive, interpret, and act on their environment in similar or mutually agreed-upon ways. Because of their lack of similarity in language, culture, and/or experience, diverse groups typically are less cohesive than homogeneous groups. Often mistrust, miscommunication, stress, and attitudinal differences reduce cohesiveness, which in turn can diminish productivity. This may be one explanation for the results of a study that showed greater turnover among store employees who feel they are greatly outnumbered by coworkers from other racial or ethnic groups.[36] In a diverse group, managers are challenged to take the lead in building cohesiveness by establishing common goals and values. Group cohesiveness will be discussed in greater detail in Chapter 14.

Communication Problems   Perhaps the most common negative effect of diversity is communication problems. These difficulties include misunderstandings, inaccuracies, inefficiencies, and slowness. Speed is lost when not all group members are fluent in the same language or when additional time is required to explain things. Sometimes diversity may decrease communication, as when white male managers feel less comfortable giving feedback to women or minorities for fear of how criticism may be received. The result may be employees who do not have a clear idea of what they need to do to improve their performance.

Diversity can also lead to errors and misunderstandings. Group members may assume they interpret things similarly when they in fact do not, or they may disagree because of their different frames of reference.[37] For example, if managers do not actively encourage and accept the expression of different points of view, some employees may be afraid to speak up at meetings, leaving the manager with a false impression that consensus has been reached. We discuss other problems in communication and how to avoid them in Chapter 15.

Mistrust and Tension   People prefer to associate with others who are like themselves. This is a normal, understandable tendency. But it can often lead to misunderstanding, mistrust, and even fear of those who are different because of a lack of contact and low familiarity. For example, if women and minority group members are routinely excluded, as they sometimes are, from joining white male colleagues at business lunches or after-hour gatherings, they may come to feel isolated from their colleagues. Similarly, tension often develops between people of different ages—for example, what one generation might see as a tasteless tattoo may be a creative example of body art for a member of a different generation. Such misunderstandings can cause stress, tension, and even resentment, making it more difficult to reach agreement on solutions to problems.

Stereotyping   We learn to see the world in a certain way on the basis of our backgrounds and experiences. Our interests, values, and cultures act as filters and distort, block, and select what we see and hear. We see and hear what we expect to see and hear. Group members often inappropriately stereotype their different colleagues rather than accurately perceiving and evaluating those individuals' contributions, capabilities, aspirations, and motivations. Such stereotypes are usually negative or condescending. Women may be stereotyped as not dedicated to their careers, older workers as unwilling to learn new skills, minority group members as less educated or capable. But even so-called positive stereotypes can be burdensome. For example, the common stereotype that Asians are good at math may leave unrecognized other attributes that a particular Asian employee might have. Many women and minorities dislike being stereotyped as members of groups that need special help or support, preferring to be treated as individuals.

Stereotypes may cost the organization dearly by stifling employees' ambition so that they don't fully contribute. Research supports the idea that people perform better when they expect that they can. In a study in which undergraduate students were purportedly pretesting a new graduate admissions test, half the subjects were told that males had greater ability in the test's subject matter. Although all subjects were told they received the same score, the females exposed to the biased message rated their abilities in the subject lower than the males who heard the message, and they set lower goals for their future performance in that area. In another study, playing off the stereotypes that males and Asians excel at math, Asian American women were given a math test after they answered a set of questions either about their Asian identity or about their gender. When asked about their ethnic background, they performed better; when asked about gender, they performed worse.[38] In a corporate setting, managers want their employees to perform to their full ability; stereotypes that dampen individual employees' ambition and performance also detract from the organization's success.

Unless managers are aware of their stereotypes, either their own or those held by others, the stereotypes can directly affect how people in their organizations are treated. Employees stereotyped as unmotivated or emotional will be given less stress-provoking (and perhaps less important) jobs than their coworkers. Those job assignments will create frustrated employees, perhaps resulting in lower commitment, higher turnover, and underused skills.[39]

TABLE 11.7   Beyond Affirmative Action: Key Practices to Leverage Employee Differences

	Key Individual Practices	Key Organizational Practices
Seeing	• Adopt a stance that relevant differences are ubiquitous. • Attend to points of conflict. • Observe silence.	• Attend to intergroup tension. • Reduce the climate of secrecy.
Understanding	Cultivate sources of information about the difference.	

	• Build skill in acquiring data.
	  – Listen.
	  – Ask questions.
	  – Learn and share your own story.
	• Include people who are different in your inner circle or network.
		• Acquire information via survey and other data gathering.
		• Create and institutionalize inclusive structures.

Valuing	• Lower the levels of unnecessary carefulness when dealing with differences. • Be willing to persist in the midst of conflict and its accompanying discomfort. • Incorporate data into your worldview.	• Reward and hold employees accountable for engaging in difference-related activities. • Recruit and develop people who add diversity to the organization.

SOURCE: M. N. Davidson, *The End of Diversity as We Know It: Why Diversity Efforts Fail and How Leveraging Difference Can Succeed* (San Francisco: Berrett-Kohler Press, 2011).

The Challenge Ahead   For all these reasons, and more, managing diversity is not easy. As illustrated by the example of NASCAR in the following "Management Connection: Progress Report," U.S. organizations are not isolated from the continuing effects of America's racial legacy or the remaining barriers to equal opportunity. Nor are managers immune to the biases, stereotypes, lack of experience, and tensions that make communication, teamwork, and leadership in a diverse workforce much more challenging. Yet managers very much need to confront these issues. They need to develop the skills and strategies diversity requires if they and their organizations are to succeed in our increasingly multicultural business environment.

One constructive way to begin is with what Martin Davidson has called "leveraging difference." This approach sees diversity not as a problem to be tolerated or solved but as a resource the organization can capitalize on, even though doing so is sometimes difficult. Leveraging difference starts with the recognition that we all bring something different to an organization. Along with surface differences such as sex and race, we contribute different ways of thinking and problem solving, different strengths and values, and so on. To capitalize on these differences, as shown in Table 11.7, people in the organization have to begin by seeing them. Then individuals must make the effort to understand the differences by asking questions and listening carefully. The next step is to value the differences not only through the organization's recruitment and recognition programs but also through willingness to persist despite conflict and to incorporate new perspectives into one's own thinking. This effort provides the information needed to leverage the differences by applying them to the whole spectrum of organization activities, such as innovating, learning, working as a team, and interacting with customers.[40] The remainder of this chapter provides further thinking on how to meet the challenges of diversity and leverage it for organizational success.

Management Connection

NASCAR'S DRIVE FOR DIVERSITY CAN BE A GRUELING RIDE

The driver development program of NASCAR's Drive for Diversity (D4D) effort aims to "give minority and female drivers the opportunity to compete with a NASCAR team." It does so by recruiting minority and female drivers, training them, and letting them compete in the K&N Pro Series East and Whelen All-American Series. Also, according to NASCAR, the program "seeks opportunities for program graduates to advance within various NASCAR series; provides media training and marketing guidance to developing drivers; and exposes participating drivers to media opportunities outside the sport."

The program is open to candidates who are between the ages of 15 and 26, citizens or those legally able to work in the United States, and female or a member of one of several minority groups: African American, Asian, Hispanic, Native Hawaiian or Pacific Islander, and American Indian. However, not just anyone in these groups qualifies. All applicants must have experience and skill in racing at the local or regional level (for example, in go-karts, sprint cars, or stock cars). Out of more than 200 applicants, NASCAR selects about 30 to compete in an evaluation program called the Combine. NASCAR observes their on-track performance and interactions with sponsors and the media. It then chooses six to ten drivers for the program, based on driving ability, physical stamina, knowledge about cars, and whether they are marketable. Drivers chosen for the 2013 class came from California, Nevada, New Mexico, North Carolina, Tennessee, Mexico, and Puerto Rico.

According to Marcus Jadotte, NASCAR's vice president of public affairs and multicultural development, NASCAR's hope is "to invite and encourage diverse participation across the sport." D4D drivers such as Kyle Larson and Darrell Wallace Jr. credit the program with giving them the kinds of experiences they need to reach their full potential and introduce the sport to a wider audience. Veteran driver Kyle Busch agrees that diversity can benefit the whole organization, saying it "widens our fan base."

Participants in the program are grateful for the experience, training, and mentoring. However, they acknowledge that there's a downside. Although few applicants make the cut and the training is rigorous, D4D drivers have admitted they hear criticism that NASCAR is giving them an unfair advantage. However, drivers such as Ryan Gifford and Katie Hagar from the 2010 class say their best answer is to learn all aspects of the sport, get out on the track, ride near the front, and win.[41]

- Does the D4D program sound more like managing diversity or affirmative action? Why?
- How should NASCAR address criticism that it gives minority and female drivers an unfair advantage?

Multicultural Organizations

To capitalize on the benefits and minimize the costs of a diverse workforce, perhaps one of the first things managers need to do is examine their organization's prevailing assumptions about people and cultures. Table 11.8 shows some of the fundamental assumptions that may exist. Based on these assumptions, we can classify organizations as one of three types and describe their implications for managers.

Some organizations are **monolithic**. This type of organization has very little cultural integration; in other words, it employs few women, minorities, or any other groups that differ from the majority. For example, in its hiring, an organization might favor alumni of the same college, perhaps even more specifically targeting members of fraternities who are enthusiastic about the school's football team. Such an organization is highly homogeneous in terms of its employee population. In monolithic organizations, if groups other than the norm are employed, they are found primarily in low-status jobs. Minority group members must adopt the norms of the majority to survive. This fact, coupled with small numbers, keeps conflicts among groups low. Discrimination and prejudice typically prevail, informal integration is almost nonexistent, and minority group members do not identify strongly with the company.

monolithic organization

An organization that has a low degree of structural integration—employing few women, minorities, or other groups that differ from the majority—and thus has a highly homogeneous employee population.

TABLE 11.8   Diversity Assumptions and Their Implications for Management

Common and Misleading Assumptions		Less Common and More Appropriate Assumptions	
Homogeneity	*Melting pot myth:* We are all the same.	**Heterogeneity**	*Image of cultural pluralism:* We are not all the same; groups within society differ across cultures.
Similarity	*Similarity myth:* "They" are all just like me.	**Similarity and difference**	*They are not just like me:* Many people differ from me culturally. Most people exhibit both cultural similarities and differences when compared with me.
Parochialism	*Only-one-way myth:* Our way is the only way. We do not recognize any other way of living or working.	**Equifinality**	*Our way is not the only way:* There are many culturally distinct ways of reaching the same goal, of working, and of living one's life.
Ethnocentrism	*One-best-way myth:* Our way is the best way. All other approaches are inferior versions of our way.	**Culture contingency**	*Our way is one possible way:* There are many and equally good ways to reach the same goal. The best way depends on the culture of the people involved.

SOURCE: From "Diversity Assumptions and Their Implications for Management" by Nancy J. Adler, *Handbook of Organization*, 1996. Reprinted courtesy of Marcel Dekker Inc., New York.

pluralistic organization

An organization that has a relatively diverse employee population and makes an effort to involve employees from different gender, racial, or cultural backgrounds.

Most large U.S. organizations made the transition from monolithic to pluralistic organizations in the 1960s and 1970s because of changing demographics as well as societal forces such as the civil rights and women's movements. **Pluralistic organizations** have a more diverse employee population and take steps to involve persons from different gender, racial, or cultural backgrounds. These organizations use an affirmative action approach to managing diversity: They actively try to hire and train a diverse workforce and to ensure against any discrimination against minority group members. They typically have much more integration than do monolithic organizations, but like monolithic organizations, they often have minority group members clustered at certain levels or in particular functions within the organization.

Because of greater cultural integration, affirmative action programs, and training programs, the pluralistic organization has some acceptance of minority group members into the informal network, much less discrimination, and less prejudice. Improved employment opportunities create greater identification with the organization among minority group members. Often the resentment of majority group members, coupled with the increased number of women and minorities, creates more conflict than exists in the monolithic organization.

multicultural organization

An organization that values cultural diversity and seeks to utilize and encourage it.

The pluralistic organization fails to address the cultural aspects of integration. In contrast, in **multicultural organizations** diversity not only exists but is valued. These organizations fully integrate gender, racial, and minority group members both formally and informally. But managers in such organizations do not focus primarily on the visible differences between employees, such as race or sex. Rather, managers value and draw on the different experience and knowledge employees bring to the organization and help it achieve agreed-upon strategies and goals.[42] The multicultural organization is marked by an absence of prejudice and discrimination and by low levels of intergroup conflict. Such an organization creates a synergistic environment in which all members contribute to their maximum potential, and the advantages of diversity can be fully realized.[43]

How Organizations Can Cultivate a Diverse Workforce

LO 6

An organization's plans for becoming multicultural and making the most of its diverse workforce should include (1) securing top management's leadership and commitment, (2) assessing the organization's progress toward goals, (3) attracting employees, (4) training employees in diversity, and (5) retaining employees. A recent study examining the performance of hundreds of companies over a 30-year period found that organizations that assigned responsibility for achieving diversity targets to certain individuals or groups made the most progress in increasing the share of female and black workers on their payrolls. Moderate change occurred in companies that set up programs for mentoring and networking, but formal diversity training programs had little effect unless the organizations also use the other methods.[44] Thus cultivating diversity needs to be a well-planned, organizationwide effort in which each element is supported by the personal commitment of individual managers, who address this issue as seriously as they do other management challenges. These managers actively seek to develop the skills, understanding, and practices that enable people of every background to do their best work in the common pursuit of the organization's goals.

Top Management's Leadership and Commitment

Obtaining top management's leadership and commitment is critical for diversity programs to succeed. Otherwise the rest of the organization will not take the effort seriously. One way to communicate this commitment to all employees—as well as to the external environment—is to incorporate the organization's attitudes toward diversity into the corporate mission statement and into strategic plans and objectives. Managerial compensation can be linked directly to accomplishing diversity goals. Adequate funding must be allocated to the diversity effort to ensure its success. Also, top management can set an example for other organization members by participating in diversity programs and making participation mandatory for all managers.

Joe Dumars is one of the high-profile minority presidents in the NBA.

As we mentioned earlier, some organizations have established corporate offices or committees to coordinate the companywide diversity effort and provide feedback to top management. Honeywell hired a director of workforce diversity, and Avon, a director of multicultural planning and design. Other companies prefer to incorporate diversity management into the function of director of affirmative action or EEO.

The work of managing diversity cannot be done by top management or diversity directors alone. Many companies rely on minority advisory groups or task forces to monitor organizational policies, practices, and attitudes; assess their impact on the diverse groups within the organization; and provide feedback and suggestions to top management.

For example, at Equitable Life Assurance Society, employee groups meet regularly with the CEO to discuss issues pertaining to women, African Americans, and Hispanics and make recommendations for improvement. At Honeywell, disabled employees formed a council to discuss their needs. They proposed and accepted an accessibility program that went beyond federal regulations for accommodations of disabilities.

As you can see, progressive companies are moving from asking managers what they think minority employees need and toward asking the employees themselves what they need.

Organizational Assessment

The next step in managing diversity is to establish an ongoing assessment of the organization's workforce, culture, policies, and practices in areas such as recruitment, promotions, benefits, and compensation. As part of this assessment, managers may evaluate whether they are attracting their share of diverse candidates from the labor pool and whether the needs of their customers are being addressed by the current composition of their workforce. The objective is to identify areas where there are problems or opportunities and to make recommendations where changes are needed. Etsy, the social commerce website for handcrafted and vintage items, determined that 80 percent of its customers are women but only about 3 percent of its engineers were women. Marc Hedlund, senior vice president of engineering, was concerned this mismatch was making it harder to attract and serve customers. Hedlund determined that Etsy needed to bring more female engineers on board and develop their skills.[45]

Many women and Asians can be at a disadvantage when aggressiveness is a valued part of an organization's culture. Analysis might reveal that this value exists and that it excludes employees who do not share it from full participation. Managers can then decide that the organizational values need to be changed so that other styles of interacting are equally acceptable. Managers can also change their own behaviors to reflect this change—for example, by calling on all individuals in a meeting for their ideas instead of letting more assertive participants dominate. Corporate values and norms should be identified and critically evaluated regarding their necessity and their impact on the diverse workforce.

Attracting Employees

Companies can attract a diverse, qualified workforce by using effective recruiting practices, accommodating employees' work and family needs, and offering alternative work arrangements.

Recruitment   A company's image can be a strong recruiting tool. Companies with reputations for hiring and promoting all types of people have a competitive advantage. Xerox gives prospective minority employees reprints of an article that rates the company as one of the best places for African Americans to work. Hewlett-Packard ensures that its female candidates are familiar with its high rating by *Working Woman* magazine.

Many employers are implementing policies to attract more women, ensure that women's talents are used to full advantage, and avoid losing their most capable female employees. Etsy's solution was to increase the pool of software engineers, at the same time positioning itself as a company that values women. It offers female engineers $5,000 scholarships to the Hacker School's three-month programming course, which brought a flood of Etsy-appreciating women to learn the kinds of skills Etsy needs. Also, it shifted its focus from hiring senior engineers to hiring junior engineers and training them to lead. The focus on diversity not only has increased the share of female engineers at Etsy, but it also has attracted the kinds of male engineers who value the company's culture and work well on group projects.

Many minorities, disabled persons, and economically disadvantaged people are physically isolated from job opportunities. Companies can bring information about job opportunities to the source of labor, or they can transport the labor to the jobs. Polycast Technology in Stamford, Connecticut, contracts with a private van company to transport workers from the Bronx in New York City to jobs in Stamford. Days Inn recruits homeless workers in Atlanta and houses them in a motel within walking distance of their jobs. Burger King has done a lot to recruit and hire immigrants in its fast-food restaurants.

In Practice

STRONG IMAGE IS A RECRUITING TOOL FOR CAESAR RIVISE

Diversity is built into the origins of the Philadelphia law firm of Caesar Rivise. The firm's founder was Abraham Caesar, an attorney specializing in intellectual property (for example, patents and trademarks). Back in 1926, Caesar could not land a job at one of the local law firms because he was Jewish. Instead he founded his own firm, joined the next year by partner Charles Rivise. Together the two attorneys built their practice and wrote important reference books on patents, establishing their reputation as experts in the field.

Given Caesar's early experiences, it's not surprising that his law firm committed itself to diversity in hiring. Stanley Cohen, now a partner, noticed that when he joined the firm in the 1960s. Back then, he recalls, his secretary was an African American man. Another Caesar Rivise employee since the 1960s is Bernice Mims. Although Mims graduated at the top of her South Philadelphia High School class, jobs were offered to other students and not Mims because she was black and the employer stipulated "no Jews or Negroes." However, Caesar hired her as a law clerk, and she remained loyal to the firm, eventually working her way up to manager of human resources.

Today Caesar Rivise builds on its historical commitment to diversity in recruiting by sponsoring diversity fellowships at Drexel University's Earle Mack School of Law. The firm assists qualified minority law students with tuition and offers them work experience. Partnering with Drexel is a good strategic fit for the firm because the university emphasizes technology and science—backgrounds that are important for working with corporate clients on technical matters. Cohen, for example, has a chemical engineering degree from Drexel.[46]

- In what ways is Caesar Rivise's image a strong recruiting tool for the firm?

Accommodating Work and Family Needs   More job seekers are putting family needs first. Corporate work and family policies are now one of the most important recruiting tools.

Employers that offer onsite child care report decreased turnover and absenteeism and improved morale. In addition to providing child care, many companies now assist with care for elderly dependents, offer time off to care for sick family members, provide parental leaves of absence, and offer a variety of benefits that can be tailored to individual family needs. Some companies are accommodating the needs and concerns of dual-career couples by limiting relocation requirements or providing job search assistance to relocated spouses.

Alternative Work Arrangements   Another way managers accommodate diversity is to offer flexible work schedules and arrangements. Stiff demand for engineering talent is motivating manufacturing companies to accommodate the needs of employees with family responsibilities. Autodesk, which sells design software, sees flexible scheduling as a way to attract and keep female employees. At Freescale Semiconductor, the focus is on meeting performance targets, not on working a set schedule. Section manager Amy Oesch says this approach has enabled her to juggle family responsibilities while moving up to positions of greater authority and earning a graduate degree.[47]

Other creative work arrangements include compressed workweeks (e.g., four 10-hour days) and job sharing, in which two part-time workers share one full-time job. Another option to accommodate working mothers and disabled employees is teleworking (working from home) or telecommuting (working from home via computer hookup to the main work site). This option has been slow to catch on, but the organizations that have tried it report favorable results.

Training Employees

As you learned in Chapter 10, employees can be developed in a variety of ways. Traditionally, most management training was based on the unstated assumption that managing means managing a homogeneous, often white-male, full-time workforce. But gender, race, culture, age, educational, and other differences create an additional layer of complexity.[48] Diversity training programs attempt to identify and reduce hidden biases and develop the skills needed to manage a diversified workforce effectively.

The majority of U.S. organizations sponsor some sort of diversity training. Typically, diversity training has two components: awareness building and skill building.

Awareness Building   Awareness building is designed to increase awareness of the meaning and importance of valuing diversity.[49] Its aim is not to teach specific skills but to sensitize employees to the assumptions they make about others and the way those assumptions affect their behaviors, decisions, and judgment. For example, male employees who have never reported to a female manager may feel awkward the first time they are required to do so. Awareness building can reveal this concern in advance and help the managers address it.

To build awareness, trainers teach people to become familiar with myths, stereotypes, and cultural differences as well as the organizational barriers that inhibit the full contributions of all employees. They develop a better understanding of corporate culture, requirements for success, and career choices that affect opportunities for advancement.

In most companies, the rules for success are ambiguous, unwritten, and perhaps inconsistent with written policy. A common problem for women, minorities, immigrants, and young employees is that they are unaware of many of the unofficial rules that are obvious to people in the mainstream. For example, organizations often have informal networks and power structures that may not be apparent or readily available to women and minority group members. As a result, these employees are less likely to know where to go when they need to get something approved or when they want to build support and alliances. For managers, valuing diversity means teaching the unwritten rules or cultural values to those who need to know them and changing the rules when necessary to benefit employees and hence the organization. It also requires inviting outsiders in and giving them access to information and meaningful relationships with people in power.

Skill Building   Diversity training that merely identifies problems without giving participants the tools they need to be able to act on what they have learned may leave participants feeling that the training was not useful or worthwhile. For this reason, many organizations include skill building as part of a diversity program. Skill building is designed to allow all employees and managers to develop the skills they need to deal effectively with one another and with customers in a diverse environment. Most of the skills taught are interpersonal, such as active listening, coaching, and giving feedback. Ideally, the skills taught are based on the organizational assessment, so the training can be tailored to the specific business issues managers have identified. For example, if too many women and minorities believe they are not getting enough helpful feedback, the skills-building program can be designed to address that issue. Likewise, training in flexible scheduling can help managers meet the company's needs while accommodating and valuing workers who want to be able to set aside time to advance their education, participate in community projects, or look after elderly parents. Tying the training to specific, measurable business goals increases its usefulness and allows managers to assess whether it is working.

Experiential exercises and videotapes, DVDs, and software often are used in the training programs to help expose stereotypes and encourage employees to discuss fears, biases, and problems. Again, the best exercises are related to the actual problems employees are likely to encounter in the workplace. For example, employees in a hospital diversity training program may practice how to handle a white patient who asks to be treated only by a white doctor or a male patient who wants to be treated only by a male doctor. Training ABC, Advanced Training Source, and American Training

TABLE 11.9
Guidelines for Diversity Training

1.	**Position training in your broad diversity strategy.** Training is one important element of managing diversity, but on its own it will probably fail. Culture change means altering underlying assumptions and systems that guide organizational behavior. Training programs must be internally consistent with, and complement, other initiatives focused on culture change.
2.	**Do a thorough needs analysis.** Do not start training prematurely. As with any training program, eagerness to "do something" may backfire unless you have assessed what specific aspects of diversity need attention first. Focus groups help identify what employees view as priority issues.
3.	**Distinguish between education and training.** Education helps build awareness and understanding but does not teach usable skills. Training involves activities that enhance skills in areas such as coaching, conducting performance appraisals, and adapting communication styles. Education and training are both important, but they're not the same.
4.	**Use a participative design process.** Tap a multitude of parties to ensure that the content and tone of the program are suitable to everyone involved. Outside consultants often provide fresh perspectives and have credibility. Insiders have specific company knowledge, sensitivity to local issues, and long-standing relationships with company members. Balance these various sources.
5.	**Test the training thoroughly before rollout.** Given the sensitivity, even volatility, of diversity issues, use diversity councils and advocacy groups to pilot the programs. Build in ample feedback time to allow these groups to address sensitive concerns and refine the training.
6.	**Incorporate diversity programs into the core training curriculum.** One-time programs do not have a lasting impact. Blend the program's content into other training programs such as performance appraisal, coaching, and so on.

SOURCE: From *Training: The Human Side of Business.* 1993. Copyright 1993. The Lakewood Media Group.

Resources are among the companies that offer such products. Table 11.9 provides a set of guidelines for designing effective diversity training.

Retaining Employees

As replacing qualified and experienced workers becomes more difficult and costly, retaining good workers will become much more important. Nationwide, turnover rates have been rising, with companies needing to replace more than 1 percent of their workers every month—and far more in the retailing and services industries. A number of policies and strategies, such as the following, can be used to increase retention of all employees, especially those who are different from the norm.[50]

Support Groups   Companies can help form minority networks and other support groups to promote information exchange and social support. Support groups, sometimes called affinity groups, provide emotional and career support for members who traditionally have not been included in the majority's informal groups. They also can help diverse employees understand work norms and the corporate culture.

At Apple headquarters in Cupertino, California, support groups include a Jewish cultural group, a gay/lesbian group, an African American group, and a technical women's group. Avon encourages employees to organize into African American, Hispanic, and Asian networks by granting them official recognition and assigning a senior manager to provide advice. These groups help new employees adjust and provide direct feedback to management on problems that concern the groups.

Mentoring   Many people have been puzzled at the apparent inability of women and minorities to move up beyond a certain point on the corporate ladder (the glass ceiling). To help these groups enter the informal network that provides exposure to top

mentors

Higher-level managers who help ensure that high-potential people are introduced to top management and socialized into the norms and values of the organization.

management and access to information about organizational politics, many companies have implemented formal mentoring programs. **Mentors** are higher-level managers who help ensure that high-potential people are introduced to top management and socialized into the norms and values of the organization.

In Canada, Ernst & Young makes mentorship an important part of employee development. In fact, the tax and consulting firm has established several mentoring programs aimed at the needs of particular employee groups, including women, minorities, and immigrants. Mentors work with employees to help them develop relevant experience, add skills, and make contact with senior leaders. Ernst & Young sees these mentorships not only as a way to increase what employees can offer but also as a way to fill its talent pipeline with future leaders. In a related but distinct effort, Ernst & Young identifies high-potential employees and has company leaders sponsor them. Sponsorship is similar to mentorship except that the sponsor is more actively involved in the employee's development. Finally, in an unusual twist on mentorship, Ernst & Young has a reverse mentoring program in which women and minority employees counsel leaders on issues related to diversity at the company.[51]

Career Development and Promotions   Because they are hitting a glass ceiling, many of the most talented women and minority group members are leaving their organizations in search of better opportunities elsewhere. In response, companies such as Deloitte & Touche and Honeywell have established teams to evaluate the career progress of women, minorities, and employees with disabilities and to devise ways to move them up through the ranks. One extremely important step is to make sure deserving employees get a chance at line positions. Women in particular are often relegated to staff positions, such as human resources, with less opportunity to demonstrate how they can earn money for their employers. Career development programs

In Practice

CHIEF DIVERSITY OFFICER AT INGERSOLL RAND

To ensure that career development succeeds and management is accountable for fostering diversity, some companies hire a chief diversity officer (CDO). At Ingersoll Rand, for example, CDO Nereida (Neddy) Perez is responsible for developing diverse leadership. Ingersoll Rand, which makes equipment for heating and cooling, food storage, and more, sees ethnically diverse management talent as a resource for building international sales. In addition, the company was concerned about failure to retain talented women in a male-dominated industry, where they saw only limited career paths.

Perez, who was born in Cuba and worked in human resources for several multinational firms, reports to Ingersoll Rand's CEO, Michael Lamach. They meet every two months to review progress toward diversity-related goals. Perez has launched leadership training for female employees in Europe and networking groups in North America for veterans, women, and African Americans. Under Perez, the company partnered with the Center for Creative Leadership to launch the Women's Leadership Program for women in middle management. The program offers these managers training, mentoring, coaching, and feedback so they build strong relationships, leadership skills, and an understanding of how to lead change.

Activities such as these are backed up by Ingersoll Rand's stated values. The company says "a diverse and inclusive culture is essential" to being innovative, adding, "It is through our behaviors and day-to-day actions that we strive to create a respectful, inclusive and open culture around the world that our colleagues, customers and suppliers want to be affiliated with." Every day, Leddy Perez is working to put those statements into action.[52]

• How well are the activities described here aligned with Ingersoll Rand's goals for diversity?

that give a wide range of employees exposure and experience in line jobs can make senior management positions more available to them.

Systems Accommodation   Managers can support diversity by recognizing cultural and religious holidays, differing modes of dress, and dietary restrictions as well as accommodating the needs of individuals with disabilities. One important disabling condition is AIDS. Under the ADA, organizations must accommodate employees with AIDS as they would persons with any other disability, permitting and even encouraging them to continue working for as long as they are able and, if warranted, allowing flexible scheduling. Also, accommodations for disability may become increasingly important in the future as the median age of the workforce continues to rise. In addition, the rise in the *weight* of the average U.S. worker may raise disability concerns. Not only are the familiar health consequences such as heart disease, joint problems, and diabetes associated with increased weight, but one study found that obese workers (with a body mass index of 40 or more) had many more workplace injury claims and absences related to injuries.[53] This pattern suggests that managers of the future will be even more concerned than in the past with keeping their workers of all sizes on the job by maintaining safe workplaces and offering benefits that encourage healthy lifestyles (possibly through company-sponsored fitness programs).

Accountability   As we noted at the beginning of this section, one of the most effective ways to ensure that diversity efforts succeed is to hold managers accountable for hiring and developing a diverse workforce. Organizations must ensure that their performance appraisal and reward systems reinforce the importance of effective diversity management. At PepsiCo, each executive reporting to the CEO is assigned responsibility for employee development of a different group—for example, the company's women or Latinos or gay and lesbian employees. The executive responsible for that group must identify leadership talent, learn group members' concerns, identify areas where support is needed, and identify plans for addressing these issues.[54]

For decades, U.S. corporations were striving to integrate their workforces because of regulatory and social responsibility pressures. Today globalization, changing demographics, and the expansion of ethnic markets at home have made managing a diverse workforce a bottom-line issue. Managers at organizations such as NASCAR realize that to remain competitive in the coming years, they will have to make managing diversity a strategic priority to attract, develop, keep, and apply the knowledge of their top talent.

Management Connection

ON DIVERSITY, NASCAR LEADERS SHOW THEY MEAN BUSINESS

Participants in NASCAR's Drive for Diversity program say it works. For example, NASCAR partners with Virginia State University (and other schools) to recruit marketing interns. One of them, Adenike Mustapha, told a reporter that the internship "exposed me to something I would never have been exposed to before." The more people who are exposed, they agree, the more who will become fans. That's also what NASCAR hopes will happen when D4D driver Daniel Suarez of Mexico uses his Twitter account to field Spanish-language questions about racing.

The commitment to diversity was tested recently when a NASCAR driver, Jeremy Clements, let slip a racial slur while talking to a blogger for MTV News. Clements was not using the ugly term to refer to a colleague; it slipped out as he made a general remark about overly aggressive drivers. Some organizations might have tried to downplay the situation, but NASCAR suspended Clements for two weeks.

Beyond punishing Clements, NASCAR directed him to meet with Richard Lapchick, cofounder of a diversity training program of the National Consortium for Academics and Sports. That program, the Teamwork Leadership Institute (TLI), provides diversity training to the National Basketball Association, Major League Baseball,

MANAGER'S BRIEF

PROGRESS REPORT

ONWARD

and many college athletics departments as well as to NASCAR employees. After the suspension, Clements said the counseling from Lapchick helped him think more carefully about himself and the impact of his words.

Lest anyone think this incident signals a weak commitment to diversity at NASCAR, Lapchick argues that the opposite is true. Over the course of a decade and a half, Lapchick says, he has consistently seen from CEO Brian France a sincere commitment to making NASCAR "look like America." Lapchick's TLI has provided more training, he says, to NASCAR "than any other [sports] league or college." It has brought in TLI to train all its employees, at a cost of more than $500,000. TLI training includes discussion and exercises related to self-identity and the use of stereotypes, using examples drawn from sports.

Besides bringing in female and minority drivers, NASCAR has hired diverse employees at its headquarters. The 26 members of its board and officers include eight women and two persons of color. Lapchick gives particular credit to the hiring of Marcus Jadotte as vice president of public affairs and multicultural development. Jadotte ensures that NASCAR's leaders have regular training and keeps the issue on the executive agenda.[55]

- Assess NASCAR's response to a driver's use of a racial slur. What did it do right? What else should it have done?
- Assess NASCAR's leadership and commitment concerning diversity. What else should it do?

KEY TERMS

affirmative action, p. 383

managing diversity, p. 370

mentors, p. 396

monolithic organization, p. 389

multicultural organization, p. 390

pluralistic organization, p. 390

sexual harassment, p. 376

SUMMARY OF LEARNING OBJECTIVES

Now that you have studied Chapter 11, you should be able to:

LO 1 Describe how changes in the U.S. workforce make diversity a critical organizational and managerial issue.

The labor force is getting older and more racially and ethnically diverse, with a higher proportion of women. In addition, the jobs that are being created frequently require higher skills than the typical worker can provide; thus we are seeing a growing skills gap. To be competitive, organizations can no longer take the traditional approach of depending on white males to form the core of the workforce. Today managers must look broadly to make use of talent wherever it can be found. As the labor market changes, organizations that can recruit, develop, motivate, and retain a diverse workforce will have a competitive advantage.

LO 2 Distinguish between affirmative action and managing diversity.

Affirmative action is designed to correct past exclusion of women and minorities from U.S. organizations. But despite the accomplishments of affirmative action, it has not eliminated barriers that prevent individuals from reaching their full potential. Managing diversity goes beyond hiring people who are different from the norm and seeks to support, nurture, and use employee differences to the organization's advantage.

LO 3 Explain how diversity, if well managed, can give organizations a competitive edge.

Managing diversity is a bottom-line issue. If managers are effective at managing diversity, they will have an easier time attracting, retaining, and motivating the best employees. They will be more effective at marketing to diverse consumer groups in the United States and globally. They will have a workforce that is more creative, more innovative, and better able to solve problems. In addition, they are likely to increase the flexibility and responsiveness of the organization to environmental change.

LO 4 Identify challenges associated with managing a diverse workforce.

The challenges for managers created by a diverse workforce include decreased group cohesiveness, communication problems, mistrust and tension, and stereotyping. These challenges can be turned into advantages by means of training and effective management.

LO 5 Define monolithic, pluralistic, and multicultural organizations.

These categories are based on the organization's prevailing assumptions about people and cultures. Monolithic organizations have a low degree of structural integration, so their population is homogeneous. Pluralistic organizations have a relatively diverse employee population and try to involve various types of employees (e.g., engaging in affirmative action and avoiding discrimination). Multicultural organizations not only have diversity but value it, and they fully integrate men and women of various racial and ethnic groups as well as people with different types of expertise. Conflict is greatest in a pluralistic organization.

 List steps managers and their organizations can take to cultivate diversity.

To be successful, organizational efforts to manage diversity must have top management support and commitment. Organizations should first undertake a thorough assessment of their cultures, policies, and practices as well as the demographics of their labor pools and customer bases. Only after this diagnosis has been completed is a company in position to initiate programs designed to attract, develop, motivate, and retain a diverse workforce.

DISCUSSION QUESTIONS

1. What opportunities do you see as a result of changes in our nation's workforce?

2. Is prejudice declining in our society? In our organizations? Why or why not?

3. What distinctions can you make between affirmative action and managing diversity?

4. How can managers overcome obstacles to diversity such as mistrust and tension, stereotyping, and communication problems?

5. How can organizations meet the special needs of different groups (e.g., work and family issues) without appearing to show favoritism to those particular sets of employees?

6. How can diversity give a company a competitive edge? Can diversity really make a difference in the bottom line? How?

EXPERIENTIAL EXERCISES

11.1   BEING DIFFERENT

OBJECTIVES

1. To increase your awareness of the feeling of being different.

2. To understand better the context of being different.

INSTRUCTIONS

1. Working alone, complete the Being Different Worksheet.

2. In small groups, compare worksheets and prepare answers to the discussion questions.

3. When the class reconvenes, group spokespersons present group findings.

DISCUSSION QUESTIONS

1. Were there students who experienced being different in situations that surprised you?

2. How would you define 'being different'?

3. How can this exercise be used to good advantage?

Being Different Worksheet

Think back to a recent situation in which you experienced 'being different' and answer the following questions:

1. Describe the situation in which you experienced 'being different'.

_____

_____

2. Explain how you felt.

_____

_____

3. What did you do as a result of 'being different'? (That is, in what way was your behavior changed by the feeling of 'being different'?)

_____

_____

4. What did others in the situation do? How do you think they felt about the situation?

_____

_____

5. How did the situation turn out in the end?

_____

_____

6. As a result of that event, how will you probably behave differently in the future? In what way has the situation changed you?

_____

_____

11.2   GENDER STEREOTYPES

PART I

Your instructor will divide the group into smaller groups based on gender, resulting in male-only and female-only groups. Groups are to brainstorm a list in response to the following statements. It is not necessary for all members to agree with everything the group generates. Add all inputs to the list.

Female groups complete the following:

- All men are _____
- Men think all women are _____

Male groups complete the following:

- All women are _____
- Women think all men are _____

PART II

After generating your lists, your groups will present a role-play to the class based on the following scenarios by switching gender roles (females portray males, and males portray females):

Two friends (of the same gender) meeting each other back at school for the first time this year.

A person flirting with a member of the opposite sex at a party. (Females play a male flirting with a female; males play a female flirting with a male.)

QUESTIONS

1. What aspects of the role-plays were accurate, distorted, or inaccurate?

2. How did you feel portraying the opposite gender, and how did it feel to see your gender portrayed?

3. On what stereotypes or experiences were these role-plays based?

PART III

Your group will now write its brainstorm lists on the board for discussion. Remember that these lists are a product of a group effort and are generally based on stereotypes and not necessarily the view of any one individual.

Analyze the lists for positive and negative results in both personal and professional settings. Generate a list of ways to dispel, reduce, or counter negative stereotypes.

QUESTIONS

1. What similarities, patterns, or trends developed from the groups?

2. How do you feel about the thoughts presented about your gender?

3. What implications do these thoughts have on actions and situations in the work environment?

4. What can you do to reduce the negative effects of these stereotypes? What can you do to help dispel these stereotypes? (Brainstorm with your group or class.)

SOURCE: Portions of this exercise were adapted from concepts in S. F. Fritz, W. Brown, J. Lunde, and E. Banset, _Interpersonal Skills for Leadership_ (Englewood Cliffs, NJ: Prentice Hall, 1999); and A. B. Shani and J. B. Lau, _Behavior in Organizations: An Experiential Approach,_ 6th ed. (New York: Irwin, 1996).

11.3 HE WORKS, SHE WORKS

INSTRUCTIONS

1. Complete the He Works, She Works Worksheet. In the appropriate spaces, write what you think the stereotyped responses would be. Do not spend too much time consid-ering any one item. Rather, respond quickly and let your first impression or thought guide your answer.

2. Compare your individual responses with those of other class members or participants. It is interesting to identify and discuss the most frequently used stereotypes.

He Works, She Works Worksheet

The family picture is on *his* desk: *He's a solid, responsible family man.*

His desk is cluttered: _____
_____

He's talking with coworkers: _____
_____

He's not at his desk: _____
_____

He's not in the office: _____
_____

The family picture is on *her* desk: *Her family will come before her career.*

Her desk is cluttered: _____
_____

She's talking with co-workers: _____
_____

She's not at her desk: _____
_____

She's not in the office: _____
_____

The family picture is on *his* desk: *He's a solid, responsible family man.*

He's having lunch with the boss: _____
_____

The boss criticized *him:* _____
_____

He got an unfair deal: _____
_____

He's getting married: _____
_____

He's going on a business trip: _____
_____

He's leaving for a better job: _____
_____

The family picture is on *her* desk: *Her family will come before her career.*

She's having lunch with the boss: _____
_____

The boss criticized *her:* _____
_____

She got an unfair deal: _____

_____

She's getting married: _____

_____

She's going on a business trip: _____

_____

She's leaving for a better job: _____

_____

SOURCE: F. Luthans, *Organizational Behavior.* 1989. Copyright © 1989 The McGraw-Hill Companies. Reproduced with permission.

CONCLUDING CASE

NICHE HOTEL GROUP

Monique Johnson was thrilled about her new position as vice president of human resources for Niche Hotel Group (NHG). The hotel chain has distinctive properties in major cities throughout the United States, attracting a young, international clientele with super-fast Wi-Fi, casual but elegant surroundings, and popular sushi bars. Besides the chance to stay at these establishments as she toured the country, Monique would have opportunities to meet the members of NHG's enthusiastic, talented, and racially diverse workforce. In addition, she was proud to advance NHG's practice of valuing employees' and customers' diversity, including respect for all people regardless of age, sex, race, ethnicity, nationality, disability status, and sexual orientation. She felt sure those values would be upheld because the commitment came from the top. In fact, NHG's chief executive, Mike Jepsen, had asked Monique to meet with him every Thursday to review the company's performance in attracting and developing talent.

For several weeks, Monique's work progressed much as she had expected. Then she heard some disturbing news. One of the hotel's managers, April Lee, called her to say she had received complaints that an assistant manager in the hotel's sushi bar had been embarrassing some of the male servers. When April met with the servers to investigate, they described being teased because they were gay, but said they had not bothered to complain. Two of the servers admitted that they believed complaining would be futile. As white, male employees, they said, they doubted they would be taken seriously, because NHG's management tended to favor its female and minority employees. April worried that the servers might quit, take legal action, or both before the situation could be sorted out. Meanwhile, she wondered

how top management would help her deal with the situation. Monique reviewed with April the basic legal requirements and company policy for handling this type of problem, and she offered to fly out to April's hotel with one of her staff members after her Thursday meeting with the CEO.

That Thursday, Monique briefed Mike about the situation at April's hotel. Mike sighed, "Here we go again." In response to Monique's puzzled look, he explained, "We've had mandatory diversity training three times for every single NHG employee. But it's never enough. Sooner or later, someone hurts someone else's feelings, and we have to bring back the trainers. I guess we just have to keep doing it until everyone respects everyone else's differences."

"You've done diversity training three times without creating a positive climate for diversity?" replied Monique. Mike nodded his head ruefully and then asked if she had a better idea. "Maybe. Hmm, maybe it's time to stop focusing so much on categorizing people and start thinking about how each of us individually is working as part of a team, how each of us is contributing to our mission. Maybe we need to train in something else—say, communication—how we talk and how well we listen."

DISCUSSION QUESTIONS

1. How can promoting a diverse workforce help Niche Hotel Group succeed as a business?

2. Why do you think diversity training has not always prevented problems at NHG?

3. What should NHG do to improve its climate for diversity?

PART THREE   SUPPORTING CASE

Zappos

At the turn of the millennium, Zappos, a Las Vegas–based Internet retailer, was a start-up struggling to survive. The company wanted to be *the* online destination for buying shoes, but customers hesitated to pick out shoes online. The company hired a

27-year-old business consultant named Tony Hsieh to figure out what would save Zappos.

Hsieh, a first-generation Taiwanese American with a degree in computer science, already had a couple of successful business start-ups under his belt. Undeterred by Zappos's weak performance, he set an ambitious goal: Zappos would become the largest shoe retailer on the Internet. How? Not by focusing on mainly price or even selection, but by enhancing a company culture designed to make employees happy. Happy employees, Hsieh believed, would deliver superior service. And when customers take a chance on picking out shoes from a website, they want to trust that the seller will ensure they are satisfied with everything about the purchase, from shoe style and fit to fast delivery and an easy returns policy.

The approach quickly began to stimulate sales, and just a year after he started advising Zappos, Hsieh was named chief executive. He works for the startlingly small salary of $36,000. That arrangement doesn't bother Hsieh because he is more motivated by creating a great organization than by earning money. After all, his previous business, LinkExchange, brought him $265 million when he sold it to Microsoft.

The Zappos culture is built on 10 core values:

1. Deliver WOW (an emotional impact and powerful story to tell) through service.
2. Embrace and drive change.
3. Create fun and a little weirdness.
4. Be adventurous, creative, and open-minded.
5. Pursue growth and learning.
6. Build open and honest relationships with communication.
7. Build a positive team and family spirit. ("Family" refers to Zappos co-workers.)
8. Do more with less.
9. Be passionate and determined.
10. Be humble.

These somewhat unconventional values are essential hiring criteria, and the company's career website directs potential applicants to read the values—which are described in whimsical terms—and apply for a job only if they want to be part of this "best thing about the Zappos family." In fact, at the end of the orientation process, employees are offered $3,000 to quit if they feel they aren't a good fit with the company values, and displaying a lack of the values is grounds for being discharged. According to Hsieh, hiring people who share the core values makes it easy to form real friendships, and those relationships, in turn, create an environment in which people think creatively.

The Zappos human resources department, under the leadership of Hollie Delaney, a Salt Lake City native, ensures that job candidates start to experience and participate in this unconventional, fun culture during the application and selection process. An online application invites them to submit video cover letters with their applications, and interviews are conducted in a room that looks like the set of a TV talk show, where candidates might answer a question such as "What's your theme song?" Employees evaluating candidates consider not only work history but also the way candidates interact during lunch. They even take into account the observations of the shuttle drivers who take visiting job candidates back to their hotel. Once on board, employees might discover that fun and a little weirdness at the company includes an opportunity to dye Hsieh's or another

manager's hair blue or shave his or her head at the annual Bald & Blue Day. And the commitment to wowing customers spills over into work relationships: Given a chance to reward colleagues' good behavior with a $50 monthly bonus, many employees held off, waiting to see exceptional behavior.

Recently performance appraisals also were brought into line with the focus on values. Employees are rated not just on task accomplishment but also on how well they represent the core values. Managers are expected to describe specific instances of employees demonstrating the values at work, and employees who score low on a measure have the chance to receive training in that value. Outside the formal appraisal process, employees also continue to receive regular feedback on task-related measures such as percentage of hours spent talking to customers.

Delaney acknowledges that the company's values result in a work environment that is loud, hardworking, and full of change—conditions that aren't for everyone. Pay also isn't necessarily high, especially for call center workers. But for those who share the values, this kind of workplace is exhilarating. There also are plenty of rewards and perks, including profit sharing, a nap room, and access to a life coach who counsels employees as they sit on a velvet throne.

With this approach to human resources management, Hsieh helped Zappos grow into a billion-dollar company, which was eventually acquired by Amazon. Hsieh negotiated a deal in which Amazon promised to let Zappos continue operating independently, in accordance with its distinctive culture.

Unfortunately, although the 2008 financial crisis didn't keep sales at Zappos from rising, the ongoing economic slowdown eventually hurt, and Zappos laid off some of its workers, letting them down as gently as it could with generous severance packages. Even so, Zappos, unlike many businesses, hasn't outsourced its call center, located in Kentucky, because those employees need to be a part of the company culture. After all, they are the ones who talk directly with customers, and they're trained to wow customers—for example, encouraging them to try multiple sizes because shipping is free in both directions. Now the company's challenge is to reassure the remaining members of the family that Zappos is a great place to work even when times are tough.

QUESTIONS

1. Evaluate whether you think Zappos is a responsive organization. How do you expect its recent downsizing to affect its responsiveness?

2. How does human resource management reinforce Zappos's core values?

3. How well do you think Zappos's human resource strategy supports the valuing of employee diversity? What diversity issues does Zappos need to address?

SOURCES: H. Blodget, "Zappos CEO Tony Hsieh Making $36,000 a Year Working for Amazon," *Yahoo Finance,* September 10, 2010, http://finance.yahoo.com; Zappos, Jobs webpage, http://about.zappos.com/jobs/; K. Gurchiek, "Delivering HR at Zappos," *HR Magazine,* June 2011, http://www.shrm.org; J. M. O'Brien, "Zappos Knows How to Kick It," *Fortune,* January 22, 2009, http://money.cnn.com; and R. Pyrillis, "The Reviews Are In," *Workforce Management,* May 1, 2011, Business & Company Resource Center, http://galenet.galegroup.com.

CHAPTER 12

Leadership

Every soldier has a right to competent command.

— Julius Caesar

Management Connection

MEG WHITMAN'S LEADERSHIP CHALLENGE AT HEWLETT-PACKARD

One of the great legends of the computer age tells of how William Hewlett and David Packard, two recent graduates with degrees in electrical engineering, set up shop in a Palo Alto, California, garage to make electronic instruments in the 1930s. Through technological expertise, management innovation, and respect for their highly skilled workers, the two founders built their garage enterprise, Hewlett-Packard Company, into a Silicon Valley leader serving businesses and individuals. Consumers have known HP's brand most for its calculators, personal computers, and printers.

Beginning in the 1990s, however, HP has struggled to live up to its earlier reputation. It remains an industry giant, ranked number 10 on the Fortune 500, but it seems to have lost its direction. Calculators, PCs, and printers have all become commodities or near-commodities. The company fell behind in innovation in the market for computers, especially mobile devices. Market share, profits, and the company's stock market valuation have been sliding for years. It announced a tablet PC and then pulled it from the market after poor initial reviews; scared off loyal PC customers by publicly flirting with the idea of selling off that product line; and tried to expand into the software business by acquiring a British company for $11 billion, a price widely viewed as too high. Meanwhile, there have been persistent reports of poor morale throughout HP and turmoil in the top ranks. In just over a decade, the company pushed out four chief executives.

Desperate for a turnaround, HP's board of directors most recently tried appointing former eBay chief executive and unsuccessful candidate for California governor, Meg Whitman. Whitman herself had been a member of HP's board for several months, so she had seen the company's difficulties from the inside. Her track record with eBay showed that she could perform well in Silicon Valley.

Can putting Whitman in the top job turn around HP's sliding performance? Although she says change will take five years, she immediately trimmed back executive perks, modeling the respect for workers that had characterized Hewlett and Packard's leadership. Whitman is doing her best to exude confidence. She declared to a *Forbes* reporter, "Problems are good, as long as you solve them quickly." She is determined to diagnose those problems and get her people working on fast solutions.[1]

Observers agree that Hewlett Packard's people need a compelling vision and inspiration to bring that vision to life. HP's directors chose Meg Whitman as a person they believe can deliver this kind of leadership. As you read this chapter, compare Whitman's approach with the kinds of practices recommended for successful leadership.

People get excited about the topic of leadership. They want to know what makes a great leader like HP's founders, Bill Hewlett and David Packard. Managers in all industries are interested in this question. They believe the answer will bring improved organizational performance and personal career success. They hope to acquire the skills that will transform an average manager into a true leader.

Based on the idea that leadership can be learned, many large organizations such as Home Depot and Union Pacific actively recruit retired military personnel in the belief that military training and experience prepare those individuals to lead. Of course you don't have to join the armed services to acquire leadership skills. According to one source, "Leadership seems to be the marshaling of skills possessed by a majority but used by a minority. But it's something that can be learned by anyone, taught to everyone, denied to no one."[2]

LO 1   What is leadership? To start, a leader is one who influences others to attain goals. The greater the number of followers, the greater the influence. And the more successful the attainment of worthy goals, the more evident the leadership. But we must explore beyond this bare definition to capture the excitement and intrigue that devoted followers and students of leadership feel when they see a great leader in action, to understand what organizational leaders really do, and to learn what it really takes to become a truly outstanding leader.

Outstanding leaders combine good strategic substance and effective interpersonal processes to formulate and implement strategies that produce results and sustainable competitive advantage.[3] They may launch enterprises, build organization cultures, win wars, or otherwise change the course of events.[4] They are strategists who seize opportunities others overlook, but "they are also passionately concerned with detail—all the small, fundamental realities that can make or mar the grandest of plans."[5]

What Do We Want from Our Leaders?

LO 2   What do people want from their leaders? Broadly speaking, they want help in achieving their goals.[6] These goals include not just more pay and promotions but support for their personal development; clearing obstacles so they can perform at high levels; and treatment that is respectful, fair, and ethical. Leaders serve people best when they help them develop their own initiative and good judgment, enable them to grow, and help them become better contributors. People want competence and proper management—the kinds of things you will read about in this chapter and that are found in other chapters in this book.

> Organizations need people at all levels to be leaders.

What do organizations need? Organizations need people at all levels to be leaders. Leaders throughout the organization are needed to do the things that their people want, but also to help create and implement strategic direction. Thus organizations place people in formal leadership roles so these leaders will achieve not their personal goals, but the organization's goals. At Illinois Tool Works (ITW), general counsel Maria Green has learned to create a listening environment so members of the legal staff contribute ideas. In the past, Green admits, she would have been eager to deliver answers showcasing her own extensive legal and business knowledge. However, a mentor helped her understand that ITW needs Green, as a leader, to draw out the full potential of the entire group.[7]

These two perspectives—what people want and what organizations need—are neatly combined in a set of five key behaviors identified by James Kouzes and Barry Posner, two well-known authors and consultants.[8] The best leaders

1. *Challenge the process.* They challenge conventional beliefs and practices, and they create constructive change.

2. *Inspire a shared vision.* They appeal to people's values and motivate them to care about an important mission.

3. *Enable others to act.* They give people access to information and give them the power to perform to their full potential.

4. *Model the way.* They don't just tell people what to do—they are living examples of the ideals they believe in.

5. *Encourage the heart.* They show appreciation, provide rewards, and use various approaches to motivate people in positive ways.

You will read about these and other aspects of leadership in this and the following chapters. The topics we discuss will not only help you become a better leader but give you benchmarks that will help you assess the competence and fairness with which your boss manages you.

Vision

"The leader's job is to create a vision," stated Robert L. Swiggett, former chair of Kollmorgen Corporation.[9] Until a few years ago, *vision* was not a word one heard managers utter. But today, having a vision for the future and communicating that vision to others are known to be essential components of great leadership. "If there is no vision, there is no business," maintains entrepreneur Mark Leslie.[10] Joe Nevin, an MIS director, described leaders as "painters of the vision and architects of the journey."[11] Practicing businesspeople are not alone in this belief; academic research shows that a clear vision and communication of that vision lead to higher venture growth in entrepreneurial firms.[12]

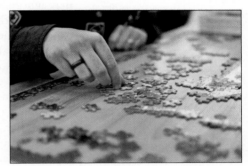

Imagine trying to complete a challenging jigsaw puzzle without the vision of what you're working toward.

vision

A mental image of a possible and desirable future state of the organization.

A **vision** is a mental image of a possible and desirable future state of the organization. It expresses the leader's ambitions for the organization.[13] A leader can create a vision that describes high performance aspirations, the nature of corporate or business strategy, or even the kind of workplace worth building. The best visions are both ideal and unique.[14] If a vision conveys an *ideal*, it communicates a standard of excellence and a clear choice of positive values. If the vision is also *unique*, it communicates and inspires pride in being different from other organizations. The choice of language is important; the words should imply a combination of realism and optimism, an action orientation, and resolution and confidence that the vision will be attained.[15]

Visions can be small or large and can exist at any organizational level as well as at the very top. The important points are that (1) a vision is necessary for effective leadership; (2) a person or team can develop a vision for any job, work unit, or organization; and (3) many people, including managers who do not develop into strong leaders, do not develop a clear vision—instead they focus on performing or surviving on a day-by-day basis.

Put another way, leaders must know what they want.[16] And other people must understand what that is. The leader must be able to articulate the vision, clearly and often. Other people throughout the organization should understand the vision and be able to state it clearly themselves. That's a start. But the vision means nothing until the leader and followers take action to turn the vision into reality.[17]

One leader who articulated and modeled a clear vision was George Buckley, chief executive of 3M Company, the innovative manufacturer best known for its Scotch tape, Post-It notes, and sandpaper. When the economy turned sour, other manufacturers slashed spending on research and development (R&D), but Buckley wanted to retain 3M's commitment to innovation. So even as he tied R&D spending to revenues (R&D spending fell, but not faster than revenues), he challenged his R&D staff to target their efforts toward making products cheaper to produce—and even convinced them that the effort could be satisfying. He accomplished this by recognizing that what drives researchers is a belief that what they do is intellectually stimulating and significant. For example, when Buckley asked the leader of 3M's abrasives business what innovations were in the pipeline, the unit's head commented that abrasives were "not considered sexy." Buckley's replied, "Why not? I think abrasives are sexy. Why can't abrasives be sexy?" Eventually, as researchers saw how their innovations were helping the company serve its markets, they grew enthusiastic about Buckley's vision.[18]

A metaphor reinforces the important concept of vision.[19] Putting a jigsaw puzzle together is much easier if you have the picture on the box cover in front of you. Without the picture, or vision, the lack of direction is likely to result in frustration and failure. That is what communicating a vision is all about: making clear where you are heading.

Not just any vision will do.

Not just any vision will do. Visions can be inappropriate, or fail, for a variety of reasons.[20] First, an inappropriate vision may reflect merely the leader's personal needs. Such a vision can be unethical, or it may fail because of lack of acceptance by the market or by those who must implement it. Second (and related to the first), an inappropriate vision may ignore stakeholder needs. Third, the leader must stay abreast of environmental changes. Although effective leaders maintain confidence and persevere despite obstacles, the time may come when the facts dictate that the vision must change. You will learn more about change and how to manage it later in the book.

Where do visions come from?[21] Leaders should be sensitive to emerging opportunities, develop the right capabilities or worldviews, and not be overly invested in the status quo. You also can capitalize on networks of insightful individuals who have ideas about the future. Some visions are accidental; a company may stumble into an opportunity, and the leader may get credit for foresight. Some leaders and companies launch many new initiatives and, through trial and error, occasionally hit home runs. If the company learns from these successes, the vision emerges.

In Practice

CORCORAN GROUP VISION

When Barbara Corcoran was running her New York real estate brokerage, the Corcoran Group, her vision was of a firm with a family spirit, of "happy people having fun." Despite the challenges of starting up New York's first female-owned real estate firm, Corcoran recalls that it was "fun building a business." In her bright-red suits, she boldly stood out from the crowd. At the office, she passed out colorful prize ribbons to top-performing agents. She set up a regular schedule of shoe shiners and massage therapists to pamper her people so they would feel loved. Her employee parties were the talk of the real estate industry. According to Corcoran, the spirit of fun and love generated innovation as well as loyalty, and it attracted highly motivated people to the firm.

At the same time, everyone knew they were at Corcoran Group to make deals. Even as she rewarded her top sellers, Corcoran was quick to dismiss her lowest-performing employees. Employees who did stay around were inspired by her vision, positive attitude, and boundless energy and determination.

Fun-loving and hard-working, Barbara Corcoran turned her real estate group into New York's largest residential brokerage firm.

Corcoran describes herself as someone who didn't have school smarts but does have a great imagination. Her ability to envision a loving, fun, hard-driving real estate firm shaped the Corcoran Group into New York's largest residential brokerage with more than 1,000 people. When Corcoran sold the business in 2001, it brought her $66 million. Today, in her role as a potential investor on ABC's *Shark Tank* competition show, Corcoran recommends a similar kind of vision to would-be entrepreneurs.[22]

- Why do you think Barbara Corcoran's vision worked well for the Corcoran Group?

Leading and Managing

Effective managers are not necessarily true leaders. Many administrators, supervisors, and even top executives perform their responsibilities successfully without being great leaders. But these positions afford an opportunity for leadership. The ability to lead effectively, then, will set the excellent managers apart from others.

Whereas management must deal with the ongoing, day-to-day complexities of organizations, true leadership includes effectively orchestrating important change.[23] Managing requires planning and budgeting routines; leading includes setting the direction (creating a vision) for the firm. Management requires structuring the organization, staffing it with capable people, and monitoring activities; leadership goes beyond these functions by inspiring people to attain the vision. Great leaders keep people focused on moving the organization toward its ideal future, motivating them to overcome whatever obstacles lie in the way.

> Good leadership, unfortunately, is all too rare.

Good leadership, unfortunately, is all too rare. Managers may focus on the activities that earn them praise and rewards, such as actions that cause a rise in the company's stock price, rather than making tough ethical choices or investing in long-term projects. Some new managers, learning that quick wins will help them establish their credibility as leaders, push a pet project while neglecting the impact on the very people they were assigned to lead. This approach tends to backfire because employees distrust this type of manager and lose any commitment they might have had to the team's long-term success. Successful leaders, in contrast, enlist the team in scoring collective wins that result from working together toward a shared vision.[24]

It is important to be clear here about several things. First, management and leadership are both vitally important. To highlight the need for more leadership is not to minimize the importance of management or managers. But leadership involves unique processes that are distinguishable from basic management processes.[25] Moreover, just because they involve different processes does not mean that they require different, separate people. The same individual can exemplify effective managerial processes, leadership processes, both, or neither.

Some people dislike the idea of distinguishing between management and leadership, maintaining that it is artificial or derogatory toward the managers and the management processes that make organizations run. An alternative distinction is between supervisory and strategic leadership.[26] **Supervisory leadership** is behavior that provides guidance, support, and corrective feedback for day-to-day activities. **Strategic leadership** gives purpose and meaning to organizations. Strategic leadership involves anticipating and envisioning a viable future for the organization and working with others to initiate changes that create such a future.[27] For example,

supervisory leadership

Behavior that provides guidance, support, and corrective feedback for day-to-day activities.

strategic leadership

Behavior that gives purpose and meaning to organizations, envisioning and creating a positive future.

Indian business leaders prioritize their top responsibilities[28] as providing input for business strategy (which you studied thoroughly in Part I of this book); keeper of the organizational culture (introduced in Chapter 2); and guiding, teaching, and serving as a role model for employees (employees being the focus of this part of the book).

Leading and Following

Organizations succeed or fail not only because of how well they are led but because of how well followers follow. Just as managers are not necessarily good leaders, people are not always good followers. One leadership scholar stated, "Executives are given subordinates; they have to earn followers."[29] But it's also true that good followers help produce good leaders.

As a manager, you will be asked to play the roles of both leader and follower. As you lead the people who report to you, you will report to your boss. You will be a member of some teams and committees, and you may head others. Although the leadership roles get the glamour and therefore are the roles that many people covet, followers must perform their responsibilities conscientiously and well. Good follow-ership doesn't mean merely obeying orders, although some bosses may view it that way. The most effective followers are capable of independent thinking and at the same time are actively committed to organizational goals.[30] Robert Townsend, who led a legendary turnaround at Avis, said that the most important characteristic of a follower may be the willingness to tell the truth.[31]

They master skills that are useful to their organizations, and they hold performance standards that are higher than required. Effective followers may not get the glory, but they know their contributions to the organization are valuable. And as they make those contributions, they study leaders in preparation for their own leadership roles.[32] Effective followers also distinguish themselves from ineffective ones by their enthusiasm and commitment to the organization and to a person or purpose—an idea, a product—other than themselves or their own interests.

Power and Leadership

Central to effective leadership is **power**—the ability to influence other people. In organizations, this influence often means the ability to get things done or accomplish one's goals despite resistance from others.

power

The ability to influence others.

In Practice

A MANAGER'S POWER TO INFLUENCE

Managers are sometimes surprised to discover that their power to influence goes far beyond the scope of their job duties because less powerful employees are eager to seek their favor. In that context, a behavior as simple as making eye contact with an employee can serve as a kind of reward that inspires the employee.

Linda Parker Hudson discovered this kind of power when she became division president for defense contractor General Dynamics. In her first week on the job, she showed up wearing a distinctively tied scarf. The next day, she spotted more than a dozen female employees wearing scarves tied into identical bows. (Male executives, of course, have similar impacts on their employees.) Hudson admits that the experience was more alarming than flattering; not everyone enjoys that level of scrutiny. But she also recognized that this kind of influence also would enable her to shape the organization's culture.

When Hudson later took charge of the U.S. division of another defense contractor, BAE Systems, she told the managers reporting to her that it was her habit to send e-mail at odd hours and she expected a "rapid response." When she had a thought at 3:00 a.m., she'd send out a message. But it took Hudson by surprise when she received immediate responses from managers who had begun sleeping with their BlackBerry phones within reach. By rapid, she had not really meant *immediate,* but her staff members were eager to do whatever they thought she wanted. It took Hudson months to persuade them she really expected them to sleep at night.[33]

• Why do you think a manager such as Linda Parker Hudson has so much ability to influence the people in her organization? What are the pros and cons to this?

Sources of Power

One of the earliest and still most useful approaches to understanding power suggests that leaders have five important potential sources of power in organizations.[34] Figure 12.1 shows those power sources.

Legitimate Power   The leader with *legitimate power* has the right, or the authority, to tell others what to do; employees are obligated to comply with legitimate orders. For example, a supervisor tells an employee to remove a safety hazard, and the employee removes the hazard because he has to obey the authority of his boss. In contrast, when a staff person lacks the authority to give an order to a line manager, the

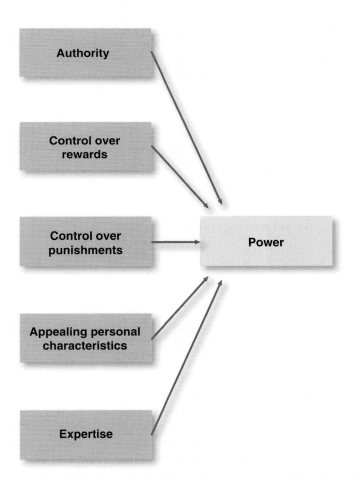

FIGURE 12.1
Sources of Power

SOURCE: Adapted from J. R. P. French and B. Raven, "The Bases of Social Power," in *Studies in Social Power,* ed. D. Cartwright (Ann Arbor, MI: Institute for Social Research, 1959).

staff person has no legitimate power over the manager. As you might guess, managers have more legitimate power over their direct reports than they do over their peers, bosses, and others inside or outside their organizations.[35]

Reward Power   The leader who has *reward power* influences others because she controls valued rewards; people comply with the leader's wishes to receive those rewards. For example, a manager works hard to achieve her performance goals to get a positive performance review and a big pay raise from her boss. On the other hand, if company policy dictates that everyone receive the same salary increase, a leader's reward power decreases because he or she is unable to give higher raises.

Coercive Power   The leader with *coercive power* has control over punishments; people comply to avoid those punishments. For instance, a manager implements an absenteeism policy that administers disciplinary actions to offending employees. A manager has less coercive power if, say, a union contract limits her ability to punish. In general, lower-level managers have less legitimate, coercive, and reward power than do middle and higher-level managers.[36]

Referent Power   The leader with *referent power* has personal characteristics that appeal to others; people comply because of admiration, personal liking, a desire for approval, or a desire to be like the leader. For example, young, ambitious managers emulate the work habits and personal style of a successful, charismatic executive. An executive who is incompetent, disliked, and less respected has little referent power.

Expert Power   The leader who has *expert power* has certain expertise or knowledge; people comply because they believe in, can learn from, or can otherwise gain from that expertise. For example, a sales manager gives her salespeople some tips on how to close a deal. The salespeople then alter their sales techniques because they respect the manager's expertise. However, this manager may lack expert power in other areas, such as finance; thus her salespeople may ignore her advice concerning financial matters.

People who are in a position that gives them the right to tell others what to do, who can reward and punish, who are well liked and admired, and who have expertise on which other people can draw will be powerful members of the organization. All of these sources of power are potentially important. Although it is easy to assume that the most powerful bosses are those who have high legitimate power and control major rewards and punishments, it is important not to underestimate the more personal sources such as expert and referent power.

Traditional Approaches to Understanding Leadership

 LO 5   Three traditional approaches to studying leadership are the trait approach, the behavioral approach, and the situational approach.

Leader Traits

trait approach

A leadership perspective that attempts to determine the personal characteristics that great leaders share.

The **trait approach** is the oldest leadership perspective; it focuses on individual leaders and attempts to determine the personal characteristics (traits) that great leaders share. What set Winston Churchill, Alexander the Great, Gandhi, and Martin Luther King Jr. apart from the crowd? The trait approach assumes the existence of a leadership personality and assumes that leaders are born, not made.

From 1904 to 1948, researchers conducted more than 100 leadership trait studies.[37] At the end of that period, management scholars concluded that no particular set of traits is necessary for a person to become a successful leader. Enthusiasm for the trait approach diminished, but some research on traits continued. By the mid-1970s, a more balanced view emerged: Although no traits ensure leadership success, certain characteristics are potentially useful. The current perspective is that some personality characteristics—many of which a person need not be born with but can strive to acquire—contribute to leader effectiveness.[38]

1. *Drive.* Drive refers to a set of characteristics that reflect a high level of effort. Drive includes high need for achievement, constant striving for improvement, ambition, energy, tenacity (persistence in the face of obstacles), and initiative. In several countries, the achievement needs of top executives have been shown to be related to the growth rates of their organizations.[39] But the need to achieve can be a drawback if leaders focus on personal achievement and get so personally involved with the work that they do not delegate enough authority and responsibility. And whereas need for achievement has been shown to predict organizational effectiveness in entrepreneurial firms, it does not predict success for division heads in larger and more bureaucratic firms.[40]

2. *Leadership motivation.* Great leaders not only have drive; they *want to lead.* In this regard, it helps to be extroverted—extroversion is consistently related to both leader emergence and leader effectiveness.[41] However—and this is a huge point—introverts have great strengths that can contribute to effective leadership, and extroversion can backfire. For example, the assertiveness of extroverted leaders can quash the contributions of group members. Extroverts sometimes should adopt a more reserved, quiet style.[42]

Also important is a high need for power, a preference to be in leadership rather than follower positions.[43] A high power need induces people to attempt to influence others and sustains interest and satisfaction in the process of leadership. When the power need is exercised in moral and socially constructive ways, rather than to the detriment of others, leaders inspire more trust, respect, and commitment to their vision.

3. *Integrity.* Integrity is the correspondence between actions and words. Honesty and credibility, in addition to being desirable characteristics in their own right, are especially important for leaders because these traits inspire trust in others.

4. *Self-confidence.* Self-confidence is important for a number of reasons. The leadership role is challenging, and setbacks are inevitable. Self-confidence allows a leader to overcome obstacles, make decisions despite uncertainty, and instill confidence in others. Of course you don't want to overdo this; arrogance and cockiness have triggered more than one leader's downfall.

5. *Knowledge of the business.* Effective leaders have a high level of knowledge about their industries, companies, and technical matters. Leaders must have the intelligence to interpret vast quantities of information. Advanced degrees are useful in a career, but ultimately less important than acquired expertise in matters relevant to the organization.[44]

Finally, one personal skill may be the most important: the ability to perceive the needs and goals of others and to adjust one's personal leadership approach accordingly.[45] Effective leaders do not rely on one leadership style; rather, they are capable of using different styles as the situation warrants.[46] This quality is the cornerstone of the situational approaches to leadership, which we will discuss shortly.

> Arrogance and cockiness have triggered more than one leader's downfall.

Leader Behaviors

The **behavioral approach** to leadership attempts to identify what good leaders do. Should leaders focus on getting the job done or on keeping their followers happy? Should they make decisions autocratically or democratically? In the behavioral approach, personal characteristics are considered less important than the actual behaviors that leaders exhibit.

behavioral approach

A leadership perspective that attempts to identify what good leaders do—that is, what behaviors they exhibit.

Bottom Line

Task performance behaviors focus on achieving work goals. *What shows you that a manager cares about task performance?*

task performance behaviors

Actions taken to ensure that the work group or organization reaches its goals.

group maintenance behaviors

Actions taken to ensure the satisfaction of group members, develop and maintain harmonious work relationships, and preserve the social stability of the group.

Three general categories of leadership behavior have received particular attention: behaviors related to task performance, group maintenance, and employee participation in decision making.

Task Performance   Leadership requires getting the job done. **Task performance behaviors** are the leader's efforts to ensure that the work unit or organization reaches its goals. This dimension is variously referred to as *concern for production, directive leadership, initiating structure,* or *closeness of supervision.* It includes a focus on work speed, quality and accuracy, quantity of output, and following the rules.[47] This type of leader behavior improves leader job performance and group and organizational performance.[48]

Group Maintenance   Leadership is inherently an interpersonal, group activity.[49] In exhibiting **group maintenance behaviors,** leaders take action to ensure the satisfaction of group members, develop and maintain harmonious work relationships, and preserve the social stability of the group. This dimension is sometimes referred to as *concern for people, supportive leadership,* or *consideration.* It includes a focus on people's feelings and comfort, appreciation of them, and stress reduction.[50] This type of leader behavior has a strong positive impact on follower satisfaction, motivation, and leader effectiveness.[51]

What specific behaviors do performance- and maintenance-oriented leadership imply? To help answer this question, assume you are asked to rate your boss on these two dimensions. If a leadership study were conducted in your organization, you would be asked to fill out a questionnaire similar to the one in Table 12.1. The behaviors indicated in the first set of questions represent performance-oriented leadership; those indicated in the second set represent maintenance-oriented leadership.

TABLE 12.1

Questions Assessing Task Performance and Group Maintenance Leadership

Task Performance Leadership
1. Is your superior strict about observing regulations?
2. To what extent does your superior give you instructions and orders?
3. Is your superior strict about the amount of work you do?
4. Does your superior urge you to complete your work by a specified time?
5. Does your superior try to make you work to your maximum capacity?
6. When you do an inadequate job, does your superior focus on the inadequate way the job is done?
7. Does your superior ask you for reports about the progress of your work?
8. How precisely does your superior work out plans for goal achievement each month?

Group Maintenance Leadership
1. Can you talk freely with your superior about your work?
2. Does your superior generally support you?
3. Is your superior concerned about your personal problems?
4. Do you think your superior trusts you?
5. Does your superior give you recognition when you do your job well?
6. When a problem arises in your workplace, does your superior ask your opinion about how to solve it?
7. Is your superior concerned about your future benefits, such as promotions and pay raises?
8. Does your superior treat you fairly?

SOURCE: Reprinted from J. Misumi and M. Peterson, "The Performance-Maintenance (PM) Theory of Leadership: Review of a Japanese Research Program," *Administrative Science Quarterly* 30, no. 2 (June 1985). Reprinted with permission of Sage Publications, Inc.

Leader–member exchange (LMX) theory highlights the importance of leader behaviors not just toward the group as a whole but toward individuals on a personal basis.[52] The focus in the original formulation, which has since been expanded, is primarily on the leader behaviors historically considered group maintenance.[53] According to LMX theory, and as supported by research evidence, maintenance behaviors such as trust, open communication, mutual respect, mutual obligation, and mutual loyalty form the cornerstone of relationships that are satisfying and perhaps more productive.[54]

Remember, though, the potential for cross-cultural differences. Maintenance behaviors are important everywhere, but the specific behaviors can differ from one culture to another. For example, in the United States, maintenance behaviors include dealing with people face to face; in Japan, written memos are preferred over giving directions face to face, thus avoiding confrontation and permitting face-saving in the event of disagreement.[55]

Participation in Decision Making   How should a leader make decisions? More specifically, to what extent should leaders involve their people in making decisions?[56] As a dimension of leadership behavior, **participation in decision making** can range from autocratic to democratic. **Autocratic leadership** makes decisions and then announces them to the group. **Democratic leadership** solicits input from others. Democratic leadership seeks information, opinions, and preferences, sometimes to the point of meeting with the group, leading discussions, and using consensus or majority vote to make the final choice.

The Effects of Leader Behavior   How the leader behaves influences people's attitudes and performance. Studies of these effects focus on autocratic versus democratic decision styles or on performance- versus maintenance-oriented behaviors.

Decision Styles   The classic study comparing autocratic and democratic styles found that a democratic approach resulted in the most positive attitudes, whereas an autocratic approach resulted in somewhat higher performance.[57] A **laissez-faire** style, in which the leader essentially made no decisions, led to more negative attitudes and lower performance. These results seem logical and probably represent the prevalent beliefs among managers about the general effects of these approaches.

Democratic styles, appealing though they may seem, are not always the most appropriate. When speed is of the essence, democratic decision making may be too slow, or people may want decisiveness from the leader.[58] Whether a decision should be made autocratically or democratically depends on the characteristics of the leader, the followers, and the situation.[59] Thus a situational approach to leader decision styles, discussed later in the chapter, is appropriate.

Performance and Maintenance Behaviors   The performance and maintenance dimensions of leadership are independent of each other. In other words, a leader can behave in ways that emphasize one, both, or neither of these dimensions.

> A leader can behave in ways that emphasize one, both, or neither of these dimensions.

Some research indicates that the ideal combination is to engage in both types of leader behaviors.

A team of Ohio State University researchers investigated the effects of leader behaviors in a truck manufacturing plant of International Harvester.[60] Generally, supervisors who were high on maintenance behaviors (which the researchers termed *consideration*) had fewer grievances and less turnover in their work units than supervisors who were low on this dimension. The opposite held for task performance behaviors (which the research team called *initiating structure*). Supervisors high on this dimension had more grievances and higher turnover rates.

---

leader–member exchange (LMX) theory

Highlights the importance of leader behaviors not just toward the group as a whole but toward individuals on a personal basis.

participation in decision making

Leader behaviors indicating the extent to which others are involved in making decisions.

autocratic leadership

A form of leadership in which the leader makes decisions on his or her own and then announces those decisions to the group.

democratic leadership

A form of leadership in which the leader solicits input from subordinates.

laissez-faire

A leadership philosophy characterized by an absence of managerial decision making.

When maintenance and performance leadership behaviors were considered together, the results were more complex. But one conclusion was clear: when a leader is high on performance-oriented behaviors, he or she should also be maintenance oriented. Otherwise, the leader will face high rates of employee turnover and grievances.

At about the same time the Ohio State studies were being conducted, a research program at the University of Michigan was studying the impact of the same leader behaviors on groups' job performance.[61] Among other things, the researchers concluded that the most effective managers engaged in what they called task-oriented behavior: planning, scheduling, coordinating, providing resources, and setting performance goals. Effective managers also exhibited more relationship-oriented behavior: demonstrating trust and confidence, being friendly and considerate, showing appreciation, keeping people informed, and so on. As you can see, these dimensions of leader behavior are essentially the task performance and group maintenance dimensions.

After the Ohio State and Michigan findings were published, it became popular to talk about the ideal leader as one who is always both performance and maintenance oriented. The best-known leadership training model to follow this style is Blake and Mouton's Leadership Grid.[62] In grid training, managers are rated on their performance-oriented behavior (called *concern for production*) and maintenance-oriented behavior (*concern for people*). Then their scores are plotted on the grid shown in Figure 12.2. The highest score is a 9 on both dimensions.

As the figure shows, joint scores can fall at any point on the grid. Managers who did not score a 9,9—for example, those who were high on concern for people but low on concern for production—would then receive training on how to become a 9,9 leader.

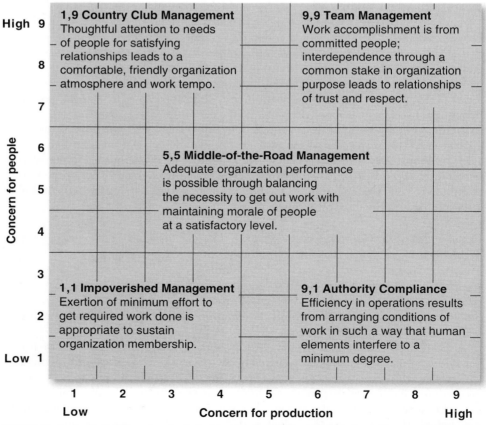

FIGURE 12.2
The Leadership Grid

For a long time, grid training was warmly received by U.S. business and industry. Later, however, it was criticized for embracing a simplistic, one-best-way style of leadership and ignoring the possibility that 9,9 is not best under all circumstances. For example, even 1,1 can be appropriate if employees know their jobs (and therefore don't need to receive directions). Also, they may enjoy their jobs and their co-workers enough that whether the boss shows personal concern for them is not very important. Nonetheless, if the manager is uncertain how to behave, it probably is best to exhibit behaviors that are related to both task performance and group maintenance.[63]

In fact, a wide range of effective leadership styles exists. Organizations that understand the need for diverse leadership styles will have a competitive advantage in the modern business environment over those that believe there is only one best way.

Situational Approaches to Leadership

According to proponents of the **situational approach** to leadership, universally important traits and behaviors don't exist. They believe effective leader behaviors vary from situation to situation. The leader should first analyze the situation and then decide what to do. In other words, look before you lead.

A head nurse in a hospital described her situational approach to leadership:

> My leadership style is a mix of all styles. In this environment I normally let people participate. But in a code blue situation where a patient is dying I automatically become very autocratic: "You do this; you do that; you, out of the room; you all better be quiet; you, get Dr. Mansfield." The staff tell me that's the only time they see me like that. In an emergency like that, you don't have time to vote, talk a lot, or yell at each other. It's time for someone to set up the order.
>
> I remember one time, one person saying, "Wait a minute, I want to do this." He wanted to do the mouth-to-mouth resuscitation. I knew the person behind him did it better, so I said, "No, he does it." This fellow told me later that I hurt him so badly to yell that in front of all the staff and doctors. It was like he wasn't good enough. So I explained it to him: "That's the way it is. A life was on the line. I couldn't give you warm fuzzies. I couldn't make you look good because you didn't have the skills to give the very best to that patient who wasn't breathing anymore."[64]

Look before you lead.

This nurse has her own intuitive situational approach to leadership. She knows the potential advantages of the participatory approach to decision making, but she also knows that in some circumstances she must make decisions herself.

The first situational model of leadership was proposed in 1958 by Tannenbaum and Schmidt. In their classic *Harvard Business Review* article, these authors described how managers should consider three factors before deciding how to lead: forces in the manager, forces in the subordinate, and forces in the situation.[65]

Forces in the manager include the manager's personal values, inclinations, feelings of security, and confidence in subordinates. Forces in the subordinate include his or her knowledge and experience, readiness to assume responsibility for decision making, interest in the task or problem, and understanding and acceptance of the organization's goals. Forces in the situation include the type of leadership style the organization values, the degree to which the group works effectively as a unit, the problem itself and the type of information needed to solve it, and the amount of time the leader has to make the decision.

situational approach

Leadership perspective proposing that universally important traits and behaviors do not exist, and that effective leadership behavior varies from situation to situation.

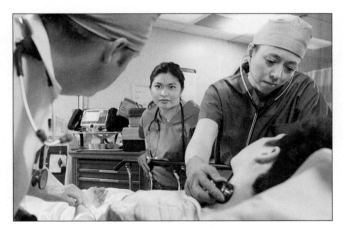

Nurses experience situational leadership on a daily basis. How would you handle a leadership role under pressure?

Consider which of these forces makes an autocratic style most appropriate and which dictates a democratic, participative style. By engaging in this exercise, you are constructing a situational theory of leadership.

Although the Tannenbaum and Schmidt article was published more than a half-century ago, most of its arguments remain valid. Since that time, other situational models have emerged. We will focus here on four: the Vroom model for decision making, Fiedler's contingency model, Hersey and Blanchard's situational theory, and path–goal theory.

The Vroom Model of Leadership   This situational model follows in the tradition of Tannenbaum and Schmidt. The **Vroom model** emphasizes the participative dimension of leadership: how leaders go about making decisions. The model uses the basic situational approach of assessing the situation before determining the best leadership style.[66]

Table 12.2 shows the situational factors used to analyze problems. Each is based on an important attribute of the problem the leader faces and should be assessed as either high or low.

The Vroom model, shown in Figure 12.3, operates like a funnel. You answer the questions one at a time, choosing high or low for each, sometimes skipping questions as you follow the appropriate path. Eventually you reach one of 14 possible endpoints. For each endpoint, the model states which of five decision styles is most appropriate. Several decision styles may work, but the style recommended is the one that takes the least amount of time.

Table 12.3 defines the five leader decision styles. The five styles indicate that there are several shades of participation, not just autocratic or democratic.

Of course not every managerial decision warrants this complicated analysis. But the model becomes less complex after you work through it a couple of times. Also, using the model for major decisions ensures that you consider the important situational factors and alerts you to the most appropriate style to use.

Fiedler's Contingency Model   According to **Fiedler's contingency model of leadership effectiveness,** effectiveness depends on two factors: the personal style of the leader and the degree to which the situation gives the leader power, control, and influence over the situation.[67] Figure 12.4 illustrates the contingency model. The upper

---

Vroom model

A situational model that focuses on the participative dimension of leadership.

Fiedler's contingency model of leadership effectiveness

A situational approach to leadership postulating that effectiveness depends on the personal style of the leader and the degree to which the situation gives the leader power, control, and influence over the situation.

TABLE 12.2
Situational Factors for Problem Analysis

Decision significance:	The significance of the decision to the success of the project or organization.
Importance of commitment:	The importance of team members' commitment to the decision.
Leader's expertise:	Your knowledge or expertise in relation to this problem.
Likelihood of commitment:	The likelihood that the team would commit itself to a decision that you might make on your own.
Group support for objectives:	The degree to which the team supports the organization's objectives at stake in this problem.
Group expertise:	Team members' knowledge or expertise in relation to this problem.
Team competence:	The ability of team members to work together in solving problems.

SOURCE: Reprinted from *Organizational Dynamics*, Vol. 28, No. 4, Victor H. Vroom, "Leadership and the Decision-Making Process," pp. 82–94. Copyright © 2000 with permission from Elsevier.

Time-Driven Model

FIGURE 12.3
Vroom's Model of
Leadership Style

Instructions: The matrix operates like a funnel. You start at the left with a specific decision problem in mind. The column headings denote situational factors which may or may not be present in that problem. You progress by selecting high or low (H or L) for each relevant situational factor. Proceed down from the funnel, judging only those situational factors for which a judgement is called for, until you reach the recommended process.

	Decision Significance	Importance of Commitment	Leader Expertise	Likelihood of Commitment	Group Support	Group Expertise	Team Competence	
P R O B L E M S T A T E M E N T	H	H	H	H	-	-	-	Decide
				L	H	H	H	Delegate
							L	Consult (group)
						L	-	Consult (group)
					L	-	-	Consult (group)
			L	H	H	H	H	Facilitate
							L	Consult (individually)
						L	-	Consult (individually)
					L	-	-	Consult (individually)
				L	H	H	H	Facilitate
							L	Consult (group)
						L	-	Consult (group)
					L	-	-	Consult (group)
		L	H	-	-	-	-	Decide
			L	-	H	H	H	Facilitate
							L	Consult (individually)
						L	-	Consult (individually)
					L	-	-	Consult (individually)
	L	H	-	H	-	-	-	Decide
				L	-	-	H	Delegate
							L	Facilitate
		L	-	-	-	-	-	Decide

SOURCE: Reprinted from *Organizational Dynamics,* Vol. 28, No. 4, Victor H. Vroom, "Leadership and the Decision-Making Process," pp. 82–94. Copyright © 2000 with permission from Elsevier.

TABLE 12.3
Vroom's Leader Decision Styles

Decide: You make the decision alone and either announce or sell it to the group. You may use your expertise in collecting information that you deem relevant to the problem from the group or others.

Consult individually: You present the problem to the group members individually, get their suggestions, and then make the decision.

Consult the group: You present the problem to the group members in a meeting, get their suggestions, and then make the decision.

Facilitate: You present the problem to the group in a meeting. You act as a facilitator, defining the problem to be solved and the boundaries within which the decision must be made. Your objective is to get concurrence on a decision. Above all, you take care to ensure that your ideas are not given any greater weight than those of others simply because of your position.

Delegate: You permit the group to make the decision within prescribed limits. The group undertakes the identification and diagnosis of the problem, developing alternative procedures for solving it and deciding on one or more alternative solutions. Although you play no direct role in the group's deliberations unless explicitly asked, your role is an important one behind the scenes, providing needed resources and encouragement.

SOURCE: Reprinted from *Organizational Dynamics,* Vol. 28, No. 4, Victor H. Vroom, "Leadership and the Decision-Making Process," pp. 82–94. Copyright © 2000 with permission from Elsevier.

half of the figure shows the situational analysis, and the lower half indicates the appropriate style. In the upper portion, three questions are used to analyze the situation:

1. Are leader–member relations good or poor? (To what extent is the leader accepted and supported by group members?)
2. Is the task structured or unstructured? (To what extent do group members know what their goals are and how to accomplish them?)
3. Is the leader's position power strong or weak (high or low)? (To what extent does the leader have the authority to reward and punish?)

These three sequential questions create a decision tree (from top to bottom in the figure) in which a situation is classified into one of eight categories. The lower the category number, the more favorable the situation is for the leader; the higher the number, the less favorable the situation. Fiedler originally called this variable "situational favorableness," and later "situational control." Situation 1 is the best: relations are good, task structure is high, and power is high. In the least favorable situation (8), in which the leader has very little situational control, relations are poor, tasks lack structure, and the leader's power is weak.

Different situations dictate different leadership styles. Fiedler measured leadership styles with an instrument assessing the leader's least preferred co-worker (LPC); that is, the attitude toward the follower the leader liked the least. This was considered an indication more generally of leaders' attitudes toward people. If a leader can single out the person she likes the least, but her attitude is not all that negative, she would receive a high score on the LPC scale. Leaders with more negative attitudes toward others would receive low LPC scores.

Based on the LPC score, Fiedler considered two leadership styles. **Task-motivated leadership** places primary emphasis on completing the task and is more likely exhibited by leaders with low LPC scores. **Relationship-motivated leadership** emphasizes maintaining good interpersonal relationships and is more likely from high-LPC leaders. These leadership styles correspond to task performance and group maintenance leader behaviors, respectively.

task-motivated leadership

Leadership that places primary emphasis on completing a task.

relationship-motivated leadership

Leadership that places primary emphasis on maintaining good interpersonal relationships.

FIGURE 12.4

Fiedler's Analysis of Situations in Which the Task- or Relationship-Motivated Leader Is More Effective

Leader–member relations	Good				Poor			
Task structure	Structured		Unstructured		Structured		Unstructured	
Leader position power	High	Low	High	Low	High	Low	High	Low
Favorable for leader → Unfavorable for leader								
Type of leader most effective in the situation	Task-motivated	Task-motivated	Task-motivated	Relation-ship-motivated	Relation-ship-motivated	Relation-ship-motivated	Relation-ship-motivated	Task-motivated

SOURCE: From Dennis Organ and Thomas Bateman, *Organizational Behavior*, 4th ed., McGraw-Hill, 1990. © 1990 by The McGraw-Hill Companies, Inc. Reprinted with permission.

The lower part of Figure 12.4 indicates which style is situationally appropriate. For situations 1, 2, 3, and 8, a task-motivated leadership style is more effective. For situations 4 through 7, relationship-motivated leadership is more appropriate.

Fiedler's theory was not always supported by research. It is better supported if three broad rather than eight specific levels of situational control are assumed: low, medium, and high. The theory was quite controversial in academic circles; among other arguable things, it assumed that leaders cannot change their styles but must be assigned to situations that suit their styles. However, the model has withstood the test of time and still receives attention. Most important, it initiated and continues to emphasize the importance of finding a fit between the situation and the leader's style.

Hersey and Blanchard's Situational Theory   Hersey and Blanchard developed a situational model that added another factor the leader should take into account before deciding whether task performance or maintenance behaviors are more important. Originally called the *life-cycle theory of leadership*, **Hersey and Blanchard's situational theory** highlights the maturity of the followers as the key situational factor.[68] **Job maturity** is the level of the follower's skills and technical knowledge relative to the task being performed; **psychological maturity** is the follower's self-confidence and self-respect. High-maturity followers have both the ability and the confidence to do a good job.

The theory proposes that the more mature the followers, the less the leader needs to engage in task performance behaviors. The required amount of maintenance behavior is a bit more complex; maintenance behaviors are not important with followers of low or high levels of maturity but are important for followers of moderate maturity. For low-maturity followers, the emphasis should be on performance-related leadership; for moderate-maturity followers, performance leadership is somewhat less important and maintenance behaviors become more important; and for high-maturity followers, neither dimension of leadership behavior is important.

Little academic research has been done on this situational theory, but the model is popular in management training seminars. Regardless of its scientific validity, Hersey and Blanchard's model provides a reminder that it is important to treat different people differently. Moreover, it suggests the importance of treating the same individual differently from time to time as he or she changes jobs or acquires more maturity in her or his particular job.[69]

Path–Goal Theory   Perhaps the most comprehensive and generally useful situational model of leadership effectiveness is path–goal theory. Developed by Robert House, **path–goal theory** gets its name from its concern with how leaders influence followers' perceptions of their work goals and the paths they follow toward goal attainment.[70]

The key situational factors in path–goal theory are (1) personal characteristics of followers and (2) environmental pressures and demands with which followers must cope to attain their work goals. These factors determine which leadership behaviors are most appropriate.

The four pertinent leadership behaviors are as follows:

1. *Directive leadership*, a form of task performance–oriented behavior.
2. *Supportive leadership*, a form of group maintenance–oriented behavior.
3. *Participative leadership*, or decision style.
4. *Achievement-oriented leadership*, or behaviors geared toward motivating people, such as setting challenging goals and rewarding good performance.

These situational factors and leader behaviors are merged in Figure 12.5. As you can see, appropriate leader behaviors—as determined by characteristics of followers and the work environment—lead to effective performance.

Hersey and Blanchard's situational theory

A life-cycle theory of leadership postulating that a manager should consider an employee's psychological and job maturity before deciding whether task performance or maintenance behaviors are more important.

job maturity

The level of the employee's skills and technical knowledge relative to the task being performed.

psychological maturity

An employee's self-confidence and self-respect.

path–goal theory

A theory that concerns how leaders influence subordinates' perceptions of their work goals and the paths they follow toward attainment of those goals.

FIGURE 12.5
The Path–Goal Framework

The theory also specifies which follower and environmental characteristics are important. There are three key follower characteristics. *Authoritarianism* is the degree to which individuals respect, admire, and defer to authority. *Locus of control* is the extent to which individuals see the environment as responsive to their own behavior. People with an *internal* locus of control believe that what happens to them is their own doing; people with an *external* locus of control believe that it is just luck or fate. Finally, *ability* is people's beliefs about their own abilities to do their assigned jobs.

Path–goal theory states that these personal characteristics determine the appropriateness of various leadership styles. For example, the theory makes the following propositions:

- A directive leadership style is more appropriate for highly authoritarian people because such people respect authority.
- A participative leadership style is more appropriate for people who have an internal locus of control because these individuals prefer to have more influence over their own lives.
- A directive style is more appropriate when subordinates' ability is low. The directive style helps people understand what has to be done.

Appropriate leadership style is also determined by three important environmental factors: people's tasks, the formal authority system of the organization, and the primary work group:

- Directive leadership is inappropriate if tasks already are well structured.
- If the task and the authority or rule system are dissatisfying, directive leadership will create greater dissatisfaction.
- If the task or authority system is dissatisfying, supportive leadership is especially appropriate because it offers one positive source of gratification in an otherwise negative situation.
- If the primary work group provides social support to its members, supportive leadership is less important.

Path–goal theory offers many more propositions. In general, the theory suggests that the functions of the leader are to (1) make the path to work goals easier to travel by providing coaching and direction, (2) reduce frustrating barriers to goal attainment, and (3) increase opportunities for personal satisfaction by increasing payoffs to people for achieving performance goals. The best way to do these things depends on your people and on the work situation. Again, analyze and then adapt your style accordingly.

Substitutes for Leadership   Sometimes leaders don't have to lead, or situations constrain their ability to lead effectively. The situation may be one in which leadership is unnecessary or has little impact. **Substitutes for leadership** can provide the same influence on people that leaders otherwise would have.

Certain follower, task, and organizational factors are substitutes for task performance and group maintenance leader behaviors.[71] For example, group maintenance behaviors are less important and have less impact if people already have a closely knit group, they have a professional orientation, the job is inherently satisfying, or there is great physical distance between leader and followers. Thus physicians who are

substitutes for leadership

Factors in the workplace that can exert the same influence on employees as leaders would provide.

strongly concerned with professional conduct, enjoy their work, and work independently do not need social support from hospital administrators.

Task performance leadership is less important and will have less of a positive effect if people have a lot of experience and ability, feedback is supplied to them directly from the task or by computer, or the rules and procedures are rigid. If these factors are operating, the leader does not have to tell people what to do or how well they are performing.

The concept of substitutes for leadership does more than indicate when a leader's attempts at influence will and will not work. It provides useful and practical prescriptions for how to manage more efficiently.[72] If the manager can develop the work situation to the point that a number of these substitutes for leadership are operating, less time will need to be spent in direct attempts to influence people. The leader will be free to spend more time on other important activities.

Research indicates that substitutes for leadership may be better predictors of commitment and satisfaction than of performance.[73] These substitutes are helpful, but you can't put substitutes in place and think you've completed your job as leader. Consider, for example, whether these substitutes would be enough to turn around performance at Hewlett-Packard (see "Management Connection: Progress Report"). And as a follower, consider this: if you're not getting good leadership, and if these substitutes are not in place, create your own substitute for leadership—self-leadership. Take the initiative to motivate yourself, lead yourself, create positive change, and lead others.

Management Connection

IS MEG WHITMAN'S LEADERSHIP STYLE RIGHT FOR HEWLETT-PACKARD?

Meg Whitman's vision for Hewlett Packard is to make it a stronger version of itself: not splitting it up, as some have advised, but holding it together by remotivating employees to do what HP does, only better. Upon taking the CEO position, she announced to the board of directors, "Rule number one is to fix what we have"—a statement that ended rumors about HP selling off its PC unit or backing out of its deal to buy Autonomy. Months later, Whitman presided over a meeting of software engineers and managers, some of whom viewed the new CEO with suspicion. When one of them challenged her by pointing out that attendees were live-blogging her comments, Whitman observed that their conduct was "a sign of an unhappy company" because it demonstrated they "wish HP ill." Her words signaled she was aware of HP's morale problem and took it seriously, thereby grabbing her audience's attention.

To improve how HP works, Whitman set about getting employees the resources they need. She restructured the company into two business units, one focusing on needs of corporate customers, such as powerful computer servers and networking systems, and the other selling hardware often purchased by consumers, including PCs, laptops, and mobile devices. A survey of HP salespeople showed they thought their sales software was abysmal. They spent weeks assembling bids that competitors could pull together in days. Whitman approved an investment in customer relationship management software from Salesforce.com, which dramatically sped up the bidding process. To compete in today's design-conscious consumer segment, HP hired a vice president for design and added designers from trendy firms. It has begun launching new laptops and tablets with more elegant features.

Whitman has further demonstrated HP's recommitment to customer service by visiting big enterprise buyers. In her first full year on the job, she met with individual customers or resellers more than 300 times and with 42 small groups in the United States, Europe, and India. This allowed her to reinforce that the company would continue to stand behind its PCs and that she understands the needs of her customers.

Whitman's reputation suggests she will be unlikely to back down and may relate well to workers in Silicon Valley, known for a work culture that is simultaneously hard-driving and playful, casual about hierarchy and respectful of knowledge. Writers for *Forbes* describe her as "blunt, folksy, and persistent" and "decisive without being abrasive." Time will show whether those are the qualities HP needs at the top.[74]

- What leader traits and behaviors has Meg Whitman used? Are they likely to be effective?
- How well suited to HP's situation is Whitman's leadership style, as described here?

MANAGER'S BRIEF

PROGRESS REPORT

ONWARD

Contemporary Perspectives on Leadership

LO 7 So far you have learned the major classic approaches to understanding leadership, all of which remain useful today. Now we will discuss a number of newer developments that are revolutionizing our understanding of this vital aspect of management.

Charismatic Leadership

Like many great leaders, Ronald Reagan had charisma. So does Barack Obama. Thomas Watson, Alfred Sloan, Steve Jobs, and Richard Branson are good examples of charismatic leaders in industry.

Martin Luther King was a brilliant, charismatic leader who had a compelling vision, a dream for a better world.

charismatic leader

A person who is dominant, self-confident, convinced of the moral righteousness of his or her beliefs, and able to arouse a sense of excitement and adventure in followers.

Charisma is a rather elusive concept; it is easy to spot but hard to define. What *is* charisma, and how does one acquire it? According to one definition, "Charisma packs an emotional wallop for followers above and beyond ordinary esteem, affection, admiration, and trust. . . . The charismatic is an idolized hero, a messiah, and a savior."[75] As you can see from this quotation, many people, particularly North Americans, value charisma in their leaders. But some people don't like the term *charisma*; it can be associated with the negative charisma of evil leaders whom people follow blindly.[76] Nevertheless, charismatic leaders who display appropriate values and use their charisma for appropriate purposes serve as ethical role models for others.[77]

Charismatic leaders are dominant and exceptionally self-confident and have a strong conviction in the moral righteousness of their beliefs.[78] They strive to create an aura of competence and success and communicate high expectations for and confidence in followers. Ultimately, charismatic leaders satisfy other peoples' needs.[79] Even people who have direct contact with a leader can perceive him or her as charismatic, because other followers spread the word.[80] And guess what: People can learn to be more charismatic.[81]

The charismatic leader articulates ideological goals and makes sacrifices in pursuit of those goals.[82] Martin Luther King Jr. had a dream for a better world, and John F. Kennedy spoke of landing a human on the moon. In other words, such leaders have a compelling vision. The charismatic leader also arouses a sense of excitement and adventure. He or she is an eloquent speaker who exhibits superior verbal skills, which help communicate the vision and motivate followers. Walt Disney mesmerized people with his storytelling; had enormous creative talent; and instilled in his organization strong values of good taste, risk taking, and innovation.[83]

Leaders who possess these characteristics or do these things inspire in their followers trust, confidence, acceptance, obedience, emotional involvement, affection, admiration, and higher performance.[84] For example, a recent study of firefighters found them to be happier when working for charismatic officers who expressed positive attitudes.[85] Having charisma not only helps CEOs inspire other employees in the organization but also may enable them to influence external stakeholders, including customers and investors.[86] Evidence for the positive effects of charismatic leadership has been found in a wide variety of groups, organizations, and management levels, and in countries including India, Singapore, the Netherlands, China, Japan, and Canada.[87]

Charisma has been shown to improve corporate financial performance, particularly under conditions of uncertainty—that is, in risky circumstances or when environments are changing and people have difficulty understanding what they should do.[88] Uncertainty is stressful, and it makes people more receptive to the ideas and actions of charismatic leaders. By the way, too, as an organization's performance improves under a person's leadership, that person becomes seen as more charismatic as a result of the higher performance.[89]

Transformational Leadership

Charisma contributes to transformational leadership. **Transformational leaders** motivate people to transcend their personal interests for the sake of the larger community.[90] They generate excitement and revitalize organizations. At Amazon, chief executive Jeff Bezos generates excitement with his zeal to create a great customer experience coupled with determination to focus on the long term, no matter how hard investors press for quick profits. His vision keeps employees innovating and gives them a sense of purpose greater than quarterly financial performance.[91]

The transformational process moves beyond the more traditional *transactional* approach to leadership. **Transactional leaders** view management as a series of transactions in which they use their legitimate, reward, and coercive powers to give commands and exchange rewards for services rendered. Unlike transformational leadership, transactional leadership is dispassionate; it does not excite, transform, empower, or inspire people to focus on the interests of the group or organization. However, transactional approaches may be more effective for individualists than for collectivists (recall Chapter 6).[92]

transformational leaders

Leaders who motivate people to transcend their personal interests for the good of the group.

transactional leaders

Leaders who manage through transactions, using their legitimate, reward, and coercive powers to give commands and exchange rewards for services rendered.

Generating Excitement   Transformational leaders generate excitement in several ways.[93] First, they are charismatic, as described earlier. Second, they give their followers individualized attention. Transformational leaders delegate challenging work to deserving people, keep lines of communication open, and provide one-on-one mentoring to develop their people. They do not treat everyone alike because not everyone *is* alike.

Third, transformational leaders are intellectually stimulating. They arouse in their followers an awareness of problems and potential solutions. They articulate the organization's opportunities, threats, strengths, and weaknesses. They stir the imagination and generate insights. Therefore, problems are recognized, and high-quality solutions are identified and implemented with the full commitment of followers.

Additional Strategies   At least four additional strategies contribute to transformational leadership.[94] First, transformational leaders have a vision—a goal, an agenda, or a results orientation that grabs people's attention. Second, they communicate their vision; through words, manner, or symbolism, they relate a compelling image of the ultimate goal. Transformational leadership is most effective in motivating followers when they can see directly the meaningful consequences of the leader's vision, such as by interacting with those who benefit from their work.[95]

> Transformational leaders strive for success rather than merely try to avoid failure.

Third, transformational leaders build trust by being consistent, dependable, and persistent. They position themselves clearly by choosing a direction and staying with it, thus projecting integrity. Finally, they have a positive self-regard. They do not feel self-important or complacent; rather, they recognize their personal strengths, compensate for their weaknesses, nurture and continually develop their talents, and know how to learn from failure. They strive for success rather than merely try to avoid failure.

Transformational leadership has been identified in industry, the military, and politics.[96] Besides Amazon's Jeff Bezos, mentioned earlier, examples of transformational leaders in business include Herb Kelleher (former CEO of Southwest Airlines), David

Neeleman (entrepreneur and founder of JetBlue), and Lee Iacocca (who led Chrysler's turnaround during the 1980s).[97] Transformational leadership exhibited by CEOs predicts firm performance, at least for small and midsized firms.[98]

As with studies of charisma, transformational leadership and its positive impact on follower satisfaction and performance have been demonstrated in countries the world over, including Egypt, Germany, China, England, and Japan.[99] A study in Korean companies found that transformational leadership predicted employee motivation, which in turn predicted creativity.[100] Under transformational leadership, people view their jobs as more intrinsically motivating (see Chapter 13 for more on this) and are more strongly committed to work goals.[101] And top management teams agree more clearly about important organizational goals, which translates into higher organizational performance.[102]

In Practice

TRANSFORMATIONAL LEADERSHIP AT LOCKERZ

An example of a manager exhibiting transformational leadership is Kathy Savitt, founder and chief executive officer of Lockerz. The company operates an e-commerce website that uses social networking tools to engage teens in shopping online. Teens who visit the site can help themselves and their friends earn points toward discounts on merchandise by clicking images of the items and viewing various kinds of promotional content. The company grew out of Savitt's passion for serving this young demographic group.

Savitt has a vision not only for the company's place as an Internet marketer but also for the kind of company it should be for its employees. Her vision is of a business in which the employees respect one another and are fearless about innovation. In hiring, Savitt seeks people who not only are highly intelligent but also listen attentively, demonstrate respect for others, and can laugh at themselves. She models her vision of the workplace by addressing problems and setbacks frankly and with a focus on solutions, saying it takes courage to work through failure.

Savitt expresses confidence that by bringing in people who have talent plus a drive to contribute, she can create a company culture that avoids cynical practices she has experienced at other companies in the past. For example, she has seen business meetings that play a kind of stump-the-chump game, in which if one employee tries to answer a question or offer an idea, others pile on with criticism. Savitt believes she can avoid that by communicating the values of courage, innovation, and results.[103]

- What kinds of behavior can help Savitt build employees' trust in her and her vision?

Bottom Line
Transformational leadership is good for people and good for the bottom line.
Why might improving employees' personal development be good for a company?

Transforming Leaders   Importantly, transformational leadership is not the exclusive domain of presidents and chief executives. In the military, leaders who received transformational leadership training had a positive impact on followers' personal development. They also were successful as indirect leaders: military recruits under the transformational leaders' direct reports were stronger performers.[104] Don't forget, though: The best leaders are those who can display both transformational and transactional behaviors.[105]

Ford Motor Company, in collaboration with the University of Michigan School of Business, put thousands of middle managers through a program designed to stimulate transformational leadership.[106] The training included analysis of the changing business environment, company strategy, and personal reflection and discussion about the need to change. Participants assessed their own leadership styles and developed a specific change initiative to implement after the training—a change that would make a needed and lasting difference for the company.

Over the next six months, the managers implemented change on the job. Almost half of the initiatives resulted in transformational changes in the organization or work unit; the rest of the changes were smaller, more incremental, or more personal. Whether managers made small or transformational changes depended on their attitude going into the training, their level of self-esteem, and the amount of support they received from others on the job for their efforts. Thus some managers did not respond as hoped. But almost half embraced the training, became more transformational in orientation, and tackled significant transformational changes for the company.

Level 5 leadership, a term well-known among executives, is considered by some to be the ultimate leadership style. Level 5 leadership is a combination of strong professional will (determination) and personal humility that builds enduring greatness.[107] Thus a Level 5 leader is relentlessly focused on the organization's long-term success while behaving with modesty, directing attention toward the organization rather than him- or herself. Examples include John Chambers, CEO of Cisco Systems, and IBM's former chief executive Louis Gerstner. Gerstner is widely credited for turning around a stodgy IBM by shifting its focus from computer hardware to business solutions. Following his retirement, Gerstner wrote a memoir that details what happened at the company but says little about himself. Level 5 leadership is seen as a way to transform organizations to make them great and requires the leader to exhibit a combination of transactional and transformational styles.[108]

> **Level 5 leadership**
>
> A combination of strong professional will (determination) and humility that builds enduring greatness.

Authenticity

Consider **authentic leadership** to be rooted in the ancient Greek philosophy "To thine own self be true."[109] In your own leadership, strive for authenticity in the form of honesty, genuineness, reliability, integrity, and trustworthiness. Authentic transformational leaders care about public interests (community, organizational, or group), not just their own.[110] They are willing to sacrifice their own interests for others, and they can be trusted. They are ethically mature; people view leaders who exhibit moral reasoning as more transformational than leaders who do not.[111] Importantly, ethical leadership flows down from one organizational level to the next[112]—your actions as a leader have an impact beyond your immediate, direct reports.

Pseudotransformational leaders are the opposite: they talk a good game, but they ignore followers' real needs as their own self-interests (power, prestige, control, wealth, fame) take precedence.[113]

> **authentic leadership**
>
> A style in which the leader is true to himself or herself while leading.
>
> **pseudotransformational leaders**
>
> Leaders who talk about positive change but allow their self-interest to take precedence over followers' needs.

In Practice

TEAM BUILDING AT YUM BRANDS

Not every manager can motivate employees by giving them a rubber chicken, as David Novak has done, but that is just the point. Novak, the chief executive of Yum Brands, says, "Nobody's going to follow you unless you're the real deal." And Novak seems genuinely excited about the fast-food business, specifically Yum's three chains: KFC, Pizza Hut, and Taco Bell.

With a compensation package nearing $30 million, Novak ranks among the highest-paid CEOs, but his tastes are aligned with his customers'. Buckets of KFC chicken were a childhood treat, and Taco Bell and Pizza Hut were big parts of his college experience. Novak speaks exuberantly of the menu extensions created to spur overseas expansion, such as the "unbelievably fiery" chicken drumsticks sold in India. The art displayed at Yum's headquarters consists of photos showing Novak with employees around the world.

In Novak's view, the most important work at Yum Brands is done by the restaurants' general managers "because they build the teams that satisfy the customers." An important part of team building is employee recognition, clearly one of Novak's passions and part of every manager's job description. When Novak was president of KFC, he tried using a rubber chicken as a recognition award, and it created a spirit of fun that Novak wants to keep. When he became president of Pizza Hut, he gave away cheese-shaped hats. Now, as CEO of the combined restaurant company, he gives out windup chattering-teeth toys, which symbolize "walking the talk" of leadership. Adding to the significance, Novak writes a personal note on each token and presents it along with a cash award.[114]

- At a fast-food company, can a manager with an eight-figure income be an authentic leader? What qualities are needed for authenticity, and does it depend on the context or kind of company?

Opportunities for Leaders

A common view of leaders is that they are superheroes acting alone, swooping in to save the day. But especially in these complex times, leaders cannot and need not act alone. Effective leadership must permeate the organization, not reside in one or two superstars at the top. The leader's job becomes one of spreading leadership abilities throughout the firm.[115] Make people responsible for their own performance. Create an environment in which each person can figure out what needs to be done and then do it well. Point the way and clear the path so that people can succeed. Give them the credit they deserve. Make heroes out of *them*.

Thus what is now required of leaders is less the efficient management of resources and more the effective unleashing of people and their intellectual capital.

This perspective uncovers a variety of nontraditional leadership roles that are emerging as vitally important.[116] The term **servant–leader** was coined by Robert Greenleaf, a retired AT&T executive. The term is paradoxical in the sense that "leader" and "servant" are usually opposites; the servant–leader's relationship with employees is more like that of serving customers. For the individual who wants to both lead and serve others, servant–leadership is a way of relating to others to serve their needs and enhance their personal growth while strengthening the organization.[117] For example, at Mississippi Health Services, CEO John Heer had himself and the other executives assessed for servant leadership qualities, including humility, honesty, integrity, and a focus on results. The executives then created action plans for improving in the areas with the lowest scores and met to share their results and plans. Asking for help with weaknesses felt uncomfortable, but the process freed everyone to be more honest and led to greater satisfaction among employees, doctors, and patients. Even market share improved.[118]

A number of other roles provide leadership opportunities. **Intergroup leaders** lead collaborative performance between different groups or organizations.[119] Examples are interdepartmental cooperation, joint ventures, public/private partnerships, and collaborations that cross national, cultural, and religious boundaries.

With work often being team-based (see Chapter 14), **shared leadership** occurs when leadership rotates to the person with the key knowledge, skills, and abilities for the issue facing the team at a particular time.[120] Shared leadership is most important when tasks are interdependent, are complex, and require creativity. High-performing teams engaged in such work exhibit more shared leadership than poorly performing teams. In consulting teams, the higher the shared leadership, the higher their clients rated the teams' performance.[121] The role of vertical leader remains important—the formal leader still designs the team, manages its external boundaries, provides task direction, emphasizes the importance of the shared leadership approach, and engages in the transactional

servant–leader

A leader who serves others' needs while strengthening the organization.

intergroup leader

A leader who leads collaborative performance between different groups or organizations.

shared leadership

Rotating leadership, in which people rotate through the leadership role based on which person has the most relevant skills at a particular time.

and transformational activities described in this chapter. But at the same time, the metaphor of geese in V-formation adds strength to the group; the lead goose periodically drops to the back, and another goose steps up and takes its place at the forefront.

Lateral leadership does not involve a hierarchical, superior–subordinate relationship but instead invites colleagues at the same level to solve problems together.[122] You alone can't provide a solution to every problem, but you can create processes through which people work collaboratively. If you can get people working to improve methods collaboratively, you can help create an endless stream of innovations. In other words, it's not about you providing solutions to problems; it's about creating better interpersonal processes for finding solutions. Strategies and tactics can be found throughout this book, including the chapters on decision making, organization structure, teams, communication, and change.

A Note on Courage

To be a good leader, you need the courage to create a vision of greatness for your unit; identify and manage allies, adversaries, and fence sitters; and execute your vision, often against opposition. This does not mean you should commit career suicide by alienating too many powerful people; it does mean taking reasonable risks, with the good of the firm at heart, to produce constructive change.

For example, Alan Mulally needed courage when he left Boeing to take charge of Ford Motor Company in 2006, a point at which a series of poor decisions had made Ford a money-losing company. Many of Ford's managers were skeptical of Mulally as their new CEO because he came from outside the automobile industry. Nevertheless, Mullaly plunged ahead with two decisions that were controversial at the time. He borrowed heavily and determined that the company would go forward with greater focus by offering fewer brands and models, with each being the best in its class. He also insisted that Ford's executives take a clear look at reality, however perilous it might be. He began calling weekly meetings at which each manager had to grade his or her group's progress. At the first such meeting, the managers all said their situation was fine, and Mulally vehemently registered his disbelief that no one had problems when the company was forecasting a loss of $17 billion. After that, the reports became more honest, and Mulally praised the honesty. Instead of competing to put the best face on what they saw, executives began collaborating for the company's sake, sharing ideas for solutions. A few years later, Mulally's courageous efforts looked brilliant; Ford's borrowing gave the company resources to draw on when other automakers were accepting government loans to survive a financial crisis, and within a few years, Ford was recording record profits.[123]

Specifically, fulfilling your vision will require some of the following acts of courage:[124] (1) seeing things as they are and facing them head-on, making no excuses and harboring no wishful illusions; (2) saying what needs to be said to those who need to hear it; and (3) persisting despite resistance, criticism, abuse, and setbacks. Courage includes stating the realities, even when they are harsh, and publicly stating what you will do to help and what you want from others. This means laying the cards on the table honestly: Here is what I want from you . . . what do you want from me?[125]

lateral leadership

Style in which colleagues at the same hierarchical level are invited to collaborate and facilitate joint problem solving.

Developing Your Leadership Skills

As with other things, you must work at developing your leadership abilities. Great musicians and great athletes don't become great on natural gifts alone. They pay their dues by practicing, learning, and sacrificing. Leaders in a variety of fields, when asked how they became the best leader possible, offered the following comments:[126]

- "I've observed methods and skills of my bosses that I respected."
- "By taking risks, trying, and learning from my mistakes."

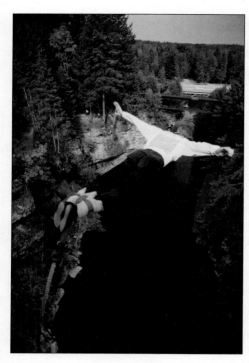

Challenges expand knowledge and experiences. Being open to new ideas allows managers to learn, grow, and succeed even though the challenge may be out of their comfort zone.

- "Reading autobiographies of leaders I admire to try to understand how they think."
- "Lots of practice."
- "By making mistakes myself and trying a different approach."
- "By being put in positions of responsibility that other people counted on."

How Do I Start?

How do you go about developing your leadership abilities? You don't have to wait until you land a management job or even finish your education. You can begin establishing credibility by behaving with integrity, learning from your mistakes, and becoming competent in your chosen field. You should look for—and then seize—opportunities to take actions that will help the groups you already belong to. Even before you are a supervisor, you can practice empowering others by listening carefully when you are in a group and by sharing what you know so that the whole group will be better informed. Finally, begin building a network of personal contacts by reaching out to others to offer help, not just to request it.[127]

When you are searching for your next job, look for a position with an employer that is committed to developing leadership talent. Ideally, leadership development is connected to opportunities to practice the skills you are learning about, so ask about chances to lead a project or a team, even for short periods of time.[128] Companies that excel at leadership development include Johnson & Johnson, Hewlett-Packard, and General Electric.[129]

More specifically, here are some developmental experiences you should seek:[130]

- *Assignments:* Building something from nothing; fixing or turning around a failing operation; taking on project or task force responsibilities; accepting international assignments.
- *Other people:* Having exposure to positive role models; increasing visibility to others; working with people of diverse backgrounds.
- *Hardships:* Overcoming ideas that fail and deals that collapse; confronting others' performance problems; breaking out of a career rut.
- *Other events:* Formal courses; challenging job experiences; supervision of others; experiences outside work.

What Are the Keys?

The most effective developmental experiences have three components: assessment, challenge, and support.[131] Assessment includes information that gives you an understanding of where you are now, what your strengths are, your current levels of performance and leadership effectiveness, and your primary development needs. You can think about what your past feedback has been, what previous successes and failures you have had, how people have reacted to your ideas and actions, what your personal goals are, and what strategies you should implement to make progress. You can seek answers from your peers at work, bosses, family, friends, customers, and anyone else who knows you and how you work. The information you collect will help clarify what you need to learn, improve, or change.[132]

The most potent developmental experiences provide challenge—they stretch you. We all think and behave in habitual, comfortable ways. This is natural and perhaps sufficient to survive. But you've probably heard people say how important it can be to get out of your comfort zone—to tackle situations that require new skills and abilities, that are confusing or ambiguous, or that you simply would rather not deal with.

Sometimes the challenge comes from lack of experience; other times, it requires changing old habits. It may be uncomfortable, but this is how great managers learn. Remember, some people don't bother to learn or refuse to learn. Make sure you think about your experiences along the way and reflect on them afterward, introspectively and in discussion with others.

You receive support when others send the message that your efforts to learn and grow are valued. Without support, challenging developmental experiences can be overwhelming. With support, it is easier to handle the struggle, stay on course, open up to learning, and actually learn from experiences. Support can come informally from other people; more formally through the procedures of the organization; and through learning resources in the forms of training, constructive feedback, talking with others, and so on.

What develops in leadership development? Through such experiences, you can acquire more self-awareness and self-confidence, a broader perspective on the organizational system, creative thinking, the ability to work more effectively in complex social systems, and the ability to learn from experience.

Management Connection

HP'S FUTURE ACCORDING TO MEG WHITMAN

A year and a half into Meg Whitman's tenure as chief executive of Hewlett-Packard, some observers doubted she could lead a successful turnaround. In a recent analysis of CEO performance, Bloomberg ranked Whitman as the "biggest CEO underachiever," based on HP's stock performance relative to the market overall. Whitman pointed to her original forecast that a turnaround would take five years and insisted that employees, customers, and business partners had said they see signs of a turnaround. Although the sliding stock price showed the doubts of investors, others interpreted her stance as evidence of courage, consistency, and an admirably long view of corporate performance.

Whitman had shown courage before joining HP. Early in her career, she was a junior partner at Bain Consulting. Colleagues were intimidated by her boss, Tom Tierney, but Whitman met with him privately and asked whether he wanted feedback from the staff about his leadership style. When Tierney said yes, she told him he was like a steamroller and inhibited his staff. After the initial shock, Tierney took her counsel to heart and now praises her courage.

At HP, Whitman has applied a similar fearlessness concerning the truth. Soon after HP lost a bid to sell Microsoft servers for its Bing search engine, she called Microsoft's CEO to find out why. Microsoft sent her a nine-page explanation of areas in which HP fell short.

Whitman assembled a team of managers to analyze how to get it right next time. When Microsoft needed more servers for Bing, HP won the order.

Whitman also has demonstrated concern for what it is like to be an HP employee. She has sought to restore a culture more like the one that prevailed under the founders—one where technology is revered and technology workers are valued. She eliminated the fenced-off executive parking lot and executive suites, working in a cubicle like everyone else. When she travels, she stays at a Courtyard Marriott, and when she works evenings, she orders from Chipotle or the local pizza company. Whitman certainly values the power of symbols. HP's renovated meeting center at headquarters in Palo Alto has a courtyard built around an oak tree planted by Bill Hewlett and Dave Packard in the 1960s. Meg told a *Bloomberg Businessweek* reporter, "This is symbolic of the rebirth of Hewlett-Packard anchored by the foundation of that oak tree."[133]

- What evidence, if any, do you see that Whitman is a charismatic leader? A transformational leader? An authentic leader? A servant–leader?
- Look up recent business news to learn how well HP is performing today and whether Whitman remains CEO. Has she been a successful leader of HP? Why or why not?

MANAGER'S BRIEF

PROGRESS REPORT

ONWARD

KEY TERMS

SUMMARY OF LEARNING OBJECTIVES

Now that you have studied Chapter 12, you should be able to

LO 1   Discuss what it means to be a leader.

A leader is one who influences others to attain goals. Leaders orchestrate change, set direction, and motivate people to overcome obstacles and move the organization toward its ideal future.

LO 2   Summarize what people want and organizations need from their leaders.

People want help in achieving their goals, and organizations need leaders at all levels. The best leaders challenge the process, inspire a shared vision, enable others to act, model the way, and encourage the heart.

LO 3   Explain how a good vision helps you be a better leader.

Outstanding leaders have vision. A vision is a mental image that goes beyond the ordinary and perhaps beyond what others thought possible. The vision provides the direction in which the leader wants the organization to move and inspiration for people to pursue it.

LO 4   Identify sources of power in organizations.

Having power and using it appropriately are essential to effective leadership. Managers at all levels of the organization have five potential sources of power. Legitimate power is the company-granted authority to direct others. Reward power is control over rewards valued by others in the organization. Coercive power is control over punishments that others in the organization want to avoid. Referent power consists of personal characteristics that appeal to others, so they model their behavior on the leader's and seek the leader's approval. Expert power is expertise or knowledge that can benefit others in the organization.

LO 5   List personal traits and skills of effective leaders.

Important leader characteristics include drive, leadership, motivation, integrity, self-confidence, and knowledge of the business. Perhaps the most important skill is the ability to perceive the situation accurately and then change behavior accordingly.

LO 6   Describe behaviors that will make you a better leader and identify when the situation calls for them.

Important leader behaviors include task performance behaviors, group maintenance, and decision making. According to the Vroom model, the leadership style should involve individual decisions, consultation with followers, facilitation, or delegation depending on qualities such as the significance of the decision and the importance of followers' commitment. Fiedler's contingency model says that a task-motivated leader is more successful when leader–member relations are good and the task is highly structured, or with an unstructured task but low position power for the leader, or with poor leader–member relations when the task structure and leader's position power are both low. In other situations, a relationship-oriented leader will perform better. Hersey and Blanchard's situational theory says that task performance behaviors become less important as the follower's job maturity and psychological maturity increase. Path–goal theory assesses characteristics of the followers, the leader, and the situation; it then indicates the appropriateness of directive, supportive, participative, or achievement-oriented leadership behaviors.

LO 7   Distinguish between charismatic and transformational leaders.

To have charisma is to be dominant and self-confident, to have a strong conviction of the righteousness of your beliefs, to create an aura of competence and success, and to communicate high expectations for and confidence in your followers. Charisma is one component of transformational leadership. Transformational leaders translate a vision into reality by inspiring people to transcend their individual interests for the good of the larger community. They do this through charisma, individualized attention to followers, intellectual stimulation, formation and communication of their vision, building of trust, and positive self-regard.

LO 8   Describe types of opportunities to be a leader in an organization.

There's plenty of opportunity to be a leader; being a manager of others who report to you is just the traditional one. You can also take or create opportunities to be a servant–leader or intergroup leader and engage in shared leadership and lateral leadership. A servant–leader serves others' needs while strengthening the organization. An intergroup leader leads collaborative performance between different groups or organizations. Shared leadership involves taking on a leadership role when your skills are most relevant to a particular situation. Lateral leadership is inspiring people to work collaboratively and solve problems together.

LO 9   Discuss how to further your own leadership development.

You can develop your own leadership skills not only by understanding what effective leadership is all about but also by seeking challenging developmental experiences. Such important life experiences come from taking challenging assignments, through exposure in working with other people, by overcoming hardships and failures, by taking formal courses, and by other actions. The most important elements of a good developmental experience are assessment, challenge, and support.

DISCUSSION QUESTIONS

1. What do you want from your leader?
2. Is there a difference between effective management and effective leadership? Explain your views and learn from others' views.
3. Identify someone you think is an effective leader. What makes him or her effective?
4. Do you think most managers can be transformational leaders? Why or why not?
5. In your own words, define courage. What is the role of courage in leadership? Give examples of acts of leadership you consider courageous.
6. Do you think men and women differ in their leadership styles? If so, how? Do men and/or women prefer different styles in their bosses? What evidence do you have for your answers?
7. Who are your heroes? What makes them heroes, and what can you learn from them?
8. Assess yourself as a leader based on what you have read in this chapter. What are your strengths and weaknesses?
9. Identify the developmental experiences you have had that may have strengthened your ability to lead. What did those experiences teach you? Also identify some developmental experiences you need to acquire and how you will seek them. Be specific.
10. Consider a couple of decisions you are facing that could involve other people. Use the Vroom model to decide what approach to use to make the decisions.
11. Consider a job you hold or held in the past. Consider how your boss managed you. How would you describe him or her as a leader? What substitutes for leadership would you have enjoyed seeing put into place?
12. Consider an organization of which you are a leader or a member. What could great transformational leadership accomplish in the organization?
13. Name some prominent leaders whom you would describe as authentic and inauthentic and discuss.
14. Name some leaders you consider servant–leaders and discuss.
15. Identify some opportunities for you to exhibit shared leadership and lateral leadership.

EXPERIENTIAL EXERCISES

12.1   POWER AND INFLUENCE

OBJECTIVE

To explore the nature of power and influence, and your attitudes toward different kinds of power and influence.

INSTRUCTIONS

Read the introductions and complete sections A, B, and C.

Power and Influence Worksheet

A. Power

Many well-known people have made statements about power and winning (e.g., P. T. Barnum, Mao Tse-tung, Leo Durocher, Lord Acton, Vince Lombardi). Some of these statements are listed in the table that follows. Indicate how you feel about each of the statements by circling number 1 if you strongly disagree and so on.

	Strongly Disagree	Disagree	Neutral	Agree	Strongly Agree
Winning is everything.	1	2	3	4	5
Nice guys finish last.	1	2	3	4	5
There can be only one winner.	1	2	3	4	5
There's a sucker born every minute.	1	2	3	4	5
You can't completely trust anyone.	1	2	3	4	5
All power rests at the end of the gun.	1	2	3	4	5
Power seekers are greedy and can't be trusted.	1	2	3	4	5
Power corrupts; absolute power corrupts absolutely.	1	2	3	4	5
You get as much power as you pay for.	1	2	3	4	5

B. Influence

During the past week or so, you have come in contact with many people. Some have influenced you positively, some negatively. Try to recall recent experiences with employers, peers, teachers, parents, clergy, and the like who may have influenced you in some way. Then try to think about how and why they influenced you as they did.

1. On the following table, list the names of all those who influenced you during the past week or so according to the kind of power that person used. The same person's name may appear under more than one type of power if that person used multiple power bases. Also indicate whether the influence was positive (+) or negative (−).

Power Base	Names and Whether (+) or (−)
Legitimate authority	_____
Reward	_____
Coercive	_____
Referent	_____
Expert	_____

2. After examining your list, check (√) the following questions.

	Yes	No
a. Was there one person who had + marks appearing under several power bases?	_____	_____
b. Was there one person who had − marks appearing under several power bases?	_____	_____
c. Did you find that most of the people with + marks tended to fall under the same power bases?	_____	_____
d. Did you find that most of the people with − marks tended to fall under the same power bases?	_____	_____

3. From your answers to the last two questions, list which power bases you found to be positive (+) and which you found to be negative (−).

+	−
_____	_____
_____	_____
_____	_____
_____	_____

Do you think you personally prefer to use those power bases you listed under + when you try to influence people? Do you actually use them?

C. Power and Influence

From the table in Part B, find the one person who you think had the strongest positive influence on you (Person I), and the one who had the strongest negative influence (Person 2). These are most likely the persons whose names appear most frequently.

In the following table, place a I on the line for each statement that best indicates how you think Person I would respond to that statement. Put a 2 on the line for each statement that reflects how you think Person 2 would respond to that item.

	Strongly Disagree	Disagree	Neutral	Agree	Strongly Agree
Winning is everything.	_____	_____	_____	_____	_____
Nice guys finish last.	_____	_____	_____	_____	_____
There can be only one winner.	_____	_____	_____	_____	_____
There's a sucker born every minute	_____	_____	_____	_____	_____
You can't completely trust anyone.	_____	_____	_____	_____	_____
All power rests at the end of the gun.	_____	_____	_____	_____	_____
Power seekers are greedy and can't be trusted.	_____	_____	_____	_____	_____
Power corrupts; absolute power corrupts absolutely.	_____	_____	_____	_____	_____
You get as much power as you pay for.	_____	_____	_____	_____	_____

Now compare your responses in Part A to those in Part C. Do you more closely resemble Person I or Person 2? Do you prefer to use the kinds of power that person uses? Which kinds of power do you use most frequently? Which do you use least frequently? When do you feel you have the greatest power? When do you have the least power? How do these answers compare to what you found in Part B3?

SOURCE: Excerpted from Laurence R. Jauch, Arthur G. Bedeian, Sally A. Coltin, and William F. Glueck, *The Managerial Experience: Cases, Exercises, and Readings*, 5th ed. Copyright © 1989. South-Western, a part of Cengage Learning, Inc. Reproduced by permission. www.cengage.com/permissions.

12.2   EVALUATING YOUR LEADERSHIP STYLE

OBJECTIVES

1. To examine your personal style of leadership.
2. To study the nature of the leadership process.
3. To identify ways to improve or modify your leadership style.

INSTRUCTIONS

1. Working alone, complete and score the Leadership Style Survey.
2. In small groups, exchange scores, compute average scores, and develop responses to the discussion questions.
3. After the class reconvenes, group spokespersons present group findings.

DISCUSSION QUESTIONS

1. In what ways did your experience or lack of experience influence your responses to the survey?
2. In what ways did student scores and student responses to survey test items converge? In what ways did they diverge?
3. What do you think accounts for differences in student leadership attitudes?
4. How can students make constructive use of the survey results?

Leadership Style Survey

This survey describes various aspects of leadership behavior. To measure your leadership style, respond to each statement according to the way you would act (or think you would act) if you were a work group leader.

	Always	Frequently	Occasionally	Seldom	Never
1. I would allow team members the freedom to do their jobs in their own way.	5	4	3	2	1
2. I would make important decisions on my own initiative without consulting the workers.	5	4	3	2	1
3. I would allow the team members to make their own decisions.	5	4	3	2	1
4. I would not try to socialize with the workers.	5	4	3	2	1
5. I would allow team members to do their jobs as they see fit.	5	4	3	2	1
6. I would consider myself to be the group's spokesperson.	5	4	3	2	1
7. I would be warm, friendly, and approachable.	5	4	3	2	1
8. I would be sure that the workers understand and follow all the rules and regulations.	5	4	3	2	1
9. I would demonstrate a real concern for the workers' welfare.	5	4	3	2	1
10. I would be the one to decide what is to be done and how it is to be done.	5	4	3	2	1
11. I would delegate authority to the workers.	5	4	3	2	1
12. I would urge the workers to meet production quotas.	5	4	3	2	1
13. I would trust the workers to use good judgment in decision making.	5	4	3	2	1
14. I would assign specific tasks to specific people.	5	4	3	2	1
15. I would let the workers establish their own work pace.	5	4	3	2	1
16. I would not feel that I have to explain my decisions to workers.	5	4	3	2	1
17. I would try to make each worker feel that his or her contribution is important.	5	4	3	2	1
18. I would establish the work schedules.	5	4	3	2	1
19. I would encourage workers to get involved in setting work goals.	5	4	3	2	1
20. I would be action oriented and results oriented.	5	4	3	2	1
21. I would get the workers involved in making decisions.	5	4	3	2	1
22. I would outline needed changes and monitor action closely.	5	4	3	2	1
23. I would help the group achieve consensus on important changes.	5	4	3	2	1
24. I would supervise closely to ensure that standards are met.	5	4	3	2	1
25. I would consistently reinforce good work.	5	4	3	2	1
26. I would nip problems in the bud.	5	4	3	2	1
27. I would consult the group before making decisions.	5	4	3	2	1

CONCLUDING CASE

BREITT, STARR & DIAMOND LLC

Josh Breitt, Rachel Starr, and Justin Diamond started an advertising agency to serve the needs of small businesses selling in and around their metropolitan area. Breitt contributed clever ideas and a talent for writing scripts and wooing clients. Starr brought a wealth of media contacts, and Diamond handled the artwork. Their quirky ad campaigns soon attracted a stream of projects from car dealers, community banks, and a carpet store. Since the agency's first year, these clients have kept the bills paid while the three win contracts from other companies. Breitt, Starr & Diamond (BS&D) prospered by helping clients keep up with the times, and the agency grew to meet the demand, adding a bookkeeper, a graphic artist, a web designer, two salespeople, a social-media expert, and a retired human resource manager, who works 10 hours per week.

As the firm grew, the three partners felt they were constantly being pulled away from their areas of expertise to answer questions and solve problems about how to coordinate work, define jobs, and set priorities. They realized that none of them had any management training—and none of them had ever wanted to be a manager. They decided to hire a manager for a position they would call general manager of operations. That person would be responsible for supervising the employees, making sure expenses didn't go over budget, and planning the resources (including people) needed for further growth.

The partners interviewed several candidates and hired Brad Howser, a longtime administrator for a four-physician medical office. Howser spent the first few weeks quietly studying BS&D's financial data and observing employees at work. Then he became more outspoken and assertive. Although the partners had never cared to monitor what time employees came or left, Howser began requiring all employees to start by 9:00 each morning. The graphic artist and one of the salespeople complained that flexible hours were necessary for their child care arrangements, but Howser was unyielding. He also questioned whether the employees had been shopping carefully for supplies, indicating that from then on, he would be making all purchases, and only after the employees submitted their requests on a form of his design. Finally, to promote what he called team spirit, Howser began scheduling weekly Monday-morning staff meetings. He would offer motivational thoughts based on his experience at his previous job and invite the employees to share any work-related concerns or ideas they might have. Generally, the employees chose not to share.

Initially, the partners were impressed with Howser's vigorous approach to his job. They felt more productive than they had been in years because Howser was handling employee concerns himself. Then the top salesperson quit, followed by the social-media expert. The bookkeeper asked if she might meet with the partners. "Is it something you should be discussing with Brad?" Rachel asked her. The bookkeeper replied that, no, it was *about* Brad. All the employees were unhappy with him, and more were likely to leave.

DISCUSSION QUESTIONS

1. Assume that hiring a general manager of operations was a good idea. What leadership style would be most effective in this position? Why?

2. What leader behaviors did Brad Howser exhibit? How well do they fit the needs of the ad agency?

3. Consider your own leadership style. What are some of your tendencies, and how might you change your perspective?

CHAPTER 13

Motivating for Performance

> The worst mistake a boss can make is not to say well done.
> — JOHN ASHCROFT, BUSINESS EXECUTIVE
>
> The reward of a thing well done is to have done it.
> — RALPH WALDO EMERSON

LEARNING OBJECTIVES

CHAPTER OUTLINE

Management Connection

WHAT MAKES SAS A GREAT PLACE TO WORK?

SAS (named after its first product, Statistical Analysis Software) has grown since its 1976 founding into the world's leader in data analytics software—a $2.8 billion company with more than 12,000 employees in 55 countries. Along the way, SAS has ranked as one of the 100 Best Companies to Work For in America every year since the Great Place to Work Institute began handing out that recognition in *Fortune* magazine—and in the top five every year since 2010. In 2012, the institute created its first list of the World's Best Multinational Workplaces, and SAS took the number one spot. Both rankings are based on a combination of employee surveys and an analysis by the institute.

What does SAS do to earn this prestigious recognition? Certainly, the company is famous for the perks it offers its employees. Along with medical insurance, vacation time, profit sharing, and retirement savings accounts, SAS employees have access to adoption assistance, parental leave, and a college scholarship program for their children. At the Cary, North Carolina, headquarters, employees can use the on-site fitness center, health clinic, and day care center. Stress management programs include yoga, massage, and exercise programs. Those seeking to juggle home and work responsibilities can seek flexibility through options such as telecommuting and job sharing.

However, if you talk to SAS's leaders, you hear less about benefits and more about the company's values, which shape its work environment. As Jack Poll, SAS's director of recreation and employee services told a reporter for *Fast Company,* "When people are treated as if they're important and truly make a difference, their loyalty and engagement soar." The kind of treatment Poll is referring to emphasizes appreciating what workers contribute, building their trust, and empowering them to make decisions in their area of responsibility. Poll and SAS's founder and chief executive, James Goodnight, believe this treatment is the primary way SAS unleashes creativity. Creativity, in the hypercompetitive world of computer software, is essential for staying relevant. That SAS gets it right is evident in the company's sales, which have risen every year of the company's existence.[1]

SAS stands out as a company that offers generous benefits to its workers. As you read this chapter, consider whether generosity is enough to bring out employees' best work, aimed at the company's goals and priorities. If not, what other efforts should managers make?

are motivated to achieve. Microsoft uses the acronym SMART to create motivating goals: specific, measurable, achievable, results-based, and time-specific.[15]

Stretch Goals

stretch goals

Targets that are particularly demanding, sometimes even thought to be impossible.

Some firms today set **stretch goals**—targets that are exceptionally demanding and that some people would never even think of. There are two types of stretch goals: vertical stretch goals, aligned with current activities including productivity and financial results, and horizontal stretch goals, which involve people's professional development such as attempting and learning new, difficult things.[16] Impossible though stretch goals may seem to some, they often are in fact attainable.

Stretch goals can generate a major shift away from mediocrity and toward tremendous achievement. But if someone tries in good faith but doesn't meet their stretch goals, don't punish—remember how difficult they are! Base your assessment on how much performance has improved, how the performance compares with others, and how much progress has been made.[17]

Limitations of Goal Setting

Goal setting is an extraordinarily powerful management technique. But even specific, challenging, attainable goals work better under some conditions than others. For example, if people lack relevant ability and knowledge, a better course to follow might be simply urging them to do their best or setting a goal to learn rather than a goal to achieve a specific performance level.[18] Individual performance goals can be dysfunctional if people work in a group and cooperation among team members is essential to team performance.[19] Individualized goals can create competition and reduce cooperation. In groups, individual goals aimed at maximizing individual performance will hurt group performance; groupcentric goals aimed at maximizing the individual's contributions to the group's performance have a positive effect.[20] If cooperation is important, performance goals should be established for the team.

Setting unprecedented goals can push an individual to reach a higher level of achievement.

Goals can generate manipulative game-playing and unethical behavior. For example, people can sometimes find ingenious ways to set easy goals and convince their bosses that they are difficult.[21] Or they may find ways to meet goals simply to receive a reward, without necessarily performing in desirable ways. In the earlier example of Quick Lane Tire & Auto Center, goals based on sales dollars are specific and measurable but reward employees for focusing on inventory and margins, not customers and their cars. Similarly, in big law firms, it's common for lawyers to keep detailed records of their time and to be rewarded for billing, say, 2,000 hours per year. This system is an invitation to work inefficiently and a dismal, demotivating environment for any lawyer who chose the profession out of concern for clients or love of the law.[22] In addition, people who don't meet their goals are more likely to engage in unethical behavior than are people who are trying to do their best but have no specific performance goals. This is true regardless of whether they have financial incentives, and it is particularly true when people fall just short of reaching their goals.[23]

Another familiar example comes from the pages of financial reports. Some executives have mastered the art of earnings management—precisely meeting Wall Street analysts' earnings estimates or beating them by a single penny.[24] The media trumpet, and investors reward, the company that meets or beats the estimates. People sometimes meet this goal by either manipulating the numbers or initiating whispering campaigns to persuade analysts to lower their estimates, making them more attainable. The marketplace wants short-term, quarterly performance, but long-term viability is ultimately more important to a company's success.

It is important *not* to establish a single productivity goal if there are other important dimensions of performance.[25] For instance, if the acquisition of knowledge and skills is important, you can also set a specific and challenging learning goal such as "identify 10 ways to develop relationships with end users of our products." Productivity goals will likely enhance productivity, but they may also cause employees to neglect other areas, such as learning, tackling new projects, or developing creative solutions to job-related problems. A manager who wants to motivate creativity can establish creativity goals along with productivity goals for individuals or for brainstorming teams.[26]

Set Your Own Goals

Goal setting works for yourself as well—it's a powerful tool for self-management. Set goals for yourself; don't just try hard or hope for the best. Create a statement of purpose for yourself comprising three elements: an inspiring distant vision, a mid-distant goal along the way (worthy in its own right), and near-term objectives to start working on immediately.[27] So if you are going into business, you might articulate your goal for the type of businessperson you want to be in five years, the types of jobs that could create the opportunities and teach you what you need to know to become that businessperson, and the specific schoolwork and job search activities that can get you moving in those directions. And on the job, apply SMART and other goal-setting advice for yourself.

law of effect

A law formulated by Edward Thorndike in 1911 stating that behavior that is followed by positive consequences will likely be repeated.

reinforcers

Positive consequences that motivate behavior.

organizational behavior modification (OB mod)

The application of reinforcement theory in organizational settings.

Reinforcing Performance

Goals are universal motivators. So are the processes of reinforcement described in this section. In 1911, psychologist Edward Thorndike formulated the **law of effect:** behavior that is followed by positive consequences probably will be repeated.[28] This powerful law of behavior laid the foundation for countless investigations into the effects of the positive consequences, called **reinforcers,** that motivate behavior. **Organizational behavior modification** (or **OB mod**) attempts to influence people's behavior, and improve performance,[29] by systematically managing work conditions and the consequences of people's actions.

Four key consequences of behavior either encourage or discourage people's behavior (see Figure 13.1):

1. **Positive reinforcement**—applying a positive consequence that increases the likelihood that the person will repeat the behavior that led to it. Examples of positive reinforcers include compliments, letters of commendation, favorable performance evaluations, and pay raises.[30]
2. **Negative reinforcement**—removing or withholding an undesirable consequence. For example, a manager takes an employee (or a school takes a student) off probation because of improved performance.

positive reinforcement

Applying consequences that increase the likelihood that a person will repeat the behavior that led to it.

negative reinforcement

Removing or withholding an undesirable consequence.

FIGURE 13.1
The Consequences of Behavior

punishment

Administering an aversive consequence.

extinction

Withdrawing or failing to provide a reinforcing consequence.

3. **Punishment**—administering an aversive consequence. Examples include criticizing or shouting at an employee, assigning an unappealing task, and sending a worker home without pay. Negative reinforcement can involve the *threat* of punishment and not delivering the punishment when employees perform satisfactorily. Punishment is the actual delivery of the aversive consequence. Managers use punishment when they think it is warranted or when they believe others expect them to, and they usually concern themselves with following company policy and procedure.[31]

4. **Extinction**—withdrawing or failing to provide a reinforcing consequence. When this occurs, motivation is reduced and the behavior is *extinguished*, or eliminated. Ways that managers may unintentionally extinguish desired behaviors include not giving a compliment for a job well done, forgetting to say thanks for a favor, and setting impossible performance goals so a person never experiences success. Extinction may be used to end undesirable behaviors, too. The manager might ignore long-winded observations during a meeting or fail to acknowledge unimportant e-mails in the hope that the lack of feedback will discourage the employee from continuing.

The first two consequences, positive and negative reinforcement, are positive for the person receiving them—the person either gains something or avoids something negative. Therefore, the person who experiences these consequences will be motivated to behave in the ways that led to the reinforcement. The last two consequences, punishment and extinction, are negative outcomes for the person receiving them: motivation to repeat the behavior that led to the undesirable results will be reduced.

Managers should be careful to match consequences to what employees will actually find desirable or undesirable. A supervisor once made the mistake of punishing an employee for tardiness by suspending him for three days during fishing season. The employee was delighted.[32]

(Mis)Managing Rewards and Punishments

You've learned about the positive effects of a transformational leadership style, but giving rewards to high-performing people is also essential.[33] Unfortunately, sometimes organizations and managers reinforce the wrong behaviors.[34] For example, compensation plans that include stock options are intended to reinforce behaviors that add to the company's value, but stock options also can reinforce decisions that artificially deliver short-term gains in stock prices, even if they hurt the company in the long run. Likewise, programs that punish employees for absenteeism beyond a certain limit may actually encourage them to be absent. People may use up all their allowable absences and fail to come to work regularly until they reach the point at which their next absence will result in punishment. Sometimes employees are reinforced with admiration for multitasking. This behavior may look efficient and send a signal that the employee is busy and valuable, but multitasking actually slows down the brain's efficiency and can contribute to mistakes.[35] Scans of brain activity show that the brain is not able to concentrate on two tasks at once; it needs time to switch among the multitasker's activities. As a result, managers who praise the hard work of multitaskers may be unintentionally reinforcing inefficiency and failure to think deeply about problems.

> Sometimes organizations and managers reinforce the wrong behaviors.

To use reinforcement effectively, managers must identify which kinds of behaviors they reinforce and which they discourage (see Table 13.1). The reward system has to support the firm's strategy, defining people's performance in ways that pursue strategic objectives.[36] Reward employees for developing themselves in strategically important ways—for building new skills that are critical to strengthening core competencies and creating value.

"The things that get rewarded get done" is what one author called The Greatest Management Principle in the World. With this in mind, Michael LeBoeuf offered prescriptions for effectively motivating high performance. Companies, and individual managers, should reward the following:

1. *Solid solutions* instead of quick fixes.
2. *Risk taking* instead of risk avoiding.
3. *Applied creativity* instead of mindless conformity.
4. *Decisive action* instead of paralysis by analysis.
5. *Smart work* instead of busywork.
6. *Simplification* instead of needless complication.
7. *Quietly effective behavior* instead of squeaky wheels.
8. *Quality work* instead of fast work.
9. *Loyalty* instead of turnover.
10. *Working together* instead of working against.

TABLE 13.1

The Greatest Management Principle in the World

SOURCE: From *The Greatest Management Principle in the World* by Michael LeBoeuf. Copyright © 1985 by Michael LeBoeuf. Reprinted with permission.

Managers should be creative in their use of reinforcers. QuikTrip, which operates a chain of convenience stores in 11 states, has a creative way of making sure new employees at headquarters feel welcome. On an employee's first day, a tub of candy appears on his or her desk. The treats reward co-workers for coming over to introduce themselves. The company also offers above-average pay for the industry and enjoys its industry's lowest rate of employee turnover.[37]

Innovative managers use nonmonetary rewards, including intellectual challenge, greater responsibility, autonomy, recognition, flexible benefits, and greater influence over decisions. These and other rewards for high-performing employees, when creatively devised and applied, can continue to motivate when pay and promotions are scarce. Employees at Brown Flynn—a firm that provides services to help companies exercise social responsibility—receive practical benefits such as profit sharing and creative ones such as jewelry and shopping sprees, but the intangibles may be what matter most. Employees describe Brown Flynn as offering challenges and rewards, mutual respect, recognition for hard work, and opportunities to exercise leadership.[38]

Managing Mistakes

How a manager reacts to people's mistakes has a big impact on motivation. Punishment is sometimes appropriate, as when people violate the law, ethical standards, safety rules, or standards of interpersonal treatment, or when they perform like a slacker. But sometimes managers punish people when they shouldn't—when poor performance isn't the person's fault or when managers take out their frustrations on the wrong people.

Managers who overuse punishment or use it inappropriately create a climate of fear in the workplace.[39] Fear causes people to focus on the short term, sometimes creating problems in the longer run. Fear also creates a focus on oneself rather than on the group and the organization. B. Joseph White, president emeritus of the University of Illinois, recalls consulting for a high-tech entrepreneur who heard a manager present a proposal and responded with brutal criticism: "That's the . . . stupidest idea I ever heard in my life. I'm disappointed in you." According to White, this talented manager was so upset she never again felt fully able to contribute.[40] To avoid such damage, managers should think about how they handle mistakes.

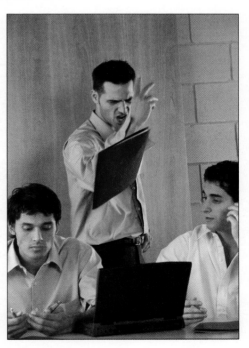

Managers who inappropriately yell at their staff or overuse punishment often create a climate of fear and anxiety in the workplace. How would you deal with a situation like this?

Recognize that everyone makes mistakes and that mistakes can be dealt with constructively by discussing and learning from them. Don't punish, but praise, people who deliver bad news to their bosses. Treat failure to act as a failure but don't punish unsuccessful, good-faith efforts. If you're a leader, talk about your failures with your people and show how you learned from them. Give people second chances and maybe third chances. (Donald Trump claims to give second chances, but never third.) Encourage people to try new things and don't punish them if what they try doesn't work out.

Providing Feedback

Most managers don't provide enough useful feedback, and most people don't ask for feedback enough.[41] As a manager, you should consider all potential causes of poor performance, pay full attention when employees ask for feedback or want to discuss performance issues, and give feedback according to the guidelines you read about in Chapter 10.

Feedback can be offered in many ways.[42] Customers sometimes give feedback directly; you also can request customer feedback and give it to the employee. You can provide statistics on work that the person has directly influenced. A manufacturing firm—high tech or otherwise—can put the phone number or website of the production team on the product so customers can contact the team directly. Performance reviews, described in Chapter 11, should be conducted regularly. And bosses should give more regular, ongoing feedback—it helps correct problems immediately, provides immediate reinforcement for good work, and prevents surprises when the formal review comes.

Try not to be afraid of receiving feedback; in fact, you should actively seek it.

For yourself, try not to be afraid of receiving feedback; in fact, you should actively seek it. But whether or not you seek the feedback, when you get it, don't ignore it. Try to avoid negative

In Practice

AUTOMATIC FEEDBACK FROM RESCUE TIME

Some employees are setting up their computers to give them automatic feedback, using tools such as RescueTime to give them auto-analytics. The idea behind auto-analytics is that people *want* to work more productively, so if they have information about what their strengths and weaknesses are, they will have ideas about what to change and will be empowered to improve. RescueTime is software that tracks how long a computer user spends on particular categories of websites and applications—say, checking e-mail and updating Facebook. It generates charts and reports of what the user is doing, such as how much time the computer is sitting idle and how often the user is switching between windows on the screen. It also lets users send themselves alerts when a given situation occurs (for example, too many minutes on social media) or block sites at particular times if they decide it might help them stay on track.

Although some companies have used RescueTime to give supervisors information about what employees are doing, advocates of auto-analytics see the greatest potential in encouraging employees to use the tool personally as a self-motivator. This frees the employees to think creatively about their time and notice what works for them personally, so it is empowering. One employee determined that he was more productive if the software reminded him to switch tasks every 20 minutes; another determined that he produced the most work during periods when he was conducting online chats with colleagues and customers.[44]

- Do you think RescueTime feedback would motivate you better if you used it on your own or with the data going to your supervisor? Why?

emotions such as anger, hurt, defensiveness, or resignation. Think, It's up to me to get the feedback I need; I need to know these things about my performance and my behavior; learning what I need to know about myself will help me identify needs and create new opportunities; it serves my interest best to know rather than not know; taking initiative on this gives me more power and influence over my career.[43]

Performance-Related Beliefs

LO 4

In contrast to reinforcement theory, which describes the processes by which factors in the work environment affect people's behavior, expectancy theory considers some of the cognitive processes that go on in people's heads. According to **expectancy theory,** the person's work efforts lead to some level of performance.[45] Then performance results in one or more outcomes for the person. This process is shown in Figure 13.2. People develop two important beliefs linking these three events: expectancy, which links effort to performance, and instrumentality, which links performance to outcomes.

expectancy theory

A theory proposing that people will behave based on their perceived likelihood that their effort will lead to a certain outcome and on how highly they value that outcome.

The Effort-to-Performance Link

The first belief, **expectancy,** is people's perceived likelihood that their efforts will enable them to attain their performance goals. An expectancy can be high (up to 100 percent), such as when a student is confident that if she studies hard, she can get a good grade on the final. An expectancy can also be low (down to a 0 percent likelihood), such as when a suitor is convinced that his dream date will never go out with him.

expectancy

Employees' perception of the likelihood that their efforts will enable them to attain their performance goals.

All else equal, high expectancies create higher motivation than do low expectancies. In the preceding examples, the student is more likely to study for the exam than the suitor is to pursue the dream date, even though both want their respective outcomes.

Expectancies can vary among individuals, even in the same situation. For example, a sales manager might initiate a competition in which the top salesperson wins a free trip to Hawaii. In such cases, the few top people, who have performed well in the past, will be more motivated by the contest than will the historically average and below-average performers. The top people will have higher expectancies—stronger beliefs that their efforts can help them win the competition.

The Performance-to-Outcome Link

The example of the sales contest illustrates how performance results in some kind of **outcome,** or consequence, for the person. Actually, it often results in several outcomes. For example, turning in the best sales performance could lead to (1) a competitive victory, (2) the free trip to Hawaii, (3) feelings of achievement, (4) recognition from the boss, (5) prestige throughout the company, and (6) resentment from other salespeople.

outcome

A consequence a person receives for his or her performance.

FIGURE 13.2
Basic Concepts of
Expectancy Theory

Winning a competition for a free trip to Hawaii would be great, but what about all the losers?

But how certain is it that performance will result in all of those outcomes? Will winning the contest really lead to resentment? Will it really lead to increased prestige?

These questions address the second key belief described by expectancy theory: instrumentality.[46] **Instrumentality** is the perceived likelihood that performance will be followed by a particular outcome. Like expectancies, instrumentalities can be high (up to 100 percent) or low (approaching 0 percent). For example, you can be fully confident that if you do a good job, you'll get a promotion; or you can feel that no matter how well you do, the promotion will go to someone else.

Also, each outcome has an associated valence. **Valence** is the value the person places on the outcome. Valences can be positive, as a Hawaiian vacation would be for most people, or negative, as in the case of the other salespeople's resentment.

instrumentality

The perceived likelihood that performance will be followed by a particular outcome.

valence

The value an outcome holds for the person contemplating it.

Impact on Motivation

For motivation to be high, expectancy, instrumentalities, and total valence of all outcomes must all be high. A person will not be highly motivated if any of the following conditions exist:

1. He believes he can't perform well enough to achieve the positive outcomes that he knows the company provides to good performers (high valence and high instrumentality but low expectancy).
2. He knows he can do the job and is fairly certain what the ultimate outcomes will be (say, a promotion and a transfer). However, he doesn't want those outcomes or believes other, negative outcomes outweigh the positive (high expectancy and high instrumentality but low valence).
3. He knows he can do the job and wants several important outcomes (a favorable performance review, a raise, and a promotion). But he believes that no matter how well he performs, the outcomes will not be forthcoming (high expectancy and positive valences but low instrumentality).

Managerial Implications of Expectancy Theory

Expectancy theory helps the manager zero in on key leverage points for influencing motivation. Three implications are crucial:

1. *Increase expectancies.* Provide a work environment that facilitates good performance and set realistically attainable performance goals. Provide training, support, required resources, and encouragement so that people are confident they can perform at the levels expected of them. Recall from Chapter 12 that some leaders excel at boosting their followers' confidence.
2. *Identify positively valent outcomes.* Understand what people want to get out of work. Think about what their jobs provide them and what is not, but could be, provided. Consider how people may differ in the valences they assign to outcomes. Know the need theories of motivation, described in the next section, and their implications for identifying important outcomes.
3. *Make performance instrumental toward positive outcomes.* Make sure that good performance is followed by personal recognition and praise, favorable performance reviews, pay increases, and other positive results. Also, make sure that working hard and doing things well will have as few negative results as possible. It is useful to realize, too, that bosses usually control rewards and punishments, but others do so as well. Peers, direct reports, customers, and others tend to provide rewards in the form of compliments, help, and social punishments.

Organizations may set up formal reward systems as well. Umpqua Bank in Rose-burg, Oregon, set up a link called Brag Box on its intranet. Employees visit the Brag Box to post comments about good things their co-workers have done. Sandy Hunt, Umpqua's vice president for rewards and recognition, regularly checks the Brag Box and notifies managers when their employees have received a compliment so the managers can further reinforce compliments with praise. In addition, every team at Umpqua has a recognition fund, which any team member can spend to recognize co-workers for going the extra mile.[47] As you read "Management Connection: Progress Report," consider whether similar ideas would motivate employees at SAS.

Management Connection

GETTING EMPLOYEES TO BACK THE MISSION OF SAS

James Goodnight, a statistician, founded SAS with colleagues from North Carolina State University. Since his first experiences of programming a computer while in college, Goodnight had recognized the joy of creating something that would benefit others. Goodnight expected that his employees too would feel rewarded by their accomplishments. On SAS's website, Goodnight describes SAS's culture as one that "rewards innovation, encourages employees to try new things and yet doesn't penalize them for taking chances."

To see how this works, consider how SAS has recently innovated in a couple of important areas of computing. One is the rapid switch of the computer industry to cloud computing. SAS grew up when big organizations invested in large, powerful computers, and its software was written for those systems. With the rise of the Internet, data has streamed in from many sources in real time, and computing systems are being reworked to process the data in parallel on multiple computers that do not necessarily reside at the organization using the data. Some observers wondered whether SAS could rewrite its software for this new era of computing. But because SAS attracts the best people (thanks to its reputation for treating employees well), hires for creativity, and makes it easy to stay on the job (thanks to corporate perks such as subsidized cafeterias and on-site haircuts), SAS has no trouble convincing

employees to push hard toward reaching ambitious goals. SAS impressed observers by announcing new, cloud-ready software with graphics that even nonexperts can view on their laptop or tablet computers.

SAS also has smoothly entered the social-media era by introducing a networking site for its employees. The company found that its employees, especially the younger ones, were sharing work information with each other on sites such as Facebook. Although some companies were cracking down on social-media use, SAS got busy creating software that would be so useful and easy to learn that employees wouldn't be able to resist. The result was the Hub, which enrolled more than 1,400 employees even before its official launch. Rather than micromanaging how the Hub would be used, SAS's information systems division showed off some relevant features, gently pointed out advantages to nonusers, and trusted them to behave professionally. Before long, about two-thirds of SAS employees were trading information on the Hub.[48]

- What kinds of reinforcement and feedback do you think would be most effective with SAS employees?
- How should SAS's managers apply the implications of expectancy theory (listed just before this case) to keep the company innovative?

Understanding People's Needs

So far, we have focused on processes underlying motivation. The manager who appropriately applies goal-setting, reinforcement, and expectancy theories is creating essential motivating elements in the work environment. But motivation also is affected by characteristics of the person. The second type of motivation theory, *content theories*, indicates the kinds of needs that people want to satisfy. People have different needs energizing and motivating them toward different goals and reinforcers. The extent to which and the ways in which a person's needs are met or not met at work affect his or her behavior on the job.

The most important theories describing the content of people's needs are Maslow's need hierarchy, Alderfer's ERG theory, and McClelland's needs.

Maslow's Need Hierarchy

Maslow's need hierarchy

A conception of human needs organizing needs into a hierarchy of five major types.

Abraham Maslow organized five major types of human needs into a hierarchy, as shown in Figure 13.3.[49] **Maslow's need hierarchy** illustrates his conception of people satisfying their needs in a specified order, from bottom to top. The needs, in ascending order, are

1. *Physiological* (food, water, sex, and shelter).
2. *Safety or security* (protection against threat and deprivation).
3. *Social* (friendship, affection, belonging, and love).
4. *Ego* (independence, achievement, freedom, status, recognition, and self-esteem).
5. *Self-actualization* (realizing one's full potential, becoming everything one is capable of being).

According to Maslow, people are motivated to satisfy the lower needs before they try to satisfy the higher needs. In today's workplace, physiological and safety needs generally are well satisfied, making social, ego, and self-actualization needs important. But safety issues are still very important in manufacturing, mining, health care, and other work environments. And long after the terrorist attacks of September 2001, employees still felt fear, denial, and anger—especially among people with children, women, and those close to the events.[50] To deal with such safety issues, managers can show what the firm will do to improve security and manage employee risk, including crisis management plans as discussed in Chapter 3.

> Safety issues are still very important in manufacturing, mining, health care, and other work environments.

Once a need is satisfied, it is no longer a powerful motivator. For example, labor unions negotiate for higher wages, benefits, safety standards, and job security. These bargaining issues relate directly to the satisfaction of Maslow's lower-level needs. Only after these needs are reasonably satisfied do the higher-level needs—social, ego, and self-actualization—become dominant concerns.

FIGURE 13.3
Maslow's Need Hierarchy

SOURCE: D. Organ and T. Bateman, *Organizational Behavior*, 4th ed., 1991. Copyright 1991. The McGraw-Hill Companies, Inc. Reprinted with permission.

Maslow's hierarchy, however, is a simplistic and not altogether accurate theory of human motivation.[51] For example, not everyone progresses through the five needs in hierarchical order. But Maslow made three important contributions. First, he identified important need categories, which can help managers create effective positive reinforcers. Second, it is helpful to think of two general levels of needs, in which lower-level needs must be satisfied before higher-level needs become important. Third, Maslow alerted managers to the importance of personal growth and self-actualization.

Self-actualization is the best-known concept arising from this theory. According to Maslow, the average person is only 10 percent self-actualized. In other words, most of us are living our lives and working at our jobs with a large untapped reservoir of potential. The implication is clear: Managers should help create a work environment that provides training, resources, autonomy, responsibilities, and challenging assignments. This type of environment gives people a chance to use their skills and abilities in creative ways and allows them to achieve more of their full potential.

So treat people not merely as a cost to be controlled but an asset to be developed. Many companies have embarked on programs that provide personal growth experiences for their people. An employee at Federal Express said, "The best I can be is what I can be here. Federal Express . . . gave me the confidence and self-esteem to become the person I had the potential to become."[52] Individual managers also can promote employee growth. Pete Wamsteeker's first supervisor, at a feed company, routinely invited him to discuss his career plans, and Wamsteeker did the same for his employees when he became general manager of Cargill Animal Nutrition. When Wamsteeker took that position, he started by learning about his employees so that he could ensure each was in the job where he or she could contribute best.[53]

Organizations gain by making full use of their human resources. Employees also gain by capitalizing on opportunities to meet their higher-order needs on the job. At Campbell Soup Company, managers are rewarded for developing their employees, and Lisa Walker, business director of Campbell USA's wellness team, rises to that challenge. She worked with one employee to help him collaborate better so that he would be seen as a team player with promotion potential. Walker's employee appreciated that her coaching gave him an opportunity for greater achievement, status, and self-esteem.[54]

Alderfer's ERG Theory

A theory of human needs that is more advanced than Maslow's is Alderfer's ERG theory.[55] Maslow's theory has general applicability, but Alderfer aims his theory expressly at understanding people's needs at work.

Alderfer's ERG theory postulates three sets of needs: existence, relatedness, and growth. Existence needs are all material and physiological desires. Relatedness needs involve relationships with other people and are satisfied through the process of mutually sharing thoughts and feelings. Growth needs motivate people to change themselves or their environment productively or creatively. Satisfaction of the growth needs comes from fully using personal capacities and developing new capacities.

What similarities do you see between Alderfer's and Maslow's needs? Roughly speaking, existence needs subsume physiological and security needs, relatedness needs are similar to social and esteem needs, and growth needs correspond to self-actualization.

ERG theory proposes that several needs can be operating at once. Thus, whereas Maslow would say that self-actualization is important to people only after other sets of needs are satisfied, Alderfer maintains that people— particularly working people in our postindustrial society—can be motivated to satisfy existence, relatedness, and growth needs at the same time.

Alderfer's ERG theory
A human needs theory postulating that people have three basic sets of needs that can operate simultaneously.

FedEx and some other companies care about and pay attention to the growth and development of their people.

Consider which theory best explains the motives identified by Diane Schumaker-Krieg to describe her successful career in the financial services industry. Schumaker-Krieg says she was "driven . . . by fear" in October 1987, when she was working for investment firm Dillon Read at the time of the stock market crash. Lay-offs were spreading throughout the industry, jobs were scarce, and she was supporting her son following a divorce. Out of determination to take care of her son, Schumaker-Krieg reacted to being laid off by writing a plan for a new business. She persuaded Dillon Read to fund the idea for a year, began building the business, moved it to Credit Suisse, and within years was earning $150 million in profits for her employer. During that time, she remarried and earned enough to retire, but she continues working, now with Wells Fargo. She sees her current motivation as enjoyment of her accomplishments, her business relationships, and opportunities to continue innovating.[56] Certainly lower-level needs dominated the early years of Schumaker-Krieg's career, but did the basis for her motivation move one step at a time through all the levels of Maslow's hierarchy?

Maslow's theory is better known to American managers than Alderfer's, but ERG theory has more scientific support.[57] Both have practical value in that they remind managers of the types of reinforcers or rewards that can be used to motivate people. Regardless of whether a manager prefers the Maslow or the Alderfer theory of needs, he or she can motivate people by helping them satisfy their needs, particularly by offering opportunities for self-actualization and growth.

McClelland's Needs

David McClelland also identified a number of basic needs that guide people. The most important needs for managers, according to McClelland, are the needs for achievement, affiliation, and power.[58] Different needs predominate for different people. As you read about these needs, think about yourself—which ones are most and least important to you?

The need for achievement is characterized by a strong orientation toward accomplishment and an obsession with success and goal attainment. Most managers and entrepreneurs in the United States have high levels of this need and like to see it in their employees.

The need for affiliation reflects a strong desire to be liked by other people. Individuals who have high levels of this need are oriented toward getting along with others and may be less concerned with performing at high levels.

The need for power is a desire to influence or control other people. This need can be a negative force—termed *personalized power*—if it is expressed through the aggressive manipulation and exploitation of others. People high on the personalized power need want power purely for the pursuit of their own goals. But the need for power also can be a positive motive—called *socialized power*—because it can be channeled toward the constructive improvement of organizations and societies.

Low need for affiliation and moderate to high need for power are associated with managerial success for both higher- and lower-level managers.[59] One reason the need for affiliation is not necessary for leadership success is that people high on this need have difficulty making tough but necessary decisions that will make some people unhappy.

Need Theories: International Perspectives

How do the need theories apply abroad?[60] Whereas managers in the United States care most strongly about achievement, esteem, and self-actualization, managers in Greece and Japan are motivated more by security. Social needs are most important in Sweden, Norway, and Denmark. "Doing your own thing"—the phrase from the 1960s that describes an American culture oriented toward self-actualization—is not even translatable into Chinese. "Achievement," too, is difficult to translate into most other languages. Researchers in France, Japan, and Sweden would have been unlikely even to conceive of McClelland's achievement motive because people of those countries traditionally tend to be more group-oriented than individually oriented.

Clearly, achievement, growth, and self-actualization are profoundly important in the United States, Canada, and Great Britain. But these needs are not universally important. Every manager must remember that need importance varies from country to country and that people may not be motivated by the same needs. One study found that employees in many countries are highly engaged at companies that have strong leadership, work/life balance, a good reputation, and opportunities for employees to contribute; another found

variations from country to country:[61] Employees in Canada were attracted by competitive pay, work/life balance, and opportunities for advancement; workers in Germany by autonomy; in Japan by high-quality co-workers; in the Netherlands by a collaborative work environment; and in the United States by competitive health benefits. Generally, no single way is best, and managers can customize their approaches by considering how individuals differ.[62]

The Japanese are more group-oriented whereas Americans are more individually oriented when it comes to motivation. How do you think this affects how these two countries do business together?

Designing Motivating Jobs

Here's an example of a company that gave a reward that didn't motivate. One of Mary Kay Ash's former employers gave her a sales award: a flounder-fishing light. Unfortunately, she didn't fish. Fortunately, she later was able to design her own organization, Mary Kay Cosmetics, around intrinsic as well as extrinsic motivators that mattered to her people.[63] **Extrinsic rewards** are given to people by the boss, the company, or some other person. An **intrinsic reward** is a reward the person derives directly from performing the job itself. An interesting project, an intriguing subject that is fun to study, a completed sale, and the discovery of the perfect solution to a difficult problem all can give people the feeling that they have done something well. This is the essence of the motivation that comes from intrinsic rewards.

Intrinsic rewards are essential to the motivation underlying creativity.[64] A challenging problem, a chance to create something new, and work that is exciting in and of itself can provide intrinsic motivation that inspires people to devote time and energy to the task. So do managers who allow people some freedom to pursue the tasks that interest them most. The opposite situations result in routine, habitual behaviors that interfere with creativity.[65] A study in manufacturing facilities found that employees initiated more applications for patents, made more novel and useful suggestions, and were rated by their managers as more creative when their jobs were challenging and their managers did not control their activities closely.[66]

Conversely, some managers and organizations create environments that quash creativity and motivation.[67] The classic example of a demotivating job is the highly specialized assembly line job; each worker performs one boring operation before passing the work along to the next worker. Such specialization, the mechanistic approach to job design, was the prevailing practice through most of the 20th century.[68] But jobs that are too simple and routine result in employee dissatisfaction, absenteeism, and turnover.

Especially in industries that depend on highly motivated knowledge workers, keeping talented employees may require letting them design their own jobs so their work

extrinsic reward

Reward given to a person by the boss, the company, or some other person.

intrinsic reward

Reward a worker derives directly from performing the job itself.

> Intrinsic rewards are essential to the motivation underlying creativity.

Bottom Line

Intrinsic rewards and the freedom to be creative are keys to innovation.

Why might an employee be more innovative when a job is intrinsically rewarding?

job rotation

Changing from one task to another to alleviate boredom.

job enlargement

Giving people additional tasks at the same time to alleviate boredom.

job enrichment

Changing a task to make it inherently more rewarding, motivating, and satisfying.

two-factor theory

Herzberg's theory describing two factors affecting people's work motivation and satisfaction.

hygiene factors

Characteristics of the workplace, such as company policies, working conditions, pay, and supervision, that can make people dissatisfied.

motivators

Factors that make a job more motivating, such as additional job responsibilities, opportunities for personal growth and recognition, and feelings of achievement.

is more interesting than it would be elsewhere.[69] Jobs can be designed in the following ways to increase intrinsic rewards and therefore motivation.

Job Rotation, Enlargement, and Enrichment

With **job rotation,** workers who spend all their time in one routine task can instead move from one task to another. Rather than dishing out the pasta in a cafeteria line all day, a person might work the pasta, then the salads, and then the vegetables or desserts. Job rotation is intended to alleviate boredom by giving people different things to do at different times.

As you may guess, however, the person may just be changing from one boring job to another. But job rotation can benefit everyone when done properly, with people's input and career interests in mind. Harrah's Entertainment uses job rotation for its IT workers, which gives them a broad knowledge of the business that enhances their value to the company at the same time it opens up opportunities for career development.[70]

Job enlargement is similar to job rotation in that people are given different tasks to do. But whereas job rotation involves doing one task at one time and changing to a different task at a different time, job enlargement means that the worker has multiple tasks at the same time. Thus an assembly worker's job is enlarged if he or she is given two tasks rather than one to perform. In a study of job enlargement in a financial services organization, enlarged jobs led to higher job satisfaction, better error detection by clerks, and improved customer service.[71]

With job enlargement, the person's additional tasks are at the same level of responsibility. More profound changes occur when jobs are enriched. **Job enrichment** means that jobs are restructured or redesigned by adding higher levels of responsibility. This practice includes giving people not only more tasks but higher-level ones, such as when decisions are delegated downward and authority is decentralized. Herzberg's two-factor theory was the first approach to job enrichment, followed by the Hackman and Oldham model.

Herzberg's Two-Factor Theory

Frederick Herzberg's **two-factor theory** distinguished between two broad categories of factors that affect people working on their jobs.[72] The first category, **hygiene factors,** are characteristics of the workplace: company policies, working conditions, pay, co-workers, supervision, and so forth. These factors can make people unhappy if they are poorly managed. If they are well managed and viewed as positive by employees, the employees will no longer be dissatisfied. However, no matter how good these factors are, they will not make people truly satisfied or motivated to do a good job.

According to Herzberg, the key to true job satisfaction and motivation to perform lies in the second category: the motivators. The **motivators** describe the job itself—that is, what people *do* at work. Motivators are the nature of the work itself, the actual job responsibilities, opportunity for personal growth and recognition, and the feelings of achievement the job provides. When these factors are present, jobs are presumed to be both satisfying and motivating for most people.

Herzberg's theory has been criticized by many scholars, and for that reason we will not go into more detail about his original theory. But Herzberg was a pioneer in the area of job design and still is a respected name among American managers. Furthermore, even if the specifics of his theory do not hold up to scientific scrutiny, he made several very important contributions. First, Herzberg's theory highlights the important distinction between extrinsic rewards (from hygiene factors) and intrinsic rewards (from motivators). Second, it reminds managers not to count solely on extrinsic rewards to motivate workers but to focus on intrinsic rewards as well. Third, it set the stage for later theories, such as the Hackman and Oldham model, that explain more precisely how managers can enrich people's jobs.

The Hackman and Oldham Model of Job Design

Following Herzberg's work, Hackman and Oldham proposed a more complete model of job design.[73] Figure 13.4 illustrates their model. As you can see, well-designed jobs lead to high motivation, high-quality performance, high satisfaction, and low absenteeism and turnover. These outcomes occur when people experience three critical psychological states (noted in the middle column of the figure):

1. They believe they are doing something meaningful because their work is important to other people.
2. They feel personally responsible for how the work turns out.
3. They learn how well they perform their jobs.

These psychological states occur when people are working on enriched jobs—that is, jobs that offer the following five core job dimensions:

1. *Skill variety*—different job activities involving several skills and talents. When cleaning employees in hospitals were given some freedom in how they carried out their work, the employees themselves added skill variety to their work through extra efforts such as engaging patients in small talk and figuring out ways they could make nurses' jobs easier. After adding this skill variety, the employees reported being more satisfied with their jobs.[74]
2. *Task identity*—the completion of a whole, identifiable piece of work. At State Farm Insurance, agents are independent contractors who sell and provide service for State Farm products exclusively. They have built and invested in their own businesses. As a result, agent retention and productivity are far better than industry norms.[75]
3. *Task significance*—an important, positive impact on the lives of others. A study of lifeguards found dramatic improvements in their performance if they were taught about how lifeguards make a difference by preventing deaths.

FIGURE 13.4
The Hackman and Oldham Model of Job Enrichment

Lifeguards in the study who simply were told that the job can be personally enriching showed no such improvements.[76] Similarly, James Perry, an expert on motivation of government employees, says these workers generally have a strong commitment to serving the public good, including public welfare and stewardship of public resources.[77]

4. *Autonomy*—independence and discretion in making decisions. In a research hospital, a department administrator told her people to do the kinds of research they wanted as long as it was within budget (and legal!). With no other guidelines—that is, complete autonomy—productivity increased sixfold in a year.[78]

5. *Feedback*—information about job performance. Many companies post charts or provide computerized data indicating productivity, number of rejects, and other data. The Parasole restaurant group, which operates a variety of casual restaurants and steakhouses in Minnesota, uses customer feedback on social media—hundreds of comments every day—as a powerful source of motivation. Employees see that today's customers comment about their experiences online and that the employees' treatment of customers has a direct impact on what they post.[79]

The most effective job enrichment increases all five core dimensions.

A person's growth need strength will help determine just how effective a job enrichment program might be. **Growth need strength** is the degree to which individuals want personal and psychological development. Job enrichment would be more successful for people with high growth need strength. But very few people respond negatively to job enrichment.[80]

Empowerment

Today one frequently hears managers talk about empowering their people. Individuals may—or may not—feel empowered, and groups can have a culture of empowerment that predicts work unit performance.[81] **Empowerment** is the process of sharing power with employees, thereby enhancing their confidence in their ability to perform their jobs and their belief that they are influential contributors to the organization. Unfortunately, empowerment doesn't always live up to its hype. One problem is that managers undermine it by sending mixed messages such as "Do your own thing—the way we tell you."[82] But empowerment can be profoundly motivating when done properly.[83]

Empowerment results in changes in employees' beliefs—from feeling powerless to believing strongly in their own personal effectiveness.[84] The result is that people take more initiative and persevere in achieving their goals and their leader's vision even in the face of obstacles.[85] Specifically, empowerment encourages the following beliefs among employees.[86] First, they perceive meaning in their work: Their job fits their values. Second, they feel competent, or capable of performing their jobs with skill. Third, they have a sense of self-determination, of having some choice in regard to the tasks, methods, and pace of their work. Fourth, they have an impact—that is, they have some influence over important strategic, administrative, or operating decisions or outcomes on the job.

When speaking of times when they felt disempowered, people mentioned the following:[87]

- I had no input into a hiring decision of someone who was to report directly to me. I didn't even get to speak to the candidate.
- They treated us like mushrooms. They fed us and kept us in the dark.
- I worked extremely hard—long hours and late nights—on an urgent project, and then my manager took full credit for it.
- My suggestions, whether good or bad, were either not solicited or, worse, ignored.

- The project was reassigned without my knowledge or input.

In contrast, people felt empowered in the following examples:

- I was able to make a large financial decision on my own. I got to write a large check without being questioned.
- After having received a memo that said, "Cut travel," I made my case about why it was necessary to travel for business reasons, and I was told to go ahead.
- I was five years old, and my dad said, "You'll make a great mechanic one day." He planted the seed. Now I'm an engineer.
- My president supported my idea without question.
- All the financial data were shared with me.

To foster empowerment,[88] management must create an environment in which all the employees feel they have real influence over performance standards and business effectiveness within their areas of responsibility.[89] An empowering work environment provides people with information necessary for them to perform at their best, knowledge about how to use the information and how to do their work, power to make decisions that give them control over their work, and the rewards they deserve for the contributions they make.[90] Such an environment reduces costs because fewer people are needed to supervise, monitor, and coordinate. It improves quality and service because high performance is inspired at the source—the people who do the work. It also allows quick action because people on the spot see problems, solutions, and opportunities for innovation on which they are empowered to act.

It is essential to give people clear strategic direction but to leave some room for flexibility and calculated risk taking. For example, Southwest Airlines' strategic principle of "meet customers' short-haul travel needs at fares competitive with the cost of automobile travel" helps employees keep strategic objectives in mind and use their discretion in making complicated decisions about service offerings, route selection, cabin design, ticketing procedures, and pricing.[91] More-specific actions include increasing signature authority at all levels; reducing the number of rules and approval steps; assigning nonroutine jobs; allowing independent judgment, flexibility, and creativity; defining jobs more broadly as projects rather than tasks; and providing more access to resources and people throughout the organization.[92]

You should not be surprised when empowerment causes some problems, at least in the short term. This often occurs with virtually any change, including changes for the better. It's important to remember that with empowerment comes responsibility, and employees don't necessarily like the accountability at first.[93] People may make mistakes at first, especially until they have had adequate training. And because more training is needed, costs are higher. Also, because people acquire new skills and make greater contributions, they may demand higher wages. But if they are well-trained and truly empowered, they will deserve them—and both they and the company will benefit.

Bottom Line

Job enrichment and empowerment don't work magic overnight; people may resist the new approaches and make mistakes along the way. But done right, their potential to achieve real results is undeniable.
Name two ways to ensure that empowerment is done right.

Achieving Fairness

Ultimately, one of the most important issues in motivation surrounds how people view their contributions to the organization and what they receive from the organization. Ideally, they will view their relationship with their employer as a well-balanced, mutually beneficial exchange. As people work and realize the outcomes or consequences of their actions, they assess how fairly the organization treats them.

The starting point for understanding how people interpret their contributions and outcomes is equity theory.[94] **Equity theory** proposes that when people assess how fairly they are treated, they consider two key factors: outcomes and inputs. Outcomes,

LO 7

equity theory

A theory stating that people assess how fairly they have been treated according to two key factors: outcomes and inputs.

Equity theory suggests that people compare the ratio of their outcomes to inputs against the outcome-to-input ratio of some comparison person. How would you deal with someone you perceive to be a slacker who gets promoted over you?

as in expectancy theory, refer to the various things the person receives on the job: recognition, pay, benefits, satisfaction, security, job assignments, punishments, and so forth. Inputs refer to the contributions the person makes to the organization: effort, time, talent, performance, extra commitment, good citizenship, and so forth. People have a general expectation that the outcomes they receive will reflect, or be proportionate to, the inputs they provide—a fair day's pay (and other outcomes) for a fair day's work (broadly defined by how people view all their contributions).

But this comparison of outcomes to inputs is not the whole story. People also pay attention to the outcomes and inputs others receive. At salary review time, for example, most people—from executives on down—try to pick up clues that will tell them who got the high raises. As described in the following section, they compare ratios, try to restore equity if necessary, and derive more or less satisfaction based on how fairly they believe they have been treated.

Assessing Equity

Equity theory suggests that people compare the ratio of their own outcomes to inputs against the outcome-to-input ratio of some comparison person. The comparison person can be a fellow student, a co-worker, a boss, or an average industry pay scale. Stated more succinctly, people compare

$$\text{Their own } \frac{\text{Outcomes}}{\text{Inputs}} \text{ versus Others' } \frac{\text{Outcomes}}{\text{Inputs}}$$

If the ratios are equivalent, people believe the relationship is equitable, or fair. Equity causes people to be satisfied with their treatment. But the person who believes his or her ratio is lower than another's will feel inequitably treated. Inequity causes dissatisfaction and leads to an attempt to restore balance to the relationship.

Inequity and the negative feelings it creates may appear anywhere. As a student, perhaps you have been in the following situation. You stay up all night and get a C on the exam. Meanwhile another student studies a couple of hours, goes out for the rest of the evening, gets a good night's sleep, and gets a B on the exam. You perceive your inputs (time spent studying) as much greater than the other student's, but your outcomes are lower. You are displeased at the seeming unfairness. In business, the same thing sometimes happens with pay raises. One manager puts in 60-hour weeks, has a degree from a prestigious university, and believes she is destined for the top. When her archrival—whom she perceives as less deserving ("she never comes into the office on weekends, and all she does when she is here is butter up the boss")—gets the higher raise or the promotion, she experiences severe feelings of inequity. Motivation problems resulting from perceived pay inequities may be the reason major league baseball teams that have great differences in their player salaries tend to win fewer games.[95]

In recent years, many people have felt inequity when they learn about large sums paid to high-profile CEOs. Fair pay will be an increasingly public issue at U.S. companies in the near future because the Dodd-Frank Wall Street Reform and Consumer Protection Act requires greater disclosure of performance-based pay details.[96]

Assessments of equity are not made objectively. They are subjective perceptions or beliefs. In the preceding examples, the person who got the higher raise probably felt she deserved it. Even if she admits she doesn't put in long workweeks, she may convince herself she doesn't need to because she's so talented. The student who got the higher grade may believe it was a fair, equitable result because (1) she kept up all semester, while the other student did not, and (2) she's smart. (Ability and experience, not just time and effort, can be seen as inputs.)

Restoring Equity

People who feel inequitably treated and dissatisfied are motivated to do something to restore equity. They have a number of options to change the ratios or reevaluate the situation and decide it is equitable after all.

The equity equation shown earlier indicates a person's options for restoring equity. People who feel inequitably treated can reduce their inputs by giving less effort, performing at lower levels, or quitting. ("Well, if that's the way things work around here, there's no way I'm going to work that hard [or stick around].") Or they can attempt to increase their outcomes. ("My boss [or teacher] is going to hear about this. I deserve more; there must be some way I can get more.") On the positive side, employees may also put forth extra effort to keep a situation equitable for the group. In the first few months of each year, many accountants face a flood of work related to annual reports and tax preparation. At Gramkow, Carnevale, Seifert & Company, an accounting firm in Oradell, New Jersey, Kenneth Benkovic works long hours during tax time. He explains, "What helps motivate me is that I look around the office and I see people who are working as hard or harder than I am. You feel guilty if you're not pulling your own weight."[97]

Other ways of restoring equity focus on changing the other person's ratio. A person can decrease others' outcomes. For example, an employee may sabotage work to create problems for his company or his boss.[98] A person can also change her perceptions of inputs or outcomes. ("That promotion isn't as great a deal as he thinks. The pay is not that much better, and the headaches will be unbelievable.") It is also possible to increase others' inputs, particularly by changing perceptions. ("The more I think about it, the more I see he deserved it. He's worked hard all year, he's competent, and it's about time he got a break.")

Thus a person can restore equity in a number of ways by behaviorally or perceptually changing inputs and outcomes.

Procedural Justice

Inevitably, managers make decisions that have outcomes more favorable for some than for others. Those with favorable outcomes will be pleased; those with worse outcomes, all else equal, will be more displeased. But managers desiring to put salve on the wounds—say, of people they like or respect or want to keep and motivate—still can take actions to reduce the dissatisfaction. The key is for people to believe that managers provide **procedural justice**—using fair process in decision making and helping others know that the process was as fair as possible. When people perceive procedural fairness, they are more likely to support decisions and decision makers.[99] For example, one year after layoffs, managers' use of procedural justice (in the form of employee participation in decisions) still predicted survivors' organizational commitment, job satisfaction, and trust toward management.[100]

Even if people believe that their outcome was inequitable and unfair, they are more likely to view justice as having been served if the process was fair. You can increase people's beliefs that the process was fair by making the process open and visible; stating decision criteria in advance rather than after the fact; making sure that the most appropriate people—those who have valid information and are viewed as trustworthy—make the decisions; giving people a chance to participate in the process; and providing an appeal process that allows people to question decisions safely and receive complete answers.[101] However, the impact of procedural justice can differ by country and culture—for instance, the impact is strongest among nations characterized by individualism, femininity, uncertainty avoidance, and low power distance (recall Chapter 6).[102]

At an elevator plant in the United States, an army of consultants arrived one day, unexplained and annoying.[103] The rumor mill kicked in; employees thought the plant was to be shut down or that some of them would be laid off. Three months later,

procedural justice

Using fair processes in decision making and making sure others know that the process was as fair as possible.

management unveiled its new plan, involving a new method of manufacturing based on teams. As the changes were implemented, management did not adequately answer questions about the purpose of the changes, employees resisted, conflicts arose, and the formerly popular plant manager lost the trust of his people. Costs skyrocketed, and quality plummeted.

Concerned, management conducted an employee survey. Employees were skeptical that the survey results would lead to any positive changes and were worried that management would be angry that people had voiced their honest opinions. But management reacted by saying, "We were wrong, we screwed up, we didn't use the right process." They went on to share with employees critical business information, the limited options available, and the dire consequences if the company didn't change. Employees saw the dilemma and came to view the business problem as theirs as well as management's, but they were scared that some of them would lose their jobs. Management retained the right to lay people off if business conditions grew worse but also made several promises: no layoffs as a result of changes made; cross-training programs for employees; no replacements of departing people until conditions improved; a chance for employees to serve in new roles as consultants on quality issues; and sharing of sales and cost data on a regular basis.

The news was bad, but people understood it and began to share responsibility with management. This was the beginning of the restoration of trust and commitment and of steady improvements in performance.

Job Satisfaction

Bottom Line

A single satisfied person doesn't necessarily produce well on every performance dimension. But an organization full of people with high job satisfaction will likely perform well in many ways.

In an organization with a strategy focused on low cost, is employee satisfaction important? Why or why not?

If people feel fairly treated from the outcomes they receive and the processes used, they will be satisfied. A satisfied worker is not necessarily more productive than a dissatisfied one; sometimes people are happy with their jobs because they don't have to work hard! But job dissatisfaction, aggregated across many individuals, creates a workforce that is more likely to exhibit (1) higher turnover; (2) higher absenteeism; (3) less good citizenship among employees;[104] (4) more grievances and lawsuits; (5) strikes; (6) stealing, sabotage, and vandalism; (7) poorer mental and physical health (which can mean higher job stress, higher insurance costs, and more lawsuits);[105] (8) more injuries;[106] (9) poor customer service;[107] and (10) lower productivity and profits.[108] All of these consequences of dissatisfaction, either directly or indirectly, are costly to organizations. Sadly, a survey of U.S. households found that a majority of workers are dissatisfied with their jobs, with the greatest amount of dissatisfaction among workers aged 25 and younger.[109]

Job satisfaction is especially important for relationship-oriented service employees such as realtors, hair stylists, and stockbrokers. Customers develop (or don't develop) a commitment to a specific service provider. Satisfied service providers are less likely to quit the company and more likely to provide an enjoyable customer experience.[110]

Quality of Work Life

quality of work life (QWL) programs

Programs designed to create a workplace that enhances employee well-being.

Quality of work life (QWL) programs create a workplace that enhances employee well-being and satisfaction. The general goal of QWL programs is to satisfy the full range of employee needs. People's needs apparently are well met at Plante Moran, an accounting firm with offices in 18 Midwestern cities. Cofounder Frank Moran's goal was for the business to be a "people firm disguised as an accounting firm," and he brought that vision to life by allowing any flexible work arrangement that is satisfactory to the employee's clients. The firm's website, which promises a "jerk-free" workplace, describes challenging jobs with varied assignments and buddies assigned to new employees so they can more wisely navigate their careers. In the end, what employees say they appreciate most are the interesting assignments that bring them into direct contact with key people at client companies.[111]

QWL has eight categories:[112]

1. Adequate and fair compensation
2. A safe and healthy environment
3. Jobs that develop human capacities
4. A chance for personal growth and security
5. A social environment that fosters personal identity, freedom from prejudice, a sense of community, and upward mobility
6. Constitutionalism, or the rights of personal privacy, dissent, and due process
7. A work role that minimizes infringement on personal leisure and family needs
8. Socially responsible organizational actions

Plante Moran promises applicants a "jerk-free" workplace on its website.

Organizations differ drastically in their attention to QWL. Critics claim that QWL programs don't necessarily inspire employees to work harder if the company does not tie rewards directly to individual performance. Advocates of QWL claim that it improves organizational effectiveness and productivity. The term *productivity*, as applied by QWL programs, means much more than each person's quantity of work output.[113] It also includes turnover, absenteeism, accidents, theft, sabotage, creativity, innovation, and especially the quality of work.

All in all, people's satisfaction and well-being have many important consequences, beneficial to both employees and employers.[114] These range from better attitudes and health to work behaviors and performance and ultimately include business outcomes.[115] In a well-managed workplace, win–win solutions are indeed possible.

In Practice

MARS ADDRESSES QUALITY OF LIFE

As the third-largest privately owned company in the United States (private meaning its stock is not traded in stock exchanges), Mars Inc. need not publish details about how it is managed. However, what information is available suggests that the company deserves its recently won spot on *Fortune*'s list of the 100 Best Companies to Work for in America.

With employee turnover near 5 percent, one reason employees stay is that they have plenty of room to develop in their careers. Although Mars is mainly known for its candy brands, including M&M's, Snickers, Twix, and Skittles, it also sells Orbit gum, Uncle Ben's rice, and Pedigree pet food. Depending on their interests, employees are encouraged to move across divisions as they advance.

The company has a distinctive management philosophy based on five values: quality, responsibility, mutuality, efficiency, and freedom. These principles, laid down by the Mars family, were published in a booklet and are often cited. They keep employees focused on serving customers, and they reinforce that each person is responsible for good results in his or her area. The freedom ideal is based on the company's private ownership. Because management does not have to answer for its stock price every quarter, mistakes can be tolerated, and it is safe to pursue ideas with a long-term payoff. This wider view also drives managers' commitment to developing and mentoring employees.

These values, more than headline-grabbing perks, are what create a distinctive work environment. However, Mars does have a fun side. The candy in the vending machines is free, and workers in the pet care division are encouraged to bring their pets to the office.[116]

• Based on the information given, how well does Mars address quality of work life?

Psychological Contracts

psychological contract

A set of perceptions of what employees owe their employers and what their employers owe them.

The relationship between individuals and employing organizations typically is formalized by a written contract. But in employees' minds, there also exists a **psychological contract**—a set of perceptions of what they owe their employers and what their employers owe them.[117] This contract, whether it is seen as being upheld or violated—and whether the parties trust one another or not—has important implications for employee satisfaction and motivation and the effectiveness of the organization. Experiencing significant breach of psychological contract also can adversely affect physical and mental health.[118]

Historically, in many companies, the employment relationship was stable and predictable. Now mergers, layoffs, and other disruptions have torn asunder the old deal.[119] As one executive put it, "The 'used-to-be's' must give way to the realities of 'What is and what will be.'"[120] The fundamental used-to-be of traditionally managed organizations was that employees were expected to be loyal, and employers would provide secure employment. Today the implicit contract goes something like this:[121] If people stay, do their own jobs plus someone else's (who has been downsized), and do additional things such as participating in task forces, the company will try to provide a job (if it can), provide gestures that it cares, and keep providing more or less the same pay (with periodic small increases). The likely result of this not-very-satisfying arrangement: uninspired people and a business trying to survive. Career advisors tell disillusioned employees to think of themselves as free agents and to change jobs when a new option beckons.

But a better deal is possible, for both employers and employees.[122] Ideally, your employer will provide continuous skill updating and an invigorating work environment in which you can use your skills and are motivated to stay even though you may have other job options.[123] The employer says, in essence, "If you make us more valuable, we'll make you more valuable," and the employee says, "If you help me grow, I'll help the company grow." The company benefits from your contributions, and you thrive in your work while you also become more marketable if and when you decide to look elsewhere. Employment is an alliance—perhaps temporary, perhaps long term—aimed at helping both employer and employee succeed.[124] The results of such a contract are much more likely to be a mutually beneficial and satisfying relationship and a high-performing, successful organization.

Consider how business coach Ram Charan assumed this new psychological contract in advising a frustrated human resource (HR) manager.[125] The manager had asked Charan for guidance in coping with bureaucratic red tape that was frustrating to him as a leader and to the employees in his group. Charan encouraged the manager to reframe the situation as a need for learning, creativity, and leadership. The manager, said Charan, should investigate what the managers in other departments need from HR so that his people would truly be serving business needs and helping to solve business problems. Charan also encouraged the manager to learn about his employees' career goals and interests so that he can focus on ways to develop his people's strengths through assignments and greater decision-making authority within the department. If the HR manager accepts Charan's guidance, he and his people will face more interesting challenges than they would by simply defining themselves as a static part of a bureaucracy.

Finally, consider how these ideas for motivation apply at SAS. Read the "Management Connection: Onward" feature and ask yourself whether old-fashioned stable employment relationships can—or should—be the norm.

Management Connection

HOW SAS MAKES WORK MOTIVATING

Jennifer Mann, SAS's vice president of human resources, says everyone there "is working toward the same vision and inspiring each other to do their best work." Mann sees this as evidence that the company's culture is yielding great results. Other signs of success include employee turnover below 3 percent (versus the industry average of more than 20 percent), tens of thousands of job applicants to fill hundreds of open positions, and steadily growing revenues.

What convinces employees that SAS values their contributions? We have already talked about employee benefits, but these are mere symbols of underlying beliefs. The managers rewarded at SAS are those who advocate for and develop their people. CEO James Goodnight (also an owner of the privately held company) puts his time and money on the line for his people. Each month, he presides at a breakfast meeting where any employee may join in and ask questions or share ideas. In 2008, as financial crisis gave way to Great Recession, other software companies announced major layoffs, and SAS employees became nervous. Goodnight spoke to all of them via webcast, saying there would be no layoffs; they just needed to be frugal. Not only did the company weather that economic downturn, it continued growing and developed new products to launch as the economy recovered.

Another quality of the SAS culture is trust in employees. The company's standard workweek is just 35 hours, and its onsite facilities and beautiful grounds make it easy for employees to take a break to work out, get a haircut or massage, or go for a hike. Managers don't worry that employees will goof off; they find that trust motivates employees to work hard to please customers and help the company succeed. In fact, great subsidized food (some of it grown on an SAS-owned organic farm) and other services can make staying at work easier than going home. A similar attitude of trust applies to sick days at SAS, which are unlimited.

Finally, SAS ensures that work is meaningful. Goodnight reminds employees that SAS software is useful to people all over the world. Programmers' work is designed so they feel ownership of their creations. Even the landscapers at headquarters are assigned to particular plots, so these employees enjoy imparting beauty to that parcel and feel the same identification with the company as any programmer does.[126]

- How does SAS make its jobs motivating? What other principles of job design could enhance motivation at SAS?
- What elements of SAS's approach to motivation do you think would contribute more to job satisfaction than to performance? Why?

KEY TERMS

Alderfer's ERG theory, p. 451

empowerment, p. 456

equity theory, p. 457

expectancy, p. 447

expectancy theory, p. 447

extinction, p. 444

extrinsic reward, p. 453

goal-setting theory, p. 441

growth need strength, p. 456

hygiene factors, p. 454

instrumentality, p. 448

intrinsic reward, p. 453

job enlargement, p. 454

job enrichment, p. 454

job rotation, p. 454

law of effect, p. 443

Maslow's need hierarchy, p. 450

motivation, p. 440

motivators, p. 454

negative reinforcement, p. 443

organizational behavior modification (OB mod), p. 443

outcome, p. 447

positive reinforcement, p. 443

procedural justice, p. 459

psychological contract, p. 462

punishment, p. 444

quality of work life (QWL) programs, p. 460

reinforcers, p. 443

stretch goals, p. 442

two-factor theory, p. 454

valence, p. 448

SUMMARY OF LEARNING OBJECTIVES

Now that you have studied Chapter 13, you should be able to:

LO 1   Identify the kinds of behaviors managers need to motivate in people.

All important work behaviors are motivated. Managers need to motivate employees to join and remain in the organization and to exhibit high attendance, job performance, and citizenship.

LO 2   List principles for setting goals that motivate employees.

Goal setting is a powerful motivator. Specific, quantifiable, and challenging but attainable goals motivate high effort and performance. Goal setting can be used for teams as well as for individuals. Care should be taken to avoid setting single goals to the exclusion of other important dimensions of performance. Managers also should keep sight of the other potential downsides of goals.

LO 3   Summarize how to reward good performance effectively.

Organizational behavior modification programs influence behavior at work by arranging consequences for people's actions. Most programs use positive reinforcement as a consequence, but other important consequences are negative reinforcement, punishment, and extinction. Care must be taken to reinforce appropriate, not inappropriate, behavior. Innovative managers use a wide variety of rewards for good performance. They also understand how to manage mistakes and provide useful feedback.

LO 4   Describe the key beliefs that affect people's motivation.

Expectancy theory describes three important work-related beliefs. Motivation is a function of people's (1) expectancies, or effort-to-performance links; (2) instrumentalities, or performance-to-outcome links; and (3) the valences people attach to the outcomes of performance. In addition, people care about equity and justice.

LO 5   Discuss ways in which people's individual needs affect their behavior.

According to Maslow, important needs arise at five levels of a hierarchy: physiological, safety, social, ego, and self-actualization needs. Focusing more on the context of work, Alderfer's ERG theory describes three sets of needs: existence, relatedness, and growth. McClelland says people vary in the extent to which they have needs for achievement, affiliation, and power. Because people are inclined to satisfy their various needs, these theories suggest to managers the kinds of rewards that motivate people.

LO 6   Define ways to create jobs that motivate.

One approach to satisfying needs and motivating people is to create intrinsic motivation through the improved design of jobs. Jobs can be enriched by building in more skill variety, task identity, task significance, autonomy, and feedback. Empowerment, the most recent development in the creation of motivating jobs, includes the perceptions of meaning, competence, self-determination, and impact. These qualities come from an environment in which people have necessary information, knowledge, power, and rewards.

LO 7   Summarize how people assess fairness and how to achieve fairness.

Equity theory states that people compare their inputs and outcomes to the inputs and outcomes of others. Perceptions of equity (fairness) are satisfying; feelings of inequity (unfairness) are dissatisfying and motivate people to change their behavior or their perceptions to restore equity. In addition to fairness of outcomes, as described in equity theory, fairness is also appraised and managed through procedural justice.

LO 8   Identify causes and consequences of a satisfied workforce.

A satisfied workforce has many advantages for the firm, including lower absenteeism and turnover; fewer grievances, lawsuits, and strikes; lower health costs; and higher-quality work. One general approach to generating higher satisfaction for people is to implement a quality of work life program. QWL seeks to provide a safe and healthy environment, opportunity for personal growth, a positive social environment, fair treatment, and other improvements in people's work lives. These and other benefits from the organization, exchanged for contributions from employees, create a psychological contract. Over time, how the psychological contract is upheld or violated, and changed unfairly or fairly, will influence people's satisfaction and motivation.

DISCUSSION QUESTIONS

1. Think of a significant mistake made by someone on a job. How did the boss handle it, and what was the effect?

2. Why do you think it is so difficult for managers to empower their people?

3. Think of a job you hold currently or held in the past. How would you describe the psychological contract? How does(did) this affect your attitudes and behaviors on the job?

4. If a famous executive or sports figure were to give a passionate motivational speech, trying to persuade people to work harder, what do you think the impact would be? Why?

5. Give some examples of situations in which you wanted to do a great job but were prevented from doing so. What was the impact on you, and what would this suggest to you in your efforts to motivate other people to perform?

6. Discuss the similarities and differences between setting goals for other people and setting goals for yourself. When does goal setting fail, and when does it succeed?

7. Identify four examples of people inadvertently reinforcing the wrong behaviors or punishing or extinguishing good behaviors.

8. Assess yourself on McClelland's three needs. On which need are you highest, and on which are you lowest? What are the implications for you as a manager? *pg 452*

9. Identify a job you have held and appraise it on Hackman and Oldham's five core job dimensions. Also describe the degree to which it made you feel empowered. As a class, choose one job and discuss together how it could be changed to be more motivating and empowering.

10. Using expectancy theory, analyze how you have made and will make personal choices, such as a major area of study, a career to pursue, or job interviews to seek.

11. Describe a time when you felt unfairly treated and explain why. How did you respond to the inequity? What other options might you have had?

12. Provide examples of how outcomes perceived as unfair can decrease motivation. Then discuss how procedural justice, or fair process, can help overcome the negative effects.

13. What are the implications for your career of, and how will you prepare for, the psychological contracts described at the end of the chapter?

14. Set some goals for yourself, considering the discussion of goal setting in the chapter.

EXPERIENTIAL EXERCISES

13.1   ASSESSING YOURSELF

Circle the response that most closely correlates with each of the following items:

	Agree		Neither Agree nor Disagree		Disagree
1. I have developed a written list of short and long-term goals I would like to accomplish.	1	2	3	4	5
2. When setting goals for myself, I give consideration to what my capabilities and limits are.	1	2	3	4	5
3. I set goals that are realistic and attainable.	1	2	3	4	5
4. My goals are based on my hopes and beliefs, not on those of my parents, friends, or significant other.	1	2	3	4	5
5. When I fail to achieve a goal, I get back on track.	1	2	3	4	5
6. My goals are based on my personal values.	1	2	3	4	5
7. I have a current mission statement and have involved those closest to me in formulating it.	1	2	3	4	5
8. I regularly check my progress toward achieving the goals I have set.	1	2	3	4	5
9. When setting goals, I strive for performance, not outcomes.	1	2	3	4	5
10. I have a support system in place—friends, family members, and/or colleagues who believe in me and support my goals.	1	2	3	4	5
11. I apply SMART characteristics to my goals.	1	2	3	4	5
12. I prioritize my goals, focusing only on the most important or valuable ones at a particular point in time.	1	2	3	4	5
13. I reward myself when I achieve a goal or even when I reach a particular milestone.	1	2	3	4	5
14. I revisit my goals periodically and add and modify goals as appropriate.	1	2	3	4	5

Sum your circled responses. If your total is 42 or higher, you might want to explore ways to improve your skill in the area of goal setting.

SOURCE: Suzanne C. de Janasz, Karen O'Dowd, and Beth Z. Schneider, *Interpersonal Skills in Organizations,* McGraw-Hill, 2002, p. 211. Copyright 2002. The McGraw-Hill Companies, Inc. Reprinted with permission.

13.2 PERSONAL GOAL SETTING

1. In the spaces provided, brainstorm your goals in the following categories. Write down as many as you wish, including goals that are short-, mid-, and long-term.

   Academic, intellectual

   Health, fitness

   Social: family, friends, significant other, community

   Career, job

   Financial

   Other

2. Of the goals you have listed, select from each of the six categories the two most important goals that you would like to pursue in the short term (next 6–12 months). Write these here.

   a. _____
   b. _____
   c. _____
   d. _____
   e. _____
   f. _____
   g. _____
   h. _____
   i. _____
   j. _____
   k. _____
   l. _____

3. From the 12 goals listed, choose the 3 that are the most important to you at this time: the 3 you commit to work on in the next few months. Write a goal statement for each one, using the following guidelines:

   Begin each with the word "To . . ."
   Be specific.

   Quantify the goal if possible.

   Each goal statement should be realistic, attainable, and within your control.

   Each goal statement should reflect your aspirations—not those of others such as parents, roommates, significant others, and the like.

   a. _____
   b. _____
   c. _____

4. On a separate sheet of paper, develop an action plan for each goal statement. For each action plan,
   List the steps you will take to accomplish the goal.

   Include dates (by when) and initials (who's responsible) for each step.

   Visualize completing the goal and, working backward, specify each step necessary between now and then to reach the goal.

   Identify any potential barriers you might experience in attaining the goal. Problem-solve around these obstacles and convert them into steps in your action plan.

   Identify the resources you will need to accomplish these goals and build in steps to acquire the necessary information into your action plan.

5. Transfer the dates of each step for each goal in your action plan to a daily calendar.

6. Keep an ongoing daily or weekly record of the positive steps you take toward meeting each goal.

SOURCE: Suzanne C. de Janasz, Karen O'Dowd, and Beth Z. Schneider, *Interpersonal Skills in Organizations*, McGraw-Hill, 2002, p. 211. Copyright 2002. The McGraw-Hill Companies, Inc. Reprinted with permission.

13.3 WHAT DO STUDENTS WANT FROM THEIR JOBS?

OBJECTIVES

1. To demonstrate individual differences in job expectations.
2. To illustrate individual differences in need and motivational structures.
3. To examine and compare extrinsic and intrinsic rewards.

INSTRUCTIONS

1. Working alone, complete the "What I Want from My Job" survey.
2. In small groups, compare and analyze differences in the survey results and prepare group responses to the discussion questions.

3. After the class reconvenes, group spokespersons present group findings.

DISCUSSION QUESTIONS

1. Which items received the highest and lowest scores from you? Why?
2. On which items were there most and least agreement among students? What are the implications?
3. Which job rewards are extrinsic, and which are intrinsic?
4. Were more response differences found in intrinsic or in extrinsic rewards?
5. In what ways do you think blue-collar workers' responses would differ from those of college students?

What I Want from My Job

Determine what you want from a job by circling the level of importance of each of the following job rewards:

	Very Important	Important	Indifferent	Unimportant	Very Unimportant
1. Advancement opportunities	5	4	3	2	1
2. Appropriate company policies	5	4	3	2	1
3. Authority	5	4	3	2	1
4. Autonomy and freedom on the job	5	4	3	2	1
5. Challenging work	5	4	3	2	1
6. Company reputation	5	4	3	2	1
7. Fringe benefits	5	4	3	2	1
8. Geographic location	5	4	3	2	1
9. Good coworkers	5	4	3	2	1
10. Good supervision	5	4	3	2	1
11. Job security	5	4	3	2	1
12. Money	5	4	3	2	1
13. Opportunity for self-development	5	4	3	2	1
14. Pleasant office and working conditions	5	4	3	2	1
15. Performance feedback	5	4	3	2	1
16. Prestigious job title	5	4	3	2	1
17. Recognition for doing a good job	5	4	3	2	1
18. Responsibility	5	4	3	2	1
19. Sense of achievement	5	4	3	2	1
20. Training programs	5	4	3	2	1
21. Type of work	5	4	3	2	1
22. Working with people	5	4	3	2	1

CONCLUDING CASE

BIG BISON RESORTS: FINDING THE KEY TO WHAT EMPLOYEES VALUE

Frank Schuman, vice president of human resources for Big Bison Resorts, heard laughter as he approached the chief executive's office door. As he stepped into the room, he saw CEO Janette Briggs seated behind her desk, regaling two other executives with a story that the three were obviously enjoying immensely.

"Oh, Frank! Good!" exclaimed Janette when she saw him enter. "I was just telling Pedro and Marlys about my great adventure in TV land." Janette had been away from the office for the past two weeks, taping the popular reality TV show *Executive in Disguise* instead of running her company, a regional chain of indoor water parks.

"How did it go?" asked Frank. "From the laughter I heard outside your door, it must have been hilarious."

"Well, funny, yes," replied Janette. "But mainly it was eye-opening. After spending all that time in our kitchens and cleaning the guest rooms and pools, I see our people and their jobs in a totally new way."

"Is that why you called me here? I was expecting you wanted to review our plans for the Employee of the Month program we're unrolling next month. That is, until I saw—" He waved his hand toward the other two people seated in the room, Pedro Gutierrez, head of operations, and finance chief Marlys Higgenbotham. "Or at least I was guessing they're not here to nominate the first employee of the month."

"No, see, that's the issue. After working directly with our frontline staff, I'm having my doubts about putting resources into

Employee of the Month," replied the CEO. Frank swallowed. Employee of the Month had been a pet idea of Janette's, so he had poured most of his time into developing the program. Each month, a manager at each resort was going to nominate a top-performing employee to be the Employee of the Month and enjoy the glory, not to mention a premium parking space and a framed photo posted in the lobby of the resort where he or she worked. Now it appeared that Janette shared what, he had to admit, were his own doubts about whether the program would really do much to improve performance or lower turnover. Janette continued, "Have a seat, Frank, and let me tell you about what I saw the past two weeks." Frank settled into a chair next to Marlys.

Janette brought Frank up to date: "I've been telling Marlys and Pedro what it was like to work in one of our kitchens. The pace is unbelievable. The workload is unbelievable. And the teamwork is out of this world. Frank, I was amazed, and you would be, too. I know how to make a grilled cheese sandwich, but these folks do a lot more than cook. They're planning and controlling on the fly: How many salads? How many pancakes? How can we make all that without any waste? There's no supervisor on the line; they're all thinking like managers—how to please customers, control costs. Honestly, our managers could take lessons from them on teamwork and quality control."

"It sounds like we have a lot of Employees of the Month," Frank said hopefully. Maybe the program wouldn't be canceled after all, and his group's efforts wouldn't have been wasted.

"No, no, no!" broke in Marlys. "The point is, we've tried so many programs to boost productivity. As you know, we were looking at bonuses last year, till the economy got so bad. We simply couldn't justify paying more when occupancy rates were diving. But we have to do something. Now that business is picking up in our market area, other hotels and resorts are going to start recruiting away our best people. The question is, what can we do that will keep employees working as hard as they are now without burning out and leaving us? We thought people would just like a little recognition, but Janette is saying she doubts it now."

"Exactly," said Janette. "And that's why I called you in. We need your expertise about human relations. What do people want? I thought it would be pay, prizes, that sort of thing. And you went along with me. But really, Frank, can that be it? The people I worked with the past two weeks—they have so much skill at what they do, and they're constantly thinking up ways to make our guests happy. They already take pride in what they accomplish. We need to decide what will make their jobs better so they can accomplish more without us getting in their way with, well, Employee of the Month ceremonies."

"OK," replied Frank, "now that you've put it that way, I have to ask if maybe what we don't want to do is decide what will make their jobs better."

As Janette and Marlys gazed at Frank quizzically, Pedro spoke up. "That's great, Frank. You're saying we shouldn't make their jobs better? I came up through the ranks at Big Bison, and I can recall that those hourly jobs aren't exactly perfect the way they are."

"What I mean," replied Frank, "is that we need to listen before we decide."

DISCUSSION QUESTIONS

1. What kinds of behavior would an Employee of the Month program, as described here, reinforce at Big Bison Resorts? How might the company apply the principles of reinforcement more effectively?

2. How might Big Bison Resorts get input from employees to make the company's jobs more motivating? What impact would this effort have on the company's performance?

3. How would Big Bison's employees perceive the equity of the Employee of the Month program? Compare their reactions to that program with the response you would expect from an effort to involve employees in improving their jobs.

4. Think about a previous job you have held or hold currently. If you had the power to make such decisions, what would you do to make the job more motivating for employees?

CHAPTER 14

Teamwork

"No one can whistle a symphony. It takes an orchestra to play it."

— HALFORD E. LUCCOCK

Management Connection

HOW TEAMS WORK AT WHOLE FOODS MARKET

Whole Foods Market has a purpose beyond profits, and even a purpose beyond selling gorgeous vegetables and great cheeses. The chain of more than 300 health-food stores in the United States, Canada, and the United Kingdom seeks to do no less than "contribute to the well-being of people and the planet." This mission shapes the selection of merchandise grown organically and sustainably, including fresh produce, meats and fish, and whole grains, all attractively displayed. It also shapes the way the company treats its 70,000-plus employees.

Management of employees is based on key values: personal responsibility, valuing diversity, and commitment to the organization's purpose. To sustain this combination of values, the company operates as a set of teams, with every employee being a team member. A team may have between six and a hundred members, with the large teams divided into subteams. The leader of each team in a store is a member of the store's leadership team, and the head of each store leadership team is a member of a regional team. At the top of the Whole Foods hierarchy is an executive team. Each employee is responsible for participating in decisions related to his or her team's work. Team members have a vote in which employees are part of the team and what benefits will be included in their compensation packages.

Team spirit and empowerment at Whole Foods has laid a strong foundation for business success. Cofounder and CEO John Mackey says living out the store's values creates a climate that frees employees to

innovate without fear, and the creative, fear-free environment feels great to shoppers. It is one of a handful of companies that has attained a spot on *Fortune*'s list of Best Companies to Work For in every year the list has been compiled. Most recently, on the global Best Companies list, Whole Foods was ranked number one among food and drug stores. Consistent with that ranking, Whole Foods reports employee turnover of just 10 percent per year (the industry average is ten times that). And after year upon year of strong growth, Whole Foods has become the world's largest supermarket chain specializing in natural and organic foods, with investors seeing far more room to grow in the future.[1]

Whole Foods Market expresses a strong commitment to its employees, empowers them to make decisions, and expects a high level of commitment to serving customers. As you read this chapter, consider whether these ingredients are enough to ensure truly effective teamwork.

Sometimes teams work, and sometimes they don't. The goal of this chapter is to help make sure that your teams (and you) succeed. Empowerment at Whole Foods Market illustrates one way a company can apply teamwork with extraordinary results.

Teams transform the ways organizations do business.[2] Almost all companies now use teams to produce goods and services, to manage projects, and to make decisions and run the company.[3] For you, this has two vital implications. First, you will be working in and perhaps managing teams. Second, the ability to work in and lead teams is valuable to your employer and important to your career. Fortunately, coursework focusing on team training can enhance students' teamwork knowledge and skills.[4]

The Contributions of Teams

Bottom Line

Well-managed teams are powerful forces that can deliver all desired results.

What do you think makes a team more powerful than a set of individuals?

Used properly, teams can be powerfully effective as a building block for organization structure. Organizations such as Semco, W. L. Gore, and Kollmorgen, manufacturer of printed circuits and electro-optic devices, are structured entirely around teams. 3M's breakthrough products emerge through the use of teams that are small entrepreneurial businesses within the larger corporation.

Teams can increase productivity, improve quality, and reduce costs. At Massachusetts-based manufacturer FLEXcon, teams of employees applying the lean principles described in Chapter 9 have significantly increased productivity and decreased energy consumption.[5] At Nucor's steel plant in Decatur, Alabama, the general manager credits teamwork for high productivity and improved safety.[6]

Teams also can enhance speed and be powerful forces for innovation, creativity,[7] and change. Boeing, 3M, and many other companies use teams to create new products faster. General Mills uses a team approach to make decisions about the packaging for its products. For product divisions such as Big G cereals, Yoplait yogurt, or Green Giant vegetables, teams bring together employees from brand design, engineering, production, research and development, and other relevant functions to figure out how packaging can reduce waste, cut costs, send a clearer marketing message, and find ways to work more efficiently with suppliers.[8]

> Teams also can enhance speed and be powerful forces for innovation, creativity, and change.

Teams also provide many benefits for their members.[9] The team is a very useful learning mechanism. Members learn about the company and themselves, and they acquire new skills and performance strategies. The team can satisfy important personal needs, such as affiliation and esteem. Other needs are met as team members receive tangible organizational rewards that they could not have achieved working alone. Moreover, teams help individuals develop their networks.[10]

Team members can provide one another with feedback; identify opportunities for growth and development; and train, coach, and mentor.[11] A marketing representative can learn about financial modeling from a colleague on a new product development team, and the financial expert can learn about consumer marketing. Experience working together in a team, and developing strong problem-solving capabilities, is a vital supplement to specific job skills or functional expertise. And the skills are transferable to new positions.

work teams

Teams that make or do things such as manufacture, assemble, sell, or provide service.

Types of Teams

Your organization may have hundreds of groups and teams, but they can be classified into just a few primary types.[12] **Work teams** make or do things such as manufacture, assemble, sell, or provide service. They typically are well defined; a clear part of the formal organizational structure; and composed of a full-time, stable membership. Work teams are what most people think of when they think of teams in organizations.[13]

Project and development teams work on long-term projects, often over a period of years. They have specific assignments, such as research or new product development, and members usually must contribute expert knowledge and judgment. These teams work toward a one-time product, disbanding once their work is completed. Then new teams are formed for new projects.

Parallel teams operate separately from the regular work structure of the firm on a temporary basis. Members often come from different units or jobs and are asked to do work that is not normally done by the standard structure. Their charge is to recommend solutions to specific problems. They usually do not have authority to act, however. Examples include task forces and quality or safety teams formed to study a particular problem. At Game Freak, the videogame studio that created the Pokémon games for Nintendo, parallel teams have a chance to become development teams. Whenever an employee has a new idea for a game, if he or she can persuade two other people to support the idea, the company will allot this team three months to develop the idea. After that time, if management sees potential, it allots another three months for the parallel team to continue its work. At the six-month mark, Game Freak determines whether to back the project with a full-fledged development team. Employees feel inspired by the chance to experiment with entirely new concepts rather than working only on small parts of today's complex game software.[14]

Management teams coordinate and provide direction to the subunits under their jurisdiction and integrate work among subunits.[15] The management team is based on authority stemming from hierarchical rank and is responsible for the overall performance of the business unit. Managers responsible for different subunits form a team together, and at the top of the organization resides the executive management team that establishes strategic direction and manages the firm's overall performance.

Transnational teams are work teams composed of multinational members whose activities span multiple countries.[16] Such teams differ from other work teams not only by being multicultural but also by often being geographically dispersed, being psychologically distant, and working on highly complex projects having considerable impact on company objectives.

Transnational teams tend to be **virtual teams,** communicating electronically more than face to face, although other types of teams may operate virtually as well. Virtual teams face difficult challenges: building trust, cohesion, and team identity, and overcoming the isolation of virtual team members.[17] Table 14.1 suggests ways that managers can improve the effectiveness of virtual teams.

project and development teams

Teams that work on long-term projects but disband once the work is completed.

parallel teams

Teams that operate separately from the regular work structure and exist temporarily.

management teams

Teams that coordinate and provide direction to the subunits under their jurisdiction and integrate work among subunits.

transnational teams

Work groups composed of multinational members whose activities span multiple countries.

virtual teams

Teams that are physically dispersed and communicate electronically more than face to face.

One example of a project and development team is the Omnica product development team. The 28-person team is responsible for producing medical and high-tech products for their clients faster and more efficiently than they could by any other means.

TABLE 14.1

Practices of Effective Virtual Team Leaders

Leadership Practices of Virtual Team Leader	How Do Virtual Team Leaders Do It?
Establish and maintain trust through the use of communication technology.	Focusing the norms on how information is communicated.
	Revisiting and adjusting the communication norms as the team evolves (virtual get-togethers).
	Making progress explicit through use of team virtual workspace.
	Equal "suffering" in the geographically distributed world.
Ensure diversity in the team is understood, appreciated, and leveraged.	Prominent team expertise directory and skills matrix in the virtual workspace.
	Virtual subteaming to pair diverse members and rotate subteam members.
Manage virtual work cycle and meetings.	Use the start of virtual meeting (each time) for social relationship building.
	During meeting—ensure through check-ins that everyone is engaged and heard from.
	End of meeting—ensure that the minutes and future work plan are posted to team repository.
Monitor team progress through the use of technology.	Make progress explicit through balanced scorecard measurements posted in the team's virtual workspace.
Enhance external visibility of the team and its members.	Frequent report-outs to a virtual steering committee (comprising local bosses of team members).
Ensure individuals benefit from participating in virtual teams.	Virtual reward ceremonies.
	Individual recognition at the start of each virtual meeting.
	Making each team member's real-location boss aware of the member's contribution.

SOURCE: From A. Malhotra, A. Majchrzak, and B. Rosen, "Leading Virtual Teams," *Academy of Management Perspectives* (February 2007), pp. 60–70. Reproduced with permission of Academy of Management via Copyright Clearance Center..

teaming:

A strategy of teamwork on the fly, with many temporary, changing teams.

traditional work groups

Groups that have no managerial responsibilities.

self-managed teams

Autonomous work groups in which workers are trained to do all or most of the jobs in a unit and make decisions previously made by frontline supervisors.

In today's fast-changing, unpredictable environment, **teaming** is a strategy of teamwork on the fly.[18] In teaming, organizations create many temporary, changing teams, and you might feel like you are in a shifting series of temporary pick-up basketball games, working with different teammates and facing different challenges. You will leave one team when it has achieved (or failed at) its goal and join new teams when new opportunities arise. Because no two projects are alike, people need to get up to speed quickly on brand-new topics again and again. Because solutions can come from anywhere, team members can, too.

Self-Managed Teams

Today many types of work teams exist, with different labels.[19] **Traditional work groups** have no managerial responsibilities. The frontline manager plans, organizes, staffs, directs, and controls them, and other groups provide support activities, including quality control and maintenance.

But the trend is toward giving teams more autonomy so that workers are trained to do all or most of the jobs in the unit, and they make decisions previously made by frontline supervisors.[20] People sometime resist **self-managed teams,** in part because they don't want so much responsibility and the change is difficult.[21] In addition, people often don't like to do performance evaluation of teammates or to fire people, and poorly managed conflict may be a particular problem in self-managed teams.[22] But compared with traditionally managed teams, self-managed teams appear to be more productive, have lower costs, provide better customer service, provide higher quality, have better safety records, and are more satisfying for members.

Autonomous work groups control decisions about and execution of a complete range of tasks—acquiring raw materials and performing operations, quality control, maintenance, and shipping. They are fully responsible for an entire product or an entire part of a production process. **Self-designing teams** do all of that and go one step further—they also have control over the design of the team. They decide themselves whom to hire, whom to fire, and what tasks the team will perform.

When teams reach the point of being truly self-managed, results have included lower costs and greater levels of team productivity, quality, and customer satisfaction.[23] Overall, autonomous teams are known to improve the organization's financial and overall performance, at least in North America.[24] For example, at Lockheed Martin's Missiles and Fire Control facility in Troy, Alabama, all members of the workforce are assigned to self-directed work teams, and many also participate in performance management teams, which set goals and monitor progress. The teams have achieved 100 percent on-time delivery, 99 percent of first-pass production meeting quality standards, and a 43 percent cut in energy consumption per unit produced.[25]

In trying to take such practices to operations outside the United States, managers need to recognize that cultural differences such as those described in Chapter 6 may affect how employees react to being given decision-making authority. As you learn more about the self-managed teams at Whole Foods Market, described in "Management Connection: Progress Report," consider whether this kind of employee empowerment would continue to be effective if the company expanded into other countries with different cultures.

autonomous work groups

Groups that control decisions about and execution of a complete range of tasks.

self-designing teams

Teams with the responsibilities of autonomous work groups and control over hiring, firing, and deciding what tasks members perform.

Teams at Lockheed Martin have achieved success in terms of on-time delivery and production standards, allowing the company to meet customer demand.

Management Connection

SELF-MANAGED TEAMS AT WHOLE FOODS MARKET

To spur innovation and strengthen commitment, Whole Foods Market empowers employees to participate in planning and decision making with their teams. Within a store, members of teams are involved in decisions concerning product selection and merchandising (the way products are displayed to entice buyers) as well as efforts to improve efficiency. They also contribute to decisions about hiring and compensation.

The company is widely known for team member involvement in hiring decisions, but employees support rather than control the entire hiring process. A human resource employee at each store or other facility screens job applications and selects candidates with the necessary skills and concern for customer service. Candidates who pass the initial screening may be interviewed by one or more store leaders. (Applicants to lead teams

generally interview with a group.) Each employee hired then begins an orientation period, during which he or she has probationary status. After the new employee has worked with the team for one to three months, the team meets to decide whether to keep the person on the team, based on whether he or she meets the job requirements, follows company policies and procedures, provides excellent customer service, and works well with the team. Two-thirds must vote in favor of the employee; otherwise, the person can try to join another team or will have to leave the company.

Whole Foods recognizes that for empowerment to succeed, employees need information and other resources to support them in carrying out their responsibilities. Managers share information about the company's financial performance, and everyone can see a list of the gross pay of

MANAGER'S BRIEF

PROGRESS REPORT

ONWARD

every team member, including top executives. The company also provides key information for decisions about benefits, starting with the total amount the company will allocate to that expense. Every three years, employees vote on which benefits they want to receive as part of their compensation package. The company provides a list of possible benefits, identifying the cost of each one. Then the employees set priorities within the spending limit.

Rewards, too, are linked to teamwork. Most incentive pay, such as bonuses, is tied to team performance. As CEO John Mackey has said, "We have a shared fate. We either succeed together or we fail together."[26]

- What advantages does teamwork offer to Whole Foods Market?
- Why do you think human resources professionals conduct the initial screening process for new hires? What might be the consequences of having the store teams carry out the entire process of hiring and rewarding team members?

How Groups Become Real Teams

The words *group* and *team* often are used interchangeably.[27] Modern managers sometimes use the word *teams* to the point that it has become a cliché; they talk about teams while skeptics perceive no real teamwork.

Therefore making a distinction between groups and teams can be useful. A *working group* is a collection of people who work in the same area or have been drawn together to undertake a task but do not necessarily come together as a unit and achieve significant performance improvements. A real **team** is formed of people (usually a small number) with complementary skills who trust one another and are committed to a common purpose, common performance goals, and a common approach for which they hold themselves mutually accountable.[28]

Groups become true teams via basic group processes, critical periods, and the management practices described throughout this chapter.

Group Processes

Assume you are the leader of a newly formed group—actually a bunch of people. What will you face as you attempt to develop your group into a high-performing team? If groups are to develop successfully, they will engage in various processes, including these broad categories:[29]

- *Forming*—group members attempt to lay the ground rules for what types of behavior are acceptable.
- *Storming*—hostilities and conflict arise, and people jockey for positions of power and status.
- *Norming*—group members agree on their shared goals, and norms and closer relationships develop.
- *Performing*—the group channels its energies into performing its tasks.

Virtual teams also go through these stages of group development.[30] The forming stage is characterized by unbridled optimism: "I believe we have a great team and will work well together. We all understand the importance of the project and intend to take it seriously." Optimism turns into reality shock in the storming stage: "No one has taken a leadership role. We have not made the project the priority that it deserves." The norming stage comes at about the halfway point in the project life cycle, in which people refocus and recommit: "You must make firm commitments to a specific time schedule." The performing stage is the dash to the finish as teammates show the discipline needed to meet the deadline.

Groups don't necessarily go through those processes in that particular sequence, but all the processes are important. From a leadership perspective, it is particularly useful to know the two most fundamental phases of team functioning: a transition phase of

team

A small number of people with complementary skills who are committed to a common purpose, set of performance goals, and approach for which they hold themselves mutually accountable.

planning and establishing the group's mission, goals, and processes, and an action phase in which the team executes the work activities that contribute directly to it performance goals.[31] Think about how often groups dive into their work without adequately tackling the transition phase and the problems that arise when they neglect that phase.

Critical Periods

Groups pass through critical periods, or times when they are particularly open to formative experiences.[32] The first such critical period is in the forming stage, at the first meeting, when rules and roles are established that set longer-lasting precedents. A second critical period is the midway point between the initial meeting and a deadline (e.g., completing a project or making a presentation). At this point, the group has enough experience to understand its work; it comes to realize that time is becoming a scarce resource and it must get on with it; and there is enough time left to change its approach if necessary.

In the initial meeting, the group should establish desired norms, roles, and other determinants of effectiveness, which are discussed throughout this chapter. At the second critical period (the midpoint), groups should renew or open lines of communication with outside constituencies. The group can use fresh information from its external environment to revise its approach to performing its task and ensure that it meets the needs of customers and clients. Without these activities, groups may get off on the wrong foot from the beginning, and members may never revise their behavior in the appropriate direction.[33]

Teaming Challenges

In today's era of teaming, fast-forming, fast-acting, temporary groups do not have the luxury of time to allow all necessary team processes to develop slowly and naturally. Practices that are particularly helpful in this context[34] include (1) emphasizing the team's purpose, including why it exists, what's at stake, and what its shared values are; (2) building psychological safety, making clear that people need to and can freely speak up, be honest, disagree, offer ideas, raise issues, share their knowledge, ask questions, or show fallibility without fear that others will think less of them or criticize them; (3) embracing failure, understanding that mistakes are inevitable, errors should be acknowledged, and learning as we go is a way to create new knowledge while we execute; and (4) putting conflict to work by explaining how we arrive at our views, expressing interest in one another's thinking and analyses, and attempting fully to understand and capitalize on others' diverse perspectives.[35]

The leader, and team members who want to help the team perform well, should ask for, expect, and model these behaviors.

Why Groups Sometimes Fail

Team building does not necessarily progress smoothly and culminate in a well-oiled team and superb performance.[36] Some groups never do work out. Such groups can be frustrating for managers and members, who may feel teams are a waste of time and that the difficulties outweigh the benefits.

It is not easy to build high-performance teams. *Teams* is often just a word management uses to describe merely putting people into groups. "Teams" sometimes are launched with little or no training or support systems. For example, both managers and group members need new skills to make a group work. These skills include negotiating goals that everyone can get behind, delivering on promises made, speaking up in groups to share ideas and build cooperation, recognizing and getting along with people's different work styles, and finding constructive ways to deal with conflict.[37] Giving up some control is very difficult for managers from traditional systems, but they have to realize they will gain control in the long run by creating stronger, better-performing units.

Teams should be empowered,[38] as discussed in Chapter 13. The benefits of teams are reduced when they are not allowed to make important decisions—in other words, when management doesn't trust them with important responsibilities. If teams must acquire permission for every innovative idea, they will revert to making safe, traditional decisions.[39]

Empowerment enhances team performance even among virtual teams.

Empowerment enhances team performance even among virtual teams. Empowerment for virtual teams includes thorough training in using the technologies and strong technical support from management. Some virtual teams have periodic face-to-face interactions, which help performance; empowerment is particularly helpful for virtual teams that don't often meet face to face.[40]

In today's fast-moving business environment, the difference between success and failure often lies with whether people can rapidly form and contribute to one team after another as new opportunities and challenges arise. Teamwork fails when individuals have not considered what they bring to a team and how to bring out the best in others. To be successful, team members must apply clear thinking and appropriate practices.[41] That is what this entire chapter is about.

In Practice

TEAMWORK AT MENLO INNOVATIONS

All work is teamwork at Menlo Innovations. The Ann Arbor, Michigan, software company assigns all tasks to pairs of employees who share a computer—and they switch partners every week. No one, not even CEO Richard Sheridan, works alone in an assigned office or even at an assigned desk—everyone works in one large room. Each project is divided into small tasks, handwritten by team members on index cards with estimates of the time required. The cards are posted on a wall to represent each project's work flow. The pairs of employees working on the same project team sit near one another for ease in asking questions and trading ideas.

The goal of this extreme teamwork is to put employees in situations in which they are constantly learning from one another. Sheridan believes ideas get stale unless new people get involved and ask questions. Some employees find that voicing problems to a partner helps them recognize solutions. Also, work on a software project that could stretch over months is more interesting when employees switch tasks and partners. Menlo's teamwork system is creating software that works well for customers without requiring overtime from employees.

To make its team structure work, Menlo selects job applicants who perform well in this kind of environment. Candidates visit the company to work in pairs on sample projects while employees observe. Afterward, the observers discuss whether they would be able to work well with each candidate. Candidates approved by a majority of the observers get a paid trial before the final hiring decision. Performance feedback also is a group process, conducted over lunch with one's peers.[42]

- Does the Menlo Innovations work system allow enough time for groups to develop into teams? What do you think of their approach?

Building Effective Teams

All the considerations just described form the building blocks of an effective work team. But what does it really mean for a team to be effective? Team effectiveness is defined by three criteria.[43]

1. The productive output of the team meets or exceeds the standards of quantity and quality; the team's output is acceptable to the customers, inside or outside the organization, who receive the team's goods or services.

2. Team members realize satisfaction of their personal needs.
3. Team members remain committed to working together again; that is, the group doesn't burn out and disintegrate after a grueling project. Looking back, the members are glad they were involved. In other words, effective teams remain viable and have good prospects for repeated success in the future.[44]

Performance Focus

The key element of effective teamwork is commitment to a common purpose.[45] The best teams are those that have been given an important performance challenge by management and then have reached a common understanding and appreciation of their purpose. Without such understanding and commitment, a group will be just a bunch of individuals.

The best teams also work hard at developing a common understanding of how they will work together to achieve their purpose.[46] They discuss and agree on such details as how tasks will be allocated and how they will make decisions. The team should examine its performance strategies and be amenable to changing them when appropriate. For example, work teams usually standardize at least some processes, but they should be willing to try creative new ideas if the situation calls for them.[47] With a clear, strong, motivating purpose and effective performance strategies, people will pull together into a powerful force that has a chance to achieve extraordinary things.

The team's general purpose should be translated into specific, measurable performance goals.[48] You learned in Chapter 13 about how goals motivate individual performance. Performance can be defined by collective end products instead of an accumulation of individual products.[49] Team-based performance goals help define and distinguish the team's product, encourage communication within the team, energize and motivate team members, provide feedback on progress, signal team victories (and defeats), and ensure that the team focuses clearly on results. It is not simple in practice, but teams with both difficult goals and incentives to attain them tend to achieve the highest performance levels.[50]

The best team-based measurement systems inform top management of the team's level of performance and help the team understand its own processes and gauge its own progress. Ideally, the team plays the lead role in designing its own measurement system. This responsibility is a great indicator of whether the team is truly empowered.[51]

Teams, like individuals, need feedback on their performance. Feedback from customers is especially crucial. Some customers for the team's products are inside the organization. Teams should be responsible for satisfying customers and should be given or should seek performance feedback.

Better yet, wherever possible, teams should interact directly with external customers who make the ultimate buying decisions about their goods and services. External customers typically provide the most honest, and most crucial and useful, performance feedback of all.[52]

Motivating Teamwork

Sometimes individuals work less hard and are less productive when they are members of a group. Such **social loafing** occurs when individuals believe that their contributions are not important, others will do the work for them, their lack of effort will go undetected, or they will be the lone sucker if they work hard but others don't. Perhaps you have seen social loafing in some of your student teams.[53] Conversely, sometimes individuals work harder when they are members of a group than when they are working alone. This **social facilitation effect** occurs because individuals usually are more motivated when others are present, they are concerned with what others think of them, and they want to maintain a positive self-image.

A social facilitation effect is maintained—and a social loafing effect can be avoided—when group members know each other, they can observe and communicate with one

social loafing

Working less hard and being less productive when in a group.

social facilitation effect

Working harder when in a group than when working alone.

another, clear performance goals exist, the task is meaningful to the people working on it, they believe that their efforts matter and others will not take advantage of them, and the culture supports teamwork.[54] Thus, under ideal circumstances, everyone works hard, contributes in concrete ways to the team's work, and is accountable to other team members. Accountability to one another, rather than just to the boss, is an essential aspect of good teamwork. Accountability inspires mutual commitment and trust.[55] Trust in your teammates—and their trust in you—may be the ultimate key to effectiveness.

> Accountability to one another, rather than just to the boss, is an essential aspect of good teamwork.

Team effort is also generated by designing the team's task to be motivating. Techniques for creating motivating tasks appear in the guidelines for job enrichment discussed in Chapter 13. Tasks are motivating when they use a variety of member skills and provide high task variety, identity, significance, autonomy, and performance feedback.

Ultimately, teamwork is motivated by tying rewards to team performance.[56] Furthermore, combining individual and shared rewards can reduce social loafing and increase team performance.[57] If team performance can be measured validly, team-based rewards can be given accordingly.

It is not easy to move from a system of rewards based on individual performance to one based on team performance and cooperation. It also may not be appropriate unless people are truly interdependent and must collaborate to attain true team goals.[58] Team-based rewards are often combined with regular salaries and rewards based on individual performance. At the National Information Solutions Cooperative, which provides utilities with accounting and billing services, rewards for teamwork include bonuses based on the company's and division's financial performance. In addition, individual performance reviews (which affect compensation decisions) include an assessment of how well employees collaborate. Although NISC meets industry standards for salaries, employees say what engages them most is experiencing NISC's supportive climate, encouragement of new ideas, and concern for helping customers.[59]

If team performance is difficult to measure validly, then desired behaviors, activities, and processes that indicate good teamwork can be rewarded. Individuals in teams can be given differential rewards based on teamwork indicated by active participation, cooperation, leadership, and other contributions to the team.

If team members are to be rewarded differentially, such decisions are better *not* left only to the boss.[60] They should be made by the team itself through peer ratings or multirater evaluation systems. Why? Team members are in a better position to observe, know, and make valid reward allocations. Finally, the more teams the organization has, and the more a full team orientation exists, the more valid and effective it will be to distribute rewards via gainsharing and other organizationwide incentives.

Member Contributions

Team members should be selected and trained so that they become effective contributors to the team. The teams themselves often hire their new members. MillerCoors Brewing Company and Eastman Chemical teams select members based on the results of tests designed to predict how well they will contribute to team success in an empowered environment. At Texas Instruments, human resources screens applicants, and then team members interview them and make selection decisions.

Generally, the skills required by teams include technical or functional expertise, problem-solving and decision-making skills, and interpersonal skills. Some managers and teams mistakenly overemphasize some skills, particularly technical or functional ones, and underemphasize the others. A recent study found that groups in which members shared sad feelings performed better at analytical tasks and difficult decisions, and groups did better at creative tasks if they shared positive emotions.[61]

Learning to share emotions appropriately can therefore be an important skill for team success. For the best team performance, all three types of skills should be represented, and developed, among team members.

Norms

Norms are shared beliefs about how people should think and behave. For example, some people like to keep information and knowledge to themselves, but teams should try to establish a norm of knowledge sharing because it can improve team performance.[62] Teams perform better when they think and talk about their tasks (duties, equipment, and resources) and about how they interact with and depend on one another.[63] From the organization's standpoint, norms can be positive or negative. In some teams, everyone works hard; in other groups, employees are antimanagement and do as little work as possible. Some groups develop norms of taking risks, others of being conservative.[64] A norm could dictate that employees speak either favorably or critically of the company. Team members may show concern about poor safety practices, drug and alcohol abuse, and employee theft, or they may not care about these issues (or may even condone such practices). Health consciousness is the norm among executives at some companies, but smoking is the norm at tobacco companies. Some groups have norms of distrust and of being closed toward one another; but as you might guess, norms of trust and open discussion about conflict are better for group performance.[65]

A professor described his consulting experiences at two companies that exhibited different norms in their management teams.[66] At Federal Express Corporation, a young manager interrupted the professor's talk by proclaiming that a recent decision by top management ran counter to the professor's point about corporate planning. He was challenging top management to defend its decision. A hot debate ensued, and after an hour everyone went to lunch without a trace of hard feelings. But at another corporation, the professor opened a meeting by asking a group of top managers to describe the company's culture. There was silence. He asked again. More silence. Then someone passed him an unsigned note that read, "Dummy, can't you see that we can't speak our minds? Ask for the input anonymously, in writing." As you can see, norms are important and can vary greatly from one group to another.

Roles

Roles are different sets of expectations for how different individuals should behave. Whereas norms apply generally to all team members, different roles exist for different members within the norm structure.

Two important sets of roles must be performed.[67] **Task specialist roles** are filled by individuals who have particular job-related skills and abilities. These employees keep the team moving toward accomplishment of the objectives. **Team maintenance roles** develop and maintain harmony within the team. They boost morale, give support, provide humor, soothe hurt feelings, and generally exhibit a concern with members' well-being.

Note the similarity between these roles and the important task performance and group maintenance leadership behaviors you learned about in Chapter 12. As suggested in that chapter, some of these roles will be more important than others at different times and under different circumstances. But these behaviors need not be carried out only by one or two leaders; any member of the team can assume them at

norms

Shared beliefs about how people should think and behave.

roles

Different sets of expectations for how different individuals should behave.

task specialist role

Role requiring stronger job-related skills and abilities.

team maintenance role

Role that develops and maintains team harmony.

The mission of Cassini Imaging Science Team is to guide the cameras that take photos of the outer reaches of space. Though the team is widely dispersed (members' locations include New York, California, and Belgium), they are united by a shared sense of purpose and a high value placed on scientific knowledge and technical excellence.

any time. Both types of roles can be performed by different individuals to maintain an effectively functioning work team.

Beyond what you read about in Chapter 12, what roles should team leaders perform? Superior leaders are better at relating, scouting, persuading, and empowering than are average team leaders.[68] Relating includes exhibiting more social and political awareness, caring for team members, and building trust. Scouting means seeking information from managers, peers, and specialists, and investigating problems systematically. Persuading means not only influencing the team members but also obtaining external support for teams. Empowerment includes delegating authority, being flexible regarding team decisions, and coaching. Leaders also should roll up their sleeves and do real work to accomplish team goals, not just supervise.[69]

Finally, recall from Chapter 12 the importance of team leadership, in which group members rotate or share leadership roles.[70]

Cohesiveness

One of the most important properties of a team is cohesiveness.[71] **Cohesiveness** refers to how attractive the team is to its members, how motivated members are to remain in the team, and the degree to which team members influence one another. In general, it refers to how tightly knit the team is.

The Importance of Cohesiveness   Cohesiveness is important for two primary reasons. First, it contributes to member satisfaction. In a cohesive team, members communicate and get along well with one another. They feel good about being a part of the team. Even if their jobs are unfulfilling or the organization is oppressive, people gain some satisfaction from enjoying their co-workers.

Second, cohesiveness has a major impact on performance. A study of manufacturing teams showed that performance improvements in both quality and productivity occurred in the most cohesive unit, whereas conflict within another team prevented any quality or productivity improvements.[72] Sports fans read about this all the time. When teams are winning, players talk about the team being close, getting along well, and knowing one another's games. In contrast, losing is attributed to infighting and divisiveness.

Cohesiveness clearly can have a positive effect on performance.[73] But this interpretation is simplistic; exceptions to this intuitive relationship occur. Tightly knit work groups can also be disruptive to the organization, such as when they sabotage the assembly line, get their boss fired, or enforce low performance norms. When does high cohesiveness lead to good performance, and when does it result in poor performance? The ultimate outcome depends on the task and on whether the group has high or low performance norms.

The Task   If the task is to make a decision or solve a problem, cohesiveness can lead to poor performance. Groupthink (discussed in Chapter 3) occurs when a tightly knit group is so cooperative that agreeing with one another's opinions and refraining from criticizing others' ideas become norms. For a cohesive group to make good decisions, it should establish a norm of constructive disagreement. This type of debating is important for groups up to the level of boards of directors.[74] In top management teams it has been shown to improve the financial performance of companies.[75]

But the effect of cohesiveness on performance can be positive, particularly if the task is to produce some tangible output. In day-to-day work groups for which decision making is not the primary task, cohesiveness can enhance performance. However, that depends on the group's performance norms.[76]

Performance Norms   Some groups are better than others at ensuring that their members behave the way the group prefers. Cohesive groups are more effective than noncohesive groups at norm enforcement. But the next question is, Do they have norms of high or low performance?

FIGURE 14.1
Cohesiveness, Performance
Norms, and Group
Performance

Performance norms

	Low	**High**
High	High goal attainment (group's perspective) and lowest task performance (management's perspective)	High goal attainment and task performance
Low	Poor goal attainment and task performance	Moderate goal attainment and task performance

Cohesiveness

As Figure 14.1 shows, the highest performance occurs when a cohesive team has high-performance norms. But if a highly cohesive group has low-performance norms, that group will have the worst performance. In the group's eyes, however, it will have succeeded in achieving its goal of poor performance. Noncohesive groups with high-performance norms can be effective from the company's standpoint. However, they won't be as productive as they would be if they were more cohesive. Noncohesive groups with low-performance norms perform poorly, but they will not ruin things for management as effectively as can cohesive groups with low-performance norms.

Building Cohesiveness and High-Performance Norms

As Figure 14.1 suggests, managers should build teams that are cohesive and have high performance norms. The following actions can help create such teams:[77]

1. *Recruit members with similar attitudes, values, and backgrounds.* Similar individuals are more likely to get along with one another. Don't do this, though, if the team's task requires heterogeneous skills and inputs. For example, a homogeneous committee or board might make poor decisions because it will lack different information and viewpoints and may succumb to groupthink. Research has shown that educational diversity and national diversity provide more benefits than limitations to groups' use and application of information.[78]
2. *Maintain high entrance and socialization standards.* Teams and organizations that are difficult to get into have more prestige. Individuals who survive a difficult interview, selection, or training process will be proud of their accomplishment and feel more attachment to the team.
3. *Keep the team small* (but large enough to get the job done). The larger the group, the less important members may feel. Small teams make individuals feel like large contributors.
4. *Help the team succeed, and publicize its successes.* You read about empowerment in the previous chapter; you can empower teams as well as individuals.[79] Be a path–goal leader who facilitates success; the experience of winning brings teams closer together. Then, if you inform superiors of your team's successes, members will believe they are part of an important, prestigious unit. Teams that get into a good performance track continue to perform well as time goes on; groups that don't often enter a downward spiral in which problems compound over time.[80]
5. *Be a participative leader.* Participation in decisions gets team members more involved with one another and striving toward goal accomplishment. Too much autocratic decision making from above can alienate the group from management.

6. *Present a challenge from outside the team.* Competition with other groups makes team members band together to defeat the enemy (witness what happens to school spirit before a big game against an archrival). Some of the greatest teams in business and in science have been focused on winning a competition.[81]

   But don't *you* become the outside threat. If team members dislike you as a boss, they will become more cohesive—but their performance norms will be against you, not with you.

7. *Tie rewards to team performance.* To a large degree, teams are motivated just as individuals are—they do the activities that are rewarded. Make sure that high-performing teams get the rewards they deserve and that poorly performing groups get fewer rewards. You read about this earlier. Bear in mind that not just monetary rewards but also recognition for good work are powerful motivators. Recognize and celebrate team accomplishments. The team will become more cohesive and perform better to reap more rewards. Performance goals will be high, the organization will benefit from higher team motivation and productivity, and the individual needs of team members will be better satisfied. Ideally, being a member of a high-performing team, recognized as such throughout the organization, will become a badge of honor.[82]

But keep in mind that strong cohesiveness encouraging agreeableness can be dysfunctional. For problem solving and decision making, the team should establish norms promoting an open, constructive atmosphere including honest disagreement over issues without personal conflict and animosity.[83]

In Practice

SU2C DREAM TEAMS BUILD COHESIVENESS

High-performance norms are a given for the ten Dream Teams funded by the Stand Up to Cancer (SU2C) campaign. These teams are doing nothing less than bringing together researchers in science and medicine to find more effective ways of defeating cancer. In the traditional approach, a donor such as the National Institutes of Health awards $500,000 to a principal investigator in a particular specialty, who becomes the lead author on the resulting research paper and perhaps also the owner of a patent. In contrast, SU2C gives out millions of dollars at a time, typically in three-year grants to cross-disciplinary teams drawn from multiple institutions and monitored by the American Association for Cancer Research.

An example is the epigenetics team, which is studying the ways enzymes affect the expression of genes, including those that trigger the formation of cancer cells. Although we cannot change the genes we are born with, intentional and unintentional exposure to environmental chemicals does affect the triggering behavior of the enzymes. Scientists on the epigenetics team include geneticists, pathologists, and biochemists; other team members are doctors (oncologists and surgeons), nurses, and technicians. The team has a pair of leaders, Johns Hopkins oncologist Stephen Baylin and Peter Jones, a biochemist and molecular biologist at the University of Southern California. Together, the team members bring their specialized knowledge to bear on the problem. They give up the prestige of independently directing achievements in their narrower specialties in exchange for the satisfaction of making faster progress on major problems.[84]

- How can the SU2C Dream Teams build cohesiveness, given that members are from different disciplines and work for different organizations?

Managing Lateral Relationships

Teams do not function in a vacuum; they are interdependent with other teams. For example, **boundary-spanning** teams are responsible for interfacing with other teams to eliminate production bottlenecks and implement new processes and for working with suppliers on quality issues.[85] Boundary-spanning activities[86] crucial to the team are those that entail dealing with people outside the group.

Managing Outward

Several vital roles link teams to their external environments—that is, to other individuals and groups both inside and outside the organization. A specific type of role that spans team boundaries is the **gatekeeper,** a team member who stays abreast of current information in scientific and other fields and informs the group of important developments. Information useful to the group can also include information about resources, trends, and political support throughout the corporation or the industry.[87]

The team's strategy dictates the team's mix of internally versus externally focused roles and how the mix changes over time. General team strategies include informing, parading, and probing.[88] The **informing** strategy entails making decisions with the team and then telling outsiders of the team's intentions. **Parading** means the team's strategy is to emphasize internal team building and achieve external visibility simultaneously. **Probing** involves a focus on external relations. This strategy requires team members to interact frequently with outsiders; diagnose the needs of customers, clients, and higher-ups; and experiment with solutions before taking action.

The appropriate balance between an internal and external strategic focus and between internal and external roles depends on how much the team needs information, support, and resources from outside. When teams have a high degree of dependence on outsiders, probing is the best strategy. Parading teams perform at an intermediate level, and informing teams are likely to fail. They are too isolated from the outside groups on which they depend.

Informing or parading strategies may be more effective for teams that are less dependent on outside groups—for example, established teams working on routine tasks in stable external environments. But for most important work teams—task forces, new product teams, and strategic decision-making teams tackling unstructured problems in rapidly changing external environments—effective performance in roles that involve interfacing with the outside will be vital.

Lateral Role Relationships

Managing relationships with other groups and teams means engaging in a dynamic give-and-take that ensures proper coordination throughout the management system. To many managers, this process often seems like a chaotic free-for-all. To help understand the process and make it more productive, we can identify and examine the different types of lateral role relationships and take a strategic approach to building constructive relationships.

> Different teams, like different individuals, have roles to perform.

Different teams, like different individuals, have roles to perform. As teams carry out their roles, several distinct patterns of working relationships develop:[89]

1. *Work flow relationships* emerge as materials are passed from one group to another. A group commonly receives work from one unit, processes it, and sends it to the next unit in the process. Your group, then, will come before some groups and after others in the process.
2. *Service relationships* exist when top management centralizes an activity to which a large number of other units must gain access. Common examples are

LO 6

boundary-spanning

Interaction between a group or group member and other people in other groups.

gatekeeper

A team member who keeps abreast of current developments and provides the team with relevant information.

informing

A team strategy that entails making decisions with the team and then informing outsiders of its intentions.

parading

A team strategy that entails simultaneously emphasizing internal team building and achieving external visibility.

probing

A team strategy that requires team members to interact frequently with outsiders, diagnose their needs, and experiment with solutions.

technology services, libraries, and clerical staff. Such units assist other people to help them accomplish their goals.

3. *Advisory relationships* are created when teams with problems call on centralized sources of expert knowledge. For example, staff members in the human resources or legal department advise work teams.

4. *Audit relationships* develop when people not directly in the chain of command evaluate the methods and performances of other teams. Financial auditors check the books, and technical auditors assess the methods and technical quality of the work.

5. *Stabilization relationships* involve auditing before the fact. In other words, teams sometimes must obtain clearance from others—for example, for large purchases—before they take action.

6. *Liaison relationships* involve intermediaries between teams. Managers often are called on to mediate conflict between two organizational units. Public relations people, sales managers, purchasing agents, and others who work across organizational boundaries serve in liaison roles as they maintain communications between the organization and the outside world.

By assessing each working relationship with another unit (from whom do we receive work, and to whom do we send work? what permissions do we control, and to whom must we go for authorizations?), teams can better understand whom to contact and when, where, why, and how to do so. Coordination throughout the working system improves, problems are avoided or short-circuited before they get too serious, and performance improves.[90]

Managing Conflict

LO 7

The complex maze of interdependencies throughout organizations provides many opportunities for conflict to arise among groups and teams. Some conflict is constructive for the organization, as we discussed in Chapter 3. Typically, conflict can foster creativity when it is about ideas rather than personalities. In contrast, team members can be committed to maintaining harmony during meetings, but unresolved differences can spill over into nasty remarks outside the office.[91]

Many factors cause great potential for destructive conflict: the sheer number and variety of contacts, ambiguities in jurisdiction and responsibility, differences in goals, competition for scarce resources, different perspectives held by members of different units, varying time horizons in which some units attend to long-term considerations and others focus on short-term needs, and others. Tensions and anxieties are likely to arise in teams that are demographically diverse, include members from different parts of the organization, or are composed of contrasting personalities. Both demographic and cross-functional heterogeneity initially lead to problems such as stress, lower cooperation, and lower cohesiveness.[92] Transformational leadership (recall Chapter 13), effective diversity management (recall Chapter 11), and constructive conflict management (see the following), can reduce the problems and help realize the often-untapped potential benefits of diversity in teams.[93]

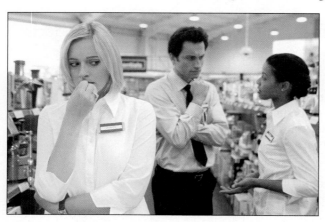

Teams inevitably face conflicts and must decide how to manage them.

Conflict Styles

Teams inevitably face conflicts and must decide how to manage them. The aim should be to make the conflict productive—that is, to make those involved believe they have benefited rather than lost from the conflict.[94] People believe they have benefited from a conflict when (1) a new solution is implemented, the problem is solved, and it is unlikely to emerge again, and (2) work relationships have been strengthened and people believe they can work together productively in the future.

People handle conflict in different ways. You have your own style; others' styles may be similar or may differ. Styles depend in part on the home country's cultural norms. For example, as you learned in Chapter 6, people from some cultures are more concerned with collective than with individual interests, and they are more likely than managers in the United States to turn to higher authorities to make decisions rather than resolve conflicts themselves.[95] But culture aside, any team or individual has several options regarding how to deal with conflicts.[96] These personal styles of dealing with conflict, shown in Figure 14.2, are distinguished based on how much people strive to satisfy their own concerns (the assertiveness dimension) and how much they focus on satisfying the other party's concerns (the cooperation dimension).

For example, a common reaction to conflict is **avoidance.** Here, people do nothing to satisfy themselves or others. They either ignore the problem by doing nothing at all or address it by merely smoothing over or deemphasizing the disagreement. This, of course, fails to solve the problem or clear the air. In a large retail company, employees in the marketing department decided they were tired of dealing with the limits placed on them by the security team of the company's information technology (IT) department. Marketing wanted more communication with consumers, while IT security was obsessed with protecting the company's data from unauthorized access. To avoid the conflict, the marketing group set up a website without telling anyone in IT security.[97]

Accommodation means cooperating on behalf of the other party but not being assertive about one's own interests. **Compromise** involves moderate attention to both parties' concerns, being neither highly cooperative nor highly assertive. This style results in satisficing but not optimizing solutions. **Competing** is a highly competitive response in which people focus strictly on their own wishes and are unwilling to recognize the other person's concerns. Finally, **collaboration** emphasizes both cooperation and assertiveness. The goal is to maximize satisfaction for both parties. At the retail company in the previous example, a consulting firm called Solutionary discovered the website secretly created by the marketing group during a routine test of the company's computer network. Using basic techniques, the consultants were able to hack into the company's network and alter information, such as store prices, very easily. Knowing this would be simple for an outsider to do, the consultants then called together the IT security people and the marketing people to work out a solution that would meet marketing goals without compromising the data in the computer system.[98]

avoidance

A reaction to conflict that involves ignoring the problem by doing nothing at all, or deemphasizing the disagreement.

accommodation

A style of dealing with conflict involving cooperation on behalf of the other party but not being assertive about one's own interests.

compromise

A style of dealing with conflict involving moderate attention to both parties' concerns.

competing

A style of dealing with conflict involving strong focus on one's own goals and little or no concern for the other person's goals.

collaboration

A style of dealing with conflict emphasizing both cooperation and assertiveness to maximize both parties' satisfaction.

FIGURE 14.2
Conflict Management Strategies

SOURCE: K. Thomas, "Conflict and Conflict Management." In *Handbook of Industrial and Organizational Psychology*, ed. M. D. Dunnette. Copyright © 1976. Reprinted by permission of the author.

So imagine you and a friend want to go to a movie together, and you have different movies in mind. If he insists that you go to his movie, he is showing the competing style. If you agree, even though you prefer another movie, you are accommodating. If one of you mentions a third movie that neither of you is excited about but both of you are willing to live with, you are compromising. If you realize you don't know all the options, do some research, and find another movie that you're both enthusiastic about, you are collaborating.

Different approaches are necessary at different times.[99] For example, competing can be necessary for cutting costs or dealing with other scarce resources. Compromise may be useful when people are under time pressure, when they need to achieve a temporary solution, or when collaboration fails. People should accommodate when they learn they are wrong or to minimize loss when they are outmatched. Even avoiding may be appropriate if the issue is trivial or resolving the conflict should be someone else's responsibility.

But when the conflict concerns important issues, when both sets of concerns are valid and important, when a creative solution is needed, and when commitment to the solution is vital to implementation, collaboration is the ideal approach. Collaboration can be achieved by airing feelings and opinions, addressing all concerns, and not letting personal attacks interfere with problem solving. An important technique is to invoke **superordinate goals**—higher-level organizational goals toward which everyone should be striving and that ultimately need to take precedence over personal or unit preferences.[100] A superordinate identity can reduce differences and enhance performance.[101] Collaboration offers the best chance of reaching mutually satisfactory solutions based on the ideas and interests of all parties and of maintaining and strengthening work relationships.

superordinate goals

Higher-level goals taking priority over specific individual or group goals.

Being a Mediator

Managers spend a lot of time trying to resolve conflict between other people. You already may have served as a **mediator,** a third party intervening to help settle a conflict between other people. Third-party intervention, done well, can improve working relationships and help the parties improve their own conflict management, communication, and problem-solving skills.[102]

Some insight comes from a study of human resource (HR) managers and the conflicts with which they deal.[103] HR managers encounter every type of conflict imaginable: interpersonal difficulties from minor irritations to jealousy to fights; operations issues, including union issues, work assignments, overtime, and sick leave; discipline over infractions ranging from drug use and theft to sleeping on the job; sexual harassment and racial bias; pay and promotion issues; and feuds or strategic conflicts among divisions or individuals at the highest organizational levels.

mediator

A third party who intervenes to help others manage their conflict.

HR managers encounter every type of conflict imaginable.

In the study, the HR managers successfully settled most of the disputes. These managers typically follow a four-stage strategy. They investigate by interviewing the disputants and others and gathering more information. While talking with the disputants, they seek both parties' perspectives, remaining as neutral as possible. The discussion should stay issue oriented, not personal. They decide how to resolve the dispute, often in conjunction with the disputants' bosses. In preparing to decide what to do, blame should not be assigned prematurely; at this point they should be exploring solutions. They take action by explaining their decisions and the reasoning, and advise or train the disputants to avoid future incidents. And they follow up by making sure everyone understands the solution, documenting the conflict and the resolution, and monitoring the results by checking back with the disputants and their bosses. Throughout, the objectives of the HR people are to be fully informed so that they understand the conflict; to be active and assertive in trying to resolve it; to be as objective, neutral, and impartial as humanly possible; and to be flexible by modifying their approaches according to the situation.

In Practice

TEAM LEADER AND MEDIATOR

In her management career at IBM, Sharon Nunes has participated in a lot of teams. Nunes, now a vice president at the company, has used her experiences to develop ideas about managing conflicts among team members.

First, Nunes has learned to value diverse viewpoints as a source of creative thinking. She saw how creativity was stifled in a work group led by a manager who preferred to hire employees who had graduated from the same business school. Although the manager and employees bonded over conversations about shared experiences, the work group never produced exceptional results because group members' similar ideas were never challenged. Nunes concluded that she would excel by including people who could deliver different outlooks and experiences.

Nunes realized, however, that diverse outlooks are beneficial only if team members share a common goal. That requires shifting attention away from individual wins in a debate and looking for areas of common ground. Nunes found that she and other team members had to accept challenges to their viewpoints gracefully. For example, when Nunes led a team that was setting up a new health care business, she discovered that team members had strong but varied opinions and different styles. Nunes recognized her logical, fact-oriented approach to thinking, which came from her science background, as an approach she sometimes needed to set aside for the sake of listening, persuading, and keeping the focus on team objectives.[104]

- How does Nunes's role as a team leader resemble the role of a mediator?

Here are some other recommendations for more effective conflict management.[105] Don't allow dysfunctional conflict to build, or hope or assume that it will go away. Address it before it escalates. Try to resolve it, and if the first efforts don't work, try others. And remember the earlier discussion (Chapter 13) of procedural justice. Even if disputants are not happy with your decisions, there are benefits to providing fair treatment, making a good-faith effort, giving them a voice in the proceedings, and so on. Caring about others' goals as well as your own will help ensure a collaborative process. Remember, too, that you may be able to ask HR specialists to help with difficult conflicts.

Electronic and Virtual Conflict

When teams are geographically dispersed, as is often the case for virtual teams, team members tend to experience more conflict and less trust.[106] Conflict management affects the success of virtual teams.[107] In a recent study, avoidance hurt performance. Accommodation—conceding to others to maintain harmony rather than assertively attempting to negotiate integrative solutions—had no effect on performance. Collaboration had a positive effect on performance. The researchers also uncovered two surprises: compromise hurt performance, and competition helped performance. Compromises hurt because they often are watered-down, middle-of-the-road, suboptimal solutions. Competitive behavior was useful because the virtual teams were temporary and under time pressure, so having some individuals behave dominantly and impose decisions to achieve efficiency was more useful than detrimental.

When people have problems in business-to-business e-commerce (e.g., costly delays), they tend to behave competitively and defensively rather than collaboratively.[108] Technical problems and recurring problems test people's patience. The conflict will escalate unless people use more cooperative, collaborative styles. Try to prevent conflicts before they arise; for example, make sure your information system is running smoothly before linking with others. Monitor and reduce or eliminate problems as soon as possible. When problems arise, express your willingness to cooperate, and then actually be cooperative. Even technical problems require the social skills of good management.

In the end, of course, conflicts are part of human relationships, whether they occur online or face to face. Members of a virtual team at a software company and members of a deli team at the nearest Whole Foods Market need relevant skills, such as the ability to communicate and cooperate. As you read "Management Connection: Onward," think about the skills needed to keep diverse employees working constructively at Whole Foods.

MANAGER'S BRIEF

PROGRESS REPORT

ONWARD

Management Connection

COHESIVENESS AND CONFLICT AT WHOLE FOODS MARKET

What unifies employees at Whole Foods Market is the sense of mission and shared values. Serving on a team fulfilling a mission gives each team member a sense of purpose, and the team monitors performance, making sure everyone contributes. In addition, unlike many retailers, Whole Foods schedules most of its employees for full-time work, which enables them to learn more about their jobs, build stronger team relationships, and develop a greater commitment to the organization.

A challenge to cohesiveness, however, is one of the very values the company espouses: appreciation of diversity. Whole Foods stresses its commitment to hiring employees from many ethnic backgrounds. Compared with other supermarkets, its dress code offers wide latitude for personal style. To counteract misunderstandings that can occur when people come from different backgrounds and express themselves differently, the company expects team members to communicate frequently and respectfully and to show appreciation for what others contribute.

CEO John Mackey sees a role for competition as well as collaboration. The company encourages teams to compete with one another to be best at what they do. For example, the produce teams might strive to have the biggest sales increase in their region or among all the company's stores. The glory of being the best Whole Foods produce team is a compelling motivator, with or without a bonus. As team members collaborate in trying to outdo

other teams, they build the sense of identity Mackey sees in what he considers the company's strongest teams. Some teams, for example, invent team names.

Beyond this kind of desirable competition among teams, conflicts do occur within teams. In one incident that recently made national news, two team members at a store in Albuquerque were suspended (with pay) after they became upset during a team meeting. At the meeting, discussion turned to the men's use of Spanish at work. The two men interpreted statements by the team leader to mean they were forbidden from speaking Spanish while on the job, and they became angry. Management saw their anger as "rude and disrespectful both in an office and in the store in front of customers," so the two were suspended. Through official statements, Whole Foods said it uses English as its "default" language, especially for safety matters, but does not forbid the speaking of other languages. It added that its leadership team would soon review the company's language policy.[109]

- How does Whole Foods promote team cohesiveness? What else can it do?
- How should Whole Foods manage the conflict in its Albuquerque store? What should it do to minimize similar conflicts in the future?
- If you were in this situation, would your conflict management styles involve avoidance, accommodation, compromise, competition, or collaboration? Why?

KEY TERMS

accommodation, p. 487

autonomous work groups, p. 475

avoidance, p. 487

boundary-spanning, p. 485

cohesiveness, p. 482

collaboration, p. 487

competing, p. 487

compromise, p. 487

gatekeeper, p. 485

informing, p. 485

management teams, p. 473

mediator, p. 488

norms, p. 481

parading, p. 485

parallel teams, p. 473

probing, p. 485

project and development teams, p. 473

roles, p. 481

self-designing teams, p. 475

self-managed teams, p. 474

social facilitation effect, p. 479

social loafing, p. 479

superordinate goals, p. 488

task specialist roles, p. 481

team, p. 476

teaming, p. 474

team maintenance roles, p. 481

traditional work groups, p. 474

transnational teams, p. 473

virtual teams, p. 473

work teams, p. 472

SUMMARY OF LEARNING OBJECTIVES

Now that you have studied Chapter 14, you should be able to:

LO 1   Discuss how teams can contribute to an organization's effectiveness.

Teams are building blocks for organization structure and forces for productivity, quality, cost savings, speed, change, and innovation. They have the potential to provide many benefits for both the organization and individual members.

LO 2   Describe different types of teams.

Compared with traditional work groups that were closely supervised, today's teams have more authority and often are self-managed. Teams now are used in many more ways, for many more purposes, than in the past. Generally, types of teams include work teams, project and development teams, parallel teams, management teams, transnational teams, and virtual teams. Types of work teams range from traditional groups with low autonomy to self-designing teams with high autonomy.

LO 3   Summarize how groups become teams.

Groups carry on a variety of important developmental processes, including forming, storming, norming, and performing. A true team has members who complement one another; who are committed to a common purpose, performance goals, and approach; and who hold themselves accountable to one another.

LO 4   Explain why groups sometimes fail.

Teams do not always work well. Some companies underestimate the difficulties of moving to a team-based approach. Teams require training, empowerment, and a well-managed transition to make them work. Groups may fail to become effective teams unless managers and team members commit to the idea, understand what makes teams work, and implement appropriate practices.

LO 5   Describe how to build an effective team.

Create a team with a high-performance focus by establishing a common purpose, translating the purpose into measurable team goals, designing the team's task so it is intrinsically motivating, designing a team-based performance measurement system, and providing team rewards.

Work to develop a common understanding of how the team will perform its task. Make it clear that everyone has to work hard and contribute in concrete ways. Establish mutual accountability and build trust among members. Examine the team's strategies periodically and be willing to adapt.

Make sure members contribute fully by selecting them appropriately, training them, and checking that all important roles are carried out. Take a variety of steps to establish team cohesiveness and high performance norms.

And don't just manage inwardly. Manage the team's relations with outsiders, too.

LO 6   List methods for managing a team's relationships with other teams.

Perform important roles such as gatekeeping, informing, parading, and probing. Identify the types of lateral role relationships you have with outsiders. This can help coordinate efforts throughout the work system.

LO 7   Identify ways to manage conflict.

Managing lateral relationships well can prevent some conflict. But conflict arises because of the sheer number of contacts, ambiguities, goal differences, competition for scarce resources, and different perspectives and time horizons. Depending on the situation, five basic interpersonal approaches to managing conflict can be used: avoidance, accommodation, compromise, competition, and collaboration. Superordinate goals offer a focus on higher-level organizational goals that can help generate a collaborative relationship. Techniques for managing conflict between other parties include acting as a mediator and managing virtual conflict.

DISCUSSION QUESTIONS

1. Why do you think some people resist the idea of working in teams? How would you deal with their resistance?

2. Consider a job you have held. To what extent did you work in teams, and how effective was the teamwork? What affected the effectiveness?

3. Experts say that teams are a means, not an end. What do you think they mean? What do you think happens in a company that creates teams just for the sake of having teams because it's a fad or because it sounds good? How can this pitfall be avoided?

4. Choose a sports team with which you are familiar. Assess its effectiveness and discuss the factors that contribute to its level of effectiveness.

5. Assess the effectiveness, as in Question 4, of a student group with which you have been affiliated. Could anything have been done to make it more effective?

6. Consider the various roles members have to perform for a team to be effective. Which roles would play to your strengths, and which to your weaknesses? How can you become a better team member?

7. Discuss personal examples of virtual conflict and how they were managed, well or poorly.

8. What do you think are your own most commonly used approaches to handling conflict? Least common? What can you do to expand your repertoire and become more effective at conflict management?

9. Generate real examples of how superordinate goals have helped resolve a conflict. Identify some current conflicts and provide some specific ideas for how superordinate goals could be used to help.

10. Have you ever been part of a group that was self-managed? What was good about it, and what not so good? Why do many managers resist this idea? Why do some people love the idea of being a member of such a team, while others don't?

11. How might self-managed teams operate differently in different cultures? What are the advantages, disadvantages, and implications of homogeneous versus highly diverse self-managed teams?

EXPERIENTIAL EXERCISES

14.1   PRISONERS' DILEMMA: AN INTERGROUP COMPETITION

INSTRUCTIONS

1. The instructor explains what will take place in this exercise and assigns people to groups. Two types of teams are formed and named Red and Blue (with no more than eight per group) and are not to communicate with the other team in any way, verbally or nonverbally, except when told to do so by the instructor. Groups are given time to study the Prisoners' Dilemma Tally Sheet.

2. (3 min.) Round 1. Each team has three minutes to make a team decision. Write your decisions when the instructor says time is up.

3. (2 min.) The choices of the teams are announced for Round 1. The scores are entered on the Tally Sheet.

4. (4–5 min.) Round 2 is conducted in the same manner as Round 1.

5. (6 min.) Round 3 is announced as a special round for which the payoff points are doubled. Each team is instructed to send one representative to chairs in the center of the room. After representatives have conferred for three minutes,

they return to their teams. Teams then have three minutes, as before, in which to make their decisions. When recording their scores, they should be reminded that points indicated by the payoff schedule are doubled for this round only.

6. (8–10 min.) Rounds 4, 5, and 6 are conducted in the same manner as the first three rounds.

7. (6 min.) Round 7 is announced as a special round, in which the payoff points are squared (multiplied by themselves: e.g., a score of 4 would be $4^2 = 16$). A minus sign would be retained (e.g., $-(3)^2 = -9$). Team representatives meet for three minutes; then the teams meet for three minutes. At the instructor's signal, the teams write their choices, and then the two choices are announced.

8. (6 min.) Round 8 is handled exactly as Round 7 was. Payoff points are squared.

9. (10–20 min.) The point total for each team is announced, and the sum of the two team totals is calculated and compared with the maximum positive or negative outcomes (+108 or −108 points).

Prisoners' Dilemma Tally Sheet

INSTRUCTIONS:

For 10 successive rounds, the Red team will choose either an A or a B and the Blue team will choose either an X or a Y. The score each team receives in a round is determined by the pattern made by the choices of both teams, according to the following schedule:

PAYOFF SCHEDULE:

AX—Both teams win 3 points.
AY—Red team loses 6 points; Blue team wins 6 points.
BX—Red team wins 6 points; Blue team loses 6 points.
BY—Both teams lose 3 points.

Scorecard:

Round	Minutes	Choice		Cumulative Points	
		Red Team	Blue Team	Red Team	Blue Team
1	3				
2	3				
3*	3 (reps.), 3(teams)				
4	3				
5	3				
6*	3 (reps.), 3(teams)				
7**	3 (reps.), 3(teams)				
8**	3 (reps.), 3(teams)				

*Payoff points are doubled for this round.
**Payoff points are squared for this round. (Retain the minus sign.)
SOURCE: Dorothy Hai, "Prisoner's Dilemma," in *Organizational Behavior: Experiences and Cases,* 1E. Copyright © 1986. South-Western, a part of Cengage Learning, Inc. Reproduced with permission. www.cengage.com/permissions

14.2 THE TRAVELER'S CHECK SCAM GROUP EXERCISE

INSTRUCTIONS

1. (3 min.) Each group selects an observer. The observer remains silent during the group problem-solving process, recording the activities of the group on the Observer's Report Form.

2. (15 min.) Group members read the following problem and proceed to solve it.

3. (2 min.) When the group has a solution to the problem upon which all members agree, it will be written on a note and handed to the instructor.

4. (5 min.) The observer briefs the group on the problem-solving processes observed during the exercise.

5. (25 min.) The small group discusses the following topics:

   a. Did the group decide on a problem solution process before it attempted to solve the problem? If so, what was it?

   b. Was the solution of the problem hindered in any way by the lack of an appropriate agreed-upon group problem-solving process? Explain.

   c. Who were the leaders of the group during the exercise? What did they do? Critique their leadership activities.

   d. What communications patterns were used by the group during the exercise? Who participated the most? Who participated the least? Describe individual behaviors.

   e. Did the group solve the problem? How many members of the group discovered the correct answer on their own?

   f. Was using the group to solve this problem better than assigning the problem to one person? Explain the rationale for your answer.

THE CASE OF MICKEY THE DIP

Mickey the Dip, an expert pickpocket and forger, liked to work the Los Angeles International Airport on busy days. His technique was to pick the pockets of prosperous-looking victims just before they boarded planes to the East Coast. This gave Mickey five hours to use stolen credit cards before the owners could report their losses.

One morning Mickey snatched a fat wallet from a traveler and left the airport to examine his loot. To his surprise he found no credit cards but instead $500 in traveler's checks. After 20 minutes of practice, Mickey could sign a perfect imitation of the victim's signature. He then proceeded to a large department store where all suits were being sold for 75 percent off the regular price. Mickey purchased a suit for $225 and paid for it with $300 in stolen traveler's checks. After the clerk who served him went to lunch, he bought another suit for $150 and paid for it with the remaining $200 of stolen traveler's checks. Later, Mickey switched the labels on the two suits and, using the receipt from the $225 suit, returned the $150 suit at a centralized return desk for a refund. The refund clerk took the suit and gave Mickey eleven $20 bills, which he stuffed into his pocket and disappeared.

When the department store deposited the traveler's checks, they were returned as forgeries. Assuming the store normally sold suits at twice their wholesale price and used 10 percent of sales as an overhead cost figure, what was the cash value of the loss suffered by the store as a result of Mickey's caper? Do not consider taxes in your computations.

THE TRAVELER'S CHECK SCAM EXERCISE OBSERVER'S REPORT

1. What happened during the first few minutes the group met after members finished reading the problem? (List behaviors of specific group members.)

2. Identify the group role played by each group member during the exercise. Give examples of the behavior of each.

3. Were there any conflicts within or among group members during the exercise? Explain the nature of the conflicts and the behavior of the individual(s) involved.

4. How were decisions made in the group? Give specific examples.

5. How could the group improve its problem-solving skills?

SOURCE: Peter P. Dawson, *Fundamentals of Organizational Behavior*. Copyright © 1985 Pearson Education, Inc. Reprinted by permission of Pearson Education, Inc., Upper Saddle River, NJ.

CONCLUDING CASE

EXCEL PRO DRILLING SYSTEMS

Based in Alabama, Excel Pro Drilling Systems sells drilling equipment around the world. Its factories in Brazil, China, the Czech Republic, India, and South Africa run three shifts to keep up with strong demand in developing nations. Excel Pro enjoys profitability, but environmental groups have expressed concern about its impact on climate change. As executives explored their response, they saw that achieving more sustainable resource use also could make the company more efficient and create a more favorable business environment for the long term.

The executives decided to form a group called the Excel Pro Green Team, made up of representatives in each of its locations. Each facility's managers chose three employees, one each from engineering, production, and finance, with leadership skills, English-language ability, and interest in the topic of environmental sustainability. These 18 employees formed the Green Team.

To save money as well as fuel, the Green Team operates as a virtual team. Its members meet by videoconferencing once a month. Between meetings, they share thoughts via e-mail and in a social-media-style page Excel Pro created for this purpose.

Initially, all the Green Team members were enthusiastic. The Czech and Brazilian representatives even came to the first meeting with specific ideas. Other team members were inspired to prepare ideas for the next meeting, but several were concerned that the team needed a plan establishing goals and a time line before the team addressed specific actions. Most of the third meeting was devoted to debating whether to establish an action plan or refine the ideas already submitted. Frustrated, the South African representatives took one idea to their facility's management for approval and began to implement it without telling the rest of the team.

By the fourth meeting, the representatives in India and the Czech Republic were openly complaining that meetings were always scheduled at times convenient for the headquarters employees. The Chinese team members agreed; in fact, one had quietly stopped attending meetings, although she did continue to participate in the exchange of e-mail ideas. The debate about whether headquarters should always schedule meetings lasted for 45 minutes, after which no one was in any mood to discuss sustainability.

Two of the Alabama team representatives took their frustration to their managers. The executive team investigated and decided the team needed to be unified behind a common goal. They directed the team to present three resource-saving ideas by the end of the year, and they offered a reward system to promote teamwork. The team members are each allocated 100 points a month. Whenever one team member appreciates another's actions, he or she gives that person points. All team members' point scores are viewable by the whole team at a shared website. At the end of the year, the points earned by each employee will be exchanged for cash rewards in the local currency. The executives hope the program will motivate greater cooperation.

DISCUSSION QUESTIONS

1. What went wrong in the formation of the Green Team? What should Excel Pro have done differently?

2. What conditions contribute to this team's cohesiveness? What reduces cohesiveness?

3. What do you think of the points plan? How should Excel Pro's management help the Green Team manage its conflict?

CHAPTER 15

Communicating

The single biggest problem with communication is the illusion that it has taken place.

— G. B. Shaw

LEARNING OBJECTIVES

After studying Chapter 15, you will be able to:

LO 1   Discuss important advantages of two-way communication. p. 498

LO 2   Identify communication problems to avoid. p. 499

LO 3   Describe when and how to use the various communication channels. p. 501

LO 4   Summarize ways to become a better sender and receiver of information. p. 506

LO 5   Explain how to improve downward, upward, and horizontal communication. p. 512

LO 6   Summarize how to work with the company grapevine. p. 516

LO 7   Describe the boundaryless organization and its advantages. p. 517

CHAPTER OUTLINE

Interpersonal Communication
One-Way versus Two-Way Communication
Communication Pitfalls
Mixed Signals and Misperception
Oral and Written Channels
Electronic Media
Media Richness

Improving Communication Skills
Improving Sender Skills
Nonverbal Skills
Improving Receiver Skills

Organizational Communication
Downward Communication
Upward Communication
Horizontal Communication
Informal Communication
Boundarylessness

Management Connection

HOW YAHOO'S MARISSA MAYER TRIED TO GET EMPLOYEES TALKING

Before Google, there was Yahoo, one of the most popular Internet search engines of the 1990s. The company, founded by two Stanford graduate students, was innovative and fun, its employees calling themselves Yahoos. But then Yahoo became—at least in Internet years—a stodgy old-timer. Despite hanging onto 700 million users, Yahoo had falling revenues and market share and a shrinking workforce. It was launching no hit products for mobile devices or social media.

To bring new life to Yahoo, its board of directors turned to today's most popular Internet search firm, Google, and recruited away Marissa Mayer. Mayer, Google's vice president of location and local services, was one of its original employees (its first female engineer). She has a reputation for being brilliant, hardworking, and highly successful at developing people.

One of Mayer's chief concerns when she arrived at Yahoo was that employees seemed detached and demoralized. At other big-name Internet companies and hot start-ups, employees labor through the night, but Yahoo's parking lots emptied out promptly at five. Mayer was determined to reignite the company's former enthusiasm. She started with a memo announcing her longstanding respect for Yahoo and determination to make it "the absolute best place to work," and she set up weekly Friday meetings to bring everyone up to speed on her plans and Yahoo's performance. Yahoo also began offering free food in its cafeteria and gave its employees new smartphones.

Mayer's next move sparked controversy. She decided to bring people close together by requiring their presence in the workplace. In a memo from HR director Jackie Reses, Yahoo announced that employees would

> "People are more collaborative and innovative when they're together."
>
> Marissa Mayer, Yahoo CEO

no longer be allowed work-from-home arrangements; they must be at the office with their colleagues. Reses wrote, "We need to be one Yahoo!, and that starts with physically being together."

Some employees were angry enough to leak the memo, though it was labeled confidential. Within days, people inside and outside Yahoo were furiously questioning the end of telecommuting. Most critics predicted demotivation or saw hypocrisy in a CEO who had recently given birth imposing restrictions that could make scheduling more difficult for working parents. However, Mayer insisted the new policy is not about motivation or child care, but about bringing employees close together so they can communicate more easily. Employees who happen to pass by each other's desks or sit near one another at lunch are likelier to build ties, ask questions, and trade ideas. Those interactions, Mayer believes, will open the door to more innovation and camaraderie.[1]

Marissa Mayer values spontaneous workplace conversations so much that she risked criticism by banning the practice of working from home. As you read this chapter, consider how communication among employees can build commitment and nourish creativity.

As Yahoo's Marissa Mayer is well aware, effective communication is a fundamental component of work performance and organizational effectiveness.[2] It is a primary means by which managers carry out the responsibilities described throughout this book, such as making group decisions, sharing a vision, coordinating individuals and work groups, hiring and motivating employees, and leading teams. In these and other areas, managers have to be able to share thoughts clearly and convincingly, and they have to listen effectively to others. In this chapter, we present important communication concepts and some practical guidelines for improving your effectiveness. We also discuss communication at the organizational level.

Interpersonal Communication

communication

The transmission of information and meaning from one party to another through the use of shared symbols.

Communication is the transmission of information and meaning from one party to another through the use of shared symbols. Figure 15.1 shows a general model of how one person communicates with another.

The sender initiates the process by conveying information to the receiver—the person for whom the message is intended. The sender has a meaning he or she wishes to communicate and encodes the meaning into symbols (the words chosen for the message). Then the sender transmits, or sends, the message through some channel, such as a verbal or written medium.

The receiver decodes the message (e.g., reads it) and attempts to interpret the sender's meaning. The receiver may provide feedback to the sender by encoding a message in response to the sender's message.

The communication process often is hampered by noise, or interference in the system, that blocks perfect understanding. Noise could be anything that interferes with accurate communication: ringing telephones, thoughts about other things, or simple fatigue or stress. The model in Figure 15.1 is more than a theoretical treatment of the communication process: it points out the key ways in which communications can break down. Mistakes can be made at each stage of the model. A manager who is alert to potential problems can perform each step carefully to ensure more effective communication. The model also helps explain the topics discussed next: the differences between one-way and two-way communication, communication pitfalls, misperception, and the various communication channels.

one-way communication

A process in which information flows in only one direction—from the sender to the receiver, with no feedback loop.

One-Way versus Two-Way Communication

 LO 1

In **one-way communication**, information flows in only one direction—from the sender to the receiver, with no feedback loop. A manager sends an e-mail to a subordinate without asking for a response. An employee phones the information technology (IT) department and leaves a message requesting repairs for her computer. A supervisor scolds a production worker about defects and then storms away.

two-way communication

A process in which information flows in two directions—the receiver provides feedback, and the sender is receptive to the feedback.

When receivers respond to senders—Person B becomes the sender and Person A the receiver—**two-way communication** has occurred. One-way communication in situations like those just described can become two-way if the manager's e-mail invites the receiver to reply with any questions, the IT department returns the employee's call and asks for details about the computer problem, and the supervisor calms down and listens to the production worker's explanation of why defects are occurring.

FIGURE 15.1
A Model of One-Way Communication

True two-way communication means not only that the receiver provides feedback but also that the sender is receptive to the feedback. In these constructive exchanges, information is shared between both parties rather than merely delivered from one person to the other.

Because it is faster and easier for the sender, one-way communication is much more common than it should be. A busy executive finds it easier to dash off an e-mail message than to discuss a nagging problem with a subordinate. Also, he doesn't have to deal with questions or be challenged by someone who disagrees.

Two-way communication is more difficult and time-consuming than one-way communication. However, it is more accurate; fewer mistakes occur, and fewer problems arise. When receivers have a chance to ask questions, share concerns, and make suggestions or modifications, they understand more precisely what is being communicated and what they should do with the information.[3] Effectively sharing information among teammates is a prime contributor to performance.[4]

These advantages of two-way communication are why Cisco manager Randy Pond wants to see and hear the people he is meeting with. If some participants are in remote locations, Pond, who is Cisco's executive vice president of operations, processes, and systems, uses a videoconference. During one such meeting, when Pond made a statement, he watched his colleagues on his computer screen and noticed that one put his head in his hands. Pond reminded the participants that he could see them, adding, "If you disagree, tell me." This prodding opened up a fuller discussion of the ideas under consideration.[5]

Communication Pitfalls

As we know from personal experience, the sender's intended message does not always get across to the receiver. You are operating under an illusion if you think there is a perfect correlation between what you say and what people hear.[6] Errors can occur in all stages of the communication process. In the encoding stage, words can be misused, decimal points entered in the wrong places, facts left out, or ambiguous phrases inserted. In the transmission stage, a message may get lost on a cluttered desk, the words on the screen could be too small to read from the back of the room, or words might be spoken with ambiguous inflections.

Decoding problems arise when the receiver doesn't listen carefully or reads too quickly and overlooks a key point. And of course receivers can misinterpret the message: A reader draws the wrong conclusion from an unclear text message, a listener takes a general statement by the boss too personally, or a sideways glance is taken the wrong way.

More generally, people's perceptual and filtering processes create misinterpretations. **Perception** is the process of receiving and interpreting information. As you know, such processes are not perfectly objective. They are subjective because people's self-interested motives and attitudes toward the sender and toward the message create biased interpretations. People often assume that others share their views and naturally pay more attention to their own views than to those of others.[7] But perceptual differences get in the way of shared consensus. To remedy this situation, it helps to remember that others' viewpoints are legitimate and to incorporate others' perspectives into your interpretation of issues.[8] Generally, adopting another person's viewpoint is fundamental to working collaboratively. And your ability to take others' perspectives—for instance, really to understand the viewpoints of customers or suppliers—can result in higher assessments of your performance.[9]

Filtering is the process of withholding, ignoring, or distorting information. Senders do this, for example, when they tell the boss what they think the boss wants to hear or give unwarranted compliments rather than honest criticism. Receivers also filter information; they may fail to recognize an important message or attend to some aspects of the message but not others.

A manager at a magazine who tended to phrase the assignments she gave her reporters as questions—"How would you like to do the X project with Y?" and "I was thinking of putting you on the X project; is that okay?"—was criticized by her male boss, who told her she did not assume the proper demeanor with her staff.[10] Another,

Bottom Line

Don't expect to deliver results without communicating effectively in all directions of the compass.

How can two-way communication with your supervisor help you deliver results as an employee?

perception

The process of receiving and interpreting information.

filtering

The process of withholding, ignoring, or distorting information.

the owner of a retail operation, told one of her store managers to do something by saying, "The bookkeeper needs help with the billing. How would you feel about helping her out?" He said fine but didn't do it. Whereas the boss thought he meant he would do it, he said he meant to indicate how he would feel about helping. He decided he had better things to do.[11]

Because of such filtering and perceptual differences, you cannot assume the other person means what you think he means or understands the meanings you intend. Managers need to excel at reading interactions and adjusting their communication styles and perceptions to the people with whom they interact.[12] The very human tendencies to filter and perceive subjectively underlie much of the need for more effective communication practices that you will read about in the rest of this chapter.

Mixed Signals and Misperception

A common thread underlying the discussion so far is that people's perceptions can undermine attempts to communicate. People do not pay attention to everything going on around them. They inadvertently send mixed signals that can undermine the intended messages. Different people attend to different things, and people interpret the same thing in different ways. All of this creates problems in communication.

If the communication is between people from different cultures, these problems are magnified.[13] Communication breakdowns often occur when business transactions take place between people from different countries.[14] Chapter 6 introduced you to the importance of these cultural issues.

The following example highlights the operation of mixed signals and misperceptions. A bank CEO knew that to be competitive he had to downsize his organization, and the employees who remained would have to commit to customer service, become more empowered, and really earn customer loyalty.[15] Knowing that his employees would have doubts and concerns about the coming reorganization, he decided to make a promise to them that he would do his best to guarantee employment to the survivors.

What signals did the CEO communicate to his people by his promises? One positive signal was that he cared about his people. But he also signaled that *he* would

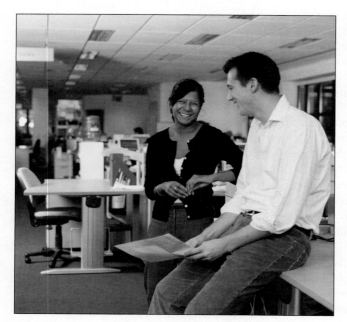

Any interpersonal situation holds potential for perceptual errors, filtering, and other communication breakdowns.

take care of *them*, thus undermining his goal of giving them more responsibility and empowering them. The employees wanted management to take responsibility for the market challenge that *they* needed to face—to handle things for them when in fact *they* needed to learn the new ways of doing business. Inadvertently, the CEO spoke to their backward-looking need for security when he had meant to make them see that the bank's future depended on their efforts. However, the CEO did avoid one common pitfall at companies that announce plans for downsizing or outsourcing: ignoring the emotional significance of the message.[16] Sometimes managers are so intent on delivering the business rationale for the changes that they fail to acknowledge the human cost of layoffs. When employees hear a message that neglects to address their feelings, they generally interpret the message to mean that managers don't care.

Consider how many problems can be avoided—and how much more effective communication can be—if people take the time to (1) ensure that the receivers attend to the message they are sending, (2) consider the other party's frame of reference and attempt to convey the message with that viewpoint in mind, (3) take concrete steps to minimize perceptual errors and improper signals in both sending and receiving, and (4) send consistent messages. You should make an effort to predict people's interpretations of your messages and think in terms of how they could misinterpret your messages. It helps to say not only what you mean but also what you don't mean. Every time you say "I am not saying X, I am saying Y," you eliminate a possible misinterpretation.[17]

Oral and Written Channels

LO 3

Communication can be sent through a variety of channels (step 3 in the Figure 15.1 model), including oral, written, and electronic. Each channel has advantages and disadvantages.

Oral communication includes face-to-face discussion, telephone conversations, and formal presentations and speeches. Advantages are that questions can be asked and answered, feedback is immediate and direct, the receiver(s) can sense the sender's sincerity (or lack thereof), and oral communication is more persuasive and sometimes less expensive than written. However, oral communication also has disadvantages: it can lead to spontaneous, ill-considered statements (and regret), and there is no permanent record of it (unless an effort is made to record it).

Written communication includes e-mail, memos, letters, reports, computer files, and other written documents. Advantages to using written messages are that the message can be revised several times, it is a permanent record that can be saved, the message stays the same even if relayed through many people, and the receiver has more time to analyze the message. Disadvantages are that the sender has no control over where, when, or if the message is read; the sender does not receive immediate feedback; the receiver may not understand parts of the message; and the message must be longer to contain enough information to answer anticipated questions.[18]

You should weigh these considerations when deciding whether to communicate orally or in writing. Also, sometimes use both channels, such as following up a meeting with a confirming memo or writing an e-mail to prepare someone for your phone call.

Electronic Media

Among other things, electronic media provide opportunities for individuals to multi-communicate: engage in more than one conversation at the same time.[19] In electronic decision rooms, software supports simultaneous access to shared files and allows people to share views and do work collectively.[20] Other means of electronic communication include teleconferencing, in which groups of people in different locations interact over telephone lines and perhaps also see one another on television monitors as they participate in group discussions (videoconferencing). And you probably are intimately familiar with e-mail, instant messaging, text messaging, and blogging.

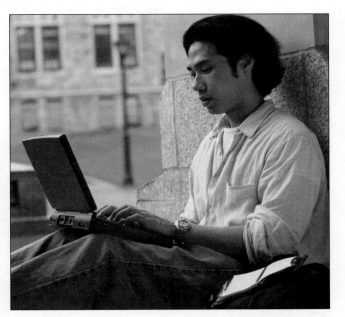

Recently, as we shall see, social media have made their way into the workplace as well.

E-mail is a fundamental tool of workplace communication. In fact, for some kinds of work, employees spend a substantial part of each workday reading and replying to e-mail messages. For short messages and to get a quick reply, workers also may use text messages or instant messaging (IMing). And employers are catching up with consumers in their use of social media. Close to four in ten companies communicate on video-sharing sites and blogs, and roughly a quarter use wikis (publications with contributions from many authors and users) and micro-blogging (such as Twitter).[21] Generally, social media invite comments from an entire network of users. Suppose a company uses a blog to communicate with the external environment (for example, sharing information about products or corporate social responsibility) or with employees (for example, posts about company initiatives or employee accomplishments). The blog's audience typically can comment in reply to each blog post.

E-mail is one of the most convenient forms of communication, but what are some of the pitfalls? How often have you sent an e-mail, whether personal or professional, and found that someone misinterpreted the message?

Bottom Line

Imagine how much time you would lose if you couldn't communicate electronically; imagine the savings of money and natural resources you could create if your company and its people sought and used the most cost-effective ways to communicate.

What forms of electronic communication do you use (on the job or for personal use)?

Advantages   Advantages of electronic communication are numerous and dramatic. Within firms, the advantages include the sharing of more information and speed and efficiency in delivering routine messages to large numbers of people across vast geographic areas. Discussing ideas with colleagues in other cities is much faster and less expensive with teleconferencing or corporate social media than when the colleagues must travel to be at the same location. Business-related wikis such as Socialtext let project teams post their ideas in one forum for others to add contributions. Socialtext allows project leaders to grant users access based on their need to know and participate. Web Crossing uses wikis for product development. The wikis save the company "untold amounts of paper, postage, meetings, travel budgets, conference calls, and the time required to coordinate it all."[22]

Some companies, including Boeing, use brainstorming software that allows anonymous contributions, presuming it will add more honesty to internal discussions. Some research indicates more data sharing and critical argumentation, and higher-quality decisions, with a group decision support system than is found in face-to-face meetings.[23] Others are concerned that anonymity tempts participants to make careless, rude, or ill-advised statements, so they require identities to be revealed, or they limit access to social networking technologies. However, a growing number of companies see services such as LinkedIn, Twitter, and Facebook as necessary for staying in touch with the hundreds of millions of people who use these services—especially the younger generations of co-workers and customers, who are likelier to check tweets and texts than voice mail and e-mail.[24]

Disadvantages   Disadvantages of electronic communication include the difficulty of solving complex problems that require more extended, face-to-face interaction and the inability to pick up subtle, nonverbal, or inflectional clues about what the communicator is thinking or conveying. Perhaps partly for this reason, people are more willing to lie online.[25] In online bargaining—even before it begins—negotiators distrust one another more than in face-to-face negotiations. After the negotiation (compared with face-to-face negotiators), people usually are less satisfied with their outcomes, even when the outcomes are economically equivalent.[26]

Although organizations rely heavily on computer-aided communication for group decision making, face-to-face groups generally take less time, make higher-quality decisions, and are more satisfying for members.[27] E-mail is most appropriate for routine messages that do not require the exchange of large quantities of complex information. It is less suitable for confidential information, resolving conflicts, or negotiating.[28] Employees have reported being laid off via e-mail and even text messages.[29] Not only do these more impersonal forms of communication cause hurt feelings, but an upset employee can also easily forward messages, and forwarding often has a snowball effect that can embarrass everyone involved.

Companies are worried about leaks and negative portrayals, and they may require employees to agree to specific guidelines before they post information on

Cisco employees in New York, left, and San Jose, California, on screen, meeting via monitor. What are the advantages and disadvantages to using this type of technology to communicate?

blogs or networking sites or use a microblogging service such as Twitter. IBM handled this challenge by inviting employees to draft guidelines for using social media. The employees' ideas were reviewed by members of the company's human resources, marketing, finance, communications, and legal departments and then became company policy. When IBM employees use social media, they are expected to follow company rules for business conduct, identify themselves, be respectful, speak for themselves (not say they represent the company), and avoid disclosing company secrets or defaming competitors. The company has concluded that using this policy to train employees is less risky than either trying to keep people away from networking altogether or failing to train them in appropriate conduct.[30]

Two results of electronic communication are a proliferation of negative and nasty messages, and misinterpretations. People hurl insults, vent frustration, snitch on coworkers to the boss, and otherwise breach protocol. The lack of nonverbal cues can result in kidding remarks being taken seriously, causing resentment and regret.[31] People see negative meanings in neutral messages[32] and are more likely to lie electronically and to feel justified in doing so.[33] Also, it is not unheard of for confidential messages—including details about people's personal lives and insulting, embarrassing remarks—to become public knowledge through electronic leaks.

Other downsides to electronic communication are important to know.[34] Different people and sometimes different working units latch onto different channels as their medium of choice. For example, many Generation Y workers and customers (born in 1980 or later) tend to ignore voice mail and infrequently check e-mail because they expect these messages to be mostly spam.[35] Another disadvantage is that electronic messages sometimes are seen by those for whom they are not intended. Be careful with whether you click Reply or Reply to All, set your message notifications not to pop up when you're using your computer for a presentation, and remember that any message you put online might be reposted or forwarded to others. Many companies use software to monitor electronic messages. And the messages can be used in court cases to indict individuals or companies. Electronic messages sent from work and on company-provided devices are private property—but they are private property of the system's owner, not of the sender.

> Electronic messages are private property of the system's owner, not of the sender.

Here's a golden rule (like the sunshine rule in the ethics chapter): Don't hit Send or post a comment unless you'd be comfortable having the contents on the front page of a newspaper, being read by your mother or a competitor.

Managing the Electronic Load   Electronic communication media are essential these days, but the sheer volume of communication can be overwhelming.[36] Fortunately, a few rules of thumb can help; by one estimate, workers can improve their productivity in e-mail use alone by as much as 30 percent.[37] For the problem of information overload, the challenge is to separate the truly important from the routine. Take control over your time by deciding how often you need to check e-mail, texts, and tweets and turn off the notifications when you are doing other things.[38] When you check messages, reply immediately if you can, so you only handle each message once, and use the organizational tools such as file folders that come with the software. And, of course, avoid burdening others by copying them on messages they do not need to see. Some employees are finding that social media offer more efficient communication tools than e-mail. At IBM Software Group, for example, Luis Suarez posts answers to business questions on a social media site, where it is far simpler to address the usual follow-up questions and forwarding of information that accompany e-mail discussions.[39]

Of course, management also has a role to play. Often employees check messages constantly because they believe (perhaps correctly) that this is what their bosses expect of them. Managers can help employees by limiting and communicating the times during which they expect a prompt response.[40]

Some companies are recognizing the downsides of electronic media overuse. At U.S. Cellular, an executive vice president took the step of banning e-mail altogether on

Fridays. After some resistance, employees found that they were building deeper working relationships through phone calls and face-to-face visits.[41] And at PBD Worldwide Fulfillment Services, Fridays without e-mail have taught new (or old) communication habits that spilled over into the rest of the week. E-mail volume at PBD dropped 75 percent and translated into greater efficiency.[42]

The Virtual Office   Based on the philosophy that management's focus should be on what people do, not where they are, the **virtual office** is a mobile office in which people can work anywhere—their home, car, airport, customers' offices—as long as they have the tools to communicate with customers and colleagues.

In the short run, at least, the benefits of virtual offices appear substantial. Saving money on rent and utilities is an obvious advantage. A virtual office also gives employees access to whatever information they need from the company, whether they are in a meeting, visiting a client, or working from home.[43] Hiring and retaining talented people is easier because virtual offices support scheduling flexibility and may make it possible to keep an employee who wants to relocate—for example, with a spouse taking a new job in another city.

But what will be the longer-term impact on productivity and morale? We may be in danger of losing too many human moments, those authentic encounters that happen only when two people are physically together.[44] Some people hate working at home. Some send texts, e-mail, and tweets in the middle of the night—and others receive them. Some work around the clock and still feel they are not doing enough. The long hours of being constantly close to the technical tools of work can cause burnout. And some companies are learning that direct supervision at the office is necessary to maintain the quality of work, especially when employees are inexperienced and need guidance. The virtual office requires changes in human beings and presents technical challenges; so although it is much hyped and useful, it will not completely replace real offices and face-to-face work.

virtual office

A mobile office in which people can work anywhere as long as they have the tools to communicate with customers and colleagues.

In Practice

COMMUNICATING AT AUTOMATTIC INC.

Automattic Inc. takes the virtual office to an extreme, and its people love it. The company, which provides web hosting and other services for blogs on WordPress, has its headquarters in San Francisco. However, most of its employees are not there but working at their homes in 28 U.S. states plus more than two dozen other countries.

Automattic's corporate culture shows it believes in social media—and its people. Its About Us web page consists of photos of all its employees, arranged alphabetically and accompanied by lighthearted self-descriptions. For keeping tabs on projects, brainstorming new ideas, and making announcements, employees use internal blogs. For meetings, participants sign in to the Skype or Google+ Hangouts video chat service. If a topic is sensitive or a misunderstanding occurs, employees place a phone call (the traditional way or using Skype). For an informal chat, they often use the ICQ instant-messaging system.

To verify that job candidates have the right skills to thrive in this culture, the company assigns potential new employees to work on a project for several weeks before it makes a hiring decision. Also, every new employee starts out by working in customer service, so the whole team has shared experiences and customer knowledge.

Automattic has not abandoned face-to-face communication. Teams are encouraged to meet at least once a year in mutually agreed-on locations. And at a different location each year, the company hosts a week-long grand meetup for everyone to gather, get acquainted, and talk strategy.[45]

- Could you communicate effectively in a work environment like Automattic's? Why or why not?

Media Richness

Some communication channels convey more information than others. The amount of information a medium conveys is called **media richness**.[46] The more information or cues a medium sends to the receiver, the richer the medium is.[47] The richest media are more personal than technological, provide quick feedback, allow lots of descriptive language, and send different types of cues. Thus face-to-face communication is the richest medium because it offers a variety of cues in addition to words: tone of voice, facial expression, body language, and other nonverbal signals. It also allows more descriptive language than, say, a memo does. In addition, it affords more opportunity for the receiver to give feedback to and ask questions of the sender, turning one-way into two-way communication.

The telephone is less rich than face-to-face communication, and electronic mail is less rich yet. In general, you should send difficult and unusual messages through richer media, transmit simple and routine messages through less rich media, and use multiple media for important messages that you want to ensure people attend to and understand.[48] You should also consider factors such as which medium your receiver prefers, the preferred communication style in your organization, and cost.[49] Also, as you read "Management Connection: Progress Report," consider how Yahoo's policy requiring employees to work at company facilities affects the media richness of their communications.

media richness

The degree to which a communication channel conveys information.

Management Connection

GOING FACE TO FACE AT YAHOO

Marissa Mayer's decision to insist that employees work together, not from home, was an endorsement of the value of face-to-face communication. Ironically, it also pointed to the limitations of the very channels of communication that Yahoo provides, e-mail and instant messaging as well as other forms of electronic communication. The assumption is that workers who encounter one another in physical space will share more ideas than workers who don't make those physical connections. As Jackie Reses's message stated, "Some of the best decisions and insights come from hallway and cafeteria discussions, meeting new people, and impromptu team meetings."

When Yahoo's memo was leaked to the media, it opened the way to a flood of comments. Some people acknowledged research supporting Mayer's decision. One professor told a reporter that teams with face-to-face contact experience greater cohesiveness and trust, and another said that most of the information people receive in a spoken message comes from facial expressions and the speaker's tone of voice. A research scientist who runs Sociometric Solutions has collected detailed data about people's interactions and learned that people who have the most face-to-face communication and friendships at work are not only more productive but also happier.

Nevertheless, critics of Mayer's decision note that telecommuters have been shown to work longer hours than in-office workers. (However, this points to a downside of telecommuting; if these workers are spending *more* time on the job, working from home does not actually help with work–life balance, as is popularly believed.) Others point to the strangeness of an Internet company not trusting its employees to communicate effectively through electronic channels. To some, the change in policy looked like a step backward by a company trying to signal it was finally moving forward.

Another aspect of this decision, of course, was the way Yahoo's management implemented it. Mayer could have presented the idea to employees at one of her Friday meetings, or she could have held a conversation about policy ideas on social media. Instead, she arranged for the head of human resources to send all employees a memo announcing the decision via e-mail.[50]

- What impacts on communication would most likely result from Yahoo's directive to end work-at-home arrangements?
- Was an e-mailed memo the most appropriate communication channel to use for sending this message? Why or why not?

MANAGER'S BRIEF

PROGRESS REPORT

ONWARD

Improving Communication Skills

 Employers are dismayed by college graduates' poor communication skills. A demonstrated ability to communicate effectively makes a job candidate more attractive and distinguishes him or her from others. You can do many things to improve your communication skills, both as a sender and as a receiver.

Improving Sender Skills

To start, be aware that honest, direct, straight talk is important but all too rare. CEOs are often coached on how to slant their messages for different audiences—the investment community, employees, or the board. That's not likely to be straight talk. The focus of the messages can differ, but they can't be inconsistent. People should be able to identify your perspective, your reasoning, and your intentions.[51]

Beyond this basic point, senders can improve their skills in making persuasive presentations, writing, language use, and sending nonverbal messages. Table 15.1 offers some useful tips on formal presentations; the following discussion focuses more on other keys to persuasion.

Presentation and Persuasion Skills Throughout your career, you will be called on to state your case on a variety of issues. You will have information and perhaps an opinion or proposal to present to others. Typically, your goal will be to sell your idea. In other words, your challenge will be to persuade others to go along with your personal recommendation. As a leader, you will find that some of your toughest challenges arise when people do not want to do what has to be done. Leaders have to be persuasive to get people on board.[52]

> Persuasion is not what many people think.

Your attitude in presenting ideas and persuading others is important. Persuasion is not what many people think: merely selling an idea or convincing others to see things your way. Don't assume that it takes a "my way or the highway" approach, with a one-shot effort to make a hard sell and resisting compromise.[53] It usually is more constructive to consider persuasion a process of learning from each other and negotiating a shared solution. Persuasive speakers are seen as authentic, which happens when speakers are open with the audience, make a connection, demonstrate passion, and show they are listening as well as speaking. As a speaker, you can practice this kind of authenticity by noticing and adopting the type of body language you use when you're around people you're comfortable with, planning how to engage directly with your listeners, identifying the reasons you care about your topic, and watching for nonverbal cues as well as fully engaging yourself when you listen to audience comments and questions.[54]

The most powerful and persuasive messages are simple and informative, are told with stories and anecdotes, and convey excitement.[55] People are more likely to remember and buy into your message if you can express it as a story that is simple, unexpected, concrete, and credible and that includes emotional content. For example, the Chicago energy company Exelon wanted to build employee support for its corporate values. To teach about diversity, the company posted videos of its executives making personal statements about what diversity means to them. A finance executive told about being from a working-class family in England and feeling like an outsider when he took a job in a bank where most of the employees came from the upper class. When this manager asserted, "I never want anyone else to feel that way," his openness about his own life made his statement more powerful.[56] Then, to be credible, a communicator backs up the message with actions consistent with the words.

TABLE 15.1
Ten Ways to Add Power to
Your Presentations

"All the great speakers were bad speakers at first." Ralph Waldo Emerson

1. *Spend adequate time on the **content** of your presentation.* It's easy to get so distracted with PowerPoint slides or concern about delivery skills that the actual content of a presentation is neglected. Know your content inside and out; you'll be able to discuss it conversationally and won't be tempted to memorize. If you believe in what you're saying and *own* the material, you will convey enthusiasm and will be more relaxed.

2. *Clearly understand the **objective** of your presentation.* Answer this question with one sentence: "What do I want the audience to believe following this presentation?" Writing down your objective will help you focus on your bottom line. Everything else in a presentation—the structure, the words, the visuals—should support your objective.

3. ***Tell** the audience the **purpose** of the presentation.* As the saying goes, "Tell them what you're going to tell them, then tell them, then tell them what you've told them." Use a clear preview statement early on to help the audience know where you're taking them.

4. *Provide **meaning**, not just data.* Today information is widely available; you won't impress people by overloading them with data. People have limited attention spans and want presenters to help clarify the meaning of data.

5. ***Practice, practice, practice.*** Appearing polished and relaxed during a presentation requires rehearsal time. Practice making your points in a variety of ways. Above all, don't memorize a presentation's content.

6. *Remember that a presentation is more like a **conversation** than a speech.* Keep your tone conversational, yet professional. Audience members will be much more engaged if they feel you are talking with them rather than at them. Rely on PowerPoint slides or a broad outline to jog your memory.

7. *Remember the incredible power of **eye contact**.* Look at individual people in the audience. Try to have a series of one-on-one conversations with people in the room. This will calm you and help you connect with your audience.

8. ***Allow imperfection.*** If you forget what you were going to say, simply pause, look at your notes, and go on. Don't break character and effusively apologize or giggle or look mortified. Remember that an audience doesn't know your material nearly as well as you do and won't notice many mistakes.

9. *Be prepared to **answer tough questions**.* Try to anticipate the toughest questions you might receive. Plan your answers in advance. If you don't have an answer, acknowledge the fact and offer to get the information later.

10. *Provide a **crisp wrap-up** to a question-and-answer session.* Whenever possible, follow the Q&A period with a brief summary statement. Set up the Q&A session by saying, "We'll take questions for 10 minutes and then have a few closing remarks." This prevents your presentation from just winding down to a weak ending. Also, if you receive hostile or hard-to-answer questions, you'll have a chance to have the final word.

SOURCE: Lynn Hamilton, class handout (with permission).

Writing Skills   Effective writing is more than correct spelling, punctuation, and grammar (although these help). Good writing above all requires clear, logical thinking.[57] The act of writing can be a powerful aid to thinking because you have to think about what you really want to say and what the logic is behind your message.[58]

You want people to find your e-mail and reports readable and interesting. Strive for clarity, organization, readability, and brevity.[59] Brevity is much appreciated by readers who are overloaded with documents, including e-mail. Help e-mail recipients manage the flood of information by providing specific subject lines, putting your main point at the beginning of the message, limiting paragraphs to five lines or less, and avoiding sarcasm or caustic humor (which can be misinterpreted, especially when readers are scanning messages in a hurry).[60]

Your first draft rarely is as good as it could be. If you have time, revise it. Take the reader into consideration. Go through your entire letter, memo, or report and delete all unnecessary words, sentences, and paragraphs. Use specific, concrete words rather than abstract phrases. Instead of saying, "A period of unfavorable weather set in," say, "It rained every day for a week."

Language   Word choice can enhance or interfere with communication effectiveness. For example, jargon is actually a form of shorthand and can make communication more effective when both the sender and the receiver know the buzzwords. But when the receiver is unfamiliar with the jargon, misunderstandings result. When people from different functional areas or disciplines communicate with one another, misunderstandings often occur because of language barriers. As in writing, simplicity usually helps.

Therefore, whether speaking or writing, you should consider the receiver's background—cultural as well as technical—and adjust your language accordingly. When you are receiving, don't assume that your understanding is the same as the speaker's intentions. Cisco CEO John Chambers, whose background is in business, simply asks the engineering managers in his high-tech company to explain any jargon. He says, "They do it remarkably well."[61] At the same time, Chambers shows respect and enhances his credibility by being truly interested in their work. Whenever Chambers travels with or reviews engineers, he asks them to teach him a topic—and he listens.

In Practice

POSITIVE COMMUNICATION AT KAISER PERMANENTE

George Halvorson, chief executive officer of Kaiser Permanente, is committed to a communication style that is sensitive to his readers. Several years ago, Halvorson adopted the habit of sending the health care company's employees personal notes every Friday. In each note, Halvorson "celebrates" (his word) something people in the organization are doing right and, as he told a reporter, he strives to do this with "absolute honesty," avoiding jargon and any attempt to spin a story to make the institution look better than it is.

Given that hospital or clinic employees have widely differing levels of education and areas of specialty, Halvorson takes care to explain whatever situation he is praising. For example, in one message, Halvorson wrote about employees' efforts at reducing pressure ulcers (bedsores), a painful, potentially dangerous skin condition that can result when patients are unable to move around and are left in one position too long. Halvorson explained the condition, detailed what employees are doing to prevent it, and included charts of data. He also explained why the efforts matter: "Consistency is golden. Being consistent with best practices saves lives. Look at the chart. Lives are being saved. . . . So my letter this week celebrates the really smart and practical caregivers who figured out what we needed to do."

These words of appreciation are simple and specific. They come from the top of the organization. It is easy to imagine a Kaiser Permanente employee reading a message like this one and feeling proud to work for the organization. As it turns out, Halvorson also came to enjoy writing them because the practice caused him to look for good work being done every day.[62]

- What are the impacts of communications like these? Why do they have so much impact?

The meaning of word choices also can vary by culture. Japanese people use the simple word *hai* (yes) to convey that they understand what is being said; it does not necessarily mean that they agree. Asian businesspeople rarely use the direct "no," using more subtle or tangential ways of disagreeing.[63] Similarly, Japanese speakers apologize more often than Americans; the Japanese focus on the potential of an apology to repair damage in relationships, whereas U.S. speakers interpret apologies as admissions of guilt and therefore avoid them. Global teams fail when members have difficulties communicating because of language, cultural, and geographic barriers. Heterogeneity harms team functioning at first. But when they develop ways to interact and communicate, teams develop a common identity and perform well.[64]

Global teams fail when members have difficulty communicating because of language, cultural, and geographic barriers. What could you do to overcome these barriers?

When conducting business overseas, try to learn something about the other country's language and customs. Americans are less likely to do this than people from some other cultures; most Americans do not consider a foreign language necessary for doing business abroad, and a significant majority of U.S. firms do not require employees sent abroad to know the local language.[65] But those who do will have a big edge over their competitors who do not.[66] Making the effort to learn the local language builds rapport, sets a proper tone for doing business, aids in adjustment to culture shock, and especially can help you get inside the other culture.[67] You will learn more about how people think, feel, and behave, both in their lives and in their business dealings.

> Those who learn local languages and customs will have a big edge over their competitors who do not.

Nonverbal Skills

As you know, people send and interpret signals other than those that are spoken or written. Nonverbal messages can support or undermine the stated message. Often nonverbal cues make a greater impact than other signals. In employees' eyes, managers' actions often speak louder than the words managers choose. Project manager Steve Bailey had already given many presentations when he attended a presentation skills workshop. There a facilitator pointed out Bailey's habit of clasping and unclasping his hands as he spoke. The behavior was distracting and made him appear less authoritative. When Bailey stopped making that gesture, he discovered that his audiences tended to be more convinced by his presentations.[68]

In conversation, except when you intend to convey a negative message, you should give nonverbal signals that express warmth, respect, concern, a feeling of equality, and a willingness to listen. Negative nonverbal signals show coolness, disrespect, lack of interest, and a feeling of superiority.[69] The following suggestions can help you send positive nonverbal signals.

First, use time appropriately. Avoid keeping your employees waiting to see you. Devote sufficient time to your meetings with them and communicate frequently with them to signal your interest in their concerns. Second, make your office arrangement conducive to open communication. A seating arrangement that avoids separation of people helps establish a warm, cooperative atmosphere (in contrast, an arrangement in which you sit behind your desk and your subordinate sits before you creates a more intimidating, authoritative environment).[70] Third, remember your body language. Facial expression and tone of voice can account for much of the communication between two people.[71] Several nonverbal body signals convey a positive attitude toward the other person: assuming a position close to the person; gesturing frequently; maintaining eye contact; smiling; having an open body orientation, such as facing the other person directly; uncrossing the arms; and leaning forward to convey interest in what the other person is saying.

Silence is an interesting nonverbal signal. The average American is said to spend about twice as many hours per day in conversation as the average Japanese.[72] North Americans tend to talk to fill silences. Japanese allow long silences to develop, believing they can get to know people better. Japanese believe that two people with good rapport will know each other's thoughts. The need to use words implies a lack of understanding.

Improving Receiver Skills

Once you become effective at sending oral, written, and nonverbal messages, you are halfway toward becoming a complete communicator. However, you must also develop adequate receiving capabilities. Receivers need good listening, reading, and observational skills.

Listening   In today's demanding work environment, managers need excellent listening skills. Although people frequently assume that good listening is easy and natural, in fact it is difficult and not nearly as common as needed. Consultant Bernard Ferrari saw this challenge in a meeting of an industrial company's chief marketing officer and the team that had introduced a new product. The new product was not selling, even though the engineers on the team described it as delivering many important benefits. The CMO listened carefully to the engineers and then asked, given that the product was great and the engineers convincingly described its worth, what customers were saying that might explain the lack of orders. The engineers admitted they had not spoken with any customers; rather, they had been careful not to leak any information while the product was under development and assumed that customers would plainly see its value. Because the CMO took time to listen to the engineers, instead of jumping to conclusions about the source of the problem, she and the engineers could arrive at a plan for them to begin talking to technical people at the customer firms, and orders soon began flowing in.[73]

reflection

Process by which a person states what he or she believes the other person is saying.

A basic technique called *reflection* will help a manager listen effectively.[74] **Reflection** is a process by which a person states what he or she believes the other person is saying. This technique places a greater emphasis on listening than on talking, and the result is more accurate two-way communication.

Besides using reflection, you can improve how well you listen by practicing the techniques described in Table 15.2. (Note the date of the citation; some things don't change!) For managers, the stakes are high; failure to listen not only causes managers to miss good ideas but can even drive employees away.[75]

Listening begins with personal contact. Staying in the office, keeping the door closed, and eating lunch at your desk are sometimes necessary to get pressing work done, but that is no way to stay on top of what's going on. Better to walk the halls, initiate conversations and go to lunch even with people outside your area, have coffee in a popular gathering place, and maybe even move your desk onto the factory floor.[76]

When a manager takes time to really listen to and get to know people, those same people think, "She's showing an interest in me" or "He's letting me know that I matter" or "She values my ideas and contributions." Trust develops. Listening and learning from others are even more important for innovation than for routine work. Successful change and innovation come through lots of human contact.

Reading   Illiteracy is a significant problem in the United States as well as in other countries. Even if illiteracy is not a problem in your organization, reading mistakes are common and costly. As a receiver, for your own benefit, read memos and e-mail as soon as possible, before it's too late to respond. You may skim most of your reading materials, but read important messages, documents, and passages slowly and carefully. Note important points for later referral. Consider taking courses to increase your

1. *Find an area of interest.* Even if you decide the topic is dull, ask yourself, "What is the speaker saying that I can use?"
2. *Judge content, not delivery.* Don't get caught up in the speaker's personality, mannerisms, speaking voice, or clothing. Instead, try to learn what the speaker knows.
3. *Hold your fire.* Rather than getting immediately excited by what the speaker seems to be saying, withhold evaluation until you understand the speaker's message.
4. *Listen for ideas.* Don't get bogged down in all the facts and details; focus on central ideas.
5. *Be flexible.* Have several systems for note taking and use the system best suited to the speaker's style. Don't take too many notes or try to force everything said by a disorganized speaker into a formal outline.
6. *Resist distraction.* Close the door, shut off the radio, move closer to the person talking, or ask him or her to speak louder. Don't look out the window or at papers on your desk.
7. *Exercise your mind.* Some people tune out when the material gets difficult. Develop an appetite for a good mental challenge.
8. *Keep your mind open.* Many people get overly emotional when they hear words referring to their most deeply held convictions—for example, *union, subsidy, import, Republican* or *Democrat,* and *big business.* Try not to let your emotions interfere with comprehension.
9. *Capitalize on thought speed.* Take advantage of the fact that most people talk at a rate of about 125 words per minute, but most of us think at about four times that rate. Use those extra 400 words per minute to think about what the speaker is saying rather than turning your thoughts to something else.
10. *Work at listening.* Spend some energy. Don't just pretend you're paying attention. Show interest. Good listening is hard work, but the benefits outweigh the costs.

TABLE 15.2

Ten Keys to Effective Listening

SOURCE: Ralph G. Nichols, "Listening Is a 10-Part Skill," *Nation's Business* 45 (July 1957), pp. 56–60. Cited in R. C. Huseman, C. M. Logue, and D. L. Freshley, eds., *Readings in Interpersonal and Organizational Communication* (Boston: Allyn & Bacon, 1977).

reading speed and comprehension skills. Finally, don't limit your reading to items about your particular job skill or technical expertise; read materials that fall outside your immediate concerns. You never know when a creative idea that will help you in your work will be inspired by a novel, a biography, a sports story, or an article about a problem in another business or industry.

Observing   Effective communicators are also capable of observing and interpreting nonverbal communications. (As Yogi Berra said, "You can observe a lot by watching.") For example, by reading nonverbal cues, a presenter can determine how her talk is going and adjust her approach if necessary. Some companies train their sales forces to interpret the nonverbal signals of potential customers. People can also decode nonverbal signals to determine whether a sender is being truthful or deceitful. Deceitful communicators tend to maintain less eye contact, make either more or fewer body movements than usual, and smile either too much or too little. Verbally, they offer fewer specifics than do truthful senders.[77]

A vital source of useful observations comes from personally visiting people, plants, and other locations to get a firsthand view.[78] Many corporate executives rely heavily on reports from the field and don't travel to remote locations to observe firsthand what is going on. Reports are no substitute for actually seeing things happen in practice. Frequent visits to the field and careful observation can help a manager develop deep understanding of current operations, future prospects, and ideas for how to exploit capabilities fully.[79]

Of course, you must accurately interpret what you observe. A Canadian conducting business with a high-ranking official in Kuwait was surprised that the meeting was held in an open office and was interrupted constantly.[80] He interpreted the lack of a big, private office and secretary to mean that the Kuwaiti was of low rank and uninterested in doing business, and he lost interest in the deal. The Canadian observed the facts accurately, but his perceptual biases and lack of awareness regarding how norms differ across cultures caused him to misinterpret what he saw.

The Japanese are particularly skilled at interpreting every nuance of voice and gesture, putting most Westerners at a disadvantage.[81] When one is conducting business in Asia or other countries, local guides can be invaluable not only to interpret language but to decode behavior at meetings, what subtle hints and nonverbal cues mean, who the key people are, and how the decision-making process operates.

Organizational Communication

Being a skilled communicator is essential to being a good manager and team leader. But communication must also be managed throughout the organization. Every minute of every day, countless bits of information are transmitted through an organization. The flow of information affects how well people and units perform. Communications travel downward, upward, horizontally, and informally within the organization.

Downward Communication

downward communication

Information that flows from higher to lower levels in the organization's hierarchy.

Downward communication refers to the flow of information from higher to lower levels in the organization's hierarchy. Examples include a manager giving an assignment to an assistant, a supervisor making an announcement to his subordinates, and a company president delivering a talk to her management team. Downward communication that provides relevant information enhances employee identification with the company, supportive attitudes, and decisions consistent with the organization's objectives.[82]

People must receive the information they need to perform their jobs and become—and remain—loyal members of the organization. But they often lack adequate information.[83] One problem is information overload; they are bombarded with so much information that they fail to absorb everything. Much of the information is not very important, but its volume causes a lot of relevant information to be lost.

A second problem is a lack of openness between managers and employees. Managers may believe "No news is good news," "I don't have time to keep them informed of everything they want to know," or "It's none of their business, anyway." Some managers withhold information even if sharing it would be useful.

A third problem is filtering, introduced earlier in the chapter. When messages are passed from one person to another, some information is left out. When a message passes through many people, each transmission may cause further information losses. The message can also be distorted as people add their own words or interpretations.

Filtering poses serious problems in organizations. As messages are communicated downward through many organizational levels, much information is lost. The data in Figure 15.2 suggest that by the time messages reach the people for whom they are intended, the receivers may get very little useful information. The smaller the number of authority levels through which communications must pass, the less information will be lost or distorted. Flatter organization offers the advantage of fewer problems caused by filtering of information as it cascades through many layers.

> As messages are communicated downward through many organizational levels, much information is lost.

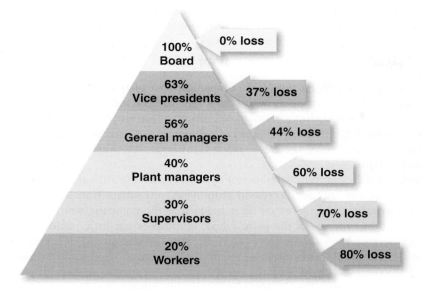

FIGURE 15.2

Information Loss in Downward Communication

Coaching   Some of the most important downward communications occur when managers give performance feedback to their direct reports. We discussed earlier the importance of giving feedback and positive reinforcement when it is deserved. It is also important to discuss poor performance explicitly and areas that can be improved.

Coaching is dialogue with a goal of helping another be more effective and achieve his or her full potential on the job.[84] When done properly, coaching develops executives and enhances performance.[85] When people have performance problems or exhibit behaviors that need to be changed, coaching is often the best way to help a person change and succeed. And coaching is not just for poor performers; as even the greatest athletes know, it is for anyone who is good and aspires to excellence. Although coaches for executives sometimes are hired from the outside, coaches from outside your organization may not understand fully the context in which you are working.[86] So don't take advice automatically. The best use of coaches is as sounding boards, helping you think through the potential impact of your ideas, generate new options, and learn from experience.

Companies such as Coca-Cola use coaching as an essential part of their executive development process. When done well, coaching is true dialogue between two committed people engaged in joint problem solving. Thus it is far more than an occasion for highlighting poor performance, delivering reprimands, or giving advice. Good coaching requires achieving real understanding of the problem, the person, and the situation; jointly generating ideas for what to do; and encouraging the person to improve. Good coaches ask a lot of questions, listen well, provide input, and encourage others to think for themselves. Effective coaching requires honesty, calmness, and supportiveness—all aided by a sincere desire to help. The ultimate and longest-lasting form of help is to help people think through and solve their own problems.

Downward Communication in Difficult Times   Managers frequently need to deliver bad news,[87] and proper downward communication can be particularly valuable during difficult times. During corporate mergers and acquisitions, employees are anxious as they wonder how the changes will affect them. Ideally—and ethically—top management should communicate with employees about the change as early as possible.

But some argue against that approach, maintaining that informing employees about the reorganization might cause them to quit too early. Then too, top management

coaching

Dialogue with a goal of helping another be more effective and achieve his or her full potential on the job.

often cloisters itself, prompting rumors and anxiety. CEOs and other senior execs are surrounded by lawyers, investment bankers, and so on—people who are paid merely to make the deal happen, not to make it work.

Yet with the people who are affected by the deal, you must increase, not decrease, communication.[88]

In a merger of two *Fortune* 500 companies, two plants received very different information.[89] All employees at both plants received the initial letter from the CEO announcing the merger. But after that, one plant was kept in the dark while the other was continually filled in on what was happening. Top management gave employees information about layoffs; transfers; promotions and demotions; and changes in pay, jobs, and benefits.

Which plant do you think fared better as the difficult transitional months unfolded? In both plants, the merger decreased employees' job satisfaction and commitment to the organization and increased their belief that the company was untrustworthy, dishonest, and uncaring. In the plant whose employees got little information, these problems persisted for a long time. But in the plant where employees received complete information, the situation stabilized and attitudes improved toward their normal levels. Full communication not only helped employees survive an anxious period but also served a symbolic value by signaling care and concern for employees. Without such communications, employee reactions to a merger or acquisition may be so negative that they undermine the corporate strategy and performance.

Open-Book Management   Executives often are proud of their newsletters, staff meetings, videos, and other vehicles of downward communication. More often than not, the information provided concerns company sports teams, birthdays, and new copy machines. But here is a more unconventional philosophy. **Open-book management** is the practice of sharing with employees at all levels of the organization vital information previously meant for management's eyes only. This information includes financial goals, income statements, budgets, sales, forecasts, and other relevant data about company performance and prospects. This practice is dramatically different from the traditional closed-book approach in which people may or may not have a clue about how the company is doing, may or may not believe the things that management tells them, and may or may not believe that their personal performance makes a difference.

Open-book management is controversial because many managers prefer to keep such information to themselves. Sharing strategic plans and financial information with employees could lead to leaks to competitors or to employee dissatisfaction with compensation. Father of scientific management Frederick Taylor, early in the 20th century, would have considered opening the books to all employees idiotic.[90]

But then Jack Stack tried it at Springfield ReManufacturing Corporation, which was on the brink of collapse.[91] The results? Workers were highly motivated and understood the ins and outs of the business. Similarly, at Hilcorp Energy Company, senior managers assemble the 280-plus employees once a month to share data about the company's performance and listen to ideas from the workers. Greg Lalicker, a Hilcorp executive vice president, explains that when employees understand how their work affects profits, they "pull together, not competing against each other."[92]

Upward Communication

Upward communication travels from lower to higher ranks in the hierarchy. Adequate upward communication is important for several reasons.[93] First, managers learn what's going on. Management gains a more accurate picture of subordinates' work, accomplishments, problems, plans, attitudes, and ideas. Second, employees gain from the opportunity to communicate upward. People can relieve some of their frustrations and achieve a stronger sense of participation in the enterprise. Third, effective upward communication facilitates downward communication as good listening becomes a two-way street.

open-book management
Practice of sharing with employees at all levels of the organization vital information previously meant for management's eyes only.

Bottom Line
The more management communicates cost, quality, sustainability, and other data, the more people will care about and pay attention to performance and find new ways to improve.
For employees to be motivated by open-book management, what kinds of information would they need besides sales and profit numbers?

upward communication
Information that flows from lower to higher levels in the organization's hierarchy.

The problems common in upward communication are similar to those for downward communication. Managers, like their subordinates, are bombarded with information and may neglect or miss information from below. Furthermore, some employees are not always open with their bosses; in other words, filtering occurs upward as well as downward. People tend to share only good news with their bosses and suppress bad news because they (1) want to appear competent; (2) mistrust their boss and fear that if he or she finds out about something they have done they will be punished; (3) fear the boss will punish the messenger, even if the reported problem is not that person's fault; or (4) believe they are helping their boss if they shield him or her from problems.

For these and other reasons, managers may not learn about important problems. As one leadership expert put it, "If the messages from below say you are doing a flawless job, send back for a more candid assessment."[94]

Managing Upward Communication Generating useful information from below requires managers to both facilitate and motivate upward communication. For example, they could have an open-door policy and encourage people to use it, have lunch or coffee with employees, use surveys, institute a program for suggestions, or have town hall meetings. They can ask for advice, make informal visits to plants, really think about and respond to employee suggestions, and distribute summaries of new ideas and practices inspired by employee suggestions and actions.[95]

Some executives practice MBWA (management by wandering around). That term, coined by Ed Carlson of United Airlines, refers simply to getting out of the office, walking around, and talking frequently and informally with employees.[96] At the headquarters of Secura Insurance in Appleton, Wisconsin, CEO John Bykowski makes a habit of walking through the building to talk with and listen to employees.[97] And in the offices of the *South Florida Sun-Sentinel*, recently retired editor Earl Maucker was known for dropping in to employees' offices and cubicles and for being accessible and frank, so his editorial staff trusted what he said.[98]

Useful upward communication must be reinforced and not punished. The person who tries to talk to the manager about a problem must not be brushed off consistently. An announced open-door policy must truly be open-door. Also, people must trust their supervisor and know that the manager will not hold a grudge if they deliver negative information. To get honesty, managers must truly listen, not punish the messenger for being honest, and act on valid comments.

Horizontal Communication

Much information needs to be shared among people on the same hierarchical level. Such **horizontal communication** can take place among people in the same work team or in different departments. For example, a purchasing agent discusses a problem with a production engineer, and a task force of department heads meets to discuss a particular concern. Communicating with others outside the firm, including potential investors, is another vital type of horizontal communication.[99]

Horizontal communication has several important functions.[100] First, it allows sharing of information, coordination, and problem solving among units. Second, it helps solve conflicts. Third, by allowing interaction among peers, it provides social and emotional support to people. All these factors contribute to morale and effectiveness. For example, National Public Radio has brought together groups of a few dozen employees from different departments to share ideas for new projects. On one of these Serendipity Days, the employees put together a program for training staff members in using social media. And a study at the University of Michigan found that researchers were significantly more likely to collaborate on research projects with a colleague if they both worked in the same building and had walking patterns that overlapped.[101]

horizontal communication

Information moving between people on the same hierarchical level.

Managing Horizontal Communication   The need for horizontal communication is similar to the need for integration, discussed in Chapter 8. Particularly in complex environments, in which decisions in one unit affect another, information must be shared horizontally. As examples of good horizontal communication, Motorola holds an annual conference for sharing best learnings across functional and business groups throughout the company. NASA collocates scientists from different disciplines. Hewlett-Packard uses common databases for different product groups to share information and ideas.[102]

Applied Materials, a semiconductor equipment manufacturer in Santa Clara, California, took a sophisticated approach to managing horizontal communication. To improve the caliber and efficiency of its information technology (IT) group, the company outsourced routine tasks, cut the in-house IT workforce, and focused the remaining IT employees on supporting strategy. As a result, the IT workers were expected to collaborate with each other (and with customers) to develop and implement creative projects. To improve this kind of collaboration, Applied Materials conducted a survey of the IT staff to determine the existing patterns of communication. Survey results showed that about half of the IT employees were, in effect, communication hubs—many of their colleagues consulted with them for ideas and questions. Those highly networked employees weren't necessarily managers; they were people at all levels whom others trusted and respected. The company assembled a team of 12 highly networked IT employees and had them share insights about what conditions affected collaboration in the company. This team identified barriers, and Applied Materials used that information to provide coaching in better communication. A follow-up survey showed that more employees had become highly networked.[103]

Informal Communication

LO 6

Organizational communications differ in formality. Formal communications are official, organization-sanctioned episodes of information transmission. They can move upward, downward, or horizontally and often are prearranged and necessary for performing some task.

Informal communication is more unofficial. People gossip; employees complain about their bosses; people talk about their favorite sports teams; work teams tell newcomers how to get by.[104]

grapevine

Informal communication network.

The **grapevine** is the social network of informal communications. Informal networks provide people with information, help them solve problems, and teach them how to do their work successfully. You should develop a good network of people willing and able to help.[105] However, the grapevine can be destructive when irrelevant or erroneous gossip and rumors proliferate and harm operations.[106]

What does this mean for you personally? Don't engage in e-gossip. Embarrassing episodes become public, and lawsuits based on defamation of character and invasion of privacy have used e-mail evidence. But don't avoid the grapevine, either.[107] Listen, but evaluate before believing what you hear. Who is the source? How credible is he or she? Does the rumor make sense? Is it consistent or inconsistent with other things you know or have heard? Seek more information. Don't stir the pot.

Managing Informal Communication   Rumors start over any number of topics, including who's leaving, who's getting a promotion, salaries, job security, and costly mistakes. Rumors can destroy people's faith and trust in the company—and in each other. But the grapevine cannot be eliminated. Therefore, managers need to work with the grapevine.

The grapevine can be managed in several ways.[108] First, if a manager hears a story that could get out of hand, he or she should talk to the key people involved to get the facts and their perspectives. Don't allow malicious gossip.

Second, suggestions for preventing rumors from starting include explaining events that are important but have not been explained, dispelling uncertainties by providing facts, and working to establish open communications and trust over time. These efforts are especially important during times of uncertainty, such as after a merger or layoff or when sales slow down, because rumors increase along with anxiety.

Third, neutralize rumors once they have started. Disregard a rumor if it is ridiculous; openly confirm any parts that are true; make public comments ("no comment" is seen as a confirmation of the rumor); deny the rumor if the denial is based in truth (don't make false denials); make sure communications about the issue are consistent; select a spokesperson of appropriate rank and knowledge; and hold town meetings if needed.[109]

It's hard to know how rumors get started, but we do know they happen. The grapevine can be managed if you talk to the key people involved and neutralize rumors once they've started.

Boundarylessness

Many executives and management scholars today consider free access to information in all directions to be an organizational imperative. Jack Welch, when he was CEO of General Electric, coined the term *boundarylessness*. A **boundaryless organization** is one in which no barriers to information flow exist. Instead of separating people, jobs, processes, and places with boundaries, ideas, information, decisions, and actions move to where they are most needed.[110] This free flow does not imply a random free-for-all of unlimited communication and information overload. It implies information available *as needed* moving quickly and easily enough that the organization functions far better as a whole than as separate parts.

GE's chief learning officer used the metaphor of the organization as a house having three kinds of boundaries: the floors and ceilings, the walls that separate the rooms, and the outside walls. These barriers correspond in organizations to the boundaries between different organizational levels, different units and departments, and the organization and its external stakeholders—for example, suppliers and customers. GE adds a fourth wall: global boundaries separating domestic from global operations.[111]

GE's famous Workout program is a series of meetings for business members across multiple hierarchical levels, characterized by extremely frank, tough discussions that break down vertical boundaries. Workout has involved hundreds of thousands of GE people; in any given week thousands may be participating in a Workout program.[112] Workout is also done with customers and suppliers, breaking down outside boundaries. GE has also reached out to the community by providing this expertise to nonprofits, such as CommonBond Communities, a provider of affordable housing. A GE employee led a Workout session in which CommonBond employees identified how to improve processes and horizontal communication.[113]

GE uses plenty of other techniques to break down boundaries as well. It relentlessly benchmarks competitors and companies in other industries to learn best practices all over the world. GE places different functions together physically, such as engineering and manufacturing. It shares services across units. And it sometimes shares physical locations with its customers.

Boundaryless organizations intentionally create dialogue across boundaries, turning barriers into permeable membranes. As the GE people put it, people from different parts of the organization need to learn "how to talk."[114] They must also learn "how to walk." That is, dialogue is essential, but it must be followed by commensurate action. As you read "Management Connection: Onward," consider whether Yahoo under Marissa Mayer meets the description of a boundaryless organization.

LO 7

boundaryless organization

Organization in which there are no barriers to information flow.

Management Connection

FORMAL AND INFORMAL COMMUNICATION AT YAHOO

Marissa Mayer's first months at Yahoo showed her to be concerned about formal and informal communication. Some of her earliest actions established downward communication and invited upward communication. For example, upon arriving, she sent employees a memo expressing her excitement to be at Yahoo, encouraging them to "keep moving" on their "important work," and inviting them to share their ideas with her. Soon after, she set up Friday town hall meetings. At one, she announced an initiative with the lighthearted name PB&J, for streamlining *process*, reducing *bureaucracy*, and removing *jams*. As part of the initiative, Mayer described a company website for employees to add and vote on ideas. The site ranks the ideas by popularity, and management promised to implement the best ideas.

The announcement of the policy ending work-at-home arrangements was aimed at increasing informal communication. Aiming for a positive tone, HR executive Jackie Reses started by recalling some of the benefits Yahoo had previously delivered and said, "We want everyone to participate in our culture and contribute to the positive momentum." The memo next explained the rationale for the decision: fostering communication and collaboration so Yahoo could "become the absolute best place to work." Addressing questions that might come from employees wondering whether they could work from home even for brief periods, Reses said, "For the rest of us who occasionally have to stay at home for the cable guy, please use your best judgment in the spirit of collaboration."

The announcement also generated unintended informal communication when angry employees shared the memo with journalists, even though it was marked "proprietary and confidential." One employee affected by the decision called it "outrageous and a morale killer." A possible reason for the anger was that employees received an order to come to the workplace, rather than incentives or a message encouraging them. Also, the decision may have come as a surprise, given that it reversed earlier policy and stands in contrast to flexible work arrangements allowed at Google, Facebook, LinkedIn, Hewlett-Packard, IBM, Microsoft, and Cisco, among other companies. At those companies, working at home is not necessarily encouraged, but it is available with the assumption that workers and their managers can take responsibility for being productive. One Silicon Valley observer suggested that Yahoo made the policy change to shake up the culture and revitalize communication but will likely relax the rules eventually.[115]

- How could Mayer make her downward communication more effective?
- How could Yahoo make informal communication among employees more constructive?

KEY TERMS

boundaryless organization, p. 517	grapevine, p. 516	perception, p. 499
coaching, p. 513	horizontal communication, p. 515	reflection, p. 510
communication, p. 498	media richness, p. 505	two-way communication, p. 498
downward communication, p. 512	one-way communication, p. 498	upward communication, p. 514
filtering, p. 499	open-book management, p. 514	virtual office, p. 504

SUMMARY OF LEARNING OBJECTIVES

Now that you have studied Chapter 15, you should be able to:

 Discuss important advantages of two-way communication.

One-way communication flows from the sender to the receiver with no feedback loop. In two-way communication, each person is both a sender and a receiver as both parties provide and react to information. One-way communication is faster and easier but less accurate than two-way; two-way communication is slower and more difficult but is more accurate and results in better performance.

 Identify communication problems to avoid.

The communication process involves a sender who conveys information to a receiver. Problems in communication can occur in all stages: encoding, transmission, decoding, and interpreting. Noise in the system further complicates communication, creating more distortion. Moreover, feedback may be unavailable or misleading. Subjective perceptions and filtering add to the possibility of error.

LO 3 Describe when and how to use the various communication channels.

Communications are sent through oral, written, and electronic channels. All have important advantages and disadvantages that should be considered before choosing a channel. Electronic media have a huge impact on interpersonal and organizational communications and make possible the virtual office. Key advantages of electronic media are speed, cost, and efficiency, but the downsides are also significant, including information overload. Media richness, or how much and what sort of information a channel conveys, is one factor to consider as you decide which channels to use and how to use them both efficiently and effectively.

LO 4 Summarize ways to become a better sender and receiver of information.

Practice writing, be critical of your work, and revise. Train yourself as a speaker. Use language carefully and well and work to overcome cross-cultural language differences. Be alert to the nonverbal signals that you send, including your use of time as perceived by other people. Know the common bad listening habits and work to overcome them. Read widely and engage in careful, firsthand observation and interpretation.

LO 5 Explain how to improve downward, upward, and horizontal communication.

Actively manage communications in all directions. Engage in two-way communication more than one-way. Make information available to others. Useful approaches to downward communication include coaching, special communications during difficult periods, and open-book management. You should also both facilitate and motivate people to communicate upward. Many mechanisms exist for enhancing horizontal communications.

LO 6 Summarize how to work with the company grapevine.

The informal flow of information can contribute as much as formal communication can to organizational effectiveness and morale. Managers must understand that the grapevine cannot be eliminated and should be managed actively. Many of the suggestions for managing formal communications apply also to managing the grapevine. Moreover, managers can take steps to prevent rumors or neutralize the ones that arise.

LO 7 Describe the boundaryless organization and its advantages.

Boundaries—psychological if not physical—exist between different organizational levels, units, and organizations and external stakeholders. The ideal boundaryless organization is one in which no barriers to information flow exist. Ideas, information, decisions, and actions move to where they are most needed. Information is available as needed and freely accessible so that the organization as a whole functions far better than as separate parts.

DISCUSSION QUESTIONS

1. Think of an occasion when you faced a miscommunication problem. What do you think caused the problem? How do you think it should have been handled better?

2. Have you ever *not* given someone information or opinions that perhaps you should have? Why? Was it the right thing to do? Why or why not? What would cause you to be glad that you provided (or withheld) negative or difficult information? What would cause you to regret providing/withholding it?

3. Think back to discussions you have heard or participated in. Consider the differences between one-way and two-way communication. How can two one-ways be turned into a true two-way?

4. Share with the class some of your experiences—both good and bad—with electronic media.

5. Report examples of mixed signals you have received (or sent). How can you reduce the potential for misunderstanding and misperception as you communicate with others?

6. What makes you want to say to someone, "You're not listening"?

7. What do you think about the practice of open-book management? What would you think about it if you were running your own company?

8. Discuss organizational rumors you have heard: what they were about, how they got started, how accurate they were, and how people reacted to them. What lessons can you learn from these episodes?

9. Refer to the "The Virtual Office section". What do you think will be the long-term impact of the mobile office on job satisfaction and performance? If you were a manager, how would you maximize the benefits and minimize the drawbacks? If you worked in this environment, how would you manage yourself to maximize your performance and avoid burnout?

10. Have you ever made or seen mistakes due to people not speaking a common language well? How do you or will you deal with others who do not speak the same language as you?

11. Have you ever tried to coach someone? What did you do well, and what mistakes did you make? How can you become a better coach?

12. Have you ever been coached by someone? What did he or she do well, and what mistakes were made? How was it for you to be on the receiving end of the coaching, and how did you respond? What is required to be successful as the receiver of someone else's coaching attempts?

13. Think about how companies communicate with Wall Street and the media and how analysts on TV communicate with viewers. What concepts from the chapter apply, and how can you become a more astute consumer of such information?

EXPERIENTIAL EXERCISES

15.1   NONVERBAL COMMUNICATION

OBJECTIVE

To become more conscious of nonverbal messages.

INSTRUCTIONS

Following is a list of nonverbal communication methods. Pick a day on which you will attempt to keep track of these methods.

Think back at the end of the day to three people with whom you communicated in some way. Record how you responded to these people in terms of their nonverbal communication methods. Identify those that had the greatest and least effect on your behavior.

Nonverbal Communication Worksheet

Medium	What Was the Message?	How Did You Respond?	Which Affected Your Behavior Most and Least?
How they shook hands			
Their posture			
Their facial expressions			
Their appearance			
Their voice tones			
Their smiles			
The expressions in their eyes			
Their confidence			
The way they moved			
The way they stood			
How close they stood to you			
How they smelled			
Symbols or gestures they used			
How loudly they spoke			

SOURCE: Excerpted from Laurence R. Jauch, Arthur G. Bedian, Sally A. Coltin, and William F. Glueck, *The Managerial Experience: Cases, Exercises, and Readings,* 5th ed. Copyright © 1989. South-Western, a part of Cengage Learning, Inc. Reproduced by permission. www.cengage.com/permissions

15.2 LISTENING SKILLS SURVEY

OBJECTIVES

1. To measure your skills as a listener.

2. To gain insight into the factors that determine good listening habits.

3. To demonstrate how you can become a better listener.

INSTRUCTIONS

1. Working alone, complete the Listening Skills Survey.

2. In small groups, compare scores, discuss survey test items, and prepare responses to the discussion questions.

3. After the class reconvenes, group spokespersons present group findings.

DISCUSSION QUESTIONS

1. In what ways did students' responses on the survey agree or disagree?

2. What do you think accounts for the differences?

3. How can the results of this survey be put to practical use?

Listening Skills Survey

To measure your listening skills, complete the following survey by circling the degree to which you agree with each statement.

	Strongly Agree	Agree	Neither Agree nor Disagree	Disagree	Strongly Disagree
1. I tend to be patient with the speaker, making sure she or he is finished speaking before I respond in any fashion.	5	4	3	2	1
2. When listening, I don't doodle or fiddle with papers and things that might distract me from the speaker.	5	4	3	2	1
3. I attempt to understand the speaker's point of view.	5	4	3	2	1
4. I try not to put the speaker on the defensive by arguing or criticizing.	5	4	3	2	1
5. When I listen, I focus on the speaker's feelings.	5	4	3	2	1
6. I let a speaker's annoying mannerisms distract me.	5	4	3	2	1
7. While the speaker is talking, I watch carefully for facial expressions and other types of body language.	5	4	3	2	1
8. I never talk when the other person is trying to say something.	5	4	3	2	1
9. During a conversation, a period of silence seems awkward to me.	5	4	3	2	1
10. I want people to just give me the facts and allow me to make up my own mind.	5	4	3	2	1
11. When the speaker is finished, I respond to his or her feelings.	5	4	3	2	1
12. I don't evaluate the speaker's words until she or he is finished talking.	5	4	3	2	1

15.3 ACTIVE LISTENING

This exercise involves triads. Each triad counts off into threes: 1, 2, 3, 1, 2, 3, and so on. In the first round, all the 1s in their respective triads take the pro position (see the topics given later in exercise), all the 2s take the con position, and all the 3s act as observers. After a topic is given, two individuals representing opposing viewpoints have one minute to collect their thoughts and then five to seven minutes to arrive at a mutually agreeable position on that topic.

The observer should use the form here to capture actual examples of what the individuals said or did that indicated active and less-than-active listening. When time is called, the pro individuals share their opinion of which listening behaviors they performed well and which ones they'd like to improve. Then the con individuals do the same. Finally, the observers share their observations and insights, using examples to reinforce their feedback.

If additional rounds are used, rotate the roles so that each person plays a speaking role and, if possible, an observing role.

Round 1:
Topic selected: _____
Notes:

Round 2:
Topic selected: _____
Notes:

Listening Feedback Form

Indicators of Active Listening	Pro	Con
1. Asked questions for clarification		
2. Paraphrased the opposing view		
3. Responded to nonverbal cues (e.g., body posture, tone of voice)		
4. Appeared to move toward a mutually satisfying solution		
Indicators of Less-Than-Active Listening		
5. Interrupted before allowing the other person to finish		
6. Was defensive about her or his position		
7. Appeared to dominate the conversation		
8. Ignored nonverbal cues		

Potential topics to be used:

1. Gun control
2. Capital punishment
3. Race as a criterion for college admission
4. Prison reform
5. U.S. intervention in wars outside of the United States
6. Legalization of marijuana
7. Mandatory armed forces draft
8. Interracial adoption
9. Premarital and extramarital sex
10. Prayer in schools
11. Diversity in the workplace
12. Pornography on the Internet

QUESTIONS

1. Did you arrive at a mutually agreeable solution? What helped you get there?

2. What were some factors that hindered this process?

3. How comfortable did you feel arguing the position you were given? How did this influence your ability to listen actively?

4. If the position you were given was exactly opposite your values or beliefs, do you see this topic differently now than before the exercise?

5. What steps can you take to improve your ability to listen actively to friends or associates, especially when you don't agree with their viewpoint?

CONCLUDING CASE

BEST TRUST BANK

Best Trust Bank attracts accounts from households and businesses based on its broad name recognition and reputation for integrity. In this way, Best Trust has grown to one of the world's top 25 banks. Its 73,000 employees work at headquarters and in facilities located in 47 countries.

One of those employees is Paul Wysinsky, who in the 1970s took an entry-level job as a bank teller. As he developed a track record of satisfying customers, working efficiently, and cooperating well with others on his team, Paul moved up to teller supervisor, branch manager, and operations manager. He took business courses during the evening, earned a master's degree, and worked his way up through middle management positions.

Twenty years later, he was offered a vice president's job in the human resources division, responsible for recruiting and retaining Best Trust's employees in Houston. Eager to learn about a new part of the company, Paul tackled the new responsibilities so well that when there was an opening for a new executive vice president in charge of corporate human resources, Paul was tapped to run all of HR.

The nature of Paul's work communications changed considerably as he rose through the ranks. When Paul was a teller, he looked forward to chatting with his co-workers during breaks; their enjoyment of each other's company made the days pass pleasantly. His supervisor checked in with him regularly to make sure Paul understood his job. His favorite responsibility, though, was greeting customers and listening to them carefully, trying to guess the unspoken needs that Best Trust might be able to meet. When customers were upset about a problem, he used to get nervous; but with experience, he became an expert at listening attentively, helping the customer find the best possible solution, and speaking in a respectful tone that almost always soothed any frayed nerves.

Now that Paul is an executive vice president, he rarely talks with Best Trust's customers, and more of his communications are structured and formal. Although he cares about attracting, motivating, and retaining employees in all positions, he knows he cannot possibly have a dialogue with 73,000 people in dozens of countries. In fact, he can't even have personal conversations with all of the HR employees—Best Trust has more than 800 of them, including several at each facility.

Consequently, Paul looks for a variety of ways to communicate. He meets weekly with all the department and functional heads involved in formulating strategy. The meeting's agenda includes reviewing HR issues such as leadership development, succession planning, diversity management, and employee satisfaction. Paul is well prepared because he meets at least weekly with each of the managers who report directly to him. In these one-on-one meetings, Paul and the manager review progress on the issues handled by that manager. Paul also uses those meetings to learn what challenges the manager is facing so he can offer coaching and encouragement. And Paul looks for ways to meet with as many employees outside HR as he can. For example, he attends an annual employee recognition gathering held to honor the company's 800 top-performing employees. There he talks to as many people as he can. He asks open-ended questions such as "What are you happy about at Best Trust? What could we do better?"

Talking one on one to employees can feel like an escape from one of the chief annoyances of his job: poorly written messages from many of the bank's middle managers. It seems that Best Trust has excelled at finding people with strong analytic and customer service skills, but many of these people stumble at presenting an idea or summarizing their progress in e-mails and reports. Paul feels intense time pressure, and if he gets a suggestion but

can't figure out the main idea in the first couple of sentences, he simply passes it to one of his managers for a possible follow-up. Paul suspects that good ideas and real problems are being missed. Rambling reports and presentations loaded with jargon seem to have become a norm at Best Trust, and Paul is thinking about adding a new training program to improve writing skills.

To get out the word about the bank's policies, benefits, and other initiatives, Paul uses a variety of media. He gives presentations at events such as the employee recognition gathering and at branches around the world. Four times a year, he records a video that is posted on the bank's intranet. Topics range from a summary of HR resources to interviews with key leaders at Best Trust. Also on the intranet, Paul leads regular town hall meetings, a live video feed that allows employees to post questions and ideas, which Paul and other executives answer immediately on the video.

Promotions to the executive level are not the only reason communication has changed for Paul at Best Trust. Another source of change is technology. When Paul was a teller, the Internet was just a concept, and transmitting data online was a major undertaking that required computer experts. Now the Internet is a basic tool. On the plus side, it helps Paul deliver information efficiently and keep up with far-flung colleagues. But Paul also has a whole set of policy concerns related to the Internet, such as whether to allow employees to access social networking sites and how closely to monitor blogs and other public information for company-related posts. When Paul thinks about it, he realizes that his communication skills have barely grown as fast as the communication demands of his work.

QUESTIONS

1. How has the media richness of Paul's communications changed since the days when he was a teller?

2. What sender and receiver skills are described in this case? Which ones need improvement? Offer one suggestion for improving the weak skills.

3. How might Paul improve upward communication and the communication culture more generally at Best Trust?

PART FOUR SUPPORTING CASE

Leading and Motivating When Disaster Strikes: Magna Exteriors and Interiors

The name of Magna Exteriors and Interiors Corporation captures its product mix of vehicle components that give each car or truck model its distinctive look. Some of Magna's exterior products are trim, roof systems, body panels, and front and rear end fascia; interior products include trim, cockpit systems, and cargo management systems. Nowadays auto companies don't make all these components but, instead, create the designs and handle the final assembly of components from suppliers such as

Magna, delivered to the auto company as needed to meet production plans.

Magna Exteriors and Interiors is a unit of Magna International, which describes itself as "the most diversified automotive supplier in the world." Magna has 263 manufacturing operations plus sales and engineering centers in 26 countries of North America, South America, Africa, Europe, and Asia. These meet the needs of more than two dozen customers, including General Motors,

Ford, Chrysler, Toyota, Mack, Harley Davidson, Freightliner, and Volkswagen. The customers sell very different kinds of vehicles, and it is expensive to build and transport large components, so Magna's factories need to be close to customers both geographically and in their working relationships.

Meeting these requirements suddenly became a problem for Magna's factory in Howell, Michigan, on a recent Wednesday evening in March. A fire started on an assembly line at the facility, which makes interior trim such as rear window trays, door panels, and skins for instrument panels. Fortunately the hundred workers who were finishing up the afternoon shift all escaped safely.

The Howell facility employs about 450 workers. Its customers include 16 GM, Ford, Chrysler, Nissan, and Mazda assembly plants. Forecasting a shortage of parts, some of its customers slowed production and canceled shifts in the days immediately after the fire. Magna's managers knew they needed to scramble, or employees would be out of work and important customers would be lost. Robert Brownlee, president of Magna Exteriors and Interiors North America, decided the Howell facility should be running again within just two days. Meeting that goal would require an all-out effort.

While the firefighters were still battling the blaze, Brownlee conferred by phone with his top managers, figuring out what they should do first. Because they couldn't yet assess the extent of the damages, they had to work with a worst-case scenario: destruction of the entire building. They identified four Magna facilities making similar products, where they could ship the Howell plant's tooling on flatbed trucks if need be. That night, Brownlee directed all four of the plants to increase production and build up their inventories in case they would be needed for the Howell plant's customers.

Next the managers set up a reconstruction team, including electricians, pipe fitters, millwrights, mechanics, toolmakers, and information technology specialists. The team assembled in Howell with a structural engineer, awaiting permission to enter the damaged building. On Thursday night, about 24 hours after the fire, the fire department let the team enter the plant. The structural engineer determined that the fire had been contained in one part of the plant. About 30 percent of the plant, representing one out of four production sectors, was destroyed beyond repair. One of the four remaining production sectors had largely escaped damage.

Now the clock was ticking on Brownlee's two-day recovery goal. On Friday morning, workers pulled damaged tooling out of the rubble and had it moved to Brighton, a city 12 miles away, where they cleaned it and set up a temporary assembly line in a Magna warehouse. Back in Howell, the reconstruction team was building a temporary wall to seal off the undamaged part of the facility and repairing the roof. The heating and electrical systems were destroyed, so they brought in a dozen diesel generators to power heaters and lighting. Until the roof was repaired, they coped with Michigan's wintry March weather by wearing snowmobile suits while clearing out debris and damaged products, working around the clock.

The next morning, spirits rose when power was restored to the least-damaged sector, and the lights came back on. Workers continued to repair, clean, and rewire the tooling. By Saturday night, workers were able to restart some of the machinery and do test runs. Unfortunately they ran into problems with each attempt. Managers were scrambling to keep on top of the plant reconstruction and the attempts to restart machinery. Brownlee saw that this was too much responsibility. He called together the managers, put each one in charge of relaunching one product line, and directed them to put a subordinate in charge of every other duty, including reconstruction.

The efforts to restart continued as representatives from every customer monitored the progress. Magna gave customers daily updates, and as each assembly line resumed, the relevant customer's representative signed off as part of the quality-control practices. By Sunday, limited production had begun at the Howell plant. Six days after the fire department determined that the fire was extinguished, the Howell plant was running at 80 percent of capacity, and its temporary line in Brighton handled the remaining production.

In a statement to the media, the company publicly thanked "the Magna Howell employees who continue to do whatever it takes to meet customer requirements; the Magna group office employees and Magna employees from numerous other divisions who have come to support the effort," the company's contractors and customers, the community's firefighters, and others who helped after the fire.

QUESTIONS

1. As a leader, what vision did Robert Brownlee offer? What combination of task performance and group maintenance behaviors did he use? Was this the appropriate combination after the fire? Why or why not?

2. What do you think the Magna managers and employees were motivated by most after the fire? Why?

3. Management set up a cross-functional reconstruction team, but there is no evidence that this was a self-managed team. Would a self-managed team have been more effective? Why or why not?

SOURCES: D. Sedgwick, "Five-Alarm Planning," *Crain's Detroit Business,* April 18, 2011, Business & Company Resource Center, http://galenet.galegroup.com; Magna International, "About Magna Exteriors and Interiors," http://www.magna.com; T. Van Alphen, "Magna Plant Resumes Full Deliveries after Fire," *Toronto Star,* March 10, 2011, http://www.thestar.com; and Magna International, "Magna Atreum Howell Plant Back in Business Six Days after Fire," news release, March 9, 2011, http://www.magna.com.

CHAPTER 16

Managerial Control

> More than at any time in the past, companies will not be able to hold themselves together with the traditional methods of control: hierarchy, systems, budgets, and the like. . . . The bonding glue will increasingly become ideological.
>
> — COLLINS AND PORRAS[1]
>
> Use your good judgment in all situations. There will be no additional rules.
>
> — NORDSTROM'S EMPLOYEE MANUAL

LEARNING OBJECTIVES

After studying Chapter 16, you will be able to:

LO 1 Explain why companies develop control systems for employees. p. 528

LO 2 Summarize how to design a basic bureaucratic control system. p. 529

LO 3 Describe the purposes for using budgets as a control device. p. 538

LO 4 Define basic types of financial statements and financial ratios used as controls. p. 541

LO 5 List procedures for implementing effective control systems. p. 546

LO 6 Identify ways in which organizations use market control mechanisms. p. 551

LO 7 Discuss the use of clan control in an empowered organization. p. 553

CHAPTER OUTLINE

Bureaucratic Control Systems

The Control Cycle

Approaches to Bureaucratic Control

Management Audits

Budgetary Controls

Financial Controls

The Downside of Bureaucratic Control

Designing Effective Control Systems

The Other Controls: Markets and Clans

Market Control

Clan Control: The Role of Empowerment and Culture

Management Connection

CAN BETTER CONTROLS HELP BEST BUY SURVIVE IN THE INTERNET AGE?

Best Buy once had other stores' managers running scared. Founder Richard Schulze built a St. Paul, Minnesota, electronics store into a retailing giant; today more than 100,000 employees sell $50 billion of merchandise a year. Consumers who once bought a television set at a department or discount store flocked to Best Buy for its wide selection and knowledgeable salespeople. Today, however, consumers have alternatives. They can find product specifications and reviews online, from the comfort of their homes. Those who bother to visit a store are likely to be just taking a look at preselected items; after making their choice, they will return to the Internet and order from the lowest-priced seller.

Best Buy is struggling to stay relevant in this environment. Its revenues at stores open a year or more have been sliding, and it has posted one unprofitable quarter after another. Its market share, though it represents close to one-third of U.S. sales of consumer electronics, is falling. Competing on price with online retailers such as Amazon is difficult because Best Buy has many large stores to maintain.

Management has tried several responses. Trying to keep prices low, the company launched a program to match prices available online. It cut costs by laying off employees. It lured in younger shoppers with low-priced items such as CDs and expanded into services with the Geek Squad. It pressed customers to buy extended warranties, which are very profitable. To its credit, Best Buy has stayed in business while its main store competitor, Circuit City, declared bankruptcy.

One of management's most attention-getting efforts was the decision to abandon a policy called Results Only

Work Environment (ROWE). The policy granted employees at headquarters freedom to set work hours; managers evaluated these employees only on their achievements, not their attendance. The policy had been announced to great fanfare, with its sponsors saying ROWE helped the company save money that would have been lost to employee turnover. However, CEO Hubert Joly saw ROWE as a failure to lead decisively at a time when Best Buy needs all hands on deck. Not only did Joly insist that headquarters employees show up on a standard schedule, he also asked, during the December 2012 holiday season, that office employees spend extra hours helping out in stores. Advocates for employee empowerment howled, but that year, the company at least temporarily halted the downward slide of holiday revenues.[2]

Survival is difficult in the retailing industry because consumer tastes and habits can change abruptly. Best Buy won over a huge base of customers and is now struggling to keep them without sacrificing profits. As you read this chapter, think about the kinds of control measures and processes that can help a company manage in a turbulent environment.

control

Any process that directs the activities of individuals toward the achievement of organizational goals.

Financial measures are signaling Best Buy's managers that they need to make changes to improve performance. Another company that uses measurements to help it improve is La-Z-Boy, where teams of employees constantly find ways to improve productivity and quality. La-Z-Boy also uses systems to prevent problems. It assigns a production engineer to design teams to make sure that new products can be produced efficiently, reducing defects as well as costs.[3] These examples are two sides of one coin: control—a means or mechanism for regulating the behavior of organization members. Left on their own, people may act in ways that they perceive to be beneficial to them individually but that may work to the detriment of the organization as a whole. Even well-intentioned people may not know whether they are directing their efforts toward the activities that are most important. Thus control is one of the fundamental forces that keep the organization together and heading in the right direction.

Control is defined as any process that directs the activities of individuals toward the achievement of organizational goals. It is how effective managers make sure that activities are going as planned. Some managers don't want to admit it (see Table 16.1), but control problems—the lack of controls or the wrong kinds of controls—frequently cause irreparable damage to organizations. Ineffective control systems result in problems ranging from employee theft to peeling tire tread problems. BP has spent billions of dollars to repair damage to the Gulf of Mexico following the Deepwater Horizon disaster; years later, it was still in court, defending charges of negligence. The damage to its reputation could hardly help the company as it more recently responded to safety questions related to an oil leak in Norway.[4] Employees simply wasting time cost U.S. employers billions of dollars each year![5]

Control has been called one of the conjoined twins of management. The other twin is planning. Some means of control are necessary because once managers form plans and strategies, they must ensure that the plans are carried out. They must make sure that other people are doing what needs to be done and not doing inappropriate things. If plans are not carried out properly, management must take steps to correct the problem. This process is the primary control function of management. By ensuring creativity, enhancing quality, and reducing cost, managers must figure out ways to control the activities in their organizations.

> *Control has been called one of the conjoined twins of management.*

Not surprisingly, effective planning facilitates control, and control facilitates planning. Planning lays out a framework for the future and, in this sense, provides a blueprint for control. Control systems, in turn, regulate the allocation and use of resources and, in so doing, facilitate the process of the next phases of planning. In today's complex organizational environment, both functions have become more difficult to implement while they have become more important in every department of

TABLE 16.1

Symptoms of an Out-of-Control Company

• **Lax top management**—senior managers do not emphasize or value the need for controls, or they set a bad example.
• **Absence of policies**—the firm's expectations are not established in writing.
• **Lack of agreed-upon standards**—organization members are unclear about what needs to be achieved.
• **"Shoot the messenger" management**—employees feel their careers would be at risk if they reported bad news.
• **Lack of periodic reviews**—managers do not assess performance on a regular, timely basis.
• **Bad information systems**—key data are not measured and reported in a timely and easily accessible way.
• **Lack of ethics in the culture**—organization members have not internalized a commitment to integrity.

the organization. Managers today must control their people, inventories, quality, and costs, to mention just a few of their responsibilities.

According to William Ouchi of the University of California at Los Angeles, managers can apply three broad strategies for achieving organizational control: bureaucratic control, market control, and clan control.[6] **Bureaucratic control** is the use of rules, regulations, and formal authority to guide performance. It includes such items as budgets, statistical reports, and performance appraisals to regulate behavior and results. **Market control** involves the use of pricing mechanisms to regulate activities in organizations as though they were economic transactions. Business units may be treated as profit centers and trade resources (services or goods) with one another via such mechanisms. Managers who run these units may be evaluated on the basis of profit and loss. **Clan control,** (also known as *cultural control),* unlike the first two types, does not assume that the interests of the organization and individuals naturally diverge. Instead clan control is based on the idea that employees may share the values, expectations, and goals of the organization and act in accordance with them. When members of an organization have common values and goals—and trust one another—formal controls may be less necessary. Clan control is based on many of the interpersonal processes described in the organization culture section of Chapter 2, in Chapter 12 on leadership, and in Chapter 14 on groups and teams (e.g., group norms and cohesiveness).

Table 16.2 summarizes the main features of bureaucratic, market, and clan controls. We use this framework as a foundation for our discussions throughout the chapter.

bureaucratic control

The use of rules, regulations, and authority to guide performance.

market control

Control based on the use of pricing mechanisms and economic information to regulate activities within organizations.

clan control

Control based on the norms, values, shared goals, and trust among group members.

Bureaucratic Control Systems

Bureaucratic (or formal) control systems are designed to measure progress toward set performance goals and, if necessary, to apply corrective measures to ensure that performance achieves managers' objectives. Control systems detect and correct significant variations, or discrepancies, in the results of planned activities.

The Control Cycle

As Figure 16.1 shows, a typical control system has four major steps:

1. Setting performance standards.
2. Measuring performance.
3. Comparing performance against the standards and determining deviations.
4. Taking action to correct problems and reinforce successes.

System Control	Features and Requirements
Bureaucratic control	Uses formal rules, standards, hierarchy, and legitimate authority. Works best where tasks are certain and workers are independent.
Market control	Uses prices, competition, profit centers, and exchange relationships. Works best where tangible output can be identified and a market can be established between parties.
Clan control	Involves culture, shared values, beliefs, expectations, and trust. Works best where there is no one best way to do a job, and employees are empowered to make decisions.

TABLE 16.2
Characteristics of Controls

SOURCES: W. G. Ouchi, "A Conceptual Framework for the Design of Organizational Control Mechanisms," *Management Science* 25 (1979), pp. 833–48; W. G. Ouchi, "Markets, Bureaucracies, and Clans," *Administrative Science Quarterly* 25 (1980), pp. 129–41; and R. D. Robey and C. A. Sales, *Designing Organizations* (Burr Ridge, IL: Richard D. Irwin, 1994).

FIGURE 16.1
The Control Process

standard

Expected performance
for a given goal: a target
that establishes a desired
performance level, motivates
performance, and serves as
a benchmark against which
actual performance is assessed.

Bottom Line

Standards must be set for all
bottom-line practices.
*Give an example of a standard
for sustainability.*

Step 1: Setting Performance Standards   Every organization has goals: profitability, innovation, satisfaction of customers and employees, and so on. A **standard** is the level of expected performance for a given goal. Standards are targets that establish desired performance levels, motivate performance, and serve as benchmarks against which to assess actual performance. Standards can be set for any activity—financial activities, operating activities, legal compliance, charitable contributions, and so on.[7]

We have discussed setting performance standards in other parts of the text. For example, employee goal setting for motivation is built around the concept of specific, measurable performance standards. Such standards should be challenging and should aim for improvement over past performance. Typically, performance standards are derived from job requirements, such as increasing market share by 10 percent, reducing costs 20 percent, and answering customer complaints within 24 hours. But performance standards don't apply just to people in isolation—they frequently reflect the integration of both human and system performance. HealthPartners, a Bloomington, Minnesota, nonprofit organization that operates clinics and a hospital and offers health insurance plans, sets ambitious standards for patient care. To achieve a goal of reducing diabetes complications by 30 percent, HealthPartners measured existing practices and results and then set up a standard protocol for exams and treatments, including the requirement that any abnormal results receive an immediate response. To encourage its physicians to follow the protocol, HealthPartners offers financial incentives for compliance. In little more than a decade, HealthPartners exceeded its goal for improved diabetes care. HealthPartners has similar programs for treatment of cardiovascular disease and depression and for improving the health status of patients who are obese or smoke.[8] In a recent year, HealthPartners estimated it saved more than $3.6 million through programs aimed at eliminating health complications that bring patients back to the hospital after being discharged.

Performance standards can be set with respect to (1) quantity, (2) quality, (3) time used, and (4) cost. For example, production activities include volume of output (quantity), defects (quality), on-time availability of finished goods (time use), and dollar expenditures for raw materials and direct labor (cost). Many important aspects of performance, such as customer service, can be measured by the same standards—adequate supply and availability of products, quality of service, speed of delivery, and so forth.

One word of caution: The downside of establishing performance targets and standards is that they may not be supported by other elements of the control system. Each piece of the system is important and depends on the others. Otherwise the system can get terribly out of balance.

Step 2: Measuring Performance   The second step in the control process is to measure performance levels. For example, managers can count units produced, days absent, papers filed, samples distributed, and dollars earned. Performance data commonly are obtained from three sources: written reports, oral reports, and personal observations.

Written reports include computer printouts and on-screen reports. Thanks to computers' data-gathering and analysis capabilities and decreasing costs, both large and small companies can gather huge amounts of performance data.

One common example of oral reports occurs when a salesperson contacts his or her immediate manager at the close of each business day to report the accomplishments, problems, or customers' reactions during the day. The manager can ask questions to gain additional information or clear up any misunderstandings. When necessary, tentative corrective actions can be worked out during the discussion.

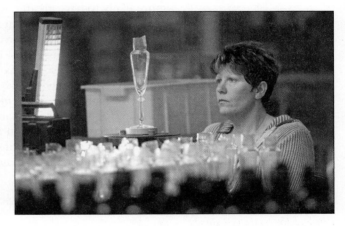

Personal observation involves going to the area where activities take place and watching what is occurring. The manager can directly observe work methods, employees' nonverbal signals, and the general operation. Personal observation gives a detailed picture of what is going on, but it also has some disadvantages. It does not provide accurate quantitative data; the information usually is general and subjective. Also, employees can misunderstand the purpose of personal observation as mistrust or lack of confidence. Still, many managers believe in the value of firsthand observation. As you learned in earlier chapters, personal contact can increase leadership visibility and upward communication. It also provides valuable information about performance to supplement written and oral reports.

At the Baccarat factory in France, the workers in the quality control area are responsible for the quality and selection of these fine cut crystal glasses.

Regardless of the performance measure used, the information must be provided to managers on a timely basis. For example, consumer goods companies such as General Foods carefully track new product sales in selected local markets first so they can make any necessary adjustments well before a national rollout. Information that is not available is of little or no use to managers.

Step 3: Comparing Performance with the Standard   The third step in the control process is comparing performance with the standard. In this process, the manager evaluates the performance. For some activities, relatively small deviations from the standard are acceptable, whereas in others a slight deviation may be serious. In many manufacturing processes, a significant deviation in either direction (e.g., drilling a hole that is too small or too large) is unacceptable. In other cases, a deviation in one direction, such as sales or customer satisfaction that fall below the target level, is a problem, but a deviation in the other, exceeding the sales target or customer expectations, is a sign employees are getting better-than-expected results. As a result, managers who perform the oversight must analyze and evaluate the results carefully.

> Managers can save much time and effort if they apply the principle of exception.

The managerial **principle of exception** states that control is enhanced by concentrating on the exceptions to, or significant deviations from, the expected result or standard. In other words, in comparing performance with the standard, managers need to direct their attention to the exception—for example, a handful of defective components produced on an assembly line or the feedback from customers who are upset or delighted with a service. Atlanta-based US Security Associates uses information technology to gather performance data on its uniformed security guards and dispatches supervisors to investigate any variances from performance norms, such as a failure of a guard to sign in at a client's location on time.[9]

principle of exception

A managerial principle stating that control is enhanced by concentrating on the exceptions to or significant deviations from the expected result or standard.

With the principle of exception, only exceptional cases require corrective action. This principle is important in controlling. The manager is not concerned with performance that equals or closely approximates the expected results. Managers can save much time and effort if they apply the principle of exception.

Step 4: Taking Action to Correct Problems and Reinforce Successes The last step in the control process is to take appropriate action when there are significant deviations. This step ensures that operations are adjusted to achieve the planned results—or to continue exceeding the plan if the manager determines that is possible. In cases in which significant variances are discovered, the manager usually takes immediate and vigorous action.

When corrective action is needed to solve a systemic problem, such as major delays in work flow, often a team approach is most effective. A corrective action is more likely to have greater acceptance in the organization if it is based on a common effort and takes into account multiple points of view. As we discussed in Chapter 14, teams often bring a greater diversity of resources, ideas, and perspectives to problem solving. Knowledgeable team members can often prevent managers from implementing simplistic solutions that don't address the underlying causes of a problem. They are more likely to take into account the effects of any solution on other parts of the organization, preventing new problems from arising later. And they may well develop solutions that managers might not have considered on their own. As a result, any corrective action that is finally adopted will probably be more effective. An important added benefit of bringing employees together to develop corrective actions is that it helps managers build and reinforce an organizationwide culture of high standards.

In Practice

TEAM APPROACH AT MCDONALD'S

McDonald's has an extra challenge in introducing corrective action: When it identifies a problem in its restaurants, it has to persuade franchise owners that they should make changes. Most McDonald's restaurants have independent owners (franchisees), so the company cannot simply direct them as it would direct employees.

Recently, McDonald's addressed the problem that its sales had begun to fall after years of solid growth. In looking for the source of the problem, management observed that the data it gathers about customer satisfaction showed an increase in complaints about speed and quality of service. Also, in independent surveys of fast-food customer service by *QSR* magazine, the company trailed its competitors in server friendliness and average service time.

McDonald's responded by sharing this information with its franchisees. It told them that a survey by the National Restaurant Association showed that customers care almost as much about high-quality service as about value for the price. McDonald's urged franchisees to schedule more employees for peak hours, and it began providing equipment and training for a new dual-point ordering system. Under the system, one employee takes a customer's order and provides a receipt showing an order number. The customer moves to the other end of the counter to pick up the order when the order number displays on a monitor. An employee there scans the receipt, thanks the customer, and invites him or her to return. A new, third employee, called a runner, fetches items such as juice, sauces, and cups. In the past, one employee tried to handle all of these tasks, and the activity could seem chaotic.[10]

- How can a team approach help McDonald's improve customer service in this situation?

The selection of the corrective action depends on the nature of the problem. The corrective action may involve a shift in marketing strategy (if, say, the problem is lower-than-expected sales), a disciplinary action, a new way to check the accuracy of manufactured parts, or a major modification to a process or system. Sometimes managers learn they can get better results if they adjust their own practices. Yum Brands, whose franchise restaurants include KFC, Taco Bell, Pizza Hut, and Long John Silver's, conducts regular surveys to learn whether employees feel strong commitment to their jobs. These data are shared with managers to help them measure their performance as leaders and motivators. Jonathan McDaniel, a Houston KFC manager, once learned that his employees were unhappy with their work hours. He began asking them ahead of time whether they wanted particular days off each month—information that helped him create better schedules and end a cause of employee dissatisfaction.[11]

After trying corrective action, a growing number of organizations conduct an **after-action review,** a frank and open-minded discussion of the four questions shown in Figure 16.2, aimed at continuous improvement.[12] The process was developed by the U.S. Army to help soldiers learn from their experiences, and many companies find that the method applies equally well to businesses that want to improve. Employees at the J. M. Huber Corporation conduct a review after every planned project and major unplanned event and then post the lessons learned in a database available online. In the public sector, emergency response teams have improved their performance as a result of using after-action reviews. This type of review is most effective if the reviews are scheduled consistently, participation is mandatory, and all participants in the project are included.

Approaches to Bureaucratic Control

The three approaches to bureaucratic control are feedforward, concurrent, and feedback. **Feedforward control** takes place before operations begin and includes policies, procedures, and rules designed to ensure that planned activities are carried out properly. Examples include inspection of raw materials and proper selection and training of employees. **Concurrent control** takes place while plans are being carried out. It includes directing, monitoring, and fine-tuning activities as they occur. **Feedback control** focuses on the use of information about results to correct deviations from the acceptable standard after they arise.

Feedforward Control   Feedforward control (sometimes called *preliminary control*) is future oriented; its aim is to prevent problems before they arise. Instead of waiting for results and comparing them with goals, a manager can exert control by limiting activities in advance. For example, companies have policies defining the scope within which decisions are made. A company may dictate that managers must adhere to clear ethical and legal guidelines when making decisions. Formal rules and procedures also prescribe people's actions before they occur. For example, legal experts advise companies to establish policies forbidding disclosure of proprietary information or making clear that employees are not speaking for the company when they

---

after-action review

A frank and open-minded discussion of four basic questions aimed at continuous improvement.

feedforward control

The control process used before operations begin, including policies, procedures, and rules designed to ensure that planned activities are carried out properly.

concurrent control

The control process used while plans are being carried out, including directing, monitoring, and fine-tuning activities as they are performed.

feedback control

Control that focuses on the use of information about previous results to correct deviations from the acceptable standard.

FIGURE 16.2

Questions for an After-Action Review

post messages on blogs, microblogging sites such as Twitter, or social networking sites such as Facebook. Human resource policies defining what forms of body art are acceptable to display at work can avoid awkward case-by-case conversations about a tattoo that offends co-workers or piercings that are incompatible with the company's image.[13]

Recently more managers have grown concerned about the organizational pitfalls of workplace romances, and some have sought a solution in feedforward controls. As wonderful as it is to find love, problems can arise if romantic activities between a supervisor and subordinate create a conflict of interest or charges of sexual harassment. Other employees might interpret the relationship wrongly—that the company sanctions personal relationships as a path to advancement. In addition, romantic ups and downs can spill over into the workplace and affect everyone's mood and motivation. Controls aimed at preventing such problems in an organization include training in appropriate behavior (including how to avoid sexual harassment) and even requiring executives and their romantic interests to sign love contracts in which they indicate that the relationship is voluntary and welcome. A copy of the contract goes into the company's personnel files in case the attachment disintegrates and an unhappy employee wants to blame the company for having allowed it in the first place.[14]

Concurrent Control   Concurrent control, which takes place while plans are carried out, is the heart of any control system. On a manufacturing floor, all efforts are directed toward producing the correct quantity and quality of the right products in the specified amount of time. In an airline terminal, the baggage must get to the right airplanes before flights depart. In factories, materials must be available when and where needed, and breakdowns in the production process must be repaired immediately. Concurrent control also is in effect when supervisors watch employees to ensure they work efficiently and avoid mistakes.

Advances in information technology have created powerful concurrent controls. Computerized systems give managers immediate access to data from the most remote corners of their companies. For example, managers can update budgets instantly based on a continuous flow of performance data. In production facilities, monitoring systems that track errors per hour, machine speeds, and other measures allow managers to correct small production problems before they become disasters. Point-of-sale terminals in store checkout lines send sales data back to a retailer's headquarters to show which products are selling in which locations.

Concurrent control also can be applied to service settings. As part of its efforts to transform safety, quality, and efficiency, Virginia Mason Medical Center authorized employees to issue personal safety alerts (PSAs). If any employee has a concern or question about a patient's safety, that employee may call an alert. The PSA system not only has improved the hospital's safety performance, it also has lowered its costs for professional liability insurance.[15]

Timing is an important aspect of feedback control.

Feedback Control   Feedback control is involved when performance data have been gathered and analyzed and the results have been returned to someone (or something) in the process to make corrections. When supervisors monitor behavior, they are exercising concurrent control. When they point out and correct improper performance, they are using feedback as a means of control.

Timing is an important aspect of feedback control. Long time lags often occur between performance and feedback, such as when actual spending is compared with the quarterly budget, instead of weekly or monthly, or when some aspect of performance is compared with the projection made a year earlier. Yet if feedback on performance is not timely, managers cannot quickly identify and eliminate the problem and prevent more serious harm.[16]

Some feedback processes are under real-time (concurrent) control, such as a computer-controlled robot on an assembly line. Such units have sensors that continually determine whether they are in the correct position to perform their functions. If they are not, a built-in control device makes immediate corrections.

In other situations, feedback processes require more time. The feedback used by Hertz includes customer ratings of the company's service and the quality of the cars it rents. Patterns of praise and complaints can help the company reinforce or correct practices at particular facilities or throughout the organization, and if a customer is upset about something, Hertz wants to know as soon as possible so it can correct the problem. In the past, gathering and interpreting customer feedback from surveys and online comments could take about three weeks. Now, however, analytic software collects and tallies data as it flows into the company, and it delivers daily reports to local managers. Armed with the information, the managers are expected to respond to any problems within 24 hours. With these changes, customer satisfaction with Hertz has been rising consistently.[17]

In Practice

FEEDBACK AT FAMILY PRACTICE ASSOCIATES

Family Practice Associates (FPA) discovered that the feedback from establishing and using performance standards is a prerequisite for improvement. Without this feedback, the five-doctor medical practice in Wilmington, Delaware, didn't even know how badly it needed to improve, much less what to change.

Several years ago, the physicians at FPA decided to apply for the National Committee for Quality Assurance (NCQA) award for quality of care for diabetes patients. To do that, they would have to submit data summarizing the care they provided. When the doctors began compiling the data, they were shocked to see that test results were sadly out of date. Out of the more than 900 patients with diabetes, hundreds were missing appointments, not receiving follow-up calls, and not scheduling appointments with specialists. Before FPA could even apply for the quality award, it would have to start following up with patients so that FPA could deliver the care they needed.

Once the office staff began contacting patients, the doctors could begin collecting data. Every month, doctors meet to review reports of their progress against the NCQA's quality standards and other quality measures. By becoming more methodical, the practice earned the NCQA award and then was surprised with a bonus from Medicaid—a $10,000 incentive for providing superior care. Buoyed by the recognition, FPA continued to improve by converting from paper to electronic health records. The electronic system lets FPA quickly generate reports that identify additional areas for improvement.[18]

• How might feedforward control supplement these efforts at quality improvement?

The Role of Six Sigma   One of the most important quality control tools to emerge is six sigma, which we first discussed in Chapter 9. It is a particularly robust and powerful application of feedback control. Six sigma is designed to reduce defects in all organization processes—not just product defects but anything that may result in customer dissatisfaction. The system was developed at Motorola in the late 1980s, when the company found it was being beaten consistently in the competitive marketplace by foreign firms that were able to produce higher-quality products at a lower cost. Since then, the technique has been widely adopted and even improved on by many companies, such as GE, AlliedSignal, Ford, and Xerox.

Bottom Line

Six sigma aims for defect-free performance.

What impact would achieving six sigma quality have on a company's costs?

Sigma is the Greek letter used in statistics to designate the estimated standard deviation, or variation, in a process. It indicates how often defects in a process are likely to occur. The higher the sigma number, the lower the level of variation or defects. For example, as you can see in Table 16.3, a two-sigma-level process has more than 300,000 defects per million opportunities (DPMO)—not a very well-controlled process. A three-sigma-level process has 66,807 DPMO, which is roughly a 93 percent level of accuracy. Many organizations operate at this level, which on its face does not sound too bad, until we consider its implications—for example, 7 items of airline baggage lost for every 100 processed. The additional costs to organizations of such inaccuracy are enormous. As you can see in the table, even at just above a 99 percent defect-free rate, or 6,210 DPMO, the accuracy level is often unacceptable.[19]

At a six-sigma level, a process is producing fewer than 3.4 defects per million, which we saw in Chapter 9 is a 99.99966 percent level of accuracy. Six-sigma companies have not only close to zero product or service defects but also substantially lower production costs and cycle times and much higher levels of customer satisfaction. The methodology isn't just for the factory floor, either. Accountants have used six sigma to improve the quality of their audits investigating risks faced by their clients.[20]

The six-sigma approach is based on an intense statistical analysis of business processes that contribute to customer satisfaction. For example, a business process could be assembling a product or delivering products to customers. For the given process, the effort begins by defining the outputs and information that flow through each stage of the process and then measuring performance at each stage. A variety of tools are available for analyzing the results. These might include looking for all the root causes of any problem. Suppose some customers are dissatisfied with a company's customer service. Asking "why?" over and over could reveal that customers are dissatisfied because phone calls go unanswered, which happens because support staff cannot keep up with the call volume, which happens because the department is understaffed, which is the result of frozen hiring levels, the result of budget cuts. Any solution will have to address the budget restrictions, either by increasing the budget or by finding a way that a small department can satisfy customers. After the problems are analyzed, process improvements are identified and implemented, and the new process is evaluated again. This cycle continues until the desired quality level is achieved. In this way, the six-sigma process leads to continuous improvement in an organization's operations.

Six sigma has come under some criticism for not always delivering business results.[21] One likely reason six sigma doesn't always improve the bottom line is that it focuses only on how to eliminate defects in a process, not whether the process is the best one for the organization. So, for example, at 3M, a drive to improve efficiency through six sigma has been blamed for slowing the flow of innovative ideas. At Home Depot, six sigma has been credited with improving such processes as customer checkout and

TABLE 16.3

Relationship between Sigma Level and Defects per Million Opportunities

Sigma Level	DPMO	Is Four Sigma Good Enough?
2σ	308,537	Consider these everyday examples of four-sigma quality . . .
3σ	66,807	• 20,000 lost articles of mail per hour.
4σ	**6,210**	• Unsafe drinking water 15 minutes per day.
5σ	233	• 5,000 incorrect surgical operations per week.
6σ	3.4	• 200,000 wrong prescriptions each year.
		• No electricity for 7 hours each month.

SOURCE: Tom Rancour and Mike McCracken, "Applying 6 Sigma Methods for Breakthrough Safety Performance," *Professional Safety* 45, no. 10 (October 2000), pp. 29–32. Reprinted with permission.

deciding where to place products in stores, but some say the effort took store workers away from customers. One way managers can apply the strengths of six sigma and minimize the drawbacks is by setting different goals and control processes for the company's mature products than for its areas of innovation.

Management Audits

Over the years, **management audits** have developed as a means of evaluating the effectiveness and efficiency of various systems within an organization, from social responsibility programs to accounting control. Management audits may be external or internal. Managers conduct external audits of other companies and internal audits of their own companies. Some of the same tools and approaches are used for both types of audit.[22]

External Audits   An **external audit** occurs when one organization evaluates another organization. Typically an external body such as a CPA firm conducts financial audits of an organization (accounting audits are discussed later). But any company can conduct external audits of competitors or other companies for its own strategic decision-making purposes. This type of analysis (1) investigates other organizations for possible merger or acquisition, (2) determines the soundness of a company that will be used as a major supplier, or (3) discovers the strengths and weaknesses of a competitor to maintain or better exploit the competitive advantage of the investigating organization. Publicly available data usually are used for these evaluations.[23]

External audits provide essential feedback control when they identify legal and ethical lapses that could harm the organization and its reputation. They also are useful for preliminary control because they can prevent problems from occurring. If a company seeking to acquire other businesses gathers adequate, accurate information about possible candidates, it is more likely to acquire the most appropriate companies and avoid unsound acquisitions.

Internal Audits   An organization may assign a group to conduct an **internal audit** to assess (1) what the company has done for itself and (2) what it has done for its customers or other recipients of its goods or services. The company can be evaluated on a number of factors, including financial stability, production efficiency, sales effectiveness, human resources development, earnings growth, energy use, public relations, civic responsibility, and other criteria of organizational effectiveness. The audit reviews the company's past, present, and future, including any risks the organization should be prepared to face.[24] A recent study found that the stock prices of companies with highly rated audit committees tended to rise faster than shares of companies with lower-rated internal auditors. It is likely that the higher-rated audit committees do a better job of finding and eliminating undesirable practices.[25]

To perform a management audit, auditors compile a list of desired qualifications and weight each qualification. Among the most common undesirable practices uncovered by a management audit are the performance of unnecessary work, duplication of work, poor inventory control, uneconomical use of equipment and machines, procedures that are more costly than necessary, and wasted resources. At Capital One Financial Corporation, the human resources (HR) department performed an audit of facilities usage. Over several months, staff members walked through headquarters, noting which desks were occupied. The audit determined that more than 4 out of 10 desks were unused each day, and another 3 out of 10 were unused at least part of the day. Employees were away at meetings, visiting clients, or working flexible schedules. The HR staff developed a plan for Capital One to operate more efficiently in one-third of its space. Now most employees keep their work items in a cart, which they take to a desk when they need one. The change saves the company $3 million a year.[26]

---

management audit

An evaluation of the effectiveness and efficiency of various systems within an organization.

---

external audit

An evaluation conducted by one organization, such as a CPA firm, on another.

---

internal audit

A periodic assessment of a company's own planning, organizing, leading, and controlling processes.

Sustainability Audits and the Triple Bottom Line   Companies that are serious about goals for sustainability conduct audits to evaluate how effectively they are serving all stakeholders and protecting the environment. These sustainability audits typically evaluate performance in terms of a triple bottom line—that is, the company's financial performance, environmental impact, and impact on people in the company and the communities where it operates. Adapting a slogan coined by Shell in the 1990s, an easy way to remember the three bottom lines is with the terms *profit*, *planet*, and *people*.[27] In practice, reporting a triple bottom line is not standardized and regulated the way financial reporting is. A company might report its profitability in the traditional way, its environmental impact in terms of trends in efficiency of resource use, and its human impact in terms of general policies. As we saw Chapter 13, we can expect the impact of a sustainability audit to be greatest where there are specific goals and rewards for achieving them. However, committing to issue a report based on a sustainability audit can be a first step toward measuring and reinforcing sustainable business practices.

Budgetary Controls

Budgetary control is one of the most widely recognized and commonly used methods of managerial control. It ties together feedforward control, concurrent control, and feedback control, depending on the point at which it is applied. Budgetary control is the process of finding out what's being done and comparing the results with the corresponding budget data to verify accomplishments or remedy differences. Budgetary control is commonly called **budgeting.**

budgeting

The process of investigating what is being done and comparing the results with the corresponding budget data to verify accomplishments or remedy differences; also called *budgetary controlling.*

Fundamental Budgetary Considerations   In private industry, budgetary control begins with an estimate of sales and expected income. Table 16.4 shows a budget with a forecast of expected sales (the sales budget) on the top row, followed by several categories of estimated expenses for the first three months of the year. In the bottom row, the profit estimate is determined by subtracting each month's budgeted expenses from the sales in that month's sales budget. Columns next to each month's budget provide space to enter the actual accomplishments so that managers can readily compare expected amounts and actual results.

Although this discussion of budgeting focuses on the flow of money into and out of the organization, budgeting information is not confined to finances. The entire enterprise and any of its units can create budgets for their activities, using units other than dollars if appropriate. For example, many organizations use production budgets forecasting physical units produced and shipped, and labor can be budgeted in skill levels or hours of work required.

TABLE 16.4   A Sales Expense Budget

	January		February		March	
	Estimate	Actual	Estimate	Actual	Estimate	Actual
Sales	$1,200,000		$1,350,000		$1,400,000	
Expenses						
General overhead	310,000		310,000		310,000	
Selling	242,000		275,000		288,000	
Producing	327,000		430,500		456,800	
Research	118,400		118,400		115,000	
Office	90,000		91,200		91,500	
Advertising	32,500		27,000		25,800	
Estimated gross profit	80,100		97,900		112,900	

A primary consideration of budgeting is the length of the budget period. All budgets are prepared for a specific time period. Many budgets cover one, three, or six months or one year. The length of time selected depends on the primary purpose of the budgeting. The period chosen should include the enterprise's complete normal cycle of activity. For example, seasonal variations should be included for production and for sales. The budget period commonly coincides with other control devices such as managerial reports, balance sheets, and statements of profit and loss. In addition, the extent to which reasonable forecasts can be made should be considered in selecting the length of the budget period.

Budgetary control proceeds through several stages. Establishing *expectancies* starts with the broad plan for the company and the estimate of sales, and it ends with budget approval and publication. Next, the budgetary operations stage deals with finding out what is being accomplished and comparing the results with expectancies. The last stage, as in any control process, involves responding appropriately with some combination of reinforcing successes and correcting problems.

Although practices differ widely, a member of top management often serves as the chief coordinator for formulating and using the budget. Usually the chief financial officer (CFO) has these duties. He or she needs to be less concerned with the details than with resolving conflicting interests, recommending adjustments when needed, and giving official sanction to the budgetary procedures. In a small company, budgeting responsibility generally rests with the owner.

Types of Budgets   There are many types of budgets. Some of the more common types are as follows:

- *Sales budget.* Usually data for the sales budget include forecasts of sales by month, sales area, and product.
- *Production budget.* The production budget commonly is expressed in physical units. Required information for preparing this budget includes types and capacities of machines, economic quantities to produce, and availability of materials.
- *Cost budget.* The cost budget is used for areas of the organization that incur expenses but no revenue, such as human resources and other support departments. Cost budgets may also be included in the production budget. Costs may be fixed, or independent of the immediate level of activity (such as rent), or variable, rising or falling with the level of activity (such as raw materials).
- *Cash budget.* The cash budget is essential to every business. It should be prepared after all other budget estimates are completed. The cash budget shows the anticipated receipts and expenditures, the amount of working capital available, the extent to which outside financing may be required, and the periods and amounts of cash available.
- *Capital budget.* The capital budget is used for the cost of fixed assets such as plants and equipment. Such costs are usually treated not as regular expenses but as investments because of their long-term nature and importance to the organization's productivity.
- *Master budget.* The master budget includes all the major activities of the business. It brings together and coordinates all the activities of the other budgets and can be thought of as a budget of budgets.

Traditionally, budgets were often imposed top-down, with senior management setting specific targets for the entire organization at the beginning of the budget process. In today's more complex organizations, the budget process is much more likely to be bottom-up, with top management setting the general direction but with lower-level and middle-level managers actually developing the budgets and submitting them for approval. When the budgets are consolidated, senior managers can then determine whether the budget objectives of the organization are being met. The budget will then be either approved or sent back down the organization for additional refinement.

accounting audits

Procedures used to verify accounting reports and statements.

Accounting records must be inspected periodically to ensure they were properly prepared and are correct. **Accounting audits,** which are designed to verify accounting reports and statements, are essential to the control process. This audit is performed by members of an outside firm of public accountants. Knowing that accounting records are accurate, true, and in keeping with generally accepted accounting practices (GAAP) creates confidence that a reliable base exists for sound overall controlling purposes.

Activity-Based Costing   Traditional methods of cost accounting may be inappropriate in today's business environment because they are based on outdated methods of rigid hierarchical organization. Instead of assuming that organizations are bureaucratic machines that can be separated into component functions such as human resources, purchasing, and maintenance, companies such as Hewlett-Packard and GE have used **activity-based costing (ABC)** to allocate costs across business processes.

activity-based   costing (ABC)

A method of cost accounting designed to identify streams of activity and then to allocate costs across particular business processes according to the amount of time employees devote to particular activities.

ABC starts with the assumption that organizations are collections of people performing many different but related activities to satisfy customer needs. The ABC system is designed to identify those streams of activity and then to allocate costs across particular business processes. The basic procedure involves assigning expenses to particular processes or areas of activity. In a manufacturing company, for example, a group of employees might process sales orders, buy parts, and request engineering changes. The expenses for their salaries and fringe benefits would be divided among these activities according to the amount of time spent on each activity. A similar approach, illustrated in Figure 16.3, is to allocate expenses of providing support services to the functions served. In this example, a medical clinic, administrative expenses such as office workers' salaries, rent, and utilities are divided among the doctors' practices and the clinic's laboratory and radiology services. Options for allocating these expenses include the number of employees served in each group, the number of patients seen, and the square footage occupied by each group. Traditional and ABC systems reach the same bottom line. However, because the ABC method allocates costs across business processes, it provides a more accurate picture of how costs should be charged to products and services.[28]

This heightened accuracy can give managers a more realistic picture of how the organization is actually allocating its resources. It can highlight where wasted activities are occurring or whether activities cost too much relative to the benefits provided. Managers can then take action to correct the problem.

Bottom Line

Activity-based costing can highlight overspending.

If one activity costs the most, how would you decide whether this is a case of overspending?

FIGURE 16.3
Activity-Based Costing Example: ABC Medical Clinic

Administrative expenses			Laboratory	Radiology	Dr. Kent (240 visits)	Dr. Olson (200 visits)	Dr. Lane (160 visits)
Office salaries							
Direct	1,500				600	500	400
Payroll and personnel	1,000		119	39	337	254	251
Supervision	2,000		238	79	673	508	502
Unutilized*	500	**Expenses allocated to services provided**					
Advertising	600				200	200	200
Rent	1,000		125	125	250	250	250
Utilities	200		25	25	50	50	50
Office supplies	300				100	100	100
Building insurance	100		12	13	25	25	25
Telephone	600				200	200	200
Depreciation	300				100	100	100
Total	8,100		519	281	2,535	2,187	2,078
*Not allocated.							

Source: Based on Pam Schuneman, "Master the 'ABCs' of Activity-Based Costing," *Managed Care,* May 1997, http://www.managedcaremag.com.

Financial Controls

In addition to budgets, businesses commonly use other statements for financial control. Two financial statements that help control overall organizational performance are the balance sheet and the profit and loss statement.

The Balance Sheet   The **balance sheet** shows the financial picture of a company at a given time. This statement itemizes three elements: (1) assets, (2) liabilities, and (3) stockholders' equity. **Assets** are the values of the various items the corporation owns. **Liabilities** are the amounts the corporation owes to various creditors. **Stockholders' equity** is the amount accruing to the corporation's owners. The relationship among these three elements is as follows:

$$\text{Assets} = \text{Liabilities} + \text{Stockholders' equity}$$

Table 16.5 shows an example of a balance sheet. During the year, the company grew because it enlarged its building and acquired more machinery and equipment by means of long-term debt in the form of a first mortgage. Additional stock was sold to help finance the expansion. At the same time, accounts receivable were increased, and work in process was reduced. Observe that Total assets ($3,053,367) = Total liabilities ($677,204 + $618,600) + Stockholders' equity ($700,000 + $981,943 + $75,620).

Summarizing balance sheet items over a long period of time uncovers important trends and gives a manager further insight into overall performance and areas in which adjustments need to be made. For example, at some point, the company might decide that it would be prudent to slow down its expansion plans.

The Profit and Loss Statement   The **profit and loss statement** is an itemized financial statement of the income and expenses of a company's operations. Table 16.6 shows a comparative statement of profit and loss for two consecutive years. In this illustration, the operating revenue of the enterprise has increased. Expense also has increased but at a lower rate, resulting in a higher net income. Some managers draw up tentative profit and loss statements and use them as goals. Then performance is measured against these goals or standards. From comparative statements of this type, a manager can identify trouble areas and correct them.

Controlling by profit and loss is most commonly used for the entire enterprise and, in the case of a diversified corporation, its divisions. However, if controlling is by departments, as in a decentralized organization in which department managers have control over both revenue and expense, a profit and loss statement is used for each department. Each department's output is measured, and a cost, including overhead, is charged to each department's operation. Expected net income is the standard for measuring a department's performance.

Financial Ratios   An effective approach for checking on the overall performance of an enterprise is to use key financial ratios. Ratios help indicate possible strengths and weaknesses in a company's operations. Key ratios are calculated from selected items on the profit and loss statement and the balance sheet. We will briefly discuss three categories of financial ratios—liquidity, leverage, and profitability:

- *Liquidity ratios.* Liquidity ratios indicate a company's ability to pay short-term debts. The most common liquidity ratio is *current assets to current liabilities*, called the **current ratio** or *net working capital ratio*. This ratio indicates the extent to which current assets can decline and still be adequate to pay current liabilities. Some analysts set a ratio of 2 to 1, or 2.00, as the desirable minimum. For example, referring back to Table 16.5, the liquidity ratio there is about 2.86 ($1,918,455/$667,204). The company's current assets are more than capable of supporting its current liabilities.

---

balance sheet

A report that shows the financial picture of a company at a given time and itemizes assets, liabilities, and stockholders' equity.

---

assets

The values of the various items the corporation owns.

---

liabilities

The amounts a corporation owes to various creditors.

---

stockholders' equity

The amount accruing to the corporation's owners.

---

profit and loss statement

An itemized financial statement of the income and expenses of a company's operations.

---

current ratio

A liquidity ratio that indicates the extent to which short-term assets can decline and still be adequate to pay short-term liabilities.

TABLE 16.5
A Comparative Balance
Sheet

Comparative Balance Sheet for the Years Ending December 31		
	This Year	**Last Year**
Assets		
Current assets:		
Cash	$161,870	$119,200
U.S. Treasury bills	250,400	30,760
Accounts receivable	825,595	458,762
Inventories:		
Work in process and finished products	429,250	770,800
Raw materials and supplies	251,340	231,010
Total current assets	1,918,455	1,610,532
Other assets:		
Land	157,570	155,250
Building	740,135	91,784
Machinery and equipment	172,688	63,673
Furniture and fixtures	132,494	57,110
Total other assets before depreciation	1,202,887	367,817
Less: Accumulated depreciation and amortization	67,975	63,786
Total other assets	1,134,912	304,031
Total assets	$3,053,367	$1,914,563
Liabilities and stockholders' equity		
Current liabilities:		
Accounts payable	$287,564	$441,685
Payrolls and withholdings from employees	44,055	49,580
Commissions and sundry accruals	83,260	41,362
Federal taxes on income	176,340	50,770
Current installment on long-term debt	85,985	38,624
Total current liabilities	667,204	622,021
Long-term liabilities:		
15-year, 9 percent loan, payable in each of the years 2002–2015	210,000	225,000
5 percent first mortgage	408,600	
Registered 9 percent notes payable		275,000
Total long-term liabilities	618,600	500,000
Stockholders' equity:		
Common stock: authorized 1,000,000 shares, outstanding last year 492,000 shares, outstanding this year 700,000 shares at $1 par value	700,000	492,000
Capital surplus	981,943	248,836
Earned surplus	75,620	51,706
Total stockholders' equity	1,757,563	792,542
Total liabilities and stockholders' equity	$3,053,367	$1,914,563

Comparative Statement of Profit and Loss for the Years Ending June 30	This Year	Last Year	Increase or Decrease
Income:			
Net sales	$253,218	$257,636	$4,418*
Dividends from investments	480	430	50
Other	1,741	1,773	32*
Total	255,439	259,839	4,400*
Deductions:			
Cost of goods sold	180,481	178,866	1,615
Selling and administrative expenses	39,218	34,019	5,199
Interest expense	2,483	2,604	121*
Other	1,941	1,139	802
Total	224,123	216,628	7,495
Income before taxes	31,316	43,211	11,895*
Provision for taxes	3,300	9,500	6,200*
Net income	$ 28,016	$ 33,711	$5,695*

* Decrease

TABLE 16.6
A Comparative Statement of Profit and Loss

- *Leverage ratios.* Leverage ratios show the relative amount of funds in the business supplied by creditors and shareholders. An important example is the **debt–equity ratio,** which indicates the company's ability to meet its long-term financial obligations. If this ratio is less than 1.5, the amount of debt is not considered excessive. In Table 16.5, the debt–equity ratio is only 0.35 ($618,600/$1,757,563). The company has financed its expansion almost entirely by issuing stock rather than by incurring significant long-term debt.

- *Profitability ratios.* Profitability ratios indicate management's ability to generate a financial return on sales or investment. For example, **return of investment (ROI)** is a ratio of profit to capital used, or a rate of return from capital (equity plus long-term debt). This ratio allows managers and shareholders to assess how well the firm is doing compared with other investments. For example, if the net income of the company in Table 16.5 were $300,000 this year, its return on capital would be 12.6 percent [$300,000/($1,757,563/$618,600)]—normally a very reasonable rate of return.

debt–equity ratio

A leverage ratio that indicates the company's ability to meet its long-term financial obligations.

return on investment (ROI)

A ratio of profit to capital used, or a rate of return from capital.

Using Financial Ratios   Although ratios provide both performance standards and indicators of what has occurred, exclusive reliance on financial ratios can have negative consequences. Because ratios usually are expressed in compressed time horizons (monthly, quarterly, or yearly), they often cause **management myopia**—managers focus on short-term earnings and profits at the expense of their longer-term strategic obligations.[29] Control systems using long-term (e.g., three− to six-year) performance targets can reduce management myopia and focus attention further into the future.

A second negative outcome of ratios is that they relegate other important considerations to a secondary position. Research and development, management development, progressive human resource practices, and other considerations may receive insufficient attention. Therefore, the use of ratios should be supplemented with other control measures. Organizations can hold managers accountable for market share, number of patents granted, sales of new products, human resource development,

management myopia

Focusing on short-term earnings and profits at the expense of longer-term strategic obligations.

Management Connection

BEST BUY AIMS FOR BETTER NUMBERS

Best Buy's financial numbers have raised concern. The company has recently posted losses, with flat sales and falling market share, even after Circuit City closed. A key measure in retailing is same-store sales, the total sales made only at the company's stores that have been open at least one year. By ignoring any other stores, managers can see whether performance has changed within stores, in contrast to sales growth or declines from opening or closing stores. At Best Buy, same-store sales have been falling. Managers are digging for the reasons and trying to improve performance.

To sell more, Best Buy cut prices, but to preserve profits, it must cut costs, too. On the price side, the company promised to match the lowest price charged by any competitor, and it increased the value of rewards issued to customers with loyalty cards. On the cost side, CEO Hubert Joly announced a decision to cut spending by $725 million, starting with layoffs of 400 employees at headquarters, designed to save $150 million. Despite the cost cutting, driving down prices has shrunk profit margins. Also, in competing with online retailers, Best Buy remains at a disadvantage. Selling from a warehouse is cheaper than selling from a store, and most of Best Buy's customers shop in its stores, not at its website.

Another way to sell more is to use persuasive salespeople. In its early years, Best Buy was known for skillful selling, and managers emphasized sales targets. Best Buy recently increased training and began offering incentive pay linked to sales. The ratio of closed to attempted sales did not improve, but surveys showed greater customer satisfaction.

Customer service may be another key to sales. Before Joly became CEO, Best Buy had an embarrassing December shopping season in which it lacked inventory needed to fill all its orders and waited to admit the problem until a few days before Christmas, when it was difficult for customers who had placed orders to find substitutes quickly. The next December, Joly asked territory and district managers, their staff members, and headquarters employees to volunteer to help local stores outside of their regular work hours. That year, U.S. same-store sales did not slide; they were close to the previous year's numbers.

Management also considered geography. The worst performance has been in Best Buy's European stores, so the company arranged to sell its European operations.[30]

- How well do you think Best Buy's management has analyzed and corrected its performance? Why?
- Besides the measures described here, what other financial measures could help with controlling performance at Best Buy?

and other performance indicators. As you read "Management Connection: Progress Report," consider the advantages and limits of financial ratios in helping Best Buy's managers figure out how to improve performance.

The Downside of Bureaucratic Control

So far you have learned about control from a mechanical viewpoint. But organizations are not strictly mechanical; they are composed of people. Although control systems are used to constrain people's behavior and make their future behavior predictable, people

> A control system cannot be effective without consideration of how people will react to it.

are not machines that automatically fall into line as the designers of control systems intend. In fact, control systems can lead to dysfunctional behavior. A control system cannot be effective without consideration of how people will react to it. For effective control of employee behavior, managers should consider three types of potential responses to control: rigid bureaucratic behavior, tactical behavior, and resistance.[31]

Rigid Bureaucratic Behavior Often people act in ways that will help them look good on the control system's measures. This tendency can be useful because it focuses people on the behaviors management requires. But it can result in rigid, inflexible behavior geared toward doing *only* what the system requires. For example, in the earlier discussion of six sigma, we noted that this control process emphasizes efficiency over innovation. After 3M began using six sigma extensively, it slipped from its goal of having at least one-third of sales come from newly released products. When George Buckley took the CEO post, only one-fourth of sales were coming from new products, and Buckley began relying less extensively on efficiency controls. Buckley explained to a reporter, "Invention is by its very nature a disorderly process."[32] The control challenge, of course, is for 3M to be both efficient and creative.

Rigid bureaucratic behavior occurs when control systems prompt employees to stay out of trouble by following the rules. Unfortunately, such systems often lead to poor customer service and make the entire organization slow to act. (Recall the discussion of bureaucracy in Chapter 10.) General Motors is notorious for having a lumbering bureaucracy, which has often been blamed for making the company unresponsive to changes in consumer tastes. For example, several years ago, GM kept engineers at work on the design for a new Hummer SUV even though many of them doubted the vehicles would ever be built. Their pessimism was correct; GM shut down the Hummer group. The company has been trying to change. For its head of vehicle development, GM selected Mary Barra, who has a background in both manufacturing and human resources as well as a reputation for speaking out and pressing for action. She quickly eliminated layers of management between herself and the top engineer and aggressively supports designers who want to make changes consumers are asking for.[33]

We have all been victimized at some time by rigid bureaucratic behavior. Reflect for a moment on this now classic story of a nightmare at a hospital:

> At midnight, a patient with eye pains enters an emergency room at a hospital. At the reception area, he is classified as a nonemergency case and referred to the hospital's eye clinic. Trouble is, the eye clinic doesn't open until the next morning. When he arrives at the clinic, the nurse asks for his referral slip, but the emergency room doctor had forgotten to give it to him. The patient has to return to the emergency room and wait for another physician to screen him. The physician refers him back to the eye clinic and to a social worker to arrange payment. Finally, a third doctor looks into his eye, sees a small piece of metal, and removes it—a 30-second procedure.[34]

Stories such as these have, of course, given bureaucracy a bad name. Some managers will not even use the term *bureaucratic control* because of its potentially negative connotation. That is unfortunate because the control system itself is not the problem. The problems occur when the systems are no longer viewed as tools for running the business but instead as rules for dictating rigid behavior.

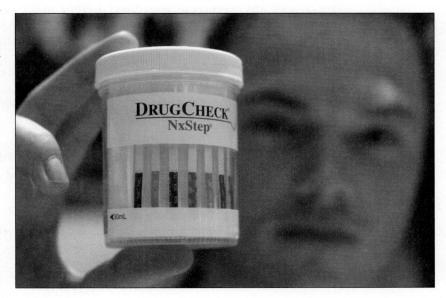

Drug testing is one of the ways organizations monitor employees. Some people favor the control measure but change their minds when personally asked to submit a urine specimen.

Tactical Behavior Control systems will be ineffective if employees engage in tactics aimed at beating the system. The most common type of tactical behavior is to manipulate information or report false performance data. People may produce two kinds of invalid data: about what *has* been done and about what *can* be done. False reporting about the past is less common because it is easier to identify someone who misreports what happened than someone who gives an erroneous prediction or estimate of what might happen. Still, managers sometimes change their accounting systems to smooth out the numbers. Also, people may intentionally feed false information into a management information system to cover up errors or poor performance. A few years ago, several customs inspectors at Orlando Sanford International Airport said their supervisors had pressured them to speed up the processing of passengers by entering generic data instead of actually questioning the passengers. According to the inspectors, when the system flagged passengers for additional screening during busy periods, they were told to guess at the information, such as race and length of stay, rather than asking the passengers to provide the information. The justification for this behavior was that time pressure gave them no more than a minute to screen each passenger and keep the line moving, so that the public would be satisfied with their agency's work.[35]

More commonly, people falsify their predictions or requests for the future. When asked to give budgetary estimates, employees usually ask for larger amounts than they need. On the other hand, they sometimes submit unrealistically *low* estimates when they believe a low estimate will help them get a budget or a project approved. Budget-setting sessions can become tugs of war between subordinates trying to get slack in the budget and superiors attempting to minimize slack. Similar tactics are exhibited when managers negotiate unrealistically low performance standards so that subordinates will have little trouble meeting them; when salespeople project low forecasts so that they will look good by exceeding them; and when workers slow down the work pace while time-study analysts are setting work pace standards. In these and other cases, people are concerned only with their own performance figures rather than with the overall performance of their departments or companies.

Resistance to Control   Often people strongly resist control systems. They do so for several reasons. First, comprehensive control systems increase the accuracy of performance data and make employees more accountable for their actions. Control systems uncover mistakes, threaten people's job security and status, and decrease people's autonomy.

Second, control systems can change expertise and power structures. For example, management information systems can make the costing, purchasing, and production decisions previously made by managers much quicker. Those individuals may fear a loss of expertise, power, and decision-making authority as a result.

Third, control systems can change the social structure of an organization. They can create competition and disrupt social groups and friendships. People may end up competing against those with whom they formerly had comfortable, cooperative relationships. Because people's social needs are so important, they will resist control systems that reduce social need satisfaction.

Fourth, control systems may be seen as an invasion of privacy, lead to lawsuits, and cause low morale.

Designing Effective Control Systems

Effective control systems maximize potential benefits and minimize dysfunctional behaviors. To achieve this, management needs to design control systems that

1. Establish valid performance standards.
2. Provide adequate information to employees.
3. Ensure acceptability to employees.
4. Maintain open communication.
5. Use multiple approaches.

Establish Valid Performance Standards   An effective control system must be based on valid and accurate performance standards. The most effective standards, as discussed earlier, tend to be expressed in quantitative terms; they are objective rather than subjective. Also, the measures should not be capable of being easily sabotaged or faked. Moreover, the system must incorporate all important aspects of performance.

For example, a company that just focused on sales volume without also looking at profitability might soon go out of business. As you learned earlier, unmeasured behaviors are neglected. Often performance standards for delivering training and other HR programs emphasize trainee satisfaction as reported on surveys. But the Philadelphia Department of Licenses and Inspections instead verified that its training actually improved employee performance. The department was notorious for its long lines and rude workers, so it turned for help to the Philadelphia Ritz-Carlton Hotel—part of a chain known for its superb customer service. The hotel's area general manager provided training initially to 40 department workers in how to improve their service skills. As part of its posttraining measurement process, the department checked the wait times for license applicants, which dropped from 82 minutes to 14 minutes. The department is continuing its partnership program with Ritz-Carlton through additional employee training and attendance at each other's management meetings.[36]

But management also must defend against another problem: too many measures that create overcontrol and employee resistance. To make many controls tolerable, managers can devote attention to a few key areas while setting satisfactory performance standards in others. Or they can establish simple priorities. The purchasing agent may have to meet targets in the following sequence: quality, availability, cost, inventory level. Finally, managers can set tolerance ranges. For example, in financial budgeting, optimistic, expected, and minimum levels sometimes are specified.

Many companies' budgets set cost targets only. This causes managers to control spending but also to neglect earnings. At Emerson Electric, profit and growth are key measures. If an unanticipated opportunity to increase market share arises, managers can spend what they need to go after it. The phrase "it's not in the budget" is less likely to stifle people at Emerson than it is at most other companies.

This principle applies to nonfinancial aspects of performance as well. At many customer service call centers, control aims to maximize efficiency by focusing on the average amount of time each agent spends handling each phone call. But the business objectives of call centers should also include other measures such as cross-selling products or improving customer satisfaction and repeat business. Carlson Leisure Travel Services is one of a growing number of companies using new technology to analyze the content—not just the duration—of each call and capture information about the amount call center agents sell.[37]

Business consultant Michael Hammer summarizes these points in terms of what he calls seven "deadly sins" of performance measurement to avoid:[38]

1. *Vanity*—using measures that are sure to make managers and the organization look good. For example, a company might measure order fulfillment in terms of whether products are delivered by the latest date promised by the organization, rather than by the tougher and more meaningful measure of when the customers request to receive the products.
2. *Provincialism*—limiting measures to functional or departmental responsibilities rather than the organization's overall objectives. If a company's transportation department measures only shipping costs, it won't have an incentive to consider that shipping reliability (delivery on a given date) will affect performance at the company's stores or distribution centers.
3. *Narcissism*—measuring from the employee's, manager's, or company's point of view, rather than the customer's. For example, a maker of computer systems measured on-time shipping of each component; if 90 percent of the system's components arrived at the customer on time, it was 90 percent on time. But from the customer's point of view, the system wasn't on time at all because the customer needed *all* the components to use the system.
4. *Laziness*—not expending the effort to analyze what is important to measure. An electric power company simply assumed customers cared about installation speed, but in fact, customers really cared more about receiving an accurate installation schedule.

5. *Pettiness*—measuring just one component of what affects business performance. An example would be clothing manufacturers that assume they should consider just manufacturing cost rather than the overall costs of making exactly the right products available in stores when customers demand them.

6. *Inanity*—failing to consider the way standards will affect real-world human behavior and company performance. A fast-food restaurant targeted waste reduction and was surprised when restaurant managers began slowing down operations by directing their employees to hold off on cooking anything until orders were placed.

7. *Frivolity*—making excuses for poor performance rather than taking performance standards seriously. In some organizations, more effort goes to blaming others than to correcting problems.

According to Hammer, the basic correction to these "sins" is to select standards carefully that look at entire business processes, such as product development or order fulfillment, and identify which actions make those processes succeed. Then managers should measure performance against these standards precisely, accurately, and practically, making individuals responsible for their achievement and rewarding success.

Provide Adequate Information   Management must communicate to employees the importance and nature of the control system. Then people must receive feedback about their performance. Feedback motivates people and provides information that enables them to correct their own deviations from performance standards. Allowing people to initiate their own corrective action encourages self-control and reduces the need for outside supervision. Open-book management, described in Chapter 15, is a powerful use of this control principle.

Information should be as accessible as possible, particularly when people must make decisions quickly and frequently. For example, a national food company with its own truck fleet had a difficult problem. The company wanted drivers to go through customer sales records every night, insert new prices from headquarters every morning, and still make their rounds—an impossible set of demands. To solve this control problem, the company installed personal computers in more than 1,000 delivery trucks. Now drivers use their PCs for constant communication with headquarters. Each night drivers send information about the stores, and each morning headquarters sends prices and recommended stock mixes.

In general, a manager designing a control system should evaluate the information system in terms of the following questions:

1. Does it provide people with data relevant to the decisions they need to make?
2. Does it provide the right amount of information to decision makers throughout the organization?
3. Does it provide enough information to each part of the organization about how other, related parts of the organization are functioning?[39]

In Practice

QUALITY STANDARDS AT RITZ-CARLTON

Ritz-Carlton sets performance measures for maintaining its impressive reputation and ensures that employees see how they contribute. The measures are based on the key factors behind the company's success: its mystique, employee engagement, customer engagement, product service excellence, community involvement, and financial performance. Financial performance is viewed as the result of achieving the other goals. For each success factor, cross-functional teams identify targets as detailed as the number of scuff marks on elevator doors or the percentage of satisfied employees at a location. The teams include frontline employees, so that early in the control process, employees already feel their input matters.

At each location, at the beginning of every shift, all employees gather for a meeting to discuss activities, issues, and Ritz-Carlton's business philosophy. They compare recent performance against the company's targets in each area. These conversations reinforce the key performance factors and help employees appreciate the importance of what they do.

Each business unit has up to three priorities to focus on, with each employee working to improve customer, employee, or financial results. Even the training department measures its success by its impact on customer satisfaction. Employees appreciate their role in giving each guest a special experience. One recent guest noted how hotel employees learned his name and looked for ways to meet his needs even before he expressed them. For example, a concierge noticed him preparing to answer a phone call in the lobby and guided him to a quiet room with great cell phone reception. All employees have the authority to spend up to $2,000 to satisfy an unhappy customer, but because they are so attentive and well trained in problem solving, they rarely need to spend any of it.[40]

- How does Ritz-Carlton ensure that hotel employees have adequate information for meeting quality standards?

Ensure Acceptability to Employees Employees are less likely to resist a control system and exhibit dysfunctional behaviors if they accept the system. They are more likely to accept systems that have useful performance standards but are not overly controlling. Employees also will find systems more acceptable if they believe the standards are possible to achieve.

The control system should emphasize positive behavior rather than focusing on controlling negative behavior alone. In more than two decades, Johnson & Johnson's Ethicon San Lorenzo facility has never had to recall a product. The company makes sutures, meshes, and other supplies for surgery—an industry in which quality must be perfect but recalls have been all too common. To achieve these outstanding results, the company set up a system it calls the Do It Right Framework, which includes training, employee involvement in process improvements, and open communication about company objectives and the reasons for changes. Most important, employees understand that their work matters. Every employee sees a video about Ethicon's work, highlighted by a cardiovascular surgeon describing how he uses the products and why their quality affects patients' recovery. Thus, doing the job right is something employees genuinely care about.[41]

One of the best ways to establish reasonable standards and thus gain employee acceptance of the control system is to set standards participatively. As we discussed in Chapter 4, participation in decision making secures people's understanding and cooperation and results in better decisions. Allowing employees to collaborate in control system decisions that affect their jobs directly will help overcome resistance and foster acceptance of the system. In addition, employees on the front line are more likely to know which standards are most important and practical, and they can inform a manager's judgment on these issues. Finally, if standards are established in collaboration with employees, managers will more easily obtain cooperation on solving the problem when deviations from standards occur.

Maintain Open Communication When deviations from standards occur, it is important for employees to feel able to report the deviations so that the problem can be addressed. If employees come to feel that their managers want to hear only good news or, worse, if they fear reprisal for reporting bad news, even if it is not their fault, then any controls that are in place will be much less likely to be effective. Problems may go unreported or, even worse, may reach the point at which they become much more expensive or difficult to solve. But if managers create an environment of openness and honesty, one in which employees feel comfortable sharing even negative information and are appreciated for doing so in a timely fashion, then the control system is much more likely to work effectively.

Nevertheless, managers may sometimes need to discipline employees who are failing to meet important standards. In such cases, an approach called *progressive discipline* is usually most effective. In this approach, clear standards are established, but failure to meet them is dealt with in a progressive or step-by-step process. For example, the first time an employee's sales performance has been worse than it should have been, the supervising manager may offer verbal counseling or coaching. If problems persist, the next step might be a written reprimand. This type of reasonable and considered approach signals to all employees that the manager is interested in improving their performance, not in punishing them.

Use Multiple Approaches   Multiple controls are necessary. For example, banks need controls on risk so that they don't lose a lot of money from defaulting borrowers, as well as profit controls including sales budgets that aim for growth in accounts and customers.

As you learned earlier in this chapter, control systems generally should include both financial and nonfinancial performance targets and incorporate aspects of preliminary, concurrent, and feedback control. In recent years, a growing number of companies have combined targets for managers into a **balanced scorecard,** a combination of four sets of performance measures: (1) financial, (2) customer satisfaction, (3) business processes (quality and efficiency), and (4) learning and growth.[42] The goal is generally to broaden management's horizon beyond short-term financial results so that the company's long-term success is more likely. For example, Hyde Park Electronics had been using a variety of financial controls when it adopted a business scorecard that added metrics such as on-time delivery, employee satisfaction, and sales impact of marketing activities. Profits under the balanced scorecard reached record levels.[43] The balanced scorecard also is adaptable to nonprofit settings. Ocean-Monmouth Legal Services, which provides legal services to poor people in New Jersey, uses a balanced scorecard to track progress in meeting strategic, operational, financial, and client satisfaction goals. The organization's executive director, Harold E. Creacy, credits the approach with helping to cope with the rising costs and tight resources that so often plague nonprofits.[44]

Effective control will also require managers and organizations to use many of the other techniques and practices of good management. For example, compensation systems will grant rewards for meeting standards and impose consequences if they are not met. And to gain employee acceptance, managers may also rely on many of the other communication and motivational tools that we discussed in earlier chapters, such as persuasion and positive reinforcement.

balanced scorecard

Control system combining four sets of performance measures: financial, customer, business process, and learning and growth.

The Other Controls: Markets and Clans

Although the concept of control has always been a central feature of organizations, the principles and philosophies underlying its use are changing. In the past, control was focused almost exclusively on bureaucratic (and market) mechanisms. Generations of managers were taught that they could maximize productivity by regulating what employees did on the job—through standard operating procedures, rules, regulations, and close supervision. To increase output on an assembly line, for example, managers in the past tried to identify the one best way to approach the work and then to monitor

Although formal bureaucratic control systems are perhaps the most pervasive in organizations, they are not always the most effective.

employees' activities to make certain that they followed standard operating procedures. In short, they controlled work by dividing and simplifying tasks, a process we referred to in Chapter 1 as *scientific management*.

Although formal bureaucratic control systems are perhaps the most pervasive in organizations (and the most talked about in management textbooks), they are not always the most effective. Market controls and clan controls may both represent more flexible, though no less potent, approaches to regulating performance.

Market Control

In contrast to bureaucratic controls, market controls involve the use of economic forces—and the pricing mechanisms that accompany them—to regulate performance. The system works like this: when output from an individual, department, or business unit has value to other people, a price can be negotiated for its exchange. As a market for these transactions becomes established, two effects occur:

- Price becomes an indicator of the value of the good or service.
- Price competition has the effect of controlling productivity and performance.

The basic principles that underlie market controls can operate at the corporate level, the business unit (or department) level, and the individual level. Figure 16.4 shows a few ways in which market controls are used in an organization.

Market Controls at the Corporate Level   In large, diversified companies, market controls often are used to regulate independent business units. Particularly in large conglomerate firms that act as holding companies, business units typically are treated as profit centers that compete with one another. Top executives may place very few bureaucratic controls on business unit managers but use profit and loss data for evaluating performance. Although decision making and power are decentralized to the business units, market controls ensure that business unit performance is in line with corporate objectives.

FIGURE 16.4

Examples of Market Control

Use of market control mechanisms in this way has been criticized by those who insist that economic measures do not reflect the complete value of an organization adequately. Employees often suffer as diversified companies are repeatedly bought and sold based on market controls.

Market Controls at the Business Unit Level   Market control also can be used within business units to regulate exchanges among departments and functions. Transfer pricing is one method that organizations use to try to reflect market forces for internal transactions. A **transfer price** is the charge by one unit in the organization for a good or service that it supplies to another unit of the same organization. For example, in automobile manufacturing, a transfer price may be affixed to components and subassemblies before they are shipped to subsequent business units for final assembly. Ideally, the transfer price reflects the price that the receiving business unit would have to pay for that product or service in the marketplace.

As organizations have more options to outsource goods and services to external partners, market controls such as transfer prices provide natural incentives to keep costs down and quality up. Managers stay in close touch with prices in the marketplace to make sure their own costs are in line, and they try to improve the service they provide to increase their department's value to the organization. Consider the situation in which training and development activities can be done internally by the human resources department or outsourced to a consulting firm. If the human resources department cannot supply quality training at a reasonable price, there may be no reason for that department to exist inside the firm. Similarly, Penske Truck Leasing Company began outsourcing many of its finance processes to a company called Genpact, not only for lower prices but also for the expertise developed by that specialized firm to compete in the marketplace. Penske's senior vice president of finance, Frank Cocuzza, says the department spends $20 million less per year than it did to perform the same functions in-house while it has improved its rate of collections and learned thousands of ways to make his own operation more efficient, modeled after Genpact's lean practices.[45]

Market Controls at the Individual Level   Market controls also are used at the individual level. For example, when organizations are trying to hire employees, the supply and demand for particular skills influence the wages employees can expect to receive and the rate organizations are likely to pay. Employees or job candidates who have more valuable skills tend to be paid a higher wage. Of course, wages don't always reflect market rates—sometimes they are based (perhaps arbitrarily) on internal resource considerations—but the market rate is often the best indicator of an employee's potential worth to a firm.

Market-based controls such as these are important in that they provide a natural incentive for employees to enhance their skills and offer them to potential firms. Even after individuals gain employment, market-based wages are important as controls in that persons with higher economic value may be promoted faster to higher positions in the organization.

Market controls often are used by boards of directors to manage CEOs of major corporations. Ironically, CEOs usually are seen as the

---

transfer price

Price charged by one unit for a good or service provided to another unit within the organization.

As much as it would seem that market controls play a significant role in the salary of a professional baseball player or any other professional athlete, are the sometimes ridiculously high salaries that are paid for players today truly indicative of a player's skill—or something else? If the player doesn't live up to the expectation of the previously perceived skill level or, put another way, has a bad year, should the organization be allowed to cut his pay?

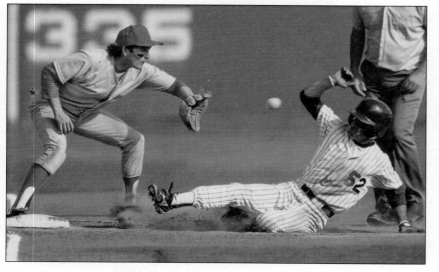

ones controlling everyone else in the company; but the CEO is accountable to the board of directors, and the board must devise ways to ensure that the CEO acts in its interest. Absent board control, CEOs may act in ways that make them look good personally (such as making the company bigger or more diversified) but that do not lead to higher profits for the firm. And as recent corporate scandals have shown, without board control, CEOs may also artificially inflate the firm's earnings or not fully declare expenses, making the firm look much more successful than it really is.

Traditionally, boards have tried to control CEO performance mainly through the use of incentive plans in addition to base salary. These typically include some type of bonus tied to short-term profit targets. In large U.S. companies, most CEO compensation is now at risk, meaning it depends mainly on the performance of the company. In addition to short-term incentives, boards use some type of long-term incentives linked to the firm's share price, usually through stock options, which we discussed in Chapter 10. Also, balanced scorecards are intended to keep CEOs focused on the company's longer-term health. And under the Sarbanes-Oxley Act, described in Chapter 5, board members are expected to exercise careful control over the company's financial performance, including oversight of the CEO's compensation package.

Clan Control: The Role of Empowerment and Culture

Increasingly, managers are discovering that control systems based solely on bureaucratic and market mechanisms are insufficient for directing today's workforce. There are several reasons for this:

- *Employees' jobs have changed.* The nature of work is evolving. Employees working with computers, for example, have more variability in their jobs, and much of their work is intellectual and therefore invisible. Because of this, there is no one best way to perform a task, and programming or standardizing jobs becomes extremely difficult. Close supervision is also unrealistic because it is nearly impossible to supervise activities such as reasoning and problem solving.
- *The nature of management has changed.* The role of managers is evolving, too. Managers used to know more about the job than employees did. Today it is typical for employees to know more about their jobs than anyone else does. We refer to this as the shift from touch labor to knowledge work. When real expertise in organizations exists at the very lowest levels, hierarchical control becomes impractical.[46]
- *The employment relationship has changed.* The social contract at work is being renegotiated. It used to be that employees were most concerned about issues such as pay, job security, and the hours of work. Today, however, more and more employees want to be more fully engaged in their work, taking part in decision making, devising solutions to unique problems, and receiving assignments that are challenging and involving. They want to use their brains.

For these three reasons, the concept of *empowerment* not only has become more popular in organizations but has become a necessary aspect of a manager's repertoire of control. With no one best way to approach a job and no way to scrutinize what employees do every day, managers must empower employees to make decisions and trust that they will act in the best interests of the firm. But this does not mean giving up control. It means creating a strong culture of high standards and integrity so that employees will exercise effective control on their own.

Recall our extensive discussion of organization culture in Chapter 2. If the organization's culture encourages the wrong behaviors, then an effort to impose effective

(ROWE) was inconsistent with "all hands on deck." If employees could work wherever and whenever they wanted, perhaps they would not be at the office when needed or would be unavailable in a crisis. Ending ROWE would put employees "in the office as much as possible," to quote Best Buy spokesman Matt Furman. Joly also said ROWE delegates decisions that managers should be involved in making.

The creators of the ROWE policy dispute this understanding. Cali Ressler and Jody Thompson, former Best Buy employees, came up with the idea as a way to improve efficiency while motivating workers. They say Best Buy saved more than $2 million in the first two years of ROWE because employee turnover plummeted and productivity

Perhaps more ROWE-style flexibility would have made Best Buy nimbler; clearly, Joly disagrees. In contrast to the bottom-up creation of ROWE, the program's elimination was a swift, top-down decision.

In the months since Joly's announcement, Best Buy's revenues stopped falling, and its stock price took a long-awaited upward turn.[50]

- How well did ROWE meet the criteria of an effective performance system? Will eliminating it be more or less effective? Why?
- How can clan control help Best Buy improve its performance?

controls will be severely hindered. But if managers create and reinforce a strong culture that encourages correct behavior, one in which everyone understands management's values and expectations and is motivated to act in accordance with them, then
clan control can be a very effective control tool.[47] As we noted at the beginning of
this chapter, clan control involves creating relationships built on mutual respect and
encouraging each individual to take responsibility for his or her actions. Employees
work within a guiding framework of values, and they are expected to use good judgment. For example, at NetApp, an IT company specializing in data storage and protection, a commitment to employee empowerment prompted the switch from a 12-page
travel policy to some simple guidelines for employees who need to go on a business
trip: "We are a frugal company. But don't show up dog-tired to save a few bucks. Use
your common sense."[48] The emphasis in an empowered organization is one of its

Bottom Line

Clan control empowers
employees to meet

KEY TERMS

SUMMARY OF LEARNING OBJECTIVES

Now that you have studied Chapter 16, you should be able to:

LO 1   Explain why companies develop control systems for employees.

Left to their own devices, employees may act in ways that do
not benefit the organization. Control systems are designed to
eliminate idiosyncratic behavior and keep employees directed
toward achieving the goals of the firm. Control systems are a
steering mechanism for guiding resources and for helping each
individual act on behalf of the organization.

LO 2   Summarize how to design a basic bureaucratic control system.

The design of a basic control system involves four steps:
(1) setting performance standards, (2) measuring performance,
(3) comparing performance with the standards, and (4) eliminating unfavorable deviations by taking corrective action. Performance standards should be valid and should cover issues
such as quantity, quality, time, and cost. Once performance is
compared with the standards, the principle of exception suggests that the manager needs to direct attention to the exceptional cases that have significant deviations. Then the manager
takes the action most likely to solve the problem.

LO 3   Describe the purposes for using budgets as a control device.

Budgets combine the benefits of feedforward, concurrent, and
feedback controls. They are used as an initial guide for allocating resources, a reference point for using funds, and a feedback
mechanism for comparing actual levels of sales and expenses with
their expected levels. Recently companies have modified their
budgeting processes to allocate costs over basic processes (such
as customer service) rather than to functions or departments. By
changing the way they prepare budgets, many companies have discovered ways to eliminate waste and improve business processes.

LO 4   Define basic types of financial statements and financial ratios used as controls.

The basic financial statements are the balance sheet and the
profit and loss statement. The balance sheet compares the
value of company assets to the obligations the company owes
to owners and creditors. The profit and loss statement shows

company income relative to costs incurred. In addition to these
statements, companies look at liquidity ratios (whether the
company can pay its short-term debts), leverage ratios (the
extent to which the company is funding operations by going
into debt), and profitability ratios (profit relative to investment).
These ratios provide a goal for managers as well as a standard
against which to evaluate performance.

LO 5   List procedures for implementing effective control systems.

To maximize the effectiveness of controls, managers should
(1) establish valid performance standards, (2) provide adequate
information to employees, (3) ensure acceptability, (4) maintain
open communication, and (5) see that multiple approaches are
used (such as bureaucratic, market, and clan control).

LO 6   Identify ways in which organizations use market control mechanisms.

Market controls can be used at the level of the corporation, the
business unit or department, or the individual. At the corporate
level, business units are evaluated against one another based on
profitability. At times, less profitable businesses are sold while
more profitable businesses receive more resources. Within
business units, transfer pricing may be used to approximate
market mechanisms to control transactions among departments. At the individual level, market mechanisms control the
wage rate of employees and can be used to evaluate the performance of individual managers.

LO 7   Discuss the use of clan control in an empowered organization.

Approaching control from a centralized, mechanistic viewpoint
is increasingly impractical. In today's organizations, it is difficult
to program one best way to approach work, and it is often difficult to monitor performance. To be responsive to customers,
companies must harness the expertise of employees and give
them the freedom to act on their own initiative. To maintain
control while empowering employees, companies should (1)
use self-guided teams, (2) allow decision making at the source
of the problems, (3) build trust and mutual respect, (4) base
control on a guiding framework of norms, and (5) use incentive
systems that encourage teamwork.

DISCUSSION QUESTIONS

1. What controls can you identify in the management of your school or at a company where you now work (or recently worked)? If you can, interview a manager or employee of the organization to learn more about the controls in use there. How might the organization's performance change if those controls were not in place?

2. How are leadership and control different? How are planning and control different? How are structure and control different?

3. Imagine you are the sales manager of a company that sells medical supplies to hospitals nationwide. You have 10 salespeople reporting to you. You are responsible for your department achieving a certain level of sales each year. In general terms, how might you go about taking each step in the control cycle?

4. In the situation described in Question 3, what actions would you need to take if sales fell far below the budgeted level? What, if any, actions would you need to take if sales far exceeded the sales budget? If sales are right on target, does effective controlling require any response from you? (Would your answer differ if the department were on target overall, but some salespeople fell short and others exceeded their targets?)

5. Besides sales and expenses, identify five other important control measures for a business. Include at least one nonfinancial measure.

6. What are the pros and cons of bureaucratic controls such as rules, procedures, and supervision?

7. Suppose a company at which executives were rewarded for meeting targets based only on profits and stock price switches to a balanced scorecard that adds measures for customer satisfaction, employee engagement, employee diversity, and ethical conduct. How, if at all, would you expect executives' performance to change in response to the new control system? How, if at all, would you expect the company's performance to change?

8. Google offers Google Apps, such as Gmail, Google Calendar, and Docs & Spreadsheets, as collaboration tools for employees. Describe how the company could use market controls to determine whether Google employees will use these software programs or competing software (e.g., Word and Excel).

9. How effective is clan control as a control mechanism? What are its strengths? Its limitations? When would a manager rely on clan control the most?

10. Does empowerment imply the loss of control? Why or why not?

11. Some people use the concept of personal control to describe the application of business control principles to individual careers. Thinking about your school performance and career plans, which steps of the control process (Figure 16.1) have you been applying effectively? How do you keep track of your performance in meeting your career and life goals? How do you measure your success? Does clan control help you meet your personal objectives?

EXPERIENTIAL EXERCISES

16.1   SAFETY PROGRAM

OBJECTIVE

To understand some of the specific activities that fall under the management functions of planning, organizing, controlling and staffing, and directing.

INSTRUCTIONS

Read the following case and then evaluate the likely success of this managerial control effort. Specifically, how well did the manager review the source of the problems? How well designed is the new control system? How effectively is the manager building employee commitment to using the control mechanisms? How could this manager improve the control process? Summarize your findings and recommendations in a paragraph or two.

MANAGING THE VAMP CO. SAFETY PROGRAM

If there are specific things that a manager does, how are they done? What does it look like when one manages? The following describes a typical situation in which a manager performs managerial functions:

As production manager of the Vamp Stamping Company, you've become quite concerned over the metal stamping shop's safety record. Accidents that resulted in operators' missing time on the job have increased quite rapidly in the past year. These more serious accidents have jumped from 3 percent of all accidents reported to a current level of 10 percent.

Because you're concerned about your workers' safety as well as the company's ability to meet its customers' orders, you want to reduce this downtime accident rate to its previous level or lower within the next six months.

You call the accident trend to the attention of your production supervisors, pointing out the seriousness of the situation and their continuing responsibility to enforce the gloves and safety goggles rules. Effective immediately, every supervisor will review his or her accident reports for the past year, file a report summarizing these accidents with you, and state their intended actions to correct recurring causes of the accidents. They will make out weekly safety reports as well as meet with you every Friday to discuss what is being done and any problems they are running into.

You request the union steward's cooperation in helping the safety supervisor set up a short program on shop safety practices.

Because the machine operators are having the accidents, you encourage your supervisors to talk to their workers and find out what they think can be done to reduce the downtime accident rate to its previous level.

While the program is going on, you review the weekly reports, looking for patterns that will tell you how effective the program is and where the trouble spots are. If a supervisor's operators are not decreasing their accident rate, you discuss the matter in considerable detail with the supervisor and his or her key workers.

SOURCE: From Theodore T. Herbert, *The New Management: Study Guide*, 4th ed., p. 41.

16.2 PRELIMINARY, CONCURRENT, AND FEEDBACK CONTROL

OBJECTIVES

1. To demonstrate the need for control procedures.

2. To gain experience in determining when to use preliminary, concurrent, and feedback controls.

INSTRUCTIONS

1. Read the text materials on preliminary, concurrent, and feedback control.

2. Read the Control Problem Situation and be prepared to resolve those control problems in a group setting.

3. Your instructor will divide the class into small groups. Each group completes the Preliminary, Concurrent, and Feedback Control Worksheet by achieving consensus on the types of control that should be applied in each situation. The group also develops responses to the discussion questions.

4. After the class reconvenes, group spokespersons present group findings.

DISCUSSION QUESTIONS

1. For which control(s) was it easier to determine application? For which was it harder?

2. Would this exercise be better assigned to groups or to individuals?

CONTROL PROBLEM SITUATION

Your management consulting team has just been hired by Technocron International, a rapidly growing producer of electronic surveillance devices that are sold to commercial and government end users. Some sales are made through direct selling, and some through industrial resellers. Direct-sale profits are being hurt by what seem to be exorbitant expenses paid to a few of the salespeople, especially those who fly all over the world in patterns that suggest little planning and control. There is trouble among the resellers because standard contracts have not been established and each reseller has an entirely different contractual relationship. Repayment schedules vary widely from customer to customer. Also, profits are reduced by the need to customize most orders, making mass production almost impossible. However, no effort has been made to create interchangeable components. There are also tremendous inventory problems. Some raw materials and parts are bought in such small quantities that new orders are being placed almost daily. Other orders are so large that there is hardly room to store everything. Many of these purchased components are later found to be defective and unusable, causing production delays. Engineering changes are made that make large numbers of old components still in storage obsolete. Some delays result from designs that are very difficult to assemble, and assemblers complain that their corrective suggestions are ignored by engineering. To save money, untrained workers are hired and assigned to experienced worker-buddies who are expected to train them on the job. However, many of the new people are too poorly educated to understand their assignments, and their worker-buddies wind up doing a great deal of their work. This, along with the low pay and lack of consideration from engineering, is causing a great deal of worker unrest and talk of forming a union. Last week alone nine new worker grievances were filed, and the U.S. Equal Employment Opportunity Commission has just announced intentions to investigate two charges of discrimination on the part of the company. There is also a serious cash flow problem because a number of long-term debts are coming due at the same time. The cash flow problem could be relieved somewhat if some of the accounts payable could be collected.

The CEO manages corporate matters through five functional divisions: operations, engineering, marketing, finance, and human resources management and general administration.

Preliminary, Concurrent, and Feedback Control Worksheet

Technocron International is in need of a variety of controls. Complete the following matrix by noting the preliminary, concurrent, and feedback controls that are needed in each of the five functional divisions.

Divisions	Preliminary Controls	Concurrent Controls	Feedback Controls
HRM and general administration	_____	_____	_____
Operations	_____	_____	_____
Engineering	_____	_____	_____
Marketing	_____	_____	_____
Finance	_____	_____	_____

CONCLUDING CASE

THE GRIZZLY BEAR LODGE

Diane and Rudy Conrad own a small lodge outside Yellowstone National Park. Their lodge has 15 rooms that can accommodate up to 40 guests, with some rooms set up for families. Diane and Rudy serve a continental breakfast on weekdays and a full breakfast on weekends, included in the room rates they charge. Their busy season runs from May through September, but they remain open until Thanksgiving and reopen in April for a short spring season. They currently employ one cook and two waitpersons for the breakfasts on weekends, handling the other breakfasts themselves. They also have several housekeeping staff members, a groundskeeper, and a front-desk employee. The Conrads take pride in the efficiency of their operation, including the loyalty of their employees, which they attribute to their own form of clan control. If a guest needs something—whether it's a breakfast catered to a special diet or an extra set of towels—Grizzly Bear workers are empowered to supply it.

The Conrads are considering expanding their business. They have been offered the opportunity to buy the property next door, which would give them the space to build an annex containing an additional 20 rooms. Currently their annual sales total $300,000. With expenses running at $230,000—including mortgage, payroll, maintenance, and so forth—the Conrads' annual income is $70,000. They want to expand and make improvements without cutting back on the personal service they offer to their guests. In fact, in addition to hiring more staff

to handle the larger facility, they are considering collaborating with more local businesses to offer guided rafting, fishing, hiking, and horseback riding trips. They also want to expand their food service to include dinner during the high season, which means renovating the restaurant area of the lodge and hiring more kitchen and wait staff. Ultimately, the Conrads would like the lodge to be open year-round, offering guests opportunities to cross-country ski, ride snowmobiles, or hike in the winter. They hope to offer holiday packages for Thanksgiving, Christmas, and New Year's celebrations in the great outdoors. The Conrads report that their employees are enthusiastic about their plans and want to stay with them through the expansion process. "This is our dream business," says Rudy. "We're only at the beginning."

QUESTIONS

1. Discuss how Rudy and Diane can use feedforward, concurrent, and feedback controls both now and in the future at the Grizzly Bear Lodge to ensure their guests' satisfaction.

2. What might be some of the fundamental budgetary considerations the Conrads would have as they plan the expansion of their lodge?

3. Describe how the Conrads could use market controls to plan and implement their expansion.

CHAPTER 17

Managing Technology and Innovation

> The imperatives of technology and organization, not the images of ideology, are what determine the shape of economic society.
>
> —John Kenneth Galbraith

Management Connection

HOW TESLA MOTORS DRIVES IN TECHNOLOGY'S FAST LANE

For the average manager, competing against the dominant car makers with a start-up would be unthinkable, but Elon Musk is far from average. Musk, who made his fortune starting the Internet ventures Zip2 and PayPal, believes he can compete by offering better vehicles—that run on electricity. To do so, his company, Tesla Motors, must overcome technological hurdles and convince car buyers to imagine driving in a new way. According to Musk, the vehicle industry someday must switch from gasoline to battery power, and he wants to drive that change.

As Musk sees it, being outside the auto-making establishment gives Tesla an advantage. Whereas the established car companies have labored to redesign vehicles to run on electrical power along with or in place of gasoline, Tesla's pure goal is to build an electric vehicle that is a pleasure to drive. Its first vehicle, the $109,000 Roadster sports car, sold few units but provided lessons for Tesla's more competitively priced entrant into the luxury market, the Model S sedan. The engineers placed the Model S's battery pack in the base of the vehicle, adding stability and safety while freeing up space for other uses—a spacious trunk, a storage compartment under the front hood, and room for seats to fold down in the back, allowing the car to carry seven people. In place of a gear shift console, a 17-inch touch screen displays controls and maps. And the super-efficient engine can take the car from 0 to 60 miles per hour in a few seconds.

Even as Musk persisted, observers doubted, seeing Tesla struggle with delays and quarterly losses while developing and troubleshooting its vehicles. Recently, however, developments suggest Tesla can succeed financially by leaving the competition in the dust technologically. By December 2012, the company reached full production of the Model S. Soon glowing reviews made news: *Motor Trend* named it Car of the Year, calling it "a truly remarkable automobile." *Road and Track* said of the Model S, "For the first time since automobiles had fins, the world stands in awe of a car from the United States." And *Consumer Reports* said it was the best car it had ever tested.

In the first quarter of 2013, Tesla delivered 4,750 units of the Model S and recorded its first quarterly profit. This reaches Tesla's desired pace of 20,000 cars per year, but that is far from the hundreds of thousands of hybrids sold by Honda and Toyota. Even so, investors—and drivers—are beginning to believe Tesla can make the electric car the vehicle of choice.[1]

Although more companies are introducing electric vehicles, most cars still run on gasoline. As you read this chapter, think about the issues that Tesla's managers must consider as they decide how to make electric vehicles an attractive and affordable option.

Although some visionaries such as Tesla's Elon Musk seem fearless, technological innovation is daunting in its complexity and pace of change. Nevertheless, it also is vital for a firm's competitive advantage. Not long ago, new products took years to plan and develop, were standardized and mass produced, and were pushed onto the market through extensive selling and promotional campaigns. With sales lives for these products measured in decades, production processes used equipment dedicated to making only those standardized products and achieved savings through economies of scale. But today's customers often demand products that have yet to be designed. Product development is now a race to become the first to introduce innovative products—products whose lives often are measured in months as they are quickly replaced by other, even more technologically sophisticated products.

Today's managers and organizations depend on effective management of technology not only to carry out their basic tasks but, even more important, to ensure the continuing competitiveness of their goods or services. In a marketplace where technology and rapid innovation are critical for success, managers must understand how technologies emerge, develop, and change the ways organizations compete and the ways people work. This chapter discusses how technology can affect an organization's competitiveness and how to integrate technology into the organization's competitive strategy. Then we assess the technological needs of the organization and the means by which these needs can be met.

Bottom Line

Innovation is a key to competitiveness

Why does innovation matter for a service business?

Technology and Innovation

technology

The systematic application of scientific knowledge to a new product, process, or service.

innovation

A change in method or technology; a positive, useful departure from previous ways of doing things.

In Chapter 9, we defined **technology** as the methods, processes, systems, and skills used to transform resources into products. More broadly speaking, we can think of technology as the commercialization of science: the systematic application of scientific knowledge to a new product, process, or service. In this sense, technology is embedded in every product, service, and procedure used or produced.[2]

When technology is used to create a new product or service to sell or a new way of working, what has taken place is a form of innovation. Innovation differs from invention, or making a new idea manifest, which may or may not add value to any organization. In the context of management, **innovation** is any new way of working that creates value. Innovation can result from combining things that are new or from combining existing things in new ways. The resulting innovation can be any one of these three fundamental types:[3]

1. *Product innovation* is a change in the outputs (goods or services) the organization produces. If BP's research into biofuels resulted in a new kind of fuel to sell, this would be an example of product innovation.
2. *Process innovation* is a change in the way outputs (goods or services) are produced. If BP's research into biofuels resulted in a more efficient way to produce fuel from sugarcane, this would be an example of process innovation. Other examples of process innovation are flexible manufacturing processes discussed in Chapter 9, including mass customization, just-in-time, and concurrent engineering.
3. *Business model innovation* refers to a change in the way the organization creates and delivers value. The change may affect any element of a company's business model: its customer value proposition (the basic problem it solves, such as ecofriendly fuel for about the same cost as fossil fuels), its profit formula (the financial road map for its success), its key resources (people, technology, facilities, brand, etc.), and its key processes. Examples of business model innovation include Amazon (bookselling), Netflix (video rental), and NetJets (business travel).

These categories cover a multitude of creative new ideas, which in businesses can involve changes in product offerings, the basic platforms or common features and processes that underlie product creation, the customer problems the organization can solve, the types of customers the organization serves, the nature of the experience provided by the organization, the way the organization earns money from what it does, the efficiency and effectiveness of its processes, the structure of the organization, the supply chain through which it delivers goods and services, the physical or virtual points at which it interacts with customers, the ways the organization communicates, and the brand associated with the organization and its products.[4]

There are definable and predictable patterns in the way technologies emerge, develop, and are replaced. Critical forces converge to create new technologies, which then follow well-defined life cycle patterns. Understanding the forces driving technological development and the patterns they follow can help a manager anticipate, monitor, and manage technologies more effectively.

1. There must be a need, or demand, for the technology. Without this need driving the process, there is no reason for technological innovation to occur.
2. Meeting the need must be theoretically possible, and the knowledge to do so must be available from basic science.
3. We must be able to convert the scientific knowledge into practice in both engineering and economic terms. If we can theoretically do something but doing it is economically impractical, the technology cannot be expected to emerge.
4. The funding, skilled labor, time, space, and other resources needed to develop the technology must be available.
5. Entrepreneurial initiative is needed to identify and pull all the necessary elements together.

In Practice

FORCES DRIVING INNOVATION AT PRATT & WHITNEY

These forces have driven technological development and product innovation at Pratt & Whitney, a leading aerospace company. In the market for jet engines, Pratt & Whitney has a strong presence in the military sector but has lagged the competition in selling engines for commercial aircraft. Management decided that its competitive edge would come from offering aircraft companies a far more efficient engine.

It was a daring move. Designing a completely new engine and finding a customer to incorporate it into the design of a plane would take two decades. Management pulled together R&D funds from every source they could tap, eventually spending $1.5 billion before they had signed a single sales contract. Talented engineers and scientists created Pratt's Pure-Power engine, which uses a technology called a geared turbo fan (GTF). The GTF technology incorporates three product innovations: a lightweight but powerful gearbox, a bigger fan, and a lighter-weight engine housing. Together, these improve fuel efficiency by 16 percent, or roughly three times the improvement engine makers have offered in the past. It also cuts the engine's noise level in half.

Meanwhile, Pratt's sales team found their first customer, Bombardier, a Canadian company that was designing a new line of aircraft called the CSeries, which it hoped would compete with the Boeing 737 and Airbus A319/A320. Bombardier was hoping that offering airlines greater efficiency would enable it to capture 50 percent of the market for jets seating 100 to 150 passengers. Pratt's GTF engine was just what it needed to meet that goal.[5]

- Which forces were driving this innovation at Pratt & Whitney?

Technology Life Cycle

technology life cycle

A predictable pattern followed by a technological innovation from its inception and development to market saturation and replacement.

Technological innovations typically follow a relatively predictable pattern called the **technology life cycle**. Figure 17.1 depicts the pattern. The cycle begins with the recognition of a need and a perception of a means by which the need can be satisfied through applied science or knowledge. The knowledge and ideas are brought together and developed, culminating in a new technological innovation. Early progress can be slow in these formative years as competitors continually experiment with product design and operational characteristics to meet consumer needs. This stage is where the rate of product innovation tends to be highest. For example, during the early years of the auto industry, companies tried a wide range of machines, including electric and steam-driven cars, to determine which product would be most effective. Eventually the internal combustion engine emerged as the dominant design, and the number of product innovations leveled off.

> Once early problems are resolved and a dominant design emerges, improvements come more from process innovations.

Once early problems are resolved and a dominant design emerges, improvements come more from process innovations to refine the technology. At this point managers can gain an advantage by pursuing process efficiencies and cost competitiveness. In the auto example, as companies settled on a product standard, they began leveraging the benefits of mass production and vertical integration to improve productivity. These process innovations were instrumental in lowering production costs and bringing the price of automobiles in line with consumer budgets.[6]

Eventually the new technology begins to reach the upper limits of both its performance capabilities and the spread of its usage. Development slows and becomes increasingly costly, and the market becomes saturated (i.e., there are few new customers). The technology can remain in this mature stage for some time—as in the case of autos—or can be replaced quickly by another technology offering superior performance or economic advantage. The life cycles can take decades or even centuries, as in the case of iron- and steel-making technologies. A dramatic example of technology evolution can be found in the recorded music industry, which moved from the relatively primitive device Thomas Edison invented through the vinyl record to the cassette tape to the digitally recorded CD and then to highly miniaturized but memory-intensive MP3 players such as the iPod, which are now being challenged by services, such as Pandora or Rhapsody, that allow users to stream songs from the Internet on their cell phones or computers.

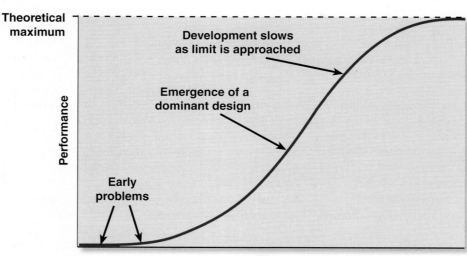

FIGURE 17.1
The Technology Life Cycle

As this example shows, a technology life cycle can be made up of many individual product life cycles. Each of these products performs a similar task—delivering recorded music to a listener—yet each product is an improvement over its predecessors. In this way, technological development involves significant innovations, often representing entirely new technologies, followed by a large number of small, incremental innovations. Ongoing development of a technology increases the benefits gained through its use, makes the technology easier to use, and allows more applications. In the process, the use of the technology expands to new adopters.

Diffusion of Technological Innovations

Like the technology life cycle, the adoption of new technology over time follows an S-shaped pattern (see the top line in Figure 17.2). The percentage of people using the technology is small in the beginning but increases dramatically as the technology succeeds and spreads through the population. Eventually the number of users peaks and levels off when the market for the technology is saturated. This pattern, first observed in 1903, has been verified with many new technologies and ideas in a wide variety of industries and settings.[7]

The adopters of a new technology fall into five groups (see the bottom line in Figure 17.2). Each group presents different challenges and opportunities to managers who want to market a new technology or product innovation.

The first group, representing approximately 2.5 percent of adopters, consists of the *innovators*. Typically, innovators are adventurous and willing to take risks. They are willing to pay a premium for the latest and newest technology or product to come along and to champion it if it meets with their approval. The enthusiasm of innovator–adopters is no guarantee of success—for example, the product may still be too expensive for the general market. But a lack of enthusiasm among this group is often a sign that the new technology has serious problems and more development is needed.

The next 13.5 percent of adopters are *early adopters*. This group is critical to the success of a new technology because its members include well-respected opinion leaders. Early adopters often are the people or organizations to which others look for leadership, ideas, and up-to-date technological information. Innovators and early adopters are extremely important in new product launches, and marketing managers often spend heavily in promotion among these groups to generate a groundswell of enthusiasm.

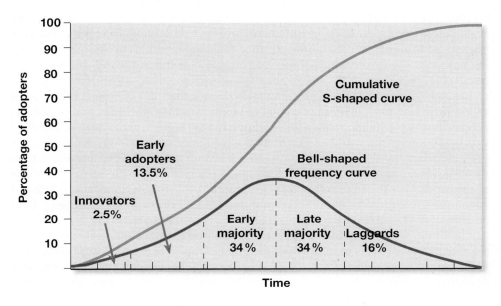

FIGURE 17.2

Technology Dissemination Pattern and Adopter Categories

The next group, representing 34 percent of adopters, is the *early majority*. These adopters are more deliberate and take longer to decide to use something new. Often they are important members of a community or industry, but typically not the leaders. It may take a while for the technology or new product to spread to this group, but once it does, use will begin to proliferate into the mainstream.

Representing the next 34 percent are the *late majority*. Members of this group are more skeptical of technological change and approach innovation with great caution, often adopting only out of economic necessity or increasing social pressure.

The final 16 percent are *laggards*. Often isolated and highly conservative in their views, laggards are extremely suspicious of innovation and change.

The speed with which an innovation spreads depends largely on five attributes. An innovation will spread quickly if it

- Has a great advantage over its predecessor.
- Is compatible with existing systems, procedures, infrastructures, and ways of thinking.
- Has less rather than greater complexity.
- Can be tried or tested easily without significant cost or commitment.
- Can be observed and copied easily.

Designing products with these technological considerations in mind can make a critical difference in their success.

Technological Innovation in a Competitive Environment

 LO 3

Discussions about technology life cycles and diffusion patterns may imply that technological change occurs naturally or automatically. Just the opposite is true: Change is neither easy nor natural in organizations. (We discuss change more fully in the next chapter.) Decisions about technology and innovation are very strategic, and managers need to approach them in a systematic way.

In Chapter 4, we discussed two generic strategies a company can use to position itself in the market: low cost and differentiation. With low-cost leadership, the company maintains an advantage because it has a lower cost than its competitors. With a differentiation strategy, the advantage comes from having a unique good or service for which customers are willing to pay a premium price.[8] Technological innovations can support either of these strategies: They can be used to gain cost advantage through pioneering lower-cost product designs and creating low-cost ways to perform needed operations, or they can support differentiation by pioneering unique goods or services that increase buyer value and thus command premium prices.

In some cases, technology can completely change the rules of competition within an industry. Clayton Christensen coined the term *disruptive innovation* to describe situations in which a simple application is adopted at the lower end of a market and then swiftly takes over the market.[9] For example, computer users initially mocked tablet computers because they offer less computing power than a laptop and more bulk than a smartphone. Nevertheless, Apple's iPad quickly helped tablets carve out a big share of the market for portable computers. The power of disruptive innovation creates a dilemma for companies: Should they continue on with the superior technology (and possibly lose the advantages of early adoption) or switch over to the new technology (and find themselves with an inferior product that may or may not succeed)? In practice, the tendency is to innovate to the point that products or services become too sophisticated or expensive for buyers' tastes, creating new opportunities for the next disruptive innovation. To be a disruptive innovator, focus on the users of a product

Bottom Line

Innovation can improve any bottom-line practice. *How can innovation support a low-cost strategy?*

and look for customers whose needs are being ignored—say, because they want something that costs less or is easier to use.

But industries seldom are transformed overnight. Typically, signals of a new technology's impact are visible well in advance, leaving time for companies and people to respond. For example, almost every competitor in the telecommunications industry fully understood the value of cellular technology. Often the key issue is not whether to adopt a new technology but when to adopt it and how to integrate the change with the organization's operating practices and strategies.

Technology Leadership

The adage "timing is everything" is applied to many things, ranging from financial investments to telling jokes. It also applies to the development and exploitation of new technologies. Industry leaders such as 3M, Amazon, Nike, and Merck

> Often the key issue is not whether to adopt a new technology but when to adopt it.

built and now maintain their competitive positions through early development and application of new technologies. However, technology leadership imposes costs and risks, and it is not the best approach for every organization (see Table 17.1).[10] Apple is well known for its technology leadership, beginning with its Macintosh computer, which pioneered the use of a mouse and graphical desktop icons instead of strings of typed computer commands, and advancing through the wildly popular iPod and iPhone.

Advantages of Technology Leadership   What makes innovators and technology leadership attractive is the potential for high profits and first-mover advantages. Being the first to market with new technologies can provide significant competitive advantage. If technology leadership increases an organization's efficiency relative to competitors, it achieves a cost advantage. The organization can use the advantage to reap greater profits than competitors or attract more customers by charging lower prices. Similarly, if a company is first to market with a new technology, it may be able to charge a premium price because it faces no competition. Higher prices and greater profits can defray the costs of developing new technologies.

This one-time advantage of being the technology leader can be turned into a sustainable advantage. Sustainability of a lead depends on competitors' ability to duplicate the technology and the organization's ability to keep building on the lead quickly enough to outpace competitors. It can do this in several ways. The reputation for being an innovator can create an ongoing advantage and even spill over to the

Advantages	Disadvantages
First-mover advantage	Greater risks
Little or no competition	Cost of technology development
Greater efficiency	Costs of market development and customer education
Higher profit margins	Infrastructure costs
Sustainable advantage	Costs of learning and eliminating defects
Reputation for innovation	Possible cannibalization of existing products
Establishment of entry barriers	
Occupation of best market niches	
Opportunities to learn	

TABLE 17.1

Advantages and Disadvantages of Technology Leadership

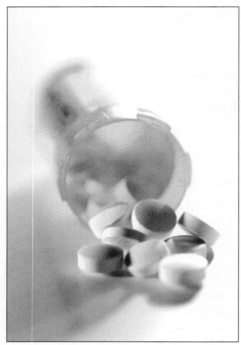

Top pharmaceutical companies depend on patents to allow them several years of selling new drugs without competition before cheaper generic versions of their drugs are released. Their competitive strategy is to develop new drugs in the meantime to sustain their success.

company's other products. For example, 3M's reputation for innovation and quality differentiates some of its standard products, such as adhesive tape, and allows a product to command a premium price. A competitor may be able to copy the product but not the reputation. Patents and other institutional barriers also can be used to block competitors and maintain leadership. The big players in the pharmaceutical industry invest heavily in research and development; they depend on patents to give them several years of selling new drugs without competition before generic versions of their drugs are permitted. For example, the blood thinner Plavix, which has the second-largest level of sales in the world, was protected by patent until 2011. In that year and the next, the patents for one-fifth of current drugs were set to expire, so pharmaceutical companies faced a tremendous challenge to develop new drugs.[11]

The first mover can also preempt competitors by occupying the best market niches. If it can establish high switching costs (recall Chapter 2) for repeat customers, these positions can be difficult for competitors to capture. Microsoft dominates the software market with its Windows operating system because of the large library of software that is packaged with it. Although other companies can offer more advanced software, their products are not as attractive because they are not bundled as the Windows-based systems is.

Technology leadership can provide a significant learning advantage. Although competitors may be able to copy or adopt a new technology, ongoing learning by the technology leader can keep a company ahead by generating minor improvements that are difficult to imitate. Many Japanese manufacturers use several small, incremental improvements generated with their *kaizen* programs (recall Chapter 9) to upgrade the quality of their products and processes continuously. All these minor improvements cannot be copied easily by competitors, and collectively they can provide a significant advantage.[12]

> The first mover can also preempt competitors by occupying the best market niches.

Disadvantages of Technology Leadership

Being the first to develop or adopt a new technology does not always lead to immediate advantage and high profits, however. Although such potential may exist, technology leadership does impose high costs and risks that followers do not have to bear. Being the leader thus can be more costly than being the follower. (There's good reason the forefront of technology is often called the bleeding edge.) These costs include educating buyers unfamiliar with the new technology, building an infrastructure to support the technology, and developing complementary products to achieve the technology's full potential. For example, when the personal computer was first developed in the 1970s, dozens of computer companies entered the market. Almost all of them failed, usually because they lacked the financial, marketing, and sales ability required to attract and service customers. Also, many new products require regulatory approval. For example, developing a new drug, including testing and obtaining FDA approval, can take 10 years or more and cost upward of $60 million to $1 billion or more. After that, developers enjoy a profitable period of patent protection until competitors move in with low-cost generics. Although these followers do not get the benefits of being first to market, they can copy the drug for a fraction of the cost once the original patents expire. This strategy can be highly profitable.[13]

Being a pioneer carries other risks. If raw materials and equipment are new or have unique specifications, a ready supply at a reasonable cost may not be available. Or the technology may not be fully developed and may have problems yet to be resolved. In addition, the unproved market for the technology creates uncertainty in demand. Finally, the new technology may have an adverse impact on existing structures or business. It may cannibalize current products or make existing investments obsolete.

Technology Followership

Not all organizations are equally prepared to be technology leaders, nor would leadership benefit each organization equally. In deciding whether to be a technology leader or follower, managers will consider their company's competitive strategy, the benefits gained through use of the technology, and the characteristics of their organization.[14]

Interestingly, technology followership also can be used to support both low-cost and differentiation strategies. If the follower learns from the leader's experience, it can avoid the costs and risks of technology leadership, thereby establishing a low-cost position. The makers of generic drugs use this type of strategy. Followership also can support differentiation. By learning from the leader, the follower can adapt the products or delivery systems to fit buyers' needs more closely. Microsoft is famous for having built a successful company on this type of followership. The company's products, including music players, video game consoles, spreadsheet and word-processing software, and web browsers, have been launched after technology leaders have paved the way. Likewise, Facebook came to dominate the realm of social networking only after other services such as Friendster and MySpace had burned through money introducing the concept. Newer competitors, such as Google, continue to enter the market with the hope that they can lure away users with a service that improves on Facebook's strengths while avoiding its weaknesses. This follower strategy is more challenging once an industry leader has established widespread customer loyalty.

A manager's decision on when to adopt new technology also depends on the potential benefits of the new technology as well as the organization's technology skills. As discussed earlier, technologies do not emerge in their final state; rather, they exhibit ongoing development (see Figure 17.3). Such development eventually makes the technology easier to use and more adaptable to various strategies. For example, the development of high-bandwidth communication networks has enabled many more companies to work with suppliers located abroad. At the same time, complementary products and technologies may be developed and introduced that make the main technology more useful. For example, tablet computers are becoming more of an asset at work—and therefore more common—as wireless speeds increase and developers offer business-friendly apps and adapt popular business software for use on mobile devices.

Bottom Line

Following the technology leader can save development expense.
How can being a follower help reduce costs?

SOURCE: D. M. Schroeder, "A Dynamic Perspective on the Impact of Process Innovation upon Competitive Strategies," *Strategic Management Journal* 11 (January 1990), pp. 25–42. Reprinted with permission.

FIGURE 17.3
Dynamic Forces of a Technology's Competitive Impact

These complementary products and technologies combine with the gradual diffusion of the technology to form a shifting competitive impact from the technology. The appropriate time for an organization to adopt technological innovations is when the costs and risks of switching to the technology are outweighed by the benefits. This point will be different for each organization, with some organizations benefiting from a leadership, early adopter role, and others from a followership role, depending on each organization's characteristics and strategies.[15]

Assessing Technology Needs

The biggest industry sector in the U.S. economy is health care services, where spending is soaring, much to the dismay of the insurers and patients paying the medical bills. One reason U.S. health care costs so much is that the industry has been slower than others to adopt types of technology that can make day-to-day operations more efficient. According to a RAND Corporation study, Americans could save $162 billion a year if health care providers made better investments in information technology. For example, fewer than one out of five hospitals are using a complete bar code system for dispensing medicine, which could save money and reduce medication errors.[16]

In today's increasingly competitive environment, failure to assess the technology needs of the organization correctly can fundamentally impair the organization's effectiveness. Assessing the technology needs of the organization involves measuring current technologies as well as external trends affecting the industry.

Measuring Current Technologies

technology audit

Process of clarifying the key technologies on which an organization depends.

Before organizations can devise strategies for developing and exploiting technological innovation, they must gain a clear understanding of their current technology base. A **technology audit** helps clarify the key technologies on which an organization depends. The most important dimension of a new technology is its competitive value. One technique for measuring competitive value categorizes technologies as emerging, pacing, key, and base:[17]

- *Emerging technologies* are still under development and thus are unproved. They may, however, significantly alter the rules of competition in the future. Managers will want to monitor the development of emerging technologies but may not yet need to invest in them until they have been more fully developed.
- *Pacing technologies* have yet to prove their full value but have the potential to alter the rules of competition by providing significant advantage. For example, when first installed, computer-aided manufacturing (see Chapter 9) was a pacing technology. Its full potential was not yet widely realized, but companies that used it effectively developed significant speed and cost advantages. Managers will want to focus on developing or investing in pacing technologies because of the competitive advantages they can provide.
- *Key technologies* have proved effective, but they also provide a strategic advantage because not everyone uses them. Knowledge and dissemination of these technologies are limited, and they continue to provide some first-mover advantages. For example, a more powerful, proprietary processing chip by Intel is a key technology for that organization. Eventually, alternatives to key technologies can emerge. But until then key technologies can give organization managers a significant competitive edge and make it much more difficult for new entrants to threaten the organization.

The most important dimension of a new technology is its competitive value.

- *Base technologies* are those that are commonplace in the industry; everyone must have them to be able to operate. Thus they provide little competitive advantage. Managers have to invest only to ensure their organization's continued competence in the technology.

Technologies can evolve rapidly through these categories. For example, electronic word processing was considered an emerging technology in the late 1970s. By the early 1980s, it could have been considered pacing. Although promising advantages, the technology's cost and capabilities restricted its usefulness to a limited number of applications. With continued improvements and more powerful computer chips, electronic word processing quickly became a key technology. Its costs dropped, its usage spread, and it demonstrated the capacity to enhance productivity. By the late 1980s, it was considered a base technology in most applications. Word-processing technology is now used so widely that it is viewed as a routine activity in almost every office.

In Practice

TECHNOLOGY AT SQUARE

A basic technology decision for retailers is how to accept payments. The traditional methods of paying with cash or check have become less common as consumers prefer to whip out a credit or debit card. More recently, some retailers are switching to a method shoppers find even more convenient: using the mobile device they already have in their hand or tucked into a pocket.

A company called Square, for example, created software that lets consumers pay automatically. To use the Pay With Square app, you enter credit card information into your phone and authorize the app to communicate with specific retailers' checkout registers. You tell the clerk, "Charge it to [your name]," and the store register processes the transaction wirelessly with your phone. For retailers, Square offers software called Register, which processes sales, collects customer data, and keeps track of inventory from an iPad or other Apple mobile device. Square made inroads with independent shops by charging a modest flat rate of $275 per month. It has since grown to process more than $10 billion in transactions a year, including online at Square Marketplace and at the U.S. Starbucks locations.

Retailers love the efficiency of accepting mobile payments, and consumers eventually should be able to enjoy the advantage of having a phone hold all their coupons, frequent-shopper IDs, and payment information. One challenge holding back more widespread adoption of services such as Square is that various payment systems and devices are not always compatible. For mobile payments to become the mainstream form of payment, companies providing the services will have to establish common technology standards and software platforms.[18]

- Is Square's mobile payment technology an emerging, pacing, key, or base technology? Why?

Assessing External Technological Trends

Just as with any planning, decisions about technology must balance internal capabilities (strengths and weaknesses) with external opportunities and threats. Managers can use several techniques to understand better how technology is changing within an industry.

Benchmarking   As mentioned in Chapter 4, benchmarking is the process of comparing the organization's practices and technologies with those of other companies. The ability to benchmark technologies against those of competitors varies among industries. Although competitors understandably are reluctant to share their secrets, information trading for benchmarking is not uncommon and can prove highly valuable. For example, Harley-Davidson's recovery of its reputation for manufacturing quality motorcycles began only after company executives toured Honda's plant and witnessed firsthand the weaknesses of Harley's manufacturing technologies and the vast potential for improvement.

Benchmarking against potential competitors in other nations is also important. Companies may find key or pacing technologies in use that can be imported easily and offer significant advantage. Also, overseas firms may be more willing to share their knowledge if they are not direct competitors and if they are eager to exchange information to benefit both companies.

Scanning   Whereas benchmarking focuses on what is being done currently, scanning focuses on what can be done and what is being developed. In other words, benchmarking examines key and perhaps some pacing technologies, whereas scanning seeks out pacing and emerging technologies—those just being introduced and still in development.

Scanning typically involves a number of tactics, many of them the same as those used in benchmarking. However, scanning places greater emphasis on identifying and monitoring the sources of new technologies for an industry. It also may dictate that executives read more cutting-edge research journals and attend research conferences and seminars. The extent to which scanning is done depends largely on how close to the cutting edge of technology an organization needs to operate.

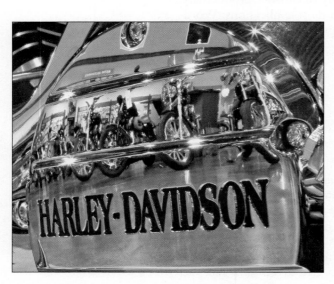

After Harley-Davidson executives toured a Honda plant, they were able to identify the weaknesses within their own company and use that knowledge to improve and boost their reputation.

Key Factors to Consider in Technology Decisions

LO 5   Once managers have thoroughly analyzed their organization's current technological position, they can plan how to either develop or exploit emerging technological innovations for the future. Managers must balance many interrelated factors in their decisions, such as the technology's potential to support the organization's strategic needs and the organization's skills and capabilities to exploit the technology successfully. The organization's competitive strategy, the technical abilities of its employees to deal with the new technology, the fit of the technology with the company's operations, and the company's ability to deal with the risks and ambiguities of adopting a new technology all must be considered in conjunction with the dynamic forces of a developing technology. This process does not always mean waiting for the technology to develop. Often it requires changing the capabilities and strategies of the organization to match the needs of the technology, including hiring new people, training existing employees, changing internal policies and procedures, and changing strategies. These considerations are discussed next.

Anticipated Market Receptiveness

The first consideration that needs to be addressed in developing a strategy around technological innovation is market potential. In many cases, innovations are stimulated by external demand for new goods and services. For example, a Boston company called Rethink Robotics believes the problem of repetitive-motion injuries will drive demand for robots that can safely work near humans to perform repetitive tasks such as picking, sorting, and arranging items. The company has responded by developing its Baxter robot with plastic, padded arms and sensors in the joints so workers can safely stand nearby and program the six-foot-tall robot. To help production workers control the robot, Baxter has a display screen on which expressive eyes signal the robot's status.[19]

In assessing market receptiveness, executives need to make two determinations:

1. In the short run, the new technology should have an immediate, valuable application.
2. In the long run, the technology must be able to satisfy market needs.

For example, retailers are always looking for ways to get the right goods on their shelves at the right time at a lower cost. They were therefore immediately interested in the introduction of a new technology for tracking inventory, radio frequency identification (RFID). As we saw in Chapter 9's discussion of logistics, RFID tags on pallets of merchandise are an efficient method by which retailers can keep track of inventory moving to warehouses and stores. They provide both cost savings and up-to-the-minute data for measuring demand. With this track record, makers of RFID tags are able to sell additional benefits to existing and new customers. Walmart has begun putting RFID tags on individual products so store employees can measure exactly what is in stock with the wave of a scanner. Hospitals are beginning to place RFID tags on equipment, supplies, and even patients' bracelets so they can ensure adequate supplies and efficiently deliver the right services. And when art collectors transport valuable pieces, they often mark each work with an RFID tag as one of their many security measures.[20]

Technological Feasibility

In addition to market receptiveness, managers must consider the feasibility of technological innovations. Visions can stay unrealized for a long time. Technical obstacles may represent barriers to progress. For example, security experts have for years wanted reliable face recognition systems; if a computer can correctly associate a face with the correct person's identity, this would prevent many of the problems that arise from stolen ID cards, passwords, and other fallible protection systems. But a recent study by the National Research Council found that face recognition technology cannot be improved to the point of making zero errors. Some of the stumbling blocks that are too complex for the computer systems of today and the foreseeable future are picking out facial features from a picture with other details, accounting for differences in a person's posture or facial expression, and accounting for differences in lighting levels and time (because people's faces change as they age). Improving performance in one of these areas tends to reduce performance in another. Even testing these systems is difficult; if, say, the lighting is adjusted, the results will diverge from test results under different conditions. At a recent NFL Super Bowl, face recognition technology was tested as a means to spot terrorists in a crowd, but the trial results were disappointing.[21]

Other industries face technological hurdles as well. In the oil industry, for example, technological barriers prevent exploration and drilling in the deepest parts of the ocean. In medicine, scientists and doctors work continuously to identify the causes of and cures for diseases such as cancer and AIDS. Makers of electronic devices are constantly challenged by how to keep their processors cool enough to function properly even as they get smaller and more powerful. GE recently applied jet engine technology to send high-velocity jets of air across electronic components, replacing fans with a system that can be as small as 4 millimeters high.[22] As time passes, however, electronics manufacturers will surely be looking for something even smaller. Each of these potentially valuable innovations is slowed by the technical limits of currently available technologies.

Economic Viability

Closely related to technological feasibility is economic viability. Apart from whether a firm can pull off a technological innovation, executives must consider whether there is a good financial incentive for doing so. The use of hydrogen-powered fuel cell technology for automobiles is almost feasible technically, but its costs are still too high. In addition, even if those costs were brought down to more acceptable levels, the absence of a supporting infrastructure in the society as a whole—such as the lack of hydrogen refueling stations—would represent another barrier to economic viability. However, if organizations can find niche markets for a high-priced new technology, they often can advance the technology to the point that applications become more affordable. For example, three-dimensional (3D) printers can read plans and translate them into physical objects by spraying out extremely thin layers of plastic or other materials to create the physical object. With advances in computer software, a skilled designer can create a 3D model of a part in a matter of hours and then direct the printer to finish the job. If the design disappoints, changes are easy to make with the software's commands, and no machinery needs to be retooled. A factory might invest in a high-end printer for $100,000 or more, but the price of basic printers has fallen below $1,500, putting them in reach of entrepreneurs and inventors.[23]

Less futuristic innovations also require a careful assessment of economic viability and costs. New technologies often represent an expensive and long-term commitment of resources. And integrating them effectively within an organization can require a great deal of management time. Once an organization commits to a technological innovation, a change in direction becomes extremely difficult and costly. For these reasons, a careful,

> Closely related to technological feasibility is economic viability.

In Practice

3D PRINTING

As 3D printer capabilities advance and prices fall, this technology is finding uses at all levels of business. Big manufacturers use 3D printing to create prototypes and make certain parts. Ford uses 3D printers to make prototype parts for its test vehicles much faster than it could by using traditional production methods. General Electric prints complex parts such as fuel injectors because 3D printing more precisely re-creates the complex designs used for efficient air flow. Biomedical companies use the technology to make custom-fit hearing aids.

Small companies and even independent inventors also are applying this technology. Some, such as Shapeways, offer 3D printing as a service; Shapeways can print items made of ceramics, sandstone, plastics, and metals. Inventors and would-be entrepreneurs can join TechShop or Fab Labs to use 3D printers and other equipment to bring their ideas to reality.

People familiar with 3D printing call it a disruptive innovation that will transform the nature of manufacturing. More and more products can be customized, with complex designs as simple to build as basic objects. Product users can become product makers, printing replacements for broken drawer handles or kitchen gadgets or scanning an online bar code to order replacement auto parts. The technology's relatively low cost offers potential for manufacturing in poor and underserved areas—say, printing tent stakes near the site of a disaster or parts for water pumps in villages of a developing nation. Small-scale, local manufacturing facilities could replace huge factories in low-wage areas. Most dramatically, 3D printing printer jets can actually spray cells to grow human tissue such as skin, cartilage, and muscle. Early tests at Wake Forest Baptist Medical Center have made human ears.[24]

- What characteristics of 3D printing could make it economically viable for an auto mechanic?

objective analysis of technology costs versus benefits is essential. Of course, benefits can be substantial as well. Fast-food restaurants can adopt a system called Hyperactive Bob. The system scans the parking lot to count vehicles that are arriving; compiles that data with information about time of day, cooking times, ordering patterns, and so on; and then issues orders to employees, telling them which items and how many to begin cooking. Employees touch a screen to indicate when they accept a task and when they are finished. The system, made by Hyperactive Technologies, costs $5,000 to install and $3,000 a year for software licensing, but it saves thousands a year in reduced food waste plus much more in reduced employee turnover—because Bob is an alternative to being shouted at by an anxious supervisor.[25]

The issue of economic viability takes us back to our earlier discussion of adoption timing. Earlier adopters may have first-mover advantages, but costs are associated with this strategic approach. The development costs of a particular technological innovation may be quite high, as in pharmaceuticals, chemicals, and software. Patents and copyrights often help organizations recoup the costs of their investments in technological innovations. Without such protection, the investments in research and development might not be justifiable.

Hyperactive Bob applies robotics technology (computer vision and artificial intelligence) to fast-food operations to make them more efficient. Using this technology is economically feasible because it reduces waste, improves customer satisfaction, and reduces employee turnover.

Unfortunately, the exploding growth in piracy or even fakery of patented pharmaceuticals, software, and other products has added new barriers to economic viability. Globalization has created a worldwide market for goods produced by low-cost counterfeiters and pirates overseas, who have the added advantage that they do not have to incur research and development expense. In addition, technology has made it easy to copy software without paying for it. Ugg boots, iPhones, Pfizer's anti-impotence drug Viagra, Rolex watches, Prada handbags, LEGO building sets, and countless music and movie recordings—all these and much more have been counterfeited or illegally copied and sold. In one year alone, U.S. Customs and Border Protections seized counterfeit or pirated goods worth $1.1 billion in lost sales, and that amount does not count the goods that slipped through customs undetected. A major contributor to the problem is China, which in recent years has accounted for more than three-quarters of the fake or pirated goods seized by the U.S. government. All these measures are designed to help organizations—and countries—maintain the economic viability of their innovations.[26]

Anticipated Capability Development

We have stated repeatedly in this text that organizations should (and do) build their strategies based on core capabilities. This advice applies to technology and innovation strategies as well. Frequently we can view technological innovations that are the tangible product of intangible—or tacit—knowledge and skill that make up a firm's core capabilities. Merck and Intel are examples of companies in which core capabilities in research and development lead to new technological innovations. Even in these cases, research capabilities are not always a good match with market opportunities. Pharmaceutical companies such as Merck are finding that many of the best new opportunities for fighting disease are in biotechnology, but the companies had developed expertise in chemistry-based drugs. Often these companies add new capabilities by acquiring or setting up ventures with biotechnology start-ups.

Some innovations are competency enhancing, exploiting or strengthening a core capability, whereas others are competency destroying. Continuing the example of Merck, biotechnology is changing the pharmaceutical industry. Currently, most core capabilities in the industry are in chemistry-based drugs. The shift to biotech requires firms to

Bottom Line
Innovation requires financial feasibility.
Say an innovation is exciting but unprofitable. What are the risks of pursuing it anyway?

develop or acquire a capability in biology-based therapeutics. For most firms, that is not an easy shift.[27]

A firm may not be technology oriented, but it still must pay attention to changing technology because it sometimes will need new capabilities to survive. For example, when Amazon.com changed the face of e-retailing in the 1990s, traditional brick-and-mortar bookstores had to adapt quickly. To regain competitiveness, they had to bolster their information technology capabilities, which wasn't always an easy thing to do.

The upshot of this is that although certain technologies may have tremendous market applicability, managers must have (or develop) the internal capabilities needed to execute their technology strategies. Without the skills needed to implement an innovation, even promising technological advances may prove disastrous.

Organizational Suitability

The final issues that tend to be addressed in deciding on technological innovations have to do with the culture of the organization, the interests of managers, and the expectations of stakeholders. Companies such as 3M and Google, which are seen as proactive technology-push innovators, tend to have cultures that are more outward-looking and opportunistic. Executives in these *prospector* firms give considerable priority to developing and exploiting technological expertise, and decision makers tend to have bold intuitive visions of the future. Typically they have technology champions who articulate competitively aggressive, first-mover technological strategies. In many cases, executives are more concerned about the opportunity costs of not taking action than they are about the potential to fail.

By contrast, *defender* firms, such as Kroger and Safeway, tend to adopt a more circumspect posture toward innovation. These firms tend to operate in stable environments. As a result, their strategies are focused more on deepening their capability base through complementary technologies that extend rather than replace their current ones. Strategic decisions are likely to be based on careful analysis and experience in the industry setting. In the United States, supermarkets have competed for decades by emphasizing low-cost distribution over large distances. That strategy has helped the companies survive low-cost pressure from Walmart but has not always translated well when U.S.-based supermarket chains have tried to expand into other parts of the world.[28]

A hybrid *analyzer* firm, such as Microsoft, needs to stay technologically competitive but tends to allow others to demonstrate solid demand in new arenas before it responds. Microsoft's Xbox game console, Office software, and Zune music player all contain innovations, but other companies pioneered the original path-breaking product concepts. As we noted earlier, these types of firms tend to adopt an early follower strategy to grab a dominant position more from their strengths in marketing and manufacturing than through technological innovation.

Every company has different capabilities to deal with new technology. As discussed previously, early adopters have characteristics different from those of late adopters. Early adopters of new technologies tend to be larger, more profitable, and more specialized. Therefore, they are in an economic position to absorb the risks associated with early adoption while profiting more from its advantages. In addition, the people involved in early adoption are more highly educated, have a greater ability to deal with abstraction, can cope with uncertainty more effectively, and have strong problem-solving capabilities. Thus early adopters can more effectively manage the difficulties and uncertainty of a less fully developed technology.[29]

One additional consideration managers need to take into account when introducing new technology is the impact the new technology will have on employees. Often new technology brings with it work flow and other changes that directly affect the organization's work environment. If the organization does not endorse and implement innovation, these changes may create anxiety and even resistance among employees, making integration of the technology more difficult. When managers communicate well in advance about the new technology, explain its purpose, and provide the necessary training, the process of integrating the new technology into the organization's existing processes becomes easier. The cooperation of employees is often a major factor in determining how difficult and costly the introduction of new technology will be. We discuss the issue of managing change in more detail in the next chapter.

Table 17.2 briefly summarizes the five major factors we have been discussing: market receptiveness, technological feasibility, economic viability, anticipated competence development, and organizational suitability. All of these considerations jointly influence the decisions managers will make about technology innovations. A lack in even one of them can derail an otherwise promising project. For example, consider how these factors apply to Tesla Motors' introduction of a luxury electric car as you read "Management Connection: Progress Report."

Considerations	Examples
Market receptiveness—assess external demand for the technology (short/long run).	Cell phones, MP3, personal digital assistants (PDAs), HDTV
Technological feasibility—evaluate technical barriers to progress.	Deep-sea oil exploration, physical size of PC microprocessors
Economic viability—examine any cost considerations and forecast profitability.	Solar fusion, fuel cells for automobiles, missile defense systems
Competence development—determine whether current capabilities are sufficient.	Information technology in hospitals, digital technology in cameras
Organizational suitability—assess the fit with culture and managerial systems.	Steel companies focusing on creativity and innovation

TABLE 17.2

Framing Decisions about Technological Innovation

Management Connection

THE CHALLENGING ROAD FOR TESLA MOTORS

The ecstatic reviews of the Model S suggest that Tesla Motors has mastered electric car technology. But business success requires more. For Tesla to continue leading in what founder and CEO Elon Musk sees as the future of driving, it must sell enough electric vehicles at a sufficient profit, something other start-ups failed to do. Therefore, Tesla is innovating in marketing, distribution, and access to recharging stations.

Initial orders for the Model S arrived faster than Tesla could make them. Emphasizing luxury and performance, rather than eco-friendliness, created excitement justifying a premium price (around $70,000). Now Tesla is making 20,000 Model S cars a year, a profitable pace at its Fremont, California, factory—a vacant auto plant acquired at far less than the cost of building new. Next, Tesla must persuade more drivers to go electric. The federal government helped with a tax credit of $7,500 on the purchase of an electric vehicle (it also loaned Tesla $465 million). Still, to broaden its customer base, Tesla needs a more affordable vehicle. By 2017, after its introduction of the Model X sport utility vehicle, Tesla intends to offer a car for about half the price of the Model S.

As a start-up in a mature industry, Tesla needed a plan for getting cars to consumers. Instead of approaching auto dealerships, Tesla opened stores in upscale shopping centers. Each store lovingly displays a Model S surrounded by exhibits about its features. At touch screens, shoppers can learn what they can save on gas by driving a Model S, as well as select options and see an image of their car. Tesla pays salespeople a flat rate, not commissions, to motivate them to develop customer relationships, not just move merchandise. However, dealer franchises have sued Tesla for violating state franchise laws, so Tesla is spending money to defend its stores state by state. Where it loses, drivers must travel elsewhere to see the car (they can order one online).

Another roadblock to adoption of all-electric vehicles is that stations for recharging a car are few, and fully recharging can take hours. Tesla developed battery technology that takes a car farther—about 200 miles in the case of the Model S. It also is building a network of Superchargers, which deliver free recharging; 20 minutes will charge the battery halfway. The company plans Superchargers for most U.S. metropolitan areas by the end of 2013, conveniently sited near roadside diners and shopping centers.[30]

- What are the advantages and disadvantages to Tesla Motors in being a technology leader?
- How has Tesla Motors addressed market receptiveness, technological feasibility, and economic viability?

MANAGER'S BRIEF

PROGRESS REPORT

ONWARD

Sourcing and Acquiring New Technologies

Developing new technology may conjure up visions of scientists and product developers working in research and development (R&D) laboratories like that of Bell Labs. However, new technology also can come from many other sources, including suppliers, manufacturers, users, other industries, universities, the government, and overseas companies. Although every source of innovation should be explored, each industry usually has specific sources for most of its new technologies. For example, because of the limited resources of most farming operations, innovations in farming most often come from manufacturers, suppliers, and government extension services. Seed manufacturers develop and market new, superior hybrids; chemical producers improve pesticides and herbicides; and equipment manufacturers design improved farm equipment. Land grant universities develop new farming techniques, and extension agents spread their usage.

In many industries, however, the primary sources of new technology are the organizations that use it. For instance, more than three-fourths of scientific innovations are developed by the users of the scientific instruments being improved and subsequently may be licensed or sold to manufacturers or suppliers.[31]

Essentially, the question of how to acquire new technology is a **make-or-buy decision**. In other words, should the organization develop the technology itself or acquire it from an outside source? However, the decision is not that simple. There are many alternatives, and each has advantages and disadvantages. Some of the most common options are discussed in the following sections.

make-or-buy decision

The question an organization asks itself about whether to acquire new technology from an outside source or develop it itself.

Internal Development

Developing a new technology within the company has the potential advantage of keeping the technology proprietary—exclusive to the organization. This provides an important advantage over competitors. The disadvantage of internal development is that it usually requires additional staff and funding for an extended period. Even if the development succeeds, considerable time may elapse before practical benefits are realized. Managers must carefully weigh the potential benefits of proprietary technology against the cost of developing it. Intel balances these risks and benefits by operating research and development laboratories in several locations, including Oregon, Israel, India, and China. Engineers in the various labs have come up with breakthrough ideas in the projects they have tackled, and labs in offshore locations can get around legal restrictions on technology imports as well as save money relative to the cost of hiring talent in the United States.[32]

Purchase

Most technology already is available in products or processes that can be purchased openly. For example, a bank that needs sophisticated information-processing equipment need not develop the technology itself. It can simply purchase the technology from manufacturers or suppliers. In most situations, this is the simplest, easiest, and most cost-effective way to acquire new technology. However, in this case, the technology itself will not offer a competitive advantage.

Bottom Line

Purchasing may be faster and cheaper than internal development.

What is the main downside of this way to acquire technology?

Contracted Development

If the technology is not available and a company lacks the resources or time to develop it internally, it may choose to contract the development from outside sources. Possible contractors include other companies, independent research laboratories, and university and government institutions. Usually outside contracting involves an agreed-upon series of objectives and timetables for the project, with payments made as each part of the project is tested and achieved.

Licensing

Certain technologies that are not easily purchased as part of a product can be licensed for a fee. Companies that develop video games often license technology, including the software that models the physics behind the activities depicted in the game. The artwork, characters, and music for a particular game may be unique, but the basic laws of real-world physics apply to the action shown in most of today's sophisticated games, so there is no advantage to programming that aspect of each game. Licensing is more economical.[33]

Technology Trading

Another way to gain access to new technologies is with technology trading. Representatives from Scotsman Ice Systems have studied other manufacturers' information technology applications. Whether or not those companies were in the same industry, their experiences have provided Scotsman with lessons that would have been expensive to learn from trial and error. Similarly, Mary Jo Cartwright, a director of manufacturing operations for Batesville Casket Company, toured a John Deere farm equipment plant and took note of a technology called visual management screens, which display how-to information for production workers. Although the technology wasn't worthwhile for Batesville at the time, when it later became involved in more customization, the company introduced visual management screens to give workers detailed and understandable assembly instructions.[34]

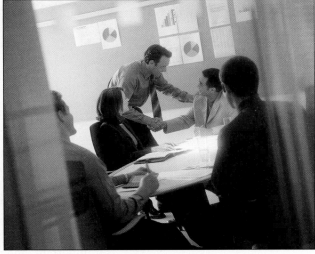

Being open to collaboration can result in ideas to achieve greater success.

Sometimes even rival companies use technology trading. Not all industries are amenable to this kind of sharing, but technology trading is becoming increasingly common because of the high cost of developing advanced technologies independently.[35]

Research Partnerships and Joint Ventures

Research partnerships are arrangements designed to pursue specific new technology development jointly. Typically each member enters the partnership with different skills or resources needed for development to succeed. One effective combination is an established company and a start-up. Joint ventures are similar in most respects to research partnerships, but they tend to have greater permanence, and their outcomes result in entirely new companies.[36] But as we described in our discussion on strategic alliances in Chapter 9,

> Sometimes even powerful competitors collaborate on projects.

sometimes even powerful competitors collaborate on projects. An example is the strategic alliance formed by Tyson Foods, the giant meat producer, and ConocoPhillips, one of the big U.S. oil companies, to develop a renewable diesel fuel that includes beef, pork, and poultry fat discarded during meat processing. This alliance brings together Tyson's knowledge in applying protein chemistry and Conoco's knowledge of refinery technology.[37]

Acquisition of an Owner of the Technology

If a company lacks the needed technology but wishes to acquire proprietary ownership of it, one option is to purchase the company that owns the technology. This transaction can take a number of forms, ranging from an outright purchase of the entire company to a minority interest sufficient to gain access to the technology. Twitter has recently been buying privately owned tech companies at a rapid clip. Among its recent acquisitions were Vine, creator of a service that lets people post short videos;

FIGURE 17.4

Technology Acquisition Options

Lucky Sort, which built software for identifying patterns in live data streams such as social-media posts and news reports; and Bluefin Labs, which developed a service that gathers data from social media to measure what TV shows and ads people are talking about.[38] Each acquisition gave Twitter new technological capabilities related to its main service of hosting microblogs and delivering ads to users.

Choosing among these alternatives is simpler if managers ask the following basic questions:

1. Is it important (and possible) in terms of competitive advantage for the technology to remain proprietary?
2. Are the time, skills, and resources for internal development available?
3. Is the technology readily available outside the company?

As Figure 17.4 illustrates, the answers to these questions guide the manager to the most appropriate technology acquisition option.

If the preferred decision is to acquire a company, managers take additional steps to ensure the acquisition will make sense for the long term. For example, they try to make sure that key employees will remain with the firm instead of leaving and perhaps taking essential technical expertise with them. Similarly, as with any large investment, managers carefully assess whether the financial benefits of the acquisition will justify the purchase price.

Technology and Managerial Roles

chief information officer (CIO)

Executive in charge of information technology strategy and development.

In organizations, technology traditionally has been the responsibility of vice presidents for research and development. These executives are directly responsible for corporate and divisional R&D laboratories. Typically their jobs have a functional orientation. But increasingly companies have the position of **chief information officer (CIO),** often also called the chief technology officer (CTO). The CIO is a senior position at the corporate level with broad, integrative responsibilities. CIOs coordinate the technological efforts of the various business units; act as a voice for technology in the top management team; identify ways that technology can support the company's strategy; supervise new technology development; and assess the technological implications of major strategic initiatives such as acqui-sitions, new ventures, and strategic alliances. They also manage their organization's information technology (IT) group.[39]

In organizations that value the agility resulting from continuous learning, this position sometimes is a varia-tion on the CTO known as a *chief innovation officer*. The chief innovation officer not only ensures that technology advances in line with the company's strategy, but also ensures that ideas and knowledge freely flow between R&D and other employees as well as between research-ers and the company's management.[40]

Without the CIO's integrative role, different departments in an organization could easily adopt dif-ferent technology tools and standards, leading to much higher equipment and maintenance expense and diffi-culties in connecting the different parts of the organi-zation. Also, because organization technologists often have very specialized expertise, managers without such expertise may have difficulty supervising them effec-tively. A CIO can help managers ensure that the work technologists do is aligned with the strategic goals of the organization.

Sophie Vandebroek, chief technology officer of Xerox, took on this role with the goal of making Xerox's systems simpler, speedier, smaller, smarter, more secure, and socially responsible—what she calls the "six S's."

Chief technology officers also perform an important boundary role: they work directly with outside organizations. For example, they work with universities for fund-ing research to stay abreast of technical developments and with regulatory agencies to ensure compliance with regulations, identify trends, and influence the regulatory process.

Other people play a variety of critical roles in developing new technology. Recall from Chapter 7 that it is the entrepreneur who, in an effort to exploit untried technologies, invents new products or finds new ways to produce old prod-ucts. The entrepreneur opens up new possibilities that change the competitive structure of entire industries. For example, Steve Jobs started Apple Computer in his garage, helping to popularize the personal computer and years later the MP3 music player.

Key roles in acquiring and developing new technologies are the technical innova-tor, product champion, and executive champion.[41] The **technical innovator** develops the new technology or has the key skills needed to install and operate the technology. This person possesses the requisite technical skills, but he or she may not have the managerial skills needed to push the idea forward and secure acceptance within the organization. This is where the product champion gets involved. Introducing new technology into an organization requires someone to promote the idea. The **product champion**—often at the risk of his or her position and prestige—promotes the idea throughout the organization, searching for support and acceptance. The champion can be a high-level manager but often is not. If the champion lacks the power and financial resources to make the required changes independently, she or he must con-vince people who have such authority to support the innovation. In other words, product champions must get sponsorship.

Sponsorship comes from the **executive champion,** who has the status, author-ity, and financial resources to support the project and protect the product champion. Without this support and protection, the product champion, and thus the new tech-nology, could not succeed. Resources needed to develop the innovation would be unavailable, and without protection, the champion would not be allowed to continue promoting the change.

technical innovator

A person who develops a new technology or has the key skills to install and operate the technology.

product champion

A person who promotes a new technology throughout the organization in an effort to obtain acceptance of and support for it.

executive champion

An executive who supports a new technology and protects the product champion of the innovation.

In Practice

INNOVATION IN THE MILITARY

In the hierarchical culture of the military, executive champions are essential to clear the way for innovation. This was the case with the introduction of solar technology to U.S. forces fighting in Iraq and Afghanistan.

Even as technological advances have made U.S. armed forces formidable, they have increased the need for energy to power all the high-tech gear. Supply lines are loaded with batteries and portable generators in addition to food and medical supplies. The supply convoys face danger as they deliver these goods along routes planted with roadside bombs. Particularly perilous is the transportation of fuel, and in Afghanistan, 30 percent of that fuel is used for powering generators.

Since 2001, the U.S. military has been exploring alternative energy options, but these needed an advocate. In Iraq in 2006, Major General Richard Zilmer, commander of the first Marine Expeditionary Force, requested renewable energy gear for forward bases. Nothing came of that request.

Two years later, when marines made a similar request, Navy Secretary Ray Mabus had established a goal for half of the navy's energy to come from nonfossil fuels by 2020. (The Marine Corps is part of the U.S. Navy.) Also, the Marine Expeditionary Energy Office was in place to figure out how to apply the navy's energy innovations to marines on active duty. With leaders pushing for innovation, scientists got to work and within months had developed a small solar- and battery-power generator that could be transported on Humvees. They also created small solar panels for marines to carry and open up to recharge their equipment. It was a welcome relief; marines had been carrying up to 20 pounds of batteries in their gear. Best of all, reducing the need for helicopter pilots and truck drivers to deliver batteries and fuel to troops in remote locations can literally save lives.[42]

- What would be the challenges of trying to be a product champion in this situation?

Organizing for Innovation

Successful innovation is a lot more than a great idea. A study by the Boston Consulting Group found that lack of good ideas is hardly ever the obstacle to profitable innovation. More often, ideas fail to generate financial returns because the organization isn't set up to innovate. The culture is risk averse, projects get bogged down, efforts aren't coordinated, and management can't figure out where to direct the company's money.[43] In contrast, as shown in Figure 17.5, innovation has a chance to flourish when positive values are in place, when the organization integrates internal and external knowledge, and when its people are encouraged to own and solve problems and to experiment continuously.

> More often, ideas fail to generate financial returns because the organization isn't set up to innovate.

In Chapter 9 we introduced the concept of learning organizations—companies that excel at solving problems, seeking and finding new approaches, and sharing new knowledge with all members of an organization. Such learning organizations are particularly well positioned to develop useful innovations. The innovations may involve a kind of ambidexterity, or doing two things at once. Some innovations are about exploiting existing capabilities—to improve production speed or product quality, for example. Or the innovation may involve exploring new knowledge—seeking to develop new products or services.[44] Both innovation processes are necessary. Innovative learning organizations use their existing strengths

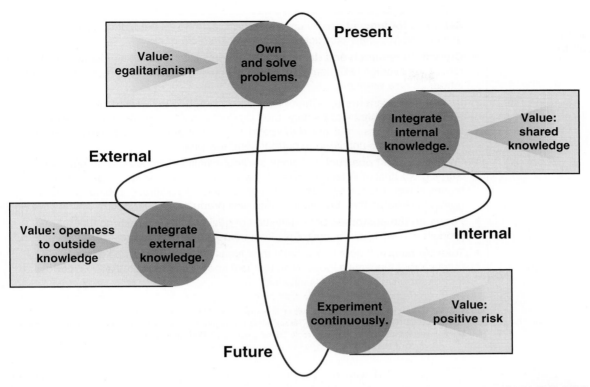

SOURCE: Dorothy Leonard Barton, "The Factory as Learning Laboratory," *Sloan Management Review* (1992), p 34.

FIGURE 17.5
Requirements for Innovation

to improve their operations and thus improve their bottom lines. But they also learn to unleash people's creative energies and capabilities to develop new products and processes that will ensure their long-term competitiveness. In this section, we discuss some of the approaches managers use to organize for innovation.

Unleashing Creativity

3M has a strong orientation toward intrapreneurship and derives about one-third of its revenues from new products. 3M, Google, Apple, and IBM have well-established histories of producing many successful new technologies and products. What sets these and other continuous innovators apart? The one thing these companies have in common is an organizational culture that encourages innovation.[45]

> Failure is the essence of learning, growing, and succeeding.

Consider the 3M legend from the early 1920s of inventor Francis G. Okie. Okie dreamed up the idea of using sandpaper instead of razor blades for shaving. The aim was to reduce the risk of nicks and avoid sharp instruments. The idea failed, but rather than being punished for the failure, Okie was encouraged to champion other ideas, which included 3M's first blockbuster success: waterproof sandpaper. A culture that permits failure is crucial for fostering the creative thinking and risk taking required for innovation.

As strange as it may seem, celebrating failure can be vital to the innovation process.[46] Failure is the essence of learning, growing, and succeeding. Innovative companies have many balls in the air at all times, with many people trying many new ideas. A majority of the ideas will fail, but it is only through this process that the few big hits will emerge that make a company an innovative star. Madison Mount, who leads the design work for food and beverage clients of IDEO, says, "If I'm not taking risks, I feel uncomfortable, because I'm not learning."[47] This type of attitude from a manager can foster creative thinking throughout the ranks.

TABLE 17.3
3M's Rules for an
Innovative Culture

• **Set goals for innovation.** By corporate decree, 25 to 30 percent of annual sales must come from new products that are five years old or newer.
• **Commit to research and development.** 3M invests in R&D at almost double the rate of the average U.S. company. One R&D goal is to cut in half the time it takes to introduce new products.
• **Inspire intrapreneurship.** Champions are encouraged to run with new ideas, and they get a chance to manage their products as if they were running their own businesses. 3Mers are allowed to spend 15 percent of their time pursuing personal research interests unrelated to current company projects.
• **Facilitate, don't obstruct.** Divisions are kept small and are allowed to operate with a great deal of independence but have constant access to information and technical resources. Researchers with good ideas are awarded $50,000 Genesis grants to develop their brainstorms into new products.
• **Focus on the customer.** 3M's definition of quality is to demonstrate that the product can do what the customer—not some arbitrary standard—dictates.
• **Tolerate failure.** 3Mers know that if their ideas fail, they still will be encouraged to pursue other innovative ideas. Management knows that mistakes will be made and that destructive criticism kills initiative.

SOURCES: Company reports; R. Mitchell, "Masters of Innovation: How 3M Keeps Its New Products Coming," *BusinessWeek*, April 10, 1989, pp. 58–63; T. Katauskas, "Follow-Through: 3M's Formula for Success," *R&D*, November 1990; and T. J. Martin, "Ten Commandments for Managing Creative People," *Fortune*, January 16, 1995, pp. 135–36.

A culture that permits failure is crucial for fostering the creative thinking and risk taking required for innovation. If 3M hadn't kept Francis G. Okie on board after a few failed inventions, Okie would never have come up with 3M's first success—waterproof sandpaper.

Bottom Line

Bureaucracy busting encourages innovation.

Name one way to bust bureaucracy.

3M uses the simple set of rules listed in Table 17.3 to help foster innovation. These rules can be—and are—copied by other companies. But 3M has an advantage in that it has followed these rules since its inception and has ingrained them in its culture. This culture is shared and passed on in part through stories. One such legend is about the 3M engineer who was fired because he refused to stop working on a project that his boss thought was wasting resources. Despite being fired, the engineer came to work as usual, finished the project, and demonstrated the value of his innovation. The engineer eventually was promoted to head a new division created to manufacture and market the innovation.

Bureaucracy Busting

Bureaucracy is an enemy of innovation. Although bureaucracy is useful to maintain orderliness and gain efficiencies, it also can work directly against innovation. Developing radically different technologies requires a more fluid and flexible (organic) structure that does not restrict thought and action. Although "fluid and flexible" can sometimes feel more like "chaotic and uncertain," companies take this approach because it is necessary in an environment of rapid change. Elmer's Products, which makes a variety of adhesives and presentation materials as well as the famous white glue, has established a policy of open innovation. A cross-functional team of seven employees is responsible for sharing ideas about innovation, and all employees are encouraged to submit ideas. About a dozen employees in another group are assigned to spend 25 to 50 percent of their time exploring ideas from sources outside the organization, including inventors, suppliers, other companies, and researchers at universities.[48]

To balance innovation with other business goals, companies often establish special temporary project structures that are isolated from the rest of the organization and allowed to operate under different rules. These units go by many names, including skunkworks (recall Chapter 7), greenhouses, and reserves. At Google, for example, Google X is a division set up to identify futuristic ideas and develop them; its projects include the self-driving car and the Google Glass wearable computer.

To foster a culture that values innovation, software maker Intuit set up a program called Innovation Lab. Adapting a policy that Google made famous, the company allows employees to spend 10 percent of their time on unstructured activities aimed at generating and developing new ideas. They can choose an idea they personally feel passionate about or can devote the time to learning about new technologies. Intuit also sponsors idea jams—days set aside for employees with an idea to assemble a team to develop the idea. Idea jams are one-day events that take place every three months. Employees also have access to workgroup software called Brainstorm, which helps them share ideas and recruit team members to work on the ideas during the idea jams and their unstructured time. Review groups and mentors ensure that ideas are practical and successful. Intuit provides cash awards for winning ideas, but the excitement of Innovation Lab and idea jams is what really motivates Intuit employees to contribute to innovations such as the mobile version of QuickBooks Online.[49]

Bureaucracy-busting managerial systems that encourage collaboration can facilitate innovation. At steel companies such as Chaparral and Nucor, for example, employees work in cross-functional teams to solve problems and create innovative solutions. These flat structures help create an environment that encourages creativity and cooperation. Teams focus on current issues and problems as well as future concerns and opportunities. In addition, teams collaborate with outside partners to bring knowledge into the organization so it can be integrated with existing ideas and information to create innovations. All the while, teams are supported by values of egalitarianism, information sharing, openness to outside ideas, and positive risk. The aim is to destroy the traditional boundaries between functions and departments to create collaborative, less bureaucratic learning laboratories.[50]

Implementing Development Projects

A powerful tool for managing technology and innovations is the **development project**.[51] A development project is a focused organizational effort to create a new product or process via technological advances. For example, when MTV launched channels aimed at various Asian American markets, the company used development projects embedded in a culture that values innovation.

Development projects typically feature a special cross-functional team that works together on an overall concept or idea. Like most cross-functional teams, its success depends on how well individuals work together to pursue a common vision. And in the case of development projects, teams must interact with suppliers and customers frequently, making the complexity of their task that much greater. Because of their urgency and strategic importance, most development projects are conducted under intense time and budget pressures, thus presenting a real-time test of the company's ability to innovate.

Managers should recognize that development projects have multiple benefits. Not only are they useful for creating new products and processes, but they frequently cultivate skills and knowledge that can be used for future endeavors. In other words, the capabilities that companies derive from a development project frequently can be turned into a source of competitive advantage. For example, when Ford created a development project to design an air-conditioning compressor to outperform its Japanese rival, executives also discovered that they had laid the foundation for new processes that Ford could use in future projects. Their new capability in integrated design and manufacturing helped Ford reduce the costs and lead times for other product developments. Thus organizational learning had become an equally important criterion for evaluating the success of the project.

For development projects to achieve their fullest benefit, they should build on core capabilities (recall Chapters 4 and 9); have a guiding vision about what must be accomplished and why (Chapter 12); have a committed team (Chapters 12 and 14); instill a philosophy of continuous improvement (Chapter 9); and generate integrated, coordinated efforts across all units (Chapters 8 and 9).

development project

A focused organizational effort to create a new product or process via technological advances.

Technology, Job Design, and Human Resources

Adopting a new technology typically requires changes in the way jobs are designed. Often the way the task is redefined fits people to the demands of the technology to maximize the technology's operation. But this often fails to maximize total productivity because it ignores the human part of the equation. The social relationships and human aspects of the task may suffer, lowering overall productivity.

sociotechnical systems

An approach to job design that attempts to redesign tasks to optimize operation of a new technology while preserving employees' interpersonal relationships and other human aspects of the work.

The **sociotechnical systems** approach to work redesign specifically addresses this problem. This approach redesigns tasks in a manner that jointly optimizes the social and technical efficiency of work. Beginning with studies on the introduction of new coal-mining technologies in 1949, the sociotechnical systems approach to work design focused on small, self-regulating work groups.[52] Later it was found that such work arrangements could operate effectively only in an environment in which bureaucracy was limited. Today's trends in bureaucracy bashing, lean and flat organizations, work teams, and an empowered workforce are logical extensions of the sociotechnical philosophy of work design. At the same time, the technologies of the information age—in which people at all organizational levels have access to vast amounts of information—make these leaner and less bureaucratic organizations possible.

Managers face several choices regarding how to apply a new technology. Technology can be used to limit the tasks and responsibilities of workers and "de-skill" the workforce, thus turning workers into servants of the technology. Alternatively, managers can select and train workers to master the technology, using it to achieve great accomplishments and improve the quality of their lives. Technology, when managed effectively, can empower workers as it improves the competitiveness of organizations.[53]

However, as managers make decisions about how to design jobs and manage employees, they also need to consider other human resource systems that complement the introduction of new technology. Table 17.4, for example, shows how compensation systems can be changed to facilitate the implementation of advanced manufacturing technology. In the contemporary setting, the use of group incentives, salary, and skill-based pay systems helps reinforce the collective effort (recall the use of cross-functional teams), professionalism, empowerment, and flexibility required for knowledge work. If a company's pay system is not aligned with the new technologies, it may not reward

TABLE 17.4   Compensation Practices in Traditional and Advanced Manufacturing Firms

Type of Compensation Practice	Traditional Factory	Integrated Manufacturing
Performance-contingent	Focus on individual incentives reflects division of labor and separation of stages and functions.	Extensive use of group incentives to encourage teamwork, cooperation, and joint problem solving.
Job-contingent	Use of hourly wage assumes that differences in employee contribution are captured in job classifications and that performance is determined largely by the production system.	Use of salary assumes that the employees' contributions transcend the job per se to affect output substantially. The distinctions between classes of employment are diminished.
Person-contingent	Seniority pay rewards experience as a surrogate for knowledge and skill in a stable environment and rewards loyalty to reduce uncertainty within the system.	Skill-based pay rewards continuous learning and the value added from increased flexibility in a dynamic environment.

SOURCE: S. A. Snell and J. W. Dean Jr., "Strategic Compensation for Integrated Manufacturing: The Moderating Effects of Jobs and Organizational Inertia," *Academy of Management Journal* 37 (1994), pp. 1109–40.

behavior that is needed to make the changes work. Worse, existing reward systems actually may reinforce old behaviors that run counter to what is needed for the new technology.

Taken as a whole, these ideas provide a set of guidelines for managing the strategic and organizational issues associated with technology and innovation. The issues are relevant whether a company is simply automating an activity or, as in the case of Tesla Motors, entering a new high-tech business (see "Management Connection: Onward"). In Chapter 18, we expand this discussion to focus on how organizations can reshape themselves to adapt to a dynamic marketplace. Managing change and organizational learning are central elements of what it takes to become a world-class organization.

Management Connection

TESLA MOTORS AS INNOVATOR AND TECHNOLOGY PARTNER

MANAGER'S BRIEF

PROGRESS REPORT

ONWARD

Being a relatively tiny start-up in an industry of giants has posed risks for Tesla Motors because operating an auto company requires an enormous amount of money for product design and development, factories, and distribution networks. But in some ways, Tesla's situation as an upstart with a visionary founder has also been an advantage. The company can concentrate on electric vehicles without lines of already-popular cars stealing management's attention. And as a young 3,000-employee business, it doesn't have to cover labor and other expenses that became entrenched at Ford, General Motors, and Chrysler. It operates more like a high-tech firm, with employees lured to the company to do something extraordinary. Elon Musk holds weekly meetings to review progress on each model and critique designs.

The factory where Tesla builds the Model S has a history of innovation. General Motors built the plant and operated it until the 1980s, when U.S. managers began to realize that quality initiatives in Japan were leaving them behind. GM arranged with Toyota to operate the plant jointly. That venture ended, and the plant closed. When Tesla purchased it, Musk was able to hire experienced auto workers from the community. To make 2,000 Model S sedans every year, it needs only one-fourth of the space, so there is plenty of room to grow.

According to Tesla's head of manufacturing, the time that elapsed from the Model S's initial design to production of the car was a little more than two years, in contrast to a norm of five or six years at a major auto maker. Because of Musk's determination to engineer the Model S from scratch, the company is more directly involved in making parts than is typical today. It makes the cars' battery packs and touch screen control panels, for example. Tesla also has built on its reputation as an electric-car innovator by making deals to supply its well-designed parts to other companies, including Toyota and Daimler, maker of the Mercedes-Benz.

Success will inevitably bring growth. Tesla is spending heavily to expand and staff its factory and network of stores, set up a service network, and build charging stations. It wants to pursue growth in Europe and Asia as well. The challenge will be to continue managing innovation as effectively in a bigger company.[54]

- How does Tesla Motors source and acquire new technologies? What are the advantages of this approach?
- How would you advise Tesla's managers to continue unleashing creativity as the company grows?

KEY TERMS

chief information officer (CIO), p. 580

development project, p. 585

executive champion, p. 581

innovation, p. 562

make-or-buy decision, p. 578

product champion, p. 581

sociotechnical systems, p. 586

technical innovator, p. 581

technology, p. 562

technology audit, p. 570

technology life cycle, p. 564

SUMMARY OF LEARNING OBJECTIVES

Now that you have studied Chapter 17, you should be able to:

LO 1 List the types of processes that spur development of new technologies.

Forces that compel the emergence of a new technology include (1) a need for the technology, (2) the requisite scientific knowledge, (3) the technical convertibility of this knowledge, (4) the capital resources to fund development, and (5) the entrepreneurial insight and initiative to pull the components together.

LO 2 Describe how technologies proceed through a life cycle.

New technologies follow a predictable life cycle. First, a workable idea about how to meet a market need is developed into a product innovation. Early progress can be slow as competitors experiment with product designs. Eventually a dominant design emerges as the market accepts the technology, and further refinements to the technology result from process innovations. As the technology begins to approach both the theoretical limits to its performance potential and market saturation, growth slows and the technology matures. At this point, the technology can remain stable or be replaced by a new technology.

LO 3 Discuss ways to manage technology for competitive advantage.

Adopters of new technologies are categorized according to the timing of their adoption: innovators, early adopters, the early majority, the late majority, and laggards. Technology leadership has many first-mover advantages but also poses significant disadvantages. The same may be said for followership. After that, technology that helps improve efficiency will support a low-cost strategy, whereas technologies that help make products more distinctive or unique will support a differentiation strategy. Determining an appropriate technology strategy depends on the degree to which the technology supports the organization's competitive requirements and, if a technology leadership strategy is chosen, the company's ability, in terms of skills, resources, and commitment, to deal with the risks and uncertainties of leadership.

LO 4 Summarize how to assess technology needs.

Assessing the technology needs of a company begins by benchmarking, or comparing, the technologies it employs with those of both competitors and noncompetitors. Benchmarking should be done on a global basis to understand practices used worldwide. Technology scanning helps identify emerging technologies and those still under development in an effort to project their eventual competitive impact.

LO 5 Identify alternative methods of pursuing technological innovation.

New technologies can be acquired or developed. Options include internal development, purchase, contracted development, licensing, trading, research partnerships and joint ventures, and acquisition. The approach used depends on the existing availability of the technology; the skills, resources, and time available; and the importance of keeping the technology proprietary.

LO 6 Define key roles in managing technology.

People play many roles in managing technology. For example, the chief information officer is the person with broad, integrative responsibility for technological innovation. In addition, the entrepreneur is the person who recognizes the competitive potential of the technology and finds new ways to exploit opportunities. The technical innovator has the key skills needed to develop or install and operate the technology. The product champion is the person who promotes the new idea(s) to gain support throughout the organization. The executive champion is the person with the status and resources to support the project.

LO 7 Describe the elements of an innovative organization.

Organizing for innovation involves unleashing the creative energies of employees while directing their efforts toward meeting market needs in a timely manner. Companies can unleash creativity by establishing a culture that values intrapreneurship; accepts and even celebrates failure as a sign of innovation; and reinforces innovation through goal setting, rewards, and stories of creative employees. The organization's structure should balance bureaucracy for controlling existing processes with a flexibility that allows innovation to take place. Development projects provide an opportunity for cross-functional teamwork aimed at innovation. Job design should take into account both social relationships and the technical efficiency of work so that jobs are within employees' ability but also empower them to work cooperatively and creatively.

LO 8 List characteristics of successful development projects.

For development projects to achieve the fullest benefit, they should (1) build on core capabilities; (2) have a guiding vision about what must be accomplished and why; (3) have a committed team; (4) instill a philosophy of continuous improvement; and (5) generate integrated, coordinated efforts across all teams and units.

DISCUSSION QUESTIONS

1. According to Francis Bacon, "A wise man will make more opportunities than he finds." What does this have to do with technology and innovation? What does it have to do with competitive advantage?

2. What examples of technological innovation can you identify? What forces led to the commercialization of the science behind those technologies? Did the capability exist before the market demand, or was the demand there before the technology was available?

3. Thomas Edison once said that most innovations are 10 percent inspiration and 90 percent perspiration. How does this match what you know about technology life cycles?

4. Why would a company choose to follow rather than lead technological innovations? Is the potential advantage of technological leadership greater when innovations are occurring rapidly, or is it better in this case to follow?

5. If you were in the grocery business, whom would you benchmark for technological innovations? Would the companies be inside or outside your industry? Why?

6. How would you see the executive champion, the chief information officer, and the product champion working together? Could the roles all be played by the same individual? Why or why not?

EXPERIENTIAL EXERCISES

17.1   PLANNING FOR INNOVATION

OBJECTIVES

1. To brainstorm innovative ideas for a company that has become stagnant.

2. To explore the elements of a good innovation plan.

INSTRUCTIONS

1. Read the Hallmark Cards scenario.

2. Individually or in small groups, offer a plan for encouraging innovation at Hallmark Cards. Discuss staffing, rewards, organizational structure, work design, and any other facets of organizational behavior that apply.

3. In small groups, or with the entire class, share the plans you developed.

HALLMARK CARDS SCENARIO

Recognized as a leader in greeting cards, Hallmark Cards is constantly pushed to avoid stagnancy or decline of a mature product. They've done a lot over the recent years to drive innovation, including developing cards with sound (2006), recordable cards (2008), and countdown cards (2012). However, this year, Hallmark is closing its Topeka production center, in part because of excess capacity arising from declines in production volume affected by the rise of social media. How can Hallmark plan for further innovation to keep it at the forefront?

DISCUSSION QUESTIONS

1. What elements do these plans have in common?

2. How well do the plans follow the innovation process?

3. Do the plans incorporate provisions for fulfilling the various roles required for innovation?

4. What are the strengths and weaknesses of each plan?

5. What should be the components of an effective plan?

Source: Hallmark Company website, "Innovative Cards from Hallmark," http://www.corporate.hallmark.com.

17.2 INNOVATION FOR THE FUTURE

OBJECTIVE

To look ahead into the future.

INSTRUCTIONS

Choose a partner. Together, develop an innovative product or service that will be popular in the year 2025. As you develop your product or service, ask yourselves the following questions:

1. What trends lead you to believe that this product or service will be successful?

2. What current technologies, services, or products will your idea replace?

Present your idea to the class for discussion.

CONCLUDING CASE

WORLDWIDE GAMES

Players of video games often purchase their fun from Worldwide Games, which develops and markets game consoles, portable game devices, and software for playing games either on the company's hardware or on personal computers. Game enthusiasts are always on the lookout for game-playing experiences that are more intense, more lifelike, or more complex, so satisfying them drives constant innovation at Worldwide. The company has developed major and minor advances in screen resolution, processor speed, new kinds of controllers, creative story lines,

and more. Its console division focuses on hardware technology, and its online division focuses on powerful new gaming software, often involving elaborate story lines played by subscribers around the world, using the Internet to collaborate or compete. Continuous innovation in both divisions essentially keeps Worldwide on a par with its major competitors, who also are constantly on the lookout for the best new idea.

In recent years, two related areas of technology have been essential for the growth of Worldwide and its competitors:

social networking and the ability of broadband Internet connections to deliver fast audio and video streams for playing elaborate games online. Worldwide's console division has adopted this technology by inviting purchasers of its latest console to join its Players Network. Those who join the Players Network can use their console to make an Internet connection and play games with other members anywhere in the network. Each player uses his or her controller, console, and television display and sees all the participants' actions on the display. In addition, Worldwide's online division continues to push the limits of online games played with the processing power of the latest personal computers. For the most popular programs, gamers who pay a subscription fee create their own characters, or avatars, to act out the parts in the game. Although the personal data of the players are kept private, players can use the avatars' names to look up other players' track records and invite selected avatars to join their team.

Because a necessary component of both kinds of games—console based and computer based—is for players to register and pay a fee or join the Players Network, Worldwide collects not only money from customers but also information about them. That system came under real risk when hackers recently broke into first the Players Network database and then the registration records of Worldwide Online's subscribers.

As soon as the company detected an intrusion into the Players Network, it shut down the network. When the company's security employees realized they couldn't immediately prevent intrusions within a day or two, Worldwide announced that hackers had obtained the names and possibly the credit card numbers of its tens of millions of network members. Until the problem was fixed, they would be able to play games from disks loaded into their consoles but would not be able to use the network.

While the company was investigating the original security breach, it discovered that the Worldwide Online user database also had been hacked. The company immediately announced that breach, including the fact that some credit card accounts might have been accessed. It shut down that network as well until the security hole could be plugged.

Fixing the problem, which took about a month, included adding firewalls and encryption to the existing security measures. Afterward the company reopened both networks, apologized to consumers, and offered a month of free access to paid services. Returning customers had to download upgraded security software before they could resume play. The entire incident cost the company hundreds of millions of dollars for the investigation, upgrades, and lost sales.

As operations returned to normal, Worldwide tried to minimize the risk of future intrusions by putting an executive in charge of security. The company announced that it had hired a chief information security officer. This manager reports to the company's chief information officer, who reports to the chief transformation officer, who reports to the chief executive officer.

QUESTIONS

1. Is Worldwide Games a technology leader or a technology follower? What are the risks and benefits of staking out this position?

2. What opportunities might Worldwide be missing by not having its chief information officer report directly to the CEO?

3. What makes innovation important for Worldwide? Following the hacking incident, how might bureaucracy be expected to interfere with innovation? How should Worldwide engage in bureaucracy busting?

Operations Management in the New Economy

The business of a company—any company—is to transform certain inputs, by means of a process, into outputs. Bringing these outputs (the product) to market cost effectively will ensure the company's continued existence and well-being. The methods, systems, and mental framework by which a company transforms its inputs into outputs characterize its operations. A company maintains the health of its transformation process through management of these operations. Operations management is the analysis and implementation of this process.

Many factors impinge on a company's operations and managers. As company size increases, so do the number of variables. Effective management of the operation and its variables contributes in no small measure to the company's success, whether the company is small or large, diversified or devoted to core businesses, a network organization or a highly structured, centralized body. It holds true whether the company sells a tangible product (goods) or an intangible one (services) because in both cases the customer is buying the object of a desire or the satisfaction of a need.

EFFECTS OF CHANGE

We often read that operations management is in transition today. In actuality, it has always been in transition because the world is always changing. Changes may take the form of new products (imagine the first traders bringing spices to Europe in the early Middle Ages), new distribution channels (FedEx completely revamped our expectations about package delivery), alterations in the labor pool (women assumed many factory jobs during World War II when men were at war), or new technologies (gunpowder altered all the rules of war in 14th century Europe).

Characteristic of the current age is the quickening rate at which change occurs, placing pressure on individuals to adapt quickly and rewarding those able to shift mental gears, personal habits, and priorities easily. Indeed, survival of the fittest applies not only to physical attributes but also to mental agility. Operations managers must be among the most fit to function effectively in today's world.

THE CONTEXT OF OPERATIONS MANAGEMENT

What does it mean to be an effective manager of an operation? It means responding to the needs of diverse parties within the company, ensuring smooth movement through all stages of the transformation process. We can even take the viewpoint that, within the process, the customer is the department receiving the result of the preceding stage. For example, in a printing company, the operator of the press is the customer of the prepress area. An effective manager works with this awareness, ensuring that each area supplies what the next one expects.

Operations management also means satisfying parties in the larger arena. For example, investors may want to know how well a new product line is faring in the market or whether a new manufacturing process is delivering as promised. The community may want assurances that wastes from the production process will not cause quality of life to suffer. The government may demand an accounting of any number of activities covered by regulations. Thus the manager of an operation does not exist in isolation but is part of an ongoing interaction among any number of parties.

In ages past, the world was home to many societies or cultures, which were mostly different one from another, but each was more homogeneous than is the case today. Buyers in a given community needed the same products. Everyone knew what those products were, and common agreement on quality prevailed. Also prevalent was a common understanding of the entitlements of various social levels. (What goods of what quality were the prerogative of the wealthy, for example.) Because items were individually made, customization was the norm; there was no other way to do business.

As the industrial age dawned in the 19th century, this situation changed. Suddenly the customer was no longer a few identifiable individuals but a growing mass of less well-defined persons, any of whom, with money, could have what was formerly the prerogative of the few. With industrialization came mass production, and one product for all buyers became the norm because there was no other cost-effective way to do business.

The modern-day corporation took shape against this background, and marketing was born. Now in the digital age we are witnessing a phenomenon that once would have sounded like an oxymoron: mass customization. What are the implications for today's managers?

When the product is static or has few variations, operations management quite justifiably focuses on the product (and its cost). This perspective has produced the orientation of traditional operations management. With the ability to manufacture many variations of the same product, with access to increasing amounts of information, the focus today has shifted to the customer's experience of the product: how he or she perceives to have been served by the vendor. The customer assesses whether the product contains the desired characteristics and quality at the best price. Management of an operation with this awareness probably will spell the success or failure of the company in today's environment.

But is today's customer truly different? Yes and no. Despite the fact that things change, things also stay the same. Human beings still engage in the same activities. They create community; they raise the next generation; they trade; they provide for themselves; and in the process, they learn, fight, and play. And today's managers still shuttle inputs through the transformation process into successful outputs. Most of the traditional notions about human activity still apply.

To explain any activity, however, one may use a variety of lenses (Galileo's lens was different from Ptolemy's, so he derived a different explanation of the universe). A manager may view the process from the standpoint of product specifications, cost limitations, customer satisfaction, or any number of viewpoints. The lens chosen will reflect a particular view of the world and its priorities and of the company's priorities.

Sometimes there are no right or wrong choices, only consequences. The lens that adequately explained a given phenomenon at one time may not serve today. What is reflected through the lens will form the guidelines for decisions, however, so the choice has far-reaching repercussions.

NEW PERSPECTIVES

From time to time, particular orientations or viewpoints burst onto the stage, altering perceptions and leaving changed priorities in their wake. Such is the case with W. Edwards Deming's total quality management, now an article of faith for many of today's managers. The Japanese readily embraced Deming's principles, taking an enviable and now imitated approach to customer satisfaction (see Chapter 9 of the text for Deming's 14 points). Western nations paid scant attention until they saw the results of offering quality in a customer-oriented operation.

For most of us, quality is what we see in the result (does the product meet manufacturing specifications?). In his lengthy essay *Zen and the Art of Motorcycle Maintenance,* Robert Pirsig associated achievement of quality with a state of mind: "Skilled mechanics and machinists of a certain sort . . . have patience, care and attentiveness to what they're doing, a kind of inner peace of mind that isn't contrived but results from a kind of harmony with the work . . . [1] More characteristic of the Eastern mind-set, this statement means that quality (good or bad) is not an attribute of the end product but, rather, is inherent in the way an individual interacts with the subject of his or her attention.

To achieve good quality requires knowing what is good and then having the mind-set suitable for achieving it. This attentiveness is related to the Japanese *kaizen,* a willingness and desire to improve constantly. Since the 1980s, Japanese business practices have been the object of study and implementation by Westerners, from specific procedures (such as *kanban,* the basis of just-in-time inventory management) to general philosophies (the *kaizen* that is part of Japanese general operations strategy). A manager anywhere today would be ill served by neglect of these concepts.

Likewise, companies that involve employees in the process are on the way to understanding that the people who interface with the product are crucial to its success. We will see how important this view is in a few pages.

CORPORATE ORGANIZATION

There are many ways to structure a company, and some of today's companies have taken their present form as a result of trends in the economy: mergers or acquisitions, diversification, alliances. With all, certain functions are still identifiable in most corporate organizations. The operation of that function is what commands the attention of its managers. Let us consider how some of these common functions support the operations management system.

Strategic Planning On the highest level, guiding the corporation from the broadest perspective is strategic, or long-range, planning. The firm's upper-level managers provide the corporation's direction, defining and refining its mission in the process. Management of this function entails answering questions such as these: What business are we in? What business should or will we be in? Who are our customers? How can or should we serve them? Do we want to focus on core businesses or diversify? Answers to these questions will help develop corporate goals, which, filtered through the company's management levels, give direction to its operation.

As stated earlier, the world is always changing. Good strategic planning seeks to anticipate change and then plan for it. Good planners also foster a feeling of confidence about what is likely to produce success. During the 1990s, when the rallying cry of much of corporate management was to stick to core businesses, GE chief Jack Welch built a successful conglomerate of widely diverse businesses, finding people with the mind-set to operate well within that structure and achieving effective coordination of all functions through its many divisions.

Marketing Of all the company's functions, marketing is closest to the customer. Its job is to identify customer needs (latent or manifest) and translate them back to the firm for its reaction. Its role in supporting the operations management system is therefore critical. Operations managers must then restate what marketing has communicated in terms that will bring about the needed response from the production mechanism. To support its efforts, marketing works with advertising to state the company's offerings in terms that are attractive to the buyer. Sales is part of the marketing function also; salespeople are those who take action to sell within an identified market. This is the front line, where information about customer needs and desires penetrates and gains the attention of the company.

A story told in sales circles is about the ABC Company (a shoe manufacturer), whose marketing head visited a remote area of the world to assess the market. He returned to report to his boss, "There's no market; they don't wear shoes." The marketing head of competitor XYZ Company made the same trip for the same purpose, reporting to his boss, "It's a terrific market! They've got no shoes!" Marketing's response to a circumstance can take a firm into new areas.

Research and Engineering Suppose the marketing function has identified a new need or potential market. Enter the design and engineering people, whose function is the development and refinement of the product and the processes that manufacture it. They design, develop, and test the product through all stages until it is ready for market launch. They interact with customers who participate in the testing of a new product prior to launching. They also interact with operations—the product attributes and the processes required to make them will become the responsibility of the operations management system. Even as a product is still on the drawing board, its design may change based on customer response, manufacturing procedures (i.e., what is feasible in the current setup), or prices of material or labor.

As researchers and developers, this part of the company is most in touch with what will be available in the future, and one of its functions is identification and implementation of solutions not currently in use. The result of the designers' work will affect purchasing (of parts, equipment, materials), inventory management (quantities of items to keep on hand), shop floor operation (equipment may need rearrangement), capacity requirements (maximum rate of production), and human resources (human skills needed and cost of acquisition).

Human Resources This brings us to the next function: human resources. A company is its people. They form the culture, produce the product, and deliver it. The human resources function must seek, attract, and keep individuals having the skills, human qualities, and experience required by the operations management system. Effective management of human resources thus directly affects the entire production process. Any company wishing to build a plant in a geographically desirable area would be foolish not to take into account the human component: educational level, work ethic, habits, and expectations of the labor pool.

Some believe that there are no bad employees, only employees placed in wrong positions. Effective use of employees will provide operations managers with a valuable source of innovation and productivity gains because the employees are actually in contact with the product (and with the customer, in the case of a service business). They are the interface where quality is born. It cannot be stressed too heavily that one of the most valuable attributes of any employee is the ability to communicate: to articulate what's right about the work experience, what's wrong, and how to improve it. Dissatisfaction unexpressed is potential trouble; ideas not presented represent lost potential.

Purchasing Just as human inputs matter, so do materials. Selecting inputs that will support the company's orientation and vision is the crucial role played by the purchasing function. Optimally, it is a source of expertise for the operations management system, providing information about the variety of materials and systems available for use by the production process. The performance of any operating division is ultimately dependent on goods and services supplied to it by purchasing. Will the materials produce the result intended by the design of the product? Will they allow themselves to be molded as intended by the production process? Will they support the level of quality promised?

Cost-effective supply of the right materials potentially represents enormous savings for the company. A purchasing manager was once heard to say, "The sales division would have to close $500,000 in new business to produce the money I just saved by changing suppliers."

Logistics The logistics of moving inputs through transformation may or may not benefit from an overview of the entire process; the flow may take different names, depending on its location in the process. It may be called *inventory management* as inputs arrive, *scheduling* while in the transformation process, and *distribution* when outputs are en route to the customer. Smooth or poor coordination of the flow from supplier of materials to delivery to the customer has repercussions throughout the channel. If materials are not ready for a specific section of the production apparatus at the right time, equipment and machinery sit idle (a drain on profitability). Delays in delivery to customers mean delays in payment received, and that has an impact on the company's cash flow.

Finance This brings us to the finance area. This function serves as an interface between the firm's managers and the financial community: banks, investment firms, and stockholders. These entities have a stake in the company's success or failure and at all times are poised to assist, advise, provide support, or withdraw it. Finance must explain the company's performance adequately to elicit the maximum amount of support from financial institutions. In so doing, it makes use of the accounting department. Not merely a mechanism for tracking costs, the accounting department provides information useful to managers in understanding

the cost implications of their decisions. Such cost-monitoring information can help managers understand how their own costs compare with standard costs, for example. Accounting also can help derive the cost implications of introducing new equipment or technologies.

In another of its roles, the finance function must be knowledgeable about the firm's creditworthiness. Any decline in the company's ability to pay its bills will weaken its position vis-á-vis competitors. Finance also must monitor the creditworthiness of suppliers. If suppliers are not financially able to deliver what they promise, the operations management system will feel the impact immediately. The financial community watches the impact of all these decisions, basing its ratings (and therefore support) on the wisdom of the decision makers.

A Team Operation The fineness with which one breaks down the preceding functions can vary, but it should be clear at this point that the operations management system is only one of those operating within the corporate context. In the best of all possible worlds, operations management works hand in glove with the other functions, alert to any harmful fragmentation or lack of communication. Communication is, of course, a two-way street, and just as operations people must be aware of the workings of the other functions, the latter must know what the operations management system perceives, needs, and expects.

Satisfying customer expectations is a corporate activity, the work of one body (from *corpus,* Latin for "body"), with the whole dependent on how well its parts work individually and how well they work together. Neglect of any one organ affects the body's ability to perform at optimum level.

PREPARING FOR THE FUTURE IN THE NEW ECONOMY

In addition to awareness of how the company is operating at present, every good manager will give thought to what could happen, what is likely to happen, and what is possible, both for the company as a whole and for his or her own sphere of influence. Stated another way, an effective manager has a sense of vision. This means being aware of changes or potential changes in customer demands and changes in the company's resources (technology, labor pool, financial support). A good manager must listen, being attentive to all facts, and then select the useful facts from among the many supplied. A manager must constantly ask, "What if . . .?"

With good vision and a healthy curiosity, a manager will more adequately handle factors impinging on the operations management system. The objective is to develop a sense of vision adequate to anticipate conceivable consequences. Let us consider some of today's challenges in what is often referred to as the **new economy.**

Globalization A company's sphere of activity has always been what could be reached easily by current means of communication and transportation. What is reachable has constantly expanded. The entire world is today's operating arena, both for buying inputs and for selling outputs. This circumstance presents the operations management system with a new range of possibilities.

The possibility of outsourcing has always been present. That is, do we make a particular component of the product, or do we send it out for manufacture pursuant to our specifications? Today a manager may outsource locally or to any facility in the world offering the capability of supplying the need. It takes a lot of information, as well as sound judgment, to know which part of the process would benefit from being handled out of house.

The success of producing elsewhere depends in part on the characteristics of the elsewhere. In the 20th century, U.S. companies based in northern states sometimes would move certain manufacturing operations to the southern part of the country, taking advantage of lower labor costs. Although this required some adjustment in expectations, the adjustment is slight compared to manufacturing in Pacific Rim countries or Latin America, for example. The reason is simple: Each culture handles things in a particular way. A wise manager will not assume that a different culture will respond to expectations in the same manner as an American labor force would, and this circumstance may work to one's advantage or to one's detriment. Those who can anticipate potential problem areas are ahead of the game in the decision to manufacture offshore.

Then there is the globe as marketplace. To sell globally requires product design that accounts for differing tastes throughout the world's cultures. A small manufacturer of skin care products based on formulas from India began marketing her line in America some years ago. She reports that she had to make alterations to account for the fact that Americans would not use a product with an unusual smell, no matter how beneficial for the skin.[2] Nescafe markets its products all over the globe, but the instant coffee sold in Brazil does not taste like that sold in the United States—in each instance, the product must satisfy the taste of a different culture.[3]

The ease with which the operations management system can make these alterations has increased dramatically in the last few decades. Digital technology has made flexibility in manufacturing a much more attainable situation than was previously the case, offering enormous potential to vary the product.

Environment Another challenge facing today's manager is the environment, meaning both the world and the milieu in which the company operates. In an earlier time, negative effects from a manufacturing process were absorbed unobtrusively by the surroundings. As population density increased and consumption skyrocketed, particularly in the Western nations, this ceased to be true. What occurs in one place on the planet has an impact on the rest of it. The manager's challenge is to care enough about the future without imperiling today's operations, and the decisions are not simple.

It is unfortunate that the issue of environmental responsibility traditionally has been cast in ethical terms. Although this stance is valid, and ultimately the reason for being good stewards of the planet, it does not help managers handle all the information required to make good decisions or quantify what is needed for decision making. In addition, consumers are often inconsistent, demanding recycled paper, for instance, and then choosing to buy whiter paper that is not recycled.

Certainly the past few decades have witnessed significant progress in the handling of the most blatantly offensive effects of manufacturing processes (waste streaming, emissions control). But making the right decision is not a clear-cut path. Consider the simple example of the supermarket checkout stand. "Would you like paper or plastic for your groceries?" The environmentally responsible buyer must choose between less than desirable alternatives. Paper (even if recycled) uses trees; plastic uses hydrocarbons and is not as easy to recycle. Decisions faced by operations managers are infinitely more complex.

Furthermore, if managers do not see to their societal responsibility, others will demand compliance. A corporation is not its own island in community waters because others are affected by its decisions: property owners, investors, the larger public, and tomorrow's adults. Surely we have learned by now that groups that do not police their own ranks effectively are sure targets for policing by others, whether governmental agencies or community organizations.

The alternatives for an operations manager are therefore to react or to take a leadership role, becoming knowledgeable about potential negative effects of the process managed by him or her and proposing ways to handle them. In the long term, if we are to manage our economy's activities for tomorrow rather than today, responsibility for the environment is not a choice.

Knowledge and Information One of the features of the new economy is that in the transformation process, the major input is intellectual property: knowledge, research, information, and design. These inputs have supplanted (in value) the material inputs required to build physical units. When knowledge is the major raw material, launching the first unit of a product represents millions of dollars; the cost of the second and thereafter is minuscule.

The products themselves are of a different nature, and it often takes greater sophistication to use a new-economy product—thus, for example, people's reluctance to switch from a PC to a Mac or vice versa. As a result, customers are not as likely to be swayed by advertising as by their increasing knowledge of the product and its technology. Successful companies will be those that increase a customer's knowledge base in general and skill with their own products in particular.

As the information explosion continues to feed today's consumers and today's workforce, the knowledge acquired gives rise to expectations. As we will discuss later, today's consumers are far from being locked into only a few sources for their information. Rather, they swim in an ocean of facts, figures, perspectives, and opportunities.

Nor are today's employees like those of yesteryear. It is instead the case that, depending on his or her own personal needs or aspirations, an employee is drawn to (and will stay with) a specific job in a given company for two reasons: (1) the possibility of experiencing personal satisfaction or growth and (2) satisfaction in the human interaction prevalent at that company. The balance of these factors varies with the individual, but everyone draws from these two wells. Today's managers therefore must provide more than the means for an employee to put bread on the table. The company must offer ongoing professional development, opportunity for increased responsibility in the firm, and a satisfying place to work. Today's employees do not expect to be supervised, but rather coached along the path of success. Clearly the manager also must be knowledgeable and continue to grow, increasing in value as a mentor.

Technology The challenge of technology will occupy us for the rest of these pages. Technology has always existed and has always been neutral. That is, just as a knife serves to feed the family or to kill an adversary, new technologies can be used to help or harm. As with any challenge, managers can view technological innovation as something to react to, something to anticipate, something to plan for, or something from which to derive potential improvements and growth.

Technologies exist in various stages of development; that is, some are ready and available for use by the operations management system, some will be cost-effective in 5 or 10 years, and some are in embryo. Any forward-looking manager will be aware of all three. Technology companies (those that market the latest of a given technology, such as cellular phones) must monitor technology on two fronts. They must be aware of similar products on the market, constantly assessing the limits of their own products. They also must be aware of technologies potentially usable by their own operations, just as any nontechnology company would.

In its development, a technology tends to move to the hands of the user. Take the clock as an example. At one time in history, the only clock in the community was the one in the town square. Then wealthier people could purchase large timepieces known as grandfather clocks. By the middle of the 20th century, most adults owned a wristwatch, often a special gift received at graduation. Today children and adults have access to many timepieces, from those on their wrists to the many in the home, office, or car. We could trace a similar progression for other technologies, such as engines and, of course, computers (where the transition from mainframes to portable PCs occurred within a few decades of the last century).

The shift of a technology to the user is not always smooth. One of the potential stumbling blocks when a company embraces a technology is to discount the human factor involved in its use. We see this in small businesses constantly. The local copy shop brings in the latest copying and finishing equipment, offering everything from double-sided, spiral-bound reports graced with photos to personalized, artistic party invitations. The resulting product, however, is in part dependent on the skill and experience of the operator and the availability of sufficient personnel to work with customers.

Larger industrial equipment offers a similar scenario. At an earlier time in history, the operator of, for example, a multistory printing press would have 30 years to become familiar with the operation of that equipment before a new generation came on stream. In today's offices, employees barely become proficient at using the current popular software before a new or different version of it comes out. These improvements provide fertile ground for inefficiencies in the final analysis; technology can advance only at the rate at which human beings can use it effectively.

With this knowledge, any effective operations manager will have some type of formal technology management in place—some means of looking ahead, preparing for the effects of new technologies. When envisioning the potential of new technology (or technology in embryo), the best human characteristics to bring to the table are

1. Awareness (information plus perspective).
2. Imagination (the ability to create new scenarios from existing ones).

Awareness is the easiest to acquire. In fact, it can be bought from the many consultants standing ready to assist corporations

in preparing for the future. One must cultivate powers of imagination within oneself.

THE INTERNET

That brings us to the current challenge for one's imaginative powers: the Internet. Opportunities and pitfalls abound on the web. What follows are some noteworthy experiences gained from successful and unsuccessful uses of the Internet. By the time this material sees print, much will have changed.

Several methods have emerged as options for exploiting an Internet operation. A regular **bricks and mortar** business can create its own in-house web group, or it can partner with a dot-com company that will operate the web end of its business for it. For example, when the three largest retailers in the country decided to jump on the **e-tailing** bandwagon in the late 1990s, their strategies differed. JC Penney and Sears formed their own in-house website divisions; Kmart, in contrast, contracted with a subsidiary, bluelight.com, to get its site up and running. Last, a business can elect to sell its products only on the Internet. Internet-only companies are referred to as **pure-play** operations. Amazon.com is an example.

Managers also have to figure out how to integrate web activities seamlessly into their operations. Poorly integrated systems can wreak havoc within an organization. For instance, the first Christmas Toys 'R' Us did business on the web, the company had to turn away customers because it couldn't fill the number of orders the site generated. To solve the problem, Toys 'R' Us formed an alliance with Amazon.com. Amazon handled the website and the online ordering process, and Toys 'R' Us managed inventory and shipping. Each company had expertise the other needed to sell toys online.

Alongside web sales, retailers are in various stages of deploying new technologies to offer the benefits of online shopping at the retail site. For example, a kiosk on the shopping floor can make information available electronically, providing shoppers the information they need to make a buying decision. Lamps Plus gives its customers access to high-resolution images they can zoom in on and manipulate to review fabric textures and sample different colors and products in a **360-degree view**. Pacific

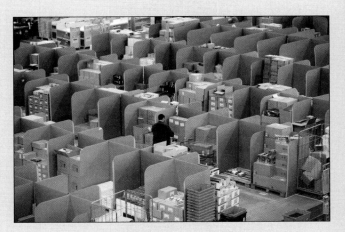

Amazon.com was slow to make a profit because of its initial start-up costs—for product and warehouses, for example. However, e-tailers offering travel products, software, and financial services have low overhead and can see a profit much faster.

Sunwear lets its customers search for and display clothing for boys or girls by item, color, and price. Other sites, such as eBags and Amazon, offer online guides or customer reviews to help buyers make decisions.

These retailers, along with others such as Nordstrom, Eddie Bauer, and Radio Shack, are building on brand-name presence and a familiarity already created at the mall, in the dealership, and through catalog sales—an advantage not enjoyed by companies operating exclusively on the web.

Not long ago, the online auctioneer eBay and a few companies that built e-stores for other firms were the only ones operating in the black. However, pure-play companies can be successful. Approximately one-quarter of the 200 public Internet companies that survived the dot-bomb shakeout are profitable now under standard accounting rules. The biggest moneymakers are online travel, software, and financial services. Why? Because they sell pure information products—there are no products to store or ship. But even Amazon.com, which has long operated in the red, is finally showing a profit despite the fact that every time someone buys a book on Amazon, the company must turn around and purchase a copy from the publisher. Also, once pure-play companies recoup their initial start-up costs, they don't need to spend much more money as sales rise. No additional stores need to be built to reach consumers, for example.[4]

Nonetheless, technology tricks and novel business ideas are not enough. Customers still want speed, convenience, quality, and good service. In this regard, the web is no different from conventional stores and catalogs. Customers ultimately will cast their votes for the companies that provide the best product experience whether they see the product on the web or can touch it in stores.

COMPANYWIDE RESONANCE

Sales and marketing data collection is turned on its head by the Internet as companies record information about a user's habits during a website visit. For instance, if you buy a product on Amazon.com, during future visits, the site will make suggestions about similar products in which you might be interested. Many retailers are of the opinion that this type of **data mining** will make or break the operation in the future. That is, the ability to collect and use information from online customers will be crucial to successful marketing decisions.

Moreover, a company's web page can make it easy or hard for the customer to get the information leading to a purchase. As some have learned the hard way, it is not enough simply to place images that are successful in print on the web; each medium has its own characteristics.

The design of the company's website has a companywide impact. For example, if a customer on the web can verify that an item is available, the chances of closing the sale are increased. If a customer can find out the expected delivery date of the product and the means, the chances of a sale are increased even more. In this scenario, front- and back-end operations touch, and delivering the goods is still key to success.

Mountains of Data The purchasing function benefits from the web through sheer availability of information as well as ease of response to questions. Today a purchasing manager need not wait for a visit from a sales representative. In fact, under the impact of the web, businesses are seeing a realignment of the traditional relationships among producers, wholesalers, distributors, and retailers. In the business-to-business world, buyers previously faced a number of obstacles to getting the best deal: Suppliers were distant, research time was scarce, and intermediaries controlled most of the information. Enter Ariba, a web-based marketplace for industrial goods. Purchasing need only put out a contract on the web, and a flood of bids from suppliers may be the response. In a sense, web-based companies are becoming the new intermediaries, the conduit between producers and buyers.

Purchasing managers can go online to Ariba for industrial goods, National Transportation Exchange for trucking, Chemdex for biochemical supplies, and IMX Exchange for mortgage brokers to find loans, and this is only the start.

The Internet has also become the intermediary between employers and employees. Human resources departments can avail themselves of numerous web-based tools to find candidates. Not only are there gigantic job exchanges such as Monster.com, but intranets exist to keep job searches within companies. Job seekers and potential employers can access one another's information based on geographic preference, salary range, or skill sets.

Logistics, scheduling, and distribution tasks increasingly are plugged into web-based networks, benefiting from the ease of gathering weather data, traffic patterns, and late-breaking news. Tracking information about shipments can be downloaded from FedEx. Zip codes are available online from the U.S. postal service. These factors affect the company's ability to deliver the product on time and the availability of materials from suppliers, effects ultimately felt by the operations management system.

Changing Information Patterns To reduce printing costs and make documents widely available, companies are digitizing information. In some instances, they are posting it on the web. Different people residing in distant places can view the same information this way. Still, digitizing information is not without its obstacles. Not all people have the same hardware and software used for viewing and printing out information. Additionally, miscommunications can occur that otherwise might not if all employees were working under one roof.

Corporations must take these circumstances into account when deciding how to use the web because the decisions affect each of the company's functioning units. Posting certain kinds of information does not usually cause problems. For example, providing company address(es), phone numbers, hours of operation, and the like is more economically done on the web than by a live employee answering the telephone. Many inquiries that in the print age were handled by mailing out an annual report, for example, may be handled more cost effectively on the web.

Supplying other types of information, however, might not be as free of repercussions as in the preceding examples. Depending on whether the company is a business-to-business or a business-to-consumer operation, buyers will want product information, forms and terms of payment, special sales, return policies, status of an order, shipping rates and turnaround, possibility of changing a current order, tracking information, or status of an order.

Companies can easily track their shipments by downloading the information directly from FedEx.

Providing and maintaining only one piece of this information—for example, change in an order—affects at least three departments: accounting, distribution, and marketing. Each department supplying the information must be aware of the consequences of making the information available and have a mechanism for handling changes. Coordination becomes an issue as well. For example, charges to a credit card account must not occur before the merchandise is shipped. Whether selling to another business or to consumers, online operation requires new networks. Companies forge ahead nonetheless in this burgeoning technology, realizing that the potential advantages are well worth the temporary discomforts.

INTELLECTUAL PROPERTY

We have mentioned that a characteristic of the new economy is the nature of the product: knowledge, design, and engineering, rather than hard manufacturing. Let us look at an environmental engineering firm and how the web affects its operation. The business of such a firm might include devising solutions to improve power plant operation. The activities of firms involved in the planning of any such industrial facility are subject to compliance with government regulations. Handling engineering projects, such as a new power plant, requires submission of an enormous amount of data to demonstrate that the firm has complied with and planned for all impacts on the community. A requirement might be, for example, that notification be given to every property owner within a certain radius of the plant. Downloading that information from title companies and then monitoring the notification process is only one of a multitude of tasks potentially manageable on the web.

The firm must provide the information to the various parties in certain forms, which gives rise to new information needs. For example, one way to verify that it has indeed shipped the requisite print or CD-ROM copies is by downloading tracking information from FedEx. It also can make its compliance documentation available in a read-only format on the web, allowing printing of sections by those who wish to do so.

In preparing to build a plant, all federal, state, and local regulations must be accounted for. The firm must provide information on how its power plant will affect traffic patterns,

cultural resources, schools, water supply, flora and fauna, and air quality. It also must state its plans for handling hazardous materials generated during the construction and operation of the plant.

Managing the enormous body of information to respond in the ways illustrated would have been a near impossibility before computer management of data.

PITFALLS

What have been the experiences of those who have succeeded in e-commerce and those who have failed, and what can we learn from them? We already mentioned Toys 'R' Us and its inability to fill its orders on the web. In addition to losing business, it, along with other retailers such as Macys.com and CDNow, was subject to Federal Trade Commission investigation and fines regarding rules for order fulfillment. The FTC regulation states that if retailers cannot meet promised deadlines, they must notify customers, giving them the option of canceling the order. Could the management of these companies have foreseen the inability to fill orders and, if so, how?

Confidentiality of information is an issue. A recent Gallup poll revealed that 66 percent of Americans favor new laws to protect their privacy amid the high-tech revolution.[5] Amazon.com found itself under fire after it began charging different consumers different prices on the basis of information it had collected on them. Toys 'R' Us was hit with a class-action lawsuit claiming that it allowed market researchers to access consumer data from its website. The retailer responded that it had hired the firm to analyze customers' data to improve their shopping experience. Although breach of confidentiality predates the web, the enormity of any breach is compounded by the staggering amounts of digital data available for tapping. The Federal Trade Commission and Congress are attempting to pass laws and institute regulations to protect consumers.

Customer familiarity with the web is another issue. Despite what seems to be a flurry of online buying, media reports suggest that many customers are not buying online at all, or only infrequently, or only certain products. As with catalog shopping, the online industry will mature as consumers become more familiar with offerings and as web retailers improve in presentation and fulfillment.

Some customers are concerned about credit card data transmitted online and are therefore hesitant to shop. The misuse of credit card data is present, however, every time a clerk in a store records the data during a purchase. Although this is more a perception than a real problem, perception motivates people's actions, preventing some from making the leap into cybershopping.

Circumstances such as these are forcing the formation of new business models as companies grapple with all the variables, spurred on by the potential benefits.

NEW NEEDS AND DESIRES

Customers themselves are changing as it becomes possible to satisfy latent needs or desires. We have alluded to mass customization. Here are some specific examples of varying product features.

Setting up an assembly line or installing production equipment is part of the cost of manufacturing. Speaking of color choice in automobiles, Henry Ford once said, "They can have any color they want, as long as it's black." Alteration of a manufacturing process to vary a product feature was very costly. With the flexible manufacturing available in the digital age, manufacturers have the option of producing multiple flavors of bottled water, blue jeans tailored for different bodies, and a veritable artist's palette for automobile colors. Levi Strauss and Brooks now offer machine-customized garments, accommodating a vast array of body measurements. Barbie's friends can have hair and skin color, clothing, and even personalities picked by their young owners. Digital technology fuels the manufacturing capability; the web spurs demand.

The result is that customers' desire for customization and personalization has been moved to a new level. Shoppers previously settled for a product that was mostly, or approximately, what they wanted. They are now beginning to see that sometimes they can have a product endowed with precisely the features they want. The experience of product acquisition is therefore changing.

THE VALUE OF HUMAN ATTRIBUTES

What are the implications of all this change for traditional operations management? Changes are remembered as negative or positive, depending on how well one has survived them. There is no reason to believe that technological change is any more threatening than other kinds of change. Traditional human qualities still serve: vision, awareness, alertness, imagination, courage, steadfastness, persistence, flexibility, attentiveness, and goodwill.

Today's managers must be aware, noticing shifts in trends, habits and customs, possibilities, and ground rules. They must have or develop the vision to foresee the range of possibilities and then the imagination to create solutions. They must have the courage to strike out in new directions and be alert to adjustments required by the new direction. An effective manager will be flexible enough to make an adjustment and steadfast in the face of misunderstandings and mistakes. A manager will need to be persistent in following the chosen path, with attentiveness to all facets of the surroundings. Chances of success in any challenge are enhanced by goodwill.

Finally, he or she will need luck. Some say "it comes to you," and some say "you make your own." Most think that both are true.

KEY TERMS

bricks and mortar,   p. 595
data mining,   p. 596
e-tailing,   p. 595
new economy,   p. 593
pure-play,   p. 595
360-degree view,   p. 596

DISCUSSION QUESTIONS

1. What is mass customization? How can products be mass-produced yet still be differentiated to appeal to individual market sectors? How has mass customization affected management's focus on the product?

2. Why was Deming's total quality management embraced by the Japanese long before Deming's philosophy became key to U.S. operations management? How does it relate to operations management?

3. How has the new economy changed operations management? What is the major input in the operations process as a result?

4. What must businesses consider in deciding to take advantage of new technology? How does new technology affect operations management decisions?

5. Why were many dot-com companies so short-lived at the end of the 20th century? Why would Amazon and Toys 'R' Us form an alliance? Which firm is likely to benefit more? Explain.

6. How can the Internet improve a firm's operations management?

7. What are the implications for operations management of customers being able to satisfy purchasing needs immediately by using the Internet? Have e-business functions fundamentally changed the way firms do business? Explain.

CHAPTER 18

Creating and Leading Change

> The world hates change, yet that is the only thing that has brought progress.
> — CHARLES KETTERING

> My interest is in the future because I am going to spend the rest of my life there.
> — CHARLES KETTERING

Management Connection

HOW TIME WARNER SURFS A TIDAL WAVE OF CHANGE

Most managers would say that their industries are undergoing major transformations, and managers of media companies are seeing some of the greatest turbulence. Consumers continue to read, watch, and listen to news and entertainment, but tastes change quickly—not only for particular shows or magazines, but for entire formats and technologies. Managers cannot simply define themselves as being in the television business or the magazine business. Today a magazine, for example, likely has an Internet presence, where it offers videos as well as articles. Then it must consider how consumers want to watch those videos—perhaps not on a magazine website but on YouTube, discovered via a friend's recommendation on Twitter.

This is the kind of environment Time Warner must contend with. For over a decade, the company sought to master it by building a media empire extending into all technologies as they gained popularity. In 1989, the merger of the Time Inc. magazine powerhouse with Warner Communications created a single company offering the major media of the day: magazines, films, and cable television. In 2001, the company bought AOL to add a role on the Internet.

That strategy has not walled off Time Warner from change, however. Consumers move out of as well as into new media, sometimes leaving Time Warner in shrinking sectors. Time Warner sold off Warner Music in 2004 as music downloads sucked away profits. In 2009, it sold AOL and Time Warner Cable after consumers abandoned the

former service in favor of broadband, and cable service providers struggled with competition from satellite and Internet alternatives. More recently, its magazine group, Time Inc., has experienced steady, steep declines in ad revenue and newsstand sales, despite being the largest U.S. magazine publisher, with titles including *Time, Sports Illustrated,* and *People.* So Time Warner decided to spin off Time Inc. According to Time Warner CEO Jeff Bewkes, this change would enable Time Warner to enjoy stronger growth while Time Inc. could become a more flexible, focused publishing company. Time Warner's remaining operations also represent a more focused company, involved mainly in films (the Warner Bros. film studio) and cable television (including HBO, CNN, and TNT).

Of course, cable television and movies also are challenged by new forms of Internet competition. The question for Bewkes is how Time Warner, after it trims down by spinning off Time Inc., can ride atop the wave of change in its two remaining media.[1]

Changes like the ones faced by, and required of, Time Warner and other media companies are not easy, do not happen automatically, and often require managers to overcome a host of obstacles. As you study this chapter, think about why the ability to change is both challenging and essential.

An ever-changing world is full of uncertainty and risk.[2] Now and in the foreseeable future, just a sampling of the many disruptive forces in play includes a fragile financial system, breakdowns in global trade, growing income inequality, environmental degradation, declining public health and education, and underperforming institutions.[3] These and other dynamic forces make it essential for organizations (and people) to cope, anticipate, adapt, and change.

Lest the preceding paragraph sound like gloom and doom, one useful perspective is to view problems as opportunities.[4] As but one example, manufacturing was presumed in recent years to be virtually dead in the United States, but global circumstances are changing, and visionary leaders and optimistic entrepreneurs are spearheading a manufacturing comeback.[5]

As you can imagine, currently and forevermore, some organizations and people deal with change more effectively than others. The challenge for organizations is not just to produce innovative new products but to balance a culture that is innovative and that builds a sustainable business. And for individuals, the ability to cope with change is related to their job performance, the rewards they receive,[6] and their career success.

But coping with change isn't enough. Managers and their organizations need to create change and improve constantly to achieve world-class excellence and competitive advantage for the future. For Time Warner and its leaders, change in the media industry is something in the environment that they must respond to by making their own changes.

Becoming World Class

LO 1

Managers today want, or *should* want, their organizations to become world class.[7] Being world class requires applying the best and latest knowledge and ideas and having the ability to operate at the highest standards of any place anywhere.[8] Thus becoming world class does not mean merely improving. It means becoming one of the very best in the world at what you do. To some people, striving for world-class excellence seems a lofty, impossible, unnecessary goal. But it is a goal that helps one survive and succeed in today's intensely competitive business world.

Bottom Line

It's a worthy aspiration: becoming world class at every one of your competitive goals. *What does it mean to be world class at a goal such as quality or sustainability?*

World-class companies create high-value products and earn superior profits over the long run. They demolish the obsolete methods, systems, and cultures of the past that impeded their progress and apply more effective organizational strategies, structures, processes, and management of human resources. And increasingly, companies are vehicles for accomplishing societal purposes. Business is an intrinsic part of society, and value can be measured not just in short-term profits but sustainable profits and contributions to society over time.[9] Great leaders, collaborating with others, build enduring institutions that can compete successfully on a global basis.[10]

Sustainable, Great Futures

Two Stanford professors, James Collins and Jerry Porras, studied 18 corporations that had achieved and maintained greatness for half a century or more.[11] The companies included Sony, American Express, Motorola, Marriott, Johnson & Johnson, Disney, 3M, Hewlett-Packard, Citicorp, and Walmart. Over the years, these companies have been widely admired, been considered the premier institutions in their industries, and made a real impact on the world. Although every company goes through periodic downturns—and these firms are no exceptions over their long histories—these companies have consistently prevailed across the decades. They turn in extraordinary performance over the long run, rather than fleeting greatness.

The researchers sought to identify the essential characteristics of enduringly great companies. These great companies have strong core values in which they believe deeply, and they express and live the values consistently. They are driven by goals— not just incremental improvements or business-as-usual goals, but stretch goals (recall Chapter 13). They change continuously, driving for progress via adaptability, experimentation, trial and error, entrepreneurial thinking, and fast action. And they do not focus on beating the competition; they focus primarily on beating themselves. They continually ask, "How can we improve ourselves to do better tomorrow than we did today?"

But underneath the action and the changes, the core values and vision remain steadfast and uncompromised. Table 18.1 displays the core values of several companies that were built to last. Note that the values are not all the same. In fact, no set of common values consistently predicted success. Instead the critical factor is that great companies *have* core values, *know* what they are and what they mean, and *live* by them—year after year.

3M	Innovation—"Thou shalt not kill a new product idea."	
	Absolute integrity.	
	Respect for individual initiative and personal growth.	
	Tolerance for honest mistakes.	
	Product quality and reliability.	
	"Our real business is solving problems."	
Sony	To experience the sheer joy that comes from the advancement, application, and innovation of technology that benefits the general public.	
	To elevate the Japanese culture and national status.	
	Being pioneers—not following others, but doing the impossible.	
	Respecting and encouraging each individual's ability and creativity.	
Walmart	"We exist to provide value to our customers"—to make their lives better via lower prices and greater selection; all else is secondary.	
	Swim upstream, buck conventional wisdom.	
	Be in partnership with employees.	
	Work with passion, commitment, and enthusiasm.	
	Run lean.	
	Pursue ever-higher goals.	
Walt Disney	No cynicism allowed.	
	Fanatical attention to consistency and detail.	
	Continuous progress via creativity, dreams, and imagination.	
	Fanatical control and preservation of Disney's "magic" image.	
	"To bring happiness to millions" and to celebrate, nurture, and promulgate "wholesome American values."	

TABLE 18.1
Core Ideologies in Built-to-Last Companies

SOURCE: From *Built to Last* by James C. Collins and Jerry I. Porras, Copyright © 1997 by James C. Collins and Jerry I. Porras. Reprinted by permission of the authors, HarperCollins Publishers, Inc. and Random House Group Limited.

The Tyranny of the *Or*

tyranny of the *or*

The belief that things must be either A or B and cannot be both; that only one goal and not another can be attained.

Many companies, and individuals, are plagued by the **tyranny of the or.** This refers to the belief that things must be either A or B and cannot be both. The authors of *Built to Last* provide many common examples: beliefs that you must choose either change or stability; be conservative or bold; have control and consistency or creative freedom; do well in the short term or invest for the future; plan methodically or be opportunistic; create shareholder wealth or do good for the world; be pragmatic or idealistic.[12] Such beliefs, that only one goal but not another can be attained, often are invalid and certainly are constraining—unnecessarily so.

The Genius of the *And*

genius of the *and*; organizational ambidexterity

Ability to achieve multiple objectives simultaneously.

In contrast to the tyranny of the *or*, the **genius of the *and***—more academically, **organizational ambidexterity**—refers to being able to achieve multiple objectives at the same time.[13] It develops via the actions of many individuals throughout the organization. We discussed earlier in the book the importance of delivering multiple competitive values to customers, performing all the management functions, reconciling hard-nosed business logic with ethics, leading and empowering, and others. Authors Collins and Porras have their own list:[14]

- Purpose beyond profit *and* pragmatic pursuit of profit.
- Relatively fixed core values *and* vigorous change and movement.
- Conservatism with the core values *and* bold business moves.
- Clear vision and direction *and* experimentation.
- Stretch goals *and* incremental progress.
- Control based on values *and* operational freedom.
- Long-term thinking and investment *and* demand for short-term results.
- Visionary, futuristic thinking *and* daily, nuts-and-bolts execution.

You have learned about all of these concepts throughout this course and should not lose sight of any of them—either in your mind or in your actions. To achieve them requires the continuous and effective management of change.

Achieving Sustained Greatness

A study of 200 management techniques employed by 160 companies over 10 years identified the specific management practices that lead to sustained, superior performance.[15] The authors boiled their findings down to four key factors:

1. *Strategy*—focused on customers, continually fine-tuned based on marketplace changes, and clearly communicated to employees.
2. *Execution*—good people, with decision-making authority on the front lines, doing quality work and cutting costs.
3. *Culture*—one that motivates, empowers people to innovate, rewards people appropriately (psychologically as well as economically), entails strong values, challenges people, and provides a satisfying work environment.
4. *Structure*—making the organization easy to work in and easy to work with, characterized by cooperation and the exchange of information and knowledge throughout the organization.

You have been learning about these concepts throughout this course.

Becoming world class doesn't apply only to the private sector. People worry about globalization's negative effects on local communities as plants shut down and people lose their jobs to overseas workers. But local communities do have options—not easy ones, but doable. A locality can strive to become a world-class center of *thinkers, makers,* or *traders.*[16] Thus Boston creates new ideas and technologies that often dominate world markets; Spartanburg–Greenville,

Becoming world class doesn't apply only to the private sector.

South Carolina, is a world-class manufacturing region that is home to more than 80 international firms representing 18 countries; and Miami, Florida, connects Latino and Anglo cultures the way Hong Kong and Singapore have historically bridged Chinese and British cultures. The keys to creating world-class local communities include visionary leadership, a climate friendly to business, a commitment to training workers, and collaboration among businesses and between business and local government.[17]

Organization Development

How do organizations become more ambidextrous and move in the other positive directions described throughout this book? This chapter discusses several general approaches that will create positive change. We begin here with an umbrella concept called organization development.

Probably the single most widely-used approach to organizational change in the Western world, applied increasingly on a global scale,[18] is **organization development (OD).** OD is a systemwide application of behavioral science knowledge to develop, improve, and reinforce the strategies, structures, and processes that lead to organization effectiveness.[19] Throughout this course, you have acquired knowledge about behavioral science and the strategies, structures, and processes that help organizations become more effective. The systemwide component of the definition means that OD is not a narrow improvement in technology or operations but a broader approach to changing organizations, units, or people. The behavioral science component means that OD is not *directly* concerned with economic, financial, or technical aspects of the organization—although they may benefit through changes in the behavior of the people in the organization. The other key part of the definition—to develop, improve, and reinforce—refers to the actual process of changing for the better and for the long term.

organization development (OD)

The systemwide application of behavioral science knowledge to develop, improve, and reinforce the strategies, structures, and processes that lead to organizational effectiveness.

The strategy of Cirque du Soleil is one of constant innovation: combining circus and theater and studying other industries such as car design, fashion, and restaurants to get ideas for new shows.

Two features of organization development are important to note.[20] First, it aims to increase organizational effectiveness—improving the organization's ability to deal with customers, stockholders, governments, employees, and other stakeholders, which results in better-quality products, higher financial returns, and high quality of work life. Second, OD has an important underlying value orientation: It supports human potential, development, and participation in addition to performance and competitive advantage.

Many specific OD techniques fit under this philosophical umbrella.[21] The basic types are strategic interventions, including helping organizations conduct mergers and acquisitions, change their strategies, and develop alliances; technostructural interventions relating to organization structure and design, employee involvement, and work design; human resources management interventions, including attracting good people, setting goals, and appraising and rewarding performance; and human process interventions, including conflict resolution, team building, communication, and leadership. You learned about these topics throughout your management course. You also will learn more about the process of creating change in the rest of this chapter.

Managing Change

People are the key to successful change.[22] For an organization to be great, or even just to survive, people have to care about its fate and know how they can contribute. But typically leadership lies with only a few people at the top. Too few take on the burden of change; the number of people who care deeply, and who make innovative contributions, is too small. People throughout the organization need to take a greater interest and a more active role in helping the business as a whole. They have to identify with the entire organization, not just with their unit and close colleagues.

Shared leadership is crucial to the success of most change efforts—people must be not just supporters of change but also implementers.[23]

This shared responsibility for change is not unusual in start-ups and very small organizations. But too often it is lost with growth and over time. In large, traditional corporations, it is all too rare. Organizations need to rekindle individual creativity and responsibility permanently, instituting a true change in the behavior of people throughout the ranks. The essential task is to motivate people fully to keep changing in response to new business challenges.

Motivating People to Change

People must be motivated to change. But often they resist changing. Some people resist change more than others, but managers tend to underestimate the amount of resistance they will encounter.[24]

People at all levels of their organizations, from entry-level workers to top executives, resist change. For example, many banks and credit unions are switching from specialized roles in branches, such as tellers and personal bankers, to employing employees who are universal agents, able to process transactions, open accounts, and sell products. When they make this change, the main source of resistance is that the new jobs involve selling (identifying unmet customer needs and suggesting products and services). A typical branch employee is unaccustomed to selling and may even have a negative opinion of a salesperson's role, especially in a bank.[25]

At IBM, executives learned that lower-level managers were getting bogged down because they had to invest so much time and effort in obtaining approval from higher-ups. CEO Sam Palmisano announced that he would give first-level managers authority to spend $5,000 without prior approval—a daring move, considering that the authority applied to 30,000 managers. However, the managers felt uncomfortable with their new authority, and in the first year of the new program, they spent only $100,000 of the $150 million Palmisano had entrusted to them.[26] In other words, they were reluctant to change the way they worked, even though it stood to make their job easier.

Many people (and organizations) settle for mediocrity rather than aspire to excellence. They resist the idea of striving mightily for excellence. When told by their managers, "We have to become world class," their reactions resemble the following statements:

- "Those world-class performance numbers are ridiculous! I don't believe them, they are impossible! Maybe in some industries, some companies . . . but ours is unique . . ."
- "Sure, maybe some companies achieve those numbers, but there's no hurry . . . We're doing all right. Sales were up 5 percent this year, costs were down 2 percent. And we've got to keep cutting corners . . ."
- "We can't afford to be world class like those big global companies; we don't have the money or staff . . ."
- "We don't need to expand internationally. One of our local competitors tried that a few years ago and lost its shirt."
- "It's not a level playing field . . . the others have unfair advantages . . ."

General reasons for resistance

Inertia   Timing   Surprise   Peer pressure

Resistance to change

Self-interest   Misunderstanding   Different assessments   Management tactics

Change-specific reasons for resistance

FIGURE 18.1
Reasons for Resistance to Change

To deal with such reactions and successfully implement positive change, managers must understand why people often resist change. Many factors go into people's resistance to, ambivalence toward, and readiness for change.[27] Figure 18.1 shows some common reasons for resistance. Some reasons are general and arise in most change efforts. Other reasons for resistance relate to the specific nature of a particular change.

General Reasons for Resistance   Several reasons for resistance arise regardless of the actual content of the change:[28]

- *Inertia.* Usually people don't want to disturb the status quo. The old ways of doing things are comfortable and easy, so people don't want to shake things up and try something new. For example, it is easier to keep living in the same apartment or house than to move to another.
- *Timing.* People often resist change because of poor timing. Maybe you would like to move to a different place to live, but do you want to move this week? Even if a place were available, you probably couldn't take the time. If managers or employees are unusually busy or under stress, or if relations between management and workers are strained, the timing is wrong for introducing new proposals. Where possible, managers should introduce change when people are receptive.
- *Surprise.* One key aspect of timing and receptivity is surprise. If the change is sudden, unexpected, or extreme, resistance may be the initial—almost reflexive—reaction. Suppose your school announced an increase in tuition, effective at the beginning of next term. Wouldn't you at least want more warning so you might be prepared? Managers or others initiating a change often forget that others haven't given the matter much thought; the change leaders need to allow time for others to prepare for the change.
- *Peer pressure.* Sometimes work teams resist new ideas. Even if individual members do not strongly oppose a change suggested by management, the team may band together in opposition. Peer pressure will cause individuals to resist even reasonable changes, especially if a group is highly cohesive and has antimanagement norms (recall Chapter 14). Of course peer pressure can be a positive force, too. Change leaders who invite—and listen to—ideas from team members may find that peer pressure becomes a driving force behind the change's success.

Change-Specific Reasons for Resistance   Other causes of resistance arise from the specific nature of a proposed change. Change-specific reasons for resistance include[29]

- *Self-interest.* Most people care less about the organization's best interest than they do about their own best interests. They will resist a change if they think it will cause them to lose something of value. What could people fear to lose? At worst, their jobs, if management is considering closing down a plant. A merger, reorganization, or technological change could create the same fear. Other possible fears include loss of the feeling of being competent in a familiar job, expectations that the job will become more difficult or time-consuming, and concerns about the organization's future, given that management wasn't satisfied with the status quo.

- *Misunderstanding.* Even when management proposes a change that will benefit everyone, people may resist because they don't fully understand it. People may not see how the change fits with the firm's strategy, or they simply may not see the change's advantage over current practices.[30] One company met resistance to the idea of introducing flexible working hours, a system in which workers have some say regarding the hours they work. This system can benefit employees, but a false rumor circulated among plant employees that people would have to work evenings, weekends, or whenever their supervisors wanted. The employees' union demanded that management drop the flexible hours idea. The president was caught completely off guard by this unexpected resistance and complied with the union's demand.

- *Different assessments.* Employees receive different—and usually less—information than management receives. Even within top management ranks, some executives know more than others do. Such discrepancies cause people to develop different assessments of proposed changes. Some may be aware that the benefits outweigh the costs, whereas others may see only the costs and not the advantages. This is a common problem when management announces a change, say, in work procedures, and doesn't explain to employees why the change is needed. Management expects advantages in terms of increased efficiency, but workers may see the change as another arbitrary, ill-informed management rule that causes headaches for those who must carry it out.

- *Management tactics.* Management may attempt to force the change and may fail to address concerns. Or it may fail to provide the necessary resources, knowledge, or leadership to help the change succeed. Sometimes a change receives so much exposure and glorification that employees resent it and resist. Managers who overpromise what they, or the change, can deliver may discover that the next time they want to introduce a change, they have lost credibility, so employees resist.

It is important to recognize that employees' assessments can be more accurate than management's; employees may know a change won't work even if management doesn't. In this case, resistance to change is beneficial for the organization. Thus, even though management typically considers resistance a challenge to be overcome, it may actually represent an important signal that a proposed change requires further, more open-minded scrutiny.[31]

In Practice

FLEXIBLE WORKSPACES AT AMERICAN EXPRESS

An increasingly common change that can spark a wide variety of reactions is the switch from offices or cubicles to open workspaces. Shared workspaces are intended not only to save money but also to stimulate conversations that might lead to sharing ideas or answering questions. In a twist on this idea, some companies have noticed that many employees do not even come into the office every day; they may be traveling to meet with customers, or perhaps they work from home or another remote location for part of the week. These companies save space (and therefore money) by setting up unassigned workspaces, often in open arrangements. Whoever comes to the office on a given day selects a place to work and sets up for that day. Companies using flexible workspaces include American Express, GlaxoSmithKline, Eli Lilly, and PricewaterhouseCoopers.

At American Express, flexible workspaces are tied to flexible work arrangements. Based on data from employee surveys, the company classifies each employee into one of four groups: (1) *Hub* employees have jobs requiring them to work face to face with their colleagues; (2) *club* employees work in a hub office fewer than four days a week because they work part-time or do some work from another location; (3) *roam* employees mainly work away from the office, usually because they visit clients; and (4) *home*-based employees have made arrangements to work from home. Hub employees have their own desk at the office; others share desks in open spaces when they go in. American Express trains managers to work with employees at remote locations and has measured improvements in costs and productivity.[32]

- Which of the reasons given for resistance to change might you have expected to see in response to American Express's introduction of flexible workspaces? Why?

A General Model for Managing Resistance

Motivating people to change often requires three basic stages, shown in Figure 18.2: unfreezing, moving to institute the change, and refreezing.[33]

Unfreezing In the **unfreezing** stage, management realizes that its current practices are no longer appropriate and the company must break out of (unfreeze) its present mold by doing things differently. People must come to recognize that some of the past ways of thinking, feeling, and doing things are obsolete.[34] A direct and sometimes effective way to do this is to communicate the negative consequences of the old ways by comparing the organization's performance with that of its competitors. As discussed in Chapter 15, management can share with employees data about costs, quality, and profits.[35] Sometimes an organization can open minds by easing employees into the transition gently and letting the more flexible employees deliver the message favoring change. When Washington State Employees Credit Union rewrote job descriptions to staff its branches with universal agents, it didn't force all the employees to change jobs. Rather, those who wanted to remain tellers or in other traditional roles could do so as long as they demonstrated a supportive attitude. In addition, the company selected and trained a group of branch employees to answer questions about the new universal-agent position.[36]

When managers communicate the need to change, they need to take care not to arouse people's defensiveness. Instead of unfreezing resistance, managers are likely to place employees on the defensive when they pin the blame for shortcomings directly and entirely on the workers.[37] Similarly, bombarding employees with facts aimed at inducing fear may only add to their resistance. When a problem seems huge, people often decide it is hopeless and don't face it. In these difficult situations, leaders more effectively unfreeze negative behavior with a message of hope and a commitment to collaborate so that they can accomplish successful change together.

unfreezing

Realizing that current practices are inappropriate and that new behavior is necessary.

FIGURE 18.2
Motivating People to Change

The gap is between what is and what
could be.

performance gap

The difference between actual
performance and desired
performance.

Bottom Line

A useful tactic for innovating
toward a positive future is to
imagine the difference between
what *is* and what *could be*

moving

Instituting the change.

force-field analysis

An approach to implementing
the unfreezing/moving/refreezing
model by identifying the forces
that prevent people from
changing and those that will
drive people toward change.

An important contributor to unfreezing is the recognition of a performance gap, which can be a precipitator of major change. A **performance gap** is the difference between actual performance and the performance that should or could exist.[38] As an impetus for change, a performance gap can apply to the organization as a whole; it also can apply to departments, groups, and individuals.

A gap typically implies poor performance; for example, sales, profits, stock price, or other financial indicators are down. This situation attracts management's attention, and management introduces changes to try to correct things. But another, very important form of performance gap can exist. This type of gap can occur when performance is good but someone realizes that it could be better. Thus the gap is between what is and what could be. Important changes can and should be made even when performance is good.[39]

In the realm of change management, employees are particularly motivated by situations that combine the sense of urgency that comes from identifying a problem with the sense of excitement that comes from identifying an opportunity. Furthermore, managers communicating a performance gap should keep in mind that employees care about more than market share and revenues. Employees want to know how making a change can help them have a positive impact on their work group, their customers, their company, their community, and themselves. For example, a financial services company met resistance when it tried to persuade employees that a change would enhance the company's competitive position. Employees got on board only after the change leaders also started talking about how the change would help employees reduce errors, enable teams to avoid duplication of effort, make jobs more interesting, and help the organization fulfill its mission to deliver affordable housing.[40]

Moving   The next step, **moving** to institute the change, begins with establishing a vision of where the company is heading. You learned about vision in the leadership chapter. The vision can be realized through strategic, structural, cultural, and individual change. Strategic ideas are discussed throughout the book. Changes in structure may involve moving to the divisional, matrix, or some other appropriate form (discussed in Chapters 8 and 9). Cultural changes (Chapter 2) are institutionalized through effective leadership (Chapters 12 through 15). Individuals will change as new people join the company (Chapters 10 and 11) and as people throughout the organization adopt the leader's new vision for the future.

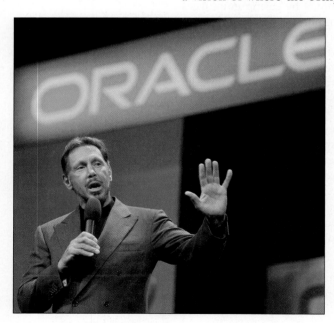

Lawrence Ellison, CEO of Oracle,
is well-versed in what it takes to
convey a vision of change within
his organization. Oracle has often
acquired other companies, bringing
tumultuous change for individual
employees and managers within
both organizations.

One technique that helps to manage the change process, **force-field analysis,** involves identifying the specific forces that prevent people from changing and the specific forces that will drive people toward change.[41] Managers operating under this concept investigate forces acting in opposite directions. Eliminating the restraining forces helps people unfreeze, and increasing the driving forces helps and motivates them to move forward.

The great social psychologist Kurt Lewin developed force-field analysis (and the unfreezing/moving/refreezing model). Lewin theorized that although driving forces may be more easily changed, shifting them may increase opposition (tension and/or conflict) within the organization and add restraining forces. Therefore, to create change, it is crucial to remove restraining forces. An exercise at the end of the chapter provides an example and takes you through this process.

Refreezing   Finally, **refreezing** means strengthening the new behaviors that support the change. Refreezing involves implementing control systems that support the change (Chapter 16), applying corrective action when necessary, and reinforcing behaviors and performance (Chapter 13) that support the agenda. Management should consistently support and reward evidence of movement in the right direction.[42]

In today's organizations, refreezing is not always the best third step if it creates new behaviors that are as rigid as the old ones. The ideal new culture is one of continuous change. Refreezing is appropriate when it permanently installs behaviors that focus on important business results and maintain essential core values. But refreezing should not create new rigidities that might become dysfunctional as the business environment continues to change.[43] The behaviors that should be refrozen are those that promote continued adaptability, flexibility, experimentation, assessment of results, and continuous improvement—in other words, lock in key values, capabilities, and strategic mission but not necessarily specific practices and procedures.

> **refreezing**
>
> Strengthening the new behaviors that support the change.

Specific Approaches to Enlist Cooperation

You can try to command people to change, but the key to long-term success is to use other approaches.[44] Developing true support is better than driving a program forward.[45] How, specifically, can managers motivate people to change?

Most managers underestimate the variety of ways they can influence people during a period of change.[46] Several effective approaches to managing resistance and enlisting cooperation are available, as described in Table 18.2 and expanded here.

TABLE 18.2   Methods for Managing Resistance to Change

Approach	Commonly Used in Situations	Advantage	Drawbacks
Education and communication	When there is a lack of information or inaccurate information and analysis.	Once persuaded, people will often help with the implementation of the change.	Can be very time-consuming if lots of people are involved.
Participation and involvement	When the initiators do not have all the information they need to design the change and when others have considerable power to resist.	People who participate will be committed to implementing change, and any relevant information they have will be integrated into the change plan.	Can be very time-consuming if participators design an inappropriate change.
Facilitation and support	When people are resisting because of adjustment problems.	No other approach works as well with adjustment problems.	Can be time-consuming and expensive and still fail.
Negotiation and rewards	When someone or some group will clearly lose out in a change and when that group has considerable power to resist.	Sometimes it is a relatively easy way to avoid major resistance.	Can be too expensive in many cases if it alerts others to negotiate for compliance.
Manipulation and cooptation	When other tactics will not work or are too expensive.	It can be a relatively quick and inexpensive solution to resistance problems.	Can lead to future problems if people feel manipulated.
Explicit and implicit coercion	When speed is essential, and the change initiators possess considerable power.	It is speedy and can overcome any kind of resistance.	Can be risky if it leaves people angry at the initiators.

Education and Communication   Management should educate people about upcoming changes before they occur. It should communicate not only the nature of the change but its logic. This process can include one-on-one discussions, presentations to groups, and reports and memos. As we discussed in Chapter 15, effective communication includes feedback and listening. That provides an environment in which management can explain the rationale for the change—and perhaps improve it.

Participation and Involvement   The people who are affected by the change should be involved in the change's design and implementation. For major, organizationwide change, participation in the process can extend from the top to the very bottom of the organization.[47] When feasible, management should use the advice of people throughout the organization.

As you learned in Chapter 3, people who are involved in decisions understand them more fully and are more committed to them. People's understanding and commitment are important ingredients in the successful implementation of a change. Participation also provides an excellent opportunity for education and communication.

Facilitation and Support   Management should make the change as easy as possible for employees and support their efforts. Facilitation involves providing the training and other resources people need to carry out the change and perform their jobs under the new circumstances. This step often includes decentralizing authority and empowering people—that is, giving them the power to make the decisions and changes needed to improve their performance.

Offering support involves listening patiently to problems, being understanding if performance drops temporarily or the change is not perfected immediately, and generally being on the employees' side and showing consideration during a difficult period.

Negotiation and Rewards   When necessary and appropriate, management can offer concrete incentives for cooperation with the change. Perhaps job enrichment is acceptable only with a higher wage rate, or a work rule change is resisted until management agrees to a concession on some other rule (say, regarding taking breaks). Even among higher-level managers, one executive might agree to another's idea for a policy change only in return for support on some other issue of more personal importance. Rewards such as bonuses, wages and salaries, recognition, job assignments, and perks can be examined and perhaps restructured to reinforce the direction of the change.[48]

When people trust one another, change is easier. But change is further facilitated by demonstrating its benefits to people.[49] Describing benefits can take place in the context of negotiation or working together to find a mutually acceptable way to implement the change. A Colorado nonprofit agency called Envision did this when the state government slashed its funding, reducing the agency's budget by 7.5 percent. Envision provides a variety of services to adults and children with developmental disabilities and depends on employees' commitment to its mission. Executive director Mary Lu Walton set up a team of employees to figure out how to cut costs, and she encouraged them to focus on eliminating the tasks employees dislike. The team members restructured work, sparing seven of the ten jobs originally targeted for layoffs. Within a few months, Envision was a leaner organization with employees fully committed to the change.[50]

Manipulation and Cooptation   Sometimes managers use more subtle, covert tactics to implement change. One form of manipulation is cooptation, which involves giving a resisting individual a desirable role in the change process. The leader of a resisting group often is coopted. For example, management might invite a union leader to be a member of an executive committee or ask a key member of an outside organization to join the company's board of directors. As a person becomes involved in the change, he or she may become less resistant to the actions of the coopting group or organization.

Explicit and Implicit Coercion   Some managers apply punishment or the threat of punishment to those who resist change. With this approach, managers use force to make people comply with their wishes. For example, a manager might insist that subordinates cooperate with the change and threaten them with job loss, denial of a promotion, or an unattractive work assignment. Sometimes you just have to lay down the law.

Each approach to managing resistance has advantages and drawbacks and, like many of the other situational management approaches described in this book, each is useful in different situations. Look back at Table 18.2, which summarizes the advantages, drawbacks, and appropriate circumstances for these approaches to managing resistance to change. As the table implies, managers should not use just one or two general approaches, regardless of the circumstances. Effective change managers are familiar with the various approaches and know how to apply them according to the situation.

Throughout the process, change leaders need to build in stability. Recall from the companies that were built to last that they all have essential core characteristics of which they don't lose sight. In the midst of change, turmoil, and uncertainty, people need anchors onto which they can latch.[51] Making an organization's values and mission constant and visible can often serve this stabilizing function. In addition, strategic principles can be important anchors during change.[52] Maintaining the visibility of key people, continuing key assignments and projects, and making announcements about which organizational components will *not* change can also promote stability. Such anchors will reduce anxiety and help overcome resistance. As you read "Management Connection: Progress Report," consider how the managers of Time Warner's magazine spin-off should apply these methods.

Management Connection

CHANGE MANAGEMENT CHALLENGES OF THE TIME INC. SPIN-OFF

In Time Warner's announcement that it would spin off the Time Inc. magazine business, CEO Jeff Bewkes expressed the change positively. According to Bewkes, Time Warner would strengthen its "growth profile," and Time Inc. would benefit because it would have the "flexibility and focus of being a stand-alone public company." In an e-mail to Time Inc. employees, Bewkes acknowledged that change "can be unsettling" and expressed confidence that employees "have the fortitude to stay focused on what Time Inc. does better than anyone: produce great journalism that your readers and audiences love."

Bewkes did *not* say, however, that the change would be easy. In fact, the magazine company would face challenges such as finding leadership and restoring morale even as it struggled to cope with a world in which print magazines have become less relevant. On the leadership front, Time Inc. had already experienced turnover at the top. A CEO hired in 2010 was dismissed months later for his management style, and nine months passed before Time Warner found a replacement, Laura Lang, who brought a background in direct advertising. After Time Warner announced the spin-off, Lang said she intended to resign but would stay through the transition long enough to help with the search for the next CEO.

Even before the announcement of the spin-off, the magazine group's struggles had been hurting morale.

Employees could see the declines in revenue, and Time Inc. had recently said it would lay off 6 percent of employees—the third layoff in four years. Pay rates were frozen, and bonuses were eliminated. Time Warner also had explored selling the magazine group to a company in Des Moines, a possible change in location or management style that displeased some of the New York employees. Some questioned whether the Time Warner CEO even cared about the magazine business.

To restore morale, Time Inc.'s managers needed to offer a positive vision of the future. Although the magazine group lost access to a bigger company's cash, it could choose to invest more in the future of digital magazine content rather than competing for resources with more-profitable divisions. And within the magazine business, Time Inc. is the biggest publisher. Soon after the spin-off announcement, *Time* magazine's managing editor, Richard Stengel, told a reporter that operating independently presented a chance to "test that hypothesis that people will pay for great content and great journalism."[53]

- Of the methods for managing resistance to change (Table 18.2), which are potentially relevant to Time Inc.? How and why?
- Imagine you were brought in to lead Time Inc. What would you say and do to restore morale? What ideas could you include from the genius of the *and?*

MANAGER'S BRIEF   PROGRESS REPORT   ONWARD

Harmonizing Multiple Changes

total organization change

Introducing and sustaining multiple policies, practices, and procedures across multiple units and levels.

There are no silver bullets or single-shot methods of changing organizations successfully. Single shots rarely hit a challenging target. Usually many issues need simultaneous attention, and any single, small change will be absorbed by the prevailing culture and disappear. **Total organization change** involves introducing and sustaining multiple policies, practices, and procedures across multiple units and levels.[54] Such change affects the thinking and behavior of everyone in the organization, can enhance the organization's culture and success, and can be sustained over time.

A survey at a Harvard Business School conference found that the average attendee's company had five major change efforts going on at once.[55] The problem is, these efforts usually are simultaneous but not coordinated. As a result, changes get muddled; people lose focus.[56] The people involved suffer from confusion, frustration, low morale, and low motivation.

Because companies introduce new changes constantly, many people complain about their companies' "flavor of the month" approach to change. That is, employees often see many change efforts as just the company's jumping on the latest bandwagon or fad. The more these change fads come and go, the more cynical people become, and the more difficult it is to get them committed to making the change a success.[57]

> Many people complain about their companies' "flavor of the month" approach to change.

So an important question is, Which change efforts are really worth undertaking? Here are some specific questions to ask before embarking on a change project:[58]

- What is the evidence that the approach really can produce positive results?
- Is the approach relevant to your company's strategies and priorities?
- Can you assess the costs and potential benefits?
- Does it really help people add value through their work?
- Does it help the company focus better on customers and the things they value?
- Can you go through the decision-making process described in Chapter 3, understand what you're facing, and feel that you are taking the right approach?

Management also needs to connect the dots—that is, integrate the various efforts into a coherent picture that people can see, understand, and get behind.[59] You connect the dots by understanding each change program and its goals, by identifying similarities among the programs and their differences, and by dropping programs that don't meet priority goals or demonstrate clear results. Most important, you do it by communicating to everyone concerned the common themes among the various programs: their common rationales, objectives, and methods. You show them how the various parts fit the strategic big picture and how the changes will make things better for the company and its people. You must communicate these benefits thoroughly, honestly, and frequently.[60]

Leading Change

Successful change requires managers to lead it actively. The essential activities of leading change are summarized in Figure 18.3.

The companies that lead change most effectively establish a sense of urgency.[61] To do so, managers must examine current realities and pressures in the marketplace and the competitive arena, identify both crises and opportunities, and be frank and honest about them. In this sense, urgency is a reality-based sense of determination, not just fear-based busyness. The immediacy of the need for change is an important component, in part because so many large companies grow complacent.

Figure 18.4 shows some common reasons for complacency. To stop complacency and create urgency, a manager can talk candidly about the organization's weaknesses compared with competitors, making a point to back up statements with data. Other tactics include setting stretch goals, putting employees in direct contact with unhappy

FIGURE 18.3
Leading Change

1 Establishing a sense of urgency

2 Creating the guiding coalition

3 Developing a vision and strategy

4 Communicating the change vision

5 Empowering broad-based action

6 Generating short-term wins

7 Consolidating gains and producing more change

8 Anchoring new approaches in the culture

customers and shareholders, distributing worrisome information to all employees instead of merely engaging in management happy talk, eliminating excessive perks, and highlighting to everyone the future opportunities that exist but that the organization so far has failed to pursue.

Ultimately, urgency is driven by compelling business reasons for change. Survival, competition, and winning in the marketplace are compelling; they provide a sense of direction and energy around change. Change becomes not a hobby, a luxury, or something nice to do, but a business necessity.[62]

To create a guiding coalition means putting together a group with enough power to lead the change. Change efforts fail when a sufficiently powerful coalition is not formed.[63] Major organization change requires leadership from top management, working as a team. But over time, the support must gradually expand outward and downward throughout the organization. Middle managers and supervisors are essential. Groups at all levels are the glue that can hold change efforts together, the medium for communicating about the changes, and the means for enacting new behaviors.[64]

Developing a vision and strategy, as discussed in earlier chapters, directs the change effort. This process involves determining the idealized, expected state of affairs after the change is implemented. Because confusion is common during major organizational

FIGURE 18.4
Sources of Complacency

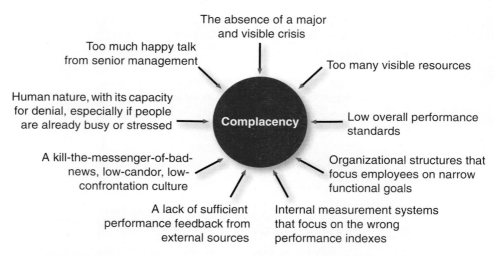

change, the clearest possible image of the future state must be developed and conveyed to everyone.[65] This image, or vision, is a target or guideline that can clarify expectations, dispel rumors, and mobilize people's energies. The portrait of the future also should communicate how the transition will occur, why the change is being implemented, and how people will be affected by the change. The power of a compelling vision is one of the most important aspects of change and should not be underestimated or underused.

Communicating the change vision requires using every possible channel and opportunity to talk up and reinforce the vision and required new behaviors. It is said that aspiring change leaders undercommunicate the vision by a factor of 10, or even 100 or 1,000, seriously undermining the chances of success.[66] In delivering more messages, however, do not forget that communication is a two-way street. When consultant Steve Schumacher was hired to improve the performance of a division in which quality, productivity, and customer service had been declining, he started by setting up meetings in which employees described what they saw as the underlying problems. His message to them was simply that the company cared about their views and wouldn't make changes until they had been heard. Schumacher and his team then compiled a list of all the issues and shared it with every employee. Only then did he ask for volunteers to participate in planning solutions. The consulting team was flooded with volunteers. Not only were employees willing to change, but they were excited to be included in planning, and they hungered for a better understanding of where the company wanted to go and how they could contribute to that vision. Before long, as a result of this team effort, performance measures began to rise across the board.[67]

Empowering broad-based action means getting rid of obstacles to success, including systems and structures that constrain rather than facilitate. Encourage risk taking and experimentation and empower people by providing information, knowledge, authority, and rewards, as described in Chapter 13.

Generate short-term wins. Don't wait for the ultimate grand realization of the vision. You need results. As small victories accumulate, you make the transition from an isolated initiative to an integral part of the business.[68] Plan for and create small victories that indicate to everyone that progress is being made. Recognize and reward the people who made the wins possible, doing it visibly so that people notice and the positive message permeates the organization.

Make sure you consolidate gains and produce more change. With the well-earned credibility of previous successes, keep changing things in ways that support the vision.

Hire, promote, and develop people who will further the vision. Reinvigorate the organization and your change efforts with new projects and change agents.

Finally, anchor new approaches in the culture.[69] Highlight positive results, communicate the connections between the new behaviors and the improved results, and keep developing new change agents and leaders. Continually increase the number of people joining you in taking responsibility for change.[70]

The conventional way in which organizations apply these eight steps of leading change has been to set up strategy or project teams to conduct annual strategy reviews or launch new projects over the course of months or years. However, this approach can be too slow for seizing the opportunities popping up in today's business environment. Therefore, John Kotter, who proposed the eight steps, now advises companies to become more agile in leading change by empowering networks of employees to accelerate change.[71] These networks bring together volunteers from all levels and functions of the organization who are excited about the change vision and have the skills needed to implement it. When someone in the organization sees a problem or opportunity, any member of the network can share the issue and invite others to join a team developing a solution. The teamwork is in addition to the employee's usual responsibilities, so the network requires highly committed people who experience the rewards of making a significant, visible contribution.

Shaping the Future

Most change is reactive. A better way to change is to be proactive. **Reactive change** means responding to pressure after a problem has arisen. It also implies being a follower. **Proactive change** means anticipating and preparing for an uncertain future. It implies being a leader and creating the future you want.

The road to the future includes drivers, passengers, and road kill. Put another way: on the road to the future, who will be the windshield, and who will be the bug?[72] Needless to say, it's best to be a driver.[73] How do you become a driver? By being proactive more than merely reactive, by really thinking about the future, and by *creating* futures.

reactive change

A change effort that occurs under pressure; problem-driven change.

proactive change

A change effort that is initiated before a performance gap has occurred.

Thinking about the Future

If you think only about the present or wallow in the uncertainties of the future, your future is just a roll of the dice. It is far better to exercise foresight, set an agenda for the future, and pursue it with everything you've got. So contemplate and envision the future.

Before the 20th century, people lived without antibiotics, automobiles, airplanes, tractors, and air conditioning. Imagine how this combination of inventions has revolutionized where and how well people live. And in just the past few decades, we have seen the invention and spread of personal computers, cell phones, and the mapping of the human genome. These innovations are still shaping how we learn, communicate, and treat disease.

> On the road to the future, who will be the windshield, and who will be the bug?

Will the 21st century bring transformations that are just as dramatic? Some people think the potential for innovation and growth is unprecedented in areas such as information technology, the biological sciences, agriculture, water supply, and clean energy technologies.[74] Futurist Richard Watson sees the cell phone as the device that will most transform how we live in the 21st century. He foresees a cashless society in which consumers use signals from their phones to make payments as well as send

BE FEARLESS.

symantec

Don't think taking risks and being fearless is only for companies; think of your own quest for personal advantage in the same way. Ultimately where you go, what you do, who you become are up to you.

adapters

Companies that take the current industry structure and its evolution as givens and choose where to compete.

shapers

Companies that try to change the structure of their industries, creating a future competitive landscape of their own design.

messages. Futurist Cynthia Wagner sees career opportunities stemming from researchers' growing knowledge of processes in the human brain. In the future, Wagner surmises, this knowledge will help bioengineers develop microelectrodes to translate paralyzed patients' brain signals into words and movements, and computer scientists will apply the knowledge to make advances in artificial intelligence.[75] Just as technologies change, so do additional trends rise and fall, recently including a (temporary, most likely) damper on globalization, rising distrust of business, a growing role of government, strains on natural resources, and changing patterns of global consumption.[76] Vast new markets exist, new kinds of companies are ready to be created, and new business models will emerge.[77] All offer prime opportunity to those who create the future.

Creating the Future

Companies can try different strategic postures to prepare to compete in an uncertain future. **Adapters** take the current industry structure and its future evolution as givens. They choose where to compete. This posture is taken by most companies by conducting standard strategic analysis and choosing how to compete within given environments. In contrast, **shapers** try to change the structure of their industries, creating a future competitive landscape of their own design.[78]

Researchers studying corporate performance over a 10-year period found that 17 companies in the *Fortune* 1000 grew total shareholder return by 35 percent or more per year.[79] How did they do it? They completely reinvented industries. Harley-Davidson turned around by selling not just motorcycles but nostalgia. Amgen broke the rules of the biotech industry by focusing not on what customers wanted but on great science. Starbucks began selling a commodity in trendy stores. CarMax and other companies reinvented the auto industry.

You need to create advantages. The challenge is not to maintain your position in the current competitive arena but to create new competitive arenas, transform your industry, and imagine a future that others don't see. Creating advantage is better than playing catch-up. At best, doing things to catch up buys time; it cannot get you out ahead of the pack or buy world-class excellence.[80] To create new markets or transform industries—these are perhaps the ultimate forms of proactive change.[81]

Figure 18.5 illustrates the vast opportunity to create new markets. Articulated needs are those that customers acknowledge and try to satisfy. Unarticulated needs are those that customers have not yet experienced. Served customers are those to whom your company is now selling, and unserved customers are untapped markets.

Business as usual concentrates on the lower-left quadrant. The leaders who re-create the game are constantly trying to create new opportunities in the other three quadrants.[82] For example, as a middle class emerges in populous and fast-developing nations such as India, China, and Brazil, some see problems in the strain this puts on the planet's resources. Others see unexploited opportunities to serve new customers with new kinds of products that are made more sustainably or enable consumers to live a more sustainable lifestyle.[83]

Other companies hope to meet unarticulated needs by developing and exploiting cutting-edge technology. The nanometer—one-billionth of a meter, 1/100,000 the width of a human hair, or about the size of 10 hydrogen atoms in a row—is the building block of a new industry, nanotechnology. The nanometer is so important because matter at this scale often behaves differently—speeding electrons through circuits faster, conducting heat better, or offering qualities such as greater strength, durability, or reactivity.[84] Large and small companies are beginning to rush nano-based products into the marketplace. Current applications include nanotech silver (which has antimicrobial properties) in grooming products and odor-resistant socks, nanoscale features in semiconductors, and the use of nanoparticles as catalysts in making chemicals for

FIGURE 18.5
Vast Opportunity

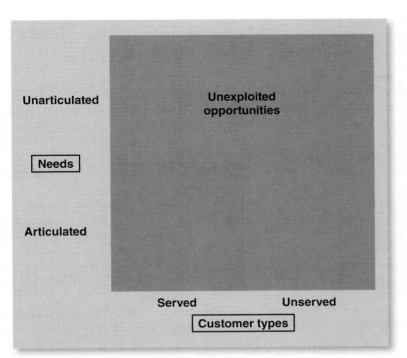

use in coatings, paints, sunscreens, and other products.[85] Applications under development include high-performance rechargeable batteries that can store hydrogen and other high-energy gases, nano-biochips that can detect cancer in a patient within minutes, and a nanotechnology material called graphene that can be used to produce a computer touchscreen one one atom thick.[86]

Is nanotech—for that matter, are most industries of the future—being overhyped? By some estimates, products using nanotech materials could achieve sales of $3.3 trillion by 2018; others say $49 billion in 2017 would be a more realistic figure. Either way, the expansion of this technology has been impressive, given that it is still under development. Sales of products applying nanotechnology have grown by more than 18 percent a year over the past few years.[87] However, there are concerns that the technology is untested and perhaps risky.[88] The particles are so small that they can pass through most manufactured filters as well as through cell walls, and their ability to react at the atomic level could cause unforeseen chemical and biological consequences. At the heart of the problem is a lack of experience with these materials, coupled with the fact that their properties are different from the same materials at a larger scale. Scientists have measured inhaled particles in the respiratory tract, for example, but have only begun to study whether cells' functions are impaired by contact with nanoparticles. Thus industry is challenged to apply this exciting new technology while protecting its workers and customers against the possibility of risks that aren't yet known.[89]

Who can meet such a challenge best? As you've read, technological change is a central part of the changing landscape, and competition often arises between newcomers and established companies.

All things considered, which should you and your firm do?

- Preserve old advantages or create new advantages?
- Lock in old markets or create new markets?
- Take the path of greatest familiarity or the path of greatest opportunity?
- Be only a benchmarker or a pathbreaker?
- Place priority on short-term financial returns or on making a real, long-term impact?

- Do only what seems doable or what is difficult and worthwhile?
- Change what is or create what isn't?
- Look to the past or live for the future?[90]

Shaping Your Own Future

If you are an organizational leader and your organization operates in traditional ways, your key goal should be to create a revolution, genetically reengineering your company before it becomes a dinosaur of the modern era.[91] What should be the goals of the revolution? You've been learning about them throughout this course.

But maybe you are not going to lead a revolution. Maybe you just want a successful career and a good life. You still must be able to choose and pursue long-term goals[92] and deal with an economic environment that is highly competitive and fast-moving.[93] Creating the future you want for yourself requires setting high personal standards. Don't settle for mediocrity; don't assume that good is necessarily good enough—for yourself or for your employer. Think about how not just to meet expectations but to exceed them; not merely to live with apparent constraints but break free of the unimportant, arbitrary, or imagined ones; and to seize opportunities instead of letting them pass by.[94]

> Look for positions that stretch you and for bosses who develop their protégés.

The most successful individuals take charge of their own development the way an entrepreneur takes charge of a business.[95] More specific advice from the leading authors on career management:[96] Consciously and actively manage your own career. Develop marketable skills and keep developing more. Make career choices based on personal growth, development, and learning opportunities. Look for positions that stretch you and for bosses who develop their protégés. Seek environments that provide training and the opportunity to experiment and innovate. And know yourself; assess your strengths and weaknesses, your true interests, and ethical standards. If you are not already thinking in these terms and taking commensurate action, you should start now.

Additionally, become indispensable to your organization. Be enthusiastic in your job and committed to doing great work, but don't be blindly loyal to one company. Be prepared to leave if necessary. View your job as an opportunity to prove what you can do and increase what you can do, not as a comfortable niche for the long term.[97] Go out on your own if it meets your skills and temperament.

This points out the need to maintain your options. More and more, contemporary careers can involve leaving behind a large organization and going entrepreneurial, becoming self-employed in the postcorporate world.[98] In such a career, independent individuals are free to make their own choices. They can flexibly and quickly respond to demands and opportunities. Developing start-up ventures, consulting, accepting temporary employment, doing project work for one organization and then another, working in professional partnerships, being a constant deal maker—these can be the elements of a successful career. Ideally, this self-employed model can help provide a balanced approach to working and to living life at home and with family because people have more control over their work activities and schedules.

This go-it-alone approach can sound ideal, but it also has downsides. Independence can be frightening, the future unpredictable. It can isolate road warriors who are always on the go, working from their cars and airports, and interfere with social and family life.[99] Effective self-management is needed to keep career and family obligations in perspective and in control.

Coping with uncertainty and change is easier if you develop resilience. To become more resilient, practice thinking of the world as complex but full of opportunities; expect change, but see it as interesting and potentially rewarding, even if changing is difficult. Also, keep a sense of purpose, set priorities for your time, be flexible when facing uncertainty or a need to change, and take an active role in the face of change rather than waiting for change to happen to you.[100]

Learning and Leading

Continuous learning is a vital route to renewable competitive advantage.[101] People in your organization—and you, personally—should constantly explore, discover, and take action, as illustrated in Figure 18.6. With this approach, you can learn what is effective and what is not and adjust and improve accordingly. The philosophy of continuous learning helps your company achieve lower cost, higher quality, better service, superior innovation, greater sustainability, and greater speed—and helps you grow and develop on a personal level.

Commit to lifelong learning. Lifelong learning requires occasionally taking risks, moving outside your comfort zone, honestly assessing the reasons behind your successes and failures, asking for and listening to other people's information and opinions, and being open to new ideas.[102]

Through a career, a person can inhabit and grow through the hierarchy of stages illustrated in Figure 18.7 from Jim Collins's book *Good to Great*. The descriptions in the hierarchy suggest not only that you should do these things, but that you should do them well. Your first job may not include managerial responsibilities, but it will require you to be an individual contributor and probably to be part of a team. Level 3 is where managerial capabilities are required, whereas Level 4 distinguishes true leadership from competent management. Level 5 represents a leadership style that you read about briefly in Chapter 12, which combines strong will and determination with personal humility. The figure shows that Level 5 leadership represents a peak achievement, the ultimate

Bottom Line

Continuous learning provides a fundamental competitive advantage by helping you and your organization achieve difficult goals.

What are the three phases in the process of continuous learning?

Commit to lifelong learning.

FIGURE 18.6
Learning Cycle: Explore, Discover, Act

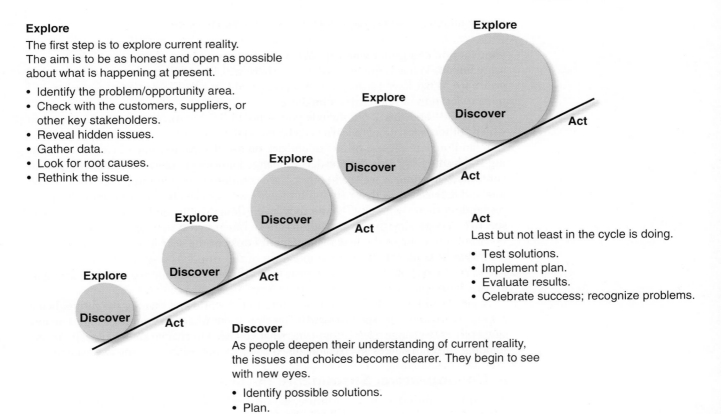

Explore

The first step is to explore current reality. The aim is to be as honest and open as possible about what is happening at present.

- Identify the problem/opportunity area.
- Check with the customers, suppliers, or other key stakeholders.
- Reveal hidden issues.
- Gather data.
- Look for root causes.
- Rethink the issue.

Act
Last but not least in the cycle is doing.

- Test solutions.
- Implement plan.
- Evaluate results.
- Celebrate success; recognize problems.

Discover
As people deepen their understanding of current reality, the issues and choices become clearer. They begin to see with new eyes.

- Identify possible solutions.
- Plan.
- Anticipate problems.

SOURCE: From *Leaning into the Future: Changing the Way People Change Organizations* by George Binney and Collin Williams; published by Nicholas Brealey Publishing Ltd., 1997. Reprinted by permission.

FIGURE 18.7
Level 5 Hierarchy

LEVEL 5   **LEVEL 5 EXECUTIVE**
Builds enduring greatness through a
paradoxical blend of personal humility
and professional will.

LEVEL 4   **EFFECTIVE LEADER**
Catalyzes commitment to and vigorous
pursuit of a clear and compelling vision,
stimulating higher performance standards.

LEVEL 3   **COMPETENT MANAGER**
Organizes people and resources toward the
effective and efficient pursuit of predetermined
objectives.

LEVEL 2   **CONTRIBUTING TEAM MEMBER**
Contributes individual capabilities to the
achievement of group objectives and works
effectively with others in a group setting.

LEVEL 1   **HIGHLY CAPABLE INDIVIDUAL**
Makes productive contributions through talent,
knowledge, skills, and good work habits.

SOURCE: From *Good to Great.* Copyright © 2001 by Jim Collins. Reprinted from Jim Collins.

contribution of a leader who can turn a good company into a great one.[103] You might ask yourself, What is my level now (or where will I be after graduation)? What do I aspire to? What have I learned to this point that can help me progress, and what do I need to learn to develop myself further?

A leader—and this could include you—should be able to create an environment in which "others are willing to learn and change so their organizations can adapt and innovate [and] inspire diverse others to embark on a collective journey of continual learning and leading."[104] Learning leaders exchange knowledge freely; commit to their own continuous learning as well as to others'; are committed to examining their own behaviors and defensiveness that may inhibit their learning; devote time to their colleagues, suspending their own beliefs while they listen thoughtfully; and develop a broad perspective, recognizing that organizations are an integrated system of relationships.[105]

Honored as one of the best management books of the year in Europe, *Leaning into the Future* gets its title from a combination of the words *leading* and *learning*.[106] The two perspectives, on the surface, appear very different. But they are powerful and synergistic when pursued in complementary ways.

A successful future derives from adapting to the world *and* shaping the future; being responsive to others' perspectives *and* being clear about what you want to change; encouraging others to change *while* recognizing what you need to change about yourself; understanding current realities *and* passionately pursuing your vision; learning *and* leading.

A Collaborative, Sustainable Future?

As you lead and learn into the future, we urge you to (1) bear in mind the long run, in addition to the immediate demands you must face, and (2) consider collaboration as a key to sustained success. At the outset of this chapter and throughout this book, you learned about many of today's big challenges. The good news is that new business models and new forms of collaboration are taking root, and others are waiting to be created.[107] Entrepreneurs with societal goals are driving new approaches to commerce. The private sector is tackling social and environmental issues, the public sector is enacting market-based approaches to delivering service, and nonprofits now pursue sustainable business models.

Business and tomorrow's leaders in every sector are vitally important for determining what the future will be. It would be naïve to think that, without more forward thinking and appropriate action, long-term considerations will overpower the many short-term pressures for immediate results. And there still is the enduring controversy over the obligations of business. But a long-term focus and perspective, balanced with prudent financial considerations, is required to achieve sustainable financial success and the corporate purpose enduringly over time.

It would be erroneous to assume that collaboration will replace competition. Competition has upsides and downsides, and although new competitors enter every field, former competitors sometimes become collaborators. Certainly at local levels and sometimes at regional and global levels, multisector clusters of businesses, schools, universities, nonprofits, and governments are collaborating in mutually beneficial and effective ways. People are learning to work more effectively together— not just within but across organizations and sector boundaries—to produce new models for action that revitalize business and change the world.[108]

Management Connection

SHAPING THE FUTURE OF TIME WARNER

For Time Warner CEO Jeff Bewkes, the spin-off of Time Inc. is a key part of keeping the company focused on the businesses where it can increase its profits and value to shareholders. The magazine business had brought in 12 percent of Time Warner's revenue, but after expenses, it contributed a smaller share of profits, and its earnings were falling. With the magazine unit gone, Bewkes can focus all employees' attention on creating and selling video content—what Bewkes calls "strategic clarity."

The future of Time Inc. looks more uncertain to many observers. It will start off already in debt at least $500 million, and it needs people who can figure out how to increase revenues in a business that has been shrinking. Even on some of its websites, including those for *Sports Illustrated* and *People*, the number of unique visitors has declined. On the upside, any earnings the magazine publisher generates can be directed toward modernizing its offerings for the digital age. Four of the company's magazines (*People*, *Sports Illustrated*, *Time*, and *InStyle*) reportedly are among the top ten U.S. magazines in terms of revenue.

To meet these challenges, Time Inc. will need leaders able to inspire employees who are worried about cutbacks and changing technology. This need comes at a time when the top position of the company has been in flux for years. Critics of CEO Laura Lang pointed out that her background was not in magazines, and she was unable to express a clear strategy. In July 2013, Time Inc. announced Joe Ripp as its new CEO. Time Warner's CEO told employees that Mr. Ripp is "a highly respected executive with a distinguished record of taking on difficult challenges and delivering financial results."

Despite previous concerns, Bewkes expresses little worry about the future of either company. He calls digital media "just another platform," insisting that the creation of desirable content is what drives customers to any medium. In Bewkes's view, Time Warner is "very stable and steady" while many investors scurry to and from whatever looks like the next big online innovation. History suggests that if Time Warner is like many other companies, both it and Time Inc. can grow stronger; analysts reviewing data from the past decade found that in 80 spin-offs at U.S. companies, both the parent companies and the ones spun off delivered returns higher than those for companies overall.[109]

- How should the managers of Time Warner and Time Inc. carry out the essential activities for leading change (Figure 18.3)?
- Imagine you are a manager for Time Inc. How can this chapter's advice for shaping the future help you succeed?

KEY TERMS

adapters, p. 618

force-field analysis, p. 610

genius of the *and,* p. 604

moving, p. 610

organization development (OD), p. 605

organizational ambidexterity, p. 604

performance gap, p. 610

proactive change, p. 617

reactive change, p. 617

refreezing, p. 611

shapers, p. 618

total organization change, p. 614

tyranny of the *or,* p. 604

unfreezing, p. 609

SUMMARY OF LEARNING OBJECTIVES

Now that you have studied Chapter 18, you should be able to:

 Discuss what it takes to be world class.

You should strive for world-class excellence, which means using the very best and latest knowledge and ideas to operate at the highest standards of any place anywhere. Sustainable greatness comes from, among other things, having strong core values, living those values constantly, striving for continuous improvement, experimenting, and always trying to do better tomorrow than today. It is essential not to fall prey to the tyranny of the *or*—that is, the belief that one important goal can be attained only at the expense of another. The genius of the *and* is that multiple important goals can be achieved simultaneously and synergistically.

 Describe how to manage and lead change effectively.

Effective change management occurs when the organization moves from its current state to a desired future state without excessive cost to the organization or its people. People resist change for a variety of reasons, including inertia, poor timing, surprise, peer pressure, self-interest, misunderstanding, different information about (and assessments of) the change, and management's tactics.

Motivating people to change requires a general process of unfreezing, moving, and refreezing, with the caveat that appropriate and not inappropriate behaviors be refrozen. More specific techniques to motivate people to change include education and communication, participation and involvement, facilitation and support, negotiation and rewards, manipulation and cooptation, and coercion. Each approach has strengths, weaknesses, and appropriate uses, and multiple approaches can be used. It is important to harmonize the multiple changes that are occurring throughout the organization.

Effective change requires active leadership, including creating a sense of urgency, forming a guiding coalition, developing a vision and strategy, communicating the change vision, empowering broad-based action, generating short-term wins, consolidating gains and producing more change, and anchoring the new approaches in the culture.

LO 3 Describe strategies for creating a successful future.

Preparing for an uncertain future requires a proactive approach. You can proactively forge the future by being a shaper more than an adapter, creating new competitive advantages, actively managing your career and your personal development, and becoming an active leader and a lifelong learner.

DISCUSSION QUESTIONS

1. Why do some people resist the goal of becoming world class? How can this resistance be overcome?

2. Generate specific examples of world-class business that you have seen as a consumer. Also, generate examples of poor business practice. Why and how do some companies inspire world-class practices while others do not?

3. How might blogging and other social forms of communication via social media affect the process of managing change? What are the professional and career implications of blogging for you?

4. Generate and discuss examples of problems and opportunities that have inspired change, both in businesses and in you personally.

5. Review the methods for dealing with resistance to change. Generate specific examples of each that you have seen and analyze why they worked or failed to work.

6. Choose some specific types of changes you would like to see happen in groups or organizations with which you are familiar. Imagine that you were to try to bring about these changes. What sources of resistance should you anticipate? How would you manage the resistance?

7. Develop a specific plan for becoming a continuous learner.

8. In your own words, what does the idea of creating the future mean to you? How can you put this concept to good use? Again, generate some specific ideas that you can really use.

9. In what ways do you think the manager's job will be different in 20 years from what it is today? How can you prepare for that future?

EXPERIENTIAL EXERCISES

18.1   A FORCE-FIELD ANALYSIS

OBJECTIVE

To introduce you to force-field analysis for managing organizational change.

INSTRUCTIONS

Read the following force-field analysis and come up with an organizational problem of your own to analyze.

FORCE-FIELD ANALYSIS

As described in the chapter, a force-field analysis is one way to assess change in an organization. The change leader identifies the driving and restraining forces at work at a particular time, assesses organizational strengths, and selects forces to add or remove to create change. Using force-field analysis demonstrates the range of forces pressing on an organization at a particular time and can increase optimism that change is possible.

Example—trying to increase student participation in student government.

Driving Forces	Restraining Forces
More money allocated for student government activities. ⟶	⟵ High emphasis on grades—a need to study more.
Better publicity and public relations programs for student government. ⟶	⟵ Other activities—cultural, social, sports— divert interest.
Student government representatives go to classes and explain positive effects of student decisions. ⟶	⟵ Not much public relations work in the past.
Special career programs offered for student government participants. ⟶	⟵ Students do not see student government as effective or helping them get a job.

Present balance point

Force-Field Analysis Worksheet

1. Choose an organizational change in process, complete the Problem Analysis section, and fill in the model. (10–15 min.)

2. In groups of three or four, discuss the driving and restraining forces in each person's problem. (20 min.)

3. Class discussion: (10 min.)
   a. Why is it useful to break up a problem situation into driving and restraining forces?
   b. Would the model be applied any differently to an individual or organizational problem?

PROBLEM ANALYSIS

1. Describe the problem in a few words.

   _____

   _____

   _____

   _____

   _____

2. A list of forces driving toward change would include these:
   a. _____

   b. _____

   c. _____

   d. _____

   e. _____

   f. _____

3. A list of forces restraining change would include these:

a. _____

b. _____

c. _____

d. _____

e. _____

f. _____

4. Put the driving and restraining forces of the problem on this force-field analysis, according to their degree of impact on change.

Driving Forces	Restraining Forces
→————————————→	←————————————←

Present balance point

18.2 NETWORKING SCENARIOS

1. Working on your own, develop a networking strategy for the following three scenarios. (10 min.)

2. Working with your partner or small group, collaborate on identifying the best strategy for dealing with each of the three scenarios. Each group should develop one best strategy for each scenario. (20 min.)

3. Each group reports, sharing its best strategies for each of the three scenarios (or at least one if not enough time is available). (2–3 min. per group per strategy)

4. The large group or class engages in discussion, using the questions at the end. (10 min.)

SCENARIOS

I. You are running for student government president. What steps would you take to make your candidacy a success?

1. _____

2. _____

3. _____

4. _____

5. _____

6. _____

II. You are in an internship and are interested in becoming a permanent full-time employee at the organization. What people would you approach and what steps could you take to obtain an offer?

1. _____

2. _____

3. _____

4. _____

5. _____

6. _____

III. You just moved to a new community, and your company's business growth relies heavily on referrals. How do you make contacts in a place where you don't know anyone? How can you build a client base?

1. _____

2. _____

3. _____

4. _____

5. _____

6. _____

QUESTIONS

1. What was difficult about this exercise?
2. What creative means were devised to build networks of contacts in these scenarios?
3. Which of these ideas would be easy to implement? Which would be difficult? What makes some strategies easier to do than others?
4. What personal qualities are needed actually to use these strategies?
5. How can someone who is shy about approaching new people use (some or all of) these strategies successfully?
6. What did you learn about yourself and others from this exercise?

SOURCE: Suzanne C. de Janasz, Karen O'Dowd, and Beth Z. Schneider, *Interpersonal Skills in Organizations,* McGraw-Hill/Irwin, 2002, p. 212. © 2002 The McGraw-Hill Companies. Reprinted with permission.

CONCLUDING CASE

EATWELL TECHNOLOGIES

Cristina Muñoz and P. R. (Pete) Prakash started EatWell Technologies as a result of conversations they held while they were graduate students in bioengineering. Both scientists were interested in how to develop crops offering superior nutrition in developing countries, and both believe that business innovation can and should drive social change. They focused their research on a genetically modified strain of rice that is drought tolerant and high in vitamin A and iron. Upon completing their studies, they wrote a business plan and formed EatWell Technologies to commercialize their new rice. Their aim was to sell first in Africa, where nutrition is an urgent problem and the potential for economic development presents huge opportunities for business. They selected Nigeria as their first target market.

Working through the government and with nongovernmental development organizations and local farmers, Cristina and Pete established a reputation for integrity and a desirable product. As farmers began purchasing their rice, the two owners hired research assistants, office staff, and sales representatives. They began to enjoy modest profits and started paying themselves a monthly salary—far from what they could earn as scientists in a large corporation but enough to live on. They began discussing what products to offer next. Cristina suggested they develop improved leafy greens to provide variety in local diets; Pete was inclined to add new strains of rice, their area of greatest knowledge.

The two entrepreneurs also realized that as their venture grew, it needed management expertise beyond their skills as scientists. They hired an experienced office manager, and the office staff appreciated her tactful guidance. They also interviewed Bill Jensen, a recently retired vice president of a community bank. Bill was impressed with the company's mission and thought an interesting retirement project would be to help EatWell become financially stronger. Pete, Cristina, and Bill reached an agreement by which Bill would become a third partner in exchange for investing $450,000. The partners met daily, and Bill helped the scientists track cash flow, choose suppliers, and meet experts who can help the business expand into new markets.

At one of their strategy meetings, Pete and Cristina agreed it is time to settle on the direction for product development: Will EatWell be a rice company, or should it diversify into green vegetables? Bill surprised them with a few PowerPoint slides about his idea. Bill pointed out that rice and leafy greens are commodities, and EatWell will never get much of a return from investing in commodities. Instead, he pointed out the value of the rice as a brand. Imagine where EatWell could go by incorporating the rice into other products, such as energy bars and breakfast cereal. They could go beyond farming into the cities and sell to Africa's rapidly growing middle class, who could pay a premium. They could even start paying themselves salaries in line with their expertise and the risks they took on by forming the company. Pete and Cristina were shocked. From their viewpoint, Bill had lost sight of the company's purpose.

DISCUSSION QUESTIONS

1. Review the first section of the chapter, about becoming world class. How can EatWell Technologies fulfill its social mission and be profitable?
2. In this case, where do you see resistance to change? How can leaders overcome the resistance? How should they?
3. Suppose you are coaching Pete and Cristina. What advice would you give them about shaping their future?

PART FIVE   SUPPORTING CASE

Technology Helps Dollar General Pinch Pennies

More and more consumers determined to save money are winding up at deep-discount retailers popularly known as dollar stores. These relatively small stores—including Dollar General, Family Dollar, and Dollar Tree—offer food, clothing, and household items at deep discounts. Discounters such as Target and Walmart offer a wider selection, but more consumers are trading down to find the best possible prices.

Competing with Walmart on price is hardly an easy strategy. When Kathleen Guion took charge of store operations and store development for Dollar General, she got to work initiating a whole host of changes. Many of these were aimed at controlling costs and helping the stores run more efficiently, and many of the changes involved improving the technology used by store employees, bringing it more in line with industry standards.

Guion found that Dollar General used some truly low-tech approaches to activities involved in running the stores. When trucks pulled up with deliveries, for example, store employees pulled cartons out of the truck one by one and carried them into the store for stocking the shelves. And whenever items languished on shelves too long, the same employees would repack them in boxes and carry them into the back room for storage. Not only were these methods slow, but employees hated lugging the boxes around. Calling her change program EZ Store, Guion simplified those jobs. She bought large wheeled bins called rolltainers, which employees use to move products from the trucks to back rooms to the sales floor. And when products don't sell as expected, the EZ Store plan calls for marking down the price low enough that the products do get sold. Not only does EZ Store make working for Dollar General more enjoyable by eliminating undesirable chores, but the greater efficiency gives employees more time to serve customers.

Under Guion's direction, Dollar General also upgraded its computer systems to deliver better information faster. The company introduced handheld scanners connected to an inventory management system so employees can quickly and accurately see which items need to be replenished and when. Computers linked to headquarters have been installed in the back rooms of all the stores. (Surprising as it may sound, until 2009, headquarters sent messages to stores via postal mail.) The company introduced computer-based training programs to improve employees' skills, as well as software for screening job candidates to identify which of them have qualities associated with success. And to reduce thefts in the stores, the company installed closed-circuit television systems.

Managers also have been given better technology. Dollar General bought district managers personal computers with software that monitors performance and flags exceptions to standards. It also gave them BlackBerry handheld devices so they can keep in touch with their people and keep up to date on store performance while they travel. The technology has enabled Dollar General to widen the district managers' span of control because fewer managers can keep up with more stores. More efficient management, in turn, has supported the company's program of rapidly opening new stores. (It now has more than 9,500 in 35 states.)

These efficiency improvements are essential in the difficult retailing industry because Walmart and Target as well as other dollar stores recognize that consumers will move elsewhere if one store doesn't remain competitive. All low-price retailers are constantly looking for ways to improve efficiency. Furthermore, in recent months, costs of transportation and basic goods such as food have been rising, which limits the amount by which retailers can mark up their prices and still offer the best deal. Dollar General CEO Richard Dreiling recently noted that the stores were carrying more than 220 items priced at $1, and that raising the price by even 15 cents would discourage some of the company's regular customers. As Dollar General tries to maintain profitability, it will keep looking for ways to change how it does business, and technology will continue to play a role in the solutions. So far, it's a strategy that has fueled tremendous growth at Dollar General even as other retailers are struggling to maintain sales volume.

QUESTIONS

1. What types of control are important at Dollar General? Why are these important?

2. What technological innovations did Kathleen Guion introduce at Dollar General? How did these innovations support the company's strategy?

3. What challenges would you have expected Guion to face in introducing these changes? What principles of managing change would you have suggested she apply?

SOURCES: Based on "Operational Improvements Benefit Employees, Customers," *MMR*, May 17, 2010, Business & Company Resource Center, http://galenet.galegroup.com; J. Jannarone, "Will Dollar General Lead Retailers into Battle?" *The Wall Street Journal*, June 6, 2011, http://online.wsj.com; A. Zimmerman, "Dollar Stores Find Splurges Drying Up," *The Wall Street Journal*, July 11, 2011, http://online.wsj.com; C. Burritt, "Dollar Stores: More Brands, More Customers," *Bloomberg Businessweek*, July 29, 2010, http://www.businessweek.com; M. Jarzemsky, "Dollar General's Earnings Gain 15%," *The Wall Street Journal*, June 1, 2011, http://online.wsj.com; Dollar General, "About Us," http://dollargeneral.com; and Dollar General, "Dollar General Announces Kathleen Guion, Division President of Store Operations and Store Development, Will Transition to Retirement," news release, July 25, 2011, http://newscenter.dollargeneral.com.

CASE INCIDENTS

Robot Repercussion

Victor Principal, vice president of industrial relations for General Manufacturing, Inc., sat in his office reviewing the list of benefits the company expected to realize from increasing its use of industrial robots. In a few minutes, he would walk down to the labor management conference room for a meeting with Ralph McIntosh, president of the labor union local representing most of the company's industrial employees. The purpose of this meeting would be to exchange views and positions informally preliminary to the opening for formal contract negotiations later in the month, which would focus on the use of computer-integrated robotics systems and the resulting impact on employment, workers, and jobs.

Experts concluded that the impact of robot installation on employment would be profound, although the extent of the worker replacement was not clear. The inescapable conclusion was that robot usage had the capacity to increase manufacturing performance and decrease manufacturing employment.

Principal walked down to the conference room. Finding McIntosh already there, Principal stated the company's position regarding installation of industrial robots: "The company needs the cooperation of the union and our workers. We don't wish to be perceived as callously exchanging human workers for robots." Then Principal listed the major advantages associated with robots: (1) improved quality of product as a result of the accuracy of robots; (2) reduced operating costs because the per-hour operational cost of robots was about one-third of the per-hour cost of wages and benefits paid to an average employee; (3) reliability improvements because robots work tirelessly and don't require behavioral support; and (4) greater manufacturing flexibility because robots are readily reprogrammable for different jobs. Principal concluded that these advantages would make the company more competitive, which would allow it to grow and increase its workforce.

McIntosh's response was direct and strong: "We aren't Luddites racing around ruining machines. We know it's necessary to increase productivity and that robotic technology is here. But we can't give the company a blank check. We need safeguards and protection." McIntosh continued, "We intend to bargain for the following contract provisions:

1. Establishment of labor–management committees to negotiate in advance about the labor impact of robotics technology

and, of equal importance, to have a voice in deciding how and whether it should be used.

2. Rights to advance notice about installation of new technology.

3. Retraining rights for workers displaced, to include retraining for new positions in the plant, the community, or other company plants.

4. Spreading the work among workers by use of a four-day workweek or other acceptable plan as an alternative to reducing the workforce."

McIntosh's final sentence summed up the union's position: "We in the union believe the company is giving our jobs to robots to reduce the labor force."

Their meeting ended amiably, but Principal and McIntosh each knew that much hard bargaining lay ahead. As Principal returned to his office, the two opposing positions were obvious. On his yellow tablet, Principal listed the requirements as he saw them: (1) A clearly stated overall policy was needed to guide negotiation decisions and actions; (2) it was critical to decide on a company position regarding each of the union's announced demands and concerns; and (3) a plan had to be developed.

As Principal considered these challenges, he idly contemplated a robot possessing artificial intelligence and vision capability that could help him in his work. Immediately a danger alarm sounded in his mind. A robot so constructed might be more than helpful and might take over this and other important aspects of his job. Slightly chagrined, Principal returned to his task. He needed help—but not from any smart robot.

SOURCE: J. Champion and J. James, *Critical Incidents in Management: Decision and Policy Issues*, 6th ed. McGraw-Hill/Irwin, 1989. © 1989 The McGraw-Hill Companies.

Implementing Strategic Change

James Fulmer, chief executive officer of Allied Industries, reviewed three notes he had exchanged with Frank Curtis, director of fiscal affairs, now president of a company owned by Allied. The two executives were going to meet in a few minutes to discuss problems that had recently surfaced. During the past decade, Allied had aggressively pursued a growth objective based on a conglomerate strategy of acquiring companies in distress. CEO Fulmer's policy was to appoint a new chief operating officer for each acquisition with instructions to facilitate a turnaround. Fulmer reviewed two of the notes he had written to Curtis.

Date: January 15

Memorandum

To: Frank Curtis, Director of Fiscal Affairs, Allied Industries

From: James Fulmer, Chairman, Allied Industries

Subject: Your Appointment as President, Lee Medical Supplies

You are aware that Allied Industries recently acquired Lee Medical Supplies. Mr. John Lee, founder and president of the company, has agreed to retire, and I am appointing you to replace him. Our acquisitions group will brief you on the company, but I want to warn you that Lee Medical Supplies has a history of mismanagement. As a distributor of medical items, the company's sales

last year totaled approximately $300 million, with net earnings of only $12 million. Your job is to make company sales and profits compatible with Allied standards. You are reminded that it is my policy to call for an independent evaluation of company progress and your performance as president after 18 months.

Date: September 10

Memorandum

To: Frank Curtis, President, Lee Medical Supplies

From: James Fulmer, Chairman, Allied Industries

Subject: Serious Problems at Lee Medical Supplies

In accord with corporate policy, consultants recently conducted an evaluation of Lee Medical Supplies. In a relatively short period of time, you have increased sales and profits to meet Allied's standards, but I am alarmed at other aspects of your performance. I am told that during the past 18 months, three of your nine vice presidents have resigned and that you have terminated four others. An opinion survey conducted by the consultants indicates that a low state of morale exists and that your managerial appointees are regarded by their subordinates as hard-nosed perfectionists obsessed with quotas and profits. Employees report that ruthless competition now exists between divisions, regions, and districts. They also note that the collegial, family-oriented atmosphere fostered by Mr. Lee has been replaced by a dog-eat-dog situation characterized by negative management attitudes toward employee feelings and needs. After you have studied the enclosed report from the consultants, we will meet to discuss their findings. I am particularly concerned with their final conclusion that "a form of corporate cancer seems to be spreading throughout Lee Medical Supplies."

As Fulmer prepared to read the third note, written by Frank Curtis, he reflected on his interview with the consultants. Although Fulmer considered Curtis a financial expert and a turnaround specialist, his subordinates characterized Curtis as an autocrat better suited to be a marine boot camp commander.

Date: September 28
Memorandum
To: James Fulmer
From: Frank Curtis
Subject: The So-Called Serious Problems at Lee Medical Supplies

I have received your memorandum dated September 10, and reviewed the consultants' report. When you appointed me to my present position, I was instructed to take over an unprofitable company and make it profitable. I have done so in 18 months, although I inherited a family-owned business that by your own admission had been mismanaged for years. I found a group of managers and salespeople with an average company tenure of 22 years. Mr. Lee had centralized all personnel decisions so that only he could terminate an employee. He tolerated mediocre performance. All employees were paid on a straight salary basis, with seniority the sole criterion for advancement. Some emphasis was given to increasing sales each year, but none was given to reducing costs and increasing profits. Employees did indeed find the company a fun place to work, and the feeling of being a part of a family did permeate the company. Such attitudes were, however, accompanied by mediocrity, incompetence, and poor performance.

I found it necessary to implement immediate strategic changes in five areas: the organization's structure, employee rewards and incentives, management information systems, allocation of resources, and managerial leadership style. As a result, sales areas were reorganized into divisions, regions and districts. Managers who I felt were incompetent and/or lacking in commitment to my objectives and methods were replaced. Unproductive and

mediocre employees were encouraged to find jobs elsewhere. Authority for staffing and compensation decisions was decentralized to units at the division, region, and district levels. Managers of those units were informed that along with their authority went responsibility for reducing costs and for increasing sales and profits. Each unit was established as a profit center. A new department was established and charged with reviewing performance of those units. Improved accounting and control systems were implemented. A program was developed to establish standards and monitor performance. Performance appraisals are now required for all employees. To encourage more aggressive action, bonuses and incentives are offered to managers of units showing increased profits. A commission plan based on measurable sales and profit performances has replaced straight salaries. Resources are allocated to units based on their performance.

My own leadership style has probably represented the most traumatic change for employees. Internal competition is a formally mandated policy throughout the company. It has been responsible for much of the progress achieved to date. Progress, however, is never made without costs, and I recognize that employees are not having as much fun as in the past. I was employed to achieve results and not to ensure that employees remain secure and happy in their work. Don't let a few crybabies unable to adjust to changes lead you to believe that problems take precedence over profits. Does it mean that I am not people oriented if I believe it is unlikely that a spirit of aggressiveness and competitiveness can coexist with an atmosphere of cooperativeness and family orientation? Do you feel that we are obligated to employees because of past practices? Frankly, I thought I had your support to do whatever was necessary to get this company turned around. In our meeting, tell me if you think my approaches have been wrong and, if so, tell me what I should have done differently.

Just as Fulmer finished reviewing the third memorandum, his secretary informed him that Curtis had arrived for their scheduled meeting. He realized he was undecided about how to communicate to Curtis his ideas and beliefs regarding how changes in an organization can best be implemented. One thing he did know: He didn't appreciate how Curtis had expressed his views in his memorandum, but he recognized that he probably should set aside emotions and respond to the questions Curtis posed.

SOURCE: J. Champion and J. James, *Critical Incidents in Management: Decision and Policy Issues,* 6th ed. McGraw-Hill/Irwin, 1989. © 1989 The McGraw-Hill Companies.

NOTES

Chapter 1

1. Morten T. Hansen, Herminia Ibarra, and Urs Peyer, "The Best-Performing CEOs in the World," *Harvard Business Review*, January–February 2013, pp. 82–92; Adam Lashinsky, "Amazon's Jeff Bezos: The Ultimate Disrupter," *Fortune*, November 16, 2012, http://management.fortune.cnn.com; Adam Hartung, "Why Jeff Bezos Is Our Greatest Living CEO," *Forbes*, January 8, 2013, http://www.forbes.com.

2. Hansen, Ibarra, and Peyer, "The Best-Performing CEOs."

3. S. Green, F. Hassan, J. Immelt, M. Marks, and D. Meiland, "In Search of Global Leaders," *Harvard Business Review*, August 2003, pp. 38–45.

4. "World's Most Admired Companies," *Fortune*, March 19, 2012, http://money.cnn.com/magazines/fortune/.

5. John Christoffersen, "Global Ambition: GE Looks Outside U.S. for Growth," *Cincinnati Post*, January 18, 2007, downloaded from Business & Company Resource Center, http://galenet.galegroup.com.

6. Staff writer, "Bigger Abroad," *The Economist*, February 17, 2011, http://www.economist.com; David Germain, "Overseas Slice of 'Pi' Flips Hollywood Formula," *Associated Press*, February 17, 2013, http://entertainment.inquirer.net; Mfonobong Nsehe, "Hollywood, Meet Nollywood," *Forbes*, April 19, 2011, http://www.forbes.com.

7. Betsy Morris, "The Pepsi Challenge," *Fortune*, February 19, 2008, http://money.cnn.com.

8. Duane Stanford, "Africa: Coke's Last Frontier," *Bloomberg Businessweek*, October 28, 2010, http://www.businessweek.com; and Geoffrey Colvin, "The Great Shakeout," *Fortune*, March 21, 2011, pp. 111–112.

9. T. Bisoux, "Corporate CounterCulture," *BizEd*, November/December 2004, pp. 16–20, quoted on p. 19.

10. G. Huber, *The Necessary Nature of Future Firms* (Thousand Oaks, CA: Sage, 2004).

11. Jay Greene and Cliff Edwards, "Desktops Are So Twentieth Century," *BusinessWeek*, December 8, 2006, http://www.businessweek.com.

12. F. Cairncross, *The Company of the Future* (Cambridge, MA: Harvard Business School Press, 2002).

13. Jessi Hempel, "Web 2.0: The Party's Over," *Fortune*, June 1, 2010, http://tech.fortune.cnn.com.

14. Robert Austin, "Managing Knowledge Workers," *Science*, July 21, 2006, accessed at ScienceCareers.org, http://sciencecareers.sciencemag.org.

15. David Raths, "Hospital IT Departments Prescribe Portals for Physicians," *KMWorld*, February 2007, downloaded from Business & Company Resource Center, http://galenet.galegroup.com.

16. M. Hansen and B. von Oetinger, "Introducing T-Shaped Managers: Knowledge Management's Next Generation," *Harvard Business Review*, March 2001, pp. 106–16.

17. John Teresko, "Toyota's Real Secret," *Industry Week*, February 2007, downloaded from Business & Company Resource Center, http://galenet.galegroup.com.

18. Shelly Banjo, "Firms Take Online Reviews to Heart," *The Wall Street Journal*, July 29, 2012, http://online.wsj.com.

19. B. Kowitt, "Dunkin' Brands' Kitchen Crew," *Fortune*, May 24, 2010, pp. 72–74.

20. "Home and Abroad," *The Economist*, February 10, 2007, Business & Company Resource Center, http://galenet.galegroup.com; A. Wooldridge, "The World Turned Upside Down," *The Economist*, April 17, 2010, pp. 1–3.

21. Neal E. Boudette, "New U.S. Car Plants Signal Renewal for Manufacturing," *The Wall Street Journal*, January 26, 2012, http://online.wsj.com.

22. R. I. Sutton, "The Weird Rules of Creativity," *Harvard Business Review*, September 2001, pp. 94–103.

23. Laura Landro, "Hospitals Take Consumers' Advice," *The Wall Street Journal*, February 7, 2007, http://online.wsj.com.

24. O. Port, "The Kings of Quality," *BusinessWeek*, August 30, 2004, p. 20.

25. Karla Ward, "Attracting Opposites," *Lexington Herald-Leader*, December 12, 2006; and Lisa McTigue Pierce, "How to Do It 'My Way,'" *Food & Drug Packaging*, January 2007, both downloaded from Business & Company Resource Center, http://galenet.galegroup.com.

26. Pierce, "How to Do It 'My Way'"; and MyJones website, http://www.myjones.com, accessed March 9, 2007.

27. D. A. Garvin, "Manufacturing Strategic Planning," *California Management Review*, Summer 1993, pp. 85–106.

28. Bureau of Labor Statistics, "Projections Overview," *Occupational Outlook Handbook*, March 29, 2012, http://www.bls.gov.

29. Sherri Begin, "The Art of Service," *Crain's Detroit Business*, February 12, 2007, downloaded from Business & Company Resource Center, http://galenet.galegroup.com.

30. Adam Lashinsky, "Chaos by Design," *Fortune*, October 2, 2006, http://money.cnn.com.

31. Teresko, "Toyota's Real Secret."

32. Ibid.

33. Gary McWilliams, "Wal-Mart's Radio-Tracked Inventory Hits Static," *The Wall Street Journal*, February 15, 2007, http://online.wsj.com.

34. Kris Maher, "Wal-Mart Seeks New Flexibility in Worker Shifts," *The Wall Street Journal*, January 3, 2007, http://online.wsj.com.

35. S. Cendrowski, "Singapore Airlines," *Fortune*, June 14, 2010, p. 22.

36. F. Gillette, "The Duke of Discomfort," *Bloomberg Businessweek*, September 6, 2010, pp. 58–61.

37. J. Pfeffer, "Building Sustainable Organizations: The Human Factor," *Academy of Management Perspectives*, 24, pp. 34–45 (2010).

38. S. L. Hart, *Capitalism at the Crossroads*, 3rd ed., (Upper Saddle River, NJ: Wharton School Publishing, 2010).

39. P. Bisson, E. Stephenson, and S. P. Vigueire, "Global Forces: An Introduction," *McKinsey Quarterly*, June 2010, pp. 1–4.

40. Hansen, Ibarra, and Peyer, "The Best-Performing CEOs," p. 90.

41. Ben Johnson, "GE's CTO Mark Little on Tech Leaps in 2013, and 2012's Christmas Netflix Outage," *Marketplace Tech Report*, December 27, 2012, http://www.marketplace.org; Joseph Walker, "The Upside of a Demotion from Jack Welch," *FINS Technology*, January 19, 2012, http://it-jobs.fins.com; GE, "Corporate Executives: Mark M. Little," http://www.ge.com,; GE Ecomagination, "GE Electrifies the SAE 2012 World Congress," May 1, 2012, http://www.ecomagination.com.

42. B. Dumaine, "Searching for Profits in Patagonia," *Fortune*, March 21, 2011, pp. 97–105.

43. B. Doppelt, *Leading Change toward Sustainability* (Sheffield, UK: Greenleaf, 2010).

44. Vanessa Fuhrmans, "A Novel Plan Helps Hospital Wean Itself off Pricey Tests," *The Wall Street Journal*, January 12, 2007, http://online.wsj.com.

45. J. W. Cortada, *21st Century Business* (London: Financial Times/Prentice Hall, 2001).

46. D. Lepak, K. Smith, and M. S. Taylor, "Value Creation and Value Capture: A Multilevel Perspective," *Academy of Management Review* 23 (2007), pp. 180–94.

47. R. Webber, "General Management Past and Future," *Financial Times Mastering Management*, 1997.

48. Lashinsky, "Amazon's Jeff Bezos"; Debbie Hazel, "Retail's Power Players," *Chain Store Age*, January 2013, Business Insights: Essentials, http://bi.galegroup.com; Matt Warman, "Amazon: Don't Blame Us for the Revolution on the High Street," *Telegraph (London)*, October 12, 2012, Business Insights: Essentials, http://bi.galegroup.com.

49. M. Menz, "Functional Top Management Team Members: A Review, Synthesis, and Research Agenda," *Journal of Management* 38 (2012) pp. 45–80.

50. D. Kreeger, "Is Your Organization Positioned to Meet the Challenge of Climate Change?" *World Climate Change Report*, October 22, 2009, pp. 1–7.

51. C. Ren and C. Guo, "Middle Managers' Strategic Role in the Corporate Entrepreneurial Process:

Attention-based Effects," *Journal of Management* 37 (2011) pp. 1586–1610.

52. A. Raes, M. Heijltjes, U. Glunk, et al., "The Interface of the Top Management Team and Middle Managers: A Process Model," *Academy of Management Review* 36 (2011), pp. 102–126.

53. Q. N. Huy, "In Praise of Middle Managers," *Harvard Business Review*, September 2001, pp. 72–79.

54. L. A. Hill, "New Manager Development for the 21st Century," *Academy of Management Executive*, August 2004, pp. 121–26.

55. C. Bartlett and S. Goshal, "The Myth of the Generic Manager: New Personal Competencies for New Management Roles," *California Management Review* 40, no. 1 (1997), pp. 92–116.

56. Ray Fisman, "In Defense of Middle Management," *Slate*, October 13, 2010, http://www.slate.com; and Nicholas Bloom, Benn Eifert, Aprajit Mahajan, et al., "Does Management Matter? Evidence from India," NBER Working Paper 16658 (Cambridge, MA: National Bureau of Economic Research, January 2011), http://www.nber.org/papers/w16658.

57. L. R. Sayles, "Doing Things Right: A New Imperative for Middle Managers," *Organizational Dynamics*, Spring 1993, pp. 5–14.

58. H. Mintzberg, *The Nature of Managerial Work* (New York: Harper & Row, 1973).

59. R. Katz, "Skills of an Effective Administrator," *Harvard Business Review* 52 (September–October), pp. 90–102.

60. Hill, "New Manager Development for the 21st Century."

61. H. Mintzberg, "The Manager's Job: Folklore and Fact," *Harvard Business Review* 53 (July–August 1975), pp. 49–61.

62. Colin Stewart, "Program Teaches Corporate Skills to Cure What Ails Them," *Orange County Register*, December 28, 2006, downloaded from Business & Company Resource Center, http://galenet.galegroup.com.

63. "Nontraditional Path: From Pre-Med Dropout to Next Aetna CEO," *DiversityInc.*, October 28, 2010, http://diversityinc.com; and Aetna, "Executive Biographies: Mark T. Bertolini," *About Us: Corporate Profile*, http://www.aetna.com, accessed February 25, 2011.

64. Hill, "New Manager Development for the 21st Century."

65. D. Goleman, R. Boyatzis, and A. McKee, *Primal Leadership: Realizing the Power of Emotional Intelligence* (Boston: Harvard Business School Press, 2002).

66. J. Antonakis, N. Ashkanasy, and M. Dasborough, "Does Leadership Need Emotional Intelligence?" *Leadership Quarterly* 20 (2009), pp. 247–261.; E. A. Locke, "Why Emotional Intelligence Is an Invalid Concept," *Journal of Organizational Behavior* 26 (2005), pp. 425–431.; F. Walter, M. Cole, and R. Humphrey, "Emotional Intelligence:

Sine Qua Non of Leadership or Folderol?" *Academy of Management Perspectives* (2011), pp. 45–49.

67. R. Boyatzis, "Get Motivated," *Harvard Business Review*, January 2004, p. 30.

68. W. George, "Find Your Voice," *Harvard Business Review*, January 2004, p. 35.

69. Stephen Xavier, "Control Yourself: What Role Does Emotional Intelligence Play in Executive Leadership?" *US Business Review*, March 2006, downloaded from Business & Company Resource Center, http://galenet.galegroup.com.

70. Ibid.

71. W. Kiechel III, "A Manager's Career in the New Economy," *Fortune*, April 4, 1994, pp. 68–72.

72. K. Inkson and M. B. Arther, "How to Be a Successful Career Capitalist," *Organizational Dynamics*, Summer 2001, pp. 48–60.

73. Geoffrey Colvin, "What It Takes to Be Great," *Fortune*, October 19, 2006, http://money.cnn.com.

74. L. M Roberts, J. Dutton, G. Spreitzer, E. Heaphy, and R. Quinn, "Composing the Reflected Best-Self Portrait: Building Pathways for Becoming Extraordinary in Work Organizations," *Academy of Management Review* 30 (2005), pp. 712–36.

75. L. M. Roberts, "Changing Faces: Professional Image Construction in Diverse Organizational Settings," *Academy of Management Review* 30 (2005), pp. 685–711.

76. M. E. P. Seligman, *Authentic Happiness: Using the New Positive Psychology to Realize Your Potential for Lasting Fulfillment* (New York: Free Press, 2002).

77. Joann S. Lublin, "Climbing the Ladder? Join a Group," *The Wall Street Journal*, December 13, 2012, http://online.wsj.com; BlackRock Careers page, http://www2.blackrock.com; "Anne F. Ackerley: Executive Profile," *Bloomberg Businessweek Company Insight Center*, http://investing.businessweek.com.

78. E. W. Morrison, "Newcomers' Relationships: The Role of Social Network Ties during Socialization," *Academy of Management Journal* 45 (2002), pp. 1149–60.

79. R. Cotton, Y. Shen, and R. Llvne-Tarandach, "On Becoming Extraordinary: The Content and Structure of the Developmental Networks of Major League Baseball Hall of Famers," *Academy of Management Journal* 54 (2011), pp. 15–46.

80. P. Adler and S. Kwon, "Social Capital: Prospects for a New Concept," *Academy of Management Review* 27 (2002), pp. 17–40.

81. Jessi Hempel, "How LinkedIn Will Fire Up Your Career," *Fortune*, April 12, 2010, pp. 74–82.; C. Galunic, G. Ertug, and M. Gargiulo, "The Positive Externalities of Social Capital:

Benefiting from Senior Brokers," *Academy of Management Journal*, 55, 1213-1231 (2012).

82. T. Peters, *Liberation Management* (New York: Alfred A. Knopf, 1992).

83. P. Drucker, "What Makes an Effective Executive?" *Harvard Business Review*, June 2004, pp. 58–63.

84. Lashinsky, "Amazon's Jeff Bezos"; Hazel, "Retail's Power Players"; Erika Andersen, "How the Best Leaders Are Kicking Everyone Else's . . . Results," *Forbes*, February 11, 2013, http://www.forbes.com.

Appendix A

1. C. George, *The History of Management Thought* (Englewood Cliffs, NJ: Prentice-Hall, 1972).

2. Ibid.

3. A. D. Chandler, *Scale and Scope: The Dynamic of Industrial Capitalism* (Cambridge, MA: Belknap Press of Harvard University Press, 1990).

4. Ibid.

5. J. Baughman, *The History of American Management* (Englewood Cliffs, NJ: Prentice-Hall, 1969), chap. 1.

6. George, *The History of Management Thought*, chaps. 5–7; F. Taylor, *The Principles of Scientific Management* (New York: Harper & Row, 1911).

7. J. Case, "A Company of Businesspeople," *Inc.*, April 1993, pp. 70–93.

8. Schlosser and Florian, "*Fortune* 500 Amazing Facts!"

9. H. Fayol, *General and Industrial Management*, trans. C. Storrs (Marshfield, MA: Pitman Publishing, 1949).

10. George, *The History of Management Thought*, chap. 9; J. Massie, "Management Theory," in *Handbook of Organizations*, ed. J. March (Chicago: Rand McNally, 1965), pp. 387–422.

11. C. Barnard, *The Functions of the Executive* (Cambridge, MA: Harvard University Press, 1938).

12. George, *The History of Management Thought*; Massie, "Management Theory."

13. E. Mayo, *The Human Problems of Industrial Civilization* (New York: Macmillan, 1933): F. Roethlisberger and W. Dickson, *Management and the Worker* (Cambridge, MA: Harvard University Press, 1939).

14. A. Maslow, "A Theory of Human Motivation," *Psychological Review* 50 (July 1943), pp. 370–96.

15. A. Carey, "The Hawthorne Studies: A Radical Criticism," *American Sociological Review* 32, no.3 (1967), pp. 403–16.

16. M. Weber, *The Theory of Social and Economic Organizations*, trans. T. Parsons and A. Henderson (New York: Free Press, 1947).

17. George, *The History of Management Thought*, chap. 11.

18. D. McGregor, *The Human Side of Enterprise* (New York: McGraw-Hill, 1960).

19. C. Argyris, *Personality and Organization* (New York: Harper & Row, 1957).

20. R. Likert, *The Human Organization* (New York: McGraw-Hill, 1967).

21. L. von Bertalanffy, "The History and Status of General Systems Theory," *Academy of Management Journal* 15 (1972), pp. 407–26; D. Katz and R. Kahn, *The Social Psychology of Organizations*, 2nd ed. (New York: John Wiley & Sons, 1978).

22. J. Thompson, *Organizations in Action* (New York: McGraw-Hill, 1967); J. Galbraith, *Organization Design* (Reading, MA: Addison-Wesley, 1977); D. Miller and P. Friesen, *Organizations: A Quantum View* (Englewood Cliffs, NJ: Prentice-Hall, 1984).

23. R. E. Wright, " Teaching History in Business Schools: An Insider's View," *Academy of Management Learning & Education* 9 (2010), pp. 697–700.

24. S. Cummings and T. Bridgman, "The Relevant Past: Why the History of Management Should Be Critical for Our Future," *Academy of Learning & Education* 10 (2011), pp. 77–93.

Chapter 2

1. Farhad Manjoo, "The Great Tech War of 2012," *Fast Company*, October 19, 2011, http://www.fastcompany.com; Facebook, "Key Facts," Facebook newsroom, http://newsroom.fb.com; Christopher Williams, "Is Facebook Really a Mobile Company?" *Telegraph (London)*, January 31, 2013, Business Insights: Essentials, http://bi.galegroup.com; "Facebook's Flotation," *The Economist*, May 21, 2012, http://www.economist.com; "Live and Unplugged," *The Economist*, November 21, 2012, http://www.economist.com.

2. K. Galbraith, "Economy Shifts, and the Ethanol Industry Reels," *The New York Times*, November 4, 2008, http://www.nytimes.com.

3. J. Fuller and M. C. Jensen, "Just Say No to Wall Street," *Journal of Applied Corporate Finance* 14, no. 4 (Winter 2002), pp. 41–46.

4. J. Mouawad, "Oil Innovations Pump New Life into Old Wells," *The New York Times*, March 5, 2007, http://www.nytimes.com.

5. Marc Levinson, "Job Creation in the Manufacturing Revival," Congressional Research Service Report for Congress R41898, June 20, 2012, available at http://www.fas.org/sqp/crs/misc/R41898.pdf.

6. U.S. Department of Health and Human Services (DHHS), "Small Employers: Top Five Things to Know," *HealthCare .gov*, http://www.healthcare.gov; Internal Revenue Service (IRS), "Small Business Health Care Tax Credit for Small Employers," http://www.irs.gov; DHHS, "Large Employers: Insurance and Tax Information," *HealthCare.gov*, http://www.healthcare.gov; IRS, "Affordable Care Act Tax Provisions," http://www.irs.gov; and DHHS, "About the Law: Provisions of the Affordable Care Act, by Year," HealthCare.gov, http://www.healthcare.gov. Jen Wieczner, "Why Your Boss Is Dumping Your Wife," *MarketWatch*, February 22, 2013, http://www.marketwatch.com.

7. "CEO Dough," *USA Today*, January 20, 2006, http://www.usatoday.com.

8. Bureau of Labor Statistics, "Employment Projections—2008–18," news release, December 10, 2009, http://www.bls.gov/emp.

9. M. M. Hamilton, "Age 65 and Not Ready or Able to Go," *Washington Post*, January 14, 2007, http://www.washingtonpost.com.

10. Bureau of Labor Statistics, "Charting the U.S. Labor Market in 2005," June 2006, http://www.bls.gov/cps/labor2005/home.htm; and Bureau of Labor Statistics, "Back to College," *BLS Spotlight on Statistics*, September 2010, http://www.bls.gov/spotlight.

11. See, for example, B. Arnoldy, "Too Prosperous, Massachusetts Is Losing Its Labor Force," *Christian Science Monitor*, January 9, 2007, http://www.csmonitor.com.

12. Bureau of Labor Statistics, "Foreign-Born Workers: Labor Force Characteristics—2009," news release, March 19, 2010, http://www.bls.gov/cps; and BLS, "Employment Projections—2008–18."

13. Bureau of Labor Statistics, "Women in the Labor Force: A Databook," Report 1026, December 2010, http://www.bls.gov/cps/wlf-databook-2010.pdf.

14. Michael M. Grynbaum, "Health Panel Approves Restriction on Sale of Large Sugary Drinks," *New York Times*, September 13, 2012, http://www.nytimes.com; Mike Esterl, "Is This the End of the Soft-Drink Era?" *The Wall Street Journal*, January 18, 2013, http://online.wsj.com; Angela Hanson, "Middle of the Road," *Convenience Store News*, October 1, 2012, Business Insights: Essentials, http://bi.galegroup.com; Stephanie Strom, "PepsiCo, Shifting Aim, Sees Promise in Yogurt," *New York Times*, July 8, 2012, http://www.nytimes.com; Alan Richman, "Refreshing Revival," *International Food Ingredients*, Autumn 2012, Business Insights: Essentials, http://bi.galegroup.com.

15. T. Webb, "BP to Cut Production Amid Impact of Deepwater Horizon Spill," *The Observer*, January 30, 2011, http://www.guardian.co.uk; "The Shores of Recovery," *The Economist*, April 23, 2011, Business & Company Resource Center, http://galenet.galegroup.com; and C. Prentice, "Doing Business on the Gulf Coast, Post-Spill," *Bloomberg Businessweek*, April 19, 2011, http://www.businessweek.com.; Suzanne Goldenberg, "Justice Department Deal Reduces BP's Deepwater Horizon Fine by $3.4 Billion," *Guardian (London)*, February 20, 2013, http://www.guardian.co.uk.

16. Esterl, "Is This the End of the Soft-Drink Era?"; "Cola Wars, Continued: Good for You, Not for Shareholders," *The Economist*, March 17, 2012, http://www.economist.com; Alan Rappeport, "Pepsi Calls for Ceasefire in Cola Wars," *Financial Times*, April 30, 2012, http://www.ft.com.

17. "Cola Wars, Continued"; Rappeport, "Pepsi Calls for Ceasefire."

18. "Cola Wars, Continued"; Strom, "PepsiCo, Shifting Aim"; Martha C. White, "Coke and Pepsi May Be Readying Another Cola War," *NBC News*, February 14, 2012, http://www.nbcnews.com.

19. D. J. Collis and C. A. Montgomery, *Corporate Strategy: Resources and Scope of the Firm* (New York: McGraw-Hill/Irwin, 1997).

20. J. DeGaspari, "Pfizer Retrenches," *MMR*, February 12, 2007, Business & Company Resource Center, http://galenet.galegroup.com.

21. M. J. Eyring, "Learning from Tata Motors' Nano Mistakes," *Bloomberg Businessweek*, January 11, 2011, http://www.businessweek.com; and S. Philip, "Tata Motors Profit Rises 100-Fold on Jaguar Land Rover Sales," *Bloomberg Businessweek*, November 10, 2010, http://www.businessweek.com.

22. Strom, "PepsiCo, Shifting Aim"; Esterl, "Is This the End of the Soft-Drink Era?"

23. PepsiCo website, http://www.pepsico.com; Strom, "PepsiCo, Shifting Aim."

24. Danielle Kucera, "Inkling Builds a Better (and Pricier) E-Book," *Bloomberg Businessweek*, February 12, 2013, http://www.businessweek.com.

25. Richman, "Refreshing Revival."

26. Adapted from H. L. Lee and C. Billington, "The Evolution of Supply-Chain-Management Models and Practice at Hewlett-Packard," *Interfaces* 25, no. 5 (September–October 1995), pp. 42–63. See also Edward W. Davis and Robert E. Spekman, *The Extended Enterprise: Gaining Competitive Advantage through Collaborative Supply Chains* (Upper Saddle River, NJ: Prentice Hall, 2004).

27. T. Maylett and K. Vitasek, "For Closer Collaboration, Try Education," *Supply Chain Management Review*, January–February 2007, Business & Company Resource Center, http://galenet.galegroup.com.

28. M. Ramsey and S. Moffett, "Japan Parts Shortage Hits Auto Makers," *The Wall Street Journal*, March 24, 2011, http://online.wsj.com; A. Hesseldahl, "Short Supply of Japanese Electronic

Parts Hitting Global Car Industry," *All Things Digital*, March 24, 2011, http://newenterprise.allthingsd.com; and J. Bennett, "Quake Spurs Supplier," *The Wall Street Journal*, March 31, 2011, http://online.wsj.com.

29. Connie Bensen, "When Brand Advocates Become Employees: IdeaStorm PM Cy Jervis Shares Tips for Businesses," Dell Community: Social Business Connection, January 7, 2013, http://en.community.dell.com.

30. Mike Snider, "Social Media Is Latest Front of Cola Wars," *USA Today*, April 30, 2012, http://usatoday30.usatoday.com.

31. Manjoo, "The Great Tech War of 2012"; Shaaydi Raice, "Facebook Defends Ads as Quiet Period Ends," *The Wall Street Journal*, June 12, 2012, http://online.wsj.com; "Facebook: Search Me," *The Economist*, January 19, 2013, http://www.economist.com.

32. P. Kotler, *Marketing Management: Analysis, Planning, Implementation and Control*, 9th ed. (Englewood Cliffs, NJ: Prentice Hall, 1990).

33. A. A. Buchko, "Conceptualization and Measurement of Environmental Uncertainty: An Assessment of the Miles and Snow Perceived Environmental Uncertainty Scale," *Academy of Management Journal* 37, no. 2 (April 1994), pp. 410–25.

34. A. F. Hagen, "Corporate Executives and Environmental Scanning Activities: An Empirical Investigation," *SAM Advanced Management Journal* 60, no. 2 (Spring 1995), pp. 41–47; R. L. Daft, "Chief Executive Scanning, Environmental Characteristics, and Company Performance: An Empirical Study," *Strategic Management Journal* 9, no. 2 (March/April 1988), pp. 123–39; and M. Yasai-Ardekani, "Designs for Environmental Scanning Systems: Tests of a Contingency Theory," *Management Science* 42, no. 2 (February 1996), pp. 187–204.

35. S. Ghoshal, "Building Effective Intelligence Systems for Competitive Advantage," *Sloan Management Review* 28, no. 1 (Fall 1986), pp. 49–58; and K. D. Cory, "Can Competitive Intelligence Lead to a Sustainable Competitive Advantage?" *Competitive Intelligence Review* 7, no. 3 (Fall 1996), pp. 45–55.

36. P. J. H. Schoemaker, "Multiple Scenario Development: Its Conceptual and Behavioral Foundation," *Strategic Management Journal* 14, no. 3 (March 1993), pp. 193–213.

37. R. R. Peterson, "An Analysis of Contemporary Forecasting in Small Business," *Journal of Business Forecasting Methods & Systems* 15, no. 2 (Summer 1996), pp. 10–12; and S. Makridakis. "Business Forecasting for Management: Strategic Business Forecasting," *International Journal of Forecasting* 12, no. 3 (September 1996), pp. 435–37.

38. R. A. D'Aveni, *Hypercompetition—Managing the Dynamics of Strategic Maneuvering* (New York: Free Press, 1994); and M. A. Cusumano, "Strategic Maneuvering and Mass-Market Dynamics: The Triumph of VHS over Beta," *Business History Review* 66, no. 1 (Spring 1992), pp. 51–94.

39. Model adapted from C. Zeithaml and V. Zeithaml, "Environmental Management: Revising the Marketing Perspective," *Journal of Marketing*, Spring 1984. Published by the American Marketing Association.

40. Strom, "PepsiCo, Shifting Aim."

41. R. King and A. Satariano, "Apple Gets Corporate Sales Backup at Unisys," *Bloomberg Businessweek*, October 25, 2010, http://www.businessweek.com.

42. "Bayer to Axe 6,100 Jobs Worldwide after Schering Takeover," news release, March 2, 2007, *Agence France Presse*, http://www.afp.com.

43. Strom, "PepsiCo, Shifting Aim."

44. S. McGrath and J. D. Stoll, "Ford to Sell Aston Martin Unit in Deal Valued at $848 Million," *The Wall Street Journal*, March 12, 2007, http://online.wsj.com.

45. R. Miles and C. Snow, *Organizational Strategy, Structure, and Process* (New York: McGraw-Hill, 1978).

46. C. Zeithaml and V. Zeithaml, "Environmental Management: Revising the Marketing Perspective," *Journal of Marketing* 48 (Spring 1984), pp. 46–53.

47. "Washington Wire," *The Wall Street Journal*, March 16, 2007, http://blogs.wsj.com/washwire/.

48. W. P. Burgers, "Cooperative Strategy in High Technology Industries," *International Journal of Management* 13, no. 2 (June 1996), pp. 127–34; and J. E. McGee, "Cooperative Strategy and New Venture Performance: The Role of Business Strategy and Management Experience," *Strategic Management Journal* 16, no. 7 (October 1995), pp. 565–80.

49. A. Bluestein, L. Buchanan, M. Chafkin, J. Del Rey, A. Joyner, and R. McCarthy, "The Ultimate Business Tune-Up for Times Like These," *Inc.*, January 2009, http://www.inc.com.

50. Bureau of Labor Statistics, "Contingent and Alternative Employment Arrangements, February 2005," news release, July 27, 2005, http://www.bls.gov/cps/.

51. M. B. Meznar, "Buffer or Bridge? Environmental and Organizational Determinants of Public Affairs Activities in American Firms," *Academy of Management Journal* 38, no. 4 (August 1995), pp. 975–96.

52. Tammy Erickson, "The Rise of the New Contract Worker," *Harvard Business Review*, September 7, 2012, http://blogs.hbr.org; Adecco, "2012 Job Market Perspectives," http://www.adeccousa.com; "Integrating Contingent Workers," *Baseline*, January 19, 2012, Business

Insights: Essentials, http://bi.galegroup.com; "Tech Talk," *Workforce Management*, August 1, 2012, Business Insights: Essentials, http://bi.galegroup.com.

53. D. Lei, "Advanced Manufacturing Technology: Organizational Design and Strategic Flexibility," *Organization Studies* 17, no. 3 (1996), pp. 501–23; and J. W. Dean Jr. and S. A. Snell, "The Strategic Use of Integrated Manufacturing: An Empirical Examination," *Strategic Management Journal* 17, no. 6 (June 1996), pp. 459–80.

54. R. H. Kilmann, M. J. Saxton, and R. Serpa, *Gaining Control of the Corporate Culture* (San Francisco: Jossey-Bass, 1985); and K. S. Cameron and R. E. Quinn, *Diagnosing and Changing Organizational Culture: Based on the Competing Values Framework* (Englewood Cliffs, NJ: Addison-Wesley, 1998).

55. Farhad Manjoo, "How Google Became Such a Great Place to Work," *Slate*, January 21, 2013, http://www.slate.com; Nancy M. Davis, "Google's Top Recruiter," *HR Magazine*, July 2012, Business Insights: Essentials, http://bi.galegroup.com; Caitlin Kelly, "OK, Google, Take a Deep Breath," *New York Times*, February 20, 2013, Business Insights: Essentials, http://bi.galegroup.com.

56. C. Hymowitz, "In Deal-Making, Keep People in Mind," *The Wall Street Journal*, May 12, 2008, http://online.wsj.com.

57. Cameron and Quinn, *Diagnosing and Changing Organizational Culture*.

58. S. Desmidt and A. Heene, "Mission Statement Perception: Are We All on the Same Wavelength? A Case Study in a Flemish Hospital," *Health Care Management Review*, January–March 2007, Business & Company Resource Center, http://galenet.galegroup.com.

59. C. Gallo, "How Ritz-Carlton Maintains Its Mystique," *BusinessWeek*, February 13, 2007, http://www.businessweek.com.

60. R. Leifer and P. K. Mills, "An Information Processing Approach for Deciding upon Control Strategies and Reducing Control Loss in Emerging Organizations," *Journal of Management* 22, no. 1 (1996), pp. 113–37; S. A. Dellana and R. D. Hauser, "Toward Defining the Quality Culture," *Engineering Management Journal* 11, no. 2 (June 1999), pp. 11–15; and D. Cohen and L. Prusak, *In Good Company: How Social Capital Makes Organizations Work* (Cambridge, MA: Harvard Business School Press, 2001).

61. J. Koob, "Early Warnings on Culture Clash," *Mergers & Acquisitions*, July 1, 2006, Business & Company Resource Center, http://galenet.galegroup.com.

62. The Kennedy Group Ltd., "Culture vs. Climate," Kennedy Group Executive Strategies, http://thekennedygroup.com; R. L. Manning, "Development

of the Psychological Climate Scale for Small Business," *Journal of New Business Ideas and Trends* 8, no. 1 (2010), pp. 50–65, OCLC FirstSearch, http://newfirstsearch.org; and Grapevine Solutions, "Job Climate Surveys," http://www.grapevinesurveys.com.

63. Manjoo, "The Great Tech War of 2012"; *Economist*, "Live and Unplugged"; *Economist*, "Facebook: Search Me"; Mike Shields, "ESPN.com Enables Facebook's Automated Sharing," *Adweek*, March 29, 2012, http://www.adweek.com; Laurie Segall, "Facebook Charges $100 to Message Mark Zuckerberg," *CNN Money*, January 11, 2013, http://money.cnn.com; Loretta Chao, "Brazil: The Social Media Capital of the Universe," *The Wall Street Journal*, February 4, 2013, http://online.wsj.com.

Chapter 3

1. Daniel Michaels, "Innovation Is Messy Business," *The Wall Street Journal*, January 24, 2013, http://online.wsj.com; Clive Irving, "How Boeing's Dreamliner Was Grounded," *Daily Beast*, January 29, 2013, http://www.thedailybeast.com; Jon Ostrower and Joann S. Lublin, "The Two Men behind the 787," *The Wall Street Journal*, January 24, 2013, http://online.wsj.com.
2. Ann Zimmerman, "The New Logistics of Christmas," *The Wall Street Journal*, December 13, 2012, http://online.wsj.com.
3. M. Blenko, M. Mankins, and P. Rogers, "The Decision-Driven Organization," *Harvard Business Review*, June, 2010, pp. 54–62.
4. M. Magasin and F. L. Gehlen, "Unwise Decisions and Unanticipated Consequences," *Sloan Management Review* 41 (1999), pp. 47–60.
5. M. McCall and R. Kaplan, *Whatever It Takes: Decision Makers at Work* (Englewood Cliffs, NJ: Prentice-Hall, 1985); and Luda Kopeikina, "The Elements of a Clear Decision," *MIT Sloan Management Review* 47 (Winter 2006), pp. 19–20.
6. B. Bass, *Organizational Decision Making* (Homewood, IL: Richard D. Irwin, 1983).
7. J. March, "Bounded Rationality, Ambiguity, and the Engineering of Choice," *Bell Journal of Economics* 9 (1978), pp. 587–608.
8. D. Messick and M. Bazerman, "Ethical Leadership and the Psychology of Decision Making," *Sloan Management Review* (Winter 1996), pp. 9–22.
9. I., Katz and B. Willis, "A CEO's Dilemma: When Is It Safe to Hire Again?" *Bloomberg Businessweek*, 2011. pp. 22–24.
10. Alex Taylor III, "The Greatest Business Decisions of All Time: Ford," *Fortune*, October 1, 2012, http://money.cnn.com/gallery/news/companies/2012/10/01/greatest-business-decisions.fortune/index.html.

11. Susumu Ogawa and Frank T. Piller, "Reducing the Risks of New Product Development," *MIT Sloan Management Review* 47 (Winter 2006), pp. 65–71.
12. McCall and Kaplan, *Whatever It Takes*.
13. Amy Barrett, "The Case for User Reviews," *Inc.*, September 1, 2010, http://www.inc.com.
14. Barrett, "The Case for User Reviews."
15. Q. Spitzer and R. Evans, *Heads, You Win! How the Best Companies Think* (New York: Simon & Schuster, 1997).
16. C. Gettys and S. Fisher, "Hypothesis Plausibility and Hypotheses Generation," *Organizational Behavior and Human Performance* 24 (1979), pp. 93–110.
17. E. R. Alexander, "The Design of Alternatives in Organizational Contexts: A Pilot Study," *Administrative Science Quarterly* 24 (1979), pp. 382–404.
18. Ogawa and Piller, "Reducing the Risks," p. 68.
19. A. R. Rao, M. E. Bergen, and S. Davis, "How to Fight a Price War," *Harvard Business Review*, March–April 2000, pp. 107–16.
20. Barrett, "The Case for User Reviews."
21. Barrett, "The Case for User Reviews."
22. Rachel Emma Silverman, "Big Data Upends the Way Workers Are Paid," *The Wall Street Journal*, September 19, 2012, http://online.wsj.com.
23. Spitzer and Evans, *Heads, You Win!*
24. Morrill, "Sound of an IPO"; Gray, "Pandora Pulls Back the Curtain"; Bruno, "Thinking Outside the Box"; Antony Bruno, "Dashboard Confessional," *Billboard*, January 22, 2011, Business & Company Resource Center, http://galenet.galegroup.com; Clint Cooper, "Music in Motion," *Chattanooga Times/Free Press*, September 30, 2010, Business & Company Resource Center, http://galenet.galegroup.com; John Moe, "Sony's New Music Service: A Good Deal or Not?" *Marketplace*, February 17, 2011, http://www.publicradio.org; Matthew Lasar, "The Perils of Being Pandora," *Ars Technica*, February 15, 2011, http://arstechnica.com; and Andrew Hampp, "Why Pandora Is on Virtually Every Device," *Advertising Age*, January 17, 2011, http://adage.com.
25. Barrett, "The Case for User Reviews."
26. McCall and Kaplan, *Whatever It Takes*.
27. Chenda Ngak, "Report: Apple, Google Maps Debacle Sparked by Voice Navigation Disagreement," *CBS News*, September 27, 2012, http://www.cbsnews.com; Dave Thier, "The Most Hilarious Fails of Apple Maps," *Forbes*, September 21, 2012, http://www.forbes.com; Elan Dekel, "Why Did Apple Fire the Maps Product Manager?" *Forbes*, November 28, 2012, http://www.forbes.com; Caroline Henshaw, "Australia Police Warn Apple Maps Pose Danger," *The Wall Street Journal*, December 11, 2012, http://blogs.wsj.com; Nick Wingfield, "While Apple Regroups,

Google Offers a Maps App," *New York Times*, December 12, 2012, http://www.nytimes.com.
28. Barrett, "The Case for User Reviews."
29. J. Pfeffer and R. Sutton, *The Knowing–Doing Gap* (Boston: Harvard Business School Press, 2000).
30. D. Siebold, "Making Meetings More Successful," *Journal of Business Communication* 16 (Summer 1979), pp. 3–20.
31. Barrett, "The Case for User Reviews."
32. I. Janis and L. Mann, *Decision Making* (New York: Free Press, 1977); and Bass, *Organizational Decision Making*.
33. Kopeikina, "The Elements of a Clear Decision."
34. Michaels, "Innovation Is Messy Business"; Ostrower and Lublin, "The Two Men behind the 787."
35. J. W. Dean Jr. and M. Sharfman, "Does Decision Process Matter? A Study of Strategic Decision-Making Effectiveness," *Academy of Management Journal* 39 (1996), pp. 368–96.
36. R. Nisbett and L. Ross, *Human Inference: Strategies and Shortcomings* (Englewood Cliffs, NJ: Prentice-Hall, 1980).
37. Messick and Bazerman, "Ethical Leadership."
38. Phred Dvorak, "Dangers of Clinging to Solutions of the Past," *The Wall Street Journal*, March 2, 2009, http://online.wsj.com.
39. T. Bateman and C. Zeithaml, "The Psychological Context of Strategic Decisions: A Model and Convergent Experimental Findings," *Strategic Management Journal* 10 (1989), pp. 59–74.
40. Erin White, "Why Good Managers Make Bad Decisions," *The Wall Street Journal*, February 12, 2009, http://online.wsj.com.
41. D. Barton, "Capitalism for the Long Term," *Harvard Business Review*, March, 2011 pp. 84–91.
42. Messick and Bazerman, "Ethical Leadership."
43. N. Adler, *International Dimensions of Organizational Behavior* (Boston: Kent, 1990).
44. Joann S. Lublin, "Recall the Mistakes of Your Past Bosses, So You Can Do Better," *The Wall Street Journal*, January 2, 2007, http://online.wsj.com.
45. L. Perlow, G. Okhuysen, and N. Repenning, "The Speed Trap: Exploring the Relationship between Decision Making and Temporal Context," *Academy of Management Journal* 45 (2002), pp. 931–55.
46. K. M. Esenhardt, "Speed and Strategic Choice: How Managers Accelerate Decision Making," *California Management Review* 32 (Spring 1990), pp. 39–54.
47. Stephen Power and Ben Casselman, "BP, Industry Both Blamed in Gulf Spill," *The Wall Street Journal*, January 5, 2011, http://online.wsj.com; Russell Gold and Ben Casselman, "Far Offshore, a Rash of Close Calls," *The Wall Street*

Journal, December 8, 2010, http://online.wsj.com; Ben Casselman and Spencer Swartz, "BP: No Single Factor Caused Gulf Spill," *The Wall Street Journal*, September 8, 2010, http://online.wsj.com; and Russell Gold and Ben Casselman, "On Doomed Rig's Last Day, a Divisive Change of Plan," *The Wall Street Journal*, August 26, 2010, http://online.wsj.com.

48. Q. Spitzer and R. Evans, "New Problems in Problem Solving," *Across the Board*, April 1997, pp. 36–40.

49. G. W. Hill, "Group versus Individual Performance: Are $n + 1$ Heads Better than 1?" *Psychological Bulletin* 91 (1982), pp. 517–39.

50. N. R. F. Maier, "Assets and Liabilities in Group Problem Solving: The Need for an Integrative Function," *Psychological Review* 74 (1967), pp. 239–49.

51. Martin Harrysson, Estelle Metayer, and Hugo Sarrazin, "How 'Social Intelligence' Can Guide Decisions," *McKinsey Quarterly* (November 2012), https://www.mckinseyquarterly.com; "Twitter-sphere to Stratosphere," *Business Traveller*, February 27, 2013, http://www.businesstravelerusa.com; General Electric, "Virgin America and GE LEAP Forward towards the Future of Flight," *Storify*, 2011, http://storify.com.

52. Maier, "Assets and Liabilities in Group Problem Solving."

53. D. A. Garvin and M. A. Roberto, "What You Don't Know about Making Decisions," *Harvard Business Review*, September 2001, pp. 108–16.

54. Christopher Borrelli, "'Brave' Co-Director, Producer Take Up Arms to Promote Pixar's Latest," *Chicago Tribune*, June 21, 2012, http://www.chicagotribune.com.

55. A. Amason, "Distinguishing the Effects of Functional and Dysfunctional Conflict on Strategic Decision Making: Resolving a Paradox for Top Management Teams," *Academy of Management Journal* 39 (1996), pp. 123–48; and R. Dooley and G. Fyxell, "Attaining Decision Quality and Commitment from Dissent: The Moderating Effects of Loyalty and Competence in Strategic Decision-Making Teams," *Academy of Management Journal* (August 1999), pp. 389–402.

56. C. De Dreu and L. Weingart, "Task versus Relationship Conflict, Team Performance, and Team Member Satisfaction: A Meta-Analysis," *Journal of Applied Psychology* 88 (2003), pp. 741–49.

57. Cosier and Schwenk, "Agreement and Thinking Alike."

58. Ibid.

59. P. LaBerre, "The Creative Revolution," *Industry Week*, May 16, 1994, pp. 12–19.

60. J. V. Anderson, "Weirder Than Fiction: The Reality and Myths of Creativity," *Academy of Management Executive* (November 1992), pp. 40–47; J. Krohe Jr., "Managing Creativity," *Across the Board* (September 1996), pp. 17–21;

and R. I. Sutton, "The Weird Rules of Creativity," *Harvard Business Review* (September 2001), pp. 94–103.

61. K. DeStobbeleir, S. Ashford, and D. Buyens, "Self-Regulation of Creativity at Work: The Role of Feedback-Seeking Behavior in Creative Performance," *Academy of Management Journal* 54 (2011), pp. 811–831; Y. Gong, S. Cheung, M. Wang, and J. Huang, "Unfolding the Proactive Process for Creativity: Integration of the Employee Proactivity, Information Exchange, and Psychological Safety Perspectives," *Journal of Management* 38 (2010), pp. 1611–633.

62. M. Bear, "Putting Creativity to Work: The Implementation of Creative Ideas in Organizations," *Academy of Management Journal* 55 (2012), pp. 1102–1119. J. Perry-Smith and C. Shalley, "The Social Side of Creativity: A Static and Dynamic Social Network Perspective," *Academy of Management Review* 28 (2003), pp. 89–106; and J. Perry-Smith, "Social yet Creative: The Role of Social Relationships in Facilitating Individual Creativity," *Academy of Management Journal* 49 (2006), pp. 85–101.

63. "Innovation from the Ground Up," *Industry Week*, March 7, 2007, http://www.industryweek.com (interview of Erika Andersen); T. M. Amabile, "A Model of Creativity and Innovation in Organizations," in *Research in Organizational Behavior*, ed. B. Straw and L. Cummings, vol. 10 (Greenwich, CT: JAI Press, 1988), pp. 123–68.

64. T. Amabile, C. Hadley, and S. Kramer, "Creativity under the Gun," *Harvard Business Review* (August 2002), pp. 52–61.

65. Rachel Emma Silverman, "Doodling for Dollars," *The Wall Street Journal*, April 24, 2012, http://online.wsj.com.

66. S. Farmer, P. Tierney, and K. Kung-McIntyre, "Employee Creativity in Taiwan: An Application of Role Identity Theory," *Academy of Management Journal* 46 (2003), pp. 618–30.

67. "Innovation from the Ground Up."

68. L. Thompson, "Improving the Creativity of Organizational Work Groups," *Academy of Management Executive* 17 (2003), pp. 96–109.

69. J. Walter, F. Fellermanns, and C. Lechner, "Decision Making within and between Organizations: Rationality, Politics, and Alliance Performance," *Journal of Management* 38 (2012), pp. 1582–1610.

70. T. Levitt, "Creativity Is Not Enough," *Harvard Business Review* (August 2002), pp. 137–44.

71. Dean and Sharfman, "Does Decision Process Matter?"

72. K. Eisenhardt, J. Kahwajy, and L. J. Bourgeois III, "How Management Teams Can Have a Good Fight," *Harvard Management Review*, July–August 1997, pp. 77–85.

73. C. M. Pearson and I. I. Mitroff, "From Crisis Prone to Crisis Prepared: A Framework for Crisis Management," *Academy of Management Executive* (February 1993), pp. 48–59.

74. Jordan Robertson and Eileen Sullivan, "U.S. Power Grid Hacked, Officials Say," *Chicago Tribune*, April 9, 2009, http://www.chicagotribune.com.

75. S. Moore, "Disaster's Future: The Prospects for Corporate Crisis Management and Communication," *Business Horizons*, January–February 2004, pp. 29–36.

76. G. Meyers with J. Holusha, *When It Hits the Fan: Managing the Nine Crises of Business* (Boston: Houghton Mifflin, 1986); and S. Bacharach and P. Bamberger, "9/11 and New York City Firefighters' Post Hoc Unit Support and Control Climates: A Context Theory of the Consequences of Involvement in Traumatic Work-Related Events," *Academy of Management Journal* 50 (2007), pp. 849–68.

77. McCall and Kaplan, *Whatever It Takes*.

78. Leigh Buchanan, "How I Handled Myself during a Prison Riot," *Inc.*, September 1, 2010, http://www.inc.com (interview with Jerry B. Heftler).

79. J. Dutton, P. Frost, M. Worline, J. Lilius, and J. Kanov, "Leading in Times of Trauma," *Harvard Business Review* (January 2002), pp. 54–61.

80. Michaels, "Innovation Is Messy Business"; Andy Pasztor, "U.S. Sees Extended 787 Inquiry," *The Wall Street Journal*, January 24, 2013, http://online.wsj.com; Andy Pasztor, Yoree Koh, and Yoshio Takahashi, "Needed: Battery Expertise for 787 Probe," *The Wall Street Journal*, February 26, 2013, http://online.wsj.com; The Week, "Is the Boeing Dreamliner Back in Business?" *MSN Money*, February 25, 2013, http://money.msn.com.

Chapter 4

1. Jennifer Reingold, "Bob Iger: Disney's Fun King," *Fortune*, May 9, 2012, http://management.fortune.cnn.com; "Fortune 500: 66, Walt Disney," *Fortune*, May 21, 2012, http://money.cnn.com; Walt Disney Company, "Company Overview," http://thewaltdisneycompany.com; "Walt Disney Co., Burbank, CA," *ReferenceUSA*, http://referenceusa.com.

2. J. Bracker and J. Pearson, "Planning and Financial Performance of Small Mature Firms," *Strategic Management Journal* 7 (1986), pp. 503–22; and P. Waalewijn and P. Segaar, "Strategic Management: The Key to Profitability in Small Companies," *Long Range Planning* 26, no. 2 (April 1993), pp. 24–30.

3. P. Glader, "GE Taps Veteran Rice to Lead Global Operations," *The Wall Street Journal*, November 9, 2010, http://online.wsj.com.

4. S. Terlep, "GM Caps Profitable Year," *The Wall Street Journal*, February 24, 2011, http://online.wsj.com; B. Cox, "For Big Three Automakers, an Unlikely Time for a Turnaround," *Fort Worth Star-Telegram*, April 15, 2011, http://www.star-telegram.com; and D. Barkholz, "Dealers: We Want More Cars!" *Automotive News*, August 23, 2010, Business & Company Resource Center, http://galenet.galegroup.com.

5. A. Murray, "JetBlue: Now Just Another Airline in a Lousy Business," *The Wall Street Journal*, February 21, 2007, http://online.wsj.com.

6. Jennifer J. Salopek, "Investing in Ideal Customer Service," *T+D*, October 2012, Business Insights: Essentials, http://bi.galegroup.com.

7. "Measurement Takes Center Stage in Bill Gates' 2013 Letter," *NTEN Blog*, January 30, 2013, http://www.nten.org; Bill and Melinda Gates Foundation, "Who We Are: Foundation Fact Sheet," http://www.gatesfoundation.org; Bill and Melinda Gates Foundation, "Annual Letter from Bill Gates," 2013, http://annualletter.gatesfoundation.org; Bill and Melinda Gates Foundation, "A Guide to Actionable Measurement," 2010, http://docs.gatesfoundation.org.

8. D. C. Hambrick and J. W. Fredrickson, "Are You Sure You Have a Strategy?" *Academy of Management Executive* 19, no. 4 (2005), pp. 51–62.

9. Brendan Byrnes, "Playing to Win: How Procter & Gamble Increased Its Market Cap by $100 Billion," *Motley Fool*, February 27, 2013, http://www.fool.com (interview with Roger Martin); unsigned review of *Playing to Win: How Strategy Really Works*, by A. G. Lafley and Roger Martin, *The Economist*, January 12, 2013, http://www.economist.com; Dan Schawbel, "A. G. Lafley: Develop a Strategy to Win at Business," *Forbes*, February 5, 2013, http://www.forbes.com (interview with A. G. Lafley).

10. J. L. Bower and C. G. Gilbert, "How Managers' Everyday Decisions Create or Destroy Your Company's Strategy," *Harvard Business Review*, February 2007, pp. 72–79.

11. R. Kaplan and D. Norton, "Plotting Success with 'Strategy Maps,'" *Optimize*, February 2004, http://www.optimizemag.com; and R. S. Kaplan and D. P. Norton, "Having Trouble with Your Strategy? Then Map It," *Harvard Business Review*, September–October 2000.

12. Walt Disney Company, "Company Overview"; Brooks Barnes, "Disney, Struggling to Find Its Digital Footing, Overhauls Disney.com," *New York Times*, October 21, 2012, http://www.nytimes.com; Derrik J. Lang, "Disney Closing 'Epic Mickey' Video Game Developer," *Bloomberg Businessweek*, January 29, 2013, http://www.businessweek.com; Associated Press, "Disney to Shutter Online Movie Store, Website," *Bloomberg Businessweek*, November 19, 2012, http://www.businessweek.com.

13. Bower and Gilbert, "Managers' Everyday Decisions"; and "Business: Fading Fads," *The Economist*, April 22, 2000, pp. 60–61.

14. S. W. Floyd and P. J. Lane, "Strategizing throughout the Organization: Management Role Conflict in Strategic Renewal," *Academy of Management Review* 25, no. 1 (January 2000), pp. 154–77.

15. Mission statements quoted from the corporate websites: McDonald's, "Student Research," http://www.mcdonalds.com; Google, "Company," http://www.google.com; U.S. Air Force, "Our Mission," http://www.airforce.com.

16. Vision statements quoted from the organizations' websites: DuPont, "Our Company: DuPont Vision," http://www2.dupont.com; City of Redmond, "City of Redmond Vision Statement," http://www.ci.redmond.wa.us; and Great Lakes Naval Museum Association, "Vision Statement," http://www.greatlakesnavalmuseum.org.

17. A. Martin, "The Happiest Meal: Hot Profits," *The New York Times*, January 11, 2009, http://www.nytimes.com.

18. A. A. Thompson and A. J. Strickland III, *Strategic Management: Concepts and Cases*, 8th ed. (New York: Richard D. Irwin, 1995), p. 23; R. Edward Freeman, J. S. Harrison, and A. C. Wicks, *Managing for Stakeholders* (New Haven, CT: Yale University Press, 2007).

19. R. Gobel, "Inspiring Innovation," *Success*, April 2009, pp. 24–26.

20. M. Kanelios, "Full Steam Ahead for Nevada Solar Project," *CNet News.com*, March 20, 2007, http://news.com.com.

21. D. Porter, "One Man's Garbage Becomes Another's Power Plant," *Yahoo News*, October 28, 2008, http://news.yahoo.com.

22. A. Loten, "Running a Business in a Disaster Zone," *The Wall Street Journal*, December 30, 2010, http://online.wsj.com.

23. D. J. Collis and C. A. Montgomery, *Corporate Strategy: A Resource-Based Approach*, 2nd ed. (New York, McGraw-Hill/Irwin, 2005).

24. R. L. Priem, "A Consumer Perspective on Value Creation," *Academy of Management Review* 32, no. 1 (2007), pp. 219–35.

25. Jim Edwards, "Check Out the Insane Lengths Zappos Customer Service Reps Will Go To," *Business Insider*, January 9, 2012, http://articles.businessinsider.com; Zappos.com, "About," http://about.zappos.com; Mig Pascual, "Zappos: Five Out-of-the-Box Ideas for Keeping Employees Engaged," *U.S. News & World Report*, October 30, 2012, http://money.usnews.com.

26. A. Wilcox King, "Disentangling Interfirm and Intrafirm Causal Ambiguity: A Conceptual Model of Causal Ambiguity and Sustainable Competitive Advantage," *Academy of Management Review* 32, no. 1 (2007), pp. 156–78.

27. "Beware of Benchmarking Pitfalls Warns AXA Chief," *Europe Intelligence Wire*, May 13, 2010, Business & Company Resource Center, http://galenet.galegroup.com.

28. Erica Driver, "QlikTech Comes Out Strong in Gartner SWOT Analysis," *QlikCommunity Business Discovery Blog*, October 15, 2010, http://community.qlikview.com; Erica Driver, "QlikTech: A Leader in the Gartner MQ for Third Year in a Row," *QlikCommunity Business Discovery Blog*, February 28, 2013, http://community.qlikview.com; QlikView, "Gartner Research Report: 2013 Magic Quadrant for Business Intelligence and Analytics Platforms," analyst report, http://www.qlikview.com.

29. D. G. Sirmon, M. A. Hitt, and R. D. Ireland, "Managing Firm Resources in Dynamic Environments to Create Value: Looking inside the Black Box," *Academy of Management Review* 32, no. 1 (2007), pp. 273–92.

30. A. Bluestein, "The Success Gene," *Inc.*, April 2008, pp. 83–94.

31. P. Haspeslagh, "Portfolio Planning: Uses and Limits," *Harvard Business Review* 60, no. 1 (1982), pp. 58–67; R. Hamermesh, *Making Strategy Work* (New York: John Wiley & Sons, 1986); and R. A. Proctor, "Toward a New Model for Product Portfolio Analysis," *Management Decision* 28, no. 3 (1990), pp. 14–17.

32. Scott Malone, "GE to Return $18 Billion to Shareholders after Early NBC Deal," Reuters, February 13, 2013, http://www.reuters.com; Associated Press, "GE Energy and Other Firms Buy Wind Farms in France," *Bloomberg Businessweek*, January 2, 2013, http://www.businessweek.com; Julia Werdigier, "General Electric to Buy Avio for $4.3 Billion," *New York Times*, December 21, 2012, http://dealbook.nytimes.com; General Electric, "Avio Acquisition Could Create Growth Opportunities beyond Aviation: Shipping and Oil and Gas Beckon," *GE Reports*, December 21, 2012, http://www.gereports.com; General Electric, "Investor Relations," http://www.ge.com.

33. S. Higginbotham, "Cisco: What Went Wrong and What Needs to Be Fixed," *Bloomberg Businessweek*, April 7, 2011, http://www.businessweek.com; V. Heiskanen and K. Hoffmann, "Cisco to Close Flip Video-Camera Business as Part of Revamp," *Bloomberg Businessweek*, April 12, 2011, http://www.businessweek.com; I. Sidhu, *Doing Both: Capturing Today's Profit and Driving Tomorrow's Growth*, FT Press, 2010; and Associated Press, "Cisco Share Climb after CEO Promises Changes,"

Bloomberg Businessweek, April 6, 2011, http://www.businessweek.com.

34. M. Porter, *Competitive Advantage* (New York: Free Press, 1985), pp. 11–14.

35. K. Talley, "Wal-Mart Sees Shoppers' Pain," *The Wall Street Journal*, April 28, 2011, http://online.wsj.com.

36. Ben Kuchera, "How Valve 'Devalued' Video Games, and Why That's Great News for Developers and Players," *Penny Arcade Report*, April 16, 2012, http://penny-arcade.com; Dave Thier, "What Both Microsoft and Sony Can Learn from Valve's Steam Sales," *Forbes*, January 23, 2013, http://www.forbes.com; Valve, "Brazilian Payment Methods and Pricing Live on Steam," news release, November 6, 2012, http://sotre.steampowered.com; Valve, "About" page for Steam, http://store.steampowered.com/about/.

37. R. Varadarajan, "Think Small," *The Wall Street Journal*, February 14, 2007, http://online.wsj.com.

38. F. F. Suarez and G. Lanzolla, "The Role of Environmental Dynamics in Building a First Mover Advantage Theory," *Academy of Management Review* 32, no. 2 (2007), pp. 377–92.

39. Robert Trigaux, "Now Public, Outback Parent Bloomin' Brands Sets Ambitious Expansion Plan," *Tampa Bay Times*, September 5, 2012, http://www.tampabay.com.

40. J. Scheck and P. Glader, "R&D Spending Holds Steady in Slump," *The Wall Street Journal*, April 6, 2009, http://online.wsj.com.

41. R. A. Eisenstat, "Implementing Strategy: Developing a Partnership for Change," *Planning Review*, September–October 1993, pp. 33–36.

42. Jack Nicas, "Flying Spirit's 'Dollar Store in the Sky' to Profit," *The Wall Street Journal*, November 20, 2012, http://online.wsj.com.

43. Reingold, "Bob Iger"; Barnes, "Disney Struggling to Find Its Digital Footing"; Walt Disney Company, "Investor Relations," http://thewaltdisneycompany.com/investors; Daniel Rasmus, "Defining Your Company's Vision," *Fast Company*, February 28, 2012, http://www.fastcompany.com; Matthew Panzarino, "Disney and Netflix Just Pushed Streaming Video into Its Next Era," *Next Web*, December 4, 2012, http://thenextweb.com; Ethan Smith, "Disney CEO Turns Slump into a Springboard," *The Wall Street Journal*, November 8, 2010, http://online.wsj.com; Ethan Smith and Erica Orden, "Mickey, Darth Vader Join Forces in $4.05 Billion Deal," *The Wall Street Journal*, October 31, 2012, http://online.wsj.com; Associated Press, "Disney Rolls Out More Live TV Apps with Comcast," *Bloomberg Businessweek*, June 14, 2012, http://www.businessweek.com.

Chapter 5

1. Bill George, "How IBM's Sam Palmisano Redefined the Global Corporation," *HBR Blog Network: HBS Faculty*, January 18, 2012, http://blogs.hbr.org; IBM, "What Is a Smarter Planet?" http://www.ibm.com; Ann Bednarz, "IBM's Rometty Nets $16.2 Million in First Year as CEO," *Network World*, March 13, 2013, http://www.networkworld.com; Steve Lohr, "IBM's Rometty on the Data Challenge to the Culture of Management," *New York Times*, March 7, 2013, http://bits.blogs.nytimes.com; Steve Lohr, "The 2012 Patent Rankings: IBM on Top (Again), Google and Apple Surging," *New York Times*, January 10, 2013, http://bits.blogs.nytimes.com.

2. V. Anand, B. Ashforth, and M. Joshi, "Business as Usual: The Acceptance and Perpetuation of Corruption in Organizations," *Academy of Management Executive* (May 2004), pp. 39–53; and B. Ashforth, D. Gioia, S. Robinson, and L. Trevino, "Re-viewing Organizational Corruption," *Academy of Management Review* 33 (July 2008), 670–684.

3. Edelman Berland, "2013 Edelman Trust Barometer: Executive Summary," http://www.edelman.com.

4. M. Banaji, M. Bazerman, and D. Chugh, "How (Un)Ethical Are You?" *Harvard Business Review*, December 2003, pp. 56–64.

5. S. L. Grover, "The Truth, the Whole Truth, and Nothing but the Truth: The Causes and Management of Workplace Lying," *Academy of Management Executive* 19 (May 2005), pp. 148–57.

6. D. Gelles, "Blogs That Spin a Web of Deception," *Financial Times*, February 12, 2009, Business & Company Resource Center, http://galenet.galegroup.com.

7. M. E. Guy, *Ethical Decision Making in Everyday Work Situations* (New York: Quorum Books, 1990).

8. O. C. Ferrell and J. Fraedrich, *Business Ethics: Ethical Decision Making and Cases*, 3rd ed. (Boston: Houghton Mifflin, 1997).

9. Ibid.

10. Guy, *Ethical Decision Making*.

11. This fictional example is based on ideas from Business Ethics Alliance, "Practice Ethical Scenario: Moral Courage," Creighton University Collect of Business, February 26, 2013, http://www.businessethicsalliance.org; Michael Josephson, "Business Ethics Insight: The Power of Integrity," Josephson Institute blog, November 3, 2012, http://josephsoninstitute.org; Alina Tugend, "Doing the Right Thing, Whatever That Is," *New York Times*, September 21, 2012, http://www.nytimes.com.

12. Ferrell and Fraedrich, *Business Ethics*.

13. J. Hechinger and D. Armstrong, "Universities Resolve Kickback Allegations," *The Wall Street Journal*, April 3, 2007, http://online.wsj.com; J. Hechinger, "Probe into College–Lender Ties Widens," *The Wall Street Journal*, April 5, 2007, http://online.wsj.com; and Associated Press, "CIT Executives Placed on Leave Amid Student Loan Investigation," *The Wall Street Journal*, April 9, 2007, http://online.wsj.com.

14. Hechinger and Armstrong, "Universities Resolve Kickback Allegations"; and AP, "CIT Executives."

15. A. Spicer, T. Dunfee, and W. Biley, "Does National Context Matter in Ethical Decision Making? An Empirical Test of Integrative Social Contracts Theory," *Academy of Management Journal* 47 (2004), pp. 610–20; W. Bailey and A. Spicer, "When Does National Identity Matter? Convergence and Divergence in International Business Ethics," *Academy of Management Journal*, 2007, 1462–80; and K. Martin, J. Cullen, J. Johnson, and K. Parboteeah, "Deciding to Bribe: A Cross-Level Analysis of Firm and Home Country Influences on Bribery Activity," *Academy of Management Journal*, 2007, 1401–22.

16. L. Kohlberg and D. Candee, "The Relationship of Moral Judgment to Moral Action" in *Morality, Moral Behavior, and Moral Development*, ed. W. M. Kurtines and J. L. Gerwitz (New York: John Wiley & Sons, 1984).

17. L. K. Trevino, "Ethical Decision Making in Organizations: A Person–Situation Interactionist Model," *Academy of Management Review*, 1992, pp. 601–17.

18. S. Hannah, B. Avolio, and D. May, "Moral Maturation and Moral Conation: A Capacity Approach to Explaining Moral Thought and Action," *Academy of Management Review* 36 (2011), pp. 663–685.

19. For more in-depth discussion of the ethical alternatives, see Josephson, "Business Ethics Insight"; Tugend, "Doing the Right Thing."

20. A. Crane, "Modern Slavery as a Management Practice: Exploring the Conditions and Capabilities for Human Exploitation," *Academy of Management Review* 38 (2013), pp. 49–69.

21. J. Badarocco Jr. and A. Webb, "Business Ethics: A View from the Trenches," *California Management Review*, Winter 1995, pp. 8–28; and G. Laczniak, M. Berkowitz, R. Brookes, and J. Hale, "The Business of Ethics: Improving or Deteriorating?" *Business Horizons*, January–February 1995, pp. 39–47.

22. "Survey: Managers Rate High on Ethics, Professionalism," *Chief Learning Officer*, October 16, 2012, http://clomedia.com

23. J. Kammeyer-Mueller, L. Simon, and B. Rich, "The Psychic Cost of Doing Wrong: Ethical Conflict, Divestiture Socialization, and Emotional Exhaustion," *Journal of Management* 38 (2012), pp. 784–808.

24. Anand, Ashforth, and Joshi, "Business as Usual."
25. S. Glover, "SOX Compliance Proves Beneficial to Organizations, Fuels Risk Consciousness," *National Underwriter Property & Casualty*, November 15, 2010, pp. 34, 36; and P. Sweeney, "Will New Regulations Deter Corporate Fraud?" *Financial Executive*, January–February 2011, pp. 54–57.
26. R. E. Allinson, "A Call for Ethically Centered Management," *Academy of Management Executive*, February 1995, pp. 73–76.
27. R. T. De George, *Business Ethics*, 3rd ed. (New York: Macmillan, 1990).
28. B. W. Heineman Jr., "Avoiding Integrity Land Mines," *Harvard Business Review*, April 2007, pp. 100–108.
29. Leslie Kwoh, "Go Ahead and Take Off, for as Long as You Like," *The Wall Street Journal*, October 26, 2012, http://online.wsj.com; Plante Moran, "Red Frog Events," Perspectives, February 20, 2013, http://www.plantemoran.com; Joe Reynolds, "Give Your Employees Unlimited Vacation Days," *Inc.*, January 5, 2012, http://www.inc.com; "Red Frog Events," Inc. 500 Profiles, *Inc.*, http://www.inc.com; Illinois State University, "Red Frog Events," *News and Views*, September 2011, http://blogs.ilstu.edu.
30. R. A. Cooke, "Danger Signs of Unethical Behavior: How to Determine If Your Firm Is at Ethical Risk," *Journal of Business Ethics*, April 1991, pp. 249–53.
31. L. K. Trevino and M. Brown, "Managing to Be Ethical: Debunking Five Business Ethics Myths," *Academy of Management Executive*, May 2004, pp. 69–81.
32. Ibid.
33. Heineman, "Avoiding Integrity Land Mines."
34. D. Messick and M. Bazerman, "Ethical Leadership and the Psychology of Decision Making," *Sloan Management Review*, Winter 1996, pp. 9–22.
35. C. Handy, *Beyond Uncertainty: The Changing Worlds of Organizations* (Boston: Harvard Business School Press, 1996).
36. J. Stevens, H. Steensma, D. Harrison, and P. Cochran, "Symbolic or Substantive Document? The Influence of Ethics Codes on Financial Executives' Decisions," *Strategic Management Journal* 26 (2005), pp. 181–95; and J. Weber, "Does It Take an Economic Village to Raise an Ethical Company?" *Academy of Management Executive* 19 (May 2005), pp. 158–59.
37. J. B. Ciulla, "Why Is Business Talking about Ethics? Reflections on Foreign Conversations," *California Management Review*, Fall 1991, pp. 67–80.
38. R. J. Zablow, "Creating and Sustaining an Ethical Workplace: Ethics Resource Center (ERC)," "Code Construction and Content," *The Ethics Resource Center Toolkit*, http://www.ethics.org; and J. Brown, "Ten Writing Tips for Creating an Effective Code of Conduct," Ethics Resource Center, http://www.ethics.org.
39. G. R. Weaver, L. K. Trevino, and P. L. Cochran, "Corporate Ethics Programs as Control Systems: Influences of Executive Commitment and Environmental Factors," *Academy of Management Journal* 42 (1999), pp. 41–57.
40. L. S. Paine, "Managing for Organizational Integrity," *Harvard Business Review*, March–April 1994, pp. 106–17.
41. F. Hall and E. Hall, "The ADA: Going beyond the Law," *Academy of Management Executive*, February 1994, pp. 7–13; and A. Farnham, "Brushing Up Your Vision Thing," *Fortune*, May 1, 1995, p. 129.
42. Trevino and Brown, "Managing to Be Ethical," p. 70.
43. Ibid.
44. Banaji, Bazerman, and Chugh, "How (Un)Ethical Are You?"
45. B. Gunia, L. Wang, L. Huang, J. Wang, and K. Murnighan, "Contemplation and Conversation: Subtle Influences on Moral Decision Making," *Academy of Management Journal* 55 (2012), pp. 13–33.
46. Anand, Ashforth, and Joshi, "Business as Usual"; and Remi Trudel and June Cotte, "Does Being Ethical Pay?" *The Wall Street Journal*, May 12, 2008, http://online.wsj.com.
47. T. Thomas, J. Schermerhorn Jr. and J. Dienhart, "Strategic Leadership of Ethical Behavior in Business," *Academy of Management Executive*, May 2004, pp. 56–66.
48. Trevino and Brown, "Managing to Be Ethical."
49. B. Rokos and J. Katzanek, "325 Could Lose Jobs When Hemet Call Center Closes," *Press-Enterprise (Riverside, Calif.)*, August 5, 2010, Business & Company Resource Center, http://galenet.galegroup.com; and B. Rokos, "Hilton Call Center Employees in Hemet Trained Overseas Workers before Losing Jobs," *Press-Enterprise (Riverside, Calif.)*, August 13, 2010, Business & Company Resource Center, http://galenet.galegroup.com.
50. M. E. Schreiber and D. R. Marshall, "Reducing the Risk of Whistleblower Complaints," *Risk Management* 53, no. 11 (November 2006), OCLC FirstSearch, http://firstsearch.oclc.org.
51. George, "How IBM's Sam Palmisano Redefined the Global Corporation"; Leigh Nakanishi, "Technology's Achilles' Heel," Edelman Conversations: Global Practices, January 28, 2013, http://www.edelman.com; IBM, "IBM Policies," About IBM, http://www.ibm.com; IBM, "Our Values," IBM Employment, http://www-03.ibm.com; Christopher M. Matthews, "Judge Limits Requirements to IBM, SEC Settlement," *The Wall Street Journal*, February 4, 2013, http://blogs.wsj.com.
52. R. Bies, J. Bartunek, T. Fort, and M. Zald, "Corporations as Social Change Agents: Individual, Interpersonal, Institutional, and Environmental Dynamics," *Academy of Management Review*, 2007, pp. 788–93. B. Liodice, "10 Companies with Social Responsibility at the Core," *AdvertisingAge* (April 19, 2010).
53. L. Preston and J. Post, eds., *Private Management and Public Policy* (Englewood Cliffs, NJ: Prentice-Hall, 1975).
54. Ferrell and Fraedrich, *Business Ethics*.
55. H. Aguinis and A. Glavas, "What We Know and Don't Know about Corporate Social Responsibility: A Review and Research Agenda," *Journal of Management* (2012), pp. 932–968.
56. D. Matten and J. Moon, "'Implicit' and 'Explicit' CSR: A Conceptual Framework for a Comparative Understanding of Corporate Social Responsibility," *Academy of Management Review*, 2008, pp. 404–24.
57. A. Carroll, "Managing Ethically with Global Stakeholders: A Present and Future Challenge," *Academy of Management Executive*, May 2004, pp. 114–20.
58. L. Etter, "Smithfield to Phase Out Crates," *The Wall Street Journal*, January 25, 2007, http://online.wsj.com.
59. P. C. Godfrey, "The Relationship between Corporate Philanthropy and Shareholder Wealth: A Risk Management Perspective," *Academy of Management Review* 30 (2005), pp. 777–98. H. Wang and C. Qian, "Corporate Philanthropy and Corporate Financial Performance: The Roles of Stakeholder Response and Political Access," *Academy of Management Journal* 54 (2011), pp. 1159–1181.
60. R. Giacalone, "A Transcendent Business Education for the 21st Century," *Academy of Management Learning & Education*, 2004, pp. 415–20.
61. M. Witzel, "Not for Wealth Alone: The Rise of Business Ethics," *Financial Times Mastering Management Review*, November 1999, pp. 14–19.
62. D. C. Korten, *When Corporations Ruled the World* (San Francisco: Berrett-Koehler, 1995).
63. Handy, *Beyond Uncertainty*.
64. D. Barton, "Capitalism for the Long Term," *Harvard Business Review*, March 2011, pp. 84–91.
65. D. Quinn and T. Jones, "An Agent Morality View of Business Policy," *Academy of Management Review* 20 (1995), pp. 22–42.
66. B. McKay, "Why Coke Aims to Slake Global Thirst for Safe Water," *The Wall Street Journal*, March 15, 2007, http://online.wsj.com.

67. N. Varchaver, "Chemical Reaction," *Fortune*, April 2, 2007, Business & Company Resource Center, http://galenet.galegroup.com.
68. D. Schuler and M. Cording, "A Corporate Social Performance–Corporate Financial Performance Behavioral Model for Consumers," *Academy of Management Review* 31 (2006), pp. 540–58.
69. M. Orlitzky, F. Schmidt, and S. Rynes, "Corporate Social and Financial Performance: A Meta-Analysis," *Organization Studies*, 24 (2003), pp. 403–41. J. Peloza, "The Challenge of Measuring Financial Impacts from Investments in Corporate Social Performance," *Journal of Management* 35 (2009), pp. 1518–1541.
70. D. Turban and D. Greening, "Corporate Social Performance and Organizational Attractiveness to Prospective Employees," *Academy of Management Journal* 40 (1997), pp. 658–72.
71. A. McWilliams and D. Siegel, "Corporate Social Responsibility: A Theory of the Firm Perspective," *Academy of Management Review* 26 (2001), pp. 117–27.
72. S. L. Hart and M. B. Milstein, "Global Sustainability and the Creative Destructions of Industries," *Sloan Management Review*, Fall 1999, pp. 23–33.
73. P. M. Senge and G. Carstedt, "Innovating Our Way to the Next Industrial Revolution," *Sloan Management Review*, Winter 2001, pp. 24–38.
74. C.K. Prahalad and M.R. Rangaswami, "Why Sustainability Is Now the Key Driver of Innovation," *Harvard Business Review*, September 2009, pp. 56–64.
75. Y. Chouinard, J. Ellison, and R. Ridgeway, "The Sustainable Economy," *Harvard Business Review* (October 2011), pp. 52–62.
76. C. Holliday, "Sustainable Growth, the DuPont Way," *Harvard Business Review*, September 2001, pp. 129–34. P. Bansal and K. Roth, "Why Companies Go Green: A Model of Ecological Responsiveness," *Academy of Management Journal* 43 (2000), pp. 717–736.
77. D. Lubin and D. Esty, "The Sustainability Imperative," *Harvard Business Review*, May 2010, pp. 42–50. R. Nidumolu, C. K. Prahalad, and M. R. Rangaswami, "Why Sustainability Is Now the Key Driver of Innovation," *Harvard Business Review* (September 2009), pp. 57–64.
78. P. Shrivastava, "Ecocentric Management for a Risk Society," *Academy of Management Review* 20 (1995), pp. 118–37.
79. Ibid.
80. Ibid.
81. "3M Deploys ChargePoint Electric Vehicle Charging Station at HQ," *Manufacturing Close-Up*, February 16, 2011, Business & Company Resource Center, http://galenet.galegroup.com.
82. M. Herbst, "Gore Rings a Green Alarm," *BusinessWeek*, March 22, 2007;

E. Osnos, "In China's Toxic Air, Winds of Change," *Chicago Tribune*, March 13, 2007; and Xinhua News Agency, "Unclean Drinking Water Threatens Health of 320M Chinese: Report," *BBC Monitoring International Reports*, March 13, 2007, all downloaded from Business & Company Resource Center, http://galenet.galegroup.com.
83. K. Haanaes, D. Michael, J. Jurgens, and S. Rangan, "Making Sustainability Profitable," *Harvard Business Review* (March 2013), pp. 110–114.
84. Shrivastava, "Ecocentric Management."
85. M. Gunther, "Green Is Good," *Fortune*, March 22, 2007, http://money.cnn.com;
86. S. Waddock, "Leadership Integrity in a Fractured Knowledge World," *Academy of Management Learning & Education*, 2007, pp. 543–57.
87. R. Martin and A. Kemper, "Saving the Planet: A Tale of Two Strategies," *Harvard Business Review* (April 2012), pp. 48–56.
88. J. O'Toole, "Do Good, Do Well: The Business Enterprise Trust Awards," *California Management Review*, Spring 1991, pp. 9–24 and Shrivastava, "Ecocentric Management."
89. B. Doppelt, *Leading Change toward Sustainability* (Sheffield, UK: Greenleaf, 2010).
90. Ibid.
91. M. Russo and P. Fouts, "A Resource-Based Perspective on Corporate Environmental Performance and Profitability," *Academy of Management Journal* 40 (1997), pp. 534–59; and R. D. Klassen and D. Clay Whybark, "The Impact of Environmental Technologies on Manufacturing Performance," *Academy of Management Journal* 42 (1999), pp. 599–615.
92. G. Unruh and R. Etternson, "Growing Green," *Harvard Business Review*, June 2010, pp. 94–100.
93. Ibid.
94. Ibid.
95. Ibid.
96. Siemens USA, "Energy Efficiency," http://www.usa.siemens.com; Devan Schwartz, "Sky Lakes, Siemens Team Up for Energy Efficiency," *Herald and News (Klamath Falls, OR)*, January 30, 2013, http://www.heraldandnews.com.
97. G. Colvin, "The King of Water," *Fortune*, July 5, 2010, pp. 52–59.
98. "Water as a Scarce Resource: An Interview with Nestle's Chairman," *McKinsey Quarterly*, 2010, Issue 1, pp. 76–80.
99. J. Ball, "Green Goal of 'Carbon Neutrality' Hits Limit," *The Wall Street Journal*, December 30, 2008, http://online.wsj.com; and Google Inc., "Going Green at Google," Corporate Overview: Green Initiatives, Google Corporate home page, http://www.google.com/corporate/green/.
100. J. Rogers, "The CEO of Duke Energy on Learning to Work with

Green Activists," *Harvard Business Review* (May 2011), pp. 51–54; and M. Tercek and J. Adams, *Nature's Fortune* (New York: Basic Books, 2013).
101. G. Pinchot and E. Pinchot, *The Intelligent Organization* (San Francisco: Berrett-Koehler, 1996). S. L. Hart, *Capitalism as the Crossroads*, 3rd ed. (Upper Saddle River, NJ: Wharton School Publishing, 2010).
102. M. Tercek and J. Adams, *Nature's Fortune*.
103. Chouinard et al., "The Sustainable Economy."
104. Ibid.
105. Ibid.
106. B. McKibben, "Global Warming's Terrifying Math," Rolling Stone (2012) http://www.rollingstone.com/politics/news/global-warmings-terrifying-new-math-20120719; B. Smit and J. Wandel, "Adaptation, Adaptive Capacity and Vulnerability," *Global Environmental Change* 16 (2006), pp. 282–292; Tercek and Adams, *Nature's Fortune*; E. Weber and P. Stern, "Public Understanding of Climate Change in the United States," *American Psychologist* 66 (2011), pp. 315–328.
107. S. L. Hart, "Beyond Greening: Strategies for a Sustainable World," *Harvard Business Review*, January–February 1997, pp. 66–76.
108. IBM, "Responsibility at IBM," About IBM, http://www.ibm.com; IBM, "IBM Policies"; Jen Crozier, "Urban Challenges," *Citizen IBM Blog*, November 14, 2012, http://citizenibm.com; IBM, "EPA Recognizes IBM for Climate Change Leadership," news release, March 1, 2013, http://www.ibm.com; IBM, "Sustainability on a Smarter Planet," Smarter Planet: Sustainability, http://www.ibm.com; Nick Zieminski, "IBM's 'Building Whisperer' Sees Retrofit Boom," *Chicago Tribune*, May 8, 2012, http://articles.chicagotribune.com; Verne Kopytoff, "The Complex Business of Recycling E-Waste," *Bloomberg Businessweek*, January 8, 2013, http://www.businessweek.com; IBM, "IBM's Energy Program Saves $43 Million and Avoids 175,000 Metric Tons of CO^2 Emissions," news release, July 2, 2012, http://www-03.ibm.com.

Appendix B

1. P. Hawken, A. Lovins, and L. Hunter Lovins, *Natural Capitalism* (Boston: Little Brown, 1999).
2. F. Rice, "Who Scores Best on the Environment?" *Fortune*, July 26, 1993, p. 114–22.
3. Stavins, "The Challenge of Going Green."
4. F. B. Cross, "The Weaning of the Green: Environmentalism Comes of Age in the 1990s," *Business Horizons*, September–October 1990, pp. 40–46.
5. Stavins, "The Challenge of Going Green."

6. J. Singh, "Making Business Sense of Environmental Compliance," *Sloan Management Review*, Spring 2000, pp. 91–100.

7. H. Ellison, "Saving Nature While Earning Money," *International Herald Tribune*, June 23, 1997, p. 18.

8. E. Smith and V. Cahan, "The Greening of Corporate America," *BusinessWeek*, April 23, 1990, pp. 96–103.

9. M. E. Porter, "America's Green Strategy," *Science*, April 1991, p. 168.

10. A. Kleiner, "What Does It Mean to Be Green?" *Harvard Business Review*, July–August 1991, pp. 38–47.

11. D. C. Kinlaw, *Competitive and Green: Sustainable Performance in the Environmental Age* (Amsterdam: Pfeiffer & Co., 1993).

12. Rice, "Who Scores Best on the Environment?"

13. Rice, "Who Scores Best on the Environment?"; J. O'Toole, "Do Good, Do Well: The Business Enterprise Trust Awards," *California Management Review*, Spring 1991, pp. 9–24.

14. O'Toole, "Do Good, Do Well."

15. G. Hardin, "The Tragedy of the Commons," *Science* 162 (1968), pp. 1243–48.

16. D. Kirkpatrick, "Environmentalism: The New Crusade," *Fortune*, February 12, 1990, pp. 44–55.

17. Ibid.

18. R. Carson, *Silent Spring* (Boston: Houghton Mifflin, 1962); R. Paehlke, *Environmentalism and the Future of Progressive Politics* (New Haven, CT: Yale University Press, 1989), pp. 13–41, 76–143; R. Nash, ed., *The American Environment* (Reading, MA: Addison-Wesley, 1968); R. Revelle and H. Landsberg, eds., *America's Changing Environment* (Boston: Beacon Press, 1970); L. Caldwell, *Environment: A Challenge to Modern Society* (Garden City, NY: Anchor Books, 1971); and J. M. Petulla, *Environmental Protection in the United States* (San Francisco: San Francisco Study Center, 1987).

19. B. Commoner, *Science and Survival* (New York: Viking Press, 1963); and B. Commoner, *The Closing Circle: Nature, Man and Technology* (New York: Bantam Books; 1971).

20. R. Paehlke, *Environmentalism and the Future of Progressive Politics* (New Haven: Yale University Press, 1989).

21. P. Shrivastava, "Ecocentric Management for a Risk Society," *Academy of Management Review* 20 (1995), pp. 118–37.

22. Commoner, *The Closing Circle*.

23. Paehlke, *Environmentalism*.

24. Ibid.

25. Ibid.

26. P. Hawken, J. Ogilvy, and P. Schwartz, *Seven Tomorrows: Toward a Voluntary History* (New York: Bantam Books, 1982); and Paehlke, *Environmentalism*.

27. Porter, "America's Green Strategy."

28. R. Y. K. Chan, "An Emerging Green Market in China: Myth or Reality?" *Business Horizons*, March–April 2000, pp. 55–60.

29. S. Waddock and N. Smith, "Corporate Responsibility Audits: Doing Well by Doing Good," *Sloan Management Review*, Winter 2000, pp. 75–83.

30. C. Morrison, *Managing Environmental Affairs: Corporate Practices in the U.S., Canada, and Europe* (New York: Conference Board, 1991).

31. Ibid.

32. Kleiner, "What Does It Mean to Be Green?"

33. K. Fischer and J. Schot, *Environmental Strategies for Industry* (Washington, DC: Island Press, 1993).

34. J. Howard, J. Nash, and J. Ehrenfeld, "Standard or Smokescreen? Implementation of a Voluntary Environmental Code," *California Management Review*, Winter 2000, pp. 63–82.

35. Rice, "Who Scores Best on the Environment?"

36. C. Lockwood, "Building the Green Way," *Harvard Business Review* (June 2006), pp. 129–137.

37. G. Unruh, "The Biosphere Rules," *Harvard Business Review* (February 2008), pp. 111–117.

38. Rice, "Who Scores Best on the Environment?"

39. Ibid.

40. W. S. Laufer, "Social Accountability and Corporate Greenwashing," *Journal of Business Ethics* 43 (2003), pp. 253–61.

41. S. Hart and M. Milstein, "Global Sustainability and the Creative Destruction of Industries," *Sloan Management Review*, Fall 1999, pp. 23–32; Ellison, "Saving Nature While Earning Money."

42. J. Elkington and T. Burke, *The Green Capitalists* (London: Victor Gullanez, 1989); and M. Zetlin, "The Greening of Corporate America," *Management Review*, June 1990, pp. 10–17.

43. Smith and Cahan, "The Greening of Corporate America."

44. J. Carey, "Global Warming," *BusinessWeek*, August 16, 2004, pp. 60–69.

45. J. Stevens, "Assessing the Health Risks of Incinerating Garbage," *EURA Reporter*, October 1989, pp. 6–10.

46. Carey, "Global Warming."

47. A. Lovins, L. Hunter Lovins, and P. Hawken, "A Road Map for Natural Capitalism," *Harvard Business Review*, May–June 1999, pp. 145–58.

48. A. Kolk, "Green Reporting," *Harvard Business Review*, January–February 2000, pp. 15–16.

49. L. Blumberg and R. Gottlieb, "The Resurrection of Incineration" and "The Economic Factors," in *War on Waste*, ed. L. Blumberg and R. Gottlieb (Washington, DC: Island Press, 1989).

50. Carey, "Global Warming."

51. L. Blumberg and R. Gottlieb, "Recycling's Unrealized Promise," in *Business Horizons*, March–April 2000, pp. 55–60.

52. Carey, "Global Warming."

53. Lovins, Lovins, and Hawken, "A Road Map for Natural Capitalism."

54. J. Elkington, "Towards the Sustainable Corporation: Win-Win-Win Business Strategies for Sustainable Development," *California Management Review*, Winter 1994, pp. 90–100.

55. Lovins, Lovins, and Hawken, "A Road Map for Natural Capitalism."

56. R. Nidumolu, C. K. Prahalad, and M. R. Rangaswami, "Why Sustainability Is Now the Key Driver of Innovation," *Harvard Business Review* (September 2009), pp. 57–64.

57. Carey, "Global Warming."

58. Dechant and Altman, "Environmental Leadership."

59. H. Ellison, "Joint Implementation Promotes Cooperation on World Climate," *International Herald Tribune*, June 23, 1997, p. 21.

60. Corbett and Van Wassenhove, "The Green Fee."

61. Polansky and Rosenberger, "Reevaluating Green Marketing."

62. Carey, "Global Warming."

63. D. Lubin and D. Esty, "The Sustainability Imperative," *Harvard Business Review* 42 (May 2010), pp. 42–50.

64. R. D. Klassen and D. Clay Whybark, "The Impact of Environmental Technologies on Manufacturing Performance," *Academy of Management Journal* 42 (1999), pp. 599–615.

65. D. Machalaba, "New Recyclables Market Emerges: Plastic Railroad Ties," *The Wall Street Journal*, October 19, 2004, p. B1.

66. Hart and Milstein, "Global Sustainability."

67. Ibid.

68. Ibid.

69. D. Lubin and D. Esty, "The Sustainability Imperative," *Harvard Business Review*, May 2010, pp. 42–50.

70. Martin and Kemper, "Saving the Planet," pp. 48–56.

71. Nidumolu et al., "Why Sustainability Is Now the Key Driver of Innovation."

72. Polansky and Rosenberger, "Reevaluating Green Marketing."

73. Hart and Milstein, "Global Sustainability."

74. A. Beard and R. Hornik, "It's Hard to Be Good," *Harvard Business Review* (November 2011), pp. 88–96.

75. Nidumolu et al., "Why Sustainability Is Now the Key Driver of Innovation."

76. Martin and Kemper, "Saving the Planet."

77. Hart and Milstein, "Global Sustainability."

78. M. Fong, "Soy Underwear? China Targets Eco-Friendly Clothes Market," *The Wall Street Journal*, December 17, 2004, pp. B1, B4.

79. Polansky and Rosenberger, "Reevaluating Green Marketing."

80. Nidumolu et al., "Why Sustainability Is Now the Key Driver of Innovation."

81. Polansky and Rosenberger, "Reevaluating Green Marketing."

82. Elkington, "Towards the Sustainable Corporation."

83. F. S. Rowland, "Chlorofluorocarbons and the Depletion of Stratospheric Ozone," *American Scientist*, January–February 1989, pp. 36–45.

84. Elkington, "Towards the Sustainable Corporation."

85. Y. Chouinard, J. Ellison, and R. Ridgeway, "The Sustainable Economy," *Harvard Business Review* (October 2011), pp. 52–62.

86. M. Lubber, "Sustainability: Ending the 'Tyranny of Short-Termism,'" April 1, 2011, www.ceres.org.

87. Ibid.

88. H. Ellison, "The Balance Sheet," *International Herald Tribune*, June 23, 1997, p. 21.

89. P. B. Gray and D. Devlin, "Heroes of Small Business," *Fortune Small Business*, November 2000, pp. 50–64.

Chapter 6

1. Loretta Chao, "As Rivals Outsource, Lenovo Keeps Production In-House," *The Wall Street Journal*, July 9, 2012, http://online.wsj.com; Saabira Chaudhuri, "Is the End of the PC Market Closer than We Think?" *The Wall Street Journal*, January 14, 2013, http://blogs.wsj.com; Bruce Einhorn, "Lenovo's Persistent PC Strategy in India," *Bloomberg Businessweek*, November 6, 2012, http://www.businessweek.com; Joe McDonald, "Lenovo Profit Boosted by Smartphones, Tablets," *Bloomberg Businessweek*, January 30, 2013, http://www.businessweek.com; Paul Mozur, "Lenovo Profit Rose in Latest Quarter," *The Wall Street Journal*, January 30, 2013, http://online.wsj.com; Loretta Chao, "Chinese Tech Titans Eye Brazil," *The Wall Street Journal*, January 8, 2013, http://online.wsj.com; Tom Orlik and Paul Mozur, "Lenovo Says Phones Are in the Black in China," *The Wall Street Journal*, January 23, 2013, http://online.wsj.com.

2. D. Wessel, "Big U.S. Firms Shift Hiring Abroad," *The Wall Street Journal*, April 19, 2011, http://online.wsj.com.

3. E. Smith and J. T. Areddy, "Disney to Begin Shanghai Park," *The Wall Street Journal*, April 4, 2011, http://online.wsj.com.

4. M. S. Malone, "Living in a Bipolar Business World," *ABC News*, November 13, 2009, http://abcnews.go.com.

5. World Trade Organization, "World Trade Developments," *International Trade Statistics 2012*, p. 14, available at http://www.wto.org; World Trade Organization, "Trade Growth to Slow in 2012 after Strong Deceleration in 2011," news release, May 10, 2012, http://

www.wto.org; Mark Dorns, "Growing Appetite for American-Made Goods Overseas," Economics and Statistics Administration, March 22, 2011, http://www.esa.doc.gov.

6. See, for example, M. Mandel, "What Spending Slowdown?" *BusinessWeek*, April 23, 2007, http://www.businessweek.com.

7. Bureau of the Census, *Statistical Abstract of the United States: 2011*, table 1290, p. 797, http://www.census.gov; UN Conference on Trade and Development (UNCTAD), "Inward and Outward Foreign Direct Investment Flows," UnctadStat, http://unctadstat.unctad.org.

8. Reuters, "Deutsche Boerse Set for NYSE Deal as Nasdaq Bows Out," LiveMint.com, May 16, 2011, http://www.livemint.com; and F. Yan and A. Leung, "China's Geely Completes Volvo Buy," LiveMint.com, August 2, 2010, http://www.livemint.com.

9. C. Zappone, "China Poised for Global Shopping Spree," *CNNMoney*, March 30, 2007, http://money.cnn.com.

10. R. Rodriguez, "Peach Growers in Valley, China Fight for Market Share," *Fresno (Calif.) Bee*, January 31, 2011, http://www.fresnobee.com; and "AIADA: Imports Increase Market Share," *Auto Remarketing*, December 7, 2010, http://www.autoremarketing.com.

11. Joseph B. White, "What Is an American Car?" *The Wall Street Journal*, January 26, 2009, http://online.wsj.com.

12. T. Heston, "Fitting into the Global Puzzle," *Fabricating and Metalworking*, February 2007, Business & Company Resource Center, http://galenet.galegroup.com.

13. N. Sandler, "Software That Will This Sentence Fix," *BusinessWeek*, February 22, 2007, Business & Company Resource Center, http://galenet.galegroup.com.

14. D. W. Drezner, "The Outsourcing Bogeyman," *Foreign Affairs*, May/June 2004.

15. D. Wessel and B. Davis, "Pain from Free Trade Spurs Second Thoughts," *The Wall Street Journal*, March 28, 2007, http://online.wsj.com.

16. Wessel, "Big U.S. Firms Shift Hiring Abroad."

17. Wessel and Davis, "Pain from Free Trade"; P. Levy, "Trade Truths for Turbulent Times: A Reply to Vladimir Masch," *BusinessWeek*, February 14, 2007, Business & Company Resource Center, http://galenet.galegroup.com; P. Restuccia, "Profs Claim the Threat of Outsourcing Is Overblown," *Boston Herald*, February 12, 2007, http://galenet.galegroup.com; and D. Blanchard, "Compete or Retreat," *Industry Week*, January 2007, http://galenet.galegroup.com.

18. D. Whitford, "Where in the World Is Cheap Labor?" *Fortune*, March 22, 2011, http://money.cnn.com.

19. C. Lombardi, "Survey: Software Companies Increasing Offshoring Work," *C/Net News*, January 12, 2007, http://news.com.com.

20. "When Staying Put Trumps Offshoring," *McKinsey Quarterly*, December 7, 2004, online; and C. Koepfer, "A Look at Total Cost Can Change the View," *Production Machining*, January 2011, p. 6.

21. Koepfer, "A Look at Total Cost"; and Whitford, "Where in the World Is Cheap Labor?"

22. European Union, "About the EU," http://europa.eu; Central Intelligence Agency, "European Union," *The World Factbook*, http://www.cia.gov.

23. "Irish Welcome Portuguese to the 'Debt Club,'" *The Wall Street Journal*, April 7, 2011, http://blogs.wsj.com; S. Rastello and R. Christie, "IMF Will Work on Portugal Bailout Plan with European Union," *Bloomberg Businessweek*, April 8, 2011, http://www.businessweek.com; P. Kowsmann, "Portugal Reaches a Deal on Bailout," *The Wall Street Journal*, May 4, 2011, http://online.wsj.com; and M. Elliott, "Global Crises? Don't Panic," *Fortune*, April 21, 2011, http://money.cnn.com.

24. Liz Alderman, "Foreign Investment in Europe Starts Anew," *New York Times*, March 4, 2012.

25. R. Casert, "EU Waves New Fines in Face of Microsoft," *Seattle Times*, March 2, 2007; and D. Litterick, "Regulation EU Losing Patience with Reluctant Microsoft," *Daily Telegraph (London)*, March 2, 2007, Business & Company Resource Center, http://galenet.galegroup.com.

26. World Trade Organization, "World Trade Developments," p. 15.

27. Alex Frangos, "Behind China's Switch to High-End Exports," *The Wall Street Journal*, March 24, 2013, http://online.wsj.com; Yajun Zhang, "China Begins to Lose Edge as World's Factory Floor," *The Wall Street Journal*, January 16, 2013, http://online.wsj.com.

28. "Three Snapshots of Chinese Innovation," *McKinsey Quarterly*, February 2012, http://www.mckinseyquarterly.com.

29. J. T. Areddy and P. Sanders, "Chinese Learn English the Disney Way," *The Wall Street Journal*, April 20, 2009, http://online.wsj.com.

30. Bureau of Labor Statistics, "International Comparisons of Hourly Compensation Costs in Manufacturing, 2007," news release, March 26, 2009, http://www.bls.gov/ilc.

31. G. Anand, "India Graduates Millions, but Too Few Are Fit to Hire," *The Wall Street Journal*, April 5, 2011, http://online.wsj.com.

32. "Citigroup Plans More Branches in India," *Associated Press*, March 26, 2007, http://my.earthlink.net.

33. A. van Agtmael, "Industrial Revolution 2.0," *Foreign Policy*, January–February

2007, Business & Company Resource Center, http://galenet.galegroup.com.

34. Asia-Pacific Economic Cooperation, "About Us," http://www.apec.org.

35. Agtmael, "Industrial Revolution 2.0"; CEMEX website, http://www.cemex.com.

36. C. Simoes and I. Dantas, "Brazil's Economy: Growth May Have a Downside," *Bloomberg Businessweek*, June 10, 2010, http://www.businessweek.com; A. Ragir and D. Kopecki, "Brazil's Credit Boom Could End in Tears," *Bloomberg Businessweek*, January 6, 2011, http://www.businessweek.com; and S. Nielsen, "Wind Power: Brazil's Second Act," *Bloomberg Businessweek*, October 7, 2010, http://www.businessweek.com; Polya Lesova and Michael Molinski, "Latin America's New Tigers Forge Ahead," *MarketWatch*, July 25, 2012, http://www.marketwatch.com.

37. Agtmael, "Industrial Revolution 2.0."

38. Office of the United States Trade Representative, "Free Trade Agreements," http://www.ustr.gov.

39. U.S. Energy Information Administration, "How Dependent Are We on Foreign Oil?" *Energy in Brief*, July 13, 2012, http://www.eia.gov; World Trade Organization, "World and Regional Export Profiles 2011, *International Trade Statistics 2012*, http://www.wto.org.

40. F. Aquila, "Africa's Biggest Score: A Thriving Economy," *Bloomberg Businessweek*, June 28, 2010, http://www.businessweek.com; Sarah Frier, "For IBM, Africa Is Risky and Rife with Opportunity," *Bloomberg Businessweek*, February 21, 2013, http://www.businessweek.com.

41. E. Markowitz, "A Dating Site Thrives in Delhi," *Inc.*, February 14, 2011, http://www.inc.com; and H. Seligson, "Jilted in the U.S., a Site Finds Love in India," *The New York Times*, February 19, 2011, http://www.nytimes.com.

42. See, for example, "India's Bharti Says to Sign Wal-Mart Deal in April," *Reuters*, April 11, 2007, http://news.yahoo.com.

43. Leslie Kwoh, "Cinnabon Finds Sweet Success in Russia, Mideast," *The Wall Street Journal*, December 25, 2012, http://online.wsj.com.

44. P. B. Kavilanz, "U.S. Slaps Tariffs on Chinese Imports," *CNNMoney.com*, March 30, 2007, http://money.cnn.com.

45. Heineken International website, http://www.henekeninternational.com; and Heineken N.V. profile, Vintners.com, http://www.vintners.com.

46. S. Elliott, "Ford Tries a Global Campaign for Its Global Car," *The New York Times*, February 25, 2011, Business & Company Resource Center, http://galenet.galegroup.com.

47. A.-W. Harzing, "An Empirical Analysis and Extension of the Bartlett and Ghoshal Typology of Multinational Companies," *Journal of International Business Studies* 31, no. 1 (2000), pp. 101–20; Sucheta Nadkarni, Pol Herrmann, Pedro David Perez, "Domestic Mindsets and Early International Performance: The Moderating Effect of Global Industry Conditions," *Strategic Management Journal* 32, no. 5 (May 2011), pp. 510–31; S. M. Morris and S. A. Snell, "Intellectual Capital Configurations and Organizational Capability: An Empirical Examination of Human Resource Subunits in the Multinational Enterprise," *Journal of International Business Studies* 42, no. 6 (2011), pp. 805–27; Elaine Ferndale, Jaap Paauwe, Shad S. Morris, Günther K. Stahl, Philip Stiles, Jonathan Trevor, Patrick M. Wright, "Context-Bound Configurations of Corporate HR Functions in Multinational Corporations," *Human Resource Management* 49, no. 1 (Jan/Feb 2010), pp. 45–66.

48. Julie Jargon, "Starbucks in Europe Imports U.S. Tactics," *The Wall Street Journal*, December 27, 2012, http://online.wsj.com; Laurie Burkitt, "Starbucks Plays to Local Chinese Tastes," *The Wall Street Journal*, November 26, 2012, http://online.wsj.com; Liz Alderman, "In Europe, Starbucks Adjusts to a Cafe Culture," *New York Times*, March 30, 2012, http://www.nytimes.com.

49. J. Sandberg, "How Long Can India Keep Office Politics out of Outsourcing?" *The Wall Street Journal*, February 27, 2007, http://online.wsj.com.

50. Toshiro Wakayama, Junjiro Shintaku, and Tomofumi Amano, "What Panasonic Learned in China," *Harvard Business Review*, December 2012, pp. 109–113; Daisuke Wakabayashi, "Panasonic to Pare Unprofitable Units," *The Wall Street Journal*, March 28, 2013, http://online.wsj.com.

51. Chao, "As Rivals Outsource"; Chao, "Chinese Tech Titans Eye Brazil"; Orlik and Mozur, "Lenovo Says Phones Are in the Black"; Juro Osawa, "Made in the USA by Apple and Lenovo," *The Wall Street Journal*, December 6, 2012, http://blogs.wsj.com; Ian Sherr, "Lenovo Aims Higher in U.S.," *The Wall Street Journal*, January 10, 2013, http://online.wsj.com.

52. C. H. Moon, "The Choice of Entry Modes and Theories of Foreign Direct Investment," *Journal of Global Marketing* 11, no. 2 (1997), pp. 43–64; and I. Maignan and B. A. Lukas, "Entry Mode Decisions: The Role of Managers' Mental Models," *Journal of Global Marketing* 10, no. 4 (1997), pp. 7–22.

53. Diane Cardwell and Keith Bradsher, "U.S. Will Place Tariffs on Chinese Solar Panels," *New York Times*, October 10, 2012, http://www.nytimes.com; Charles Riley, "Major Chinese Solar Company Goes Bankrupt," *CNNMoney*, March 21, 2013, http://money.cnn.com.

54. P. Jitpleecheep, "Auntie Anne's Aims to Double Asia Outlets," *Bangkok Post*, April 10, 2007, Business & Company Resource Center, http://galenet.galegroup.com.

55. M. Prewitt, "Breaking Down the Great Wall to Franchising in China," *Nation's Restaurant News*, March 12, 2007, Business & Company Resource Center, http://galenet.galegroup.com.

56. "Hershey's Global Gambit," *BusinessWeek*, April 4, 2007, http://www.businessweek.com.

57. S. Oster, N. Shirouzu, and P. Glader, "China Squeezes Foreigners for Share of Global Riches," *The Wall Street Journal*, December 28, 2010, http://online.wsj.com.

58. R. C. Beasley, "Reducing the Risk of Failure in the Formation of Commercial Partnerships," *Licensing Journal* 24, no. 4 (April 2004), p. 71; Elie Chrysostome, Roli Nigam, Chaire Stephen Jarilowski, "Revisiting Strategic Learning in International Joint Ventures: A Knowledge Creation Perspective," *International Journal of Management* 30, no. 1 (March 2013), pp. 88–98.

59. J. T. Areddy, "In China, Tire-Espionage Suit Treads Loudly," *The Wall Street Journal*, April 28, 2011, http://online.wsj.com; Bryan Vogel, "ITC Foreign-Based Misappropriation of Trade Secrets Actions," *InsideCounsel*, July 31, 2012, http://www.insidecounsel.com; Julie Juan Li, Laura Poppo, Kevin Zheng Zhou, "Relational Mechanisms, Formal Contracts, and Local Knowledge Acquisition by International Subsidiaries," *Strategic Management Journal* 31, no. 4 (April 2010), pp. 349–70.

60. K. Hille, "Western Faces Are Vital to China," *Financial Times*, December 9, 2010, Business & Company Resource Center, http://galenet.galegroup.com; and J. S. Lublin, "Finding Top Talent in China, India, Brazil," *The Wall Street Journal*, April 11, 2011, http://online.wsj.com.

61. A. W. Andreason, "Expatriate Adjustment to Foreign Assignments," *International Journal of Commerce and Management* 13, no. 1 (Spring 2003), pp. 42–61.

62. P. Capell, "Know before You Go: Expats' Advice to Couples," *Career Journal Europe*, May 2, 2006, htp://www.careerjournaleurope.com; Mila Lazarova, Mina Westman, Margaret A. Shaffer, "Elucidating the Positive Side of the Work-Family Interface on International Assignments: A Model of Expatriate Work and Family Performance," *Academy of Management Review* 35, no. 1 (January 2010), pp. 93–117.

63. R. A. Swaak, "Expatriate Failures: Too Many, Too Much Cost, Too Little Planning," *Compensation & Benefits Review*, November/December 1995, pp. 50–52.

64. Capell, "Know before You Go."
65. G. M. Sprietzer, M. W. McCall, and J. D. Mahoney, "Early Identification of International Executive Potential," *Journal of Applied Psychology* 82, no. 1 (1997), pp. 6–29; R. Mortensen, "Beyond the Fence Line," *HRMagazine*, November 1997, pp. 100–9; "Expatriate Games," *Journal of Business Strategy*, July/August 1997, pp. 4–5; and "Building a Global Workforce Starts with Recruitment," *Personnel Journal* (special supplement), March 1996, pp. 9–11; Ming Li, William H. Mobley, Aidan Kelly, "When Do Global Leaders Learn Best to Develop Cultural Intelligence? An Investigation of the Moderating Role of Experiential Learning Style," *Academy of Management Learning & Education* 12, no. 1 (March 2013), pp. 32–50; Nicola M. Pless, Thomas Maak, Günther K. Stahl, "Developing Responsible Global Leaders through International Service-Learning Programs: The Ulysses Experience," *Academy of Management Learning & Education* 10, no. 2 (June 2011), pp. 237–60.
66. A. Paul, "How the Internet Shrinks the Distance between Us," *The Wall Street Journal*, March 16, 2007, http://online .wsj.com.
67. G. A. Fowler, "In China's Offices, Foreign Colleagues Might Get an Earful," *The Wall Street Journal*, February 13, 2007, http://online.wsj.com.
68. John Slocum, "Coming to America," *Human Resource Executive*, October 2, 2008, http://www.hrexecutive.com.
69. J. Brett, K. Behfar, and M. C. Kern, "Managing Multicultural Teams," *Harvard Business Review*, November 2006, pp. 84–91.
70. D. Stamps, "Welcome to America," *Training*, November 1996, pp. 23–30.
71. L. K. Trevino and K. A. Nelson, *Managing Business Ethics: Straight Talk about How to Do It Right* (New York: John Wiley & Sons, 1995).
72. Transparency International, "Leading Exporters Undermine Development with Dirty Business Overseas," news release, October 4, 2006, http://www. transparency.org.
73. Mo Ibrahim, "Celtel's Founder on Building a Business on the World's Poorest Continent," *Harvard Business Review*, October 2012, pp. 41–44; Zain, "About Zain: Overview," http://www.zain.com; Bharti Airtel, "About Bharti Airtel," http://www. airtel.in.
74. J. G. Longnecker, J. A. McKinney, and C. W. Moore, "The Ethical Issues of International Bribery: A Study of Attitudes among U.S. Business Professionals," *Journal of Business Ethics* 7 (1988), pp. 341–46.
75. D. Searcey, "U.K. Law on Bribes Has Firms in a Sweat," *The Wall Street Journal*, December 28, 2010, http:// online.wsj.com.

76. Ibid.; and J. Holzer and S. Raice, "IBM Settles Bribery Charges," *The Wall Street Journal*, March 19, 2011, http://online. wsj.com.
77. UPS, "The UPS Code of Business Conduct: Leading with Integrity," UPS Pressroom, http://www.pressroom.ups .com; and i-Sight, "International Code of Conduct: United Parcel Service," Best Practices, June 17, 2010, http://i-sight .com.
78. A. B. Desai and T. Rittenburg, "Global Ethics: An Integrative Framework for MNEs," *Journal of Business Ethics* 16 (1997), pp. 791–800; and P. Buller, J. Kohls, and K. Anderson, "A Model for Addressing Cross-Cultural Ethical Conflicts," *Business & Society* 36, no. 2 (June 1997), pp. 169–93.
79. Chao, "As Rivals Outsource"; Einhorn, "Lenovo's Persistent PC Strategy"; Chao, "Chinese Tech Titans Eye Brazil"; Sherr, "Lenovo Aims Higher in U.S."; Bruce Einhorn, "In China's Smartphone Market, Lenovo Gets Busy," *Bloomberg Businessweek*, January 3, 2013, http://www.businessweek. com.

Chapter 7

1. Meghan Casserly, "Popchips: The Next $1 Billion Snack Food or Just Full of Hot Air?" *Forbes*, January 24, 2013, http://www.forbes.com; Nicole Hong, "New Kind of Chip Pops on the Scene," *The Wall Street Journal*, February 20, 2013, http://online.wsj.com; Laura Petrecca, "Popchips CEO Keith Belling Is 'Poptimist' on Healthy Snacks," *USA Today*, April 12, 2010, http://usatoday30 .usatoday.com; Stacy Finz, "Popchips Doing Healthy Sales, Expanding to Britain," *San Francisco Chronicle*, March 1, 2012, http://www.sfgate.com.
2. S. Shane and S. Venkataraman, "The Promise of Entrepreneurship as a Field of Research, *Academy of Management Review* 25 (2000), pp. 217–26.
3. J. A. Timmons, *New Venture Creation* (Burr Ridge, IL: Richard D. Irwin, 1994).
4. S. Shane and S. Venkataraman, "The Promise of Entrepreneurship As a Field of Research," *Academy of Management Review* 25 (2000), pp. 271–26.
5. M. A. Hitt, R. D. Ireland, D. Sirmon, and C. Trahms, "Strategic Entrepreneurship: Creating Value for Individuals, Organizations, and Society," *Academy of Management Perspectives* (May 2011), pp. 57–75.
6. W. Megginson, M. J. Byrd, S. R. Scott Jr., and L. Megginson, *Small Business Management: An Entrepreneur's Guide to Success*, 2nd ed. (Boston: Irwin McGraw-Hill, 1997).
7. J. Timmons and S. Spinelli, *New Venture Creation: Entrepreneurship for the 21st Century*, 6th ed. (New York: McGraw-Hill/Irwin, 2004), p. 3.

8. J. A. Timmons, *The Entrepreneurial Mind* (Andover, MA: Brick House, 1989).
9. B. Casselman, "Risk-Averse Culture Infects U.S. Workers, Entrepreneurs," *Wall Street Journal*, June 2, 2013. A.1
10. D. J. Isenberg, "The Global Entrepreneur," *Harvard Business Review*, December 2008, pp. 107–11.
11. Timmons and Spinelli, *New Venture Creation*.
12. A. Loten, "Start-Ups Key to States' Economic Success," *Inc.*, February 7, 2007, http://www.inc.com.
13. Timmons and Spinelli, *New Venture Creation*.
14. Ibid.
15. D. Bricklin, "Natural-Born Entrepreneur," *Harvard Business Review* (September 2001), pp. 53–59, p. 58.
16. Alexandra Levit, "'Insider' Entrepreneurs," *The Wall Street Journal*, April 6, 2009, http://online.wsj.com.
17. M. A. Hitt, R. D. Ireland, D. Sirmon, and C. Trahms, "Strategic Entrepreneurship: Creating Value for Individuals, Organizations, and Society," *Academy of Management Perspectives* (May 2011), pp. 57–75.
18. "For Zappos, the Next Trend Is More Customized Pages for Customers," *InternetRetailer*, February 12, 2009, http://www.internetretailer.com; M. Chafkin, "How I Did It: Tony Hsieh, CEO, Zappos.com," *Inc.*, September 2006, http://www.inc.com.
19. C. Conner, "Who's Starting America's New Businesses? And Why?" *Forbes* (July 22, 2012).
20. "Coolest College Start-Ups: Where Are They Now?" *Inc.*, March 2011, http://www.inc.com; E. Lee, "The Small-Business Numbers Cruncher," *San Francisco Chronicle*, January 3, 2011, Business & Company Resource Center, http://galenet.galegroup.com; M. Chafkin, "InDinero Fixes Money Management," *Inc.*, December 2010, http://www.inc.com; and A. Gardella, "Can a 20-Year-Old Help You Track Your Finances?" *The New York Times*, September 29, 2010, http://boss.blogs .nytimes.com.
21. L. Kanter, "The Eco-Advantage," *Inc.*, November 2006, pp. 78–103 (NaturaLawn example on page 84).
22. H. Aldrich, *Ethnic Entrepreneurs: Immigrant Business in Industrial Societies* (Newbury Park, CA: Sage, 1990).
23. R. Flandez, "Immigrants Gain Edge Doing Business Back Home," *The Wall Street Journal*, March 20, 2007, http:// online.wsj.com.
24. Timmons and Spinelli, *New Venture Creation*.
25. J. Collins and J. Porras, *Built to Last* (London: Century, 1996).
26. Collins and Porras, *Built to Last*.
27. K. H. Vesper, *New Venture Mechanics* (Englewood Cliffs, NJ: Prentice Hall, 1993).

28. "Entrepreneur of 2012: Limor Fried," *Entrepreneur*, December 18, 2012, http://www.entrepreneur.com.

29. Vesper, *New Venture Mechanics*.

30. J. Berg, "Entrepreneurs Develop Errand Service," *Patriot-News (Harrisburg, PA)*, January 23, 2007, http://galenet.galegroup.com.

31. Timmons and Spinelli, *New Venture Creation*.

32. P. J. Sauer, "Serving Up Success," *Inc.*, January 2007, http://www.inc.com.

33. K. Spors, "Franchised versus Nonfranchised Businesses," *The Wall Street Journal*, February 27, 2007, http://online.wsj.com.

34. Timmons and Spinelli, *New Venture Creation*.

35. "The Biggest Trends in Business for 2013," *Entrepreneur*, December 3, 2012, http://www.entrepreneur.com.

36. D. Fenn, "30 Under 30," *Inc.* July 2, 2012.

37. "Innovation: Inside the Space Station," *Inc.*, April 1, 2013, http://www.inc.com; Andy Pasztor, "Never-Wracking Space Drama Swirls around Unmanned Cargo Capsule," *The Wall Street Journal*, March 1, 2013, http://online.wsj.com.

38. *Entrepreneur*, "The Biggest Trends in Business for 2013"; April Joyner, "Thinking of Starting a Business? Check Out Consumer Health Technology," *Inc.*, April 8, 2013, http://www.inc.com; General Electric, "GE and Startup Health Select 13 Consumer Health Companies for Entrepreneurship Program," news release, April 4, 2013, http://www.genewscenter.com.

39. J. J. Colao, "America's Most Promising Company Is Redefining Mobile: Meet 3Cinteractive," *Forbes*, January 23, 2013, http://www.forbes.com; Justine Griffin, "John Duffy, Small Business Leader, Palm Beach County," *South Florida Sun-Sentinel*, April 26, 2012, http://www.sun-sentinel.com; 3Cinteractive, "About 3Cinteractive," http://www.3cinteractive.com/About/.

40. J. E. Lange, "Entrepreneurs and the Continuing Internet: The Expanding Frontier," in Timmons and Spinelli, *New Venture Creation*, pp. 183–220.

41. Ibid.

42. J. E. Vascellaro, "Selling Your Designs Online," *The Wall Street Journal*, April 5, 2007, http://online.wsj.com.

43. J. Short, T. Moss, and G. Lumpkin, "Research in Social Entrepreneurship: Past, Contributions and Future Opportunities," *Strategic Entrepreneurship Journal* 3 (2009), pp. 161–94. S. Zahra and M. Wright, "Entrepreneur's Next Act," *Academy of Management Perspectives* (2011), pp. 67–83.

44. P. Dacin, M.T. Dacin, and M. Matear, "Social Entrepreneurship: Why We Don't Need a New Theory and How We Move Forward from Here," *Academy of Management Perspectives* 24 (2010), pp. 37–57.

45. T. Miller, M. Grimes, J. McMullen, and T. Vogus, "Venturing for Others with Heart and Head: How Compassion Encourages Social Entrepreneurship," *Academy of Management Review* 37 (2012), pp. 616–40.

46. J. Mair and I. Marti, "Social Entrepreneurship Research: A Source of Explanation, Prediction, and Delight," *Journal of World Business* 41 (2006), pp. 36–44.

47. D. Bornstein and S. Davis, *Social Entrepreneurship: What Everyone Needs to Know* (Oxford, UK: Oxford University Press, 2010).

48. D. Bornstein, *How to Change the World: Social Entrepreneurs and the Power of New Ideas* (Oxford, UK: Oxford University Press, 2004).

49. B. Dumaine, "Lighting Up Africa," *Fortune*, July 5, 2010, p. 22.

50. J. Thompson and I. MacMillan, "Making Social Ventures Work," *Harvard Business Review*, September, 2010, pp. 66–73.

51. Ibid.

52. Ibid.

53. M. Driver, "An Interview with Michael Porter: Social Entrepreneurship and the Transformation of Capitalism," *Academy of Management Learning & Education* 11 (2012), pp. 421–31.

54. M. Porter and M. Kramer, "Creating Shared Value," *Harvard Business Review* (January-February 2011), pp. 62–77.

55. H. Sabeti, "The For-Benefit Enterprise," *Harvard Business Review* (November 2011), pp. 98–194.

56. P. Omidyar, "eBay's Founder on Innovating the Business Model of Social Change," *Harvard Business Review* (September 2011), pp. 41–44.

57. Timmons, *New Venture Creation*.

58. M. Cardon, J. Wincent, J. Singh, and M. Drnovsek, "The Nature and Experience of Entrepreneurial Passion," *Academy of Management Review* 34 (2009), pp. 511–32.

59. J. R. Baum and E. A. Locke, "The Relationship of Entrepreneurial Traits, Skill, and Motivation to Subsequent Venture Growth," *Journal of Applied Psychology* 89 (2004), pp. 587–98.

60. M. Sonfield and R. Lussier, "The Entrepreneurial Strategy Matrix: A Model for New and Ongoing Ventures," *Business Horizons*, May–June 1997, pp. 73–77.

61. C. Lagorio, "Solved! Hands-Free Door Opening," *Inc.*, March 2011, http://www.inc.com; "Coolest College Start-Ups 2011," *Inc.*, March 2011, http://www.inc.com; and Toepener website, http://www.toepener.com.

62. Lange, "Entrepreneurs and the Continuing Internet."

63. S. Venkataraman and M. Low, "On the Nature of Critical Relationships: A Test of the Liabilities and Size Hypothesis," in *Frontiers of Entrepreneurship Research* (Babson Park, MA: Babson College, 1991), p. 97.

64. Timmons and Spinelli, *New Venture Creation*.

65. Cari Tuna, "Tough Call: Deciding to Start a Business," *The Wall Street Journal*, January 8, 2009, http://online.wsj.com.

66. H. Dietrich, "Worried about Future Viaduct Construction Woes, Sound Sports Is Planning Ahead," *Minneapolis–St. Paul Business Journal*, http://twincities.bizjournals.com.

67. L. Buchanan, "Create Jobs, Eliminate Waste, Preserve Value," *Inc.*, December 2006, pp. 94–106.

68. M. V. Copeland, "A Studio System for Startups," *Business 2.0*, May 2007, Business & Company Resource Center, http://galenet.galegroup.com.

69. R. Price, "The Role of Service Providers in Establishing Networked Regional Business Accelerators in Utah," *International Journal of Technology Management* 27 (2004), pp. 465–74.

70. Norm Brodsky, "Street Smarts: Our Irrational Fear of Numbers," *Inc.*, January 2009, http://www.inc.com.

71. Jeremy Quittner, "Robin Chase: How I Survived a Huge Screw-Up," *Inc.*, February 28, 2013, http://www.inc.com.

72. D. McGinn, "Why Size Matters," *Inc.*, Fall 2004, pp. 32–36.

73. S. E. Needleman, "When It's Time to Take On Help," *The Wall Street Journal*, January 16, 2011, http://online.wsj.com.

74. Kanter, "The Eco-Advantage."

75. W. Harris, "Team Players," *Black Enterprise*, January 2007, Business & Company Resource Center, http://galenet.galegroup.com.

76. S. Finkelstein, "The Myth of Managerial Superiority in Internet Startups: An Autopsy," *Organizational Dynamics*, Fall 2001, pp. 172–85.

77. S. E. Needleman, "Management Flubs Made by Rookie Bosses," *The Wall Street Journal*, January 3, 2011, http://online.wsj.com.

78. R. Weisman, "Bootstrappers Avoid Outside Money Ties," *Boston Globe*, February 5, 2007, Business & Company Resource Center, http://galenet.galegroup.com.

79. Cordeiro, "Sweet Returns."

80. G. Stalk and H. Foley, "Avoid the Traps That Can Destroy Family Businesses," *Harvard Business Review* (January-February), pp. 25–27.

81. P. F. Drucker, "How to Save the Family Business," *The Wall Street Journal*, August 19, 1994, p. A10.

82. D. Gamer, R. Owen, and R. Conway, *The Ernst & Young Guide to Raising Capital* (New York: John Wiley & Sons, 1991).

83. Ibid.

84. J. H. Ostdick, "Elevating the Bottom Line," *Success*, December 2010, pp. 59–64.

85. Casserly, "Popchips: The Next $1 Billion Snack Food?"; Hong, "New

Kind of Chip"; Petrecca, "Popchips CEO Keith Belling"; Breeanna Hare, "Amidst Complaints, Popchips CEO Apologizes for Ashton Kutcher Ad," *CNN Wire*, May 3, 2012, Business Insights: Essentials, http://bi.galegroup.com; Bridget Goldschmidt, "Pop Go the Snacks," *Progressive Grocer*, April 1, 2013, Business Insights: Essentials, http://bi.galegroup.com; Hoover's, "Snack Foods Manufacturing Industry Profile," First Research Industry Profiles, http://www.firstresearch.com, last updated March 18, 2013.

86. R. D. Hisrich and M. P. Peters, *Entrepreneurship: Starting, Developing, and Managing a New Enterprise* (Burr Ridge, IL: Irwin, 1994).

87. Ibid.

88. Small Business Administration, "Frequently Asked Questions about Small Business Finance," SBA Office of Advocacy, September 2011, http://www.sba.gov; Ewing Marion Kauffman Foundation, "Six Myths about Venture Capital Offer Dose of Reality to Startups in *Harvard Business Review* Article," news release, April 16, 2013, http://www.kauffman.org.

89. Aaron Task, "Janitor Turned Owner Rescues Failing Ohio Factory," *Yahoo News*, February 29, 2012, http://news.yahoo.com.

90. "JOBS Act, One Year Later: Hang Tight, Equity Crowdfunding Is Coming," *Entrepreneur*, April 5, 2013, http://www.entrepreneur.com; "Crowdfunding Industry on Fire: Trends to Watch," *Entrepreneur*, April 8, 2013, http://www.entrepreneur.com; Becky Yerak, "Is Promise Worth Peril?" *Chicago Tribune*, February 24, 2013, sec. 2, pp. 1, 3; Sarah E. Needleman and Lora Kolodny, "Site Unseen: More 'Angels' Invest via Internet," *The Wall Street Journal*, January 23, 2013, http://online.wsj.com.

91. W. A. Sahlman, "How to Write a Great Business Plan," *Harvard Business Review*, July–August 1997, pp. 98–108.

92. Ibid.

93. Copeland, "Start Last, Finish First."

94. Sahlman, "How to Write a Great Business Plan."

95. R. D. Atkinson and D. K. Correa, *The 2007 State New Economy Index* (Ewing Marion Kauffman Foundation and Information Technology and Innovation Foundation, 2007), http://www.kauffman.org; and J. Gangemi, "Ranking the States for the New Economy," *BusinessWeek*, February 27, 2007, http://www.businessweek.com.

96. M. Zimmerman and G. Zeitz, "Beyond Survival: Achieving New Venture Growth by Building Legitimacy," *Academy of Management Review*, 27 (2002), pp. 414–21.

97. A. L. Stinchcombe, "Social Structure and Organizations," in J. G. March,

ed., *Handbook of Organizations* (Chicago: Rand McNally, 1965), pp. 142–93.

98. L. Taylor, "Want Your Start-Up to Be Successful? Appearance Is Everything," *Inc.*, February 23, 2007, http://www.inc.com.

99. Ibid.

100. Rob Walker, "Can Tumblr's David Karp Embrace Ads without Selling Out?" *New York Times*, July 12, 2012, http://www.nytimes.com; Jeff Bercovici, "Tumblr: David Karp's $800 Million Art Project," *Forbes*, January 2, 2013, http://www.forbes.com; Josh Halliday, "David Karp, Founder of Tumblr, on Realising His Dream," *Guardian*, January 29, 2012, http://www.guardian.co.uk.

101. R. A. Baron and G. D. Markman, "Beyond Social Capital: How Social Skills Can Enhance Entrepreneurs' Success," *Academy of Management Executive*, February 2000, pp. 106–16.

102. J. Florin, M. Lubatkin, and W. Schulze, "A Social Capital Model of High-Growth Ventures," *Academy of Management Journal* 46 (2003), pp. 374–84.

103. J. Gangemi, "Young, Fearless, and Smart," *BusinessWeek*, October 30, 2006, http://www.businessweek.com.

104. Harris, "Team Players."

105. R. M. Kanter, The Change Masters (New York: Simon & Schuster, 1983).

106. Collins and Porras, *Built to Last.*

107. R. M. Kanter, C. Ingols, E. Morgan, and T. K. Seggerman, "Driving Corporate Entrepreneurship," *Management Review* 76 (April 1987), pp. 14–16.

108. J. Argenti, *Corporate Collapse: The Causes and Symptoms* (New York: John Wiley & Sons, 1979).

109. Kanter et al., "Driving Corporate Entrepreneurship."

110. Y. Ling, Z. Simsek, M. Lubatkin, and J. Veiga, "Transformational Leadership's Role in Promoting Corporate Entrepreneurship: Examining the CEO–TMT Interface," *Academy of Management Journal*, 2008, pp. 557–76.

111. G. T. Lumpkin and G. G. Dess, "Clarifying the Entrepreneurial Orientation Construct and Linking It to Performance," *Academy of Management Review* 21 (1996), pp. 135–72.

112. H. J. Sapienza, E. Autio, G. George, and S. A. Zahra, "A Capabilities Perspective on the Effects of Early Internationalization on Firm Survival and Growth," *Academy of Management Review* 31, no. (2006), pp. 914–33.

113. T. Bateman and J. M. Crant, "The Proactive Dimension of Organizational Behavior," *Journal of Organizational Behavior* (1993), pp. 103–18.

114. Lumpkin and Dess, "Clarifying the Entrepreneurial Orientation Construct."

115. C. Pinchot and E. Pinchot, *The Intelligent Organization* (San Francisco: Barrett-Koehler, 1996).

116. Casserly, "Popchips: The Next $1 Billion Snack Food?"; Hong, "New Kind of Chip"; Petrecca, "Popchips CEO Keith Belling."

Chapter 8

1. General Motors, Annual Report 2012, www.gm.com; Tim Higgins and Jeff Green, "GM Seen Planning Global Reorganization against 'Fiefdoms,'" Bloomberg, August 17, 2012, http://www.bloomberg.com; Qineqt, "General Motors Reorganization: Will the Glory Days Be Back?" *Seeking Alpha*, September 3, 2012, http://seekingalpha.com; Paul A. Eisenstein, "Big Management Shake-Up on the Horizon at GM," *NBC News*, August 22, 2012, http://www.nbcnews.com; Ben Klayman, "Car Guy or Bean Counter?" Reuters, July 19, 2012, http://www.reuters.com; "Government in March Sold $621M Worth of GM Stock," *CBS News*, April 10, 2013, http://www.cbsnews.com; Yuri Kageyama, "Toyota Top Selling Automaker Despite China Fall," *Detroit Free Press*, April 24, 2013, http://www.freep.com.

2. R. N. Ashkenas and S. C. Francis, "Integration Managers: Special Leaders for Special Times," *Harvard Business Review* 78, no. 6 (November–December 2000), pp. 108–16.

3. A. West, "The Flute Factory: An Empirical Measurement of the Effect of the Division of Labor on Productivity and Production Cost," *American Economist* 43, no. 1 (Spring 1999), pp. 82–87.

4. P. Lawrence and J. Lorsch, *Organization and Environment* (Homewood, IL: Richard D. Irwin, 1969).

5. Ibid.; and B. L. Thompson, *The New Manager's Handbook* (New York: McGraw-Hill, 1994). See also S. Sharifi and K. S. Pawar, "Product Design as a Means of Integrating Differentiation," *Technovation* 16, no. 5 (May 1996), pp. 255–64; and W. B. Stevenson and J. M. Bartunek, "Power, Interaction, Position, and the Generation of Cultural Agreement in Organizations," *Human Relations* 49, no. 1 (January 1996), pp. 75–104.

6. P. Puranam, H. Singh, and M. Zollo, "Organizing for Innovation: Managing the Coordination-Autonomy Dilemma in Technology Acquisitions," *Academy of Management Journal* 49, no. 2 (2006), pp. 263–80.

7. M. S. Burns, "Taming the Wild West," *Game Developer*, March 1, 2010, Business & Company Resource Center, http://galenet.galegroup.com.

8. A. J. Ali, R. C. Camp, and M. Gibbs, "The Ten Commandments Perspective on Power and Authority in Organizations," *Journal of Business Ethics* 26, no. 4 (August 2000), pp. 351–61; and R. F. Pearse, "Understanding Organizational Power and Influence

Systems," *Compensation & Benefits Management* 16, no. 4 (Autumn 2000), pp. 28–38.

9. J. Pfeffer, *Power: Why Some People Have It—and Others Don't* (New York: HarperCollins, 2010).

10. S. F. Shultz, *Board Book: Making Your Corporate Board a Strategic Force in Your Company's Success* (New York: AMACOM, 2000); and R. D. Ward, *Improving Corporate Boards: The Boardroom Insider Guidebook* (New York: John Wiley & Sons, 2000).

11. T. Perkins, "The 'Compliance Board,'" *The Wall Street Journal*, March 2, 2007, http://online.wsj.com.

12. Mike Esterl and Joann S. Lublin, "Coke Refreshes Aging Board," *The Wall Street Journal*, April 23, 2013, http://online.wsj.com; Duane D. Stanford, "Coca-Cola Woman Board Nominee Bucks Slowing Diversity Trend," *Bloomberg Businessweek*, February 22, 2013, http://www.businessweek.com; Reuters, "Coca-Cola Looks to More Diverse Board," April 24, 2013, http://www.reuters.com.

13. Margaret Heffernan, "You *Really* Need Outside Directors: Here's Why," *Inc.*, October 15, 2012, http://www.inc.com; Kingston Smith LLP, "Lessons Learned: Surviving the Recession," news release, February 20, 2009, http://www.kingstonsmithw1.co.uk; Karl Stark and Bill Stewart, "Why You Need an Advisory Board," *Inc.*, January 24, 2012, http://www.inc.com.

14. C. M. Daily and D. R. Dalton, "CEO and Board Chair Roles Held Jointly or Separately: Much Ado about Nothing?" *Academy of Management Executive* 11, no. 3 (August 1997), pp. 11–20.

15. T. Simons, L. H. Pelled, and K. A. Smith, "Making Use of Difference: Diversity, Debate, and Decision Comprehensiveness in Top Management Teams," *Academy of Management Journal* 42, no. 6 (December 1999), pp. 662–73; and C. Carl Pegels, Y. I Song, and B. Yang, "Management Heterogeneity, Competitive Interaction Groups, and Firm Performance," *Strategic Management Journal* 21, no. 3 (September 2000), pp. 911–21.

16. S. Vickery, C. Droge, and R. Germain, "The Relationship between Product Customization and Organizational Structure," *Journal of Operations Management* 17, no. 4 (June 1999), pp. 377–91. See also N. Nohria, W. Joyce, and B. Roberson, "What Really Works," *Harvard Business Review* (July 2003).

17. Andrew R. McIlvaine, "Flat, Fast and . . . Risky?" *Human Resource Executive Online*, March 6, 2012, http://www.hreonline.com.

18. D. Van Fleet and A. Bedeian, "A History of the Span of Management," *Academy of Management Review* 2 (1977), pp. 356–72. Results of Corporate Executive Board survey reported in McIlvaine, "Flat, Fast and . . . Risky?"

19. P. Jehiel, "Information Aggregation and Communication in Organizations," *Management Science* 45, no. 5 (May 1999), pp. 659–69; and A. Altaffer, "First-Line Managers: Measuring Their Span of Control," *Nursing Management* 29, no. 7 (July 1998), pp. 36–40.

20. "Span of Control vs. Span of Support," *Journal for Quality and Participation* 23, no. 4 (Fall 2000), p. 15; J. Gallo and P. R. Thompson, "Goals, Measures, and Beyond: In Search of Accountability in Federal HRM," *Public Personnel Management* 29, no. 2 (Summer 2000), pp. 237–48; C. O. Longenecker and T. C. Stansfield, "Why Plant Managers Fail: Causes and Consequences," *Industrial Management* 42, no. 1 (January/February 2000), pp. 24–32.

21. Z. X. Chen and S. Aryee, "Delegation and Employee Work Outcomes: An Examination of the Cultural Context of Mediating Processes in China," *Academy of Management Journal* 50, no. 1 (2007), pp. 226–38.

22. "How to Delegate More Effectively," *Community Banker*, February 2009, p. 14; B. Nefer, "Don't Be Delegation-Phobic," *Supervision*, December 2008, Business & Company Resource Center, http://galenet.galegroup.com; J. Mahoney, "Delegating Effectively," *Nursing Management* 28, no. 6 (June 1997), p. 62; and J. Lagges, "The Role of Delegation in Improving Productivity," *Personnel Journal*, November 1979, pp. 776–79.

23. G. Matthews, "Run Your Business or Build an Organization?" *Harvard Management Review*, March–April 1984, pp. 34–44.

24. N. Siggelkow and J. W. Rivkin, "When Exploration Backfires: Unintended Consequences of Multilevel Organizational Search," *Academy of Management Proceedings*, 2006, pp. BB1–BB6.

25. "Missing Its Targets," *Delaney Report*, November 26, 2012, Business Insights: Essentials, http://bi.galegroup.com.

26. J. R. Hollenbeck, A. P. J. Ellis, S. E. Humphrey, A. S. Garza, and D. R. Ilgen, "Asymmetry in Structural Adaptation: The Differential Impact of Centralizing versus Decentralizing Team Decision-Making Structures," *Organizational Behavior and Human Decision Processes* 114 (2011), pp. 64–74.

27. R. Forrester, "Empowerment: Rejuvenating a Potent Idea," *Academy of Management Executive* 14, no. 3 (August 2000), pp. 67–80; and M. L. Perry, C. L. Pearce, and H. P. Sims Jr., "Empowered Selling Teams: How Shared Leadership Can Contribute to Selling Team Outcomes," *Journal of Personal Selling & Sales Management* 19, no. 3 (Summer 1999), pp. 35–51.

28. L. Gard, "Growth Trifecta," *Construction Today*, January 2009, Business & Company Resource Center, http://galenet.galegroup.com; and

Environmental Systems Design, "About ESD," corporate website, http://www.esdesign.com.

29. E. E. Lawler III, "New Roles for the Staff Function: Strategic Support and Services," in *Organizing for the Future*, J. Galbraith, E. E. Lawler III, & Associates (San Francisco: Jossey-Bass, 1993).

30. N. D. Kho, "Embedded Librarianship: Building Relational Roles," *Information Today*, March 2011, pp. 1, 35–36.

31. R. Cross and L. Baird, "Technology Is Not Enough: Improving Performance by Building Organizational Memory," *Sloan Management Review* 41, no. 3 (Spring 2000), pp. 69–78; and R. Duncan, "What Is the Right Organizational Structure?" *Organizational Dynamics* 7 (Winter 1979), pp. 59–80.

32. Michael Bartlett, "Expanding Horizons," *Credit Union Journal*, November 26, 2012, Business Insights: Essentials, http://bi.galegroup.com.

33. G. S. Day, "Creating a Market-Driven Organization," *Sloan Management Review* 41, no. 1 (Fall 1999), pp. 11–22.

34. R. Boehm and C. Phipps, "Flatness Forays," *McKinsey Quarterly* 3 (1996), pp. 128–43.

35. B. T. Lamont, V. Sambamurthy, K. M. Ellis, and P. G. Simmonds, "The Influence of Organizational Structure on the Information Received by Corporate Strategists of Multinational Enterprises," *Management International Review* 40, no. 3 (2000), pp. 231–52.

36. L. A. Johnson, "Pfizer Planning to Redraw Its Battle Lines," *America's Intelligence Wire*, October 8, 2008, Business & Company Resource Center, http://galenet.galegroup.com.

37. T. Stynes and P. Ziobro, "Avon Plans Restructuring," *The Wall Street Journal*, February 24, 2011, http://online.wsj.com.

38. General Motors, Annual Report 2012; Higgins and Green, "GM Seen Planning Global Reorganization"; Eisenstein, "Big Management Shake-Up"; Klayman, "Car Guy or Bean Counter?"; Sharon Terlep, "GM's Chief Labors to Get Rebuilt Car Maker into Gear," *The Wall Street Journal*, June 11, 2012, http://online.wsj.com; "Mary Barra: GM's Next CEO?" *Fortune*, December 17, 2012, http://management.fortune.cnn.com.

39. W. Bernasco, P. C. de WeerdNederhof, H. Tillema, and H. Boer, "Balanced Matrix Structure and New Product Development Process at Texas Instruments Materials and Controls Division," *R&D Management* 29, no. 2 (April 1999), pp. 121–31; J. K. McCollum, "The Matrix Structure: Bane or Benefit to High Tech Organizations?" *Project Management Journal* 24, no. 2 (June 1993), pp. 23–26; R. C. Ford, "Cross-Functional Structures: A Review and Integration of Matrix," *Journal of Management* 18, no. 2 (June 1992), pp. 267–94; and

H. Kolodny, "Managing in a Matrix," *Business Horizons*, March–April 1981, pp. 17–24.

40. D. Cackowski, M. K. Najdawi, and Q. B. Chung, "Object Analysis in Organizational Design: A Solution for Matrix Organizations," *Project Management Journal* 31, no. 3 (September 2000), pp. 44–51; J. Barker, "Conflict Approaches of Effective and Ineffective Project Managers: A Field Study in a Matrix Organization," *Journal of Management Studies* 25, no. 2 (March 1988), pp. 167–78; G. J. Chambers, "The Individual in a Matrix Organization," *Project Management Journal* 20, no. 4 (December 1989), pp. 37–42, 50; and S. Davis and P. Lawrence, "Problems of Matrix Organizations," *Harvard Business Review*, May–June 1978, pp. 131–42.

41. A. Ferner, "Being Local Worldwide: ABB and the Challenge of Global Management Relations," *Industrielles* 55, no. 3 (Summer 2000), pp. 527–29; and C. Bartlett and S. Ghoshal, "Matrix Management: Not a Structure, a Frame of Mind," *Harvard Business Review* 68 (July–August 1990), pp. 138–45.

42. J. Tata, S. Prasad, and R. Thorn, "The Influence of Organizational Structure on the Effectiveness of TQM Programs," *Journal of Managerial Issues* 11, no. 4 (Winter 1999), pp. 440–53; and Davis and Lawrence, "Problems of Matrix Organizations."

43. R. E. Miles and C. C. Snow, *Fit, Failure, and the Hall of Fame* (New York: Free Press, 1994); and G. Symon, "Information and Communication Technologies and Network Organization: A Critical Analysis," *Journal of Occupational and Organizational Psychology* 73, no. 4 (December 2000), pp. 389–95.

44. D. Dahl, "A Radical Take on the Virtual Company," *Inc.*, March 1, 2011, http://www.inc.com.

45. Miles and Snow, *Fit, Failure, and the Hall of Fame*.

46. S. C. Kang, S. S. Morris, and S. A. Snell, "Relational Archetypes, Organizational Learning, and Value Creation: Extending the Human Resource Architecture," *Academy of Management Review* 32, no. 1 (2007), pp. 236–56.

47. J. G. March and H. A. Simon, *Organizations* (New York: John Wiley & Sons, 1958); and J. D. Thompson, *Organizations in Action* (New York: McGraw-Hill, 1967).

48. P. S. Adler, "Building Better Bureaucracies," *Academy of Management Executive* 13, no. 4 (November 1999), pp. 36–49.

49. J. Galbraith, "Organization Design: An Information Processing View," *Interfaces* 4 (Fall 1974), pp. 28–36. See also S. A. Mohrman, "Integrating Roles and Structure in the Lateral Organization," in *Organizing for the Future*, ed.

J. Galbraith, E. E. Lawler III, & Associates (San Francisco: Jossey-Bass, 1993); and B. B. Flynn and F. J. Flynn, "Information-Processing Alternatives for Coping with Manufacturing Environment Complexity," *Decision Sciences* 30, no. 4 (Fall 1999), pp. 1021–52.

50. Galbraith, "Organization Design," and Mohrman, "Integrating Roles and Structure."

51. Rik Kirkland, "Making Internal Collaboration Work: An Interview with Don Tapscott," *McKinsey Quarterly*, January 2013, http://www.mckinseyquarterly.com; Darryl K. Taft, "IBM Tops Social Business Software Market Four Years in a Row," *eWeek*, April 23, 2013, http://www.eweek.com; Deloitte LLP, "Enterprise Social Networks: Useful Tool, Not a Panacea," *CIO Journal*, February 21, 2013, http://deloitte.wsj.com/cio/.

52. General Motors, Annual Report 2012; Higgins and Green, "GM Seen Planning Global Reorganization"; Qineqt, "General Motors Reorganization"; Eisenstein, "Big Management Shake-Up"; Klayman, "Car Guy or Bean Counter?"; Terlep, "GM's Chief Labors"; *Fortune*, "Mary Barra"; David Shepardson, "U.S. Sells Nearly 20 Percent of Remaining GM Shares," *Detroit News*, April 25, 2013, http://www.detroitnews.com; *CBS News*, "Government in March Sold $621M."

Chapter 9

1. General Electric 2012 Annual Report, http://www.ge.com/ar/2012/; General Electric, "Fact Sheet," http://www.ge.com/company/fact-sheet; Geoff Colvin, "Grading Jeff Immelt," *Fortune*, February 10, 2011, http://management.fortune.cnn.com; Kate Linebaugh, "GE Feels Its Own Cuts," *The Wall Street Journal*, September 17, 2012, http://online.wsj.com; Michal Lev-Ram, "Why GE Is Betting on Software," *Fortune*, April 25, 2013, http://tech.fortune.cnn.com.

2. C. O'Reilly and M. Tushman, "Ambidexterity as a Dynamic Capability: Resolving the Innovator's Dilemma," Research Paper no. 1963, Stanford Graduate School of Business, March 2007, http://ssrn.com/abstract=978493.

3. P. M. Wright, L. Dyer, and M. G. Takla, "What's Next? Key Findings from the 1999 State-of-the-Art and Practice Study," *Human Resource Planning* 22, no. 4 (1999), pp. 12–20; and Donald Sull, "How to Thrive in Turbulent Markets," *Harvard Business Review*, February 2009, pp. 78–88.

4. T. Burns and G. Stalker, *The Management of Innovation* (London: Tavistock, 1961).

5. D. Krackhardt and J. R. Hanson, "Information Networks: The Company

behind the Chart," *Harvard Business Review*, July–August 1993, pp. 104–11.

6. G. Hamel and C. K. Prahalad, "Competing for the Future," *Harvard Business Review*, July–August 1994, pp. 122–28.

7. G. Hamel and C. K. Prahalad, *Competing for the Future* (Boston: Harvard Business School Press, 1994).

8. D. G. Sirmon, M. A. Hitt, and R. D. Ireland, "Managing Firm Resources in Dynamic Environments to Create Value: Looking inside the Black Box," *Academy of Management Review* 32, no. 1 (2007), pp. 273–92.

9. J. Cohen, "Getting Rid of the Busy Work So You Can Get to Work," *Management Innovation eXchange*, June 25, 2010, http://www.managementexchange.com; and G. Hamel with P. Labarre, "Improving Our Capacity to Manage," *The Wall Street Journal*, April 6, 2011, http://blogs.wsj.com.

10. "Monster, NYT Form Online Jobs Alliance," *Reuters*, February 14, 2007, http://news.yahoo.com.

11. G. Slowinski, E. Hummel, A. Gupta, and E. R. Gilmont, "Effective Practices for Sourcing Innovation," *Research-Technology Management*, January–February 2009, pp. 27–34.

12. R. C. Sampson, "R&D Alliances and Firm Performance: The Impact of Technological Diversity and Alliance Organization on Innovation," *Academy of Management Journal* 50, no. 2 (2007), pp. 364–86.

13. R. M. Kanter, "Collaborative Advantage: The Art of Alliances," *Harvard Business Review*, July–August 1999, pp. 96–108; J. B. Cullen, J. L. Johnson, and T. Sakano, "Success through Commitment and Trust: The Soft Side of Strategic Alliance Management," *Journal of World Business* 35, no. 3 (Fall 2000), pp. 223–40; and P. Kale, H. Singh, and H. Perlmutter, "Learning and Protection of Proprietary Assets in Strategic Alliances: Building Relational Capital," *Strategic Management Journal* 21, no. 3 (March 2000), pp. 217–37.

14. P. Senge, *The Fifth Discipline* (New York: Doubleday Currency, 1990).

15. D. A. Garvin, "Building a Learning Organization," *Harvard Business Review*, July–August 1993, pp. 78–91; D. A. Garvin, *Learning in Action: A Guide to Putting the Learning Organization to Work* (Boston: Harvard Business School Press, 2000); and V. J. Marsick and K. E. Watkins, *Facilitating Learning Organizations: Making Learning Count* (Aldershot, Hampshire: Gower, 1999).

16. Ibid.; and N. Anand, H. K. Gardner, and T. Morris, "Knowledge-Based Innovation: Emergence and Embedding of New Practice Areas in Management Consulting Firms," *Academy of Management Journal* 50, no. 2 (2007), pp. 406–28.

17. J. G. March, "Exploration and Exploitation in Organizational Learning," *Organization Science* 2, no. 1 (February 1991), pp. 71–87; and S.-C. Kang and S. A. Snell, "Intellectual Capital Architectures and Ambidextrous Learning: A Framework for Human Resource Management," *Journal of Management Studies* 46, no. 1 (2009), pp. 65–92.

18. R. J. Vandenberg, H. A. Richardson, and L. J. Eastman, "The Impact of High Involvement Work Process on Organizational Effectiveness: A Second-Order Latent Variable Approach," *Group & Organization Management* 24, no. 3 (September 1999), pp. 300–39; G. M. Spreitzer and A. K. Mishra, "Giving Up Control without Losing Control: Trust and Its Substitutes' Effects on Managers' Involving Employees in Decision Making," *Group & Organization Management* 24, no. 2 (June 1999), pp. 155–87; and S. Albers Mohrman, G. E. Ledford, and E. E. Lawler III, *Strategies for High Performance Organizations—The CEO Report: Employee Involvement, TQM, and Reengineering Programs in Fortune 1000 Corporations* (San Francisco: Jossey-Bass, 1998).

19. R. Pagnamenta, "Transformation That Could Rescue Unilever from the Slippery Slope," *The Times (London)*, January 3, 2007; and "Unilever on Revival Track after Top Managers Culled," *Evening Standard (London)*, May 3, 2007, Business & Company Resource Center, http://galenet.galegroup.com.

20. "Alfred Chandler," *The Economist*, May 17, 2007, http://www.economist.com; C. Farrell, "Alfred Chandler: Big Business' Big Loss," *Bloomberg Businessweek*, May 14, 2007, http://www.businessweek.com.

21. Renee Dudley, "Walmart Faces the Cost of Cost-Cutting: Empty Shelves," *Bloomberg Businessweek*, March 28, 2013, http://www.businessweek.com.

22. Pagnamenta, "Transformation That Could Rescue Unilever."

23. L. L. Hellofs and R. Jacobson, "Market Share and Customers' Perceptions of Quality: When Can Firms Grow Their Way to Higher versus Lower Quality?" *Journal of Marketing* 63, no. 1 (January 1999), pp. 16–25.

24. J. Dean, "The Greatly Improbable, Highly Enjoyable, Increasingly Profitable Life of Michael Kobold," *Inc.*, May 2007, pp. 126–34.

25. V. Vara, "After GE," *The Wall Street Journal*, April 12, 2007, http://online.wsj.com.

26. Arik Hesseldahl, "Seven Questions for the Man Shaking Up HP's Operations, John Hinshaw," *All Things D*, March 19, 2013, http://allthingsd.com; Clint Boulton, "H-P Chief Counting on Tech Exec to Whip Cost Structure into Shape," *The Wall Street Journal*,

January 11, 2013, http://blogs.wsj.com/cio/; Bob Brown, "What the Man behind HP's New Internal IT Plan Has in Mind," *CIO*, April 23, 2013, http://www.cio.com.

27. W. F. Cascio, "Downsizing: What Do We Know? What Have We Learned?" *Academy of Management Executive* 7 (February 1993), pp. 95–104; and S. J. Freeman, "The Gestalt of Organizational Downsizing: Downsizing Strategies as Package of Change," *Human Relations* 52, no. 12 (December 1999), pp. 1505–41.

28. Erica Orden, "DreamWorks Weighs Layoffs," *The Wall Street Journal*, February 7, 2013, http://online.wsj.com; Paul Bond, "DreamWorks Animation Reports Healthy Quarter," *Hollywood Reporter*, April 30, 2013, http://www.hollywoodreporter.com.

29. W. F. Cascio, "Strategies for Responsible Restructuring," *Academy of Management Executive* 19, no. 4 (2005), pp. 39–50; Cascio, "Downsizing: What Do We Know?"; Freeman, "The Gestalt of Organizational Downsizing"; and M. Hitt, B. Keats, H. Harback, and R. Nixon, "Rightsizing: Building and Maintaining Strategic Leadership and Long-Term Competitiveness," *Organizational Dynamics*, Fall 1994, pp. 18–31.

30. C. D. Zatzick and R. D. Iverson, "High-Involvement Management and Workforce Reduction: Competitive Advantage or Disadvantage?" *Academy of Management Journal* 49, no. 5 (2006), pp. 999–1015.

31. Cascio, "Strategies for Responsible Restructuring"; Cascio, "Downsizing"; and J. Ciancio, "Survivor's Syndrome," *Nursing Management* 31, no. 5 (May 2000), pp. 43–45.

32. General Electric 2012 Annual Report; Lev-Ram, "Why GE Is Betting on Software"; Kate Linebaugh, "The New GE Way: Go Deep, Not Wide," *The Wall Street Journal*, March 7, 2012, http://online.wsj.com; Beth Kowitt, "How a Top GE Exec Engineered Himself out of a Job," *Fortune*, August 3, 2012, http://management.fortune.cnn.com; Kate Linebaugh, "GE Shake-Up Will Audition New Leaders," *The Wall Street Journal*, July 20, 2012, http://online.wsj.com; Ashlee Vance, "GE Tries to Make Its Machines Cool and Connected," *Bloomberg Businessweek*, http://www.businessweek.com; Peter Coy, "GE Builds a Better Battery," *Bloomberg Businessweek*, July 11, 2012, http://www.businessweek.com.

33. T. Wailgum, "CRM Definition and Solutions," *CIO*, March 6, 2007, http://www.cio.com; M. Burns, "CRM Survey 2011," *CA Magazine*, May 2011, http://www.camagazine.com; and M. Burns, "CRM Survey 2010," *CA Magazine*, April 2010, http://www.camagazine.com.

34. C. Dawson, "Toyota, Salesforce.com to Create Social Media Network for Vehicles," *The Wall Street Journal*, May 23, 2011, http://online.wsj.com; A. Eichler, "Prius Drivers Will Get Their Own Social Network," *The Atlantic*, May 23, 2011, http://www.theatlanticwire.com; C. Chiappinelli, "Toyota Taps Salesforce CRM Technology to Link Customers to Their Cars," *Managing Automation*, May 24, 2011, http://www.managingautomation.com; and A. Censky, "Toyota Wants You to Friend Your Car. Really," *CNNMoney*, May 23, 2011, http://money.cnn.com.

35. "Salesforce.com Offers Twitter Customer-Service App," *Information Week*, March 23, 2009, Business & Company Resource Center, http://galenet.galegroup.com; and E. Beck, "Daptiv's Greenhouse: Collaboration Grows," *BusinessWeek Online*, June 12, 2008, Business & Company Resource Center, http://galenet.galegroup.com.

36. K. Ishikawa, *What Is Total Quality Control? The Japanese Way*, trans. D. J. Lu (Englewood Cliffs, NJ: Prentice-Hall, 1985); and J. Seibert and J. Lingle, "Internal Customer Service: Has It Improved?" *Quality Progress* 40, no. 3 (March 2007), OCLC FirstSearch, http://firstsearch.oclc.org.

37. M. Porter, *Competitive Advantage: Creating and Sustaining Superior Performance* (New York: Free Press, 1985); and Internet Center for Management and Business Administration, "The Value Chain," Strategy pages, *NetMBA*, http://www.netmba.com.

38. B. Creech, *The Five Pillars of TQM: How to Make Total Quality Management Work for You* (New York: Plume Publishing, 1995); and J. R. Evans and W. M. Lindsay, *Management and Control of Quality* (Mason, OH: South-Western College Publishing, 1998).

39. National Institute of Standards and Technology, "Seven U.S. Organizations Honored with the 2010 Baldrige National Quality Award," news release, November 23, 2010, http://www.nist.gov.

40. International Organization for Standardization, "ISO 9000—Quality Management," http://www.iso.org.

41. J. Champy, *Reengineering Management* (New York: HarperBusiness, 1995). See also M. Hammer and J. Champy, *Reengineering the Corporation* (New York: HarperCollins, 1992).

42. J. Woodward, *Industrial Organization: Theory and Practice* (London: Oxford University Press, 1965).

43. J. H. Gilmore and B. J. Pine, eds., *Markets of One: Creating Customer-Unique Value through Mass Customization* (Cambridge, MA: Harvard Business Review Press, 2000); and B. J. Pine, *Mass Customization: The New Frontier in*

Business Competition (Cambridge, MA: Harvard Business School Press, 1992).

44. Christina Binkley, "Liberation from the Size Tag," *The Wall Street Journal*, January 30, 2013, http://online.wsj.com; eShakti, "About Us," http://www.eshakti.com. Patricia Fletcher, "Your Brand: What Customers Say behind Your Back," *Inc.*, March 29, 2013, http://www.inc.com; Lorraine Sanders, "Bow & Drape Takes On Bespoke E-Commerce with an Approach Tailor-Made for Women," *Fast Company*, November 8, 2012, http://www.fastcompany.com.

45. F. Sahin, "Manufacturing Competitiveness: Different Systems to Achieve the Same Results," *Production and Inventory Management Journal* 41, no. 1 (First Quarter 2000), pp. 56–65.

46. S. Wadhwa and K. S. Rao, "Flexibility: An Emerging Meta-Competence for Managing High Technology," *International Journal of Technology Management* 19, no. 7–8 (2000), pp. 820–45.

47. B. A. Peters and L. F. McGinnis, "Strategic Configuration of Flexible Assembly Systems: A Single Period Approximation," *IIE Transaction* 31, no. 4 (April 1999), pp. 379–90.

48. J. K. Liker and J. M. Morgan, "The Toyota Way in Services: The Case of Lean Product Development," *Academy of Management Perspectives* 20, no. 2 (May 2006), pp. 5–20; "Strategic Reconfiguration: Manufacturing's Key Role in Innovation," *Production and Inventory Management Journal* (Summer–Fall 2001), pp. 9–17; J. Jusko, "Lean Confusion," *Industry Week*, September 2010, pp. 32–34; and Sahin, "Manufacturing Competitiveness."

49. Travis Hessman, "Lean's High-Tech Makeover," *Industry Week*, November 14, 2012, http://www.industryweek.com.

50. Sahin, "Manufacturing Competitiveness"; and G. S. Vasilash, "Flexible Thinking: How Need, Innovation, Teamwork & a Whole Bunch of Machining Centers Have Transformed TRW Tillsonburg into a Model of Lean Manufacturing," *Automotive Manufacturing & Production* 111, no. 10 (October 1999), pp. 64–65.

51. T. Aeppel and J. Lahart, "Lean Factories Find It Hard to Cut Jobs Even in a Slump," *The Wall Street Journal*, March 9, 2009, http://online.wsj.com.

52. C. H. Chung, "Balancing the Two Dimensions of Time for Time-Based Competition," *Journal of Managerial Issues* 11, no. 3 (Fall 1999), pp. 299–314; and D. R. Towill and P. McCullen, "The Impact of Agile Manufacturing on Supply Chain Dynamics," *International Journal of Logistics Management* 10, no. 1 (1999), pp. 83–96. See also G. Stalk and T. M. Hout, *Competing against Time: How Time-Based Competition Is Reshaping Global Markets* (New York: Free Press, 1990).

53. M. Hayes Weier, "Best Buy Sees a Growth Future in RFID," *EE Times*, March 27, 2007, http://www.eetimes.com.

54. A. M. Field, "Where Have All the Flowers Gone?" *Journal of Commerce*, April 16, 2007, Business & Company Resource Center, http://galenet.galegroup.com.

55. M. Settle, "How to Use Virtualization to Save Money and Improve Service Quality," *eWeek*, August 23, 2010, Business & Company Resource Center, http://galenet.galegroup.com.

56. Patrice Novotny, "Japan Manufacturers in Post-Tsunami Rethink," *Industry Week*, March 5, 2012, http://www.industryweek.com; Kelly Marchese, Siva Paramasivam, and Michael Held, "Bouncing Back: Supply Chain Risk Management Lessons from Post-Tsunami Japan," *Industry Week*, March 9, 2012, http://www.industryweek.com.

57. R. Miel and D. Sedgwick, "Just-in-Time Seats Die Out," *Automotive News*, August 4, 2010, Business & Company Resource Center, http://galenet.galegroup.com.

58. J. E. Ettlie, "Product Development—Beyond Simultaneous Engineering," *Automative Manufacturing & Production* 112, no. 7 (July 2000), p. 18; U. Roy, J. M. Usher, and H. R. Parsaei, eds. *Simultaneous Engineering: Methodologies and Applications* (Newark, NJ: Gordon and Breach, 1999); and M. M. Helms and L. P. Ettkin, "Time-Based Competitiveness: A Strategic Perspective," *Competitiveness Review* 10, no. 2 (2000), pp. 1–14.

59. Richard J. Schonberger, "DFMA—a Potent Lean Methodology," *Assembly*, April 2013, http://www.assemblymag.com.

60. R. Ashkenas, D. Ulrich, T. Jick, and S. Kerr, *The Boundaryless Organization: Breaking the Chains of Organizational Structure* (San Francisco: Jossey-Bass, 1995); R. W. Keidel, "Rethinking Organizational Design," *Academy of Management Executive*, November 1994, pp. 12–27; and R. Ashkenas, T. Jick, D. Ulrich, and C. Paul-Chowdhury, *The Boundaryless Organization Field Guide: Practical Tools for Building the New Organization* (San Francisco: Jossey-Bass, 1999).

61. Guy Boulton, "GE Healthcare Systems CEO Sees Challenges, Opportunities," *Milwaukee Journal-Sentinel*, December 4, 2011, http://www.jsonline.com; General Electric, "What Is Six Sigma? The Roadmap to Customer Impact," n.d., http://www.ge.com/sixsigma/SixSigma.pdf; Ed Crooks, "Lean Cuts Fat off GE's Production Line," *Financial Times*, April 2, 2012, http://www.ft.com; Rachel King, "GE Becomes More Agile," *CIO Journal*, May 30, 2012, http://blogs.wsj.com; General Electric, "GE Aviation Delivers Its First Production Wing Components for the Airbus A350 XWB," news release, March 7, 2013, http://www.businesswire.com.

Chapter 10

1. J. Light, "Google Is No. 1 on List of Desired Employers," *The Wall Street Journal*, March 21, 2011, http://online.wsj.com; R. Waters, "Google Tries New Angle on Hiring," *Financial Times*, February 7, 2011, Business & Company Resource Center, http://galenet.galegroup.com; Digits, "Want to Work for Google? Here's How," *The Wall Street Journal*, June 8, 2011, http://online.wsj.com (video; interview with Joseph Walker); M. Liedtke and B. Ortutay, "Google Wants to Be Cool Again," *Houston Chronicle*, January 22, 2011, Business & Company Resource Center, http://galenet.galegroup.com; "100 Best Companies to Work for 2012," *Fortune*, February 6, 2012; Farhad Manjoo, "How Google Became Such a Great Place to Work," *Slate*, January 21, 2013, http://www.slate.com; Meghan Casserly, "Here's What Happens to Google Employees When They Die," *Forbes*, August 8, 2012, http://www.forbes.com.

2. N. Gardner, D. McGranahan, and W. Wolf, "Question for Your HR Chief: Are We Using Our 'People Data' to Create Value?" *McKinsey Quarterly*, March 2011, https://www.mckinseyquarterly.com.

3. "HR's Impact on Shareholder Value," *Workforce Management*, December 11, 2006, Business & Company Resource Center, http://galenet.galegroup.com.

4. P. M. Wright and S. A. Snell, "Partner or Guardian? HR's Challenge in Balancing Value and Values," *Human Resource Management* 44, no. 2 (2005), pp. 177–82.

5. E. Pofeldt, "Empty Desk Syndrome: How to Handle a Hiring Freeze," *Inc.*, May 2008, pp. 39–40; and C. Tuna, "Some Employers See Hiring Opportunity," *The Wall Street Journal*, April 3, 2009, http://online.wsj.com.

6. R. Mullins, "They're Loving It," *Tampa (Fla.) Tribune*, March 20, 2011, Business & Company Resource Center, http://galenet.galegroup.com; and J. R. Hagerty, "Help Wanted on Factory Floor," *The Wall Street Journal*, May 6, 2011, http://online.wsj.com.

7. Kristina Peterson, "Bill to Boost Visas Cheers Tech Firms," *The Wall Street Journal*, January 29, 2013, http://online.wsj.com; Jessica Cook, "The Clock Is Ticking: Timing on Foreign Visas Is Essential," *Employee Benefit News*, April 15, 2013, p. 10; Jonathan Rothwell and Neil G. Ruiz, "H-1B Visas and the STEM Shortage," Brookings Institution research paper, May 10, 2013, http://www.brookings.edu.

8. D. E. Hartley, *Job Analysis at the Speed of Reality* (Amherst, MA: HRD Press, 1999); F. P. Morgeson and M. A. Campion, "Accuracy in Job Analysis: Toward an Inference-Based Model," *Journal of Organizational*

Behavior 21, no. 7 (November 2000), pp. 819–27; and J. S. Shippmann, R. A. Ash, L. Carr, and B. Hesketh, "The Practice of Competency Modeling," *Personnel Psychology* 53, no. 3 (Autumn 2000), pp. 703–40.

9. J. S. Schippmann, *Strategic Job Modeling: Working at the Core of Integrated Human Resources* (Mahwah, NJ: Lawrence Erlbaum Associates, 1999).

10. D. E. Terpstra, "The Search for Effective Methods," *HR Focus*, May 1996, pp. 16–17; H. G. Heneman III and R. A. Berkley, "Applicant Attraction Practices and Outcomes among Small Businesses," *Journal of Small Business Management* 37, no. 1 (January 1999), pp. 53–74; and J.-M. Hiltrop, "The Quest for the Best: Human Resource Practices to Attract and Retain Talent," *European Management Journal* 17, no. 4 (August 1999), pp. 422–30.

11. G. Crispin and M. Mehler, "10th Annual CareerXroads Source of Hire Report: by the Numbers," CareerXroads, March 2011, http://www.careerxroads.com; and J. Light, "Recruiters Rethink Online Playbook," *The Wall Street Journal*, January 18, 2011, http://online.wsj.com.

12. F. Hansen, "Employee Referral Programs, Selective Campus Recruitment Could Touch Off Bias Charges," *Workforce Management*, June 26, 2006, General Reference Center Gold, http://find.galegroup.com.

13. R. Myers, "Interviewing Techniques: Tips from the Pros," *Journal of Accountancy* (August 2006), Business & Company Resource Center, http://galenet.galegroup.com; M. McDaniel, D. L. Whetzel, F. L. Schmidt, and S. D. Maurer, "The Validity of Employment Interviews: A Comprehensive Review and Meta-Analysis," *Journal of Applied Psychology* 79, no. 4 (August 1994), pp. 599–616; M. A. Campion, J. E. Campion, and P. J. Hudson Jr., "Structured Interviewing: A Note on Incremental Validity and Alternative Question Types," *Journal of Applied Psychology* 79, no. 6 (December 1994), pp. 998–1002; and R. A. Fear, *The Evaluation Interview* (New York: McGraw-Hill, 1984).

14. Myers, "Interviewing Techniques."

15. U.S. Merit Systems Protection Board, "The Federal Selection Interview: Unrealized Potential," February 2003, mspb.gov/studies/interview.htm; Lauren Weber, "Now Hiring? Tips for Conducting Interviews," *The Wall Street Journal*, December 4, 2012, http://online.wsj.com; Frederick P. Morgeson, "The Science of Talent Selection," *Health Management Technology*, April 2012, EBSCOhost, http://web.ebscohost.com.

16. T. Lewin, "Dean at M.I.T. Resigns, Ending a 28-Year Lie," *New York Times*, April 27, 2007, http://www.nytimes.com.

17. D. Meinert, "Seeing behind the Mask," *HR Magazine*, February 2011, pp. 31–37.

18. Ibid., p. 37.

19. T. Ackerman, "Does Psych Testing Result in Better Hires?" *Houston Chronicle*, June 21, 2010, Business & Company Resource Center, http://galenet.galegroup.com; Center for Advanced Human Resource Studies, "Should Personality Testing Be Part of the Hiring Process?" CAHRS ResearchLink, no. 12, November 2010, http://digitalcommons.ilr.cornell.edu; and E. Frauenheim, "Personality Tests Adapt to the Times," *Workforce Management*, February 1, 2010, Business & Company Resource Center, http://galenet.galegroup.com.

20. R. E. Ployhart, J. A. Weekley, and K. Baughman, "The Structure and Function of Human Capital Emergence: A Multilevel Examination of the Attraction-Selection-Attrition Model," *Academy of Management Journal* 49, no. 4 (2006), pp. 661–77.

21. R. Zeidner, "Putting Drug Screening to the Test," *HR Magazine*, November 2010, ProQuest, http://proquest.umi.com.

22. C. Rubin, "Medical Marijuana Laws Leave Employers Dazed and Confused," *Inc.*, February 12, 2010, http://www.inc.com.

23. P. M. Wright, M. K. Kacmar, G. C. McMahan, and K. Deleeuw, "$P = f(M \times A)$: Cognitive Ability as a Moderator of the Relationship between Personality and Job Performance," *Journal of Management* 21, no. 6 (1995), pp. 1129–2063; P. R. Sackett and D. J. Ostgaard, "Job-Specific Applicant Pools and National Norms for Cognitive Ability Tests: Implications for Range Restriction Corrections in Validation Research," *Journal of Applied Psychology* 79, no. 5 (October 1994), pp. 680–84; F. L. Schmidt and J. E. Hunter, "Tacit Knowledge, Practical Intelligence, General Mental Ability, and Job Knowledge," *Current Directions in Psychological Science* 2, no. 1 (1993), pp. 3–13; M. Roznowski, D. N. Dickter, L. L. Sawin, V. J. Shute, and S. Hong, "The Validity of Measures of Cognitive Processes and Generability for Learning and Performance on Highly Complex Computerized Tutors: Is the G Factor of Intelligence Even More General?" *Journal of Applied Psychology* 85, no. 6 (December 2000), pp. 940–55; and J. M. Cortina, N. B. Goldstein, S. C. Payne, H. K. Davison, and S. W. Gilliland, "The Incremental Validity of Interview Scores over and above Cognitive Ability and Conscientiousness Scores," *Personnel Psychology* 53, no. 2 (Summer 2000), pp. 325–51.

24. W. Arthur Jr., D. J. Woehr, and R. Maldegen, "Convergent and Discriminant Validity of Assessment Center Dimensions: A Conceptual and Empirical Reexamination of the Assessment Center Construct-Related Validity Paradox," *Journal of Management* 26, no. 4 (2000), pp. 813–35; and R. Randall, E. Ferguson, and F. Patterson, "Self-Assessment Accuracy and Assessment Center Decisions," *Journal of Occupational and Organizational Psychology* 73, no. 4 (December 2000), p. 443.

25. L. A. McFarland and A. M. Ryan, "Variance in Faking across Noncognitive Measures," *Journal of Applied Psychology* 85, no. 5 (October 2000), pp. 812–21. D. E. Terpstra, R. B. Kethley, R. T. Foley, and W. Limpaphayom, "The Nature of Litigation Surrounding Five Screening Devices," *Public Personnel Management* 29, no. 1 (Spring 2000), pp. 43–54.

26. D. S. Ones, C. Viswesvaran, and F. L. Schmidt, "Comprehensive Meta-Analysis of Integrity Test Validities: Findings and Implications for Personnel Selection and Theories of Job Performance," *Journal of Applied Psychology* 78 (August 1993), pp. 679–703.

27. S. Hananel, "Jobless People Need Not Apply?" *Houston Chronicle*, February 17, 2011, Business & Company Resource Center, http://galenet.galegroup.com.

28. Joseph Walker, "Meet the New Boss: Big Data," *The Wall Street Journal*, September 20, 2012, http://online.wsj.com; Steven Rosenbush and Michael Totty, "How Big Data Is Changing the Whole Equation for Business," *The Wall Street Journal*, March 8, 2013, http://online.wsj.com; Kathleen Koster, "Hiring Managers Turn to Software," *Employee Benefit News*, August 2012, pp. 26, 28.

29. R.-L. DeWitt, "The Structural Consequences of Downsizing," *Organization Science* 4, no. 1 (February 1993), pp. 30–40; and P. P. Shah, "Network Destruction: The Structural Implications of Downsizing," *Academy of Management Journal* 43, no. 1 (February 2000), pp. 101–12.

30. See *Adair v. United States*, 2078 U.S. 161 (1908): and D. A. Ballam, "Employment-at-Will; The Impending Death of a Doctrine," *American Business Law Journal* 37, no. 4 (Summer 2000), pp. 653–87.

31. J. A. Segal, "A Warning about Warnings," *HR Magazine*, February 2009, pp. 67–70; International Public Management Association for Human Resources (IPMA-HR), "Progressive Discipline," IPMA-HR Website, http://www.ipma-hr.org; U.S. Chamber of Commerce, "Progressive Discipline," http://business.uschamber.com; and D. Grote, "Positive Approach to Employee Discipline," *ManagerNewz*, March 12, 2007, http://archive.managernewz.com.

32. J. W. Bucking, "Employee Terminations: Ten Must-Do Steps When Letting Someone Go," *Supervision*, May 2008, Business & Company Resource Center, http://galenet.galegroup.com; and M. Price, "Employee Termination Process Is Tough for Those on Both Sides," *Journal Record (Oklahoma City, OK)*,

October 23, 2008, Business & Company Resource Center, http://galenet.galegroup.com.

33. *Employer EEO Responsibilities* (Washington, DC: Equal Employment Opportunity Commission, U.S. Government Printing Office, 1996); N. J. Edman and M. D. Levin-Epstein, *Primer of Equal Employment Opportunity*, 6th ed. (Washington, DC: Bureau of National Affairs, 1994).

34. Reuters, "Wal-Mart Settles Lawsuit on Hiring," *New York Times*, February 21, 2009, http://www.nytimes.com; T. L. Gallagher, "UP Settles Discrimination Suit," *Traffic World*, February 4, 2009, Business & Company Resource Center, http://galenet.galegroup.com; and A. Martinez, "Nordstrom Agrees to Pay to Settle Harassment Suit," *Seattle Times*, April 18, 2009, Business & Company Resource Center, http://galenet.galegroup.com.

35. R. Gatewood and H. Field, *Human Resource Selection*, 3rd ed. (Chicago: Dryden Press, 1994), pp. 36–49; and R. A. Baysinger, "Disparate Treatment and Disparate Impact Theories of Discrimination: The Continuing Evolution of Title VII of the 1964 Civil Rights Act," in *Readings in Personnel and Human Resource Management*, ed. R. S. Schuler, S. A. Youngblood, and V. L. Huber (St. Paul, MN: West Publishing, 1987).

36. L. Patel, "2010 State of the Industry: Continued Dedication to Workplace Learning," *T + D*, November 2010, pp. 48–53.

37. A. P. Carnevale, *America and the New Economy: How New Competitive Standards Are Radically Changing American Workplaces* (San Francisco: Jossey-Bass, 1991); M. Hequet, "Doing More with Less," *Training* 31 (October 1995), pp. 77–82; and R. M. Fulmer, P. A. Gibbs, and M. Goldsmith, "Developing Leaders: How Winning Companies Keep on Winning," *Sloan Management Review* 42, no. 1 (Fall 2000), pp. 49–59.

38. Lorri Freifeld, "Verizon's #1 Calling," *Training*, January/February 2013, EBSCOhost, http://web.ebscohost.com.

39. Ibid.

40. University of Colorado Denver, "Study Shows Employees Learn Best from Video Games," news release, October 19, 2010, http://www.ucdenver.edu.

41. J. Gordon, "Building Brand Champions: How Training Helps Drive a Core Business Process at General Mills," *Training*, January–February 2007, General Reference Center Gold, http://find.galegroup.com.

42. Light, "Google Is No. 1"; Waters, "Google Tries New Angle"; Digits, "Want to Work for Google?"; A. Fisher, "So You Want to Work at Google," *Fortune*, April 7, 2011, http://management.fortune.cnn.com; A. Bryant, "The Quest to Build a Better Boss," *New York Times*, March 13, 2011, Business & Company Resource Center, http://galenet.galegroup.com; Manjoo, "How Google Became Such a Great Place to Work"; Joseph Walker, "School's in Session at Google," *The Wall Street Journal*, July 5, 2012, http://online.wsj.com.

43. For more information, see K. Wexley and G. Latham, *Increasing Productivity through Performance Appraisal* (Reading, MA: Addison-Wesley, 1994).

44. F. Shipper, R. C. Hoffman, and D. M. Rotondo, "Does the 360 Feedback Process Create Actionable Knowledge Equally across Cultures?" *Academy of Management Learning & Education* 6, no. 1 (2007), pp. 33–50.

45. G. Toegel and J. Conger, "360 Degree Assessment: Time for Reinvention," *Academy of Management Learning and Education* 2, no. 3 (September 2003), p. 297; L. K. Johnson, "Retooling 360s for Better Performance," *Harvard Business School Working Knowledge*, February 23, 2004, online.

46. M. Edwards and A. J. Ewen, "How to Manage Performance and Pay with 360-Degree Feedback," *Compensation and Benefits Review* 28, no. 3 (May/June 1996), pp. 41–46. See also S. Crabtree, "What Your Employees Need to Know," *Gallup Management Journal*, April 13, 2011, Business & Company Resource Center, http://galenet.galegroup.com; and R. S. Schuler, *Personnel and Human Resource Management* (St. Paul, MN: West Publishing, 1984).

47. Bureau of Labor Statistics, "Employer Costs for Employee Compensation—March 2011," news release, June 8, 2011, http://www.bls.gov.

48. D. Darlin, "Using the Web to Get the Boss to Pay More," *New York Times*, March 3, 2007, http://www.nytimes.com.

49. A. Colella, R. L. Paetzold, A. Zardkoohi, and M. J. Wesson, "Exposing Pay Secrecy," *Academy of Management Review* 32, no. 1 (2007), pp. 55–71; Lauren Weber and Rachel Emma Silverman, "Workers Share Their Salary Secrets," *The Wall Street Journal*, April 16, 2013, http://online.wsj.com.

50. S. Gross and J. Bacher, "The New Variable Pay Programs: How Some Succeed, Why Some Don't," *Compensation and Benefits Review* 25, no. 1 (January–February 1993), p. 51; and G. T. Milkovich and J. M. Newman, *Compensation* (New York: McGraw-Hill/Irwin, 1999).

51. K. Maher and K. Hudson, "Wal-Mart to Sweeten Bonus Plans for Staff," *The Wall Street Journal*, March 22, 2007, http://online.wsj.com.

52. T. Welbourne and L. Gomez-Mejia, "Gainsharing: A Critical Review and a Future Research Agenda," *Journal of Management* 21, no. 3 (1995), pp. 559–609; L. P. Gomez-Mejia, T. M. Welbourne, and R. M. Wiseman, "The Role of Risk Sharing and Risk Taking under Gainsharing," *Academy of Management Review* 25, no. 3 (July 2000), pp. 492–507; D. Collins, *Gainsharing and Power: Lessons from Six Scanlon Plans* (Ithaca, NY: ILR Press, 1998); and P. K. Zingheim and J. R. Schuster, *Pay People Right!* (San Francisco: Jossey-Bass, 2000).

53. E. Krell, "All for Incentives, Incentives for All," *HR Magazine*, January 2011, pp. 35–38.

54. E. Grossfield, "Superintendent Gets a Good Review and Partial Bonus," *Post-Bulletin (Rochester, MN)*, July 13, 2006, Business & Company Resource Center, http://galenet.galegroup.com. See also D. W. Meyers, *Human Management: Principles and Practice* (Chicago: Commerce Clearing House, 1986); and J. P. Guthrie, "Alternative Pay Practices and Employee Turnover: An Organization Economics Perspective," *Group & Organization Management* 25, no. 4 (December 2000), pp. 419–39.

55. Lawrence Mishel and Natalie Sabadish, "CEO Pay and the Top 1%," Economic Policy Institute, May 2, 2012, http://www.epi.org; Stephen Miller, "Executive Pay: How Much Is Too Much?" Society of Human Resource Management, October 2, 2012, http://www.shrm.org; Nuno Fernandes, Miguel A. Ferreira, Pedro Matos, and Kevin J. Murphy, "Are U.S. CEOs Paid More? New International Evidence," *Review of Financial Studies* 26, no. 2 (2013), pp. 323–67.

56. M. J. Conyon, "Executive Compensation and Incentives," *Academy of Management Perspectives* 20, no. 1 (February 2006), pp. 25–44.

57. C. Forelle and J. Bandler, "The Perfect Payday," *The Wall Street Journal*, March 18, 2006, http://online.wsj.com.

58. Conyon, "Executive Compensation and Incentives."

59. J. D. Glater, "Stock Options Are Adjusted after Many Share Prices Fall," *New York Times*, March 27, 2009, http://www.nytimes.com; Carol Bowie, "Post-Crisis Trends in U.S. Executive Pay," Harvard Law School Forum on Corporate Governance and Financial Regulation, February 27, 2012, https://blogs.law.harvard.edu; Scott Thurm, "Pay for Performance' No Longer a Punchline," *The Wall Street Journal*, March 20, 2013, http://online.wsj.com.

60. Employee Benefit Research Institute, "Employer Spending on Health Insurance," in *EBRI Databook on Employee Benefits*, updated May 2011, http://www.ebri.org.

61. D. Cauchon, "Pension Gap Divides Public and Private Workers," *USA Today*, February 21, 2007, http://www.usatoday.com.

62. E. C. Kearns and M. Gallagher, eds., *The Fair Labor Standards Act* (Washington, DC: BNA, 1999).

63. C. Fay and H. W. Risher, "Contractors, Comparable Worth and the New OFCCP: Deja Vu and

More," *Compensation and Benefits Review* 32, no. 5 (September/October 2000), pp. 23–33; and G. Flynn, "Protect Yourself from an Equal-Pay Audit," *Workforce* 78, no. 6 (June 1999), pp. 144–46.

64. G. W. Bohlander, S. A. Snell, and A. W. Sherman Jr., *Managing Human Resources*, 12th ed. (Mason, OH: South-Western Publishing, 2001).

65. K. Maher, "Mine Probe Faults Massey," *The Wall Street Journal*, May 20, 2011, http://online.wsj.com.

66. Mine Safety and Health Administration, "Coal Fatalities for 1990 through 2010," Mining Fatality Statistics, http://www.msha.gov/stats/centurystats/coalstats.asp.

67. "U.S. Teens Work Late, Long and in Danger, Study," *Reuters*, March 5, 2007, http://news.yahoo.com; and C. K. Johnson, "Teens Tell about On-the-Job Dangers," *Chicago Tribune*, March 5, 2007, http://www.chicagotribune.com.

68. Dave Johnson, "Respect the Rules," *Industrial Safety & Hygiene News*, March 2013, pp. 34, 36; Royal Dutch Shell, "Strengthening Our Safety Culture," Environment & Society, http://www.shell.com/global/environment-society/safety/culture.html; Jon Birger, "Why Shell Is Betting Billions to Drill for Oil . . . Here," *Fortune*, June 11, 2012, EBSCOhost, http://web.ebscohost.com.

69. L. Kahn, *Primer of Labor Relations*, 25th ed. (Washington, DC: Bureau of National Affairs Books, 1994); and A. Sloane and F. Witney, *Labor Relations* (Englewood Cliffs, NJ: Prentice-Hall, 1985).

70. S. Premack and J. E. Hunter; "Individual Unionization Decisions," *Psychological Bulletin* 103 (1988), pp. 223–34; L. Troy, *Beyond Unions and Collective Bargaining* (Armonk, NY: M. E. Sharpe, 1999); and J. A. McClendon, "Members and Nonmembers: Determinants of Dues-Paying Membership in a Bargaining Unit," *Relations Industrielles* 55, no. 2 (Spring 2000), pp. 332–47.

71. R. Sinclair and L. Tetrick, "Social Exchange and Union Commitment: A Comparison of Union Instrumentality and Union Support Perceptions," *Journal of Organizational Behavior* 16, no. 6 (November 1995), pp. 669–79. See also Premack and Hunter, "Individual Unionization Decisions."

72. D. Lewin and Richard B. Peterson, *The Modern Grievance Procedure in the United States* (Westport, CT: Quorum Books, 1998).

73. G. Bohlander and D. Blancero, "A Study of Reversal Determinants in Discipline and Discharge Arbitration Awards: The Impact of Just Cause Standards," *Labor Studies Journal* 21, no. 3 (Fall 1996), pp. 3–18.

74. Light, "Google Is No. 1"; Liedtke and Ortutay, "Google Wants to Be Cool Again"; Bryant, "The Quest to Build a Better Boss"; A. Efrati and P. W. Tam, "Google Battles to Keep Talent," *The Wall Street Journal*, November 11, 2010, http://online.wsj.com; M. Ahmed, "Why Sensible Uncle Is Being Consigned to the Back Seat," *Times (London)*, January 22, 2011, Business & Company Resource Center, http://galenet.galegroup.com; C. C. Miller, "New Stage, New Skills," *New York Times*, January 22, 2011, Business & Company Resource Center, http://galenet.galegroup.com; Manjoo, "How Google Became Such a Great Place to Work"; Casserly, "Here's What Happens to Google Employees."

Chapter 11

1. Louis Llovio, "Diversity Making Inroads in NASCAR," *Richmond (Va.) Times Dispatch*, April 22, 2013, http://www.timesdispatch.com; Bill Speros, "Class Set for NASCAR's Drive for Diversity," *ESPN.com*, January 16, 2013, http://espn.go.com; Richard E. Lapchick, "NASCAR's Chairman Puts Talk of Diversity into Action," *Sports Business Journal*, May 13–19, 2013, http://www.sportsbusinessdaily.com; Al Pearce, "NASCAR Continues Drive for Diversity with '13 Class," *Autoweek*, January 16, 2013, http://www.autoweek.com; NASCAR, "Frequently Asked Questions," NASCAR Diversity, http://www.nascardiversity.com.

2. B. Eisenberg and M. Ruthsdotter, "Living the Legacy: The Women's Rights Movement 1848–1998," National Women's History Project, http://www.legacy98.org/move-hist.html.

3. Ibid.; and Bureau of Labor Statistics, "Labor Force Statistics from the Current Population Survey," http://www.bls.gov/cps.

4. Shung J. Shin, Tae-Yeol Kim, Jeong-Yeon Lee, and Lin Bian, "Cognitive Team Diversity and Individual Team Member Creativity: A Cross-Level Interaction," *Academy of Management Journal* 55 (February 2012), pp. 197–212; David A. Harrison and Katherine J. Klein, "What's the Difference? Diversity Constructs as Separation, Variety, or Disparity in Organizations," *Academy of Management Review* 32 (October 2007), pp. 1199–1228; and Scott E. Page, "Making the Difference: Applying a Logic of Diversity," *Academy of Management Perspectives* 21 (November 2007), pp. 6–20.

5. Bureau of Labor Statistics, "Employment Projections: 2006–16," news release, December 4, 2007, http://www.bls.gov.

6. U.S. Bureau of the Census, "Minority Population Tops 100 Million," news release, May 17, 2007, http://www.census.gov.

7. Bureau of Labor Statistics, "Household Data: Annual Averages," *Labor Force Statistics from the Current Population Survey*, http://www.bls.gov/cps/demographis.htm; and Bureau of Labor Statistics, *Women in the Labor Force: A Databook*, Report 1011, December 2008, http://www.bls.gov/cps/wlf-databook-2008.pdf.

8. C. Hymowitz, "Bend without Breaking: Women Executives Discuss the Art of Flex Schedules," *The Wall Street Journal*, March 6, 2007, http://online.wsj.com.

9. Bureau of Labor Statistics (BLS), "Labor Force Characteristics by Race and Ethnicity, 2011," Report 1036, August 2012, http://www.bls.gov; AAUW, "The Simple Truth about the Gender Pay Gap," 2013, http://www.aauw.org; Jessica Bennett, "How to Attack the Gender Wage Gap? Speak Up," *New York Times*, December 15, 2012, http://www.nytimes.com.

10. Catalyst, "Women CEOs of the *Fortune* 1000," May 2011, http://www.catalyst.org; and Alliance for Board Diversity, "Women and Minorities Lose Ground on *Fortune* 500 Corporate Boards, Alliance for Board Diversity Census Shows," news release, May 2, 2011, http://theabd.org.

11. Robi Ludwig, "Bad Female Boss? She May Have Queen Bee Syndrome," *Today*, April 12, 2011, http://www.today.com; Peggy Drexler, "The Tyranny of the Queen Bee," *The Wall Street Journal*, March 6, 2013, http://online.wsj.com.

12. A. Selko, "Gender Still a Large Hurdle to Career Advancement Say Women Execs," *Industry Week*, March 8, 2007, http://www.industryweek.com.

13. D. Carvajal, "The Codes That Need to Be Broken," *New York Times*, January 26, 2011, http://www.nytimes.com.

14. S. Armour, "Companies Try to Educate Teen Workers about Harassment," *USA Today*, October 19, 2006, http://www.usatoday.com.

15. G. Bohlander, S. Snell, and A. Sherman, *Managing Human Resources*, 12th ed. (Mason, OH: South-Western Publishing, 2001); and W. Petrocelli and B. K. Repa, *Sexual Harassment on the Job: What It Is and How to Stop It* (Berkeley, CA: Nolo Press, 1998).

16. Bureau of Labor Statistics (BLS), "Employment Projections, 2010–20," news release, February 1, 2012, http://www.bls.gov; BLS, "Foreign-Born Workers: Labor Force Characteristics, 2012," news release, May 22, 2013, http://www.bls.gov; Carol Morello and Ted Mellnik, "Census: Minority Babies Are Now Majority in United States," *Washington Post*, May 17, 2012, http://articles.washingtonpost.com.

17. "The United States of Entrepreneurs," *The Economist*, March 14, 2009, http://www.kauffman.org.

18. BLS, "Labor Force Characteristics by Race and Ethnicity, 2011."

19. M. Bertrand and S. Mullainathan, "Are Emily and Greg More Employable than Lakisha and Jamal?" NBER Working Paper No. 9873, July 2003, http://www.nber.org.

20. M. P. McQueen, "Workplace Disabilities Are on the Rise," *The Wall Street Journal*, May 1, 2007, http://online.wsj.com.

21. U.S. Bureau of the Census, "Anniversary of Americans with Disabilities Act: July 26," Facts for Features CB11-FF.14, May 31, 2011, http://www.census.gov; and Bureau of Labor Statistics, "Persons with a Disability: Labor Force Characteristics—2009," news release, August 25, 2010, http://www.bls.gov/cps.

22. Equal Employment Opportunity Commission (EEOC), "Disability Discrimination," http://www.eeoc.gov; EEOC, "Notice Concerning the Americans with Disabilities Act (ADA) Amendments Act of 2008," http://www.eeoc.gov; and EEOC, "ADA Charge Data by Impairments/Bases: Resolutions, FY1997–FY2008," http://www.eeoc.gov.

23. Daniel de Vise, "Number of U.S. Adults with College Degrees Hits Historic High," *Washington Post*, February 23, 2012, http://articles.washingtonpost.com; Bureau of the Census, "Kurt Bauman, Chief of the Education and Social Stratification Branch, Appeared on C-SPAN's 'Washington Journal' to Discuss Educational Attainment in the United States," newsroom, February 24, 2012, http://www.census.gov/newsroom/cspan/educ/; BLS, "Foreign-Born Workers."

24. U.S. Bureau of the Census, *Statistical Abstract of the United States: 2007*, table 574, p. 373; and AARP, "Workforce Trends," Money and Work pages of AARP website, http://www.aarp.org.

25. S. F. Gale, "Phased Retirement," *Workforce Management*, n.d., http://www.workforce.com.

26. Karen Aho, "Why Some Love Hiring Older Workers," *MSN Money*, April 9, 2013, http://money.msn.com; Francine M. Tishman, Sara Van Looy, and Susanne M. Bruyère, "Employer Strategies for Responding to an Aging Workforce," National Technical Assistance and Research (NTAR) Leadership Center, March 2012, http://www.dol.gov/odep; CVS Caremark, "Growing Career Opportunities," http://info.cvscaremark.com; Sloan Center for Aging and Work, "CVS Caremark Snowbird Program," case study, 2012, http://capricorn.bc.edu/agingandwork/database.

27. N. A. Hira, "Attracting the Twentysomething Worker," *Fortune*, May 15, 2007, http://money.cnn.com.

28. T. Hoffman, "Eight New Ways to Target Top Talent in '08," *Computerworld*, January 28, 2008, pp. 34, 36; and A. Kingsbury, "The CIA and NSA Want You to Be Their Friend on Facebook," *U.S. News & World Report Online*, February 5, 2009, Business & Company Resource Center, http://galenet.galegroup.com.

29. See, for example, C. Francoeur, R. Labelle, and B. Sinclair-Desgangné, "Gender Diversity in Corporate Governance and Top Management," *Journal of Business Ethics* 81, no. 1 (2008), pp. 83–95; A. McMillan-Capehart, J. R. Aaron, and B. N. Cline, "Investor Reactions to Diversity Reputation Signals," *Corporate Reputation Review* 13 (2010), pp. 184–97; P. Wang and J. L. Schwarz, "Stock Price Reactions to GLBT Nondiscrimination Policies," *Human Resource Management* 49, no. 2 (2010), pp. 195–216; R. C. Anderson, D. M. Reeb, A. Upadhyay, and W. Zhao, "The Economics of Director Heterogeneity," *Financial Management* 40, no. 1 (2011), pp. 5–38; and M. Davidson, "Leveraging Difference for Organizational Excellence: Managing Diversity Differently," technical note UVA-OB-0767 (Charlottesville, VA: Darden Business Publishing, 2002); Eric Kearney, Diether Gebert, and Sven C. Voelpel, "When and How Diversity Benefits Teams: The Importance of Team Members' Need for Cognition," *Academy of Management Journal* 52 (June 2009), pp. 581–598.

30. N. Adler, *International Dimensions of Organizational Behavior*, 3rd ed. (Boston: PWS-Kent, 1997); and T. Cox and S. Blake, "Managing Cultural Diversity: Implications for Organizational Competitiveness," *Academy of Management Executives* 5 (August 1991), pp. 45–56.

31. J. P. Morgan, "Diversity," corporate Careers page, http://careers.jpmorgan.com.

32. Procter & Gamble, "Diversity," corporate Careers website, http://www.pg.com/en_US/careers/diversity.shtml; Procter & Gamble, "Fulfilling Our Potential," corporate website, http://www.pg.com/en_US/company/; P. Sellers, "P&G Rates an 'A' for Board Diversity," *Fortune*, May 5, 2011, http://postcards.blogs.fortune.cnn.com; D. Holthaus, "'My Black' Campaign Helps P&G Diversify Workforce," *Cincinnati.com*, July 11, 2010, http://news.cincinnati.com; and A. Beckett, "P&G Appoints Picou as Its Supply Chain Director," *The Grocer*, August 21, 2010, p. 60.

33. See, for example, S. J. Tribble, "Cisco Accused of Bias in Hiring," *San Jose Mercury News*, May 10, 2007, http://www.mercurynews.com; G. Appleson, "Baby Boomers, Often Targeted in Layoffs, Fight Age Discrimination," *St. Louis Post-Dispatch*, April 29, 2007, Business & Company Resource Center, http://galenet.galegroup.com; "Class Action Suits in the Workplace Are on the Rise," *HR Focus*, April 2007, http://galenet.galegroup.com; and M. Schoeff Jr., "Walgreen Suit Reflects EEOC's Latest Strategies," *Workforce Management*, March 26, 2007, http://

galenet.galegroup.com; Erika Hayes James and Lynn Perry Wooten, "Diversity Crises: How Firms Manage Discrimination Lawsuits," *Academy of Management Journal* 49 (December 2006), pp. 1103–1118.

34. R. R. Thomas Jr., "From Affirmative Action to Affirming Diversity," *Harvard Business Review*, March–April 1990.

35. K. Jesella, "Mom's Mad, and She's Organized," *New York Times*, February 22, 2007, http://www.nytimes.com.

36. G. Avalos, "Study Looks at Diversity, Turnover," *Contra Costa Times (Walnut Creek, CA)*, October 13, 2006, Business & Company Resource Center, http://galenet.galegroup.com; Aparna Joshi and Hyuntak Roh, "The Role of Context in Work Team Diversity Research: A Meta-Analytic Review," *Academy of Management Journal* 52 (June 2009), pp. 559–627.

37. Adler, *International Dimensions of Organizational Behavior*; Cox and Blake, "Managing Cultural Diversity"; Brian Blume, Timothy Baldwin, and Katherine Ryan, "Communication Apprehension: A Barrier to Students' Leadership, Adaptability, and Multicultural Appreciation," *Academy of Management Learning and Education*, 12 September 12, 2012, pp.158–172.

38. J. D. Nordell, "Positions of Power: How Female Ambition Is Shaped," *Slate*, November 21, 2006, http://www.slate.com.

39. Adler, *International Dimensions of Organizational Behavior*.

40. Davidson, "Leveraging Difference for Organizational Excellence."

41. Llovio, "Diversity Making Inroads in NASCAR"; Speros, "Class Set for NASCAR's Drive for Diversity"; Pearce, "NASCAR Continues Drive for Diversity"; NASCAR, "Frequently Asked Questions"; Tom Bowles, "Drive for Diversity Drivers Talk Race and Gender in NASCAR," *SI.com (Sports Illustrated)*, July 30, 2010, http://sportsillustrated.cnn.com.

42. K. A. Jehn, "Workplace Diversity, Conflict, and Productivity: Managing in the 21st Century," SEI Center for Advanced Studies in Management, Wharton School, University of Pennsylvania, Diversity, http://mktg-sun.wharton.upenn.edu/SEI/diversity.html; Anne Nederveen Pieterse, Daan van Knippenberg, and Dirk van Dierendonck, "Cultural Diversity and Team Performance: The Role of Team Member Goal Orientation," *Academy of Management Journal*, 56 July 20, 2012, pp. 782–804.

43. A. J. Murrell, F. J. Crosby, and R. J. Ely, *Mentoring Dilemmas: Developmental Relationships within Multicultural Organizations* (Mahwah, NJ: Lawrence Erlbaum Associates, 1999). See a review of this book by

M. L. Lengnick-Hall, "Mentoring Dilemmas: Developmental Relationships within Multicultural Organizations," *Personnel Psychology* 53, no. 1 (Spring 2000), pp. 224–27.

44. A. Kalev, F. Dobbin, and E. Kelly, "Best Practices or Best Guesses? Assessing the Efficacy of Corporate Affirmative Action and Diversity Policies," *American Sociological Review* 71 (2006), pp. 589–617.

45. Brett Berson, Jack Zenger, Kellan Elliott-McCrea, and Joseph Folkman, "Why Recruiting Women Requires Creativity," *Build*, February 25, 2013, http://thebuildnetwork.com.

46. M. Y. Kinney, "Firm Makes a Case for Loyalty," *Philadelphia Inquirer*, April 5, 2009, Business & Company Resource Center, http://galenet.galegroup.com; R. Hightower, "Law Firm to Celebrate Employee's 50-Year Mark," *Philadelphia Tribune*, April 9, 2009, http://www.phillytrib.com; Caesar, Rivise, Bernstein, Cohen & Pokotilow, "About Us," http://www.crbcp.com; Drexel University, "Drexel at a Glance," http://www.drexel.edu; and Drexel University Earle Mack School of Law, "Diversity Initiatives," http://www.drexel.edu/law/diversity.asp.

47. A. Selko, "The Changing Faces of the Workplace," *Industry Week*, April 1, 2007, http://www.industryweek.com; and M. D. Lee, S. M. MacDermid, and M. L. Buck, "Organizational Paradigms of Reduced-Load Work: Accommodation, Elaboration, and Transformation," *Academy of Management Journal* 43, no. 6 (December 2000), pp. 1211–34.

48. L. E. Overmyer Day, "The Pitfalls of Diversity Training," *Training and Development* 49, no. 12 (December 1995), pp. 24–29; S. Rynes and B. Rosen, "A Field Survey of Factors Affecting the Adoption and Perceived Success of Diversity Training," *Personnel Psychology* 48, no. 2 (Summer 1995), pp. 247–70; L. Ford, "Diversity: From Cartoons to Confrontations," *Training & Development* 54, no. 8 (August 2000), pp. 70–71; and J. M. Ivancevich and J. A. Gilbert, "Diversity Management: Time for a New Approach," *Public Personnel Management* 29, no. 1 (Spring 2000), pp. 75–92; Katerina Bezrukova, Karen A. Jehn, and Chester S. Spell, "Reviewing Diversity Training: Where We Have Been and Where We Should Go," *Academy of Management Learning and Education* 11 (June 2012), pp. 207–227.

49. M. Burkart, "The Role of Training in Advancing a Diversity Initiative," *Diversity Factor* 8, no. 1 (Fall 1999), pp. 2–5.

50. "How Bad Is the Turnover Problem?" *HR Focus*, March 2007, Business & Company Resource Center, http://galenet.galegroup.com; B. Thomas, "Black Entrepreneurs Win, Corporations Lose," *BusinessWeek*, September 20, 2006, General Reference Center Gold, http://find.galegroup.com; and P. Shurn-Hannah, "Solving the Minority Retention Mystery," *The Human Resource Professional* 13, no. 3 (May/June 2000), pp. 22–27.

51. Ernst & Young, "Mentorship, Sponsorship Keys to Building a Strong and Committed Workforce," news release, April 12, 2011, http://www.ey.com/CA/en/.

52. Leslie Kwoh, "Firms Hail New Chiefs (of Diversity)," *The Wall Street Journal*, January 5, 2012, http://online.wsj.com; Center for Creative Leadership, "Ingersoll Rand: Using Gender Diversity as a Lever for Operational Excellence, Global Growth and Innovation," May 2013, http://www.ccl.org; Ingersoll Rand, "About Us" and "Company Information," http://company.ingersollrand.com; International Society of Diversity and Inclusion Professionals, "Champion: Nereida (Neddy) Perez," http://diversityandinclusionrprofessionals.org.

53. C. K. Johnson, "Study: Fat Workers Cost Employers More," *Associated Press*, April 23, 2007, http://news.yahoo.com.

54. R. Rodriguez, "Diversity Finds Its Place," *HRMagazine*, August 2006, Business & Company Resource Center, http://galenet.galegroup.com.

55. Llovio, "Diversity Making Inroads in NASCAR"; Speros, "Class Set for NASCAR's Drive for Diversity"; Lapchick, "NASCAR's Chairman Puts Talk of Diversity into Action"; Associated Press, "Jeremy Clements Looking for Redemption," *SI.com (Sports Illustrated)*, March 15, 2013, http://sportsillustrated.cnn.com; Heather Tucker, "Jeremy Clements' Racial Remark Revealed," *USA Today*, March 1, 2013, http://www.usatoday.com; George Diaz, "Suspension for Racial Slur Reflects NASCAR's Commitment to Diversity," *Chicago Tribune*, March 6, 2013, http://articles.chicagotribune.com; National Consortium for Academics and Sports, "Teamwork Leadership Institute," http://ncasports.org.

Chapter 12

1. George Anders, "Meg Whitman Jolts HP as Its Reluctant Savior," *Forbes*, May 22, 2013, http://www.forbes.com; James Bandler and Doris Burke, "How HP Lost Its Way," *Fortune*, May 21, 2012, EBSCOhost, http://web.ebscohost.com; Ashlee Vance and Aaron Ricade La, "Mark Hurd, Leo Apotheker, Meg Whitman in Hewlett-Packard's Vertigo," *Bloomberg Businessweek*, January 14, 2013, EBSCOhost, http://web.ebscohost.com; Dean Takahashi, "Meg Whitman Says 'You Can Feel the Turnaround Taking Place at HP' (but Not at Dell)," *VentureBeat*, May 22, 2013, http://venturebeat.com; Kevin McLaughlin, "HP Is Losing Some Rock Star Big Engineers," *Business Insider*, May 20, 2013, http://www.businessinsider.com.

2. W. Bennis and B. Nanus, *Leaders* (New York: Harper & Row, 1985), p. 27.

3. J. Petrick, R. Schere, J. Brodzinski, J. Quinn, and M. Fall Ainina, "Global Leadership Skills and Reputational Capital: Intangible Resources for Sustainable Competitive Advantage," *Academy of Management Executive*, February 1999, pp. 58–69.

4. Bennis and Nanus, *Leaders*.

5. Ibid., p. 144.

6. E. E. Lawler III, *Treat People Right! How Organizations and Individuals Can Propel Each Other into a Virtual Spiral of Success* (San Francisco: Jossey-Bass, 2003).

7. Alejandra Cancino, "Deliberate Change of Pace Works for ITW Attorney," *Chicago Tribune*, May 6, 2013, sec. 2, pp. 1, 4.

8. J. Kouzes and B. Posner, *The Leadership Challenge*, 2nd ed. (San Francisco: Jossey-Bass, 1995).

9. J. Kouzes and B. Posner, *The Leadership Challenge*, 1st ed. (San Francisco: Jossey-Bass, 1987).

10. Ibid.

11. Ibid.

12. J. Baum, E. A. Locke, and S. Kirkpatrick, "A Longitudinal Study of the Relation of Vision and Vision Communication to Venture Growth in Entrepreneurial Firms," *Journal of Applied Psychology* 83 (1998), pp. 43–54.

13. E. C. Shapiro, *Fad Surfing in the Boardroom* (Reading, MA: Addison-Wesley, 1995).

14. Kouzes and Posner, *The Leadership Challenge* (1995).

15. Ibid.

16. W. Bennis and R. Townsend, *Reinventing Leadership* (New York: William Morrow, 1995).

17. Ibid.

18. D. Mattioli and K. Maher, "At 3M, Innovation Comes in Tweaks and Snips," *The Wall Street Journal*, March 1, 2010, http://online.wsj.com.

19. Kouzes and Posner, *The Leadership Challenge* (1987).

20. J. A. Conger, "The Dark Side of Leadership," *Organizational Dynamics* 19 (Autumn 1990), pp. 44–55.

21. J. Conger, "The Vision Thing: Explorations into Visionary Leadership," in *Cutting Edge Leadership 2000*, ed. B. Kellerman and L. Matusak (College Park, MD: James MacGregor Burns Academy of Leadership, 2000).

22. Christopher Hann, "A Leading Personality," *Entrepreneur*, March 2012, pp. 59–62; Dinah Eng, "Barbara Corcoran: From Waitress to Real Estate Queen," *Fortune*, May 23, 2013, http://money.cnn.com; Barbara Corcoran, "My Favorite Mistake," *Newsweek*, January 16, 2012, http://www.thedailybeast.com/newsweek/.

23. J. P. Kotter, "What Leaders Really Do," *Harvard Business Review* 68 (May–June 1990) pp. 103–11.

24. M. E. Van Buren and T. Safferstone, "Collective Quick Wins," *Computerworld*, January 26, 2009, pp. 24–25.

25. G. Yukl, *Leadership in Organizations*, 3rd ed. (Englewood Cliffs, NJ: Prentice Hall, 1994).

26. R. House and R. Aditya, "The Social Scientific Study of Leadership: Quo Vadis?" *Journal of Management* 23 (1997), pp. 409–73.

27. R. D. Ireland and M. A. Hitt. "Achieving and Maintaining Strategic Competitiveness in the 21st Century. The Role of Strategic Leadership," *Academy of Management Executive*, February 1999, pp. 43–57.

28. P. Cappelli, H. Singh, J. V. Singh, and M. Useem, "Leadership Lessons from India," *Harvard Business Review*, March 2010, pp. 90–97.

29. J. Gardner, "The Heart of the Matter: Leader–Constituent Interaction," pp. 239–244, quote at p. 240. *Leading & Leadership*, ed. T. Fuller (Notre Dame, IN: University of Notre Dame Press, 2000).

30. R. E. Kelly, "In Praise of Followers," *Harvard Business Review* 66 (November–December 1988), pp. 142–48.

31. Bennis and Townsend, *Reinventing Leadership*.

32. Kelly, "In Praise of Followers."

33. J. S. Lublin, "Bosses' Small Gestures Send Big Signals," *The Wall Street Journal*, December 2, 2010, http://online.wsj.com; and R. I. Sutton, "Why Good Bosses Tune In to Their People," *McKinsey Quarterly*, August 2010, https://www.mckinseyquarterly.com.

34. J. R. P. French and B. Raven, "The Bases of Social Power," in *Studies in Social Power*, ed. D. Cartwright (Ann Arbor, MI: Institute for Social Research, 1959).

35. G. Yukl and C. Falbe, "Importance of Different Power Sources in Downward and Lateral Relations," *Journal of Applied Psychology* 76 (1991), pp. 416–23.

36. Ibid.

37. R. M. Stogdill, "Personal Factors Associated with Leadership: A Survey of the Literature," *Journal of Psychology* 25 (1948), pp. 35–71.

38. S. Kirkpatrick and E. Locke, "Leadership: Do Traits Matter?" *The Executive* 5 (May 1991), pp. 48–60.

39. G. A. Yukl, *Leadership in Organizations*, 2nd ed. (Englewood Cliffs, NJ: Prentice-Hall, 1989).

40. R. Heifetz and D. Laurie, "The Work of Leadership," *Harvard Business Review*, January–February 1997, pp. 124–34.

41. T. Judge, J. Bono, R. Ilies, and M. Gerhardt, "Personality and Leadership: A Qualitative and Quantitative Review," *Journal of Applied Psychology* 87 (2002), pp. 765–80.

42. A. Grant, F. Gino, and D. Hofmann, "Reversing the Extroverted Leadership Advantage: The Role of Employee Proactivity," *Academy of Management Journal* 54 (2011), pp. 528–550.

43. R. Foti and N. M. A. Hauenstein, "Pattern and Variable Approaches in Leadership Emergence and Effectiveness," *Journal of Applied Psychology* 92 (2007), pp. 347–55.

44. J. P. Kotter, *The General Managers* (New York: Free Press, 1982).

45. S. Zaccaro, R. Foti, and D. Kenny, "Self-Monitoring and Trait-Based Variance in Leadership: An Investigation of Leader Flexibility across Multiple Group Situations," *Journal of Applied Psychology* 76 (1991), pp. 308–15.

46. D. Goleman, "Leadership That Gets Results," *Harvard Business Review*, March–April 2000, pp. 78–90.

47. J. Misumi and M. Peterson, "The Performance-Maintenance (PM) Theory of Leadership: Review of a Japanese Research Program," *Administrative Science Quarterly* 30 (June 1985), pp. 198–223.

48. T. Judge, R. Piccolo, and R. Ilies, "The Forgotten Ones? The Validity of Consideration and Initiating Structure in Leadership Research," *Journal of Applied Psychology* 89 (2004), pp. 36–51.

49. G. Thomas, R. Martin, and R. Riggio, "Leading Groups: Leadership as a Group Process," *Group Processes & Intergroup Relations* 16 (2013), pp. 3–16.

50. Misumi and Peterson, "The Performance-Maintenance (PM) Theory."

51. Judge, Piccolo, and Ilies, "The Forgotten Ones?"

52. G. Graen and M. Uhl-Bien, "Relationship-Based Approach to Leadership: Development of Leader-Member Exchange (LMX) Theory of Leadership over 25 Years: Applying a Multi-Level Multidomain Perspective," *Leadership Quarterly* 6, no. 2 (1995), pp. 219–47.

53. House and Aditya, "The Social Scientific Study of Leadership."

54. C. R. Gerstner and D. V. Day, "Meta-Analytic Review of Leader-Member Exchange Theory: Correlates and Construct Issues," *Journal of Applied Psychology* 82 (1997), pp. 827–44.

55. House and Aditya, "The Social Scientific Study of Leadership."

56. J. Wagner III, "Participation's Effect on Performance and Satisfaction: A Reconsideration of Research," *Academy of Management Review*, April 1994, pp. 312–30.

57. R. White and R. Lippitt, *Autocracy and Democracy: An Experimental Inquiry* (New York: Harper & Brothers, 1960).

58. J. Muczyk and R. Steel, "Leadership Style and the Turnaround Executive," *Business Horizons*, March–April 1999, pp. 39–46.

59. A. Tannenbaum and W. Schmidt, "How to Choose a Leadership Pattern," *Harvard Business Review* 36 (March–April 1958), pp. 95–101.

60. E. Fleishman and E. Harris, "Patterns of Leadership Behavior Related to Employee Grievances and Turnover," *Personnel Psychology* 15 (1962), pp. 43–56.

61. R. Likert, *The Human Organization: Its Management and Value* (New York: McGraw-Hill, 1967).

62. R. Blake and J. Mouton, *The Managerial Grid* (Houston: Gulf, 1964).

63. Misumi and Peterson, "The Performance-Maintenance (PM) Theory."

64. J. Wall, *Bosses* (Lexington, MA: Lexington Books, 1986), p. 103.

65. Tannenbaum and Schmidt, "How to Choose a Leadership Pattern."

66. V. H. Vroom, "Leadership and the Decision-Making Process," *Organizational Dynamics*, Spring 2000, pp. 82–93.

67. F. E. Fiedler, *A Theory of Leadership Effectiveness* (New York: McGraw-Hill, 1967).

68. P. Hersey and K. Blanchard, *The Management of Organizational Behavior* (Englewood Cliffs, NJ: Prentice Hall, 1984).

69. Yukl, *Leadership in Organizations*.

70. R. J. House, "A Path Goal Theory of Leader Effectiveness," *Administrative Science Quarterly* 16 (1971), pp. 321–39.

71. J. Howell, J. Bowen, P. Dorfman, S. Kerr, and P. Podsakoff, "Substitutes for Leadership: Effective Alternatives to Ineffective Leadership," *Organizational Dynamics* 19 (Summer 1990), pp. 21–38.

72. R. G. Lord and W. Gradwohl Smith, "Leadership and the Changing Nature of Performance," in *The Changing Nature of Performance*, ed. D. R. Ilgen and E. D. Pulakos (San Francisco: Jossey-Bass, 1999).

73. S. Dionne, F. Yammarino, L. Atwater, and L. James, "Neutralizing Substitutes for Leadership Theory: Leadership Effects and Common-Source Bias," *Journal of Applied Psychology* 87 (2002), pp. 454–64.

74. Anders, "Meg Whitman Jolts HP"; Bandler and Burke, "How HP Lost Its Way"; Vance and La, "Mark Hurd, Leo Apotheker, Meg Whitman."

75. B. M. Bass, *Leadership and Performance Beyond Expectations* (New York: Free Press, 1985).

76. Y. A. Nur, "Charisma and Managerial Leadership: The Gift That Never Was," *Business Horizons*, July–August 1998, pp. 19–26; and R. J. House, "A 1976 Theory of Charismatic Leadership," in *Leadership: The Cutting Edge*, ed. J. G. Hunt and L. L. Larson (Carbondale, IL: Southern Illinois University Press, 1977).

77. M. Brown and L. Trevino, "Socialized Charismatic Leadership, Values Congruence, and Deviance in Work

Groups," *Journal of Applied Psychology* 91 (2006), pp. 954–62.

78. M. Potts and P. Behr, *The Leading Edge* (New York: McGraw-Hill, 1987).

79. J. Howell and B. Shamir, "The Role of Followers in the Charismatic Leadership Process: Relationships and Their Consequences," *Academy of Management Review* 30 (2005), pp. 96–112.

80. B. Galvin, P. Balkundi, and D. Waldman, *Academy of Management Review* 35 (2010), pp. 477–494.

81. J. Antonakis, M. Fenley, and S. Liechti, *Academy of Management Learning & Education* 10 (2011), pp. 374–396.

82. S. Yorges, H. Weiss, and O. Strickland, "The Effect of Leader Outcomes on Influence, Attributions, and Perceptions of Charisma," *Journal of Applied Psychology* 84 (1999), pp. 428–36.

83. Potts and Behr, *Leading Edge.*

84. D. A. Waldman and F. J. Yammarino, "CEO Charismatic Leadership: Levels-of-Management and Levels-of-Analysis Effects," *Academy of Management Review* 24 (1999), pp. 266–85.

85. A. Erez, V. F. Misangyi, D. E. Johnson, M. A. LePine, and K. C. Halverson, "Stirring the Hearts of Followers: Charismatic Leadership as the Transferral of Affect," *Journal of Applied Psychology* 93 (2008), pp. 602–16.

86. A. Fanelli and V. Misangyi, "Bringing Out Charisma: CEO Charisma and External Stakeholders," *Academy of Management Review* 31 (2006), pp. 1049–61.

87. House and Aditya, "The Social Scientific Study of Leadership."

88. D. A. Waldman, G. G. Ramirez, R. J. House, and P. Puranam, "Does Leadership Matter? CEO Leadership Attributes and Profitability under Conditions of Perceived Environmental Uncertainty," *Academy of Management Journal* 44 (2001), pp. 134–43.

89. B. Agle, N. Nagarajan, J. Sonnenfeld, and D. Srinivasan, "Does CEO Charisma Matter? An Empirical Analysis of the Relationships among Organizational Performance, Environmental Uncertainty, and Top Management Team Perceptions of CEO Charisma," *Academy of Management Journal* 49 (2006), pp. 161–74.

90. J. M. Howell and K. E. Hall-Merenda, "The Ties That Bind: The Impact of Leader-Member Exchange, Transformational and Transactional Leadership, and Distance on Predicting Follower Performance," *Journal of Applied Psychology* 84 (1999), pp. 680–94; and B. M. Bass, "Leadership: Good, Better, Best," *Organizational Dynamics,* Winter 1985, pp. 26–40.

91. Adam Lashinsky, "Amazon's Jeff Bezos: The Ultimate Disrupter," *Fortune,* November 16, 2012, http://management.fortune.cnn.com.

92. D. I. Jung and B. J. Avolio, "Effects of Leadership Style and Followers' Cultural Orientation on Performance in Group and Individual Task Conditions," *Academy of Management Journal* 42 (1999), pp. 208–18.

93. Bass, *Leadership.*

94. Bennis and Nanus, *Leaders.*

95. A. M. Grant, "Leading with Meaning: Beneficiary Contact, Prosocial Impact, and the Performance Effects of Transformational Leadership," *Academy of Management Journal* 55 (2012), pp. 458–476.

96. B. Bass, B. Avolio, and L. Goodheim, "Biography and the Assessment of Transformational Leadership at the World-Class Level," *Journal of Management* 13 (1987), pp. 7–20.

97. K. Albrecht and R. Zemke, *Service America* (Homewood, IL: Dow Jones Irwin, 1985).

98. Y. Ling, Z. Simisek, M. Lubatkin, and J. F. Veiga, "The Impact of Transformational CEOs on the Performance of Small to Medium-Sized Firms: Does Organizational Context Matter?" *Journal of Applied Psychology* 93 (2008), pp. 923–34.

99. T. A. Judge and J. E. Bono, "Five-Factor Model of Personality and Transformational Leadership," *Journal of Applied Psychology* 85 (2000), pp. 751–65; and B. Bass, "Does the Transactional-Transformational Paradigm Transcend Organizational and National Boundaries?" *American Psychologist* 22 (1997), pp. 130–42.

100. S. J. Shin and J. Zhou, "Transformational Leadership, Conservation, and Creativity: Evidence from Korea," *Academy of Management Journal* 46 (2003), pp. 703–14.

101. R. Piccolo and J. Colquitt, "Transformational Leadership and Job Behaviors: The Mediating Role of Core Job Characteristics," *Academy of Management Journal* 49 (2006), pp. 327–40.

102. A. Colbert, A. Kristof-Brown, B. Bradley, and M. Barrick, "CEO Transformational Leadership: The Role of Goal Importance Congruence in Top Management Teams," *Academy of Management Journal* 51 (2008), pp. 81–96.

103. A. Bryant, "The Dangers of Cynicism at the Office," *The New York Times,* December 4, 2010, http://www.nytimes.com; and T. Duryee, "How Lockerz Is Making Shopping a Lot More Fun for the 19 and Under Crowd," *All Things Digital,* February 3, 2011, http://emoney.allthingsd.com.

104. T. Dvir, D. Eden, B. Avolio, and B. Shamir, "Impact of Transformational Leadership on Follower Development and Performance: A Field Experiment," *Academy of Management Journal* 45 (2002), pp. 735–44.

105. B. M. Bass, *Transformational Leadership: Industry, Military, and Educational Impact* (Mahwah, NJ: Lawrence Erlbaum Associates, 1998). T. Judge and R. Piccolo, "Transformational and Transactional Leadership: A Meta-analytic Test of Their Relative Validity," *Journal of Applied Psychology* 89 (2004), pp. 755–768.

106. G. Spreitzer and R. Quinn, "Empowering Middle Managers to Be Transformational Leaders," *Journal of Applied Behavioral Science* 32 (1996), pp. 237–61.

107. J. Collins, "Level 5 Leadership," *Harvard Business Review* 1 (2001), pp. 66–76; and J. Kline Harrison and M. William Clough, "Characteristics of 'State of the Art' Leaders: Productive Narcissism versus Emotional Intelligence and Level 5 Capabilities," *Social Science Journal* 43 (2006), pp. 287–92.

108. D. Vera and M. Crossan, "Strategic Leadership and Organizational Learning," *Academy of Management Review* 29 (2004), pp. 222–40.

109. F. Luthans, *Organizational Behavior,* 10th ed. (New York: McGraw-Hill/Irwin, 2005). F. Luthans and B. Avolio, "Authentic Leadership Development," in *Positive Organizational Scholarship,* eds. K. Cameron, J. Dutton, and R. Quinn (San Francisco: Berrett-Koehler, 2003), pp. 241–258.

110. B. M. Bass, "Thoughts and Plans," in *Cutting Edge Leadership 2000,* ed. B. Kellerman and L. R. Matusak (College Park, MD: James MacGregor Burns Academy of Leadership, 2000), pp. 5–9.

111. N. Turner, J. Barling, O. Epitropaki, V. Butcher, and C. Milner, "Transformational Leadership and Moral Reasoning," *Journal of Applied Psychology* 87 (2002), pp. 304–11.

112. D. M. Mayer, M. Kuenzi, R. Greenbaum, M. Bardes, and R. Salvador, "How Low Does Ethical Leadership Flow? Test of a Trickle-Down Model," *Organizational Behavior and Human Decision Processes* 108 (2009), pp. 1–13.

113. Bass, "Thoughts and Plans."

114. Tiffany Hsu, "Yum CEO David Novak on Rubber Chickens, China and Taco Bell," *Los Angeles Times,* March 30, 2012, http://articles.latimes.com; J. P. Donlon, "CEO of the Year David Novak: The Recognition Leader," *Chief Executive,* June 27, 2012, http://chiefexecutive.net; Tony Bingham and Pat Galagan, "Taking People with You: David C. Novak's Leadership Philosophy Pays Off in Big Results for Yum Brands," *T + D,* April 2012, Business Insights: Essentials, http://bi.galegroup.com.

115. W. Bennis, "The End of Leadership: Exemplary Leadership Is Impossible without Full Inclusion, Initiatives, and Cooperation of Followers," *Organizational Dynamics,* Summer 1999, pp. 71–79.

116. Robert K. Greenleaf Center for Servant Leadership, "What Is Servant Leadership?" https://www.greenleaf.org; Larry W. Boone and Sanya Makhani, "Five Necessary Attitudes of a Servant Leader," *Review of Business* 83, no. 1 (Winter 2012), pp. 83–96.

117. D. Van Dierendonck, "Servant Leadership: A Review and Synthesis," *Journal of Management* 37 (2011), pp. 1228–1261.

118. Emma Johnson, "How to Become a Servant Leader," *Success*, December 5, 2011, http://www.success.com.

119. M. Hogg, D. van Knippenberg, and D. E. Rasst III, "Intergroup Leadership in Organizations: Leading across Group and Organizational Boundaries," *Academy of Management Review* 37 (2012), pp. 232–255; T. Pittinsky (ed.), *Crossing the Divide: Intergroup Leadership in a World of Difference* (Cambridge, MA: Harvard Business Publishing, 2009); T. Pittinsky and S. Simon, "Intergroup Leadership," *Leadership Quarterly* 18 (2007), pp. 586–605.

120. C. L. Pearce, "The Future of Leadership: Combining Vertical and Shared Leadership to Transform Knowledge Work," *Academy of Management Executive*, February 2004, pp. 47–57.

121. J. Carson, P. Tesluk, and J. Marrone, "Shared Leadership in Teams: An Investigation of Antecedent Conditions and Performance," *Academy of Management Journal* 50 (2007), pp. 1217–34.

122. R. Fisher and A. Sharp, *Getting It Done* (New York: HarperCollins, 1998).

123. J. Reed and B. Simon, "Adroit in Detroit," *Financial Times*, January 25, 2011, Business & Company Resource Center, http://galenet.galegroup.com; "Epiphany in Dearborn: Ford," *The Economist*, December 11, 2010, Business & Company Resource Center, http://galenet.galegroup.com; and J. LaReau, "Ford Slashes Debt, Spends on Operations," *Automotive News*, January 31, 2011, Business & Company Resource Center, http://galenet.galegroup.com.

124. P. Block, *The Empowered Manager* (San Francisco: Jossey-Bass, 1991).

125. Ibid.

126. Kouzes and Posner, *The Leadership Challenge* (1995).

127. L. W. Boone and M. S. Peborde, "Developing Leadership Skills in College and Early Career Positions," *Review of Business*, Spring 2008, Business & Company Resource Center, http://galenet.galegroup.com.

128. A. Gaines, "Straight to the Top," *American Executive*, August 2008, Business & Company Resource Center, http://galenet.galegroup.com; and S. J. Allen and N. S. Hartman, "Leadership Development: An Exploration of Sources of Learning," *SAM Advanced Management Journal*, Winter 2008, pp. 10–19, 62–63.

129. R. Fulmer, P. Gibbs, and M. Goldsmith, "Developing Leaders: How Winning Companies Keep on Winning," *Sloan Management Review* (Fall 2000), pp. 49–59.

130. M. McCall, *High Flyers* (Boston: Harvard Business School Press, 1998).

131. E. Van Velsor, C. D. McCauley, and R. Moxley, "Our View of Leadership Development," in *Center for Creative Leadership Handbook of Leadership Development*, ed. C. D. McCauley, R. Moxley, and E. Van Velsor (San Francisco: Jossey-Bass, 1998), pp. 1–25.

132. D. S. DeRue and N. Wellman, "Developing Leaders via Experience: The Role of Developmental Challenge, Learning Orientation, and Feedback Availability," *Journal of Applied Psychology* 94 (2009), pp. 859–75.

133. Anders, "Meg Whitman Jolts HP"; Bandler and Burke, "How HP Lost Its Way"; Vance and La, "Mark Hurd, Leo Apotheker, Meg Whitman"; Takahashi, "Meg Whitman Says 'You Can Feel the Turnaround'"; Bloomberg, "Biggest CEO Underachievers: Executives," Bloomberg Visual Data, http://www.bloomberg.com, last updated May 1, 2013; Henry Blodget, "Top CEOs Ranked by Their (Lousy) Stock Performance," *Yahoo Finance*, May 24, 2013, http://finance.yahoo.com.

Chapter 13

1. Mark C. Crowley, "How SAS Became the World's Best Place to Work," *Fast Company*, January 22, 2013, http://www.fastcompany.com; Omar Akhtar, "Best Companies: All-Stars," *Fortune*, January 24, 2013, http://money.cnn.com; "100 Best Companies to Work For 2013," *Fortune*, February 4, 2013, http://money.cnn.com; Great Place to Work, "World's Best Multinational Workplaces 2012," http://www.greatplacetowork.com; Nigel Barber, "What Makes Workers Happy? Lessons from the Best Company to Work For," *Psychology Today*, June 1, 2011, http://www.psychologytoday.com; Leigh Buchanan, "How SAS Continues to Grow," *Inc.*, August 23, 2011, http://www.inc.com; David Ranii, "SAS Rated World's Best Workplace," *News & Observer* (Raleigh, NC), November 14, 2012, http://www.newsobserver.com; SAS, "SAS Ranks No. 1 in the World for Best Workplaces," news release, November 14, 2012, http://www.sas.com; SAS website, http://www.sas.com; Nicola Leske, "SAS Says Spurned IBM and Others for Independence," Reuters, June 21, 2012, http://in.reuters.com.

2. R. Kreitner and F. Luthans, "A Social Learning Approach to Behavioral Management: Radical Behaviorists 'Mellowing Out,'" *Organizational Dynamics*, Autumn 1984, pp. 47–65.

3. D. Katz and R. L. Kahn, *The Social Psychology of Organizations* (New York: John Wiley & Sons, 1966).

4. C. A. Bartlett and S. Ghoshal, "Building Competitive Advantage through People," *Sloan Management Review*, Winter 2002, pp. 34–41.

5. E. Locke, "Toward a Theory of Task Motivation and Incentives," *Organizational Behavior and Human Performance* 3 (1968), pp. 157–89.

6. W. F. Cascio, "Managing a Virtual Workplace," *Academy of Management Executive*, August 2000, pp. 81–90.

7. E. A. Locke, "Guest Editor's Introduction: Goal-Setting Theory and Its Applications to the World of Business," *Academy of Management Executive* 4 (November 2004), pp. 124–25.

8. G. P. Latham, "The Motivational Benefits of Goal-Setting," *Academy of Management Executive* 4 (November 2004), pp. 126–29.

9. E. A. Locke, "Linking Goals to Monetary Incentives," *Academy of Management Executive* 4 (November 2004), pp. 130–33.

10. E. E. Lawler III, *Treat People Right!* (San Francisco: Jossey-Bass, 2003).

11. Ibid.

12. J. Bono and T. Judge, "Self-Concordance at Work: Toward Understanding the Motivational Effects of Transformational Leaders," *Academy of Management Journal* 46 (2003), pp. 554–71.

13. C. Crossley, C. Cooper, and T. Wernsing, "Making Things Happen through Challenging Goals: Leader Proactivity, Trust, and Business-Unit Performance," *Journal of Applied Psychology* (2013), pp. 540–549.

14. A. Wilson, "Kansas Quick Lane Operation Is Well-Tuned," *Automotive News*, April 5, 2010, Business & Company Resource Center, http://galenet.galegroup.com.

15. K. N. Shaw, "Changing the Goal-Setting Process at Microsoft," *Academy of Management Executive* 4 (November 2004), pp. 139–43.

16. S. Kerr and S. Laundauer, "Using Stretch Goals to Promote Organizational Effectiveness and Personal Growth: General Electric and Goldman Sachs," *Academy of Management Executive* 4 (November 2004), pp. 134–38.

17. Ibid.

18. Latham, "Motivational Benefits of Goal-Setting."

19. T. Mitchell and W. Silver, "Individual and Group Goals When Workers Are Interdependent: Effects on Task Strategies and Performance," *Journal of Applied Psychology* 75 (1990), pp. 185–93.

20. A. Kleingeld, H. van Mierlo, and L. Arends, "The Effect of Goal Setting on Group Performance: A Meta-Analysis,"

Journal of Applied Psychology 96 (2011), pp. 1289–1304.

21. Latham, "Motivational Benefits of Goal-Setting."

22. D. H. Pink, *Drive: The Surprising Truth about What Motivates Us* (New York: Riverhead Books, 2009), pp. 98–99.

23. M. Schweitzer, L. Ordonez, and B. Douma, "Goal Setting as a Motivator of Unethical Behavior," *Academy of Management Journal* 47 (2004), pp. 422–32.

24. M. A. Duran, "Norm-Based Behavior and Corporate Malpractice," *Journal of Economic Issues* 41, no. 1 (March 2007), Business & Company Resource Center, http://galenet.galegroup.com; and D. Durfee, "Management or Manipulation?" *CFO*, December 2006, http://galenet.galegroup.com.

25. G. Seijts and G. Latham, "Learning versus Performance Goals: When Should Each Be Used?" *Academy of Management Executive* 19 (February 2005), pp. 124–31; P. C. Early, T. Connolly, and G. Ekegren, "Goals, Strategy Development, and Task Performance: Some Limits on the Efficacy of Goal Setting," *Journal of Applied Psychology* 74 (1989), pp. 24–33; and C. E. Shalley, "Effects of Productivity Goals, Creativity Goals, and Personal Discretion on Individual Creativity," *Journal of Applied Psychology* 76 (1991), pp. 179–85.

26. R. C. Litchfield, "Brainstorming Reconsidered: A Goal-Based View," *Academy of Management Review* 33 (2008), pp. 649–668.

27. R. Fisher and A. Sharp, *Getting It Done* (New York: HarperCollins, 1998).

28. E. Thorndike, *Animal Intelligence* (New York: Macmillan, 1911).

29. A. D. Stajkovic and F. Luthans, "Differential Effects of Incentive Motivators on Work Performance," *Academy of Management Journal* 44 (2001), pp. 580–90.

30. J. Zaslow, "The Most-Praised Generation Goes to Work," *The Wall Street Journal*, April 20, 2007, http;//online.wsj.com.

31. K. Butterfield, L. K. Trevino, and G. Ball, "Punishment from the Manager's Perspective: A Grounded Investigation and Inductive Model," *Academy of Management Review* 39 (1996), pp. 1479–512.

32. Adam Madison, "Positive Results," *Rock Products*, September 1, 2008, Business & Company Resource Center, http://galenet.galegroup.com.

33. T. Judge and R. Piccolo, "Transformational and Transactional Leadership: A Meta-Analytic Test of Their Relative Ability," *Journal of Applied Psychology* 89 (2004), pp. 755–68.

34. S. Kerr, "On the Folly of Rewarding A While Hoping for B," *Academy of Management Journal* 18 (1975), pp. 769–83.

35. S. Lohr, "Science Finds Advantage in Focusing, Not Multitasking," *Chicago Tribune*, March 25, 2007, sec. 1, p. 10.

36. E. E. Lawler III, *Rewarding Excellence* (San Francisco: Jossey-Bass, 2000).

37. Colleen Leahey, "11 Top Perks from Best Companies," *Fortune*, January 18, 2013, http://money.cnn.com; "100 Best Companies to Work For: QuikTrip," *Fortune*, February 4, 2013, http://money.cnn.com.

38. J. H. Cho, "Lessons in Employee Appreciation," *Star-Ledger* (Newark, NJ), February 8, 2007, Business & Company Resource Center, http://galenet.galegroup.com.

39. J. Pfeffer and R. Sutton, *The Knowing–Doing Gap* (Boston: Harvard Business School Press, 2000).

40. J. S. Lublin, "Recall the Mistakes of Your Past Bosses, So You Can Do Better," *The Wall Street Journal*, January 2, 2007, http://online.wsj.com.

41. S. Moss and J. Sanchez, "Are Your Employees Avoiding You? Managerial Strategies for Closing the Feedback Gap," *Academy of Management Executive* 18, no. 1 (February 2004), pp. 32–44.

42. Lawler, *Treat People Right!*

43. S. B. Silverman, C. E. Pogson, and A. B. Cober, "When Employees at Work Don't Get It: A Model for Enhancing Individual Employee Change in Response to Performance Feedback," *Academy of Management Executive* 19, no. 2 (May 2005), pp. 135–47; and J. Jackman and M. Strober, "Fear of Feedback," *Harvard Business Review*, April 2003, pp. 101–7.

44. H. James Wilson, "Employees, Measure Yourselves," *The Wall Street Journal*, April 2, 2012, http://online.wsj.com; Sue Shellenbarger, "How Productivity Tools Can Waste Your Time," *The Wall Street Journal*, January 29, 2013, http://online.wsj.com; Bill Winterberg, "Maximize Your Technology Spending in 2012," *Journal of Financial Planning*, January 2012, pp. 34–35; Marguerite McNeal, "What's Your Number?" *Marketing Research*, Winter 2012, p. 3.

45. V. H. Vroom, *Work and Motivation* (New York: John Wiley & Sons, 1964).

46. R. E. Wood, P. W. B. Atkins, and J. E. H. Bright, "Bonuses, Goals, and Instrumentality Effects," *Journal of Applied Psychology* 84 (1999), pp. 703–20.

47. Melanie Scarborough, "The Rewards of Recognition: Six Strategies for Successful Employee Programs," *Community Banker*, January 2009, pp. 24–27.

48. Crowley, "How SAS Became the World's Best Place to Work"; Buchanan, "How SAS Continues to Grow"; Steve Lohr, "The Nimble Dance of a Rich Legacy Software Company," *New York Times*, March 28, 2013, http://bits.blogs.nytimes.com; Kristin Burnham, "Five Tips for Social Business Adoption: How SAS Succeeded," *CIO*, May 21, 2012, http://www.cio.com.

49. A. H. Maslow, "A Theory of Human Motivation," *Psychological Review*, July 1943, pp. 370–96.

50. L. Mainicro and D. Gibson, "Managing Employee Trauma: Dealing with the Emotional Fallout from 9-11," *Academy of Management Executive*, August 2003, pp. 130–43.

51. M. Wahba and L. Birdwell, "Maslow Reconsidered: A Review of Research on the Need Hierarchy Theory," *Organizational Behavior and Human Performance* 15 (1976), pp. 212–40.

52. G. Dessler, "How to Earn Your Employees' Commitment," *Academy of Management Executive*, May 1999, pp. 58–67, quoted on p. 63.

53. C. Hymowitz, "Managers Lose Talent When They Neglect to Coach Their Staffs," *The Wall Street Journal*, March 19, 2007, http://online.wsj.com.

54. Ibid.

55. C. Alderfer, *Existence, Relatedness, and Growth: Human Needs in Organizational Settings* (Glencoe, IL: Free Press, 1972).

56. C. Hymowitz, "When the Paycheck Isn't Optional, Ambition Is Less Complicated," *The Wall Street Journal*, April 26, 2007, http://online.wsj.com.

57. C. Pinder, *Work Motivation* (Glenview, IL: Scott, Foresman, 1984).

58. D. McClelland, *The Achieving Society* (New York: Van Nostrand Reinhold, 1961).

59. D. McClelland and R. Boyatzis, "Leadership Motive Pattern and Long-Term Success in Management," *Journal of Applied Psychology* 67 (1982), pp. 737–43.

60. N. Adler, *International Dimensions of Organizational Behavior*, 2nd ed. (Boston: Kent, 1991); and G. Hofstede, *Cultures and Organizations* (London: McGraw-Hill, 1991).

61. N. R. Lockwood, "Leveraging Employee Engagement for Competitive Advantage: HR's Strategic Role," *HRMagazine*, March 2007, Business & Company Resource Center, http://galenet.galegroup.com.

62. E. E. Lawler III and D. Finegold, "Individualizing the Organization: Past, Present, and Future," *Organizational Dynamics*, Summer 2000, pp. 1–15.

63. Ibid.

64. T. M. Amabile, "A Model of Creativity and Innovation in Organizations," in *Research in Organizational Behavior*, ed. B. M. Staw and L. L. Cummings (Greenwich, CT: JAI Press, 1988), pp. 10, 123–67.

65. C. M. Ford, "A Theory of Individual Creative Action in Multiple Social Domains," *Academy of Management Review* 21 (1996), pp. 1112–42.

66. G. Oldham and A. Cummings, "Employee Creativity: Personal and Contextual Factors at Work," *Academy of Management Journal* 39 (1996), pp. 607–34.

67. T. Amabile, R. Conti, H. Coon, J. Lazenby, and M. Herron, "Assessing

the Work Environment for Creativity," *Academy of Management Journal* 39 (1996), pp. 1154–84.

68. M. Campion and G. Sanborn, "Job Design," in *Handbook of Industrial Engineering*, ed. G. Salvendy (New York: John Wiley & Sons, 1991).

69. Lawler and Finegold, "Individualizing the Organization."

70. R. Garretson, "Job Rotation Pays Dividends," *Network World*, February 26, 2007, OCLC FirstSearch, http://firstsearch.oclc.org.

71. M. Campion and D. McClelland, "Interdisciplinary Examination of the Costs and Benefits of Enlarged Jobs: A Job Design Quasi-Experiment," *Journal of Applied Psychology* 76 (1991), pp. 186–98.

72. F. Herzberg, *Work and the Nature of Men* (Cleveland: World, 1966).

73. J. R. Hackman, G. Oldham, R. Janson, and K. Purdy, "A New Strategy for Job Enrichment," *California Management Review* 16 (Fall 1975), pp. 57–71.

74. Pink, *Drive*, p. 119.

75. R. Rechheld, "Loyalty-Based Management" *Harvard Business Review*, March–April 1993, pp. 64–73.

76. "Motivation in Today's Workplace: The Link to Performance," *HR Magazine*, July 2010, pp. 1–9.

77. B. Trahant, "Recruiting and Engaging the Federal Workforce," *Public Manager*, Spring 2008, Business & Company Resource Center, http://galenet.galegroup.com.

78. T. Peters and N. Austin, *A Passion for Excellence* (New York: Random House, 1985).

79. Ashish Gambhir, "Use Online Feedback to Motivate, Engage Employees," *QSRweb.com*, April 16, 2012, http://www.qsrweb.com; Parasole website, http://www.parasole.com.

80. Campion and Sanborn, "Job Design."

81. S. Seibert, S. Silver, and W. A. Randolph, "Taking Empowerment to the Next Level: A Multiple-Level Model of Empowerment, Performance, and Satisfaction," *Academy of Management Journal* 47 (2004), pp. 332–49.

82. C. Argyris, "Empowerment: The Emperor's New Clothes," *Harvard Business Review*, May–June 1998, pp. 98–105.

83. R. Forrester, "Empowerment: Rejuvenating a Potent Idea," *Academy of Management Executive*, August 2000, pp. 67–80; N. Lorinkova, M. Pearsall, and H. P. Sims, Jr., "Examining the Differential Longitudinal Performance of Directive versus Empowering Leadership in Teams," *Academy of Management Journal* 56 (2012), pp. 573–96; D. Liu, S. Zhang, L. Wang, and T. Lee, "The Effects of Autonomy and Empowerment on Employee Turnover: Test of a Multilevel Model in Teams," *Journal of Applied Psychology* 96 (2011), pp. 1305–16; M. T. Maynard, L. Gilson, and

J. Mathieu, "Empowerment—Fad or Fab? A Multilevel Review of the Past Two Decades of Research," *Journal of Management* 38 (2012), pp. 1231–81; X. Zhang and K. Bartol, "Linking Empowering Leadership and Employee Creativity: The Influence of Psychological Empowerment, Intrinsic Motivation, and Creative Process Engagement," *Academy of Management Journal* 53 (2010), pp. 107–28.

84. R. C. Liden, S. J. Wayne, and R. T. Sparrowe, "An Examination of the Mediating Role of Psychological Empowerment on the Relations between the Job, Interpersonal Relationships, and Work Outcomes," *Journal of Applied Psychology* 85 (2000), pp. 407–16.

85. Peters and Austin, A *Passion for Excellence*.

86. K. Thomas and B. Velthouse, "Cognitive Elements of Empowerment: An 'Interpretive' Model of Intrinsic Task Motivation," *Academy of Management Review* 15 (1990), pp. 666–81.

87. J. Kouzes and B. Posner, *The Leadership Challenge*, 2nd ed. (San Francisco: Jossey-Bass, 1995).

88. M. M. Butts, R. J. Vandenberg, D. M. DeJoy, B. S. Schaffer, and M. G. Wilson, "Individual Reactions to High Involvement Work Processes: Investigating the Role of Empowerment and Perceived Organizational Support," *Journal of Occupational Health Psychology* 14 (2009), pp. 122–36.

89. Price Waterhouse Change Integration Team, *Better Change* (Burr Ridge, IL: Richard D. Irwin, 1995).

90. E. E. Lawler III, *The Ultimate Advantage: Creating the High Involvement Organization* (San Francisco: Jossey-Bass, 1992).

91. O. Gadiesh and J. L. Gilbert, "Transforming Corner-Office Strategy into Frontline Action," *Harvard Business Review*, May 2001, pp. 72–79.

92. Kouzes and Posner, *The Leadership Challenge*.

93. W. A. Randolph and M. Sashkin, "Can Organizational Empowerment Work in Multinational Settings?" *Academy of Management Executive* 16 (2002), pp. 102–15.

94. J. Adams, "Inequality in Social Exchange," in *Advances in Experimental Social Psychology*, ed. L. Berkowitz (New York: Academic Press, 1965).

95. M. Bloom, "The Performance Effects of Pay Dispersion of Individuals and Organizations," *Academy of Management Journal* 42 (1999), pp. 25–40.

96. T. Jackson, "Dodd-Frank Will Only Deepen Corporate Pay Envy," *Financial Times*, March 21, 2011, Business & Company Resource Center, http://galenet.galegroup.com; and M. E. Podmolik, "Kraft CEO Sees Bonus Cut as Goals Go Unmet," *Chicago Tribune*, April 1, 2011, sec. 1, pp. 21, 23; Emily Chasan, "Executive Pay Gets

New Spin," *The Wall Street Journal*, September 25, 2012, http://online.wsj.com.

97. D. Prial, "Crunch Time for CPAs," *The Record (Bergen County, NJ)*, April 17, 2007, Business & Company Resource Center, http://galenet.galegroup.com.

98. D. Skarlicki, R. Folger, and P. Tesluk, "Personality as a Moderator in the Relationships between Fairness and Retaliation," *Academy of Management Journal* 42 (1999), pp. 100–108.

99. J. Brockner, "Making Sense of Procedural Fairness: How High Procedural Fairness Can Reduce or Heighten the Influence of Outcome Favorability," *Academy of Management Review* 27 (2002), pp. 58–76; and D. De Cremer and D. van Knippenberg, "How Do Leaders Promote Cooperation? The Effects of Charisma and Procedural Fairness," *Journal of Applied Psychology* 87 (2002), pp. 858–66.

100. M. Kernan and P. Hanges, "Survivor Reactions to Reorganization: Antecedents and Consequences of Procedural, Interpersonal, and Informational Justice," *Journal of Applied Psychology* 87 (2002), pp. 916–28.

101. Lawler, *Treat People Right!*

102. R. Shao, D. Rupp, D. Skarlicki, and K. Jones, "Employee Justice across Cultures: A Meta-Analytic Review," *Journal of Management* 39 (2013), pp. 263–301.

103. W. C. Kim and R. Mauborgne, "Fair Process: Managing in the Knowledge Economy," *Harvard Business Review*, July–August 1997, pp. 65–75.

104. T. Bateman and D. Organ, "Job Satisfaction and the Good Sold: The Relationship between Affect and Employee 'Citizenship,'" *Academy of Management Journal* (1983), pp. 587–95.

105. D. Henne and E. Locke, "Job Dissatisfaction: What Are the Consequences?" *International Journal of Psychology* 20 (1985), pp. 221–40.

106. J. Barling, E. K. Kelloway, and R. Iverson, "High-Quality Work, Job Satisfaction, and Occupational Injuries," *Journal of Applied Psychology* 88 (2003), pp. 276–83.

107. D. Bowen, S. Gilliland, and R. Folger, "HRM and Service Fairness: How Being Fair with Employees Spills Over to Customers," *Organizational Dynamics* (Winter 1999), pp. 7–23.

108. J. Harter, F. Schmidt, and T. Hayes, "Business-Unit-Level Relationship between Employee Satisfaction, Employee Engagement, and Business Outcomes: A Meta-Analysis," *Journal of Applied Psychology* 87 (2002), pp. 268–79.

109. T. Schweitzer, "U.S. Workers Hate Their Jobs More Than Ever," *Inc.*, March 6, 2007, http://www.inc.com.

110. Heiner Evanschitzky, Christopher Groening, Vikas Mittal, and Maren Wunderlich, "How Employer

and Employee Satisfaction Affect Customer Satisfaction: An Application to Franchise Services," *Journal of Service Research* 14, no. 2 (May 2011), pp. 136–48; and "Motivation in Today's Workplace," pp. 1–2, 4.

111. Erika Fry, "Low Key, High Quirk," *Fortune*, January 17, 2013, http://management.fortune.cnn.com; PlanteMoran, "Careers at Plante Moran," http://www.plantemoran.com.

112. R. E. Walton, "Improving the Quality of Work Life," *Harvard Business Review* (May–June 1974), pp. 12, 16, 155.

113. E. E. Lawler III, "Strategies for Improving the Quality of Work Life," *American Psychologist* 37 (1982), pp. 486–93; and J. L. Suttle, "Improving Life at Work: Problems and Prospects," in *Improving Life at Work*, ed. J. R. Hackman and J. L. Suttle (Santa Monica, CA: Goodyear, 1977); B. Erdogan, T. Bauer, D. Truxillo, et al., "Whistle while You Work: A Review of the Life Satisfaction Literature," *Journal of Management* 38 (2012), pp. 1038–83.

114. P. B. Warr, "Well-Being and the Workplace," in D. Kahneman, E. Diener, and N. Schwarz (eds.), *Well-Being: The Foundations of Hedonic Psychology* (New York: Russell Sage Foundation, 1999); and T. A. Wright and R. Cropanzano, "The Role of Psychological Well-Being in Job Performance: A Fresh Look at an Age-Old Quest." *Organizational Dynamics* 33 (2004), pp. 338–51.

115. J. K. Harter, F. L. Schmidt, and C. L. M. Keyes, "Well-Being in the Workplace and Its Relationship to Business Outcomes: A Review of the Gallup Studies," in C.L.M. Keyes and J. Haidt (eds.), *Flourishing: The Positive Person and the Good Life* (Washington DC: American Psychological Association, 2003), pp. 205–24.

116. David A. Kaplan, "Mars Incorporated: A Pretty Sweet Place to Work," *Fortune*, January 17, 2013, http://management.fortune.cnn.com; Anne VanderMey and David A. Kaplan, "A Workplace Gone to the Dogs," *Fortune*, January 17, 2013, http://management.fortune.cnn.com; Mars, "Careers That Mean More," http://www.mars.com; Noelle McElhatton, "Bruce McColl, Mars," *Marketing*, July 2012, pp. 25–27.

117. S. L. Robinson, "Trust and Breach of the Psychological Contract," *Administrative Science Quarterly* 41 (1996), pp. 574–99.

118. J. Robbins, M. Ford, and L. Tetrick, "Perceived Unfairness and Employee Health: A Meta-Analytic Integration," *Journal of Applied Psychology* 97 (2012), pp. 235–72.

119. D. Rousseau, "Changing the Deal While Keeping the People," *Academy of Management Executive* 10 (1996), pp. 50–58.

120. E. Ridolfi, "Executive Commentary," *Academy of Management Executive* 10 (1996), pp. 59–60.

121. E. E. Lawler III, *From the Ground Up* (San Francisco: Jossey-Bass, 1996).

122. Ibid.

123. S. Ghoshal, C. Bartlett, and P. Moran, "Value Creation: The New Management Manifesto," *Financial Times Mastering Management Review*, November 1999, pp. 34–37.

124. R. Hoffman, B. Casnocha, and C. Yen, "Tours of Duty: The New Employer-Employee Contract," *Harvard Business Review* (June 2013), pp. 48–58.

125. Ram Charan, "Stop Whining, Start Thinking," *BusinessWeek*, August 14, 2008, http://www.businessweek.com.

126. Crowley, "How SAS Became the World's Best Place to Work"; Buchanan, "How SAS Continues to Grow"; Great Place to Work, "World's Best Multinational Workplaces 2012"; *Fortune*, "100 Best Places to Work For 2013"; Barber, "What Makes Workers Happy?"; Jenn Mann, "The Best Place to Work . . . in the World!" *SAS Voices*, November 14, 2012, http://blogs.sas.com; Roberta Matuson, "Why Most Recruitment Strategies Are Failing and What You Can Do to Fix This," *Forbes*, March 13, 2013, http://www.forbes.com.

Chapter 14

1. John Mackey and Raj Sisodia, "Want to Hire Great People? Hire Consciously," *Fortune*, January 17, 2013, http://management.fortune.cnn.com; Andrea Davis, "Benefits Democracy: Whole Foods Takes Benefits to a Vote," *Employee Benefit News*, May 2012, p. 11; Jessica Rohman, "Whole Foods Market," Great Place to Work blog, March 6, 2013, http://www.greatplacetowork.com; Anne VanderMey, "World's Most Admired Companies 2013: Whole Foods Market," *Fortune*, March 18, 2013, http://money.cnn.com; Whole Foods Market, "Careers," http://www.wholefoodsmarket.com/careers; "Groups Wield Power at Whole Foods," *Executive Leadership*, May 2013, Business Insights: Essentials, http://bi.galegroup.com; Vance Cariaga, "Whole Foods Market Calms Street's Nerves over Growth," *Investors.com*, June 10, 2013, http://news.investors.com.

2. E. C. Wenger and W. M. Snyder, "Communities of Practice: The Organizational Frontier," *Harvard Business Review*, January–February 2000, pp. 139–45.

3. S. Cohen and D. Bailey, "What Makes Teams Work: Group Effectiveness Research from the Shop Floor to the Executive Suite," *Journal of Management* 23 (1997), pp. 239–90.

4. G. Chen, L. Donahue, and R. Klimoski, "Training Undergraduates to Work in Organizational Teams," *Academy of*

Management Learning and Education 3 (2004), pp. 27–40.

5. Steve Minter, "Better Together," *Industry Week*, February 2012, Business Insights: Global, http://bi.galegroup.com.

6. E. Fleischauer, "Nucor Manager Says Teamwork Key to Success; Q1 Earnings Up," *Decatur (AL) Daily*, April 20, 2007, http://www.decaturdaily.com.

7. A. Somech and A. Drach-Zahavy, "Translating Team Creativity to Innovation Implementation: The Role of Team Composition and Climate for Innovation," *Journal of Management* 39 (2013).

8. P. Demetrakakes, "Packaging a Big Part of General Success," *Food and Beverage Packaging*, October 2008, Business & Company Resource Center, http://galenet.galegroup.com.

9. D. Nadler, J. R. Hackman, and E. E. Lawler III, *Managing Organizational Behavior* (Boston: Little, Brown, 1979).

10. A. C. Edmondson, "Teamwork on the Fly," *Harvard Business Review* (April), pp. 72–80.

11. M. Cianni and D. Wnuck, "Individual Growth and Team Enhancement: Moving toward a New Model of Career Development," *Academy of Management Executive* 11 (1997), pp. 105–15.

12. S. Cohen, "New Approaches to Teams and Teamwork," in J. Galbraith, E. E. Lawler III, and Associates, *Organizing for the Future* (San Francisco: Jossey-Bass, 1993).

13. Cohen and Bailey, "What Makes Teams Work."

14. Satoru Iwata, "Iwata Asks: HarmoKnight," http://www.nintendo.co.uk; Ishaan, "How the Pokémon Studio's New Platformer, HarmoKnight, Came to Be," *Siliconera*, March 6, 2013, http://www.siliconera.com.

15. L. Mullins, "Integration Crew for Maryland Bank," *American Banker*, February 13, 2007, General Reference Center Gold, http://find.galegroup.com.

16. C. Snow, S. Snell, S. Davison, and D. Hambrick, "Use Transnational Teams to Globalize Your Company," *Organizational Dynamics*, Spring 1996, pp. 50–67.

17. B. Kirkman, B. Rosen, C. Gibson, P. Tesluk, and S. McPherson, "Five Challenges to Virtual Team Success: Lessons from Sabre, Inc.," *Academy of Management Executive* 16 (2002), pp. 67–80.

18. A. C. Edmondson, "Teamwork on the Fly," *Harvard Business Review* (April), pp. 72–80.

19. R. Banker, J. Field, R. Schroeder, and K. Sinha, "Impact of Work Teams on Manufacturing Performance: A Longitudinal Field Study," *Academy of Management Journal* 39 (1996), pp. 867–90.

20. D. Yeatts, M. Hipskind, and D. Barnes, "Lessons Learned from Self-Managed

Work Teams," *Business Horizons*, July–August 1994, pp. 11–18.

21. B. Kirkman and D. Shapiro, "The Impact of Cultural Values on Job Satisfaction and Organizational Commitment in Self-Managing Work Teams: The Mediating Role of Employee Resistance," *Academy of Management Journal* 44 (2001), pp. 557–69.

22. C. Langfred, "The Downside of Self-Management: A Longitudinal Study of the Effects of Conflict on Trust, Autonomy, and Task Interdependence in Self-Managing Teams," *Academy of Management Journal*, 2007, pp. 885–900.

23. B. Kirkman and D. Shapiro, "The Impact of Cultural Values on Employee Resistance to Teams: Toward a Model of Globalized Self-Managing Work Team Effectiveness," *Academy of Management Review* 22 (1997), pp. 730–57.

24. B. Macy and H. Isumi, "Organizational Change, Design, and Work Innovation: A Meta-Analysis of 131 North American Field Studies—1961–1991," *Research in Organizational Change and Development* 7 (1993), pp. 235–313.

25. Jill Jusko, "2012 IW Best Plants Winner: Engaged Teams Keep Lockheed Martin Delivering on Time, Every Time," *Industry Week*, January 17, 2013, http://www.industryweek.com.

26. Mackey and Sisodia, "Want to Hire Great People?"; Davis, "Benefits Democracy"; Rohman, "Whole Foods Market"; Whole Foods Market, "Careers"; *Executive Leadership*, "Groups Wield Power."

27. Cohen and Bailey, "What Makes Teams Work."

28. J. Katzenbach and D. Smith, "The Discipline of Teams," *Harvard Business Review*, March–April 1993, pp. 111–20.

29. B. W. Tuckman, "Developmental Sequence in Small Groups," *Psychological Bulletin* 63 (1965), pp. 384–99.

30. S. Furst, M. Reeves, B. Rosen, and R. Blackburn, "Managing the Life Cycle of Virtual Teams," *Academy of Management Executive*, May 2004, pp. 6–20. Quotes in this paragraph are from pp. 11 and 12.

31. M. Marks, J. Mathieu, and S. Zaccaro, "A Temporally Based Framework and Taxonomy of Team Processes," *Academy of Management Review* 26 (2011), pp. 356–76; F. Morgeson, D. S. DeRue, and E. Karam, "Leadership in Teams: A Functional Approach to Understanding Leadership Structures and Processes," *Journal of Management* 36 (2010), pp. 5–39.

32. C. J. G. Gersick, "Time and Transition in Work Teams: Toward a New Model of Group Development," *Academy of Management Journal* 31 (1988), pp. 9–41.

33. J. R. Hackman, *Groups That Work (and Those That Don't)*. (San Francisco: Jossey-Bass, 1990).

34. Ibid; "Teamwork on the Fly."

35. I. Hoever, D. van Knippenberg, W. van Ginkel, and H. Barkema, "Fostering Team Creativity: Perspective Taking as Key to Unlocking Diversity's Potential," *Journal of Applied Psychology* 97 (2012), pp. 982–96.

36. R. Cross, "Looking before You Leap: Assessing the Jump to Teams in Knowledge-Based Work," *Business Horizons*, September–October 2000, pp. 29–36.

37. Geoff Colvin, "The Art of the Self-Managing Team," *Fortune*, December 5, 2012, http://management.fortune.cnn.com; Chana R. Schoenberger, "How to Get People to Work Together," *Wall Street Journal*, September 7, 2012, http://blogs.wsj.com; John Baldoni, "The Secret to Team Collaboration: Individuality," *Inc.*, January 18, 2012, http://www.inc.com.

38. N. Lorinkova, M. Pearsall, and H. P. Sims Jr., "Examining the Differential Longitudinal Performance of Directive versus Empowering Leadership in Teams," *Academy of Management Journal* 56 (2013), pp. 573–96; M. T. Maynard, L. Gilson, and J. Mathieu, "Empowerment—Fad or Fab? A Multilevel Review of the Past Two Decades of Research," *Journal of Management* 38 (2012), pp. 1231–81; S. Seibert, G. Wang, and S. Courtright, "Antecedents and Consequences of Psychological and Team Empowerment in Organizations: A Meta-Analytic Review," *Journal of Applied Psychology* 96 (2011), pp. 981–1003; G. Chen, P. N. Sharma, S. Edinger, D. Shapiro, and J-L. Farh, "Motivating and Demotivating Forces in Teams: Cross-Level Influences of Empowering Leadership and Relationship Conflict," *Journal of Applied Psychology* 96 (2011), pp. 541–57.

39. A. Nahavandi and E. Aranda, "Restructuring Teams for the Reengineered Organization," *Academy of Management Executive*, November 1994, pp. 58–68.

40. B. Kirkman, B. Rosen, P. Tesluk, and C. Gibson, "The Impact of Team Empowerment on Virtual Team Performance: The Moderating Role of Face-to-Face Interaction," *Academy of Management Journal* 47 (2004), pp. 175–92.

41. J. R. Katzenbach and D. K. Smith, *The Wisdom of Teams* (Boston: Harvard Business School Press, 1993); and Maggie Starvish, "Why Leaders Need to Rethink Teamwork," *Forbes*, December 28, 2012, http://www.forbes.com.

42. Leigh Buchanan, "Taking Teamwork to the Extreme," *Inc.*, April 18, 2013, http://www.inc.com; David Brandt, "A Lean Take on Edison's Lab," *Industrial Engineer*, March 2012, pp. 50–52; Katherine Reynolds Lewis, "A Software Company Takes a Page from Toyota's Playbook," *Fortune*, October 6, 2011,

http://management.fortune.cnn.com; Menlo Innovations, "Our Story," http://www.menloinnovations.com.

43. Nadler et al., *Managing Organizational Behavior*.

44. Ibid.

45. Katzenbach and Smith, "The Discipline of Teams."

46. Ibid.

47. L. Gibson, J. Mathieu, C. Shalley, and T. Ruddy, "Creativity and Standardization: Complementary or Conflicting Drivers of Team Effectiveness?" *Academy of Management Journal* 48 (2005), pp. 521–31.

48. C. Meyer, "How the Right Measures Help Teams Excel," *Harvard Business Review*, May–June 1994, pp. 95–103.

49. J. R. Katzenbach and J. A. Santamaria, "Firing Up the Front Line," *Harvard Business Review*, May–June 1999, pp. 107–17.

50. D. Knight, C. Durham, and E. Locke, "The Relationship of Team Goals, Incentives, and Efficacy to Strategic Risk, Tactical Implementation, and Performance," *Academy of Management Journal* 44 (2001), pp. 326–38. A. Kleingeld, H. van Mierlo, and L. Arends, "The Effect of Goal Setting on Group Performance: A Meta-Analysis," *Journal of Applied Psychology* 96 (2011), pp. 1289–1304; C. Barnes, J. Hollenbeck, D. Jundt, D. S. De Rue, and S. Harmon, "Mixing Individual Incentives and Group Incentives: Best of Both Worlds or Social Dilemma?" *Journal of Management* 37 (2011), pp. 1611–35.

51. B. L. Kirkman and B. Rosen, "Powering Up Teams," *Organizational Dynamics* (Winter 2000), pp. 48–66.

52. Lawler, *From the Ground Up*.

53. A. Jassawalla, H. Sashittal, and A. Maishe, "Students' Perceptions of Social Loafing: Its Antecedents and Consequences in Undergraduate Business Classroom Teams," *Academy of Management Learning and Education*, 2009, pp. 42–54.

54. M. Erez, "Is Group Productivity Loss the Rule or the Exception? Effects of Culture and Group-Based Motivation," *Academy of Management Journal* 39 (1996), pp. 1513–37.

55. Katzenbach and Smith, "The Discipline of Teams."

56. Nanama Acheampong, "The Power of Positive Employee Recognition," *HR Focus*, December 2012, Business Insights: Global, http://bi.galegroup.com; Mark Funkhouser, "How to Insult Government Workers: Pay for Performance Sends All the Wrong Messages," *Governing*, April 2013, Business Insights: Global, http://bi.galegroup.com; and M. Johnson, J. Hollenbeck, S. Humphrey, D. Ilgen, D. Jundt, and C. Meyer, "Cutthroat Cooperation: Asymmetrical Adaptation to Changes in Team Reward Structures,"

Academy of Management Journal, 2006, 103–19.

57. M. J. Pearsall, M. S. Christian, and A. P. J. Ellis, "Motivating Interdependent Teams: Individual Rewards, Shared Rewards, or Something In Between?" *Journal of Applied Psychology* 95 (2010), pp. 183–91.

58. R. Wageman, "Interdependence and Group Effectiveness," *Administrative Science Quarterly* 40 (1995), pp. 145–80.

59. Mary K. Pratt, "Best Places Spotlight: NISC Supports Team Relationships," *Computerworld*, June 18, 2012, http://www.computerworld.com; "100 Best Places to Work in IT 2012: Employer Profile," *Computerworld*, June 18, 2012, http://www.computerworld.com; National Information Solutions Cooperative, "Careers: Benefits and Compensation," http://www.nisc.coop.

60. Lawler, *From the Ground Up.*

61. R. Preidt, "Work Teams Who Share Negative Emotions Better at Problem-Solving," *Bloomberg Businessweek*, November 23, 2010, http://www.businessweek.com.

62. A. Srivastava, K. Bartol, and E. Locke, "Empowering Leadership in Management Teams: Effects on Knowledge Sharing, Efficacy, and Performance," *Academy of Management Journal*, 2006, pp. 1239–51.

63. L. A. DeChurch and J. R. Mesmer-Magnus, "The Cognitive Underpinnings of Effective Teamwork: A Meta-Analysis." *Journal of Applied Psychology* 95 (2010), pp. 32–53.

64. J. M. Levine, E. T. Higgins, and H. Choi, "Development of Strategic Norms in Groups," *Organizational Behavior and Human Decision Processes* 82 (2000), pp. 88–101.

65. K. Jehn and E. Mannix, "The Dynamic Nature of Conflict: A Longitudinal Study of Intragroup Conflict and Group Performance," *Academy of Management Journal* 44 (2001), pp. 238–51.

66. J. O'Toole, *Vanguard Management: Redesigning the Corporate Future* (New York: Doubleday, 1985).

67. R. F. Bales, *Interaction Process Analysis: A Method for the Study of Small Groups* (Reading, MA: Addison-Wesley, 1950).

68. V. U. Druskat and J. Wheeler, "Managing from the Boundary: The Effective Leadership of Self-Managing Work Teams," *Academy of Management Journal* 46 (2003), pp. 435–57.

69. Katzenbach and Smith, *The Wisdom of Teams.*

70. J. Carson, P. Tesluk, and J. Marrone, "Shared Leadership in Teams: An Investigation of Antecedent Conditions and Performance," *Academy of Management Journal*, 2007, pp. 1217–34.

71. S. E. Seashore, *Group Cohesiveness in the Industrial Work Group* (Ann Arbor, MI: University of Michigan Press, 1954).

72. Banker et al., "Impact of Work Teams on Manufacturing Performance."

73. B. Mullen and C. Cooper, "The Relation between Group Cohesiveness and Performance: An Integration," *Psychological Bulletin* 115 (1994), pp. 210–27.

74. D. P. Forbes and F. J. Milliken, "Cognition and Corporate Governance: Understanding Boards of Directors as Strategic Decision-Making Groups," *Academy of Management Review* 24 (1999), pp. 489–505.

75. T. Simons, L. H. Pelled, and K. A. Smith, "Making Use of Difference: Diversity, Debate, and Decision Comprehensiveness in Top Management Teams," *Academy of Management Journal* 42 (1999), pp. 662–73.

76. Seashore, *Group Cohesiveness in the Industrial Work Group.*

77. B. Lott and A. Lott, "Group Cohesiveness as Interpersonal Attraction: A Review of Relationships with Antecedent and Consequent Variables," *Psychological Bulletin*, October 1965, pp. 259–309.

78. K. Dahlin, L. Weingart, and P. Hinds, "Team Diversity and Information Use," *Academy of Management Journal* 48 (2005), pp. 1107–23.

79. B. L. Kirkman and B. Rosen, "Beyond Self-Management: Antecedents and Consequences of Team Empowerment," *Academy of Management Journal* 42 (1999), pp. 58–74.

80. Hackman, *Groups That Work.*

81. W. Bennis, *Organizing Genius* (Reading, MA: Addison-Wesley, 1997).

82. Cianni and Wnuck, "Individual Growth and Team Enhancement."

83. K. Jehn, "A Multimethod Examination of the Benefits and Detriments of Intragroup Conflict," *Administrative Science Quarterly* 40 (1995), pp. 245–82.

84. Bill Saporito, "Cancer Dream Teams: Road to a Cure?" *Time*, March 21, 2013, http://healthland.time.com; Bill Saporito and Alice Park, "The Conspiracy to End Cancer," *Time*, April 1, 2013, EBSCOhost, urlhttp://web.ebscohost.com; Stand Up to Cancer, "SU2C Dream Teams," http://www.standup2cancer.org.

85. Wellins et al., *Inside Teams.*

86. J. A. Marrone, "Team Boundary Spanning: A Multilevel Review of Past Research and Proposals for the Future," *Journal of Management* 36 (2010), pp. 911–40.

87. D. G. Ancona, "Outward Bound: Strategies for Team Survival in an Organization," *Academy of Management Journal* 33 (1990), pp. 334–65.

88. Ibid.

89. L. Sayles, *Leadership: What Effective Managers Really Do, and How They Do It* (New York: McGraw-Hill, 1979).

90. Ibid.

91. P. Lencioni, "How to Foster Good Conflict," *The Wall Street Journal*, November 13, 2008, http://online.wsj.com; and D. Schachter, "Learn

to Embrace Opposition for Improved Decision Making," *Information Outlook*, October 2008, Business & Company Resource Center, http://galenet.galegroup.com.

92. J. Chatman and F. Flynn, "The Influence of Demographic Heterogeneity on the Emergence and Consequences of Cooperative Norms in Work Teams," *Academy of Management Journal* 44 (2001), pp. 956–74; and R. T. Keller, "Cross-Functional Project Groups in Research and New Product Development: Diversity, Communications, Job Stress, and Outcomes," *Academy of Management Journal* 44 (2001), pp. 547–55.

93. J-L. Farh, C. Lee, and C. Farh, "Task Conflict and Team Creativity: A Question of How Much and When," *Journal of Applied Psychology* (2010), pp. 1173–80; J. Shaw, J. Zhu, M. Duffy, K. Scott, H. A. Shih, and E. Susanto, "A Contingency Model of Conflict and Team Effectiveness," *Journal of Applied Psychology* 96 (2011), pp. 391–400; F. R. C. de Wit, L. Greer, and K. Jehn, "The Paradox of Intergroup Conflict: A Meta-Analysis," *Journal of Applied Psychology* 97 (2012), pp. 360–90; S. Thatcher and P. Patel, "Group Faultlines: A Review, Integration, and Guide for Research," *Journal of Management* 38 (2012), pp. 969–1009; Ibid.; "Fostering Team Creativity."

94. D. Tjosvold, *Working Together to Get Things Done* (Lexington, MA: Lexington Books, 1986).

95. C. Tinsley and J. Brett, "Managing Workplace Conflict in the United States and Hong Kong," *Organizational Behavior and Human Decision Processes* 85 (2001), pp. 360–81.

96. K. W. Thomas, "Conflict and Conflict Management," in *Handbook of Industrial and Organizational Psychology*, ed. M. D. Dunnette (Chicago: Rand McNally, 1976).

97. D. Tynan, "IT Turf Wars," *InfoWorld.com*, February 14, 2011, Business & Company Resource Center, http://galenet.galegroup.com.

98. Ibid.

99. K. W. Thomas, "Toward Multidimensional Values in Teaching: The Example of Conflict Behaviors," *Academy of Management Review*, 1977, pp. 484–89.

100. C. O. Longenecker and M. Neubert, "Barriers and Gateways to Management Cooperation and Teamwork," *Business Horizons*, September–October 2000, pp. 37–44.

101. M. Johnson, J. Hollenbeck, S. Humphrey, D. Algen, D. Jundt, and C. Meyer, "Cutthroat Cooperation: Asymmetrical Adaptation to Changes in Team Reward Structures," *Academy of Management Journal* 49 (2006), pp. 103–119.

102. P. S. Nugent, "Managing Conflict: Third-Party Interventions for Managers," *Academy of Management Executive* 16 (2002), pp. 139–54.

103. M. Blum and J. A. Wall Jr., "HRM: Managing Conflicts in the Firm," *Business Horizons*, May–June 1997, pp. 84–87.

104. S. Nunes, "How to Work outside Your Comfort Zone," *Bloomberg Businessweek*, July 6, 2010, http://www.businessweek.com.

105. J. A. Wall Jr. and R. R. Callister, "Conflict and Its Management," *Journal of Management* 21 (1995), pp. 515–58.

106. J. Polzer, C. B. Crisp, S. Jarvenpaa, and J. Kim, "Extending the Faultline Model to Geographically Dispersed Teams: How Collocated Subgroups Can Impair Group Functioning," *Academy of Management Journal* 49 (2006), pp. 679–92.

107. M. Montoya-Weiss, A. Massey, and M. Song, "Getting It Together: Temporal Coordination and Conflict Management in Global Virtual Teams," *Academy of Management Journal* 44 (2001), pp. 1251–62.

108. R. Standifer and J. A. Wall Jr., "Managing Conflict in B2B Commerce," *Business Horizons*, March–April 2003, pp. 65–70.

109. Mackey and Sisodia, "Want to Hire Great People?"; Rohman, "Whole Foods Market"; Whole Foods Market, "Careers"; *Executive Leadership*, "Groups Wield Power"; Mike Sunnucks, "Language Dispute Puts Whole Foods in Workplace Spotlight," *Phoenix Business Journal*, June 6, 2013, http://www.bizjournals.com/phoenix; Susanna Kim, "Whole Foods Says It Does Not Forbid Employees from Speaking Foreign Languages," *ABC News*, June 7, 2013, http://abcnews.go.com.

Chapter 15

1. Rachel Emma Silverman, "At Yahoo, Working from Home Doesn't Work," *The Wall Street Journal*, February 25, 2013, http://blogs.wsj.com; Kara Swisher, "'Physically Together': Here's the Internal Yahoo No-Work-from-Home Memo for Remote Workers and Maybe More," *All Things D*, February 22, 2013, http://allthingsd.com; Kara Swisher, "Survey Says: Despite Yahoo Ban, Most Tech Companies Support Work-from-Home for Employees," *All Things D*, February 25, 2013, http://allthingsd.com; Amanda Enayati, "A Work-from-Home Mom Defends Yahoo's Mayer," *CNN.com*, February 27, 2013, http://www.cnn.com; Yuki Noguchi, "Experts Boil Telecommuting Decisions Down to Flexibility vs. Serendipity," *Morning Edition*, February 28, 2013, http://www.npr.org; Patricia Sellers, "Marissa Mayer: Ready to Rumble at Yahoo," *Fortune*, October 11, 2012, http://postcards. blogs.fortune.cnn.com; "Softening Yahoo's Image? Company Rolls Out Parental Leave, Other Benefits," *HR Focus*, June 2013, p. 7; Stephanie Mlot, "Marissa Mayer Addresses Yahoo Staff in First Memo," *PC Magazine*, July 2012, EBSCOhost, http://web.ebscohost.com; "Mayer Brings Some Google to Yahoo, including Free Lunch," *PC Magazine*, July 2012, EBSCOhost, http://web.ebscohost.com; Brad Stone, Brian Womack, and Emily Chang, "Reading the Mind of Marissa Mayer," *Bloomberg Businessweek*, July 23, 2012, EBSCOhost, http://web.ebscohost.com.

2. L. Penley, E. Alexander, I. E. Jernigan, and C. Henwood, "Communication Abilities of Managers: The Relationship to Performance," *Journal of Management* 17 (1991), pp. 57–76.

3. W. V. Haney, "A Comparative Study of Unilateral and Bilateral Communication," *Academy of Management Journal* 7 (1964), pp. 128–36.

4. J. R. Mesmer-Magnus and L. A. DeChurch, "Information Sharing and Team Performance: A Meta-Analysis." *Journal of Applied Psychology* 94 (2009), pp. 535–46.

5. Boris Groysberg and Michael Slind, "Leadership Is a Conversation," *Harvard Business Review*, June 2012, pp. 76–84.

6. M. McCormack, "The Illusion of Communication," *Financial Times Mastering Management Review*, July 1999, pp. 8–9.

7. R. Cross and S. Brodt, "How Assumptions of Consensus Undermine Decision Making," *Sloan Management Review* 42 (2001), pp. 86–94.

8. S. Mohammed and E. Ringseis, "Cognitive Diversity and Consensus in Group Decision Making: The Role of Inputs, Processes, and Outcomes," *Organizational Behavior and Human Decision Processes* 85 (2001), pp. 310–35.

9. S. Parker and C. Axtell, "Seeing Another Viewpoint: Antecedents and Outcomes of Employee Perspective Taking," *Academy of Management Journal* 44 (2001), pp. 1085–100.

10. D. Tannen, "The Power of Talk: Who Gets Heard and Why," *Harvard Business Review*, September–October 1995, pp. 138–48.

11. Ibid.

12. Ibid.

13. L. K. Larkey, "Toward a Theory of Communicative Interactions in Culturally Diverse Workgroups," *Academy of Management Review*, April 1996, pp. 463–91.

14. L. A. Liu, C.H. Chua, and G. Stahl, "Quality of Communication Experience: Definition, Measurement, and Implications for Intercultural Negotiations," *Journal of Applied Psychology* 95 (2010), pp. 469–87.

15. C. Argyris, "Good Communication That Blocks Learning," *Harvard Business Review*, July–August 1994, pp. 77–85.

16. E. Krell, "The Unintended Word," *HRMagazine*, August 2006, General Reference Center Gold, http://find.galegroup.com.

17. C. Deutsch, "The Multimedia Benefits Kit," *The New York Times*, October 14, 1990, sec.3, p. 25.

18. T. W. Comstock, *Communicating in Business and Industry* (Albany, NY: Delmar, 1985).

19. N. L. Reinsch Jr., J. W. Turner, and C. H. Tinsley, "Multicommunicating: A Practice Whose Time Has Come?" *Academy of Management Review* 33 (2008), pp. 391–403.

20. J. Taylor and W. Wacker, *The 500 Year Delta: What Happens after What Comes Next* (New York: HarperCollins, 1997).

21. Michael Chui, James Manyika, Jacques Bughin, et al., "The Social Economy: Unlocking Value and Productivity through Social Technologies," McKinsey Global Institute, July 2012, http://www.mckinsey.com.

22. J. Dye, "Collaboration 2.0: Make the Web Your Workspace," *EContent*, January– February 2007, General Reference Center Gold, http://find.galegroup.com.

23. S. S. K. Lam and J. Schaubroeck, "Improving Group Decisions by Better Pooling Information: A Comparative Advantage of Group Decision Support Systems," *Journal of Applied Psychology* 85 (2000), pp. 565–73.

24. M. Schmulen, "Memo to the Boss: Twitter's Not a Time Suck," *Fortune*, January 19, 2010, http://tech.fortune.cnn.com; D. Lindorff, "Facing Up to Facebook," *Treasury & Risk*, April 2011, Business & Company Resource Center, http://galenet.galegroup.com; and S. Ali, "Why No One under 30 Answers Your Voicemail," *DiversityInc*, August 27, 2010, http://www.diversityinc.com.

25. C. Naquin, T. Kurtzberg, and L. Belkin, "The Finer Points of Lying Online: E-Mail versus Pen and Paper," *Journal of Applied Psychology* 95 (2010), pp. 387–94.

26. C. Naquin and G. Paulson, "Online Bargaining and Interpersonal Trust," *Journal of Applied Psychology* 88 (2003), pp. 113–20.

27. B. Baltes, M. Dickson, M. Sherman, C. Bauer, and J. LaGanke, "Computer-Mediated Communication and Group Decision Making: A Meta-Analysis," *Organizational Behavior and Human Decision Processes* 87 (2002), pp. 156–79.

28. R. Rice and D. Case, "Electronic Message Systems in the University: A Description of Use and Utility," *Journal of Communication* 33 (1983), pp. 131–52; and C. Steinfield, "Dimensions of Electronic Mail Use in an Organizational Setting," *Proceedings of the Academy of Management*, San Diego, 1985.

29. M. Gardner, "You've Got Mail: 'We're Letting You Go,'" *Christian Science Monitor*, September 18, 2006, http://www.csmonitor.com; and Linton Weeks,

"Read the Blog: You're Fired," *National Public Radio*, December 8, 2008, http://www.npr.org.

30. Lindorff, "Facing Up to Facebook."

31. Reuters, "Is That Really What Your E-mail Meant to Say?" *Yahoo News*, February 14, 2007, http://news.yahoo.com.

32. K. Byron, "Carrying Too Heavy a Load? The Communication and Miscommunication of Emotion by Email," *Academy of Management Review* 33 (2008), pp. 309–27.

33. C. E. Naquin, T. R. Kurtzberg, and L. Y. Belkin, "The Finer Points of Lying Online: E-mail versus Pen and Paper," *Journal of Applied Psychology* 95 (2010), pp. 387–94.

34. B. Glassberg, W. Kettinger, and J. Logan, "Electronic Communication: An Ounce of Policy Is Worth a Pound of Cure," *Business Horizons*, July–August 1996, pp. 74–80.

35. Ali, "Why No One under 30 Answers Your Voicemail."

36. M. Totty, "Rethinking the Inbox," *The Wall Street Journal*, March 26, 2007, http://online.wsj.com. Reuters, "BlackBerrys, Laptops Blur Work/Home Balance: Poll," *Yahoo News*, April 5, 2007, http://news.yahoo.com; and M. Locher, "BlackBerry Addiction Starts at the Top," *PC World*, March 6, 2007, http://www.pcworld.com.

37. Chui et al., "The Social Economy," p. 47.

38. Robby Macdonell, "Can We Talk for a Minute about Why Email Sucks So Much?" *RescueTime Blog*, February 16, 2013, http://blog.rescuetime.com.

39. Chui et al., "The Social Economy," p. 29.

40. Locher, "BlackBerry Addiction."

41. E. Horng, "No E-mail Fridays Transform Office," *ABC News*, March 10, 2007, http://abcnews.go.com.

42. Ibid.

43. T. Mackintosh, "Is This the Year You Move to a Virtual Office?" *Accounting Technology*, May 2007, General Reference Center Gold, http://find.galegroup.com.

44. E. M. Hallowell, "The Human Moment at Work," *Harvard Business Review*, January–February 1999, pp. 58–66.

45. Rachel Emma Silverman, "Step into the Office-less Company," *The Wall Street Journal*, September 4, 2012, http://online.wsj.com; Verne Kopytoff, "Why Some Company Offices Are Virtual," *Businessweek*, September 10, 2012, EBSCOhost, http://web.ebscohost.com; Automattic, "Work with Us," http://automattic.com.

46. R. Lengel and R. Daft, "The Selection of Communication Media as an Executive Skill," *Academy of Management Executive* 2 (1988), pp. 225–32.

47. J. R. Carlson and R. W. Zmud, "Channel Expansion Theory and the Experiential Nature of Media Richness Perceptions," *Academy of Management Journal* 42 (1999), pp. 153–70.

48. L. Trevino, R. Daft, and R. Lengel, "Understanding Managers' Media Choices: A Symbolic Interactionist Perspective," in *Organizations and Communication Technology*, ed. J. Fulk and C. Steinfield (London: Sage, 1990).

49. J. Fulk and B. Boyd, "Emerging Theories of Communication in Organizations," *Journal of Management* 17 (1991), pp. 407–46.

50. Silverman, "At Yahoo, Working from Home Doesn't Work"; Swisher, "'Physically Together'"; Enayati, "A Work-from-Home Mom"; Noguchi, "Experts Boil Telecommuting Decisions Down"; Mary C. Noonan and Jennifer L. Glass, "The Hard Truth about Telecommuting," *Monthly Labor Review*, June 2012, pp. 38–45; Claire Suddath, "Why Won't Yahoo! Let Employees Work from Home?" *Bloomberg Businessweek*, February 25, 2013, http://www.businessweek.com; Claire Suddath, "The Right Way for a CEO to Deliver Bad News," *Bloomberg Businessweek*, May 9, 2013, EBSCOhost, http://web.ebscohost.com.

51. L. Bossidy and R. Charan, *Confronting Reality: Doing What Matters to Get Things Right* (New York: Crown Business, 2004).

52. M. McCall, M. Lombardo, and A. Morrison, *The Lessons of Experience: How Successful Executives Develop on the Job* (Lexington, MA: Lexington, 1988).

53. J. A. Conger, "The Necessary Art of Persuasion," *Harvard Business Review*, May–June 1998, pp. 84–95.

54. N. Morgan, "How to Become an Authentic Speaker," *Harvard Business Review*, November 2008, pp. 115–19.

55. N. Nohria and B. Harrington, *Six Principles of Successful Persuasion* (Boston: Harvard Business School Publishing Division, 1993).

56. Groysberg and Slind, "Leadership Is a Conversation," pp. 79–80.

57. H. K. Mintz, "Business Writing Styles for the 70's," *Business Horizons*, August 1972. Cited in *Readings in Interpersonal and Organizational Communication*, ed. R. C. Huseman, C. M. Logue, and D. L. Freshley (Boston: Allyn & Bacon, 1977).

58. C. D. Decker, "Writing to Teach Thinking," *Across the Board*, March 1996, pp. 19–20.

59. M. Forbes, "Exorcising Demons from Important Business Letters," *Marketing Times*, March–April 1981, pp. 36–38.

60. T. Flood, "Top Ten Mistakes Managers Make with Email," *The Wall Street Journal*, February 3, 2010, http://online.wsj.com.

61. D. Jones, "Cisco CEO Sees Tech as Integral to Success," *USA Today*, March 19, 2007, p. 4B (interview with John Chambers).

62. Rex W. Huppke, "Boss Shows How to Come Across as Human in Emails," *Chicago Tribune*, February 4, 2013, sec.2, pp. 1, 3; "Kaiser Permanente CEO's Personal Letters to Staff Celebrate Successes and Encourage Future Achievements," *Managed Care Weekly Digest*, April 1, 2013, Business Insights: Global, http://bi.galegroup.com; Jim Gardner, "Boss Talk (and Book) from Kaiser," *San Francisco Business Times*, May 16, 2013, http://www.bizjournals.com/sanfrancisco.

63. G. Ferraro, "The Need for Linguistic Proficiency in Global Business," *Business Horizons*, May–June 1996, pp. 39–46; William W. Maddux, Peter H. Kim, Tetsushi Okumura, and Jeanne M. Brett, "Why 'I'm Sorry' Doesn't Always Translate," *Harvard Business Review*, June 2012, p. 26.

64. P. C. Early and E. Mosakowski, "Creating Hybrid Team Cultures: An Empirical Test of Transnational Team Functioning," *Academy of Management Journal* 43 (2000), pp. 26–49.

65. Ferraro, "The Need for Linguistic Proficiency."

66. C. Chu, *The Asian Mind Game* (New York: Rawson Associates, 1991).

67. Ferraro, "The Need for Linguistic Proficiency."

68. J. S. Lublin, "Improv Troupe Teaches Managers How to Give Better Presentations," *Career Journal*, February 7, 2007, http://www.careerjournal.com.

69. Comstock, *Communicating in Business and Industry*.

70. M. Korda, *Power: How to Get It, How to Use It* (New York: Random House, 1975).

71. A. Mehrabian, "Communication without Words," *Psychology Today*, September 1968, p. 52. Cited in M. B. McCaskey, "The Hidden Message Managers Send," *Harvard Business Review*, November–December 1979, pp. 135–48.

72. Ferraro, "The Need for Linguistic Proficiency."

73. Bernard T. Ferrari, "The Executive's Guide to Better Listening," *McKinsey Quarterly*, February 2012, https://www.mckinseyquarterly.com.

74. A. Athos and J. Gabarro, *Interpersonal Behavior* (Englewood Cliffs, NJ: Prentice-Hall, 1978).

75. M. K. Pratt, "Five Ways to Drive Your Best Workers out the Door," *Computerworld*, August 25, 2008, pp. 26–27, 30.

76. J. Kouzes and B. Posner, *The Leadership Challenge* (San Francisco: Jossey-Bass, 1995).

77. G. Graham, J. Unruh, and P. Jennings, "The Impact of Nonverbal Communication in Organizations: A Survey of Perceptions," *Journal of Business Communications* 28 (1991), pp. 45–62.

78. Ibid.

79. D. Upton and S. Macadam, "Why (and How) to Take a Plant Tour," *Harvard Business Review*, May–June 1997, pp. 97–106.

80. N. Adler, *International Dimensions of Organizational Behavior*, 2nd ed. (Boston: Kent, 1991).

81. Chu, *The Asian Mind Game*.

82. A. Smidts, A. T. H. Pruyn, and C. B. M. van Riel, "The Impact of Employee Communication and Perceived External Prestige on Organizational Identification," *Academy of Management Journal* 49 (2001), pp. 1051–62.

83. J. W. Koehler, K. W. E. Anatol, and R. L. Applebaum, *Organizational Communication: Behavioral Perspectives* (Orlando, FL: Holt, Rinehart & Winston, 1981).

84. J. Waldroop and T. Butler, "The Executive as Coach," *Harvard Business Review*, November–December 1996, pp. 111–17.

85. D. T. Hall, K. L. Otazo, and G. P. Hollenbeck, "Behind Closed Doors: What Really Happens in Executive Coaching," *Organizational Dynamics*, Winter 1999, pp. 39–53.

86. T. Judge and J. Cowell, "The Brave New World of Coaching," *Business Horizons*, July–August 1997, pp. 71–77; E. E. Lawler III, *Treat People Right!* (San Francisco: Jossey-Bass, 2003); and L. A. Hill, "New Manager Development for the 21st Century," *Academy of Management Executive*, August 2004, pp. 121–26.

87. R. J. Bies, "The Delivery of Bad News in Organizations: A Framework for Analysis," *Journal of Management* 39 (2013), pp. 136–62.

88. J. Gutknecht and J. B. Keys, "Mergers, Acquisitions, and Takeovers: Maintaining Morale of Survivors and Protecting Employees," *Academy of Management Executive*, August 1993, pp. 26–36.

89. D. Schweiger and A. DeNisi, "Communication with Employees Following a Merger: A Longitudinal Field Experiment," *Academy of Management Journal* 34 (1991), pp. 110–35.

90. J. Case, "Opening the Books," *Harvard Business Review*, March–April 1997, pp. 118–27.

91. T. R. V. Davis, "Open-Book Management: Its Promise and Pitfalls," *Organization Dynamics*, Winter 1997, pp. 7–20.

92. P. Patel, "Houston's Top Workplaces 2010: No. 1 Midsize Company, Hilcorp Energy Company," *Houston Chronicle*, November 7, 2010, Business & Company Resource Center, http://galenet.galegroup.com; and P. Patel, "Houston's Top Workplaces 2010 Q&A," *Houston Chronicle*, November 7, 2010, Business & Company Resource Center, http://galenet.galegroup.com.

93. W. V. Ruch, *Corporate Communications* (Westport, CT: Quorum, 1984).

94. J. Gardner, "The Heart of the Matter: Leader-Constituent Interaction," in *Leading & Leadership*, ed. T. Fuller (Notre Dame, IN: Notre Dame University Press, 2000), pp. 239–44.

95. R. Ashkenas, D. Ulrich, T. Jick, and S. Kerr, *The Boundaryless Organization* (San Francisco: Jossey-Bass, 1995).

96. Ruch, *Corporate Communications*.

97. P. Bach, "Staying in Touch: A Changing Picture," *Post-Crescent* (Appleton, WI), April 18, 2006, General Reference Center Gold, http://find.galegroup.com.

98. M. Fitzgerald, "The Earl of Florida," *Editor & Publisher*, February 1, 2007, General Reference Center Gold, http://find.galegroup.com.

99. A. Hutton, "Four Rules for Taking Your Message to Wall Street," *Harvard Business Review*, May 2001, pp. 125–32.

100. Koehler et al., *Organizational Communication*.

101. Rachel Emma Silverman, "The Science of Serendipity in the Workplace," *The Wall Street Journal*, April 30, 2013, http://online.wsj.com.

102. Ashkenas et al., *The Boundaryless Organization*.

103. T. Harbert, "Teamwork for Techies," *Computerworld*, December 20, 2010, pp. 24–27.

104. N. B. Kurland and L. H. Pelled, "Passing the Word: Toward a Model of Gossip and Power in the Workplace," *Academy of Management Review* 25 (2000), pp. 428–38.

105. L. Abrams, R. Cross, E. Lesser, and D. Levin, "Nurturing Interpersonal Trust in Knowledge-Sharing Networks," *Academy of Management Executive* 17 (November 2003), pp. 64–77.

106. R. L. Rosnow, "Rumor as Communication: A Contextual Approach," *Journal of Communication* 38 (1988), pp. 12–28.

107. L. Burke and J. M. Wise, "The Effective Care, Handling, and Pruning of the Office Grapevine," *Business Horizons*, May–June 2003, pp. 71–76.

108. K. Davis, "The Care and Cultivation of the Corporate Grapevine," *Dun's Review*, July 1973, pp. 44–47.

109. N. Difonzo, P. Bordia, and R. Rosnow, "Reining in Rumors," *Organizational Dynamics*, Summer 1994, pp. 47–62.

110. Ashkenas et al., *The Boundaryless Organization*.

111. R. M. Hodgetts, "A Conversation with Steve Kerr," *Organizational Dynamics*, Spring 1996, pp. 68–79.

112. R. M. Fulmer, "The Evolving Paradigm of Leadership Development," *Organizational Dynamics*, Spring 1997, pp. 59–72.

113. General Electric, "GE Shares Skills, Intellectual Capital with CommonBond Communities," news release, December 4, 2006, http://www.genewscenter.com.

114. Ashkenas et al., *The Boundaryless Organization*.

115. Swisher, "'Physically Together'"; Swisher, "Survey Says"; Enayati, "A Work-from-Home Mom"; Sellers, "Marissa Mayer"; Mlot, "Marissa Mayer Addresses Yahoo Staff"; "Yahoo! Telecommuting Ban May Be Unique, but Revisiting Arrangements Recommended," *HR Focus*, April 2013, pp. 1–3.

Chapter 16

1. J. C. Collins and J. I. Porras, *Built to Last: Successful Habits of Visionary Companies* (New York: HarperBusiness, 1994).

2. Thomas Lee, "Best Buy Ends Flexible Work Program," *Minneapolis Star Tribune*, March 5, 2013, http://www.startribune.com; Lee Schafer, "Pitching In Is the New Rule at Best Buy," *Minneapolis Star Tribune*, February 16, 2013, http://www.startribune.com; Thomas Lee, David Shaffer, and Paul McEnroe, "Lost Empire: Can Best Buy Make a Comeback?" *Minneapolis Star Tribune*, March 25, 2013, http://www.startribune.com; Larry Downes, "Why Best Buy Is Going out of Business . . . Gradually," *Forbes*, January 2, 2012; Ann Zimmerman, "Can This Former Clerk Save Best Buy?" *The Wall Street Journal*, April 25, 2013; Matthew Rocco, "Best Buy Cuts Headcount at HQ by 400," *Fox Business*, February 26, 2013, http://www.foxbusiness.com; Joan E. Solsman, "Best Buy Increases Loyalty Rewards in Move to Spur Sales," *The Wall Street Journal*, April 3, 2013, http://online.wsj.com; Venessa Wong, "How Best Buy Has Changed Its Tune on Flexible Work," *Bloomberg Businessweek*, March 7, 2013, http://www.businessweek.com.

3. Steve Minter, "La-Z-Boy Never Rests on Continuous Improvement," *Industry Week*, January 2013, Business Insights: Essentials, http://bi.galegroup.com.

4. Tom Fowler, "BP Promotes a New Approach to Safety," *The Wall Street Journal*, February 13, 2013, http://blogs.wsj.com; Kjetil Malkenes Hovland, "Norway Orders BP Safety Review after Leak," *The Wall Street Journal*, April 29, 2013, http://online.wsj.com.

5. W. G. Ouchi, "Markets, Bureaucracies, and Clans," *Administrative Science Quarterly* 25 (1980), pp. 129–41.

6. R. Simons, A. Davila, and R. S. Kaplan, *Performance Measurement & Control Systems for Implementing Strategy* (Englewood Cliffs, NJ: Prentice Hall, 2000).

7. E. D. Pulakos, S. Arad, M. A. Donovan, and K. E. Plamondon, "Adaptability in the Workplace: Development of a Taxonomy of Adaptive Performance," *Journal of Applied Psychology* 85, no. 4 (August 2000), pp. 12–24; and K. A. Merchant and T. Sandino, "Four Options for Measuring Value Creation: Strategies for Managers to Avoid Potential Flaws in Accounting Measures of Performance," *Journal of Accountancy* 208, no. 2 (2009), pp. 34–38.

8. E. Gardner, "High-Quality Information," *Modern Healthcare*, March 5, 2007, General Reference Center Gold, http://find.galegroup.com; HealthPartners/Regions Hospital, "HealthPartners, Regions Partner to Prevent More than 380 Readmissions in 2012," news release, March 13, 2013, http://online.wsj.com.

9. J. T. Burr, "Keys to a Successful Internal Audit," *Quality Progress* 30, no. 4 (April 1997), pp. 75–77; and J. Zorabedian, "Uniform Security," *American Executive*, June 2008, Business & Company Resource Center, http://galenet.galegroup.com.

10. Julie Jargon, "McDonald's Tackles Repair of 'Broken' Service," *The Wall Street Journal*, April 10, 2013, http://online.wsj.com; Julie Jargon, "Your McDonald's Ordering Ritual Is About to Change," *The Wall Street Journal*, April 10, 2013, http://blogs.wsj.com; Martha C. White, "McDonald's Executive Says 'Service Is Broken,'" *NBC News*, April 12, 2013, http://www.nbcnews.com.

11. E. White, "How Surveying Workers Can Pay Off," *The Wall Street Journal*, June 18, 2007, http://online.wsj.com.

12. Todd Henshaw, "Nano Tools for Leaders: After Action Reviews," *Wharton@Work*, April 2012, http://executiveeducation.wharton.upenn.edu; John Kello, "Upon Further Review: Benefits of Brief Post-Shift Huddles," *Industrial Safety & Hygiene News*, August 2012, p. 30; Stephen C. Harper, "Survival of the Swiftest," *Industrial Management*, January 2012, pp. 16–20.

13. B. Roberts, "Stay Ahead of the Technology Use Curve," *HRMagazine*, October 2008, Business & Company Resource Center, http://galenet.galegroup.com; and K. A. Carr, "Broaching Body Art," *Crain's Cleveland Business*, September 29, 2008, http://galenet.galegroup.com.

14. T. Hals, "Beware the Pitfalls of Office Romance," *Yahoo News*, February 13, 2007, http://news.yahoo.com; and M. Selvin, "'Love Contract'? It's Office Policy," *Los Angeles Times*, February 13, 2007, http://www.latimes.com.

15. Gary S. Kaplan, "Pursuing the Perfect Patient Experience," *Frontiers of Health Services Management*, Spring 2013, pp. 16–27. For an additional example in another type of organization, see David T. Goomas, Stuart M. Smith, and Timothy D. Ludwig, "Business Activity Monitoring: Real-Time Group Goals and Feedback Using an Overhead Scoreboard in a Distribution Center," *Journal of Organizational Behavior Management* 31 no. 3 (2011), pp. 196–209.

16. V. U. Druskat, "Effects and Timing of Developmental Peer Appraisals in Self-Managing Work Groups," *Journal of Applied Psychology* 84, no. 1 (February 1999), p. 58; Baard Kuvaas, "The Interactive Role of Performance Appraisal Reactions and Regular Feedback," *Journal of Managerial Psychology* 26 no. 2 (2011), pp. 123–137.

17. "Business Analytics: Numbers and Nuance," *CIO Insight*, January 12, 2011, Business & Company Resource Center, http://galenet.galegroup.com.

18. M. Lewis Jr., "Eyes on the Prize," *Medical Economics*, February 10, 2011, pp. 34–42.

19. S. Waddock and N. Smith, "Corporate Responsibility Audits: Doing Well by Doing Good," *Sloan Management Review* 41, no. 2 (Winter 2000), pp. 75–83; L. L. Bergeson, "OSHA Gives Incentives for Voluntary Self-Audits," *Pollution Engineering* 32, no. 10 (October 2000), pp. 33–34; Scott M. Shafer and Sara B. Moeller, "The Effects of Six Sigma on Corporate Performance: An Empirical Investigation," *Journal of Operations Management* 30 no. (7–8) (November 1, 2012): 521–32.

20. S. Aghili, "A Six Sigma Approach to Internal Audits," *Strategic Finance*, February 2009, Business & Company Resource Center, http://galenet.galegroup.com.

21. See, for example, B. Hindo, "At 3M, a Struggle between Efficiency and Creativity," *BusinessWeek*, June 11, 2007, General Reference Center Gold, http://find.galegroup.com; B. Hindo and B. Grow, "Six Sigma; So Yesterday?" *BusinessWeek*, June 11, 2007, http://find.galegroup.com; and J. Rae, "Viewpoint: Have It Both Ways," *BusinessWeek*, June 11, 2007, http://find.galegroup.com.

22. T. Rancour and M. McCracken, "Applying 6 Sigma Methods for Breakthrough Safety Performance," *Professional Safety* 45, no. 10 (October 2000), pp. 29–32; and G. Eckes, "Making Six Sigma Last," *Ivey Business Journal*, January–February 2002, p. 77.

23. J. L. Colbert, "The Impact of the New External Auditing Standards," *Internal Auditor* 5, no. 6 (December 2000), pp. 46–50.

24. Aghili, "A Six Sigma Approach"; Y. Giard and Y. Nadeau, "Improving the Processes," *CA Magazine*, December 2008, Business & Company Resource Center, http://galenet.galegroup.com; and G. Cheney, "Connecting the Dots to the Next Crisis," *Financial Executive*, April 2009, pp. 30–33.

25. J. D. Glater, "The Better the Audit Panel, the Higher the Stock Price," *New York Times*, April 8, 2005, p. C4; and M. Alic and B. Rusjan, "Contribution of the ISO 9001 Internal Audit to Business Performance," *International Journal of Quality and Reliability Management* 27, no. 8 (2010), pp. 916–37.

26. B. Roberts, "Data-Driven Human Capital Decisions," *HRMagazine*, March 2007, General Reference Center Gold, http://find.galegroup.com. See also

Ceren Atilgan and Peter McCullen, "Improving Supply Chain Performance through Auditing: A Change Management Perspective," *Supply Chain Management* 16 no. 1 (2011), pp. 11–19.

27. Jan Tullberg, "Triple Bottom Line—a Vaulting Ambition?" *Business Ethics: A European Review* 21 no. 3 (June 2012), pp. 310–24; Grant Davis, "The Triple Bottom Line Goal of Sustainable Businesses," *Entrepreneur*, April 24, 2013, http://www.entrepreneur.com; Rebecca Coons, "Corporate Social Responsibility: Pursuing the Triple Bottom Line," *IHS Chemical Week*, May 27–June 3, 2013, pp. 21–23.

28. Pam Schuneman, "Master the 'ABCs' of Activity-Based Costing," *Managed Care*, May 1997, http://www.managedcaremag.com; Ivana Drazic Lutilsky and Martina Dragija, "Activity Based Costing as a Means to Full Costing: Possibilities and Constraints for European Universities," *Management* 17 no. 1 (June 2012), pp. 33–57.

29. K. Merchant, *Control in Business Organizations* (Boston: Pitman, 1985); and C. W. Chow, Y. Kato, and K. A. Merchant, "The Use of Organizational Controls and Their Effects on Data Manipulation and Management Myopia," *Accounting, Organizations, and Society* 21, nos. 2/3 (February/April 1996), pp. 175–92.

30. Lee, "Best Buy Ends Flexible Work Program"; Schafer, "Pitching In Is the New Rule"; Lee et al., "Lost Empire"; Downes, "Why Best Buy Is Going out of Business"; Zimmerman, "Can This Former Clerk Save Best Buy?"; Rocco, "Best Buy Cuts Headcount"; Solsman, "Best Buy Increases Loyalty Rewards"; Drew Fitzgerald, "Best Buy Posts Loss as Revenue Falls," *The Wall Street Journal*, May 21, 2013, http://online.wsj.com; Dan Newman, "Where's Best Buy Heading in 2013?" *Motley Fool*, January 8, 2013, http://www.fool.com; Best Buy, "Best Buy Reports Better-than-Expected First Quarter Results," news release, May 21, 2013, http://phx.corporate-ir.net; Best Buy, "Best Buy Reports Fourth Quarter and Fiscal Year Results," news release, March 1, 2013, http://phx.corporate-ir.net.

31. E. E. Lawler III and J. Rhode, *Information and Control in Organizations* (Pacific Palisades, CA: Goodyear, 1976); A. Ferner, "The Underpinnings of 'Bureaucratic' Control Systems: HRM in European Multinationals," *Journal of Management Studies* 37, no. 4 (June 2000), pp. 521–39; and M. S. Fenwick, "Cultural and Bureaucratic Control in MNEs: The Role of Expatriate Performance Management," *Management International Review* 39 (1999), pp. 107–25.

32. Hindo, "At 3M, a Struggle between Efficiency and Creativity." See also Jason J. Dahling, Samantha L. Chau,

and Alison O'Malley, "Correlates and Consequences of Feedback Orientation in Organizations," *Journal of Management* 38 no. 2 (2012), pp. 531–46.

33. S. Terlep, "GM's Latest Change Agent Tackles Designs, Red Tape," *The Wall Street Journal*, June 15, 2011, http://online.wsj.com.

34. J. Veiga and J. Yanouzas, *The Dynamics of Organization Theory*, 2nd ed. (St. Paul, MN: West, 1984).

35. P. R. Gutierrez, "Airport Workers Report Breach," *Orlando Sentinel*, May 26, 2007, General Reference Center Gold, http://find.galegroup.com.

36. M. Gelbart, "L&I Gets Ritz-Carlton Image Tips," *Philadelphia Inquirer*, March 10, 2009, http://www.philly.com.

37. J. Fleischer, "New Methods to Measure Performance," *Call Center*, February 1, 2007, General Reference Center Gold, http://find.galegroup.com.

38. M. Hammer, "The Seven Deadly Sins of Performance Measurement and How to Avoid Them," *MIT Sloan Management Review* 48, no. 3 (Spring 2007), pp. 19–28.

39. Lawler and Rhode, *Information and Control in Organizations;* and J. A. Gowan Jr. and R. G. Mathieu, "Critical Factors in Information System Development for a Flexible Manufacturing System," *Computers in Industry* 28, no. 3 (June 1996), pp. 173–83.

40. Peter Pronovost, "A Method to the Mystique," blog of the Armstrong Institute for Patient Safety and Quality, Johns Hopkins Medicine, February 19, 2013, http://armstronginstitute.blogs.hopkinsmedicine.org; Kimberly Maul, "The Human Touch," *Marketing News*, May 2013, pp. 6–7; Ashley Furness, "The Secret to Ritz-Carlton's Customer Service Mojo," *Bill Quiseng: Deliver the World's Best Customer Experience*, November 19, 2012, http://billquiseng.com.

41. Adrienne Selko, "Ethicon: Employee Engagement Results in Zero Product Recalls," *Industry Week*, January 17, 2013, http://www.industryweek.com.

42. R. S. Kaplan and D. P. Norton, *The Balanced Scorecard: Translating Strategy into Action* (Boston: Harvard Business School Press, 1996); and A. Gumbus and R. N. Lussier, "Entrepreneurs Use a Balanced Scorecard to Translate Strategy into Performance Measures," *Journal of Small Business Management* 44, no. 3 (July 2006), General Reference Center Gold, http://find.galegroup.com.

43. Gumbus and Lussier, "Entrepreneurs Use a Balanced Scorecard."

44. M. A. Reed-Woodard, "The Business of Nonprofit," *Black Enterprise*, June 2007, General Reference Center Gold, http://find.galegroup.com.

45. R. Myers, "Going Away," *CFO*, May 2007, General Reference Center Gold, http://find.galegroup.com.

46. K. Moores and J. Mula, "The Salience of Market, Bureaucratic, and Clan Controls in the Management of Family Firm Transitions: Some Tentative Australian Evidence," *Family Business Review* 13, no. 2 (June 2000), pp. 91–106; and A. Walker and R. Newcombe, "The Positive Use of Power on a Major Construction Project," *Construction Management and Economics* 18, no. 1 (January/February 2000), pp. 37–44.

47. P. H. Fuchs, K. E. Mifflin, D. Miller, and J. O. Whitney, "Strategic Integration: Competing in the Age of Capabilities," *California Management Review* 42, no. 3 (Spring 2000), pp. 118–47; M. A. Lando, "Making Compliance Part of Your Organization's Culture," *Healthcare Executive* 15, no. 5 (September/October 1999), pp. 18–22; K. A. Frank and K. Fahrbach, "Organization Culture as a Complex System: Balance and Information in Models of Influence and Selection," *Organization Science* 10, no. 3 (May/June 1999), pp. 253–77; Serge A. Rijsdijk and Jan van den Ende, "Control Combinations in New Product Development Projects," *Journal of Product Innovation Management* 28 no. 6 (November 2011), pp. 868–80.

48. R. J. Grossman, "Tough Love at Netflix," *HR Magazine*, April 2010, http://galenet.galegroup.com.

49. "100 Best Companies to Work For, 2009," *Fortune*, February 2, 2009, http://money.cnn.com.

50. Lee, "Best Buy Ends Flexible Work Program"; Schafer, "Pitching In Is the New Rule"; Lee et al., "Lost Empire"; Wong, "How Best Buy Has Changed Its Tune"; Thomas Lee, "Best Buy's CEO Hubert Joly Shines at His First Annual Meeting," *Minneapolis Star Tribune*, June 21, 2013, http://www.startribune.com; Hubert Joly, "Best Buy CEO on Leadership," *Minneapolis Star Tribune*, March 17, 2013, http://www.startribune.com; Jody Thompson, "ROWE Creators Set the Record Straight: Best Buy CEO Doesn't Understand ROWE," *Cali and Jody Blog* (CultureRx), March 18, 2013, http://www.gorowe.com.

Chapter 17

1. Michael Levi, "How Tesla Pulled ahead of the Electric-Car Pack," *The Wall Street Journal*, June 20, 2013, http://online.wsj.com; Ashlee Vance, "Elon Musk, Man of Tomorrow," *Bloomberg Businessweek*, September 17, 2012, EBSCOhost, http://web.ebscohost.com; Tesla Motors, "Model S Innovations: Technology," http://www.teslamotors.com; George Blankenship, "Inside Tesla," Tesla Motors blog, March 21, 2013, http://www.teslamotors.com; "General Electric Motors," *The Economist*, April 20, 2013, http://www.economist.com; Angus MacKenzie, "2013 Motor Trend Car of the Year: Tesla Model S," *Motor Trend*, January 2013, http://www.motortrend.com; Jason Cammisa, "Return to Power: The 2013 Tesla Model S," *Road & Track*, February 25, 2013, http://www.roadandtrack.com; Peter Valdes-Dapena, "Tesla: Consumer Reports' Best Car Ever Tested," *CNNMoney*, May 9, 2013, http://money.cnn.com; Mike Ramsey, "Tesla Motors Approaches Crossroad," *The Wall Street Journal*, February 10, 2013, http://online.wsj.com.

2. R. A. Burgelman, M. A. Maidique, and S. C. Wheelwright, *Strategic Management of Technology and Innovation* (New York: McGraw-Hill, 2000); Panagiotis Ganotakis and James H. Love, "The Innovation Value Chain in New Technology-Based Firms," *Journal of Product Innovation Management* 29, no. 5 (September 2012): 839–60.

3. D. C. L. Prestwood and P. A. Schumann Jr., "Revitalize Your Organization," *Executive Excellence* 15, no. 2 (February 1998), p. 16; C. Y. Baldwin and K. B. Clark, "Managing in an Age of Modularity," *Harvard Business Review* 75, no. 5 (September–October 1997), pp. 84–93; S. Gopalakrishnan, P. Bierly, and E. H. Kessler, "A Reexamination of Product and Process Innovations Using a Knowledge-Based View," *Journal of High Technology Management Research* 10, no. 1 (Spring 1999), pp. 147–66; J. Pullin, "Bombardier Commands Top Marks," *Professional Engineering* 13, no. 3 (July 5, 2000), pp. 40–46; M. Johnson, C. Christensen, and H. Kagermann, "Reinventing Your Business Model," *Harvard Business Review* (December 2008), pp. 50–59; C. M. Christensen, *The Innovator's Dilemma* (Boston: Harvard Business Publishing, 1997); and C. M. Christensen, S. D. Anthony, and E. A. Roth, *Seeing What's Next* (Boston: Harvard Business Publishing, 2004).

4. M. Sawhney, R. C. Wolcott, and I. Arroniz, "The 12 Different Ways for Companies to Innovate," *MIT Sloan Management Review* 47, no. 3 (Spring 2006), pp. 75–81; Julian Birkinshaw, Gary Hamel, and Michael J. Mol, "Management Innovation," *Academy of Management Review* 33 (October 2008): 825–45.

5. B. Saporito, "How to Build a Job Engine," *Time*, May 19, 2011, http://www.time.com.

6. G. P. Pisano, *The Development Factory: Unlocking the Potential of Process Innovation* (Boston: Harvard Business School Press, 1996); and R. Leifer, C. M. McDermott, G. C. O'Connor, L. S. Peters, M. Rice, and R. W. Veryzer, *Radical Innovation: How Mature Companies Can Outsmart Upstarts* (Cambridge MA: Harvard Business School Press, 2000).

7. H. M. O'Neill, R. W. Pounder, and A. K. Buchholtz, "Patterns in the Diffusion of Strategies across Organizations: Insights from the Innovation, Diffusion Literature," *Academy of Management Review* 23, no. 1

(January 1998), pp. 98–114;
E. M. Rogers, *Diffusion of Innovations* (New York: Free Press, 1995); and
B. Guilhon, ed., *"Technology and Markets for Knowledge: Knowledge Creation, Diffusion and Exchange within a Growing Economy," Economics of Science, Technology and Innovation* 22 (Dordrecht, Netherlands: Kluwer Academic Publishing, 2000).

8. M. E. Porter, *Competitive Strategy* (New York: Free Press, 1980).

9. Clayton M. Christensen, Scott D. Anthony, and Erik A. Roth, *Seeing What's Next* (Boston: Harvard Business School Publishing, 2004); Clayton Christensen, "Key Concepts: Disruptive Innovation," http://www.claytonchristensen.com; Innosight, "Expertise: Driving New Growth through Disruptive Innovation," http://www.innosight.com; Matthew Yglesias, "Stop 'Disrupting' Everything," *Slate*, May 1, 2013, http://www.slate.com.

10. S. A. Zahra, S. Nash, and D. J. Bickford, "Transforming Technological Pioneering in Competitive Advantage," *Academy of Management Executive* 9, no. 1 (1995), pp. 17–31; and M. Sadowski and A. Roth, "Technology Leadership Can Pay Off," *Research Technology Management* 42, no. 6 (November/December 1999), pp. 32–33.

11. A. Weintraub, "Who Might Be Eyeing Bristol?" *BusinessWeek*, June 20, 2007, General Reference Center Gold, http://find.galegroup.com; and D. Cust, "Pharma Sector Faces 'Perfect Storm,'" *Acquisitions Monthly*, June 2007, http://find.galegroup.com.

12. M. Imai and G. Kaizen, *A Commonsense, Low-Cost Approach to Management* (New York: McGraw-Hill, 1997); and M. Imai and G. Kaizen, *The Key to Japan's Competitive Success* (New York: McGraw-Hill, 1986).

13. M. Hiltzik, "How Big Pharma Distorts the Costs of Developing New Drugs," *Los Angeles Times*, April 3, 2011, http://articles.latimes.com; "Brand Drugs Soar as Generics Rise," *Journal of Nursing*, April 1, 2011, http://www.asrn.org; and J. J. Castellani, "The Role of Innovation in Addressing Global Health," remarks from the Under Secretary for Economic, Energy and Agricultural Affairs, U.S. Department of State, March 17, 2011, http://www.state.gov.

14. See Matthew Semadeni and Brian S. Anderson, "The Follower's Dilemma: Innovation and Imitation in the Professional Services Industry," *Academy of Management Journal* 53 (October 2010): 1175–1193.

15. P. A. Geroski, "Models of Technology Diffusion," *Research Policy* 29, no. 4/5 (April 2000), pp. 603–25; and L. A. Thomas, "Adoption Order of New Technologies in Evolving Markets," *Journal of Economic Behavior & Organization* 38, no. 4 (April 1999), pp. 453–82.

16. G. Colvin, "McKesson: Wiring the Medical World," *Fortune*, February 5, 2007, http://money.cnn.com.

17. R. E. Oligney and M. I. Economides, "Technology as an Asset," *Hart's Petroleum Engineer International* 71, no. 9 (September 1998), p. 27.

18. Dan Slater, "Most Innovative Companies 2013: Square," *Fast Company*, February 11, 2013, http://www.fastcompany.com; Miguel Helft, "The Death of Cash," *Fortune*, July 23, 2012, EBSCOhost, http://web.ebscohost.com; Angus Loten and Emily Maltby, "Mobile Payments Brighten Cash Flow for Small Business," *The Wall Street Journal*, February 27, 2013, http://online.wsj.com; "Square Creates 'Square Market,' an Ecommerce Service for Businesses," *Entrepreneur*, June 25, 2013, http://www.entrepreneur.com.

19. Ameet Sachdev, "Bewitched by Baxter: Robot Draws Admirers," *Chicago Tribune*, January 22, 2013, sec. 2, pp. 1, 3.

20. M. Bustillo, "Wal-Mart Radio Tags to Track Clothing," *The Wall Street Journal*, July 23, 2010, http://online.wsj.com; "RFID: Challenges and Opportunities," *MoreRFID*, June 30, 2011, http://www.morerfid.com; and D. Steinberg, "The $25 Billion Art Move," *The Wall Street Journal*, June 24, 2011, http://online.wsj.com.

21. "Not Dead Yet? Maybe Face Recognition Just Needs Re-purposing," *Security Director's Report*, June 2011, pp. 2–5.

22. General Electric, "GE Cooling Technology, as Thin as a Credit Card, Enables Ultra-Thin Tablets, Laptops," news release, December 11, 2012, http://www.genewscenter.com.

23. Clint Boulton, "Printing Out Barbies and Ford Cylinders," *The Wall Street Journal*, June 5, 2013, http://online.wsj.com; Elizabeth Royte, "The Printed World," *Smithsonian*, May 2013, pp. 50–57.

24. Boulton, "Printing Out Barbies"; Royte, "The Printed World"; Geoffrey A. Fowler, "Build a Better Mousetrap—Fast," *The Wall Street Journal*, June 10, 2013, http://online.wsj.com; Robert MacPherson, "3D Printing a Major Theme of SXSW," *Industry Week*, March 10, 2013, http://www.industryweek.com.

25. M. Kanellos, "For Fast-Food Help, Call in the Robots," *CNet News*, March 26, 2007, http://news.com.com.

26. J. Jusko, "Foiling Fakes," *Industry Week*, May 2007, General Reference Center Gold, http://find.galegroup.com.

27. Lynda Aiman-Smith and Stephen G. Green, "Implementing a New Manufacturing Technology: The Related Effects of Technology Characteristics and User Learning Activities," *Academy of Management Journal* 45 (April 2002): 421–430.

28. "Fresh, but Far from Easy," *The Economist*, June 23, 2007, General Reference Center Gold, http://find.galegroup.com.

29. R. Dewan, B. Jing, and A. Seidmann, "Adoption of Internet-Based Product Customization and Pricing Strategies," *Journal of Management Information Systems* 17, no. 2 (Fall 2000), pp. 9–28; P. A. Geroski, "Models of Technology Diffusion," *Research Policy* 29, no. 4/5 (April 2000), pp. 603–25; Rogers, *Diffusion of Innovations*.

30. Levi, "How Tesla Pulled Ahead"; Vance, "Elon Musk, Man of Tomorrow"; Blankenship, "Inside Tesla"; *The Economist*, "General Electric Motors"; MacKenzie, "2013 Motor Trend Car of the Year"; Cammisa, "Return to Power"; Valdes-Dapena, "Tesla: Consumer Reports' Best Car"; Ramsey, "Tesla Motors Approaches Crossroad"; Tesla Motors, "Supercharger," http://www.teslamotors.com; Ina Fried, "Musk: Mainstream Tesla Model 3–4 Years Out, Will Be 20 Percent Smaller than Model S," *All Things D*, May 29, 2013, http://allthingsd.com; Mike Ramsey and Tess Stynes, "Tesla Sees First-Ever Quarterly Profit," *The Wall Street Journal*, April 1, 2013, http://online.wsj.com; Mike Ramsey and Valerie Bauerlein, "Tesla Clashes with Car Dealers," *The Wall Street Journal*, June 18, 2013, http://online.wsj.com; Joseph B. White, "Tesla Has a Fresh $1 Billion—and Lots of Ways to Spend It," *The Wall Street Journal*, May 17, 2013, http://blogs.wsj.com.

31. E. Von Hippel, *The Sources of Innovation* (Oxford, UK: Oxford University Press, 1994); and D. Leonard, *Wellsprings of Knowledge: Building and Sustaining the Sources of Innovation* (Cambridge, MA: Harvard Business School Press, 1998); Melissa E. Graebner, Kathleen M. Eisenhardt, and Philip T. Roundy, "Success and Failure in Technology Acquisitions: Lessons for Buyers and Sellers," *Academy of Management Perspectives* 24 (3), no. 3 (August 2010): 73–92.

32. T. Krazit, "Intel R&D on Slow Boat to China," *CNet News*, April 16, 2007, http://news.com.com.

33. "Online Gaming's Netscape Moment?" *The Economist*, June 9, 2007, http://find.galegroup.com.

34. T. Purdum, "Benchmarking Outside the Box: Best Practices Can Rise from Where You Least Expect Them," *Industry Week*, March 2007, General Reference Center Gold, http://find.galegroup.com.

35. Von Hippel, *The Sources of Innovation*; and Leonard, *Wellsprings of Knowledge*.

36. J. Hagedoorn, A. N. Link, and N. S. Vonortas, "Research Partnerships," *Research Policy* 29, no. 4/5 (April 2000), pp. 567–86; S.-S. Yi, "Entry, Licensing and Research Joint

Ventures," *International Journal of Industrial Organization* 17, no. 1 (January 1999), pp. 1–24; Satish Nambisan and Mohanbir Sawhney, "Orchestration Processes in Network-centric Innovation: Evidence from the Field," *Academy of Management Perspectives* 25 (August 2011), pp. 40–57; Ulrich Lichtenthaler, "Open Innovation: Past Research, Current Debates, and Future Directions," *Academy of Management Perspectives* 25 (February 2011), pp. 75–93; Esteve Almirall and Ramon Casadesus-Masanell, "Open versus Closed Innovation: A Model of Discovery and Divergence," *Academy of Management Review* 35 (January 2010), pp. 27–47; Corey C. Phelps, "A Longitudinal Study of the Influence of Alliance Network Structure and Composition on Firm Exploratory Innovation," *Academy of Management Journal* 53 (August 2010), pp. 890–913.

37. R. Dorn, "Chicken, Pork or Beef?" *Fleet Equipment*, May 2007, General Reference Center Gold, http://find.galegroup.com; and "One of the Nation's Largest Producers of Animal Fat and a Major Oil Company Have Decided to Make Diesel Fuel Together," *Diesel Progress*, North American ed., May 2007, http://find.galegroup.com.

38. Chris Dieterich, "Facebook, Google Lead Private Tech Acquisitions," *MarketWatch*, February 12, 2013, http://www.marketwatch.com; Sarah Perez, "Twitter Acquires Big Data Visualization Startup Luck Sort, Service to Shutter in Months Ahead," *TechCrunch*, May 13, 2013, http://techcrunch.com; Keach Hagey, "Twitter Cozies Up to Television with New Ad Products," *The Wall Street Journal*, May 23, 2013, http://blogs.wsj.com.

39. T. Hoffman, "Change Agents," *ComputerWorld*, April 23, 2007, General Reference Center Gold, http://find.galegroup.com; Center for CIO Leadership, "Center for CIO Leadership Unveils 2008 Survey Results," news release, November 18, 2008, http://www.marketwire.com; and Center for CIO Leadership, "CIO Leadership Survey Executive Summary," abstract, 2008, http://www.cioleadershipcenter.com; and G. H. Anthes, "The CIO/CTO Balancing Act," *ComputerWorld* 34, no. 25 (June 19, 2000), pp. 50–51.

40. "Information Resources: The Evolution of R&D," *Research-Technology Management*, May–June 2011, pp. 65–66; and J. C. Spender and B. Strong, "Who Has Innovative Ideas? Employees," *The Wall Street Journal*, August 23, 2010, http://online.wsj.com.

41. D. L. Day, "Raising Radicals: Different Processes for Championing Innovative Corporate Ventures," *Organization Science* 5, no. 2 (May 1994), pp. 148–72; C. Siporin, "Want Speedy FDA Approval? Hire a 'Product Champion,'"

Medical Marketing & Media, October 1993, pp. 22–28; C. Siporin, "How You Can Capitalize on Phase 3B," *Medical Marketing & Media*, October 1994, pp. 72–72; and E. H. Kessler, "Tightening the Belt: Methods for Reducing Development Costs Associated with New Product Innovation," *Journal of Engineering and Technology Management* 17, no. 1 (March 2000), pp. 59–92.

42. K. Johnson, "Solar Updates Marines' Arsenal," *The Wall Street Journal*, May 9, 2011, http://online.wsj.com.

43. J. P. Andrew, K. Haanæs, D. C. Michael, H. L. Sirkin, and A. Taylor, *Innovation 2009: Making Hard Decisions in the Downturn*, Boston Consulting Group Senior Management Survey, http://www.bcg.com.

44. J. G. March, "Exploration and Exploitation in Organizational Learning," *Organization Science* 2, no. 1 (1991), pp. 71–87; and S. C. Kang and S. A. Snell, "Intellectual Capital Architectures and Ambidextrous Learning: A Framework for Human Resource Management," *Journal of Management Studies* 46, no. 1 (2009), pp. 65–92.

45. Jeff DeGraff, "Why the 'Most Innovative Companies' Aren't," *Fortune*, March 13, 2013, http://management.fortune.com; Henry Chesbrough, "Why Bad Things Happen to Good Technology," *The Wall Street Journal*, June 19, 2012, http://online.wsj.com; Steven Levy, "Google's Larry Page on Why Moon Shots Matter," *Wired*, January 17, 2013, http://www.wired.com.

46. D. A. Fields, "How to Stop the Dumbing Down of Your Company," *Industry Week*, March 7, 2007, http://www.industryweek.com; L. K. Gundry, J. R. Kickul, and C. W. Prather, "Building the Creative Organization," *Organizational Dynamics* 22, no. 2 (Spring 1994), pp. 22–36; and T. Kuczmarski, "Inspiring and Implementing the Innovation Mind-Set," *Planning Review*, September–October 1994, pp. 37–48.

47. D. Rodriguez and R. Jacoby, "Embracing Risk to Grow and Innovate," *BusinessWeek*, May 16, 2007, http://www.businessweek.com.

48. Steve Minter, "Priming the Supply Chain of Ideas," *Industry Week*, February 2013, Business Insights: Essentials, http://bi.galegroup.com.

49. D. Tsuruoka, "Intuit Innovation Lab, 'Idea Jams' Aim to Spur Creativity," *Investor's Business Daily*, April 14, 2009, Business & Company Resource Center, http://galenet.galegroup.com.

50. D. Leonard, *Wellsprings of Knowledge: Building and Sustaining the Sources of Innovation* (Cambridge MA: Harvard Business School Press, 1998); D. Leonard-Barton, "The Factory as a Learning Laboratory," *Sloan Management Review*, Fall

1992, pp. 23–38; and A. K. Gupta and V. Govindarajan, "Knowledge Management's Social Dimension: Lessons from Nucor Steel," *Sloan Management Review* 42, no. 1 (Fall 2000), pp. 71–80.

51. H. K. Bowen, K. B. Clark, C. A. Holloway, and S. C. Wheelwright, "Development Projects: The Engine of Renewal," *Harvard Business Review*, September–October 1994, pp. 110–20; C. Eden, T. Williams, and F. Ackermann, "Dismantling the Learning Curve: The Role of Disruptions on the Planning of Development Projects," *International Journal of Project Management* 16, no. 3 (June 1998), pp. 131–38; and M. V. Tatikonda and S. R. Rosenthal, "Technology Novelty, Project Complexity, and Product Development Project Execution Success: A Deeper Look at Task Uncertainty in Product Innovation," *IEEE Transactions on Engineering Management* 47, no. 1 (February 2000), pp. 74–87.

52. E. Trist, "The Evolution of Sociotechnical Systems as a Conceptual Framework and as an Action Research Program," in *Perspectives on Organizational Design and Behavior*, ed. A. Van de Ven and W. F. Joyce, pp. 19–75 (New York: John Wiley & Sons, 1981); and A. Molina, "Insights into the Nature of Technology Diffusion and Implementation: The Perspective of Sociotechnical Alignment," *Technovation* 17, nos. 11/12 (November/December 1997), pp. 601–26.

53. Lynda Aiman-Smith and Stephen G. Green, "Implementing New Manufacturing Technology: The Related Effects of Technology Characteristics and User Learning Activities," *Academy of Management Journal* 45 (April 2002), pp. 421–30; Terri L. Griffith, "Technology Features as Triggers for Sensemaking," *Academy of Management Review* 24 (July 1999), pp. 472–88.

54. Levi, "How Tesla Pulled Ahead"; Vance, "Elon Musk, Man of Tomorrow"; *The Economist*, "General Electric Motors"; White, "Tesla Has a Fresh $1 Billion"; Ben Rooney, "Tesla Shares Pop on $100 Million Toyota Deal," *CNNMoney*, July 20, 2011, http://money.cnn.com; David Herron, "Tesla's Technology inside the Mercedes-Benz B-Class Electric Drive," *Long Tail Pipe*, March 27, 2013, http://www.longtailpipe.com; Dana Hull, "Tesla Gears Up to Hire Manufacturing Workers," *Los Angeles Times*, January 17, 2012, http://articles.latimes.com.

Appendix D

1. R. M. Pirsig, *Zen and the Art of Motorcycle Maintenance* (New York: William Morrow and Company, 1974).

2. P. Raichur, *Absolute Beauty* (New York: HarperPerennial, 1986).

3. Nescafe: Nestle (verified by T. Haywood via 1/16/01 e-mail that Nescafe and Nesquik flavors are modified for the market in which they are sold).

4. T. J. Mullaney and R. D. Hof, "Information Technology Annual Report," *BusinessWeek Online*, June 24, 2002.

5. J. Black, "The Fight for Privacy Has Just Begun," *BusinessWeek Online*, January 10, 2002.

Chapter 18

1. Keach Hagey and Martin Peers, "Time Warner Opts to Spin Off All Magazines," *The Wall Street Journal*, March 6, 2013, http://online.wsj.com; Jill Goldsmith, "Time Warner to Split with Magazines," *Variety*, March 6, 2013, http://variety.com; Christine Haughney, "Spinoff of Time Inc. Rattles Employees," *New York Times*, March 13, 2013, http://www.nytimes.com; Amy Chozick, "Time Inc. Will Be Spun Off," *New York Times*, March 6, 2013, Business Insights: Global, http://bi.galegroup.com; Julianne Pepitone, "Time Warner to Spin Off Time Inc. Magazines," *CNN Wire*, March 7, 2013, Business Insights: Global, http://bi.galegroup.com; Diane Brady, "Time Warner Makes Strides in Digital Media," *Bloomberg Businessweek*, February 14, 2013, http://www.businessweek.com.

2. M. Reeves and M. Deimler, "Adaptability: The New Competitive Advantage," *Harvard Business Review*, July–August 2011, pp. 135–41.

3. J. Bower, H. Leonard, and L. Paine, "Global Capitalism at Risk: What Are You Doing about It?" *Harvard Business Review*, September 2011, pp. 105–12.

4. Ibid.

5. J. R. Immelt, "The CEO of General Electric on Sparking an American Manufacturing Renewal," *Harvard Business Review*, March 2012, pp. 43–46.

6. T. A. Judge, C. J. Thoresen, V. Pucik, and T. M. Welbourne, "Managerial Coping with Organizational Change: A Dispositional Perspective," *Journal of Applied Psychology* 84 (1999), pp. 107–22.

7. C. Giffi, A. Roth, and G. Seal, *Competing in World-Class Manufacturing: America's 21st Century Challenge* (Homewood, IL: Business One Irwin, 1990).

8. R. M. Kanter, *World Class: Thriving Locally in the Global Economy* (New York: Touchstone, 1995).

9. R. M. Kanter, "How Great Companies Think Differently," *Harvard Business Review*, November 2011, pp. 66–78.

10. Giffi, Roth, and Seal, *Competing in World-Class Manufacturing*.

11. J. Collins and J. Porras, *Built to Last* (London: Century, 1996).

12. Collins and Porras, *Built to Last*.

13. C. Gibson and J. Birkinshaw, "The Antecedents, Consequences, and Mediating Role of Organizational Ambidexterity," *Academy of Management Journal* 47 (2004), pp. 209–26.

14. Collins and Porras, *Built to Last*.

15. N. Nohria, W. Joyce, and B. Roberson, "What Really Works," *Harvard Business Review*, July 2003, pp. 42–52.

16. R. M. Kanter, "Thriving Locally in the Global Economy," *Harvard Business Review*, August 2003, pp. 119–27.

17. Ibid.; R. M. Kanter, "How Great Companies Think Differently," *Harvard Business Review*, November 2011, pp. 66–78.

18. B. Burnes and B. Cooke, "The Past, Present and Future of Organization Development: Taking the Long View," *Human Relations* 65 (2012), pp. 1395–1429.

19. T. Cummings and C. Worley, *Organization Development and Change*, 8th ed. (Mason, OH: Thomson/South-Western, 2005).

20. Ibid.

21. Ibid.

22. D. R. Conner, *Managing at the Speed of Change* (New York: Random House, 2006); and R. Teerlink, "Harley's Leadership U-Turn," *Harvard Business Review*, July–August 2000, pp. 43–48.

23. E. E. Lawler III, *Treat People Right!* (San Francisco: Jossey-Bass, 2003).

24. P. Zigarmi and J. Hoekstra, "Leadership Strategies for Making Change Stick," *Perspectives* (Ken Blanchard Companies, 2008), http://www.kenblanchard.com.

25. Kevin Wack, "Reinventing the Branch Employee: A How-to Guide," *American Banker*, June 2013, Business Insights: Global, http://bi.galegroup.com.

26. Conner, *Managing at the Speed of Change*; and S. Oreg, "Resistance to Change: Developing an Individual Differences Measure," *Journal of Applied Psychology*, 2003, pp. 680–93.

27. S. Oreg and N. Sverdlik, "Ambivalence toward Imposed Change: The Conflict between Dispositional Resistance to Change and the Orientation toward the Change Agent," *Journal of Applied Psychology* 96 (2011), pp. 337–49; A. Rafferty and S. L. Restubog, "The Impact of Change Process and Context on Change Reactions and Turnover during a Merger," *Journal of Management* 36 (2010), pp. 1309–38; A. Rafferty, N. Jimmieson, and A. Armenakis, "Change Readiness: A Multilevel Review," *Journal of Management* 39 (2013), pp. 110–35.

28. J. Stanislao and B. C. Stanislao, "Dealing with Resistance to Change," *Business Horizons*, July–August 1983, pp. 74–78; and J. D. Ford and L. W. Ford, "Decoding Resistance to Change," *Harvard Business Review*, April 2009, pp. 99–103.

29. J. P. Kotter and L. A. Schlesinger, "Choosing Strategies for Change," *Harvard Business Review*, March–April 1979, pp. 106–114; Ford and Ford, "Decoding Resistance to Change"; and Zigarmi and Hoekstra, "Leadership Strategies."

30. D. Zell, "Overcoming Barriers to Work Innovations: Lessons Learned at Hewlett-Packard," *Organizational Dynamics*, Summer 2001, pp. 77–85.

31. E. B. Dent and S. Galloway Goldberg, "Challenging Resistance to Change," *Journal of Applied Behavioral Science*, March 1999, pp. 25–41; Ford and Ford, "Decoding Resistance to Change"; Zigarmi and Hoekstra, "Leadership Strategies"; and J. Ford, L. Ford, and A. D'Amelio, "Resistance to Change: The Rest of the Story," *Academy of Management Review* 33 (2008), pp. 362–77.

32. Rachel Emma Silverman and Robin Sidel, "Warming Up to the Officeless Office," *The Wall Street Journal*, April 17, 2012, http://online.wsj.com; Network of Executive Women, "American Express Marries Work Styles with Work Spaces," News and Blogs, January 20, 2010, http://www.newonline.org; Jeanne Meister, "Flexible Workspaces: Employee Perk or Business Tool to Recruit Top Talent?" *Forbes*, April 1, 2013, http://www.forbes.com; "Designing a More Work-Friendly Workspace," *Entrepreneur*, February 21, 2012, http://www.entrepreneur.com.

33. G. Johnson, *Strategic Change and the Management Process* (New York: Basil Blackwell, 1987); and K. Lewin, "Frontiers in Group Dynamics," *Human Relations* 1 (1947), pp. 5–41.

34. E. H. Schein, "Organizational Culture: What It Is and How to Change It," in *Human Resource Management in International Firms*, ed. P. Evans, Y. Doz, and A. Laurent (New York: St. Martin's Press, 1990).

35. M. Beer, R. Eisenstat, and B. Spector, *The Critical Path to Corporate Renewal* (Cambridge, MA: Harvard Business School Press, 1990).

36. Wack, "Reinventing the Branch Employee."

37. E. E. Lawler III, "Transformation from Control to Involvement," in *Corporate Transformation*, ed. R. Kilmann and T. Covin (San Francisco: Jossey-Bass, 1988).

38. D. Hellriegel and J. W. Slocum Jr., *Management*, 4th ed. (Reading, MA: Addison-Wesley, 1986).

39. F. Vermeulen, P. Puranam, and R. Gulate, "Change for Change's Sake," *Harvard Business Review* 88 (June 2010), pp. 70–76.

40. C. Aiken and S. Keller, "The Irrational Side of Change Management," *McKinsey Quarterly*, April 2009, http://www.mckinseyquarterly.com.

41. Lewin, "Frontiers in Group Dynamics."

42. Schein, "Organizational Culture."

43. E. E. Lawler III, *From the Ground Up* (San Francisco: Jossey-Bass, 1995).

44. Q. Nguyen Huy, "Time, Temporal Capability, and Planned Change," *Academy of Management Review* 26 (2001), pp. 601–23.

45. B. Sugarman, "A Learning-Based Approach to Organizational Change: Some Results and Guidelines," *Organizational Dynamics*, Summer 2001, pp. 62–75.

46. Kotter and Schlesinger, "Choosing Strategies for Change."

47. R. H. Miles, "Beyond the Age of Dilbert: Accelerating Corporate Transformations by Rapidly Engaging all Employees," *Organizational Dynamics*, Spring 2001, pp. 313–21.

48. D. A. Nadler, "Managing Organizational Change: An Integrative Approach," *Journal of Applied Behavioral Science* 17 (1981), pp. 191–211.

49. D. Rousseau and S. A. Tijoriwala, "What's a Good Reason to Change? Motivated Reasoning and Social Accounts in Promoting Organizational Change," *Journal of Applied Psychology* 84 (1999), pp. 514–28.

50. Dori Meinert, "Wings of Change," *HR Magazine*, November 2012, Business Insights: Global, http://bi.galegroup.com.

51. C. F. Leana and B. Barry, "Stability and Change as Simultaneous Experiences in Organizational Life," *Academy of Management Review* 25 (2000), pp. 753–59.

52. O. Gadiesh and J. Gilbert, "Transforming Corner-Office Strategy into Frontline Action," *Harvard Business Review*, May 2001, pp. 72–79.

53. Hagey and Peers, "Time Warner Opts to Spin Off All Magazines"; Goldsmith, "Time Warner to Split with Magazines"; Haughney, "Spinoff of Time Inc. Rattles Employees"; Chozick, "Time Inc. Will Be Spun Off"; Pepitone, "Time Warner to Spin Off Time Inc. Magazines"; Keith J. Kelly, "How Time Flies!" *New York Post*, March 7, 2013, http://www.nypost.com; "The Art of the Spin-Off," *The Economist*, May 4, 2013, Business Insights: Global, http://bi.galegroup.com; "Publishing," *Delaney Report*, February 4, 2013, Business Insights: Global, http://bi.galegroup.com.

54. B. Schneider, A. Brief, and R. Guzzo, "Creating a Climate and Culture for Sustainable Organizational Change," *Organizational Dynamics*, Spring 1996, pp. 7–19.

55. The Price Waterhouse Change Integration Team, *Better Change: Best Practices for Transforming Your Organization* (Burr Ridge, IL: Irwin, 1995).

56. M. Beer and N. Nohria, "Cracking the Code of Change," *Harvard Business Review*, May–June 2000, pp. 133–41.

57. N. Nohria and J. Berkley, "Whatever Happened to the Take-Charge Manager?" *Harvard Business Review*, January–February 1994, pp. 128–37.

58. D. Miller, J. Hartwick, and I. Le Breton-Miller, "How to Detect a Management Fad—and Distinguish It from a Classic," *Business Horizons*, July–August 2004, pp. 7–16.

59. Price Waterhouse Change Integration Team, *Better Change*.

60. Ibid.

61. John P. Kotter, "Accelerate!" *Harvard Business Review*, November 2012, pp. 46–58; Kotter International, "Our Prinicples: Urgency," http://www.kotterinternational.com.

62. Lawler, *From the Ground Up*.

63. J. Kotter, *Leading Change* (Boston: Harvard Business School Press, 1996).

64. Schneider, Brief, and Guzzo, "Creating a Climate and Culture."

65. R. Beckhard and R. Harris, *Organizational Transitions* (Reading, MA: Addison-Wesley, 1977).

66. Kotter, *Leading Change*.

67. S. Schumacher, "Waking Employees," *Rock Products*, September 1, 2010, Business & Company Resource Center, http://galenet.galegroup.com.

68. G. Hamel, "Waking Up IBM," *Harvard Business Review*, July–August 2000, pp. 137–46; and Deutschman, *Change or Die*.

69. Kotter, *Leading Change*.

70. D. Smith, *Taking Charge of Change* (Reading, MA: Addison-Wesley, 1996).

71. Kotter, "Accelerate!"

72. G. Hamel, "Killer Strategies That Make Shareholders Rich," *Fortune*, June 23, 1997, pp. 22–34.

73. G. Hamel and C. K. Prahalad, *Competing for the Future* (Boston: Harvard Business School Press, 1994).

74. Mckinley Conway, "Coming: The Biggest Boom Ever!" *The Futurist*, May–June 2010, Business & Company Resource Center, http://galenet.galegroup.com.

75. M. Cheung, "Phones to Replace the Wallet, a Smarter Internet, and More Futurist Predictions," *Computer Dealer News*, October 2010, p. 8; and C. G. Wagner, "70 Jobs for 2030," *The Futurist*, January–February 2011, pp. 30–33.

76. E. Beinhocker, I. Davis, and L. Mendenca, "The 10 Trends You Have to Watch," *Harvard Business Review* 87 (July/August 2009), pp. 5–60.

77. S. Zuboff and J. Maxim, *The Support Economy* (New York: Penguin, 2004); R. M. Kanter, "How Great Companies Think Differently," *Harvard Business Review*, November 2011, pp. 66–78.

78. H. Courtney, J. Kirkland, and P. Viguerie, "Strategy under Uncertainty," *Harvard Business Review*, November–December 1997, pp. 66–79.

79. J. O'Shea and C. Madigan, *Dangerous Company: The Consulting Powerhouses and the Business They Save and Ruin* (New York: Times Books, 1997).

80. Hamel and Prahalad, *Competing for the Future*.

81. Ibid.

82. Ibid.

83. A. Scott, "Sustainability: Building Better Practices," *Chemical Week*, October 11, 2010, pp. 24–27.

84. M. Courtney, "Small Is Beautiful," *Computing*, August 5, 2010, Business & Company Resource Center, http://galenet.galegroup.com; and G. E. King and L. Gibbs, "The Little Unknown," *Industrial Engineer*, July 2010, pp. 33–37.

85. King and Gibbs, "The Little Unknown"; P. Livingstone, "Billions of Pieces, Billions of Questions," *R&D Magazine*, October 2010, pp. 8–13; and J. Katz, "Nanotechnology: Beyond the Hype," *Industry Week*, November 2010, pp. 22–26.

86. Courtney, "Small Is Beautiful"; Livingstone, "Billions of Pieces"; and Katz, "Nanotechnology."

87. Global Information, "Global Market for Nanotechnology to Reach $3.3 Trillion by 2018," news release, PR Newswire, http://www.prnewswire.com; BCC Research, "Nanotechnology: A Realistic Market Assessment," report highlights, September 2012, http://www.bccresearch.com.

88. Julie Deardorff, "Scientists: Nanotech-Based Products Offer Great Potential but Unknown Risks," *Chicago Tribune*, July 10, 2012, http://articles.chicagotribune.com; Laura Walter, "Sizing Up Nanotechnology Safety," *EHS Today*, April 18, 2013, http://ehstoday.com; "Nanotechnology-Related Safety and Ethics Problem Emerging," *Science Daily*, April 28, 2012, http://www.sciencedaily.com.

89. Deardorff, "Scientists"; Walter, "Sizing Up Nanotechnology Safety"; "News in Nanotechnology," *EHS Today*, December 2012, p. 20.

90. Hamel and Prahalad, *Competing for the Future*.

91. J. Kotter, *The New Rules: How to Succeed in Today's Post-Corporate World* (New York: Free Press, 1995).

92. T. Bateman and B. Barry, "Masters of the Long Haul: Pursuing Long-Term Work Goals," *Journal of Organizational Behavior* (2012).

93. Kotter, *The New Rules*.

94. T. Bateman and C. Porath, "Transcendent Behavior," in *Positive Organizational Scholarship*, ed. K. Cameron, J. Dutton, and R. Quinn (San Francisco: Barrett-Koehler, 2003).

95. L. A. Hill, "New Manager Development for the 21st Century," *Academy of Management Executive*, August 2004, pp. 121–26; and D. A. Ready, J. A. Conger, L. A. Hill, "Are You a High Potential?" *Harvard Business Review* 88 (June 2010), pp. 78–84.

96. Lawler, *From the Ground Up*; and Kotter, *The New Rules*.

97. Lawler, *Treat People Right!*
98. M. Peiperl and Y. Baruck, "Back to Square Zero: The Post-Corporate Career," *Organizational Dynamics,* Spring 1997, pp. 7–22.
99. Ibid.
100. Conner, *Managing at the Speed of Change,* pp. 235–45.
101. J. W. Slocum Jr., M. McGill, and D. Lei, "The New Learning Strategy Anytime, Anything, Anywhere," *Organizational Dynamics,* Autumn 1994, pp. 33–37.
102. Kotter, *The New Rules.*
103. J. Collins, *From Good to Great* (New York: HarperBusiness, 2001).
104. Hill, "New Manager Development for the 21st Century," p. 125.
105. J. A. Raelin, "Don't Bother Putting Leadership into People," *Academy of Management Executive,* August 2004, pp. 131–35.
106. G. Binney, and C. Williams, *Leaning into the Future* (London: Nicholas Brealey, 1997).
107. P. Omidyar, "How Great Companies Think Differently: eBay's Founder on Innovating the Business Model of Social Change," *Harvard Business Review,* September 2011, pp. 41–44; M. Porter and M. Kramer, "Creating Shared Value," *Harvard Business Review,* January-February 2011, pp. 62–77; H. Sabeti, "The For-Benefit Enterprise," *Harvard Business Review,* November 2011, pp. 99–104.
108. Ibid.
109. Hagey and Peers, "Time Warner Opts to Spin Off All Magazines"; Goldsmith, "Time Warner to Split with Magazines"; Haughney, "Spinoff of Time Inc. Rattles Employees"; Brady, "Time Warner Makes Strides"; *The Economist,* "The Art of the Spin-Off"; *Delaney Report,* "Publishing"; Joann S. Lublin and Keach Hagey, "Front-Runner Emerges for Time Inc. CEO," *The Wall Street Journal,* July 2, 2013, http://online.wsj.com.

PHOTO CREDITS

B

Baby-boomers, 381
Background checks, 336
BAE Systems, 411
Bain Consulting, 431

Balance sheet   *A report that shows the financial picture of a company at a given time and itemizes assets, liabilities, and stockholders' equity,* **541–542**

Balanced scorecard   *Control system combining four sets of performance measures: financial, customer, business process, and learning and growth,* 127, **550**

Baldrige Award, 310–311
Bank Boston, 167
Bank of America, 167
Bargaining
    collective, 359–360
    online, 502
Barnes & Noble, 54, 298

Barriers to entry   *Conditions that prevent new companies from entering an industry,* **52–53**

BARS, 347–348
Base technologies, 571
Baskin-Robbins, 8
Batesville Casket Company, 579
Bayer, 61, 182, 332
BCG matrix, 139–140
Bechtel, 211, 279
Behavior, consequences of, 443–444
Behavioral appraisals, 347

Behavioral approach   *A leadership perspective that attempts to identify what good leaders do—that is, what behaviors they exhibit,* **413–417**

Behavioral description interview, 335
Behaviorally anchored rating scale (BARS), 347–348
Bell Labs, 578
Beloit Corporation, 239
Ben & Jerry's, 173, 441

Benchmarking   *The process of comparing an organization's practices and technologies with those of other companies,* **60–61,** **136–137, 572**

Benefits, for employees, 50, 355–356
Best Buy, 234, 317, 527–528, 544, 555
Best-case scenario, 59
Best-in-class, 60–61
Best practices, 136
Biases, psychological, 89–91
Bigelow Aerospace, 233
Bill and Melinda Gates Foundation, 124
BlackRock, 22
Blake and Mouton's Leadership Grid, 416
Blockbuster, 52
Blogging, 501, 503–504
Bloomin' Brands, 142
Bluefin Labs, 580
BMC Software, 318
BMW, 193
Board of directors, 267–268
Boards, advisory, 248
Body language, 509–510
Body Shop, 173
Boeing, 55–56, 79, 90, 102, 233, 279, 429, 472, 502
Bombardier, 563
Bonefish Grill, 142

Bonuses
    for innovation, 98
    for management, 353

Bootlegging   *Informal work on projects, other than those officially assigned, of employees' own choosing and initiative,* **250**

Borders Books, 372
Borrow-use-return, 172
Boston Consulting Group, 139, 582

Boundary-spanning   *Interacting with people in other groups, thus creating linkages between groups,* **485**

Boundaryless organization   *Organization in which there are no barriers to information flow,* 320, **517**

Bounded rationality   *A less-than-perfect form of rationality in which decision makers cannot be perfectly rational because decisions are complex and complete information is unavailable or cannot be fully processed,* **99**

Brainstorming   *A process in which group members generate as many ideas about a problem as they can; criticism is withheld until all ideas have been proposed,* **98,** 502, 585

Brand identification, 53
Bribery Act, 217
Bribes, 48, 158, 216–217
Bricks and mortar business, 595
Bristol-Myers Squibb Company, 182
British Petroleum, 50, 92, 100, 212, 528, 562

Broker   *A person who assembles and coordinates participants in a network,* **283**

Brooks, 598
Brown Flynn, 445
Brown v. Board of Education, 371
Browning-Ferris, 183
Budgetary controls, 538–540

Budgeting   *The process of investigating what is being done and comparing the results with the corresponding budget data to verify accomplishments or remedy differences; also called budgetary controlling,* **538**

    activity-based costing, 540
    capital, 539
    cash, 539
    cost, 539
    master, 539
    operational, 145
    production, 539
    sales expense, 538–539
    strategic, 145
    types of, 539–540

Buffering   *Creating supplies of excess resources in case of unpredictable needs,* **64**

Built to Last, 604
Bull and bear markets, 47
Bureaucracy, 37–38, 64, 584–585

Bureaucratic control   *The use of rules, regulations, and authority to guide performance,* **529;** *see also Control systems*

    approaches to, 533–537
    budgetary controls; *see Budgeting*

control cycle, 529–533
designing effective, 546–550
downside of, 544–546
financial controls, 541–544
management audits, 537–538
Burger King, 313, 392
Burt's Bees, 166, 173

Business accelerators   *Organization that provides support and advice to help young businesses grow,* **240**

Business ethics   *The moral principles and standards that guide behavior in the world of business,* **156,** 159–160; *see also Ethics*

Business failures, 7, 238–243

Business incubators   *Protected environments for new, small businesses,* **240**

Business model innovation, 562
Business models, 234

Business plan   *A formal planning step that focuses on the entire venture and describes all the elements involved in starting it,* **244–245**

Business portfolio, 139

Business strategy   *The major actions by which a business competes in a particular industry or market,* **141–142**

Business-to-business (BB) selling, 57

C

Caesar Rivise, 393
CafePress, 234

Cafeteria benefit program   *An employee benefit program in which employees choose from a menu of options to create a benefit package tailored to their needs,* **356**

CAFTA-DR, 199
CalPERS, 184
Campbell Soup, 451
Canon, 319
Capital
    human, 329–330
    intellectual, 329
    social, 23, 248
Capital budget, 539
Capital One, 537
Capterra, 83–86, 88–89

Carbon footprint   *The output of carbon dioxide and other greenhouses gases,* **172**

Care at Hand, 233
Care USA, 268
Career management
    continuous learning, 621–622
    keys to success, 20–25
    networking, 29
    Personal Assessment of Management Skills (PAMS), 27–29
    planning worksheet, 30–32
    promotions, 396–397
CareerBuilder.com, 334
Cargill Animal Nutrition, 451
Carlson Leisure Travel, 547
CarMax, 618
Carmike Cinema, 275
Carrabba's, 142–143
Carrying capacity, 180

Caux Principles *Ethical principles established by international executives based in Caux, Switzerland, in collaboration with business leaders from Japan, Europe, and the United States,* **157**

Centralized organization
An organization in which high-level executives make most decisions and pass them down to lower levels for implementation, **272–273**

Certainty *The state that exists when decision makers have accurate and comprehensive information,* **81**

Charismatic leader *A person who is dominant, self-confident, convinced of the moral righteousness of his or her beliefs, and able to arouse a sense of excitement and adventure in followers,* **424**–425

Chief information officer (CIO)
Executive in charge of information technology strategy and development, **580**–581

Clan control *Control based on the norms, values, shared goals, and trust among group members,* **529**, 553–554

Coaching *Dialogue with a goal of helping another be more effective and achieve his or her full potential on the job,* 346, **513**

Coalitional model *Model of organizational decision making in which groups with differing preferences use power and negotiation to influence decisions,* **99**

Cognitive conflict *Issue-based differences in perspectives or judgments,* **96**

Cohesiveness *The degree to which a group is attractive to its members, members are motivated to remain in the group, and members influence one another,* 386, **482**–484

Collaboration *A style of dealing with conflict emphasizing both cooperation and assertiveness to maximize both parties' satisfaction,* **487**–488

Communication *The transmission of information and meaning from one party to another through the use of shared symbols,* 496–525, **498**

Comparable worth *Principle of equal pay for different jobs of equal worth,* **356**

Competing *A style of dealing with conflict involving strong focus on one's own goals and little or no concern for the other person's goals,* **487**–488

Competitive environment
The immediate environment surrounding a firm; includes suppliers, customers, rivals, and the like, **44**

Competitive intelligence *Information that helps managers determine how to compete better,* **59**

Compliance-based ethics programs
Company mechanisms typically designed by corporate counsel to prevent, detect, and punish legal violations, **164**

Complimentary products and technologies, 569
Compressed workweek, 393

Compromise *A style of dealing with conflict involving moderate attention to both parties' concerns,* **487–488**

Computer-aided design, 314

Computer-integrated manufacturing (CIM) *The use of computer-aided design and computer-aided manufacturing to sequence and optimize a number of production processes,* **314–315**

Concentration *A strategy employed for an organization that operates a single business and competes in a single industry,* **138–139**

Concentric diversification *A strategy used to add new businesses that produce related products or are involved in related markets and activities,* **138–139**

Conceptual and decision skills *Skills pertaining to the ability to identify and resolve problems for the benefit of the organization and its members,* **19**

Concern for people, 414, 416
Concern for production, 414, 416

Concurrent control *The control process used while plans are being carried out, including directing, monitoring, and fine-tuning activities as they are performed,* **533–534**

Concurrent engineering *A design approach in which all relevant functions cooperate jointly and continually in a maximum effort aimed at producing high-quality products that meet customers' needs,* **319**

Confidentiality, of information, 597
Conflict of interest, 155, 158

Conflict *Opposing pressures from different sources, occurring on the level of psychological conflict or conflict between individuals or groups,* **82–83**

affective, 96
cognitive, 96
constructive, 96–97
managing, 486
styles, 486–488
virtual, 489–490

Conglomerate diversification *A strategy used to add new businesses that produce unrelated products or are involved in unrelated markets and activities,* **139**

ConocoPhillips, 579
Conservation, 180
Consideration, 414
Consolidated Natural Gas, 183
Constructive conflict, 96–97
Constructive feedback, 350
Consumer Protection Act, 458
Consumers, 56–57
Contemporary approaches to management, 38–39
Content theories, 449
Content validity, 339

Contingencies, 39
Contingency models of leadership, 418–421
Contingency perspective, 38–39

Contingency plans *Alternative courses of action that can be implemented based on how the future unfolds,* **85–86, 122**

Contingent workers, 64–65
Continuous improvement, 8, 308
Continuous learning, 621–622

Continuous process *A process that is highly automated and has a continuous production flow,* **313**

Contracted development, 578
Contraction, 63
Contracts
    labor, 34
    psychological, 462

Control *Any process that directs the activities of individuals toward the achievement of organizational goals,* **528**

    as a function of management, 14–15
    illusion of, 90
    market, 529, 551–553
    monitoring and, 124
    resistance to, 546
Control systems, 526–559
    bureaucratic systems
        approaches to, 533–537
        budgetary controls, 538–540
        control cycle, 529–533
        designing effective, 546–550
        downside of, 544–546
        financial controls, 541–544
        management audits, 537–538
    clan control, 529, 553–554
    concurrent, 533–534
    defined, 528
    feedback, 533–535
    feedforward, 533–534
    market control, 529, 551–553
    six sigma, 310, 535–537, 545
    span of, 269–270
    strategic, 144–145

Controlling *The management function of monitoring performance and making needed changes,* **14**

Converse, 62

Cooperative strategies *Strategies used by two or more organizations working together to manage the external environment,* **63**

Cooptation, 63, 612
Coordination and communication, 285–286

Coordination by mutual adjustment *Units interact with one another to make accommodations to achieve flexible coordination,* **285, 286**

Coordination by plan *Interdependent units are required to meet deadlines and objectives that contribute to a common goal,* **284**

Coordination by standardization, 284

Coordination *The procedures that link the various parts of an organization for the purpose of achieving the organization's overall mission,* **265**

Copyright laws, 48
CopyShark.net, 241
Corcoran Group, 408–409
Cordis Corporation, 277

Core capability *A unique skill and/or knowledge an organization possesses that gives it an edge over competitors,* **134–136, 298–299**

Core values, 603
Corning, 136, 328, 377
Corporate culture, 66–72
Corporate entrepreneurship, 249–251
Corporate Executive Board, 270

Corporate governance *The role of a corporation's executive staff and board of directors in ensuring that the firm's activities meet the goals of the firm's stakeholders,* **269**

Corporate social responsibility (CSR) *Obligation toward society assumed by business,* 166–171, **168,** 235; *see also Ethics*

Corporate strategy *The set of businesses, markets, or industries in which an organization competes and the distribution of resources among those entities,* **138–141**

Corrective action, 533
Corruption, in foreign transactions, 216–217
Cost-benefit analysis, 181
Cost budget, 539–540

Cost competitiveness *Keeping costs low to achieve profits and be able to offer prices that are attractive to consumers,* **10–11**

Costs
    activity-based, 540
    management of, 10–11
    switching, 55, 568
    transportation, 207
Counterfeit goods, 575
Courage, 166, 429
Cradle-to-cradle, 172
Cradle-to-grave, 172
Creativity, 97–98, 583–584
Credit Suisse, 452
Crisis management, 100–102
Criterion-related validity, 339
Critical incident technique, 347
Cross-cultural communication, 213–216, 508–509
Crowdfunding, 246
Cultural control, 529
Cultural integration, 389
Culture
    adhocracy, 70
    diagnosing, 68–71
    ethnocentrism, 213, 390
    group, 69–70
    hierarchical, 70
    managing, 71
    organizational, 67–72
    preference scale, 75–77
    rational, 70
    understanding, 213–216
Culture contingency, 390

Culture shock *The disorientation and stress associated with being in a foreign environment,* **213**

Current assets, 541
Current liabilities, 541

Current ratio *A liquidity ratio that indicates the extent to which short-term assets can decline and still be adequate to pay short-term liabilities,* **541**

Custom-made solutions *New, creative solutions designed specifically for the problem,* **84**

Customer division, 278
Customer goals, 127–128

Customer relationship management (CRM) *A multifaceted process focusing on creating two-way exchanges with customers to foster intimate knowledge of their needs, wants, and buying patterns,* **307–309**

Customer responsiveness, organizing for, 306–312
Customer service, 56–57
Customers, 56–57, 306–312
Customization, mass, 65, 313–315
CVS Caremark, 382
Cycle time reduction, 318

D

Danish Steel, 184
Data mining, 596
Days Inn, 392
DB Healthcare, 230
DealPerk, 241

Debt-equity ratio *A leverage ratio that indicates the company's ability to meet its long-term financial obligations,* **543**

Decentralized organization *An organization in which lower-level managers make important decisions,* 64, **272–273**

Decision making
    alternative evaluation, 85–86
    barriers to effective, 89–93
    best decision, 89
    brainstorming, 98, 502, 585
    centralized, 272–273
    characteristics of, 80–83
    coalitional model, 99
    conflict in, 82–83, 96–97
    constraints on, 98–99
    contingency plans, 85–86, 122
    creativity and, 97–98
    crisis management, 100–102
    custom-made solutions, 84
    decentralized, 64, 272–273
    ethical, 164–165
    evaluating the decision, 88–89
    garbage can model, 99–100
    in groups, 93–95, 105
    groupthink, 95, 385, 482
    implementing the decision, 87–88
    incremental model, 99
    making the choice, 86–87
    nonprogrammed, 81
    organizational, 98–102
    participation in, 415
    phases of, 83–89
    versus planning, 120–121
    problem ID, 83–84
    programmed, 80–81
    psychological biases, 89–91
    ready-made solutions, 84
    requirements for effective, 95–96
    social realities, 93
    stages of, 121

    time pressures, 91–92
    types of, 80–81
Decision skills, 19
Decision styles, 415
Decoding, 498
Defects, 8, 535–537
Defects per million opportunities (DPMO), 536

Defenders *Companies that stay within a stable product domain as a strategic maneuver,* **62,** 576

Delegation *The assignment of new or additional responsibilities to a subordinate,* 241, **270–272**

Dell Computer, 57, 198, 308, 313, 318, 333
Deloitte & Touche, 329, 396
Demand forecasts, 330–331
Deming's 14 points, 310

Democratic leadership *A form of leadership in which the leader solicits input from subordinates,* **415**

Demographics *Measures of various characteristics of the people who make up groups or other social units,* **49–50**

Departmentalization *Subdividing an organization into smaller subunits,* **274**

    customer/geographic, 278
    divisional, 276–278
    matrix, 278–282
    product approach, 277–278
Designer role, 283
Deutsche Asset Management, 184
Deutsche Boerse, 189

Development *Helping managers and professional employees learn the broad skills needed for their present and future jobs,* **344–346**

Development project *A focused organizational effort to create a new product or process via technological advances,* **585**

Devil's advocate *A person who has the job of criticizing ideas to ensure that their downsides are fully explored,* **97**

Dialectic *A structured debate comparing two conflicting courses of action,* **97**

Differential piecerate system, 35
Differentiated market, 384

Differentiation *An aspect of the organization's internal environment created by job specialization and the division of labor,* **264–265,** 566

Differentiation strategy *A strategy an organization uses to build competitive advantage by being unique in its industry or market segment along one or more dimensions,* **141–142**

Dillon Read, 452
Directive leadership, 414, 421–422
Discipline, progressive, 340–341, 550

Discounting the future *A bias weighting short-term costs and benefits more heavily than longer-term costs and benefits,* **91**

Discrimination, 370–371
Diseconomies of scale, 303
Disempowerment, 456
Disney, 231, 234, 328, 602
Disruptive innovation, 566
Distribution channels, 202

Diversification *A firm's investment in a different product, business, or geographic area,* **61,** 138–139

Diversity, 368–403
    accommodation, 397, 487–488
    accountability for, 271, 397
    versus affirmative action, 383–388
    age of workforce, 381–383
    assumptions, 386, 390
    attracting employees, 392–393
    awareness building, 394
    challenges of, 386–388
    communication problems, 386–387
    competitive advantage through, 384–385
    components of, 372
    cultivating, 391–397
    defined, 372
    gay, lesbian, bisexual, transgendered, 378
    gender issues, 373–378
    history, 370–371
    managing, 370
    mentally and physically disabled, 380–381
    minorities and immigrants, 49–50, 370–371, 378–380
    mistrust and tension, 387
    multicultural organizations, 389–391
    organizational assessment, 392
    retaining employees, 384, 395–397
    stereotyping, 387
    top management commitment for, 391–392
    women, 49–50, 370–371, 373–378
    workforce of the future, 373

Diversity training *Programs that focus on identifying and reducing hidden biases against people with differences and developing the skills needed to manage a diversified workforce,* **346,** 394–395

DiversityInc.com, 380

Divestiture *A firm selling one or more businesses,* **62**

Division managers, 281

Division of labor *The assignment of different tasks to different people or groups,* **264**

Divisional organization *Departmentalization that groups units around products, customers, or geographic regions,* **276–278**

Dodd-Frank Wall Street Reform, 458
Dogs, 139–140

Domain selection *Entering a new market or industry with an existing expertise,* **61**

Domestic partners, 50
Domino Sugar, 313
DoubleClick, 137

Forming stage, 476
Foursquare, 229
14 principles of management, 36

Framing effects *A decision bias influenced by the way in which a problem or decision alternative is phrased or presented,* **90–91**

Franchise Chat, 233

Franchising *An entrepreneurial alliance between a franchisor (an innovator who has created at least one successful store and wants to grow) and a franchisee (a partner who manages a new store of the same type in a new location),* 208, **232–233**

Freescale Semiconductor, 393
Friendster, 569
Frivolity, 548

Frontline managers *Lower-level managers who supervise the operational activities of the organization,* **17–18**

Functional managers, 281

Functional organization *Departmentalization around specialized activities such as production, marketing, and human resources,* **275–276**

Functional strategies *Strategies implemented by each functional area of the organization to support the organization's business strategy,* **142–143**

FundersClub, 246

G

Gage Products Company, 56
Gainsharing plans, 353
Game Freak, 473
Gap Incorporated, 62

Garbage can model *Model of organizational decision making depicting a chaotic process and seemingly random decisions,* **99–100**

Gatekeeper *A team member who keeps abreast of current developments and provides the team with relevant information,* **485**

Gay, lesbian, bisexual, transgendered, 378
GDF Suez, 11
Geely, 189
Gender issues, 373–378
General Dynamics, 217, 410
General Electric, 5, 11–12, 94, 118, 122, 138–139, 143, 161, 171, 182, 188, 194, 269, 295–296, 303, 306, 310, 320–321, 328, 344, 430, 517, 535, 540, 573–574, 592
General Foods, 531
General Mills, 345, 472
General Motors, 8, 10, 56, 120, 122, 182, 190, 191, 197, 209, 263–264, 273, 278, 279, 288, 302, 313, 545, 587
Generalist, 21
Generally accepted accounting principles (GAAP), 540
Generation Y, 383
Generativity, 169

Genius of the *and*; organizational ambidexterity *Ability to achieve multiple objectives simultaneously,* **604**

Genpact, 552
Genworth, 182
Geographic division, 278
Gifts, 158, 217
Glass ceiling, 374–375
GlaxoSmithKline, 6, 609
Global economy; *see also* International management
    consequences of, 188–192
    European union, 195–196
    foreign direct investment, 189–190
Global Fund, 62–63
Global Hyatt, 212
Global management; *see* International management

Global model *An organizational model consisting of a company's overseas subsidiaries and characterized by centralized decision making and tight control by the parent company over most aspects of worldwide operations; typically adopted by organizations that base their global competitive strategy on cost considerations,* **203–204**

Global Reporting Initiatives, 173
Global Research Technologies LLC, 182
Global strategic coordination, 201
Globalization, 4–5, 141, 593–594; *see also* International management

Goal *A target or end that management desires to reach,* **121**

    aligning, 127–128
    alternative, 121–122
    customer, 127–128
    evaluation of, 123
    financial, 127–128
    growth, 127–128
    hierarchy of, 125
    internal, 127–128
    learning, 127–128
    limitations of, 442–443
    performance, 479
    selection of, 123, 130–131
    setting of, 441–443
    strategic, 125–126, 131
    stretch, 442
    superordinate, 488

Goal displacement *A decision-making group loses sight of its original goal and a new, less important goal emerges,* **95**

Goal-setting theory *A motivation theory stating that people have conscious goals that energize them and direct their thoughts and behaviors toward a particular end,* **441**

Godrej Beverages and Foods, 209
Goldman Sachs, 174
Good to Great, 621
Google, 9, 14, 58, 63, 67, 87, 130, 173, 229, 300, 327–328, 332, 346, 361–362, 497, 569, 576, 583–585
Gossip, 516
Gradual diffusion, 570
Grameen Bank, 235
Gramkow, Carnvale, Seifert & Company, 459

Grapevine *Informal communication network,* **516**

Grease payments, 217
Great Lakes Naval Museum, 131

Great Recession, 46–47
Greatness, achieving, 604–605
Green Mountain Coffee, 55, 167
Greenhouses, 584
Gross domestic product (GDP), 195
Group culture, 69–70
Group Danone, 173
Group incentive plans, 353

Group maintenance behaviors *Actions taken to ensure the satisfaction of group members, develop and maintain harmonious work relationships, and preserve the social stability of the group,* **414–415,** 421

Groupon, 4
Groups; *see also* Teams
    decision making in, 93–95, 105
    development stages of, 476–478
    failure of, 477–478
    versus teams, 476
    working, 476

Groupthink *A phenomenon that occurs in decision making when group members avoid disagreement as they strive for consensus,* **95,** 385, 482

Growth goals, 127–128

Growth need strength *The degree to which individuals want personal and psychological development,* **456**

Growth/share matrix, 139–140
GS Yuasa Corporation, 102

H

Hackman and Oldham model of job design, 455–456
Half Price Books, 243
Harassment, 341–342, 376–377
Hard Rock Café, 123
Harley-Davidson, 572, 618
Harmonix Music Systems, 266
Harrah's Entertainment, 454
Hawthorne Effect, 37
Hawthorne Studies, 36–37
Health and safety, 356–357
Health insurance, 48, 355–356
HealthPartners, 530
Hefty, 184
Heineken, 203
Heinz, 202
Herman Miller, 181, 182
Hermés International, 11

Hersey and Blanchard's situational theory *A life cycle theory of leadership postulating that a manager should consider an employee's psychological and job maturity before deciding whether task performance or maintenance behaviors are more important,* **421**

Hershey, 209
Hertz, 62, 535
Herzberg's two-factor theory, 454
Heterogeneity, 390
Hewlett-Packard, 136, 182, 183, 231, 304, 392, 405–406, 423, 430, 431, 516, 540, 602
Hierarchical culture, 70

Hierarchy *The authority levels of the organizational pyramid,* **269**

Hierarchy of needs, 37, 450–451

High-involvement organization
A type of organization in which top management ensures that there is consensus about the direction in which the business is heading, **301**–302

Hilcorp, 514
Hilton International, 203, 208
Hilton Worldwide, 166
Hit Forge, 240
Hitachi, 56, 186
Home Depot, 406, 536
Homogeneity, 390
Hon Hai, 198
Honda Motor Company, 8, 136, 143, 203, 349, 572
Honeywell, 269, 391, 396

Horizontal communication   *Information shared among people on the same hierarchical level,* **515**–516

Horizontal organizational structure
  divisional, 276–278
  functional, 275–276
  matrix, 278–282
  network, 282–283
Horizontal stretch goals, 442
Horse trading, 249

Host-country nationals   *Natives of the country where an overseas subsidiary is located,* **210**

Hostile environment, 376–377
Hulu, 52, 72

Human capital   *The knowledge, skills, and abilities of employees that have economic value,* **329**–330

Human process interventions, 605
Human relations approach to management, 36–37
Human resources analysis, 132, 135

Human resources management (HRM)
Formal systems for the management of people within an organization, 326–367, **328**

  accommodating work/family needs, 393
  affirmative action, 383–388
  alternative work schedules, 393
  attracting employees, 392–393
  background checks, 336
  demand forecasts, 330–331
  discipline, 340–341, 550
  diversity; *see* Diversity
  employee benefits, 50, 355–356
  function, 592–593
  harassment, 341–342, 376–377
  health and safety issues, 356–357
  interviewing, 334–335
  job analysis, 333
  job design, 453–457, 586–587
  labor relations, 358–361
  legal issues, 341–343, 356
  mentoring, 395–396
  outplacement, 340
  performance appraisal; *see* Performance appraisal
  planning process, 330–333
  preemployment testing, 336–339
  promotions, 396–397
  recruitment, 333–334, 392
  reference checks, 335–336
  retaining employees, 384, 395–397
  reward systems, 351–357, 444–445, 453–454, 479–480, 612
  selection process, 334–339
  strategic impact of, 328–330
  termination, 340–341
  training and development; *see* Training
  workforce reduction, 340–343
Human resources management interventions, 605
Huntsman Chemical, 441
Hyde Park Electronics, 550

Hygiene factors   *Characteristics of the workplace, such as company policies, working conditions, pay, and supervision, that can make people dissatisfied,* **454**

Hyperactive Technologies, 575

I

IBM Corporation, 57, 59, 135, 153–154, 163, 166, 167, 174, 182, 186, 187, 200, 202, 217, 231, 279, 287, 302, 326, 328, 344, 349, 374, 384, 427, 489, 503, 583, 606
IDEO, 300, 583
Ignighter.com, 201
Illinois Tool Works (ITW), 406

Illusion of control   *People's belief that they can influence events even when they have no control over what will happen,* **90**

Immigrants, in the workforce, 49–50, 370–371, 378–380
Implementers, 606
Implicit coercion, 612–613
IMX Exchange, 596
Inanity, 548
Incentive plans, 353–354
Inclusion, 384–385; *see also* Diversity

Incremental model   *Model of organizational decision making in which major solutions arise through a series of smaller decisions,* **99**

Incubators, business, 240

Independent strategies   *Strategies that an organization acting on its own uses to change some aspect of its current environment,* **62**–63

India, 198
inDinero, 229
Inditex, 11
Individual incentive plans, 353
Individual pay decisions, 352
Individualism, 214–215
Individualized attention, 425
Industry analysis, 132
Informal authority, 267
Informal communication, 516–517
Informal power, 271
Information, reducing need for, 286
Information overload, 512
Information processing, 286
Information technology, 100, 581

Informing   *A team strategy that entails making decisions with the team and then informing outsiders of its intentions,* **485**

Ingersoll Rand, 396

Initial public offering (IPO)   *Sale to the public, for the first time, of federally registered and underwritten shares of stock in the company,* **242**–243

Initiating structure, 414, 415

Innovation   *The introduction of new goods and services; a change in method or technology; a positive, useful departure from previous ways of doing things,* **7**

  business model, 562
  creativity, 97–98, 583–584
  development projects, 585
  organizing for, 582–587
  process, 562
  product, 562
  spread of, 566
  technology and, **562**
Innovators, 565

Inpatriate   *A foreign national brought in to work at the parent company,* **214**

Inputs   *Goods and services organizations take in and use to create products or services,* **44**, **458**

Inside directors, 267
Instagram, 229
Instant messaging, 501

Instrumentality   *The perceived likelihood that performance will be followed by a particular outcome,* **448**

Insurance, 355–356
Intangible assets, 134
Integrated Medical Solutions, 101

Integration   *The degree to which differentiated work units work together and coordinate their efforts,* **264**

  global, 200–201
  organizational, 264–266, 283–286
  vertical, 138–139
Integrity, 413

Integrity-based ethics programs
Company mechanisms designed to instill in people a personal responsibility for ethical behavior, **164**

Integrity tests, 338
Intel Corporation, 126, 246, 575, 578
Intellectual capital, 329
Intellectual property, 575, 597
Intellectual stimulation, 93
Intellectually stimulating, 425
Intercontinental, 203

Intergroup leader   *A leader who leads collaborative performance between groups or organizations,* **428**

Intermedia, 383

Intermediary model   *Charging fees to bring buyers and sellers together,* **234**

Intermediate consumer   *A customer who purchases raw materials or wholesale products before selling them to final customers,* **57**

Internal audit   *A periodic assessment of a company's own planning, organizing, leading, and controlling processes,* **537**

Internal benchmarking, 136; *see also* Benchmarking
Internal customers, 308

Internal development, of new technology, 578
Internal goals, 127–128
Internal recruiting, 333–334
Internal resources analysis, 135
Internal strengths and weaknesses, analysis of, 134–137, 149–150
International Franchise Association, 233
International Harvester, 415
International management, 186–223; *see also* Global economy
    Africa and the Middle East, 199–200
    bribes, 48, 158, 216–217
    China/Pacific Rim, 196–198
    choosing a strategy, 202–206
    communication, 508–509
    consequences of a global economy, 188–192
    cultural issues, 213–216, 508–509
    entry mode, 206–209
    environment and, 181
    ethics, 161, 216–218
    European unification, 195–196
    expatriates, 210–212
    exporting, 207
    franchising, 208
    global strategy, 200–206
    growth in, 190
    implications, 188–192
    India, 198
    inpatriates, 214
    joint ventures, 208–209
    licensing, 207–208
    local responsiveness, 201–202
    multinational organization model, 203
    NAFTA, 52, 198–199, 207
    need theories, 452–453
    North and South America, 198–199
    offshoring, 192–194
    organizational models, 200, 202–206
    outsourcing and, 192–194, 594
    skills of global managers, 210–213
    tariffs, 202, 207
    trade imbalance, 197–198
    trading partners, 196
    transnational model, 204–206
    wholly owned subsidiaries, 209

International model *An organizational model that is composed of a company's overseas subsidiaries and characterized by greater control by the parent company over the research function and local product and marketing strategies than is the case in the multinational model,* **202–203**

International Monetary Fund, 194
International Organization for Standardization, 311
International Trade Commission (ITC), 209
Internet
    advantages of using, 502
    background checks via, 336
    blogging, 501, 503–504
    business models, 234
    business venture failure, 7, 238–243
    crowdfunding and, 246
    disadvantages of using, 502–503
    e-commerce, 595–596
    electronic communication, 501–504
    globalization, 4–5
    importance to business, 5
    instant messaging, 501
    job searching via, 334
    selling via, 595–596
    social networking, 23, 58, 72, 308, 336, 383, 501–504
    unethical use of, 156
    virtual offices, 282–283, 504
Internship programs, 380
InternshipIN, 229

Interpersonal and communication skills *People skills; the ability to lead, motivate, and communicate effectively with others,* **20**

Interpersonal communication, 498–505
Interstate Commerce Commission, 48
Interviews, for jobs, 334–335
Intolerance of ineffective humanity, 169

Intrapreneurs *New venture creators working inside big companies,* **228,** 250, 583

Intrinsic reward *Reward a worker derives directly from performing the job itself,* **453**

Intuit, 133, 303, 585
Invention, versus innovation, 562
Involvement, change management and, 612
IPOs, 242–243

ISO 9001 *A series of quality standards developed by a committee working under the International Organization for Standardization to improve total quality in all businesses for the benefit of producers and consumers,* **311**

Ispat International, 6
itMD, 233

J

J. Crew, 225
Jade Corporation, 191
Jamba Juice, 225
Japan Airlines, 102
JC Penney, 595
JetBlue, 122, 426
Jiffy Lube, 232
JIT, 318–319
JLW Homes, 241, 249
J.M. Huber Corporation, 533

Job analysis *A tool for determining what is done on a given job and what should be done on that job,* **333**

Job description, 333
Job design, 453–457, 586–587

Job enlargement *Giving people additional tasks at the same time to alleviate boredom,* **454**

Job enrichment *Changing a task to make it inherently more rewarding, motivating, and satisfying,* **454**

Job maturity *The level of the employee's skills and technical knowledge relative to the task being performed,* **421**

Job posting system, 334

Job rotation *Changing from one task to another to alleviate boredom,* 345, **454**

Job satisfaction, 460–462
Job sharing, 393
Job shop, 313
Job specification, 333
John Deere, 579
Johnson & Johnson, 100–101, 182, 277, 328, 380, 430, 441, 549, 602
Johnson Controls, 319

Joint implementation, 183
Joint ventures, 63, 141, 208–209, 579
Jones Soda Company, 9
J.P. Morgan, 385
Jumpstart Our Business Startups Act, 246

Just-in-time (JIT) *A system that calls for subassemblies and components to be manufactured in very small lots and delivered to the next stage of the production process just as they are needed,* **318–319**

Justice, procedural, 459–460
JVC, 190

K

Kaiser Permanente, 380, 508
Kaizen, 308, 568, 592
Kanban, 592
Kawasaki, 209
Kellogg Company, 62, 202
Kelly Services, 91
Kenneth Cole, 166
Keurig, 55
Key technologies, 570
KFC, 533
Kickbacks, 48, 158
Kickstarter, 246
Kmart, 595
K&N Management, 311

Knowledge management *Practices aimed at discovering and harnessing an organization's intellectual resources,* **6,** 286

Knowledge workers, 6
Kobold Watch, 303
KOC Holding, 9

Kohlberg's model of cognitive moral development *Classification of people based on their level of moral judgment,* **159**

Kollmorgen Corporation, 407, 472
Kraft Foods, 374
Kroger, 138, 384, 576
Kyosei, 157

L

La-Z-Boy, 528
Labor, division of, 264
Labor contracts, 34
Labor force, 49–50
Labor laws, 341–343, 358
Labor-Management Relations Act, 358
Labor-Management Reporting and Disclosure Act, 358

Labor relations *The system of relations between workers and management,* **358–361**

Labor supply forecasts, 331–332
Laggards, 566

Laissez-faire *A leadership philosophy characterized by an absence of managerial decision making,* **415**

Lamps Plus, 595
Landrum-Griffin Act, 358
Language, 508

Large batch *Technologies that produce goods and services in high volume,* **313**

Late majority, 566

Organizational behavior, 38

Organizational behavior modification (OB mod) *The application of reinforcement theory in organizational settings,* **443**

Organizational climate *The patterns of attitudes and behavior that shape people's experience of an organization,* **71–72**

Organizational communication, 512–517
Organizational learning, 582, 585
Organizational suitability, 576–577
Organizations
   assessment of, 392
   decision making; *see* Decision making
   high-involvement, 301–302
   learning, 300–301, 582, 585
   multicultural, 389–391
   pluralistic, 390

Organizing *The management function of assembling and coordinating human, financial, physical, informational, and other resources needed to achieve goals,* **13–14**

Orientation training *Training designed to introduce new employees to the company and familiarize them with policies, procedures, culture, and the like,* **345**

OST system, 145
Outback Steakhouse, 142–143

Outcome *A consequence a person receives for his or her performance,* **447,** 458

Outplacement *The process of helping people who have been dismissed from the company regain employment elsewhere,* **340**

Outputs *The products and services organizations create,* **44**

Outside directors, 267

Outsourcing *Contracting with an outside provider to produce one or more of an organization's goods or services,* **192–194,** 594

P

Pacific Gas & Electric, 183
Pacific Rim, 196–198
Pacific Sunwear, 595–596
Pacification, competitive, 62
Pacing technologies, 570
Packaging, 172, 174
Panasonic, 205
Paper-and-pencil honesty tests, 338
Paper-Feet, 241

Parading *A team strategy that entails simultaneously emphasizing internal team building and achieving external visibility,* **485**

Parallel teams *Teams that operate separately from the regular work structure and exist temporarily,* **473**

Paralysis by analysis, 86
Parker Hannifin Corporation, 317
Parochialism, 390

Participation, change management and, 612

Participation in decision making *Leader behaviors that managers perform in involving their employees in making decisions,* **415**

Participative leadership, 421
Participative management, 38, 301
Partnerships, 56, 63, 141, 249, 299–300, 301, 579
Passive employee, 23
Patagonia Sur, 11
Patents, 48, 53

Path-goal theory *A theory that concerns how leaders influence subordinates' perceptions of their work goals and the paths they follow toward attainment of those goals,* **421–422**

Pay level, 351
Pay structure, 352
Payless ShoeSource, 338
PayPerPost, 156
PBD Worldwide, 504
Pearson PLC, 197
Peer evaluation, 349
Peer pressure, 607
Penske Truck Leasing Company, 552
People skills, 20
PepsiCo, 5, 50, 51–55, 57, 61, 374, 397

Perception *The process of receiving and interpreting information,* **499**–500

Performance appraisal (PA) *Assessment of an employee's job performance,* **347**

   behavioral appraisal, 347
   benchmarking, 60–61, 136–137, 572
   by customers, 349
   deadly sins of, 547–548
   giving feedback, 350–351, 446–447, 456
   goal setting, 441–442
   managing mistakes, 445–446
   MBO, 347–348
   measuring performance, 531
   motivation; *see* Motivation
   by peers, 349
   by personal observation, 531
   purposes of, 347
   reinforcing, 443–447
   results appraisals, 347–348
   rewards and punishments, 351–357, 444–445, 453–454, 479–480, 612
   self-appraisals, 349
   setting standards, 530–532, 546–548
   by subordinates, 349
   by teams, 349
   of teams, 479
   360 degree appraisal, 349–350
   trait appraisal, 347
   what to appraise, 347–349
   who should appraise, 349–350
Performance behaviors, 415–417
Performance drivers, 7–11

Performance gap *The difference between actual performance and desired performance,* **610**

Performance goals, 479
Performance norms, 482–483
Performance-related beliefs, 447–449
Performance tests, 337
Performance-to-outcome link, 447–448
Performing stage, 476
Personal Assessment of Management Skills (PAMS), 27–29
Personal fulfillment, 37

Personality tests, 336–337
Personalized power, 452
Personnel management; *see* Human resources management
Persuading, 482
Persuasion skills, 506–507
Pettiness, 548
Pfizer, 53, 202, 278, 299, 575

Philanthropic responsibilities *Additional behaviors and activities that society finds desirable and that the values of the business support,* **168–169**

Philips, 8, 190, 204
Physically disabled, 380–381
Piecerate system, 35
Pillsbury, 345
Pinterest, 229, 287
Pitney Bowes, 374
Pixar, 96
Pizza Hut, 533

Planning *The management function of systematically making decisions about the goals and activities that an individual, a group, a work unit, or the overall organization will pursue,* **13**; *see also Strategic Planning*

   alignment of plans, 127–128
   alternatives, 121–122
   business plans, 244–245
   contingency plans, 85–86, 122
   control systems and, 528
   versus decision making, 120–121
   evaluation of, 123
   as a function of management, 13
   goals; *see* Goal
   human resources, 330–333
   implementation, 123–124
   key elements, 245–247
   levels of, 125–126
   monitoring of, 124
   operational, 125–127
   process of, 120–124
   scenario, 59–60, 85–86, 123
   selection of plan, 123
   selling the plan, 247
   situational analysis, 120–121
   SWOT analysis, 137–138, 149–150
   tactical, 125–127

Plans *The actions or means managers intend to use to achieve organizational goals,* **122**

Plant Closing Bill, 342
Plante Moran, 335, 460

Pluralistic organization *An organization that has a relatively diverse employee population and makes an effort to involve employees from different gender, racial, or cultural backgrounds,* **390**

Plussing, 96
PMF Industries, 313
Political and regulatory analysis, 132
Politics, organizational, 99
Polycast Technology, 392
Polygraph tests, 338
Popchips, 225, 243–244, 252
Portfolio, 139

Positive reinforcement *Applying consequences that increase the likelihood that a person will repeat the behavior that led to it,* **443–444**

Positive self-regard, 425

Power *The ability to influence others,* **410**

    informal, 271
    leadership and, 410–412
    need for, 452
    sources of, 411–412
Power distance, 214–215
PPR Group, 184
Practical Computer Applications, 242
Pratt & Whitney, 563
Preemployment testing, 336–339
Pregnancy Discrimination Act, 356
Preliminary control, 533
Presentation skills, 506–507
PriceSpective, 329–330
PricewaterhouseCoopers, 175, 184, 380, 609
Pricing, transfer, 552

Principle of exception *A managerial principle stating that control is enhanced by concentrating on the exceptions to or significant deviations from the expected result or standard,* **531–532**

Proactive change *A response that is initiated before a performance gap has occurred,* **617**

Probing *A team strategy that requires team members to interact frequently with outsiders, diagnose their needs, and experiment with solutions,* **485**

Procedural justice *Using fair process in decision making and making sure others know that the process was as fair as possible,* **459–460**

Process engineering role, 283
Process innovation, 562
Procter & Gamble, 125, 180, 182, 202, 204, 210, 231, 237, 312, 344, 380, 385

Product champion *A person who promotes a new technology throughout the organization in an effort to obtain acceptance of and support for it,* **581**

Product complements, 53–55
Product development, 7
Product divisions, 277–278
Product innovation, 562
Product life cycle, 565
Product managers, 281
Product Red, 62
Production budget, 539
Productivity, 461

Profit and loss statement *An itemized financial statement of the income and expenses of a company's operations,* **541, 543**

Profit margin, 308
Profit-sharing plans, 353
Profitability ratios, 543

Programmed decisions *Decisions encountered and made before, having objectively correct answers, and solvable by using simple rules, policies, or numerical computations,* **80–81**

Progressive discipline, 340–341, 550

Project and development teams *Teams that work on long-term projects but disband once the work is completed,* 250, **473**

Promotions, 396–397

Prospectors *Companies that continuously change the boundaries for their task environments by seeking new products and markets, diversifying and merging, or acquiring new enterprises,* **62,** 576

Protectionism, 202
Provincialism, 547
Prudential Insurance, 287

Pseudotransformational leaders *Leaders who talk about positive change but allow their self-interest to take precedence over followers' needs,* **427**

Psychological biases, 89–91

Psychological contract *A set of perceptions of what employees owe their employers, and what their employers owe them,* **462**

Psychological maturity *An employee's self-confidence and self-respect,* **421**

Public stock offering, 242–243
Puma, 184

Punishment *Administering an aversive consequence,* **444**

Purchasing function, 593
Pure Digital, 140
Pure-play operations, 595

Q

QlikTech, 137
Quaker Oats, 268

Quality *The excellence of your product (goods or services),* **8**

    awards for, 310–311
    certification of, 311
    continuous improvement, 8, 308
    defects, 8, 535–537
    ISO 9001, 311
    service, 9
    six sigma, 310, 535–537, 545
    TQM, 309, 592

Quality of work life (QWL) programs *Programs designed to create a workplace that enhances employee wellbeing,* **460–461**

Quantitative management, 38
Question marks, 139–140
Quick Lane Tire & Auto Center, 441–442
Quid pro quo harassment, 376
QuikTrip, 445
Quotas, 202

R

R.A. Jones & Company, 319
Radio frequency identification (RFID), 317–318, 573
Radio Shack, 596
Rainmaker Thinking, 383
RAND Corporation, 570

Rational culture, 70
Ratios, financial, 541–544
RCA Corporation, 204, 208

Reactive change *A response that occurs under pressure; problem-driven change,* **617**

Reading skills, 510–511

Ready-made solutions *Ideas that have been seen or tried before,* **84**

Real-time information, 92
Receiver, 498
Receiver skills, 510–512
Receptiveness, anticipated market, 572–573
Recession, Great, 46–47
Reconciliation, 170–171

Recruitment *The development of a pool of applicants for jobs in an organization,* **333–334,** 392

Red Frog Events, 162
Reductions, in workforce, 340–343
Reengineering, 311–312
Reference checks, 335–336
Referent power, 412

Reflection *Process by which a person states what he or she believes the other person is saying,* **510**

Refreezing *Strengthening the new behaviors that support the change,* **611**

Regulations, impacting business, 48
Regulators, 48
Regulatory analysis, 132

Reinforcers *Positive consequences that motivate behavior,* **443**

Relatedness needs, 451
Relating, 482

Relationship-motivated leadership *Leadership that places primary emphasis on maintaining good interpersonal relationships,* **420**

Relationship-oriented behavior, 416

Relativism *Philosophy that bases ethical behavior on the opinions and behaviors of relevant other people,* **158,** 159

Reliability *The consistency of test scores over time and across alternative measurements,* **338–339**

Rent the Runway, 229
RescueTime, 446
Research and engineering function, 592
Research partnerships, 579
Reserves, 584
Resistance
    to change, 606–611
    to control, 546

Resources *Inputs to a system that can enhance performance,* **134–136**

Responsibility *The assignment of a task that an employee is supposed to carry out,* **270–271**

Responsive organization, 296–298
Restriction of Hazardous Substances Directive, 183
Results appraisals, 347–348
Résumés, 334
Retaining employees, 384, 395–397
Rethink Robotics, 573
Retirement, 381–382

Return on investment (ROI) *A ratio of profit to capital used, or a rate of return from capital,* **543**

Reverse logistics, 183
Reverse mentoring, 396
Reward power, 412
Rewards and punishments, for performance, 351–357, 444–445, 453–454, 479–480, 612
RFID, 317–318, 573

Right-to-work *Legislation that allows employees to work without having to join a union,* **360**

Rightsizing *A successful effort to achieve an appropriate size at which the company performs most effectively,* **305**

Rigid bureaucratic behavior, 544–545
Ring Masters, 246

Risk *The state that exists when the probability of success is less than 100 percent and losses may occur,* **82**

    entrepreneurship and, 237–238, 239, 247, 250
    environment and, 171–172
Ritz-Carlton, 9, 69, 547–549
ROI, 543

Roles *Different sets of expectations for how different individuals should behave,* **481–482**

Rotation, of jobs, 345, 454
Royal Dutch Shell, 60, 182, 357
Ruby Tuesday, 208
Rugged individualism, 214
Rumors, controlling, 516–517
Russell Reynolds, 210
Ryanair, 10

S
Safety, 356–357
Safeway, 138, 225, 576
Salaries, 352
Sales expense budget, 538–539
Salesforce.com, 307–308
Samsung, 4, 198
San Francisco Federal Credit Union, 276

Sarbanes-Oxley Act *An act passed into law by Congress in to establish strict accounting and reporting rules in order to make senior managers more accountable and to improve and maintain investor confidence,* **160–161, 163, 269, 553**

SAS, 5, 439–440, 449, 463
Satisfaction, job, 460–462

Satisficing *Choosing an option that is acceptable, although not necessarily the best or perfect,* **86–87, 95**

Scale economies, 302
Scanning, environmental, 59, 572

Scenario *A narrative that describes a particular set of future conditions,* **59–60, 85–86, 123**

Schedules, flexible, 374
Schering, 61
Schott, 133
Scientific management, 34–36, 551
Scorecard, balanced, 127, 550
Scotsman Ice Systems, 579
Scott Paper, 142, 183
Scouting, 482
Sears, 278, 302, 333, 337, 595
Secura Insurance, 515
Securities and Exchange Commission (SEC), 48, 164, 184, 217, 246, 269

Selection *Choosing from among qualified applicants to hire into an organization,* **334–339**

Self-actualization, 37, 450–451
Self-appraisals, 349
Self-confidence, 413
Self-contained tasks, 286

Self-designing teams *Teams with the responsibilities of autonomous work groups, plus control over hiring, firing, and deciding what tasks members perform,* **475**

Self-managed teams *Autonomous work groups in which workers are trained to do all or most of the jobs in a unit, have no immediate supervisor, and make decisions previously made by frontline supervisors,* **474–476**

Self-reliance, 21–22
Self-SWOT, 137
Semco, 472
Sender, 498
Sender skills, 506–509

Servant-leader *A leader who serves others' needs while strengthening the organization,* **428**

Servatii Pastry Shop, 242

Service *The speed and dependability with which an organization delivers what customers want,* **9**

Service Cloud, 308
Service relationships, 485–486
Service sector, employment in, 9
ServiceMaster, 441
Seventh Generation Products, 180, 184

Sexual harassment *Conduct of a sexual nature that has negative consequences for employment,* 341–342, **376–377**

Shapers *Companies that try to change the structure of their industries, creating a future competitive landscape of their own design,* **618**

Shared leadership *Rotating leadership, in which people rotate through the leadership role based on which person has the most relevant skills at a particular time,* **428–429, 606**

Shell, 47, 269, 313, 349
Sheraton, 203
Shout! Factory, 239
SI Group, 209
Siderca, 199

Siemens, 6, 173, 209
Silent killers, of strategies, 144
Similarity, 390
Simultaneous engineering, 319
Singapore Airlines, 10

Situational analysis *A process planners use, within time and resource constraints, to gather, interpret, and summarize all information relevant to the planning issue under consideration,* **120–121**

Situational approach *Leadership perspective proposing that universally important traits and behaviors do not exist and that effective leadership behavior varies from situation to situation,* **417–423**

Situational interview, 335
Situational theory, 421

Six sigma quality *A method of systematically analyzing work processes to identify and eliminate virtually all causes of defects, standardizing the processes to reach the lowest practicable level of any cause of customer dissatisfaction,* **310, 535–537, 545**

Skill building, 394–395

Skunkworks *A project team designated to produce a new, innovative product,* **250, 584**

Slack resources, 286

Small batch *Technologies that produce goods and services in low volume,* **313**

Small business *A business having fewer than 100 employees, independently owned and operated, not dominant in its field, and not characterized by many innovative practices,* **226, 302–304**

Small Business Administration, 226, 233, 243
SMART, 121–122, 442
Smarter Planet initiative, 200
Smithfield Foods, 168

Smoothing *Leveling normal fluctuations at the boundaries of the environment,* **65**

Social analysis, 132

Social capital *Goodwill stemming from your social relationships; a competitive advantage in the form of relationships with other people and the image other people have of you,* **23, 248**

Social enterprises *Organization that applies business models and leverages resources in ways that address social problems,* **235**

Social entrepreneurship *Leveraging resources to address social problems,* **235–236**

Social facilitation effect *Working harder when in a group than when working alone,* **479–480**

Social intelligence, 94
Social issues, 50

Top-management teams, 248, 269

Total organization change *Introducing and sustaining multiple policies, practices, and procedures across multiple units and levels,* **614**

Total quality management (TQM) *An integrative approach to management that supports the attainment of customer satisfaction through a wide variety of tools and techniques that result in high-quality goods and services,* **309, 592**

Toxic Release Inventory, 180
Toyota Motor Corporation, 7, 8, 10, 173, 191, 196, 203, 210, 213, 264, 300, 307, 316, 319, 587
Toys "R" Us, 80, 595, 597
TQM, 309, 592
Trade imbalance, 197–198
Trademarks, 48
Traders, 604
Trading, technology, 579
Trading partners, 196

Traditional work groups *Groups that have no managerial responsibilities,* **474**

Tragedy of the commons, 180
Training ABC, 394

Training *Teaching lower-level employees how to perform their present jobs,* **344**

    diversity, 346, 394–395
    management programs, 346
    methods used, 345–346
    orientation, 345
    process, 344–345
    of teams, 345
Trait appraisals, 347

Trait approach *A leadership perspective that attempts to determine the personal characteristics that great leaders share,* **412–413**

Transaction fee model *Charging fees for goods and services,* **234**

Transactional leaders *Leaders who manage through transactions, using their legitimate, reward, and coercive powers to give commands and exchange rewards for services rendered,* **425**

Transcendent education *An education with five higher goals that balance self-interest with responsibility to others,* **169**

Transfer price *Price charged by one unit for a good or service provided to another unit within the organization,* **552**

Transformational leader *A leader who motivates people to transcend their personal interests for the good of the group,* **425–427**

Transition phase, 476–477

Transnational model *An organizational model characterized by centralizing certain functions in locations that best achieve cost economies; basing other functions in the company's national subsidiaries to facilitate greater local responsiveness; and fostering communication among subsidiaries to permit transfer of technological expertise and skills,* **204–206**

Transnational teams, 473
Transocean, 92
Transportation costs, 207
Tribune Company, 68
TripAdvisor, 7

Triple bottom line *Economic, social, and environmental performance,* **168**

TruGreen, 230
TRW, 279
TSG Consumer Partners, 252
Tumblr, 229, 248, 287
Twitter, 7, 94, 282, 287, 308, 502, 503, 579–580
Two-boss managers, 281

Two-factor theory *Herzberg's theory describing two factors affecting people's work motivation and satisfaction,* **454**

Two-way communication *A process in which information flows in two directions—the receiver provides feedback, and the sender is receptive to the feedback,* **498–499**

Tyranny of the or *The belief that things must be either A or B and cannot be both; that only one goal and not another can be attained,* **604**

Tyson Foods, 579

U

UberMedia, 239
Umpqua Bank, 449

Uncertainty *The state that exists when decision makers have insufficient information,* **82**

    adapting to, 64–65
    avoidance of, 214
    environmental, 58–59
    and risk, 81–82
Unemployment insurance, 355
Unexamined assumptions, 386

Unfreezing *Realizing that current practices are inappropriate and that new behavior is necessary,* **609–610**

Unification, European, 195–196
Unilever, 173, 183, 186, 204, 302, 303
Union Carbide, 59, 100–101, 179
Union Pacific, 183, 342, 406

Union shop *An organization with a union and a union security clause specifying that workers must join the union after a set period of time,* **360**

Unionization, 358–359
Unisys, 61, 163–164
United Airlines, 515
U.S. Cellular, 503
U.S. Postal Service, 299
U.S. Sentencing Commission, 217
U.S. Steel, 34
United Technologies, 217

Unity-of-command principle *A structure in which each worker reports to one boss, who in turn reports to one boss,* **279**

Universal needs, 200–201

Universalism *The ethical system stating that all people should uphold certain values that society needs to function,* **157**

Unstructured interview, 335
UPS, 156, 217

Upward communication *Information that flows from lower to higher levels in the organization's hierarchy,* **514–515**

US Airways, 140
US Security Associates, 531

Utilitarianism *An ethical system stating that the greatest good for the greatest number should be the overriding concern of decision makers,* **158, 159**

V

Valence *The value an outcome holds for the person contemplating it,* **448**

Valent outcomes, 448

Validity *The degree to which a selection test predicts or correlates with job performance,* **338–339**

Value *The monetary amount associated with how well a job, task, good, or service meets users' needs,* **13, 69**

Value-added manufacturing, 318

Value chain *The sequence of activities that flow from raw materials to the delivery of a good or service, with additional value created at each step,* **308–309**

Valve, 142
Valve Software, 266
Vanity, 547
Variable pay, 353–354
Veil of ignorance, 165
Verizon, 344–345
Verlinvest, 252

Vertical integration *The acquisition or development of new businesses that produce parts or components of the organization's product,* **138–139**

Vertical leader, 428–429
Vertical organizational structure
    authority, 267–269
    decentralization, 64, 272–273
    delegation, 241, 270–272
    hierarchical, 269
    span of control, 269–270
Vertical stretch goals, 442
Viacom, 63
Videoconferencing, 501

Vigilance *A process in which a decision maker carefully executes all stages of decision making,* **89**

Vine, 579
Virgin Airlines, 94
Virginia Commonwealth University Health System, 6
Virginia Mason Medical Center, 12, 534

Virtual conflict, 489–490

Virtual office *A mobile office in which people can work anywhere, as long as they have the tools to communicate with customers and colleagues,* 282–283, **504**

Virtual teams *Teams that are physically dispersed and communicate electronically more than face-to-face,* **473**–474, 476

Virtue ethics *Perspective that what is moral comes from what a mature person with "good" moral character would deem right,* **158**–159

Vision *A mental image of a possible and desirable future state of the organization,* 69, 130–131, **407**–408, 615–616

Vocational Rehabilitation Act, 343
Volkswagen, 4, 186, 264

Vroom model *A situational model that focuses on the participative dimension of leadership,* **418**–419

W

Wages/payment systems, 351–356, 586
Wagner Act, 358
Walgreens, 234
Walmart, 10, 127, 141, 168, 183, 202, 229, 231, 263, 302–303, 308, 317, 342, 353, 358, 573, 576, 602, 603
Walt Disney Company, 67, 119–120, 127, 129, 134, 145–146, 188, 197, 603
Ward Group, 137

WARN Act, 342
Washington State Employees Credit Union, 609
Waste elimination, 318–319
Waste Management Inc., 183, 184
Weak cultures, 67–68
Weaknesses, analysis of, 134–137, 149–150
Web 2.0, 6
Web Crossing, 502
Wellpoint, 279
Wells Fargo, 452
Western Electric, 36
Weyerhaeuser Company, 59, 62, 91, 183
Whirlpool, 211
Whistleblowing, 166, 340
WhiteSmoke, 191–192
Whole Foods Market, 127, 167, 225, 328, 471–472, 475–476, 490
Wholly owned subsidiaries, 209
WHYCO Chromium Company, 182
Wikis, 501–502
Wild Flavors, 55
Wildcat strikes, 360
Win-win, 179
Wipro, 198
W.L. Gore, 472
Women
    glass ceiling, 374–375
    in the workforce, 49–50, 370–371, 373–378
Work-flow relationship, 485

Work teams *Teams that make or do things like manufacture, assemble, sell, or provide service,* **472**–473

Worker Adjustment and Retraining Notification Act, 342
Workers' compensation, 355
Workforce
    age of, 381–383
    demographics, 49–50
    education level, 381
    immigrants in, 49–50, 370–371, 378–380

labor shortages in, 331–332
mentally and physically disabled, 380–381
minorities in, 378–380
reduction of, 340–343
women in, 49–50, 370–371, 373–378
Working groups, 476
Working leaders, 18
World class, becoming, 602–605
The World is Flat, 188
World Trade Organization (WTO), 194–195, 207
WorldCom, 160
Worst-case scenario, 59–60
Writing skills, 507–508
Written communication, 501, 531

X

Xerox Corporation, 59, 136, 202, 279, 328, 339, 349, 374, 380, 392, 535, 581

Y

Y Combinator, 229
Yahoo, 497–498, 505, 518
Yamaha Corporation, 84
Yelp, 7
YouTube, 63
Yum Brands, 427–428

Z

Zale Corporation, 335
Zappos, 7, 135, 229, 247
Zazzle.com, 234
Zenith, 204
Zero defects, 8
Zero-sum game, 12
Zipcar, 240–241

Cropanzano, R., N-31
Crosby, F. J., N-24
Cross, F. B., N-10
Cross, R., N-17, N-32, N-34, N-36
Crossan, M., N-27
Crossley, C., N-28
Crowley, Mark C., N-28, N-29, N-31
Crozier, Jen, N-10
Cullen, John B., N-8, N-18
Culpan, T., 258
Cummings, A., N-29
Cummings, S., N-3
Cummings, T., N-41
Cust, D., N-39
Cusumano, Michael A., N-4

D

Dacin, M. T., N-15
Dacin, P., N-15
Daft, Richard L., N-4, N-35
Dahl, D., N-21
Dahlin, K., N-33
Dahling, Jason J., N-37
Daily, C. M., N-17
Dalrymple, J., 258
Dalton, D. R., N-17
D'Amelio, A., N-41
Dantas, I., N-13
Darlin, D., N-22
Dasborough, M., N-2
Dash, Anil, 243
D'Aveni, Richard A., N-4
Davidson, M. N., 388, N-24
Davila, Antonio, N-36
Davis, Andrea, N-31, N-32
Davis, B., N-12
Davis, Edward W., N-3
Davis, Grant, N-37
Davis, I., N-42
Davis, Keith, 322, N-36
Davis, Nancy M., N-4
Davis, S., N-5, N-15, N-18
Davis, T. R. V., N-36
Davison, H. K., N-21
Davison, S., N-31
Dawson, C., N-19
Dawson, Peter P., 494
Day, D. L., N-40
Day, D. V., N-26
Day, G. S., N-17
De Cremer, D., N-30
De Dreu, C., N-6
De George, R. T., N-9
de Janasz, Suzanne C., 29, 178, 465–466, 627
de Vise, Daniel, N-24
de WeerdNederhof, Petra C., N-17
de Wit, F. R. C., N-33
De Witt, R. L., N-21
Dean, James W., Jr., 586, N-4, N-5, N-6
Dean, Josh, N-19
Deardorff, Julie, N-42
Dechant, K., N-11
DeChurch, L. A., N-33, N-34
Decker, C. D., N-35
Deegan, Shannon, 67
DeGaspari, John, N-3
DeGraff, Jeff, N-40
DeGroot, Christine, 373
Deimler, M., N-41
DeJoy, D. M., N-30
Dekel, Elan, N-5
Del Rey, Jason, N-4
Deleeuw, Kevin, N-21
Dellana, Scott A., N-4
Demetrakakas, P., N-31
Deming, W. Edwards, 8, 309–310, 591
DeNisi, A., N-36

Dent, E. B., N-41
DeRue, D. S., N-28, N-32
Desai, Ashay B., N-14
Desmidt, Sebastian, N-4
Dess, G. G., N-16
Dessler, G., N-29
DeStrobbeleir, K., N-6
Deutsch, Claudia H., N-34
Devlin, D., N-12
Dewan, Rajiv, N-39
Diaz, George, N-25
Dickson, M., N-34
Dickson, W., N-2
Dickter, David N., N-21
Diener, E., N-31
Dienhart, J., N-9
Dieterich, Chris, N-40
Dietrich, H., N-15
Difonzo, N., N-36
Dingle, Derek T., 379
Dionne, S., N-26
Disney, Walt, 424
Dobbin, F., N-25
Donahue, L., N-31
Donlon, J. P., N-27
Donnelly, J., Jr., 81
Donovan, Michelle A., N-36
Dooley, R., N-6
Doppelt, B., N-1, N-10
Dorfman, P., N-26
Dorn, R., N-40
Dorns, Mark, N-12
Douma, B., N-29
Dowd, Karen O., 29, 178, 465–466
Downes, Larry, N-36, N-37
Doz, Y., N-41
Drach-Zahavy, A., N-31
Dragija, Martina, N-37
Dreiling, Richard, 628
Drexler, Peggy, N-23
Drezner, Daniel W., N-12
Driver, Erica, 138, N-7
Driver, M., N-15
Drnovsek, M., N-17
Droge, Cornelia, N-17
Drucker, Peter F., 2, 24, 42, 242, N-2, N-15
Druskat, Vanessa Urch, N-33, N-37
Dudley, Renee, N-19
Duffy, John, 234
Duffy, M., N-33
Dumaine, B., N-1, N-15
Duncan, R., N-17
Dunfee, T., N-8
Dunnette, M. D., N-33
Duran, M. A., N-29
Durfee, D., N-29
Durham, C., N-32
Duryee, T., N-27
Dutton, J., N-2, N-6, N-27, N-42
Dvir, T., N-27
Dvorak, Phred, N-5
Dye, J., N-34
Dyer, Lee, N-18

E

Early, P. C., N-29, N-35
Eastman, Lorrina J., N-19
Eckes, G., N-37
Economides, Michael I., N-39
Eden, C., N-40
Eden, D., N-27
Edinger, S., N-32
Edison, Thomas, 97, 564
Edman, Nancy J., N-22
Edmondson, A. C., N-31
Edwards, Cliff, N-1
Edwards, Jim, N-7

Edwards, M., N-22
Efrati, A., N-23
Ehrenfeld, John, N-1
Eichler, A., N-19
Eifert, Benn, N-2
Einhorn, Bruce, 258, N-12, N-14
Einstein, Albert, 97
Eisenberg, B., N-23
Eisenhardt, Kathleen M., N-6, N-39
Eisenstat, R. A., 144, N-8, N-41
Eisenstein, Paul A., N-16, N-18
Ekegren, G., N-29
Elkington, J., N-11, N-12
Elliott, M., N-12
Elliott, S., N-13
Elliott-McCrea, Kellen, N-25
Ellis, A. P. J., N-17, N-33
Ellis, K. M., N-17
Ellison, H., N-11, N-12
Ellison, J., N-10
Ellison, Lawrence, 610
Ely, R. J., N-24
Emmer, Bob, 239
Enayati, Amanda, N-34, N-35, N-36
Enders, Tom, 79
Eng, Dinah, N-25
Epitropaki, O., N-27
Erdogan, B., N-31
Erez, A., N-27
Erez, M., N-32
Erickson, Tammy, N-4
Ertug, G., N-2
Esenhardt, K. M., N-5
Esterl, Mike, N-3, N-17
Esty, D., N-10, N-11
Etter, L., N-9
Etternson, R., N-10
Ettkin, L. P., N-20
Ettlie, John E., N-20
Evans, James R., N-19
Evans, R., N-5, N-6
Evanschitzky, Heiner, N-30
Ewanick, Joel, 279
Ewen, A. J., N-22
Eyring, M. J., N-3

F

Fahrbach, Kyle, N-38
Falbe, C., N-26
Fanelli, A., N-27
Farh, C., N-33
Farh, J-L., N-32, N-33
Farmer, S. M., N-6
Farnham, A., N-9
Farrell, G., N-19
Fay, Charles, N-22
Fayol, Henri, 36, N-2
Fear, R. A., N-21
Fellermanns, F., N-6
Fenley, M., N-27
Fenn, D., N-15
Fenwick, Marilyn S., N-37
Ferguson, Eammon, N-21
Fernandes, Nuno, N-22
Ferndale, Elaine, N-13
Ferner, Anthony, N-18, N-37
Ferrari, Bernard T., 510, N-35
Ferraro, G., N-35
Ferreira, Miguel A., N-22
Ferrell, O. C., N-8, N-9
Fiedler, F. E., N-26
Field, A. M., N-20
Field, H., N-22
Field, J., N-31
Fields, D. A., N-40
Finegold, D., N-29, N-30
Finkelstein, S., N-15

Hadley, C., N-6
Hagedoorn, John, N-39
Hagen, Abdalla F., N-4, N-5
Hagerty, James R., N-20
Hagey, Keach, N-40, N-41, N-42, N-43
Hai, Dorothy, 493, 626
Hale, J., N-8
Hall, D. T, N-36
Hall, E., N-9
Hall, F., N-9
Halliday, Josh, N-16
Hall-Merenda, K. E., N-27
Hallowell, E. M., N-35
Hals, T., N-37
Halverson, K. C., N-27
Halverson, George, 508
Hambrick, Donald C., N-7, N-31
Hamel, Gary, 619, N-18, N-38, N-42
Hamermesh, R., N-7
Hamilton, Lynn, 507
Hamilton, Martha M., N-3
Hammer, Michael, 547–548, N-19, N-38
Hampp, Andrew, N-5
Hananel, S., N-21
Handy, C., N-9
Haney, W. V., N-34
Hanges, P., N-30
Hann, Christopher, N-25
Hannah, S., N-8
Hansen, F., N-21
Hansen, Morten T., N-1
Hanson, Angela, N-3
Hanson, J. R., 297, N-18
Harback, H., N-19
Harbert, T., N-36
Hardin, Garrett, 180, N-11
Hare, Breeanna, N-16
Harmon, S., N-32
Harper, Stephen C., N-37
Harrington, B., N-35
Harris, E., N-26
Harris, R., N-42
Harris, W., N-15, N-16
Harrison, David A., N-9, N-23
Harrison, J. Kline, N-27
Harrison, J. S., N-7
Harrysson, Martin, N-6
Hart, S. L., N-1, N-10, N-11, N-12, N-13
Harter, J. K., N-30, N-31
Hartley, Darin E., N-20
Hartman, Nathan S., N-28
Hartung, Adam, N-1
Hartwick, J., N-42
Harzing, Anne-Wil, 200, N-13
Haspeslagh, P., N-7
Hassan, F., N-1
Hauenstein, N. M. A., N-26
Haughney, Christine, N-41, N-42, N-43
Hauser, Richard D., N-4
Hawken, P., N-10, N-11
Hayes, T., N-30
Hazel, Debbie, N-1
Healey, Melanie, 375
Heaphy, E., N-2
Hechinger, J., N-8
Hedlund, Marc, 392
Heer, John, 428
Heffernan, Margaret, N-17
Heftler, Jerry, 101
Heifetz, R., N-26
Heijltjes, M., N-2
Heineman, B. W., Jr., N-9
Heiskanen, V., N-7
Held, Michael, N-20
Helft, Miguel, N-39
Hellofs, Linda L., N-19
Hellriegel, D., N-41
Helm, Burt, 229
Helms, Marilyn M., N-20
Hempel, Jessi, N-1, N-2

Hendricks, Ken, 239–240
Heneman, Herbert G., III, N-21
Henne, A., N-4
Henne, D., N-30
Henshaw, Caroline, N-5
Henshaw, Todd, N-37
Henwood, C., N-34
Hequet, Marc, N-22
Herbert, Theodore T., 558
Herbst, M., N-10
Herrmann, Pol, N-13
Herron, David, N-40
Herron, M., N-29
Hersey, P., N-26
Hersman, Deborah, 102
Herzberg, Frederick, 454, N-30
Hesketh, Beryl, N-21
Hesse, Dan, 353
Hesseldahl, Arik, N-3, N-19
Hessman, Travis, N-20
Heston, T., N-12
Hewlett, Bill, 231, 431
Hewlett, William, 405–406
Hewson, Marilyn, 375
Higginbotham, S., N-8
Higgins, E. T., N-33
Higgins, Tim, N-16, N-17
Hightower, Robert, N-25
Hill, G. W., N-6
Hill, L. A., N-2, N-36, N-42, N-43
Hille, K., N-13
Hiltrop, Jean-Marie, N-21
Hiltzik, M., N-39
Hindo, B., N-37
Hinds, P., N-33
Hinshaw, John, 304
Hipskind, M., N-31
Hira, N. A., N-24
Hisrich, R. D., 244, N-16
Hitt, M. A., N-7, N-14, N-18, N-19, N-26
Hodgetts, R. M., N-36
Hoekstra, J., N-41
Hoever, I., N-32
Hof, Robert D., N-41
Hoffman, K., N-7
Hoffman, Reid, N-31
Hoffman, Robert C., N-22
Hoffman, T., N-24, N-40
Hofmann, D., N-26
Hofstede, Geert, 213, 215, 349, N-29
Hogg, M., N-28
Hollenbeck, G. P., N-36
Hollenbeck, J. R., N-17, N-32, N-33
Holliday, C., N-10
Holloway, Charles A., N-40
Holthaus, D., N-24
Holusha, J., N-6
Holzer, J., N-14
Hong, Nicole, N-14, N-18, N-19
Hong, Sehee, N-21
Horng, E., N-35
Hornik, R., N-11
Hosmer, L. T., 165
House, Robert J., 421, N-26, N-27
Hout, Thomas M., N-20
Hovland, Kjetil Malkenes, N-36
Howard, J., N-1
Howell, J. M., N-27
Howell, Jon P., N-26, N-27
Hsieh, Tony, 229, 247
Hsu, Tiffany, N-27
Huang, J., N-6
Huang, L., N-9
Huber, G., N-1
Huber, V. L., N-22
Hudson, K., N-22
Hudson, Linda Parker, 410–411
Hudson, Peter J., Jr., N-21
Hull, Dana, N-40
Hummel, Edward, N-18

Humphrey, R., N-2
Humphrey, S. E., N-17, N-32, N-33
Hunt, J. G., N-26
Hunt, Sandy, 449
Hunter, J. E., N-21, N-23
Hunter, L., N-10
Huppke, Rex W., N-35
Huseman, R. C., 511, N-35
Hussey, Roger, 268
Hutton, A., N-36
Huy, Q. Nguyen, N-2, N-42
Hymowitz, Carol, N-4, N-23, N-29

I

Iacocca, Lee, 426
Ibarra, Herminia, N-1
Ibrahim, Mo, 216–217, N-14
Ibuka, Masaru, 231
Iger, Roger, 119
Ilgen, D. R., N-17, N-26, N-32
Ilies, R., N-26
Imai, Masaaki, N-39
Immelt, Jeffrey R., 163, 171, 295, 306, N-1, N-41
Ingols, C., N-16
Inkson, K., N-2
Ireland, R. D., N-7, N-14, N-18, N-26
Irving, Clive, N-6
Isdell, Neville, 170
Isenberg, D. J., N-14
Ishikawa, K., N-19
Isumi, H., N-32
Ivancevich, John M., N-25
Iverson, R. D., N-19, N-30
Iwata, Satoru, N-31

J

Jackman, J., N-29
Jackson, T., N-30
Jacobs, Bert, 63
Jacobson, Robert, N-19
Jacoby, Ryan, N-40
Jadotte, Marcus, 389
James, Erika Hayes, N-24
James, J., 117, 629, 630
James, L., N-26
Jameson, Daphne A., 221
Janis, I., N-5
Jankiewicz, Beckie, 240
Jannarone, J., 628
Janson, Robert, 455, N-30
Jargon, Julie, N-13, N-37
Jariloswki, Chaire Stephen, N-13
Jarvenpa, S., N-34
Jarzemsky, M., 628
Jassawalla, A., N-32
Jauch, Lawrence R., 30, 435, 520
Jehiel, Philippe, N-17
Jehn, Karen A., N-24, N-25, N-33
Jennings, P., N-35
Jensen, Michael C., N-3
Jernigan, I. E., N-34
Jesella, K., N-24
Jick, Todd D., N-20, N-36
Jimmieson, N., N-41
Jing, Bing, N-39
Jitpleecheep, P., N-13
Jobs, Steve, 3–4, 424, 581
Johnson, Abigail, 375
Johnson, Ben, N-1
Johnson, C. K., N-23, N-25
Johnson, D. E., N-27
Johnson, Dave, N-23
Johnson, Emma, N-28
Johnson, Gerry, N-41
Johnson, Jean L., N-8, N-18
Johnson, Keith, N-40
Johnson, Komichel, 241, 249

Johnson, Lauren Keller, N-22
Johnson, Linda A., N-17
Johnson, M., N-32, N-33, N-38
Joly, Hubert, 527, 544, 555, N-38
Jones, D., N-35
Jones, K., N-30
Jones, Peter, 484
Jones, Robert A., III, 241, 249
Jones, T., N-9
Jong-Yong, Yun, 4
Josephson, Michael, N-8
Joshi, Aparna, N-24
Joshi, M., N-8, N-9
Joyce, W. F., N-17, N-40, N-41
Joyner, April, N-4, N-15
Judge, T. A., N-26, N-27, N-28, N-29, N-36, N-41
Jundt, D., N-32, N-33
Jung, D. I., N-27
Juran, J. M., 8
Jurgens, J., N-10
Jusko, Jill, N-20, N-32, N-39

K

Kacmar, Michele K., N-21
Kadlec, Dan, 21
Kagermann, H., N-38
Kageyama, Yuri, N-16
Kahn, Linda G., N-23
Kahn, R. L., N-3, N-28
Kahneman, D., N-31
Kahwajy, J., N-6
Kaizen, Gemba, N-39
Kale, Prashant, N-18
Kalev, A., N-25
Kamdar, Rakesh, 230
Kammeyer-Mueller, J., N-8
Kanellos, Michael, N-7, N-39
Kang, S. C., N-18, N-19, N-40
Kanov, J., N-6
Kanter, L., N-14
Kanter, Rosabeth Moss, 301, N-15, N-16, N-18, N-41, N-42
Kaplan, David A., N-31
Kaplan, Gary S., N-37
Kaplan, Robert S., 128, N-5, N-6, N-7, N-36, N-38
Karam, E., N-32
Karp, David, 248
Katauskas, T., 584
Kato, Y., N-37
Katz, Daniel, N-3, N-28
Katz, Ian, N-5
Katz, J., N-42
Katz, R., N-2
Katzanek, J., N-9
Katzenbach, J., N-32, N-33
Kavilanz, P. B., N-13
Kearney, E., N-24
Kearns, Ellen C., N-22
Keats, B., N-19
Keidel, R. W., N-20
Kelleher, Herb, 426
Keller, R. T., N-33
Keller, S., N-41
Kellerman, B., N-25, N-26, N-27
Kello, John, N-37
Kelloway, E. K., N-30
Kelly, Aidan, N-14
Kelly, Caitlin, N-4
Kelly, Erin, N-25
Kelly, Keith J., N-42
Kelly, R. E., N-26
Kemper, A., N-10
Kennedy, John F., 424
Kennedy, Joyce Lain, 21
Kenny, D., N-26
Kent, Muhtar, 5
Keough, Donald, 268

Kern, M. C., N-14
Kernan, M., N-30
Kerr, S., N-20, N-26, N-28, N-29, N-36
Kessler, Eric H., N-38, N-40
Kethley, R. Bryan, N-21
Kettering, Charles, 600
Kettinger, W., N-35
Keyes, C. L. M., N-31
Keys, J. B., N-36
Kho, N. D., N-17
Kickul, Jill R., N-40
Kiechel, W., III, N-2
Kilmann, Ralph H., N-4
Kim, J., N-34
Kim, Peter H., N-35
Kim, Susanna, N-34
Kim, Tae-Yeol, N-23
Kim, W. C., N-30
King, A. Wilcox, N-7
King, Art, 335
King, G. E., N-42
King, Martin Luther, 424
King, Rachael, N-4, N-20
Kingsbury, Alex, N-24
Kinicki, A., 40
Kinlaw, Dennis C., N-10
Kinney, Monica Yant, N-25
Kirkland, J., N-42
Kirkland, Rik, N-18
Kirkman, B. L., N-31, N-32, N-33
Kirkpatrick, David, N-11
Kirkpatrick, S., N-25, N-26
Klassen, R. D., N-10, N-11
Klayman, Ben, N-16, N-17, N-18
Klein, Karen E., 260
Klein, Katherine J., N-23
Kleiner, A., N-1, N-10
Kleingeld, A., N-28, N-32
Klimoski, R., N-31
Knight, D., N-32
Ko, Albert, 241
Kobold, Michael, 303
Koehler, J. W., N-36
Koepfer, C., N-12
Koh, Yoree, N-6
Kohlberg, L., N-8
Kohls, John, N-14
Kolk, A., N-11
Kolodny, H., N-18
Kolodny, Lora, N-16
Koob, John, N-5
Kopecki, D., N-13
Kopeikina, Luda, 89, N-5
Kopytoff, Verne, N-10, N-35
Korda, M., N-35
Korn, Melissa, 341
Korten, D. C., N-9
Koster, Kathleen, N-21
Kotick, Robert, 268
Kotler, Philip, N-4
Kotter, John P., 611, 615, 616, 617, N-26, N-41, N-42, N-43
Kouzes, James, 406, N-25, N-26, N-28, N-30, N-35
Kowitt, Beth, N-1, N-19
Kowsmann, P., N-12
Krackhardt, D., 297, N-18
Kramer, M., N-15, N-43
Kramer, S., N-6
Krantz, Gene, 102
Krazit, T., N-39
Krebs, Robert, 288
Kreeger, D., N-1
Kreitner, R., 40, N-28
Krell, E., 280, N-22, N-34
Kristof-Brown, A., N-27
Krohe, J., Jr., N-6
Kroos, H., 35
Kucera, Danielle, N-3
Kuchera, Ben, N-8

Kuczmarski, Thomas, N-40
Kuenzi, M., N-27
Kullman, Ellen, 375
Kung-McIntyre, K., N-6
Kurland, N. B., N-36
Kurtines, W. M., N-8
Kurtzberg, T. R., N-34, N-35
Kuvaas, Baard, N-37
Kwoh, Leslie, N-9, N-13, N-25
Kwon, S., N-2

L

La, Aaron Ricade, N-25, N-26, N-28
LaBarre, Polly, N-6, N-18
Labelle, R., N-24
Laczniak, G., N-8
Lafley, A. G., 125, N-7
LaGanke, J., N-34
Lagges, J., N-17
Lagorio, Christine, 229, N-15
Lahart, Justin, N-20
Lalicker, Greg, 514
Lam, S. S. K., N-34
Lamach, Michael, 396
Lamont, Bruce T., N-17
Lando, Mary Ann, N-38
Landro, Laura, N-1
Landsberg, H., N-11
Lane, Peter J., N-7
Lang, Derrik, J., N-7
Lang, Laura, 613, 623
Lange, J. E., N-15
Langfred, C., N-31
Lanzolla, G., N-8
Lapchick, Richard E., 369, N-23, N-25
LaReau, J., N-28
Larkey, L. K., N-34
Larson, Kyle, 369
Larson, L. L., N-26
Lasar, Matthew, N-5
Lash, R., 280
Lashinsky, Adam, N-1, N-2, N-27
Latham, Gary P., N-22, N-28, N-29
Lau, James B., 291, 323, 400
Laufer, W. S., N-11
Laundauer, S., N-28
Laurent, A., N-41
Laurie, D., N-26
Lawler, Edward E., III, N-17, N-19, N-25, N-26, N-28, N-29, N-30, N-31, N-32, N-33, N-36, N-37, N-38, N-41, N-42, N-43
Lawrence, P. R., 265–266, 286, N-16, N-18
Lazarova, Mila, N-13
Lazenby, J., N-29
Le Breton-Miller, I., N-42
Leahey, Colleen, N-29
Leana, C. F., N-42
LeBoeuf, Michael, 445
Lechner, C., N-6
Ledford, Gerald E., N-19
Lee, C., N-33
Lee, E., N-14
Lee, Hau L., N-3
Lee, Jeong-Yeon, N-23
Lee, Mary Dean, N-25
Lee, T., N-30
Lee, Thomas, N-36, N-37, N-38
Lee, Timothy, 279
Lee, Tony, 246
Lei, David, N-4, N-43
Leifer, Richard, N-4, N-38
Lencioni, P., N-33
Lengel, R., N-35
Lengnick-Hall, Mark L., N-25
Leonard, Dorothy, N-39, N-40
Leonard, H., N-41
Leonard-Barton, D., N-40
Leopold, Aldo, 180

Lepak, D., N-1
LePine, M. A., N-27
Leske, Nicola, N-28
Leslie, Mark, 407
Lesova, Polya, N-13
Lesser, E., N-36
Leung, A., N-12
Levi, Michael, N-38, N-39, N-40
Levin, D., N-36
Levine, J. M., N-33
Levin-Epstein, Michael D., N-22
Levinson, Marc, N-3
Levit, Alexandra, N-14
Levitt, T., N-6
Lev-Ram, Michal, N-18, N-19
Levy, P., N-12
Levy, Steven, N-40
Lewicki, R., 104
Lewin, D., N-23
Lewin, Kurt, 610, N-41
Lewin, T., N-21
Lewis, Katherine Reynolds, N-32
Lewis, M., Jr., N-37
Li, Julia Juan, N-13
Li, Ming, N-14
Lichtenthaler, Ulrich, N-40
Liden, R. C., N-30
Liechti, S., N-27
Liedtke, M., N-20, N-23
Lifei, Z., 258
Light, J., N-20, N-21, N-22, N-23
Liker, J. K., N-20
Likert, Rensis, 38, N-3, N-26
Lilius, J., N-6
Limpaphayom, Wanthanee, N-21
Lindorff, D., N-34, N-35
Lindsay, William M., N-19
Linebaugh, Kate, N-18, N-19
Ling, Y., N-16, N-27
Lingle, J., N-19
Link, Albert N., N-39
Liodice, B., N-9
Lippitt, R., N-26
Lippman, Jamie, 373
Litchfield, R. C., N-29
Litterick, D., N-12
Little, Mark M., 11–12, N-1
Liu, D., N-30
Liu, L. A., N-34
Liveris, Andrew, 175
Livingstone, P., N-42
Llovio, Louis, N-23, N-24, N-25
Llvne-Tarandach, R., N-2
Locher, M., N-35
Locke, E. A., N-2, N-15, N-25, N-26, N-28, N-30, N-32, N-33
Lockwood, C., N-11
Lockwood, N. R., N-29
Logan, J., N-35
Logue, C. M., 511, N-35
Lohr, Steve, N-8, N-29
Lombardi, Candace, N-12
Lombardo, M., N-35
Longenecker, Clinton O., N-17, N-33
Longnecker, J. G., N-14
Lord, R. G., N-26
Lorinkova, N., N-30, N-32
Lorsch, J. W., 265–266, 286, N-16
Loten, Angus, N-7, N-14, N-39
Lott, A., N-33
Lott, B., N-33
Love, James H., N-38
Lovelle, Hilary, 21
Lovins, Amory, N-10, N-11
Lovins, L. Hunter, N-11
Low, M., N-15
Lubatkin, Michael, N-16, N-19, N-27
Lubber, M., N-12
Lubin, D., N-10, N-11
Lublin, Joann S., N-2, N-5, N-6, N-13, N-17, N-26, N-29, N-35, N-43

Luccock, Halford E., 470
Ludwig, Robi, N-23
Ludwig, Timothy D., N-37
Lukas, Bryan A., N-13
Lumpkin, G. T., N-15, N-16
Lunde, Joyce, 400
Lussier, Robert N., 237, N-15, N-38
Luthans, F., N-27, N-28, N-29
Lutilsky, Ivana Drazic, N-37

M

Maak, Thomas, N-15
Mabus, Ray, 582
Macadam, S., N-35
MacDermid, Shelley M., N-25
Macdonell, Robby, N-35
Machalaba, D., N-11
MacKenzie, Angus, N-38, N-39
Mackey, John, 471, 476, 490, N-31, N-32, N-34
Mackintosh, T., N-35
MacMillan, I., N-15
MacPherson, Robert, N-39
Macy, B., N-32
Maddux, William W., N-35
Madigan, C., N-42
Madison, Adam, N-29
Magasin, M., N-5
Mah, Jessica, 229
Mahajan, Aprajit, N-2
Maher, Kris, N-1, N-22, N-23, N-25, N-26
Mahoney, Janet D., N-14, N-17
Mahoney, Joan D., 212
Maidique, Modesto A., N-38
Maier, N. R. F., N-6, N-7
Maignan, Isabelle, N-13
Mainicro, L., N-29
Mair, J., N-15
Maishe, A., N-32
Majchrzak, A., 474
Makhani, Sanya, N-28
Makridakis, Spyros, N-4
Maldegen, Robyn, N-21
Malhotra, A., 474
Malone, Michael S., N-12
Malone, Scott, N-7
Maltby, Emily, N-39
Mandel, M., N-12
Manjoo, Farhad, N-3, N-4, N-5, N-20, N-23
Mankins, M., N-5
Mann, Jennifer, 463, N-31
Mann, L., N-5
Manning, R. L., N-4
Mannix, E., N-33
Manyika, James, N-34
March, J. G., N-5, N-18, N-19, N-40
Marchese, Kelly, N-20
Markman, G. D., N-16
Markowitz, E., N-13
Marks, M., N-1, N-32
Marriott, J. Willard, 231
Marriott, William, 138
Marrone, J., N-28, N-33
Marsh, George Perkins, 180
Marshall, D. R., N-9
Marsick, Victoria J., N-18
Marti, I., N-15
Martin, Andrew, N-7
Martin, K., N-8
Martin, Robin, N-26
Martin, Roger, 125, N-7, N-10
Martin, Thomas J., 584
Martinez, A., N-22
Maslow, Abraham H., 37, 450–451, N-2, N-29
Mason, Andrew, 4
Massey, A., N-34
Matear, M., N-15
Mathieu, J., N-30, N-32
Mathieu, R. G., N-38
Matos, Pedro, N-22

Matten, D., N-9
Matthews, Christopher M., N-9
Matthews, G., N-17
Mattioli, Dana, N-25, N-26
Matusak, L. R., N-25, N-26, N-27
Matuson, Roberta, N-31
Mauborgne, R., N-30
Maucker, Earl, 515
Maul, Kimberly, N-38
Maule, Amy, 274
Maurer, Steven D., N-21
Maxim, Jim, N-42
May, D., N-8
Mayer, D. M., N-27
Mayer, Marissa, 375, 497–498, 505, 517–518
Mayes, Michele Coleman, 374
Maylett, Tracy, N-3
Maynard, M. T., N-30, N-32
Mayo, Elton, 36–37, N-2
McCall, Morgan W., 212, N-5, N-6, N-14, N-28, N-35
McCanse, Anne Adams, 416
McCarthy, Ryan, N-4
McCaskey, M. B., N-35
McCauley, C. D., N-28
McClelland, David, 452, N-29, N-30
McClendon, J. A., N-23
McCollum, J. K., N-17
McCormack, M., N-34
McCoy, Sherilyn, 375
McCracken, Mike, 536, N-37
McCullen, Peter, N-20, N-37
McDaniel, Jonathan, 533
McDaniel, M., N-21
McDermott, Christopher M., N-38
McDonald, Joe, N-12
McDonald, John, 78
McElhatton, Noelle, N-31
McEnroe, Paul, N-36
McFarland, Lynn A., N-21
McGee, Jeffrey E., N-4
McGill, Chris, 239
McGill, M., N-43
McGinn, D., N-15
McGinnis, Leon F., N-20
McGranahan, D., N-20
McGrath, R. R., Jr., 148, 220, 291
McGrath, Steve, N-4
McGregor, Douglas, 38, N-3
McIlvaine, Andrew R., N-17
McKay, B., N-9
McKee, A., N-2
McKibben, B., N-10
McKinney, Joseph A., N-14
McLaughlin, Kevin, N-25, N-26
McMahan, Gary C., N-21
McMillan-Capehart, A., N-21
McMullen, J., N-15
McNeal, Marguerite, N-29
McNerney, James, 90, 102
McPherson, S., N-31
McQueen, M. P., N-24
McShane, Steven L., 76
McWilliams, A., N-10
McWilliams, Gary, N-1
Megginson, L., N-14
Megginson, W., N-14
Mehler, M., N-21
Mehrabian, A., N-35
Meiland, D., N-1
Meinert, Dori, N-21, N-42
Meister, Jeanne, N-41
Mellnik, Ted, N-23
Mendenca, L., N-42
Menz, M., N-1
Merchant, K. A., N-36, N-37
Mesmer-Magnus, J. R., N-33, N-34
Messick, D., N-5, N-9
Metayer, Estelle, N-6
Meyer, C., N-32, N-33

Westman, Mina, N-13
Wexley, Kenneth, N-22
Wheeler, J., N-33
Wheelwright, Steven C., N-38, N-40
Whetten, David A., 29, 108
Whetzel, Deborah L., N-21
White, B. Joseph, 445
White, Erin, N-5, N-37
White, Joseph B., N-12, N-39, N-40
White, Martha C., N-3, N-37
White, R., N-26
Whitford, D., N-12
Whitman, Meg, 4, 375, 405, 423, 431
Whitney, John O., N-38
Whybark, D. Clay, N-10, N-11
Wicks, A. C., N-7
Wieczner, Jen, N-3
Williams, Christopher, N-3
Williams, Colin, 621, N-43
Williams, T., N-40
Willis, B., N-5
Wilson, A., N-28
Wilson, H. James, N-29
Wilson, M. G., N-30
Winblad, Ann, 184
Wincent, J., N-15
Wingfield, Nick, N-5
Winterberg, Bill, N-29
Wise, J. M., N-36
Wiseman, Robert M., N-22
Witney, F., N-23
Witzel, M., N-9
Wnuck, D., N-31, N-33
Woehr, David J., N-21
Woertz, Pat, 375
Wojcicki, Susan, 375
Wolcott, R. C., N-38
Wolf, W., N-20

Womack, Brian, N-34
Wong, Vanessa, N-36
Wood, R. E., N-29
Woodward, Joan, 313, N-19
Wooldridge, A., N-1
Wooten, Lynn Perry, N-24
Worley, C., N-41
Worline, M., N-6
Wright, M., N-15
Wright, Patrick M., N-13, N-18, N-20, N-21
Wright, R. E., N-3
Wright, Sharon Anderson, 243
Wright, T. A., N-31
Wunderlich, Maren, N-30
Wynn, Gregory, 241, 249

X

Xavier, Stephen, N-2

Y

Yammarino, F. J., N-26, N-27
Yan, F., N-12
Yang, Baik, N-17
Yanouzas, J., N-38
Yasai-Ardekani, Masoud, N-4
Yeatts, D., N-31
Yen, C., N-31
Yerak, Becky, N-16
Yglesias, Matthew, N-39
Yi, Sang-Seung, N-39
Yorges, S., N-27
Youngblood, S. A., N-22
Yuanqing, Yang, 187, 206, 218
Yukl, G., N-26
Yunus, Muhammad, 235

Z

Zablow, R. J., N-9
Zaccaro, S., N-26, N-32
Zahra, S. A., N-15, N-16, N-39
Zald, M., N-9
Zappone, C., N-12
Zardkoohi, A., N-22
Zaslow, J., N-29
Zatzick, C. D., N-19
Zeidner, R., N-21
Zeithaml, C., 62–63, N-4, N-5
Zeithaml, V., 62–63, N-4
Zeitz, G., N-16
Zell, D., N-41
Zemke, R., N-27
Zenger, Jack, N-25
Zetlin, M., N-11
Zhang, S., N-30
Zhang, X., N-30
Zhang, Yajun, N-12
Zhao, W., N-24
Zhou, J., N-27
Zhou, Kevin Zheng, N-13
Zhu, J., N-33
Zieminski, Nick, N-10
Zigarmi, P., N-41
Zilmer, Richard, 582
Zimmerman, Ann, 628, N-5, N-36, N-37
Zimmerman, M., N-16
Zingheim, P. K., N-22
Ziobro, P., N-17
Zmud, R. W., N-35
Zoellik, Robert, 175
Zollo, M., N-16
Zorabedian, J., N-37
Zuboff, Shoshana, N-42
Zuckerberg, Mark, 43, 72